7

ESSENTIAL MATHEMATICS

FOR THE VICTORIAN CURRICULUM
THIRD EDITION

DAVID GREENWOOD
BRYN HUMBERSTONE
JUSTIN ROBINSON
JENNY GOODMAN
JENNIFER VAUGHAN
STUART PALMER

CAMBRIDGE

CAMBRIDGE
UNIVERSITY PRESS & ASSESSMENT

Shaftesbury Road, Cambridge CB2 8BS, United Kingdom

One Liberty Plaza, 20th Floor, New York, NY 10006, USA

477 Williamstown Road, Port Melbourne, VIC 3207, Australia

314–321, 3rd Floor, Plot 3, Splendor Forum, Jasola District Centre, New Delhi – 110025, India

103 Penang Road, #05–06/07, Visioncrest Commercial, Singapore 238467

Cambridge University Press is part of Cambridge University Press & Assessment, a department of the University of Cambridge.

We share the University's mission to contribute to society through the pursuit of education, learning and research at the highest international levels of excellence.

www.cambridge.org

First published 2016

Second Edition 2019

Third Edition 2024

20 19 18 17 16 15 14 13 12 11 10 9 8 7 6 5 4 3 2 1

Cover designed by Denise Lane (Sardine)

Typeset by diacriTech

Printed in China by C & C Offset Printing Co., Ltd.

A catalogue record for this book is available from the National Library of Australia at www.nla.gov.au

ISBN 978-1-009-48064-2

Additional resources for this publication at www.cambridge.edu.au/GO

Contents

3 Fractions and percentages   142

Strands: Number
Measurement

4 Algebraic techniques   230

Strand: Algebra

5   Decimals   282   Strand: Number

6   Negative numbers   354   Strands: Number
                                                                         Algebra

7 Geometry 402

Strands: Space
Measurement

8 Statistics and probability 512

Strands: Statistics
Probability
Algebra

9 Equations   592

Strand: Algebra

10 Measurement   650

Strands: Measurement
Algebra

11 Algorithmic thinking (online only)

Introduction
Activity 1: Algorithms for working with data
Activity 2: Adding consecutive numbers
Activity 3: Turtle graphics

About the authors

David Greenwood is the Head of Mathematics at Trinity Grammar School in Melbourne and has 30+ years' experience mathematics from Year 7 to 12. He is the lead author for the Cambridge Essential series and has authored more than 80 titles for the Australian Curriculum and for the syllabuses of the states and territories. He specialises in analysing curriculum and the sequencing of course content for school mathematics courses. He also has an interest in the use of technology for the teaching of mathematics.

Bryn Humberstone graduated from the University of Melbourne with an Honours degree in Pure Mathematics, and has 20+ years' experience teaching secondary school mathematics. He has been a Head of Mathematics since 2014 at two independent schools in Victoria. Bryn is passionate about applying the science of learning to teaching and curriculum design, to maximise the chances of student success.

Justin Robinson is co-founder of *The Wellbeing Distillery*, an organisation committed to energising, equipping and empowering teachers. He consults with schools globally on the fields of student and educator wellbeing. Prior to this, Justin spent 25 years teaching mathematics, covering all levels of secondary education including teaching VCE, IB and A-Levels. His driving passion was engaging and challenging students within a safe learning environment. Justin is an Honorary Fellow of the University of Melbourne's Graduate School of Education.

Jenny Goodman has taught in schools for over 28 years and is currently teaching at a selective high school in Sydney. Jenny has an interest in the importance of literacy in mathematics education, and in teaching students of differing ability levels. She was awarded the Jones Medal for education at Sydney University and the Bourke Prize for Mathematics. She has written for CambridgeMATHS NSW and was involved in the Spectrum and Spectrum Gold series.

Jennifer Vaughan has taught secondary mathematics for over 30 years in New South Wales, Western Australia, Queensland and New Zealand and has tutored and lectured in mathematics at Queensland University of Technology. She is passionate about providing students of all ability levels with opportunities to understand and to have success in using mathematics. She has had extensive experience in developing resources that make mathematical concepts more accessible; hence, facilitating student confidence, achievement and an enjoyment of maths.

Stuart Palmer was born and educated in NSW. He is a fully qualified high school mathematics teacher with more than 25 years' experience teaching students from all walks of life in a variety of schools. He has been Head of Mathematics in two schools. He is very well known by teachers throughout the state for the professional learning workshops he delivers. Stuart also assists thousands of Year 12 students every year as they prepare for their HSC Examinations. At the University of Sydney, Stuart spent more than a decade running tutorials for pre-service mathematics teachers.

Acknowledgements

The author and publisher wish to thank the following sources for permission to reproduce material:

Cover: © Getty Images / Eloku

Images: © Getty Images / Daniel Rocal - PHOTOGRAPHY, p.xx / matt_scherf / Getty Images, p.xxi / Bloom image / Getty Images, p.xxii / DEV IMAGES, p.xxiii / Chapter 1 Opener / deberarr / whitemay, p.4 / © ClassicStock / Alamy, p.5 / clu, p.7 / PBNJ Productions / Getty Images, p.8 / peterfz30 / Getty Images, p.14 / AROON PHUKEED, p.15 / Mikael Vaisanen, p.18 / D4Fish, p.20 / Grant Faint, p.23(1) / Nenov, p.23(2) / Blend Images - Peathegee Inc, p.25 / gilaxia, p.28 / Daniela D'anna / EyeEm / Getty Images, p.31 / PhotoAlles / Getty Images, p.32 / Carlos. E. Serrano, p.33 / Westend61, p.35 / Ron Levine, p.40(1) / Image Source, p.40(2) / Marc Dozier, p.41 / Kathrin Ziegler, p.42 / PETER PARKS / AFP / Gety Images, p.42 / Jason Edwards, p.46 / kali9, p.48 / Dennis Fischer Photography, p.50 / Stanislaw Pytel, p.52 / imagenavi, p.54 / Vertigo3d, p.56 / majorosl / Getty Images, p.60 / apomares, p.61 / Chapter 2 Opener / TonyFeder / AlexRaths, p.64 / blue jean images, p.67 / Cyndi Monaghan / Gty, p.69 / SolStock, p.72 / Flavio Coelho, p.73 / Paul Bradbury, p.74 / Traceydee Photography, p.77 / kali9, p.79 / DieterMeyrl, p.87 / Baran azdemir E+, p.91 / Paul Bradbury, p.97 / Monty Rakusen, p.99(1) / kasto80, p.99(2) / KTSDesign/SCIENCEPHOTOLIBRARY, p.103 / Kanok Sulaiman, p.104 / Mint Images, p.105(1) / Isabelle Rozenbaum, p.105(2) / Tatyana Tomsickova Photography, p.106 / Riou, p.144 / JohnnyGreig, p.107 / Naeblys, p.115 / Peshkova, p.121 / primeimages, p.127 / Qi Yang, p.130 / Chapter 3 Opener / undefined undefined / agrobacter, p.144 / Halfpoint Images, p.148 / Halfdark, p.149 / Peter Dazeley, p.150 / Anadolu Agency / Contributor, p.155 / Bill Varie, p.156 / Martin Poole, p.161 / BRETT STEVENS, p.162 / fotokostic, p.163 / Joff Lee, p.167 / Gregory Van Gansen, p.173 / Alys Tomlinson, p.174 / Petri Oeschger, p.185(1) / 10'000 Hours, p.185(2) / izusek, p.188 / kuritafsheen, p.192 / ArtistGNDphotography, p.193 / Paul Bradbury, p.194 / Yulia Naumenko, p.197 / John Lamb, p.198 / filo, p.198 / fotostorm, p.199 / Hiroshi Watanabe, p.202(1) / Tom Werner, p.202(2) / The Good Brigade, p.203 / gece33, p.204(1) / Marko Geber, p.204(2) / Willie B. Thomas, p.205 / Martin Poole, p.206(2) / MoMo Productions, p.209 / Luke Stanton, p.211 / Elyse Spinner, p.215 / ozgurdonmaz, p.216(1) / Arctic-Images, p.216(2) / Jonas Pattyn, p.217(1) / Westend61, p.218 / Callista Images, p.219 / Jackyenjoyphotography, p.229 / Chapter 4 Opener / Pencho Chukov / Danny Lehman, p.263 / Maskot, p.237 / Monty Rakusen, p.239 / Andrew Merry, p.243 / XiXinXing, p.248 / Hinterhaus Productions, p.251 / Imgorthand, p.252 / andresr, p.255 / adventtr, p.259(1) / mrs, p.259(2) / Davidf, p.260 / irina88w, p.261 / Jonathan Kirn, p.266 / JasonDoiy, p.267 / Teera Konakan, p.272 / Yuichiro Chino, p.273 / Comezora, p.274 / Tao Xu, p.275 / Maskot, p.280 / Frank Rothe, p.281 / Chapter 5 Opener / moodboard / Andrew Brookes, p.284 / Malkovstock, p.289 / simonkr, p.292 / South_agency, p.293(1) / Goodboy Picture Company, p.293(2) / Ariel Skelley, p.294 / Andrew Fox, p.297 / simoncarter, p.298 / Monty Rakusen, p.299 / florintt, p.303 / photovideostock, p.305 / microgen, p.305 / sestovic, p.311 / Mitchell Gunn/Getty Images, p.311 / wihteorchid, p.315(1) / VioletaStoimenova, p.315(2) / South_agency, p.316 / Chris Sattlberger, p.317 / sankai, p.320 / PM Images, p.321 / Sadeugra, p.322(1) / ANDRZEJ WOJCICKI, p.322(2) / Stanislaw Pytel, p.323 / kajakki, p.324 / PeopleImages, p.327(1) / MarianneBlais, p.327(2) / brizmaker / Getty Images, p.329 / fstop123, p.333 / fotog, p.334 / Candy Pop Images, p.338 / Chapter 6 Opener / kavram / mrcmos, p.356 / Stephen Frink, p.360 / JazzIRT, p.361 / Icy Macload, p.364 / matejmo, p.365 / Bruce Yuanyue Bi, p.366 / Fajrul Islam, p.376 / dstephens, p.377 / Photo taken by Kami (Kuo, Jia-Wei), p.379 / George Lepp, p.381 / ultramarinfoto, p.382 / je33a, p.383 / deepblue4you, p.385 / PASIEKA, p.390 / Tim Platt, p.391 / supersizer, p.392 / xavierarnau, p.393 / damircudic, p.395 / guvendemir, p.396 / Ashley Cooper, p.401 / Chapter 7 Opener / 35007 / hatman12, p.404 / M_Arnold, p.406 / MaxCab, p.420 / Xinzheng, p.421 / Image Source, p.429 / Dan Reynolds Photography, p.430 / DLMcK, p.436 / imageBROKER/Helmut Meyer zur Capellen, p.442 / BrianScantlebury, p.443 / Tempura, p.453 / photovideostock, p.460(1) / Natchaphol chaiyawet, p.460(2) / Jessica Peterson, p.463 / Oscar Wong, p.475 / DigtialStorm, p.475 / Jung Getty, p.481 / hh5800, p.482 / Hero Images, p.494 / Chapter 8 Opener / Steve Bell / VCG, p.515 / Stringer / simpson33, p.516 / Artie Photography (Artie Ng), p.519 / Nitat Termmee, p.520 / Vertigo3d, p.521 / swilmor, p.522 / skynesher, p.523 / vm, p.526 / Phil Fisk, p.527 / simonkr, p.537 / Daly and Newton, p.548 / mixetto, p.549 / Nick Rains, p.550 / Walter Geiersperger, p.551 / Justin Paget, p.558 / Oliver Strewe, p.559 / Kaori Ando, p.654 / Matteo Colombo, p.566(1) / Aaron Foster, p.566(2) / ferrantraite, p.567 / Kutay Tanir, p.569 / Tetra Images, p.573 / shekhardino, p.575 (1) / Monty Rakusen, p.575(2) / Sandra Clegg, p.579 / Federico Campolattano / 500px, p.580 / Tobias Titz, p.581 / Sally Anscombe, p.582 / Pete Saloutos, p.583 /

Zero Creatives, p.584 / Svetlana Repnitskaya, p.592 / Thomas Barwick, p.593 / Chapter 9 Opener / TommL / SCIEPRO, p.596 / Juan Silva, p.601 / d3sign, p.605(1) / Ekaterina Goncharova, p.605(2) / Enrico Calderoni/Aflo, p.612 / Feverpitched, p.619 / Luis Alvarez, p.622 / Vithun Khamsong, p.629(1) / Maskot, p.629(2) / Vladimir Godnik, p.630 / PeopleImages, p.631 / Katrin Ray Shumakov, p.634 / James Braund, p.635(1) / Cameron Spencer, p.635(2) / OrnRin, p.636 / Michael Schmitt, p.640 / Clerkenwell, p.641 / William Fawcett, p.642 / Hero Images, p.643 / Trina Dopp Photography, p.644 / d3sign, p.650 / Chapter 10 Opener / RugliG / -Oxford-, p.652 / Darryl Peroni, p.656(1) / LUCKY gilhare / 500px, p.656(4) / Cyndi Monaghan / Gty, p.656(5) / AlexLMX, p.656(6) / Xiaodong Qiu, p.657 / Feng Wei Photography, p.658 / DavidCallan, p.659 / majorosl / Getty Images, p.664 / Elena Popova, p.670 / tzahiV, p.680 / valentyn semenov / 500px, p.685(1) / BanksPhotos, p.685(2) / Seb Oliver, p.687(1) / John C Magee, 687(2) / Allan Baxter, p.692 / rabbit75_ist, p.693 / Roy Rochlin / Contributor, p.706 / Rost-9D, p.707 / Richard Drury, p.713(1) / Jackyenjoyphotography, p.713(2) / wellsie82, p.71 / Matthias Kulka, p.722 / Matt Anderson Photography, p.723 / xbrchx, p.728(1) / Danita Delimont, p.728(2) / Jonathan Pow, p.732 / PASIEKA, p.734 / Wendy Cooper, p.736 / Jupiterimages, p.745; / TED 43 / Creative Commons Attribution 3.0 Unported license, p.98.

Every effort has been made to trace and acknowledge copyright. The publisher apologises for any accidental infringement and welcomes information that would redress this situation.

Introduction

The third edition of *Essential Mathematics for the Victorian Curriculum* has been significantly revised and updated to suit the teaching and learning of Version 2.0 of the Victorian Curriculum. Many of the established features of the series have been retained, but there have been some substantial revisions, improvements and new elements introduced for this edition across the print, digital and teacher resources.

New content and some restructuring

New topics have come in at all year levels. In **Year 7** there are new lessons on ratios, volume of triangular prisms, and measurement of circles, and all geometry topics are now contained in a single chapter (Chapter 4). In **Year 8**, there are new lessons on 3D-coordinates and techniques for collecting data. For **Year 9**, error in measurement is new in Chapter 5, and sampling and proportion is introduced in Chapter 9.

In **Year 10**, four lessons each on networks and combinatorics have been added, and there are new lessons on logarithmic scales, rates of change, two-way tables and cumulative frequency curves and percentiles. The Year 10 book also covers all the 10A topics from Version 2.0 of the curriculum. This content can be left out for students intending to study General Mathematics, or prioritised for students intending to study Mathematical Methods or Specialist Mathematics.

Version 2.0 places increased emphasis on **investigations** and **modelling**, and this is covered with revised Investigations and Modelling activities at the end of chapters. There are also many new elaborations covering **First Nations Peoples' perspectives** on mathematics, ranging across all six content strands of the curriculum. These are covered in a suite of specialised investigations provided in the Online Teaching Suite.

Other new features

- **Technology and computational thinking** activities have been added to the end of every chapter to address the curriculum's increased focus on the use of technology and the understanding and application of algorithms.
- **Targeted Skillsheets** – downloadable and printable – have been written for every lesson in the series, with the intention of providing additional practice for students who need support at the basic skills covered in the lesson, with questions linked to worked examples in the book.
- **Editable PowerPoint lesson summaries** are also provided for each lesson in the series, with the intention of saving the time of teachers who were previously creating these themselves.

Diagnostic Assessment tool

Also new for this edition is a flexible, comprehensive Diagnostic Assessment tool, available through the Online Teaching Suite. This tool, featuring around 10,000 new questions, allows teachers to set diagnostic tests that are closely aligned with the textbook content, view student performance and growth via a range of reports, set follow-up work with a view to helping students improve, and export data as needed.

Guide to the working programs in exercises

The suggested working programs in the exercises in this book provide three pathways to allow differentiation for Growth, Standard and Advanced students (schools will likely have their own names for these levels).

Each exercise is structured in subsections that match the mathematical proficiencies of Fluency, Problem-solving and Reasoning, as well as Enrichment (Challenge). (Note that Understanding is covered by 'Building understanding' in each lesson.) In the exercises, the questions suggested for each pathway are listed in three columns at the top of each subsection:

Growth	Standard	Advanced
FLUENCY		
1, 2, 3(½), 4	2, 3(½), 4, 5(½)	3(½), 4, 5(½)
PROBLEM-SOLVING		
6	6, 7	7, 8
REASONING		
9	9, 10	10, 11
ENRICHMENT: Adjusting concentration		
–	–	12

The working program for Exercise 3A in Year 7. The questions recommended for a Growth student are: 1, 2, 3(1/2), 4, 6 and 9. See note below.

- The left column (lightest shaded colour) is the Growth pathway
- The middle column (medium shaded colour) is the Standard pathway
- The right column (darkest shaded colour) is the Advanced pathway.

Gradients within exercises and proficiency strands

The working programs make use of the two difficulty gradients contained within exercises. A gradient runs through the overall structure of each exercise – where there is an increasing level of mathematical sophistication required from Fluency to Problem-solving to Reasoning and Enrichment – but also within each proficiency; the first few questions in Fluency, for example, are easier than the last Fluency question.

The right mix of questions

Questions in the working programs are selected to give the most appropriate mix of *types* of questions for each learning pathway. Students going through the Growth pathway should use the left tab, which includes all but the hardest Fluency questions as well as the easiest Problem-solving and Reasoning questions. An Advanced student can use the right tab, proceed through the Fluency questions (often half of each question), and have their main focus be on the Problem-solving and Reasoning questions, as well as the Enrichment questions. A Standard student would do a mix of everything using the middle tab.

Choosing a pathway

There are a variety of ways to determine the appropriate pathway for students through the course. Schools and individual teachers should follow the method that works for them. If required, the prior-knowledge pre-tests (now found online) can be used as a tool for helping students select a pathway. The following are recommended guidelines:

- A student who gets 40% or lower should complete the Growth questions
- A student who gets above 40% and below 85% should complete the Standard questions
- A student who gets 85% or higher should complete the Advanced questions.

Note: The nomenclature used to list questions is as follows:

- 3, 4: complete all parts of questions 3 and 4
- 1-4: complete all parts of questions 1, 2, 3 and 4
- 10(½): complete half of the parts from question 10 (a, c, e, ... or b, d, f, ...)
- 2-4(½): complete half of the parts of questions 2, 3 and 4
- 4(½), 5: complete half of the parts of question 4 and all parts of question 5
- —: do not complete any of the questions in this section.

Guide to this resource

PRINT TEXTBOOK FEATURES

1 **NEW** **New lessons:** authoritative coverage of new topics in the Victorian Curriculum 2.0 in the form of new, road-tested lessons throughout each book.

2 **Victorian Curriculum 2.0:** content strands and content descriptions are listed at the beginning of the chapter (see the teaching program for more detailed curriculum documents)

3 **In this chapter:** an overview of the chapter contents

4 **Working with unfamiliar problems:** a set of problem-solving questions not tied to a specific topic

5 **Chapter introduction:** sets context for students about how the topic connects with the real world and the history of mathematics

6 **Learning intentions:** sets out what a student will be expected to learn in the lesson

7 **Lesson starter:** an activity, which can often be done in groups, to start the lesson

8 **Key ideas:** summarises the knowledge and skills for the lesson

9 **Building understanding:** a small set of discussion questions to consolidate understanding of the Key ideas (replaces Understanding questions formerly inside the exercises)

10 **Worked examples:** solutions and explanations of each line of working, along with a description that clearly describes the mathematics covered by the example

11   **Now you try:** try-it-yourself questions provided after every worked example in exactly the same style as the worked example to give immediate practice

12   **Gentle start to exercises:** the exercise begins at Fluency, with the first question always linked to the first worked example in the lesson

13   **Working programs:** differentiated question sets for three ability levels in exercises

14   **Example references:** show where a question links to a relevant worked example – the first question is always linked to the first worked example in a lesson

15   **Problems and challenges:** in each chapter provides practice with solving problems connected with the topic

16   **Chapter checklist with success criteria:** a checklist of the learning intentions for the chapter, with example questions

17   **Applications and problem-solving:** a set of three extended-response questions across two pages that give practice at applying the mathematics of the chapter to real-life contexts

18   **NEW Technology and computational thinking** activity in each chapter addresses the curriculum's increased focus on the use of different forms of technology, and the understanding and implementation of algorithms

19   **Modelling activities:** an activity in each chapter gives students the opportunity to learn and apply the mathematical modelling process to solve realistic problems

20 Chapter reviews: with short-answer, multiple-choice and extended-response questions; questions that are extension are clearly signposted

21 Solving unfamiliar problems poster: at the back of the book, outlines a strategy for solving any unfamiliar problem

INTERACTIVE TEXTBOOK FEATURES

22 **NEW** **Targeted Skillsheets,** one for each lesson, focus on a small set of related Fluency-style skills for students who need extra support, with questions linked to worked examples

23 Workspaces: almost every textbook question – including all working-out – can be completed inside the Interactive Textbook by using either a stylus, a keyboard and symbol palette, or uploading an image of the work

24 Self-assessment: students can then self-assess their own work and send alerts to the teacher. See the Introduction on page xii for more information.

25 Interactive working programs can be clicked on so that only questions included in that working program are shown on the screen

26 HOTmaths resources: a huge catered library of widgets, HOTsheets and walkthroughs seamlessly blended with the digital textbook

27 A revised set of **differentiated auto-marked practice quizzes** per lesson with saved scores

28 Scorcher: the popular competitive game

29 Worked example videos: every worked example is linked to a high-quality video demonstration, supporting both in-class learning and the flipped classroom

30 Desmos graphing calculator, scientific calculator and geometry tool are always available to open within every lesson

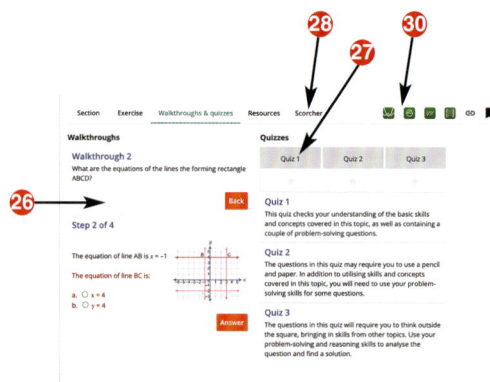

31 Desmos interactives: a set of Desmos activities written by the authors allow students to explore a key mathematical concept by using the Desmos graphing calculator or geometry tool

32 Auto-marked prior knowledge pre-test for testing the knowledge that students will need before starting the chapter

33 Auto-marked progress quizzes and chapter review multiple-choice questions in the chapter reviews can now be completed online

DOWNLOADABLE PDF TEXTBOOK

34 In addition to the Interactive Textbook, a **PDF version of the textbook** has been retained for times when users cannot go online. PDF search and commenting tools are enabled.

ONLINE TEACHING SUITE

35 NEW Diagnostic Assessment Tool included with the Online Teaching Suite allows for flexible diagnostic testing, reporting and recommendations for follow-up work to assist you to help your students to improve

36 NEW PowerPoint lesson summaries contain the main elements of each lesson in a form that can be annotated and projected in front of class

37 Learning Management System with class and student analytics, including reports and communication tools

38 Teacher view of student's work and self-assessment allows the teacher to see their class's workout, how students in the class assessed their own work, and any 'red flags' that the class has submitted to the teacher

39 Powerful test generator with a huge bank of levelled questions as well as ready-made tests

40 Revamped task manager allows teachers to incorporate many of the activities and tools listed above into teacher-controlled learning pathways that can be built for individual students, groups of students and whole classes

41 Worksheets and four differentiated chapter tests in every chapter, provided in editable Word documents

42 More printable resources: all Pre-tests, Progress quizzes and Applications and problem-solving tasks are provided in printable worksheet versions

Working with unfamiliar problems: Part 1

The questions on the next four pages are designed to provide practice in solving unfamiliar problems. Use the 'Working with unfamiliar problems' poster at the back of this book to help you if you get stuck.

In Part 1, apply the suggested strategy to solve these problems, which are in no particular order. Clearly communicate your solution and final answer.

> For questions 1–3, try starting with smaller numbers and look for a pattern.

1 How many diagonals exist for a 7-sided regular polygon? How many diagonals can be drawn from one vertex of a 30-sided regular polygon?

2 Find the value of 11111111 squared.

3 Find the sum of the first 25 odd numbers.

4 Five students have entered a race. How many different arrangements are there for first, second and third place, given that nobody ties?

> For questions 4 and 5, try making a list or table.

5 Arrange all the digits 1, 2, 3, 4 and 5 into the form ▢▢▢ × ▢▢ so that the 3-digit number multiplied by the 2-digit number gives the largest possible answer.

6 A tree surgeon charges $15 to cut a log into 4 pieces. How much would he charge, at the same rate, to cut a log into 99 pieces?

> For questions 6–8, draw a labelled diagram to help you visualise the problem.

7 How many 2-digit numbers can be written using only the digits 0, 1, 2, 3 or 4 with no repetition?

8 An 8-sided star is formed by drawing an equilateral triangle on each side of a square. Find the obtuse angle formed by adjacent sides of the star.

9 Approximately how many planes are needed to carry 76819 people if each plane holds 289 people? Give your answer to the nearest 10 planes.

> For question 9, try estimating by rounding the values in the question.

10 Approximately how many times does the word 'the' appear in this book?

11 Approximately how far would you have walked, in km, after walking 10 000 steps?

> For question 10 and 11, try working with a smaller sample first.

12 Insert operation signs between the digits 1 2 3 4 5 6 7 8 9 to make an answer of 100. The digits must be kept in ascending order.

   a Use any of the four operations and keep the digits separate.

   b Use only addition and subtraction. Also digits may be combined to form a 2- or 3-digit number.

13 A glass fish tank is a rectangular prism of width 40 cm and length 1 m. A scale is to be marked on the side of the tank showing 10-litre increases in volume. How far apart should the scale markings be? If the tank is to hold 280 litres of water and 5 cm height is allowed above the water level, what is the height of the fish tank?

> For questions 12 and 13, try using a formula or rule to find a shortcut to the answer.

> For question 14, try using algebra as a tool: define the pronumerals, form an equation and then solve it.

14 Divide $410 between Bob, Zara and Ahmed so that Bob gets $40 more than Zara and Zara has $20 more than Ahmed.

15 A sailor has a cat, a mouse and a chunk of cheese that he needs to get across the lake in his boat. The boat is very small and it can only hold the sailor and one passenger, or the cheese, at a time. The other problem the sailor faces is that if he leaves the mouse and the cat alone, the cat will eat the mouse and if he leaves the cheese with the mouse alone, the cheese will get eaten. How many trips are needed for the sailor, the cat, the mouse and the cheese to arrive safely on the other side of the lake?

16 Ethan takes 6 days to paint a house, Jack takes 8 days to paint a house and Noah takes 12 days to paint a house. Exactly how many days would it take to paint a house if all three of them worked together?

> For question 15, try using concrete, everyday materials to represent the problem.

> For question 16, try applying one or more mathematical procedures, such as a rule for adding fractions.

Working with unfamiliar problems: Part 2

For the questions in Part 2, again use the 'Working with unfamiliar problems' poster at the back of this book, but this time choose your own strategy (or strategies) to solve each problem. Clearly communicate your solution and final answer.

1 Maddie remembered her friend's house number has two digits and that they added to 8. In ascending order, list the possible house numbers that fit this description.

2 Find the smaller angle between the big hand and little hand of a clock at 2 p.m. and also at 7:10 a.m.

3 Find each 2-digit number, from 12 to 40, that has the sum of its factors greater than double the number.

4 Using grid paper, draw all the possible different arrangements of 5 equally sized connecting squares. Rotations and reflections don't count as separate arrangements. Which of your arrangements would fold up to make an open box? Mark the base square for these arrangements.

5 How many prime numbers are less than 100?

6 At the end of a soccer match, each member of the two teams of 11 players wishes to shake hands with everyone else who played. How many handshakes are needed?

7   What is the smallest number that has each of the numbers 1 to 9 as a factor?

8   A game involves rolling two 8-sided dice. The numbers shown on both dice are 1 to 8 inclusive. How many different totals are possible in this game?

9   What is the 2018th digit after the decimal point in the decimal expansion of $\frac{4}{7}$?

10 Approximately how many 20 cent coins are needed so that when placed next to each other they cover a 1-metre square? Give your answer to the nearest 100. What is their value in dollars?

11 A triangle has one angle double the smallest angle and the other angle 25° less than double the smallest angle. Find the size of the smallest angle in this triangle.

12 What is the last digit in the number 3203?

13 Find the interior angle sum of a 42-sided regular polygon.

14 How many palindromic numbers are there that are greater than 100 and less than 1000? (A palindrome is the same when written forwards and backwards.)

15 In a message that is written in secret code, what letter of the alphabet would likely be represented by the most common symbol in the message?

16 How many squares of any size are on a chess board?

1

Computation with positive integers

Maths in context: Whole numbers in the ancient world and now

Various number symbols and systems have been used over thousands of years. The Mayan people lived in Central America from 1500 BCE to the 16th century CE. They counted in 20s rather than 10s and their simplest number system used a shell for zero, a pebble for one unit, and a stick for five units.

For example:

Number	20 ($1 \times 20 + 0$)	29 ($1 \times 20 + 9$)	103 ($5 \times 20 + 3$)
20s	●	●	▬
units	🥖	● ● ● ● ● ▬	● ● ●

Here are some everyday situations where whole numbers are used now.

- Number skills are needed in algebra, which is used in numerous occupations, including coding.
- At a parkrun each runner is allocated two whole numbers: their ID bar code and a finishing place bar code. These are linked to the placement times (whole number minutes and seconds) and results uploaded onto the parkrun website.
- Builders calculate the number of pavers required around a swimming pool.
- The number of votes in an election for class representatives are tallied.

Chapter contents

Victorian Curriculum 2.0

This chapter covers the following content descriptors in the Victorian Curriculum 2.0:

NUMBER

VC2M7N02, VC2M7N08, VC2M7N10

ALGEBRA

VC2M7A02

Please refer to the curriculum support documentation in the teacher resources for a full and comprehensive mapping of this chapter to the related curriculum content descriptors.

© VCAA

Online resources

A host of additional online resources are included as part of your Interactive Textbook, including HOTmaths content, video demonstrations of all worked examples, auto-marked quizzes and much more.

1A Place value in ancient number systems

LEARNING INTENTIONS
* To understand that there are different number systems that have been used historically in different cultures
* To be able to write numbers in the Egyptian number system
* To be able to write numbers in the Babylonian number system
* To be able to write numbers in the Roman number system

Throughout the ages and in different countries, number systems were developed and used to help people count and communicate with numbers. From the ancient Egyptians to the modern day, different systems have used pictures and symbols to represent whole numbers. In Australia, the most commonly used number system is the Hindu–Arabic system (using the digits 0–9), often called the decimal system.

Lesson starter: Count like a Roman

Here are the letters used in the Roman number system for some numbers that you know.

Number	1	2	3	4	5	6
Roman numerals	I	II	III	IV	V	VI

Number	7	8	9	10	50	100
Roman numerals	VII	VIII	IX	X	L	C

* What numbers do you think XVII and XIX represent?
* Can you write the numbers 261 and 139 using Roman numerals?

The Roman numerals on this old milestone in Norfolk, England, show the distances in miles to nearby villages.

KEY IDEAS

■ **Egyptian number system**
* Records show that this number system was used from about 3000 BCE.
* **Hieroglyphics** were used to represent numbers.
* From about 1600 BCE, hieroglyphics were used to represent groups of 10, 100, 1000 etc.
* Symbols of the same type were grouped in twos or threes and arranged vertically.

Number	1	10	100	1000	10 000	100 000	1 000 000
Hieroglyphic	I	∩	℮	⌇	⌐	⌐	☥
Description	Stick or staff	Arch or heel bone	Coil of rope	Lotus flower	Bent finger or reed	Tadpole or frog	Genie

* Examples:

   3   5   21   342

- Note that the hieroglyphics with the larger value are written in front (i.e. on the left).
- There was no symbol for the number zero.

■ **Babylonian number system**
- From about 1750 BCE the ancient Babylonians used a relatively sophisticated number system and its origins have been traced to about 3000 BCE.
- Symbols called **cuneiform** (wedge shapes) were used to represent numbers.
- The symbols were written into clay tablets, which were then allowed to dry in the sun.
- The number system is based on the number 60, but a different wedge shape was used to represent groups of 10.
- The system is positional in that the position of each wedge shape helps determine its value. So ▼▼ means 2 but ▼ ▼▼ means 62.

The Hanging Gardens of Babylon, built for his wife by King Nebuchadnezzar II around 600 BCE, were one of the seven wonders of the ancient world.

Number	1	10	60
Symbol	▼	◀	▼
Description	Upright wedge shape	Sideways wedge	Upright wedge shape

- To represent zero, they used a blank space or sometimes a small slanted wedge shape for zeros inside a number.
- Examples:

5	11	72	121
▼▼▼ ▼▼	◀▼	▼ ◀▼▼	▼▼ ▼

■ **Roman number system**
- The Roman number system uses capital letters to indicate numbers. These are called Roman numerals.
- The Roman number system was developed in about the third century BCE and remained the dominant system in many parts of the world until about the Middle Ages. It is still used today in many situations.
- A smaller letter value to the left of a larger letter value indicates subtraction.
  For example, IV means $5 - 1 = 4$ and XC means $100 - 10 = 90$. Only one letter can be placed to the left for subtraction. I, X and C are the numerals that can be used to reduce the next two larger numerals. So X, for example, can be used to reduce L and C but not D.

Number	1	5	10	50	100	500	1000
Symbol	I	V	X	L	C	D	M

- Examples:

2	4	21	59	90
II	IV	XXI	LIX	XC

BUILDING UNDERSTANDING

1 Which number system uses these symbols?
  a cuneiform (wedge shapes); e.g. ▼
  b capital letters; e.g. V and L
  c hieroglyphics (pictures); e.g. ℮ and ∩

2 Write these numbers in the Egyptian number system.
  a 1   **b** 10   **c** 100   **d** 1000

3 Write these numbers in the Babylonian number system.
  a 1   **b** 10   **c** 60

4 Write these numbers in the Roman number system.
  a 1   **b** 5   **c** 10   **d** 50   **e** 100

5 In the Roman system, IV does not mean 1 + 5 to give 6. What do you think it means?

Example 1   Using ancient number systems

Write each of the numbers 3, 15 and 144 using the given number systems.
a Egyptian   **b** Babylonian   **c** Roman

SOLUTION		EXPLANATION
a 3	III	I means 1
15	∩IIII / II	∩ means 10
144	℮∩∩II / ∩∩II	℮ means 100
b 3	▼▼▼	▼ means 1
15	◀▼▼▼	◀ means 10
144	▼▼ ◀◀◀▼▼	▼ means 60
c 3	III	I means 1
15	XV	V means 5 / X means 10
144	CXLIV	C means 100 / XL means 40 / IV means 4

Now you try

Write each of the numbers 4, 23 and 142 using the given number systems.
a Egyptian   **b** Babylonian   **c** Roman

Exercise 1A

| FLUENCY | 1–5 | 1–6 | 4–6 |

Example 1a

1 Write the numbers 14 and 131 using the Egyptian number system.

Example 1b

2 Write the numbers 14 and 131 using the Babylonian number system.

Example 1c

3 Write the numbers 14 and 131 using the Roman number system.

Example 1

4 Write these numbers using the given number systems.
  a Egyptian
   i 3   **ii** 21   **iii** 114   **iv** 352
  b Babylonian
   i 4   **ii** 32   **iii** 61   **iv** 132
  c Roman
   i 2   **ii** 9   **iii** 24   **iv** 156

5 What number do these groups of symbols represent?
  a Egyptian
   i ∩∩∩lll   **ii** ℓ∩l
   iii ℓℓ∩lll   **iv** ℓℓ∩∩∩l
  b Babylonian
   i ◄▼▼   **ii** ◄◄▼▼▼
   iii ▼ ◄▼   **iv** ▼▼▼ ◄◄▼▼▼▼
  c Roman
   i IV   **ii** VIII
   iii XVI   **iv** XL

6 Work out the answer to each of these problems. Write your answer using the same number system that is given in the question.
  a XIV + XXII   **b** ℓℓ∩ll − ∩∩∩l
  c ▼ ◄▼▼▼ − ◄◄◄▼   **d** DCLXIX + IX

| PROBLEM-SOLVING | 7, 8 | 7–9 | 8–10 |

7 In ancient Babylon, a person adds ◄▼▼ goats to another group of ▼▼▼▼▼▼ goats.

How many goats are there in total? Write your answer using the Babylonian number system.

8 An ancient Roman counts the number of people in three queues. The first queue has XI, the second has LXII and the third has CXV. How many people are there in total? Write your answer using the Roman number system.

9   One Egyptian house is made from ℮℮℮∩|||||| stones and a second house is made from ℮℮∩∩∩| stones. How many more stones does the first house have? Write your answer using the Egyptian number system.

10   Which number system (Egyptian, Babylonian or Roman) uses the least number of symbols to represent these numbers?

a   55   b   60   c   3104

REASONING   11(½)   11(½), 12   11(½), 12, 13

11   In the Roman system, Is, Xs and Cs are used to reduce either of the next two larger numerals. So 9 is IX, not VIIII; and 49 is XLIX, not IL.

Also, only one numeral can be used to reduce another number. So 8 is VIII, not IIX.

Use this to write these numbers using Roman numerals.

a   4   b   9   c   14   d   19
e   29   f   41   g   49   h   89
i   99   j   449   k   922   l   3401

12   The Egyptian system generally uses more symbols to represent a number compared to other number systems.

Can you explain why? In the Egyptian system, how many symbols are used for the number 999?

13   In the Babylonian system, ▼ stands for 1, but because they did not use a symbol for zero at the end of a number, it also represents 60. People would know what it meant, depending on the situation it was used. Here is how it worked for large numbers. The dots represent empty spaces.

1   60   3600
▼   ▼.....   ▼..........

a   Write these numbers using the Babylonian system.
    i   12   ii   72   iii   120   iv   191   v   3661   vi   7224
b   Can you explain why ▼ .... represents 3600?
c   What would ▼ .... represent?

ENRICHMENT: Other number systems   –   –   14

14   Other well-known number systems include:
a   Mayan
b   modern Chinese
c   ancient Greek.
Look up these number systems on the internet or in other books. Write a brief sentence covering the points below.
i   When and where the number systems were used.
ii   What symbols were used.
iii   Examples of numbers using these symbols.

An ancient Mayan carving.

1B   Place value in Hindu–Arabic numbers

LEARNING INTENTIONS

• To understand how place value works in the Hindu–Arabic (decimal) number system
• To be able to identify the place value of digits in different numbers
• To be able to convert between basic numerals and their expanded form
• To be able to compare two positive integers by considering the digits and their place value

The commonly used number system today, called the decimal system or base 10, is also called the Hindu–Arabic number system. Like the Babylonian system, the value of the digit depends on its place in the number, but only one digit is used in each position. A digit for zero is also used. The decimal system originated in ancient India about 3000 BCE and spread throughout Europe through Arabic texts over the next 4000 years.

The famous 'Historie de la Mathematique', a French document showing the history of the Hindu–Arabic number system over thousands of years.

Lesson starter: Largest and smallest

Without using decimal points, repeated digits or a zero (0) at the start of a number, see if you can use all the digits 0, 1, 2, 3, 4, 5, 6, 7, 8, 9 to write down:

• the largest possible number
• the smallest possible number.

Can you explain why your numbers are, in fact, the largest or smallest possible?

KEY IDEAS

■ The Hindu–Arabic or **decimal system** uses base 10. This means powers of 10 (1, 10, 100, 1000, ...) are used to determine the place value of a digit in a number.

■ Indices can be used to write powers of 10.
$10 = 10^1$ $100 = 10^2$ $1000 = 10^3$ etc.

■ The symbols 0, 1, 2, 3, 4, 5, 6, 7, 8 and 9 are called **digits**.

■ Whole numbers greater than zero are called **positive integers**: 1, 2, 3, 4, …

■ The value of each digit depends on its place in the number. The **place value** of the digit 2 in the number 126, for example, is 20.

■ The **basic numeral** 3254 can be written in **expanded form** as $3 \times 1000 + 2 \times 100 + 5 \times 10 + 4 \times 1$.

thousands hundreds   tens   ones

$3\ 2\ 5\ 4 = 3 \times 1000 + 2 \times 100 + 5 \times 10 + 4 \times 1$

expanded form

■ Numbers can be written in expanded form using indices:
$$3254 = 3 \times 10^3 + 2 \times 10^2 + 5 \times 10^1 + 4 \times 1$$

■ Symbols used to compare numbers include the following:
$=$ (is equal to)	$1 + 3 = 4$	or	$10 - 7 = 3$
$\neq$ (is not equal to)	$1 + 3 \neq 5$	or	$11 + 38 \neq 50$
$>$ (is greater than)	$5 > 4$	or	$100 > 37$
$\geqslant$ (is greater than or equal to)	$5 \geqslant 4$	or	$4 \geqslant 4$
$<$ (is less than)	$4 < 5$	or	$13 < 26$
$\leqslant$ (is less than or equal to)	$4 \leqslant 5$	or	$4 \leqslant 4$
$\approx$ or $\doteq$ (is approximately equal to)	$4.02 \approx 4$	or	$8997 \doteq 9000$

BUILDING UNDERSTANDING

1 Choose one of the words 'ones', 'tens', 'hundreds' or 'thousands' to describe the 1 in each number.
a 100   **b** 1000   **c** 10   **d** 1

2 Which number using digits (next to the capital letters) matches the given numbers written in words?
A 10001   **B** 263   **C** 36015   **D** 7040201
E 7421   **F** 3615   **G** 2036   **H** 100001

a   two hundred and sixty-three

b   seven thousand four hundred and twenty-one

c   thirty-six thousand and fifteen

d   one hundred thousand and one

3 Which symbol (next to the capital letters) matches the given words?

a	is not equal to	A	$=$
b	is less than	B	$\neq$
c	is greater than or equal to	C	$>$
d	is equal to	D	$\geqslant$
e	is greater than	E	$<$
f	is less than or equal to	F	$\leqslant$
g	is approximately equal to	G	$\approx$

4 State whether each of these statements is true or false.

a $5 > 4$

b $6 = 10$

c $9 \neq 99$

d $1 < 12$

e $22 \leqslant 11$

f $126 \leqslant 126$

g $19 \geqslant 20$

h $138 > 137$

Example 2   Finding place value

Write down the place value of the digit 4 in these numbers.

a   437   b   543 910

SOLUTION

a $4 \times 100 = 400$

b $4 \times 10\,000 = 40\,000$

EXPLANATION

4 is worth 4×100

3 is worth 3×10

7 is worth 7×1

5 is worth $5 \times 100\,000$

4 is worth $4 \times 10\,000$

3 is worth 3×1000

9 is worth 9×100

1 is worth 1×10

Now you try

Write down the place value of the digit 7 in these numbers.

a   72   b   87 159

Example 3   Writing numbers in expanded form

a Write 517 in expanded form.

b Write 25 030 in expanded form.

SOLUTION

a $517 = 5 \times 100 + 1 \times 10 + 7 \times 1$

b $25\,030 = 2 \times 10\,000 + 5 \times 1000 + 0 \times 100 + 3 \times 10 + 0 \times 1$
$= 2 \times 10\,000 + 5 \times 1000 + 3 \times 10$

EXPLANATION

Write each digit separately and multiply by the appropriate power of 10.

Write each digit separately and multiply by the appropriate power of 10. Remove any term where zero is multiplied.

Now you try

a Write 2715 in expanded form.

b Write 40 320 in expanded form.

Example 4   Writing numbers in expanded form with index notation

Write the following numbers in expanded form with index notation.

a 7050

b 32 007

SOLUTION

a $7050 = 7 \times 10^3 + 5 \times 10^1$

b $32007 = 3 \times 10^4 + 2 \times 10^3 + 7 \times 1$

EXPLANATION

7050 includes 7 thousands $(7 \times 1000 = 7 \times 10^3)$, 0 hundreds, 5 tens $(5 \times 10 = 5 \times 10^1)$ and 0 ones.

The place value of the 3 is
$30\,000 = 3 \times 10\,000$
$\qquad\quad = 3 \times 10^4$

The place value of the 2 is
$2000 = 2 \times 1000$
$\qquad = 2 \times 10^3$

The place value of the 7 is $7 = 7 \times 1$.

Now you try

Write the following numbers in expanded form with index notation.

a 370

b 20 056

Exercise 1B

FLUENCY	1, 2–6(½)	2–7(½)	2–8(½)

Example 2

1 Write down the place value of the digit 4 in these numbers.
    a 943   **b** 7450

Example 2

2 Write down the place value of the digit 7 in these numbers.
    a 37   **b** 71   **c** 379   **d** 704
    e 1712   **f** 7001   **g** 45 720   **h** 170 966

Example 2

3 Write down the place value of the digit 2 in these numbers.
    a 126   **b** 2143   **c** 91 214   **d** 1 268 804

Example 3

4 Write these numbers in expanded form.
    a 17   **b** 281   **c** 935   **d** 20

Example 3

5 Write these numbers in expanded form.
    a 4491   **b** 2003   **c** 10 001   **d** 55 555

Example 4a

6 Write the following numbers in expanded form with index notation.
    a 3080   **b** 450   **c** 90 030   **d** 47 500

Example 4b

7 Write the following numbers in expanded form with index notation.
    a 42 009   **b** 3604   **c** 245   **d** 700 306

8 Write these numbers, given in expanded form, as a basic numeral.
    a $3 \times 100 + 4 \times 10 + 7 \times 1$
    b $9 \times 1000 + 4 \times 100 + 1 \times 10 + 6 \times 1$
    c $7 \times 1000 + 2 \times 10$
    d $6 \times 100\,000 + 3 \times 1$
    e $4 \times 1\,000\,000 + 3 \times 10\,000 + 7 \times 100$
    f $9 \times 10\,000\,000 + 3 \times 1000 + 2 \times 10$

PROBLEM-SOLVING	9	9(½), 10	10, 11

9 Arrange these numbers from smallest to largest.
    a 55, 45, 54, 44
    b 729, 29, 92, 927, 279
    c 23, 951, 136, 4
    d 435, 453, 534, 345, 543, 354
    e 12 345, 54 321, 34 512, 31 254
    f 1010, 1001, 10 001, 1100, 10 100

10 How many numbers can be made using the given digits? Digits are not allowed to be used more than once and all digits must be used.
    a 2, 8 and 9
    b 1, 6 and 7
    c 2, 5, 6 and 7

11 You are given three different non-zero digits, for example: 2, 5 and 8. How many three-digit numbers can be formed from your three given digits if digits can be used more than once? (For example, 522 and 825 are both possible if the original digits were 2, 5 and 8.)

REASONING		12	12	12, 13

12 The letters used here represent the digits of a number. Write each one in expanded form. For example, 7A2 means $7 \times 100 + A \times 10 + 2 \times 1$.

  a AB

  b ABCD

  c A0000A

13 By considering some of the other number systems (Egyptian, Babylonian or Roman) explained in the previous section, describe the main advantages of the Hindu–Arabic (decimal) system.

ENRICHMENT: Very large numbers		–	–	14

14 It is convenient to write very large numbers in expanded form with index notation.
Here is an example.
$50\,000\,000 = 5 \times 10\,000\,000 = 5 \times 10^7$

  a Explain why it is convenient to write large numbers in this type of expanded form.

  b 3200 can also be written in the form 32×10^2. All the non-zero digits are written down and then multiplied by a power of 10. Similarly, write each of these numbers in the same way.

   i 4100   **ii** 370 000   **iii** 21 770 000

  c Write each of these numbers as basic numerals.

   i 381×10^2 **ii** 7204×10^3 **iii** 1028×10^6

  d Write these numbers in expanded form, just as you did in the examples above. Research them if you do not know what they are.

   i 1 million

   ii 1 billion

   iii 1 trillion

   iv 1 googol

   v 1 googolplex

In 2008 in Zimbabwe, bank notes were issued in trillions of dollars, but soon became worthless due to inflation.

1C   Adding and subtracting positive integers

The process of finding the total value of two or more numbers is called addition. The words 'plus', 'add' and 'sum' are also used to describe addition.

The process for finding the difference between two numbers is called subtraction. The words 'minus', 'subtract' and 'take away' are also used to describe subtraction.

Lesson starter: Your mental strategy

A welder who is to join several lengths from a steel bar uses addition to calculate the total length, and uses subtraction to find the length of the steel that will be left over.

Many problems that involve addition and subtraction can be solved mentally without the use of a calculator or complicated written working.

Consider $98 + 22 - 31 + 29$

How would you work this out? What are the different ways it could be done mentally? Explain your method.

KEY IDEAS

■   The symbol + is used to show addition or find a sum.
    e.g. $4 + 3 = 7$

■ $a + b = b + a$ e.g. $4 + 3 = 3 + 4$
    *   This is the **commutative law** for addition, meaning that the order does not matter.

■ $a + (b + c) = (a + b) + c$ e.g. $4 + (11 + 3) = (4 + 11) + 3$
    *   This is called the **associative law** for addition, meaning that it does not matter which pair is added first.

■   The symbol − is used to show subtraction or find a difference.
    e.g. $7 - 2 = 5$

■ $a - b \neq b - a$ (in general)   e.g. $4 - 3 \neq 3 - 4$

■ $a - (b - c) \neq (a - b) - c$ (in general)   e.g. $8 - (4 - 2) \neq (8 - 4) - 2$

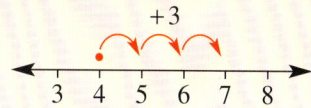

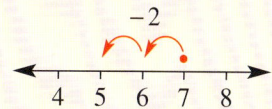

■ Mental addition and subtraction can be done using different strategies.
- **Partitioning** (grouping digits in the same position)

$$171 + 23 = 100 + (70 + 20) + (1 + 3)$$
$$= 194$$

- **Compensating** (making a 10, 100 etc. and then adjusting or compensating by adding or subtracting)

$$46 + 9 = 46 + 10 - 1$$
$$= 55$$

- **Doubling or halving** (making a double or half and then adjusting with addition or subtraction)

$$75 + 78 = 75 + 75 + 3 \qquad 124 - 61 = 124 - 62 + 1$$
$$= 150 + 3 \qquad\qquad\quad = 62 + 1$$
$$= 153 \qquad\qquad\qquad = 63$$

BUILDING UNDERSTANDING

1 **a** Give three other words that can mean the same as *addition*.
   b Give three other words that can mean the same as *subtraction*.

2 State the number which is:
   a 3 more than 7
   b 58 more than 11
   c 7 less than 19
   d 137 less than 157

3 **a** State the sum of 19 and 8.
   b State the difference between 29 and 13.

4 State whether each of these statements is true or false.
   a $4 + 3 > 6$
   b $11 + 19 \geqslant 30$
   c $13 - 9 < 8$
   d $26 - 15 \leqslant 10$
   e $1 + 7 - 4 \geqslant 4$
   f $50 - 21 + 6 < 35$

5 Give the result for each of the following.
   a 7 plus 11
   b 22 minus 3
   c the sum of 11 and 21
   d 128 add 12
   e 36 take away 15
   f the difference between 13 and 4

Example 5   Using mental strategies for addition and subtraction

Use the suggested strategy to mentally work out the answer.
a $132 + 156$ (partitioning)
b $25 + 19$ (compensating)
c $56 - 18$ (compensating)
d $35 + 36$ (doubling or halving)

SOLUTION

a $132 + 156 = 288$

EXPLANATION

$$\begin{array}{r} 100 + 30 + 2 \\ \underline{100 + 50 + 6} \\ 200 + 80 + 8 \end{array}$$

b $25 + 19 = 44$

$$25 + 19 = 25 + 20 - 1$$
$$= 45 - 1$$
$$= 44$$

c $56 - 18 = 38$

$$56 - 18 = 56 - 20 + 2$$
$$= 36 + 2$$
$$= 38$$

d $35 + 36 = 71$

$$35 + 36 = 35 + 35 + 1$$
$$= 70 + 1$$
$$= 71$$

Now you try

Use the suggested strategy to mentally work out the answer.

a $512 + 284$ (partitioning)

b $76 + 98$ (compensating)

c $42 - 19$ (compensating)

d $75 + 73$ (doubling or halving)

Exercise 1C

FLUENCY	1–5(½), 6	1–5(½), 7	2–5(½), 7(½)

Example 5a

1 Mentally find the answers to these sums. (*Hint:* Use the partitioning strategy.)

a $23 + 41$ **b** $71 + 26$ **c** $138 + 441$

d $246 + 502$ **e** $937 + 11$ **f** $1304 + 4293$

2 Mentally find the answers to these differences. (*Hint:* Use the partitioning strategy.)

a $29 - 18$ **b** $57 - 21$ **c** $249 - 137$

d $1045 - 1041$ **e** $4396 - 1285$ **f** $10\,101 - 100$

Example 5b

3 Mentally find the answers to these sums. (*Hint:* Use the compensating strategy.)

a $15 + 9$ **b** $64 + 11$ **c** $19 + 76$

d $18 + 115$ **e** $31 + 136$ **f** $245 + 52$

Example 5c

4 Mentally find the answers to these differences. (*Hint:* Use the compensating strategy.)

a $35 - 11$ **b** $45 - 19$ **c** $156 - 48$

d $244 - 22$ **e** $376 - 59$ **f** $5216 - 199$

Example 5d

5 Mentally find the answers to these sums and differences. (*Hint:* Use the doubling or halving strategy.)

a $25 + 26$ **b** $65 + 63$ **c** $121 + 123$

d $240 - 121$ **e** $482 - 240$ **f** $1006 - 504$

Example 5

6 Use the suggested strategy to mentally work out the answer.

a $123 + 145$ (partitioning)   **b** $36 + 29$ (compensating)

c $47 - 28$ (compensating)   **d** $55 + 56$ (doubling or halving)

7 Mentally find the answers to these mixed problems.

a $11 + 18 - 17$ **b** $37 - 19 + 9$ **c** $101 - 15 + 21$

d $136 + 12 - 15$ **e** $28 - 10 - 9 + 5$ **f** $39 + 71 - 10 - 10$

g $1010 - 11 + 21 - 1$ **h** $5 - 7 + 2$ **i** $10 - 25 + 18$

8   Gary worked 7 hours on Monday, 5 hours on Tuesday, 13 hours on Wednesday, 11 hours on Thursday and 2 hours on Friday. What is the total number of hours that Gary worked during the week?

9   In a batting innings, Phil hit 126 runs and Mario hit 19 runs. How many more runs did Phil hit compared to Mario?

10   A farmer reduced his cattle numbers from 86 to 54. How many cows were taken away?

11   Bag A has 18 marbles and bag B has 7 fewer marbles than bag A. What is the total number of marbles?

12   Matt has 36 cards and Andy has 35 more cards than Matt. If they combine their cards, how many do they have in total?

13   Each side on a magic triangle adds up to the same number, as shown in this example with a sum of 12 on each side.

    a   Place each of the digits from 1 to 6 in a magic triangle with three digits along each side so that each side adds up to the given number.

       i   9   **ii**   10

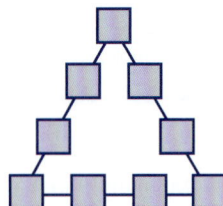

    b   Place each of the digits from 1 to 9 in a magic triangle with four digits along each side so that each side adds up to the given number.

       i   20   **ii**   23

14   **a**   The mental strategy of partitioning is easy to apply for $23 + 54$ but harder for $23 + 59$. Explain why.

      b   The mental strategy of partitioning is easy to apply for $158 - 46$ but harder for $151 - 46$. Explain why.

15   Complete these number sentences if the letters a, b and c represent numbers.

    a $a + b = c$ so $c -$ ___ $= a$ **b** $a + c = b$ so $b - a =$ ___

16   This magic triangle uses the digits 1 to 6, and has each side adding to the same total. This example shows a side total of 9.

    a   How many different side totals are possible using the same digits?

    b   Explain your method.

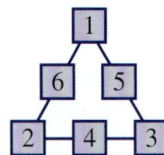

ENRICHMENT: Magic squares – – 17, 18

17 A magic square has every row, column and main diagonal adding to the same number, called the magic sum. For example, this magic square has a magic sum of 15.

4 9 2 →15
3 5 7 →15
8 1 6 →15
15 15 15 15 15

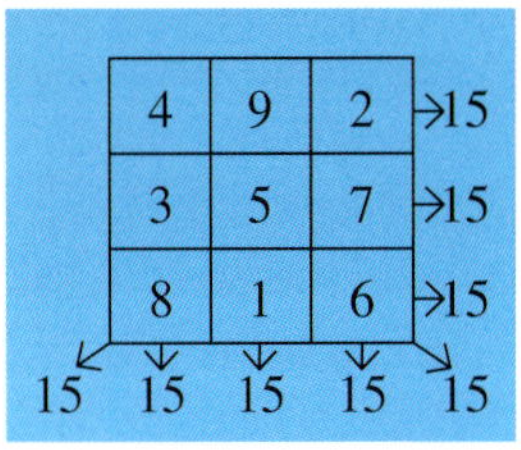

Find the magic sums for these squares, then fill in the missing numbers.

a

6		
7	5	
2		

b

10		
	11	13
		12

c

15	20	
14		
19		

d

1	15		4
	6		9
		11	
13		2	16

18 The sum of two numbers is 87 and their difference is 29. What are the two numbers?

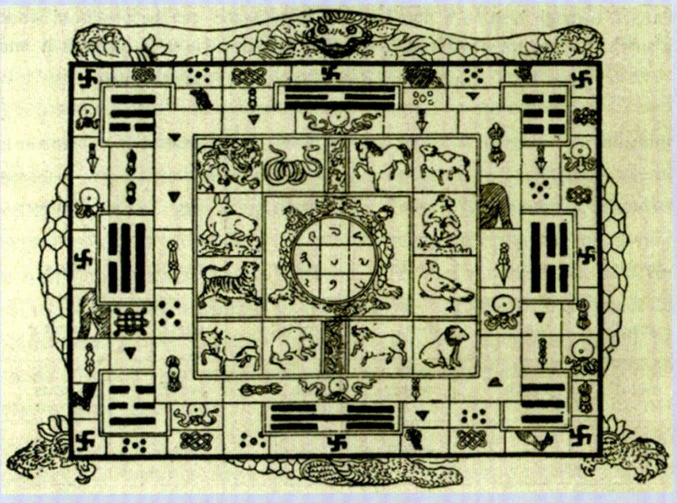

This magic square was known in ancient China as a 'Lo Shu' square and uses only the numbers 1 to 9. It is shown in the middle of this ancient design as symbols on a turtle shell, surrounded by the animals which represent the traditional Chinese names for the years.

1D Algorithms for adding and subtracting

It is not always practical to solve problems involving addition and subtraction mentally. For more complex problems a procedure involving a number of steps can be used and this helps to give the answer. Such a procedure is called an algorithm.

For the addition algorithm, if two digits add to more than 9, then the higher place value digit in the sum can be carried to the next column. For example, 10 ones can be renamed as 1 ten and carried into the tens column.

For the subtraction algorithm, if a larger digit is to be subtracted from a smaller digit in the ones column, 1 of the tens from the tens column can be renamed to form an extra 10 ones. This can be repeated where necessary in other place value columns.

A household's monthly power usage is found by subtracting consecutive end-of-month kWh (kilowatt-hour) readings, as displayed on its electricity meter. Adding these monthly amounts gives the power used per year.

Lesson starter: The missing digits

Discuss what numbers could go in the empty boxes.

Give reasons for your answers.

$$
\begin{array}{r}
1\ \square\ 4 \\
+\ 9\ 5\ \square \\
\hline
1\ \square\ 2\ 5
\end{array}
\qquad
\begin{array}{r}
\square\ 5\ \square \\
-\ 1\ \square\ 4 \\
\hline
9\ 4
\end{array}
$$

KEY IDEAS

■ An **algorithm** is a procedure involving a number of steps that eventually leads to the answer to a problem.

■ **Addition algorithm**
*   Arrange the numbers vertically so that the digits with similar place value are in the same column.
*   Add digits in the same column, starting on the right.
*   If the digits add to more than 9, carry the '10' to the next column.

$$
\begin{array}{r}
^{1}234 \\
+\ 192 \\
\hline
426
\end{array}
\qquad
\begin{array}{l}
4 + 2 = 6 \\
3 + 9 = 12 \\
1 + 2 + 1 = 4
\end{array}
$$

■ **Subtraction algorithm**
*   Arrange the numbers vertically so that the digits with similar place value are in the same column.

$$
\begin{array}{r}
^{1}\cancel{2}^{1}59 \\
-\ 1\ 82 \\
\hline
77
\end{array}
\qquad
\begin{array}{l}
9 - 2 = 7 \\
15 - 8 = 7 \\
1 - 1 = 0
\end{array}
$$

- Subtract digits in the same column top-down and starting on the right.
- If a larger digit is to be subtracted from a smaller digit in the ones column, 1 of the tens from the tens column can be renamed to form an extra 10 ones. This can be repeated where necessary in other place value columns.

■ Calculators could be used to check your answers.

BUILDING UNDERSTANDING

1 Mentally find the results to these simple sums.
   a 87 + 14   b 99 + 11   c 998 + 7   d 52 + 1053

2 Mentally find the results to these simple differences.
   a 36 − 9   b 100 − 16   c 37 − 22   d 1001 − 22

3 What is the missing number in these problems?

a
```
   3 6
 + 1 5
 ─────
   5 □
```
b
```
     4 6
 + □ 4
 ─────
   1 1 0
```
c
```
   6 7
 − 4 8
 ─────
 □ 9
```
d
```
   1 4 □ 2
 −   6 2 3
 ─────────
   8 0 9
```

Example 6   Using the addition algorithm

Give the result for each of these sums.

a
```
  26
+66
```
b
```
  439
+172
```

SOLUTION

a
```
 ¹26
+66
───
 92
```

b
```
 ¹4¹39
+1 72
─────
 6 11
```

EXPLANATION

Add the digits vertically.

6 + 6 = 12, so rename 10 of the 12 ones as 1 ten and carry this into the tens column.

9 + 2 = 11, so rename 10 of the 11 ones as 1 ten and carry this into the tens column.

1 + 3 + 7 = 11, so rename 10 of these 11 tens as 1 hundred and carry this extra 1 hundred into the hundreds column.

Now you try

Give the result for each of these sums.

a
```
  38
+54
```
b
```
  276
+459
```

Example 7   Using the subtraction algorithm

Give the result for each of these differences.

a
$$\begin{array}{r} 74 \\ -15 \\ \hline \end{array}$$

b
$$\begin{array}{r} 3240 \\ -2721 \\ \hline \end{array}$$

SOLUTION

a
$$\begin{array}{r} {}^{6}7\,{}^{1}4 \\ -1\ 5 \\ \hline 5\ 9 \end{array}$$

b
$$\begin{array}{r} {}^{2}3\,{}^{1}2\,{}^{3}4\,{}^{1}0 \\ -2\ 7\ 2\ 1 \\ \hline 5\ 1\ 9 \end{array}$$

EXPLANATION

Take 1 of the tens from 7 tens and rename it as 10 ones to make $14 - 5 = 9$.
Then subtract 1 ten from 6 tens (not 7 tens).

Take 1 of the tens from 4 tens and rename it as 10 ones to make $10 - 1 = 9$.
Subtract 2 from 3 (not 4).
Take 1 of the thousands from 3 thousands and rename it as 10 hundreds to make 12 hundreds.
12 hundreds $-$ 7 hundreds $= 5$ hundreds.
Note that 2 thousands $-$ 2 thousands $= 0$ thousands and you do not need to show a 0 before the 5.

Now you try

Give the result for each of these differences.

a
$$\begin{array}{r} 85 \\ -39 \\ \hline \end{array}$$

b
$$\begin{array}{r} 5470 \\ -3492 \\ \hline \end{array}$$

Exercise 1D

FLUENCY	1, 2–5(½)	2–6(½)	3–6(½)

Example 6

1 Give the result for each of these sums.

a
$$\begin{array}{r} 17 \\ +34 \\ \hline \end{array}$$

b
$$\begin{array}{r} 284 \\ +178 \\ \hline \end{array}$$

Example 6

2 Give the answer to each of these sums. Check your answer with a calculator.

a
$$\begin{array}{r} 36 \\ +51 \\ \hline \end{array}$$
b
$$\begin{array}{r} 74 \\ +25 \\ \hline \end{array}$$
c
$$\begin{array}{r} 17 \\ +24 \\ \hline \end{array}$$
d
$$\begin{array}{r} 47 \\ +39 \\ \hline \end{array}$$

e
$$\begin{array}{r} 129 \\ +\ 97 \\ \hline \end{array}$$
f
$$\begin{array}{r} 458 \\ +287 \\ \hline \end{array}$$
g
$$\begin{array}{r} 1041 \\ +\ 882 \\ \hline \end{array}$$
h
$$\begin{array}{r} 3092 \\ +1988 \\ \hline \end{array}$$

Example 6

3 Show your working to find the result for each of these sums.

a $85 + 76$ **b** $131 + 94$ **c** $1732 + 497$ **d** $988 + 987$

4   Give the result for each of these sums.

a
```
   17
   26
 +34
```

b
```
  126
   47
 + 19
```

c
```
  152
  247
 + 19
```

d
```
 2197
 1204
 + 807
```

e $946 + 241 + 27 + 9$

f $1052 + 839 + 7 + 84$

Example 7

5   Find the answers to these differences. Check your answer with a calculator.

a
```
  54
 −23
```

b
```
  85
 −65
```

c
```
  46
 −27
```

d
```
  94
 −36
```

e
```
  125
 − 89
```

f
```
  241
 −129
```

g
```
  358
 −279
```

h
```
  491
 −419
```

Example 7

6   Show your working to find the answer to each of these differences.

a $32 − 16$

b $124 − 77$

c $613 − 128$

d $1004 − 838$

PROBLEM-SOLVING	7, 8	8–10	9–11

7   Farmer Green owns 287 sheep, Farmer Brown owns 526 sheep and Farmer Grey owns 1041 sheep. How many sheep are there in total?

8   A car's odometer shows 12 138 kilometres at the start of a journey and 12 714 kilometres at the end of the journey. How far was the journey?

9   Two different schools have 871 and 950 students enrolled.

   a   How many students are there in total?

   b   Find the difference in the number of students between the schools.

10 Find the missing numbers in these sums.

a
```
   3 □
 + 5 3
 ─────
   □ 1
```

b
```
  1 □ 4
 +   7 □
 ───────
  □ 9 1
```

c
```
    □ □
 + □ 4 7
 ───────
   9 1 4
```

11 Find the missing numbers in these differences.

a
```
   6 □
 − 2 8
 ─────
   □ 4
```

b
```
  2 □ 5
 − □ 8 □
 ───────
    8 1
```

c
```
  3 □ □ 2
 −   9 2 □
 ─────────
  □ 1 6 5
```

REASONING   12   12, 13   12, 13

12 a Work out the answer to these simple problems.

  i $28 + 18 − 17$ **ii** $36 − 19 + 20$

  b For part **a i**, is it possible to work out $18 − 17$ and then add this total to 28?

  c For part **a ii**, is it possible to work out $19 + 20$ and then subtract this total from 36?

  d Can you suggest a good mental strategy for part **a ii** above that gives the correct answer?

13 a What are the missing digits in this sum?

  b Explain why there is more than one possible set of missing numbers in the sum given opposite. Give some examples.

```
  2 □ 3
+ □ □ □
───────
  4 2 1
```

ENRICHMENT: More magic squares   –   –   14–16

14 Complete these magic squares.

a

62	67	60
		65

b

101		114	
	106		109
	110		
113	103	102	116

15 The sum of two numbers is 978 and their difference is 74. What are the two numbers?

16 Make up some of your own problems like Question **15** and test them on a friend.

1E Multiplying small positive integers

LEARNING INTENTIONS
- To understand the commutative and associative laws for multiplication
- To be able to use mental strategies to find products
- To be able to apply the multiplication algorithm to find the product of a single digit number by a positive integer

The multiplication of two numbers represents a repeated addition.

For example, 4×2 could be thought of as 4 groups of 2 or $2 + 2 + 2 + 2$.

Similarly, 4×2 could be thought of as 2 groups of 4 or 2×4 or $4 + 4$.

4×2 ∶∶∶∶

2×4 ∶∶
∶∶
∶∶

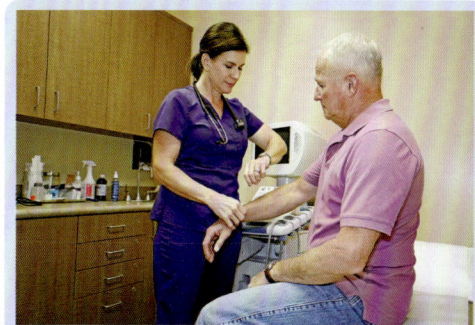

To estimate a patient's heart rate in beats per minute, a nurse counts the number of heart beats in 15 seconds and multiplies that number by 4.

Lesson starter: Are these mental strategies correct?

Three students explain their method for finding the answer to 124×8.

- Billy says that you can do 124×10 to get 1240, then subtract 2 to get 1238.
- Lea says that you halve 124 and 8 twice each to give $31 \times 2 = 62$.
- Surai says that you multiply 8 by 4 to give 32, 8 by 2 to give 16 and 8 by 1 to give 8. She says the total is therefore $32 + 16 + 8 = 56$.

Are any of the students correct and can you explain any errors in their thinking?

KEY IDEAS

■ Finding the **product** of two numbers involves multiplication. We say 'the product of 2 and 3 is 6'.

■ $a \times b = b \times a$ e.g. $2 \times 3 = 3 \times 2$
  - This is the **commutative law** for multiplication, meaning that the order does not matter.

■ $(a \times b) \times c = a \times (b \times c)$ e.g. $(3 \times 5) \times 4 = 3 \times (5 \times 4)$
  - This is the **associative law** for multiplication, meaning it does not matter which pair is multiplied first.

■ The multiplication algorithm for multiplying by a single digit involves:

$$\begin{array}{r} {}^{1}23 \\ \times\ \ 4 \\ \hline 92 \end{array}$$ $4 \times 3 = 12$
$4 \times 20 + 10 = 90$

- Multiplying the single digit by each digit in the other number, starting from the right.
- Carrying and adding any digits with a higher place value to the total in the next column.

■ Mental strategies for multiplication include:
- Knowing your multiplication tables off by heart.

$9 \times 7 = 63$ $12 \times 4 = 48$

- Using the commutative law by changing the order. For example, 43×2 might be thought of more easily as 2 groups of 43 or 2×43.
- Using the commutative and associative law by altering the order if more than one number is being multiplied.

$$\begin{aligned} 5 \times 11 \times 2 &= 5 \times 2 \times 11 \\ &= 10 \times 11 \\ &= 110 \end{aligned}$$

- Using the **distributive law** by making a 10, 100 etc. and then adjusting by adding or subtracting. The distributive law is:
$a \times (b + c) = (a \times b) + (a \times c)$ or $a \times (b - c) = (a \times b) - (b \times c)$.
This law will be used more extensively when algebra is covered.

$$\begin{aligned} 6 \times 21 &= (6 \times 20) + (6 \times 1) \\ &= 120 + 6 \\ &= 126 \end{aligned} \qquad \begin{aligned} 7 \times 18 &= (7 \times 20) - (7 \times 2) \\ &= 140 - 14 \\ &= 126 \end{aligned}$$

- Using the doubling and halving strategy by doubling one number and halving the other.
- Using factors to split a number.

$$\begin{aligned} 15 \times 18 &= 30 \times 9 \\ &= 270 \end{aligned}$$
$$\begin{aligned} 11 \times 16 &= 11 \times 8 \times 2 \\ &= 88 \times 2 \\ &= 176 \end{aligned}$$

BUILDING UNDERSTANDING

1 State the next three numbers in these patterns.
   a 4, 8, 12, 16, __   **b** 11, 22, 33, __   **c** 17, 34, 51, __

2 Are these statements true or false?
   a $4 \times 3 = 3 \times 4$ **b** $2 \times 5 \times 6 = 6 \times 5 \times 2$
   c $11 \times 5 = 10 \times 6$ **d** $3 \times 32 = 3 \times 30 + 3 \times 2$
   e $5 \times 18 = 10 \times 9$ **f** $21 \times 4 = 2 \times 42$
   g $19 \times 7 = 20 \times 7 - 19$ **h** $64 \times 4 = 128 \times 8$

3 What is the missing digit in these products?

a
$$\begin{array}{r} 2\ 1 \\ \times\ \ \ 3 \\ \hline 6\ \Box \end{array}$$

b
$$\begin{array}{r} 3\ 6 \\ \times\ \ \ 5 \\ \hline 1\ 8\ \Box \end{array}$$

c
$$\begin{array}{r} 7\ 6 \\ \times\ \ \ 2 \\ \hline 1\ \Box\ 2 \end{array}$$

d
$$\begin{array}{r} 4\ 0\ 2 \\ \times\ \ \ \ \ 3 \\ \hline 1\ \Box\ 0\ 6 \end{array}$$

Example 8   Using mental strategies for multiplication

Use a mental strategy to find the answer to each of these products.

a 7×6 **b** 3×13 **c** 4×29

d 5×24 **e** 7×14

SOLUTION

a $7 \times 6 = 42$

b $3 \times 13 = 39$

c $4 \times 29 = 116$

d $5 \times 24 = 120$

e $7 \times 14 = 98$

EXPLANATION

7×6 or 6×7 should be memorised (from multiplication tables).

$3 \times 13 = (3 \times 10) + (3 \times 3) = 30 + 9 = 39$
(The distributive law is being used.)

$4 \times 29 = (4 \times 30) - (4 \times 1) = 120 - 4 = 116$
(The distributive law is being used.)

$5 \times 24 = 10 \times 12 = 120$
(The doubling and halving strategy is being used.)

$7 \times 14 = 7 \times 7 \times 2 = 49 \times 2 = 98$
(Factors of 14 are used.)

Now you try

Use a mental strategy to find the answer to each of these products.

a 8×4 **b** 6×21 **c** 4×19

d 5×42 **e** 12×25

Example 9   Using the multiplication algorithm

Give the result for each of these products.

a 31×4 **b** 197×7

SOLUTION

a
$$\begin{array}{r} 31 \\ \times \ \ 4 \\ \hline 124 \end{array}$$

b
$$\begin{array}{r} 6\,1^{4}9\,7 \\ \times \ \ \ \ 7 \\ \hline 1\,3\,7\,9 \end{array}$$

EXPLANATION

$4 \times 1 = 4$
$4 \times 3 = 12$
$4 \times 30 = 120$
$4 + 120 = 124$

$7 \times 7 = 49$ (7 times 9 tens plus the carried 4 tens makes 67 tens. Regroup 60 tens as 6 hundreds and carry 6 into the hundreds column)

$7 \times 9 + 4 = 67$ (7 hundreds plus the carried 6 hundreds makes 13 hundreds)

$7 \times 1 + 6 = 13$

Now you try

Give the result for each of these products.

a 42×7 **b** 372×8

Exercise 1E

FLUENCY	1, 2–5(½)	2–6(½)	3–6(½)

Example 8a

1 Using your knowledge of multiplication tables, give the answer to these products.
 a 3×5 b 8×4 c 6×6 d 9×3
 e 7×4 f 4×9 g 8×7 h 5×8

Example 8b,c

2 Find the results to these products mentally. (*Hint*: Use the distributive law strategy (addition) for **a** to **d** and the distributive law strategy (subtraction) for **e** to **h**.)
 a 5×21 b 4×31 c 6×42 d 53×3
 e 3×19 f 6×29 g 4×28 h 38×7

Example 8d,e

3 Find the answer to these products mentally. (*Hint*: Use the double and halve strategy or split a number using its factors.)
 a 4×24 b 3×18 c 6×16 d 24×3

Example 8

4 Use a suitable mental strategy to find the answer to each of these products.
 a 8×7 b 4×13 c 3×29 d 4×52 e 9×14

Example 9

5 Give the result of each of these products, using the multiplication algorithm. Check your results using a calculator.

 a $\begin{array}{r} 33 \\ \times\ \ 2 \\ \hline \end{array}$ b $\begin{array}{r} 43 \\ \times\ \ \ 3 \\ \hline \end{array}$ c $\begin{array}{r} 72 \\ \times\ \ 6 \\ \hline \end{array}$ d $\begin{array}{r} 55 \\ \times\ \ 3 \\ \hline \end{array}$

 e $\begin{array}{r} 129 \\ \times\ \ 2 \\ \hline \end{array}$ f $\begin{array}{r} 407 \\ \times\ \ 7 \\ \hline \end{array}$ g $\begin{array}{r} 526 \\ \times\ \ 5 \\ \hline \end{array}$ h $\begin{array}{r} 3509 \\ \times\ \ \ \ 9 \\ \hline \end{array}$

Example 9

6 Find the answer to these products, showing your working.
 a 47×5 b 1391×3 c 9×425 d 7×4170

PROBLEM-SOLVING	7, 8	8–10	9–11

7 Eight tickets costing $33 each are purchased for a concert. What is the total cost of the tickets?

8 A circular race track is 240 metres long and Rory runs seven laps. How far does Rory run in total?

9 Reggie and Angelo combine their packs of cards. Reggie has five sets of 13 cards and Angelo has three sets of 17 cards. How many cards are there in total?

10 Sala purchases some goods for a party at an outlet store and has $100 to spend. She selects eight bottles of drink for $2 each, 13 food packs at $6 each and 18 party hats at 50 cents each. Does she have enough money to pay for all the items?

11 Find the missing digits in these products.

a
```
    3 9
  ×   7
  ─────
  2 □ 3
```

b
```
    2 5
  ×   □
  ─────
  1 2 5
```

c
```
    7 9
  ×   □
  ─────
  □ 3 7
```

d
```
  1 3 2
  ×   □
  ──────
 10 □ 6
```

e
```
    2 □
  ×   7
  ─────
  □ 8 9
```

f
```
   □ □
 ×    9
 ──────
 3 5 1
```

g
```
   2 3 □
 ×     5
 ───────
 1 □ 6 0
```

h
```
  □ □   4
 ×     □
 ────────
 □ 1 9 8
```

12 The commutative and associative laws for multiplication mean that numbers can be multiplied in any order. So $(a \times b) \times c = (b \times a) \times c = b \times (a \times c) =$ _____, where the brackets show which numbers are multiplied first. Two ways of calculating $2 \times 3 \times 5$ are $(2 \times 3) \times 5 = 6 \times 5$ and $3 \times (5 \times 2) = 3 \times 10$. Including these two ways, how many ways can $2 \times 3 \times 5$ be calculated?

13 The distributive law can help to work out products mentally.
For example, $7 \times 31 = (7 \times 30) + (7 \times 1) = 210 + 7 = 217$

Write each of the following as single products. Do not find the answer.

a $3 \times 20 + 3 \times 1$

b $9 \times 50 + 9 \times 2$

c $7 \times 30 + 7 \times 2$

d $5 \times 100 - 5 \times 3$

e $a \times 40 - a \times 2$

f $a \times 200 + a \times 3$

14 How many different ways can the two spaces be filled in this problem? Explain your reasoning.
```
   2 □ 3
 ×     4
 ───────
   8 □ 2
```

15 Find all the missing digits in these products.

a
```
   □ 1 □
 ×     7
 ───────
 □ 5 1 □
```

b
```
   2 9 □
 ×     3
 ───────
 8 □ □
```

16 The product of two numbers is 132 and their sum is 28. What are the two numbers?

Progress quiz

1A

1 Write the number 134 using the given number systems.

   a Egyptian

   b Roman

   c Babylonian

1B

2 Write the number 50862 in expanded form.

1C

3 Use the suggested strategy to mentally work out the answer.

   a $143 + 232$ (partitioning)

   b $35 + 29$ (compensating)

   c $74 - 17$ (compensating)

   d $35 + 36$ (doubling)

1D

4 Give the result for each of these problems.

   a
$$\begin{array}{r} 18 \\ +44 \\ \hline \end{array}$$

   b
$$\begin{array}{r} 124 \\ -\ 46 \\ \hline \end{array}$$

1E

5 Using your knowledge of multiplication tables, give the answer to these products.

   a 7×4 **b** 9×8

   c 12×9 **d** 5×9

1E

6 Use the distributive law strategy to find the answer to each of these products. Show your working.

   a 6×14 **b** 5×39

1E

7 Give the result of each of these products, using the multiplication algorithm. Show your working.

   a
$$\begin{array}{r} 84 \\ \times\ \ 3 \\ \hline \end{array}$$

   b
$$\begin{array}{r} 237 \\ \times\ \ 4 \\ \hline \end{array}$$

   c 2146×7

1D

8 Two different schools have 948 and 1025 students enrolled.

   a How many students are there in total?

   b Find the difference in the number of students between the schools.

1C

9 Decide if the following statements are always true (T), always false (F) or sometimes true/sometimes false (S), if a, b and c represent three different numbers.

   a $a + b = b + a$

   b $a \times b = b \times a$

   c $a - b = b - a$

   d $a \times (b + c) = a \times b + a \times c$

   e $(a + b) + c = a + (b + c)$

   f $(a - b) - c = a - (b - c)$

1F Multiplying large positive integers

LEARNING INTENTIONS

- To be able to multiply by a power of ten by adding zeros to the end of a number
- To be able to apply the multiplication algorithm to find the product of any two positive integers

There are many situations that require the multiplication of large numbers – for example, the total revenue from selling 40 000 tickets at $23 each, or the area of a rectangular park with length and width dimensions of 65 metres by 122 metres. To complete such calculations by hand requires the use of a suitable algorithm.

How much revenue came from selling tickets to this game?

Lesson starter: Spot the errors

There are three types of errors in the working shown for this problem. Find the errors and describe them.

$$
\begin{array}{r}
271 \\
\times\ \ 13 \\
\hline
613 \\
271 \\
\hline
1273
\end{array}
$$

KEY IDEAS

■ When multiplying by 10, 100, 1000, 10 000 etc. each digit appears to move to the left by the number of zeros. For example, $45 \times 1000 = 45\,000$.

■ A strategy for multiplying by multiples of 10, 100 etc. is to first multiply by the number without the zeros then insert the zeros at the end of the product.
  For example, $21 \times 3000 = 21 \times 3 \times 1000 = 63 \times 1000 = 63\,000$

■ The algorithm for multiplying large numbers involves separating the problem into smaller products and then adding the totals.

$$
\begin{array}{r}
143 \\
\times\ \ 14 \\
\hline
{}^{1}572 \quad \leftarrow 143 \times 4 \\
1430 \quad \leftarrow 143 \times 10 \\
\hline
2002 \quad \leftarrow 1430 + 572
\end{array}
$$

BUILDING UNDERSTANDING

1 What is the missing digit in these products?
  a $72 \times 10 = 7 \square 0$

  b $13 \times 100 = 130 \square$

  c $49 \times 100 = 49 \square 0$

  d $924 \times 10 = 92 \square 0$

2 What is the missing number in these products?
  a $15 \times \_\_ = 1500$

  b $329 \times \_\_ = 3290$

  c $92 \times \_\_ = 920\,000$

3 State if the following calculations are correct. If they are incorrect, find the correct answer.

How could you estimate the number of pieces of fruit and vegetables on this stall without counting them all?

a	**b**	**c**	**d**
26	39	92	102
× 4	× 14	× 24	× 24
84	156	368	408
	39	1840	240
	195	2208	648

Example 10   Multiplying large numbers

Give the result for each of these products.
  a 37×100
  b 45×70
  c 614×14

SOLUTION

a $37 \times 100 = 3700$

b $45 \times 70 = 45 \times 7 \times 10$
$= 315 \times 10$
$= 3150$

c
```
    614
 ×   14
   2456
   6140
   8596
```

EXPLANATION

Move the 3 and the 7 two places to the left, so the 3 moves into the thousands place and the 7 moves into the hundreds place. Insert two zeros at the end of the number (in the tens and ones places).

First multiply by 7 then multiply by 10 later.
```
    45
 ×   7
   315
```

First multiply 614×4.
Then multiply 614×10.
Add the totals to give the answer.

Now you try

Give the result for each of these products.
  a 23×1000
  b 73×40
  c 752×23

Exercise 1F

| FLUENCY | 1, 2–3(½), 4 | 1–3(½), 4 | 2–3(½), 4, 5 |

Example 10a

1 Give the result for each of these products.

a 4×100 b 29×10 c 183×10 d 46×100

e 50×1000 f 630×100 g 1441×10 h $2910 \times 10\,000$

Example 10b

2 Give the result for each of these products.

a 17×20 b 36×40 c 92×70 d 45×500

e 138×300 f 92×5000 g 317×200 h 1043×9000

Example 10c

3 Use the multiplication algorithm to find these products.

a $\begin{array}{r} 37 \\ \times\, 11 \\ \hline \end{array}$ b $\begin{array}{r} 72 \\ \times\, 19 \\ \hline \end{array}$ c $\begin{array}{r} 126 \\ \times\ \ 15 \\ \hline \end{array}$ d $\begin{array}{r} 428 \\ \times\ \ \ 22 \\ \hline \end{array}$

e $\begin{array}{r} 396 \\ \times\ \ \ 46 \\ \hline \end{array}$ f $\begin{array}{r} 416 \\ \times\ \ \ 98 \\ \hline \end{array}$ g $\begin{array}{r} 380 \\ \times\ \ \ 49 \\ \hline \end{array}$ h $\begin{array}{r} 1026 \\ \times\ \ \ \ 33 \\ \hline \end{array}$

Example 10a,c

4 Give the result for each of these products.

a i 43×10 ii 72×1000

b i 71×20 ii 26×300

c i 124×12 ii 382×15

5 First estimate the answers to these products, then use a calculator to see how close you were.

a 19×11 b 26×21 c 37×15 d 121×18

| PROBLEM-SOLVING | 6, 7 | 7–9 | 8–10 |

6 A pool area includes 68 square metres of paving at \$32 per square metre. Find the value of 68×32 to state the total cost of the paving.

7 Waldo buys 215 metres of pipe at \$28 per metre. What is the total cost of the piping?

8 How many seconds are there in one 24-hour day?

9 Find the missing digits in these products.

a
```
    2 ☐
  ×  1 7
   1 ☐ 1
   2 ☐ 0
  ☐☐ 1
```

b
```
    1 ☐ 3
  ×   1 ☐
   ☐ 2 9
   1 ☐ 3 ☐
  ☐☐ 5 ☐
```

c
```
    ☐☐
  ×  3 7
    3 4 3
  ☐ 4 ☐☐
  ☐☐☐☐
```

d
```
    ☐ 2 ☐
  ×   2 ☐
    1 2 6
  ☐ 5 2 ☐
  ☐ 6 ☐☐
```

10 There are 360 degrees in a full turn. How many degrees does the minute hand on a clock turn in one week?

REASONING   11   11, 12(½)   12(½), 13

11 The product of two positive integers is less than their sum. What must be true about one of the numbers?

12 If both numbers in a multiplication problem have at least three digits, then the algorithm needs to be expanded. Use the algorithm to find these products.

a 294
   × 136

b 1013
   × 916

c 3947
   × 1204

d 47126
   × 3107

13 Can you work out these computations using an effective mental strategy? Look to see if you can first simplify each question.
  a $98 \times 16 + 2 \times 16$
  b $33 \times 26 - 3 \times 26$
  c $19 \times 15 + 34 \times 17 - 4 \times 17 + 1 \times 15$
  d $22 \times 19 - 3 \times 17 + 51 \times 9 - 1 \times 9 + 13 \times 17 - 2 \times 19$

ENRICHMENT: Multiplication puzzle   –   –   14, 15

14 a What is the largest number you can make by choosing five different digits from the list 1, 2, 3, 4, 5, 6, 7, 8, 9 and placing them into the product shown at right?
  b What is the smallest number you can make by choosing five different digits from the list 1, 2, 3, 4, 5, 6, 7, 8, 9 and placing them into the product shown at right?

```
  ☐☐☐
× ☐☐
```

15 The product of two whole numbers is 14391 and their difference is 6. What are the two numbers?

1G Dividing positive integers

Division involves finding the number of equal groups into which a particular number can be divided. This can be achieved both with and without a remainder or 'left over'. Dividing 20 apples among five people and dividing $10000 between three bank accounts are examples of when division can be used.

Multiplication and division are reverse operations, and this is shown in this simple example:

$7 \times 3 = 21$ So, $21 \div 3 = 7$ and $21 \div 7 = 3$

To calculate the number of rafters needed to support a roof, a carpenter first divides the roof span (its length) by the required space between each rafter.

Lesson starter: Arranging counters

A total of 24 counters sit on a table. Using whole numbers, in how many ways can the counters be divided into equal-sized groups with no counters remaining?

- Is it also possible to divide the counters into equal-sized groups but with two counters remaining?
- If five counters are to remain, how many equal-sized groups can be formed and why?

KEY IDEAS

■ The number of equal-sized groups formed from the division operation is called the **quotient**.

■ The total being divided is called the **dividend** and the size of the equal groups is called the **divisor**.

■ Any amount remaining after division into equal-sized groups is called the **remainder**.

$7 \div 3 = 2$ and 1 remainder means
$7 = 2 \times 3 + 1$
$37 \div 5 = 7$ and 2 remainder means
$37 = 7 \times 5 + 2$

$7 \div 3 = 2$ and 1 remainder $= 2\frac{1}{3}$

total being divided
(dividend)

size of equal
groups (divisor)

quotient

■ $a \div b$ and $b \div a$ are not generally equal.
- The commutative law does not hold for division, e.g. $8 \div 2 \neq 2 \div 8$

■ $(a \div b) \div c$ and $a \div (b \div c)$ are not generally equal.
- The associative law does not hold for division, e.g. $(8 \div 4) \div 2 \neq 8 \div (4 \div 2)$

■ The short division algorithm involves first dividing into the digit with the highest place value and then carrying any remainder to the next digit, working from left to right.
$413 \div 3 = 137$ and 2 remainder
$= 137\frac{2}{3}$

$4 \div 3 = 1$ and 1 rem.

$11 \div 3 = 3$ and 2 rem.

$23 \div 3 = 7$ and 2 rem.

$$\begin{array}{r} 1\ 3\ 7 \\ 3\overline{)4^1 1^2 3} \end{array}$$

■ Mental division can be done using different strategies.
- Knowing your multiplication tables off by heart.
  $63 \div 9 = ?$ is the same as asking $9 \times ? = 63$.
- Making a convenient multiple of the divisor and then adjusting by adding or subtracting. Below is an application of the distributive law.

$$\begin{aligned} 84 \div 3 &= (60 + 24) \div 3 \\ &= (60 \div 3) + (24 \div 3) \\ &= 20 + 8 \\ &= 28 \end{aligned} \qquad \begin{aligned} 84 \div 3 &= (90 - 6) \div 3 \\ &= (90 \div 3) - (6 \div 3) \\ &= 30 - 2 \\ &= 28 \end{aligned}$$

- Halving both numbers. If both numbers in the division are even, then halve both numbers.

$$\begin{aligned} 70 \div 14 &= 35 \div 7 \\ &= 5 \end{aligned}$$

BUILDING UNDERSTANDING

1 State the number that is missing in these statements.
a $8 \div 2 = 4$ is the same as $4 \times ? = 8$.
b $36 \div 12 = 3$ is the same as $? \times 12 = 36$.
c $42 \div ? = 6$ is the same as $6 \times 7 = 42$.
d $72 \div 6 = ?$ is the same as $12 \times 6 = 72$.

2 What is the remainder when:
a   2 is divided into 7?
b   5 is divided into 37?
c   42 is divided by 8?
d   50 is divided by 9?

3 State the missing digit in each of these divisions.

a
$$\begin{array}{r} \square\,7 \\ 3\overline{)5\ \ 1} \end{array}$$

b
$$\begin{array}{r} \square\,2 \\ 7\overline{)8\ \ 4} \end{array}$$

c
$$\begin{array}{r} 2\,\square \\ 5\overline{)12\ \ 5} \end{array}$$

d
$$\begin{array}{r} 1\,\square \\ 9\overline{)13\ \ 5} \end{array}$$

Example 11   Using mental strategies for division

Use a mental strategy to find the quotient.

a $84 \div 7$ **b** $93 \div 3$ **c** $128 \div 8$

SOLUTION

a $84 \div 7 = 12$

b $93 \div 3 = 31$

c $128 \div 8 = 16$

EXPLANATION

$7 \times ? = 84$

(Use your knowledge from multiplication tables.)

$93 \div 3 = (90 \div 3) + (3 \div 3) = 30 + 1$

(This uses the distributive law.)

$128 \div 8 = 64 \div 4 = 32 \div 2 = 16$

(Halve both numbers repeatedly.)

Now you try

Use a mental strategy to find the quotient.

a $36 \div 9$ **b** $484 \div 4$ **c** $520 \div 8$

Example 12   Using the short division algorithm

Use the short division algorithm to find the quotient and remainder.

a $3\overline{)37}$ **b** $7\overline{)195}$

SOLUTION

a
$$\begin{array}{r} 12 \\ 3\overline{)37} \end{array}$$

$37 \div 3 = 12$ and 1 remainder.
$$= 12\frac{1}{3}$$

b
$$\begin{array}{r} 27 \\ 7\overline{)19^{5}5} \end{array}$$

$195 \div 7 = 27$ and 6 remainder.
$$= 27\frac{6}{7}$$

EXPLANATION

$3 \div 3 = 1$ with no remainder.

$7 \div 3 = 2$ with 1 remainder.

7 does not divide into 1.

$19 \div 7 = 2$ with 5 remainder.

$55 \div 7 = 7$ with 6 remainder.

Now you try

Use the short division algorithm to find the quotient and remainder.

a $4\overline{)93}$ **b** $6\overline{)435}$

Exercise 1G

FLUENCY	1–3($\frac{1}{2}$), 4, 6($\frac{1}{2}$)	1–3($\frac{1}{2}$), 4, 5–7($\frac{1}{2}$)	4, 5, 6–7($\frac{1}{2}$)

Example 11a

1   Use your knowledge of multiplication tables to find the quotient.
   a $28 \div 7$ b $36 \div 12$ c $48 \div 8$ d $45 \div 9$
   e $42 \div 6$ f $63 \div 7$ g $40 \div 5$ h $44 \div 4$

Example 11b

2   Find the answer to these using a mental strategy. (*Hint:* Use the distributive law strategy.)
   a $63 \div 3$ b $88 \div 4$ c $96 \div 3$ d $515 \div 5$
   e $287 \div 7$ f $189 \div 9$ g $906 \div 3$ h $305 \div 5$

Example 11c

3   Find the answers to these using a mental strategy. (*Hint:* Use the halving strategy by halving both numbers.)
   a $88 \div 4$ b $124 \div 4$ c $136 \div 8$ d $112 \div 16$

Example 11

4   Use a suitable mental strategy to find the quotient.
   a $48 \div 4$ b $81 \div 9$ c $63 \div 3$
   d $105 \div 5$ e $120 \div 4$ f $256 \div 16$

5   Write the answers to these divisions, which involve 0s and 1s.
   a $26 \div 1$ b $1094 \div 1$ c $0 \div 7$ d $0 \div 458$

Example 12

6   Use the short division algorithm to find the quotient and remainder.
   a $3\overline{)71}$ b $7\overline{)92}$ c $2\overline{)139}$ d $6\overline{)247}$
   e $4\overline{)2173}$ f $3\overline{)61\,001}$ g $5\overline{)4093}$ h $9\overline{)90\,009}$

Example 12

7   Use the short division algorithm to find the quotient and remainder.
   a $525 \div 4$ b $1691 \div 7$ c $2345 \div 6$ d $92\,337 \div 8$

PROBLEM-SOLVING	8, 9	9–12	12–14

8   If 36 food packs are divided equally among nine families, how many packs does each family receive?

9   Spring Fresh Company sells mineral water in packs of six bottles. How many packs are there in a truck containing 642 bottles?

10   A bricklayer earns \$1215 in a week.
   a   How much does he earn per day if he works Monday to Friday?
   b   How much does he earn per hour if he works 9 hours per day?

11   A straight fence has two end posts as well as other posts that are divided evenly along the fence 4 metres apart. If the fence is to be 264 metres long, how many posts are needed, including the end posts?

12   Friendly Taxis can take up to four passengers each. What is the minimum number of taxis required to transport 59 people?

13   A truck can carry up to 7 tonnes of rock in one trip. What is the minimum number of trips needed to transport 130 tonnes of rock?

14 All the rows, columns and main diagonals in the magic square multiply to give 216. Can you find the missing numbers?

	9	12
		1

REASONING   15, 16   15–17   18, 19, 20(½)

15 Write down the missing numbers.

a $37 \div 3 = 12$ and $\boxed{}$ remainder means $37 = \boxed{} \times 3 + 1$

b $96 \div 7 = \boxed{}$ and 5 remainder means $96 = 13 \times \boxed{} + 5$

c $104 \div 20 = 5$ and $\boxed{}$ remainder means $104 = \boxed{} \times 20 + 4$

16 Pies are purchased wholesale at 9 for $4. How much will it cost to purchase 153 pies?

17 Give the results to these problems, if a represents any positive integer.

a $a \div a$ b $0 \div a$ c $a \div 1$

18 A number less than 30 leaves a remainder of 3 when divided by 5 and a remainder of 2 when divided by 3. What two numbers meet the given conditions?

19 As you know $a \div b$ is not generally equal to $b \div a$. However, can you find a situation where $a \div b$ and $b \div a$ are equal? Try to find as many as possible.

20 The short division algorithm can also be used to divide by numbers with more than one digit.

e.g. $215 \div 12 = 17$ and 11 remainder.

$21 \div 12 = 1$ and 9 remainder.

$95 \div 12 = 7$ and 11 remainder.

$$\begin{array}{r} 1\ 7 \\ 12\overline{)21^95} \end{array}$$

Use the short division algorithm to find the quotient and remainder.

a $371 \div 11$ b $926 \div 17$ c $404 \div 13$

d $1621 \div 15$ e $2109 \div 23$ f $6913 \div 56$

ENRICHMENT: Long, short division   –   –   21, 22(½)

21 The magic product for this square is 6720. Find the missing numbers.

22 Instead of carrying out a complex division algorithm, you could convert the divisor into a smaller pair of factors and complete two simpler division questions to arrive at the correct answer.

1	6		56
40		2	3
14			
			10

For example:

$$\begin{aligned} 1458 \div 18 &= (1458 \div 2) \div 9 \\ &= 729 \div 9 \\ &= 81 \end{aligned}$$

Use factors to help you calculate the following.

a $555 \div 15$ b $860 \div 20$ c $3600 \div 48$

d $1456 \div 16$ e $6006 \div 42$ f $2024 \div 22$

The following problems will investigate practical situations drawing upon knowledge and skills developed throughout the chapter. In attempting to solve these problems, aim to identify the key information, use diagrams, formulate ideas, apply strategies, make calculations and check and communicate your solutions.

Vet visits

1   The following table shows the number of cats and dogs that are seen each year at Quindara Veterinary Clinic.

Year	Cats	Dogs
2018	124	111
2019	132	130
2020	118	122
2021	141	126
2022	128	122
2023	113	121

The vet owners are interested in how the number of cats and dogs compare, as well as the differences in total numbers from year to year.

a   How many more cats than dogs were seen in 2021 at Quindara Veterinary Clinic?

b   In which year was the number of cats and dogs closest?

c   In which year was the greatest number of cats and dogs seen?

d   Overall, were there more cats or dogs seen in this 6-year period?

e   What is the difference in number between the total number of cats and dogs seen over this period?

f   What was the total number of cats and dogs seen at Quindara Veterinary Clinic?

g   The vet owners hoped to see a total of 1600 cats and dogs over the 6-year period. How close did they get to their target?

Saving for a new bat

2   Zac is keen to save up to buy a $229 New Balance cricket bat. He currently has $25 and he hopes to buy the bat in 12 weeks' time, giving him enough time to knock his bat in and prepare it for the start of the new cricket season.

Zac generally earns his money from walking his neighbour's dog, where he gets $6 for taking the dog on a half-hour walk. He also gets $10 pocket money per week from his parents.

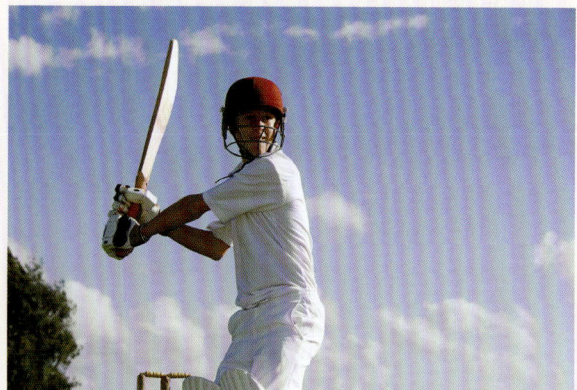

Zac wishes to explore his income and expenses to calculate the time that it will take to save for the new cricket bat.

a If Zac takes the neighbour's dog for three half-hour walks per week, how much can he earn from dog walking in 12 weeks?

b How much pocket money will Zac receive over the 12 weeks?

c Given Zac already has $25 in his wallet, he walks the dog three times per week and he receives his weekly pocket money, how much money can Zac have in 12 weeks' time?

Zac generally spends his money on food, drinks and bus fares and normally spends approximately $15 per week.

d How much money does Zac normally spend over 12 weeks?

e Given Zac's earnings and spending, how much is he likely to have saved at the end of the 12 weeks?

f If Zac does not wish to reduce his spending, how many extra dog walks would Zac have to make over the 12 weeks to have enough money to buy his chosen cricket bat?

g If Zac cannot do any more dog walks, how much less money per week would Zac need to spend if he wishes to buy his chosen bat in 12 weeks' time?

Anaya's steps

3 Anaya lives in Alice Springs and decides to keep a record of how many steps she walks each day. She discovers she walks 12 000 steps each day.

Anaya is interested in using the number of steps that she walks each day to calculate how long it will take to cover various distances.

a How many steps will she walk in a fortnight?

b If Anaya's general step length is 1 m, how many kilometres does Anaya walk in a fortnight?

c If Anaya continues to walk an average of 12 000 steps each day, how far would she walk in one year?

Alice Springs lies in the heart of Australia, and locals joke that is the only town in Australia which is the closest to every beach in Australia. The actual closest beach to Alice Springs is in Darwin and is approximately 1500 km away.

d Walking at her normal rate of 12 000 steps per day, how many days would it take Anaya to reach her closest beach in Darwin?

e Investigate your own average step length and explore how many steps you take on an average day and therefore consider how far you walk in one year.

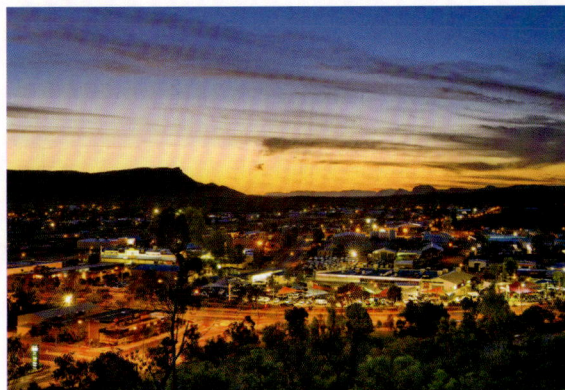

1H Estimating and rounding positive integers CONSOLIDATING

Many theoretical and practical problems do not need precise or exact answers. In such situations reasonable estimations can provide enough information to solve the problem.

The total revenue from the Australian Open tennis tournament depends on crowd numbers. Estimates would be used before the tournament begins to predict these numbers. An estimate for the total revenue might be $8 million.

An important final check before take-off is the pilot's estimate of the plane's maximum flight distance. With fuel for 4 hours and flying at 205 km/h, the maximum flight distance is 800 km, rounded to the nearest hundred km.

Lesson starter: The tennis crowd

Here is a photo of a crowd at a tennis match. Describe how you might estimate the number of people in the photo. What is your answer? How does your answer differ from those of others in your class?

How can you estimate the number of spectators?

KEY IDEAS

■ Estimates or approximations to the answers of problems can be found by **rounding** numbers to the nearest multiple of 10, 100, 1000 etc.

■ If the next digit is 0, 1, 2, 3 or 4, then round down.

■ If the next digit is 5, 6, 7, 8 or 9, then round up.

■ **Leading digit approximation** rounds the first digit up or down, resulting in a multiple of 10 or 100 or 1000 etc.
  e.g.   For 932 use 900,   For 968 use 1000,   For 3715 use 4000

■ The symbol $\approx$ means '**approximately equal to**'. The symbol $\doteqdot$ can also be used.

BUILDING UNDERSTANDING

1 State whether these numbers have been rounded up or down.
  a $59 \approx 60$ **b** $14 \approx 10$ **c** $137 \approx 140$
  d $255 \approx 260$ **e** $924 \approx 900$ **f** $1413 \approx 1000$

2 For the given estimates, decide if the approximate answer is going to give a larger or smaller result compared to the true answer.
  a $58 + 97 \approx 60 + 100$ **b** $24 \times 31 \approx 20 \times 30$
  c $130 - 79 \approx 130 - 80$ **d** $267 - 110 \approx 270 - 110$

Example 13   Rounding whole numbers

Round these numbers as indicated.
a 86 (to the nearest 10)   **b** 4142 (to the nearest 100)

SOLUTION

a $86 \approx 90$

b $4142 \approx 4100$

EXPLANATION

The digit after the 8 is greater than or equal to 5, so round up.

The digit after the 1 is less than or equal to 4, so round down.

Now you try

Round these numbers as indicated.
a 73 (to the nearest 10)   **b** 6354 (to the nearest 100)

Example 14 Using leading digit approximation

Estimate the answers to these problems by rounding each number to the leading digit.

a 42×7 **b** 95×326

SOLUTION

a $\begin{aligned} 42 \times 7 &\approx 40 \times 7 \\ &= 280 \end{aligned}$

b $\begin{aligned} 95 \times 326 &\approx 100 \times 300 \\ &= 30\,000 \end{aligned}$

EXPLANATION

The leading digit in 42 is the 4 in the 'tens' column.

The nearest 'ten' to 95 is 100, and the leading digit in 326 is in the 'hundreds' column.

Now you try

Estimate the answers to these problems by rounding each number to the leading digit.

a 63×8 **b** 185×37

Example 15 Estimating with operations

Estimate the answers to these problems by rounding both numbers as indicated.

a 115×92 (to the nearest 100)   **b** $2266 \div 9$ (to the nearest 10)

SOLUTION

a $\begin{aligned} 115 \times 92 &\approx 100 \times 100 \\ &= 10\,000 \end{aligned}$

b $\begin{aligned} 2266 \div 9 &\approx 2270 \div 10 \\ &= 227 \end{aligned}$

EXPLANATION

115 rounds to 100 and 92 rounds to 100.

2266 rounds to 2270 and 9 rounds to 10.

Now you try

Estimate the answers to these problems by rounding both numbers as indicated.

a 371×915 (to the nearest 100)   **b** $841 \div 18$ (to the nearest 10)

Exercise 1H

FLUENCY	1, 2–6(½)	2–6(½)	3–6(½)

1 Round these numbers as indicated.

Example 13a
  a i 72 (nearest 10)   **ii** 39 (nearest 10)   **iii** 153 (nearest 10)

Example 13b
  b i 362 (nearest 100)   **ii** 718 (nearest 100)   **iii** 1849 (nearest 100)

Example 13
2 Round these numbers as indicated.

  a 59 (nearest 10)   **b** 32 (nearest 10)   **c** 124 (nearest 10)

  d 185 (nearest 10)   **e** 231 (nearest 100)   **f** 894 (nearest 100)

  g 96 (nearest 10)   **h** 584 (nearest 100)   **i** 1512 (nearest 1000)

Example 14
3 Round these numbers using leading digit approximation; e.g. 385 rounds to 400 and 52 rounds to 50.

  a 21   **b** 29   **c** 136   **d** 857

  e 5600   **f** 92 104   **g** 9999   **h** 14

Example 15
4 Estimate the answers to these problems by first rounding both numbers as indicated.

  a 72 + 59 (nearest 10)   **b** 138 − 61 (nearest 10)

  c 275 − 134 (nearest 10)   **d** 841 + 99 (nearest 10)

  e 203 − 104 (nearest 100)   **f** 815 + 183 (nearest 100)

  g 990 + 125 (nearest 100)   **h** 96 + 2473 (nearest 100)

  i 1555 − 555 (nearest 1000)   **j** 44 200 − 36 700 (nearest 1000)

Example 15
5 Use leading digit approximation to estimate the answer.

  a 29 × 4   **b** 124 + 58   **c** 232 − 106   **d** 61 ÷ 5

  e 394 ÷ 10   **f** 97 × 21   **g** 1390 + 3244   **h** 999 − 888

Example 15
6 Estimate the answers to these problems by rounding both numbers as indicated.

  a 29 × 41 (nearest 10)   **b** 92 × 67 (nearest 10)

  c 124 × 173 (nearest 100)   **d** 2402 × 3817 (nearest 1000)

  e 48 ÷ 11 (nearest 10)   **f** 159 ÷ 12 (nearest 10)

  g 104 ÷ 11 (nearest 10)   **h** 2493 ÷ 103 (nearest 100)

PROBLEM-SOLVING	7, 8	8–10	8–11

7 A digger can dig 29 scoops per hour and work 7 hours per day. Approximately how many scoops can be dug over 10 days?

8 Many examples of Aboriginal art include dot paintings. Here is one example.

Estimate the number of dots it contains.

9   Most of the pens at a stockyard are full of sheep. There are 55 pens and one of the pens has 22 sheep. Give an estimate for the total number of sheep at the stockyard.

10 A whole year group of 159 students is roughly divided into 19 groups. Estimate the number in each group.

11 It is sensible sometimes to round one number up if the other number is going to be rounded down. Use leading digit approximation to estimate the answers to these problems.

a 11×19

b 129×954

c 25×36

d 1500×2500

REASONING   12(½)   12   12

12 The letters a and b represent numbers, which could be the same as each other or could be different. Use the word 'smaller' or 'larger' to complete these sentences.

a   If a and b are both rounded up, then compared to the true answer the approximate answer to:

i $a + b$ will be _____.

ii $a \times b$ will be _____.

b   If only a is rounded up, but b is left as it is, then compared to the true answer the approximate answer to:

i $a - b$ will be _____.

ii $a \div b$ will be _____.

c   If only b is rounded up, but a is left as it is, then compared to the true answer the approximate answer to:

i $a - b$ will be _____.

ii $a \div b$ will be _____.

d   If only b is rounded down, but a is left as it is, then compared to the true answer the approximate answer to:

i $a - b$ will be _____.

ii $a \div b$ will be _____.

ENRICHMENT: Maximum error   –   –   13

13 When rounding numbers before a calculation is completed, it is most likely that there will be an error. This error can be large or small, depending on the type of rounding involved.

For example, when rounding to the nearest 10, $71 \times 11 \approx 70 \times 10 = 700$.

But $71 \times 11 = 781$, so the error is 81.

a   Calculate the error if these numbers are rounded to the nearest 10 before the multiplication is calculated.

i 23×17

ii 23×24

iii 65×54

iv 67×56

b   Explain why the error in parts **i** and **iii** is much less than the error in parts **ii** and **iv**.

c   Calculate the error if these numbers are rounded to the nearest 10 before the division is calculated.

i $261 \div 9$

ii $323 \div 17$

iii $99 \div 11$

iv $396 \div 22$

d   Explain why the approximate answers in parts **i** and **ii** are less than the correct answer, and why the approximate answers in parts **iii** and **iv** are more than the correct answer.

1I Order of operations with positive integers

> **LEARNING INTENTIONS**
> * To know the convention for determining order of operations in an expression involving more than one operation
> * To be able to evaluate arithmetic expressions involving more than one operation

When combining the operations of addition, subtraction, multiplication and division, a particular order needs to be followed. Multiplication and division sit higher in the order than addition and subtraction, and this relates to how we might logically interpret simple mathematical problems put into words.

Consider these two statements.

* 2 groups of 3 chairs plus 5 chairs.
* 5 chairs plus 2 groups of 3 chairs.

In both cases, there are $2 \times 3 + 5 = 11$ chairs. This means that $2 \times 3 + 5 = 5 + 2 \times 3$.

This also suggests that for $5 + 2 \times 3$ the multiplication should be done first.

Lesson starter: Minimum brackets

* How might you use brackets to make this statement true?
$$2 + 3 \times 5 - 3 \div 6 + 1 = 2$$
* What is the minimum number of pairs of brackets needed to make it true?

> **KEY IDEAS**
>
> ■ When working with more than one operation:
>   * Deal with **brackets** (also known as parentheses) first.
>   * Do **multiplication** and **division** next, working from left to right.
>   * Do **addition** and **subtraction** last, working from left to right.
>
> $4 \times (2 + 3) - 12 \div 6$
> 1st → 5
> 2nd → 20   3rd → 2
> last → 18
>
> ■ Recall $(a + b) + c = a + (b + c)$ but $(a - b) - c \neq a - (b - c)$
> $(a \times b) \times c = a \times (b \times c)$ but $(a \div b) \div c \neq a \div (b \div c)$
>
> ■ Brackets can sit inside other brackets.
>   * Square brackets can also be used. For example, $[2 \times (3 + 4) - 1] \times 3$.
>   * Always deal with the inner brackets first.

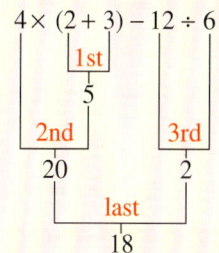

BUILDING UNDERSTANDING

1 Which operation (addition, subtraction, multiplication or division) is done first in the following?

a $2 + 5 - 3$ b $5 \div 5 \times 2$ c $2 \times 3 \div 6$

d $5 \times 2 + 3$ e $7 \div 7 - 1$ f $(6 + 2) \times 3$

g $(8 \div 4) - 1$ h $4 + 7 \times 2$ i $8 - 10 \div 5$

j $10 - 2 + 3$ k $6 + 2 \times 3 - 1$ l $5 \times (2 + 3 \div 3) - 1$

2 Classify these statements as true or false.

a $5 \times 2 + 1 = (5 \times 2) + 1$ b $10 \times (3 + 4) = 10 \times 3 + 4$

c $21 - 7 \div 7 = (21 - 7) \div 7$ d $9 - 3 \times 2 = 9 - (3 \times 2)$

A house painter uses order of operations to calculate the area to be painted on each wall and its cost.
Cost = ($/m²) × [L × W(wall) − L × W(window) − L × W(door)]

Example 16   Using order of operations

Use order of operations to answer the following.

a $5 + 10 \div 2$ b $18 - 2 \times (4 + 6) \div 5$

SOLUTION

a $5 + 10 \div 2 = 5 + 5$
$= 10$

b $18 - 2 \times (4 + 6) \div 5 = 18 - 2 \times 10 \div 5$
$= 18 - 20 \div 5$
$= 18 - 4$
$= 14$

EXPLANATION

Do the division before the addition.

Deal with brackets first.
Do the multiplication and division next, working from left to right.
Do the subtraction last.

Now you try

Use order of operations to answer the following.

a $13 + 3 \times 7$ b $100 - (4 + 8) \div 2 \times 10$

▶

Example 17   Using order of operations in worded problems

Find the answer to these worded problems by first writing the sentence using numbers and symbols.

a Double the sum of 4 and 3.

b The difference between 76 and 43 is tripled, and then the quotient of 35 and 7 is subtracted.

SOLUTION

a $2 \times (4 + 3) = 2 \times 7$
$$= 14$$

b $3 \times (76 - 43) - 35 \div 7 = 3 \times 33 - 35 \div 7$
$$= 99 - 5$$
$$= 94$$

EXPLANATION

First, write the problem using symbols and words.

Brackets are used to ensure the sum of 4 and 3 is found first.

First, write the problem using symbols and numbers.

Use brackets for the difference since this operation is to be completed first.

Now you try

Find the answer to these worded problems by first writing the sentence using numbers and symbols.

a The difference of 10 and 6 is tripled.

b The sum of 12 and 36 is doubled and then the quotient of 40 and 2 is subtracted.

Exercise 1I

FLUENCY		1–4, 7	1–5(½), 7	5–8(½)

Example 16a

1 Use order of operations to answer the following.

    a $3 + 2 \times 4$ **b** $5 + 3 \times 4$ **c** $10 - 2 \times 3$ **d** $12 - 6 \times 2$

Example 16a

2 Use order of operations to answer the following.

    a $2 \times 3 + 1 \times 2$ **b** $7 \times 2 + 1 \times 3$ **c** $6 \times 3 - 2 \times 2$ **d** $4 \times 5 - 3 \times 3$

Example 16a

3 Use order of operations to answer the following.

    a $20 \div 2 + 2$ **b** $20 + 2 \div 2$ **c** $20 - 2 \div 2$ **d** $20 \div 2 - 2$

Example 16b

4 Use order of operations to answer the following.

    a $4 \times (3 + 2)$ **b** $3 \times (4 + 2)$ **c** $(4 + 3) \times 2$ **d** $(4 - 2) \times 3$

Example 16a

5 Use order of operations to find the answers to the following.

    a $2 + 3 \times 7$ **b** $5 + 8 \times 2$ **c** $10 - 20 \div 2$

    d $22 - 16 \div 4$ **e** $6 \times 3 + 2 \times 7$ **f** $1 \times 8 - 2 \times 3$

    g $18 \div 9 + 60 \div 3$ **h** $2 + 3 \times 7 - 1$ **i** $40 - 25 \div 5 + 3$

    j $63 \div 3 \times 7 + 2 \times 3$ **k** $78 - 14 \times 4 + 6$ **l** $300 - 100 \times 4 \div 4$

Example 16b

6 Use order of operations to find the answer to the following problems.

a $2 \times (3 + 2)$
b $18 \div (10 - 4)$
c $(19 - 9) \div 5$
d $(100 + 5) \div 5 + 1$
e $2 \times (9 - 4) \div 5$
f $50 \div (13 - 3) + 4$
g $16 - 2 \times (7 - 5) + 6$
h $(7 + 2) \div (53 - 50)$
i $14 - (7 \div 7 + 1) \times 2$
j $(20 - 10) \times (5 + 7) + 1$
k $3 \times (72 \div 12 + 1) - 1$
l $48 \div (4 + 4) \div (3 \times 2)$

Example 17

7 Find the answer to these worded problems by first writing the sentence using numbers and symbols.

a Triple the sum of 3 and 6.

b Double the quotient of 20 and 4.

c The quotient of 44 and 11 plus 4.

d 5 more than the product of 6 and 12.

e The quotient of 60 and 12 is subtracted from the product of 5 and 7.

f 15 less than the difference of 48 and 12.

g The product of 9 and 12 is subtracted from double the product of 10 and 15.

8 These computations involve brackets within brackets. Ensure you work with the inner brackets first.

a $2 \times [(2 + 3) \times 5 - 1]$
b $[10 \div (2 + 3) + 1] \times 6$
c $26 \div [10 - (17 - 9)]$
d $[6 - (5 - 3)] \times 7$
e $2 + [103 - (21 + 52)] - (9 + 11) \times 6 \div 12$

PROBLEM-SOLVING	9, 10, 11(½)	10, 11(½)	11, 12

9 A delivery of 15 boxes of books arrives, each box containing eight books. The bookstore owner removes three books from each box. How many books still remain in total?

10 In a class, eight students have three televisions at home, four have two televisions, 13 have one television and two students have no television. How many televisions are there in total?

11 Insert brackets into these statements to make them true.

a $4 + 2 \times 3 = 18$
b $9 \div 12 - 9 = 3$
c $2 \times 3 + 4 - 5 = 9$
d $3 + 2 \times 7 - 3 = 20$
e $10 - 7 \div 21 - 18 = 1$
f $4 + 10 \div 21 \div 3 = 2$
g $20 - 31 - 19 \times 2 = 16$
h $50 \div 2 \times 5 - 4 = 1$
i $25 - 19 \times 3 + 7 \div 12 + 1 = 6$

12 An amount of $100 is divided into two first prizes of equal value and three second prizes of equal value. Each prize is a whole number of dollars and first prize is at least four times the value of second prize. If second prize is more than $6, find the amount of each prize.

REASONING   13(½)   13(½), 14   13(½), 14, 15

13 Decide if the brackets given in each statement are actually necessary; that is, do they make any difference to the problem?

a $2 + (3 \times 6) = 20$

b $(2 + 3) \times 6 = 30$

c $(20 \times 2) \times 3 = 120$

d $10 - (5 + 2) = 3$

e $22 - (11 - 7) = 18$

f $19 - (10 \div 2) = 14$

g $(40 \div 10) \div 4 = 1$

h $100 \div (20 \div 5) = 25$

i $2 \times (3 + 2) \div 5 = 2$

14 The letters a, b and c represent numbers. Decide if the brackets are necessary in these expressions.

a $a + (b + c)$

b $a - (b - c)$

c $a \times (b \times c)$

d $a \div (b \div c)$

15 Simplify the following. Assume $a \neq 0$ and $b \neq 0$.

a $a + b - a$

b $(a - a) \times b$

c $a + b \div b$

d $a \times b \div a$

ENRICHMENT: Operation in rules   –   –   16

16 Using whole numbers and any of the four operations $(+, -, \times, \div)$, describe how you would obtain the 'Finish' number from the 'Start' number in each of these tables. Your rule must work for every pair of numbers in its table.

a

Start	Finish
1 →	3
2 →	5
3 →	7
4 →	9

b

Start	Finish
1 →	0
2 →	3
3 →	6
4 →	9

c

Start	Finish
3 →	10
4 →	17
5 →	26
6 →	37

Make up your own table with a secret rule and test it on a friend.

Modelling

Cans and chips

At a school fundraising fair, Mike has been given $29 to spend on soft drink and chips for himself and his friends. Cans of soft drink cost $2 each and cups of chips cost $3 each.

Present a report for the following tasks and ensure that you show clear mathematical working and explanations where appropriate.

Preliminary task

a   Find the total cost of buying:
  i   5 cans of soft drink
  ii   7 cups of chips
  iii 4 cans of soft drink and 3 cups of chips
  iv   6 cans of soft drink and 5 cups of chips.

b   If 6 cups of chips and 3 cans are purchased, find the change from $29.

c   Determine the maximum number of cans of soft drink that can be purchased for $29 if:
  i   3 cups of chips are purchased
  ii   4 cups of chips are purchased.

Modelling task

Formulate

a   The problem is to find the maximum number of cans and cups of chips that Mike can purchase with the money he was given. Write down all the relevant information that will help solve this problem.

Solve

b   Choose at least two combinations for the number of cans and number of cups of chips so that the total cost is less than $29. Show your calculations to explain why your combinations are affordable.

c   Choose at least two different combinations for the number of cans and chips so that the total cost is equal to $29.

d   Determine possible combinations which would mean that Mike:
  i   maximises the number of cans purchased
  ii   maximises the number of cups of chips purchased.

Evaluate and verify

e   Determine the maximum number of items (cans and/or cups of chips) that can be purchased for $29 or less:
  i   if at least 5 cups of chips must be purchased
  ii   if there are no restrictions.

f   There are two ways of achieving the maximum number of items for part **e ii**. Explain why there are two combinations, and compare them.

Communicate

g   Summarise your results and describe any key findings.

Extension questions

a   If Mike had $67, investigate the maximum number of items (cans of soft drink and/or cups of chips) that can be purchased if at least 12 cups of chips must be included.

b   If the total amount is still $67 and the cost of chips changes to $2.50, describe how the answer to part **a** above would change. You can assume that the cost of the cans stays the same.

Making 100 dollars

Key technology: Spreadsheets

You can imagine that there are many ways in which you can make $100 from $10 and $20 notes.
Assuming you have enough of each type, you could make $100 using five $20 and no $10 notes or perhaps
three $20 notes and four $10 notes, for example.

1 Getting started

a   Without using one of the combinations mentioned in the introduction, list three different possible
combinations of $20 and $10 notes that make up a total of $100.

b   Can you find a way to make up $100 by combining $10 and $20 notes so that there is a total of
seven notes being used? If so, describe it.

c   Can you find a way to make up $100 by combining $10 and $20 notes so that there is a total of
eleven notes being used? Explain your answer.

2 Using technology

We will use a spreadsheet to explore the number of ways you can choose $10 and $20 notes to form $100.

a   Create the following spreadsheet using the given information.

- The number of $20 notes can vary and is in cell B3.
- The information in cell A7 creates the number of $10 notes selected.

	A	B	C
1	Making $100		
2			
3	Number of $20 notes	4	
4			
5	Number of $10 notes	$Total	Number of notes used
6	0	=B$3*20+A6*10	=A6+B$3
7	=A6+1		

- The information in cell B6 creates the total value of the $10 and $20 notes selected.
- The information in cell C6 creates the total number of notes selected.

b   Fill down at cells A7, B6 and C6. Fill down until ten $10 notes are used. Note that the $ sign in
cells B6 and C6 ensures that the number of $20 notes in cell B3 is used for every calculation.

c   See if your spreadsheet is working properly by altering the number of $20 notes in cell B3. All the
values should change when this cell is updated.

d   Choose two $20 notes by changing the cell B3 to equal 2. Read off your spreadsheet to answer the following.

i   How many $10 notes are required to make the total of $100?

ii   How many notes are selected in total if you make $100?

iii   Describe what happens if the number of $20 notes in cell B3 is changed to 7.

	A	B	C
1	Making $100		
2			
3	Number of $20 notes	4	
4			
5	Number of $10 notes	$Total	Number of notes used
6	0	80	4
7	1	90	5
8	2	100	6
9	3	110	7
10	4	120	8
11	5	130	9
12	6	140	10
13	7	150	11
14	8	160	12
15	9	170	13

Technology and computational thinking

3 Applying an algorithm

a   Use your spreadsheet to systematically run through and count all the ways you can make $100 using $10 and $20 notes. Apply these steps.
   - Step 1: Choose the smallest number of $20 notes possible and enter this number into cell B3.
   - Step 2: Read off the number of $10 notes needed to make $100.
   - Step 3: Increase the number of $20 used by one and repeat Step 2.
   - Step 4: Continue increasing the number of $20 notes used until you reach a maximum possible number.

b   Describe the combination of notes where a total of $100 is achieved but there are eight notes in total.

c   Is it possible to achieve a total of $100 using only six notes in total? If so, describe how.

d   How many ways were there of forming $100 from $10 and $20 notes?

4 Extension

a   Alter your spreadsheet so that a $100 total is required but this time using $5 and $20 notes. Decide if it possible to achieve a $100 total with a total of:
   i   17 notes
   ii   10 notes.

b   Alter your spreadsheet so that a $100 total is required but this time using a combination of three notes, e.g. $10, $20 and $50. What is the total number of ways this can be achieved?

The abacus

Counting boards called abacuses (or abaci) date back to 500 BCE. The abacus is a counting device that has been used for thousands of years. Abacuses were used extensively by merchants, traders, tax collectors and clerks before modern-day numeral systems were developed. These were wood or stone tablets with grooves, which would hold beans or pebbles.

The modern abacus is said to have originated in China in about the thirteenth century and includes beads on wires held in a wooden frame.

There are 5 beads on one side of a modern abacus worth 1 each and 2 beads on the opposite side worth 5 each.

- Each wire represents a different unit, e.g. ones, tens, hundreds etc.
- Beads are counted only when they are pushed towards the centre.

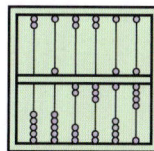

A German woodcut from 1508 showing an abacus in use by the gentleman on the right, while a mathematician (at left) writes algorithms.

thousands
hundreds
tens
ones

Here is a diagram showing the number 5716.

a What numbers are showing on the abacus diagrams below? Only the first six wires are showing.

   i   **ii**   **iii**   **iv**

b Draw abacus diagrams showing these numbers.

   i   57   **ii**   392   **iii**   6804   **iv**   290 316

c Imagine adding two numbers using an abacus by sliding beads along their wires. Clearly explain the steps taken to add these numbers.

   i **11 + 7**   **ii** **2394 + 536**

d Imagine subtracting two numbers using an abacus by sliding beads along their wires. Clearly explain the steps taken to subtract these numbers.

   i **23 − 14**   **ii** **329 − 243**

e Multiplication is calculated as a repeated addition, e.g. $3 \times 21 = 21 + 21 + 21$. Clearly explain the steps involved when using an abacus to multiply these numbers.

   i **3 × 42**   **ii** **5 × 156**

f Division is calculated as a repeated subtraction, e.g. $63 \div 21 = 3$, since $63 - 21 - 21 - 21 = 0$. Clearly explain the steps involved when using an abacus to divide these numbers.

   i **28 ÷ 7**   **ii** **405 ÷ 135**

g See if you can find a real abacus or computer abacus with which to work. Use the abacus to show how you can do the problems in parts **c** to **f** above.

Problems and challenges

1   **The extra dollar?**

The cost of dinner for two people is $45 and they both give the waiter $25 each. Of the extra $5 the waiter is allowed to keep $3 as a tip and returns $1 to each person. So the two people paid $24 each, making a total of $48, and the waiter has $3. The total is therefore $48 + $3 = $51. Where did the extra $1 come from?

> Up for a challenge? If you get stuck on a question, check out the 'Working with unfamiliar problems' poster at the end of the book to help you.

2   The sum along each line is 15. Can you place each of the digits 1, 2, 3, 4, 5, 6, 7, 8 and 9 to make this true?

3   Ethan starts at 2637 and counts backwards by eights. He stops counting when he reaches a number less than 10. What is this final number?

4   Make the total of 100 out of all the numbers 2, 3, 4, 7 and 11, using each number only once. You can use any of the operations $(+, -, \times, \div)$, as well as brackets.

5   A leaking tap loses 1 drop of water per second. If 40 of these drops of water make a volume of 10 mL, how many litres of water are wasted from this tap in mL:

a   in 1 day? (round answer to the nearest unit)

b   in 1 year? (round answer to the nearest 100).

6   When this shape is folded to make a cube, three of the sides will meet at every vertex (corner) of the cube. The numbers on these three sides can be multiplied together.

Find the smallest and largest of these products.

		7	9	11
1	3	5		

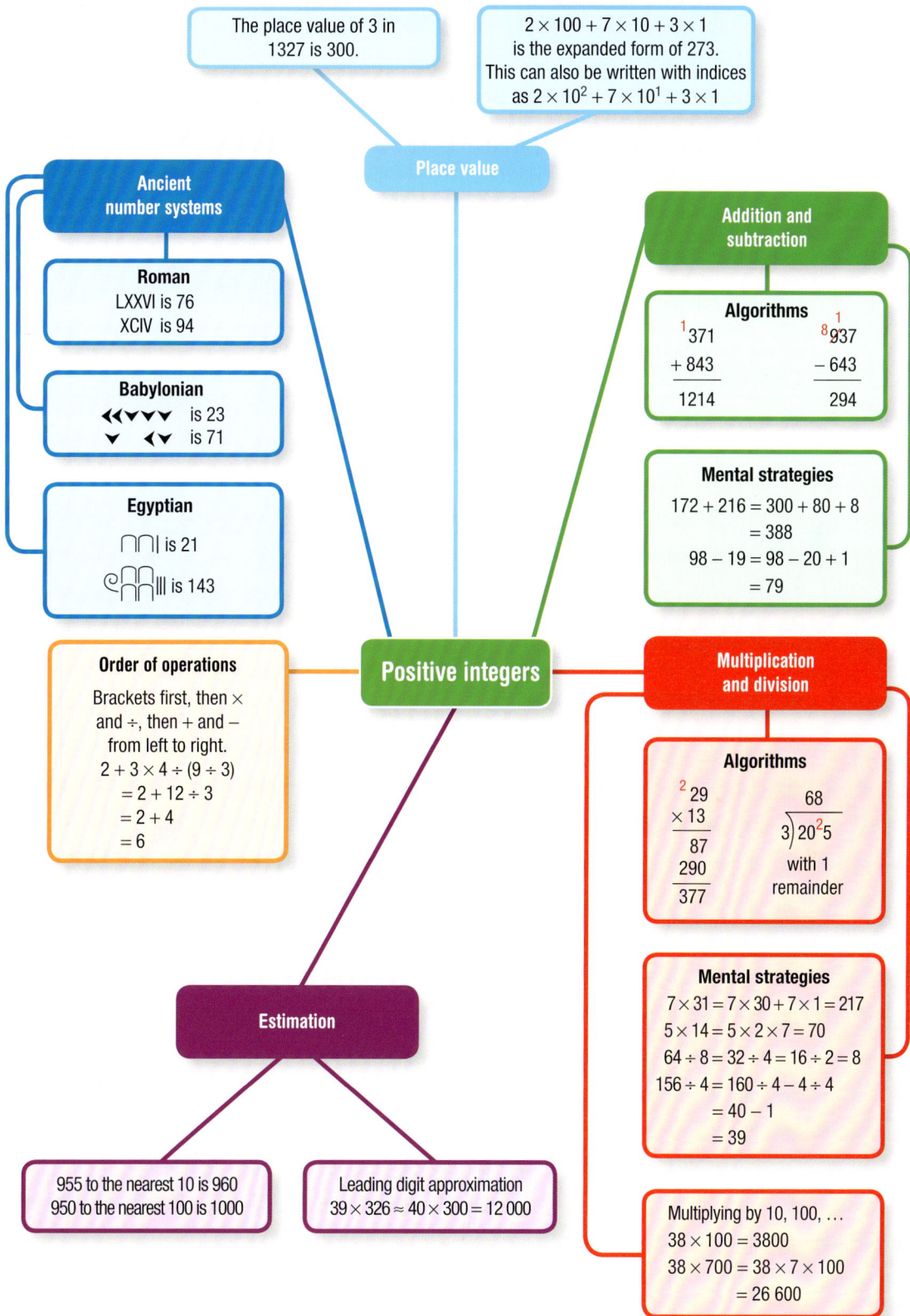

The place value of 3 in 1327 is 300.

$2 \times 100 + 7 \times 10 + 3 \times 1$ is the expanded form of 273. This can also be written with indices as $2 \times 10^2 + 7 \times 10^1 + 3 \times 1$

Place value

Ancient number systems

Roman
LXXVI is 76
XCIV is 94

Babylonian
◀◀▼▼▼ is 23
▼ ◀▼ is 71

Egyptian
∩∩| is 21
⌐∩∩||| is 143

Addition and subtraction

Algorithms

$$\begin{array}{r} {}^{1}371 \\ + 843 \\ \hline 1214 \end{array} \qquad \begin{array}{r} {}^{8}9{}^{1}37 \\ - 643 \\ \hline 294 \end{array}$$

Mental strategies
$172 + 216 = 300 + 80 + 8$
$ = 388$
$98 - 19 = 98 - 20 + 1$
$ = 79$

Order of operations
Brackets first, then $\times$ and $\div$, then $+$ and $-$ from left to right.
$2 + 3 \times 4 \div (9 \div 3)$
$= 2 + 12 \div 3$
$= 2 + 4$
$= 6$

Positive integers

Multiplication and division

Algorithms

$$\begin{array}{r} {}^{2}29 \\ \times 13 \\ \hline 87 \\ 290 \\ \hline 377 \end{array} \qquad \begin{array}{r} 68 \\ 3\overline{)20\,{}^{2}5} \end{array}$$
with 1 remainder

Mental strategies
$7 \times 31 = 7 \times 30 + 7 \times 1 = 217$
$5 \times 14 = 5 \times 2 \times 7 = 70$
$64 \div 8 = 32 \div 4 = 16 \div 2 = 8$
$156 \div 4 = 160 \div 4 - 4 \div 4$
$ = 40 - 1$
$ = 39$

Estimation

955 to the nearest 10 is 960
950 to the nearest 100 is 1000

Leading digit approximation
$39 \times 326 \approx 40 \times 300 = 12\,000$

Multiplying by 10, 100, …
$38 \times 100 = 3800$
$38 \times 700 = 38 \times 7 \times 100$
$ = 26\,600$

Chapter checklist

Chapter checklist with success criteria

A printable version of this checklist is available in the Interactive Textbook ⬇ | ✔ |

1A	**1. I can write numbers in the Egyptian, Babylonian and Roman number systems.** e.g. Write 144 in the Egyptian, Babylonian and Roman number systems.	☐
1B	**2. I can write down the place value of digits within a number.** e.g. Write the place value of the digit 4 in the number 543 910.	☐
1B	**3. I can write positive integers in expanded form with and without index notation.** e.g. Write 517 in expanded form. Rewrite 517 in expanded form with index notation.	☐
1C	**4. I can use mental addition and subtraction techniques effectively.** e.g. Mentally find 132 + 156 (with partitioning) and 56 − 18 (with compensating).	☐
1D	**5. I can use the addition algorithm.** e.g. Find 439 + 172 by first aligning the numbers vertically.	☐
1D	**6. I can use the subtraction algorithm.** e.g. Find 3240 − 2721 by first aligning the numbers vertically.	☐
1E	**7. I can use mental multiplication techniques effectively.** e.g. Mentally find 4×29.	☐
1E	**8. I can use the multiplication algorithm for single-digit products.** e.g. Find 31×4 and 197×7 using the multiplication algorithm.	☐
1F	**9. I can multiply by powers of ten.** e.g. State the value of 37×100.	☐
1F	**10. I can multiply large numbers using the multiplication algorithm.** e.g. Find 614×14 using the multiplication algorithm.	☐
1G	**11. I can use mental strategies to divide positive integers.** e.g. Mentally find $93 \div 3$.	☐
1G	**12. I can use the short division algorithm.** e.g. Find the quotient and remainder when 195 is divided by 7.	☐
1H	**13. I can round positive integers to a power of ten.** e.g. Round 4142 to the nearest 100.	☐
1H	**14. I can estimate answers using leading digit approximation.** e.g. Estimate 95×326 by rounding each number to the leading digit.	☐
1H	**15. I can estimate answers by rounding numbers.** e.g. Estimate $2266 \div 9$ by rounding both numbers to the nearest 10.	☐
1I	**16. I can use order of operations.** e.g. Find the value of $18 - 2 \times (4 + 6) \div 5$.	☐
1I	**17. I can use order of operations in worded problems.** e.g. Find the difference between 76 and 43, triple this result and, finally, subtract the quotient of 35 and 7.	☐

Short-answer questions

1A

1 Write these numbers using the given number systems.

    a Egyptian

      i 3   **ii** 31   **iii** 326

    b Babylonian

      i 12   **ii** 60   **iii** 132

    c Roman

      i 14   **ii** 40   **iii** 146

1B

2 Write down the place value of the digit 5 in these numbers.

    a 357   **b** 5249   **c** 356612

1C

3 Use a mental strategy to find these sums and differences.

    a $124 + 335$ **b** $687 - 324$ **c** $59 + 36$ **d** $256 - 39$

1D

4 Use an algorithm and show your working for these sums and differences.

    a $\begin{array}{r} 76 \\ + 52 \end{array}$ **b** $\begin{array}{r} 1528 \\ + 796 \end{array}$ **c** $\begin{array}{r} 329 \\ - 138 \end{array}$ **d** $\begin{array}{r} 2109 \\ - 1814 \end{array}$

1E/G

5 Use a mental strategy to answer the following.

    a 5×19 **b** 22×6 **c** 5×44

    d $123 \div 3$ **e** $264 \div 8$ **f** $96 \div 4$

    g 29×1000 **h** 36×300 **i** $14678 \div 1$

1F/G

6 Use an algorithm and show your working for the following.

    a $\begin{array}{r} 157 \\ \times\ 9 \end{array}$ **b** $\begin{array}{r} 27 \\ \times 13 \end{array}$ **c** $7\overline{)327}$ **d** $4\overline{)30162}$

1D/F/G

7 Find the missing digits in the following.

    a $\begin{array}{ccc} 2 & \square & 3 \\ + 7 & 3 & \square \\ \hline 9 & 6 & 1 \end{array}$ **b** $\begin{array}{ccc} \square & 2 & \square \\ - 4 & \square & 3 \\ \hline 2 & 5 & 6 \end{array}$

    c $\begin{array}{ccc} & \square & 3 \\ \times & 2 & \square \\ \hline & \square\ 7 & 1 \\ \square & 0\ 6 & 0 \\ \hline \square\ \square & 3 & 1 \end{array}$ **d** $5\overline{)\,\square\,{}^4\,1\,{}^1\,\square}$ with quotient $1\,\square\,3$ with no remainder

1H

8 Round these numbers as indicated.

    a 72 (nearest 10)   **b** 3268 (nearest 100)   **c** 951 (nearest 100)

1H

9 Use leading digit approximation to estimate the answers to the following.

    a $289 + 532$ **b** 22×19 **c** 452×11 **d** $99 \div 11$

1I

10 Use order of operations to find the answers to the following.

    a $3 \times (2 + 6)$ **b** $6 - 8 \div 4$ **c** $2 \times 8 - 12 \div 6$

    d $(5 + 2) \times 3 - (8 - 7)$ **e** $0 \times (988234 \div 3)$ **f** $1 \times (3 + 2 \times 5)$

Multiple-choice questions

1A 1 The correct Roman numerals for the number 24 are:

    A XXIII   B XXIV   C XXXLIV   D IVXX   E IXXV

1B 2 $3 \times 1000 + 9 \times 10 + 2 \times 1$ is the expanded form of:

    A 3920   B 392   C 3092   D 3902   E 329

1C/E 3 Which of the following is not true?

    A $2 + 3 = 3 + 2$ B $2 \times 3 = 3 \times 2$ C $(2 \times 3) \times 4 = 2 \times (3 \times 4)$

    D $5 \div 2 \neq 2 \div 5$ E $7 - 2 = 2 - 7$

1C 4 The sum of 198 and 103 is:

    A 301   B 304   C 299   D 199   E 95

1C 5 The difference between 378 and 81 is:

    A 459   B 297   C 303   D 317   E 299

1E 6 The product of 7 and 21 is:

    A 147   B 141   C 21   D 140   E 207

1G 7 Which of the following is the missing digit in this division?

$$7{\overline{\smash{)}\,\square\,{}^1 2\,{}^5 6}}$$

with quotient $1\ 1\ 8$

    A 6   B 1   C 9   D 8   E 7

1G 8 The remainder when 317 is divided by 9 is:

    A 7   B 5   C 2   D 1   E 0

1G 9 458 rounded to the nearest 100 is:

    A 400   B 500   C 460   D 450   E 1000

1I 10 The answer to $[2 + 3 \times (7 - 4)] \div 11$ is:

    A 1   B 5   C 11   D 121   E 0

Extended-response questions

1 A city tower construction uses 4520 tonnes of concrete trucked from a factory that is 7 kilometres from the construction site. Each concrete mixer can carry 7 tonnes of concrete, and the concrete costs $85 per truck load for the first 30 loads and $55 per load after that.

    a How many loads of concrete are needed? Add a full load for any remainder.

    b Find the total distance travelled by the concrete trucks to deliver all loads, assuming they need to return to the factory after each load.

    c Find the total cost of concrete needed for the tower construction.

    d A different concrete supplier offers a price of $65 per 8-tonne truck, no matter how many loads are needed. Find the difference in the cost of concrete for the tower by this supplier compared to the original supplier.

2   One night Ricky and her brother Micky decide to have some fun at their father's lolly shop. In the shop they find 7 tins of jelly beans each containing 135 beans, 9 packets of 121 choc buds, 12 jars of 70 smarties and 32 packets of 5 liquorice sticks.

a   Find the total number of lollies that Ricky and Micky find that night.

b   Find the difference between the number of choc buds and the number of smarties.

c   Ricky and Micky decide to divide each type of lolly into groups of 7 and then eat any remainder. Which type of lolly will they eat the most of and how many?

d   After eating the remainders, they round the total of each lolly using leading digit approximation. If they round down they put the spare lollies in their pockets. If they round up, they borrow any spare lollies from their pockets. Any left over in their pockets, they can eat. Do Ricky and Micky get to eat any more lollies?

2

Number properties and patterns

Maths in context: Number patterns around us

Mathematicians are always looking for patterns in number sequences. When a pattern is known, rules can be found, and rules can be used to predict future values.

To create a number pattern with a common difference, add or subtract an equal amount.

For example:

- When filling a swimming pool from a tap and hose, the total volume of water increases by a constant volume per minute.
- When a plane flies at a constant speed and altitude, the volume of remaining fuel decreases by an equal amount every minute.

Number patterns with a common ratio increase in value when multiplied by a number greater than 1

and decrease in value when multiplied by a number less than 1.

For example:

- A financial investment that increases each January by 3% (interest) would have a list of its January values forming a sequence of increasing numbers, with a common ratio of 1.03.
- Threatened or endangered animal species have small population numbers that are declining. Their annual population totals form a sequence of decreasing numbers, with a common ratio less than 1, e.g. 0.9. About 300 of Australia's animal species are endangered, including various possums and koalas.

Chapter contents

Victorian Curriculum 2.0

This chapter covers the following content descriptors in the Victorian Curriculum 2.0:

NUMBER

VC2M7N01, VC2M7N02

ALGEBRA

VC2M7A04, VC2M7A05

Please refer to the curriculum support documentation in the teacher resources for a full and comprehensive mapping of this chapter to the related curriculum content descriptors.

© VCAA

Online resources

A host of additional online resources are included as part of your Interactive Textbook, including HOTmaths content, video demonstrations of all worked examples, auto-marked quizzes and much more.

2A Factors and multiples   CONSOLIDATING

LEARNING INTENTIONS
- To know what factors and multiples are
- To understand that each number has infinitely many multiples
- To be able to find factors of a number
- To be able to find multiples of a number

Many famous mathematicians have studied number patterns in an attempt to better understand our world and to assist with new scientific discoveries. Around 600 BCE, the Greeks built on the early work of the Egyptians and Babylonians. Thales of Miletus, the 'father of Greek mathematics', is credited for significant advances in Number Theory. One of his students, Pythagoras of Samos, went on to become one of the most well-known mathematicians to have lived. Pythagoras was primarily a religious leader, but he believed that the understanding of the world could be enhanced through the understanding of numbers. We start this chapter on Number Properties and Patterns by explaining the concepts of factors and multiples, which are key building blocks for Number Theory.

Factors of 24 are used by nurses who dispense prescription medicines in hospitals and nursing homes. For example: four times/day is every 6 hours ($4 \times 6 = 24$); three times/day is every 8 hours ($3 \times 8 = 24$).

Imagine one dozen doughnuts packed into bags with 3 rows of 4 doughnuts each. Since $3 \times 4 = 12$, we can say that 3 and 4 are **factors** of 12.

Purchasing 'multiple' packs of one dozen doughnuts could result in buying 24, 36, 48 or 60 doughnuts, depending on the number of packs. These numbers are known as **multiples** of 12.

Lesson starter: The most factors, the most multiples

Which number that is less than 100 has the most factors?

Which number that is less than 100 has the most multiples less than 100?

KEY IDEAS

■ **Factors** of a particular number are numbers that divide exactly into that number.
- For example: The factors of 20 can be found by considering pairs of numbers that multiply to give 20 which are 1×20, 2×10 and 4×5.
  Therefore, written in **ascending** order, the factors of 20 are $1, 2, 4, 5, 10, 20$.
- Every whole number is a factor of itself and also 1 is a factor of every whole number.

■ **Multiples** of a number are found by multiplying the given number by any whole number.
  ● For example: The multiples of 20 are $20, 40, 60, 80, 100, 120, \ldots$
    Other numbers that are multiples of 20 include 480, 2000 and 68 600. Every positive integer has infinitely many multiples.

■ Given the statements above, it follows that factors are less than or equal to the particular number being considered and multiples are greater than or equal to the number being considered.

BUILDING UNDERSTANDING

1 For each of the following numbers, state whether it is a factor of 60 (F), a multiple of 60 (M) or neither (N).

a 120	**b** 14	**c** 15	**d** 40
e 6	**f** 5	**g** 240	**h** 2
i 22	**j** 600	**k** 70	**l** 1

2 For each of the following numbers, state whether it is a factor of 26 (F), a multiple of 26 (M) or neither (N).

a 2	**b** 54	**c** 52	**d** 4
e 210	**f** 27	**g** 3	**h** 182
i 1	**j** 26 000	**k** 13	**l** 39

Example 1   Finding factors

Find the complete set of factors for each of these numbers.

a 15

b 40

SOLUTION	EXPLANATION
a Factors of 15 are $1, 3, 5, 15$.	$1 \times 15 = 15$, $3 \times 5 = 15$
b Factors of 40 are: $1, 2, 4, 5, 8, 10, 20, 40$.	$1 \times 40 = 40$, $2 \times 20 = 40$
	$4 \times 10 = 40$, $5 \times 8 = 40$
	The last number you need to check is 7, but $40 \div 7 = 5$ rem. 5, so 7 is not a factor.

Now you try

Find the complete set of factors for each of these numbers.

a 21

b 30

Example 2   Listing multiples

Write down the first six multiples for each of these numbers.

a   11   b   35

SOLUTION	EXPLANATION
a 11, 22, 33, 44, 55, 66	The first multiple is always the given number. Add on the given number to find the next multiple. Repeat this process to get more multiples.
b 35, 70, 105, 140, 175, 210	Start at 35, the given number, and repeatedly add 35 to continue producing multiples.

Now you try

Write down the first six multiples for each of these numbers.

a   4   b   26

Example 3   Finding factor pairs

Express 195 as a product of two factors, both of which are greater than 10.

SOLUTION

$195 = 13 \times 15$

EXPLANATION

Systematically divide 195 by numbers greater than 10 in an attempt to find a large factor. The number 13 goes into 195 a total of 15 times with no remainder $13\overline{)19^65}$ $\overset{015}{}$.

Now you try

Express 165 as a product of two factors, both of which are greater than 10.

Exercise 2A

FLUENCY	1, 2–4(½)	2–5(½)	2–5(½)

Example 1 1 Find the complete set of factors for each of these numbers.

a   12   b   48

Example 1 2 List the complete set of factors for each of the following numbers.

a   10   b   24   c   17
d   36   e   60   f   42
g   80   h   29   i   28

Example 2

3 Write down the first six multiples for each of the following numbers.
- **a** 5
- **b** 8
- **c** 12
- **d** 7
- **e** 20
- **f** 75
- **g** 15
- **h** 100
- **i** 37

4 Fill in the gaps to complete the set of factors for each of the following numbers.
- **a** 18   1, 2, __, 6, 9, __
- **b** 25   1, __, 25
- **c** 72   __, 2, 3, ___, __, 8, __, __, 18, __, 36, 72
- **d** 120 1, 2, __, __, __, 6, __, 10, __, __, 20, __, 30, __, 60, __

5 Which number is the incorrect multiple for each of the following sequences?
- **a** 3, 6, 9, 12, 15, 18, 22, 24, 27, 30
- **b** 43, 86, 129, 162, 215, 258, 301, 344
- **c** 11, 21, 33, 44, 55, 66, 77, 88, 99, 110
- **d** 17, 34, 51, 68, 85, 102, 117, 136, 153, 170

PROBLEM-SOLVING 6, 7(½)   6–8   7–9

6 Consider the set of whole numbers from 1 to 25 inclusive.
- **a** Which number has the most factors?
- **b** Which number has the fewest factors?
- **c** Which numbers have an odd number of factors?

Example 3

7 Express each of the following numbers as a product of two factors, both of which are greater than 10.
- **a** 192
- **b** 315
- **c** 180
- **d** 121
- **e** 336
- **f** 494

8 Zane and Matt are both keen runners. Zane takes 4 minutes to jog around a running track and Matt takes 5 minutes. They start at the same time and keep running until they both cross the finish line at the same time.
- **a** How long do they run for?
- **b** How many laps did Zane run?
- **c** How many laps did Matt run?

9 Anson has invited 12 friends to his birthday party. He is making each of them a 'lolly bag' to take home after the party. To be fair, he wants to make sure that each friend has the same number of lollies. Anson has a total of 300 lollies to share among the lolly bags.
- **a** How many lollies does Anson put in each of his friends' lolly bags?
- **b** How many lollies does Anson have left over to eat himself?

Anson then decides that he wants a lolly bag for himself also.
- **c** How many lollies will now go into each of the 13 lolly bags?

After much pleading from his siblings, Anson prepares lolly bags for them also. His sister Monique notices that the total number of lolly bags is now a factor of the total number of lollies.
- **d** What are the different possible number of sibling(s) that Anson could have?
- **e** How many siblings do you expect Anson has?

10 Are the following statements true or false?
  a   A multiple of a particular number is always smaller than that number.
  b   2 is a factor of every even number.
  c   3 is a factor of every odd number.
  d   A factor is always greater than or equal to the given number.
  e   When considering a particular number, that number is both a factor and a multiple of itself.

11 60 is a number with many factors. It has a total of 12 factors and, interestingly, it has each of the
      numbers 1, 2, 3, 4, 5, 6 as a factor.
  a   What is the smallest number that has 1, 2, 3, 4, 5, 6, 7 and 8 as factors?
  b   What is the smallest number that has 1, 2, 3, 4, 5, 6, 7, 8, 9 and 10 as factors?

12 a   What numbers can claim that the number 100 is a multiple of them? (For example, 5 could claim
      that 100 is a multiple of it.)
  b   What are the factors of 100?

13 All Australian AM radio stations have frequencies that are multiples of 9. For example, a particular
      radio station has a frequency of 774 (kilohertz or kHz). Find three other AM radio stations and show
      their frequencies are, indeed, multiples of 9.

14 A particular number is a multiple of 6 and also a multiple of 15. This tells you that 6 and 15 are factors of
      the number. List all the other numbers that must be factors.

15 a   Design a spreadsheet that will enable a user to enter any number between 1 and 100 and it will
      automatically list the first 30 multiples of that number.
  b   Design a spreadsheet that will enable a user to enter any particular number between 1 and 100 and
      it will automatically list the number's factors.
  c   Improve your factor program so that it finds the sum of the factors and also states the total number
      of factors for the particular number.
  d   Use your spreadsheet program to help you find a pair of **amicable numbers**. A pair of numbers is
      said to be amicable if the sum of the factors for each number, excluding the number itself, is equal
      to the other number. Both numbers in the first pair of amicable numbers fall between 200 and 300.

   An example of a non-amicable pair of numbers:
   $12 : \text{factor sum} = 1 + 2 + 3 + 4 + 6 = 16$
   $16 : \text{factor sum} = 1 + 2 + 4 + 8 = 15$
   The factor sum for 16 would need to be 12 for the pair to be amicable numbers.

   Helpful Microsoft Excel formulas
   INT(number) – Rounds a number down to the nearest integer (whole number).
   MOD(number, divisor) – Returns the remainder after a number is divided by the divisor.
   IF(logical test, value if true, value if false) – Checks whether a condition is met and returns one
   value if true and another value if false.
   COUNTIF(range, criteria) – Counts the number of cells within a range that meet the given condition.

2B Highest common factor and lowest common multiple

LEARNING INTENTIONS
• To know the meaning of the terms highest common factor (HCF) and lowest common multiple (LCM)
• To be able to find the highest common factor of two numbers
• To be able to find the lowest common multiple of two numbers

In the previous section, factors and multiples of a number were explained. Remember that factors are less than or equal to a given number and that multiples are greater than or equal to a given number.

given number
e.g. 12

factors
≤ 12
e.g. 1, 2, 3, 4, 6, 12

multiples
≥ 12
e.g. 12, 24, 36, 48, ...

There are many applications in Mathematics for which the **highest common factor (HCF)** of two or more numbers must be determined. In particular, the skill of finding the HCF is required for the future topic of factorisation, which is an important aspect of Algebra.

Similarly, there are many occasions for which the **lowest common multiple (LCM)** of two or more numbers must be determined. Adding and subtracting fractions with different denominators requires the skill of finding the LCM.

People use HCF when calculating equivalent application rates, such as: pool owners simplifying a manufacturer's chlorine application rates; farmers calculating equivalent fertiliser rates; and nurses and chemists evaluating equivalent medication rates.

Lesson starter: You provide the starting numbers!

For each of the following answers, you must determine possible starting numbers. On all occasions, the numbers involved are less than 100.

1 The HCF of two numbers is 12.   Suggest two possible starting numbers.
2 The HCF of three numbers is 11.   Suggest three possible starting numbers.
3 The LCM of two numbers is 30.   Suggest two possible starting numbers.
4 The LCM of three numbers is 75.   Suggest three possible starting numbers.
5 The HCF of four numbers is 1.   Suggest four possible numbers.
6 The LCM of four numbers is 24.   Suggest four possible numbers.

KEY IDEAS

■ **HCF** stands for **highest common factor**. It is the highest (i.e. largest) factor that is common to the numbers provided.
  • For example, to find the HCF of 24 and 40:
    Factors of 24 are 1, 2, 3, 4, 6, 8, 12 and 24.
    Factors of 40 are 1, 2, 4, 5, 8, 10, 20 and 40.
    Therefore, common factors of 24 and 40 are 1, 2, 4 and 8.
    Therefore, the highest common factor of 24 and 40 is 8.

■ **LCM** stands for **lowest common multiple**. It is the lowest (i.e. smallest) multiple that is common to the numbers provided.
  • For example, to find the LCM of 20 and 12:
    Multiples of 20 are 20, 40, 60, 80, 100, 120, 140, …
    Multiples of 12 are 12, 24, 36, 48, 60, 72, 84, 96, 108, 120, 132, …
    Therefore, common multiples of 20 and 12 are 60, 120, 180, …
    Therefore, the lowest common multiple of 20 and 12 is 60.

■ The LCM of two numbers can always be found by multiplying the two numbers together and dividing by their HCF.
  • For example, to find the LCM of 20 and 12.
    The HCF of 20 and 12 is 4.
    Therefore, the LCM of 20 and 12 is $20 \times 12 \div 4 = 60$.

BUILDING UNDERSTANDING

1 The factors of 12 are 1, 2, 3, 4, 6 and 12, and the factors of 16 are 1, 2, 4, 8 and 16.
  a What are the common factors of 12 and 16?
  b What is the HCF of 12 and 16?

2 State the missing numbers to find out the HCF of 18 and 30.
  Factors of 18 are 1, __, 3, __, __ and 18.
  Factors of __ are 1, __, __, 5, __, 10, __ and 30.
  Therefore, the HCF of 18 and 30 is __.

3 The first 10 multiples of 8 are 8, 16, 24, 32, 40, 48, 56, 64, 72 and 80.
  The first 10 multiples of 6 are 6, 12, 18, 24, 30, 36, 42, 48, 54 and 60.
  a What are two common multiples of 8 and 6?
  b What is the LCM of 8 and 6?

4 State the missing numbers to find out the LCM of 9 and 15.
  Multiples of 9 are 9, 18, __, 36, __, __, __, __, 81 and __.
  Multiples of 15 are __, 30, __, 60, 75, __, __ and 120.
  Therefore, the LCM of 9 and 15 is __.

Example 4   Finding the highest common factor (HCF)

Find the highest common factor (HCF) of 36 and 48.

SOLUTION

Factors of 36 are:

1, 2, 3, 4, 6, 9, 12, 18 and 36.

Factors of 48 are:

1, 2, 3, 4, 6, 8, 12, 16, 24 and 48.

The HCF of 36 and 48 is 12.

EXPLANATION

$1 \times 36 = 36, \quad 2 \times 18 = 36, \quad 3 \times 12 = 36,$
$4 \times 9 = 36, \quad 6 \times 6 = 36$

$1 \times 48 = 48, 2 \times 24 = 48, 3 \times 16 = 48,$
$4 \times 12 = 48, 6 \times 8 = 48$

Common factors are 1, 2, 3, 4, 6 and 12, of which 12 is the highest.

Now you try

Find the highest common factor (HCF) of 30 and 48.

Example 5   Finding the lowest common multiple (LCM)

Find the lowest common multiple (LCM) of the following pairs of numbers.

a   5 and 11

b   6 and 10

SOLUTION

a   The LCM of 5 and 11 is 55.

b   The LCM of 6 and 10 is 30.

EXPLANATION

Note that the HCF of 5 and 11 is 1.
$5 \times 11 \div 1 = 55$
Alternatively, list multiples of 5 and 11 and then choose the lowest number in both lists.

Note that the HCF of 6 and 10 is 2.
Alternatively, list multiples of both numbers.
The LCM of 6 and 10 is $6 \times 10 \div 2 = 30$.
Multiples of 6 are 6, 12, 18, 24, 30, 36, …
Multiples of 10 are 10, 20, 30, 40, …

Now you try

Find the lowest common multiple (LCM) of the following pairs of numbers.

a   4 and 7

b   10 and 15

Exercise 2B

FLUENCY		1, 2(½), 4(½)	2–5(½)	3–6(½)

Example 4

1 Find the HCF of the following pairs of numbers.

  a 15 and 25   **b** 20 and 30

Example 4

2 Find the HCF of the following pairs of numbers.

  a 4 and 5   **b** 8 and 13   **c** 2 and 12   **d** 3 and 15
  e 16 and 20   **f** 15 and 60   **g** 50 and 150   **h** 48 and 72
  i 80 and 120   **j** 75 and 125   **k** 42 and 63   **l** 28 and 42

Example 4

3 Find the HCF of the following groups of numbers. That is, find the highest number which is a factor of all the provided numbers.

  a 20, 40, 50   **b** 6, 15, 42   **c** 50, 100, 81
  d 18, 13, 21   **e** 24, 72, 16   **f** 120, 84, 144

Example 5

4 Find the LCM of the following pairs of numbers.

  a 4 and 9   **b** 3 and 7   **c** 12 and 5
  d 10 and 11   **e** 4 and 6   **f** 5 and 10
  g 12 and 18   **h** 6 and 9   **i** 20 and 30
  j 12 and 16   **k** 44 and 12   **l** 21 and 35

Example 5

5 Find the LCM of the following groups of numbers. That is, find the lowest number which is a multiple of all the provided numbers.

  a 2, 3, 5   **b** 3, 4, 7   **c** 2, 3, 4
  d 3, 5, 9   **e** 4, 5, 8, 10   **f** 6, 12, 18, 3

6 Find the HCF of the following pairs of numbers and then use this information to help calculate the LCM of the same pair of numbers.

  a 15 and 20   **b** 12 and 24   **c** 14 and 21   **d** 45 and 27

PROBLEM-SOLVING		7, 8	8, 9	8–10

7 Find the LCM of 13 and 24.

8 Find the HCF of 45 and 72.

9 Find the LCM and HCF of 260 and 390.

10 Andrew runs laps of a circuit in 4 minutes. Bryan runs laps of the same circuit in 3 minutes. Chris can run laps of the same circuit in 6 minutes. They all start together on the starting line and run a race that goes for 36 minutes.

  a What is the first time, after the start, that they will all cross over the starting line together?

  b How many laps will each boy complete in the race?

  c How many times does Bryan overtake Andrew during this race?

2B   Highest common factor and lowest common multiple

| | 11 | 11, 12 | 12, 13 |

11 Given that the HCF of a pair of different numbers is 8, find the two numbers:
  a if both numbers are less than 20
  b when one number is in the 20s and the other in the 30s.

12 Given that the LCM of a pair of different numbers is 20, find the seven possible pairs of numbers.

13 The rule for finding the LCM of two numbers x and y is $\dfrac{x \times y}{\text{HCF}(x, y)}$. Is the rule for the LCM of three

numbers x, y and z $\dfrac{x \times y \times z}{\text{HCF}(x, y, z)}$? Explain your answer.

ENRICHMENT: LCM of large groups of numbers | – | – | 14 |

14 a Find the LCM of these single-digit numbers: 1, 2, 3, 4, 5, 6, 7, 8, 9.
   b Find the LCM of these first 10 natural numbers: 1, 2, 3, 4, 5, 6, 7, 8, 9, 10.
   c Compare your answers to parts **a** and **b**. What do you notice? Explain.
   d Find the LCM of the first 11 natural numbers.

2C   Divisibility tests   EXTENDING

LEARNING INTENTIONS
- To know the meaning of the terms divisible, divisor, dividend, quotient and remainder
- To understand that divisibility tests can be used to check if a number is divisible by another number without performing the division
- To be able to test for divisibility by 2, 3, 4, 5, 6, 8, 9 and 10

It is useful to know whether a large number is exactly divisible by another number. Although we can always carry out the division algorithm, this can be a difficult and tedious process for large numbers. There are simple divisibility tests for each of the single-digit numbers, with the exception of 7. These divisibility tests determine whether or not the number is divisible by the chosen divisor.

When a barcode is scanned, an algorithm first checks whether the code is valid. The digits are combined using a formula, then a divisibility rule is applied to test if it is a genuine barcode.

Lesson starter: Five questions in 5 minutes

In small groups, attempt to solve the following five questions in 5 minutes.

1   Some numbers greater than 1 are only divisible by 1 and themselves. What are these numbers called?
2   Is 21 541 837 divisible by 3?
3   What two-digit number is the 'most divisible' (i.e. has the most factors)?
4   Find the smallest number that is divisible by 1, 2, 3, 4, 5 and 6.
5   Find a number that is divisible by 1, 2, 3, 4, 5, 6, 7 and 8.

KEY IDEAS

■ A number is said to be **divisible** by another number if there is **no remainder** after the division has occurred. For example, 20 is divisible by 4 because $20 \div 4 = 5$ with no remainder.

■ If the divisor divides into the **dividend** exactly, then the **divisor** is said to be a factor of that number.

■ **Division notation**
The first number is called the **dividend** and the second number is called the **divisor**.
Example: $27 \div 4 = 6$ remainder 3
Another way of representing this information is
$27 = 4 \times 6 + 3$.

dividend $\longrightarrow$
divisor $\longrightarrow$
$\dfrac{27}{4} = 6 \text{ rem. } 3 = 6\dfrac{3}{4}$
remainder
quotient

■ **Key terms**
- **Dividend**   The starting number; the total; the amount you have
- **Divisor**   The number doing the dividing; the number of groups
- **Quotient**   The number of times the divisor went into the dividend, also known as 'the answer' to a division calculation
- **Remainder**   The number left over; the number remaining (sometimes written as 'rem.')

■ **Divisibility tests**

1 All numbers are divisible by 1.
2 All even numbers are divisible by 2. Last digit must be a 0, 2, 4, 6 or 8.
3 The sum of the digits must be divisible by 3.
4 The number formed from the last two digits must be divisible by 4.
5 The last digit must be a 0 or 5.
6 Must pass the divisibility tests for 2 and 3.
7 (There is no easy test for divisibility by 7.)
8 The number formed from the last three digits must be divisible by 8.
9 The sum of the digits must be divisible by 9.
10 The last digit must be 0.

BUILDING UNDERSTANDING

1 Give a reason why:
   a 8631 is not divisible by 2
   b 31 313 is not divisible by 3
   c 426 is not divisible by 4
   d 5044 is not divisible by 5
   e 87 548 is not divisible by 6
   f 214 125 is not divisible by 8
   g 3 333 333 is not divisible by 9
   h 56 405 is not divisible by 10

2 Give the remainder when:
   a 326 is divided by 3
   b 21 154 is divided into groups of four
   c 72 is divided into six groups
   d 45 675 is shared into five groups

3 Which three divisibility tests involve calculating the sum of the digits?

4 If you saw only the last digit of a 10-digit number, which three divisibility tests (apart from 1) could you still apply?

Example 6   Applying divisibility tests

Determine whether or not the following calculations are possible without leaving a remainder.
a 54 327 ÷ 3
b 765 146 ÷ 8

SOLUTION

a Digit sum = 21
   Yes, 54 327 is divisible by 3.

b
$$8\overline{)146}^{\ 6} \quad \underline{18}\ \text{rem. 2}$$
No, 765 146 is not divisible by 8.

EXPLANATION

$5 + 4 + 3 + 2 + 7 = 21$
21 is divisible by 3, therefore 54 327 must be divisible by 3.

Check whether the last three digits are divisible by 8.
They are not, therefore the original number is not divisible by 8.

Now you try

Determine whether or not the following calculations are possible without leaving a remainder. Give a reason why or why not.

a $52\,962 \div 3$ b $309\,482 \div 4$

Example 7   Testing for divisibility

Carry out divisibility tests on the given number and fill in the table with ticks or crosses.

Number	Divisible by 2	Divisible by 3	Divisible by 4	Divisible by 5	Divisible by 6	Divisible by 8	Divisible by 9	Divisible by 10
48 569 412								

SOLUTION

Number	Divisible by 2	Divisible by 3	Divisible by 4	Divisible by 5	Divisible by 6	Divisible by 8	Divisible by 9	Divisible by 10
48 569 412	✓	✓	✓	✗	✓	✗	✗	✗

EXPLANATION

48 569 412 is an even number and therefore is divisible by 2.

48 569 412 has a digit sum of 39 and therefore is divisible by 3, but not by 9.

48 569 412 is divisible by 2 and 3; therefore it is divisible by 6.

The last two digits are 12, which is divisible by 4.

The last three digits are 412, which is not divisible by 8.

The last digit is a 2 and therefore 48 569 412 is not divisible by 5 or 10.

Now you try

Carry out divisibility tests on the number 726 750 to decide which of the following numbers it is divisible by: 2, 3, 5, 6, 8, 9 and 10.

Exercise 2C

FLUENCY	1–5	1–6($\frac{1}{2}$)	6, 7

Example 6 1   Use the divisibility test for 3 to determine whether the following numbers are divisible by 3.

a   572   b   87   c   6012   d   7301

Example 6 2   Use the divisibility tests for 2 and 5 to determine whether the following calculations are possible without leaving a remainder.

a $4308 \div 2$ b $522 \div 5$ c $7020 \div 5$ d $636 \div 2$

Example 6 **3** Use the divisibility test for 9 to determine whether the following calculations are possible without leaving a remainder.

    a $363 \div 9$ **b** $702 \div 9$ **c** $2143 \div 9$ **d** $8712 \div 9$

Example 6 **4** Use the divisibility test for 6 to determine whether the following numbers are divisible by 6.

    a 332   **b** 402   **c** 735   **d** 594

Example 6 **5** Use the divisibility tests for 4 and 8 to determine whether the following calculations are possible without leaving a remainder.

    a $528 \div 4$ **b** $714 \div 4$ **c** $9200 \div 8$ **d** $5100 \div 8$

Example 6 **6** Determine whether the following calculations are possible without leaving a remainder.

    a $23\,562 \div 3$ **b** $39\,245\,678 \div 4$ **c** $1\,295\,676 \div 9$ **d** $213\,456 \div 8$

    e $3\,193\,457 \div 6$ **f** $2\,000\,340 \div 10$ **g** $51\,345\,678 \div 5$ **h** $215\,364 \div 6$

    i $9543 \div 6$ **j** $25\,756 \div 2$ **k** $56\,789 \div 9$ **l** $324\,534\,565 \div 5$

Example 7 **7** Carry out divisibility tests on the given numbers and fill in the table with ticks or crosses.

Number	Divisible by 2	Divisible by 3	Divisible by 4	Divisible by 5	Divisible by 6	Divisible by 8	Divisible by 9	Divisible by 10
243 567								
28 080								
189 000								
1 308 150								
1 062 347								

PROBLEM-SOLVING		8, 9(½)	8, 9(½), 10	11–14

8 **a** Can Julie share \$113 equally among her three children?

    b Julie finds one more dollar on the floor and realises that she can now share the money equally among her three children. How much do they each receive?

9 Write down five two-digit numbers that are divisible by:

    a 5   **b** 3

    c 2   **d** 6

    e 8   **f** 9

    g 10   **h** 4

10 The game of 'clusters' involves a group getting into smaller-sized groups as quickly as possible once a particular group size has been called out. If a year level consists of 88 students, which group sizes would ensure no students are left out of a group?

11 How many of the whole numbers between 1 and 250 inclusive are not divisible by 5?

12 How many two-digit numbers are divisible by both 2 and 3?

13 Blake is older than 20 but younger than 50. His age is divisible by 2, 3, 6 and 9. How old is he?

14 Find the largest three-digit number that is divisible by both 6 and 7.

REASONING		15	15, 16	16, 17

15 A number is divisible by 15 if it is divisible by 3 and by 5.
  a Determine if 3225 is divisible by 15, explaining why or why not.
  b Determine if 70 285 is divisible by 15, explaining why or why not.
  c The number 2 ☐ 47 ☐ is divisible by 15. Each box stands for a single missing digit and the two missing digits could be the same as each other or different digits. What could this number be? Try to list as many as possible.

16 a Is the number 968 362 396 392 139 963 359 divisible by 3?
  b Many of the digits in the number above can actually be ignored when calculating the digit sum. Which digits can be ignored and why?
  c To determine if the number above is divisible by 3, only five of the 21 digits actually need to be added together. Find this 'reduced' digit sum.

17 The divisibility test for the numeral 4 is to consider whether the number formed by the last two digits is a multiple of 4. Complete the following sentences to make a more detailed divisibility rule.
  a If the second-last digit is even, the last digit must be either a ____, ____ or ____.
  b If the second-last digit is odd, the last digit must be either a ____ or ____.

ENRICHMENT: Divisible by 11?		–	–	18

18 a Write down the first nine multiples of 11.
  b What is the difference between the two digits for each of these multiples?
  c Write down some three-digit multiples of 11.
  d What do you notice about the sum of the first digit and the last digit?

The following four-digit numbers are all divisible by 11:
1606, 2717, 6457, 9251, 9306

  e Find the sum of the odd-placed digits and the sum of the even-placed digits. Then subtract the smaller sum from the larger. What do you notice?
  f Write down a divisibility rule for the number 11.
  g Which of the following numbers are divisible by 11?
      i 2 594 669   **ii** 45 384 559   **iii** 488 220
      iv 14 641   **v** 1 358 024 679   **vi** 123 456 789 987 654 321

An alternative method is to alternate adding and subtracting each of the digits.
For example: 4 134 509 742 is divisible by 11.
Alternately adding and subtracting the digits will give the following result:
$$4 - 1 + 3 - 4 + 5 - 0 + 9 - 7 + 4 - 2 = 11$$

  h Try this technique on some of your earlier numbers.

2D Prime numbers

A **prime number** is defined as a positive whole number that has exactly two distinct factors: 1 and itself. It is believed that prime numbers (i.e. positive whole numbers with only two factors) were first studied by the ancient Greeks. More recently, the introduction of computers has allowed for huge developments in this field. Computers have allowed mathematicians to determine which large numbers are primes. Programs have also been written to automatically generate huge prime numbers that could not be calculated previously by hand.

Cryptography makes online transactions secure by secretly selecting two large prime numbers and finding their product. It would take years for a powerful computer to find the prime factors of this product, so the data is safe.

There are some interesting prime numbers that have patterns in their digits; for example, 12 345 678 901 234 567 891. This is known as an ascending prime.

You can also get palindromic primes, such as 111 191 111 and 123 494 321.

Below is a palindromic prime number that reads the same upside down or when viewed in a mirror.

$$1 8 8 8 0 8 1 8 0 8 8 8 1$$

Lesson starter: How many primes?

How many numbers from 1 to 100 are prime?

You and a classmate have 4 minutes to come up with your answer.

KEY IDEAS

- A **prime number** is a positive whole number that has exactly two distinct factors: 1 and itself.

- The prime numbers less than 20 are 2, 3, 5, 7, 11, 13, 17 and 19.

- A number that has more than two factors is called a **composite number**.

- The numbers 0 and 1 are neither prime nor composite numbers.

- The number 2 is prime. It is the only even prime number.

BUILDING UNDERSTANDING

1 The factors of 12 are 1, 2, 3, 4, 6 and 12. Is 12 a prime number?

2 The factors of 13 are 1 and 13. Is 13 a prime number?

3 State the first 10 prime numbers.

4 State the first 10 composite numbers.

5 What is the first prime number greater than 100?

6 Explain why 201 is not the first prime number greater than 200. (Hint: find another factor besides 1 and 201.)

Example 8   Determining whether a number is a prime or composite

State whether each of these numbers is a prime or composite: 22, 35, 17, 11, 9, 5.

SOLUTION	EXPLANATION
Prime: 5, 11, 17	5, 11, 17 have only two factors (1 and themselves).
Composite: 9, 22, 35	9, 22 and 35 each have more than two factors. $9 = 3 \times 3$, $22 = 2 \times 11$, $35 = 5 \times 7$

Now you try

State whether each of these numbers is prime or composite: $19, 32, 13, 79, 57, 95$.

Example 9   Finding prime factors

Find the prime factors of 30.

SOLUTION	EXPLANATION
Factors of 30 are: 1, 2, 3, 5, 6, 10, 15, 30	Find the entire set of factors first.
Prime numbers from this list of factors are 2, 3 and 5.	Include only the prime numbers in your list.

Now you try

Find the prime factors of 84.

Exercise 2D

FLUENCY	1, 2–3(½)	2–3(½), 4	2–3(⅓), 4

Example 8

1 State whether each of the following is a prime (P) or composite (C) number.

   a 7   **b** 24   **c** 29

Example 8

2 State whether each of the following is a prime (P) or composite (C) number.

   a 14   **b** 23   **c** 70   **d** 37   **e** 51   **f** 27
   g 19   **h** 3   **i** 8   **j** 49   **k** 99   **l** 59
   m 2   **n** 31   **o** 39   **p** 89   **q** 71   **r** 103

Example 9

3 Find the prime factors of:

   a 42   **b** 39   **c** 60   **d** 25   **e** 28   **f** 36

4 List the composite numbers between, but not including:

   a 30 and 50   **b** 50 and 70   **c** 80 and 100

PROBLEM-SOLVING	5	5(½), 6, 7	6–8

5 The following are not prime numbers, yet they are the product (×) of two primes. Find the two primes for each of the following numbers.

   a 55   **b** 91   **c** 143   **d** 187   **e** 365   **f** 133

6 Which one of these composite numbers has the fewest prime factors?
   12, 14, 16, 18, 20

7 Twin primes are pairs of primes that are separated from each other by only one even number; for example, 3 and 5 are twin primes. Find three more pairs of twin primes.

8 13 and 31 are known as a pair of 'reverse numbers'. They are also both prime numbers. Find any other two-digit pairs of prime reverse numbers.

REASONING	9	9, 10	10, 11

9 Many mathematicians believe that every even number greater than 2 is the sum of two prime numbers. For example, 28 is $11 + 17$. Show how each of the even numbers between 30 and 50 can be written as the sum of two primes.

10 Give two examples of a pair of primes that add to a prime number. Explain why all possible pairs of primes that add to a prime must include the number 2.

11 Find three different prime numbers that are less than 100 and which sum to a fourth different prime number. There are more than 800 possible answers. See how many you can find.

ENRICHMENT: Prime or not prime?	–	–	12

12 Design a spreadsheet that will check whether or not any number entered between 1 and 1000 is a prime number.
   If your spreadsheet is successful, someone should be able to enter the number 773 and very quickly be informed whether or not this is a prime number.
   You may choose to adapt your factor program (Enrichment activity **Exercise 2A**, Question **15**).

2E Using indices

LEARNING INTENTIONS
- To know the meaning of the terms powers, index form, basic numeral, base number and index number
- To understand what a^b means when a and b are whole numbers
- To be able to write a product in index form if there are repeated factors
- To be able to evaluate numeric expressions involving powers using multiplication

When repeated multiplication of a number occurs, the expression can be simplified using **powers**. This involves writing the repeated factor as the **base number** and then including an **index number** to indicate how many times this factor must be multiplied by itself. This is also known as writing a number in **index form**. For example, $2 \times 2 \times 2$ can be written as 2^3. The base number is 2 and the index number is 3.

Powers are also used to represent very large and very small numbers. For example, $400\,000\,000\,000\,000$ would be written as 4×10^{14}. This way of writing a number is called standard form or scientific notation, as there are some very large numbers involved in science.

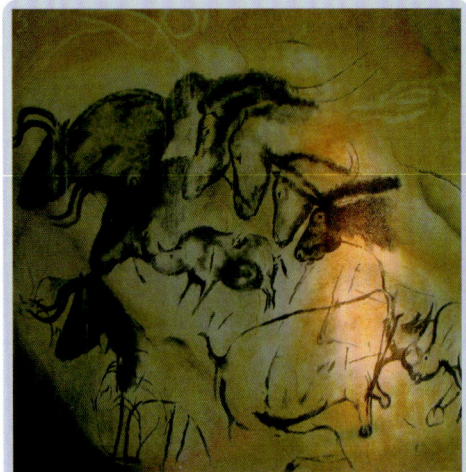

10^3 seconds $\approx$ 17 minutes; 10^6 seconds $\approx$ 12 days; 10^9 seconds $\approx$ 32 years. 10^{12} seconds ago $\approx$ 31 710 years ago, before any written language, before the pyramids of Egypt, and when prehistoric artists painted the walls of Chauvet Cave, France.

Lesson starter: A better way ...

- What is a better way of writing the calculation $2 + 2 + 2 + 2 + 2 + 2 + 2 + 2 + 2 + 2$ (that is not the answer, 20)?
- What is a better way of writing the calculation $2 \times 2 \times 2 \times 2 \times 2 \times 2 \times 2 \times 2 \times 2 \times 2$ (that is not the answer, 1024)?

You may need to access the internet to find out some of the following answers.

Computers have the capacity to store a lot of information. As you most likely know, computer memory is given in bytes.

- How many bytes (B) are in a kilobyte (kB)?
- How many kilobytes are in a megabyte (MB)?
- How many megabytes are in a gigabyte (GB)?
- How many gigabytes are in a terabyte (TB)?
- How many bytes are in a gigabyte?
  (*Hint*: It is over 1 billion and it is far easier to write this number as a power!)
- Why do computers frequently use base 2 (binary) numbers?

KEY IDEAS

- **Powers** are used to help write expressions involving repeated multiplication in a simplified form using indices.

  For example: $8 \times 8 \times 8 \times 8 \times 8$ can be written as 8^5

- When writing a **basic numeral** as a power, you need a base number and an index number. This is also known as writing an expression in **index form**.

$$\underset{\text{base number}}{8}\overset{\text{index number}}{^5} = \underset{\text{basic numeral}}{32\,768}$$

- a^b reads as 'a to the power of b'. In expanded form it would look like:

$$\underbrace{a \times a \times a \times a \times a \ldots\ldots \times a}_{\text{the factor } a \text{ appears } b \text{ times}}$$

- Powers take priority over multiplication and division in the order of operations.

  For example:
  $$3 + 2 \times 4^2 = 3 + 2 \times 16$$
  $$= 3 + 32$$
  $$= 35$$

- Note: $2^3 \neq 2 \times 3$, that is, $2^3 \neq 6$.

  Instead: $2^3 = 2 \times 2 \times 2 = 8$.

BUILDING UNDERSTANDING

1 Select the correct answer from the following alternatives.

3^7 means:

A 3×7 B $3 \times 3 \times 3$ C $7 \times 7 \times 7$

D $3 \times 7 \times 3 \times 7 \times 3 \times 7 \times 3$ E $3 \times 3 \times 3 \times 3 \times 3 \times 3 \times 3$ F 37

2 Select the correct answer from the following alternatives.

$9 \times 9 \times 9 \times 9 \times 9$ can be simplified to:

A 9×5 B 5×9 C 5^9

D 9^5 E $99\,999$ F 95

3 State the missing values in the table.

Index form	Base number	Index number	Basic numeral
2^3	2	3	8
5^2			
10^4			
2^7			
1^{12}			
12^1			
0^5			

Example 10   Converting to index form

Simplify the following expressions by writing them in index form.

a $5 \times 5 \times 5 \times 5 \times 5 \times 5$ **b** $3 \times 3 \times 2 \times 3 \times 2 \times 3$

SOLUTION	EXPLANATION
a $5 \times 5 \times 5 \times 5 \times 5 \times 5 = 5^6$	The number 5 is the repeated factor and it appears six times.
b $3 \times 3 \times 2 \times 3 \times 2 \times 3$ $= 2 \times 2 \times 3 \times 3 \times 3 \times 3$ $= 2^2 \times 3^4$	First, write the factors in increasing order (all the 2s before the 3s). The number 2 is written two times, and the number 3 is written four times.

Now you try

Simplify the following expressions by writing them in index form.

a $7 \times 7 \times 7 \times 7 \times 7$ **b** $5 \times 5 \times 11 \times 5 \times 11 \times 11 \times 5$

Example 11   Expanding a power

Expand and evaluate the following terms.

a 2^4 **b** $2^3 \times 5^2$

SOLUTION	EXPLANATION
a $2^4 = 2 \times 2 \times 2 \times 2$ $\quad = 16$	Write 2 down four times and multiply.
b $2^3 \times 5^2 = 2 \times 2 \times 2 \times 5 \times 5$ $\quad\quad\quad = 8 \times 25$ $\quad\quad\quad = 200$	Write the number 2 three times, and the number 5, two times.

Now you try

Expand and evaluate the following terms.

a 5^3 **b** $2^3 \times 10^2$

⊳

Example 12   Evaluating expression with powers

Evaluate:

a $7^2 - 6^2$

b $2 \times 3^3 + 10^2 + 1^7$

SOLUTION

a $7^2 - 6^2 = 7 \times 7 - 6 \times 6$
$= 49 - 36$
$= 13$

b $2 \times 3^3 + 10^2 + 1^7$
$= 2 \times 3 \times 3 \times 3 + 10 \times 10 + 1 \times 1 \times 1$
$\times 1 \times 1 \times 1 \times 1$
$= 54 + 100 + 1$
$= 155$

EXPLANATION

Write in expanded form (optional step).
Powers are evaluated before the subtraction occurs.

Write in expanded form (optional step).
Follow order of operation rules.
Carry out the multiplication first, then carry out the addition.

Now you try

Evaluate:

a $5^2 - 3^2$

b $5 \times 2^3 + 4^2 - 3^2$

Exercise 2E

FLUENCY	1, 2–3(½), 5–7(½)	2–3(½), 5–8(½)	2–3(⅓), 4, 5–8(⅓)

Example 10a

1 Simplify the following expressions by writing them in index form.

    a $3 \times 3 \times 3$ **b** $2 \times 2 \times 2 \times 2 \times 2$ **c** $15 \times 15 \times 15 \times 15$

    d $10 \times 10 \times 10 \times 10$ **e** 6×6 **f** $1 \times 1 \times 1 \times 1 \times 1 \times 1$

Example 10a

2 Simplify the following expressions by writing them in index form.

    a $4 \times 4 \times 5 \times 5 \times 5$ **b** $3 \times 3 \times 3 \times 3 \times 7 \times 7$ **c** $2 \times 2 \times 2 \times 5 \times 5$

Example 10b

3 Simplify the following expressions by writing them as powers.

    a $3 \times 3 \times 5 \times 5$ **b** $7 \times 7 \times 2 \times 2 \times 7$ **c** $12 \times 9 \times 9 \times 12$

    d $8 \times 8 \times 5 \times 5 \times 5$ **e** $6 \times 3 \times 6 \times 3 \times 6 \times 3$ **f** $13 \times 7 \times 13 \times 7 \times 7 \times 7$

    g $4 \times 13 \times 4 \times 4 \times 7$ **h** $10 \times 9 \times 10 \times 9 \times 9$ **i** $2 \times 3 \times 5 \times 5 \times 3 \times 2 \times 2$

Example 10b

4 Simplify by writing using powers.

    $2 \times 3 \times 5 \times 5 \times 3 \times 3 \times 2 \times 2 \times 2 \times 5 \times 3 \times 2 \times 2 \times 5 \times 3$

Example 11a

5 Expand these terms. (Do not evaluate.)

    a 2^4 **b** 17^2 **c** 9^3 **d** 3^7

    e 14^4 **f** 8^8 **g** 10^5 **h** 54^3

Example 11b   **6**   Expand these terms. (Do not evaluate.)

     a $3^5 \times 2^3$ **b** $4^3 \times 3^4$ **c** $7^2 \times 5^3$ **d** $4^6 \times 9^3$

     e 5×7^4 **f** $2^2 \times 3^3 \times 4^1$ **g** $11^5 \times 9^2$ **h** $20^3 \times 30^2$

Example 12   **7**   Evaluate:

     a 2^5 **b** 8^2 **c** 10^3 **d** $3^2 \times 2^3$

     e 10^4 **f** $2^3 \times 5^3$ **g** $1^6 \times 2^6$ **h** $11^2 \times 1^8$

Example 12   **8**   Evaluate:

     a $3^2 + 4^2$ **b** $2 \times 5^2 - 7^2$ **c** $8^2 - 2 \times 3^3$

     d $(9 - 5)^3$ **e** $2^4 \times 2^3$ **f** $2^7 - 1 \times 2 \times 3 \times 4 \times 5$

     g $1^4 + 2^3 + 3^2 + 4^1$ **h** $10^3 - 10^2$ **i** $(1^{27} + 1^{23}) \times 2^2$

PROBLEM-SOLVING

                        9–10(½)   9–10(½), 11   9–10(¼), 11, 12

9   Determine the index number for the following basic numerals.

     a $16 = 2^?$ **b** $16 = 4^?$ **c** $64 = 4^?$ **d** $64 = 2^?$

     e $27 = 3^?$ **f** $100 = 10^?$ **g** $49 = 7^?$ **h** $625 = 5^?$

10   Write one of the symbols $<$, $=$ or $>$ in the box to make the following statements true.

     a $2^6 \ \square \ 2^9$ **b** $8^3 \ \square \ 8^2$ **c** $2^4 \ \square \ 4^2$ **d** $3^2 \ \square \ 4^2$

     e $6^4 \ \square \ 5^3$ **f** $12^2 \ \square \ 3^4$ **g** $11^2 \ \square \ 2^7$ **h** $1^8 \ \square \ 2^3$

11   A text message is sent to five friends. Each of the five friends then forwards it to five other friends and each of these people also sends it to five other friends. How many people does the text message reach, not including those who forwarded the message?

12   Jane writes a chain email and sends it to five friends. Assume each person who receives the email reads it and, within 5 minutes of the email arriving, sends it to five other people who have not yet received it.

     a   Show, with calculations, why at least 156 people (including Jane) will have read the email within 15 minutes of Jane sending it.

     b   If the email always goes to a new person, and assuming every person in Australia has an email address and access to email, how long would it take until everyone in Australia has read the message? (Australian population is approx. 26 million people.)

     c   How many people will read the email within 1 hour?

     d   Using the same assumptions as above, how long would it take until everyone in the world has read the message? (World population is approx. 8 billion people.)

     e   Approximately how many people will have read the email within 2 hours?

REASONING

                              13   13, 14   13(½), 14, 15

13   Write the correct operation ($+$, $-$, $\times$, $\div$) in the box to make the following equations true.

     a $3^2 \ \square \ 4^2 = 5^2$ **b** $2^4 \ \square \ 4^2 = 4^4$ **c** $2^7 \ \square \ 5^3 = 3^1$

     d $9^2 \ \square \ 3^4 = 1^{20}$ **e** $10^2 \ \square \ 10^2 = 10^4$ **f** $10^2 \ \square \ 8^2 = 6^2$

14 The sequence 1, 2, 4, 8, 16, 32, 64, 128, 256, 512 gives the powers of 2 less than 1000.

  a Write the sequence of powers of 3 less than 1000 (starting 1, 3, 9, …)

  b Write the sequence of powers of 5 less than 1000 (starting 1, 5, 25, …)

  c **i** For the original sequence (of powers of 2), list the difference between each term and the next term (for example: $2 - 1 = 1, 4 - 2 = 2, …$)

    ii What do you notice about this sequence of differences?

  d **i** List the difference between consecutive terms in the powers of 3 sequence.

    ii What do you notice about this sequence of differences?

15 Find a value for a and for b such that $a \neq b$ and $a^b = b^a$.

ENRICHMENT: Investigating factorials –   –   16

16 In mathematics, the exclamation mark (!) is the symbol for factorials.

$4! = 4 \times 3 \times 2 \times 1 = 24$

$n! = n \times (n-1) \times (n-2) \times (n-3) \times (n-4) \times … \times 6 \times 5 \times 4 \times 3 \times 2 \times 1$

  a Evaluate $1!, 2!, 3!, 4!, 5!$ and $6!$

  Factorials can be written in prime factor form, which involves powers.

  For example: $6! = 6 \times 5 \times 4 \times 3 \times 2 \times 1$
$$= (2 \times 3) \times 5 \times (2 \times 2) \times 3 \times 2 \times 1$$
$$= 2^4 \times 3^2 \times 5$$

  b Write these numbers in prime factor form.

    i 7!   **ii** 8!   **iii** 9!   **iv** 10!

  c Write down the last digit of 12!

  d Write down the last digit of 99!

  e Find a method of working out how many consecutive zeros would occur on the right-hand end of each of the following factorials if they were evaluated. (*Hint*: Consider prime factor form.)

    i 5!   **ii** 6!   **iii** 15!   **iv** 25!

  f $10! = 3! \times 5! \times 7!$ is an example of one factorial equal to the product of three factorials. Express 24! as the product of two or more factorials.

If you could fly at the speed of light, covering 9.5×10^{12} km per year (ten trillion km/year), it would take you 10^6 years (one million years) to cross our Milky Way galaxy.

2F Prime decomposition

LEARNING INTENTIONS
- To understand that composite numbers can be broken down into a product of prime factors
- To be able to use a factor tree to find the prime factors of a number (including repeated factors)
- To be able to express a prime decomposition using powers of prime numbers

All composite numbers can be broken down (i.e. decomposed) into a unique set of prime factors. A common way of performing the decomposition into prime factors is using a factor tree. Starting with the given number, 'branches' come down in pairs, representing a pair of factors that multiply to give the number above it. This process continues until prime factors are reached.

Lesson starter: Composition of numbers from prime factors

'Compose' composite numbers by multiplying the following sets of prime factors. The first one has been done for you.

a $2 \times 3 \times 5 = 30$ b $2 \times 3 \times 7 \times 3 \times 2$ c $3^2 \times 2^3$ d $5 \times 11 \times 2^2$

e $13 \times 17 \times 2$ f $2^2 \times 5^2 \times 7^2$ g $2^5 \times 3^4 \times 7$ h $11 \times 13 \times 17$

The reverse of this process is called **decomposition**, where a number like 30 is broken down into the prime factors $2 \times 3 \times 5$.

KEY IDEAS

■ Every **composite number** can be expressed as a product of its **prime factors**.

■ A **factor tree** can be used to show the prime factors of a composite number.

■ Each 'branch' of a factor tree eventually terminates in a prime factor.

■ Powers are often used to efficiently represent composite numbers in prime factor form. For example:

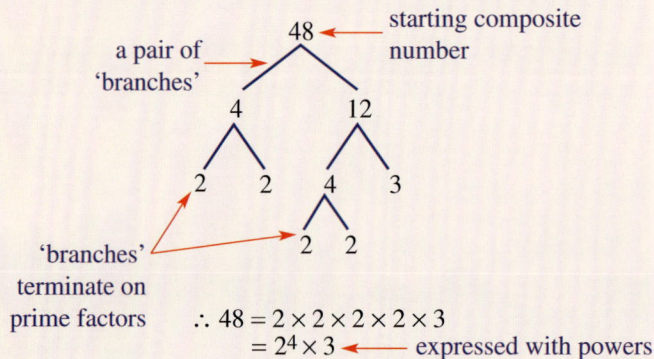

$$\therefore 48 = 2 \times 2 \times 2 \times 2 \times 3$$
$$= 2^4 \times 3 \longleftarrow \text{expressed with powers}$$

■ It does not matter which pair of factors you choose to start a factor tree. The final result of prime factors will always be the same.

■ It is conventional to write the prime factors in **ascending** (i.e. increasing) order. For example: $600 = 2^3 \times 3 \times 5^2$

BUILDING UNDERSTANDING

1 Sort the following list of numbers into two groups: composite numbers and prime numbers.
15, 13, 7, 5, 8, 9, 27, 23, 11, 4, 12, 2

2 State the missing numbers in the empty boxes to complete the following factor trees.

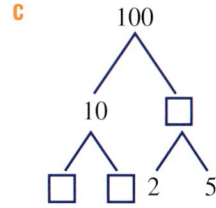

a
```
        40
       /  \
     □     8
          / \
        □    2
       / \
      2   2
```

b
```
        30
       /  \
      5    □
          / \
         □   3
```

c
```
        100
       /   \
     10     □
    / \    / \
   □   □  2   5
```

3 State the numbers on the next set of branches for each of the following factor trees.

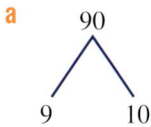

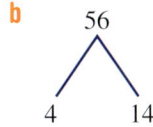

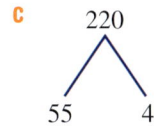

a
```
      90
     /  \
    9    10
```

b
```
      56
     /  \
    4    14
```

c
```
      220
     /   \
    55    4
```

4 State the following prime factors, using powers.

a $2 \times 3 \times 3 \times 2 \times 2$

b $5 \times 3 \times 3 \times 3 \times 3 \times 5$

c $7 \times 2 \times 3 \times 7 \times 2$

d $3 \times 3 \times 2 \times 11 \times 11 \times 2$

Example 13 Expressing composite numbers in prime factor form

Express the number 60 in prime factor form.

SOLUTION

```
        60
       /  \
      5    12
          /  \
         3    4
             / \
            2   2
```

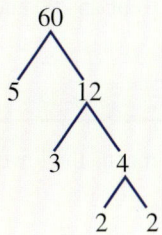

$\therefore 60 = 2 \times 2 \times 3 \times 5$

$60 = 2^2 \times 3 \times 5$

EXPLANATION

A pair of factors for 60 is 5×12.

The 5 branch terminates since 5 is a prime factor.

A pair of factors for 12 is 3×4.

The 3 branch terminates since 3 is a prime factor.

A pair of factors for 4 is 2×2.

Both these branches are now terminated.

Hence, the composite number, 60, can be written as a product of each terminating branch. The factors are listed in increasing order.

Now you try

Express the number 180 in prime factor form.

Exercise 2F

FLUENCY	1, 2(½)	2–3(½)	2–3(¼)

Example 13

1 Express the following numbers in prime factor form.

    a 36   **b** 100

Example 13

2 Express the following numbers in prime factor form.

a	72	**b**	24	**c**	38
d	44	**e**	124	**f**	80
g	96	**h**	16	**i**	75
j	111	**k**	64	**l**	56

Example 13

3 Express these larger numbers in prime factor form. Note that it can be helpful to start your factor tree with a power of 10 (e.g. 100) on one branch.

a	600	**b**	800
c	5000	**d**	2400
e	1 000 000	**f**	45 000
g	820	**h**	690

PROBLEM-SOLVING	4, 5	4–6	5–7

4 Match the correct composite number (**a** to **d**) to its set of prime factors (**A** to **D**).

a	120	**A**	$2^4 \times 3^2$
b	144	**B**	$2 \times 3 \times 5^2$
c	180	**C**	$2^2 \times 3^2 \times 5$
d	150	**D**	$2 \times 3 \times 2 \times 5 \times 2$

5 Find the smallest composite number that has the five smallest prime numbers as factors.

6 **a** Express 144 and 96 in prime factor form.

    b By considering the prime factor form, determine the highest common factor (HCF) of 144 and 96.

7 **a** Express 25 200 and 77 000 in prime factor form.

    b By considering the prime factor form, determine the highest common factor (HCF) of 25 200 and 77 000.

REASONING	8	8–10	9–12

8 The numbers 15 and 21 can be written in prime factor form as 3×5 and 3×7. This means the lowest common multiple (LCM) of 15 and 21 is $3 \times 5 \times 7$ (which is 105).

    a Use the prime factor forms to find the LCM of 14 and 21.

    b Use the prime factor forms to find the LCM of 15 and 33.

    c $60 = 2^2 \times 3 \times 5$ and $210 = 2 \times 3 \times 5 \times 7$. Use this to find the LCM of 60 and 210.

9 Represent the number 24 with four different factor trees, each resulting in the same set of prime factors. Note that simply swapping the order of a pair of factors does not qualify it as a different form of the factor tree.

10 Only one of the following is the correct set of prime factors for 424.

  A $2^2 \times 3^2 \times 5$

  B $2 \times 3^2 \times 5^2$

  C 53×8

  D $2^3 \times 53$

  a Justify why you can eliminate alternatives **A** and **B** straight away.

  b Why can option **C** be discarded as an option?

  c Show that option **D** is the correct answer.

11 a State the error in each of the following prime factor trees and/or prime decompositions.

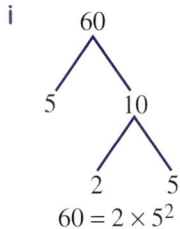

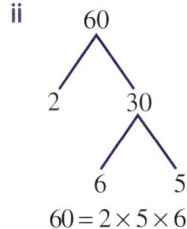

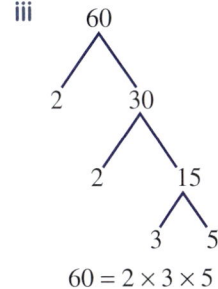

i

60 → 5, 10; 10 → 2, 5

$60 = 2 \times 5^2$

ii

60 → 2, 30; 30 → 6, 5

$60 = 2 \times 5 \times 6$

iii

60 → 2, 30; 30 → 2, 15; 15 → 3, 5

$60 = 2 \times 3 \times 5$

  b What is the correct way to express 60 in prime factor form?

12 Write 15 different (i.e. distinct) factor trees for the number 72.

ENRICHMENT: Four distinct prime factors — — 13–15

13 There are 16 composite numbers that are smaller than 1000 which have four distinct prime factors. For example: $546 = 2 \times 3 \times 7 \times 13$.

By considering the prime factor possibilities, find all 16 composite numbers and express each of them in prime factor form.

14 A conjecture is a statement that may appear to be true but has not been proved conclusively. Goldbach's conjecture states that 'Every even number greater than 2 is the sum of two prime numbers.' For example, $53 = 47 + 5$.

Challenge: Try this for every even number from 4 to 50.

15 Use the internet to find the largest known prime number.

Supercomputers like this have been used to search for prime numbers with millions of digits.

2A **1** Find the complete set of factors for each of these numbers.
  a 16
  b 70

2A **2** Write down the first four multiples for each of these numbers.
  a 7
  b 20

2B **3** Find the HCF of the following groups of numbers.
  a 15 and 10
  b 36, 54 and 72

2B **4** Find the LCM of the following groups of numbers.
  a 8 and 12
  b 3, 5 and 9

2C **5** Use divisibility rules to determine whether the following calculations are possible without
Ext   leaving a remainder. Give a reason for each answer.
  a $34\,481 \div 4$
  b $40\,827 \div 3$
  c $824\,730 \div 6$
  d $5\,247\,621 \div 9$

2C **6** The game of 'clusters' involves a group getting into smaller-sized groups as quickly as possible
Ext   once a particular group size has been called out. If a year level consists of 120 students, which
     group sizes (of more than one person) would ensure no students are left out of a group?

2D **7** State whether each of the following is a prime (P) or composite (C) number or neither (N). Give
     reasons.
  a 60   b 1   c 13   d 0

2D **8** Find the prime numbers that are factors of these numbers.
  a 35
  b 36

2E **9** Simplify the following expressions by writing them as powers.
  a $5 \times 5 \times 5 \times 5$
  b $7 \times 3 \times 7 \times 7 \times 3 \times 7 \times 7$

2E **10** Expand and evaluate the following terms.
  a 3^4
  b $1^4 \times 3^2$
  c $5^1 \times 10^4$
  d $(12 - 8)^2$
  e $9^2 - 3^3 \times 2$

2F **11** Express the following numbers in prime factor form, writing factors in ascending order.
  a 24
  b 180

2G Squares and square roots

A square number can be illustrated by considering the area of a square with a whole number as its side length.

For example:

4 cm

←4 cm→

Area of square $= 4 \text{ cm} \times 4 \text{ cm} = 16 \text{ cm}^2$

Therefore, 16 is a square number.

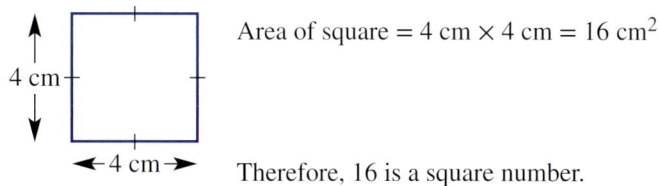

Another way of representing square numbers is through a square array of dots.

For example:

• • •

• • •

• • •

Number of dots $= 3$ rows of 3 dots
$= 3 \times 3$ dots
$= 3^2$ dots
$= 9$ dots

Therefore, 9 is a square number.

To produce a square number you multiply the number by itself. All square numbers written in index form will have a power of 2.

Finding a square root of a number is the opposite of squaring a number.

For example: $4^2 = 16$ and therefore $\sqrt{16} = 4$.

To find square roots we use our knowledge of square numbers. A calculator is also frequently used to find square roots. Geometrically, the square root of a number is the side length of a square whose area is that number.

Lesson starter: Speed squaring tests

In pairs, test one another's knowledge of square numbers.

- Ask 10 quick questions, such as '3 squared', '5 squared' etc.
- Have two turns each. Time how long it takes each of you to answer the 10 questions.
- Aim to be quicker on your second attempt.

Write down the first 10 square numbers.

- Begin to memorise these important numbers.
- Time how quickly you can recall the first 10 square numbers without looking at a list of numbers.
- Can you go under 5 seconds?

KEY IDEAS

■ Any whole number multiplied by itself produces a **square number**.

For example: $5^2 = 5 \times 5 = 25$. Therefore, 25 is a square number.

- Square numbers are also known as **perfect squares**.
- The first 12 square numbers (not including 0, which is counted as the "zero'th square number") are:

Index form	1^2	2^2	3^2	4^2	5^2	6^2	7^2	8^2	9^2	10^2	11^2	12^2
Basic numeral	1	4	9	16	25	36	49	64	81	100	121	144

- All non-zero square numbers have an odd number of factors.
- The symbol for squaring is $()^2$. The brackets are optional, but can be useful when simplifying more difficult expressions.

■ The **square root** of a given number is the 'non-negative' number that, when multiplied by itself, produces the given number.

- The symbol for square rooting is $\sqrt{9}$.
- Finding a square root of a number is the opposite of squaring a number.

  For example: $4^2 = 16$; hence, $\sqrt{16} = 4$

  We read this as: '4 squared equals 16, therefore, the square root of 16 equals 4.'
- Squaring and square rooting are 'opposite' operations.

  For example: $(\sqrt{7})^2 = 7$ also $\sqrt{(7)^2} = 7$
- A list of common square roots is:

Square root form	$\sqrt{1}$	$\sqrt{4}$	$\sqrt{9}$	$\sqrt{16}$	$\sqrt{25}$	$\sqrt{36}$	$\sqrt{49}$	$\sqrt{64}$	$\sqrt{81}$	$\sqrt{100}$	$\sqrt{121}$	$\sqrt{144}$
Basic numeral	1	2	3	4	5	6	7	8	9	10	11	12

- We can locate any square root between two positive integers by considering its square. For example, $\sqrt{31}$ must be between 5 and 6 because 31 is between $5^2 = 25$ and $6^2 = 36$.

BUILDING UNDERSTANDING

1 Consider a square of side length 6 cm. What would be the area of this shape? What special type of number is your answer?

2 State the first 15 square numbers in index form and as basic numerals.

3 We can confirm that 9 is a square number by drawing the diagram shown at right.
   a Explain using dots, why 6 is not a square number.
   b Explain using dots, why 16 is a square number.

4 Find:
   a 6^2
   b 5 squared
   c $(11)^2$
   d 10 to the power of 2
   e 7^2
   f 12×12

5 Find:
  a $\sqrt{25}$
  b the square root of 16
  c $\sqrt{100}$
  d the side length of a square that has an area of 49 cm^2

Example 14 Evaluating squares and square roots

Evaluate:
a 6^2
b $\sqrt{64}$
c $\sqrt{1600}$

SOLUTION

a $6^2 = 36$

b $\sqrt{64} = 8$

c $\sqrt{1600} = 40$

EXPLANATION

$6^2 = 6 \times 6$

$8 \times 8 = 64$
$\therefore \sqrt{64} = 8$

$40 \times 40 = 1600$
$\therefore \sqrt{1600} = 40$

Now you try

Evaluate:
a 9^2
b $\sqrt{36}$
c $\sqrt{4900}$

Example 15 Locating square roots between positive integers

State which consecutive whole numbers are either side of:
a $\sqrt{43}$
b $\sqrt{130}$

SOLUTION

a 6 and 7

b 11 and 12

EXPLANATION

$6^2 = 36$ and $7^2 = 49$
43 lies between the square numbers 36 and 49, so $\sqrt{43}$ lies between 6 and 7.

$11^2 = 121$ and $12^2 = 144$
130 lies between the square numbers 121 and 144, so $\sqrt{130}$ lies between 11 and 12.

Now you try

State which consecutive whole numbers are either side of:
a $\sqrt{11}$
b $\sqrt{109}$

Example 16   Evaluating expressions involving squares and square roots

Evaluate:

a $3^2 - \sqrt{9} + 1^2$

b $\sqrt{8^2 + 6^2}$

SOLUTION

a $3^2 - \sqrt{9} + 1^2 = 9 - 3 + 1$
$= 7$

b $\sqrt{8^2 + 6^2} = \sqrt{64 + 36}$
$= \sqrt{100}$
$= 10$

EXPLANATION

$3^2 = 3 \times 3,\ \sqrt{9} = 3,\ 1^2 = 1 \times 1$

$8^2 = 8 \times 8,\ 6^2 = 6 \times 6$
$\sqrt{100} = 10$

Now you try

Evaluate:

a $4^2 - \sqrt{25} + 7^2$

b $\sqrt{5^2 - 4^2}$

Exercise 2G

FLUENCY   1, 2–5(½)   2–6(½)   2–6(⅓)

Example 14a   **1** Evaluate:
a 4^2 **b** 7^2 **c** 3^2 **d** 10^2

Example 14a   **2** Evaluate:
a 8^2 **b** 2^2 **c** 1^2 **d** 12^2
e 6^2 **f** 15^2 **g** 5^2 **h** 0^2
i 11^2 **j** 100^2 **k** 20^2 **l** 50^2

Example 14b   **3** Evaluate:
a $\sqrt{25}$ **b** $\sqrt{9}$ **c** $\sqrt{1}$ **d** $\sqrt{121}$
e $\sqrt{0}$ **f** $\sqrt{81}$ **g** $\sqrt{49}$ **h** $\sqrt{16}$
i $\sqrt{4}$ **j** $\sqrt{144}$ **k** $\sqrt{400}$ **l** $\sqrt{169}$

Example 14c   **4** Evaluate:
a $\sqrt{2500}$ **b** $\sqrt{6400}$ **c** $\sqrt{8100}$ **d** $\sqrt{729}$

Example 15   **5** State which consecutive whole numbers are either side of:
a $\sqrt{29}$ **b** $\sqrt{40}$ **c** $\sqrt{71}$ **d** $\sqrt{50}$
e $\sqrt{85}$ **f** $\sqrt{103}$ **g** $\sqrt{7}$ **h** $\sqrt{3}$

Example 16   **6** Evaluate:
a $3^2 + 5^2 - \sqrt{16}$ **b** 4×4^2 **c** $8^2 - 0^2 + 1^2$
d $1^2 \times 2^2 \times 3^2$ **e** $\sqrt{5^2 - 3^2}$ **f** $\sqrt{81} - 3^2$
g $6^2 \div 2^2 \times 3^2$ **h** $\sqrt{9} \times \sqrt{64} \div \sqrt{36}$ **i** $\sqrt{12^2 + 5^2}$

PROBLEM-SOLVING   7, 8   7–9   8–10

7 A square floor is covered with 64 square tiles.

    a Explain why the floor length must be 8 tile lengths.

    b Hence, find the perimeter of this floor in tile lengths.

    c If a square floor is covered with 81 square tiles, what would its perimeter be?

8 The value of $\sqrt{19}$ as a decimal starts with 4 because $\sqrt{19}$ is between 4 and 5. Find the units digit for the following.

    a $\sqrt{72}$ **b** $\sqrt{83}$ **c** $\sqrt{26}$ **d** $\sqrt{34}$

9 List all the square numbers between 101 and 200 (*Hint*: There are only four.)

10 **a** Find two square numbers that add to 85.

    b Find two square numbers that have a difference of 85.

Squares and square roots are used by people who work with triangles, such as engineers, architects, builders, carpenters and designers. Electricians use a square root to calculate voltage: $V = \sqrt{PR}$, where P is power and R is resistance.

REASONING   11   11, 12   12, 13

11 The value of 74^2 can be thought of as the area of a square with width 74 units. This square can be broken into smaller areas as shown.

So $74^2 = 70^2 + 2 \times 70 \times 4 + 4^2$
           $= 4900 + 560 + 16$
           $= 5476$

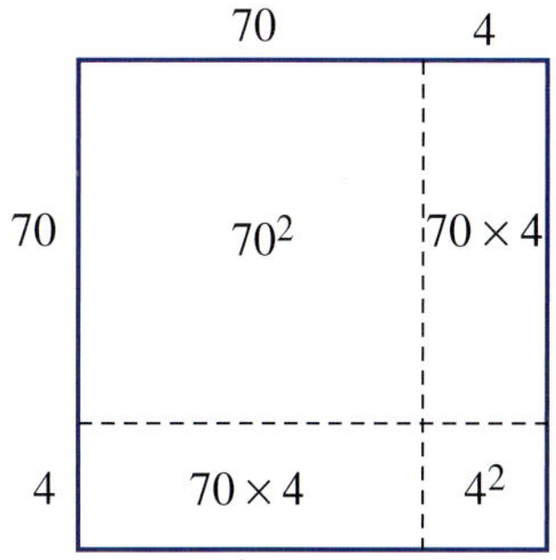

Use a diagram like the one on the right to calculate these values.

    a 34^2

    b 81^2

    c 103^2

	70	4
70	70^2	70×4
4	70×4	4^2

12 a Evaluate $3^2 \times 4^2$.

b Evaluate 12^2.

c The rule $a^2 \times b^2 = (a \times b)^2$ can be used to link $3^2 \times 4^2$ and 12^2. What are the values of a and b if $3^2 \times 4^2 = 12^2$?

d Check this formula using other numbers.

13 a Evaluate 11^2 and 111^2.

b Predict an answer for 1111^2.

c Evaluate 1111^2 and test your prediction.

ENRICHMENT: Exploring square patterns   –   –   14

14 a List the square numbers from 1^2 to 20^2 in a table like the one below.

n	1	2	3	...	20
n^2	1	4	9	...	400

b Add a new row to your table which gives the difference between each value and the previous one.

n	1	2	3	...	20
n^2	1	4	9	...	400
difference	–	3	5	...	

c What patterns do you notice in the differences between consecutive square numbers?

d Try to explain why these patterns occur. You could use a visual representation like dots arranged in square as below to help illustrate.

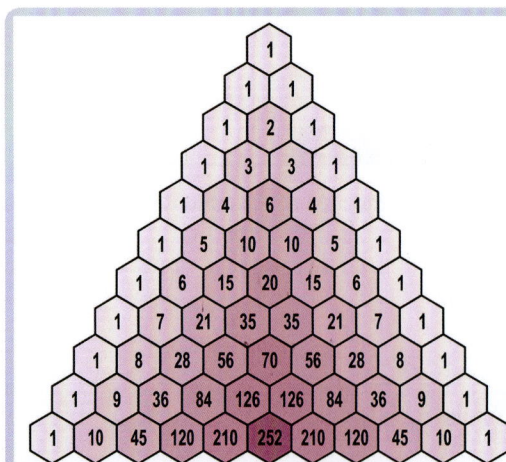

The number pattern shown here is known as Pascal's triangle, named after the French mathematician Blaise Pascal. Can you explain how the digits in each row of Pascal's triangle form the powers of 11?

2H Number patterns CONSOLIDATING

> **LEARNING INTENTIONS**
> • To understand what a number pattern (or number sequence) is
> • To be able to describe a pattern where there is a common difference (added or subtracted)
> • To be able to describe a pattern where there is a common ratio (multiplied or divided)
> • To be able to find terms in a number pattern with a common difference or ratio

Mathematicians commonly look at lists of numbers in an attempt to discover a pattern. They also aim to find a rule that describes the number pattern to allow them to predict future numbers in the sequence.

Here is a list of professional careers that all involve a high degree of mathematics and, in particular, involve looking at data so that comments can be made about past, current or future trends:

Statistician, economist, accountant, market researcher, financial analyst, cost estimator, actuary, stock broker, data scientist, research scientist, financial advisor, medical scientist, budget analyst, insurance underwriter and mathematics teacher!

People who study statistics find trends in population and employment numbers by analysing a sequence of percentage changes over previous years.

Financial analysts use sequences of previous percentage increases or decreases to forecast future earnings for various shares in the stock market.

Lesson starter: What's next?

A number sequence consisting of five terms is placed on the board. Four gaps are placed after the last number.

64, 32, 16, 8, 4, ___, ___, ___, ___

• Can you work out and describe the number pattern?
• Make up your own number pattern and test it on a class member.

KEY IDEAS

■ Number patterns are also known as **sequences**, and each number in a sequence is called a **term**.
- Each number pattern has a particular starting number and terms are generated by following a particular rule.

■ Strategies to determine the pattern involved in a number sequence include:
- Looking for a **common difference**
  Are terms increasing or decreasing by a constant amount?
  For example: 2, 6, 10, 14, 18, … Each term is increasing by 4.
- Looking for a **common ratio**
  Is each term being multiplied or divided by a constant amount?
  For example: 2, 4, 8, 16, 32, … Each term is being multiplied by 2.
- Looking for an increasing/decreasing difference
  Is there a pattern in the difference between pairs of terms?
  For example: 1, 3, 6, 10, 15, … The difference increases by 1 each term.
- Looking for two interlinked patterns
  Is there a pattern in the odd-numbered terms, and another pattern in the even-numbered terms?
  For example: 2, 8, 4, 7, 6, 6, … The odd-numbered terms increase by 2, the even-numbered terms decrease by 1.
- Looking for a special type of pattern
  Could it be a list of square numbers, prime numbers, Fibonacci numbers (1, 2, 3, 5, 8, 13, 21, …) etc.?
  For example: 1, 8, 27, 64, 125, … This is the pattern of cube numbers: $1^3, 2^3, 3^3, …$

BUILDING UNDERSTANDING

1 State the first five terms of the following number patterns.
- **a** starting number of 8, common difference of adding 3
- **b** starting number of 32, common difference of subtracting 1
- **c** starting number of 52, common difference of subtracting 4
- **d** starting number of 123, common difference of adding 7

2 State the first five terms of the following number patterns.
- **a** starting number of 3, common ratio of 2 (multiply by 2 each time)
- **b** starting number of 5, common ratio of 4
- **c** starting number of 240, common ratio of $\frac{1}{2}$ (divide by 2 each time)
- **d** starting number of 625, common ratio of $\frac{1}{5}$

3 State whether the following number patterns have a common difference (+ or −), a common ratio (× or ÷) or neither.
- **a** 4, 12, 36, 108, 324, …
- **b** 19, 17, 15, 13, 11, …
- **c** 212, 223, 234, 245, 256, …
- **d** 8, 10, 13, 17, 22, …
- **e** 64, 32, 16, 8, 4, …
- **f** 5, 15, 5, 15, 5, …
- **g** 2, 3, 5, 7, 11, …
- **h** 75, 72, 69, 66, 63, …

Example 17   Identifying patterns with a common difference

Find the next three terms for these number patterns that have a common difference.

a   6, 18, 30, 42, ___, ___, ___

b   99, 92, 85, 78, ___, ___, ___

SOLUTION	EXPLANATION
a 54, 66, 78	The common difference is 12. Continue adding 12 to generate the next three terms.
b 71, 64, 57	The pattern indicates the common difference is 7. Continue subtracting 7 to generate the next three terms.

Now you try

Find the next three terms for these number patterns that have a common difference.

a   7, 10, 13, 16, ___, ___, ___

b   187, 173, 159, 145, ___, ___, ___

Example 18   Identifying patterns with a common ratio

Find the next three terms for the following number patterns that have a common ratio.

a   2, 6, 18, 54, ___, ___, ___

b   256, 128, 64, 32, ___, ___, ___

SOLUTION	EXPLANATION
a 162, 486, 1458	The common ratio is 3. Continue multiplying by 3 to generate the next three terms.
b 16, 8, 4	The common ratio is $\frac{1}{2}$. Continue dividing by 2 to generate the next three terms.

Now you try

Find the next three terms for the following number patterns that have a common ratio.

a   5, 15, 45, ___, ___, ___

b   640, 320, 160, ___, ___, ___

Exercise 2H

FLUENCY 1, 2–5(½)   2–6(½)   2–6(¼)

1 Find the next three terms for these number patterns that have a common difference.

Example 17a

a i 5, 12, 19, ___, ___, ___
ii 32, 41, 50, ___, ___, ___

Example 17b

b i 37, 32, 27, ___, ___, ___
ii 91, 79, 67, ___, ___, ___

Example 17

2 Find the next three terms for the following number patterns that have a common difference.

a 3, 8, 13, 18, ___, ___, ___
b 4, 14, 24, 34, ___, ___, ___
c 26, 23, 20, 17, ___, ___, ___
d 106, 108, 110, 112, ___, ___, ___
e 63, 54, 45, 36, ___, ___, ___
f 9, 8, 7, 6, ___, ___, ___
g 101, 202, 303, 404, ___, ___, ___
h 75, 69, 63, 57, ___, ___, ___

Example 18

3 Find the next three terms for the following number patterns that have a common ratio.

a 2, 4, 8, 16, ___, ___, ___
b 5, 10, 20, 40, ___, ___, ___
c 96, 48, 24, ___, ___, ___
d 1215, 405, 135, ___, ___, ___
e 11, 22, 44, 88, ___, ___, ___
f 7, 70, 700, 7000, ___, ___, ___
g 256, 128, 64, 32, ___, ___, ___
h 1216, 608, 304, 152, ___, ___, ___

4 Find the missing numbers in each of the following number patterns.

a 62, 56, ___, 44, 38, ___, ___
b 15, ___, 35, ___, ___, 65, 75
c 4, 8, 16, ___, ___, 128, ___
d 3, 6, ___, 12, ___, 18, ___
e 88, 77, 66, ___, ___, ___, 22
f 2997, 999, ___, ___, 37
g 14, 42, ___, ___, 126, ___, 182
h 14, 42, ___, ___, 1134, ___, 10 206

5 Write the next three terms in each of the following sequences.

a 3, 5, 8, 12, ___, ___, ___
b 1, 2, 4, 7, 11, ___, ___, ___
c 1, 4, 9, 16, 25, ___, ___, ___
d 27, 27, 26, 24, 21, ___, ___, ___
e 2, 3, 5, 7, 11, 13, ___, ___, ___
f 2, 5, 11, 23, ___, ___, ___
g 2, 10, 3, 9, 4, 8, ___, ___, ___
h 14, 100, 20, 80, 26, 60, ___, ___, ___

6 Generate the next three terms for the following number sequences and give an appropriate name to the sequence.

a 1, 4, 9, 16, 25, 36, ___, ___, ___
b 1, 1, 2, 3, 5, 8, 13, ___, ___, ___
c 1, 8, 27, 64, 125, ___, ___, ___
d 2, 3, 5, 7, 11, 13, 17, ___, ___, ___
e 4, 6, 8, 9, 10, 12, 14, 15, ___, ___, ___
f 121, 131, 141, 151, ___, ___, ___

PROBLEM-SOLVING 7, 8   7–9   7–10

7 Complete the next three terms for the following challenging number patterns.

a 101, 103, 106, 110, ___, ___, ___
b 162, 54, 108, 36, 72, ___, ___, ___
c 3, 2, 6, 5, 15, 14, ___, ___, ___
d 0, 3, 0, 4, 1, 6, 3, ___, ___, ___

8 When making human pyramids, there is one less person on each row above, and it is complete when there is a row of only one person on the top.
Write down a number pattern for a human pyramid with 10 students on the bottom row. How many people are needed to make this pyramid?

9 The table below represents a seating plan with specific seat numbers for a section of a grandstand at a soccer ground. It continues upwards for another 20 rows.

Row 4	25	26	27	28	29	30	31	32
Row 3	17	18	19	20	21	22	23	24
Row 2	9	10	11	12	13	14	15	16
Row 1	1	2	3	4	5	6	7	8

a   What is the number of the seat directly above seat number 31?

b   What is the number of the seat on the left-hand edge of row 8?

c   What is the third seat from the right in row 14?

d   How many seats are in the grandstand?

10 Find the next five numbers in the following number pattern.

1, 4, 9, 1, 6, 2, 5, 3, 6, 4, 9, 6, 4, 8, 1, ___, ___, ___, ___, ___

REASONING   11   11, 12   12, 13

11 Jemima writes down the following number sequence: 7, 7, 7, 7, 7, 7, 7, …

Her friend Peta declares that this is not really a number pattern. Jemima defends her number pattern, stating that it is most definitely a number pattern as it has a common difference and also has a common ratio. What are the common difference and the common ratio for the number sequence above? Do you agree with Jemima or Peta?

12 Find the sum for each of the following number sequences.

a $1 + 2 + 3 + 4 + 5 + 6 + 7 + 8 + 9 + 10$

b $1 + 3 + 5 + 7 + 9 + 11 + 13 + 15 + 17 + 19$

c $1 + 2 + 3 + 4 + 5 + … + 67 + 68 + 69 + 70$

d $5 + 8 + 11 + 14 + 17 + 20 + 23 + 26 + 29 + 32 + 35 + 38$

13 **The great handshake problem**

There are a certain number of people in a room and they must all shake one another's hand. How many handshakes will there be if there are:

a   3 people in the room?

b   5 people in the room?

c   10 people in the room?

d   24 people in a classroom?

e n people in the room?

Diagram showing the possible handshakes with five people.

14 Read the following clues to work out the mystery number.

a I have three digits.

I am divisible by 5.

I am odd.

The product of my digits is 15.

The sum of my digits is less than 10.

I am less than 12×12.

b I have three digits.

The sum of my digits is 12.

My digits are all even.

My digits are all different.

I am divisible by 4.

The sum of my units and tens digits equals my hundreds digit.

c I have three digits.

I am odd and divisible by 5 and 9.

The product of my digits is 180.

The sum of my digits is less than 20.

I am greater than 30^2.

d Make up two of your own mystery number puzzles and submit your clues to your teacher.

The following problems will investigate practical situations drawing upon knowledge and skills developed throughout the chapter. In attempting to solve these problems, aim to identify the key information, use diagrams, formulate ideas, apply strategies, make calculations and check and communicate your solutions.

Prime number landscaping

1   The team at Prime Landscaping only like to plant trees, lay sleepers, or group large rocks in clumps where the number of items in the group is a prime number.

The landscaping team are interested in the prime number options available to them and the total number of objects that they might need to purchase for particular jobs.

a   Prime Landscaping want to arrange a pile of large rocks with fewer than 15 in the pile. What size groups are possible?

b   Would Prime Landscaping ever lay a group of 27 sleepers? Give a reason for your answer.

One of Prime Landscaping's clients said they only wanted trees or shrubs that were planted in even numbers as they disliked odd numbers of plants (such as a group of 3 trees or a group of 7 shrubs). Prime Landscaping felt confident they could meet the needs of their client and still stay true to their policy of planting only in groups of prime numbers.

c   What size group of plants did Prime Landscaping plant for their client?

A new client purchased 59 screening plants and wanted them to be planted in three different, but similar sized groups. Prime Landscaping said that this was possible and proceeded to plant the plants.

d   What size groups were the screening plants planted in?

Blinking rates

2   Diviesh tends to blink his eyes every four seconds, while Jordan blinks his eyes only every seven seconds. Blinking provides moisture to the eyes and prevents irritation and damage.

Diviesh and Jordan are interested in the number of times they will blink their eyes during various time intervals and how often they will blink at the same time depending on their blinking rates.

a   If Diviesh and Jordan both blink together, how long will it be until they blink together again?

b   How many times will Diviesh and Jordan blink together in one minute, and at what times will this occur?

Applications and problem-solving

Concentrated staring at a computer monitor can significantly reduce the eye blinking rate, and can result in what is known as 'gamer eye syndrome'.

Diviesh and Jordan were filmed playing a one-hour gaming session. Diviesh's blinking rate reduced to 3 blinks per minute, and Jordan's blinking rate reduced to 4 blinks per minute.

c At the start of a particular three-minute time period in their computer gaming session, Diviesh and Jordan both blinked together. If this time was referred to as 0 seconds, write down the time (in seconds) of Diviesh's next 10 blinks and Jordan's next 10 blinks.

d How frequently do Diviesh and Jordan blink together during a one-hour computer gaming session?

Excessive blinking can indicate a disorder of the nervous system. A doctor examined a particular patient and initially observed that their blink rate was 30 blinks per minute. She then decided to monitor the patient for a period of 5 minutes and was relieved to observe the patient only blinked 110 times.

e What was the average blinking rate (blinks per minute) for the patient over the 5 minute period?

A reluctant reader

3 A keen student mathematician, but reluctant reader, was encouraged by his Maths teacher to read just two pages at night on the first night and then simply add another two pages each night – so on the second night the student would have to read four pages, and then six pages on the third night and so on. The student agreed to do this.

The student is interested in how many pages he will be reading on particular nights and how long it will take to read a book of a certain size.

a How many pages would the student be reading on the 5th night?

b On what night was the student reading 16 pages?

c How many nights did it take the student to read a 182 page book?

d How big a book can the student read in a 30-day month?

e If a student wishes to read a 275 page book in 10 days, describe a different rule with a different pattern that would allow this to occur. List the number of pages the student would need to read each night.

21 Spatial patterns

Patterns can also be found in geometric shapes. Mathematicians examine patterns carefully to determine how the next term in the sequence is created. Ideally, a rule is formed that shows the relationship between the geometric shape and the number of objects (e.g. tiles, sticks, counters) required to make such a shape. Once a rule is established it can be used to make predictions about future terms in the sequence.

An architect uses spatial pattern analysis when designing open-plan offices, laboratories, museums, and seating arrangements in lecture rooms and concert halls.

Lesson starter: Stick patterns

Materials required: One box of toothpicks or a bundle of matchsticks per student.

- Generate a spatial pattern using your sticks.
- You must be able to make at least three terms in your pattern.
  For example:

- Ask your partner how many sticks would be required to make the next term in the pattern.
- Repeat the process with a different spatial design.

KEY IDEAS

■ A **spatial pattern** is a sequence of geometrical shapes that can be described by a **number pattern**.
  For example:

spatial pattern

number pattern   4   8   12

■ A spatial pattern starts with a simple geometric design. Future terms are created by adding on repeated shapes of the same design. If designs connect with an edge, the repetitive shape will be a subset of the original design, as the connecting edge does not need to be repeated.
  For example:

starting design   repeating design

■ To help describe a spatial pattern, it is generally converted to a number pattern and a common difference is observed.

■ The common difference is the number of objects (e.g. sticks) that need to be added on to create the next term.

■ A table of values shows the number of shapes and the number of sticks.

Number of squares	1	2	3	4	5
Number of sticks	4	8	12	16	20

■ A pattern rule tells how many sticks are needed for a certain number of shapes.
For example: Number of sticks = 4 × number of shapes

■ Rules can be found that connect the number of objects (e.g. sticks) required to produce the number of designs.
For example: hexagon design

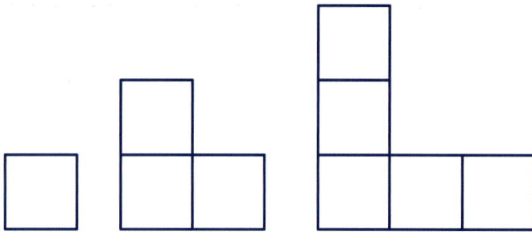

Rule: Number of sticks used = 6 × number of hexagons formed

BUILDING UNDERSTANDING

1 Describe or draw the next two terms for each of these spatial patterns.

a

b

2 For each of the following spatial patterns, describe or draw the starting geometrical design and also the geometrical design added on repetitively to create new terms. (For some patterns the repetitive design is the same as the starting design.)

a

b

c

Example 19   Drawing and describing spatial patterns

a   Draw the next two shapes in the spatial pattern shown.

b   Write the spatial pattern above as a number pattern relating the number of sticks required to make each shape.

c   Describe the pattern by stating how many sticks are required to make the first term, and how many sticks are required to make the next term in the pattern.

SOLUTION

a

b   5, 8, 11, 14, 17

c   5 sticks are required to start the pattern, and an additional 3 sticks are required to make the next term in the pattern.

EXPLANATION

Follow the pattern, by adding three sticks each time to the right-hand side.

Count the number of sticks in each term. Look for a pattern.

Now you try

a   Draw the next two shapes in the spatial pattern shown.

b   Write the spatial pattern as a number pattern relating the number of sticks required to make each shape.

c   Describe the pattern by stating how many sticks are required to make the first term, and how many sticks are required to make the next term in the pattern.

Example 20   Finding a general rule for a spatial pattern

a Draw the next two shapes in this spatial pattern.

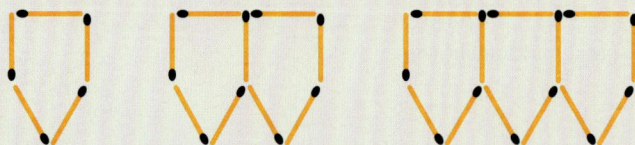

b Copy and complete the table.

Number of triangles	1	2	3	4	5
Number of sticks required	3				

c Describe a rule connecting the number of sticks required to the number of triangles.

d Use your rule to predict how many sticks would be required to make 20 triangles.

SOLUTION

a

b

Number of triangles	1	2	3	4	5
Number of sticks required	3	6	9	12	15

c Number of sticks = 3 × number of triangles

d Number of sticks = 3 × 20
   = 60
∴ 60 sticks are required.

EXPLANATION

Follow the pattern by adding one triangle each time.

An extra 3 sticks are required to make each new triangle.

3 sticks are required per triangle.

number of triangles = 20
so number of sticks = 3 × 20

Now you try

a Draw the next two shapes in this spatial pattern.

b Copy and complete the table.

Number of shapes	1	2	3	4	5
Number of sticks required	5				

c Describe a rule connecting the number of sticks required to the number of shapes.

d Use your rule to predict how many sticks would be required to make 20 shapes.

Exercise 2I

Example 19

1 **a** Draw the next two shapes in the spatial pattern shown.

   b Write the spatial pattern above as a number pattern in regard to the number of sticks required to make each shape.

   c Describe the pattern by stating how many sticks are required to make the first term, and how many sticks are required to make the next term in the pattern.

Example 19

2 For each of the spatial patterns below:

   i Draw the next two shapes.

   ii Write the spatial pattern as a number pattern.

   iii Describe the pattern by stating how many sticks are required to make the first term and how many more sticks are required to make the next term in the pattern.

   a

   b

   c

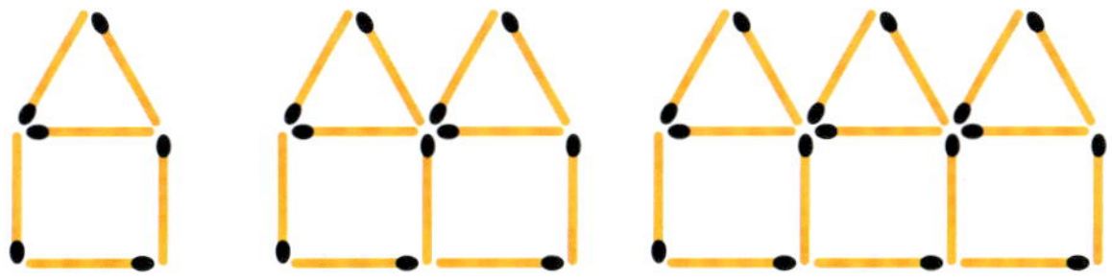

   d

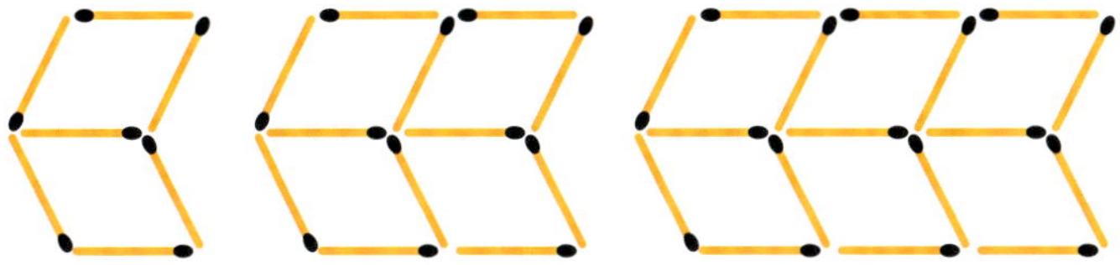

   e

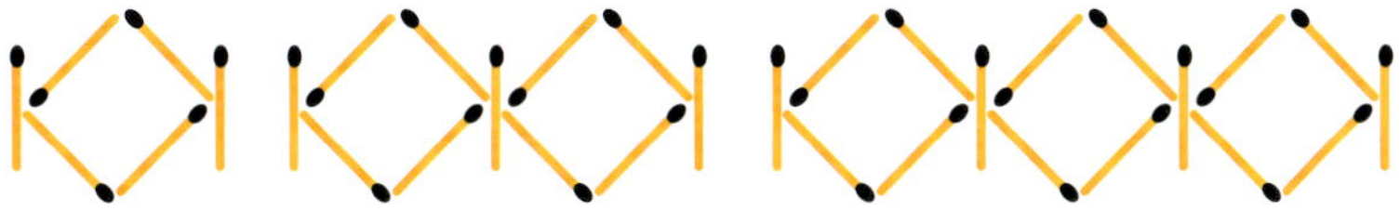

   f

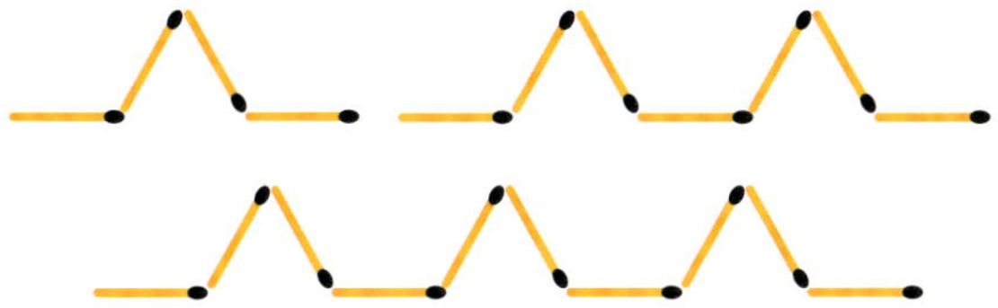

Example 20 **3 a** Draw the next two shapes in this spatial pattern.

b Copy and complete the table.

Number of crosses	1	2	3	4	5
Number of sticks required					

c Describe a rule connecting the number of sticks required to the number of crosses produced.

d Use your rule to predict how many sticks would be required to make 20 crosses.

Example 20 **4 a** Draw the next two shapes in this spatial pattern.

b Copy and complete the table. Planks are vertical and horizontal.

Number of fence sections	1	2	3	4	5
Number of planks required					

c Describe a rule connecting the number of planks required to the number of fence sections produced.

d Use your rule to predict how many planks would be required to make 20 fence sections.

PROBLEM-SOLVING	5, 6	6, 7	6–8

5 At North Park Primary School, the classrooms have trapezium-shaped tables. Mrs Greene arranges her classroom's tables in straight lines, as shown.

a Draw a table of results showing the relationship between the number of tables in a row and the number of students that can sit at the tables. Include results for up to five tables in a row.

b Describe a rule that connects the number of tables placed in a straight row to the number of students that can sit around the tables.

c The room allows seven tables to be arranged in a straight line. How many students can sit around the tables?

d There are 65 students in Grade 6 at North Park Primary School. Mrs Greene would like to arrange the tables in one straight line for an outside picnic lunch. How many tables will she need?

6 The number of tiles required to pave around a spa is related to the size of the spa. The approach is to use large tiles that are the same size as that of the smallest spa.

A spa of length 1 unit requires 8 tiles to pave around its perimeter, whereas a spa of length 4 units requires 14 tiles to pave around its perimeter.

a Complete a table of values relating length of spa and number of tiles required, for values up to and including a spa of length 6 units.

b Describe a rule that connects the number of tiles required for the length of the spa.

c The largest spa manufactured is 15 units long. How many tiles would be required to pave around its perimeter?

d A paving company has only 30 tiles left. What is the largest spa they would be able to tile around?

7 Which rule correctly describes this spatial pattern of 'hats'?

A Number of sticks = 7 × number of hats
B Number of sticks = 7 × number of hats + 1
C Number of sticks = 6 × number of hats + 2
D Number of sticks = 6 × number of hats

8 Which rule correctly describes this spatial pattern?

A Number of sticks = 5 × number of houses + 1
B Number of sticks = 6 × number of houses + 1
C Number of sticks = 6 × number of houses
D Number of sticks = 5 × number of houses

REASONING   9(½)   9(½), 10   10, 11

9 Design a spatial pattern to fit each of the following number patterns.

a 4, 7, 10, 13, …
b 4, 8, 12, 16, …
c 3, 5, 7, 9, …
d 3, 6, 9, 12, …
e 5, 8, 11, 14, …
f 6, 11, 16, 21, …

10 A rule to describe a special window spatial pattern is written as $y = 4 \times x + 1$, where y represents the number of 'sticks' required and x is the number of windows created.

a How many sticks are required to make one window?
b How many sticks are required to make 10 windows?
c How many sticks are required to make g windows?
d How many windows can be made from 65 sticks?

11 A rule to describe a special fence spatial pattern is written as $y = m \times x + n$, where y represents the number of pieces of timber required and x represents the number of fencing panels created.

a How many pieces of timber are required to make the first panel?

b What does m represent?

c Draw the first three terms of the fence spatial pattern for $m = 4$ and $n = 1$.

ENRICHMENT: Cutting up a circle   –   –   12

12 What is the *greatest* number of sections into which you can divide a circle, using only a particular number of straight line cuts?

a Explore the problem above. (*Hint*: For a given number of lines, you may need to draw several circles until you are sure that you have found the maximum number of sections.)

Note: The greatest number of sections is required and, hence, only one of the two diagrams below is correct for three straight line cuts.

Incorrect.
Not the maximum number of sections for 3 lines.

Correct.
The maximum number of sections for 3 lines.

Copy and complete this table of values.

Number of straight cuts	1	2	3	4	5	6	7
Maximum number of sections			7				

b Can you discover a pattern for the maximum number of sections created? What is the maximum number of sections that could be created with 10 straight line cuts?

c The formula for determining the maximum number of cuts is quite complex:

$$\text{sections} = \frac{1}{2} \times \text{cuts}^2 + \frac{1}{2} \times \text{cuts} + 1$$

Verify that this formula works for the values you listed in the table above.

Using the formula, how many sections could be created with 20 straight cuts?

2J Tables and rules

A rule describes a relationship between two values, often called *input* and *output*.

For example, the rule *output* = *input* + 3 describes a relationship between input and output. If the input value is 5, then the output value will be 8.

This is sometimes shown as a function machine:

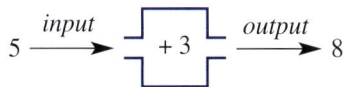

From tables of human heights and bone lengths, rules are found, e.g. height = 2.3 × femur length + 65.5 cm . By measuring bones from the Petra tombs, archaeologists calculated the height of ancient humans.

$$5 \xrightarrow{\ input\ } \boxed{+3} \xrightarrow{\ output\ } 8$$

If a different input is put in the function machine above, the output will change.

We can use a table to list a selection of input and output combinations, as below:

input	output
5	8
9	12
51	54
100	103

Another example of a rule is output = 4 × input, which we could use to create a table of values.

input	output
1	4
2	8
3	12
. . .	. . .

This can be drawn as a function machine too:

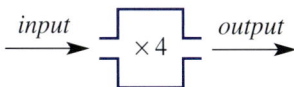

$$\xrightarrow{\ input\ } \boxed{\times 4} \xrightarrow{\ output\ }$$

Lesson starter: Guess the output

A table of values is drawn on the board with three completed rows of data.

- Additional values are placed in the *input* column. What *output* values should be in the *output* column?
- After adding *output* values, decide which rule fits (models) the values in the table and check that it works for each *input* and *output* pair.
  Four sample tables are listed below.

input	output
2	6
5	9
6	10
1	?
8	?

input	output
12	36
5	15
8	24
0	?
23	?

input	output
2	3
3	5
9	17
7	?
12	?

input	output
6	1
20	8
12	4
42	?
4	?

KEY IDEAS

■ A **rule** shows the relation between two varying quantities.

For example: *output* = *input* + 3 is a rule connecting the two quantities *input* and *output*.
The values of the *input* and the *output* can vary, but we know from the rule that the value of the *output* will always be 3 more than the value of the *input*. Rules can be thought of as function machines:

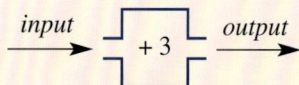

$$\text{input} \longrightarrow \boxed{+3} \longrightarrow \text{output}$$

■ A **table of values** can be created from any given rule. To complete a table of values, we start with the first *input* number and use the rule to calculate the corresponding *output* number. we do this for each of the *input* numbers in the table.

For example: For the rule *output* = *input* + 3,

$$\text{If } input = 4, \text{ then}$$
$$output = 4 + 3$$
$$= 7$$

Replacing the *input* with a number is known as **substitution**.

■ Often, a rule can be determined from a table of values. On close inspection of the values, a relationship may be observed. Each of the four operations should be considered when looking for a connection.

input	1	2	3	4	5	6
output	6	7	8	9	10	11

■ By inspection, it can be observed that every *output* value is 5 more than the corresponding *input* value. The rule can be written as: *output* = *input* + 5.

BUILDING UNDERSTANDING

1 State whether each of the following statements is true or false.
 a If *output = input × 2*, then when *input = 7*, *output = 14*.
 b If *output = input − 2*, then when *input = 5*, *output = 7*.
 c If *output = input + 2*, then when *input = 0*, *output = 2*.
 d If *output = input ÷ 2*, then when *input = 20*, *output = 10*.

2 Choose the rule (A to D) for each table of values (a to d).

Rule A: *output = input − 5*   Rule B: *output = input + 1*

Rule C: *output = 4 × input*   Rule D: *output = 5 + input*

a

input	20	14	6
output	15	9	1

b

input	8	10	12
output	13	15	17

c

input	4	5	6
output	5	6	7

d

input	4	3	2
output	16	12	8

Example 21   Completing a table of values

Copy and complete each table for the given rule.

a *output = input − 2*

input	3	5	7	12	20
output					

b *output = (3 × input) + 1*

input	4	2	9	12	0
output					

SOLUTION

a *output = input − 2*

input	3	5	7	12	20
output	1	3	5	10	18

b *output = (3 × input) + 1*

input	4	2	9	12	0
output	13	7	28	37	1

EXPLANATION

Replace each *input* value in turn into the rule.
e.g. When *input* is 3:
   output = 3 − 2 = 1

Replace each *input* value in turn into the rule.
e.g. When *input* is 4:
   output = (3 × 4) + 1 = 13

Now you try

Copy and complete each table for the given rule.

a *output = input + 4*

input	3	5	7	12	20
output					

b *output = (8 × input) − 5*

input	1	2	5	7	10
output					

Example 22   Finding a rule from a tables of values

Find the rule for each of these tables of values.

a
input	3	4	5	6	7
output	12	13	14	15	16

b
input	1	2	3	4	5
output	7	14	21	28	35

SOLUTION

a $output = input + 9$

b $output = input \times 7$ or $output = 7 \times input$

EXPLANATION

Each *output* value is 9 more than the *input* value.

By inspection, it can be observed that each *output* value is 7 times bigger than the *input* value.

Now you try

Find the rule for each of these tables of values.

a
input	10	11	12	13	14
output	5	6	7	8	9

b
input	2	3	4	5	6
output	12	18	24	30	36

Exercise 2J

FLUENCY   1–5   2–5   3–5

Example 21a

1   Copy and complete each table for the given rule.

a $output = input + 5$
input	1	3	5	10	20
output					

b $output = 2 \times input$
input	3	9	1	10	6
output					

Example 21a

2   Copy and complete each table for the given rule.

a $output = input + 3$
input	4	5	6	7	10
output					

b $output = input \times 4$
input	5	1	3	9	0
output					

c $output = input - 8$
input	11	18	9	44	100
output					

d $output = input \div 5$
input	5	15	55	0	100
output					

Example 21b

3   Copy and complete each table for the given rule.

a $output = (10 \times input) - 3$
input	1	2	3	4	5
output					

b $output = (input \div 2) + 4$
input	6	8	10	12	14
output					

c $output = (3 \times input) + 1$
input	5	12	2	9	14
output					

d $output = (2 \times input) - 4$
input	3	10	11	7	50
output					

Example 22 **4** State the rule for each of these tables of values.

a

input	4	5	6	7	8
output	5	6	7	8	9

b

input	1	2	3	4	5
output	4	8	12	16	20

Example 22 **5** State the rule for each of these tables of values.

a

input	10	8	3	1	14
output	21	19	14	12	25

b

input	6	18	30	24	66
output	1	3	5	4	11

PROBLEM-SOLVING   6, 7   6, 7   7, 8

6 A rule relating the radius and diameter of a circle is diameter = 2 × radius.
In the following table, radius is the input and diameter is the output.

a Write the rule above using input and output, rather than radius and diameter.

b Copy and complete the missing values in the table.

input	1	2	3	7				
output					20	30	100	162

7 Find a simple rule for the following tables and then copy and complete the tables.

a

input	4	10	13	6			5	11	2
output			39		24	9	15		6

b

input	12	93	14	17		10			
output	3			8	12	1	34	0	200

8 Copy and complete each table for the given rule.

a output = input × input − 2

input	3	6	8	12	2
output					

b output = (24 ÷ input) + 1

input	6	12	1	3	8
output					

c output = $input^2$ + input

input	5	12	2	9	0
output					

d output = 2 × input × input − input

input	3	10	11	7	50
output					

9   Another way of writing *output = input* + 3 is to state that $y = x + 3$. Write the rule using y and x for the following.

a
x	0	1	2	3	4
y	6	7	8	9	10

b
x	5	2	1	7	0
y	15	6	3	21	0

c
x	5	2	11	6	3
y	3	0	9	4	1

d
x	0	3	10	6	4
y	1	10	101	37	17

10 It is known that for an *input* value of 3 the *output* value is 7.
   a   State two different rules that work for these values.
   b   How many different rules are possible? Explain.

11 Many function machines can be 'reversed', allowing you to get from an output back to an input. For instance, the reverse of '+3' is '−3' because if you put a value through both machines you get this value back again, as shown:

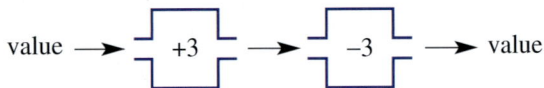

value ⟶ ┤+3├ ⟶ ┤−3├ ⟶ value

The reverse rule for *output = input* + 3 is *output = input* − 3.
Write the reverse rule for the following.
   a   *output = input* + 7
   b   *output = input* − 4
   c   *output* = 4 × *input*
   d   *output* = 2 × *input* + 1
   e   *output = input* ÷ 2 + 4

12 a   The following rules all involve two operations. Find the rule for each of these tables of values.

i
input	4	5	6	7	8
output	5	7	9	11	13

ii
input	1	2	3	4	5
output	5	9	13	17	21

iii
input	10	8	3	1	14
output	49	39	14	4	69

iv
input	6	18	30	24	66
output	3	5	7	6	13

v
input	4	5	6	7	8
output	43	53	63	73	83

vi
input	1	2	3	4	5
output	0	4	8	12	16

   b   Write three of your own two-operation rules and produce a table of values for each rule.
   c   Swap your tables of values with those of a classmate and attempt to find one another's rules.

2K The Cartesian plane and graphs

LEARNING INTENTIONS

* To know the meaning of the terms number plane (or Cartesian plane), origin and coordinates
* To be able to interpret the location of a point described by its coordinates, e.g. (2, 4)
* To be able to plot one or more points given their coordinates

We are already familiar with number lines. A number line is used to locate a position in one dimension (i.e. along the line).

A number plane is used to locate a position in two dimensions (i.e. within the plane). A number plane uses two number lines to form a grid system, so that points can be located precisely. A rule can then be illustrated visually using a number plane by forming a graph.

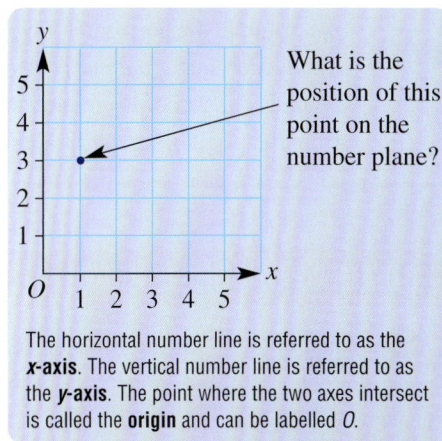

What is the position of this point on the number plane?

The horizontal number line is referred to as the *x*-axis. The vertical number line is referred to as the *y*-axis. The point where the two axes intersect is called the **origin** and can be labelled *O*.

Lesson starter: Estimate your location

Consider the door as 'the origin' of your classroom.

* Describe the position you are sitting in within the classroom in reference to the door.
* Can you think of different ways of describing your position? Which is the best way? Submit a copy of your location description to your teacher.
* Can you locate a classmate correctly when location descriptions are read out by your teacher?

A Cartesian coordinate plane is used on the touch screen of smartphones and devices to precisely locate where a touch is detected.

KEY IDEAS

■ A **number plane** is used to represent position in two dimensions, therefore it requires two coordinates.

■ In mathematics, a number plane is generally referred to as a **Cartesian plane**, named after the famous French mathematician, René Descartes (1596–1650).

■ A number plane consists of two straight perpendicular number lines, called **axes**.
   * The horizontal number line is known as the *x*-axis.
   * The vertical number line is known as the *y*-axis.

■ The point at which the two axes intersect is called the **origin**, and is often labelled *O*.

■ The position of a point on a number plane is given as a pair of numbers, known as the **coordinates** of the point. Coordinates are always written in brackets and the numbers are separated by a comma.
For example: $(2, 4)$.

- The x-coordinate (*input*) is always written first. The x-coordinate indicates how far to go from the origin in the horizontal direction.
- The y-coordinate (*output*) is always written second. The y-coordinate indicates how far to go from the origin in the vertical direction.

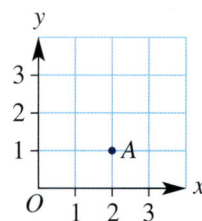

BUILDING UNDERSTANDING

1 Which of the following is the correct way to describe point A?

A 2, 1   **B** 1, 2   **C** $(2, 1)$

D $(x2, y1)$ **E** $(1, 2)$

2 Copy and complete the following sentences.

a The horizontal axis is known as the _____.

b The _____ is the vertical axis.

c The point at which the axes intersect is called the _____.

d The x-coordinate is always written _____.

e The second coordinate is always the _____.

f _____ comes before _____ in the dictionary, and the _____ coordinate comes before the _____ coordinate on the Cartesian plane.

Example 23   Plotting points on a number plane

Plot these points on a number plane: $A(2, 5)$ $B(4, 3)$ $C(0, 2)$

SOLUTION

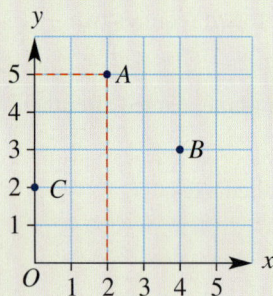

EXPLANATION

Draw a Cartesian plane, with both axes labelled from 0 to 5.

The first coordinate is the x-coordinate. The second coordinate is the y-coordinate. To plot point A, go along the horizontal axis to the number 2, then move vertically up 5 units. Place a dot at this point, which is the intersection of the line passing through the point 2 on the horizontal axis and the line passing through the point 5 on the vertical axis.

Now you try

Plot these points on a number plane: $A(1, 4)$ $B(3, 2)$ $C(4, 0)$

Example 24   Drawing graphs

For the given rule *output* = *input* + 1:

a   Copy and complete the given table of values.
b   Plot each pair of values in the table to form a graph.
c   Do these points lie in a straight line?

input (x)	output (y)
0	1
1	
2	
3	

SOLUTION

a

input (x)	output (y)
0	1
1	2
2	3
3	4

b

c   Yes

EXPLANATION

Use the given rule to find each *output* value for each *input* value. The rule is:

output = *input* + 1, so add 1 to each *input* value.

Plot each (x, y) pair.
The pairs are $(0, 1)$, $(1, 2)$, $(2, 3)$ and $(3, 4)$.

The points lie in a straight line (you could check by using a ruler to see that it is possible to draw a straight line through all the points.)

Now you try

For the given rule *output* = *input* + 4:

a   Copy and complete the given table of values.
b   Plot each pair of values in the table to form a graph.
c   Do these points lie in a straight line?

input (x)	output (y)
0	4
1	
2	
3	

Exercise 2K

| FLUENCY | 1, 3–7 | 2(½), 3–9 | 2(½), 5–10 |

Example 23

1 Plot these points on a number plane.

a $A(2, 4)$ b $B(3, 1)$ c $C(0, 1)$ d $D(2, 0)$

Example 23

2 Plot the following points on a number plane.

a $A(4, 2)$ b $B(1, 1)$ c $C(5, 3)$ d $D(0, 2)$

e $E(3, 1)$ f $F(5, 4)$ g $G(5, 0)$ h $H(0, 0)$

Example 23

3 Write down the coordinates of each of these labelled points. Your answers should be written with the point name then its coordinates, like $A(1, 4)$.

a

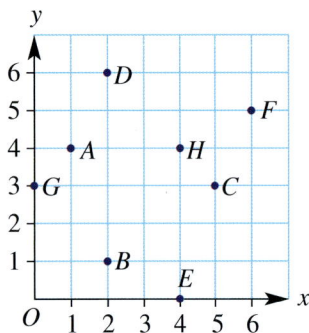

b

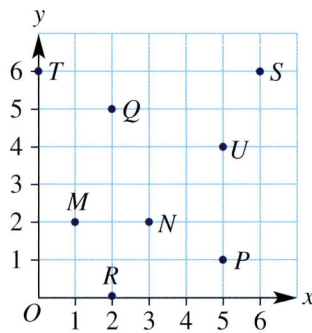

Example 24

4 For the given rule *output* = *input* + 2:

a Copy and complete the given table of values.

input (x)	output (y)
0	2
1	
2	
3	

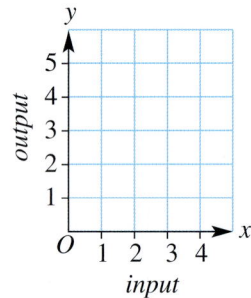

b Plot each pair of values in the table to form a graph.

c Do these points lie in a straight line?

Example 24

5 For the given rule *output* = *input* − 1:

a Copy and complete the given table of values.

input (x)	output (y)
1	
2	
3	
4	

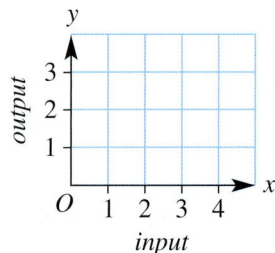

b Plot each pair of values in the table to form a graph.

c Do these points lie in a straight line?

Example 24

6 For the given rule *output* = *input* × 2:

a Copy and complete the given table of values.

input (x)	output (y)
0	
1	
2	
3	

b Plot each pair of values in the table to form a graph.

c Do these points lie in a straight line?

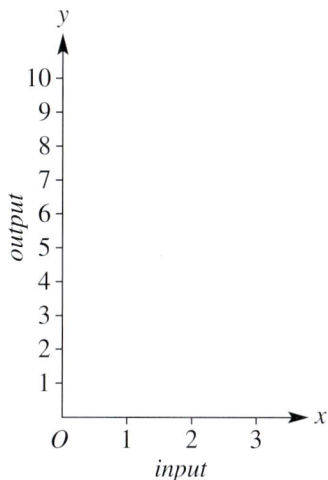

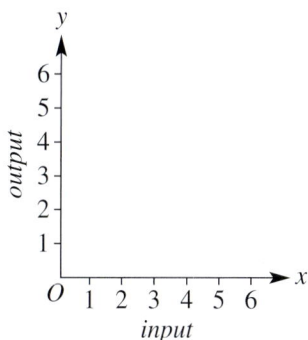

Example 24

7 For the given rule *output* = *input* × *input*:

a Copy and complete the given table of values.

input (x)	output (y)
0	0
1	
2	
3	

b Plot each pair of values in the table to form a graph.

c Do these points lie in a straight line?

Example 24

8 For the given rule *output* = 6 ÷ *input*:

a Copy and complete the given table of values.

input (x)	output (y)
1	
2	
3	
6	

b Plot each pair of values in the table to form a graph.

c Do these points lie in a straight line?

9 Draw a Cartesian plane from 0 to 5 on both axes. Place a cross on each pair of coordinates that have the same *x*- and *y*-value.

10 Draw a Cartesian plane from 0 to 8 on both axes. Plot the following points on the grid and join them in the order they are given.

(2, 7), (6, 7), (5, 5), (7, 5), (6, 2), (5, 2), (4, 1), (3, 2), (2, 2), (1, 5), (3, 5), (2, 7)

11 a Plot the following points on a Cartesian plane and join the points in the order given, to draw the basic shape of a house.

$(1,5)$, $(0,5)$, $(5,10)$, $(10,5)$, $(1,5)$, $(1,0)$, $(9,0)$, $(9,5)$

b Describe a set of four points to draw a door.

c Describe two sets of four points to draw two windows.

d Describe a set of four points to draw a chimney.

12 The perimeter of a square is its length multiplied by 4. We can write this as a rule: *perimeter* = $4 \times$ *length*.

a Copy and complete the given table of values (all values are in centimetres).

length (x)	perimeter (y)
1	4
2	
3	
4	

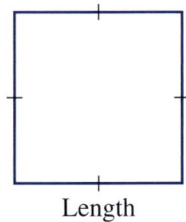

Length

b Plot each pair of values to form a graph with length on the *x*-axis and perimeter on the *y*-axis.

c Do these points lie in a straight line?

13 A grid system can be used to make secret messages. Jake decides to arrange the letters of the alphabet on a Cartesian plane in the following manner.

a Decode Jake's following message: $(3, 2)$, $(5, 1)$, $(2, 3)$, $(1, 4)$.

b Code the word SECRET.

c To increase the difficulty of the code, Jake does not include brackets or commas and he uses the origin to indicate the end of a word.
What do the following numbers mean?
1351550015434151340014535400142311435 4.

d Code the phrase: BE HERE AT SEVEN.

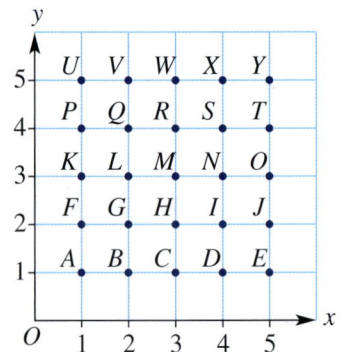

14 *ABCD* is a rectangle. The coordinates of *A*, *B* and *C* are given below. Draw each rectangle on a Cartesian plane and state the coordinates of the missing corner, *D*.

a $A(0,5)$ $B(0,3)$ $C(4,3)$ $D(?,?)$

b $A(4,4)$ $B(1,4)$ $C(1,1)$ $D(?,?)$

c $A(0,2)$ $B(3,2)$ $C(3,0)$ $D(?,?)$

d $A(4,1)$ $B(8,4)$ $C(5,8)$ $D(?,?)$

15(½)   15   15, 16

15 Write a rule (e.g. *output* = *input* × 2) that would give these graphs.

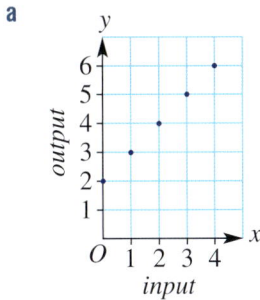

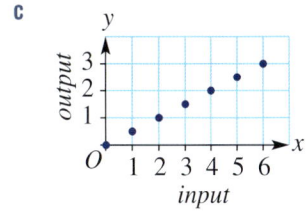

a

b

c

16 $A(1, 0)$ and $B(5, 0)$ are the base points of an isosceles triangle.

   a Find the coordinate of a possible third vertex.

   b Show on a Cartesian plane that there are infinite number of answers for this third vertex.

   c The area of the isosceles triangle is 10 square units. State the coordinates of the third vertex.

ENRICHMENT: Locating midpoints   –   –   17

17 a Plot the points $A(1, 4)$ and $B(5, 0)$ on a Cartesian plane. Draw the line segment AB. Find the coordinates of M, the midpoint of AB, and mark it on the grid. (It needs to be halfway along the line segment.)

   b Find the midpoint, M, of the line segment AB, which has coordinates $A(2, 4)$ and $B(0, 0)$.

   c Determine a method for locating the midpoint of a line segment without having to draw the points on a Cartesian plane.

   d Find the midpoint, M, of the line segment AB, which has coordinates $A(6, 3)$ and $B(2, 1)$.

   e Find the midpoint, M, of the line segment AB, which has coordinates $A(1, 4)$ and $B(4, 3)$.

   f Find the midpoint, M, of the line segment AB, which has coordinates $A(-3, 2)$ and $B(2, -3)$.

   g $M(3, 4)$ is the midpoint of AB and the coordinates of A are $(1, 5)$. What are the coordinates of B?

Plunge pool tiling

The Australian Plunge Pool Company offers a free tiled path around
each plunge pool constructed. The standard width of each plunge pool is
2 metres but the length can vary (it must be a whole number of metres).
The tiling is completed using 1 metre square tiles around all sides of the
pool. This diagram shows the tiling for a pool of length 3 metres.

*Present a report for the following tasks and ensure that you show clear
mathematical workings and explanations where appropriate.*

Preliminary task

a   Use the diagram above to count the number of tiles required for a 2 metre by 3 metre plunge pool.

b   Draw an accurate diagram of a rectangle which is 2 metres by 6 metres. If possible, use grid paper.

c   On your diagram, accurately draw 1-metre square tiles around the outside of the rectangle.

d   Use your diagram to find how many tiles would be required for a 2 metre by 6 metre plunge pool.

Modelling task

Formulate

a   The problem is to find a rule relating the *number of tiles* required to the *length of the pool*. Write
down all the relevant information that will help solve this problem, and use diagrams to illustrate
the following four pools.
i   2 m by 2 m   ii   2 m by 3 m   iii   2 m by 4 m   iv   2 m by 5 m

Solve

b   Use a table like the one shown to summarise the number of tiles required for varying pool lengths.

Pool length (m)	2	3	4	5	6
Number of tiles					

c   If the pool length increases by 1 metre, describe the effect on the number of tiles required.

d   If a pool could have a length of only 1 metre, how many tiles would need to be used?

e   Determine the rule linking the number of tiles and the length of the pool.

f   Explain why your rule correctly calculates the number of tiles required. Give a geometric reason.

Evaluate and verify

g   Using your rule from part **e** above, find the number of tiles required for a plunge pool of length:
i   8 metres   ii   15 metres.

h   Using your rule from part **e** above, find the length of a plunge pool if the number of tiles used is:
i   22   ii   44.

i   Use your rule to explain why there will always be an even number of tiles required.

Communicate

j   Summarise your results and describe any key findings.

Extension questions

a   If luxury plunge pools can have a width of 3 metres instead of 2 metres, determine the rule linking
the number of tiles and the length of these pools. Compare it to the rule found when the width is
2 metres.

b   The luxury plunge pools of width 3 metres now require the path to be two tiles wide. Investigate
how this requirement affects the rule for the number of tiles required. Use diagrams to help
communicate your solution.

Making patterns

(Key technology: Spreadsheets)

Number patterns might seem like an easy thing to generate but describing relationships within patterns is at the foundation of algorithms and complex mathematical functions. Such algorithms can help us to write computer programs and find rules to help estimate solutions to complex problems. Two key words used in this investigation are 'sequence' and 'term'. The pattern $3, 5, 7, 9, 11$, for example, is a sequence of five terms and could be described as the list of odd numbers from 5 up to 11. We will use the letter n to describe which term we are talking about. So, $n = 2$ refers to the 2nd term, which in this example is 5.

1 Getting started

a   This table shows nine terms of the even number sequence starting at 2.

n	1	2	3	4	5	6	7	8	9
Term	2	4	6	8	10	12	14	16	18

   i   What is the 4th term in the sequence of even numbers?

   ii   Which term is equal to 16?

b   **Method 1:** One way to generate the sequence of even numbers is to add 2 to the previous term. So, in this sequence, the 6th term is 12 and so the 7th term is $12 + 2 = 14$.

   i   Use this idea to find the 10th term in the sequence.

   ii   What will be the 13th term in the sequence?

c   **Method 2:** Another way to find terms is to use a rule and the value of n corresponding to the term you are finding. For example: The 5th term is $2 \times 5 = 10$ and the 7th term is $2 \times 7 = 14$ and so, in general, the nth term is given by $2 \times n$.

   i   Use this idea to find the 11th term in the sequence.

   ii   What will be the 17th term in the sequence?

   iii   What will be the 29th term in the sequence?

2 Applying an algorithm

Let's look at generating the list of odd numbers starting at 1 using **Method 1**. Look at this flow chart which generates the sequence.

a   Work through the flow chart and write the outputs into this table.

n	1	2	3		
Term, t	1				

b   Why does this algorithm only deliver 5 values for n and t?

c   Another way of generating the list of odd numbers is to use the rule: Term(t) $= 2 \times n - 1$. This is **Method 2** as described in part **1**.

   i   Check this rule by confirming the terms in the table above.

   ii   Use this rule to find the 8th term.

   iii   Draw a flow chart that outputs the first 8 terms of the odd number sequence using this rule.

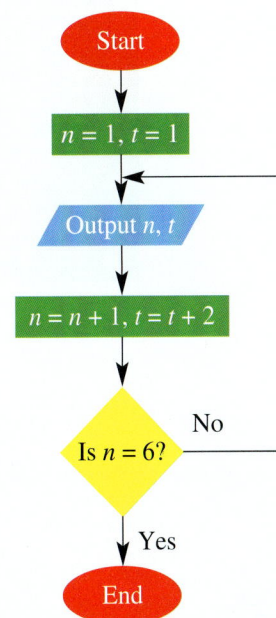

Start

$n = 1, t = 1$

Output n, t

$n = n + 1, t = t + 2$

Is $n = 6$?   No

Yes

End

Technology and computational thinking

3 Using technology

We will use a spreadsheet to generate the odd number sequence using both methods described above.

a Create a spreadsheet as follows. The *n* value is in column A and the sequence is generated in columns B and C using the two different methods.

	A	B	C
1	Generating sequences		
2			
3	n	Method 1	Method 2
4	1	1	=2*A4-1
5	=A4+1	=B4+2	
6			

b Fill down at cells A5, B5 and D4 to generate 8 terms.

c Describe the advantages and disadvantages of both methods.

d Now construct a spreadsheet to generate the following sequences using both method 1 and 2.

   i A sequence starting at 1 and increasing by 3 each time.

   ii A sequence starting at 20 and decreasing by 2 each time.

4 Extension

Use a flow chart and a spreadsheet to generate the following number sequences.

a The square numbers $1, 4, 9, \ldots$

b The triangular numbers $1, 3, 6, 10, \ldots$

c A number pattern of your choice.

Investigation

Fibonacci sequences

Leonardo Fibonacci was a famous thirteenth century mathematician who discovered some very interesting patterns of numbers in nature.

Fibonacci's rabbits

These rules determine how fast rabbits can breed in ideal circumstances.
- Generation 1: One pair of newborn rabbits is in a paddock. A pair is one female and one male.
- Generation 2: After it is 2 months old (in the third month), the female produces another pair of rabbits.
- Generation 3: After it is 3 months old (in the fourth month), this same female produces another pair of rabbits.
- Every female rabbit produces one new pair *every month* from age 2 months.
  - **a** Using the 'rabbit breeding rules', complete a drawing of the first five generations of rabbit pairs. Use it to complete the table below.
  - **b** Write down the numbers of pairs of rabbits at the end of each month for 12 months. This is the Fibonacci sequence.
  - **c** How many rabbits will there be after 1 year?
  - **d** Explain the rule for the Fibonacci sequence.

Month	1	2	3	4	5
Number of rabbits	2	2			
Number of pairs	1				

Fibonacci sequence in plants

a Count the clockwise and anticlockwise spiralling 'lumps' of some pineapples and show how these numbers relate to the Fibonacci sequence.

b Count the clockwise and anticlockwise spiralling scales of some pine cones and show how these numbers relate to the Fibonacci sequence.

Fibonacci sequence and the golden ratio

a Copy this table and extend it to show the next 10 terms of the Fibonacci sequence: $1, 1, 2, 3, 5, \ldots$

Fibonacci sequence	1	1	2	3	5	...
Ratio		1	2	1.5	...	...

$$1 \div 1 \qquad 2 \div 1 \qquad 3 \div 2$$

b Write down a new set of numbers that is one Fibonacci number divided by its previous Fibonacci number. Copy and complete this table.

c What do you notice about the new sequence (ratio)?

d Research the *golden ratio* and explain how it links to your new sequence.

1   Sticks are arranged by a student such that the first three diagrams in the pattern are:

> Up for a challenge? If you get stuck on a question, check out the 'working with unfamiliar problems' poster at the end of the book to help.

How many sticks would there be in the 50th diagram of the pattern?

2   A number is said to be a 'perfect number' if the sum of its factors equals the number. For this exercise, we must exclude the number itself as one of the factors.

The number 6 is the first perfect number.

Factors of 6 (excluding the numeral 6) are 1, 2 and 3.

The sum of these three factors is $1 + 2 + 3 = 6$. Hence, we have a perfect number.

a   Find the next perfect number. (*Hint*: It is less than 50.)

b   The third perfect number is 496. Find all the factors for this number and show that it is a perfect number.

3   Anya is a florist who is making up bunches of tulips with every bunch having the same number of tulips. Anya uses only one colour in each bunch. She has 126 red tulips, 108 pink tulips and 144 yellow tulips. Anya wants to use all the tulips.

a   What is the largest number of tulips Anya can put in each bunch?

b   How many bunches of each colour would Anya make with this number in each bunch?

4   Mr and Mrs Adams have two teenage children. If the teenagers' ages multiply together to give 252, find the sum of their ages.

5   Complete this sequence.

$2^2 = 1^2 + 3$ $3^2 = 2^2 + 5$ $4^2 = 3^2 + 7$ $5^2 =$ _____ $6^2 =$ _____

6   Use the digits 1, 9, 7 and 2, in any order, and any operations and brackets you like, to make as your answers the whole numbers 0 to 10. For example:

$1 \times 9 - 7 - 2 = 0$

$(9 - 7) \div 2 - 1 = 0$

7   The first three shapes in a pattern made with sticks are:

How many sticks make up the 100th shape?

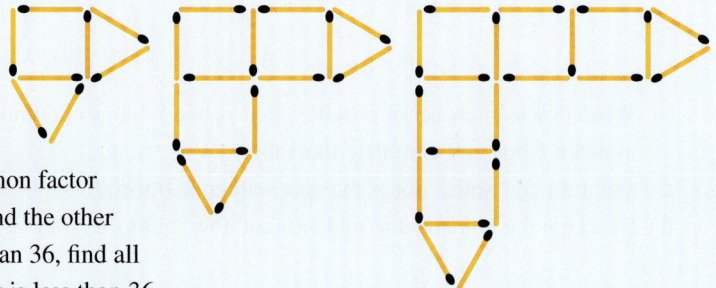

8   Two numbers have a highest common factor of 1. If one of the numbers is 36 and the other number is a positive integer less than 36, find all possible values for the number that is less than 36.

Composite numbers

A composite number has more than two factors
10: factors 1, 2, 5, 10
62: factors 1, 2, 31, 62
Composite numbers are not prime.

Multiples

Multiples are ≥ number
20: 20, 40, ⑥⓪, 80, ...
15: 15, 30, 45, ⑥⓪, 75, ...
Lowest common multiple
LCM = 60

Factor trees

90

9   10

3   3   2   5

$90 = 2 \times 3 \times 3 \times 5$
$90 = 2 \times 3^2 \times 5$

Factors

Factors are ≤ number
20: 1, 2, 4, ⑤, 10, 20
15: 1, 3, ⑤, 15
Highest common factor
HCF = 5

Number properties

Indices

$243 = \underset{\text{expanded form}}{\underline{3 \times 3 \times 3 \times 3 \times 3}} = \underset{\substack{\text{index} \\ \text{form}}}{3^5}$

$\underset{\substack{\text{basic} \\ \text{numeral}}}{}$

base number

index number

Square numbers

$16 = 4 \times 4 = 4^2$
$25 = 5 \times 5 = 5^2$

First 10 square numbers

1, 4, 9, 16, 25,
36, 49, 64, 81, 100

Prime numbers

A prime number only has two factors: 1 and itself.
5: factors 1 and 5
17: factors 1 and 17

Square roots

$\sqrt{16} = 4$
$\sqrt{25} = 5$
$\sqrt{22}$ is between 4 and 5

1 is not a prime number.

Division

$\text{dividend} \rightarrow \dfrac{52}{3} = 17\dfrac{1}{3} \leftarrow \text{remainder}$
$\text{divisor} \rightarrow$

quotient   remainder

$52 = 3 \times 17 + 1$

divisor   quotient

Divisibility tests (Ext)

2: last digit even (0, 2, 4, 6, 8)
3: sum digits ÷ 3
4: number from last two digits ÷ 4
5: last digit 0 or 5
6: ÷ by 2 and 3
8: number from last 3 digits ÷ 8
9: sum digits ÷ 9
10: last digit 0

Chapter summary

Number patterns

Sequence
2, 4, 6, 8, ...
↑ ↑ ↑ ↑
terms

Common difference of decreasing by 3:
100, 97, 94, ...

Common ratio of 2:
3, 6, 12, 24, ...

Common difference: increase of 4

Spatial pattern:

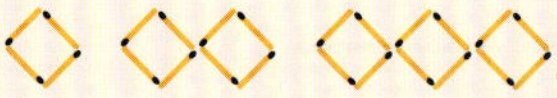

Number pattern: 4 8 12 ...

Rule: Number of sticks
$= 4 \times$ number of rhombuses

Rules, graphs and tables show a relationship between two quantities that can vary.

input	20	10	5
output	37	17	7

output $= 2 \times$ *input* $- 3$

Sam is 5 years older than his sister Mikaela

Mikaela's age	0	3	7	13
Sam's age	5	8	12	18

Graph showing a relationship

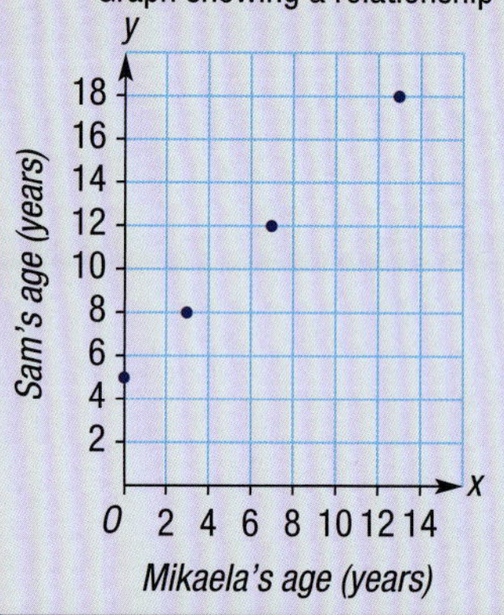

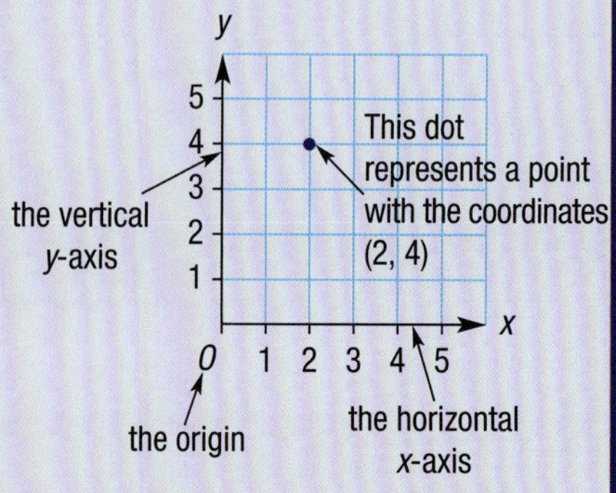

y
18
16
14
12
10
8
6
4
2
Sam's age (years)
x
O
2
4
6
8
10
12
14
Mikaela's age (years)

y
5
4
3
2
1
x
O
1
2
3
4
5
This dot represents a point with the coordinates (2, 4)
the vertical y-axis
the origin
the horizontal x-axis

Chapter checklist with success criteria

A printable version of this checklist is available in the Interactive Textbook

		✔

2A   1. **I can list the factors of a number.**
e.g. Find the complete set of factors for the number 40. ☐

2A   2. **I can list the multiples of a number (up to a certain limit).**
e.g. Write down the first six multiples of the number 11. ☐

2A   3. **I can list pairs of factors of a number.**
e.g. Express 132 as a product of two factors both of which are greater than 10. ☐

2B   4. **I can find the highest common factor (HCF) of two numbers.**
e.g. Find the highest common factor (HCF) of 36 and 48. ☐

2B   5. **I can find the lowest common multiple of two numbers.**
e.g. Find the lowest common multiple of 6 and 10. ☐

2C   6. **I can determine if a number is divisible by 2, 3, 4, 5, 6, 8, 9 and/or 10.**
e.g. Consider the number 48 569 412. State which of the following numbers are
factors of it: 2, 3, 4, 5, 6, 8, 9, 10.   (Ext) ☐

2D   7. **I can determine whether a number is prime by considering its factors.**
e.g. Explain why 17 is prime but 35 is not prime. ☐

2D   8. **I can find the prime factors of a number.**
e.g. Find the prime factors of 30. ☐

2E   9. **I can convert an expression to index form.**
e.g. Write $3 \times 3 \times 2 \times 3 \times 2 \times 3$ in index form. ☐

2E   10. **I can evaluate expressions involving powers using the order of operations.**
e.g. Evaluate $7^2 - 6^2$. ☐

2F   11. **I can express a composite number in prime factor form.**
e.g. Express the number 60 in prime factor form. ☐

2G   12. **I can find the square of a number.**
e.g. Evaluate 6^2. ☐

2G   13. **I can find the square root of a number which is a perfect square.**
e.g. Find the square root of 1600. ☐

2G   14. **I can locate square roots between consecutive whole numbers.**
e.g. State which consecutive whole numbers are either side of $\sqrt{43}$. ☐

2H   15. **I can find the common difference or common ratio in a sequence.**
e.g. Find the common ratio in the number pattern 256, 128, 64, 32, ... ☐

2H   16. **I can find the next terms in a number pattern.**
e.g. Find the next three terms in the number pattern 6, 18, 30, 42, ... ☐

Chapter checklist

		✔
2I	**17. I can describe a spatial pattern in terms of the number of objects required for the first shape, and for later shapes being added.** e.g. Describe the pattern by stating how many sticks are required to make the first term, and how many are required to make the next term in the pattern. 	☐
2I	**18. I can describe and use a rule for a spatial patterns.** e.g. Describe a rule connecting the number of sticks required to the number of triangles, and use this to find the number of sticks for 20 triangles. 	☐
2J	**19. I can complete a table of values for a given rule.** e.g. Fill out the table for the rule $output = (3 \times input) + 1$.	☐

input	4	2	9	12	0
output					

		✔
2J	**20. I can find a rule for a table of values.** e.g. Find the rule for the table of values shown.	☐

input	1	2	3	4	5
output	7	14	21	28	35

		✔
2K	**21. I can plot points on a number plane.** e.g. Plot the points $A(2, 5)$, $B(4, 3)$ and $C(0, 2)$.	☐
2K	**22. I can draw a graph of a rule by completing a table of values.** e.g. For the rule $output(y) = input(x) + 1$, construct a table of values using *input* values of 0, 1, 2 and 3. Use the table of coordinates to plot a graph.	☐

Short-answer questions

2A/D **1** **a** Find the complete set of factors of 120 and circle those that are composite numbers.

b Determine three numbers between 1000 and 2000 that each have factors $1, 2, 3, 4, 5$ and itself.

2A/D **2** **a** Write down the first 12 multiples for each of 8 and 7 and circle the odd numbers.

b Which two prime numbers less than 20 have multiples that include both 1365 and 1274?

2B **3** **a** Find the HCF of the following pairs of numbers.

   i 15 and 40   **ii** 18 and 26   **iii** 72 and 96

b Find the LCM of the following pairs of numbers.

   i 5 and 13   **ii** 6 and 9   **iii** 44 and 8

2D **4** **a** State whether each of these numbers is a prime or composite number.

   $21, 30, 11, 16, 7, 3, 2$

b How many prime multiples are there of 13?

2D/F **5** **a** State the prime factors of 770.

b Determine three composite numbers less than 100, each with only three factors that are all prime numbers less than 10.

2E **6** Simplify these expressions by writing them in index form.

   a $6 \times 6 \times 6 \times 6 \times 6 \times 6 \times 6 \times 6$ **b** $5 \times 5 \times 5 \times 5 \times 2 \times 2 \times 2 \times 2 \times 2$

2F **7** Write these numbers as a product of prime numbers. Use a factor tree and then index form.

   a 32   **b** 200   **c** 225

2F **8** Determine which number to the power of 5 equals each of the following.

   a 100 000   **b** 243   **c** 1024

2G **9** Evaluate each of the following.

   a $5^2 - 3^2$ **b** $2 \times 4^2 - 5^2$ **c** $5 \times 3^4 - 3^2 + 1^6$ **d** $12^2 - (7^2 - 6^2)$

2C **Ext** **10** Determine whether the following calculations are possible without leaving a remainder.

   a $32766 \div 4$ **b** $1136 \div 8$ **c** $2417 \div 3$

2C **Ext** **11** **a** Carry out divisibility tests on the given number and fill in the table with ticks or crosses. State the explanation for each result.

Number	Divisible by 2	Divisible by 3	Divisible by 4	Divisible by 5	Divisible by 6	Divisible by 8	Divisible by 9	Divisible by 10
84 539 424								

b Use divisibility rules to determine a 10-digit number that is divisible by $3, 5, 6$ and 9.

c Determine a six-digit number that is divisible by $2, 3, 5, 6, 9$ and 10.

Chapter review

2G

12 a Evaluate:

    i $\sqrt{25}$ **ii** $\sqrt{2500}$ **iii** $\sqrt{5^2 + 12^2}$

    iv $4^2 - \sqrt{25} + \sqrt{7^2}$ **v** $\sqrt{16 \times 49} \div \sqrt{4}$ **vi** $10^2 \div \sqrt{3^2 + 4^2}$

  b State which consecutive whole numbers are either side of:

    i $\sqrt{18}$ **ii** $\sqrt{74}$ **iii** $\sqrt{51}$

2H

13 Find the next three terms for the following number patterns that have a common difference.

  a $27, 30, 33, \ldots$

  b $67, 59, 51, \ldots$

  c $238, 196, 154, \ldots$

2H

14 Find the next three terms for the following number patterns that have a common ratio.

  a $35, 70, 140, \ldots$

  b $24\,300, 8100, 2700, \ldots$

  c $64, 160, 400, \ldots$

2H

15 Find the next six terms for each of these number patterns.

  a $21, 66, 42, 61, 84, 56, \ldots$

  b $22, 41, 79, 136, \ldots$

2I/J

16 a Draw the next two shapes in this spatial pattern of sticks.

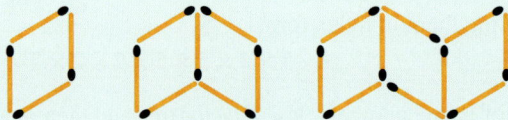

  b Copy and complete this table.

Number of rhombuses	1	2	3	4	5
Number of sticks required					

  c Describe the pattern by stating how many sticks are required to make the first rhombus and how many sticks must be added to make the next rhombus in the pattern.

2I

17 A rule to describe a special window spatial pattern is:

Number of sticks = 3 × number of windows + 2

  a How many sticks are required to make 1 window?

  b How many sticks are required to make 10 windows?

  c How many sticks are required to make g windows?

  d How many windows can be made from 65 sticks?

2J

18 Copy and complete each table for the given rule.

  a *output = input + 5*

input	3	5	7	12	20
output					

  b *output = 2 × input + 7*

input	4	2	9	12	0
output					

2J

19 Find the rule for each of these tables of values.

a

input	3	4	5	6	7
output	12	13	14	15	16

b

input	1	2	3	4	5
output	20	32	44	56	68

c

input	0	1	2	3	4
output	1	3	5	7	9

d

input	3	4	5	6	7
output	7	6	5	4	3

2K

20 a State the coordinates of each point plotted on this number plane.
  b State the coordinates on this grid of a point C so that $ABCD$ is a square.
  c State the coordinates on this grid of a point E on the x-axis so that $ABED$ is a trapezium (i.e. has only one pair of parallel sides).

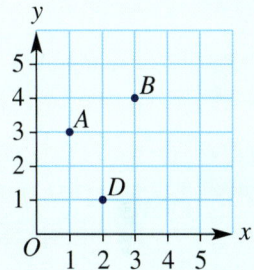

2K

21 Determine the next three terms in each of these sequences and explain how each is generated.
  a $1, 4, 9, 16, 25, \ldots$
  b $1, 8, 27, 64, \ldots$
  c $(1, 3), (2, 4), (3, 5), \ldots$
  d $31, 29, 31, 30, 31, 30, \ldots$
  e $1, \sqrt{2}, \sqrt{3}, 2, \ldots$
  f $1, 1, 2, 2, 3, 4, 4, 8, 5, 16, 6, 32, \ldots$

Multiple-choice questions

2A

1 Which number is the incorrect multiple for the following sequence?
$3, 6, 9, 12, 15, 18, 22, 24, 27, 30$
A 18 **B** 22 **C** 30 **D** 6 **E** 3

2A

2 Which group of numbers contains every factor of 60?
A $2, 3, 4, 5, 10, 12, 15, 60$
B $2, 3, 4, 5, 10, 12, 15, 20, 30$
C $1, 2, 3, 4, 5, 10, 12, 15, 20, 30$
D $2, 3, 4, 5, 10, 15, 20, 30, 60$
E $1, 2, 3, 4, 5, 6, 10, 12, 15, 20, 30, 60$

2C
(Ext)

3 Which of the following numbers is *not* divisible only by prime numbers, itself and 1?
A 21 **B** 77 **C** 110 **D** 221 **E** 65

Chapter review

2D

4   Which of the following groups of numbers include one prime and two composite numbers?

  A 2, 10, 7   B 54, 7, 11   C 9, 32, 44   D 5, 17, 23   E 18, 3, 12

2E

5   $7 \times 7 \times 7 \times 7 \times 7$ can be written as:

  A 5^7 B 7^5 C 7×5 D 75   E 77 777

2G

6   Evaluate $\sqrt{3^2 + 4^2}$.

  A 7   B 5   C 14   D 25   E 6

2B

7   The HCF and LCM of 12 and 18 are:

  A 6 and 18   B 3 and 12   C 2 and 54   D 6 and 36   E 3 and 18

2F

8   The prime factor form of 48 is:

  A $2^4 \times 3$ B $2^2 \times 3^2$ C 2×3^3 D 3×4^2 E $2^3 \times 6$

2E

9   Evaluate $4^3 - 3 \times (2^4 - 3^2)$.

  A 427   B 18   C 43   D 320   E 68

2A

10 Factors of 189 are:

  A 3, 7, 9, 18, 21, 27   B 3, 9, 18, 21   C 3, 9, 18
  D 3, 7, 9, 17, 21   E 3, 7, 9, 21, 27, 63

2C

(Ext)

11 Which number is *not* divisible by 3?

  A 25 697 403   B 31 975   C 7 297 008
  D 28 650 180   E 38 629 634 073

2K

12 Which set of points is in a horizontal line?

  A $(5, 5), (6, 6), (7, 7)$
  B $(3, 2), (3, 4), (3, 11)$
  C $(2, 4), (3, 6), (4, 8)$
  D $(5, 4), (6, 4), (8, 4), (12, 4)$
  E $(1, 5), (5, 1), (1, 1), (5, 5)$

Extended-response questions

1   For the following questions, write the answers in index notation (i.e. b^x) and simplify where possible.

  a   A rectangle has width/breadth 27 cm and length 125 cm.
    i   Write the width and the length as powers.
    ii Write power expressions for the perimeter and for the area.

  b   A square's side length is equal to 4^3.
    i   Write the side length as a power in a different way.
    ii Write power expressions in three different ways for the perimeter and for the area.

  c $5 \times 5 \times 5 \times 5 \times 7 \times 7 \times 7$

  d $4^3 + 4^3 + 4^3 + 4^3$

2   A class arranges its square desks so that the space between their desks creates rhombuses of identical size, as shown in this diagram.

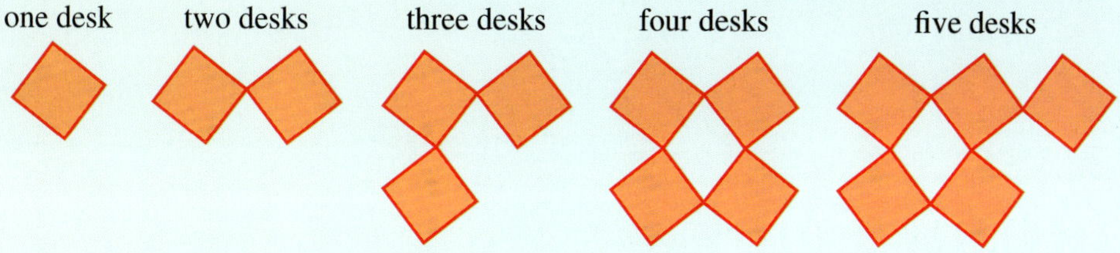

one desk   two desks   three desks   four desks   five desks

a   How many rhombuses are contained between:
   i   four desks that are in two rows (as shown in the diagram above)?
   ii   six desks in two rows?
b   Draw 12 desks in three rows arranged this way.
c   Rule up a table with columns for the number of:
   •   rows
   •   desks per row
   •   total number of desks
   •   total number of rhombuses.
   If there are four desks per row, complete your table for up to 24 desks.
d   If there are four desks per row, write a rule for the number of rhombuses in n rows of square desks.
e   Using a computer spreadsheet, complete several more tables, varying the number of desks per row.
f   Explain how the rule for the number of rhombuses changes when the number of desks, d, per row varies and also the number of rows, n, varies.
g   If the number of rows of desks equals the number of desks per row, how many desks would be required to make 10 000 rhombuses?

3

Fractions and percentages

Maths in context: Percentages and your money

Our economy relies on the exchange of money, making the profits and incomes we need for the costs of living. Most money calculations use rates, and these are always written as percentages. 'Per cent' and '%' means 'per 100'. Because one dollar contains 100 cents, a given percentage tells us the number of cents per dollar.

Stores regularly have sales and offer percentage discounts. For example, a 30% discount means 30 cents (= $(30/100) = $0.30) taken off each dollar of the original price. By using percentages to calculate discounted prices, the best deals can be found.

A pay rise is always welcomed by workers. A pay rise rate of 5% means 5 cents (= $(5/100) = $0.05) extra is added for every dollar of the employee's current pay. By using percentages, the new income can be calculated.

When you have completed your training and earn a weekly wage, you will likely want to live independently. Then it is important to prepare a budget (i.e. a saving and spending plan) and have money put aside for cost-of-living bills and personal use. To compare the proportions of income spent on each type of expense, you can calculate each as a percentage of your annual pay, totalling to 100%.

Chapter contents

Victorian Curriculum 2.0

This chapter covers the following content descriptors in the Victorian Curriculum 2.0:

NUMBER

VC2M7N03, VC2M7N05, VC2M7N06, VC2M7N07, VC2M7N09, VC2M7N10

MEASUREMENT

VC2M7M06

Please refer to the curriculum support documentation in the teacher resources for a full and comprehensive mapping of this chapter to the related curriculum content descriptors.

© VCAA

Online resources

A host of additional online resources are included as part of your Interactive Textbook, including HOTmaths content, video demonstrations of all worked examples, auto-marked quizzes and much more.

3A Introduction to fractions   CONSOLIDATING

LEARNING INTENTIONS
- To know what the numerator and denominator of a fraction represent in different situations
- To be able to represent fractions on a number line
- To be able to represent a fraction of a shape by dividing it into several regions and shading some of the regions

The word 'fraction' comes from the Latin word 'frangere', which means 'to break into pieces'.

Although the following sentences are not directly related to the mathematical use of fractions, they all contain words that are related to the original Latin term 'frangere' and they help us gain an understanding of exactly what a fraction is.

- *The fragile vase smashed into a hundred pieces when it landed on the ground.*
- *After the window was broken, several fragments were found on the floor.*
- *She fractured her leg in two places.*
- *The computer was running slowly and needed to be defragmented.*
- *The elderly gentleman was becoming very frail in his old age.*

Can you think of any other related words?

Brainstorm specific uses of fractions in everyday life. The list could include cooking, shopping, sporting, building examples and more.

Spoken time can use fractions of an hour. The digital time 6:30 can be spoken as 'half-past 6' because $\frac{30}{60} = \frac{1}{2}$; the digital time of 3:15 is the same as 'a quarter past 3' because $\frac{15}{60} = \frac{1}{4}$.

Lesson starter: What strength do you like your cordial?

Imagine preparing several jugs of different strength cordial. Samples could include $\frac{1}{4}$ strength cordial, $\frac{1}{5}$ strength cordial, $\frac{1}{6}$ strength cordial, $\frac{1}{8}$ strength cordial.

- In each case, describe how much water and how much cordial is needed to make a 1 litre mixture. Note: 1 litre (L) = 1000 millilitres (mL).
- On the label of a Cottee's cordial container, it suggests 'To make up by glass or jug: add four parts water to one part Cottee's Fruit Juice Cordial, according to taste'. What fraction of cordial do Cottee's suggest is the best?

KEY IDEAS

■ A fraction is made up of a **n**umerator (**up**) and a **d**enominator (**d**own).

For example: $\frac{3}{5}$ ← numerator
← denominator

- The **denominator** tells you how many parts the whole is divided up into.
- The **numerator** tells you how many of the divided parts you have selected.
- The horizontal line separating the numerator and the denominator is called the **vinculum.**

■ A **proper fraction** or **common fraction** is less than a whole, and therefore the numerator must be smaller than the denominator.

For example: $\frac{2}{7}$ is a proper fraction.

■ An **improper fraction** is greater than a whole, and therefore the numerator must be larger than the denominator. Some mathematicians also consider fractions equal to a whole, like $\frac{3}{3}$, to be improper fractions.

For example: $\frac{5}{3}$ is an improper fraction.

■ We can represent fractions on a number line.

This number line shows the whole numbers 0, 1 and 2. Each unit has then been divided equally into four segments, therefore creating 'quarters'.

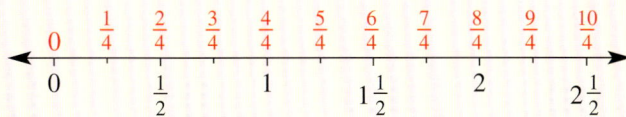

■ Whole numbers can be represented as fractions.

On the number line above we see that 1 is the same as $\frac{4}{4}$ and 2 is the same as $\frac{8}{4}$.

■ We can represent fractions using area. If a shape is divided into regions of equal areas, then shading a certain number of these regions will create a fraction of the whole shape.

For example: Fraction shaded $= \frac{3}{4}$

BUILDING UNDERSTANDING

1 **a** State the denominator of this proper fraction: $\frac{2}{9}$.

b State the numerator of this improper fraction: $\frac{7}{5}$.

2 Group the following list of fractions into proper fractions, improper fractions and whole numbers.

a $\frac{7}{6}$ **b** $\frac{2}{7}$ **c** $\frac{50}{7}$ **d** $\frac{3}{3}$ **e** $\frac{3}{4}$ **f** $\frac{5}{11}$

3 Find the whole numbers amongst the following list of fractions. (*Hint:* There are three whole numbers to find.)

a $\frac{15}{4}$ **b** $\frac{12}{5}$ **c** $\frac{30}{15}$ **d** $\frac{30}{12}$ **e** $\frac{12}{12}$ **f** $\frac{28}{7}$

Example 1   Understanding the numerator and denominator

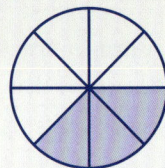

A pizza is shown in the diagram.

a Into how many pieces has the whole pizza been divided?

b How many pieces have been selected (shaded)?

c In representing the shaded fraction of the pizza:

   i   what must the denominator equal?

   ii   what must the numerator equal?

   iii write the amount of pizza selected (shaded) as a fraction.

SOLUTION		EXPLANATION
a	8	The pizza is cut into 8 equal pieces.
b	3	3 of the 8 pieces are shaded in blue.
c **i**	8	The denominator shows the number of parts the whole has been divided into.
ii	3	The numerator tells how many of the divided parts you have selected.
iii	$\frac{3}{8}$	The shaded fraction is the numerator over the denominator; i.e. 3 out of 8 divided pieces.

Now you try

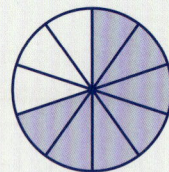

a Into how many pieces has the whole pizza been divided?

b How many pieces have been selected (shaded)?

c In representing the shaded fraction of the pizza:

   i   what must the denominator equal?

   ii   what must the numerator equal?

   iii write the amount of pizza selected (shaded) as a fraction.

Example 2   Representing fractions on a number line

Represent the fractions $\frac{3}{5}$ and $\frac{9}{5}$ on a number line.

SOLUTION

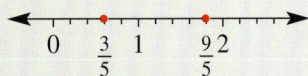

EXPLANATION

Draw a number line starting at 0 and mark on it the whole numbers 0, 1 and 2.

Divide each whole unit into five segments of equal length. Each of these segments has a length of one-fifth.

Now you try

Represent the fractions $\frac{2}{3}$ and $\frac{7}{3}$ on a number line.

Example 3   Shading areas

Represent the fraction $\frac{3}{4}$ in three different ways, using a square divided into four equal regions.

SOLUTION

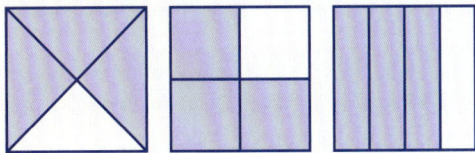

EXPLANATION

Ensure division of the square creates four equal areas. Shade in three of the four regions.

Other answers are possible.

Now you try

Represent the fraction $\frac{1}{3}$ in three different ways, using a rectangle divided into six equal regions.

Exercise 3A

FLUENCY   1, 2, 3(½), 4   2, 3(½), 4, 5(½)   3(½), 4, 5(½)

Example 1   **1** A pizza is shown to the right.
- **a** Into how many pieces has the whole pizza been divided?
- **b** How many pieces have been selected (shaded)?
- **c** In representing the shaded fraction of the pizza:
  - **i** what must the denominator equal?
  - **ii** what must the numerator equal?
  - **iii** write the amount of pizza selected (shaded) as a fraction.

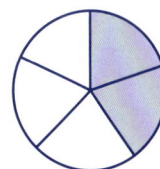

Example 1   **2** Answer the following questions for each of the pizzas (**A** to **D**) drawn below.

A 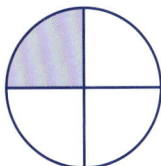   **B** 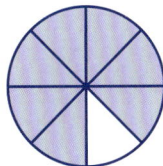   **C** 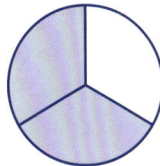   **D**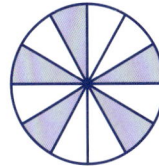

- **a** Into how many pieces has the whole pizza been divided?
- **b** How many pieces have been selected (shaded)?
- **c** In representing the shaded fraction of the pizza:
  - **i** what must the denominator equal?
  - **ii** what must the numerator equal?
  - **iii** write the amount of pizza selected (shaded) as a fraction.

Example 2   **3** Represent the following fractions on a number line.
- **a** $\frac{3}{7}$ and $\frac{6}{7}$
- **b** $\frac{2}{3}$ and $\frac{5}{3}$
- **c** $\frac{1}{6}$ and $\frac{5}{6}$
- **d** $\frac{2}{4}$ and $\frac{11}{4}$
- **e** $\frac{11}{5}$ and $\frac{8}{5}$
- **f** $\frac{5}{4}, \frac{9}{4}$ and $\frac{3}{2}$

Example 3

4   Represent each of these fractions in three different ways, using a rectangle divided into equal regions.

    a $\dfrac{1}{4}$ b $\dfrac{3}{8}$ c $\dfrac{2}{6}$

5   Write the next three fractions for each of the following fraction sequences.

    a $\dfrac{3}{5}, \dfrac{4}{5}, \dfrac{5}{5}, \dfrac{6}{5},$ ___, ___, ___   b $\dfrac{5}{8}, \dfrac{6}{8}, \dfrac{7}{8}, \dfrac{8}{8},$ ___, ___, ___   c $\dfrac{1}{3}, \dfrac{2}{3}, \dfrac{3}{3}, \dfrac{4}{3},$ ___, ___, ___

    d $\dfrac{11}{7}, \dfrac{10}{7}, \dfrac{9}{7}, \dfrac{8}{7},$ ___, ___, ___   e $\dfrac{13}{2}, \dfrac{11}{2}, \dfrac{9}{2}, \dfrac{7}{2},$ ___, ___, ___   f $\dfrac{3}{4}, \dfrac{8}{4}, \dfrac{13}{4}, \dfrac{18}{4},$ ___, ___, ___

PROBLEM-SOLVING		6	6, 7	7, 8

6   What fractions correspond to each of the red dots positioned on these number lines?

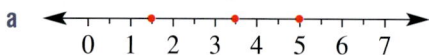

    a
    0 1 2 3 4 5 6 7

    b
    0   1   2

    c
    0   1   2   3   4

    d
    0   1   2   3   4

7   What operation (i.e. $+$, $-$, $\times$ or $\div$) does the vinculum relate to?

8   For each of the following, state what fraction of the diagram is shaded.

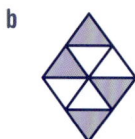

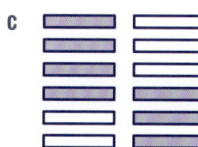

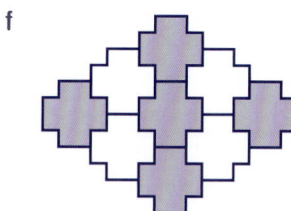

    a   b   c

    d   e   f

REASONING		9	9, 10	10, 11

9   For each of the following, write the fraction that is describing part of the total.

    a   After one day of a 43-kilometre hike, the walkers had completed 12 kilometres.

    b   Out of 15 starters, 13 runners went on and finished the race.

    c   Rainfall was below average for 11 months of the year.

    d   One egg is broken in a carton that contains a dozen eggs.

    e   Two players in the soccer team consisting of 11 players scored a goal.

    f   The lunch stop was 144 kilometres into the 475-kilometre trip.

    g   Seven members in the class of 20 have visited Australia Zoo.

    h   One of the four car tyres is worn and needs replacing.

    i   It rained three days this week.

10 **a** Explain, using diagrams, why the fractions $\frac{4}{4}$ and $\frac{6}{6}$ both have the value of 1.

   b Give some examples of fractions which would have the value of 2.

11 Which diagram has one-quarter shaded?

A   B   C   D

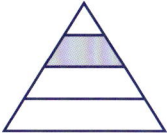

ENRICHMENT: Adjusting concentration   –   –   12

12 A 250-millilitre glass of cordial is made by mixing four parts water to one part syrup.

   a What fraction of the cordial is syrup?

   b What amount of syrup is required?

Fairuz drinks 50 millilitres of the cordial but finds it too strong. So he fills the glass back up with 50 millilitres of water.

   c How much syrup is in the cordial now?

   d What fraction of the cordial is syrup?

Fairuz drinks 50 millilitres of the cordial but still finds it too strong. So, once again, he fills the glass back up with 50 millilitres of water.

   e How much syrup is in the glass now?

   f What fraction of the cordial is syrup?

Lynn prefers her cordial much stronger compared with Fairuz. When she is given a glass of the cordial that is mixed at four parts to one, she drinks 50 millilitres and decides it is too weak. So she fills the glass back up with 50 millilitres of syrup.

   g How much syrup is in Lynn's glass now?

   h What fraction of the cordial is syrup?

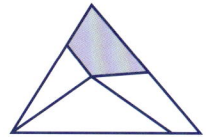

Lynn decides to repeat the process to make her cordial even stronger. So, once again, she drinks 50 millilitres and then tops the glass back up with 50 millilitres of syrup.

   i How much syrup is in Lynn's glass now?

   j What fraction of the cordial is syrup?

   k If Fairuz continues diluting his cordial concentration in this manner and Lynn continues strengthening her cordial concentration in this manner, will either of them ever reach pure water or pure syrup? Explain your reasoning.

3B   Equivalent fractions and simplified fractions

LEARNING INTENTIONS
- To understand what it means for two fractions to be equivalent
- To be able to simplify fractions by dividing by their highest common factor

Often fractions may look very different when in fact they have the same value.

For example, in an AFL football match, 'half-time' is the same as 'the end of the second quarter'. We can say that $\frac{1}{2}$ and $\frac{2}{4}$ are equivalent fractions. In both situations, the equivalent fraction of the game has been completed.

Consider a group of friends eating homemade pizzas. Each person cuts up their pizza as they like.

Trevor cuts his pizza into only two pieces, Jackie cuts hers into four pieces, Tahlia into six pieces and Jared into eight pieces. The shaded pieces are the amount that they have eaten before it is time to start the second movie.

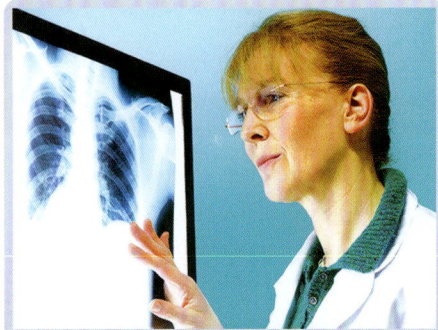

Radiologists diagnose medical conditions by using body imaging techniques such as X-rays, CT scans, MRI scans and ultrasound. They analyse the energy wave scatter fractions and how these fractions change with an illness.

By looking at the pizzas, it is clear to see that Trevor, Jackie, Tahlia and Jared have all eaten the same amount of pizza. We can therefore conclude that $\frac{1}{2}, \frac{2}{4}, \frac{3}{6}$ and $\frac{4}{8}$ are equivalent fractions.

This is written as $\frac{1}{2} = \frac{2}{4} = \frac{3}{6} = \frac{4}{8}$.

Trevor   Jackie

Tahlia   Jared

Lesson starter: Fraction clumps

Prepare a class set of fraction cards. (Two example sets are provided below.)

- Hand out one fraction card to each student.
- Students then arrange themselves into groups of equivalent fractions.
- Set an appropriate time goal by which this task must be completed.

Repeat the process with a second set of equivalent fraction cards.

Sample sets of fraction cards

Class set 1

$\frac{1}{2}, \frac{3}{12}, \frac{3}{24}, \frac{10}{80}, \frac{1}{3}, \frac{8}{40}, \frac{1}{5}, \frac{3}{6}, \frac{1}{8}, \frac{5}{40}, \frac{3}{9}, \frac{1}{4}, \frac{1000}{4000}, \frac{100}{200}, \frac{10}{50}, \frac{2}{16}, \frac{10}{30}, \frac{13}{39}, \frac{5}{10}, \frac{7}{14}, \frac{2}{6}, \frac{7}{28}, \frac{2}{10}, \frac{4}{20}, \frac{2}{8}$

Class set 2

$\frac{2}{3}, \frac{6}{14}, \frac{3}{18}, \frac{4}{10}, \frac{2}{12}, \frac{24}{64}, \frac{11}{66}, \frac{4}{6}, \frac{3}{7}, \frac{30}{70}, \frac{12}{32}, \frac{3}{8}, \frac{10}{15}, \frac{5}{30}, \frac{1}{6}, \frac{2000}{5000}, \frac{21}{49}, \frac{300}{800}, \frac{6}{9}, \frac{9}{21}, \frac{2}{5}, \frac{14}{35}, \frac{20}{30}, \frac{6}{16}, \frac{22}{55}$

KEY IDEAS

■ **Equivalent fractions** are fractions that represent the same numerical value.

For example: $\frac{1}{2}$ and $\frac{2}{4}$ are equivalent fractions.

■ Equivalent fractions are produced by multiplying the numerator and denominator by the same number.

■ Equivalent fractions can also be produced by dividing the numerator and denominator by the same number.

■ **Simplifying fractions** involves writing a fraction in its 'simplest form' in which the numerator and denominator have no common factors other than 1. To do this, the numerator and the denominator must be divided by their **highest common factor (HCF)**.

■ It is a mathematical convention to write all answers involving fractions in their simplest form.

■ A fraction wall can be helpful when comparing fractions. For example, the widths demonstrate that four-sixths and two-thirds are equivalent.

BUILDING UNDERSTANDING

1 Which of the following fractions are equivalent to $\frac{1}{2}$?

$$\frac{3}{5}, \frac{3}{6}, \frac{3}{10}, \frac{2}{4}, \frac{11}{22}, \frac{7}{15}, \frac{8}{12}, \frac{2}{1}, \frac{5}{10}, \frac{6}{10}$$

2 Which of the following fractions are equivalent to $\frac{8}{20}$?

$$\frac{4}{10}, \frac{1}{5}, \frac{6}{20}, \frac{8}{10}, \frac{16}{40}, \frac{2}{5}, \frac{4}{12}, \frac{12}{40}, \frac{80}{200}, \frac{1}{4}$$

3 Use a fraction wall or number line to give an example of three fractions that are equivalent to $\frac{2}{3}$.

4 In the following lists of equivalent fractions, choose the fraction that is in its simplest form.

a $\frac{3}{15}, \frac{10}{50}, \frac{2}{10}, \frac{1}{5}$ b $\frac{100}{600}, \frac{3}{18}, \frac{1}{6}, \frac{7}{42}$ c $\frac{4}{6}, \frac{2}{3}, \frac{16}{24}, \frac{20}{30}$

Example 4   Producing equivalent fractions with a given numerator or denominator

Fill in the missing number for the following equivalent fractions.

a $\frac{2}{3} = \frac{\square}{12}$ b $\frac{12}{20} = \frac{\square}{10}$ c $\frac{4}{5} = \frac{12}{\square}$

SOLUTION

a
$$\overset{\times 4}{\frac{2}{3} = \frac{8}{12}}\underset{\times 4}{}$$

b
$$\overset{\div 2}{\frac{12}{20} = \frac{6}{10}}\underset{\div 2}{}$$

c
$$\overset{\times 3}{\frac{4}{5} = \frac{12}{15}}\underset{\times 3}{}$$

EXPLANATION

To get from 3 to 12 using multiplication or division only, multiply by 4. The numerator must also be multiplied by 4 to make the fraction equivalent.

To get from 20 to 10, divide by 2. The numerator must also be divided by 2 to make the fraction equivalent.

Multiply by 3 to get from 4 to 12. The denominator must also be multiplied by 3 to make the fraction equivalent.

Now you try

Fill in the missing number for the following equivalent fractions.

a $\frac{3}{5} = \frac{\square}{10}$ b $\frac{18}{24} = \frac{\square}{12}$ c $\frac{5}{6} = \frac{20}{\square}$

Example 5   Converting fractions to simplest form

Write these fractions in simplest form.

a $\dfrac{12}{20}$

b $\dfrac{7}{42}$

SOLUTION

a

$$\overset{\div 4}{\underset{\div 4}{\dfrac{12}{20} = \dfrac{3}{5}}}$$

b

$$\overset{\div 7}{\underset{\div 7}{\dfrac{7}{42} = \dfrac{1}{6}}}$$

EXPLANATION

The HCF of 12 and 20 is 4.
Both the numerator and the denominator are divided by the HCF, 4.

The HCF of 7 and 42 is 7.
The 7 is 'cancelled' from the numerator and the denominator.

Now you try

Write these fractions in simplest form.

a $\dfrac{16}{20}$

b $\dfrac{14}{56}$

Example 6   Deciding if fractions are equivalent

Write either $=$ or $\neq$ between the fractions to state whether the following are equivalent or not equivalent.

a $\dfrac{8}{10} \,\square\, \dfrac{20}{25}$

b $\dfrac{2}{3} \,\square\, \dfrac{3}{12}$

SOLUTION

a

$$\overset{\div 2}{\underset{\div 2}{\dfrac{8}{10} = \dfrac{4}{5}}} \quad \text{and} \quad \overset{\div 5}{\underset{\div 5}{\dfrac{20}{25} = \dfrac{4}{5}}}$$

so $\dfrac{8}{10} = \dfrac{20}{25}$

EXPLANATION

Write each fraction in simplest form.
The numerators (4) and denominators (5) are equal, so they are equivalent.

SOLUTION

b

$$\frac{2}{6} = \frac{1}{3} \quad \text{and} \quad \frac{3}{12} = \frac{1}{4}$$

(÷2, ÷2) (÷3, ÷3)

so $\frac{2}{6} \neq \frac{3}{12}$

EXPLANATION

Write each fraction in simplest form. If they are equivalent their simplest form will have the same numerators and denominators. If not, they are not equivalent.

The denominators are different, so they are not equivalent. An alternative method is to write $\frac{2}{6} = \frac{4}{12}$ to show that when the denominators are the same (12), the numerators are different.

Now you try

By writing = or ≠ between the fractions, state whether the following pairs of fractions are equivalent or not equivalent.

a $\frac{2}{5} \square \frac{8}{20}$

b $\frac{4}{10} \square \frac{16}{30}$

Exercise 3B

FLUENCY   1–3, 5–6(½)   1–6(½)   4–6(½)

Example 4a

1   Fill in the missing number for the following equivalent fractions.

a $\frac{3}{4} = \frac{\square}{8}$

b $\frac{1}{2} = \frac{\square}{6}$

c $\frac{2}{5} = \frac{\square}{10}$

d $\frac{3}{5} = \frac{\square}{20}$

Example 4b

2   Fill in the missing number for the following equivalent fractions.

a $\frac{10}{20} = \frac{\square}{2}$

b $\frac{6}{10} = \frac{\square}{5}$

c $\frac{15}{20} = \frac{\square}{4}$

d $\frac{8}{12} = \frac{\square}{6}$

Example 4c

3   Fill in the missing number for the following equivalent fractions.

a $\frac{2}{5} = \frac{6}{\square}$

b $\frac{3}{4} = \frac{6}{\square}$

c $\frac{5}{10} = \frac{20}{\square}$

d $\frac{6}{8} = \frac{30}{\square}$

Example 4

4   Find the unknown value to make the equation true.

a $\frac{3}{4} = \frac{?}{12}$

b $\frac{5}{8} = \frac{?}{80}$

c $\frac{6}{11} = \frac{18}{?}$

d $\frac{2}{7} = \frac{16}{?}$

e $\frac{3}{?} = \frac{15}{40}$

f $\frac{?}{1} = \frac{14}{7}$

g $\frac{?}{10} = \frac{24}{20}$

h $\frac{13}{14} = \frac{?}{42}$

i $\frac{2}{7} = \frac{10}{?}$

j $\frac{19}{20} = \frac{190}{?}$

k $\frac{11}{21} = \frac{55}{?}$

l $\frac{11}{?} = \frac{44}{8}$

Example 5

5   Write the following fractions in simplest form.

a $\frac{15}{20}$

b $\frac{12}{18}$

c $\frac{10}{30}$

d $\frac{8}{22}$

e $\frac{14}{35}$

f $\frac{2}{22}$

g $\frac{8}{56}$

h $\frac{9}{27}$

i $\frac{35}{45}$

j $\frac{36}{96}$

k $\frac{120}{144}$

l $\frac{700}{140}$

Example 6

6 Write either = or ≠ between the fractions, to state whether the following pairs of fractions are equivalent or not equivalent.

a $\dfrac{1}{2} \square \dfrac{5}{8}$

b $\dfrac{4}{8} \square \dfrac{2}{4}$

c $\dfrac{3}{7} \square \dfrac{30}{70}$

d $\dfrac{5}{9} \square \dfrac{15}{18}$

e $\dfrac{11}{15} \square \dfrac{33}{45}$

f $\dfrac{1}{2} \square \dfrac{402}{804}$

g $\dfrac{12}{36} \square \dfrac{1}{3}$

h $\dfrac{18}{24} \square \dfrac{21}{28}$

i $\dfrac{6}{18} \square \dfrac{11}{33}$

PROBLEM-SOLVING	7	7, 8	8, 9

7 These lists of fractions are meant to contain only fractions in their simplest form; however, there is one mistake in each list. Find the fraction that is not in simplest form and rewrite in simplest form.

a $\dfrac{1}{3}, \dfrac{3}{8}, \dfrac{5}{9}, \dfrac{7}{14}$

b $\dfrac{2}{5}, \dfrac{12}{16}, \dfrac{16}{9}, \dfrac{13}{37}$

c $\dfrac{12}{19}, \dfrac{4}{42}, \dfrac{5}{24}, \dfrac{6}{61}$

d $\dfrac{7}{63}, \dfrac{9}{62}, \dfrac{11}{81}, \dfrac{13}{72}$

8 Four people win a competition that allows them to receive $\dfrac{1}{2}$ a tank of free petrol.

Find how many litres of petrol the drivers of these cars receive.

a Ford Territory with a 70-litre tank

b Nissan Patrol with a 90-litre tank

c Holden Commodore with a 60-litre tank

d Mazda 323 with a 48-litre tank

9 A family block of chocolate consists of 12 rows of 6 individual squares. Tania eats 16 individual squares. What fraction of the block, in simplest terms, has Tania eaten?

REASONING	10	10, 11	11, 12

10 Justin, Joanna and Jack are sharing a large pizza for dinner. The pizza has been cut into 12 equal pieces. Justin would like $\dfrac{1}{3}$ of the pizza, Joanna would like $\dfrac{1}{4}$ of the pizza and Jack will eat whatever is remaining. By considering equivalent fractions, determine how many slices each person gets served.

11 J.K. Rowling's first book, *Harry Potter and the Philosopher's Stone*, is 225 pages long. Sam plans to read the book in three days, reading the same number of pages each day.

a How many pages should Sam read each day?

b The fraction $\dfrac{75}{225}$ of the book is equivalent to what fraction in simplest form?

c By the end of the second day, Sam is on track and has read $\dfrac{2}{3}$ of the book.

How many pages of the book does $\dfrac{2}{3}$ represent?

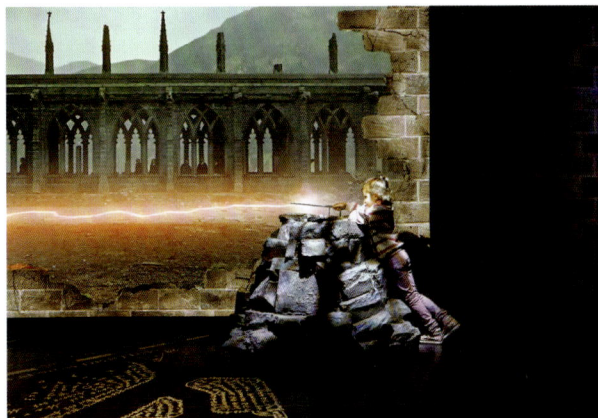

12 A fraction when simplified is written as $\frac{3}{5}$.

    a List some possibilities for what the original fraction was.

    b Explain why the sum of the original fraction's numerator and denominator must be even.

ENRICHMENT: Equivalent bars of music — — 13

13 Each piece of music has a time signature. A common time signature is called $\frac{4}{4}$ time, and is actually referred to as common time!

Common time, or $\frac{4}{4}$ time, means that there are four 'quarter notes' (or crotchets) in each bar.

Listed below are the five most commonly used musical notes.

𝆹 whole note (fills the whole bar) – semibreve

𝅗𝅥 half note (fills half the bar) – minim

♩ quarter note (four of these to a bar) – crotchet

♪ eighth note (eight to a bar) – quaver

𝅘𝅥𝅯 sixteenth note (sixteen to a bar) – semiquaver

When two or more quavers or shorter notes appear together, their 'flags' are joined together to form a horizontal bar.

    a Write six different 'bars' of music in $\frac{4}{4}$ time.

       Carry out some research on other types of musical time signatures.

    b Do you know what the time signature $\frac{12}{8}$ means?

    c Write three different bars of music for a $\frac{12}{8}$ time signature.

    d What are the musical symbols for different length rests?

    e How does a dot (or dots) written after a note affect the length of the note?

3C Mixed numerals and improper fractions   CONSOLIDATING

LEARNING INTENTIONS
- To know the meaning of the terms improper fractions and mixed numerals
- To be able to convert from a mixed numerals to an improper fraction
- To be able to convert from an improper fraction to a mixed numeral

As we have seen in this chapter, a fraction is a common way of representing part of a whole number. For example, a particular car trip may require $\frac{2}{3}$ of a tank of petrol.

On many occasions, you may need whole numbers plus a part of a whole number. For example, a long interstate car trip may require $2\frac{1}{4}$ tanks of petrol. Note that $2\frac{1}{4}$ is a way of writing $2 + \frac{1}{4}$.

When you have a combination of a whole number and a proper fraction, this number is known as a **mixed numeral**.

Nurses use many formulas requiring accurate arithmetic calculations. The time for an intravenous drip equals the total volume divided by the drip rate. The result is often a mixed numerals, such as $\frac{23}{4} = 5\frac{3}{4}$ hours.

Lesson starter: The sponge cake

With a partner, attempt to solve the following sponge cake problem. There is more than one answer.

At Pete's cake shop, small cakes are cut into four equal slices, medium cakes are cut into six equal slices and large cakes are cut into eight equal slices.

For a 70th birthday party, 13 cakes were ordered all of which were eaten. After the last slice was eaten, a total of 82 slices of cake had been eaten. How many cakes of each size were ordered?

KEY IDEAS

■ A number is said to be a **mixed numeral** when it is a mix of a whole number plus a proper fraction.

$$2\frac{3}{5} \text{ is a mixed numeral}$$

whole   proper
number   fraction

■ **Improper fractions** (fractions greater than a whole, where the numerator is greater than the denominator) can be converted to mixed numerals or whole numbers.

$$\frac{15}{4} = 3\frac{3}{4} \qquad\qquad \frac{16}{4} = 4$$

improper → mixed   improper → whole
fraction   numeral   fraction   number

■ Mixed numerals can be converted to improper fractions.

■ When improper fractions are written as mixed numerals, the fraction part should be written in simplest form.

■ A number line helps show the different types of fractions.

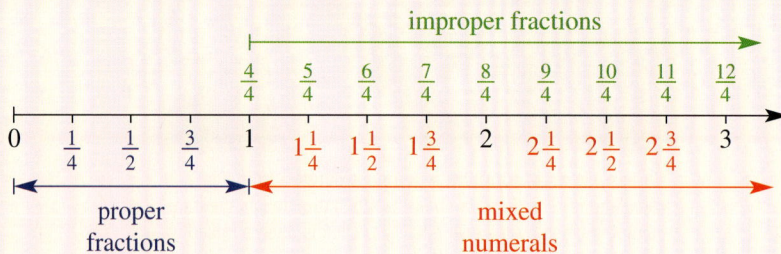

improper fractions

$$\frac{4}{4} \quad \frac{5}{4} \quad \frac{6}{4} \quad \frac{7}{4} \quad \frac{8}{4} \quad \frac{9}{4} \quad \frac{10}{4} \quad \frac{11}{4} \quad \frac{12}{4}$$

$$0 \quad \frac{1}{4} \quad \frac{1}{2} \quad \frac{3}{4} \quad 1 \quad 1\frac{1}{4} \quad 1\frac{1}{2} \quad 1\frac{3}{4} \quad 2 \quad 2\frac{1}{4} \quad 2\frac{1}{2} \quad 2\frac{3}{4} \quad 3$$

proper   mixed
fractions   numerals

BUILDING UNDERSTANDING

1 Between which two whole numbers do the following mixed numerals lie?

a $2\frac{1}{2}$ b $11\frac{1}{7}$ c $36\frac{8}{9}$

2 Work out the total number of pieces in each of these situations.

a four pizzas cut into six pieces each

b 10 Lego trucks, where each truck is made from 36 Lego pieces

c five jigsaw puzzles with 12 pieces in each puzzle

d three cakes cut into eight pieces each

3 The mixed numeral $2\frac{3}{4}$ can be represented in 'window shapes' as

$$2\frac{3}{4} = \ \blacksquare \ + \ \blacksquare \ + \ \blacksquare$$

Draw or describe the following mixed numerals using window shapes.

a $1\frac{1}{4}$ b $1\frac{3}{4}$ c $3\frac{2}{4}$ d $5\frac{2}{4}$

4 A window shape consists of four panes of glass. How many panes of glass are there in the following number of window shapes?

a 2   b 3   c 7   d 11

e $4\frac{1}{4}$ f $1\frac{3}{4}$ g $2\frac{2}{4}$ h $5\frac{4}{4}$

5 What mixed numerals correspond to the red dots on each number line?

a
```
7   8   9   10  11  12
```

b
```
0   1   2   3   4   5
```

c
```
22    23    24    25    26
```

Example 7   Converting mixed numerals to improper fractions

Convert $3\frac{1}{5}$ to an improper fraction.

SOLUTION

$3\frac{1}{5} = \dfrac{3 \times 5 + 1}{5}$

$\phantom{3\frac{1}{5}} = \dfrac{16}{5}$

EXPLANATION

$3\frac{1}{5} = 3$ wholes $+ \ \frac{1}{5}$ of a whole

Multiply the whole number by the denominator and then add the numerator.

$3 \times 5 + 1 = 16$

Now you try

Convert $2\frac{5}{6}$ to an improper fraction.

Example 8   Converting improper fractions to mixed numerals

Convert $\frac{11}{4}$ to a mixed numeral.

SOLUTION

Method 1
$$\frac{11}{4} = \frac{8+3}{4} = \frac{8}{4} + \frac{3}{4} = 2 + \frac{3}{4} = 2\frac{3}{4}$$

Method 2

$$4\overline{)11} \quad \begin{array}{c} 2 \text{ rem } 3 \end{array}$$

So $\frac{11}{4} = 2\frac{3}{4}$

EXPLANATION

$\frac{11}{4} = 11$ quarters

$$= 2\frac{3}{4}$$

Now you try

Convert $\frac{23}{7}$ to a mixed numeral.

Example 9   Writing mixed numerals in simplest form

Convert $\frac{20}{6}$ to a mixed numeral in simplest form.

SOLUTION

$$\frac{20}{6} = 3\frac{2}{6} = 3\frac{1}{3}$$

or

$$\frac{20}{6} = \frac{10}{3} = 3\frac{1}{3}$$
$\div 2$

EXPLANATION

Method 1: Convert to mixed numeral and then simplify the fraction part.

Note $\frac{2}{6} = \frac{1}{3}$
$\div 2$

Method 2: Simplify the improper fraction first and then convert to a mixed numeral.

Now you try

Convert $\frac{18}{4}$ to a mixed numeral in simplest form.

Exercise 3C

FLUENCY | 1, 2–4(½) | 2–4(⅓) | 2–4(¼)

Example 7

1 Convert the following mixed numerals to improper fractions.

a $1\frac{2}{3}$ b $2\frac{1}{5}$ c $3\frac{1}{2}$ d $1\frac{3}{4}$

Example 7

2 Convert these mixed numerals to improper fractions.

a $2\frac{1}{5}$ b $3\frac{1}{3}$ c $4\frac{1}{7}$

d $2\frac{1}{2}$ e $4\frac{2}{3}$ f $8\frac{2}{5}$

g $6\frac{1}{9}$ h $5\frac{2}{8}$ i $1\frac{11}{12}$

j $4\frac{5}{12}$ k $5\frac{15}{20}$ l $64\frac{3}{10}$

Example 8

3 Convert these improper fractions to mixed numerals.

a $\frac{7}{5}$ b $\frac{5}{3}$ c $\frac{11}{3}$

d $\frac{16}{7}$ e $\frac{12}{7}$ f $\frac{20}{3}$

g $\frac{35}{8}$ h $\frac{48}{7}$ i $\frac{37}{12}$

j $\frac{93}{10}$ k $\frac{231}{100}$ l $\frac{135}{11}$

Example 9

4 Convert these improper fractions to mixed numerals in simplest form.

a $\frac{10}{4}$ b $\frac{28}{10}$ c $\frac{16}{12}$ d $\frac{8}{6}$

e $\frac{18}{16}$ f $\frac{30}{9}$ g $\frac{40}{15}$ h $\frac{60}{25}$

PROBLEM-SOLVING | 5 | 5, 6 | 6, 7

5 Draw a number line from 0 to 5 and mark the following fractions and mixed numerals on it.

a $\frac{2}{3}, 2, \frac{5}{3}, 3\frac{1}{3}$ b $\frac{3}{4}, \frac{12}{4}, 2\frac{1}{4}, 3\frac{1}{2}$ c $\frac{4}{5}, \frac{14}{5}, 3\frac{1}{5}, \frac{10}{5}, \frac{19}{5}$

6 The number $4\frac{1}{6}$ is located between 4 and 5 on a number line, which means $\frac{25}{6}$ is also located between 4 and 5 (as it has the same value). Convert the following to mixed numerals to find the two whole numbers located either side.

a $\frac{17}{3}$ b $\frac{29}{4}$ c $\frac{50}{8}$

7 Four friends order three large pizzas for their dinner. Each pizza is cut into eight equal slices.
Simone has three slices, Izabella has four slices, Mark has five slices and Alex has three slices.

a How many pizza slices do they eat in total?

b How many pizzas do they eat in total? Give your answer as a mixed numeral.

c How many pizza slices are left uneaten?

d How many pizzas are left uneaten? Give your answer as a mixed numeral.

8   Explain, using diagrams, why $\frac{7}{4}$ and $1\frac{3}{4}$ are equal. You could use shapes split into quarters or a number line.

9   a   Patricia has three sandwiches that are cut into quarters and she eats all but one-quarter. How many quarters does she eat?

    b   Phillip has five sandwiches that are cut into halves and he eats all but one-half. How many halves does he eat?

    c   Crystal has x sandwiches that are cut into quarters and she eats all but one-quarter. How many quarters does she eat?

    d   Byron has y sandwiches that are cut into thirds and he eats all but one-third. How many thirds does he eat?

    e   Felicity has m sandwiches that are cut into n pieces and she eats them all. How many pieces does she eat?

10 A fully simplified mixed numeral between 2 and 3 is written as an improper fraction with a numerator of 17. List all the possible mixed numerals matching this description.

11 Using the digits 1, 2 and 3 only once, three different mixed numerals can be written.
    a   i   Write down the three possible mixed numerals.
        ii Find the difference between the smallest and highest mixed numerals.
    b   Repeat part a using the digits 2, 3 and 4.
    c   Repeat part a using the digits 3, 4 and 5.
    d   Predict the difference between the largest and smallest mixed numerals when using only the digits 4, 5 and 6. Check to see if your prediction is correct.
    e   Write down a rule for the difference between the largest and smallest mixed numerals when using any three consecutive integers.
    f   Extend your investigation to allow mixed numerals where the fraction part is an improper fraction.
    g   Extend your investigation to produce mixed numerals from four consecutive digits.

3D | Ordering fractions

LEARNING INTENTIONS
- To know the meaning of the terms ascending and descending
- To be able to compare two fractions and decide which one is larger
- To be able to order a list of fractions in ascending or descending order

You already know how to order a set of whole numbers.

For example: 3, 7, 15, 6, 2, 10 are a set of six different whole numbers that you could place in ascending or descending order.

In ascending order, the correct order is: 2, 3, 6, 7, 10, 15.

In descending order, the correct order is: 15, 10, 7, 6, 3, 2.

In this section, you will learn how to write different fractions in ascending and descending order. To be able to do this we need to compare different fractions and we do this through our knowledge of equivalent fractions (see **Section 3B**).

A farm mechanic maintains agricultural machinery such as harvesters and irrigation pumps. Fraction skills are essential as many components are manufactured with fractional measurements, e.g. a cover plate $6\frac{1}{4}$ inches long by $4\frac{3}{8}$ inches wide.

Remember that a number is greater than another number if it lies to the right of it on a number line.

$\frac{3}{4} > \frac{1}{2}$

0     $\frac{1}{2}$ $\frac{3}{4}$ 1

Lesson starter: The order of five

- As a warm-up activity, ask five volunteer students to arrange themselves in alphabetical order, then in height order and, finally, in birthday order.
- Each of the five students receives a large fraction card and displays it to the class.
- The rest of the class must then attempt to order the students in ascending order, according to their fraction card. It is a group decision and none of the five students should move until the class agrees on a decision.
- Repeat the activity with a set of more challenging fraction cards.

KEY IDEAS

■ To order (or arrange) fractions we must know how to compare different fractions. This is often done by considering equivalent fractions.

■ If the numerators are the same, the smallest fraction is the one with the biggest denominator, as it has been divided up into the most pieces.

For example: $\frac{1}{7} < \frac{1}{2}$

■ If the denominators are the same, the smallest fraction is the one with the smallest numerator.

For example: $\frac{3}{10} < \frac{7}{10}$

■ To order two fractions with different numerators and denominators, we can use our knowledge of equivalent fractions to produce fractions with a common denominator and then compare the numerators.

■ The **lowest common denominator (LCD)** is the lowest common multiple of the different denominators.

■ **Ascending** order is when numbers are ordered going *up*, from smallest to largest. On a number line, this means listing the numbers from left to right.

■ **Descending** order is when numbers are ordered going *down*, from largest to smallest. On a number line, this means listing the numbers from right to left.

BUILDING UNDERSTANDING

1 State the largest fraction in each of the following lists.

a $\frac{3}{7}, \frac{2}{7}, \frac{5}{7}, \frac{1}{7}$

b $\frac{4}{3}, \frac{2}{3}, \frac{7}{3}, \frac{5}{3}$

c $\frac{5}{11}, \frac{9}{11}, \frac{3}{11}, \frac{4}{11}$

d $\frac{8}{5}, \frac{4}{5}, \frac{6}{5}, \frac{7}{5}$

2 State the lowest common multiple of the following sets of numbers.

a 2, 5   b 5, 4   c 3, 6   d 4, 6

e 2, 3, 5   f 3, 4, 6   g 3, 8, 4   h 2, 6, 5

3 State the lowest common denominator of the following sets of fractions.

a $\frac{1}{3}, \frac{3}{5}$

b $\frac{2}{4}, \frac{3}{5}$

c $\frac{4}{7}, \frac{2}{3}$

d $\frac{2}{10}, \frac{1}{5}$

e $\frac{4}{6}, \frac{3}{8}$

f $\frac{5}{12}, \frac{2}{5}$

g $\frac{1}{2}, \frac{2}{3}, \frac{3}{4}$

h $\frac{4}{3}, \frac{3}{4}$

4 Find the missing numbers to produce equivalent fractions.

a $\frac{2}{5} = \frac{\square}{15}$

b $\frac{2}{3} = \frac{\square}{12}$

c $\frac{1}{4} = \frac{\square}{16}$

d $\frac{3}{7} = \frac{\square}{14}$

e $\frac{3}{8} = \frac{\square}{40}$

f $\frac{5}{6} = \frac{\square}{18}$

Example 10   Comparing fractions

Place the correct mathematical symbol <, = or >, in between the following pairs of fractions to make a true mathematical statement.

a $\dfrac{2}{5} \square \dfrac{4}{5}$

b $\dfrac{1}{3} \square \dfrac{1}{5}$

c $\dfrac{2}{3} \square \dfrac{3}{5}$

d $2\dfrac{3}{7} \square \dfrac{16}{7}$

SOLUTION

a $\dfrac{2}{5} \boxed{<} \dfrac{4}{5}$

b $\dfrac{1}{3} \boxed{>} \dfrac{1}{5}$

c $\overset{\times 5}{\underset{\times 5}{\dfrac{2}{3} = \dfrac{10}{15}}}$ and $\overset{\times 3}{\underset{\times 3}{\dfrac{3}{5} = \dfrac{9}{15}}}$

$\dfrac{10}{15} \boxed{>} \dfrac{9}{15}$. Hence, $\dfrac{2}{3} \boxed{>} \dfrac{3}{5}$.

d $2\dfrac{3}{7} \square \dfrac{16}{7}$

$\dfrac{17}{7} \boxed{>} \dfrac{16}{7}$. Hence, $2\dfrac{3}{7} \boxed{>} \dfrac{16}{7}$.

EXPLANATION

Denominators are the same, therefore compare numerators.

Numerators are the same.
Smallest fraction has the biggest denominator.

LCD of 3 and 5 is 15, so write equivalent fractions with 15 as denominator.
Denominators now the same, therefore compare numerators.

First, convert mixed numerals to improper fractions.
Now compare the two improper fractions to decide which is bigger.

Now you try

Place the correct mathematical symbol <, = or >, in between the following pairs of fractions to make a true mathematical statement.

a $\dfrac{4}{7} \square \dfrac{2}{7}$

b $\dfrac{1}{9} \square \dfrac{1}{6}$

c $\dfrac{10}{16} \square \dfrac{15}{24}$

d $2\dfrac{4}{9} \square \dfrac{25}{9}$

Example 11   Ordering fractions and mixed numerals

Place the following fractions in ascending order.

a $\dfrac{3}{4}, \dfrac{4}{5}, \dfrac{2}{3}$

b $1\dfrac{3}{5}, \dfrac{7}{4}, \dfrac{3}{2}, 2\dfrac{1}{4}, \dfrac{11}{5}$

SOLUTION

a
$$\dfrac{3}{4} \xrightarrow{\times 15} \dfrac{45}{60}, \quad \dfrac{4}{5} \xrightarrow{\times 12} \dfrac{48}{60}, \quad \dfrac{2}{3} \xrightarrow{\times 20} \dfrac{40}{60}$$

$$\dfrac{40}{60}, \dfrac{45}{60}, \dfrac{48}{60}$$

$$\dfrac{2}{3}, \dfrac{3}{4}, \dfrac{4}{5}$$

b
$$\dfrac{8}{5}, \dfrac{7}{4}, \dfrac{3}{2}, \dfrac{9}{4}, \dfrac{11}{5}$$

$$\dfrac{32}{20}, \dfrac{35}{20}, \dfrac{30}{20}, \dfrac{45}{20}, \dfrac{44}{20}$$

$$\dfrac{30}{20}, \dfrac{32}{20}, \dfrac{35}{20}, \dfrac{44}{20}, \dfrac{45}{20}$$

$$\dfrac{3}{2}, 1\dfrac{3}{5}, \dfrac{7}{4}, \dfrac{11}{5}, 2\dfrac{1}{4}$$

EXPLANATION

LCD of 3, 4 and 5 is 60. Produce equivalent fractions with denominator of 60.

Order fractions in ascending order.

Rewrite fractions back in original form.

Express all mixed numerals as improper fractions.

LCD of 2, 4 and 5 is 20. Produce equivalent fractions with a denominator of 20.

Order fractions in ascending order.

Rewrite fractions back in original form.

Now you try

Place the following fractions in ascending order.

a $\dfrac{3}{4}, \dfrac{2}{6}, \dfrac{1}{2}$

b $1\dfrac{7}{8}, \dfrac{5}{4}, 2\dfrac{1}{2}, \dfrac{3}{4}, \dfrac{9}{4}, \dfrac{23}{8}$

Exercise 3D

FLUENCY   1–3, 5   1–7($\frac{1}{2}$)   4–8($\frac{1}{2}$)

Example 10a

1 Place the correct mathematical symbol <, = or >, in between the following pairs of fractions to make a true mathematical statement.

a $\dfrac{3}{7} \square \dfrac{2}{7}$ **b** $\dfrac{4}{9} \square \dfrac{7}{9}$ **c** $\dfrac{4}{12} \square \dfrac{3}{12}$ **d** $\dfrac{5}{3} \square \dfrac{6}{3}$

Example 10b

2 Place the correct mathematical symbol <, = or >, in between the following pairs of fractions to make a true mathematical statement.

a $\dfrac{1}{5} \square \dfrac{1}{7}$ **b** $\dfrac{1}{9} \square \dfrac{1}{7}$ **c** $\dfrac{3}{6} \square \dfrac{3}{10}$ **d** $\dfrac{4}{11} \square \dfrac{4}{11}$

3 Place the correct mathematical symbol <, = or >, in between the following pairs of fractions to make a true mathematical statement.

a $\frac{2}{3} \square \frac{1}{6}$ b $\frac{4}{5} \square \frac{9}{10}$ c $\frac{3}{4} \square \frac{7}{10}$ d $\frac{2}{5} \square \frac{3}{7}$

4 Place the correct mathematical symbol <, = or >, in between the following pairs of fractions to make a true mathematical statement.

a $\frac{3}{5} \square \frac{1}{5}$ b $\frac{2}{2} \square \frac{3}{3}$ c $\frac{1}{4} \square \frac{1}{3}$ d $\frac{1}{10} \square \frac{1}{20}$

e $\frac{4}{7} \square \frac{4}{5}$ f $\frac{4}{5} \square \frac{3}{4}$ g $\frac{5}{6} \square \frac{9}{10}$ h $\frac{5}{7} \square \frac{15}{21}$

i $\frac{7}{11} \square \frac{3}{5}$ j $1\frac{2}{3} \square 1\frac{1}{2}$ k $3\frac{3}{7} \square \frac{15}{4}$ l $\frac{12}{5} \square 2\frac{3}{8}$

5 Place the following fractions in ascending order.

a $\frac{3}{5}, \frac{8}{5}, \frac{7}{5}$ b $\frac{5}{9}, \frac{1}{3}, \frac{2}{9}$

c $\frac{2}{5}, \frac{3}{4}, \frac{4}{5}$ d $\frac{5}{6}, \frac{3}{5}, \frac{2}{3}$

6 Place the following fractions and mixed numerals in ascending order.

a $2\frac{1}{4}, \frac{11}{4}, \frac{5}{2}, 3\frac{1}{3}$ b $1\frac{7}{8}, \frac{11}{6}, \frac{7}{4}, \frac{5}{3}$

c $2\frac{7}{10}, \frac{9}{4}, \frac{11}{5}, 2\frac{1}{2}, 2\frac{3}{5}$ d $4\frac{4}{9}, \frac{15}{3}, 4\frac{10}{27}, 4\frac{2}{3}, 4\frac{1}{6}$

7 Place the following fractions in descending order.

a $\frac{1}{2}, \frac{3}{5}, \frac{3}{10}, \frac{7}{10}, \frac{4}{5}$ b $\frac{3}{8}, \frac{1}{2}, \frac{5}{8}, \frac{3}{4}, \frac{1}{4}$ c $\frac{1}{3}, \frac{5}{12}, \frac{5}{6}, \frac{1}{2}, \frac{2}{3}$

8 Place the following fractions in descending order, without finding common denominators.

a $\frac{3}{5}, \frac{3}{7}, \frac{3}{6}, \frac{3}{8}$ b $\frac{1}{15}, \frac{1}{10}, \frac{1}{50}, \frac{1}{100}$

c $7\frac{1}{11}, 8\frac{3}{5}, 5\frac{4}{9}, 10\frac{2}{3}$ d $2\frac{1}{3}, 2\frac{1}{9}, 2\frac{1}{6}, 2\frac{1}{5}$

PROBLEM-SOLVING	9	9, 10	10, 11

9 Place the following cake fractions in decreasing order of size.

A sponge cake shared equally by four people $= \frac{1}{4}$ cake

B chocolate cake shared equally by eleven people $= \frac{1}{11}$ cake

C carrot and walnut cake shared equally by eight people $= \frac{1}{8}$ cake

10 Four friends, Dean, David, Andrea and Rob, all competed in the Great Ocean Road marathon. Their respective finishing times were $3\frac{1}{3}$ hours, $3\frac{5}{12}$ hours, $3\frac{1}{4}$ hours and $3\frac{4}{15}$ hours. Write down the correct finishing order of the four friends.

11 Rewrite the fractions in each set with their lowest common denominator and then write the next two fractions that would continue the pattern.

a $\dfrac{2}{9}, \dfrac{1}{3}, \dfrac{4}{9}$, _____, _____

b $\dfrac{1}{2}, \dfrac{5}{4}, 2$, _____, _____

c $\dfrac{11}{6}, \dfrac{3}{2}, \dfrac{7}{6}$, _____, _____

d $\dfrac{1}{2}, \dfrac{4}{7}, \dfrac{9}{14}$, _____, _____

REASONING	12(½)	12(½), 13	13, 14

12 For each of the following pairs of fractions, write a fraction that lies between them. Hint: convert to a common denominator first, then consider the values in between.

a $\dfrac{3}{5}, \dfrac{3}{4}$

b $\dfrac{1}{4}, \dfrac{1}{2}$

c $\dfrac{2}{7}, \dfrac{1}{6}$

d $\dfrac{17}{20}, \dfrac{7}{10}$

e $2\dfrac{1}{3}, 2\dfrac{1}{5}$

f $8\dfrac{7}{10}, 8\dfrac{3}{4}$

13 If $\dfrac{a}{b}$ is a fraction less than 1, you can always find a fraction strictly between $\dfrac{a}{b}$ and 1. For example, between $\dfrac{3}{4}$ and 1 you can find the fraction $\dfrac{7}{8}$.

a   Explain, using a common denominator of 8, why $\dfrac{3}{4}, \dfrac{7}{8}, 1$ is in ascending order.

b   Find a fraction with a denominator of 16 that lies between $\dfrac{7}{8}$ and 1.

c   Explain why you could keep going forever, finding a fraction less than 1 but greater than the second largest value.

14 Write all the whole number values that '?' can take so that $\dfrac{?}{3}$ lies strictly between:

a   2 and 3

b   5 and $5\dfrac{1}{2}$

ENRICHMENT: Shady designs	–	–	15

15 a For each of the diagrams shown, work out what fraction of the rectangle is coloured purple. Explain how you arrived at each of your answers.

i

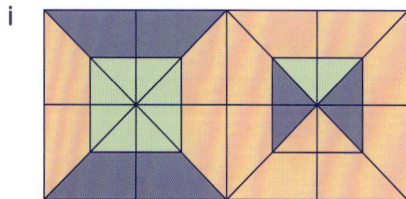

ii

iii

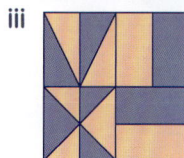

iv

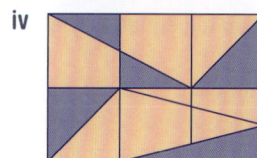

b Design and shade two more rectangle designs.

3E Adding fractions

Fractions with the same denominator can be easily added.

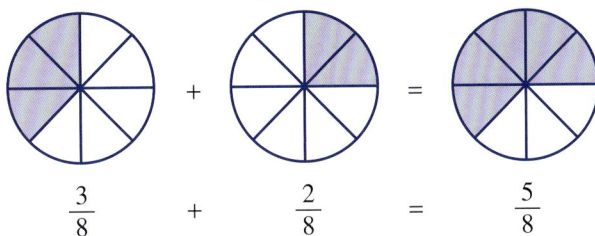

$$\frac{3}{8} + \frac{2}{8} = \frac{5}{8}$$

Fractions with different denominators cannot be added so easily.

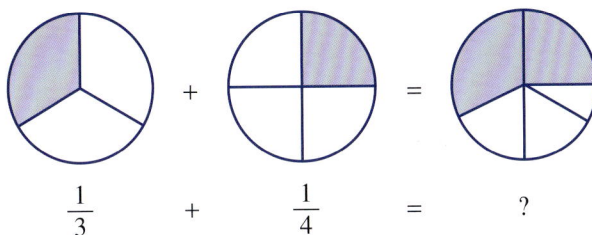

$$\frac{1}{3} + \frac{1}{4} = ?$$

Note:
$$\frac{1}{3} + \frac{1}{4} \neq \frac{1}{7}$$
$$\frac{1}{3} + \frac{1}{4} \neq \frac{2}{7}$$

But with a common denominator it is possible.

$$\frac{1}{3} + \frac{1}{4} = ?$$
$$\frac{4}{12} + \frac{3}{12} = \frac{7}{12}$$

Lesson starter: 'Like' addition

Pair up with a classmate and discuss the following.

1   Which of the following pairs of numbers can be simply added without having to carry out any form of conversion?

a   6 goals, 2 goals
b   11 goals, 5 behinds
c   56 runs, 3 wickets
d   6 hours, 5 minutes
e   21 seconds, 15 seconds
f   47 minutes, 13 seconds
g   15 cm, 3 m
h   2.2 km, 4.1 km
i   5 kg, 1680 g
j $\frac{2}{7}, \frac{3}{7}$
k $\frac{1}{4}, \frac{1}{2}$
l $2\frac{5}{12}, 1\frac{1}{3}$

Does it become clear that we can only add pairs of numbers that have the same unit? In terms of fractions, we need to have the same _____.

2   By choosing your preferred unit (when necessary), work out the answer to each of the problems above.

KEY IDEAS

■ Fractions can be simplified easily using addition if they are 'like' fractions; that is, they have the **same denominator**. This means they have been divided up into the same number of pieces.

Same denominators

■ If two or more fractions have the same denominator, to add them simply add the numerators and keep the denominator. This allows you to find the total number of divided pieces.

Different denominators

■ If the denominators are different, we use our knowledge of equivalent fractions to convert them to fractions with the same **lowest common denominator (LCD)**.

■ To do this, carry out these steps.
  1 Find the LCD (often, but not always, found by multiplying denominators).
  2 Convert fractions to their equivalent fractions with the LCD.
  3 Add the numerators and write this total above the LCD.

■ After adding fractions, always look to see if your answer needs to be simplified.

BUILDING UNDERSTANDING

1 State the missing terms in the following sentences.
  a To add two fractions, they must have the same _____.
  b When adding fractions, if they have the same _____, you simply add the _____.
  c When adding two or more fractions where the _____ are different, you must find the _____ _____ _____.
  d After carrying out the addition of fractions, you should always _____ your answer to see if it can be _____.

2 State the LCD for the following pairs of 'incomplete' fractions.
  a $\dfrac{}{5} + \dfrac{}{3}$ b $\dfrac{}{6} + \dfrac{}{3}$ c $\dfrac{}{12} + \dfrac{}{8}$ d $\dfrac{}{12} + \dfrac{}{16}$

3 Which of the following are correct?
  a $\dfrac{1}{9} + \dfrac{4}{9} = \dfrac{5}{9}$ b $\dfrac{1}{3} + \dfrac{1}{4} = \dfrac{2}{7}$ c $\dfrac{3}{5} + \dfrac{4}{5} = 1\dfrac{2}{5}$ d $\dfrac{1}{2} + \dfrac{2}{5} = \dfrac{3}{7}$

Example 12 Adding 'like' fractions

Add the following fractions.

a $\dfrac{1}{5} + \dfrac{3}{5}$

b $\dfrac{3}{11} + \dfrac{5}{11} + \dfrac{6}{11}$

SOLUTION

a $\dfrac{1}{5} + \dfrac{3}{5} = \dfrac{4}{5}$

b $\dfrac{3}{11} + \dfrac{5}{11} + \dfrac{6}{11} = \dfrac{14}{11}$

$\qquad\qquad\qquad = 1\dfrac{3}{11}$

EXPLANATION

The denominators are the same; i.e. 'like', therefore simply add the numerators.

Denominators are the same, so add numerators.

Write answer as a mixed numeral.

Now you try

Add the following fractions.

a $\dfrac{4}{7} + \dfrac{1}{7}$

b $\dfrac{4}{9} + \dfrac{2}{9} + \dfrac{5}{9}$

Example 13   Adding 'unlike' fractions

Add the following fractions.

a $\dfrac{1}{5} + \dfrac{1}{2}$

b $\dfrac{3}{4} + \dfrac{5}{6}$

SOLUTION

a $\dfrac{1}{5} + \dfrac{1}{2} = \dfrac{2}{10} + \dfrac{5}{10}$

$\qquad\qquad = \dfrac{7}{10}$

b $\dfrac{3}{4} + \dfrac{5}{6} = \dfrac{9}{12} + \dfrac{10}{12}$

$\qquad\qquad = \dfrac{19}{12}$

$\qquad\qquad = 1\dfrac{7}{12}$

EXPLANATION

LCD is 10.
Write equivalent fractions with the LCD.

$$\overset{\times 2}{\underset{\times 2}{\dfrac{1}{5} = \dfrac{2}{10}}} \qquad \overset{\times 5}{\underset{\times 5}{\dfrac{1}{2} = \dfrac{5}{10}}}$$

Denominators are the same, so add numerators.

LCD is 12.
Write equivalent fractions with the LCD.

$$\overset{\times 3}{\underset{\times 3}{\dfrac{3}{4} = \dfrac{9}{12}}} \qquad \overset{\times 2}{\underset{\times 2}{\dfrac{5}{6} = \dfrac{10}{12}}}$$

Denominators are the same, so add numerators.
Write answer as a mixed numeral.

Now you try

Add the following fractions.

a $\dfrac{1}{3} + \dfrac{1}{5}$

b $\dfrac{3}{4} + \dfrac{7}{10}$

Example 14   Adding mixed numerals

Simplify:

a $3\frac{2}{3} + 4\frac{2}{3}$

b $2\frac{5}{6} + 3\frac{3}{4}$

SOLUTION

a Method 1

$3 + 4 + \frac{2}{3} + \frac{2}{3} = 7 + \frac{4}{3}$

$\phantom{3 + 4 + \frac{2}{3} + \frac{2}{3}} = 8\frac{1}{3}$

Method 2

$\frac{11}{3} + \frac{14}{3} = \frac{25}{3}$

$\phantom{\frac{11}{3} + \frac{14}{3}} = 8\frac{1}{3}$

b Method 1

$2 + 3 + \frac{5}{6} + \frac{3}{4} = 5 + \frac{10}{12} + \frac{9}{12}$

$\phantom{2 + 3 + \frac{5}{6} + \frac{3}{4}} = 5 + \frac{19}{12}$

$\phantom{2 + 3 + \frac{5}{6} + \frac{3}{4}} = 6\frac{7}{12}$

Method 2

$\frac{17}{6} + \frac{15}{4} = \frac{34}{12} + \frac{45}{12}$

$\phantom{\frac{17}{6} + \frac{15}{4}} = \frac{79}{12}$

$\phantom{\frac{17}{6} + \frac{15}{4}} = 6\frac{7}{12}$

EXPLANATION

Add the whole number parts.

Add the fraction parts.

Noting that $\frac{4}{3} = 1\frac{1}{3}$, simplify the answer.

Convert mixed numerals to improper fractions. Have the same denominators, so add numerators.

Convert improper fraction back to a mixed numerals.

Add the whole number parts.

LCD of 6 and 4 is 12.

Write equivalent fractions with LCD.

Add the fraction parts.

Noting that $\frac{19}{12} = 1\frac{7}{12}$, simplify the answer.

Convert mixed numerals to improper fractions.

Write equivalent fractions with LCD.

Add the numerators.

Simplify answer back to a mixed numeral.

Now you try

Simplify:

a $1\frac{3}{5} + 2\frac{3}{5}$

b $2\frac{1}{10} + 1\frac{3}{4}$

Exercise 3E

FLUENCY

| | 1–5(½) | 1–4(½), 6–7(½) | 3–4(½), 6–7(½) |

Example 12a

1 Add the following fractions.

a $\frac{2}{9} + \frac{5}{9}$ **b** $\frac{1}{12} + \frac{6}{12}$ **c** $\frac{3}{15} + \frac{4}{15}$ **d** $\frac{3}{9} + \frac{2}{9}$

Example 12b

2 Add the following fractions, writing your final answers as a mixed numeral.

a $\frac{6}{7} + \frac{3}{7}$ **b** $\frac{7}{10} + \frac{6}{10}$ **c** $\frac{2}{5} + \frac{3}{5} + \frac{4}{5}$ **d** $\frac{12}{19} + \frac{3}{19} + \frac{8}{19}$

Example 13a

3 Add the following fractions.

a $\dfrac{1}{2} + \dfrac{1}{4}$ b $\dfrac{1}{3} + \dfrac{3}{5}$ c $\dfrac{1}{2} + \dfrac{1}{6}$ d $\dfrac{1}{4} + \dfrac{1}{3}$

e $\dfrac{2}{5} + \dfrac{1}{4}$ f $\dfrac{1}{5} + \dfrac{3}{4}$ g $\dfrac{2}{7} + \dfrac{1}{3}$ h $\dfrac{3}{8} + \dfrac{1}{5}$

Example 13b

4 Add the following fractions, writing your final answers as a mixed numeral.

a $\dfrac{3}{5} + \dfrac{5}{6}$ b $\dfrac{4}{7} + \dfrac{3}{4}$ c $\dfrac{8}{11} + \dfrac{2}{3}$ d $\dfrac{2}{3} + \dfrac{3}{4}$

Example 14a

5 Simplify:

a $1\dfrac{1}{5} + 2\dfrac{3}{5}$ b $3\dfrac{2}{7} + 4\dfrac{1}{7}$ c $11\dfrac{1}{4} + 1\dfrac{2}{4}$ d $1\dfrac{3}{9} + 4\dfrac{2}{9}$

e $5\dfrac{2}{3} + 4\dfrac{2}{3}$ f $8\dfrac{3}{6} + 12\dfrac{4}{6}$ g $9\dfrac{7}{11} + 9\dfrac{7}{11}$ h $4\dfrac{3}{5} + 7\dfrac{4}{5}$

Example 14b

6 Simplify:

a $2\dfrac{2}{3} + 1\dfrac{3}{4}$ b $5\dfrac{2}{5} + 1\dfrac{5}{6}$ c $3\dfrac{1}{2} + 8\dfrac{2}{3}$ d $5\dfrac{4}{7} + 7\dfrac{3}{4}$

e $8\dfrac{1}{2} + 6\dfrac{3}{5}$ f $12\dfrac{2}{3} + 6\dfrac{4}{9}$ g $17\dfrac{8}{11} + 7\dfrac{3}{4}$ h $9\dfrac{7}{12} + 5\dfrac{5}{8}$

7 Simplify:

a $\dfrac{1}{4} + \dfrac{1}{4}$ b $\dfrac{2}{9} + \dfrac{1}{3}$ c $\dfrac{7}{8} + \dfrac{1}{2}$ d $\dfrac{4}{5} + 1\dfrac{1}{4}$

e $1\dfrac{2}{3} + \dfrac{1}{6}$ f $\dfrac{10}{11} + \dfrac{3}{4}$ g $2\dfrac{1}{5} + 5\dfrac{1}{2}$ h $\dfrac{3}{8} + 2\dfrac{5}{8}$

PROBLEM-SOLVING	8, 9	9, 10	10, 11

8 Myles, Liza and Camillus work at a busy cinema complex. For a particular movie, Myles sells $\dfrac{3}{5}$ of all the tickets and Liza sells $\dfrac{1}{3}$.

a What fraction of movie tickets are sold by Myles and Liza, together?
b If all of the movie tickets are sold, what is the fraction sold by Camillus?

9 Martine loves to run and play. Yesterday, she ran for $2\dfrac{1}{4}$ kilometres, walked for $5\dfrac{2}{5}$ kilometres and skipped for $\dfrac{1}{2}$ a kilometre. What was the total distance that Martine ran, walked and skipped?

10 Jackson is working on a 1000-piece jigsaw puzzle. After 1 week, he has completed $\dfrac{1}{10}$ of the puzzle. After 2 weeks he has completed another $\dfrac{2}{5}$ of the puzzle. In the third week, Jackson completed another $\dfrac{1}{4}$ of the puzzle.

a By the end of the third week, what fraction of the puzzle has Jackson completed?
b How many pieces of the puzzle does Jackson place in the second week?
c What fraction of the puzzle is still unfinished by the end of the third week? How many pieces is this?

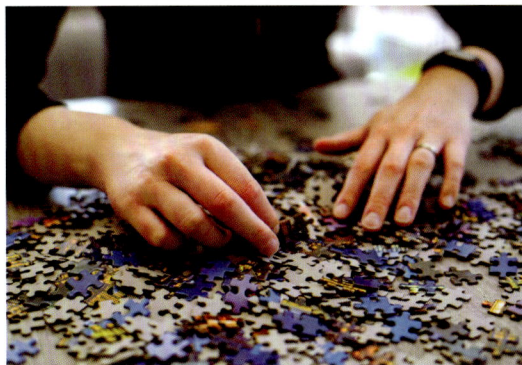

11 A survey of Year 7 students' favourite sport is carried out. A total of 180 students participate in the survey. One-fifth of students reply that netball is their favourite, one-quarter reply rugby and one-third reply soccer. The remainder of students leave the question unanswered.

   a What fraction of the Year 7 students answered the survey question?

   b What fraction of the Year 7 students left the question unanswered?

   c How many students did not answer the survey question?

REASONING	12	12, 13	13

12 Four students each read the same English novel over two nights, for homework. The table shows what fraction of the book was read on each of the two nights.

*Vesna woke up early on the third morning and read another $\frac{1}{6}$ of the novel before leaving for school.

Place the students in order, from least to most, according to what fraction of the book they had read by their next English lesson.

Student	First night	Second night
Mikhail	$\frac{2}{5}$	$\frac{1}{4}$
Jim	$\frac{1}{2}$	$\frac{1}{10}$
Vesna*	$\frac{1}{4}$	$\frac{1}{5}$
Juliet	$\frac{7}{12}$	$\frac{1}{20}$

13 Fill in the empty boxes to make the following fraction sums correct.

   a $\frac{1}{\Box} + \frac{1}{\Box} = \frac{7}{10}$

   b $\frac{1}{\Box} + \frac{1}{\Box} + \frac{1}{\Box} = \frac{7}{8}$

   c $\frac{3}{\Box} + \frac{\Box}{4} = \frac{17}{20}$

ENRICHMENT: Raise it to the max	–	–	14

14 a Using the numbers $1, 2, 3, 4, 5$ and 6 only once, arrange them in the boxes on the right to first produce the maximum possible answer, and then the minimum possible answer. Work out the maximum and minimum possible answers.

$$\frac{\Box}{\Box} + \frac{\Box}{\Box} + \frac{\Box}{\Box}$$

   b Repeat the process for four fractions using the digits 1 to 8 only once each. Again, state the maximum and minimum possible answers.

   c Investigate maximum and minimum fraction statements for other sets of numbers and explain your findings.

   d Explain how you would arrange the numbers 1 to 100 for 50 different fractions if you were trying to achieve the maximum or minimum sum.

3F Subtracting fractions

- To understand that subtracting fractions requires a common denominator
- To be able to subtract two fractions by considering their lowest common denominator
- To be able to subtract two mixed numerals

Subtracting fractions is very similar to adding fractions. You can establish the **lowest common denominator (LCD)** if one does not exist and this is done through producing equivalent fractions. Then, instead of adding numerators at the final step, you simply carry out the correct subtraction.

Complications can arise when subtracting mixed numerals and **Example 16** shows the available methods that can be used to overcome such problems.

Plumbers use fraction skills. Copper pipes for hot water have diameters in fractions of an inch, so a pipe wall thickness can be $\frac{1}{2}\left(\frac{3}{8}-\frac{1}{4}\right)=\frac{1}{16}$ of an inch. Plumbers also use wall thickness to calculate safe water pressures.

Lesson starter: Alphabet subtraction

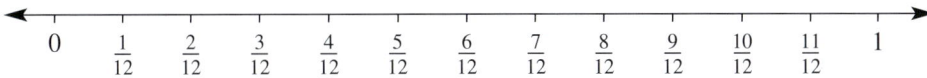

A number line from 0 to 1 marked in twelfths: $\frac{1}{12}, \frac{2}{12}, \frac{3}{12}, \frac{4}{12}, \frac{5}{12}, \frac{6}{12}, \frac{7}{12}, \frac{8}{12}, \frac{9}{12}, \frac{10}{12}, \frac{11}{12}$.

- Copy into your workbook the number line above.
- Place the following letters in the correct position on the number line.

$A=\frac{2}{3}$ $B=\frac{5}{12}$ $C=\frac{1}{2}$ $D=\frac{11}{12}$ $E=\frac{1}{12}$ $F=\frac{1}{4}$ $G=\frac{0}{12}$

$H=\frac{1}{3}$ $I=\frac{7}{12}$ $J=\frac{5}{6}$ $K=\frac{12}{12}$ $L=\frac{3}{4}$ $M=\frac{1}{6}$

- Complete the following alphabet subtractions, giving your answer as a fraction and also the corresponding alphabet letter.

a J – F   b A – G   c D – F – M   d C – B
e K – C   f L – H – E   g K – J – E   h L – I – M

- What does A + B + C + D + E + F + G + H + I – J – K – L – M equal?

KEY IDEAS

■ Fractions can be subtracted easily if they are 'like' fractions.

■ The process for subtracting fractions involves finding the lowest common denominator before subtracting the numerator. At the final step, you should also check if the result can be simplified further (for example, $\frac{3}{6}-\frac{1}{6}=\frac{2}{6}$, which simplifies to $\frac{1}{3}$).

■ When subtracting mixed numerals, you must have a fraction part that is large enough to allow the other proper fraction to be subtracted from it. If this is not the case at the start of the problem, you may choose to regroup one of the whole number parts of the first mixed numeral. For example:

$7\frac{1}{2} - 2\frac{3}{4}$ $\frac{1}{2}$ is not big enough to have $\frac{3}{4}$ subtracted from it.

$6\frac{3}{2} - 2\frac{3}{4}$ Therefore, replace 7 by $6 + 1 = 6 + \frac{2}{2}$.

■ A fail-safe method for subtracting mixed numerals is to convert to improper fractions right from the start.

For example: $7\frac{1}{2} - 2\frac{3}{4} = \frac{15}{2} - \frac{11}{4}$

BUILDING UNDERSTANDING

1 State the missing terms in these sentences.
   a To subtract one fraction from another, you must have a common _____.
   b One fail-safe method of producing a common denominator is to simply _____ the two denominators.
   c The problem with finding a common denominator that is not the lowest common denominator is that you have to deal with larger numbers and you also need to _____ your answer at the final step.
   d To find the LCD, you can _____ the denominators and then divide by the HCF of the denominators.

2 State the LCD for the following pairs of 'incomplete' fractions.
   a $\frac{}{4} - \frac{}{6}$ b $\frac{}{6} - \frac{}{9}$ c $\frac{}{8} - \frac{}{12}$ d $\frac{}{9} - \frac{}{21}$

3 Which of the following are correct?
   a $\frac{8}{10} - \frac{5}{10} = \frac{3}{10}$ b $\frac{5}{12} - \frac{5}{10} = \frac{5}{2}$
   c $\frac{8}{11} - \frac{8}{10} = \frac{0}{1} = 0$ d $\frac{3}{20} - \frac{2}{20} = \frac{1}{20}$

Example 15   Subtracting 'like' and 'unlike' fractions

Simplify:

a $\frac{7}{9} - \frac{2}{9}$ b $\frac{5}{6} - \frac{1}{4}$ c $\frac{7}{10} - \frac{8}{15}$

SOLUTION

a $\frac{7}{9} - \frac{2}{9} = \frac{5}{9}$

b $\frac{5}{6} - \frac{1}{4} = \frac{10}{12} - \frac{3}{12}$

   $= \frac{7}{12}$

EXPLANATION

Denominators are the same, therefore we are ready to subtract the second numerator from the first.

Need to find the LCD, which is 12. Write equivalent fractions with the LCD. We have the same denominators now, so subtract second numerator from the first.

c $\dfrac{7}{10} - \dfrac{8}{15} = \dfrac{21}{30} - \dfrac{16}{30}$

$= \dfrac{5}{30}$

$= \dfrac{1}{6}$

Find the LCD of 10 and 15, which is 30.
Write both fractions with a denominator of 30.
Subtract the numerators.
Simplify the result $\left(\dfrac{5}{30}\right)$ by dividing 5 and 30 by their highest common factor.

Now you try

Simplify:

a $\dfrac{8}{11} - \dfrac{3}{11}$

b $\dfrac{9}{10} - \dfrac{3}{4}$

c $\dfrac{5}{12} - \dfrac{1}{4}$

Example 16 Subtracting mixed numerals

Simplify:
a $5\dfrac{2}{3} - 3\dfrac{1}{4}$

b $8\dfrac{1}{5} - 4\dfrac{3}{4}$

SOLUTION

EXPLANATION

Method 1: Converting to an improper fraction

a $5\dfrac{2}{3} - 3\dfrac{1}{4} = \dfrac{17}{3} - \dfrac{13}{4}$

$= \dfrac{68}{12} - \dfrac{39}{12}$

$= \dfrac{29}{12}$

$= 2\dfrac{5}{12}$

Convert mixed numerals to improper fractions.
Need to find the LCD, which is 12.
Write equivalent fractions with the LCD.

We have the same denominators now, so subtract second numerator from the first and convert back to improper fraction.

b $8\dfrac{1}{5} - 4\dfrac{3}{4} = \dfrac{41}{5} - \dfrac{19}{4}$

$= \dfrac{164}{20} - \dfrac{95}{20}$

$= \dfrac{69}{20}$

$= 3\dfrac{9}{20}$

Convert mixed numerals to improper fractions.
Need to find the LCD, which is 20.
Write equivalent fractions with the LCD.
We have the same denominators now, so subtract second numerator from the first and convert back to improper fraction.

Method 2: Deal with whole numbers first, regrouping where necessary

a $5\dfrac{2}{3} - 3\dfrac{1}{4} = \left(5 + \dfrac{2}{3}\right) - \left(3 + \dfrac{1}{4}\right)$

$= (5 - 3) + \left(\dfrac{2}{3} - \dfrac{1}{4}\right)$

$= 2 + \left(\dfrac{8}{12} - \dfrac{3}{12}\right)$

$= 2\dfrac{5}{12}$

Understand that a mixed numeral is the addition of a whole number and a proper fraction.
Group whole numbers and group proper fractions.

Simplify whole numbers; simplify proper fractions.

Regrouping was not required.

Continued on next page

b $8\frac{1}{5} - 4\frac{3}{4} = \left(8 + \frac{1}{5}\right) - \left(4 + \frac{3}{4}\right)$ $\frac{3}{4}$ cannot be taken away from $\frac{1}{5}$ easily.

$= \left(7 + \frac{6}{5}\right) - \left(4 + \frac{3}{4}\right)$ Therefore, we must borrow a whole.

$= (7 - 4) + \left(\frac{6}{5} - \frac{3}{4}\right)$ Group whole numbers and group proper fractions.

$= 3 + \left(\frac{24}{20} - \frac{15}{20}\right)$ Simplify whole numbers; simplify proper fractions.

$= 3\frac{9}{20}$ Borrowing a whole was required.

Now you try

Simplify:

a $3\frac{2}{3} - 2\frac{1}{4}$

b $3\frac{2}{5} - 1\frac{3}{4}$

Exercise 3F

FLUENCY   1(½), 3(½), 5(½)   2–6(½)   3–6(½)

Example 15a
1 Simplify:

a $\frac{5}{7} - \frac{3}{7}$ **b** $\frac{4}{11} - \frac{1}{11}$ **c** $\frac{12}{18} - \frac{5}{18}$ **d** $\frac{2}{3} - \frac{1}{3}$

Example 15a
2 Simplify:

a $\frac{6}{9} - \frac{2}{9}$ **b** $\frac{5}{19} - \frac{2}{19}$ **c** $\frac{3}{5} - \frac{3}{5}$ **d** $\frac{17}{23} - \frac{9}{23}$

Example 15b
3 Simplify:

a $\frac{2}{3} - \frac{1}{4}$ **b** $\frac{3}{5} - \frac{1}{2}$ **c** $\frac{3}{5} - \frac{1}{6}$ **d** $\frac{4}{7} - \frac{1}{4}$

Example 15c
4 Simplify the following, ensuring your final answer is in simplest form.

a $\frac{5}{6} - \frac{1}{6}$ **b** $\frac{7}{10} - \frac{3}{10}$ **c** $\frac{3}{4} - \frac{1}{4}$ **d** $\frac{7}{8} - \frac{5}{8}$

e $\frac{3}{5} - \frac{1}{10}$ **f** $\frac{9}{10} - \frac{2}{5}$ **g** $\frac{5}{12} - \frac{1}{4}$ **h** $\frac{11}{20} - \frac{3}{10}$

Example 16a
5 Simplify:

a $3\frac{4}{5} - 2\frac{1}{5}$ **b** $23\frac{5}{7} - 15\frac{2}{7}$ **c** $8\frac{11}{14} - 7\frac{9}{14}$ **d** $3\frac{5}{9} - \frac{3}{9}$

e $6\frac{2}{3} - 4\frac{1}{4}$ **f** $5\frac{3}{7} - 2\frac{1}{4}$ **g** $9\frac{5}{6} - 5\frac{4}{9}$ **h** $14\frac{3}{4} - 7\frac{7}{10}$

Example 16b
6 Simplify:

a $5\frac{1}{3} - 2\frac{2}{3}$ **b** $8\frac{2}{5} - 3\frac{4}{5}$ **c** $13\frac{1}{2} - 8\frac{5}{6}$ **d** $12\frac{2}{9} - 7\frac{1}{3}$

e $8\frac{5}{12} - 3\frac{3}{4}$ **f** $1\frac{3}{5} - \frac{7}{9}$ **g** $11\frac{1}{11} - 1\frac{1}{4}$ **h** $6\frac{3}{20} - 3\frac{2}{3}$

PROBLEM-SOLVING   7, 8   8, 10   9–11

7 Tiffany poured herself a large glass of cordial. She noticed that the cordial jug has $\frac{3}{4}$ of a litre in it before she poured her glass and only $\frac{1}{5}$ of a litre in it after she filled her glass. How much cordial did Tiffany pour into her glass?

8 A family block of chocolate is made up of 60 small squares of chocolate. Marcia eats 10 blocks, Jon eats 9 blocks and Holly eats 5 blocks. What fraction of the block of chocolate is left?

9 Three friends split a restaurant bill. One pays $\frac{1}{2}$ of the bill and one pays $\frac{1}{3}$ of the bill. What fraction of the bill must the third friend pay?

10 Patty has $23\frac{1}{4}$ dollars, but owes her parents $15\frac{1}{2}$ dollars. How much money does Patty have left after she pays back her parents? Repeat this question using decimals and dollars and cents. Do you get the same answer?

11 Three cakes were served at a birthday party: an ice-cream cake, a chocolate cake and a sponge cake. Three-quarters of the ice-cream cake was eaten. The chocolate cake was cut into 12 equal pieces, of which 9 were eaten. The sponge cake was divided into 8 equal pieces, with only 1 piece remaining.
  a What fraction of each cake was eaten?
  b What fraction of each cake was left over?
  c What was the total amount of cake eaten during the party?
  d What was the total amount of cake left over after the party?

REASONING　　　　　　　　　　　12　　　　　12, 13　　　　12(½), 13, 14

12 Fill in the empty boxes to make the following fraction sums correct.

  a $\dfrac{1}{\Box} - \dfrac{1}{\Box} = \dfrac{1}{12}$

  b $\dfrac{\Box}{5} - \dfrac{\Box}{2} = \dfrac{1}{10}$

  c $2\dfrac{\Box}{3} - 1\dfrac{\Box}{3} = \dfrac{2}{3}$

  d $8\dfrac{1}{\Box} - 6\dfrac{\Box}{4} = 1\dfrac{1}{2}$

13 Today David's age is one-seventh of Felicity's age. Felicity is a teenager.
  a In 1 year's time David will be one-fifth of Felicity's age. What fraction of her age will he be in 2 years' time?
  b How many years must pass until David is one-third of Felicity's age?
  c How many years must pass until David is half Felicity's age?

14 a **Example 16** shows two possible methods for subtracting mixed numerals: 'Borrowing a whole number' and 'Converting to an improper fraction'. Simplify the following two expressions and discuss which method is the most appropriate for each question.
  i $2\dfrac{1}{5} - 1\dfrac{2}{3}$　　　　　　　　　　**ii** $27\dfrac{5}{11} - 23\dfrac{4}{5}$

  b If you have an appropriate calculator, work out how to enter fractions and check your answers to parts **i** and **ii** above.

ENRICHMENT: Letter to an absent friend　　　　–　　　　–　　　　15

15 Imagine that a friend in your class is absent for this lesson on the subtraction of fractions. They were present yesterday and understood the process involved when adding fractions. Your task is to write a letter to your friend, explaining how to subtract mixed numerals. Include some examples, discuss both possible methods but also justify your favourite method. Finish off with three questions for your friend to attempt and include the answers to these questions on the back of the letter.

3G Multiplying fractions

What does it mean to multiply two fractions?

Do you end up with a smaller amount or a larger amount when you multiply two proper fractions?

What does $\frac{1}{3} \times \frac{2}{3}$ equal?

- **'Strip' method**

  Imagine you have a strip of paper.

  You are told to shade $\frac{2}{3}$ of the strip.

  You are now told to shade in a darker colour $\frac{1}{3}$ of your $\frac{2}{3}$ strip.

  The final amount shaded is your answer.

- **'Number line' method**

  Consider the number line from 0 to 1 (shown opposite).

  It is divided into ninths.

  Locate $\frac{2}{3}$.

  Divide this position into three equal pieces (shown as ⊢←→⊣).

  To locate $\frac{1}{3} \times \frac{2}{3}$ you have only one of the three pieces.

  The final location is your answer (shown as ⊢←→⊣); i.e. $\frac{2}{9}$.

- **'Shading' method**

  Consider $\frac{1}{3}$ of a square multiplied by $\frac{2}{3}$ of a square.

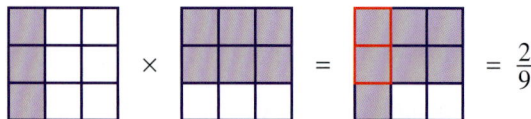

- **'The rule' method**

  When multiplying fractions, multiply the numerators and multiply the denominators.

  $$\frac{1}{3} \times \frac{2}{3} = \frac{1 \times 2}{3 \times 3} = \frac{2}{9}$$

Lesson starter: 'Clock face' multiplication

Explain and discuss the concept of fractions of an hour on the clock face.

In pairs, students match up the following 10 'clock face' multiplication questions with their correct answer. You may like to place a time limit of 5 minutes on the activity.

Discuss answers at the end of the activity.

Questions		Answers	
1	$\frac{1}{2}$ of 4 hours	A	25 minutes
2	$\frac{1}{3}$ of 2 hours	B	$1\frac{1}{2}$ hours
3	$\frac{1}{4}$ of 6 hours	C	5 minutes
4	$\frac{1}{3}$ of $\frac{1}{4}$ hour	D	$\frac{1}{4}$ hour
5	$\frac{1}{4}$ of $\frac{1}{3}$ hour	E	2 hours

Questions		Answers	
6	$\frac{1}{3}$ of $\frac{3}{4}$ hour	F	2 hours 40 minutes
7	$\frac{1}{10}$ of $\frac{1}{2}$ hour	G	$\frac{1}{12}$ hour
8	$\frac{1}{5}$ of $\frac{1}{2}$ hour	H	40 minutes
9	$\frac{2}{3}$ of 4 hours	i	$\frac{1}{10}$ hour
10	$\frac{5}{6}$ of $\frac{1}{2}$ hour	J	3 minutes

KEY IDEAS

■ Fractions do *not* need to have the same denominator to be multiplied.

■ To multiply fractions, multiply the numerators and multiply the denominators.
  - In symbols: $\frac{a}{b} \times \frac{c}{d} = \frac{a \times c}{b \times d}$

■ If possible, 'simplify', 'divide' or 'cancel' fractions before multiplying.
  - Cancelling can be done *vertically* or *diagonally*.
  - Cancelling can never be done *horizontally*.

$$\frac{3}{5} \times \frac{4^1}{8^2} \qquad \text{cancelling vertically} \qquad ✔$$

$$\frac{^1 3}{5} \times \frac{4}{6^2} \qquad \text{cancelling diagonally} \qquad ✔$$

Never do this! ⟶ $\frac{^1 3}{5} \times \frac{6^2}{7} \qquad \text{cancelling horizontally} \qquad ✘$

■ Any whole number can be written as a fraction with a denominator of 1, e.g. $4 = \frac{4}{1}$.

■ 'of', '×', 'times', 'lots of' and 'product' all refer to the same mathematical operation of multiplying.

■ Mixed numerals must be changed to improper fractions before multiplying.

■ Final answers should be written in simplest form.

BUILDING UNDERSTANDING

1 State the missing terms in these sentences.

    a A proper fraction has a value that is between _____ and _____.

    b An improper fraction is always greater than _____.

    c A mixed numeral consists of two parts, a _____ _____ part and a _____ _____ part.

2 When multiplying a whole number by a proper fraction, do you get a smaller or larger answer when compared with the whole number? Explain your answer.

3 Describe how many items you would have in these situations and use drawings to show the answer to these problems.

    a $\frac{1}{3}$ of 12 lollies
    b $\frac{2}{3}$ of 18 doughnuts
    c $\frac{3}{8}$ of 32 dots

4 One of the following four methods is the correct solution to the problem $\frac{1}{2} \times \frac{1}{5}$. Find the correct solution and copy it into your workbook.

A $\frac{1}{2} \times \frac{1}{5}$

$= \frac{1+1}{2+5}$

$= \frac{2}{7}$

B $\frac{1}{2} \times \frac{1}{5}$

$= \frac{1 \times 1}{2 \times 5}$

$= \frac{2}{10}$

C $\frac{1}{2} \times \frac{1}{5}$

$= \frac{5}{10} \times \frac{2}{10}$

$= \frac{7}{20}$

D $\frac{1}{2} \times \frac{1}{5}$

$= \frac{1 \times 1}{2 \times 5}$

$= \frac{1}{10}$

Example 17   Multiplying proper fractions

Find:

a $\frac{2}{3} \times \frac{1}{5}$
    b $\frac{3}{4} \times \frac{8}{9}$
    c $\frac{4}{8}$ of $\frac{3}{6}$

SOLUTION

a $\frac{2}{3} \times \frac{1}{5} = \frac{2 \times 1}{3 \times 5}$

$\phantom{\frac{2}{3} \times \frac{1}{5}} = \frac{2}{15}$

b $\frac{{}^1 3}{{}_1 4} \times \frac{8^2}{9_3} = \frac{1 \times 2}{1 \times 3}$

$\phantom{\frac{{}^1 3}{{}_1 4} \times \frac{8^2}{9_3}} = \frac{2}{3}$

c $\frac{4}{8}$ of $\frac{3}{6} = \frac{{}^1 4}{{}_2 8} \times \frac{3^1}{6_2}$

$\phantom{\frac{4}{8} of \frac{3}{6}} = \frac{1 \times 1}{2 \times 2}$

$\phantom{\frac{4}{8} of \frac{3}{6}} = \frac{1}{4}$

EXPLANATION

Multiply the numerators.
Multiply the denominators.
The answer is in simplest form.

Cancel first.
Then multiply numerators and denominators.

Change 'of' to multiplication sign.
Cancel and then multiply the numerators and the denominators.
The answer is in simplest form.

Now you try

Find:

a $\frac{1}{5} \times \frac{2}{7}$
    b $\frac{4}{5} \times \frac{15}{16}$
    c $\frac{3}{4}$ of $\frac{5}{9}$

Example 18   Multiplying proper fractions by positive integers

Find:

a $\quad \frac{1}{3} \times 21$

b $\quad \frac{2}{5}$ of 32

SOLUTION

a $\quad \frac{1}{3} \times 21 = \frac{1}{^1 3} \times \frac{21^7}{1}$

$\qquad = \frac{7}{1}$

$\qquad = 7$

b $\quad \frac{2}{5}$ of $32 = \frac{2}{5} \times \frac{32}{1}$

$\qquad = \frac{64}{5}$

$\qquad = 12\frac{4}{5}$

EXPLANATION

Rewrite 21 as a fraction with a denominator equal to 1.
Cancel and then multiply numerators and denominators.
$7 \div 1 = 7$

Rewrite 'of' as a multiplication sign.
Write 32 as a fraction.
Multiply numerators and denominators.
Convert answer to a mixed numeral.

Now you try

Find:

a $\quad \frac{2}{5} \times 35$

b $\quad \frac{5}{6}$ of 16

Example 19   Multiplying improper fractions

Find:

a $\quad \frac{5}{3} \times \frac{7}{2}$

b $\quad \frac{8}{5} \times \frac{15}{4}$

SOLUTION

a $\quad \frac{5}{3} \times \frac{7}{2} = \frac{5 \times 7}{3 \times 2}$

$\qquad = \frac{35}{6} = 5\frac{5}{6}$

b $\quad \frac{8}{5} \times \frac{15}{4} = \frac{^2 8 \times 15^3}{^1 5 \times 4^1}$

$\qquad = \frac{6}{1} = 6$

EXPLANATION

Multiply the numerators.
Multiply the denominators.
Convert the answer to a mixed numeral.

Cancel first.
Multiply 'cancelled' numerators and 'cancelled' denominators.
Write the answer in simplest form.

Now you try

Find:

a $\quad \frac{4}{3} \times \frac{10}{7}$

b $\quad \frac{30}{7} \times \frac{49}{10}$

Example 20   Multiplying mixed numerals

Find:

a $2\frac{1}{3} \times 1\frac{2}{5}$

b $6\frac{1}{4} \times 2\frac{2}{5}$

SOLUTION

a $2\frac{1}{3} \times 1\frac{2}{5} = \frac{7}{3} \times \frac{7}{5}$

$= \frac{49}{15}$

$= 3\frac{4}{15}$

b $6\frac{1}{4} \times 2\frac{2}{5} = \frac{^5 25}{^1 4} \times \frac{12^3}{5^1}$

$= \frac{15}{1}$

$= 15$

EXPLANATION

Convert mixed numerals to improper fractions.
Multiply numerators.
Multiply denominators.

Write the answers in the simplest form.

Convert to improper fractions.
Simplify fractions by cancelling.
Multiply numerators and denominators.
Write the answer in simplest form.

Now you try

Find:

a $2\frac{1}{5} \times 4\frac{1}{2}$

b $3\frac{1}{5} \times 3\frac{3}{4}$

Exercise 3G

FLUENCY	1, 2–5(½)	2–6(½)	2–6(½)

Example 17a

1 Find:

a $\frac{1}{2} \times \frac{1}{3}$ **b** $\frac{1}{3} \times \frac{1}{5}$ **c** $\frac{2}{3} \times \frac{5}{7}$ **d** $\frac{2}{5} \times \frac{3}{7}$

e $\frac{3}{4} \times \frac{1}{5}$ **f** $\frac{2}{7} \times \frac{1}{3}$ **g** $\frac{1}{4} \times \frac{5}{6}$ **h** $\frac{2}{9} \times \frac{2}{5}$

Example 17b

2 Multiply the following, remembering to cancel common factors in the numerator and denominators.

a $\frac{4}{7} \times \frac{1}{4}$ **b** $\frac{9}{10} \times \frac{10}{27}$ **c** $\frac{20}{40} \times \frac{80}{100}$ **d** $\frac{7}{15} \times \frac{30}{49}$

Example 17

3 Find:

a $\frac{2}{3} \times \frac{3}{5}$ **b** $\frac{3}{6} \times \frac{5}{11}$ **c** $\frac{8}{11} \times \frac{3}{4}$ **d** $\frac{2}{5} \times \frac{10}{11}$

e $\frac{2}{7}$ of $\frac{3}{5}$ **f** $\frac{3}{4}$ of $\frac{2}{5}$ **g** $\frac{5}{10}$ of $\frac{4}{7}$ **h** $\frac{6}{9}$ of $\frac{3}{12}$

Example 18

4 Find:

a $\frac{1}{3} \times 18$ **b** $\frac{1}{5} \times 45$ **c** $\frac{2}{3} \times 24$ **d** $\frac{3}{5} \times 25$

e $\frac{2}{7}$ of 42 **f** $\frac{1}{4}$ of 16 **g** $\frac{4}{5}$ of 100 **h** $\frac{3}{7}$ of 77

Example 19

5 Find:

a $\dfrac{5}{2} \times \dfrac{7}{3}$

b $\dfrac{6}{5} \times \dfrac{11}{7}$

c $\dfrac{6}{4} \times \dfrac{11}{5}$

d $\dfrac{9}{6} \times \dfrac{13}{4}$

e $\dfrac{8}{5} \times \dfrac{10}{3}$

f $\dfrac{21}{4} \times \dfrac{8}{6}$

g $\dfrac{10}{7} \times \dfrac{21}{5}$

h $\dfrac{14}{9} \times \dfrac{15}{7}$

Example 20

6 Find:

a $1\dfrac{3}{5} \times 2\dfrac{1}{3}$

b $1\dfrac{1}{7} \times 1\dfrac{2}{9}$

c $3\dfrac{1}{4} \times 2\dfrac{2}{5}$

d $4\dfrac{2}{3} \times 5\dfrac{1}{7}$

PROBLEM-SOLVING	7, 8	8, 9	8–10

7 At a particular school, the middle consists of Year 7 and Year 8 students only. $\dfrac{2}{5}$ of the middle school students are in Year 7.

a What fraction of the middle school students are in Year 8?

b If there are 120 middle school students, how many are in Year 7 and how many are in Year 8?

8 To paint one classroom, $2\dfrac{1}{3}$ litres of paint are required. How many litres of paint are required to paint five identical classrooms?

9 A scone recipe requires $1\dfrac{3}{4}$ cups of self-raising flour and $\dfrac{3}{4}$ of a cup of cream. James is catering for a large group and needs to quadruple the recipe. How much self-raising flour and how much cream will he need?

10 Julie has finished an injury-plagued netball season during which she was able to play only $\dfrac{2}{3}$ of the matches. The season consisted of 21 matches. How many games did Julie miss as a result of injury?

REASONING   11   11, 12   12, 13

11 Not all of the following fraction equations are correct. Copy them into your workbook, then place a tick beside those that are correct and a cross beside those that are wrong. Provide the correct solution for those you marked as incorrect.

a $\frac{1}{3} + \frac{1}{4} = \frac{1}{7}$ b $\frac{1}{3} + \frac{1}{4} = \frac{1}{12}$ c $\frac{1}{3} \times \frac{1}{4} = \frac{2}{7}$

d $\frac{1}{3} \times \frac{1}{4} = \frac{1}{12}$ e $\frac{1}{3} - \frac{1}{4} = \frac{1}{12}$ f $\frac{1}{3} - \frac{1}{4} = \frac{0}{-1}$

12 Circle the correct alternative for the following statement and justify your answer. Using an example, explain why the other alternatives are incorrect.

When multiplying a proper fraction by another proper fraction the answer is:

A a whole number.

B a mixed numeral.

C an improper fraction.

D a proper fraction.

13 Write two fractions that:

a multiply to $\frac{3}{5}$

b multiply to $\frac{3}{4}$

c multiply to $\frac{1}{7}$

ENRICHMENT: Who are we?   –   –   14

14 a Using the clues provided, work out which two fractions are being discussed.
   • We are two proper fractions.
   • Altogether we consist of four different digits.
   • When added together our answer will still be a proper fraction.
   • When multiplied together you could carry out some cancelling.
   • The result of our product, when simplified, contains no new digits from our original four.
   • Three of our digits are prime numbers and the fourth digit is a cube number.

   b Design your own similar question and develop a set of appropriate clues. Have a classmate try to solve your question.

   c Design the ultimate challenging 'Who are we?' question. Make sure there is only one possible answer.

3A

1 Consider the fraction $\frac{3}{4}$.

    a Represent this fraction on a diagram.

    b State the denominator of this fraction.

    c State the numerator of this fraction.

    d Represent this fraction on a number line.

    e Is this a proper fraction, an improper fraction or a mixed numeral?

3A

2 What fraction is represented on the number line shown?
Write it as an improper fraction and as a mixed numeral.

3B

3 Write three equivalent fractions for $\frac{2}{5}$.

3B

4 Write these fractions in simplest form.

    a $\frac{4}{10}$ **b** $\frac{15}{30}$ **c** $\frac{14}{6}$ **d** $\frac{24}{8}$

3C

5 Convert $1\frac{3}{5}$ to an improper fraction.

3C

6 Convert $\frac{13}{4}$ to a mixed numeral.

3D

7 Place the correct mathematical symbol <, = or > between the following pairs of fractions to make true mathematical statements.

    a $\frac{2}{3}\square\frac{5}{9}$ **b** $\frac{4}{5}\square\frac{24}{30}$ **c** $1\frac{1}{5}\square\frac{12}{10}$ **d** $\frac{5}{9}\square\frac{18}{20}$

3D

8 Write the following fractions in ascending order: $\frac{1}{2}, \frac{2}{3}, \frac{9}{4}, \frac{4}{9}$.

3E

9 Add the following fractions.

    a $\frac{4}{7}+\frac{2}{7}$ **b** $\frac{2}{5}+\frac{3}{10}$ **c** $\frac{3}{4}+\frac{2}{5}$ **d** $1\frac{3}{4}+3\frac{1}{2}$

3F

10 Simplify:

    a $\frac{5}{12}-\frac{1}{3}$ **b** $\frac{5}{6}-\frac{1}{4}$ **c** $5\frac{1}{2}-3\frac{1}{5}$

3G

11 Find:

    a $\frac{3}{5}$ of \$560   **b** $\frac{2}{3}\times\frac{7}{11}$ **c** $\frac{2}{3}\times\frac{9}{10}$ **d** $1\frac{1}{3}\times\frac{9}{16}$

3H Dividing fractions

LEARNING INTENTIONS
- To be able to find the reciprocal of a fraction or a mixed numeral
- To understand that dividing fractions can be done by multiplying by a reciprocal
- To be able to divide fractions, mixed numerals and/or whole numbers, giving an answer in simplest form

Remember that division used to be referred to as 'how many'.

Thinking of division as 'how many' helps us to understand dividing fractions.

For example, to find $\frac{1}{2} \div \frac{1}{4}$, think of $\frac{1}{2}$ how many $\frac{1}{4}$ s?   or   how many $\frac{1}{4}$ s are in a $\frac{1}{2}$?

Consider this strip of paper that is divided into four equal sections.

In our example of $\frac{1}{2} \div \frac{1}{4}$, we have only $\frac{1}{2}$ a strip, so we will shade in half the strip.

By thinking of the $\div$ sign as 'how many', the question is asking how many quarters are in half the strip. From our diagram, we can see that the answer is 2. Therefore, $\frac{1}{2} \div \frac{1}{4} = 2$.

In a game of football, when it is half-time, you have played two quarters. This is another way of confirming that $\frac{1}{2} \div \frac{1}{4} = 2$.

Lesson starter: 'Divvy up' the lolly bag

Aircraft engineers assemble new planes and aircraft mechanics maintain, service and repair planes. Fraction skills are essential as most aircraft parts use imperial measurements, usually in fractions of an inch.

To 'divvy up' means to divide up, or divide out, or share equally.

Consider a lolly bag containing 24 lollies. In pairs, students answer the following questions.

- How many lollies would each person get if you divvy up the lollies between three people?
- If you got $\frac{1}{3}$ of the lollies in the bag, how many did you get?
- Can you see that 'divvying up' by 3 is the same as getting $\frac{1}{3}$? Therefore, $\div 3$ is the same as $\times \frac{1}{3}$.
- How many lollies would each person get if you divvy up the lollies between eight people?
- If you got $\frac{1}{8}$ of the lollies in the bag, how many did you get?
- Can you see that 'divvying up' by 8 is the same as getting $\frac{1}{8}$? Therefore, $\div 8$ is the same as $\times \frac{1}{8}$.
- What do you think is the same as dividing by n?
- What do you think is the same as dividing by $\frac{a}{b}$?

KEY IDEAS

■ To find the **reciprocal** of a fraction, you must **invert** the fraction. This is done by swapping the numerator and the denominator. 'Inverting' is sometimes known as turning the fraction upside down, or flipping the fraction.
- The reciprocal of $\frac{a}{b}$ is $\frac{b}{a}$.

   For example: The reciprocal of $\frac{3}{5}$ is $\frac{5}{3}$.

■ Dividing by a number is the same as multiplying by its reciprocal.

   For example: $15 \div 3 = 5$ and $15 \times \frac{1}{3} = 5$.
- Dividing by 2 is the same as multiplying by $\frac{1}{2}$.

■ When asked to divide by a fraction, instead choose to multiply by the fraction's reciprocal.

   Therefore, to divide by $\frac{a}{b}$ we multiply by $\frac{b}{a}$.

■ When dividing, mixed numerals must be changed to improper fractions.

BUILDING UNDERSTANDING

1 Which of the following is the correct first step for finding $\frac{3}{5} \div \frac{4}{7}$?

   A $\frac{3}{5} \times \frac{7}{4}$ B $\frac{5}{3} \times \frac{4}{7}$ C $\frac{5}{3} \times \frac{7}{4}$

2 State the correct first step for each of these division questions. (Do not find the final answer.)

   a $\frac{5}{11} \div \frac{3}{5}$ b $\frac{1}{3} \div \frac{1}{5}$ c $\frac{7}{10} \div \frac{12}{5}$ d $\frac{8}{3} \div 3$

3 When dividing mixed numerals, the first step is to convert to improper fractions and the second step is to multiply by the reciprocal of the divisor. State the correct first and second steps for each of the following mixed numeral division questions. (Do not find the final answer.)

   a $2\frac{1}{2} \div 1\frac{1}{3}$ b $24 \div 3\frac{1}{5}$ c $4\frac{3}{11} \div 5\frac{1}{4}$ d $\frac{8}{3} \div 11\frac{3}{7}$

4 Make each sentence correct, by choosing the word *more* or *less* in the gap.

   a $10 \div 2$ gives an answer that is _____ than 10

   b $10 \div \frac{1}{2}$ gives an answer that is _____ than 10

   c $\frac{3}{4} \div \frac{2}{3}$ gives an answer that is _____ than $\frac{3}{4}$

   d $\frac{3}{4} \times \frac{3}{2}$ gives an answer that is _____ than $\frac{3}{4}$

   e $\frac{5}{7} \div \frac{8}{5}$ gives an answer that is _____ than $\frac{5}{7}$

   f $\frac{5}{7} \times \frac{5}{8}$ gives an answer that is _____ than $\frac{5}{7}$

Example 21   Finding reciprocals

State the reciprocal of the following.

a $\dfrac{2}{3}$

b   5

c $1\dfrac{3}{7}$

SOLUTION

a   Reciprocal of $\dfrac{2}{3}$ is $\dfrac{3}{2}$.

b   Reciprocal of 5 is $\dfrac{1}{5}$.

c   Reciprocal of $1\dfrac{3}{7}$ is $\dfrac{7}{10}$.

EXPLANATION

The numerator and denominator are swapped.

Think of 5 as $\dfrac{5}{1}$ and then invert.

Convert $1\dfrac{3}{7}$ to an improper fraction, i.e. $\dfrac{10}{7}$, and then invert.

Now you try

State the reciprocal of the following.

a $\dfrac{6}{7}$

b   3

c $3\dfrac{2}{3}$

Example 22   Dividing a fraction by a whole number

Find:

a $\dfrac{5}{8} \div 3$

b $2\dfrac{3}{11} \div 5$

SOLUTION

a $\dfrac{5}{8} \div 3 = \dfrac{5}{8} \times \dfrac{1}{3}$

$\quad = \dfrac{5}{24}$

b $2\dfrac{3}{11} \div 5 = \dfrac{25}{11} \div \dfrac{5}{1}$

$\quad = \dfrac{{}^{5}25}{11} \times \dfrac{1}{5^{1}}$

$\quad = \dfrac{5}{11}$

EXPLANATION

Change the $\div$ sign to a $\times$ sign and invert the 3 $\left(\text{or } \dfrac{3}{1} \right)$.
Multiply the numerators and denominators.

Convert the mixed numeral to an improper fraction.
Write 5 as an improper fraction.
Change the $\div$ sign to a $\times$ sign and invert the divisor.
Simplify by cancelling.
Multiply numerators and denominators.

Now you try

Find:

a $\dfrac{3}{4} \div 5$

b $3\dfrac{3}{5} \div 2$

Example 23   Dividing a whole number by a fraction

Find:

a $6 \div \frac{1}{3}$

b $24 \div \frac{3}{4}$

SOLUTION

a $6 \div \frac{1}{3} = \frac{6}{1} \times \frac{3}{1}$

$= \frac{18}{1} = 18$

b $24 \div \frac{3}{4} = \frac{\overset{8}{24}}{1} \times \frac{4}{3_1}$

$= 32$

EXPLANATION

Instead of $\div \frac{1}{3}$, change to $\times \frac{3}{1}$.
Simplify.

Instead of $\div \frac{3}{4}$, change to $\times \frac{4}{3}$.
Cancel and simplify.

Now you try

Find:

a $8 \div \frac{1}{5}$

b $20 \div \frac{4}{9}$

Example 24   Dividing fractions by fractions

Find:

a $\frac{3}{5} \div \frac{3}{8}$

b $2\frac{2}{5} \div 1\frac{3}{5}$

SOLUTION

a $\frac{3}{5} \div \frac{3}{8} = \frac{3}{5} \times \frac{8}{3}$

$= \frac{8}{5} = 1\frac{3}{5}$

b $2\frac{2}{5} \div 1\frac{3}{5} = \frac{12}{5} \div \frac{8}{5}$

$= \frac{\overset{3}{12}}{5_1} \times \frac{\overset{1}{5}}{8_2}$

$= \frac{3}{2} = 1\frac{1}{2}$

EXPLANATION

Change the $\div$ sign to a $\times$ sign and invert the divisor.
(Note: The divisor is the second fraction.)
Cancel and simplify.

Convert mixed numeral to improper fractions.
Change the $\div$ sign to a $\times$ sign and invert the divisor.
Cancel, multiply and simplify.

Now you try

Find:

a $\frac{2}{3} \div \frac{5}{8}$

b $4\frac{1}{5} \div 2\frac{3}{10}$

Exercise 3H

FLUENCY   1–4(½), 7(½)   1–7(½)   4–8(½)

Example 21a

1   State the reciprocal of the following proper fractions.

a $\dfrac{2}{5}$ b $\dfrac{5}{7}$ c $\dfrac{3}{5}$ d $\dfrac{4}{9}$

Example 21b

2   State the reciprocal of the following whole numbers.

a   2   b   6   c   10   d   4

Example 21c

3   State the reciprocal of the following mixed numerals. Remember to convert them to improper fractions first.

a $1\dfrac{5}{6}$ b $2\dfrac{2}{3}$ c $3\dfrac{1}{2}$ d $8\dfrac{2}{3}$

Example 22a

4   Find:

a $\dfrac{3}{4} \div 2$ b $\dfrac{5}{11} \div 3$ c $\dfrac{8}{5} \div 4$ d $\dfrac{15}{7} \div 3$

Example 22b

5   Find:

a $2\dfrac{1}{4} \div 3$ b $5\dfrac{1}{3} \div 4$ c $12\dfrac{4}{5} \div 8$ d $1\dfrac{13}{14} \div 9$

Example 23

6   Find:

a $5 \div \dfrac{1}{4}$ b $7 \div \dfrac{1}{3}$ c $10 \div \dfrac{1}{10}$ d $24 \div \dfrac{1}{5}$

e $12 \div \dfrac{2}{5}$ f $15 \div \dfrac{3}{8}$ g $14 \div \dfrac{7}{2}$ h $10 \div \dfrac{3}{2}$

7   Find:

Example 24a

a $\dfrac{2}{7} \div \dfrac{2}{5}$ b $\dfrac{1}{5} \div \dfrac{1}{4}$ c $\dfrac{3}{7} \div \dfrac{6}{11}$ d $\dfrac{2}{3} \div \dfrac{8}{9}$

Example 24b

e $2\dfrac{1}{4} \div 1\dfrac{1}{3}$ f $4\dfrac{1}{5} \div 3\dfrac{3}{10}$ g $12\dfrac{1}{2} \div 3\dfrac{3}{4}$ h $9\dfrac{3}{7} \div 12\dfrac{4}{7}$

Example 24

8   Find:

a $\dfrac{3}{8} \div 5$ b $22 \div \dfrac{11}{15}$ c $2\dfrac{2}{5} \div 1\dfrac{3}{4}$ d $\dfrac{3}{4} \div \dfrac{9}{4}$

e $7 \div \dfrac{1}{4}$ f $2\dfrac{6}{15} \div 9$ g $7\dfrac{2}{3} \div 1\dfrac{1}{6}$ h $\dfrac{3}{5} \div \dfrac{2}{7}$

PROBLEM-SOLVING   9, 10   10–12   11–13

9   If $2\dfrac{1}{4}$ leftover pizzas are to be shared between three friends, what fraction of pizza will each friend receive?

10   A property developer plans to subdivide $7\dfrac{1}{2}$ acres of land into blocks of at least $\dfrac{3}{5}$ of an acre. Through some of the land runs a creek, where a protected species of frog lives. How many complete blocks can the developer sell if two blocks must be reserved for the creek and its surroundings?

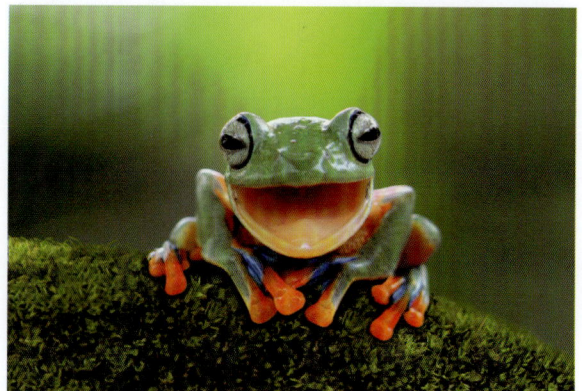

11 Miriam cuts a 10-millimetre thick sisal rope into four equal pieces. If the rope is $3\frac{3}{5}$ metres long before it is cut, how long is each piece?

12 A carpenter takes $\frac{3}{4}$ of an hour to make a chair. How many chairs can he make in 6 hours?

13 Justin is a keen runner and runs at a pace of $3\frac{1}{2}$ minutes per kilometre. Justin finished a Sunday morning run in 77 minutes. How far did he run?

| REASONING | 14 | 14, 15 | 15, 16 |

14 Use diagrams of circles split into equal sectors to explain the following.

a $\frac{3}{4} \div 2 = \frac{3}{8}$

b $3 \div \frac{1}{2} = 6$

15 Pair up the equivalent expressions and state the simplified answer.

$\frac{1}{2}$ of 8 $12 \div 4$ $10 \times \frac{1}{2}$ $10 \div 2$

$3 \div \frac{1}{2}$ $12 \times \frac{1}{4}$ $\frac{1}{2} \div \frac{1}{8}$ 3×2

16 a A car travels 180 kilometres in $1\frac{1}{2}$ hours. How far will it travel in 2 hours if it travels at the same speed?

b A different car took $2\frac{1}{4}$ hours to travel 180 kilometres. How far did it travel in 2 hours, if it maintained the same speed?

| ENRICHMENT: You provide the question | – | – | 17(½) |

17 Listed below are six different answers.
You are required to make up six questions that will result in the following answers.
All questions must involve a division sign. Your questions should increase in order of difficulty by adding extra operation signs and extra fractions.

a $\frac{3}{5}$ b $2\frac{1}{3}$ c $\frac{7}{1}$

d 0   e $\frac{1}{100}$ f $4\frac{4}{5}$

3I Fractions and percentages

We come across percentages in many everyday situations. Interest rates, discounts, test results and statistics are just some of the common ways in which we deal with percentages. Percentages are closely related to fractions. A percentage is another way of writing a fraction with a denominator of 100. Therefore, 87% means that if something is divided into 100 pieces you would have 87 of them.

A project manager calculates the fraction of a construction's total cost for wages, building materials, tax, etc. To easily compare these fractions, they are changed to percentages of the total cost.

Lesson starter: Student ranking

Five students completed five different Mathematics tests. Each of the tests was out of a different number of marks. The results are shown below. Your task is to rank the five students in descending order, according to their test result.

- Matthew scored 15 out of a possible 20 marks.
- Mengna scored 36 out of a possible 50 marks.
- Maria scored 33 out of a possible 40 marks.
- Marcus scored 7 out of a possible 10 marks.
- Melissa scored 64 out of a possible 80 marks.

Change these test results to equivalent scores out of 100, and therefore state the percentage test score for each student.

KEY IDEAS

■ The symbol % means 'per cent'. This comes from the Latin *per centum*, which means out of 100. Therefore, 75% means 75 out of 100.

■ We can write percentages as fractions by changing the % sign to a denominator of 100 (meaning out of 100).

For example: $37\% = \frac{37}{100}$

■ We can convert fractions to percentages through our knowledge of equivalent fractions.

For example: $\frac{1}{4} = \frac{25}{100} = 25\%$

■ To convert any fraction to a percentage, multiply by 100.

For example: $\frac{3}{8} \times 100 = \frac{3}{8} \times \frac{100}{1} = \frac{75}{2} = 37\frac{1}{2}$. Therefore $\frac{3}{8} = 37\frac{1}{2}\%$

■ Common percentages and their equivalent fractions are shown in the table below. It is useful to know these.

Fraction	$\frac{1}{2}$	$\frac{1}{3}$	$\frac{1}{4}$	$\frac{1}{5}$	$\frac{1}{8}$	$\frac{2}{3}$	$\frac{3}{4}$
Percentage	50%	$33\frac{1}{3}\%$	25%	20%	$12\frac{1}{2}\%$	$66\frac{2}{3}\%$	75%

BUILDING UNDERSTANDING

1 Change these test results to equivalent scores out of 100, and therefore state the percentage.

  a 7 out of 10 = _____ out of 100 = _____%

  b 12 out of 20 = _____ out of 100 = _____%

  c 80 out of 200 = _____ out of 100 = _____%

2 Write these fraction sequences into your workbook and write beside each fraction the equivalent percentage value.

  a $\frac{1}{4}, \frac{2}{4}, \frac{3}{4}, \frac{4}{4}$ **b** $\frac{1}{5}, \frac{2}{5}, \frac{3}{5}, \frac{4}{5}, \frac{5}{5}$ **c** $\frac{1}{3}, \frac{2}{3}, \frac{3}{3}$

3 If 14% of students in Year 7 are absent due to illness, what percentage of Year 7 students are at school?

Example 25   Converting percentages to fractions

Express these percentages as fractions or mixed numerals in their simplest form.
  a 17%   **b** 36%   **c** 140%

SOLUTION

a $17\% = \frac{17}{100}$

b
$$36\% = \frac{36}{100} \overset{\div 4}{=} \frac{9}{25} \quad (\div 4)$$

c
$$140\% = \frac{140}{100} \overset{\div 20}{=} \frac{7}{5} \text{ or } 1\frac{2}{5} \quad (\div 20)$$

EXPLANATION

Change % sign to a denominator of 100.

Change the % sign to a denominator of 100 then divide the numerator and the denominator by the HCF of 4. The answer is now in simplest form.

Change the % sign to a denominator of 100 then divide the numerator and the denominator by the HCF of 20. You can convert to a mixed numeral.

Now you try

Express these percentages as fractions or mixed numerals in their simplest form.
  a 39%   **b** 42%   **c** 220%

Example 26   Converting to percentages through equivalent fractions

Convert the following fractions to percentages.

a $\dfrac{5}{100}$

b $\dfrac{11}{25}$

SOLUTION

a $\dfrac{5}{100} = 5\%$

b

$$\dfrac{11}{25} \overset{\times 4}{\underset{\times 4}{=}} \dfrac{44}{100}$$

$$= 44\%$$

EXPLANATION

Denominator is already 100, therefore simply write number as a percentage

Require denominator to be 100.
Therefore, multiply numerator and denominator by 4 to get an equivalent fraction.

Now you try

Convert the following fractions to percentages.

a $\dfrac{9}{100}$

b $\dfrac{11}{20}$

Example 27   Converting to percentages by multiplying by 100

Convert the following fractions to percentages.

a $\dfrac{3}{8}$

b $3\dfrac{3}{5}$

SOLUTION

a $\dfrac{3}{8} \times 100 = \dfrac{3}{{}^2 8} \times \dfrac{100^{25}}{1}$

$\qquad = \dfrac{75}{2} = 37\dfrac{1}{2}$

$\qquad \therefore \dfrac{3}{8} = 37\dfrac{1}{2}\%$

b $3\dfrac{3}{5} \times 100 = \dfrac{18}{{}^1 5} \times \dfrac{100^{20}}{1}$

$\qquad = 360$

$\qquad \therefore 3\dfrac{3}{5} = 360\%$

EXPLANATION

Multiply by 100.
Simplify by cancelling HCF. Write your answer as a mixed numeral.

Convert mixed numeral to improper fraction.
Cancel and simplify.

Now you try

Convert the following fractions to percentages.

a $\dfrac{7}{40}$

b $2\dfrac{1}{4}$

Exercise 3I

| FLUENCY | 1, 2–4(½) | 2–5(½) | 2–5(¼) |

1 Express these percentages as fractions or mixed numerals in their simplest form.

mple 25a
a i   19%   ii   29%   iii 57%

mple 25b
b i   70%   ii   45%   iii 48%

ple 25a,b
2 Express these percentages as fractions in their simplest form.

a 11%   b 71%   c 43%   d 49%

e 25%   f 30%   g 15%   h 88%

mple 25c
3 Express these percentages as mixed numerals in their simplest form.

a 120%   b 180%   c 237%   d 401%

e 175%   f 110%   g 316%   h 840%

ample 26
4 Convert these fractions to percentages, using equivalent fractions.

a $\dfrac{8}{100}$ b $\dfrac{15}{100}$ c $\dfrac{97}{100}$ d $\dfrac{50}{100}$

e $\dfrac{7}{20}$ f $\dfrac{8}{25}$ g $\dfrac{43}{50}$ h $\dfrac{18}{20}$

i $\dfrac{56}{50}$ j $\dfrac{27}{20}$ k $\dfrac{20}{5}$ l $\dfrac{16}{10}$

ample 27
5 Convert these fractions to percentages by multiplying by 100%.

a $\dfrac{1}{8}$ b $\dfrac{1}{3}$ c $\dfrac{4}{15}$ d $\dfrac{10}{12}$

e $1\dfrac{3}{20}$ f $4\dfrac{1}{5}$ g $2\dfrac{36}{40}$ h $\dfrac{13}{40}$

| PROBLEM-SOLVING | 6, 7 | 7, 8 | 7–9 |

6 A bottle of lemonade is only 25% full.

a What fraction of the lemonade has been consumed?

b What percentage of the lemonade has been consumed?

c What fraction of the lemonade is left?

d What percentage of the lemonade is left?

7 A lemon tart is cut into eight equal pieces. What percentage of the tart does each piece represent?

8 Petrina scores 28 out of 40 on her Fractions test. What is her score as a percentage?

9 The Heathmont Hornets basketball team have won 14 out of 18 games. They still have two games to play. What is the smallest and the largest percentage of games the Hornets could win for the season?

10 Lee won his tennis match with the score
    6–4, 6–2, 6–1. Therefore, he won 18 games
    and lost 7.
    a   What fraction of games did he win?
    b   What percentage of games did he win?

11 How many percentages between 1% and 99%
    can be written as a simplified fraction with a
    denominator of 10? (For example, $30\% = \dfrac{3}{10}$,
    which would count as one possible answer.)

12 Scott and Penny have just taken out a home
    loan, with an interest rate of $5\dfrac{1}{2}\%$. Write this interest rate as a simplified fraction.

13 Give an example of a fraction that would be placed between 8% and 9% on a number line.

14 Conduct research on a major lottery competition to answer the following, if possible.
    a   Find out, on average, how many tickets are sold each week.
    b   Find out, on average, how many tickets win a prize each week.
    c   Determine the percentage chance of winning a prize.
    d   Determine the percentage chance of winning the various divisions.
    e   Work out the average profit the lottery competition makes each week.

3J Finding a percentage of a number

LEARNING INTENTIONS
- To understand that finding percentages of a number can be found by multiplying by a fraction
- To be able to find a percentage of a number
- To be able to apply percentages to worded problems

A common application of percentages is to find a certain percentage of a given number. Throughout life, you will come across many examples where you need to calculate percentages of a quantity. Examples include retail discounts, interest rates, personal improvements, salary increases, commission rates and more.

In this exercise, we will focus on the mental calculation of percentages.

Customers, retail assistants, accountants and managers all use percentage calculations when finding a discounted price. This is the original price reduced by a percentage of its value

Lesson starter: Percentages in your head

It is a useful skill to be able to quickly calculate percentages mentally.

Calculating 10% or 1% is often a good starting point. You can then multiply or divide these values to arrive at other percentage values.

- In pairs, using mental arithmetic only, calculate these 12 percentages.

  a 10% of $120   **b** 10% of $35   **c** 20% of $160   **d** 20% of $90
  e 30% of $300   **f** 30% of $40   **g** 5% of $80   **h** 5% of $420
  i 2% of $1400   **j** 2% of $550   **k** 12% of $200   **l** 15% of $60

- Check your answers with a classmate or your teacher.
- Design a quick set of 12 questions for a classmate.
- Discuss helpful mental arithmetic skills to increase your speed at calculating percentages.

KEY IDEAS

■ To find the percentage of a number we:

1 Express the required percentage as a fraction.
2 Change the word 'of' to a multiplication sign.
3 Express the number as a fraction.
4 Follow the rules for multiplication of fractions or look for a mental strategy to complete the multiplication.

$$25\% \text{ of } 60 = \frac{25}{100} \times \frac{60}{1}$$
$$= 15$$

$$25\% \text{ of } 60 = \frac{1}{4} \text{ of } 60$$
$$= 60 \div 4$$
$$= 60 \div 2 \div 2$$
$$= 15$$

■ Percentage of a number $= \dfrac{\text{percentage}}{100} \times \text{number}$

■ Useful mental strategies
- To find 50%, divide by 2
- To find 10%, divide by 10
- To find 25%, divide by 4
- To find 1%, divide by 100
- Swap the two parts of the problem around if the second number is easier to work with, e.g. find 28% of 50, find 50% of 28

BUILDING UNDERSTANDING

1 State the missing number in the following sentences.
  a Finding 10% of a quantity is the same as dividing the quantity by _____ .
  b Finding 1% of a quantity is the same as dividing the quantity by _____ .
  c Finding 50% of a quantity is the same as dividing the quantity by _____ .
  d Finding 100% of a quantity is the same as dividing the quantity by _____ .
  e Finding 20% of a quantity is the same as dividing the quantity by _____ .
  f Finding 25% of a quantity is the same as dividing the quantity by _____ .

2 Without calculating the exact values, determine which alternative (**i** or **ii**) has the highest value.
  a i   20% of $400   **ii**   25% of $500
  b i   15% of $3335   **ii**   20% of $4345
  c i   3% of $10 000   **ii**   2% of $900
  d i   88% of $45   **ii**   87% of $35

Example 28   Finding the percentage of a number

Find:
a 30% of 50   **b**   15% of 400

SOLUTION

a $30\% \text{ of } 50 = \dfrac{30}{{}_2 100} \times \dfrac{50^1}{1}$

$= \dfrac{30}{2} = 15$

Mental arithmetic:
10% of 50 = 5
Hence, 30% of 50 = 15.

b $15\% \text{ of } 400 = \dfrac{15}{{}_1 100} \times \dfrac{400^4}{1}$

$= \dfrac{15 \times 4}{1} = 60$

Mental arithmetic:
10% of 400 = 40, 5% of 400 = 20
Hence, 15% of 400 = 60.

EXPLANATION

Write % as a fraction.
Cancel and simplify.

Multiply by 3 to get 30%.

Write % as a fraction.
Cancel and simplify.

Halve to get 5%.
Multiply by 3 to get 15%.

Now you try

Find:

a   40% of 90

b   12% of 500

Example 29   **Solving a worded percentage problem**

Jacqueline has saved up $50 to purchase a new pair of jeans. She tries on many different pairs but only likes two styles, Evie and Next. The Evie jeans are normally $70 and are on sale with a 25% discount. The Next jeans retail for $80 and have a 40% discount for the next 24 hours. Can Jacqueline afford either pair of jeans?

SOLUTION

Evie jeans

Discount = 25% of $70

$$= \frac{25}{100} \times \frac{70}{1} = \$17.50$$

Sale price = $70 − $17.50

$$= \$52.50$$

Next jeans

Discount = 40% of $80

$$= \frac{40}{100} \times \frac{80}{1} = \$32$$

Sale price = $80 − $32

$$= \$48$$

Jacqueline can afford the Next jeans but not the Evie jeans.

EXPLANATION

Calculate the discount on the Evie jeans.

Find 25% of $70.

Find the sale price by subtracting the discount.

Calculate the discount on the Next jeans.

Find 40% of $80.

Find the sale price by subtracting the discount.

Now you try

Two shops sell the same jumper. In Shop A the retail price is $80 but there is currently a 30% off sale. In Shop B the retail price is $90 but there is currently a 40% off sale. In which shop is the jumper cheaper and by how much?

Exercise 3J

FLUENCY	1, 2–3(½), 4	2–3(½), 4, 5(½)	2–3(¼), 5(⅓)

Example 28   **1**   Find:

     a   50% of 20   **b**   50% of 40   **c**   10% of 60   **d**   20% of 80

Example 28   **2**   Find:

     a   50% of 140   **b**   10% of 360   **c**   20% of 50   **d**   30% of 90

     e   25% of 40   **f**   25% of 28   **g**   75% of 200   **h**   80% of 250

     i   5% of 80   **j**   4% of 1200   **k**   5% of 880   **l**   2% of 9500

     m   11% of 200   **n**   21% of 400   **o**   12% of 300   **p**   9% of 700

3 Find the following values involving percentages greater than 100%.

 a 120% of 80   b 150% of 400   c 110% of 60   d 400% of 25
 e 125% of 12   f 225% of 32   g 146% of 50   h 3000% of 20

4 Match the questions with their correct answer.

Questions	Answers
10% of $200	$8
20% of $120	$16
10% of $80	$20
50% of $60	$24
20% of $200	$25
5% of $500	$30
30% of $310	$40
10% of $160	$44
1% of $6000	$60
50% of $88	$93

5 Find:

 a 30% of $140   b 10% of 240 millimetres   c 15% of 60 kilograms
 d 2% of 4500 tonnes   e 20% of 40 minutes   f 80% of 500 centimetres
 g 5% of 30 grams   h 25% of 12 hectares   i 120% of 120 seconds

PROBLEM-SOLVING   6, 7   7–9   9–11

6 Harry scored 70% on his Percentages test. If the test is out of 50 marks, how many marks did Harry score?

7 Grace wants to purchase a new top and has $40 to spend. She really likes a red top that was originally priced at $75 and has a 40% discount ticket on it. At another shop, she also likes a striped hoody, which costs $55. There is 20% off all items in the store on this day. Can Grace afford either of the tops?

Example 29

8 In a student survey, 80% of students said they received too much homework. If 300 students were surveyed, how many students felt they get too much homework?

9 25% of teenagers say their favourite fruit is watermelon. In a survey of 48 teenagers, how many students would you expect to write watermelon as their favourite fruit?

10 At Gladesbrook College, 10% of students walk to school, 35% of students catch public transport and the remainder of students are driven to school. If there are 1200 students at the school, find how many students:

 a walk to school   b catch public transport   c are driven to school.

11 Anthea has just received a 4% salary increase. Her wage before the increase was $2000 per week.

 a How much extra money does Anthea receive due to her salary rise?
 b What is Anthea's new salary per week?
 c How much extra money does Anthea receive per year?

REASONING   12, 13   12–14   14–17

12 Sam has 2 hours of 'free time' before dinner
    is ready. He spends 25% of that time playing
    computer games, 20% playing his drums, 40%
    playing outside and 10% reading a book.
    a How long does Sam spend doing each of the
       four different activities?
    b What percentage of time does Sam have
       remaining at the end of his four activities?
    c Sam must set the table for dinner, which
       takes 5 minutes. Does he still have time to get
       this done?

13 Gavin mows 60% of the lawn in 48 minutes. How long will it take him to mow the entire lawn if he
    mows at a constant rate?

14 Find:
    a 20% of (50% of 200)   b 10% of (30% of 3000)
    c 5% of (5% of 8000)   d 80% of (20% of 400)

15 Which is larger: 60% of 80 or 80% of 60? Explain your answer.

16 Tom did the following calculation: $120 \div 4 \div 2 \times 3$. What percentage of 120 did Tom find?

17 a If 5% of an amount is $7, what is 100% of the amount?
    b If 25% of an amount is $3, what is $12\frac{1}{2}$% of the amount?

ENRICHMENT: Waning interest   –   –   18

18 When someone loses interest or motivation in a task, they can be described as having a 'waning
    interest'. Jill and Louise are enthusiastic puzzle makers, but they gradually lose interest when tackling
    very large puzzles.
    a Jill is attempting to complete a 5000-piece jigsaw puzzle in 5 weeks. Her interest drops off,
       completing 100 fewer pieces each week.
       i   How many pieces must Jill complete in the first week to ensure that she finishes the puzzle in
           the 5-week period?
       ii What percentage of the puzzle does Jill complete during each of the 5 weeks?
       iii What is the percentage that Jill's interest wanes each week?
    b Louise is attempting to complete an 8000-piece jigsaw puzzle in 5 weeks. Her interest drops off at
       a constant rate of 5% of the total jigsaw size per week.
       i   What percentage of the puzzle must Louise complete in the first week to ensure she finishes the
           puzzle in the 5-week period?
       ii Record how many pieces of the puzzle Louise completes each week and the corresponding
           percentage of the puzzle.
       iii Produce a table showing the cumulative number of pieces completed and the cumulative
           percentage of the puzzle completed over the 5-week period.

The following problems will investigate practical situations drawing upon knowledge and skills developed throughout the chapter. In attempting to solve these problems, aim to identify the key information, use diagrams, formulate ideas, apply strategies, make calculations and check and communicate your solutions.

Completing a new tunnel

1   A major new tunnel is to be built in a capital city to improve traffic congestion. The tunnel will be able to take three lanes of traffic in each direction. The project manager has established a detailed plan for the job which is scheduled to take 30 months to complete. The overall distance of the tunnel is 5 km. One year into the job, 2 km of the tunnel is complete.
To estimate if they are on schedule to finish the project on time, the project manager wants to calculate the fraction of time the job has been going, and the fraction of the length of the tunnel completed.

   a   What fraction of the time of the job has passed?
   b   What fraction of the distance of the tunnel has been completed?
   c   At the one year mark, is the job on track, in front or behind schedule?
   d   At the two year mark, what distance of the tunnel needs to have been completed for the project to be on track?
   e   With two months to go, how much of the tunnel should have been completed for the project to be on track?
   f   What is the average rate (in metres per month) that needs to be completed for the tunnel project to remain on schedule? Give your answer as a fraction and as a number to the nearest metre per month.

Cutting down on screen time

2   Wasim is a student who spends a quite a bit a time in the day looking at a screen.
Wasim is concerned about the increasing fraction of his day that he is on 'screen time' and wants to compare the amount of screen time against the time spent on other activities.

   a   His first rule for himself is that he must spend less than $\frac{1}{8}$ of an entire day watching a screen. Following this rule, what is the maximum time Wasim can watch a screen?

His parents suggest that Wasim should only take into account his waking hours. Wasim knows he needs to sleep on average 9 hours/day.
   b   If Wasim still wants to spend the same total amount of time watching a screen, what fraction of his waking day is now dedicated to screen time?

Wasim decides that he should not have to count screen time for any of the 7 hours he is at school, and chooses to look at the fraction of his leisure time he devotes to watching a screen.

c   Given Wasim still wants to spend 3 hours/day, outside of school, watching a screen, what fraction of Wasim's leisure time is screen time?

Wasim thinks that his leisure time should be spent evenly between:

- screen time
- outside time (which includes walking to and from school)
- family time (which includes meals and chores), and
- commitments time (which includes homework, music practice, sports practice on some nights).

With this new guideline:

d   what fraction of Wasim's leisure time is screen time?

e   what fraction of Wasim's waking time is screen time?

f   what fraction of Wasim's entire day is screen time?

g   how much time per day can Wasim spend, outside of school, watching a screen?

h   how many hours per year can Wasim spend watching a screen?

Isla's test scores

3   Isla has set herself the goal of achieving a score of at least 75% on each of her classroom tests for the upcoming term.

Isla in interested in what raw scores need to be achieved on future tests to achieve her goal, as well as what scores need to be obtained so that a particular average can be achieved for the term.

Determine what minimum score Isla needs to achieve on each of the following tests to reach her goal.

a   Maths test with 100 marks

b   French test with 80 marks

c   Science test with 50 marks

d   Geography test with 20 marks

The actual marks Isla achieved for the above four tests were: Maths 76 marks, French 52 marks, Science 42 marks and Geography 12 marks.

e   In which tests did Isla achieve her goal?

Isla still has one test remaining for the term and has now changed her goal to *averaging* a score of 75% across all her tests for the term. The remaining test is out of 30 marks.

f   Given that each test is equally important, what score does Isla need on her remaining test to achieve her new goal?

g   Given that each test is not equally important, but each mark is equally important, what score does Isla need on her remaining test to achieve her new goal?

3K Introduction to ratios

LEARNING INTENTIONS
- To understand that a ratio compares two or more related quantities in a given order
- To be able to write a ratio from a description
- To be able to use a common factor to simplify a ratio

Ratios are used to show the relationship between two or more related quantities. They compare quantities of the same type using the same units. The numbers in the ratio are therefore written without units.

When reading or writing ratios, the order is very important. In a sport, a team's win-loss ratio during the season could be written as 5 : 2 meaning that a team has won 5 games and only lost 2 games. This is very different from a win-loss ratio of 2 : 5 which would mean that 2 games were won and 5 games were lost.

A sporting team's win-loss performance could be expressed as a ratio.

Lesson starter: Impossible cupcakes

Liam is baking cupcakes for a group of friends and plans to make banana cupcakes and chocolate cupcakes in the ratio 2 to 3. This means that for every 2 banana cupcakes there are 3 chocolate cupcakes.

a How many chocolate cupcakes would Liam make if he makes the following number of banana cupcakes?
   i 4   ii 6   iii 8
b How many banana cupcakes would Liam make if he makes the following number of chocolate cupcakes?
   i 9   ii 15   iii 18
c How many cupcakes will Liam make in total if he makes:
   i 2 banana cupcakes?
   ii 6 chocolate cupcakes?
d Given Liam's cupcake ratio, is it possible that he could make 7 cupcakes? Explain why or why not.

KEY IDEAS

■ A ratio compares two or more related quantities.
- Ratios are expressed using whole numbers in a given order.
- A colon is used to separate the parts of a ratio.
- Ratios are expressed without units.

■ A ratio can be simplified in a similar way to a fraction.
- The fraction $\frac{4}{6}$ can be simplified to $\frac{2}{3}$.
- The ratio 4 : 6 can be simplified to 2 : 3.
- A ratio can be simplified if the numbers that make up the ratio have a common factor.
- Dividing all numbers in a ratio by their highest common factor will lead to the simplest form.

BUILDING UNDERSTANDING

1 Of a group of 5 counters, 2 of them are red and 3 of them are blue.

   a Which ratio would describe the number of red counters compared to the number of blue counters?

   A 2 : 5
   B 2 : 3
   C 3 : 2
   D 3 : 5
   E 1 : 2

   b Which ratio would describe the number of blue counters compared to the number of red counters?

   A 2 : 5   **B** 2 : 3
   C 3 : 2   **D** 3 : 5
   E 1 : 2

   c True or false? The fraction of red counters out of the total is $\frac{2}{3}$.

   d True or false? The fraction of blue counters out of the total is $\frac{3}{5}$.

2 This rectangle is divided up into 12 squares, 4 of which are shaded.

   a How many squares are unshaded?

   b A ratio which describes the ratio of shaded to unshaded squares could be:

   A 3 : 9   **B** 4 : 7
   C 4 : 8   **D** 5 : 7
   E 4 : 6

   c True or false? The correct ratio from part **b** above could also be written as 8 : 4.

   d True or false? The correct ratio from part **b** above could also be written as 1 : 2.

   e True or false? The correct ratio from part **b** above could also be written as 2 : 1.

Example 30   Expressing as a ratio

a A box contains 3 white and 4 dark chocolates. Write each of the following as a ratio.
  i the ratio of white chocolates to dark chocolates
  ii the ratio of dark chocolates to white chocolates
b A shop shelf contains 2 cakes, 5 slices and 9 pies. Write each of the following as a ratio.
  i the ratio of cakes to slices
  ii the ratio of cakes to slices to pies
  iii the ratio of pies to cakes

SOLUTION	EXPLANATION
a i $3 : 4$	The order is white to dark and there are 3 white and 4 dark chocolates.
ii $4 : 3$	The order is dark to white and there are 4 dark and 3 white chocolates.
b i $2 : 5$	We are only concerned with the ratio of cakes to slices and the order is cakes then slices.
ii $2 : 5 : 9$	Three quantities can also be compared using ratios. The order is important.
iii $9 : 2$	We are only concerned with pies and cakes and the order is pies then cakes.

Now you try

a A container has 2 clear and 5 grey marbles. Write each of the following as a ratio.
  i the ratio of clear to grey marbles
  ii the ratio of grey marbles to clear marbles.
b A computer shop has 3 laptops, 4 tablets and 7 phones on a display table. Write each of the following as a ratio.
  i the ratio of laptops to phones
  ii the ratio of laptops to tablets to phones
  iii the ratio of tablets to laptops.

Example 31 Simplifying a ratio

Simplify the following ratios.

a 4 : 10   **b** 3 : 12 : 15   **c** 15 points to 10 points

SOLUTION

a $\div 2 \left(\begin{array}{c} 4 : 10 \\ 2 : 5 \end{array}\right) \div 2$

b $\div 3 \left(\begin{array}{c} 3 : 12 : 15 \\ 1 : 4 \ : 5 \end{array}\right) \div 3$

c $\div 5 \left(\begin{array}{c} 15 : 10 \\ 3 : 2 \end{array}\right) \div 5$

EXPLANATION

The highest common factor of 4 and 10 is 2 so dividing both numbers by 2 will give the ratio in simplest form.

The highest common factor of 3, 12 and 15 is 3 so dividing all numbers by 3 will give the ratio in simplest form.

First use the numbers to write the information as a ratio without units. Then divide both numbers by the highest common factor 5.

Now you try

Simplify the following ratios.

a 15 : 5   **b** 4 : 8 : 16   **c** 18 goals to 6 goals

Exercise 3K

FLUENCY 1, 2, 4–6(½)   2, 3, 4–6(½)   3, 4–6(⅓)

Example 30

1 a A box contains 5 white and 3 dark chocolates. Write each of the following as a ratio.
   i the ratio of white chocolates to dark chocolates
   ii the ratio of dark chocolates to white chocolates

b A toy shop window contains 3 cars, 7 trucks and 4 motorcycles. Write each of the following as a ratio.
   i the ratio of cars to trucks
   ii the ratio of cars to trucks to motorcycles
   iii the ratio of motorcycles to cars

2 a A pencil case has 8 pencils and 5 pens. Write each of the following as a ratio.
   i the ratio of pencils to pens
   ii the ratio of pens to pencils

b A coffee shop produces 6 lattes, 7 cappuccinos and 5 flat white coffees in one hour. Write the following as a ratio.
   i the ratio of cappuccinos to flat whites
   ii the ratio of lattes to cappuccinos to flat whites
   iii the ratio of flat whites to lattes

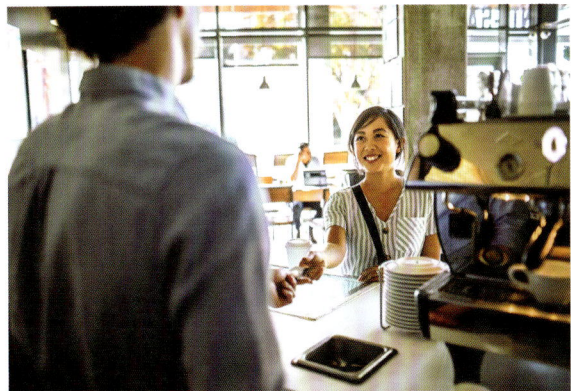

3   Each hour, a new radio station plans to play 3 songs from the 70s, 4 songs from the 80s, 7 songs from the 90s and just one song from the 60s. Write each of the following as a ratio.

   a   80s songs to 70s songs

   b   70s songs to 90s songs

   c   60s songs to 80s songs

   d   70s songs to 60s songs

   e   90s songs to 80s songs to 70s songs

   f   60s songs to 70s songs to 80s songs to 90s songs

Example 31a   4   Simplify the following ratios.

   a $3 : 6$ b $4 : 16$ c $10 : 5$ d $9 : 3$

   e $20 : 15$ f $35 : 45$ g $24 : 18$ h $110 : 90$

   i $120 : 140$ j $72 : 56$ k $99 : 22$ l $132 : 72$

Example 31b   5   Simplify the following ratios.

   a $2 : 4 : 10$ b $5 : 10 : 30$ c $12 : 6 : 18$ d $28 : 14 : 21$

   e $36 : 48 : 12$ f $2 : 90 : 16$ g $75 : 45 : 30$ h $54 : 27 : 36$

Example 31c   6   Simplify the following ratios.

   a   6 points to 3 points   b   4 goals to 16 goals

   c   20 metres to 15 metres   d   16 cm to 10 cm

   e   130 mm to 260 mm   f   48 litres to 60 litres

   g   18 kg to 12 kg to 30 kg   h   24 seconds to 48 seconds to 96 seconds

PROBLEM-SOLVING   7–8(½)   7–9(½)   8–10(½)

7   Write a ratio of shaded squares to white squares in these diagrams. Simplify your ratio if possible.

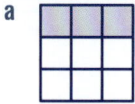

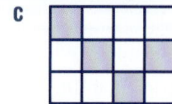

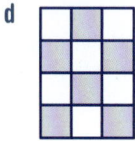

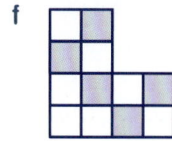

   a   b   c

   d   e   f

8   Find the missing number.

   a $\_\_ : 4 = 6 : 12$ b $\_\_ : 8 = 5 : 4$

   c $3 : 2 = \_\_ : 14$ d $9 : 4 = \_\_ : 8$

   e $26 : 39 = 2 : \_\_$ f $120 : \_\_ = 2 : 5$

9   Simplify the following ratios by firstly expressing the fractions using a common denominator if necessary.

   a $\dfrac{3}{5} : \dfrac{4}{5}$ b $\dfrac{5}{7} : \dfrac{3}{7}$ c $\dfrac{9}{11} : \dfrac{4}{11}$ d $\dfrac{7}{3} : \dfrac{13}{3}$

   e $\dfrac{1}{3} : \dfrac{1}{2}$ f $\dfrac{1}{5} : \dfrac{1}{3}$ g $\dfrac{1}{7} : \dfrac{1}{3}$ h $\dfrac{1}{4} : \dfrac{1}{8}$

   i $\dfrac{2}{5} : \dfrac{1}{10}$ j $\dfrac{1}{9} : \dfrac{2}{5}$ k $\dfrac{3}{4} : \dfrac{4}{5}$ l $\dfrac{7}{8} : \dfrac{3}{2}$

10 a Show how $1\frac{2}{3} : 2$ can be simplified to $5 : 6$.

   b Simplify these ratios that also include mixed numerals.

   i $1\frac{1}{2} : 3$ **ii** $4 : 1\frac{1}{2}$ **iii** $1\frac{2}{3} : 2\frac{1}{2}$ **iv** $3\frac{4}{5} : 2\frac{2}{3}$

REASONING		11, 12	11–13	12–14

11 George simplifies $4 : 2$ to $1 : \frac{1}{2}$. Explain his error and write the correct ratio.

12 A shade of orange is created by mixing yellow and red in the ratio $2 : 3$.

   a Explain why this is the same as mixing 4 litres of yellow paint with 6 litres of red paint.

   b Decide if the following ratios of yellow paint to red paint will make the colour more yellow or more red compared to the given ratio above:

   i $1 : 2$ **ii** $2 : 1$ **iii** $3 : 4$

13 The following compare quantities with different units. Write them using a ratio in simplest form by first writing them using the same units.

   a 50 cm to 2 metres
   b 30 mm to 5 cm
   c $4 to 250 cents
   d 800 grams to 1 kg
   e 45 minutes to 2 hours
   f 1 day to 18 hours

14 A friend says that the ratio of a number n to the same number squared n^2 is equal to $1 : 2$. Explain why the friend is incorrect unless $n = 2$.

15 The three primary colours are red, blue and yellow. Mixing them together in different ways forms a variety of colours. The primary, secondary and tertiary colours are shown in this chart.

a The secondary colours are formed by mixing the primary colours. What colour do you think will be formed if the following pairs of primary colours are mixed into the ratio 1 : 1?
  i yellow and red
  ii yellow and blue
  iii red and blue

b The tertiary colours are formed by mixing a primary colour and secondary colour. What colour do you think will be formed if the following pairs of colours are mixed into the ratio 1 : 1?
  i yellow and orange
  ii blue and violet
  iii green and yellow

c If secondary colours are formed by mixing primary colours in the ratio 1 : 1, and the tertiary colours are formed by mixing primary and secondary colours in the ratio 1 : 1, give the following ratios.
  i the ratio of yellow to red in the colour red orange.
  ii the ratio of yellow to blue in the colour yellow green.

d In a special colour mix red is mixed with blue in the ratio 2:1. This new mix is then mixed with more blue in the ratio 3 : 2. What is the ratio of red to blue in the final mix?

3L Solving problems with ratios

When considering the make up of a material like concrete, it is important to correctly balance the proportions of sand, water, cement and gravel. These ingredients could be thought of as parts of the whole, fractions or the whole or as a ratio. You might say, for example, that a particular cement mix has sand, water, cement and gravel in the ratio $3 : 2 : 1 : 4$. This means that out of a total of 10 parts, 3 of them are sand, 2 are water, 1 is cement and 4 are gravel. Similarly, you could say that the proportion or fraction of sand in the mix is $\frac{3}{10}$ and so if a load of concrete is 40 tonnes, then the proportion of sand is $\frac{3}{10} \times 40 = 12$ tonnes.

Lesson starter: Making bread

The two main ingredients in bread are flour and water. A commonly used ratio of flour to water is $5 : 3$.

- How would you describe the proportion of flour in a bread mix?
- How would you describe the fraction of water in a bread mix?
- If the ratio of flour to water is $5 : 3$, does that mean that all bread loaves that are made must have a total of 8 cups of ingredients? Explain.
- If a bread mix consisted of a total of 16 cups of bread and water, describe a method for working out the total number of cups of flour or water required.
- Is it possible to make a loaf of bread using a total of 12 cups of flour and water? Describe how you would calculate the number of cups of flour or water needed.

KEY IDEAS

- Ratios can be considered as a collection of parts.
  The ratio of vinegar to water for example might be $3 : 4$, which means that for every 3 parts of vinegar there are 4 parts of water.

- The total number of parts can be calculated by adding up all the numbers in the ratio.
  The total number of parts in the example above is $3 + 4 = 7$.

- Ratio problems can be solved by considering the proportion of one quantity compared to the whole.
  The proportion of vinegar is $\frac{3}{7}$ and so a 210 mL bottle contains $\frac{3}{7} \times 210 = 90$ mL of vinegar.

- To divide a quantity into a given ratio:
  - calculate the total number of parts (e.g. $3 + 4 = 7$)
  - calculate the proportion of the desired quantity (e.g. $\frac{3}{7}$)
  - use fractions to calculate the amount (e.g. $\frac{3}{7} \times 210 = 90$)

BUILDING UNDERSTANDING

1 A cordial mix is made up of 1 part syrup to 9 parts water.

   a Write the cordial to water mix as a ratio.

   b What is the total number of parts in the ratio?

   c What proportion of the cordial mix is syrup? Write your answer as a fraction.

   d What proportion of the cordial mix is water? Write your answer as a fraction.

   e If 400 millilitres of cordial mix is made up, how much of it is:

      i syrup?   **ii** water?

2 $150 is to be divided into two parts using the ratio 2 : 3 for Jacob and Sally, in that order.

   a What is the total number of parts in the ratio?

   b What fraction of the money would Jacob receive?

   c What fraction of the money would Sally receive?

   d Calculate the amount of money received by:

      i Jacob   **ii** Sally.

Example 32   Finding amounts given a ratio

Dry mix cement is combined with water in a given ratio to produce concrete.

a If the dry mix to water ratio is 3 : 5, write the proportion of the following as a fraction.

   i dry mix   **ii** water

b If $\frac{3}{7}$ of the concrete is dry mix, write the ratio of dry mix to water.

c If 8 litres of dry mix is used using a dry mix to water ratio of 2 : 3, what amount of water is required?

SOLUTION	EXPLANATION
a **i** $\dfrac{3}{8}$	The total number of parts is 8 and the number of parts relating to dry mix is 3.
ii $\dfrac{5}{8}$	The number of parts relating to water is 5 out of a total of 8.
b $\dfrac{3}{7} : \dfrac{4}{7} = 3 : 4$	If $\frac{3}{7}$ of the concrete is dry mix, then $\frac{4}{7}$ is water. Multiply both fraction by the common denominator to produce the simplified ratio.
c dry mix water $\times 4 \left(\begin{array}{c} 2 : 3 \\ 8 : 12 \end{array} \right) \times 4$ $\therefore$ 12 litres of water required.	Multiply both numbers in the ratio by 4 to see what amount of water corresponds to 8 litres of dry mix.

Now you try

Juice concentrate is to be combined with water in a given ratio to produce a drink.

a If the concentrate to water ratio is 2 : 7, write the proportion of the following as a fraction.

   i concentrate   **ii** water

b If $\frac{1}{5}$ of the drink is concentrate, write the ratio of concentrate to water.

c If 100 mL of concentrate is mixed using a concentrate to water ratio of 2 : 9, what amount of water is required?

Example 33 Dividing an amount into a given ratio

Divide 15 kg into the ratio 2 : 1.

SOLUTION

Total number of parts = 2 + 1 = 3

Fractions are $\frac{2}{3}$ and $\frac{1}{3}$

Amounts are $\frac{2}{3} \times 15 = 10$ and $\frac{1}{3} \times 15 = 5$

10 kg and 5 kg

EXPLANATION

First find the total number of parts in the ratio.
Calculate the proportions for each number in the ratio.
Multiply each fraction by the amount given to find the amounts corresponding to each portion.
Answer the question with the appropriate units.

Now you try

Divide 60 seconds into the ratio 3 : 1.

Exercise 3L

FLUENCY　　　　　1–5, 6(½)　　　2–5, 6(½)　　　2, 3, 5, 6(⅓)

Example 32

1 Powder is to be combined with water in a given weight ratio to produce glue.
 a If the powder to water ratio is 2 : 3, write the proportion of the following as a fraction.
  i powder　　　　　　　　　　　　ii water
 b If the powder to water ratio is 1 : 5, write the proportion of the following as a fraction.
  i powder　　　　　　　　　　　　ii water
 c If the powder to water ratio is 3 : 4, write the proportion of the following as a fraction.
  i powder　　　　　　　　　　　　ii water

Example 32

2 Flour is to be combined with water in the ratio 4 : 3 to produce damper.
 a Write the proportion of the following as a fraction.
  i flour　　　　　　　　　　　　ii water
 b If $\frac{2}{3}$ of the damper is flour, write the ratio of flour to water.
 c If 60 grams of flour is mixed using a flour to water ratio of 3 : 2, what amount of water is required?

Example 32

3 A number of hockey teams have various win-loss ratios for a season.
 a The Cats have a win-loss ratio of 5 : 3. What fraction of the games in the season did the Cats win?
 b The Jets won $\frac{3}{4}$ of their matches. Write down their win-loss ratio.
 c The Eagles lost 5 of their matches with a win-loss ratio of 2 : 1. How many matches did they win?
 d The Lions have a win-loss ratio of 2 : 7. What fraction of the games in the season did the Lions lose?
 e The Dozers lost $\frac{2}{5}$ of their matches. Write down their win-loss ratio.
 f The Sharks won 6 of their matches with a win-loss ratio of 3 : 2. How many matches did they lose?

Example 33 **4** Divide 24 kg into the ratio 1 : 3.

Example 33 **5** Divide 35 litres into the ratio 3 : 4.

Example 33 **6** Divide the following into the given ratios.

    a $40 in the ratio 2 : 3   **b** $100 in the ratio 3 : 7

    c 32 kg in the ratio 3 : 5   **d** 72 kg in the ratio 5 : 1

    e 54 litres in the ratio 5 : 4   **f** 66 litres in the ratio 2 : 9

    g 96 metres in the ratio 7 : 5   **h** 150 metres in the ratio 8 : 7

PROBLEM–SOLVING	7, 8	8, 9(½), 10	9(½), 10, 11

7 Micky is making up a spray for his fruit orchard and mixes chemical with water using a ratio of 2 : 13.

    a How much chemical should he use if making a spray with the following total number of litres?

      i 15 litres

      ii 45 litres

      iii 120 litres

    b If he uses 20 litres of chemical, how much spray will he make?

    c If he uses 39 litres of water, how much chemical does he use?

    d If he makes 60 litres of spray, how much chemical did he use?

8 Mohammad has $72 to divide amongst three children in the ratio 1 : 2 : 3.

    a How much money is given to the first child listed?

    b How much money is given to the third child listed?

9 Divide the following into the given ratios.

    a $180 into the ratio of 2 : 2 : 5   **b** 750 grams into the ratio of 5 : 3 : 7

    c 165 litres into the ratio 2 : 10 : 3   **d** 840 kg into the ratio 2 : 7 : 3

10 The ratio of cattle to sheep on a farm is 2 : 7.

    a How many sheep are there if there are 50 cattle?

    b How many cattle are there if there are 84 sheep?

    c How many sheep are there if there are 198 cattle and sheep in total?

    d How many cattle are there if there are 990 cattle and sheep in total?

11 The three angles in a triangle are in the ratio 1 : 2 : 3. What is the size of the largest angle?

REASONING 12, 13 12–14 13–15

12 Sisi divides 30 beads into a ratio of 1 : 3 to make two piles. How many beads make up the remainder?

13 Mal tips out his collection of 134 one dollar coins and divides them using the ratio 2 : 5. Will Mal be able to complete the division without leaving a remainder? Give a reason.

14 A sporting squad is to be selected for a training camp with attacking, midfielder and defence players in the ratio 3 : 5 : 2. Currently, the coach has selected 4 attacking players, 5 midfielders and 3 defence players. Find the minimum number of extra players the coach needs to select to have the correct ratio.

15 There are initially 14 lions in an enclosure at a zoo and the ratio of male to female lions is 4 : 3. Some of the male lions escaped and the ratio of male to female lions is now 2 : 3. How many male lions escaped?

ENRICHMENT: Slopes as ratios – – 16

16 The steepness of a slope can be regarded as the ratio of the vertical distance compared to the horizontal distance. So a slope with ratio 1 : 4 would mean for every 1 metre vertically you travel 4 metres horizontally.

a Describe the following slopes as ratios of vertical distance to horizontal distance.
    i vertical 20 metres and horizontal 80 metres
    ii vertical 120 metres and horizontal 40 metres

b A slope has a ratio of 2 : 9.
    i Find the horizontal distance travelled if the vertical distance is 12 metres.
    ii Find the vertical distance travelled if the horizontal distance is 36 km.

c What would be the slope ratio if $20\frac{1}{2}$ metres is climbed vertically and $5\frac{1}{2}$ is climbed horizontally?

Modelling

Pricing plants

Andrew owns a nursery and normally sells flower pots for $15 each and on average he sells 100 of these pots per day. The cost to produce each flower pot is $5, so the profit per pot under normal conditions is $10 per pot.

To attract more customers to the nursery, he considers lowering the price with one of the following deals.

- Deal 1: Lowering the selling price to $12, where he predicts he will sell $1\frac{1}{2}$ times as many pots per day.
- Deal 2: Lowering the selling price to $11, where he predicts selling $1\frac{4}{5}$ times as many pots per day.

Present a report for the following tasks and ensure that you show clear mathematical workings and explanations where appropriate.

Preliminary task

a   Under normal conditions, what is the total profit for Andrew's shop after selling 100 flower pots?

b   Using Deal 1, find the following amounts.

  i   the profit made on each pot sold

  ii   the expected number of pots to be sold

  iii   the expected total profit for Andrew's nursery for one day

c   Compared to normal conditions, by how much does Andrew's profit increase if he uses Deal 1?

d   Write the profit increase as a percentage of the original profit (found in part **a**).

Modelling task

Formulate

a   The problem is to create a deal for Andrew that will cause the profit to increase by at least 10%. Write down all the relevant information that will help solve this problem.

Solve

b   Repeat Preliminary task part **b**, but use Deal 2 instead of Deal 1.

c   Compared to normal conditions, by how much does Andrew's profit increase if he uses Deal 2? Express your answer as a percentage of the original profit with no deals.

d   Andrew considers a third deal where the selling price is reduced to $8. This will cause the number of pots sold to triple. Compare this deal with the other two, considering the total profit for a day.

Evaluate and verify

e   By considering the deals above, compare the profits for one day's trade for Andrew's nursery. Sort the deals from most profitable to least profitable for Andrew.

f   Construct your own scenario for Andrew's nursery which will cause the overall profit for one day to be at least 10% more than that of the normal conditions.

  i   Describe the scenario in terms of the price sold and the number of flower pots sold.

  ii   Show that the profit is increased by at least 10% by finding the expected total profit.

Communicate

g   Summarise your results and describe any key findings.

Extension questions

a   Is it possible to find a deal that produces exactly a 20% increase in profit for Andrew's nursery? If so, find it and explain whether or not it is a realistic deal to offer.

b   Suppose Andrew keeps the regular price at $15 per pot, but allows people to buy 5 pots for the price of 4. Explain how the results would compare with charging $12 per flower pot.

Adding to infinity

(Key technology: Spreadsheets)

It would be natural to think that a total sum would increase to infinity if we continually added on numbers to the total, however, this is not always the case. Just like in this image, we could continually zoom in adding more and more spirals but we know that the total size of the image never gets larger.

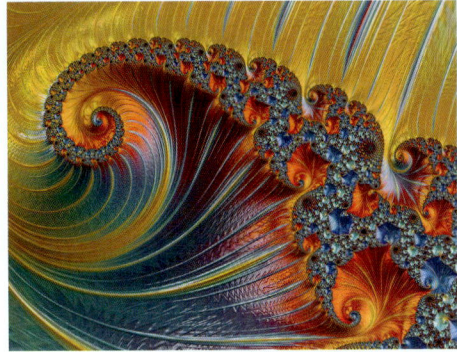

1 Getting started

a Consider a sequence of numbers where each number is double the previous number in the sequence.
Then the total sum is obtained by adding each new number to the previous total.

   i Copy and complete this table using the above description.

Sequence	1	2	4	8	16	32		
Sum	1	3	7					

   ii What do you notice about the total sum? Is it increasing more or less rapidly as more numbers are being added? Give a reason.

b Now consider finding a total sum from a sequence of numbers where each number is one half of the previous number.

   i Copy and complete this table using the above description.

Sequence	1	$\frac{1}{2}$	$\frac{1}{4}$	$\frac{1}{8}$	$\frac{1}{16}$			
Sum	1	$\frac{3}{2}$	$\frac{7}{4}$					

   ii What do you notice about the total sum? Is it increasing more or less rapidly as more numbers are being added? Give a reason.

   iii What number does your sum appear to be approaching?

2 Applying an algorithm

Here is an algorithm which finds a total sum of a sequence of n numbers starting at 1. Note that S stands for the total sum, t stands for the term in the sequence and i counts the number of terms produced.

a Copy and complete this table for $n = 6$, writing down the values for t and S from beginning to end.

t	1	$\frac{1}{2}$	$\frac{1}{4}$			
S	1	$\frac{3}{2}$				

b Describe this sequence and sum compared to the sequence studied in part **1**.

Start

↓

Input n

↓

$i = 1, t = 1, S = 1$

↓

Output t, S

↓

Is $i = n$?

No → $t = \frac{t}{2}$
$S = S + t$
$i = i + 1$

Yes ↓

End

Technology and computational thinking

c   Describe the parts of the algorithm that make the following happen.

   i   Each term is being halved each time.

   ii   The sum is increased each time by adding on the new term.

   iii   The algorithm knows when to end.

d   Write an algorithm that adds up all the numbers in a sequence but this time:

- the sequence starts at 2
- the sum is obtained by adding one third of the previous number each time.

3 Using technology

We will use a spreadsheet to generate the sums studied above.

a   Create a spreadsheet as shown.

b   Fill down at cells A5, B5 and C5 to generate 10 terms. Check that the numbers you produce match the numbers you found in parts **1b** and **2a**.

	A	B	C
1	Adding half of	previous term	
2			
3	n	Term	Sum
4	1	1	=B4
5	=A4+1	=B4/2	=C4+B5

c   Fill down further. What do you notice about the total sum?

d   Experiment with your spreadsheet by changing the rule in B5. Divide B4 by different numbers and also try multiplying B4 by a number.

e   Find a rule for cell B4 where the total sum moves closer and closer to $\frac{3}{2}$ as n increases.

4 Extension

a   Find a rule for cell B4 where the total sum moves closer and closer to 3 as n increases.

b   Describe the circumstances and the way in which the terms t are generated that make S approach closer and closer to a fixed sum rather than increasing to infinity.

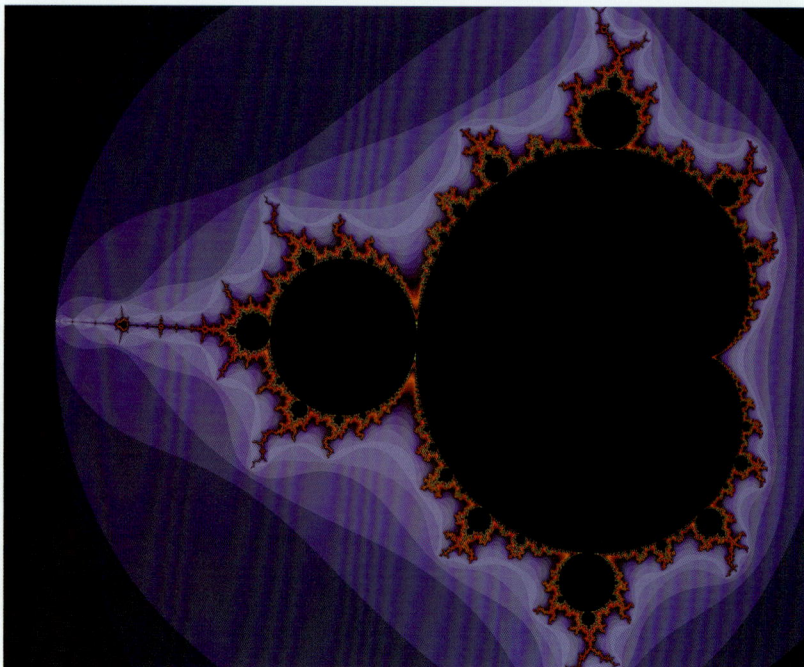

Egyptian fractions

The fractions in the ancient Egyptian Eye of Horus were used for dividing up food and land, as well as portions of medicine. They are called **unitary** fractions because all the numerators are 1.

Clearly, the ancient Egyptians had no calculators or precise measuring instruments; nevertheless, by repeatedly dividing a quantity in half, the fractions $\frac{1}{2}, \frac{1}{4}, \frac{1}{8}, \frac{1}{16}$ or $\frac{1}{32}$ were combined to estimate other fractions.

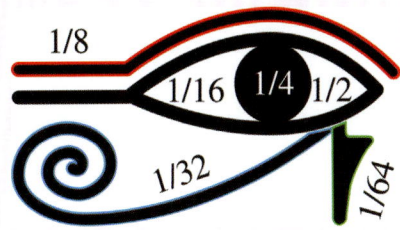

Using ancient Egyptian fractions, how could three loaves be divided equally between five people?

First, cut the loaves in half and give each customer $\frac{1}{2}$ ($\triangleright$) a loaf. The remaining half loaf can be cut into eight parts and each person is given $\frac{1}{8}$ of $\frac{1}{2} = \frac{1}{16}$ ($\triangleleft$) of a loaf. There is a small portion left

$\left(3 \text{ portions of } \frac{1}{16}\right)$, so these portions can be divided in half and each customer given $\frac{1}{2}$ of $\frac{1}{16} = \frac{1}{32}$ ($\odot$) of a loaf.

Each customer has an equal share $\frac{1}{2} + \frac{1}{16} + \frac{1}{32}$ (symbol) of the loaf and the baker will have the small $\frac{1}{32}$ (symbol) of a loaf left over.

If each loaf is divided *exactly* into five parts, the three loaves would have 15 equal parts altogether and each customer could have three parts of the 15; $\frac{3}{15} = \frac{1}{5}$ of the total or $\frac{3}{5}$ of one loaf. $\frac{3}{5} = 0.6$ and $\frac{1}{2} + \frac{1}{16} + \frac{1}{32} = 0.59375 \approx 0.6$ ($\approx$ means approximately equal).

So even without calculators or sophisticated measuring instruments, the ancient Egyptian method of repeated halving gives quite close approximations to the exact answers.

Task

Using diagrams, explain how the following portions can be divided equally using only the ancient Egyptian unitary fractions of $\frac{1}{2}, \frac{1}{4}, \frac{1}{8}, \frac{1}{16}$ and $\frac{1}{32}$.

   a   three loaves of bread shared between eight people

   b   one loaf of bread shared between five people

   c   two loaves of bread shared between three people

Include the Egyptian Eye of Horus symbols for each answer, and determine the difference between the exact answer and the approximate answer found using the ancient Egyptian method.

1   Find the sum of all fractions in the form $\frac{a}{b}$, where the numerator a is less than the denominator b, and b is an integer from 2 to 10 inclusive. Fractions that are equivalent, e.g. $\frac{1}{2}$ and $\frac{2}{4}$, should each be counted towards the sum.

> Up for a challenge? If you get stuck on a question, check out the 'Working with unfamiliar problems' poster at the end of the book to help you.

2   At the end of each practice session, Coach Andy rewards his swim team by distributing 30 pieces of chocolate according to effort. Each swimmer receives a *different* number of whole pieces of chocolate. Suggest possible numbers (all different) of chocolate pieces for each swimmer attending practice when the chocolate is shared between:

   a   4 swimmers

   b   5 swimmers

   c   6 swimmers

   d   7 swimmers.

3   In this magic square, the sum of the fractions in each row, column and diagonal is the same. Find the value of each letter in this magic square.

$\frac{2}{5}$	A	$\frac{4}{5}$
B	C	D
E	$\frac{1}{2}$	1

4   You are given four fractions: $\frac{1}{3}, \frac{1}{4}, \frac{1}{5}$ and $\frac{1}{6}$. Using any three of these fractions, complete each number sentence below.

   a $\_\_ + \_\_ \times \_\_ = \frac{7}{30}$

   b $\_\_ \div \_\_ - \_\_ = \frac{7}{6}$

   c $\_\_ + \_\_ - \_\_ = \frac{13}{60}$

5   When a \$50 item is increased by 20%, the final price is \$60. Yet when a \$60 item is reduced by 20%, the final price is not \$50. Explain.

6   \$500 is divided in the ratio 13 : 7 : 5. How much money is the largest portion?

proper fraction $\frac{3}{4}$

improper fraction $\frac{10}{7}$

mixed numeral $5\frac{3}{4}$

---

mixed $\longrightarrow$ improper

$2\frac{3}{5} = \frac{10}{5} + \frac{3}{5} = \frac{13}{5}$

improper $\longrightarrow$ mixed

$\frac{40}{15} = 2\frac{10}{15} = 2\frac{2}{3}$

or $\frac{40}{15} = \frac{5 \times 8}{5 \times 3} = \frac{8}{3} = 2\frac{2}{3}$

---

2 parts selected $\to \frac{2}{5}$ numerator denominator

5 parts in the whole

Fractions

Equivalent fractions

$\frac{50}{100} = \frac{30}{60} = \frac{21}{42} = \frac{8}{16} = \left(\frac{1}{2}\right)$

simplest form $\to$

Percentages

$1\% = \frac{1}{100}$ $50\% = \frac{50}{100} = \frac{1}{2}$

$10\% = \frac{10}{100} = \frac{1}{10}$ $75\% = \frac{75}{100} = \frac{3}{4}$

$20\% = \frac{20}{100} = \frac{1}{5}$ $80\% = \frac{80}{100} = \frac{4}{5}$

$25\% = \frac{25}{100} = \frac{1}{4}$ $100\% = \frac{100}{100} = 1$

Expressing as a proportion

$12 out of $50 = \frac{12}{50}$

$= \frac{6}{25}$

$= 24\%$

Recall

$\frac{7}{7} = 7 \div 7 = 1$

Simplify

$\frac{42}{63} = \frac{7 \times 6}{7 \times 9} = \frac{6}{9} = \frac{3 \times 2}{3 \times 3} = \frac{2}{3}$

or

$\frac{42}{63} = \frac{21 \times 2}{21 \times 3} = \frac{2}{3}$

HCF of 42 and 63 is 21.

Ratios

Simplest form uses whole numbers.

$10 : 8 = 5 : 4$

3 red and 2 blue

Ratio of red to blue is $3 : 2$.

$\frac{3}{5}$ are red, $\frac{2}{5}$ are blue

Comparing fractions

$\frac{5}{8}$? $\frac{3}{4}$

$\frac{5}{8}$ < $\frac{6}{8}$

8 is the lowest common denominator (LCD) which is the lowest common multiple (LCM) of 4 and 8.

Operating with fractions

Adding fractions

$\frac{4}{5} + \frac{2}{3}$

$= \frac{12}{15} + \frac{10}{15}$

$= \frac{22}{15} = 1\frac{7}{15}$

Subtracting fractions

$3\frac{1}{4} - 1\frac{2}{3}$ $3\frac{1}{4} - 1\frac{2}{3}$

$= 2\frac{5}{4} - 1\frac{2}{3}$ $= \frac{13}{4} - \frac{5}{3}$

$= (2 - 1) + \left(\frac{5}{4} - \frac{2}{3}\right)$ $= \frac{39}{12} - \frac{20}{12}$

$= 1 + \left(\frac{15}{12} - \frac{8}{12}\right)$ $= \frac{39 - 20}{12}$

$= 1\frac{7}{12}$ $= \frac{19}{12} = 1\frac{7}{12}$

Multiplying fractions

$\frac{5}{10}$ of $\frac{20}{50}$ $3\frac{1}{5} \times 2\frac{1}{4}$

$= \frac{5^1}{10_2} \times \frac{20^2}{50_5}$ $= \frac{16^4}{5} \times \frac{9}{4_1}$

$= \frac{1}{5}$ $= \frac{36}{5} = 7\frac{1}{5}$

Percentage of a quantity

25% of $40   120% of 50 minutes

$= \frac{1}{4} \times 40$ $= \frac{120}{100_2} \times \frac{50^1}{1}$

$= \$10$ $= 60$ minutes

$= 1$ hour

Dividing fractions

$4\frac{1}{6} \div 1\frac{1}{9}$

$= \frac{25}{6} \div \frac{10}{9}$ Reciprocal

$= \frac{25^5}{6_2} \times \frac{9^3}{10_2}$ of $\frac{10}{9}$ is $\frac{9}{10}$

$= \frac{15}{4}$

$= 3\frac{3}{4}$

Chapter checklist with success criteria

Chapter checklist

A printable version of this checklist is available in the Interactive Textbook

		✔
3A	**1. I can identify the numerator and denominator of a fraction.** e.g. A pizza has been cut into eight pieces, with three of them selected. Write the selection as a fraction and state the numerator and denominator.	☐
3A	**2. I can represent fractions on a number line.** e.g. Represent the fractions $\frac{3}{5}$ and $\frac{9}{5}$ on a number line.	☐
3A	**3. I can represent a fraction by shading areas.** e.g. Represent the fraction $\frac{3}{4}$ in three different ways, using a square divided into four equal regions.	☐
3B	**4. I can produce equivalent fractions with a given numerator or denominator.** e.g. Fill in the missing numbers for $\frac{2}{3} = \frac{?}{12}$ and $\frac{4}{5} = \frac{12}{?}$.	☐
3B	**5. I can write fractions in simplest form.** e.g. Write the fraction $\frac{12}{20}$ in simplest form.	☐
3B	**6. I can decide if two fractions are equivalent.** e.g. Are $\frac{4}{5}$ and $\frac{20}{25}$ equivalent? Explain your answer.	☐
3C	**7. I can convert mixed numerals to improper fractions.** e.g. Convert $3\frac{1}{5}$ to an improper fraction.	☐
3C	**8. I can convert from an improper fraction to a mixed numeral, simplifying if required.** e.g. Convert $\frac{11}{4}$ and $\frac{20}{6}$ to mixed numerals in simplest form.	☐
3D	**9. I can compare two fractions to decide which is bigger.** e.g. Decide which of $\frac{2}{3}$ and $\frac{3}{5}$ is bigger, and write a statement involving > or < to summarise your answer.	☐
3D	**10. I can order fractions in ascending or descending order.** e.g. Place the following fractions in ascending order: $\frac{3}{4}, \frac{4}{5}, \frac{2}{3}$.	☐
3E	**11. I can add two fractions by converting to a common denominator if required.** e.g. Find the value of $\frac{3}{4} + \frac{5}{6}$.	☐
3E	**12. I can add two mixed numerals.** e.g. Find the sum of $3\frac{2}{3}$ and $4\frac{2}{3}$.	☐
3F	**13. I can subtract fractions by converting to a common denominator if required.** e.g. Find the value of $\frac{5}{6} - \frac{1}{4}$.	☐

	✔

14. I can subtract mixed numerals. `3F`

e.g. Find the value of $5\frac{2}{3} - 3\frac{1}{4}$.

☐

15. I can multiply fractions (proper and/or improper fractions). `3G`

e.g. Find $\frac{3}{4} \times \frac{8}{9}$.

☐

16. I can multiply mixed numerals and fractions by whole numbers `3G`

e.g. Find $6\frac{1}{4} \times 2\frac{2}{5}$ and $\frac{1}{3} \times 21$.

☐

17. I can find the reciprocal of a fraction, whole number or mixed numeral. `3H`

e.g. Find the reciprocal of $1\frac{3}{7}$.

☐

18. I can divide fractions (proper and/or improper fractions). `3H`

e.g. Find $\frac{3}{5} \div \frac{3}{8}$.

☐

19. I can divide mixed numerals. `3H`

e.g. Find $2\frac{2}{5} \div 1\frac{3}{5}$.

☐

20. I can convert a percentage to a fraction or mixed numeral. `3I`

e.g. Express 36% as a fraction in simplest form.

☐

21. I can convert a fraction to a percentage. `3I`

e.g. Convert $\frac{11}{25}$ and $\frac{3}{8}$ to percentages.

☐

22. I can find the percentage of a number. `3J`
e.g. Find 15% of 400.

☐

23. I can express related quantities as a ratio. `3K`
e.g. A box contains 3 white and 4 dark chocolates. Write the ratio of dark chocolates to white chocolates.

☐

24. I can simplify a ratio. `3K`
e.g. Simplify 4 : 10

☐

25. I can find amount given a ratio. `3L`
e.g. If the ratio of dry mix cement to water is 2 : 3, what amount of water is mixed with 8 litres of dry mix cement?

☐

26. I can divide an amount into a given ratio. `3L`
e.g. Divide 15 kg into the ratio 2 : 1.

☐

Short-answer questions

3A

1 Write the following diagrams as fractions (e.g. $\frac{1}{6}$) and list them in ascending order.

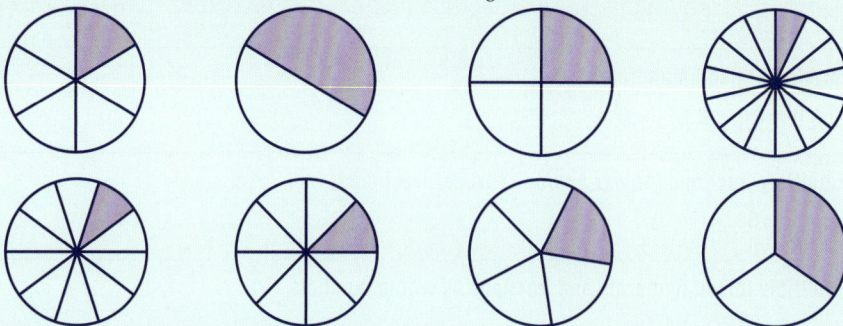

3B

2 Write four fractions equivalent to $\frac{3}{5}$ and write a sentence to explain why they are equal in value.

3B

3 Write the following fractions in simplest form.

a $\frac{18}{30}$ b $\frac{8}{28}$ c $\frac{35}{49}$

3C

4 Convert each of the following to a mixed numeral in simplest form.

a $\frac{15}{10}$ b $\frac{63}{36}$ c $\frac{45}{27}$ d $\frac{56}{16}$

3D

5 Place the correct mathematical symbol $<$, $=$ or $>$, in between the following pairs of fractions to make true mathematical statements.

a $\frac{2}{7} \square \frac{4}{7}$ b $\frac{3}{8} \square \frac{1}{8}$

c $1\frac{2}{3} \square 1\frac{3}{5}$ d $3\frac{1}{9} \square \frac{29}{9}$

3D

6 State the largest fraction in each list.

a $\frac{3}{7}, \frac{2}{7}, \frac{5}{7}, \frac{1}{7}$ b $\frac{3}{8}, \frac{2}{8}, \frac{5}{8}, \frac{1}{8}$

3D

7 State the lowest common multiple for each pair of numbers.

a 2, 5   b 3, 7   c 8, 12

3D

8 State the lowest common denominator for each set of fractions.

a $\frac{1}{2}, \frac{3}{5}$ b $\frac{2}{3}, \frac{3}{7}$ c $\frac{3}{8}, \frac{5}{12}$

3D

9 Rearrange each set of fractions in descending order.

a $1\frac{3}{5}, \frac{9}{5}, 2\frac{1}{5}$

b $\frac{14}{8}, \frac{11}{6}, \frac{9}{4}, \frac{5}{3}$

c $5\frac{2}{3}, \frac{47}{9}, 5\frac{7}{18}, 5\frac{1}{9}, 5\frac{1}{3}$

3E/F

10 Determine the simplest answer for each of the following.

a $\frac{3}{8} + \frac{1}{8}$ b $\frac{1}{3} + \frac{1}{2}$ c $\frac{3}{8} + \frac{5}{6}$

d $2\frac{7}{15} + 3\frac{3}{10}$ e $\frac{7}{8} - \frac{3}{8}$ f $5\frac{1}{4} - 2\frac{3}{4}$

g $\frac{3}{4} - \frac{2}{5} + \frac{7}{8}$ h $8\frac{7}{12} - 4\frac{7}{9} + 2\frac{1}{3}$ i $13\frac{1}{2} + 5\frac{7}{10} - 6\frac{3}{5}$

3G

11 Find:

a $\dfrac{1}{3} \times 21$

b $\dfrac{4}{5}$ of 100

c $\dfrac{3}{4}$ of 16

d $\dfrac{8}{10} \times \dfrac{25}{4}$

e $\dfrac{2}{3}$ of $\dfrac{1}{4}$

f $3\dfrac{1}{8} \times 2\dfrac{2}{5}$

3H

12 Determine the reciprocal of each of the following.

a $\dfrac{3}{4}$

b $\dfrac{7}{12}$

c $2\dfrac{3}{4}$

d $5\dfrac{1}{3}$

3H

13 Perform these divisions.

a $\dfrac{6}{10} \div 3$

b $64 \div 3\dfrac{1}{5}$

c $6\dfrac{2}{5} \div 1\dfrac{6}{10}$

d $\dfrac{3}{8} \div 1\dfrac{1}{4} \div 1\dfrac{1}{2}$

3I

14 Copy the table into your workbook and complete.

Percentage form	36%			140%		18%
Fraction		$2\dfrac{1}{5}$	$\dfrac{5}{100}$		$\dfrac{11}{25}$	

3J

15 Determine which alternative (i or ii) is the larger discount.

a   i   25% of $200

     ii   20% of $260

b   i   5% of $1200

     ii   3% of $1900

3K

16 A shop shelf displays 3 cakes, 5 slices and 4 pies. Write the following as ratios.

a   cakes to slices

b   slices to pies

c   pies to cakes

d   slices to pies to cakes

3K

17 Express these ratios in simplest form.

a   21 : 7

b   3.2 : 0.6

c $2.30 : 50 cents

3L

18 Divide $80 into the following ratios.

a   7 : 1

b   2 : 3

Multiple-choice questions

3A

1 Which set of fractions corresponds to each of the red dots positioned on the number line?

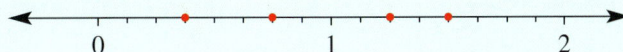

A $\dfrac{3}{8}, \dfrac{6}{8}, 1\dfrac{3}{8}, \dfrac{12}{8}$

B $\dfrac{3}{8}, \dfrac{3}{4}, 1\dfrac{1}{4}, \dfrac{12}{8}$

C $\dfrac{1}{2}, \dfrac{3}{4}, \dfrac{9}{8}, 1\dfrac{5}{8}$

D $\dfrac{2}{8}, \dfrac{3}{4}, 1\dfrac{3}{8}, 1\dfrac{1}{2}$

E $\dfrac{3}{8}, \dfrac{3}{4}, 1\dfrac{1}{2}, \dfrac{14}{8}$

3B

2 Which of the following statements is not true?

A $\dfrac{3}{4} = \dfrac{9}{12}$ B $\dfrac{6}{11} = \dfrac{18}{33}$ C $\dfrac{3}{10} = \dfrac{15}{40}$

D $\dfrac{13}{14} = \dfrac{39}{42}$ E $\dfrac{2}{7} = \dfrac{16}{56}$

3C

3 Which set of mixed numerals corresponds to the red dots on the number line?

A $1\dfrac{1}{5}, 1\dfrac{3}{5}, 2\dfrac{2}{5}, 3\dfrac{1}{5}$ B $1\dfrac{2}{5}, 1\dfrac{3}{5}, 2\dfrac{3}{5}, 3\dfrac{1}{5}$

C $1\dfrac{1}{5}, 1\dfrac{2}{5}, 2\dfrac{2}{5}, 3\dfrac{2}{5}$ D $1\dfrac{2}{5}, 1\dfrac{4}{5}, 2\dfrac{2}{5}, 3\dfrac{2}{5}$

E $1\dfrac{1}{5}, 1\dfrac{3}{5}, 2\dfrac{3}{5}, 3\dfrac{1}{5}$

3D

4 Which is the lowest common denominator for this set of fractions? $\dfrac{7}{12}, \dfrac{11}{15}, \dfrac{13}{18}$

A 60   B 120   C 180   D 3240   E 90

3D

5 Which of the following fraction groups is in correct descending order?

A $\dfrac{1}{5}, \dfrac{1}{3}, \dfrac{2}{2}$ B $\dfrac{3}{4}, \dfrac{3}{5}, \dfrac{3}{8}, \dfrac{3}{7}$

C $\dfrac{5}{8}, \dfrac{4}{5}, \dfrac{3}{8}, \dfrac{2}{3}$ D $\dfrac{1}{10}, \dfrac{1}{20}, \dfrac{1}{50}, \dfrac{1}{100}$

E $2\dfrac{1}{5}, 2\dfrac{8}{15}, 2\dfrac{2}{3}, 2\dfrac{3}{4}$

3E

6 Which problem has an incorrect answer?

A $\dfrac{1}{6} + \dfrac{3}{6} = \dfrac{4}{6}$ B $\dfrac{3}{4} + \dfrac{5}{12} = \dfrac{5}{16}$

C $\dfrac{3}{4} \times \dfrac{5}{12} = \dfrac{5}{16}$ D $5\dfrac{2}{3} - 3\dfrac{1}{4} = 2\dfrac{5}{12}$

E $\dfrac{3}{4} \times \dfrac{4}{5} = \dfrac{3}{5}$

3F

7 Three friends share a pizza. Kate eats $\dfrac{1}{5}$ of the pizza, Archie eats $\dfrac{1}{3}$ of the pizza and Luke eats the rest. What fraction of the pizza does Luke eat?

A $\dfrac{4}{12}$ B $\dfrac{2}{3}$ C $\dfrac{14}{15}$ D $\dfrac{7}{15}$ E $\dfrac{8}{15}$

3D/I

8 Which list is in correct ascending order?

A $0.68, \dfrac{3}{4}, 0.76, 77\%, \dfrac{1}{3}, 40$

B $\dfrac{7}{8}, 82\%, 0.87, \dfrac{12}{15}, 88\%$

C $21\%, 0.02, 0.2, 0.22, \dfrac{22}{10}$

D $\dfrac{14}{40}, 0.36, 0.3666, 37\%, \dfrac{93}{250}$

E $0.76, 72\%, \dfrac{3}{4}, 0.68, \dfrac{13}{40}$

3C

9 $\dfrac{60}{14}$ can be written as:

A $4\dfrac{2}{7}$ B $2\dfrac{4}{7}$ C $4\dfrac{2}{14}$ D $7\dfrac{4}{7}$ E $5\dfrac{1}{7}$

3G

10 $\dfrac{17}{25}$ of a metre of material is needed for a school project. How many centimetres is this?

A 65 cm   B 70 cm   C 68 cm   D 60 cm   E 75 cm

Extended-response questions

1 Evaluate each of the following.

a $3\frac{1}{4} + 1\frac{3}{4} \times 2\frac{1}{2}$

b $5 \div 3\frac{1}{3} + 4\frac{3}{8} - \frac{5}{12}$

c $7\frac{2}{5} + 2\frac{1}{10} \div 2\frac{4}{5} \times 3\frac{3}{4}$

d $3\frac{5}{7} + 6\frac{1}{4} \div \left(3\frac{3}{8} - \frac{3}{4}\right)$

2 The length of one side of a triangle is $\frac{5}{12}$ of the perimeter and a second side has length $\frac{5}{28}$ of the perimeter.

a If these two sides have a total length of 75 centimetres, determine the triangle's perimeter.

b Find the lengths of each of the three sides.

3 a A sale on digital cameras offers 20% discount. Determine the sale price of a camera that was originally priced at $220.

b The sale price of a DVD is $18. This is 25% less than the original marked price. Determine the original price of this DVD.

4 Perform the following calculations.

a Increase $440 by 25%. (*Hint*: first find 25% of $440.)

b Decrease 300 litres by 12%.

c Increase $100 by 10% and then decrease that amount by 10%. Explain the reason for the answer.

d When $A is increased by 20%, the result is $300. Calculate the result if $A is decreased by 20%.

5 When a Ripstick is sold for $200, the shop makes 25% profit on the price paid for it.

a If this $200 Ripstick is now sold at a discount of 10%, what is the percentage profit of the price at which the shop bought the Ripstick?

b At what price should the Ripstick be sold to make 30% profit?

6 At Sunshine School there are 640 primary school students and 860 secondary students.

For their Christmas family holiday, 70% of primary school students go to the beach and 45% of secondary students go to the beach.

Determine the overall percentage of students in the whole school that has a beach holiday for Christmas. Write this percentage as a mixed numeral.

4

Algebraic techniques

Maths in context: Apps for agriculture

Algebra is important in many occupations, including for gaming and app developers. Australian farmers now have some very useful apps to help improve food production, efficiency, and profits. This technology has been developed by the scientists and programmers at CSIRO (Commonwealth Scientific and Industrial Research Organisation).

Soilmapp is an app based on CSIRO's soil data base. Australian soils are critical to our food production and farmers need to know how well their soil holds water, and its clay content and acidity.

Yield Prophet is an app that gives grain farmers a probability for higher or lower yields based on virtual choices of nitrogen fertilisers, irrigation and grain crop varieties. Using this app, farmers can adjust their plans and save large amounts of money.

Wheatcast is a website that uses technology to forecast the harvest volumes for Australia's 30 000 grain farmers. By relating current BOM weather data to CSIRO soil moisture maps, fortnightly forecasts of harvest volumes are provided for most locations.

Chapter contents

Victorian Curriculum 2.0

This chapter covers the following content descriptors in the Victorian Curriculum 2.0:

ALGEBRA

VC2M7A01, VC2M7A02, VC2M7A06

Please refer to the curriculum support documentation in the teacher resources for a full and comprehensive mapping of this chapter to the related curriculum content descriptors.

© VCAA

Online resources

A host of additional online resources are included as part of your Interactive Textbook, including HOTmaths content, video demonstrations of all worked examples, auto-marked quizzes and much more.

The EweWatch app keeps track of the mother sheep (the ewe) before, during and after giving birth to a lamb. The ewe wears a device to track her movements. This information helps farmers to locate any ewes that have birthing problems and need help.

4A   Introduction to algebra

LEARNING INTENTIONS
- To know the basic terminology of algebra
- To be able to identify coefficients, terms and constant terms within expressions
- To be able to write expressions from word descriptions

A *pronumeral* is a letter that can represent a number. The choice of letter used is not significant mathematically, but can be used as an aid to memory. For instance, s might stand for the number of goals scored and w kg might stand for someone's weight. Remember that each pronumeral stands in place of a number (e.g. the *number* of goals, the *number* of kilograms).

The table shows the salary Petra earns for various hours of work if she is paid $12 an hour.

Using pronumerals we can work out a total salary for any number of hours of work.

Numbers of hours	Salary earned ($)
1	$12 \times 1 = 12$
2	$12 \times 2 = 24$
3	$12 \times 3 = 36$
n	$12 \times n = 12n$

Rather than writing $12 \times n$, we write $12n$ because multiplying a pronumeral by a number is common and this notation saves space. We can also write $18 \div n$ as $\frac{18}{n}$.

Lesson starter: Pronumeral stories

Ahmed has a jar with b biscuits. He eats 3 biscuits and then shares the rest equally among 8 friends. Each friend receives $\frac{b-3}{8}$ biscuits. This is a short story for the expression $\frac{b-3}{8}$. (Note that b does not stand for '*biscuits*'. It stands in place of 'the *number* of biscuits'.)

- Try to create another story for $\frac{b-3}{8}$, and share it with others in the class.
- Can you construct a story for $2t + 12$? What about $4(k + 6)$?

KEY IDEAS

■ In algebra, letters can be used to stand for numbers. A **pronumeral** is a letter that stands for a number. If a pronumeral could represent *any* number rather than just a single number, it is also called a **variable**.

■ $a \times b$ is written as ab and $a \div b$ is written as $\frac{a}{b}$.

■ A **term** consists of numbers and variables/pronumerals combined with multiplication or division. For example, 5 is a term, x is a term, $9a$ is a term, abc is a term, $\frac{4xyz}{3}$ is a term.

■ A term that does not contain any variables/pronumerals is called a **constant term**. All numbers by themselves are constant terms.

■ An (**algebraic**) **expression** consists of numbers and variables/pronumerals combined with any mathematical operations. For example, $3x + 2yz$ is an expression and $8 \div (3a - 2b) + 41$ is also an expression.

■ A **coefficient** is the number in front of a variables/pronumerals. For example, the coefficient of y in the expression $8x + 2y + z$ is 2. If there is no number in front, then the coefficient is 1, since $1z$ and z are always equal, regardless of the value of z.

BUILDING UNDERSTANDING

1 The expression $4x + 3y + 24z + 7$ has four terms.
   a State all the terms.
   b What is the constant term?
   c What is the coefficient of x?
   d Which letter has a coefficient of 24?

2 Match each of the word descriptions on the left with the correct mathematical expression on the right.
   a the sum of x and 4   **A** $x - 4$
   b 4 less than x **B** $\frac{x}{4}$
   c the product of 4 and x **C** $4 - x$
   d one-quarter of x **D** $4x$
   e the result from subtracting x from 4 **E** $\frac{4}{x}$
   f 4 divided by x **F** $x + 4$

Example 1   Using the terminology of algebra

a State the individual terms in the expression $3a + b + 13c$.
b State the constant term in the expression $4a + 3b + 5$.
c State the coefficient of each pronumeral in the expression $3a + b + 13c$.

SOLUTION

a There are three terms: $3a$, b and $13c$.

b 5

c The coefficient of a is 3, the coefficient of b is 1 and the coefficient of c is 13.

EXPLANATION

Each part of an expression is a term. Terms are added (or subtracted) to make an expression.

The constant term is 5 because it has no pronumerals (whereas $4a$ and $3b$ both have pronumerals).

The coefficient is the number in front of a pronumeral. For b, the coefficient is 1 because b is the same as $1 \times b$.

Now you try

a List the individual terms in the expression $4q + 10r + s + 2t$.
b State the constant term in the expression $4q + 7r + 6$
c State the coefficient of each pronumeral in $4q + 10r + s + 2t$.

Example 2   Writing expressions from word descriptions

Write an expression for each of the following.
a 5 more than k b 3 less than m c the sum of a and b
d double the value of x e the product of c and d

SOLUTION

a $k + 5$

b $m - 3$

c $a + b$

d $2 \times x$ or $2x$

e $c \times d$ or cd

EXPLANATION

5 must be added to k to get 5 more than k.

3 is subtracted from m.

a and b are added to obtain their sum.

x is multiplied by 2. The multiplication sign is optional.

c and d are multiplied to obtain their product.

Now you try

Write an expression for each of the following.
a 10 more than p b the product of a and b c triple the value of k
d half the value of z e 4 less than b

Example 3   Writing expressions involving more than one operation

Write an expression for each of the following without using the × or ÷ symbols.

a p is halved, then 4 is added.

b   The sum of x and y is taken and then divided by 7.

c x is added to one-seventh of y.

d   5 is subtracted from k and the result is tripled.

SOLUTION

a $\dfrac{p}{2} + 4$

b $(x + y) \div 7 = \dfrac{x + y}{7}$

c $x + \dfrac{y}{7}$ or $x + \dfrac{1}{7}y$

d $(k - 5) \times 3 = 3(k - 5)$

EXPLANATION

p is divided by 2, then 4 is added.

x and y are added. This whole expression is divided by 7. By writing the result as a fraction, the brackets are no longer needed.

x is added to one-seventh of y, which is $\dfrac{y}{7}$.

5 subtracted from k gives the expression $k - 5$. Brackets must be used to multiply the whole expression by 3.

Now you try

Write an expression for each of the following without using the × or ÷ symbols.

a m is tripled and then 5 is added.

b   The sum of a and b is halved.

c   3 is subtracted from the product of p and q.

d   5 less than m is multiplied by 7.

Exercise 4A

FLUENCY   1–2(½), 3, 4– 5(½)   3–6(½)   4–7(½)

1   List the individual terms in the following expressions.

   a $3x + 2y$ **b** $4a + 2b + c$ **c** $5a + 3b + 2$ **d** $2x + 5$

2   State the constant term in the following expressions.

   a $7a + 5$ **b** $2x + 3y + 6$ **c** $8 + 3x + 2y$ **d** $5a + 1 + 3b$

3   **a**   State the coefficient of each pronumeral in the expression $2a + 3b + c$.

     b   State the coefficient of each pronumeral in the expression $4a + b + 6c + 2d$.

Example 1

4 For each of the following expressions, state:

    i the number of terms

    ii the coefficient of n.

a $17n + 24$ **b** $31 - 27a + 15n$

c $15nw + 21n + 15$ **d** $15a - 32b + 2n + \frac{4}{3}xy$

e $n + 51$ **f** $5bn - 12 + \frac{d}{5} + 12n$

Example 2

5 Write an expression for each of the following without using the × or ÷ symbols.

  a 1 more than x **b** the sum of k and 5

  c double the value of u **d** 4 lots of y

  e half of p **f** one-third of q

  g 12 less than r **h** the product of n and 9

  i t is subtracted from 10   **j** y is divided by 8

Example 3

6 Write an expression for each of the following without using the × or ÷ symbols.

  a 5 is added to x, then the result is doubled.

  b a is tripled, then 4 is added.

  c k is multiplied by 8, then 3 is subtracted.

  d 3 is subtracted from k, then the result is multiplied by 8.

  e The sum of x and y is multiplied by 6.

  f x is multiplied by 7 and the result is halved.

  g p is halved and then 2 is added.

  h The product of x and y is subtracted from 12.

7 Describe each of these expressions in words.

  a $7x$ **b** $a + b$ **c** $(x + 4) \times 2$ **d** $5 - 3a$

PROBLEM-SOLVING	8, 9	9–11	8–12

8 Nicholas buys 10 bags of lollies from a supermarket.

  a If there are 7 lollies in each bag, how many lollies does he buy in total?

  b If there are n lollies in each bag, how many lollies does he buy in total?

    (*Hint*: Write an expression involving n.)

9 Mikayla is paid $x per hour at her job. Write an expression for each of the following amounts (in $).

  a How much does Mikayla earn if she works 8 hours?

  b If Mikayla gets a pay rise of $3 per hour, what is her new hourly wage?

  c If Mikayla works for 8 hours at the increased hourly rate, how much does she earn?

10 Recall that there are 100 centimetres in 1 metre and 1000 metres in 1 kilometre. Write expressions for each of the following.
  a How many metres are there in x km?
  b How many centimetres are there in x metres?
  c How many centimetres are there in x km?

11 A group of people go out to a restaurant, and the total amount they must pay is $A. They decide to split the bill equally. Write expressions to answer the following questions.
  a If there are 4 people in the group, how much do they each pay?
  b If there are n people in the group, how much do they each pay?
  c One of the n people has a voucher that reduces the total bill by $20. How much does each person pay now?

12 There are many different ways of describing the expression $\dfrac{a+b}{4}$ in words. One way is: 'The sum of a and b is divided by 4.' What is another way?

REASONING	13	13, 15	14, 15

13 If x is a whole number between 10 and 99, classify each of these statements as true or false.
  a x must be smaller than $2 \times x$.
  b x must be smaller than $x + 2$.
  c $x - 3$ must be greater than 10.
  d $4 \times x$ must be an even number.
  e $3 \times x$ must be an odd number.

14 If b is an even number greater than 3, classify each of these statements as true or false.
  a $b + 1$ must be even.
  b $b + 2$ could be odd.
  c $5 + b$ could be greater than 10.
  d $5b$ must be greater than b.

15 If c is a number between 10 and 99, sort the following in ascending order (i.e. smallest to largest):
  $3c, 2c, c - 4, c \div 2, 3c + 5, 4c - 2, c + 1, c \times c$.

ENRICHMENT: Many words compressed	–	–	16

16 One advantage of writing expressions in symbols rather than words is that it takes up less space. For instance, 'twice the value of the sum of x and 5' uses eight words and can be written as $2(x + 5)$. Give an example of a worded expression that uses more than 10 words and then write it as a mathematical expression.

4B Substituting numbers into algebraic expressions

LEARNING INTENTIONS
- To understand that variables/pronumerals can be replaced with numbers
- To be able to substitute numbers for variables/pronumerals
- To be able to evaluate an expression using order of operations once all variable/pronumeral values are known

Evaluation of expressions involves replacing pronumerals (like x and y) with numbers and obtaining a single number as a result. For example, we can evaluate $4 + x$ when x is 11, to get 15.

Lesson starter: Sum to 10

The pronumerals x and y could stand for any number.

- What numbers could x and y stand for if you know that $x + y$ must equal 10? Try to list as many pairs as possible.
- If $x + y$ must equal 10, what values could $3x + y$ equal? Find the largest and smallest values.

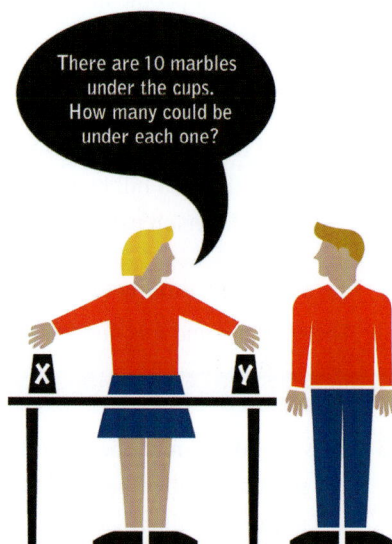

There are 10 marbles under the cups. How many could be under each one?

KEY IDEAS

■ To **evaluate** an expression or to **substitute** values means to replace each variable/pronumeral in an expression with a number to obtain a final value. For example, if $x = 3$ and $y = 8$, then $x + 2y$ evaluated gives $3 + 2 \times 8 = 19$.

■ A term like $4a$ means $4 \times a$. When substituting a number we must consider the multiplication operation, since two numbers written as 42 is very different from the product 4×2.

■ Once an expression contains no pronumerals, evaluate using the normal order of operations seen in Chapter 1:
- brackets
- multiplication and division from left to right
- addition and subtraction from left to right.

  For example:
$$(4 + 3) \times 2 - 20 \div 4 + 2 = 7 \times 2 - 20 \div 4 + 2$$
$$= 14 - 5 + 2$$
$$= 9 + 2$$
$$= 11$$

BUILDING UNDERSTANDING

1 Use the correct order of operations to evaluate the following.
   a $4 + 2 \times 5$
   b $7 - 3 \times 2$
   c $3 \times 6 - 2 \times 4$
   d $(7 - 3) \times 2$

2 What number would you get if you replaced b with 5 in the expression $8 + b$?

3 What number is obtained when $x = 3$ is substituted into the expression $5 \times x$?

4 What is the result of evaluating $10 - u$ if u is 7?

5 Calculate the value of $12 + b$ if:
   a $b = 5$
   b $b = 8$
   c $b = 60$
   d $b = 0$

Engineers, welders and metal workers regularly substitute values into formulas. A circular steel plate, used when constructing a large airduct, can have an area of: $A = \pi r^2 = \pi \times 0.7^2 = 1.5 \text{m}^2$ (using one decimal place).

Example 4   Substituting a variable/pronumeral

Given that $t = 5$, evaluate:
a $t + 7$ **b** $8t$ **c** $\dfrac{10}{t} + 4 - t$

SOLUTION

a $t + 7 = 5 + 7$
        $= 12$

b $8t = 8 \times t$
     $= 8 \times 5$
     $= 40$

c $\dfrac{10}{t} + 4 - t = \dfrac{10}{5} + 4 - 5$
              $= 2 + 4 - 5$
              $= 1$

EXPLANATION

Replace t with 5 and then evaluate the expression, which now contains no pronumerals.

Insert $\times$ where it was previously implied, then substitute 5 for t. If the multiplication sign is not included, we might get a completely incorrect answer of 85.

Replace all occurrences of t with 5 before evaluating. Note that the division $(10 \div 5)$ is calculated before the addition and subtraction.

Now you try

Given that $u = 3$, evaluate:
a $4u$ **b** $8 - u$ **c** $2u + \dfrac{12}{u} - 3$

Example 5   Substituting multiple variables/pronumerals

Substitute $x = 4$ and $y = 7$ to evaluate these expressions.

a $5x + y + 8$

b $80 - (2xy + y)$

SOLUTION	EXPLANATION
a $\begin{aligned} 5x + y + 8 &= 5 \times x + y + 8 \\ &= 5 \times 4 + 7 + 8 \\ &= 20 + 7 + 8 \\ &= 35 \end{aligned}$	Insert the implied multiplication sign between 5 and x before substituting the values for x and y.
b $\begin{aligned} 80 - (2xy + y) &= 80 - (2 \times x \times y + y) \\ &= 80 - (2 \times 4 \times 7 + 7) \\ &= 80 - (56 + 7) \\ &= 80 - 63 \\ &= 17 \end{aligned}$	Insert the multiplication signs, and remember the order in which to evaluate. Note that both occurrences of y are replaced with 7.

Now you try

Substitute $p = 3$ and $q = 10$ to evaluate these expressions.

a $4p - q + 2$

b $pq + 3 \times (q - 2p)$

Example 6   Substituting with powers and roots

If $p = 4$ and $t = 5$, find the value of:

a $3p^2$

b $t^2 + p^3$

c $\sqrt{p^2 + 3^2}$

SOLUTION	EXPLANATION
a $\begin{aligned} 3p^2 &= 3 \times p \times p \\ &= 3 \times 4 \times 4 \\ &= 48 \end{aligned}$	Note that $3p^2$ means $3 \times p \times p$ not $(3 \times p)^2$.
b $\begin{aligned} t^2 + p^3 &= 5^2 + 4^3 \\ &= 5 \times 5 + 4 \times 4 \times 4 \\ &= 25 + 64 \\ &= 89 \end{aligned}$	t is replaced with 5, and p is replaced with 4. Remember that 4^3 means $4 \times 4 \times 4$.
c $\begin{aligned} \sqrt{p^2 + 3^2} &= \sqrt{4^2 + 3^2} \\ &= \sqrt{25} \\ &= 5 \end{aligned}$	Recall that the square root of 25 is 5 because $5 \times 5 = 25$.

Now you try

If $x = 3$ and $y = 8$, find the value of:

a $4x^2$

b $x^3 + y^2$

c $\sqrt{10^2 - y^2}$

Exercise 4B

FLUENCY	1–3($\frac{1}{2}$), 6–7($\frac{1}{2}$)	1–7($\frac{1}{2}$)	4–8($\frac{1}{2}$)

Example 4a,b

1 Given $t = 5$, evaluate:

   a $t + 2$ **b** $t - 1$ **c** $t \times 2$ **d** $t \times 3$

Example 4a,b

2 Given $x = 7$, evaluate:

   a $x - 3$ **b** $x + 5$ **c** $2x$ **d** $10x$

Example 4

3 If $k = 4$, evaluate:

   a $3k + 1$ **b** $2k - 3$ **c** $10 - k$ **d** $12 - 2k$

Example 4

4 If $x = 5$, evaluate each of the following.

   a $2(x + 2) + x$ **b** $30 - (4x + 1)$

   c $\dfrac{20}{x} + 3$ **d** $(x + 5) \times \dfrac{10}{x}$

   e $\dfrac{x + 7}{4}$ **f** $\dfrac{10 - x}{x}$

   g $7x + 3(x - 1)$ **h** $40 - 3x - x$

   i $x + x(x + 1)$ **j** $\dfrac{30}{x} + 2x(x + 3)$

   k $100 - 4(3 + 4x)$ **l** $\dfrac{6(3x - 8)}{x + 2}$

Example 5

5 Substitute $a = 2$ and $b = 3$ into each of these expressions and evaluate.

   a $a + b$ **b** $3a + b$

   c $5a - 2b$ **d** $7ab + b$

   e $ab - 4 + b$ **f** $2 \times (3a + 2b)$

   g $\dfrac{8}{a} - \dfrac{12}{b}$ **h** $\dfrac{12}{a} + \dfrac{6}{b}$

Example 5

6 Evaluate the expression $5x + 2y$ when:

   a $x = 3$ and $y = 6$ **b** $x = 4$ and $y = 1$

   c $x = 7$ and $y = 3$ **d** $x = 0$ and $y = 4$

   e $x = 2$ and $y = 0$ **f** $x = 10$ and $y = 10$

7 Copy and complete each of these tables.

   a

n	1	2	3	4	5	6
$n + 4$	5			8		

   b

x	1	2	3	4	5	6
$12 - x$			9			

   c

b	1	2	3	4	5	6
$2(b - 1)$						

   d

q	1	2	3	4	5	6
$10q - q$						

Example 6   **8**   Evaluate each of the following, given $a = 9$, $b = 3$ and $c = 5$.

a $3c^2$

b $5b^2$

c $a^2 - 3^3$

d $2b^2 + \dfrac{a}{3} - 2c$

e $\sqrt{a} + \sqrt{3ab}$

f $\sqrt{b^2 + 4^2}$

g $24 + \dfrac{2b^3}{6}$

h $(2c)^2 - a^2$

PROBLEM-SOLVING	9	9, 11	10, 11

9   A number is substituted for b in the expression $7 + b$ and gives the result 12. What is the value of b?

10   A whole number is substituted for x in the expression $3x - 1$. If the result is a two-digit number, what value might x have? Try to describe all the possible answers.

11   Copy and complete the table.

x	5	9	12			
$x + 6$	11		7			
$4x$	20			24	28	

REASONING	12	12, 13	13, 14

12   Assume x and y are two numbers, where $xy = 24$.

   a   What values could x and y equal if they are whole numbers? Try to list as many as possible.

   b   What values could x and y equal if they can be decimals, fractions or whole numbers?

13   Dugald substitutes different whole numbers into the expression $5 \times (a + a)$. He notices that the result always ends in the digit 0. Try a few values and explain why this pattern occurs.

14   Values of x and y are substituted into the expression $x + 2y$ and the result is 100.

   a   Find a possible value for x and y to make $x + 2y$ equal 100.

   b   If the same values of x and y are substituted into the expression $3x + 6y$, what is the result?

   c   Explain why your answer to part **b** will always be the same, regardless of which pair you chose in part **a**.

ENRICHMENT: Missing numbers	–	–	15

15   **a**   Copy and complete the following table. Note that x and y are whole numbers (0, 1, 2, 3, …) for this table.

x	5	10	7			
y	3	4		5		
$x + y$			9	14	7	
$x - y$	2				3	8
xy		40			10	0

   b   If x and y are two numbers where $x + y$ and $x \times y$ are equal, what values might x and y have? Try to find at least three (they do not have to be whole numbers).

4C Equivalent algebraic expressions

LEARNING INTENTIONS
• To know what it means for two expressions to be equivalent
• To be able to determine whether two expressions are equivalent using substitution
• To be able to generalise number facts using algebra

Like using words from a language, there are often many ways in algebra to express the same thing. For example, we can write 'the sum of x and 4' as $x + 4$ or $4 + x$, or even $x + 1 + 1 + 1 + 1$.

No matter what number x is, $x + 4$ and $4 + x$ will always be equal. We say that the expressions $x + 4$ and $4 + x$ are equivalent because of this.

By substituting different numbers for the pronumerals it is possible to see whether two expressions are equivalent. Consider the four expressions in this table.

When identical houses are built, a window supplier can multiply the number of windows, w, ordered for one house by the number of houses. This is equivalent to adding all the windows. For example, for four houses, $4w = w + w + w + w$.

	$3a + 5$	$2a + 6$	$7a + 5 - 4a$	$a + a + 6$
$a = 0$	5	6	5	6
$a = 1$	8	8	8	8
$a = 2$	11	10	11	10
$a = 3$	14	12	14	12
$a = 4$	17	14	17	14

From this table it becomes apparent that $3a + 5$ and $7a + 5 - 4a$ are equivalent, and that $2a + 6$ and $a + a + 6$ are equivalent.

Lesson starter: Equivalent expressions

Consider the expression $2a + 4$.

• Write as many different expressions as possible that are equivalent to $2a + 4$.
• How many equivalent expressions are there?
• Try to give a logical explanation for why $2a + 4$ is equivalent to $4 + a \times 2$.

$$= a + a + a + 6$$
$$= 3a + 3 + 3$$
$$= 2a + 6 + a$$
$$= \dots$$

This collection of pronumerals and numbers can be arranged into many different equivalent expressions.

KEY IDEAS

■ Two expressions are called **equivalent** when they are always equal, regardless of what numbers are substituted for the pronumerals.
  For example:
  • $x + 12$ is equivalent to $12 + x$, because the order in which numbers are added is not important.
  • $3k$ is equivalent to $k + k + k$, because multiplying by a whole number is the same as adding repeatedly.

■ The rules of algebra are used to prove that two expressions are equivalent, but a table of values can be helpful to test whether expressions are likely to be equivalent.

BUILDING UNDERSTANDING

1 **a** State the missing numbers in this table.

  b State the missing word: $2x + 2$ and $(x + 1) \times 2$ are _____ expressions.

	$x = 0$	$x = 1$	$x = 2$	$x = 3$
$2x + 2$				
$(x + 1) \times 2$				

2 **a** State the missing numbers in this table.

  b Are $5x + 3$ and $6x + 3$ equivalent expressions?

	$x = 0$	$x = 1$	$x = 2$	$x = 3$
$5x + 3$				
$6x + 3$				

Example 7   Identifying equivalent expressions

Which two of these expressions are equivalent: $3x + 4$, $8 - x$, $2x + 4 + x$?

SOLUTION

$3x + 4$ and $2x + 4 + x$ are equivalent.

EXPLANATION

By drawing a table of values, we can see straight away that $3x + 4$ and $8 - x$ are not equivalent, since they differ for $x = 2$.

	$x = 1$	$x = 2$	$x = 3$
$3x + 4$	7	10	13
$8 - x$	7	6	5
$2x + 4 + x$	7	10	13

$3x + 4$ and $2x + 4 + x$ are equal for all values, so they are equivalent.

Now you try

Which two of these expressions are equivalent: $2a + 6$, $6a + 2$, $(a + 3) \times 2$, $8a$?

Example 8   Generalising number facts with algebra

Generalise the following number facts to find two equivalent expressions.

a $5 + 5 = 2 \times 5$, $7 + 7 = 2 \times 7$, $10 + 10 = 2 \times 10$ (Use x to stand for the number.)

b $2 + 7 = 7 + 2$, $4 + 5 = 5 + 4$, $12 + 14 = 14 + 12$ (Use a and b to stand for the numbers.)

SOLUTION

a $x + x = 2x$

b $a + b = b + a$

EXPLANATION

Each of the statements is in the form $\boxed{} + \boxed{} = 2 \times \boxed{}$, where the value of $\boxed{}$ is the same.

Use x to stand for the number in $\boxed{}$, and recall that $2 \times x$ is written $2x$.

Here there are two numbers which vary, but the pattern is always $a + b = b + a$.

For example, if $a = 2$ and $b = 7$, we get the fact $2 + 7 = 7 + 2$.

Now you try

Generalise the following number facts to find two equivalent expressions.

a $10 \times 5 \times 10 = 5 \times 100$, $10 \times 7 \times 10 = 7 \times 100$, $10 \times 3 \times 10 = 3 \times 100$ (Use x to stand for the number.)

b $4 \times 7 = 7 \times 4$, $3 \times 9 = 9 \times 3$, $12 \times 4 = 4 \times 12$ (Use a and b to stand for the numbers.)

Exercise 4C

FLUENCY	1, 2(½), 3, 5	2–5(½), 6	3–5(½), 6

Example 7

1 Decide if the following pairs of expression are equivalent (E) or not equivalent (N).

a $3x$, $2x + 4$

b $5 + a$, $a + 5$

c $2d$, $d + d$

Example 7

2 Pick the two expressions that are equivalent.

a $2x + 3$, $2x - 3$, $x + 3 + x$
b $5x - 2$, $3x - 2 + 2x$, $2x + 3x + 2$
c $4x$, $2x + 4$, $x + 4 + x$
d $5a$, $4a + a$, $3 + a$
e $2k + 2$, $3 + 2k$, $2(k + 1)$
f $b + b$, $3b$, $4b - 2b$

Example 8a

3 Generalise the following number facts to find two equivalent expressions. In each case, use x to stand for the number.

a $4 + 4 + 4 = 3 \times 4$, $7 + 7 + 7 = 3 \times 7$, $10 + 10 + 10 = 3 \times 10$

b $2 \times 7 \times 2 = 4 \times 7$, $2 \times 12 \times 2 = 4 \times 12$, $2 \times 15 \times 2 = 4 \times 15$

c $5 + 99 = 5 - 1 + 100$, $7 + 99 = 7 - 1 + 100$, $12 + 99 = 12 - 1 + 100$

d $2 \times (10 + 1) = 20 + 2 \times 1$, $2 \times (10 + 4) = 20 + 2 \times 4$, $2 \times (10 + 7) = 20 + 2 \times 7$

Example 8b

4   Generalise the following number facts to find two equivalent expressions. In each case, use a and b to stand for the numbers.

   a Fact 1: $10 \times (1 + 4) = 10 \times 1 + 10 \times 4$
       Fact 2: $10 \times (3 + 9) = 10 \times 3 + 10 \times 9$
       Fact 3: $10 \times (7 + 2) = 10 \times 7 + 10 \times 2$

   b Fact 1: $5 + 100 + 3 = 3 + 100 + 5$
       Fact 2: $9 + 100 + 8 = 8 + 100 + 9$
       Fact 3: $17 + 100 + 2 = 2 + 100 + 17$

   c Fact 1: $(3 + 1)(3 - 1) = 3^2 - 1^2$
       Fact 2: $(5 + 2)(5 - 2) = 5^2 - 2^2$
       Fact 3: $(9 + 4)(9 - 4) = 9^2 - 4^2$

   d Fact 1: $3 \times 4 + 4 \times 3 = 2 \times 3 \times 4$
       Fact 2: $7 \times 8 + 8 \times 7 = 2 \times 7 \times 8$
       Fact 3: $12 \times 5 + 5 \times 12 = 2 \times 12 \times 5$

5   Match up the equivalent expressions below.

a	$3x + 2x$	**A**	$6 - 3x$
b	$4 - 3x + 2$	**B**	$2x + 4x + x$
c	$2x + 5 + x$	**C**	$5x$
d	$x + x - 5 + x$	**D**	$4 - x$
e	$7x$	**E**	$3x + 5$
f	$4 - 3x + 2x$	**F**	$3x - 5$

6   Demonstrate that $6x + 5$ and $4x + 5 + 2x$ are likely to be equivalent by completing the table.

	$6x + 5$	$4x + 5 + 2x$
$x = 1$		
$x = 2$		
$x = 3$		
$x = 4$		

PROBLEM-SOLVING   7   7, 8   8, 9

7   Write two different expressions that are equivalent to $4x + 2$.

8   The rectangle shown below has a perimeter given by $w + l + w + l$.
   Write an equivalent expression for the perimeter.

9   There are many expressions that are equivalent to $3a + 5b + 2a - b + 4a$.
   Write an equivalent expression with as few terms as possible.

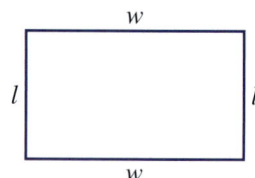

REASONING   10   11, 12   11–13

10 Prove that no pair of these four expressions is equivalent: $4 + x$, $4x$, $x - 4$, $x \div 4$. (*Hint:* substitute a value for x, like $x = 8$.)

11 Generalise each of the following patterns in numbers to give two equivalent expressions. In each case, choose pronumerals starting at 'a' (as many as required to handle the observation provided). The first one has been done for you.

   a Observation: $3 + 5 = 5 + 3$ and $2 + 7 = 7 + 2$ and $4 + 11 = 11 + 4$.

      Generalised: The two expressions $a + b$ and $b + a$ are equivalent.

   b Observation: $2 \times 5 = 5 \times 2$ and $11 \times 5 = 5 \times 11$ and $3 \times 12 = 12 \times 3$.

   c Observation: $4 \times (10 + 3) = 4 \times 10 + 4 \times 3$ and $8 \times (100 + 5) = 8 \times 100 + 8 \times 5$.

   d Observation: $100 - (4 + 6) = 100 - 4 - 6$ and $70 - (10 + 5) = 70 - 10 - 5$.

   e Observation: $20 - (4 - 2) = 20 - 4 + 2$ and $15 - (10 - 3) = 15 - 10 + 3$.

   f Observation: $100 \div 5 \div 10 = 100 \div (5 \times 10)$ and $30 \div 2 \div 3 = 30 \div (2 \times 3)$.

12 From two equivalent expressions, you can substitute values for the pronumerals to get particular number facts. For example, because $x + 4$ and $4 + x$ are equivalent, we can get number facts like $2 + 4 = 4 + 2$ and $103 + 4 = 4 + 103$ (and others). Use the following pairs of equivalent expressions to give three particular number facts.

   a $x + 12$ and $12 + x$ **b** $2(q + 1)$ and $2 + 2q$ **c** $(a + b)^2$ and $a^2 + 2ab + b^2$

13 **a** Show that the expression $4 \times (a + 2)$ is equivalent to $8 + 4a$, using a table of values for a between 1 and 4.

   b Write an expression using brackets that is equivalent to $10 + 5a$.

   c Write an expression without brackets that is equivalent to $6 \times (4 + a)$.

ENRICHMENT: Thinking about equivalence   –   –   14, 15

14 $3a + 5b$ is an expression containing two terms. List two expressions containing three terms that are equivalent to $3a + 5b$.

15 Three expressions are given: expression A, expression B and expression C.

   a If expressions A and B are equivalent, and expressions B and C are equivalent, does this mean that expressions A and C are equivalent? Try to prove your answer.

   b If expressions A and B are not equivalent, and expressions B and C are not equivalent, does this mean that expressions A and C are not equivalent? Try to prove your answer.

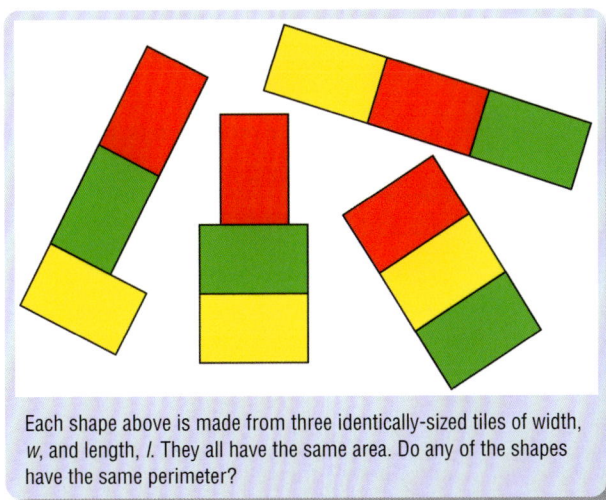

Each shape above is made from three identically-sized tiles of width, w, and length, l. They all have the same area. Do any of the shapes have the same perimeter?

4D Like terms

Whenever we have terms with exactly the same pronumeral parts, they are called 'like terms' and can be collected. For example, $3x + 5x$ can be simplified to $8x$. If the two terms do not have exactly the same pronumerals, they must be kept separate; for example, $3x + 5y$ cannot be simplified – it must be left as it is.

Recall from arithmetic that numbers can be multiplied in any order (e.g. $5 \times 3 = 3 \times 5$). This means pronumerals can appear in a different order within a term and give equivalent expressions (e.g. ab and ba are equivalent).

A vet has 3 rows of animal cages with 4 cages per row. Each cage is L cm by H cm. The total length of the cages in centimetres is $L + L + L + L = 4L$ and total height in centimetres is $H + H + H = 3H$. If another row is added, the height is $3H + H = 4H$.

Lesson starter: Simplifying expressions

- Try to find a simpler expression that is equivalent to

$$1a + 2b + 3a + 4b + 5a + 6b + \ldots + 19a + 20b$$

- What is the longest possible expression that is equivalent to $10a + 20b + 30c$? Assume that all coefficients must be whole numbers greater than zero.
- Compare your expressions to see who has the longest one.

KEY IDEAS

■ **Like terms** are terms containing exactly the same pronumerals, although not necessarily in the same order.

Like	Not like
$3x$ and $5x$	$3x$ and $5y$
$-12a$ and $7a$	$11d$ and $4c$
$5ab$ and $6ba$	$-8ab$ and $5a$
$4x^2$ and $3x^2$	x^2 and x

■ Like terms can be combined within an expression to create a simpler expression that is equivalent. For example, $5ab + 3ab$ can be simplified to $8ab$.

■ If two terms are not like terms (such as $4x$ and $5y$), they can still be added to get an expression like $4x + 5y$, but this expression cannot be simplified further.

BUILDING UNDERSTANDING

1 For each of the following terms, state all the pronumerals that occur in it.

    a $4xy$ **b** $3abc$ **c** $2k$ **d** pq

2 State the missing words or expressions to make the sentences true. More than one answer might be possible.

    a $3x$ and $5x$ are _____ terms.

    b $4x$ and $3y$ are not _____ _____.

    c $4xy$ and $4yx$ are like _____.

    d $4a$ and _____ are like terms.

    e $x + x + 7$ and $2x + 7$ are _____ expressions.

    f $3x + 2x + 4$ can be written in an equivalent way as _____.

Example 9   Identifying like terms

Classify the following pairs as like terms or not like terms.

a $3x$ and $2x$ **b** $3a$ and $3b$ **c** $2ab$ and $5ba$

d $4k$ and k **e** $2a$ and $4ab$ **f** $7ab$ and $9aba$

SOLUTION

a $3x$ and $2x$ are like terms.

b $3a$ and $3b$ are not like terms.

c $2ab$ and $5ba$ are like terms.

d $4k$ and k are like terms.

e $2a$ and $4ab$ are not like terms.

f $7ab$ and $9aba$ are not like terms.

EXPLANATION

The pronumerals are the same.

The pronumerals are different.

The pronumerals are the same, even though they are written in a different order (one a and one b).

The pronumerals are the same.

The pronumerals are not exactly the same (the first term contains only a and the second term has a and b).

The pronumerals are not exactly the same (the first term contains one a and one b, but the second term contains two copies of a and one b).

Now you try

Classify the following pairs as like terms or not like terms.

a $4x$ and $3y$ **b** $7a$ and $9a$ **c** $3xy$ and $4xyx$

d $4j$ and j **e** $8bc$ and $9cb$ **f** $9pq$ and $10p$

Example 10   Simplifying using like terms

Simplify the following by collecting like terms.

a $7b + 2 + 3b$

b $12d - 4d + d$

c $5 + 12a + 4b - 2 - 3a$

d $13a + 8b + 2a - 5b - 4a$

e $12uv + 7v - 3vu + 3v$

SOLUTION	EXPLANATION
a $7b + 2 + 3b = 10b + 2$	$7b$ and $3b$ are like terms, so they are added. They cannot be combined with the term 2 because it is not 'like' $7b$ or $3b$.
b $12d - 4d + d = 9d$	All the terms here are like terms. Remember that d means $1d$ when combining them.
c $\quad 5 + 12a + 4b - 2 - 3a$ $= 12a - 3a + 4b + 5 - 2$ $= 9a + 4b + 3$	$12a$ and $3a$ are like terms, so we first bring them to the front of the expression. We subtract $3a$ because it has a minus sign in front of it. We can also combine the 5 and the 2 because they are like terms.
d $\quad 13a + 8b + 2a - 5b - 4a$ $= 13a + 2a - 4a + 8b - 5b$ $= 11a + 3b$	First, rearrange to bring like terms together. Combine like terms, remembering to subtract any term that has a minus sign in front of it.
e $\quad 12uv + 7v - 3vu + 3v$ $= 12uv - 3vu + 7v + 3v$ $= 9uv + 10v$	Combine like terms. Remember that $12uv$ and $3vu$ are like terms (i.e. they have the same pronumerals), so $12uv - 3uv = 9uv$.

Now you try

Simplify the following by collecting like terms.

a $3a + 4 + 12a$

b $10q + 3q - 9q$

c $4x + 13y + 2x + 3 + 5y$

d $9a + 4b - 3a - 3b + a$

e $10uv + 3u - 2vu + 7u + 2v$

Exercise 4D

| FLUENCY | 1, 2–4(½) | 2–5(½) | 2(½), 4–5(½) |

Example 9

1 Classify the following pairs as like terms (L) or not like terms (N).

a $6x$ and $3x$ b $5a$ and $7b$ c $3d$ and $9d$ d $2x$ and $2y$

Example 9

2 Classify the following pairs as like terms (L) or not like terms (N).

a $7a$ and $4b$ b $3a$ and $10a$ c $18x$ and $32x$ d $4a$ and $4b$

e 7 and $10b$ f x and $4x$ g $5x$ and 5 h $12ab$ and $4ab$

i $7cd$ and $12cd$ j $3abc$ and $12abc$ k $3ab$ and $2ba$ l $4cd$ and $3dce$

Example 10

3 Simplify the following by collecting like terms.

a $a + a$ b $3x + 2x$ c $4b + 3b$ d $12d - 4d$

e $15u - 3u$ f $14ab - 2ab$ g $8ab + 3ab$ h $4xy - 3xy$

Example 10

4 Simplify the following by collecting like terms.

a $2a + a + 4b + b$ b $5a + 2a + b + 8b$ c $3x - 2x + 2y + 4y$

d $4a + 2 + 3a$ e $7 + 2b + 5b$ f $3k - 2 + 3k$

g $7f + 4 - 2f + 8$ h $4a - 4 + 5b + b$ i $3x + 7x + 3y - 4x + y$

j $10a + 3 + 4b - 2a$ k $4 + 10h - 3h$ l $10x + 4x + 31y - y$

m $10 + 7y - 3x + 5x + 2y$ n $11a + 4 - 3a + 9$ o $3b + 4b + c + 5b - c$

Example 10

5 Simplify the following by collecting like terms.

a $7ab + 4 + 2ab$ b $9xy + 2x - 3xy + 3x$ c $2cd + 5dc - 3d + 2c$

d $5uv + 12v + 4uv - 5v$ e $7pq + 2p + 4qp - q$ f $7ab + 32 - ab + 4$

| PROBLEM-SOLVING | 6, 7 | 8, 9(½) | 7, 8, 9(½) |

6 Josh and Caitlin each work for n hours per week. Josh earns \$27 per hour and Caitlin earns \$31 per hour.

a Write an expression for the amount Josh earns in one week (in dollars).

b Write an expression for the amount Caitlin earns in one week (in dollars).

c Write a simplified expression for the total amount Josh and Caitlin earn in one week (in dollars).

7 The length of the line segment shown could be expressed as $a + a + 3 + a + 1$.

$$a \quad a \quad 3 \quad a \quad 1$$

a Write the length in the simplest form.

b What is the length of the segment if a is equal to 5?

8   Let x represent the number of marbles in a
     standard-sized bag. Xavier bought 4 bags
     and Cameron bought 7 bags. Write simplified
     expressions for:
   a   the number of marbles Xavier has
   b   the number of marbles Cameron has
   c   the total number of marbles that Xavier and
       Cameron have
   d   the number of *extra* marbles that Cameron
       has compared to Xavier.

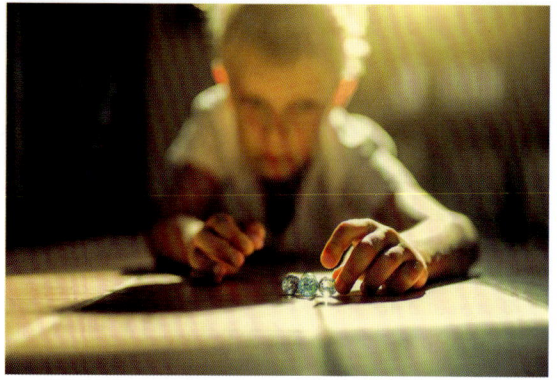

9   Simplify the following expressions as much as
     possible.
   a $3xy + 4xy + 5xy$ b $4ab + 5 + 2ab$ c $5ab + 3ba + 2ab$
   d $10xy - 4yx + 3$ e $10 - 3xy + 8xy + 4$ f $3cde + 5ecd + 2ced$
   g $4 + x + 4xy + 2xy + 5x$ h $12ab + 7 - 3ab + 2$ i $3xy - 2y + 4yx$

REASONING	10	10, 11	11, 12

10 a   Demonstrate, using a table of values, that $3x + 2x$ is equivalent to $5x$.
    b   Prove that $3x + 2y$ is not equivalent to $5xy$.

11 a   Demonstrate that $5x + 4 - 2x$ is equivalent to $3x + 4$.
    b   Prove that $5x + 4 - 2x$ is not equivalent to $7x + 4$.
    c   Prove that $5x + 4 - 2x$ is not equivalent to $7x - 4$.

12 a   Generalise the following number facts, using x to stand for the variable number.
        Fact 1: $18 \times 10 - 15 \times 10 = 3 \times 10$
        Fact 2: $18 \times 7 - 15 \times 7 = 3 \times 7$
        Fact 3: $18 \times 11 - 15 \times 11 = 3 \times 11$
    b   Explain how to find $18 \times 17 - 15 \times 17$ in the least number of calculations. You should also explain
        why your method will work.
    c   State the value of $18 \times 17 - 15 \times 17$.

ENRICHMENT: How many rearrangements?	–	–	13

13 The expression $a + 3b + 2a$ is equivalent to $3a + 3b$.
    a   List two other expressions with three terms that are equivalent to $3a + 3b$.
    b   How many expressions, consisting of exactly three terms added together, are equivalent to $3a + 3b$?
        All coefficients must be whole numbers greater than 0.

4A

1 For the expression $7a + 4b + c + 9$, answer the following.
  a State the number of terms.
  b List the individual terms.
  c State the coefficient of b.
  d What is the constant term?

4A

2 Write an expression for each of the following.
  a the product of m and p
  b the sum of a and k
  c 8 more than t
  d 4 less than w

4A

3 Write an expression for each of the following without using the ÷ or × symbols.
  a m is halved, then 7 is added.
  b 7 is added to m and then the result is halved.
  c The sum of a and k is taken and then divided by 3.
  d a is added to one-third of k.
  e 12 is subtracted from d and the result is tripled.
  f d is tripled and 12 is subtracted from the result.

4B

4 If $x = 4$, evaluate each of the following.
  a $3x + 7$
  b $\frac{20}{x} + 2 - x$
  c $18 - (2x + 1)$

4B

5 Substitute $a = 5$ and $b = 2$ into each of these expressions and evaluate.
  a $3a + b + 7$
  b $20 - (a + 2b)$
  c $\frac{35}{a + b}$
  d $5 + a^2 - 2b^2$
  e $\sqrt{a^2 - 16}$

4C

6 Which two of the following expressions are equivalent?
$3a + 4, 4a + 3, 4 + 3a, 7a$

4C

7 Generalise the following number facts to find two equivalent expressions.
  a Use x to stand for the number.
    Fact 1: $2 + 10 = 10 + 2$
    Fact 2: $5 + 10 = 10 + 5$
    Fact 3: $11 + 10 = 10 + 11$

  b Use a and b to stand for the numbers.
    Fact 1: $2 \times 3 + 2 \times 5 = 2 \times (3 + 5)$
    Fact 2: $2 \times 7 + 2 \times 9 = 2 \times (7 + 9)$
    Fact 3: $2 \times 11 + 2 \times 4 = 2 \times (11 + 4)$

4D

8 Classify the following pairs as like terms (L) or not like terms (N).
  a $3a$ and $8a$
  b $3x$ and $3xy$
  c 6 and $6a$
  d $4mp$ and $5pm$

4D

9 Simplify the following by collecting like terms.
  a $7a + 2b + 5 + a + 3b$
  b $2cd + 4c + 8d + 5dc - c + 4$

4C

10 Archie has two part-time jobs each paying \$8 per hour. He works x hours at one job and y hours at the other. Write two equivalent expressions for the total amount of money, in dollars, that he earns.

4E Multiplying and dividing expressions

When multiplying a number by a pronumeral, we have already seen we can write them next to each other. For example, $7a$ means $7 \times a$, and $5abc$ means $5 \times a \times b \times c$. The order in which numbers or pronumerals are multiplied is unimportant, so $5 \times a \times b \times c = a \times 5 \times c \times b = c \times a \times 5 \times b$. When writing a product without $\times$ signs, the numbers are written first.

We write $\dfrac{7xy}{3xz}$ as shorthand for $(7xy) \div (3xz)$.

We can simplify fractions like $\dfrac{10}{15}$ by dividing by common factors such as $\dfrac{10}{15} = \dfrac{5 \times 2}{5 \times 3} = \dfrac{2}{3}$.

Similarly, common pronumerals can be cancelled in a division like $\dfrac{7xy}{3xz}$, giving $\dfrac{7xy}{3xz} = \dfrac{7y}{3z}$.

Lesson starter: Rearranging terms

$5abc$ is equivalent to $5bac$ because the order of multiplication does not matter. In what other ways could $5abc$ be written?

$5 \times a \times b \times c = ?$

KEY IDEAS

- $a \times b$ is written as ab.

- $a \div b$ is written as $\dfrac{a}{b}$.

- $a \times a$ is written as a^2.

- Because of the commutative property of multiplication (e.g. $2 \times 7 = 7 \times 2$), the order in which values are multiplied is not important. So $3 \times a$ and $a \times 3$ are equivalent.

- Because of the associative property of multiplication (e.g. $3 \times (5 \times 2)$ and $(3 \times 5) \times 2$ are equal), brackets are not required when only multiplication is used. So $3 \times (a \times b)$ and $(3 \times a) \times b$ are both written as $3ab$.

- Numbers should be written first in a term and pronumerals are generally written in alphabetical order. For example, $b \times 2 \times a$ is written as $2ab$.

- When dividing, any common factor in the numerator and denominator can be cancelled.

  For example: $\dfrac{^2\cancel{4}a^1\cancel{b}}{^1\cancel{2}^1\cancel{b}c} = \dfrac{2a}{c}$

BUILDING UNDERSTANDING

1 Chen claims that $7 \times d$ is equivalent to $d \times 7$.

   a If $d = 3$, find the values of $7 \times d$ and $d \times 7$.

   b If $d = 5$, find the values of $7 \times d$ and $d \times 7$.

   c If $d = 8$, find the values of $7 \times d$ and $d \times 7$.

   d Is Chen correct in his claim?

2 Classify each of the following statements as true or false.

   a $4 \times n$ can be written as $4n$.

   b $n \times 3$ can be written as $3n$.

   c $4 \times b$ can be written as $b + 4$.

   d $a \times b$ can be written as ab.

   e $a \times 5$ can be written as $50a$.

   f $a \times a$ can be written as $2a$.

3 **a** Simplify the fraction $\frac{12}{18}$. (Note: This is the same as $\frac{2 \times 6}{3 \times 6}$.)

   b Simplify the fraction $\frac{2000}{3000}$. (Note: This is the same as $\frac{2 \times 1000}{3 \times 1000}$.)

   c Simplify $\frac{2a}{3a}$. (Note: This is the same as $\frac{2 \times a}{3 \times a}$.)

4 Match up these expressions with the correct way to write them.

a	$2 \times u$	**A**	$3u$
b	$7 \times u$	**B**	$\frac{5}{u}$
c	$5 \div u$	**C**	$2u$
d	$u \times 3$	**D**	$\frac{u}{5}$
e	$u \div 5$	**E**	$7u$

To tile a shopping mall floor area, a tiler is using rectangular tiles each l cm by w cm. There are 60 rows of tiles with 40 tiles per row. The tiler needs enough tile glue for area: $A = 60w \times 40l = 2400wl$ square centimetres.

Example 11   Simplifying expressions with multiplication

a Write $4 \times a \times b \times c$ without multiplication signs.

b Simplify $4a \times 2b \times 3c$, giving your final answer without multiplication signs.

c Simplify $3w \times 4w$.

SOLUTION	EXPLANATION
a $4 \times a \times b \times c = 4abc$	When pronumerals are written next to each other they are being multiplied.
b $\begin{aligned} 4a \times 2b \times 3c &= 4 \times a \times 2 \times b \times 3 \times c \\ &= 4 \times 2 \times 3 \times a \times b \times c \\ &= 24abc \end{aligned}$	First, insert the missing multiplication signs. Rearrange to bring the numbers to the front. $4 \times 2 \times 3 = 24$ and $a \times b \times c = abc$, giving the final answer.
c $\begin{aligned} 3w \times 4w &= 3 \times w \times 4 \times w \\ &= 3 \times 4 \times w \times w \\ &= 12w^2 \end{aligned}$	First, insert the missing multiplication signs. Rearrange to bring the numbers to the front. $3 \times 4 = 12$ and $w \times w$ is written as w^2.

Now you try

a Write $d \times 5 \times e \times f$ without multiplication signs.

b Simplify $3x \times 5y \times 2z$, giving your final answer without multiplication signs.

c Simplify $2a \times 5a$.

Example 12   Simplifying expressions with division

a Write $(3x + 1) \div 5$ without a division sign.

b Simplify the expression $\dfrac{8ab}{12b}$.

SOLUTION	EXPLANATION
a $(3x + 1) \div 5 = \dfrac{3x + 1}{5}$	The brackets are no longer required as it becomes clear that all of $3x + 1$ is being divided by 5.
b $\begin{aligned} \dfrac{8ab}{12b} &= \dfrac{8 \times a \times b}{12 \times b} \\ &= \dfrac{2 \times 4 \times a \times b}{3 \times 4 \times b} \\ &= \dfrac{2a}{3} \end{aligned}$	Insert multiplication signs to help spot common factors. 8 and 12 have a common factor of 4. Cancel out the common factors of 4 and b.

Now you try

a Write $(3x + 2) \div (2x + 1)$ without a division sign.

b Simplify the expression $\dfrac{12pqr}{15pr}$.

Exercise 4E

FLUENCY

1–5($\frac{1}{2}$)	2–5($\frac{1}{2}$)	3–5($\frac{1}{2}$)

1 Write the following without multiplication signs.

a $2 \times a \times b$ b $5 \times x \times y \times z$ c $8 \times q \times r$ d $12 \times s \times t \times u \times v$

e $2 \times x$ f $5 \times p$ g $8 \times a \times b$ h $3 \times 2 \times a$

i $7 \times 4 \times f$ j $5 \times 2 \times a \times b$ k $2 \times b \times 5$ l $x \times 7 \times z \times 4$

2 Simplify these expressions.

a $3a \times 12$ b $7d \times 9$ c $2 \times 4e$ d $3 \times 5a$

e $4a \times 3b$ f $7e \times 9g$ g $8a \times bc$ h $4d \times 7af$

i $a \times 3b \times 4c$ j $2a \times 4b \times c$ k $4d \times 3e \times 5fg$ l $2cb \times 3a \times 4d$

3 Simplify these expressions.

a $w \times w$ b $a \times a$ c $3d \times d$ d $2k \times k$

e $p \times 7p$ f $q \times 3q$ g $6x \times 2x$ h $9r \times 4r$

4 Write each expression without a division sign.

a $x \div 5$ b $z \div 2$ c $a \div 12$

d $b \div 5$ e $2 \div x$ f $5 \div d$

g $x \div y$ h $a \div b$ i $(4x + 1) \div 5$

j $(2x + y) \div 5$ k $(2 + x) \div (1 + y)$ l $(x - 5) \div (3 + b)$

5 Simplify the following expressions by dividing by any common factors. Remember that $\frac{a}{1} = a$.

a $\dfrac{2x}{5x}$ b $\dfrac{5a}{9a}$ c $\dfrac{9ab}{4b}$ d $\dfrac{2ab}{5a}$

e $\dfrac{2x}{4}$ f $\dfrac{9x}{12}$ g $\dfrac{10a}{15a}$ h $\dfrac{30y}{40y}$

i $\dfrac{4a}{2}$ j $\dfrac{21x}{7x}$ k $\dfrac{4xy}{2x}$ l $\dfrac{9x}{3xy}$

PROBLEM-SOLVING

6, 7	7, 9	7–9

6 Write a simplified expression for the area of the following rectangles. Recall that for rectangles, *Area = width × length*.

a k / 3 b 6 / x c $3x$ / $4y$

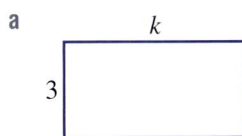

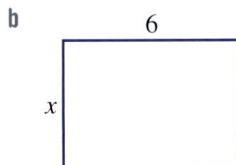

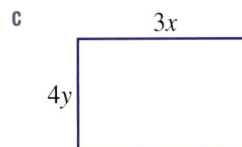

7 The weight of a single muesli bar is x grams.

a What is the weight of 4 bars? Write an expression.

b If Jamila buys n bars, what is the total weight of her purchase?

c Jamila's cousin Roland buys twice as many bars as Jamila. What is the total weight of Roland's purchase?

8 Five friends go to a restaurant. They split the bill evenly, so each spends the same amount.

a If the total cost is $100, how much do they each spend?

b If the total cost is $C, how much do they each spend? Write an expression.

9 Replace the question marks with algebraic terms to make these equivalence statements true.

   a $4c \times ? \times b = 12abc$

   b $2a \times 2b \times ? = 28abc$

   c $\dfrac{14ab}{?} = 2a$

   d $\dfrac{12xy}{?} = x$

   e $\dfrac{50x}{?} \times y = 5y$

REASONING	10	10, 11	11–13

10 The expression $3 \times 2p$ is the same as the expression $\underset{(1)}{2p} + \underset{(2)}{2p} + \underset{(3)}{2p}$.

   a What is a simpler expression for $2p + 2p + 2p$? (*Hint*: Combine like terms.)

   b $3 \times 2p$ is shorthand for $3 \times 2 \times p$. How does this relate to your answer in part **a**?

11 The area of the rectangle shown is $3a$. The length and width of this rectangle are now doubled.

   a Draw the new rectangle, showing its dimensions.

   b Write a simplified expression for the area of the new rectangle.

   c Divide the area of the new rectangle by the area of the old rectangle. What do you notice?

   d What happens to the area of the original rectangle if you triple both the length and the width?

a

3

12 Consider the expression $5a \times 4b \times 5c$.

   a Simplify the expression.

   b If $a = 3$, $b = 7$ and $c = 2$ find the value of $5a \times 4b \times 5c$ without a calculator.

   c Explain why it is easier to evaluate the simplified expression.

13 We can combine like terms after simplifying any multiplication and division. For example, $3a \times 8b - 2a \times 7b$ simplifies to $24ab - 14ab$, which simplifies to $10ab$. Use this strategy to simplify the following as much as possible.

   a $7a \times 4b - 6a \times 2b$ **b** $10a \times 5b - 4b \times 9a$ **c** $5a \times 12b - 6a \times 10b$

ENRICHMENT: Managing powers	–	–	14

14 The expression $a \times a$ can be written as a^2 and the expression $a \times a \times a$ can be written as a^3.

   a What is $3ab^2$ when written in full with multiplication signs?

   b Write $7 \times x \times x \times x \times y \times y \times y$ without any multiplication signs.

   c Simplify $2a \times 3b \times 4c \times 5a \times b \times 10c \times a$.

   d Simplify $4a^2 \times 3ab^2 \times 2c^2$.

The following problems will investigate practical situations drawing upon knowledge and skills developed throughout the chapter. In attempting to solve these problems, aim to identify the key information, use diagrams, formulate ideas, apply strategies, make calculations and check and communicate your solutions.

Comparing printing costs

1 Glenn doesn't currently own a home printer and looks into the costs of purchasing a printer, toner cartridges and paper.
Glenn finds out the following information:
- Black and white laser printer (23 pages per minute) = $98
- Toner cartridge (lasts for 1000 pages) = $72
- Reams of paper (500 pages in a ream) = $5

Another option for Glenn is to print at school, but the school charges 10 cents per A4 page of black and white printing.

Glenn is interested in comparing the cost of printing on his home printer compared to the cost of printing on one of the school's printers.

a What is the cost of Glenn printing 2000 pages at school over the course of the year?

b If Glenn wishes to print 2000 pages at home over the course of the year, how many toner cartridges and how many reams of paper will he need to purchase?

c What will it cost Glenn to buy a printer and print 2000 pages at home?

d What is the total cost of Glenn's printing at home per page including the cost of the printer?

e What is the total cost of Glenn's printing at home per page excluding the cost of the printer?

f Do you recommend Glenn prints at home or at school?

g What is the cost of Glenn printing n pages at school?

h What is the cost of Glenn printing n pages at home, excluding the cost of the printer?

i Find a value of n for which it is cheaper to print:
  i at home, including the cost of the printer
  ii at school, including the cost of the printer.

Calculating walking distance

2 Carmen determines her average stride length by walking a distance of 100 m and taking 125 steps to do so.

Carmen is curious about how far she walks in various time intervals including a whole year.

a What is Carmen's average stride length? Give your answer in metres and in centimetres.

b Write an expression for the distance in kilometres that Carmen walks in x steps.

Carmen is determined to walk at least 10 000 steps every day.

c   How far will Carmen walk on a day when she takes 10 000 steps? Give your answer in metres and in kilometres.

d   If Carmen averages 10 000 steps per day over an entire year (non-leap year), how far will Carmen walk in the year? Give your answer in kilometres.

e   How many steps per day would Carmen have to average over the year if she wanted to be able to say she had walked the 'length of Australia', a distance equivalent to walking from Melbourne to Darwin (3740 km)?

f   How many steps per day would Carmen have to average over the year if she wanted to be able to say she had walked the 'width of Australia', a distance equivalent to walking from Perth to Sydney (3932 km)?

g   How many steps per day would a student have to average over a year if they have a stride length of s metres and want to walk n kilometres?

Earning money from dog-walking

3   Eskander is keen to earn some money from offering to take their neighbours' dogs for a walk.
Eskander is interested in the total amount of money that can be earned depending on the size of the fee charge per walk, the duration of the walks and the total number of walks.

Eskander initially thinks they will simply charge $5 per dog walk and writes down the rule $M = 5 \times w$.

a   What do you think M and w stand for?

b   How much will Eskander earn from 20 dog walks?

Eskander then thinks that it makes more sense to charge a different rate for 20-minute walks and 40-minute walks. They decide to charge $4 for 20-minute walks and $8 for 40-minute walks.

c   Using a to represent the number of 20-minute walks, and b to represent the number of 40-minute walks, write a rule for the money Eskander will earn.

d   How much will Eskander earn from ten 20-minute walks and ten 40-minute walks?

Eskander realises that they are really charging the same rate per minute for the 20- and 40-minute walks.

e   How much does Eskander earn per minute of dog walking? Give your answer in dollars and also in cents.

f   Write an equation for the amount of money Eskander will earn per t minutes of walking.

g   Using this new equation, how much will Eskander earn from 600 minutes of walking? Check if this is the same amount as your answer to part d.

4F Expanding brackets   EXTENDING

LEARNING INTENTIONS
• To understand what it means to expand brackets
• To be able to expand brackets using repeated terms or rectangle areas
• To be able to expand brackets using the distributive law

We have already seen that there are different ways of writing two equivalent expressions. For example, $4a + 2a$ is equivalent to $2 \times 3a$, even though they look different.

Note that $3(7 + a) = 3 \times (7 + a)$, which is equivalent to 3 lots of $7 + a$.

So, $3(7 + a) = 7 + a + 7 + a + 7 + a$
$\qquad\qquad = 21 + 3a$

It is sometimes useful to have an expression that is written with brackets, like $3 \times (7 + a)$, and sometimes it is useful to have an expression that is written without brackets, like $21 + 3a$.

A builder designs a low-set house, 15 m long by 10 m wide. Customers can select the option of adding a deck of variable width, **x** m. The total floor area is:
$A = 15(10 + x) = \underset{\text{(house)}}{150} + \underset{\text{(deck)}}{15x}$

Lesson starter: Total area

What is the total area of the rectangle shown at right? Try to write two expressions, only one of which includes brackets.

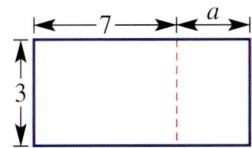

KEY IDEAS

■ **Expanding** (or **eliminating**) brackets involves writing an equivalent expression without brackets. This can be done by writing the bracketed portion a number of times or by multiplying each term.

$2(a + b) = a + b + a + b$ or $2(a + b) = 2 \times a + 2 \times b$
$\qquad\quad = 2a + 2b$ $\qquad\qquad\qquad\qquad = 2a + 2b$

■ To eliminate brackets, you can use the **distributive law**, which states that:

$a(b + c) = ab + ac$ and $a(b - c) = ab - ac$

■ The distributive law is used in arithmetic.
For example:

$5 \times 27 = 5(20 + 7)$
$\qquad\quad = 5 \times 20 + 5 \times 7$
$\qquad\quad = 100 + 35$
$\qquad\quad = 135$

■ The process of removing brackets using the distributive law is called **expansion**.

■ When expanding, every term inside the brackets must be multiplied by the term outside the brackets.

BUILDING UNDERSTANDING

1 The expression $3(a + 2)$ can be written as $(a + 2) + (a + 2) + (a + 2)$.

   a Simplify this expression by collecting like terms.

   b State $2(x + y)$ in full without brackets and simplify the result.

   c State $4(p + 1)$ in full without brackets and simplify the result.

   d State $3(4a + 2b)$ in full without brackets and simplify the result.

2 The area of the rectangle shown can be written as $4(x + 3)$.

   a What is the area of the green rectangle?

   b What is the area of the red rectangle?

   c State the total area as an expression, without using brackets.

3 State the missing parts in the following calculations which use the distributive law.

   a
$$3 \times 21 = 3 \times (20 + 1)$$
$$= 3 \times 20 + 3 \times 1$$
$$= \underline{\quad} + \underline{\quad}$$
$$= \underline{\quad}$$

   b
$$7 \times 34 = 7 \times (30 + 4)$$
$$= 7 \times \underline{\quad} + 7 \times \underline{\quad}$$
$$= \underline{\quad} + \underline{\quad}$$
$$= \underline{\quad}$$

   c
$$5 \times 19 = 5 \times (20 - 1)$$
$$= 5 \times \underline{\quad} - 5 \times \underline{\quad}$$
$$= \underline{\quad} - \underline{\quad}$$
$$= \underline{\quad}$$

4 **a** State the missing results in the following table. Remember to follow the rules for correct order of operations.

	$4(x + 3)$	$4x + 12$
$x = 1$	$= 4(1 + 3)$ $= 4(4)$ $= 16$	$= 4(1) + 12$ $= 4 + 12$ $= 16$
$x = 2$		
$x = 3$		
$x = 4$		

   b State the missing word. The expressions $4(x + 3)$ and $4x + 12$ are _____.

Example 13 Expanding brackets using rectangle areas

Write two equivalent expressions for the area of each rectangle shown, only one of which includes brackets.

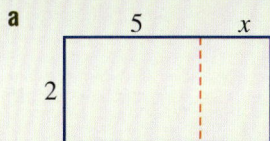

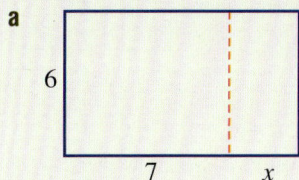

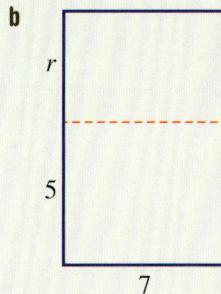

a

5	x

2

b

12

a

3

SOLUTION

a Using brackets: $2(5 + x)$

Without brackets: $10 + 2x$

b Using brackets: $12(a + 3)$

Without brackets: $12a + 36$

EXPLANATION

The whole rectangle has width 2 and length $5 + x$.
The smaller rectangles have area $2 \times 5 = 10$ and
$2 \times x = 2x$, so they are added.

The dimensions of the whole rectangle are 12 and $a + 3$.
Note that, by convention, we do not write $(a + 3)12$.
The smaller rectangles have area $12 \times a = 12a$ and
$12 \times 3 = 36$.

Now you try

Write two equivalent expressions for the area of each rectangle shown, only one of which includes brackets.

a

6

7	x

b

r

5

7

Example 14   Expanding using the distributive law

Expand the following expressions.

a $5(x + 3)$ **b** $8(a - 4)$ **c** $3(5a + 2)$ **d** $5a(3p - 7q)$

SOLUTION

a $5(x + 3) = 5 \times x + 5 \times 3$
$\qquad\qquad\;\; = 5x + 15$

b $8(a - 4) = 8 \times a - 8 \times 4$
$\qquad\qquad\;\; = 8a - 32$

c $3(5a + 2) = 3 \times 5a + 3 \times 2$
$\qquad\qquad\;\;\; = 15a + 6$

d $5a(3p - 7q) = 5a \times 3p - 5a \times 7q$
$\qquad\qquad\qquad\;\; = 15ap - 35aq$

EXPLANATION

Use the distributive law: $5(x + 3) = 5x + 5 \times 3$
Simplify the result.
Alternative method

	x	$+3$
5	$5x$	$+15$

so $5(x + 3) = 5x + 15$

Use the distributive law with subtraction:

$8(a - 4) = 8a - 8 \times 4$

Simplify the result.

Alternative method

	a	-4
8	$8a$	-32

so $8(a - 4) = 8a - 32$

Use the distributive law:

$3(5a + 2) = 3 \times 5a + 3 \times 2$

Simplify the result, remembering that $3 \times 5a = 15a$.

Alternative method

	$5a$	$+2$
3	$15a$	$+6$

so $3(5a + 2) = 15a + 6$

Expanding: $5a(3p - 7q) = 5a \times 3p - 5a \times 7q$

Simplify the result, remembering that $5a \times 3p = 15ap$
and $5a \times 7q = 35aq$.

Alternative method

	$3p$	$-7q$
$5a$	$15ap$	$-35aq$

so $5a(3p - 7q) = 15ap - 35aq$.

Now you try

Expand the following expressions.

a $4(b + 7)$ **b** $9(k - 5)$ **c** $5(2p + 5)$ **d** $9x(3z - 2)$

Exercise 4F

FLUENCY

| 1, 2, 3–4(½) | 2, 3–5(½) | 3–5(⅓) |

1 Write two equivalent expressions for the area of each rectangle shown, only one of which includes brackets.

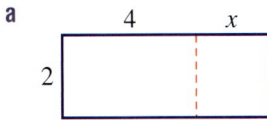

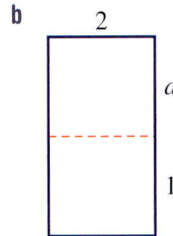

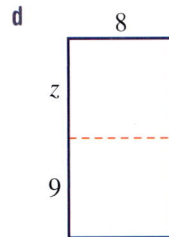

a

b

c

d

2 Use the distributive law to expand the following.

   a $6(y + 8)$ **b** $7(l + 4)$ **c** $8(s + 7)$

   d $4(2 + a)$ **e** $7(x + 5)$ **f** $3(6 + a)$

3 **a** $4(x - 3)$ **b** $5(j - 4)$ **c** $8(y - 8)$

   d $8(e - 7)$ **e** $6(3 - e)$ **f** $10(8 - y)$

4 Use the distributive law to expand the following.

   a $10(6g - 7)$ **b** $5(3e + 8)$ **c** $5(7w + 10)$

   d $5(2u + 5)$ **e** $7(8x - 2)$ **f** $3(9v - 4)$

   g $7(q - 7)$ **h** $4(5c - v)$ **i** $2(2u + 6)$

   j $6(8l + 8)$ **k** $5(k - 10)$ **l** $9(o + 7)$

5 Use the distributive law to expand the following.

   a $6i(t - v)$ **b** $2d(v + m)$ **c** $5c(2w - t)$

   d $6e(s + p)$ **e** $d(x + 9s)$ **f** $5a(2x + 3v)$

   g $5j(r + 7p)$ **h** $i(n + 4w)$ **i** $8d(s - 3t)$

   j $f(2u + v)$ **k** $7k(2v + 5y)$ **l** $4e(m + 10y)$

PROBLEM-SOLVING

| 6, 7 | 7, 8 | 7–9 |

6 Write an expression for each of the following and then expand it.

   a A number, x, has 3 added to it and the result is multiplied by 5.

   b A number, b, has 6 added to it and the result is doubled.

   c A number, z, has 4 subtracted from it and the result is multiplied by 3.

   d A number, y, is subtracted from 10 and the result is multiplied by 7.

7 At a school assembly there are a number of teachers and a number of students. Let t stand for the number of teachers and s stand for the number of students.

   a Write an expression for the total number of people at the assembly (assume there are just teachers and students in attendance).

   b If all people at the assembly are wearing two socks, write two equivalent expressions for the total number of socks being worn (one expression with brackets and one without).

8 When expanded, $4(3x + 6y)$ gives $12x + 24y$. Find two other expressions that expand to $12x + 24y$.

9 The distance around a rectangle is given by the expression $2(l + w)$, where l is the length and w is the width. What is an equivalent expression for this distance?

REASONING	10	10, 11	11, 12

10 **a** Use a diagram of a rectangle like that in Example 13 to demonstrate that $5(x + 3) = 5x + 15$.

   b Use a diagram of a rectangle to prove that $(a + 2)(b + 3) = ab + 2b + 3a + 6$.

   c Use a diagram to find an expanded form for $(a + 3)(b + 5)$.

11 To multiply a number by 99, you can multiply it by 100 and then subtract the original number. For example, $17 \times 99 = 1700 - 17 = 1683$. Explain, using algebra, why this method always works (not just for the number 17).

12 When expanded, $5(2x + 4y)$ gives $10x + 20y$.

   a How many different ways can the missing numbers be filled with whole numbers for the equivalence $\square\,(\square\,x + \square\,y) = 10x + 20y$?

   b How many different expressions expand to give $10x + 20y$ if fractions or decimals are included?

ENRICHMENT: Expanding sentences	–	–	13

13 Using words, people do a form of expansion. Consider these two statements:

   Statement A: 'John likes tennis and football.'

   Statement B: 'John likes tennis and John likes football.'

Statement B is an 'expanded form' of statement A, which is equivalent in its meaning but more clearly shows that two facts are being communicated. Write an 'expanded form' of the following sentences.

   a Rosemary likes Maths and English.

   b Priscilla eats fruit and vegetables.

   c Bailey and Lucia like the opera.

   d Frank and Igor play video games.

   e Pyodir and Astrid like fruit and vegetables.

(Note: There are four facts being communicated in part **e**.)

4G Applying algebra

LEARNING INTENTIONS
- To know that algebra can model a variety of situations
- To be able to apply an expression in a modelling situation
- To be able to construct an expression from a problem description

Algebraic expressions can be used to describe problems relating to many different areas, including costs, speeds and sporting results. Much of modern science relies on the application of algebraic rules and formulas. It is important to be able to convert word descriptions of problems to mathematical expressions in order to solve these problems mathematically.

A standard Uber fare is calculated by adding a base fare to a cost for t minutes and a cost for d km. For example, a fare in dollars could be $2.55 + 0.38t + 1.15d$.

Lesson starter: Garden bed area

The garden shown below has an area of $34\,\text{m}^2$, but the width and length are unknown.

- What are some possible values that w and l could equal?
- Try to find the dimensions of the garden that make the fencing around the outside as small as possible.

KEY IDEAS

■ Many different situations can be modelled with algebraic expressions.
  For example, an algebraic expression for perimeter is $2l + 2w$

■ To apply an expression, the pronumerals should be defined clearly. Then known values should be substituted for the pronumerals.
  For example: If $l = 5$ and $w = 10$, then

$$\text{perimeter} = 2 \times 5 + 2 \times 10$$
$$= 30$$

BUILDING UNDERSTANDING

1 The area of a rectangle is given by the expression $w \times l$, where w is its width and l is its length in metres.

    a Find the area in square metres if $w = 5$ and $l = 7$.

    b Find the area in square metres if $w = 2$ and $l = 10$.

2 The perimeter of a square with width w cm is given by the expression $4w$ cm.

    a Find the perimeter of a square with width 6 cm (i.e. $w = 6$).

    b Find the perimeter of a square with width 10 m (i.e. $w = 10$).

3 Consider the equilateral triangle shown.

    a State an expression that gives the perimeter of this triangle.

    b Use your expression to find the perimeter if $x = 12$.

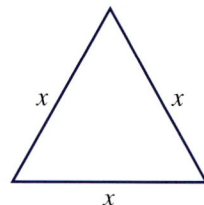

Example 15   Applying an expression

The perimeter of a rectangle is given by the expression $2w + 2l$, where w is the width and l is the length.

a Find the perimeter of a rectangle if $w = 5$ and $l = 7$.

b Find the perimeter of a rectangle with width 3 cm and length 8 cm.

SOLUTION	EXPLANATION
a $\begin{aligned} 2w + 2l &= 2(5) + 2(7) \\ &= 10 + 14 \\ &= 24 \end{aligned}$	To apply the rule, we substitute $w = 5$ and $l = 7$ into the expression. Evaluate using the normal rules of arithmetic (i.e. multiplication before addition).
b $\begin{aligned} 2w + 2l &= 2(3) + 2(8) \\ &= 6 + 16 \\ &= 22 \text{ cm} \end{aligned}$	Substitute $w = 3$ and $l = 8$ into the expression. Evaluate using the normal rules of arithmetic, remembering to include appropriate units (cm) in the answer.

Now you try

The area of a triangle is given by the expression $\dfrac{bh}{2}$ where b is the base width and h is the height.

a Find the area of a triangle if $b = 7$ and $h = 10$.

b Find the area of a triangle with base 20 cm and height 12 cm.

Example 16   Constructing expressions from problem descriptions

Write expressions for each of the following.
a   The total cost, in dollars, of 10 bottles, if each bottle costs $x.
b   The total cost, in dollars, of hiring a plumber for n hours. The plumber charges a $30 call-out fee plus $60 per hour.
c   A plumber charges a $60 call-out fee plus $50 per hour. Use an expression to find how much an 8-hour job would cost.

SOLUTION	EXPLANATION
a $10x$	Each of the 10 bottles costs $x, so the total cost is $10 \times x = 10x$.
b $30 + 60n$	For each hour, the plumber charges $60, so must pay $60 \times n = 60n$. The $30 call-out fee is added to the total bill.
c Expression for cost: $60 + 50n$ If $n = 8$, then cost is $60 + 50 \times 8 = \$460$	Substitute $n = 8$ to find the cost for an 8-hour job. Cost will be $460.

Now you try

Write expressions for each of the following.
a   The total volume, in litres, of soft drink in n bottles, if each bottle contains 2 litres.
b   The total time, in minutes, it takes to paint k square metres of fencing, given that it takes 20 minutes to set up the painting equipment and then 5 minutes per square metre.
c   Hiring a car costs $80 hiring fee plus $110 per day. Use an expression to find the cost of hiring the car for seven days.

Exercise 4G

FLUENCY	1–6	2–7	3–7

1   The perimeter of a rectangle is given by the expression $2w + 2l$ where w is the width and l is the length.
a   Find the perimeter of a rectangle if $w = 4$ and $l = 10$.
b   Find the perimeter of a rectangle with width $7\,\text{cm}$ and length $15\,\text{cm}$.

2   The perimeter of an isosceles triangle is given by the expression $x + 2y$ where x is the base length and y is the length of the other sides.
a   Find the perimeter if $x = 3$ and $y = 5$.
b   Find the perimeter of an isosceles triangle if the base length is $4\,\text{m}$ and the other sides are each $7\,\text{m}$.

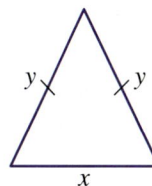

Example 16a   **3**   If pens cost $2 each, write an expression for the cost, in dollars, of n pens.

Example 16   **4**   If pencils cost $x each, write an expression for the cost, in dollars, of:
  a   10 pencils
  b   3 packets of pencils, if each packet contains 5 pencils
  c k pencils

5   A car travels at 60 km/h, so in n hours it has travelled $60n$ kilometres.
  a   How far does the car travel in 3 hours (i.e. $n = 3$)?
  b   How far does the car travel in 30 minutes?
  c   Write an expression for the total distance (in km) travelled in n hours for a motorbike with speed 70 km/h.

6   A carpenter charges a $40 call-out fee and then $80 per hour. This means the total cost, in dollars, for x hours of work is $40 + 80x$.
  a   How much would it cost for a 2-hour job (i.e. $x = 2$)?
  b   How much would it cost for a job that takes 8 hours?
  c   The call-out fee is increased to $50. What is the new expression for the total cost, in dollars, of x hours?

Example 16b   **7**   Match up the word problems with the expressions (**A** to **E**) below.
  a   The area of a rectangle with length 5 and width x.   **A** $10 + 2x$
  b   The perimeter of a rectangle with length 5 and width x.   **B** $5x$
  c   The total cost, in dollars, of hiring a DVD for x days if the price is $1 per day.   **C** $5 + x$
  d   The total cost, in dollars, of hiring a builder for 5 hours if the builder charges a   **D** x
      $10 call-out fee and then $x per hour.
  e   The total cost, in dollars, of buying a $5 magazine and a book that costs $x.   **E** $10 + 5x$

PROBLEM-SOLVING	8, 9	9–11	10–12

8   A plumber charges a $50 call-out fee and $100 per hour.
  a   Copy and complete the table below.

Number of hours	1	2	3	4	5
Total costs ($)					

  b   Find the total cost if the plumber works for t hours. Give an expression.
  c   Substitute $t = 30$ into your expression to find how much it will cost for the plumber to work 30 hours.

9   To hire a tennis court, you must pay a $5 booking fee plus $10 per hour.
  a   What is the cost of booking a court for 2 hours?
  b   What is the cost of booking a court for x hours? Write an expression.
  c   A tennis coach hires a court for 7 hours. Substitute $x = 7$ into your expression to find the total cost.

10   Adrian's mobile phone costs 30 cents to make a connection, plus 60 cents per minute of talking. This means that a t-minute call costs $30 + 60t$ cents.
  a   What is the cost of a 1-minute call?
  b   What is the cost of a 10-minute call? Give your answer in dollars.
  c   Write an expression for the cost of a t-minute call in dollars.

11 In Australian Rules football a goal is worth 6 points and a 'behind' is worth 1 point. This means the total score for a team is $6g + b$, if g goals and b behinds are scored.

   a What is the score for a team that has scored 5 goals and 3 behinds?

   b What are the values of g and b for a team that has scored 8 goals and 5 behinds?

   c If a team has a score of 20, this could be because $g = 2$ and $b = 8$. What are the other possible values of g and b?

12 In a closing-down sale, a shop sells all CDs for $\$c$ each, books cost $\$b$ each and DVDs cost $\$d$ each. Claudia buys 5 books, 2 CDs and 6 DVDs.

   a What is the cost, in dollars, of Claudia's order? Give your answer as an expression involving b, c and d.

   b Write an expression for the cost, in dollars, of Claudia's order if CDs doubled in price and DVDs halved in price.

   c As it happens, the total price Claudia ends up paying is the same in both situations. Given that CDs cost $12 and books cost $20 (so $c = 12$ and $b = 20$), how much do DVDs cost?

REASONING	13	13	13, 14

13 A shop charges $\$c$ for a box of tissues.

   a Write an expression for the total cost, in dollars, of buying n boxes of tissues.

   b If the original price is tripled, write an expression for the total cost, in dollars, of buying n boxes of tissues.

   c If the original price is tripled and twice as many boxes are bought, write an expression for the total cost in dollars.

14 Hiring a basketball court costs $10 for a booking fee, plus $30 per hour.

   a Write an expression for the total cost in dollars to hire the court for x hours.

   b For the cost of $40, you could hire the court for 1 hour. How long could you hire the court for the cost of $80? Assume that the time does not need to be rounded to the nearest hour.

   c Explain why it is *not* the case that hiring the court for twice as long costs twice as much.

   d Find the average cost per hour if the court is hired for a 5 hour basketball tournament.

   e Describe what would happen to the *average* cost per hour if the court is hired for many hours (e.g. more than 50 hours).

ENRICHMENT: Mobile phone mayhem	–	–	15

15 Rochelle and Emma are on different mobile phone plans, as shown below.

	Connection	Cost per minute
Rochelle	20 cents	60 cents
Emma	80 cents	40 cents

   a Write an expression for the cost of making a t-minute call using Rochelle's phone.

   b Write an expression for the cost of making a t-minute call using Emma's phone.

   c Whose phone plan would be cheaper for a 7-minute call?

   d What is the length of call for which it would cost exactly the same for both phones?

   e Investigate current mobile phone plans and describe how they compare to those of Rochelle's and Emma's plans.

Modelling

Internet service provider

A small internet service provider is exploring a number of pricing structures for its customers. Three structures that it is considering are listed below.

- Structure 1: No initial connection fee plus $40 per month
- Structure 2: $80 initial connection plus $30 per month
- Structure 3: $150 initial connection plus $25 per month

Present a report for the following tasks and ensure that you show clear mathematical workings and explanations where appropriate.

Preliminary task

a   Find the total cost of purchasing 12 months' service using:

   i   pricing structure 1   ii   pricing structure 2   iii   pricing structure 3.

b   How many months' service will $380 provide using pricing structure 2?

c   Which pricing structure is cheapest for 6 months of service? Give reasons.

Modelling task

Formulate

a   The problem is to find the pricing structure that provides the best and worst value for money for customers, depending on how long they use the service. Write down all the relevant information that will help solve this problem.

b   If a customer receives n months of service, write expressions for the total cost in dollars using:

   i   pricing structure 1   ii   pricing structure 2   iii   pricing structure 3.

Solve

c   Use your expressions to find the total cost of 3, 6, 9, 12 and 15 months of service using the three different pricing structures. Summarise your results using a table like the one shown.

Months	3	6	9	12	15
Structure 1 cost ($)					
Structure 2 cost ($)					
Structure 3 cost ($)					

d   Determine the pricing structure that produces most money for the internet provider for:

   i   9 months of service   ii   15 months of service.

e   For how many months will the overall cost of the following pricing structures be the same?

   i   1 and 2   ii   2 and 3   iii   1 and 3

Evaluate and verify

f   Describe the pricing structure(s) which deliver(s) the cheapest service for customers. If it depends on the number of months of service, explain how this affects the answers.

Communicate

g   Summarise your results and describe any key findings.

Extension questions

a   Construct a possible pricing structure which has a higher connection fee, but is cheaper than the above pricing structures for 12 months of service. Justify your choice.

b   Construct a possible pricing structure with a $100 connection fee that has a total cost of $520 for 12 months of service. Justify your answer with calculations.

Making microchips

Key technology: Spreadsheets and graphing

One of the key components of computers is the microchip processor. It is the nerve centre of the system which can hold a large amount of information and perform mathematical operations. The cost of making microchips involves significant set up costs and an ongoing cost per chip. These costs are passed on to the computer companies that buy and install the chips into their machines.

1 Getting started

Firstly, consider two computer chip making companies, Mybot and iChip. Their cost structures are given as follows.

- Mybot: Set-up costs: $100 000, Cost per item: $32
- iChip: Set-up costs: $50 000, Cost per item: $55

   a Find the total cost of producing 2000 chips from:

      i Mybot   **ii** iChip.

   b Find the total cost of producing 3000 chips from:

      i Mybot   **ii** iChip.

   c Which company has the least overall cost for making:

      i 2000 chips?   **ii** 3000 chips?

   d If x is the number of chips produced, write an expression for the total cost of producing chips for:

      i Mybot   **ii** iChip.

2 Using technology

   a Create a spreadsheet as shown to help find the overall costs for each company.

   b Fill down at cells A5, B4 and C4 to show the production costs of making 1 through to 10 chips.

   c Which company has the least costs for producing somewhere between 1 and 10 chips?

   d Alter the starting number in cell A4 to 1500 and compare the costs of producing 1500 to 1509 chips. Which company has the least overall cost of producing chips in this range?

   e Alter the starting number in cell A4 to 2500 and compare the costs of producing 2500 to 2509 chips. Which company has the least overall cost of producing chips in this range?

	A	B	C
1	Making chips		
2			
3	Number	Mybot	iChip
4	1	=100000+32*A4	=50000+55*A4
5	=A4+1		

3 Applying an algorithm

a   Apply the following algorithm to help search for the number of chips produced where the costs for both companies are very close.

	A	B	C
1	Making chips		
2			
3	Number	Mybot	iChip
4	2170	169440	169350
5	2171	169472	169405
6	2172	169504	169460
7	2173	169536	169515
8	2174	169568	169570
9	2175	169600	169625
10	2176	169632	169680
11	2177	169664	169735
12	2178	169696	169790
13	2179	169728	169845

- Step 1: Alter the starting number in cell A4 to 2000 and compare the costs of producing 2000 chips.
- Step 2: Note which company has the least costs.
- Step 3: Increase or decrease the number in cell A4 until your answer to the question in step 2 changes.
- Step 4: Repeat from step 3 until you have found the number of chips where the cost of production for the companies is the closest.

b   Add a graph by inserting a chart into your spreadsheet showing where the costs of production for the companies intersect. Investigate how changing the value of x in cell A4 changes the graph.

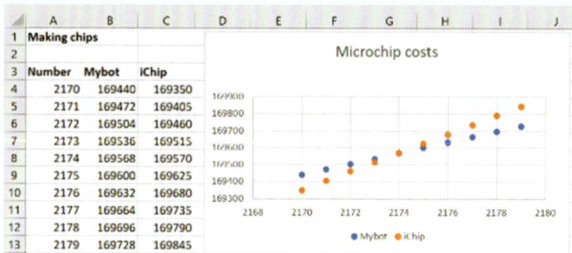

4 Extension

a   Upgrade your spreadsheet to include editable upfront costs and per chip costs for each company as shown. Note that the $ sign is used to ensure that the rules in cell B8 and C8 always refer to the upfront and per chip cost information while you fill down.

	A	B	C	D
1	Making chips			
2				
3	Mybot		iChip	
4	Upfront	100000	Upfront	50000
5	Per chip	32	Per chip	55
6				
7	Number	Mybot	iChip	
8	1	=B$4+B$5*A8	=D$4+D$5*A8	
9	=A8+1			

b   Vary these costs, and in each case, change the number in A8 to help find the number of chips where the overall costs for both companies are very similar.

Investigation

Fencing paddocks

A farmer is interested in fencing off a large number of 1 m × 1 m foraging regions for his chickens. Consider the pattern shown at right.

$n = 1$

$n = 2$

$n = 3$

a   For $n = 2$, the outside perimeter is 8 m, the area is 4 m² and the total length of fencing required is 12 m. Copy and complete the following table.

n	1	2	3	4	5	6
Outside perimeter (m)		8				
Area (m²)		4				
Fencing required (m)		12				

b   Write an expression for:
   i   the total outside perimeter of the fenced section
   ii   the total area of the fenced section.

c   The farmer knows that the expression for the total amount of fencing is one of the following. Which one is correct? Prove to the farmer that the others are incorrect.
   i $6n$
   ii $(n + 1)^2$
   iii $n \times 2 \times (n + 1)$

d   Use the correct formula to work out the total amount of fencing required if the farmer wants to have a total area of 100 m² fenced off.

In a spreadsheet application, these calculations can be made automatically. Set up a spreadsheet as follows.

	A	B	C	D
1	n	Perimeter	Area	Total fencing
2	0	0	0	0
3	=A2+1	=A3*4	=A3*A3	=A3*2*(A3+1)

Drag down the cells until you have filled all the rows from $n = 0$ to $n = 30$.

e   Find the amount of fencing needed if the farmer wants the total area to be at least:
   i   25 m²
   ii   121 m²
   iii   400 m²
   iv   500 m².

f   If the farmer has 144 m of fencing, what is the maximum area his grid could have?

g   For each of the following lengths of fencing, give the maximum area, in m², that the farmer could contain in the grid.
   i   50 m
   ii   200 m
   iii   1 km
   iv   40 km

1 If $x + y = 8$ and $y + m = 17$ find the value of $x + 2y + m$.

Up for a challenge? If you get stuck on a question, check out the 'Working with unfamiliar problems' poster at the end of the book to help you.

2 A square is cut in half and the two identical rectangles are joined to form a rectangle as shown in this diagram.

Find an expression for the perimeter of the rectangle if the square has a side length of:

a $2m$
b $4(x + 3)$
c $w + y$

3 These two identical 'L' shapes are to be joined along identical (matching) sides without any overlap. Find a simplified algebraic expression for the largest and smallest possible perimeters of the joined shapes and also for the difference between these two perimeters.

Calculate this difference when $x = 10$. The diagrams are not drawn to scale.

4 In a list of five consecutive integers, the middle integer is $3a + 2$. Find two equivalent expressions for the sum of these five integers: one expanded and simplified, and one factorised. (Note that consecutive integers are whole numbers that follow each other. For example, 3, 4, 5 and 6 are four consecutive integers.)

5 Find the values of the pronumerals below in the following sum/product tables.

a

			Sum
	a	b	c
	d	24	32
Sum	12	e	48

b

			Product
	a	b	18
	2	c	d
Product	12	e	180

6 What is the coefficient of x once the expression $x + 2(x + 1) + 3(x + 2) + 4(x + 3) + ... + 100(x + 99)$ is simplified completely?

7 Think of any number and then perform the following operations. Add 5, then double the result, then subtract 12, then subtract the original number, then add 2. Use algebra to explain why you now have the original number again. Then design a puzzle like this yourself and try it on friends.

Creating expressions

6 more than k: $k + 6$
Product of 4 and x: $4x$
10 less than b: $b - 10$
Half of q: $\frac{q}{2}$
The sum of a and b is tripled: $3(a + b)$

Multiplying and dividing expressions

$2 \times a \times 3 \times a \times b = 6a^2b$

$6xy \div 12x = \dfrac{6xy}{12x}$

$\qquad = \dfrac{y}{2}$

Pronumerals

are letters used to represent numbers
g: number of grapes in a bunch
d: distance travelled (in metres)

Terms

Terms are pronumerals and numbers combined with $\times$, $\div$
e.g. $4x$, $10y$, $\frac{a}{3}$, 12
$3a$ means $3 \times a$
$\frac{b}{10}$ means $b \div 10$

Algebraic expressions

Combination of numbers, pronumerals and operations, e.g. $2xy + 3yz$, $\frac{12}{x} - 3$

Like terms

Like terms have exactly the same pronumerals.
$5a$ and $3a$ ✓
$2ab$ and $12ba$ ✓
$7ab$ and $2a$ ✗

Equivalent expressions

Always equal when pronumerals are substituted.
e.g. $2x + 3$ and $3 + 2x$ are equivalent.
$4 \times 3a$ and $12a$ are equivalent.

Algebra

Substitution

Replacing pronumerals with values.
e.g. $5x + 2y$ when $x = 10$ with and $y = 3$
becomes $5 \times 10 + 2 \times 3 = 50 + 6 = 56$
e.g. q^2 when $q = 7$ becomes $7^2 = 49$

Combining like terms

Combining like terms gives a way to simplify.
e.g. $4a + 2 + 3a = 7a + 2$
$3b + 4c + 2b - c = 5b + 4c$
$12xy + 3x - 5yx = 7xy + 3x$

To **simplify** an expression, find a simpler expression that is equivalent.

Expanding brackets (Ext)

$3(a + 4) = 3a + 12$

	a	$+4$
3	$3a$	$+12$

$5k(10 - 2j) = 50k - 10kj$

	10	$-2j$
$5k$	$50k$	$-10kj$

Using the distributive law gives an equivalent expression.

Applications

Commonly used expressions
$A = l \times w$
$P = 2l + 2w$

Cost is $50 + 90x$
↗ call-out fee   ↖ hourly rate

Chapter checklist

Chapter checklist with success criteria

A printable version of this checklist is available in the Interactive Textbook

		✔
4A	**1. I can state the coefficients of pronumerals within an expressions.** e.g. What is the coefficient of c in $3a + b + 13c$?	☐
4A	**2. I can list terms within expressions, and identify constant terms.** e.g. List the terms in $3a + b + 13$ and circle the constant term.	☐
4A	**3. I can write algebraic expressions from word descriptions.** e.g. Write an expression for 'the sum of a and b'.	☐
4B	**4. I can substitute a number for a pronumeral and evaluate.** e.g. Given that $t = 5$, evaluate $8t$.	☐
4B	**5. I can substitute multiple numbers for multiple pronumerals and evaluate.** e.g. Substitute $x = 4$ and $y = 7$ to evaluate $80 - (2xy + y)$.	☐
4B	**6. I can substitute into expressions involving powers and roots.** e.g. If $p = 4$ find the value of $3p^2$.	☐
4C	**7. I can decide whether two expressions are equivalent.** e.g. Indicate the two expressions which are equivalent: $3x + 4$, $8 - x$, $2x + 4 + x$.	☐
4C	**8. I can generalise number facts using algebra.** e.g. Write an equation involving x to generalise the following: $1 + 1 = 2 \times 1$, $7 + 7 = 2 \times 7$, $15 + 15 = 2 \times 15$	☐
4D	**9. I can decide whether two terms are like terms.** e.g. Decide whether $2ab$ and $5ba$ are like terms, giving reasons.	☐
4D	**10. I can simplify using like terms.** e.g. Simplify $5 + 12a + 4b - 2 - 3a$ by collecting like terms.	☐
4E	**11. I can simplify expressions involving multiplication.** e.g. Simplify $4a \times 2b \times 3c$, giving your final answer without multiplication signs.	☐
4E	**12. I can simplify expressions involving division.** e.g. Simplify the expression $\frac{8ab}{12b}$.	☐
4F	**13. I can expand brackets.** (Ext) e.g. Expand $3(a + 2b)$.	☐
4G	**14. I can apply an expression in a modelling problem.** e.g. Given the perimeter of a rectangle is $2w + 2l$, find the perimeter of a rectangle with length 8 cm and width 3 cm.	☐
4G	**15. I can construct an expression from a problem description.** e.g. Write an expression for the total cost in dollars of hiring a plumber for n hours, if they charge \$30 callout fee plus \$60 per hour.	☐

Short-answer questions

4A

1 a List the four individual terms in the expression $5a + 3b + 7c + 12$.

 b What is the constant term in the expression above?

 c What is the coefficient of c in the expression above?

4A

2 Write an expression for each of the following.

 a 7 is added to u

 b k is tripled

 c 7 is added to half of r

 d 10 is subtracted from h

 e the product of x and y

 f x is subtracted from 12

4B

3 If $u = 12$, find the value of:

 a $u + 3$ **b** $2u$ **c** $\dfrac{24}{u}$ **d** $3u - 4$

4B

4 If $p = 3$ and $q = 5$, find the value of:

 a pq **b** $p + q$ **c** $2(q - p)$ **d** $4p + 3q$

4B

5 If $t = 4$ and $u = 10$, find the value of:

 a t^2 **b** $2u^2$ **c** $3 + \sqrt{t}$ **d** $\sqrt{10tu}$

4C

6 For each of the following pairs of expressions, state whether they are equivalent (E) or not equivalent (N).

 a $5x$ and $2x + 3x$ **b** $7a + 2b$ and $9ab$

 c $3c - c$ and $2c$ **d** $3(x + 2y)$ and $3x + 2y$

4D

7 Classify the following pairs as like terms (L) or not like terms (N).

 a $2x$ and $5x$ **b** $7ab$ and $2a$ **c** $3p$ and p **d** $9xy$ and $2yx$

 e $4ab$ and $4aba$ **f** $8t$ and $2t$ **g** $3p$ and 3 **h** $12k$ and $120k$

4D

8 Simplify the following by collecting like terms.

 a $2x + 3 + 5x$ **b** $12p - 3p + 2p$ **c** $12b + 4a + 2b + 3a + 4$

 d $12mn + 3m + 2n + 5nm$ **e** $1 + 2c + 4h - 3o + 5c$ **f** $7u + 3v + 2uv - 3u$

4E

9 Simplify the following expressions involving products.

 a $3a \times 4b$ **b** $2xy \times 3z$ **c** $12f \times g \times 3h$ **d** $8k \times 2 \times 4lm$

4E

10 Simplify the following expressions involving quotients.

 a $\dfrac{3u}{2u}$ **b** $\dfrac{12y}{20y}$ **c** $\dfrac{2ab}{6b}$ **d** $\dfrac{12xy}{9yz}$

4F

(Ext)

11 Expand the following expressions using the distributive law.

 a $3(x + 2)$ **b** $4(p - 3)$ **c** $7(2a + 3)$ **d** $12(2k + 3l)$

4F

(Ext)

12 Give two examples of expressions that expand to give $12b + 18c$.

4G

13 If a single tin of paint weighs 9 kg, write an expression for the weight in kg of t tins of paint.

4G

14 If there are c cats and d dogs at a vet, write an expression for the total number of animals at the vet (assume this vet only has cats and dogs present).

4G

15 Write an expression for the total number of books that Analena owns if she has x fiction books and twice as many non-fiction books.

Multiple-choice questions

4A

1 In the expression $3x + 2y + 4xy + 7yz$, the coefficient of y is:

   A 3   B 2   C 4   D 7   E 16

4B

2 If $t = 5$ and $u = 7$, then $2t + u$ is equal to:

   A 17   B 32   C 24   D 257   E 70

4B

3 If $x = 2$, then $3x^2$ is equal to:

   A 32   B 34   C 12   D 25   E 36

4C

4 Which one of the following equivalences best generalises the number facts
$2 \times 7 + 7 = 3 \times 7$, $\quad 2 \times 12 + 12 = 3 \times 12$, $\quad 2 \times 51 + 51 = 3 \times 51$?

   A $7x + 7 = 3x$ B $x + x = 2x$ C $x \times x \times x = 3x$

   D $2x + x = 3x$ E $2x + 7 = 3x$

4D

5 Which of the following pairs does *not* consist of two like terms?

   A $3x$ and $5x$ B $3y$ and $12y$ C $3ab$ and $2ab$

   D $3cd$ and $5c$ E $3xy$ and yx

4D

6 A fully simplified expression equivalent to $2a + 4 + 3b + 5a$ is:

   A 4   B $5a + 5b + 4$ C $10ab + 4$

   D $7a + 3b + 4$ E $11ab$

4E

7 The simplified form of $4x \times 3yz$ is:

   A $43xyz$ B $12xy$ C $12xyz$ D $12yz$ E $4x3yz$

4E

8 The simplified form of $\dfrac{21ab}{3ac}$ is:

   A $\dfrac{7b}{c}$ B $\dfrac{7ab}{ac}$ C $\dfrac{21b}{3c}$ D 7   E $\dfrac{b}{7c}$

4F

9 When brackets are expanded, $4(2x + 3y)$ becomes:

   A $8x + 3y$ B $2x + 12y$ C $8x + 8y$ D $24x$ E $8x + 12y$

(Ext)

4A

10 A number is doubled and then 5 is added. The result is then tripled. If the number is represented by k, then an expression for this description is:

   A $3(2k + 5)$ B $6(k + 5)$ C $2k + 5$ D $2k + 15$ E $30k$

Extended-response questions

1   A taxi driver charges \$3.50 to pick
    up passengers and then \$2.10 per
    kilometre travelled.
    a   State the total cost if the trip
        length is:
        i 10 km
        ii 20 km
        iii 100 km.
    b   Write an expression for the
        total cost, in dollars, of travelling
        a distance of d kilometres.
    c   Use your expression to find the total cost of travelling 40 km.
    d   Prove that your expression is not equivalent to $2.1 + 3.5d$ by substituting in a value for d.
    e   Another taxi driver charges \$6 to pick up passengers and then \$1.20 per kilometre. Write an
        expression for the total cost (in dollars) of travelling d kilometres in this taxi.

2   An architect has designed a room, shown below, for which x and y are unknown.
    (All measurements are in metres.)

    a   Find the perimeter of this room if $x = 3$ and $y = 2$.
    b   It costs \$3 per metre to install skirting boards around the perimeter of the room. Find the
        total cost of installing skirting boards if $x = 3$ and $y = 2$.
    c   Write an expression for the perimeter (in metres) of the room and simplify it completely.
    d   Write an expanded expression for the total cost, in dollars, of installing skirting boards along
        the room's perimeter.
    e   Write an expression for the total floor area in m^2.

5

Decimals

Maths in context: Decimal times and sport

Decimal numbers and sport go together. From recording the times to reporting the statistics, decimals can be responsible for sponsorship funding and sporting fame. Olympic medals and sporting champions are often decided by tenths or hundredths of a second.

The challenging 400 m freestyle women's swimming event has had its world record (WR) times topped recently. In 2016, Katie Ledecky of USA made a WR time of 3:56.46 s. In 2022, Australia's Ariarne Titmus beat that time by 0.06 s, swimming a WR time of 3:56.40 s. Early 2023, Canadian Summer McIntosh swam 0.32 s faster again, making a new WR time of 3:56.08 s.

Major athletic track events now use an individual electronic starter beep, replacing the pistol sound that took 0.15 s to the farthest athlete. A camera scans the finish line 2000 times per second, signalling the digital timer the instant athletes cross the line. Exact times are recorded in milliseconds, then rounded to hundredths.

The Gold Coast 500 records times to four decimal places of a second. The previous lap time record for the S5000 race was 1:10.0499 s, set in 2013. However, in October 2022, Australia's Nathan Herne broke this record with a qualifying lap time of 1:09.6681 s, exactly 0.3818 s faster. Herne went on to win his first ever S5000 race. Then, at Fukuoka 2023 World Aquatics Championships, Ariarne Titmus beat her 400 m rivals in an awesome new WR time of 3:55.38 s.

Chapter contents

Victorian Curriculum 2.0

This chapter covers the following content descriptors in the Victorian Curriculum 2.0:

NUMBER

VC2M7N03, VC2M7N04, VC2M7N05, VC2M7N06, VC2M7N07, VC2M7N10

Please refer to the curriculum support documentation in the teacher resources for a full and comprehensive mapping of this chapter to the related curriculum content descriptors.

© VCAA

Online resources

A host of additional online resources are included as part of your Interactive Textbook, including HOTmaths content, video demonstrations of all worked examples, auto-marked quizzes and much more.

5A   Place value and decimals   CONSOLIDATING

Some quantities change by whole number amounts, such as the number of people in a room, but there are many quantities that increase or decrease continuously, such as your height, weight and age. We often talk about age as a whole number (e.g. Mike is 12 years old) but, in reality, our age is an ever-increasing (continuous) quantity. For example, if Mike is 12 years, 4 months, 2 weeks, 3 days, 5 hours, 6 minutes and 33 seconds old, then Mike is actually 12.380621 47 years old!

There are many numbers in today's society that are not whole numbers. For example, it is unusual to buy an item in a supermarket that is simply a whole number of dollars. The price of almost all shopping items involves both dollars and cents. A chocolate bar may cost $1.95, which is an example of a decimal number.

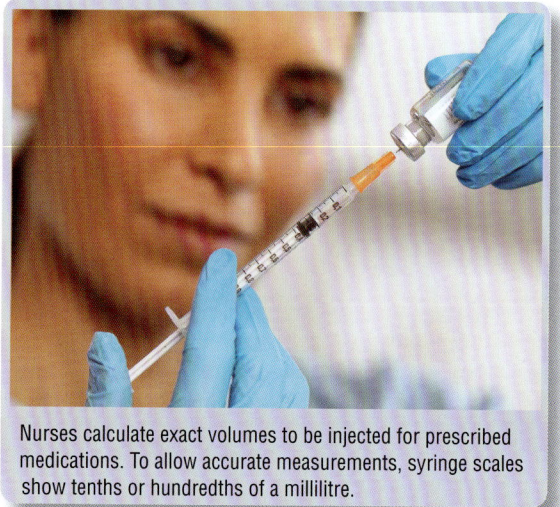

Nurses calculate exact volumes to be injected for prescribed medications. To allow accurate measurements, syringe scales show tenths or hundredths of a millilitre.

Lesson starter: Split-second timing

Organise students into pairs and use a digital stopwatch. Many students' watches will have a suitable stopwatch function.

• Try to stop the stopwatch on exactly 10 seconds. Have two attempts each.
  Were you able to stop it exactly on 10.00 seconds? What was the closest time?
• Try these additional challenges with your partner.
  a Stop the watch exactly on:
  i $12\frac{1}{2}$ seconds   **ii** 8.37 seconds   **iii** $9\frac{7}{10}$ seconds   **iv** 14.25 seconds
  b How quickly can you start and stop the stopwatch?
  c How accurately can you time 1 minute without looking at the stopwatch?

KEY IDEAS

■ A **decimal point** is used to separate the whole number from the decimal or fraction part.

■ When dealing with decimal numbers, the place value table must be extended to involve tenths, hundredths, thousandths etc.
The number 428.357 means:

Decimal point

Hundreds	Tens	Ones	.	Tenths	Hundredths	Thousandths
4	2	8	.	3	5	7
4×100	2×10	8×1	.	$3 \times \frac{1}{10}$	$5 \times \frac{1}{100}$	$7 \times \frac{1}{1000}$
400	20	8	.	$\frac{3}{10}$	$\frac{5}{100}$	$\frac{7}{1000}$

BUILDING UNDERSTANDING

1 For the number 58.237, give the value of the following digits.
a 2 **b** 3 **c** 7

2 A stopwatch is stopped at 36.57 seconds.
a What is the digit displayed in the tenths column?
b What is the digit displayed in the ones column?
c What is the digit displayed in the hundredths column?
d Is this number closer to 36 or 37 seconds?

3 Write the following number phrases as decimals.
a seven and six-tenths
b twelve and nine-tenths
c thirty-three and four-hundredths
d twenty-six and fifteen-hundredths
e eight and forty-two hundredths
f ninety-nine and twelve-thousandths

Example 1 Understanding decimal place value

What is the value of the digit 8 in the following numbers?
a 12.85 **b** 6.1287

SOLUTION	EXPLANATION
a $\frac{8}{10}$	The 8 is in the first column after the decimal point, which is the tenths column.
b $\frac{8}{1000}$	The 8 is in the third column after the decimal point, which is the thousandths column.

Now you try

What is the value of the digit 3 in the following numbers?

a 15.239

b 9.3508

▷ **Example 2   Converting simple fractions (with denominator 10, 100 etc) to decimals**

Express each of the following proper fractions and mixed numerals as decimals.

a $\dfrac{7}{10}$

b $\dfrac{5}{100}$

c $3\dfrac{17}{100}$

SOLUTION

a $\dfrac{7}{10} = 0.7$

b $\dfrac{5}{100} = 0.05$

c $3\dfrac{17}{100} = 3.17$

EXPLANATION

$\dfrac{7}{10}$ means seven-tenths, so put the 7 in the tenths column.

$\dfrac{5}{100}$ means five-hundredths, so put the 5 in the hundredths column.

$3\dfrac{17}{100}$ means 3 ones and 17 one-hundredths. 17 hundredths is one-tenth and seven-hundredths.

Now you try

Express each of the following proper fractions and mixed numerals as decimals.

a $\dfrac{9}{10}$

b $\dfrac{3}{100}$

c $4\dfrac{307}{1000}$

▷ **Example 3   Comparing and sorting decimals**

Place the correct mathematical symbol < or >, in between the following pairs of decimals to make a true mathematical statement.

a 3.5 ☐ 3.7

b 4.28 ☐ 4.263

c 0.00102 ☐ 0.01001

SOLUTION

a 3.5 < 3.7

b 4.28 > 4.263

EXPLANATION

The first digit from left-to-right where the decimals are different is in the tenths position. 5 is less than 7, so 3.5 is less than 3.7.

The ones digits (4) and tenths digits (2) are equal, so look at the hundredths digit.

8 > 6, so 4.28 > 4.263

Note: even though the thousandths digits (0 and 3) are in the opposite order, the hundredths digit is more important, so no further comparison is needed.

c $0.00102 < 0.01001$ The first digit where the decimals differ is the hundredths digit. The number 0.00102 has 0 and the number 0.01001 has 1, which is greater.

↑   ↑
hundredth   hundredth

Now you try

Place the correct mathematical symbol < or > between the following pairs of decimals to make a true mathematical statement.

a 8.7 ☐ 8.44

b 10.184 ☐ 10.19

c 0.0401 ☐ 0.00928

Exercise 5A

FLUENCY		1, 2, 3–5(½)	2–5(½)	2–6(⅓)

Example 1

1 What is the value of the digit 3 in the following numbers?
   a 1.37   b 4.213   c 10.037

Example 1

2 What is the value of the digit 6 in the following numbers?
   a 23.612   b 17.46   c 80.016
   d 0.693   e 16.4   f 8.568 13
   g 2.3641   h 11.926

Example 2a,b

3 Express each of the following proper fractions as a decimal.
   a $\frac{3}{10}$ b $\frac{8}{10}$ c $\frac{15}{100}$

   d $\frac{23}{100}$ e $\frac{9}{10}$ f $\frac{2}{100}$

   g $\frac{121}{1000}$ h $\frac{74}{1000}$

Example 2c

4 Express each of the following mixed numerals as a decimal.
   a $6\frac{4}{10}$ b $5\frac{7}{10}$ c $212\frac{3}{10}$

   d $1\frac{16}{100}$ e $14\frac{83}{100}$ f $7\frac{51}{100}$

   g $5\frac{7}{100}$ h $18\frac{612}{1000}$

Example 3

5 Place the correct mathematical symbol < or > between the following pairs of decimals to make a true mathematical statement.
   a 4.7 ☐ 4.2   b 3.65 ☐ 3.68   c 1.05 ☐ 1.03   d 5.32 ☐ 5.4

   e 6.17 ☐ 6.2   f 8.25 ☐ 8.19   g 2.34 ☐ 2.3   h 5.002 ☐ 5.01

   i 6.03 ☐ 6.00   j 8.21 ☐ 7.3   k 9.204 ☐ 8.402   l 4.11 ☐ 4.111

6 State whether each of the following statements is true or false.

a $7.24 < 7.18$ b $21.32 < 20.89$ c $4.61 > 4.57$ d $8.09 > 8.41$

e $25.8 \leqslant 28.5$ f $2.1118 \leqslant 2.8001$ g $7.93 \geqslant 8.42$ h $11.11 \geqslant 11.109$

i $\frac{3}{10} = \frac{30}{100}$ j $\frac{7}{10} = \frac{70}{100}$ k $\frac{5}{10} \neq 5$ l $\frac{2}{10} \neq \frac{20}{100}$

PROBLEM-SOLVING   7(½), 8   8, 9   8–10

7 Find the difference between each of the following decimal numbers and their nearest whole number.

a 6.9   b 7.03   c 18.98   d 16.5

e 17.999   f 4.99   g 0.85   h 99.11

8 Arrange these groups of numbers in ascending order (i.e. smallest to largest).

a 3.52, 3.05, 3.25, 3.55

b 30.6, 3.06, 3.6, 30.3

c 17.81, 1.718, 1.871, 11.87

d 26.92, 29.26, 29.62, 22.96, 22.69

9 The batting averages for five retired Australian Cricket test captains are: Adam Gilchrist 47.60, Steve Waugh 51.06, Mark Taylor 43.49, Allan Border 50.56 and Kim Hughes 37.41.

a List the five players in descending order of batting averages (i.e. largest to smallest).

b Ricky Ponting's test batting average is 56.72. Where does this rank him in terms of the retired Australian test captains listed above?

10 The depth of a river at 9:00 am on six consecutive days was:

Day 1: 1.53 m   Day 2: 1.58 m   Day 3: 1.49 m

Day 4: 1.47 m   Day 5: 1.52 m   Day 6: 1.61 m

a On which day was the river level highest?

b On which day was the river level lowest?

c On which days was the river level higher than the previous day?

REASONING   11   11, 12   12, 13

11 You can insert the digit '0' in some parts of the number 12.34 without changing the value (e.g. 12.340, 012.34) but not others (e.g. 102.34, 12.304). Explain why this is the case.

12 A, B and C are digits and A > B > C in decimal numbers. Write these numbers from smallest to largest. Note that the dot represents the decimal point.

a A.B, B.C, A.C, C.C, C.A, B.A

b A.BC, B.CA, B.BB, C.AB, C.BC, BA.CA, AB.AB, A.AA, A.CA

13 Write the following as decimals, if A is a digit.

a $\frac{A}{10}$ b $\frac{A}{100}$ c $\frac{A}{10} + \frac{A}{100}$ d $A + \frac{A}{10} + \frac{A}{1000}$

ENRICHMENT: Different decimal combinations   –   –   14

14 a Write as many different decimal numbers as you can and place them in ascending order using:

i   the digits 0, 1 and a decimal point. Each digit can be used only once.

ii the digits 0, 1, 2 and a decimal point. Each digit can be used only once.

iii the digits 0, 1, 2, 3 and a decimal point. Each digit can be used only once.

b Calculate the number of different decimal numbers that could be produced using the digits 0, 1, 2, 3, 4 and a decimal point.

5B Rounding decimals

LEARNING INTENTIONS
- To understand that rounding involves approximating a decimal number to fewer decimal places
- To be able to round decimals to a given number of decimal places

Decimal numbers sometimes contain more decimal places than we need. It is important that we are able to round decimal numbers when working with money, measuring quantities, including time and distance, or writing answers to some division calculations.

For example, the distance around the school oval might be 0.39647 km, which rounded to 1 decimal place is 0.4 km. The rounded figure, although not precise, is accurate enough for most applications.

Running events are electronically measured in seconds and rounded to 2 decimal places. Usain Bolt has repeatedly broken his own world records. In August 2009, he set a new world record of 9.58 seconds over 100 m at the World Championships in Germany, which was

A car's engine capacity is calculated by finding the total volume of its cylinders. This is given in litres, rounded to the nearest tenth. A 3.6 L engine is generally more powerful than a 2.5 L engine.

11-hundredths (0.11) of a second faster than his Beijing Olympic Games (August 2008) record of 9.69 seconds.

Lesson starter: Rounding brainstorm

1   In small groups, brainstorm occasions when it may be useful to round or estimate decimal numbers. Aim to get more than 10 common applications.
2   In pairs one person states a decimal number and the partner needs to state another decimal number that would allow the two numbers to add up to a whole number. Use mental arithmetic only. Start with 1 decimal place and try to build up to 3 or 4 decimal places.

KEY IDEAS

■ **Rounding** involves approximating a decimal number to fewer decimal places.

■ To round a decimal:
- Cut the number after the required decimal place; e.g. round to 2 decimal places.
- To determine whether you should round your answer up or down, consider only the digit *immediately* to the right of the specified place. For rounding purposes, this can be referred to as the **critical digit**.

'cut'

2 is the critical digit in this example

15.63|27

- If the critical digit is *less than* 5 (i.e. 0, 1, 2, 3 or 4), then you *round down*. This means write the original number to the place required, leaving off all other digits.
- If the critical digit is 5 *or more* (i.e. 5, 6, 7, 8 or 9), then you *round up*. This means write the original number to the place required, but increase this digit by 1, carrying if necessary. Leave off all other digits.

BUILDING UNDERSTANDING

1 For each of the following, select the closer alternative.

   a Is 5.79 closer to 5.7 or 5.8?   **b** Is 6.777 closer to 6.77 or 6.78?

2 To round correctly to a specified number of places, you must know which digit is the critical digit.

   a State the critical digit in each of the following numbers.

      i 25.8174 rounded to 1 decimal place.   Critical digit =_____

      ii 25.8174 rounded to 2 decimal places.   Critical digit =_____

      iii 25.8174 rounded to 3 decimal places.   Critical digit =_____

      iv 25.8174 rounded to the nearest whole number.   Critical digit =_____

   b State the correct rounded numbers for the numbers in parts i to iv above.

Example 4   Rounding decimals to 1 decimal place

Round both of the following to 1 decimal place.

a 25.682   **b** 13.5458

SOLUTION

a 25.7

b 13.5

EXPLANATION

The critical digit is 8 and therefore the tenths column must be rounded up from a 6 to a 7.

The critical digit is 4 and therefore the tenths column remains the same, in effect rounding the original number down to 13.5.

Now you try

Round both of the following to 1 decimal place.

a 53.741   **b** 4.1837

Example 5   Rounding decimals to different decimal places

Round each of the following to the specified number of decimal places.

a Round 18.34728 to 3 decimal places.

b Round 0.43917 to 2 decimal places.

c Round 7.59967 to 3 decimal places.

SOLUTION	EXPLANATION
a 18.347	The critical digit is 2, therefore round down.
b 0.44	The critical digit is 9, therefore round up.
c 7.600	The critical digit is 6, therefore round up. Rounding up has resulted in digits being carried over, since rounding up 7.599 in the thousandths digit means adding 0.001, giving the result of 7.600, correct to 3 decimal places.

Now you try

Round each of the following to the specified number of decimal places.

a Round 18.62109 to 2 decimal places.

b Round 3.14159 to 4 decimal places.

c Round 0.1397 to 3 decimal places.

Exercise 5B

FLUENCY	1, 2–7($\frac{1}{2}$)	2–7($\frac{1}{2}$)	3–7($\frac{1}{4}$)

1 Round each of the following to 1 decimal place.

Example 4a

   a **i** 32.481   **ii** 57.352

Example 4b

   b **i** 19.7431   **ii** 46.148

Example 4

2 Round each of the following to 1 decimal place.

a 14.82	**b** 7.38	**c** 15.62	**d** 0.87
e 6.85	**f** 9.94	**g** 55.55	**h** 7.98

Example 5

3 Write each of the following correct to 2 decimal places.

a 3.7823	**b** 11.8627	**c** 5.9156	**d** 0.93225
e 123.456	**f** 300.0549	**g** 3.1250	**h** 9.849
i 56.2893	**j** 7.121 999	**k** 29.9913	**l** 0.8971

Example 5a,b

4 Round each of the following to the specified number of decimal places, given as the number in the brackets.

a 15.913 (1)	**b** 7.8923 (2)	**c** 235.62 (0)	**d** 0.5111 (0)
e 231.86 (1)	**f** 9.3951 (1)	**g** 9.3951 (2)	**h** 34.712 89 (3)

Example 5c

5 Round each of the following to the specified number of decimal places.

   a 23.983 (1)   **b** 14.8992 (2)   **c** 6.95432 (0)   **d** 29.999731 (3)

6 Round each of the following to the nearest whole number; that is, round them to 0 decimal places.

   a 27.612   **b** 9.458   **c** 12.299   **d** 123.72

   e 22.26   **f** 117.555   **g** 2.6132   **h** 10.7532

7 Round each of the following amounts to the nearest dollar.

   a $12.85   **b** $30.50   **c** $7.10   **d** $1566.80

   e $120.45   **f** $9.55   **g** $1.39   **h** $36.19

PROBLEM-SOLVING	8	8, 9	8, 9

8 Some wise shoppers have the habit of rounding all items to the nearest dollar as they place them in their shopping basket. They can then keep a running total and have a close approximation as to how much their final bill will cost. Use this technique to estimate the cost of the following.

   a Jeanette purchases 10 items:

      $3.25, $0.85, $4.65, $8.99, $12.30, $7.10, $2.90, $1.95, $4.85, $3.99

   b Adam purchases 12 items:

      $0.55, $3.00, $5.40, $8.90, $6.90, $2.19, $3.20, $5.10, $3.15, $0.30, $4.95, $1.11

   c Jeanette's actual shopping total is $50.83 and Adam's is $44.75. How accurate were Jeanette's and Adam's estimations?

9 Electronic timing pads are standard in National Swimming competitions. In a recent 100 m freestyle race, Edwina receives a rounded time of 52.83 seconds and Jasmine a time of 53.17 seconds.

   a If the timing pads could only calculate times to the nearest second, what would be the time difference between the two swimmers?

   b If the timing pads could only calculate times to the nearest tenth of a second, what would be the time difference between the two swimmers?

   c What is the time difference between the two swimmers, correct to 2 decimal places?

   d If the timing pads could measure in seconds to 3 decimal places, what would be the quickest time in which Edwina might have swum the race?

REASONING   10   10, 11   10–12

10 Henry and Jake each go to a petrol
    station to refuel their cars.

    a   Henry buys 31.2 litres of petrol at a
        cost of 158.9 cents per litre.
        Given that $31.2 \times 158.9 = 4957.68$,
        round $49.5768 to two decimal
        places to state the total price for the
        petrol.

    b   If the price per litre had first been
        rounded to $1.59, find the total
        price for 31.2 litres.

    c   Jake buys 52.8 litres of premium
        petrol at a cost of 171.6 cents per
        litre. Find the total price he pays. (Remember to round your final answer to the nearest cent.)

    d   How much extra would Jake have to pay if the cost per litre were rounded to the nearest cent before
        Jake bought 52.8 litres?

11 Without using a calculator, evaluate $15.735629 \div 7$, correct to 2 decimal places. What is the least
    number of decimal places you need to find in the quotient to ensure that you have rounded correctly to
    2 decimal places?

12 Samara believes 0.449999 should be rounded up to 0.5, but Cassandra believes it should be rounded
    down to 0.4. Make an argument to support each of their statements, but then show the flaw in one girl's
    logic and clearly indicate which girl you think is correct.

ENRICHMENT: Rounding with technology   –   –   13, 14

13 Most calculators are able to round
    numbers correct to a specified
    number of places. Find out how to do
    this on your calculator and check
    your answers to Questions **3** and **4**.

14 Spreadsheet software packages can
    also round numbers correct to a
    specified number of places. Find out
    the correct syntax for rounding cells
    in a spreadsheet program, such as
    Microsoft Excel, and then check your
    answers to Questions **5** and **6**.

5C Adding and subtracting decimals

Addition and subtraction of decimals follows the same procedures as those for whole numbers. To add or subtract whole numbers you must line up the ones, tens, hundreds and so on, and then you add or subtract each column. When dealing with the addition or subtraction of decimals the routine is the same.

Consider how similar the following two sums are:

$$
\begin{array}{r}
5\,^{1}1\;4 \\
2\;7\;2 \\
1\;0\;6 \\
\hline
8\;9\;2
\end{array}
\qquad
\begin{array}{r}
5\,^{1}1\,.\,4 \\
2\;7\,.\,2 \\
1\;0\,.\,6 \\
\hline
8\;9\,.\,2
\end{array}
$$

Lesson starter: What's the total?

Each student thinks of three coins (gold or silver) and writes their total value on a sheet of paper. Each student in the class then estimates the total value of the amounts written down in the classroom. Record each student's estimated total.

- Each student then writes the value of the three coins they thought of on the board (e.g. $2.70, $0.80 etc.).
- Students copy down the values into their workbooks and add the decimal numbers to determine the total value of the coins in the classroom.
- Which student has the closest estimated total?

Accountants, financial planners and auditors are some of the finance professionals for whom adding and subtracting with decimals is an everyday calculation.

KEY IDEAS

■ When adding or subtracting decimals, the decimal points and each of the decimal places must be aligned under one another.

■ The location of the decimal point in the answer is directly in line with the location of each of the decimal points in the question.

■ Once the numbers are correctly aligned, proceed as if completing whole number addition or subtraction.

■ If the numbers of decimal places in the numbers being added or subtracted are different, it can be helpful to place additional zeros in the number(s) with fewer digits to the right of the decimal point to prevent calculation errors.

BUILDING UNDERSTANDING

1 7.12, 8.5 and 13.032 are added together. Which of the following is the best way to prepare these numbers ready for addition?

A	**B**	**C**	**D**
7.12	7.12	7.120	7.12
8.5	8.5	8.500	8.5
+ 13.032	+ 13.032	+ 13.032	+ 13.032
———	———	———	———

2 Which of the following is the correct way to present and solve the subtraction problem $77.81 - 6.3$?

A	**B**	**C**	**D**
77.81	77.81	77.81	77.81
− 6.3	− 6.30	− 6.3	− 6.3
84.11	71.51	14.81	77.18

Example 6   Adding decimals

Find the value of:

a $8.31 + 5.93$

b $64.8 + 3.012 + 5.94$

SOLUTION

a
$$\begin{array}{r} {}^{1}8.31 \\ + 5.93 \\ \hline 14.24 \end{array}$$

b
$$\begin{array}{r} {}^{1}6{}^{1}4.800 \\ 3.012 \\ + 5.940 \\ \hline 73.752 \end{array}$$

EXPLANATION

Make sure all decimal points and decimal places are correctly aligned directly under one another.

Align decimal points directly under one another. Fill in missing decimal places with additional zeros.

Carry out addition, following the same procedure as that for addition of whole numbers.

Now you try

Find:

a $12.52 + 23.85$

b $4.28 + 5.9 + 2.152$

Example 7   Subtracting decimals

Find the value of:

a $5.83 - 3.12$

b $146.35 - 79.5$

SOLUTION

a
```
    5.83
  − 3.12
  ──────
    2.71
```

b
```
   13 15 1
  1̶4̶ 6̶.35
 −   79.50
 ─────────
    66.85
```

EXPLANATION

Make sure all decimal points and decimal places are correctly aligned directly under one another.

Align decimal points directly under one another and fill in missing decimal places with additional zeros.
Carry out subtraction, following the same procedure as that for subtraction of whole numbers.

Now you try

Find:

a $9.48 - 4.16$

b $12.294 - 5.41$

Exercise 5C

FLUENCY   1, 2–4(½)   2–4(½)   2(½), 4(½)

Example 6a 1 Find the value of the following.

a
```
    2.14
  + 3.61
```

b
```
    3.40
  + 1.35
```

c
```
   10.053
 + 24.124
```

d
```
    5.813
  + 2.105
```

e
```
    3.12
  + 4.29
```

f
```
    2.38
  + 4.71
```

g
```
    8.90
  + 3.84
```

h
```
    2.179
  + 8.352
```

Example 6 2 Find each of the following.

a $12.45 + 3.61$

b $5.37 + 13.81 + 2.15$

c $3.6 + 4.11$

d $2.35 + 7.5$

e $312.5 + 31.25$

f $1.567 + 3.4 + 32.6$

g $5.882 + 3.01 + 12.7$

h $323.71 + 3.4506 + 12.9$

Example 7 3 Find:

a
```
    17.2
  −  5.1
```

b
```
   128.63
 −  14.50
```

c
```
    23.94
  − 17.61
```

d
```
   158.32
 −  87.53
```

Example 7

4 Find:

   a $14.8 - 2.5$ b $234.6 - 103.2$ c $25.9 - 3.67$

   d $31.657 - 18.2$ e $412.1 - 368.83$ f $5312.271 - 364.93$

PROBLEM-SOLVING	5–7	5, 7, 9	5, 8, 10

5 Find the missing numbers in the following sums.

a
```
   3 . □
 + 4 . 6
 ─────────
   □ . 3
```

b
```
   8 . □ 9
 + □ . 7 5
 ─────────
 □ 4 . 4 □
```

c
```
     1 . □ 1
 + □ □ . 1 1
 ───────────
   1 1 . 1 □
```

d
```
   □ . 3 □ 6
   2 . □ 4 3
 + 1 . 8 9 □
 ───────────
 □ 1 . 3 9 5
```

6 How much greater is 262.5 than 76.31?

7 Stuart wants to raise $100 for the Rainbow Club charity. He already has three donations of $30.20, $10.50 and $5.00. How much does Stuart still need to raise?

8 Daily rainfalls for 4 days over Easter were 12.5 mm, 3.25 mm, 0.6 mm and 32.76 mm. What was the total rainfall over the 4-day Easter holiday?

9 Copy and complete the addition table below.

+	0.01	0.05	0.38	1.42
0.3				1.72
0.75			1.13	
1.20	1.21		1.58	
1.61				3.03

10 Michelle earned $3758.65 working part-time over a 1-year period. However, she was required to pay her parents $20 per week for board for 52 weeks. Michelle also spent $425.65 on clothing and $256.90 on presents for her family and friends during the year. She placed the rest of her money in the bank. How much did Michelle bank for the year?

REASONING	11	11, 12	12, 13

11 An addition fact can be converted into two subtraction facts. For example, because $2.1 + 4.7 = 6.8$ we know that $6.8 - 2.1 = 4.7$ and $6.8 - 4.7 = 2.1$ must be true. Write two subtraction facts for each of the following.

    a $3.2 + 4.95 = 8.15$ **b** $2.8 + 3.7 = 6.5$ **c** $8.3 + 1.8 = 10.1$ **d** $2.51 + 3.8 = 6.31$

12 a Is it possible to add two decimal numbers together and get a whole number?
    If so, give an example, if not, explain why not.

    b Is it possible to subtract a decimal number from a different decimal number and get a whole number? Explain why or why not.

13 a Write down three numbers between 1 and 10, each with 2 decimal places, that would add to 11.16.

    b Can you find a solution to part **a** that uses each digit from 1 to 9 exactly once each?

ENRICHMENT: Money, money, money ...	–	–	14

14 Investigate the following procedures and share your findings with a friend.

    a Choose an amount of money that is less than \$10.00 (e.g. \$3.25).

    b Reverse the order of the digits and subtract the smaller number from the larger number (e.g. \$5.23 − \$3.25 = \$1.98).

    c Reverse the order of the digits in your new answer and now add this number to your most recent total (e.g. \$1.98 + \$8.91 = \$10.89).

    Did you also get \$10.89? Repeat the procedure using different starting values.

    Try to discover a pattern or a rule. Justify your findings.

5D Multiplying and dividing decimals by 10, 100, 1000 etc.

Powers of 10 include 10^1, 10^2, 10^3, 10^4, …, which correspond to the numbers 10, 100, 1000, 10 000, … Note that the number of zeros in the number is the same as the power of 10 for that number. For example, $10^4 = 10\,000$, the number ten thousand has four zeros and it is equal to ten to the power of four.

Lesson starter: Dynamic leap frog

A set of large number cards, enough for one card per student in the class, is required.

The set of cards should include the following digits, numbers and symbols:

0, 1, 2, 3, 4, 5, 6, 7, 8, 9, ., ×, ÷, 1, 10, 100, 1000, 10 000, 1 00 000, 1 000 000

The decimal place card is vital! Cards should be big enough to be read from the back of the classroom. Any of the digits can be doubled up to increase the total number of cards. Each student receives one card.

• Four students with one of the 0 to 9 digit cards stand up at the front and make a 4-digit number.
• The student with the decimal place card then positions themselves somewhere within this number or on either end.
• Now a student with the × or ÷ operation comes up the front.
• Finally, a student with a power of 10 card comes up and performs the actual calculation by gently moving the decimal place!
• Repeat a number of times with students swapping cards on several occasions.

Engineers, scientists and trade workers frequently multiply and divide by powers of 10. Medical researchers use microscopes to study viruses, bacteria and cells such as human red blood cells, $\frac{8}{1000}$ mm = 0.008 mm in diameter.

KEY IDEAS

■ Every number can be written so it contains a decimal point but it is usually not shown in integers.
For example: 345 and 345.0 are equivalent.

■ Extra zeros can be added in the column to the right of the decimal point without changing the value of the decimal.
For example: 12.5 = 12.50 = 12.500 = 12.5000 etc.

■ When multiplying by powers of 10, follow these rules.
  • Move the decimal point to the *right* the same number of places as there are zeros in the multiplier.
    For example, if multiplying by 1000, move the decimal point 3 places to the right.

    $5.7839 \times 1000 = 5783.9$

    (Note: The decimal point actually stays still and all the digits move three places to the left, but this is harder to visualise.)

■ When dividing by powers of 10, follow these rules.
  • Move the decimal point to the *left* the same number of places as there are zeros in the multiplier.
    For example, if dividing by 100, move the decimal point 2 places to the left.

    $2975.6 \div 100 = 29.756$

    (Note: The decimal point actually stays still and all the digits move two places to the right, but this is harder to visualise.)

BUILDING UNDERSTANDING

1 State the missing power of 10, (10, 100, 1000, etc.)

a $56.321 \times \boxed{} = 5632.1$ b $0.03572 \times \boxed{} = 3.572$

2 State the missing power of 10, (10, 100, 1000, etc.)

a $2345.1 \div \boxed{} = 2.3451$ b $0.00367 \div \boxed{} = 0.000367$

3 a   How many places and in what direction does the decimal point in the number appear to move if the following operations occur?

   i $\times 100$ ii $\times 1\,000\,000$ iii $\div 1000$ iv $\div 10\,000\,000$

  b   If all of the operations above had taken place on a number, one after the other, what would be the final position of the decimal place relative to its starting position?

Example 8   Multiplying by 10, 100, 1000 etc.

Calculate:

a 36.532×100 b $4.31 \times 10\,000$

SOLUTION	EXPLANATION
a $36.532 \times 100 = 3653.2$	100 has two zeros, therefore decimal point appears to move 2 places to the right. 36.532

b $4.31 \times 10\,000 = 43\,100$

Decimal point appears to move 4 places to the right and additional zeros are inserted as necessary. 4.3100

Now you try

Calculate:

a 51.0942×1000

b 3.9×100

Example 9   Dividing by 10, 100, 1000 etc.

Calculate:

a $268.15 \div 10$

b $7.82 \div 1000$

SOLUTION

a $268.15 \div 10 = 26.815$

b $7.82 \div 1000 = 0.00782$

EXPLANATION

10 has one zero, therefore decimal point is moved 1 place to the left. 268.15

Decimal point is moved 3 places to the left and additional zeros are inserted as necessary. $.00782$

Now you try

Calculate:

a $392.807 \div 10$

b $8.12 \div 100$

Example 10   Working with the 'missing' decimal point

Calculate:

a $567 \times 10\,000$

b $23 \div 1000$

SOLUTION

a $567 \times 10\,000 = 5\,670\,000$

b $23 \div 1000 = 0.023$

EXPLANATION

If no decimal point is shown in the question, it must be at the very end of the number.
Four additional zeros must be inserted to move the invisible decimal point 4 places to the right. $5670000.$

Decimal point is moved 3 places to the left. 0.023

Now you try

Calculate:

a 289×1000

b $78 \div 10\,000$

Example 11   Evaluating using order of operations

Evaluate this expression, using the order of operations: $426 \div 100 + 10(0.43 \times 10 - 1.6)$

SOLUTION

$426 \div 100 + 10(0.43 \times 10 - 1.6)$
$= 4.26 + 10(4.3 - 1.6)$
$= 4.26 + 10 \times 2.7$
$= 4.26 + 27$
$= 31.26$

EXPLANATION

First, we must calculate the brackets. The division by 100 can also be done in the first step.
$10(4.3 - 2.6)$ means $10 \times (4.3 - 2.6)$.

Now you try

Evaluate $32.5 - 47 \div 10 + (3.1 + 5.4) \times 100$

Exercise 5D

FLUENCY	1, 2–5($\frac{1}{2}$)	2–5($\frac{1}{2}$)	2–5($\frac{1}{3}$)

Example 8

1   Calculate:
   a 24.327×100
   b 43.61×10
   c 1.84×1000

Example 8

2   Calculate:
   a 4.87×10
   b 35.283×10
   c 422.27×10
   d 14.304×100
   e 5.69923×1000
   f 1.25963×100
   g 12.7×1000
   h 154.23×1000
   i $0.34 \times 10\,000$
   j 213.2×10
   k $867.1 \times 100\,000$
   l $0.00516 \times 100\,000\,000$

Example 9

3   Calculate:
   a $42.7 \div 10$
   b $353.1 \div 10$
   c $24.422 \div 10$
   d $5689.3 \div 100$
   e $12\,135.18 \div 1000$
   f $93\,261.1 \div 10\,000$
   g $2.9 \div 100$
   h $13.62 \div 10\,000$
   i $0.54 \div 1000$
   j $36.7 \div 100$
   k $0.02 \div 10\,000$
   l $1000.04 \div 100\,000$

Example 9

4   Calculate:
   a 22.913×100
   b $0.031\,67 \times 1000$
   c $4.9 \div 10$
   d $22.2 \div 100$
   e $6348.9 \times 10\,000$
   f $1.0032 \div 1000$

Example 10

5   Calculate:
   a 156×100
   b 43×1000
   c $2251 \div 10$
   d $16 \div 1000$
   e 2134×100
   f $2134 \div 100$
   g $7 \div 1000$
   h $99 \times 100\,000$
   i $34 \div 10\,000$

| PROBLEM-SOLVING | 6(½), 7 | 6(½), 8, 9 | 6(¼), 8–10 |

6 Evaluate the following, using the order of operations.

a $1.56 \times 100 + 24 \div 10$

b $16 \div 100 + 32 \div 10$

c $3 + 10(24 \div 100 + 8)$

d $10(6.734 \times 100 + 32)$

e $35.4 + 4.2 \times 10 - 63.4 \div 10$

f $4.7 - 24 \div 10 + 0.52 \times 10$

g $14 \div 100 + 1897 \div 1000$

h $78.1 - 10(64 \div 100 + 5)$

7 A service station charges \$1.87 per litre of petrol. How much will it cost Tanisha to fill her car with 100 litres of petrol?

8 A large bee farm produces 1200 litres of honey per day.

a If there are 1000 millilitres in 1 litre, how many millilitres of honey can the farm's bees produce in one day?

b The farm's honey is sold in 100 millilitre jars. How many jars of honey can the farm's bees fill in one day?

9 Wendy is on a mobile phone plan that charges her 3 cents per text message. On average, Wendy sends 10 text messages per day. What will it cost Wendy for 100 days of sending text messages at this rate? Give your answer in cents and then convert your answer to dollars.

10 Darren wishes to purchase 10 000 shares at \$2.12 per share. Given that there is also an additional \$200 brokerage fee, how much will it cost Darren to purchase the shares?

| REASONING | 11 | 11, 12 | 12, 13 |

11 The weight of a matchstick is 0.00015 kg. Find the weight of 10 000 boxes of matches, with each box containing 100 matches. The weight of one empty match box is 0.0075 kg.

12 Complete the table below, listing at least one possible combination of operations that would produce the stated answer from the given starting number.

Starting number	Answer	Possible two-step operations
12.357	1235.7	× 1000, ÷10
34.0045	0.0340045	
0.003601	360.1	
BAC.DFG	BA.CDFG	÷100, ×10
D.SWKK	DSWKK	
FWY	F.WY	

13 The number 12 345.6789 undergoes a series of multiplication and division operations by different powers of 10. The first four operations are: ÷1000, × 100, × 10 000 and ÷10. What is the fifth and final operation if the final number is 1.234 567 89?

14 Extremely large numbers and extremely small numbers are often written in a more practical way, known as standard form or scientific notation.

For example, the distance from Earth to the Sun is 150 000 000 kilometres! The distance of 150 million kilometres can be written in standard form as 1.5×10^8 kilometres.

On a calculator, 150 000 000 can be represented as 1.5E8.

1.5×10^8 and 1.5E8 represent the same large number and indicate that the decimal place needs to be moved 8 places to the right.

$$1.5E8 = 1.5 \times 10^8 = 1.5 \times 100 000 000$$
$$= 150000000$$

a Represent these numbers in standard form.
  i 50 000 000 000 000
  ii 42 000 000
  iii 12 300 000 000 000 000

b Use a calculator to evaluate the following.
  i 40 000 000 000 × 500 000 000
  ii 9 000 000 × 120 000 000 000 000

c The distance from Earth to the Sun is stated above as 150 million kilometres. The more precise figure is 149 597 892 kilometres. Research how astronomers can calculate the distance so accurately. (*Hint*: It is linked to the speed of light.)

d Carry out further research on very large numbers. Create a list of ten very large numbers (e.g. distance from Earth to Pluto, the number of grains in 1 kg of sand, the number of stars in the galaxy, the number of memory bytes in a terabyte…). List your ten large numbers in ascending order.

e How are very small numbers, such as 0.000000000035, represented in standard form? You can research this question if you do not know.

f Represent the following numbers in standard form.
  i 0.000001
  ii 0.0000000009
  iii 0.000000000007653

5E Multiplying decimals

LEARNING INTENTIONS
• To be able to multiply decimals
• To understand that it is helpful to estimate to check the position of the decimal point in the final answer

There are countless real-life applications that involve the multiplication of decimal numbers. For example, finding the area of a block of land that is 34.5 m long and 5.2 m wide, or pricing a 4.5-hour job at a rate of $21.75 per hour. In general, the procedure for multiplying decimal numbers is the same as multiplying whole numbers. There is, however, one extra final step, which involves placing the decimal point in the correct position in the answer.

Lesson starter: Multiplication musings

Consider the following questions within your group.

To score a synchronised dive, the sum of the execution and synchronisation scores is multiplied by the degree of difficulty and then by 0.6, to match the scoring of individual dives. For example: $39.5 \times 3.2 \times 0.6 = 75.84$.

• What happens when you multiply by a number that is less than 1?
• Consider the product of 15×0.75. Will the answer be more or less than 15? Why?
• Estimate an answer to 15×0.75.
• What is the total number of decimal places in the numbers 15 and 0.75?
• Calculate 15×0.75. How many decimal places are there in the answer?

KEY IDEAS

■ When multiplying decimals, start by ignoring any decimal points and perform the multiplication as you would normally. On arriving at your answer, place the decimal point in the correct position.

■ The correct position of the decimal point in the answer is found by following the rule that the total number of decimal places in the numbers in the question must equal the number of decimal places in the answer.

For example:

3 decimal places in the question

$5.34 \times 1.2 = 6.408$

3 decimal places in the answer

$$\begin{array}{r} 534 \\ \times\ 12 \\ \hline 1068 \\ 5340 \\ \hline 6408 \end{array}$$

decimal points ignored here

■ It is always worthwhile estimating your answer. This allows you to check that your decimal point is in the correct place and that your answer makes sense.

■ Answers can be estimated by first rounding each value to the nearest whole number.

e.g. $2.93 \times 5.17 \approx 3 \times 5$ ($\approx$ means approximately equal to)

$\qquad\qquad\quad = 15$

■ When multiplying by multiples of 10, initially ignore the zeros in the multiplier and any decimal points and perform routine multiplication. On arriving at your answer, position your decimal point, remembering to move your decimal point according to the rules of multiplying by powers of 10.

BUILDING UNDERSTANDING

1 State out the total number of decimal places in each of the following product statements.

   a 4×6.3 **b** 3.52×76

   c 42×5.123 **d** 8.71×11.2

   e 5.283×6.02 **f** 0.00103×0.0045

2 State where the decimal point should be inserted into each of the following answers so that the multiplication is true.

   a $6.4 \times 3 = 192$ **b** $6.4 \times 0.3 = 192$ **c** $0.64 \times 0.3 = 192$

3 Why is it worthwhile to estimate an answer to a multiplication question involving decimals?

4 **a** What is the difference between a decimal point and a decimal place?

     b How many decimal points and how many decimal places are in the number 423.1567?

5 State the missing words for the rule for multiplying decimal numbers (see the **Key ideas** in this section). The total number of decimal places _____ must equal the number of _____ in the answer.

⏵

Example 12   Estimating decimal products

Estimate the following by first rounding each decimal to the nearest whole number.

a 4.13×7.62 **b** 2.8×12.071

SOLUTION

a $4.13 \times 7.62 \approx 4 \times 8$
                     $= 32$

b $2.8 \times 12.071 \approx 3 \times 12$
                     $= 36$

EXPLANATION

Round each value to the nearest whole number (0 decimal places).

$4.13 \approx 4, 7.62 \approx 8$

Multiply the rounded values to obtain an estimate.

$2.8 \approx 3$ and $12.071 \approx 12$

Multiply the rounded values to obtain an estimate.

Now you try

Estimate the following by first rounding each decimal to the nearest whole number.

a 2.9×4.18 **b** 7.05×10.9

Example 13   Multiplying decimals

Calculate the following and check your answer.

a 12.31×7

b 3.63×6.9

SOLUTION

a
```
  1231
×    7
 8617
```

$12.31 \times 7 = 86.17$

b
```
   363
×   69
  3267
 21780
 25047
```

$3.63 \times 6.9 = 25.047$

EXPLANATION

Perform multiplication, ignoring the decimal point. There are 2 decimal places in the numbers in the question, so there will be 2 decimal places in the answer.

Check that this value is close to the estimated value ($\approx 12 \times 7 = 84$), which it is.

Ignore both decimal points.
Perform routine multiplication.
Total of 3 decimal places in the numbers in the question, so there must be 3 decimal places in the answer.

Check that this value is close to the estimated value ($\approx 4 \times 7 = 28$), which it is.

Now you try

Calculate:

a 32.15×9

b 2.6×1.78

Example 14   Multiplying decimals by multiples of 10

Calculate:

a $2.65 \times 40\,000$

b 0.032×600

SOLUTION

a $2.65 \times 40\,000 = 106\,000$
```
  265
×   4
 1060
```
$\therefore 10.60 \times 10\,000 = 106000.$
$\qquad\qquad\quad = 106000$

EXPLANATION

Ignore the decimal point and zeros.
Multiply 265×4.

Position the decimal point in your answer. There are 2 decimal places in 2.65, so there must be 2 decimal places in the answer.

Move the decimal point 4 places to the right, to multiply 10.60 by 10 000.

Continued on next page

SOLUTION	EXPLANATION
b $0.032 \times 600 = 19.2$	Ignore the decimal point and zeros.
$\begin{array}{r} 32 \\ \times\ \ 6 \\ \hline 192 \end{array}$	Multiply 32×6.
	Position the decimal point in the answer.
$\therefore 0.192 \times 100 = 19.2$	Shift the decimal point 2 places to the right to multiply 0.192 by 100.

Now you try

Calculate:

a 52.9×3000 \qquad\qquad\qquad **b** 0.0061×700

Exercise 5E

FLUENCY

1, 2–4($\frac{1}{2}$)	1, 3–5($\frac{1}{2}$)	1($\frac{1}{2}$), 3–5($\frac{1}{3}$)

Example 12

1 Estimate the following by first rounding each decimal to the nearest whole number.

  a 3.6×2.1
  b 4.9×8.31
  c 7.2×10.3
  d 2.95×7.832

Example 13a

2 Calculate:

  a 13.51×7
  b 2.84×6
  c 5.13×6
  d 7.215×3

Example 13

3 Calculate:

  a 5.21×4
  b 3.8×7
  c 22.93×8
  d 14×7.2
  e 3×72.82
  f 1.293×12
  g 3.4×6.8
  h 5.4×2.3
  i 0.34×16
  j 43.21×7.2
  k 0.023×0.042
  l 18.61×0.071

Example 14

4 Calculate:

  a 2.52×40
  b 6.9×70
  c 31.75×800
  d 1.4×7000
  e 3000×4.8
  f $7.291 \times 50\,000$
  g 0.0034×200
  h $0.0053 \times 70\,000$
  i 3.004×30

5 Calculate and then round your answer to the nearest dollar.

  a $5 \times \$6.30$
  b $3 \times \$7.55$
  c $4 \times \$18.70$
  d $\$1.45 \times 12$
  e $\$30.25 \times 4.8$
  f $7.2 \times \$5200$
  g $34.2 \times \$2.60$
  h $0.063 \times \$70.00$
  i $0.085 \times \$212.50$

PROBLEM-SOLVING

6	6–8	7–9

6 Use decimal multiplication to answer the following.

  a Anita requires 4.21 m of material for each dress she is making. She is planning to make a total of seven dresses. How much material does she need?

  b The net weight of a can of spaghetti is 0.445 kg. Find the net weight of eight cans of spaghetti.

  c Jimbo ran 5.35 km each day for the month of March. How many kilometres did he run for the month?

7 Bernard is making a cubby house for his children. He needs 32 lengths of timber, each 2.1 m long.

  a What is the total length of timber needed to build the cubby house?

  b What is the cost of the timber if the price is $2.95 per metre?

8 A lawyer charges $125.00 per hour to assist her client. How much does the lawyer charge the client if she works on the job for 12.25 hours?

9 According to its manufacturer, a particular car can travel 14.2 km on 1 litre of petrol.
  a How far could the car travel on 52 litres of petrol?
  b The car has 23.4 litres of fuel in the tank and must complete a journey of 310 km. Will it make the journey without refuelling?
  c If the car does make the journey, how much petrol is left in the tank at the end of the trip? If the car does not make the journey, how many extra litres of fuel are needed?

REASONING		10	10, 11	11–13

10 When estimating a decimal product, the actual answer is usually higher or lower than the estimated value. For example, $3.8 \times 2.1 = 7.98$, which is lower than the estimate of $4 \times 2 = 8$.
  a Without calculating the actual value, explain why 3.92×6.85 will be lower than the estimated value of $4 \times 7 = 28$.
  b Explain why 4.21×7.302 is higher than the estimated product.
  c Give an example of a situation where one value rounds up, and the other rounds down but the actual product is higher than the estimate.

11 Write down two numbers, each with 2 decimal places, that when multiplied by 1.83 will give an answer between 0.4 and 0.5.

12 Write down one number with 4 decimal places that when multiplied by 345.62 will give an answer between 1 and 2.

13 a If $68 \times 57 = 3876$, what is the answer to 6.8×5.7? Why?
  b If $23 \times 32 = 736$, what is the answer to 2.3×32? Why?
  c If $250 \times 300 = 75\,000$, what is the answer to 2.5×0.3? Why?
  d What is 7×6? What is the answer to 0.7×0.6? Why?

ENRICHMENT: Creating a simple cash register		–	–	14

14 Using a spreadsheet (e.g. Microsoft Excel, Google sheets, Apple numbers), design a user-friendly cash register interface. You must be able to enter up to 10 different items into your spreadsheet. You will need a quantity column and a cost per item column.

Using appropriate formulas, the total cost of the bill should be displayed, and there should then be room to enter the amount of money paid and, if necessary, what change should be given.

When your spreadsheet is set up, enter the following items.

4 chocolate bars @ $1.85 each   toothpaste @ $4.95
3 loaves of bread @ $3.19 each   2 kg sausages @ $5.99 per kg
newspaper @ $1.40   tomato sauce @ $3.20
2 × 2 litres of milk @ $3.70 each   washing powder @ $8.95
2 packets of Tim Tams @ $3.55 each   5 × 1.25 litres of soft drink @ $0.99 each
Money paid = $80.00

If your program is working correctly, the amount of change given should be $13.10.

Progress quiz

5A

1 What is the place value of the digit 6 in the following numbers?

a   3.5678   b   126.872

5A

2 Express each of the following fractions as a decimal.

a $\dfrac{9}{10}$ b $\dfrac{19}{1000}$ c $3\dfrac{1}{4}$

5A

3 Place the correct mathematical symbol < or > in between the following pairs of decimals to make a true mathematical statement.

a   4.02 $\boxed{}$ 4.1   b   3.719 $\boxed{}$ 3.71

c   8.2 $\boxed{}$ 8.19   d   14.803 $\boxed{}$ 14.8005

5B

4 Round each of the following to the specified number of decimal places.

a   16.8765 to 2 decimal places

b   2.34999 to 3 decimal places

c   0.66667 to 1 decimal place

5C

5 Find:

a $0.9 + 4.5$ b $12.56 + 3.671 + 0.8$

c $12.89 - 9.37$ d $8.06 - 2.28$

5D

6 Evaluate:

a 3.45×1000 b $65.345 \div 100$

5E

7 Estimate the following products by first rounding each value to the nearest whole number.

a 3.28×4.7 b 9.12×2.04 c 3.81×5.12

5E

8 Calculate:

a 45×2000 b 23.8×5

c 4.78×0.4 d $4.56 \times 30\,000$

5C/E

9 Insert the decimal point in the answer so that each mathematical sentence is true.

a $12 - 3.989 = 8011$

b $1.234 \times 0.08 \times 2000 = 19\,744$

5C/E

10 It costs $59.85 for a large bottle of dog shampoo. Find:

a   the change from paying with one $50 note and one $20 note

b   the cost of buying three bottles.

5F Dividing decimals

Similar to multiplication of decimal numbers, there are countless real-life applications that involve the division of decimal numbers. However, unlike multiplying decimal numbers, where we basically ignore the decimal points until the very end of the calculation, with division we try to manipulate the numbers in the question in such a way as to prevent dividing by a decimal number.

Division using decimal places is required in many calculations of an average. One example is calculating a batting average in cricket, where Australia's highest Test cricket batting average is 99.94, held by Sir Donald Bradman.

Lesson starter: Division decisions

Consider the following questions within your group.

- What happens when you divide by a number that is less than 1 but greater than 0?
- Consider the answer of $10 \div 0.2$. Will the answer be more or less than 10? Why?
- Estimate an answer to $10 \div 0.2$.
- Calculate the answer of $100 \div 2$. How does this compare to the answer of $10 \div 0.2$?
- Can you think of an easier way to calculate $21.464 \div 0.02$?

KEY IDEAS

■ **Division of decimal numbers by whole numbers**
- Complete as you would normally with any other division question.
- The decimal point in the quotient (answer) goes directly above the decimal point in the dividend.
  For example: $60.524 \div 4$

$$\begin{array}{r} 1\,5.131 \\ \hline 4)6^2 0.5^1 24 \end{array}$$

■ **Division of decimal numbers by other decimals**
- Change the divisor into a whole number.
- Whatever change is made to the divisor must also be made to the dividend.
  For example: $24.524 \div 0.02$

$$24.562 \div 0.02 = 2456.2 \div 2$$

- When dividing by multiples of 10, initially ignore the zeros in the divisor and perform routine division. On arriving at your answer, you must then re-position your decimal point according to the rules of dividing by powers of 10. For each zero in the divisor that you ignored initially, the decimal point must move 1 place to the left.

BUILDING UNDERSTANDING

1 For the question $36.52 \div 0.4 = 91.3$, which of the following options uses the correct terminology?

A 36.52 is the divisor, 0.4 is the dividend and 91.3 is the quotient.

B 36.52 is the dividend, 0.4 is the divisor and 91.3 is the quotient.

C 36.52 is the quotient, 0.4 is the dividend and 91.3 is the divisor.

D 36.52 is the divisor, 0.4 is the quotient and 91.3 is the dividend.

2 Explain where you place the decimal point in the quotient (i.e. answer), when dividing a decimal by a whole number.

3 Calculate:

    a $1200 \div 20$ **b** $120 \div 2$ **c** $12 \div 0.2$ **d** $1.2 \div 0.02$

    e Explain why these questions all give the same answer.

4 For each of the following pairs of numbers, move the decimal points the same number of places so that the second number becomes a whole number.

    a 3.2456, 0.3   **b** 120.432, 0.12   **c** 0.00345, 0.0001   **d** 1234.12, 0.004

Example 15   Dividing decimals by whole numbers

Calculate:

a $42.837 \div 3$ **b** $0.0234 \div 4$

SOLUTION

a 14.279

$$3 \overline{)4\,2.8\,^1 3\,^2 7\,^2}$$
   1 4.2 7 9

b 0.00585

$$4 \overline{)0.02\,^2 3\,^3 4\,^2 0}$$
   0.00 5 8 5

EXPLANATION

Carry out division, remembering that the decimal point in the answer is placed directly above the decimal point in the dividend.

Remember to place zeros in the answer every time the divisor 'doesn't go'. Again, align the decimal point in the answer directly above the decimal point in the question.

An additional zero is required at the end of the dividend to terminate the decimal answer.

Now you try

Calculate:

a $15.184 \div 4$ **b** $0.413 \div 5$

Example 16   Dividing decimals by decimals

Calculate:

a $62.316 \div 0.03$

b $0.03152 \div 0.002$

SOLUTION

a $62.316 \div 0.03$
   $= 6231.6 \div 3 = 2077.2$

$$
\begin{array}{r}
20\ 7\ 7.2 \\
3\overline{)62\,^{2}3\,^{2}1.6}
\end{array}
$$

b $0.03152 \div 0.002$
   $= 31.52 \div 2 = 15.76$

$$
\begin{array}{r}
1\ 5.7\ 6 \\
2\overline{)3\,^{2}1.^{1}5\,^{1}2}
\end{array}
$$

EXPLANATION

Need to divide by a whole number.

$62.316 \div 0.03$

Move each decimal point 2 places to the right.
Carry out the division question $6231.6 \div 3$.

Multiply the divisor and dividend by 1000.

$0.03152 \div 0.002$

Move each decimal point 3 places to the right.

Carry out the division question $31.52 \div 2$.

Now you try

Calculate:

a $47.188 \div 0.04$

b $0.2514 \div 0.003$

Example 17   Dividing decimals by multiples of 10

Calculate $67.04 \div 8000$.

SOLUTION

$$
\begin{array}{r}
08.38 \\
8\overline{)67.04}
\end{array}
$$

$8.38 \div 1000 = 0.00838$
$67.04 \div 8000 = 0.00838$

EXPLANATION

Ignore the three zeros in the 8000.
Divide 67.04 by 8.

Now divide by 1000, resulting in moving the
decimal point 3 places to the left.

Now you try

Calculate $149.8 \div 7000$.

Example 18   Evaluating using order of operations

Calculate using the order of operations:
$3.8 - 1.6 \times 0.45 + 5 \div 0.4$

SOLUTION

$3.8 - 1.6 \times 0.45 + 5 \div 0.4$
$= 3.8 - 0.72 + 12.5$
$= 3.08 + 12.5$
$= 15.58$

EXPLANATION

First carry out $\times$ and $\div$, working from left to right.
Then carry out $+$ and $-$, working from left to right.

Now you try

Calculate using the order of operations:
$9.3 + 1.3 \times 4.05 - 1.2 \div 0.25$

Exercise 5F

FLUENCY	1, 2–5(½)	1, 2–3(⅓), 4–6(½)	2–4(¼), 5–6(⅓)

Example 15a

1   Calculate:

  a $7.02 \div 2$ b $15.57 \div 3$ c $17.48 \div 4$ d $45.565 \div 5$

Example 15

2   Calculate:

  a $8.4 \div 2$ b $30.5 \div 5$ c $64.02 \div 3$ d $2.822 \div 4$
  e $4.713 \div 3$ f $2.156 \div 7$ g $38.786 \div 11$ h $1491.6 \div 12$
  i $0.0144 \div 6$ j $234.21 \div 2$ k $3.417 \div 5$ l $0.01025 \div 4$

Example 16a

3   Calculate:

  a $6.14 \div 0.2$ b $23.25 \div 0.3$ c $2.144 \div 0.08$ d $5.1 \div 0.6$
  e $45.171 \div 0.07$ f $10.78 \div 0.011$ g $4.003 \div 0.005$ h $432.2 \div 0.0002$

Example 16b

4   Calculate:

  a $0.3996 \div 0.009$ b $0.0032 \div 0.04$ c $0.04034 \div 0.8$ d $0.948 \div 1.2$

Example 17

5   Calculate:

  a $236.14 \div 200$ b $413.35 \div 50$ c $3.71244 \div 300$
  d $0.846 \div 200$ e $482.435 \div 5000$ f $0.0313 \div 40$

6   Calculate the following, rounding your answers to 2 decimal places.

  a $35.5\,\text{kg} \div 3$ b $\$213.25 \div 7$ c $182.6\,\text{m} \div 0.6$
  d $287\,\text{g} \div 1.2$ e $482.523\,\text{L} \div 0.5$ f $\$5235.50 \div 9$

PROBLEM-SOLVING   7(½), 8   7(½), 8–10   8, 10–12

Example 18

7 Calculate the following, using the order of operations.

   a $3.68 \div 2 + 5.7 \div 0.3$ **b** $6(3.7 \times 2.8 + 5.2)$

   c $17.83 - 1.2(8.1 - 2.35)$ **d** $9.81 \div 0.9 + 75.9 \div 10$

   e $(56.7 - 2.4) \div (0.85 \div 2 + 0.375)$ **f** $34.5 \times 2.3 + 15.8 \div (0.96 - 0.76)$

8 Find the missing digits in these division questions.

   a $0.\square\square$ **b** $0.\,6\,4$ **c** $2.\square\,5$ **d** $2.\,1\,4\,\square$

       $3\overline{)2.\,6\,\,\,7}$ $3\overline{)1.\square\,2}$ $\square\overline{)10.\,7\,\square}$ $\square\overline{)15.\square\,2\,9}$

9 Charlie paid $12.72 to fill his ride-on lawnmower with 8 L of fuel. What was the price per litre of the fuel that he purchased?

10 Dibden is a picture framer and has recently purchased 214.6 m of timber. The average-sized picture frame requires 90 cm (0.9 m) of timber. How many average picture frames could Dibden make with his new timber?

11 A water bottle can hold 600 mL of water. How many water bottles can be filled from a large drink container that can hold 16 L?

12 Six friends go out for dinner. At the end of the evening, the restaurant's bill is $398.10.

   a   As the bill is split equally among the six friends, how much does each person pay?

   b   Given that they are happy with the food and the service, they decide to round the amount they each pay to $70. What is the waiter's tip?

REASONING   13   13, 14   14, 15

13 Clara purchases 1.2 kg of apples for $3.90. Her friend Sophia buys 900 g of bananas for $2.79 at the same shop. Find the cost per kilogram of each fruit. Which type of fruit is the best value in terms of price per kilogram?

14 A police radar gun measures a car to be 231.5 m away. Exactly 0.6 seconds later, the radar gun measures the same car to be 216.8 m away.
    a   Determine the speed of the car in metres per second (m/s).
    b   Multiply your answer to part a by 3.6 to convert your answer to km/h.
    c   The car is travelling along an 80 km/h stretch of road. Is the car speeding?

15 Given that $24.53 \times 1.97 = 48.3241$, write down the value of each of the following divisions, without using a calculator.
    a $48.3241 \div 1.97$ b $48.3241 \div 2.453$ c $4832.41 \div 1.97$
    d $483.241 \div 245.3$ e $0.483241 \div 0.197$ f $483\,241 \div 2453$

ENRICHMENT: What number am I?   –   –   16

16 In each of the following, I am thinking of a number. Given the following clues for each, find each number.
    a   When I add 4.5 to my number and then multiply by 6, the answer is 30.
    b   When I divide my number by 3 and then add 2.9, the answer is 3.
    c   When I multiply my number by 100 and then add 9, the answer is 10.
    d   When I multiply my number by 5 and then add a half, the answer is 6.
    e   When I subtract 0.8 from my number, then divide by 0.2 and then divide by 0.1, the answer is 200.
    f   Make up three of your own number puzzles to share with the class.

5G Connecting decimals and fractions

LEARNING INTENTIONS
- To be able to convert decimals to fractions
- To be able to convert fractions to decimals
- To understand the symbols to indicate recurring decimals

Decimals and fractions are both commonly used to represent numbers that are not simply whole numbers. It is important that we know how to convert a decimal number to a fraction, and how to convert a fraction to a decimal number.

Lesson starter: Match my call

- In pairs, nominate one student to be 'Fraction kid' and the other to be 'Decimal expert'. 'Fraction kid' starts naming some common fractions and 'Decimal expert' tries to give the equivalent decimal value. Start with easy questions and build up to harder ones.

A civil engineer can design a tunnel for an underground railway having an upward slope with a gradient of 0.03. By converting 0.03 to 3/100 the engineer then knows that for every horizontal 100 m, the tunnel must rise by 3 m.

- After 10 turns, swap around. This time 'Decimal expert' will name some decimal numbers and 'Fraction kid' will attempt to call out the equivalent fraction.
- Discuss the following question in pairs:
  Which is easier, converting fractions to decimals or decimals to fractions?

KEY IDEAS

■ **Converting decimals to fractions**
- Using your knowledge of place value, express the decimal places as a fraction whose denominator is 10, 100, 1000 etc. Remember to simplify the fraction whenever possible.

  e.g. $0.25 = \dfrac{25}{100} = \dfrac{1}{4}$

■ **Converting fractions to decimals**
- When the denominator is 10, 100, 1000 etc. we can simply change the fraction to a decimal through knowledge of place value.

  e.g. $\dfrac{37}{100} = 0.37$

- When the denominator is *not* 10, 100, 1000 etc. try to find an equivalent fraction whose denominator is 10, 100, 1000 etc. and then convert to a decimal.

  e.g. $\dfrac{2}{5} = \dfrac{4}{10} = 0.4$

- A method that will always work for converting fractions to decimals is to divide the numerator by the denominator.

  e.g. $\dfrac{5}{8} = 8\overline{)5.^{5}0^{2}0^{4}0} = 0.625$

  $\quad\quad\ \ 0.\ 6\ \ 2\ \ 5$

■ **Recurring decimals** are decimals with a repeated pattern.
  • A dot, dots or a bar above a number or numbers indicates a repeated pattern.

e.g. $\frac{1}{3} = 0.33333\ldots = 0.\dot{3}$ $\frac{13}{11} = 1.181818\ldots = 1.\dot{1}\dot{8}$ or $1.\overline{18}$

$\frac{12}{7} = 1.714285714285\ldots = 1.\dot{7}1428\dot{5}$ or $1.\overline{714285}$

BUILDING UNDERSTANDING

1 State the missing numbers in each of these statements, which convert common fractions to decimals.

a $\frac{1}{2} = \dfrac{\boxed{}}{10} = 0.5$

b $\frac{1}{4} = \dfrac{25}{\boxed{}} = 0.25$

c $\frac{3}{4} = \dfrac{\boxed{}}{100} = 0.\boxed{}5$

d $\frac{2}{\boxed{}} = \dfrac{4}{10} = 0.\boxed{}$

2 State the missing numbers in each of these statements, which convert decimals to fractions, in simplest form.

a $0.2 = \dfrac{\boxed{}}{10} = \frac{1}{5}$

b $0.15 = \dfrac{\boxed{}}{100} = \dfrac{3}{\boxed{}}$

c $0.8 = \dfrac{8}{\boxed{}} = \dfrac{\boxed{}}{5}$

d $0.64 = \dfrac{64}{100} = \dfrac{\boxed{}}{25}$

3 State whether each of the following is true or false. Use the examples in the **Key ideas** to help.

a $0.333\ldots = 0.3$
b $0.1111\ldots = 0.\dot{1}$
c $3.2222\ldots = 3.\dot{2}$
d $1.7272\ldots = 1.7\dot{2}$
e $3.161616\ldots = 3.1\dot{6}$
f $4.216216\ldots = 4.\overline{216}$

Example 19   Converting decimals to fractions

Convert the following decimals to fractions or mixed numerals in their simplest form.
a 0.239 **b** 10.35

SOLUTION

a $\dfrac{239}{1000}$

b $10\dfrac{35}{100} = 10\dfrac{7}{20}$

EXPLANATION

$0.239 = 239$ thousandths

Note $\dfrac{239}{1000}$ cannot be simplified further.

$0.35 = 35$ hundredths, which can be simplified further by dividing the numerator and denominator by the highest common factor of 5.

Now you try

Convert the following decimals to fractions in their simplest form.

a 0.407   **b** 7.45

Example 20   Converting fractions to decimals

Convert the following fractions to decimals.

a $\dfrac{17}{100}$ **b** $5\dfrac{3}{5}$ **c** $\dfrac{7}{12}$

SOLUTION

a $\dfrac{17}{100} = 0.17$

b $5\dfrac{3}{5} = 5\dfrac{6}{10} = 5.6$

c $\dfrac{7}{12} = 0.58333\ldots$ or $0.58\dot{3}$

EXPLANATION

17 hundredths

$\dfrac{6}{10}$ is an equivalent fraction of $\dfrac{3}{5}$, whose denominator is a power of 10.

$$\begin{array}{r} 0.5\ 8\ 3\ 3\ 3\ldots \\ \hline 12\overline{)7.0\ ^{10}0\ ^{4}0\ ^{4}0\ ^{4}0} \end{array}$$

Now you try

Convert the following fractions to decimals.

a $\dfrac{123}{1000}$ **b** $19\dfrac{3}{4}$ **c** $\dfrac{5}{6}$

Exercise 5G

FLUENCY		1, 2–6(½)	2–6(½), 7	2–6(⅓), 7

Example 19a

1 Convert the following decimals to fractions in their simplest form.
  a 0.3   **b** 0.41   **c** 0.201   **d** 0.07

Example 19

2 Convert the following decimals to fractions in their simplest form.
  a 0.4   **b** 0.22   **c** 0.15   **d** 0.75

Example 19

3 Convert the following decimals to fractions or mixed numerals in their simplest form.
  a 0.5   **b** 6.4   **c** 10.15   **d** 18.12
  e 3.25   **f** 0.05   **g** 9.075   **h** 5.192

Example 20a

4 Convert each of these fractions to decimals.
  a $\dfrac{7}{10}$ **b** $\dfrac{9}{10}$ **c** $\dfrac{31}{100}$ **d** $\dfrac{79}{100}$
  e $\dfrac{121}{100}$ **f** $3\dfrac{29}{100}$ **g** $\dfrac{123}{1000}$ **h** $\dfrac{3}{100}$

Example 20b

5 Convert the following fractions to decimals, by first changing the fraction to an equivalent fraction whose denominator is a power of 10.

a $\dfrac{4}{5}$
b $\dfrac{1}{2}$
c $\dfrac{7}{20}$
d $\dfrac{23}{50}$

e $\dfrac{19}{20}$
f $3\dfrac{1}{4}$
g $\dfrac{5}{2}$
h $\dfrac{3}{8}$

Example 20c

6 Convert the following fractions to decimals, by dividing the numerator by the denominator.

a $\dfrac{1}{2}$
b $\dfrac{3}{6}$
c $\dfrac{3}{4}$
d $\dfrac{2}{5}$

e $\dfrac{1}{3}$
f $\dfrac{3}{8}$
g $\dfrac{5}{12}$
h $\dfrac{3}{7}$

7 Copy and complete the following fraction/decimal tables. The quarters table (part **c**) has already been done for you. It is worth trying to memorise these fractions and their equivalent decimal values.

a halves

Fraction	$\dfrac{0}{2}$	$\dfrac{1}{2}$	$\dfrac{2}{2}$
Decimal			

b thirds

Fraction	$\dfrac{0}{3}$	$\dfrac{1}{3}$	$\dfrac{2}{3}$	$\dfrac{3}{3}$
Decimal				

c quarters

Fraction	$\dfrac{0}{4}$	$\dfrac{1}{4}$	$\dfrac{2}{4}$	$\dfrac{3}{4}$	$\dfrac{4}{4}$
Decimal	0	0.25	0.5	0.75	1

d fifths

Fraction	$\dfrac{0}{5}$	$\dfrac{1}{5}$	$\dfrac{2}{5}$	$\dfrac{3}{5}$	$\dfrac{4}{5}$	$\dfrac{5}{5}$
Decimal						

PROBLEM-SOLVING   8, 9   8, 9   9, 10, 11

8 Arrange the following from smallest to largest.

a $\dfrac{1}{2}$, 0.75, $\dfrac{5}{8}$, 0.4, 0.99, $\dfrac{1}{4}$

b $\dfrac{3}{7}$, 0.13, $\dfrac{1}{9}$, 0.58, 0.84, $\dfrac{4}{5}$

9 Tan and Lillian are trying to work out who is the better chess player. They have both been playing chess games against their computers. Tan has played 37 games and beaten the computer 11 times. Lillian has played only 21 games and has beaten the computer 6 times.

a Using a calculator and converting the appropriate fractions to decimals, determine who is the better chess player.

b Lillian has time to play another four games of chess against her computer. To be classified as a better player than Tan, how many of these four games must she win?

10 To estimate the thickness of one sheet of A4 paper, Christopher measures a ream of paper, which consists of 500 sheets of A4 paper. He determines that the pile is 55 mm thick. How thick is one sheet of A4 paper? Express your answer as a decimal number and also as a fraction.

11 When $\frac{4}{7}$ is expressed in decimal form, find the digit in the 23rd decimal place. Give a reason for your answer.

| REASONING | 12 | 12, 14 | 13–15 |

12 a Copy and complete the following fraction/decimal table.

Fraction	$\frac{1}{2}$	$\frac{1}{3}$	$\frac{1}{4}$	$\frac{1}{5}$	$\frac{1}{6}$	$\frac{1}{7}$	$\frac{1}{8}$	$\frac{1}{9}$	$\frac{1}{10}$
Decimal									

  b Comment on the trend in the decimal values as the *denominator* increases.
  c Try to explain why this makes sense.

13 a Copy and complete the following decimal/fraction table.

Decimal	0.1	0.2	0.25	0.4	0.5	0.6	0.75	0.8	0.9
Fraction									

  b Comment on the trend in the fractions as the *decimal value* increases.
  c Try to explain why this makes sense.

14 Write three different mixed numerals with different denominators that are between the decimal values of 2.4 and 2.5.

15 A decimal that is not a recurring decimal is called a *terminating* decimal.
  For example, $3.\overline{71}$ and $2.\dot{4}$ are recurring decimals, but 12.432 and 9.07 are terminating decimals.
  a Can all fractions be converted to terminating decimals? Explain why or why not.
  b Can all terminating decimals be converted to fractions? Explain why or why not.

| ENRICHMENT: Design a decimal game for the class | – | – | 16 |

16 Using the skill of converting decimals to fractions and vice versa, design an appropriate game that students in your class could play. Ideas may include variations of Bingo, Memory, Dominoes etc. Try creating a challenging set of question cards.

The following problems will investigate practical situations drawing upon knowledge and skills developed throughout the chapter. In attempting to solve these problems, aim to identify the key information, use diagrams, formulate ideas, apply strategies, make calculations and check and communicate your solutions.

Average height of a group of friends

1   The following table shows the name and height of six friends.

Name	Height
Sam	1.45 m
Ellie	1.53 m
Leo	1.71 m
Cammo	1.54 m
Sabina	1.44 m
Felix	1.87 m

The friends are interested in comparing their heights, calculating the average height and looking at how the average might be impacted by the addition of another friend to the group.

a   Place the friends in ascending height order.

b   How much taller is Felix than Sam?

c   What is the total height of the six friends?

d   What is the average height of the six friends?

e   When a seventh friend joins the group, the new average height becomes 1.62 m. What is the height of the new friend?

A drive to the moon?

2   Linh learns that the approximate distance from Earth to the Moon is 384 400 km and that an average car cruising speed is 100 km/h.

Linh is curious about how long it would take her and her family to drive to the Moon. While she of course knows this is not possible, she does wonder how long it would take if it was.

a   Given the above information, how many hours would it take Linh and her family to drive to the Moon?

b   Convert your answer to days, giving your answer:

   i   correct to two decimal places

   ii   in exact form using decimals

   iii   in exact form using fractions

   iv   in exact form using days and hours.

c   Investigate how long would it take Linh and her family to drive to the Sun.

Changing a pool's dimensions

3 A local swimming pool is a rectangular prism and has the following dimensions:
length $= 15.2$ m, width $= 4.8$ m, depth $= 1.2$ m.

The council are interested in changing the size of the pool by a certain factor and want to be clear about the impact of such changes on its depth and perimeter.

a Aiko works for the local council and has put in a submission for increasing each of the dimensions of the pool by a factor of 1.25. What are the dimensions of the pool in Aiko's submission?

b Kaito wishes to make a scale model of Aiko's new pool, where the dimensions are $\frac{1}{10}$th of the real size. What would be the dimensions of Kaito's model pool?

c The local council decide to increase the size of the pool, but they are concerned about the pool being too deep and only want to increase the depth of the pool by a factor of 1.1. They are happy to increase the width by a factor of 1.25, but because of the available room they are actually keen to increase the length of the pool by a factor of 1.75. What are the dimensions of the new council approved pool?

d A different local councillor argued that the original perimeter of the pool must remain the same. If Aiko still wishes to increase the length of the pool by a factor of 1.25, what would the reduced width of the new pool need to be?

5H Connecting decimals and percentages

LEARNING INTENTIONS
• To understand the meaning of 'per cent' (%).
• To be able to convert between percentages and decimals

Percentages are commonly used in today's society. **Per cent** is derived from the Latin words *per centum*, meaning 'out of 100'.

Percentages give an idea of proportion. For example, if a newspaper states that 2000 people want a council swimming pool constructed, then we know how many want a pool but we do not know what proportion of the community that is. However, if there are 2500 people in this community, the newspaper can state that 80% want a swimming pool. This informs us that a majority of the community (i.e. 80 out of every 100 people) want a swimming pool constructed.

A restaurant uses only parts of some vegetables such as broccoli, capsicum and cabbage. The vegetable order can be increased by 15%, so 1.15 kg is purchased for each 1 kg of vegetables that are cooked.

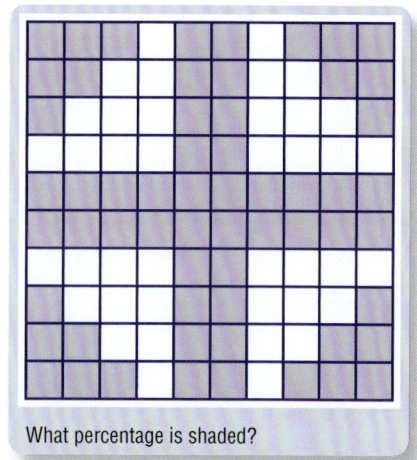

Lesson starter: Creative shading

• Draw a square of side length 10 cm and shade exactly 20% or 0.2 of this figure.
• Draw a square of side length 5 cm and shade exactly 60% or 0.6 of this figure.
• Draw another square of side length 10 cm and creatively shade an exact percentage of the figure. Ask your partner to work out the percentage you shaded.

What percentage is shaded?

KEY IDEAS

■ The symbol, %, means **per cent**. It comes from the Latin words *per centum*, which translates to 'out of 100'.
For example: 23% means 23 out of 100 which equals $\frac{23}{100} = 0.23$

■ To convert a percentage to a decimal, divide by 100. This is done by moving the decimal point 2 places to the left.
For example: $42\% = 42 \div 100 = 0.42$.

■ To convert a decimal to a percentage, multiply by 100. This is done by moving the decimal point 2 places to the right.

For example: $0.654 \times 100 = 65.4$. Therefore $0.654 = 65.4\%$

(Note: As in **Section 5D**, it is not actually the decimal point that moves; rather, it is the digits that move around the stationary decimal point.)

BUILDING UNDERSTANDING

1 72.5% is equivalent to which of the following decimals?
A 72.5   B 7.25   C 0.725   D 725.0

2 1452% is equivalent to which of the following decimals?
A 0.1452   B 14.52   C 145 200   D 145.20

3 0.39 is equivalent to which of the following percentages?
A 39%   B 3.9%   C 0.39%   D 0.0039%

4 Prue answered half the questions correctly for a test marked out of 100.
   a What score did Prue get on the test?
   b What percentage did Prue get on the test?
   c What score would you expect Prue to get if the test was out of:
     i 10   **ii** 200   **iii** 40   **iv** 2
   d What percentage would you expect Prue to get if the test was out of:
     i 10   **ii** 200   **iii** 40   **iv** 2

5 State the missing numbers or symbols in these numbers sentences.

   a $58\% = 58 \text{ out of } \boxed{} = 58 \boxed{} 100 = \dfrac{58}{\boxed{}} = 0\boxed{}58$

   b $35\% = \boxed{} \text{ out of } 100 = 35 \div \boxed{} = \dfrac{\boxed{}}{100} = \boxed{}.35$

Example 21   Converting percentages to decimals

Express the following percentages as decimals.
a 30%   **b** 3%   **c** 240%   **d** 12.5%   **e** 0.4%

SOLUTION

a $30\% = 0.3$

b $3\% = 0.03$

EXPLANATION

$30 \div 100 = 0.3$

$3 \div 100 = 0.03$
Note that 3 can be written as 003.
before moving the decimal point: 003.

Continued on next page

c 240% = 2.4   240 ÷ 100 = 2.4

d 12.5% = 0.125   Decimal point moves 2 places to the left.

e 0.4% = 0.004   Decimal point moves 2 places to the left.

Now you try

Express the following percentages as decimals.

a 92%   **b** 4%   **c** 150%   **d** 7.6%   **e** 0.05%

Example 22   Converting decimals to percentages

Express the following decimals as percentages.

a 0.045   **b** 7.2

SOLUTION   **EXPLANATION**

a 0.045 = 4.5%   Multiplying by 100 moves the decimal point 2 places to the right.

b 7.2 = 720%   Multiply 7.2 by 100.

Now you try

Express the following decimals as percentages.

a 0.703   **b** 23.1

Exercise 5H

FLUENCY   1–3(½), 5(½)   1–6(½)   3–6(½)

Example 21a **1** Express the following percentages as decimals.

a 70%   **b** 40%   **c** 50%   **d** 20%

e 48%   **f** 32%   **g** 71%   **h** 19%

Example 21b **2** Express the following percentages as decimals.

a 8%   **b** 2%   **c** 3%   **d** 5%

3 Express the following percentages as decimals.

a 32%	b 27%	c 68%	d 54%
e 6%	f 9%	g 100%	h 1%
i 218%	j 142%	k 75%	l 199%

4 Express the following percentages as decimals.

a 22.5%	b 17.5%	c 33.33%	d 8.25%
e 112.35%	f 188.8%	g 150%	h 520%
i 0.79%	j 0.025%	k 1.04%	l 0.95%

5 Express the following decimals as percentages.

a 0.8	b 0.3	c 0.45	d 0.71

6 Express the following decimals as percentages.

a 0.416	b 0.375	c 2.5	d 2.314
e 0.025	f 0.0014	g 12.7	h 1.004

PROBLEM-SOLVING	7, 8	7–9	8–10

7 Place the following values in order from highest to lowest. (*Hint*: Convert all percentages to decimals first.)

  a 86%, 0.5%, 0.6, 0.125, 22%, 75%, 2%, 0.78

  b 124%, 2.45, 1.99%, 0.02%, 1.8, 55%, 7.2, 50

8 At a hockey match, 65% of the crowd supports the home team. What percentage of the crowd does not support the home team?

9 Last Saturday, Phil spent the 24 hours of the day in the following way: 0.42 of the time was spent sleeping, 0.22 was spent playing sport and 0.11 was spent eating. The only other activity Phil did for the day was watch TV.

  a What percentage of the day did Phil spend watching TV?

  b What percentage of the day did Phil spend not playing sport?

10 Sugarloaf Reservoir has a capacity of 96 gigalitres. However, as a result of the drought it is only 25% full. How many gigalitres of water are in the reservoir?

REASONING   11   11, 12   12, 13

11 A, B, C and D are digits. Write the following decimal numbers as percentages.
  a   0.ABCD
  b   A.AC
  c   AB.DC
  d   0.0DD
  e   C.DBA
  f   0.CCCDDD

12 A, B, C and D are digits. Write the following percentages as decimal numbers.
  a   A.B%
  b   BCD%
  c   AC%
  d   0.DA%
  e   ABBB%
  f   DD.D%

13 Trudy says that it is impossible to have more than 100%. She supports her statement by saying that if you get every question correct in a test, then you get 100% and you cannot get any more.
  a   Do you agree with Trudy's statement?
  b   Provide four examples of when it makes sense that you cannot get more than 100%.
  c   Provide four examples of when it is perfectly logical to have more than 100%.

ENRICHMENT: AFL ladder   –   –   14

14 The Australian Rules football ladder has the following column headings.

Pos	Team	P	W	L	D	F	A	%	Pts
6	Brisbane Lions	22	13	8	1	2017	1890	106.72	54
7	Carlton	22	13	9	0	2270	2055	110.46	52
8	Essendon	22	10	11	1	2080	2127	97.79	42
9	Hawthorn	22	9	13	0	1962	2120	92.55	36
10	Port Adelaide	22	9	13	0	1990	2244	88.68	36

  a   Using a calculator, can you determine how the percentage column is calculated?
  b   What do you think the 'F' and the 'A' column stand for?
  c   In their next match, Essendon scores 123 points for their team and has 76 points scored against them. What will be their new percentage?
  d   By how much do Hawthorn need to win their next game to have a percentage of 100?
  e   If Port Adelaide plays Hawthorn in the next round and the final score is Port Adelaide 124 beats Hawthorn 71, will Port Adelaide's percentage become higher than Hawthorn's?

5I Expressing proportions using decimals, fractions and percentages

Sometimes we want to know the proportion of a certain quantity compared to a given total or another quantity. This may be done using a fraction, percentage or ratio. Earth's surface, for example, is about 70% ocean. So, the proportion of land could be written as 30% (as a percentage) or $\frac{3}{10}$ (as a fraction) or 0.3 (as a decimal). For different situations, it could make more sense represent a proportion as a percentage, a fraction or as a decimal.

A bricklayer can mix 4 parts of sand to 1 part of cement to make a dry mortar mix. These proportions can also be expressed as fractions and percentages:

i.e. sand $\frac{4}{5} = 80\%$, cement $\frac{1}{5} = 20\%$.

Lesson starter: Municipal parkland

A municipal area is set aside in a new suburb and is to be divided into three main parts. The total area is $10\,000\,\text{m}^2$ and the three parts are to be divided as follows.

  Parkland: $6000\,\text{m}^2$

  Shops: $2500\,\text{m}^2$

  Playground and skate park: $1500\,\text{m}^2$

- Express each area as a proportion of the total, first as a fraction and then as a percentage and finally as a decimal.

- If $\frac{3}{5}$ of the parkland is to be a lake, what percentage of the total area is the lake?

KEY IDEAS

■ To express one quantity as a proportion of the other, start with the fraction:

$$\text{fraction} = \frac{\text{amount}}{\text{total}} \quad \left(\text{e.g. } \frac{\text{red parts}}{\text{total parts}} = \frac{2}{5} \right)$$

■ This fraction can be converted to a decimal $\left(\text{e.g. } \frac{2}{5} = \frac{4}{10} = 0.4 \right)$

■ The decimal or fraction can be converted to a percentage by multiplying by 100,

  e.g. $0.4 \times 100 = 40$ so $0.4 = 40\%$, $\frac{2}{5} \times 100 = 40$ so $\frac{2}{5} = 40\%$

■ An object or quantity divided into parts can be analysed using fractions, decimals or percentages.

Shaded proportion as a fraction: $\frac{2}{5}$

Shaded proportion as a decimal: 0.4

Shaded proportion as a percentage: 40%

■ Compare proportions using the same type of number (e.g., by converting all the proportions to percentages).

e.g. Use percentages to compare the scores 17 out of 20, 0.65 and 82%

$\frac{17}{20} = \frac{85}{100} = 85\%$ and $0.65 = \frac{65}{100} = 65\%$

BUILDING UNDERSTANDING

1 This square shows some coloured triangles and some white triangles.

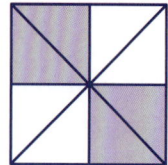

a   How many triangles are coloured?

b   How many triangles are white?

c   What fraction of the total is coloured?

d   What percentage of the total is coloured?

e   What fraction of the total is white?

f   What percentage of the total is white?

2 A farmer's pen has 2 black sheep and 8 white sheep.

a   How many sheep are there in total?

b   What fraction of the sheep are black?

c   What fraction of the sheep are white?

d   What percentage of the sheep are black?

e   What percentage of the sheep are white?

3 a   What fraction of the diagram is shaded?

b   convert your answer to part **a** into a decimal.

c   What percentage of the diagram is shaded?

Example 23   Expressing proportions as fractions, decimals and percentages

Express the proportion $40 out of a total of $200:

a   as a fraction   **b**   as a decimal   **c**   as a percentage

SOLUTION

a   Fraction: $\dfrac{40}{200} = \dfrac{1}{5}$

$\div 40$ (numerator)
$\div 40$ (denominator)

EXPLANATION

Write the given amount and divide by the total. Then simplify the fraction by dividing the numerator and denominator by the common factor (40).

b Decimal: $\dfrac{1}{5} \overset{\times 2}{\underset{\times 2}{=}} \dfrac{2}{10}$

$= 0.2$

Convert the simplified fraction to a decimal by making a 10, 100, 1000, etc.

c Percentage: $\dfrac{40}{200} \times \dfrac{100}{1} = 20$

therefore $\dfrac{40}{200} = 20\%$

Multiply the fraction by 100 to convert to a percentage, or convert the decimal to a percentage.

Alternative method: $\dfrac{40}{200} \overset{\div 2}{\underset{\div 2}{=}} \dfrac{20}{100} = 20\%$

Now you try

Express the proportion $30 out of a total of $120:

a as a fraction   **b** as a decimal   **c** as a percentage

Example 24   Finding fractions and percentages from parts

A glass of cordial is 3 parts syrup to 7 parts water.
a Express the amount of syrup as a fraction of the total.
b Express the proportion of syrup as a decimal.
c Express the amount of water as a percentage of the total.

SOLUTION

a Fraction $= \dfrac{3}{10}$

b $\dfrac{3}{10} = 0.3$

c Percentage $= \dfrac{7}{10} \times \dfrac{100\%}{1}$

$= 70\%$

EXPLANATION

There is a total of 10 parts, including 3 parts syrup.

Convert the fraction to a decimal.

There is a total 7 parts water in a total of 10 parts.

Now you try

A mixture of cordial is 2 parts syrup to 3 parts water.
a Express the amount of syrup as a fraction of the total.
b Express the proportion of water as a decimal.
c Express the amount of water as a percentage of the total.

Example 25   Comparing proportions

On a test, Jenny scored $\frac{16}{25}$, Brendan managed to get 0.6 of the questions correct and Raj received a score of 61%. Use percentages to compare the three test scores and decide who scored the highest.

SOLUTION

Jenny: $\frac{16}{25} = \frac{64}{100} = 64\%$

Brendan: $0.6 = \frac{60}{100} = 60\%$

Raj: 61%

So Jenny scored the highest

EXPLANATION

Convert Jenny's fraction to a percentage and Brendan's decimal to a percentage.
Then compare the three percentages.

Now you try

Millie, Adam and Yoe are all completing the same hike. Millie has completed $\frac{7}{20}$ of the hike, Adam has completed 0.4 of the hike and Yoe has completed 39% of the hike. Use percentages to compare the three proportions and decide who has completed the largest proportion of the hike.

Exercise 5I

FLUENCY	1–5(½), 6–9	1–5(½), 6, 8	4, 6–9

Example 23a

1 Express the following proportions as a fraction of the total. Remember to simplify all fractions.

   a 4 out of 10
   b 5 out of 20
   c $30 out of $300
   d 15 sheep out of a total of 25 sheep

Example 23b

2 Express the following proportions as a decimal.

   a 3 out of 10
   b 7 out of 10
   c 29 out of 100
   d 5 out of 100

Example 23c

3 Express the following proportions as a percentage.

   a 25 out of 100
   b 7 out of 10
   c 23 out of 50
   d 13 out of 20

Example 23

4 Express the following proportions as a fraction, a decimal and a percentage of the total.

   a 30 out of a total of 100
   b 3 out of a total of 5
   c $10 out of a total of $50
   d $60 out of a total of $80
   e 2 kg out of a total of 40 kg
   f 30 mL out of a total of 200 mL

Example 24

5 Write the shaded proportions of each shape's total area as a decimal and as a percentage.

   a   **b**   **c**

d   e   f

mple 24   **6**   A jug of lemonade is made up of 2 parts lemon juice to 18 parts water. Express the proportion of the total that is lemon juice as:

  a   a fraction   **b**   a decimal   **c**   a percentage.

mple 24   **7**   A mix of concrete is made up of 1 part cement to 4 parts sand.

  a   Express the amount of cement as a fraction of the total.

  b   Express the amount of cement as a percentage of the total.

  c   Express the proportion of the total that is sand as a decimal.

mple 25   **8**   On a test, Val scored $\frac{7}{10}$, Mel managed to get 0.67 of the questions correct and Wendy received a score of 69%. Use percentages to compare the three test scores and decide who scored the highest.

9   Three siblings walk home from school. By 4:00 pm Wally has completed $\frac{29}{50}$ of the walk, Su has completed 0.55 of the walk and Drew has completed 53% of the walk. Use percentages to compare the three proportions and decide who has walked the most.

PROBLEM-SOLVING	10, 11	10–12	11–13

10   In a new subdivision involving $20\,000\,\text{m}^2$, specific areas are set aside for the following purposes.

  • Dwellings: $12\,000\,\text{m}^2$
  • Shops: $1000\,\text{m}^2$
  • Roads/Paths: $3000\,\text{m}^2$
  • Park: $2500\,\text{m}^2$
  • Factories: Remainder

  a   What area is set aside for factories?

  b   Express the area of the following as both a fraction and a percentage of the total area.

  i   shops   **ii**   dwellings   **iii**   park

  c   What fraction of the total area is either dwellings, shops or factories?

  d   What percentage of the total area is park or roads/paths?

11   Gillian pays $80 tax out of her income of $1600. What percentage of her income does she keep? Also state this proportion as a decimal.

12   Express the following proportions as a fraction, percentage and decimals of the total. Remember to ensure the units are the same first.

  a   20 cents of $5

  b   14 days out of 5 weeks

  c   15 centimetres removed from a total length of 3 metres

  d   3 seconds taken from a world record time of 5 minutes

  e   180 grams of a total of 9 kilograms

  f   1500 centimetres from a total of 0.6 kilometres

13 Of 20 students, 10 play sport and 12 play a musical instrument, with some of these students playing both sport and music. Two students do not play any sport or musical instrument.

   a What fraction of the students play both sport and a musical instrument?

   b What percentage of the students play a musical instrument but not a sport?

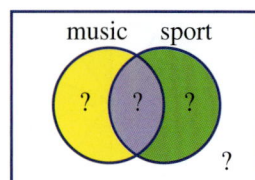

REASONING | 14, 15 | 14–16 | 15–17

14 For recent class tests, Ross scored 45 out of 60 and Maleisha scored 72 out of 100. Use percentages or decimals to show that Ross got a higher proportion of questions correct.

15 The prices of two cars are reduced for sale. A hatch priced at $20 000 is now reduced by $3000 and a 4WD priced at $80 000 is now reduced by $12 800. Determine which car has the largest percentage reduction, giving reasons.

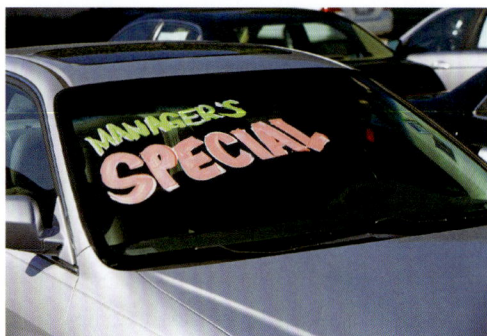

16 A yellow sports drink has 50 g of sugar dissolved in fluid that weighs 250 g, including the weight of the sugar. A blue sports drink has 57 g of sugar dissolved in fluid that weighs 300 g, including the weight of the sugar. Which sports drink has the least percentage of sugar? Give reasons.

17 A mixture of dough has a parts flour to b parts water.

   a Write an expression for the fraction of flour within the mixture.

   b Write an expression for the percentage of water within the mixture.

ENRICHMENT: Transport turmoil | – | – | 18

18 A class survey of 30 students reveals that the students use three modes of transport to get to school: bike, public transport and car. All of the students used at least one of these three modes of transport in the past week.

Twelve students used a car to get to school and did not use any of the other modes of transport. One student used all three modes of transport and one student used only a bike for the week. There were no students who used both a bike and a car but no public transport. Five students used both a car and public transport but not a bike. Eight students used only public transport.

Use this diagram to help answer the following.

   a How many students used both a bike and public transport but not a car?

   b What fraction of the students used all three modes of transport?

   c What fraction of the students used at least one mode of transport, with one of their modes being a bike?

   d What fraction of the students used at least one mode of transport, with one of their modes being public transport?

   e What percentage of students used public transport and a car during the week?

   f What percentage of students used either public transport or a car or both during the week?

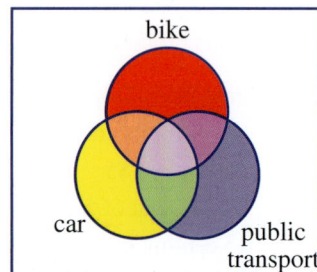

ASX share market game

Seven friends join together in a share market game and buy a total of 10 000 shares at $1.40 each. In the game they pay a brokerage fee of 2% of the value of the shares whenever they buy or sell shares. They plan to sell the shares at the end of the year.

They consider three possible investment scenarios for the year.

Scenario 1: 10% share price growth.
Scenario 2: 25% share price growth.
Scenario 3: 5% share price fall.

Present a report for the following tasks and ensure that you show clear mathematical workings and explanations where appropriate.

Preliminary task

a State the total cost of buying the 10 000 shares not including the brokerage fee.

b Find the value of the brokerage fee for buying the 10 000 shares.

c If the share price of $1.40 increased by 10%, what would be the new value of a single share?

d If the share price of $1.40 decreased by 5%, what would be the new value of a single share?

Modelling task

rmulate

a The problem is to decide if the friends will earn a profit of at least $500 each at the end of the year, after all fees are considered. Write down all the relevant information to help solve this problem.

Solve

b Assume the shares increase in value by 10% as in scenario 1.

   i What would be the value of the shares at the end of the year?

   ii Find the value of the brokerage fee for selling the 10 000 shares at the end of the year.

   iii If the friends sell the shares after a year, what is the total profit after all the buy/sell fees are paid?

   iv How much profit does each of the seven friends receive? (Assume they share the profits equally.)

c Assume the shares increase in value by 25% as in scenario 2. Find the resulting profit per person.

d If scenario 3 occurs and the shares decrease in value by 5%, find the resulting loss per person.

ate and verify

e By comparing your results from above, decide if the friends earn more than $500 each from any of the three scenarios.

f By increasing the expected growth rate, construct a scenario so that the profit per person is greater than $500 after one year. Justify your choice by showing workings.

unicate

g Summarise your results and describe any key findings.

Extension questions

a Construct a scenario that delivers exactly $500 profit per person after one year, when rounded to the nearest dollar.

b Investigate the effect on the profit per person in the following cases:

   i if the fee paid on each purchase or sale of shares is reduced

   ii if the number of friends involved is changed from seven.

Approximating $\sqrt{2}$

Key technology: Spreadsheets

We know that decimals can be used to write numbers which are of equal value to certain fractions and percentages. 1.6 for example is equal to $\frac{8}{5}$, $2.\dot{3}$ is equal to $\frac{7}{3}$ and 0.57 is equal to 57%. Such decimals are either terminating or infinitely recurring. The are other numbers, however, that cannot be described using a terminating or infinitely recurring decimal. π is one such number and is introduced in the Measurement chapter and you will have already seen numbers like $\sqrt{2}$ and $\sqrt[3]{5}$ which also fit in this category. The square root of 2 has been studied since the ancient times and is the diagonal distance across a square of side length one unit. A Babylonian clay tablet dated approximately 1700 BC shows an approximation of $\sqrt{2}$ which is correct to 6 decimal places.

1 Getting started

One way to approximate numbers which have infinitely recurring decimals uses continued fractions. $\sqrt{2}$ as a continued fraction is shown here. $1 + \cfrac{1}{2 + \cfrac{1}{2 + \cfrac{1}{2 + \cfrac{1}{2 + \ddots}}}}$

a   Find an approximation of $\sqrt{2}$ by evaluating the following. Write your answer as a decimal each time.

    i $1 + \frac{1}{2}$

    ii $1 + \cfrac{1}{2 + \frac{1}{2}}$

    iii $1 + \cfrac{1}{2 + \cfrac{1}{2 + \frac{1}{2}}}$

    iv $1 + \cfrac{1}{2 + \cfrac{1}{2 + \cfrac{1}{2 + \frac{1}{2}}}}$

b   Describe how the next continued fraction is obtained from the previous one.

2 Applying an algorithm

Here is an algorithm which finds an approximation to $\sqrt{2}$ using a continued fraction with n calculations.

a Complete this table for $n = 5$ writing down the values for i and f from beginning to end.

i	0	1	2	3		
f	2	2.5	2.4			

b What is the value of d outputted near the end of the program? Check that this value is close to the value of $\sqrt{2}$ obtained using a calculator.

c Describe the parts of the algorithm that make the following happen.

   i The f value is updated each time to a new f value.

   ii The algorithm knows when to end.

d Why do you think the rule $d = f - 1$ is used at the end to deliver the final result? *Hint*: Look at the continued fraction for $\sqrt{2}$.

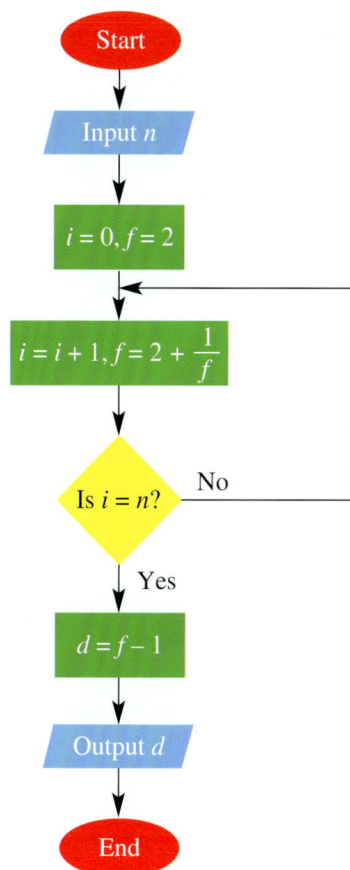

Start

Input n

$i = 0, f = 2$

$i = i + 1, f = 2 + \dfrac{1}{f}$

Is $i = n$?   No

Yes

$d = f - 1$

Output d

End

3 Using technology

Let's now use a spreadsheet to apply the above algorithm.

	A	B	C
1	Root 2 approximation		
2			
3	i	f	root 2 approximation
4	0	2	=B4-1
5	=A4+1	=2+1/B4	

a Construct a spreadsheet to calculate the continued fraction for $\sqrt{2}$ using the information provided here.

b Fill down at cells A5, B5 and C4 for about 10 rows.

c What do you notice about the approximation of $\sqrt{2}$ as you go down the list?

d Use your result to write $\sqrt{2}$ correct to:

   i 3 decimal places   **ii** 7 decimal places.

4 Extension

a Use the above technique to find an approximation for:

   i $\sqrt{5}$ **ii** $\sqrt{3}$

b You can also use dynamic geometry to estimate the value of $\sqrt{2}$ by constructing a special triangle and measuring the length of the diagonal as shown. Try this technique. Then try constructing another number like $\sqrt{3}$ or $\sqrt{5}$.

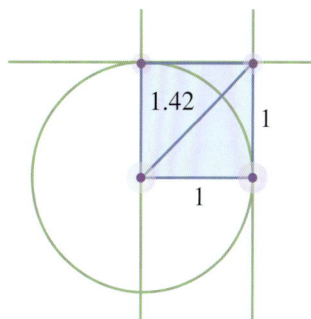

1.42

1

1

Best buy

The concept of a 'best buy' relates to purchasing a product that is the best value for money. To determine the 'best buy' you can compare the prices of similar products for the same weight.

Converting units

a Convert the following to a price per kg.
   i 2 kg of apples for $3.40
   ii 5 kg of sugar for $6.00
   iii 1.5 kg of cereal for $4.50
   iv 500 g of butter for $3.25

b Convert the following to a price per 100 g.
   i 300 g of grapes for $2.10
   ii 1 kg of cheese for $9.60
   iii 700 g of yoghurt for $7.49
   iv 160 g of dip for $3.20

STRAWBERRY	STRAWBERRY
JAM jar 375 g	JAM jar 250 g
$3.95	$2.95
$10.53 per kg	$11.80 per kg

Finding 'best buys'

a By converting to a price per kg, determine which is the best buy.
   i 2 kg of sauce A for $5.20 or 1 kg of sauce B for $2.90
   ii 4 kg of pumpkin A for $3.20 or 3 kg of pumpkin B for $2.70
   iii 500 g of honey A for $5.15 or 2 kg of honey B for $19.90
   iv 300 g of milk A for $0.88 or 1.5 kg of milk B for $4.00

b By converting to a price per 100 g, determine which is the best buy.
   i 500 g of paper A for $3.26 or 200 g of paper B for $1.25
   ii 250 g of salami A for $4.50 or 150 g of salami B for $3.10
   iii 720 g of powder A for $3.29 or 350 g of powder B for $1.90
   iv 1.1 kg of shampoo A for $12.36 or 570 g of shampoo B for $6.85

Applications of 'best buys'

a Star Washing Liquid is priced at $3.85 for 600 g, while Best Wash Liquid is priced at $5.20 for 1 kg. Find the difference in the price per 100 g, correct to the nearest cent.

b Budget apples cost $6.20 per 5 kg bag. How much would a 500 g bag of Sunny apples have to be if it was the same price per 100 g?

c 1.5 kg of cheddar cheese costs $11.55, and 800 g of feta cheese costs $7.25. Sally works out the best value cheese, then buys $5 worth of it. How much and what type of cheese did Sally buy?

1 **a** When $\frac{3}{7}$ is written as a decimal, state the digit in the 20th decimal place.

> Up for a challenge? If you get stuck on a question check out the 'Working with unfamiliar problems' poster at the end of the book to help you.

   b Given that $A \times 2.75 = 10.56$, write an expression for $1.056 \div 0.00275$.

   c Find this product:
   $(1 - 0.5)(1 - 0.\dot{3})(1 - 0.25)(1 - 0.2)$

   d Write the recurring decimal $1.4\overline{51}$ as an improper fraction.

   e Callum pays \$4.10 for his coffee using eight coins. They are made up of \$1 coins and 50 and 20 cent pieces. How many of each coin did Callum use?

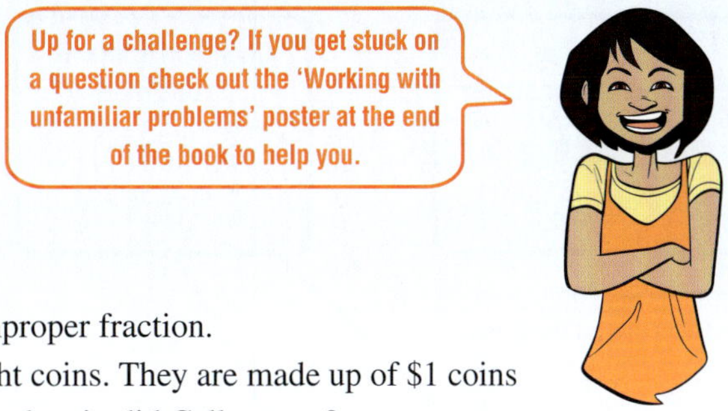

2 Consider the ladder in the diagram. The heights of each rung on the ladder are separated by an equally sized gap. Determine the heights for each rung of the ladder.

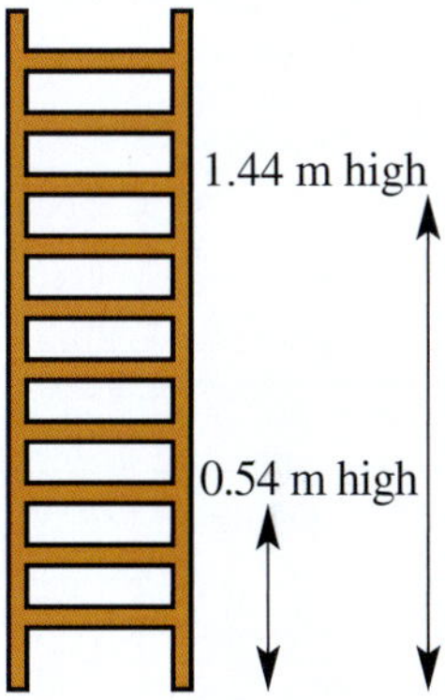

1.44 m high

0.54 m high

3 Find the digits represented by the letters in these decimal problems.

   a
   $$\begin{array}{r} A.2B \\ +\,9.C5 \\ \hline 11.12 \end{array}$$

   b
   $$\begin{array}{r} 2A.43 \\ -\,9.B4 \\ \hline C7.8D \end{array}$$

   c $3.A \times B.4 = 8.16$

   d
   $$\begin{array}{r} 0.757 \\ A\overline{)2.2B1} \end{array}$$

4 We know that $\sqrt{9}$ is 3 since $3^2 = 9$, but what about $\sqrt{2}$?

   a Find the value of:
   i 1.4^2 **ii** 1.5^2 **iii** 1.45^2

   b Now try to find the value of $\sqrt{3}$ correct to:
   i two decimal places   **ii** three decimal places.

5 Find a fraction equal to the following decimals.
   a $0.\dot{4}$ **b** $3.\dot{2}$ **c** $0.\overline{17}$ **d** $4.7\overline{28}$

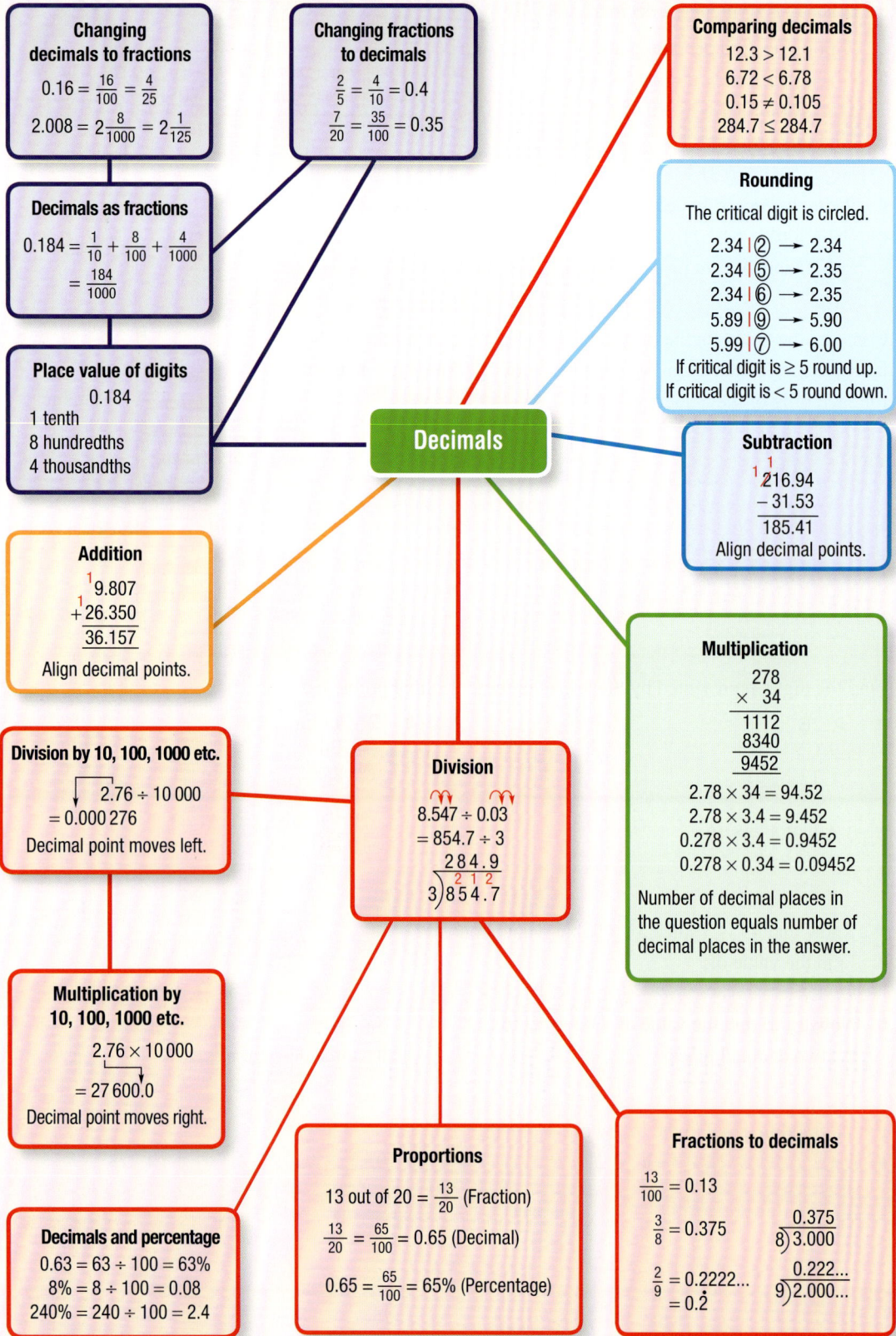

Chapter summary

Changing decimals to fractions

$0.16 = \frac{16}{100} = \frac{4}{25}$

$2.008 = 2\frac{8}{1000} = 2\frac{1}{125}$

Changing fractions to decimals

$\frac{2}{5} = \frac{4}{10} = 0.4$

$\frac{7}{20} = \frac{35}{100} = 0.35$

Comparing decimals

$12.3 > 12.1$

$6.72 < 6.78$

$0.15 \neq 0.105$

$284.7 \leq 284.7$

Decimals as fractions

$0.184 = \frac{1}{10} + \frac{8}{100} + \frac{4}{1000}$

$= \frac{184}{1000}$

Rounding

The critical digit is circled.

$2.34\,|②\;\longrightarrow\;2.34$
$2.34\,|⑤\;\longrightarrow\;2.35$
$2.34\,|⑥\;\longrightarrow\;2.35$
$5.89\,|⑨\;\longrightarrow\;5.90$
$5.99\,|⑦\;\longrightarrow\;6.00$

If critical digit is ≥ 5 round up.
If critical digit is < 5 round down.

Place value of digits

0.184
1 tenth
8 hundredths
4 thousandths

Decimals

Subtraction

$$\begin{array}{r} {}^1\!2\overset{1}{1}6.94 \\ -\ 31.53 \\ \hline 185.41 \end{array}$$

Align decimal points.

Addition

$$\begin{array}{r} {}^1\!9.807 \\ {}^1\!+26.350 \\ \hline 36.157 \end{array}$$

Align decimal points.

Multiplication

$$\begin{array}{r} 278 \\ \times\ \ 34 \\ \hline 1112 \\ 8340 \\ \hline 9452 \end{array}$$

$2.78 \times 34 = 94.52$
$2.78 \times 3.4 = 9.452$
$0.278 \times 3.4 = 0.9452$
$0.278 \times 0.34 = 0.09452$

Number of decimal places in the question equals number of decimal places in the answer.

Division by 10, 100, 1000 etc.

$2.76 \div 10\,000$
$= 0.000\,276$
Decimal point moves left.

Division

$8.547 \div 0.03$
$= 854.7 \div 3$

$$\begin{array}{r} 284.9 \\ 3{\overline{\smash{)}\,85^24^1.^27}} \end{array}$$

Multiplication by 10, 100, 1000 etc.

$2.76 \times 10\,000$

$= 27\,600.0$
Decimal point moves right.

Proportions

13 out of $20 = \frac{13}{20}$ (Fraction)

$\frac{13}{20} = \frac{65}{100} = 0.65$ (Decimal)

$0.65 = \frac{65}{100} = 65\%$ (Percentage)

Fractions to decimals

$\frac{13}{100} = 0.13$

$\frac{3}{8} = 0.375$

$$\begin{array}{r} 0.375 \\ 8{\overline{\smash{)}\,3.000}} \end{array}$$

$\frac{2}{9} = 0.2222...$
$= 0.\dot{2}$

$$\begin{array}{r} 0.222... \\ 9{\overline{\smash{)}\,2.000...}} \end{array}$$

Decimals and percentage

$0.63 = 63 \div 100 = 63\%$
$8\% = 8 \div 100 = 0.08$
$240\% = 240 \div 100 = 2.4$

Chapter checklist with success criteria

A printable version of this checklist is available in the Interactive Textbook ⬇️

		✔
5A	**1. I can state the value of a digit after the decimal point in a number.** e.g. What is the value of the digit 8 in the number 6.1287?	☐
5A	**2. I can convert fractions to decimals (if the denominator is 10, 100, 1000 etc.).** e.g. Convert $\frac{317}{100}$ to a decimal.	☐
5A	**3. I can compare two or more numbers written as decimals.** e.g. Decide which is smallest out of 2.37, 2.72, 3.27.	☐
5B	**4. I can determine the critical digit in a rounding operation.** e.g. The number 23.5398 is to be rounded to two decimal places. Circle the critical digit.	☐
5B	**5. I can round decimals to a given number of decimal places.** e.g. Round 0.43917 to 2 decimal places.	☐
5C	**6. I can add decimals.** e.g. Find $64.8 + 3.012 + 5.94$.	☐
5C	**7. I can subtract decimals.** e.g. Find $146.35 - 79.5$.	☐
5D	**8. I can multiply a decimal by a power of 10.** e.g. Evaluate $4.31 \times 10\,000$.	☐
5D	**9. I can divide a decimal by a power of 10.** e.g. Evaluate $7.82 \div 1000$.	☐
5D	**10. I can multiply and divide a whole number by a power of 10, introducing a decimal place if required.** e.g. Evaluate $23 \div 1000$.	☐
5E	**11. I can estimate decimal products using whole number approximations** e.g. Estimate 4.13×7.62 by first rounding each decimal to the nearest whole number.	☐
5E	**12. I can multiply decimals.** e.g. Calculate 3.63×6.9 and 0.032×600.	☐
5F	**13. I can divide decimals.** e.g. Calculate $2.3 \div 1.1$ and $67.04 \div 8000$.	☐
5G	**14. I can convert decimals to fractions.** e.g. Convert 10.35 to a mixed numeral in simplest form.	☐
5G	**15. I can convert fractions to decimals.** e.g. Convert $\frac{53}{5}$ to a decimal.	☐
5G	**16. I can convert fractions to recurring decimals.** e.g. Convert $\frac{7}{12}$ to a decimal.	☐

Chapter checklist

		✔
5H	**17. I can convert a percentage to a decimal.** e.g. Convert 12.5% to a decimal.	☐
5H	**18. I can convert a decimal to a percentage.** e.g. Convert 0.045 to a percentage.	☐
5I	**19. I can write a value as a proportion of a total, giving the proportion as a fraction, decimal or percentage.** e.g. Write the proportion $40 out of $200 as a fraction, a decimal and a percentage.	☐
5I	**20. I can compare proportions by converting to percentages.** e.g. By first writing the proportions as percentages, compare the scores $\frac{8}{10}$, 0.78 and 82% and decide which is largest.	☐

Short-answer questions

5A   **1**   Arrange each group in descending order, from largest to smallest.
- **a**   0.4, 0.04, 0.44
- **b**   2.16, 2.016, 2.026
- **c**   0.932, 0.98, 0.895

5G   **2**   Write each fraction as a decimal.
- **a** $\dfrac{81}{10}$
- **b** $\dfrac{81}{100}$
- **c** $\dfrac{801}{100}$
- **d** $\dfrac{801}{1000}$

5A   **3**   What is the place value of the digit 3 in the following numbers?
- **a**   12.835
- **b**   6.1237
- **c**   13.5104

5A   **4**   State whether each of the following is true or false.
- **a** $8.34 < 8.28$
- **b** $4.668 > 4.67$
- **c** $8.2 > 8.182$
- **d** $3.08 \leqslant \dfrac{308}{100}$
- **e** $\dfrac{62}{100} \geqslant 6.20$
- **f** $\dfrac{7}{10} = \dfrac{70}{100}$

5B   **5**   List all possible numbers with 3 decimal places that, when rounded to 2 decimal places, result in 45.27.

5B   **6**   Round each of the following to the specified number of decimal places (which is given in brackets).
- **a** $423.46\,(1)$
- **b** $15.8892\,(2)$
- **c** $7.254\,32\,(1)$
- **d** $69.999\,531\,(3)$
- **e** $2\dfrac{3}{4}\,(1)$
- **f** $\dfrac{2}{3}\,(2)$
- **g** $\dfrac{5}{11}\,(3)$
- **h** $\dfrac{1}{81}\,(44)$ (*Hint*: Look for a shortcut!)

5C   **7**   Evaluate:
- **a** $13.85 - 4.32$
- **b** $19.12 - 14.983$
- **c** $27.6 + 15.75$
- **d** $204.708\,37 + 35.7902$
- **e** $472.427 - 388.93$
- **f** $210.8 - (26.3 - 20.72)$

5A/B/D   **8**   State whether each of the following is true or false.
- **a** $10.34 \div 100 = 0.1034$
- **b** $3.125 \times 0.1 = 31.25$
- **c** $115.23 \div 10 = 1.1523 \times 1000$
- **d**   115.23 has 3 decimal places
- **e** $24.673 = 24.7$ when rounded to 1 decimal place

5D   **9**   Solve each of the following, using the order of operations.
- **a** 1.37×100
- **b** 0.79×1000
- **c** $225.1 \div 10$
- **d** $96.208 \div 1000$
- **e** $75.68 + 6.276 \times 100 - 63.24 \div 10$
- **f** $3.56 \times 100 + 45 \div 10$
- **g** $100 \times (56.34 \times 100 + 0.893)$

Chapter review

5E

10 Estimate the following products by first rounding each decimal to the nearest whole number.
   a 3.8×7.1 b 5.3×9.2 c 7.24×1.94
   d 9.97×3.17 e 4.94×8.7 f 3.14×2.72

5E/F

11 Calculate the following.
   a 2.4×8 b 9×7.11 c 2.3×8.4
   d $3.8 \div 4$ e $12.16 \div 8$ f $3 \div 0.5$
   g $4 \div 0.25$ h $1.2 \div 0.4$ i $3.42 \div 1.1$

5F/G/H

12 Copy and complete this table, stating fractions both with the denominator 100 and in their simplest form.

Decimal	Fraction	Percentage
0.45		
	$\frac{?}{100} = \frac{7}{10}$	
		32%
0.06		
	$\frac{79}{100}$	
1.05		
	$\frac{?}{100} = \frac{7}{20}$	
		65%
	$\frac{?}{1000} = \frac{1}{8}$	

5I

13 Write each of the following proportions as a fraction, a decimal and a percentage.
   a $3 out of $10
   b   12 litres out of 15 litres
   c   6 km out of 8 km
   d   180 mL out of 1 litre

5I

14 On a test, Dillon scored $\frac{15}{20}$, Judy managed to get 0.8 of the questions correct and Jon received a score of 78%. Use percentages to compare the test scores and decide who scored the highest.

Multiple-choice questions

5A

1 The next number in the pattern 0.023, 0.025, 0.027, 0.029 is:
   A   0.0003   B   0.030   C   0.0031   D   0.031   E   0.033

5G

2 0.05 is equivalent to:
   A $\frac{5}{10}$ B $\frac{5}{100}$ C $\frac{5}{1000}$ D $\frac{5}{500}$ E   5

5A

3 The smallest number out of 0.012, 10.2, 0.102, 0.0012 and 1.02 is:
   A   0.012   B   0.102   C   0.0012   D   1.02   E   10.2

5F

4 $0.36 \div 1000$ is equal to:
   A   3.6   B   360   C   0.036   D   0.0036   E   0.00036

5E

5 6.2×0.2 is equal to:

A 1.24   B 12.4   C 0.124   D 124   E 0.0124

5E

6 What is the answer to 0.08×0.6?

A 0.48   B 4.8   C 0.0048   D 0.048   E 48

5B

7 When rounded to 1 decimal place, 84.553 becomes:

A 80   B 84   C 84.5   D 84.6   E 84.55

5G

8 As a decimal, $\frac{23}{90}$ is equal to:

A 0.2   B $0.2\dot{5}$ C 0.26   D $0.2\dot{5}$ E $0.25\dot{6}$

5B/C

9 $7 + 0.7 + 0.07 + 0.007$, to 2 decimal places, is:

A 7.78   B 7.77   C 7   D 7.7   E 7.777

5G

10 $5.\overline{624}$ means:

A 5.62444…   B 6.6242424…   C 5.624624624…

D 5.6246464…   E 5.62456245624…

Extended-response questions

1 Find the answer in these practical situations.

  a Jessica is paid $125.70 for 10 hours of work and Jaczinda is paid $79.86 for 6 hours of work. Who receives the higher rate of pay per hour, and by how much?

  b Petrol is sold for 124.9 cents per litre. Jacob buys 30 L of petrol for his car. Find the total price he pays, to the nearest 5 cents.

  c The Green family are preparing to go to the Great Barrier Reef for a holiday. For each of the four family members, they purchase a goggles and snorkel set at $37.39 each, fins at $18.99 each and rash tops at $58.48 each. How much change is there from $500?

  d For her school, a physical education teacher buys 5 each of basketballs, rugby union and soccer balls. The total bill is $711.65. If the rugby balls cost $38.50 each and the basketballs cost $55.49 each, what is the price of a soccer ball?

2 A car can use 25% less fuel per km when travelling at 90 km/h than it would when travelling at 110 km/h. Janelle's car uses 7.8 litres of fuel per 100 km when travelling at 110 km/h, and fuel costs 155.9 cents per litre.

  a How much money could Janelle save on a 1000-km trip from Sydney to Brisbane if she travels at a constant speed of 90 km/h instead of 110 km/h?

  b During a 24-hour period, 2000 cars travel the 1000-km trip between Sydney and Brisbane. How much money could be saved if 30% of these cars travel at 90 km/h instead of 110 km/h?

3 Siobhan is on a 6-week holiday in the United Kingdom, and is using her phone to keep in contact with her friends and family in Australia. The phone charge for voice calls is $0.40 'flagfall' and $0.65 per 45 seconds; text messages are $0.38 each.

During her holiday, Siobhan makes 27 voice calls and sends 165 text messages to Australia. If her phone bill is $832.30, determine the average length of Siobhan's voice calls.

Computation with positive integers

Short-answer questions

1   Write the number seventy-four in:
  a   Babylonian numerals   b   Roman numerals   c   Egyptian numerals.

2   Write the numeral for:
  a $6 \times 10000 + 7 \times 1000 + 8 \times 100 + 4 \times 10 + 9 \times 1$
  b $7 \times 100\,000 + 8 \times 100 + 5 \times 10$

3   Calculate:
  a $96\,481 + 2760 + 82$ b $10\,963 - 4096$ c 147×3
  d 980×200 e $4932 \div 3$ f $9177 \div 12$

4   State whether each of the following is true or false.
  a $18 < 20 - 2 \times 3$ b $9 \times 6 > 45$ c $23 = 40 \div 2 + 3$

5   How much more than 17×18 is 18×19?

6   Calculate:
  a $7 \times 6 - 4 \times 3$ b $8 \times 8 - 16 \div 2$ c $12 \times (6 - 2)$
  d $16 \times [14 - (6 - 2)]$ e $24 \div 6 \times 4$ f $56 - (7 - 5) \times 7$

7   State whether each of the following is true or false.
  a $4 \times 25 \times 0 = 1000$ b $0 \div 10 = 0$ c $8 \div 1 = 1$
  d $8 \times 7 = 7 \times 8$ e $20 \div 4 = 20 \div 2 \div 2$ f $8 + 5 + 4 = 8 + 9$

8   Insert brackets to make $18 \times 7 + 3 = 18 \times 7 + 18 \times 3$ true.

9   How many times can 15 be subtracted from 135 before an answer of zero occurs?

10 Write $3\,859\,643$ correct to the nearest:
  a   10   b   thousand   c   million.

Multiple-choice questions

1   Using numerals, thirty-five thousand, two hundred and six is:
  A   350\,260   B   35\,260   C   35\,000\,206   D   3526   E   35\,206

2   The place value of 8 in $2\,581\,093$ is:
  A   8 thousand   B   80 thousand   C   8 hundred
  D   8 tens   E   8 ones

3   The remainder when $23\,650$ is divided by 4 is:
  A   0   B   4   C   1   D   2   E   3

4   $18 - 3 \times 4 + 5$ simplifies to:
  A   65   B   135   C   11   D   1   E   20

5   $800 \div 5 \times 4$ is the same as:
  A 160×4 B $800 \div 20$ C $800 \div 4 \times 5$ D   40   E $4 \times 5 \div 800$

Extended response question

Tom works as a labourer, earning $25 an hour on weekdays and $60 an hour on weekends.

a   During a particular week, Tom works 7:00 a.m. to 2:00 p.m. Monday to Thursday. How many hours does he work that week?

b   How much does Tom earn for this work?

c   If Tom works 5 hours on Saturday in the same week, what is his total income for the week?

d   How many more hours on a Friday must Tom work to earn the same amount as working 5 hours on a Saturday?

Number properties and patterns

Short-answer questions

1   List the factors of:

   a   15   b   30   c   100

2   List the first five multiples of:

   a   3   b   7   c   11

3   List all factors common to 30 and 36.

4   What is the highest factor common to 36 and 40?

5   Find the value of:

   a 11^2 b $6^2 \times 2^2$ c $33 - 2^3$

6   What is the square root of 14 400?

7   Is the equation $\sqrt{3^2 + 4^2} = 3 + 4$ true or false?

(Ext)   8   Find the smallest number that must be added to 36 791 so that it becomes divisible by:

   a   2   b   3   c   4

9   A pattern is shown using matchsticks.

   term 1   term 2   term 3

   a   How many matchsticks are needed to build the 12th term in this pattern?

   b   Which term in this pattern uses exactly 86 matchsticks?

10   Find the missing values in the table.

input	4	5	6			
output	19	23		39	47	403

11 Write down the coordinates of each point.

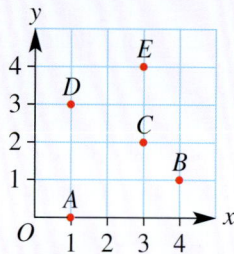

Multiple-choice questions

1   The first prime number after 20 is:
    A 21   B 22   C 23   D 24   E 25

2   The highest common factor (HCF) of 12 and 18 is:
    A 6   B 12   C 4   D 2   E 9

3   $2 \times 2 \times 2 \times 3$ is the same as:
    A 6×3 B $2^3 \times 3$ C 8^3 D 6^3 E 4^3

4   Evaluating $3^2 - \sqrt{25} + 3$ gives:
    A 8   B 5   C 4   D 17   E 7

5   The number 48 in prime factor form is:
    A $2^4 \times 5$ B $2 \times 3 \times 5$ C $2^3 \times 3^2$ D $2^4 \times 3$ E $2^3 \times 3$

Extended-response question

        term 1   term 2   term 3

The diagrams above show the tile pattern being used around the border of an inground swimming pool.

a   Draw the fourth term in the pattern.
b   How many coloured tiles are used in term 4 of the pattern?
c   Which term uses 41 coloured tiles in its construction?
d   If each coloured tile costs $1 and each white tile costs 50 cents, what is the cost of completing the pattern using 41 coloured tiles?

Fractions and percentages

Short-answer questions

1   Arrange $\frac{1}{2}, \frac{1}{3}, \frac{2}{5}$ and $\frac{3}{10}$ in *ascending* order.

2   Express $5\frac{2}{3}$ as an improper fraction.

3 Find each of the following.

a $\frac{2}{3} + \frac{1}{4}$ b $4 - 1\frac{1}{3}$ c $2\frac{1}{2} + 3\frac{3}{4}$

d $\frac{2}{5} \times \frac{1}{2}$ e $\frac{2}{3} \div \frac{1}{6}$ f $1\frac{1}{5} \times \frac{5}{12}$

4 Write 15% as a simple fraction.

5 Find 25% of $480.

6 Find $12\frac{1}{2}$% of $480.

7 State whether each of the following is true or false.

a   25% of $x = x \div 4$ b   10% of $w = \frac{w}{10}$

c   20% of 50 = 50% of 20   d   1% of $x = 100x$

8 Simplify the following ratios.

a   7:21   b   4:12:16   c   24 points to 10 points

9 Divide $60 in the given ratios.

a   5:1   b   2:3

Multiple-choice questions

1 Which of the following is equivalent to $\frac{12}{7}$?

A $\frac{24}{7}$ B $1\frac{5}{7}$ C $1\frac{5}{12}$ D $\frac{112}{17}$ E $\frac{7}{12}$

2 $\frac{1}{2} + \frac{1}{3}$ is equal to:

A $\frac{2}{5}$ B $\frac{2}{6}$ C $\frac{5}{6}$ D $\frac{1}{5}$ E $\frac{7}{6}$

3 $\frac{350}{450}$ in simplest form is:

A $\frac{35}{45}$ B $\frac{4}{5}$ C $\frac{3}{4}$ D $\frac{3.5}{4.5}$ E $\frac{7}{9}$

4 What fraction of $2 is 40 cents?

A $\frac{1}{20}$ B $\frac{20}{1}$ C $\frac{5}{1}$ D $\frac{1}{5}$ E $\frac{1}{40}$

5 $2\frac{1}{2} \div \frac{3}{4}$ is the same as:

A $\frac{5}{2} \times \frac{4}{3}$ B $\frac{5}{2} \times \frac{3}{4}$ C $\frac{2}{5} \div \frac{3}{4}$ D $\frac{2}{5} \times \frac{4}{3}$ E $\frac{3}{2} \times \frac{3}{4}$

Extended-response question

Caleb's cold and flu prescription states: 'Take two pills three times a day with food.' The bottle contains 54 pills.

a   How many pills does Caleb take each day?

b   What fraction of the bottle remains after Day 1?

c   How many days will it take for the pills to run out?

d   If Caleb takes his first dose on Friday night before going to bed, on what day will he take his last dose?

Algebraic techniques

Short-answer questions

1 Consider the expression $5x + 7y + 3x + 9$.
   a How many terms are in this expression?
   b Can the expression be simplified?
   c What is the value of the constant term?
   d What is the coefficient of y?

2 Write an algebraic expression for each of the following.
   a the sum of x and 3
   b the product of a and 12
   c the sum of double x and triple y
   d w divided by 6
   e double x taken from y

3 Find how many:
   a cents in $\$m$ b hours in x days
   c millimetres in p kilometres   d days in y hours.

4 If $m = 6$, find the value of each of the following.
   a $m + 7$ b $2m - 1$ c $6m + 3$
   d $2(m - 3)$ e $\dfrac{m + 6}{2}$ f $\dfrac{m}{2} + 4m - 3$

5 Evaluate the expression $3(2x + y)$ when $x = 5$ and $y = 2$.

6 Simplify each of the following.
   a $6a + 4a$ b $7x - 3x$ c $9a + 2a + a$
   d $m + m - m$ e $6 + 2a + 3a$ f $x + y + 3x + y$

7 a Write an expression for the perimeter of rectangle $ABCD$.
   b Write an expression for the area of rectangle $ABCD$.

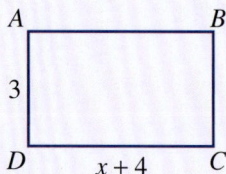

8 Find the missing term.
   a $3a \times \underline{\quad} = 18abc$ b $10ab \div \underline{\quad} = 2a$ c $2p + 2p + 2p = 6\underline{\quad}$

Ext 9 Expand:
   a $2(a + 3)$ b $12(a - b)$ c $8(3m + 4)$

10 Write the simplest expression for the perimeter of this figure.

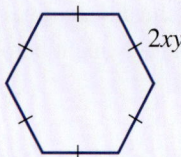

Multiple-choice questions

1 $12 - x$ means:

   A 12 less than x **B** x less than 12   **C** x has the value of 12

   D x is less than 12   **E** x is more than 12

2 Double the sum of x and y is:

   A $2(x + y)$ **B** $2x + y$ **C** $x + 2y$ **D** $(x + y)^2$ **E** $x + y + 2$

3 Half the product of a and b is:

   A $2ab$ **B** $\frac{a+b}{2}$ **C** $\frac{ab}{2}$ **D** $\frac{1}{2}a + \frac{1}{2}b$ **E** $\frac{a}{2} + b$

4 $4a + 3b + c + 5b - c$ is the same as:

   A $32ab$ **B** $4a + 8b + 2c$ **C** $8a + 4b$

   D $64abc$ **E** $4a + 8b$

5 If $a = 3$ and $b = 7$, then $3a^2 + 2b$ is equal to:

   A 66   **B** 95   **C** 23   **D** 41   **E** 20

Extended-response question

A bottle of soft drink costs \$3 and a pie costs \$2.

a Find the cost of:

   i 2 bottles of soft drink and 3 pies

   ii x bottles of soft drink and 3 pies

   iii x bottles of soft drink and y pies.

b If Anh has \$50, find his change if he buys x bottles of soft drink and y pies.

Decimals

Short-answer questions

1 Write each of the following as a decimal.

    a   two-tenths   b $\dfrac{13}{100}$ c $\dfrac{17}{10}$

2 In the decimal 136.094:

    a   what is the value of the 6?

    b   what is the value of the 4?

    c   what is the decimal, correct to the nearest tenth?

3 Round 18.398741 correct to:

    a   the nearest whole number

    b   1 decimal place

    c   2 decimal places.

4 Evaluate:

    a $15 - 10.93$ b $19.7 + 240.6 + 9.03$ c $20 - 0.99$

    d 0.6×0.4 e $(0.3)^2$ f $\dfrac{12}{0.2}$

5 Find:

    a $1.24 - 0.407$

    b $1.2 + 0.6 \times 3$

    c $1.8 \times 0.2 \div 0.01$

6 If $369 \times 123 = 45\,387$, write down the value of:

    a 3.69×1.23

    b 0.369×0.123

    c $45.387 \div 36.9$

7 Find:

    a 36.49×1000

    b $1.8 \div 100$

    c 19.43×200

8 For each of the following, state the larger of each pair.

    a $\dfrac{4}{5}, 0.79$

    b $1.1, 11\%$

    c $\dfrac{2}{3}, 0.6$

9 State if each of the following is true or false.

    a $0.5 = 50\%$ b $0.15 = \dfrac{2}{20}$ c $38\% = 0.19$

    d $126\% = 1.26$ e $\dfrac{4}{5} = 0.08$ f $1\dfrac{3}{4} = 1.75$

Multiple-choice questions

1. $80 + \frac{6}{10} + \frac{7}{1000}$ is the same as:

   A 8067   B 867   C 80.67   D 80.067   E 80.607

2. Select the incorrect statement.

   A $0.707 > 0.7$ B $0.770 = \frac{77}{100}$ C $0.07 \times 0.7 = 0.49$

   D $0.7 \times \frac{1}{10} = 0.07$ E $0.7 \times 10 = 7$

3. The best estimate for 23.4×0.96 is:

   A 234   B 230   C 0.234   D 23   E 20

4. $\frac{3}{8}$ is the same as:

   A 0.375   B 3.8   C 0.38   D $2.\dot{6}$ E 38%

5. $6.8 \div 0.04$ is the same as:

   A $68 \div 4$ B $680 \div 4$ C 17   D $\frac{4}{68}$ E $7 \div 0.05$

Extended-response question

The cost of petrol is 116.5 cents per litre.

a Find the cost of 55 L of petrol, correct to the nearest cent.

b Mahir pays cash for his 55 L of petrol. What is the amount that he pays, correct to the nearest 5 cents?

c If the price of petrol per litre is rounded to the nearest cent before the cost is calculated, how much would 55 L of petrol cost now?

d By how much is Mahir better off if the total cost is rounded rather than rounding the price per litre of the petrol?

e If the price drops to 116.2 cents per litre, is the comparison between rounding at the end versus rounding at the beginning the same as it was above?

6

Negative numbers

Maths in context: Positive and negative measurements

The Antarctic has the coldest climate on Earth. Near the coast, the temperature can range from +10°C in summer to −60°C in winter, making winter up to 70°C colder than summer. High in the mountains, temperatures average −30°C in summers and −80°C in winters, 50°C colder than summer.

Antarctic icebergs start out as huge broken ice shelves. Measuring from sea level, the top of an iceberg could be at +50 m and the bottom at −350 m, making a total height of 400 m. These gigantic icebergs are many kilometres across and weigh millions of tonnes.

When measured from its base, on the ocean floor, the Hawaiian mountain of Mauna Kea is the highest mountain in the world. The top is at +4205 m and the base at −6000 m making a total height of over 10 200 m from the base. That is much higher than Mt Everest at 8848 m above sea level.

There are several places on the Earth's continents that are below sea level. Examples include Australia's Lake Eyre at −15 m, California's Death Valley at −86 m, Israel's Sea of Galilee with its shores at −212 m and the very salty Dead Sea (pictured) with its shores at −423 m, the lowest dry land on Earth.

Chapter contents

Victorian Curriculum 2.0

This chapter covers the following content descriptors in the Victorian Curriculum 2.0:

NUMBER

VC2M7N03, VC2M7N08, VC2M7N10

ALGEBRA

VC2M7A05

Please refer to the curriculum support documentation in the teacher resources for a full and comprehensive mapping of this chapter to the related curriculum content descriptors.

© VCAA

Online resources

A host of additional online resources are included as part of your Interactive Textbook, including HOTmaths content, video demonstrations of all worked examples, auto-marked quizzes and much more.

6A   Introduction to negative integers

LEARNING INTENTIONS
- To understand that integers can be negative, positive or zero
- To be able to represent integers on a number line
- To be able to compare two integers and decide which is greater

The numbers 1, 2, 3, ... are considered to be positive because they are greater than zero (0). Negative numbers extend the number system to include numbers less than zero. Integers can be positive, zero or negative.

The winning golf score above is −7, shown in the left column. Golf scores are positive and negative integers giving the number of strokes above or below the par, the total strokes of an expert golfer.

The use of negative numbers dates back to 100 BCE when the Chinese used black rods for positive numbers and red rods for negative numbers in their rod number system. These coloured rods were used for commercial and tax calculations. Later, a great Indian mathematician named Brahmagupta (598–670) set out the rules for the use of negative numbers, using the word *fortune* for positive and *debt* for negative. Negative numbers were used to represent loss in a financial situation.

An English mathematician named John Wallis (1616–1703) invented the number line and the idea that numbers have a direction. This helped define our number system as an infinite set of numbers extending in both the positive and negative directions. Today, negative numbers are used in all sorts of mathematical calculations and are considered to be an essential part of our number system.

Lesson starter: Simple applications of negative numbers

- Try to name as many situations as possible in which negative numbers are used.
- Give examples of the numbers in each case.

KEY IDEAS

- **Negative** numbers are numbers less than zero.

- **Integers** can be negative, zero or positive and include
    ..., − 4, −3, −2, −1, 0, 1, 2, 3, 4, ...
  - The number −3 is read as 'negative 3'.
  - The number 3 is sometimes written as +3 and is sometimes read as 'positive 3'.

- A **number line** shows:
  - positive numbers to the right of zero.
  - negative numbers to the left of zero.

- Each negative number has a positive **opposite** and each positive number has a negative opposite. 3 and −3 are examples of opposite numbers.

■ Numbers can be thought of as having a *sign* (+ or −) and a *magnitude*, so numbers like 3 and −3 both have a magnitude of 3 but have opposite signs. The + sign is rarely used, as +3 is generally written as 3.

■ Negative fractions that are not integers can also be located on a number line.

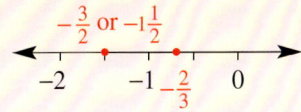

■ A number is greater than another number if it occurs to the right of it on a number line. For example, −2 is greater than −4. This can be written as −2 > −4 or −4 < −2.

BUILDING UNDERSTANDING

1 What are the missing numbers on these number lines?

a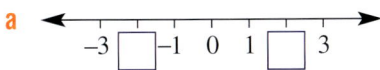

b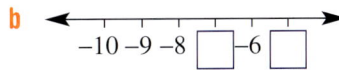

2 −5 is the opposite number of 5, and 5 is the opposite number of −5. State the opposite of these numbers.

a 2   b −7   c 21   d −1071

3 Select from the words *greater* or *less* to complete these sentences.

a 5 is _____ than 0

b −3 is _____ than 0

c 0 is _____ than −6

d 0 is _____ than 1

Example 1   Drawing a number line including integers

Draw a number line, showing all integers from −4 to 2.

SOLUTION

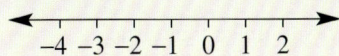

EXPLANATION

Use equally spaced markings and put −4 on the left and 2 on the right.

Now you try

Draw a number line, showing all integers from −6 to 1.

⊳

Example 2   Comparing integers using inequality symbols

Insert the symbol < (less than) or > (greater than) into these statements to make them true.

a −2 ☐ 3

b −1 ☐ −6

SOLUTION	EXPLANATION
a −2 < 3	−2 is to the left of 3 on a number line, so it is less than 3.
	←———————————→ −2 −1 0 1 2 3
b −1 > −6	−1 is to the right of −6 on a number line, so it is greater than −6.
	←———————————→ −6 −5 −4 −3 −2 −1 0

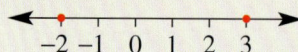

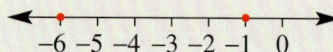

Now you try

Insert the symbol < (less than) or > (greater than) into these statements to make them true.

a 5 ☐ −7

b −4 ☐ −1

Exercise 6A

FLUENCY	1, 3–6(½)	2, 3–6(½)	3–6(½)

Example 1

1 Draw a number line, showing all integers from −2 to 3.

Example 1

2 Draw a number line for each description, showing all the given integers.
  a from −2 to 2
  b from −10 to −6

3 List all the integers that fit the description.
  a from −2 up to 4
  b greater than −3 and less than 2
  c greater than −5 and less than 1
  d less than −3 and greater than −10

Example 2

4 Insert the symbol < (less than) or > (greater than) into these statements to make them true.
  a 7 ☐ 9
  b 3 ☐ 2
  c 0 ☐ −2
  d −4 ☐ 0
  e −1 ☐ 5
  f −7 ☐ −6
  g −11 ☐ −2
  h −9 ☐ −13
  i −3 ☐ 3
  j 3 ☐ −3
  k −130 ☐ 1
  l −2 ☐ −147

5 State the temperature indicated on these thermometers.

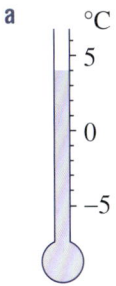

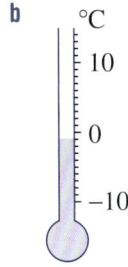

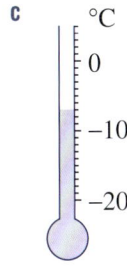

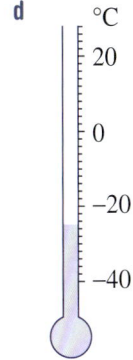

a °C
5
0
−5

b °C
10
0
−10

c °C
0
−10
−20

d °C
20
0
−20
−40

6 Write down the negative fraction or negative mixed numeral illustrated by the dot on these number lines.

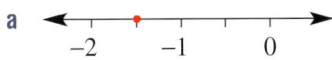

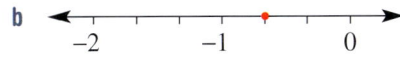

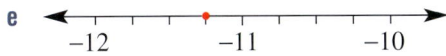

a
−2   −1   0

b
−2   −1   0

c
−5   −4

d
−10   −9

e
−12   −11   −10

f
−20   −19

PROBLEM-SOLVING   7, 8   8(½), 9   8(½), 9

7 Arrange these numbers in *ascending* order. Each number should be less than the next number in the list.
a −3, −6, 0, 2, −10, 4, −1
b −304, 126, −142, −2, 1, 71, 0

8 Write the next three numbers in these simple patterns.
a 3, 2, 1, ___,___,___
b −8, −6, −4, ___, ___, ___
c 10, 5, 0, ___,___,___
d −38, −40, −42, ___,___,___
e −91, −87, −83, ___, ___, ___
f 199, 99, −1, ___,___,___

9 These lists of numbers show deposits (positive numbers) and withdrawals (negative numbers) for a month of bank transactions. Find the balance at the end of the month.

a Start balance $200
                         −$10
                        −$130
                          $25
                        −$100
                          $20
   Final balance   _____

b Start balance $0
                          $50
                         −$60
                        −$100
                         $200
                        −$100
   Final balance   _____

REASONING   10   10, 11(½)   11(½), 12

10 If the height above sea level for a
plane is a positive number, then the
height for a submarine could be
written as a negative number. What
is the height relative to sea level for
a submarine at these depths?

   a 50 m

   b 212.5 m

   c 0 m

11 The difference between two numbers could be thought of as the
distance between the numbers on a number line. For example, the
difference between −2 and 1 is 3.

By considering them on a number line, find the difference between these pairs of numbers.

   a −1 and 1   **b** −2 and 2

   c −3 and 1   **d** −4 and 3

   e −3 and 0   **f** −4 and −1

   g −10 and −4   **h** −30 and 14

12 The opposite of any number other than 0 has the same magnitude but a different sign. (For example,
5 and −5 are opposites.)

   a Draw a number line to show 4 and its opposite, and use this to find the difference between the two
numbers.

   b State a number that has a difference of 9 with its opposite.

   c If numbers are listed in ascending order, explain by using a number line why their opposites would
be in descending order. (For example, −4, 2, 7 are ascending so 4, −2, −7 are descending.)

ENRICHMENT: The final position   –   –   13

13 For these sets of additions and subtractions, an addition means to
move to the right and a subtraction means to move left. Start at
zero each time and find the final position.

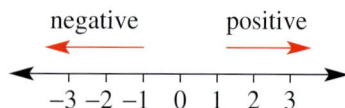

   a −1, 4, −5

   b 3, −5, −1, 4

   c −5, −1, 3, 1, −2, −1, 4

   d −10, 20, −7, −14, 8, −4

   e −250, 300, −49, −7, 36, −81

   f −7001, 6214, −132, 1493, −217

6B Adding and subtracting positive integers

Adding and subtracting a positive integer can give both positive and negative answers. For example, when a newly installed fridge at 20°C is switched on, the temperature inside the freezer might fall by 25°C. The final temperature is −5°C; i.e. $20 - 25 = -5$. If a temperature of −10°C rises by 5°C, the final temperature is −5°C; i.e. $-10 + 5 = -5$.

When food goes into a fridge or freezer its temperature begins to change, sometimes reaching temperatures below zero.

Lesson starter: Positive and negative possibilities

Decide if it is possible to find an example of the following. If so, give a specific example.

- A positive number added to a positive number gives a positive number.
- A positive number added to a positive number gives a negative number.
- A positive number added to a negative number gives a positive number.
- A positive number added to a negative number gives a negative number.
- A positive number subtracted from a positive number gives a positive number.
- A positive number subtracted from a positive number gives a negative number.
- A positive number subtracted from a negative number gives a positive number.
- A positive number subtracted from a negative number gives a negative number.

KEY IDEAS

■ If a positive number is added to any number, you move right on a number line.

$2 + 3 = 5$ Start at 2 and move right by 3.

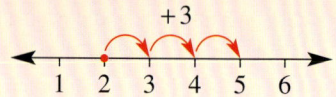

$-5 + 2 = -3$ Start at -5 and move right by 2.

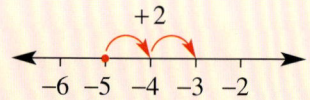

■ If a positive number is subtracted from any number, you move left on a number line.

$2 - 3 = -1$ Start at 2 and move left by 3.

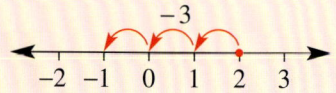

$-4 - 2 = -6$ Start at -4 and move left by 2.

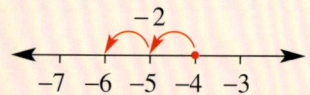

BUILDING UNDERSTANDING

1 In which direction (i.e. right or left) on a number line do you move for the following calculations?

   a 2 is added to -5 **b** 6 is added to -4

   c 4 is subtracted from 2   **d** 3 is subtracted from -4

2 Match up the problems **a** to **d** with the number lines **A** to **D**.

   a $5 - 6 = -1$ **A**

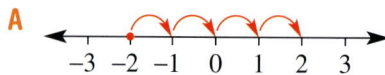

   b $-2 + 4 = 2$ **B**

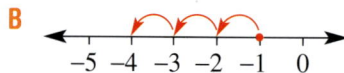

   c $-1 - 3 = -4$ **C**

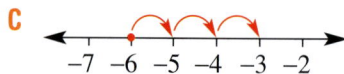

   d $-6 + 3 = -3$ **D**

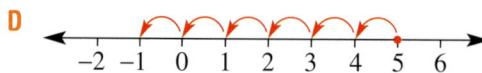

Example 3   Adding and subtracting positive integers

Calculate the answer to these additions and subtractions.

a $-2 + 3$ **b** $-8 + 1$ **c** $5 - 7$ **d** $-3 - 3$

SOLUTION

a $-2 + 3 = 1$

b $-8 + 1 = -7$

c $5 - 7 = -2$

d $-3 - 3 = -6$

EXPLANATION

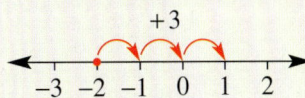

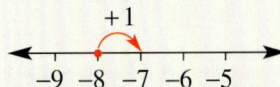

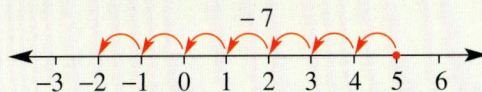

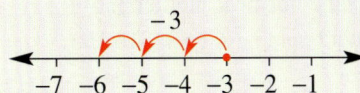

Now you try

Calculate the answer to these additions and subtractions.

a $-4 + 7$ **b** $-8 + 3$ **c** $4 - 8$ **d** $-6 - 4$

Exercise 6B

FLUENCY   1, 2–4(½)   2–5(½)   2–5(¼)

Example 3a,b

1 Calculate the answers to these additions.

    a $-2 + 5$ **b** $-6 + 2$ **c** $-4 + 3$ **d** $-3 + 8$

Example 3a,b

2 Calculate the answers to these additions.

    a $-1 + 2$ **b** $-1 + 4$ **c** $-3 + 5$ **d** $-10 + 11$

    e $-4 + 3$ **f** $-5 + 2$ **g** $-11 + 9$ **h** $-20 + 18$

    i $-4 + 0$ **j** $-8 + 0$ **k** $-30 + 29$ **l** $-39 + 41$

    m $-130 + 132$ **n** $-181 + 172$ **o** $-57 + 63$ **p** $-99 + 68$

Example 3c,d

3 Calculate the answers to these subtractions.

    a $4 - 6$ **b** $7 - 8$ **c** $3 - 11$ **d** $1 - 20$

    e $-3 - 1$ **f** $-5 - 5$ **g** $-2 - 13$ **h** $-7 - 0$

    i $-37 - 4$ **j** $39 - 51$ **k** $62 - 84$ **l** $-21 - 26$

    m $-100 - 200$ **n** $100 - 200$ **o** $328 - 421$ **p** $-496 - 138$

4   Find the missing number.

a $2 + \square = 7$

b $-2 + \square = 7$

c $-2 + \square = 3$

d $-4 + \square = -2$

e $5 - \square = 0$

f $3 - \square = -4$

g $-9 - \square = -12$

h $-20 - \square = -30$

i $-6 + \square = -1$

j $-8 - \square = -24$

k $\square + 1 = -3$

l $\square + 7 = 2$

m $\square - 4 = -10$

n $\square - 7 = -20$

o $\square + 6 = -24$

p $\square - 100 = -213$

5   Evaluate the following. Remember to work from left to right.

a $3 - 4 + 6$

b $2 - 7 - 4$

c $-1 - 4 + 6$

d $-5 - 7 - 1$

e $-3 + 2 - 7 + 9$

f $-6 + 1 - 20 + 3$

g $0 - 9 + 7 - 30$

h $-15 - 20 + 32 - 1$

PROBLEM-SOLVING	6, 7	7, 8	7–9

6   Determine how much debt remains in these financial situations.

a   owes $300 and pays back $155

b   owes $20 and borrows another $35

c   owes $21 500 and pays back $16 250

7   a   The reading on a thermometer measuring temperature rises 18°C from -15°C. What is the final temperature?

b   The reading on a thermometer measuring temperature falls 7°C from 4°C. What is the final temperature?

c   The reading on a thermometer measuring temperature falls 32°C from -14°C. What is the final temperature?

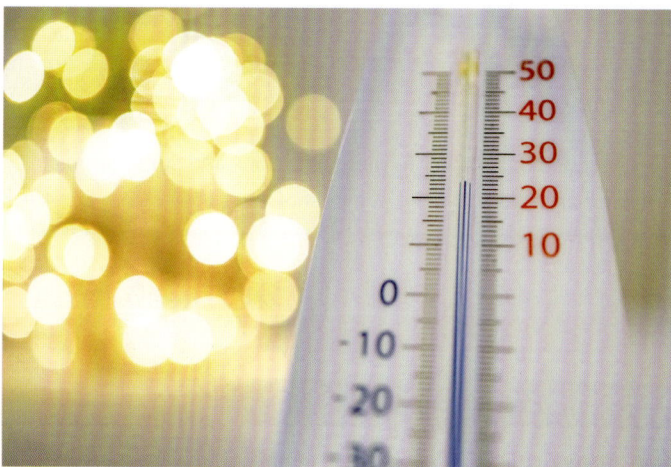

8   For an experiment, a chemical solution starts at a temperature of 25°C, falls to -3°C, rises to 15°C and then falls again to -8°C. What is the total change in temperature? Add all the changes together for each rise and fall.

9   An ocean sensor is raised and lowered to different depths in the sea. Note that -100 m means 100 m below sea level.

a   If the sensor is initially at -100 m and then raised to -41 m, how far does the sensor rise?

b   If the sensor is initially at -37 m and then lowered to -93 m how far is the sensor lowered?

10 Give an example that suits the description.

   a A positive number subtract a positive number equals a negative number.

   b A negative number subtract a positive number equals a negative number.

   c A negative number add a positive number equals a positive number.

   d A negative number add a positive number equals a negative number.

11 **a** a is a positive integer, b is a positive integer and $a > b$. For each of the following, decide if the result will be positive, negative or zero.

     i $a + b$　　　　**ii** $a - b$　　　　**iii** $b - a$　　　　**iv** $a - a$

   b a is a negative integer and b is a positive integer. Decide if each of the following is *always* true.

     i $a + b$ is positive　　　　　　　**ii** $a - b$ is negative

12 Insert + or − signs into these statements to make them true.

   a 3 ☐ 4 ☐ 5 = 4

   b 1 ☐ 7 ☐ 9 ☐ 4 = −5

   c −4 ☐ 2 ☐ 1 ☐ 3 ☐ 4 = 0

   d −20 ☐ 10 ☐ 7 ☐ 36 ☐ 1 ☐ 18 = −4

   e −a ☐ b ☐ a ☐ b = 0

   f −a ☐ a ☐ 3a ☐ b ☐ b = a − 2b

Positive and negative numbers are used to show the changes in international money exchange rates.

6C   Adding and subtracting negative integers

By observing patterns in number calculations, we can see the effect of adding and subtracting negative integers.

Addition

$2 + 3 = 5$
$2 + 2 = 4$ -1
$2 + 1 = 3$ -1
$2 + 0 = 2$ -1
$2 + (-1) = 1$ -1
$2 + (-2) = 0$ -1
$2 + (-3) = -1$ -1

Subtraction

$2 - 3 = -1$
$2 - 2 = 0$ $+1$
$2 - 1 = 1$ $+1$
$2 - 0 = 2$ $+1$
$2 - (-1) = 3$ $+1$
$2 - (-2) = 4$ $+1$
$2 - (-3) = 5$ $+1$

There are places where negative temperatures can occur daily in winter. Temperature differences are found by subtracting negative numbers. Finding an average temperature requires adding negative numbers.

So adding -3 is equivalent to subtracting 3, and subtracting -3 is equivalent to adding 3.

Lesson starter: Dealing with debt

Let $-\$10$ represent $10 of debt. Write a statement (e.g. $5 + (-10) = -5$) to represent the following financial situations.

- $10 of debt is added to a balance of $5.
- $10 of debt is added to a balance of $-\$5$.
- $10 of debt is removed from a balance of $-\$15$.

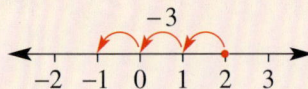
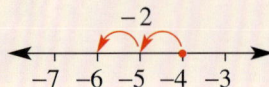

■ Subtracting a negative number is equivalent to adding its opposite.

$a - (-b) = a + b$

$5 - (-2) = 5 + 2 = 7$

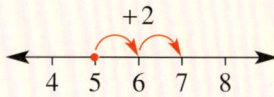

$-2 - (-3) = -2 + 3 = 1$

■ On a number line, the effect of adding or subtracting a negative number is to reverse the direction of the operation.

BUILDING UNDERSTANDING

1 State the missing numbers in these sentences. The first one has been done for you.

a $2 + 5$ means that $\boxed{5}$ is added to $\boxed{2}$.

b $-3 + 6$ means that $\boxed{}$ is added to $\boxed{}$.

c $1 + (-3)$ means that $\boxed{}$ is added to $\boxed{}$.

d $-7 + (-11)$ means that $\boxed{}$ is added to $\boxed{}$.

e $5 - 3$ means that $\boxed{}$ is subtracted from $\boxed{}$.

f $-2 - 6$ means that $\boxed{}$ is subtracted from $\boxed{}$.

g $7 - (-3)$ means that $\boxed{}$ is subtracted from $\boxed{}$.

h $-7 - (-11)$ means that $\boxed{}$ is subtracted from $\boxed{}$.

2 State the missing number or phrase to complete these sentences.

a Adding -4 is equivalent to subtracting $\boxed{}$.

b Adding -6 is equivalent to _____ 6.

c Adding 5 is equivalent to subtracting $\boxed{}$.

d Adding -11 is equivalent to _____ 11.

e Subtracting -2 is equivalent to adding $\boxed{}$.

f Subtracting -7 is equivalent to _____ 7.

3 State whether each of the following is true or false.

a $2 + (-3) = 5$

b $10 + (-1) = 9$

c $-5 + (-3) = -8$

d $-6 + (-2) = -4$

e $5 - (-1) = 4$

f $3 - (-9) = 12$

g $2 - (-3) = 1$

h $-11 - (-12) = -1$

Example 4   Adding and subtracting negative integers

Calculate the answer to these additions and subtractions.

a $7 + (-2)$ **b** $-2 + (-3)$ **c** $1 - (-3)$ **d** $-6 - (-2)$

SOLUTION	EXPLANATION
a $7 + (-2) = 7 - 2$ $= 5$	Adding -2 is equivalent to subtracting 2.
b $-2 + (-3) = -2 - 3$ $= -5$	Adding -3 is equivalent to subtracting 3.
c $1 - (-3) = 1 + 3$ $= 4$	Subtracting -3 is equivalent to adding 3.
d $-6 - (-2) = -6 + 2$ $= -4$	Subtracting -2 is equivalent to adding 2.

Now you try

Calculate the answer to these additions and subtractions.

a $9 + (-3)$ **b** $-4 + (-5)$ **c** $3 - (-7)$ **d** $-11 - (-6)$

Exercise 6C

FLUENCY	1, 2–4(½)	2–5(⅓)	2–5(¼)

Example 4a

1 Calculate the answer to these additions.

a $5 + (-3)$ **b** $7 + (-4)$ **c** $3 + (-5)$ **d** $5 + (-9)$

Example 4a,b

2 Calculate the answer to these additions.

a $3 + (-2)$ **b** $8 + (-3)$ **c** $12 + (-6)$ **d** $9 + (-7)$
e $1 + (-4)$ **f** $6 + (-11)$ **g** $20 + (-22)$ **h** $0 + (-4)$
i $-2 + (-1)$ **j** $-7 + (-15)$ **k** $-5 + (-30)$ **l** $-28 + (-52)$
m $-7 + (-3)$ **n** $-20 + (-9)$ **o** $-31 + (-19)$ **p** $-103 + (-9)$

Example 4c,d

3 Calculate the answer to these subtractions.

a $2 - (-3)$ **b** $5 - (-6)$ **c** $20 - (-30)$ **d** $29 - (-61)$
e $-5 - (-1)$ **f** $-7 - (-4)$ **g** $-11 - (-6)$ **h** $-41 - (-7)$
i $-4 - (-6)$ **j** $-9 - (-10)$ **k** $-20 - (-20)$ **l** $-96 - (-104)$
m $5 - (-23)$ **n** $28 - (-6)$ **o** $-31 - (-19)$ **p** $-104 - (-28)$

4 Find the missing number.

a $2 + \square = -1$ **b** $3 + \square = -7$ **c** $-2 + \square = -6$
d $\square + (-3) = 1$ **e** $\square + (-10) = -11$ **f** $\square + (-4) = 0$
g $5 - \square = 6$ **h** $2 - \square = 7$ **i** $-1 - \square = 3$
j $\square - (-3) = 7$ **k** $\square - (-10) = 12$ **l** $\square - (-4) = -20$
m $5 - \square = 11$ **n** $\square - (-2) = -3$ **o** $-2 - \square = -4$
p $\square + (-5) = -1$

5 Calculate the answer, working from left to right.

a $3 + (-2) + (-1)$ b $2 + (-1) + (-6)$ c $3 - (-1) - (-4)$

d $10 - (-6) + (-4)$ e $-7 - (-1) + (-3)$ f $-20 - (-10) - (-15)$

g $-9 - (-19) + (-16)$ h $-15 - (-20) + (-96)$ i $-13 - (-19) + (-21)$

j $-2 - (-3) - (-5)$ k $-18 - (-16) - (-19)$ l $5 + (-20) - (-26)$

PROBLEM-SOLVING	6, 7	7–9	8–10

6 An ocean sensor is initially at -90 m; i.e. 90 m below sea level. The sensor is raised 50 m, lowered 138 m and then raised again by 35 m. What is the probe's final position?

7 A small business has a bank balance of $-\$50\,000$. An amount of $\$20\,000$ of extra debt is added to the balance and, later, $\$35\,000$ is paid back. What is the final balance?

8 $\$100$ of debt is added to an existing balance of $\$50$ of debt. Later, $\$120$ of debt is removed from the balance. What is the final balance?

9 Here is a profit graph showing the profit for each month of the first half of the year for a bakery shop.

a What is the profit for:

  i February?

  ii April?

b What is the overall profit for the 6 months?

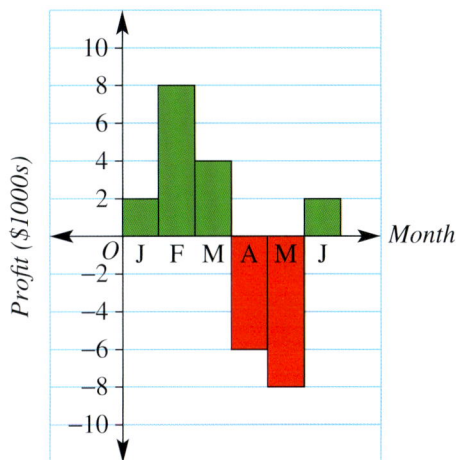

10 Complete these magic squares, using addition. The sum of each row, column and diagonal should be the same.

a

-2		5
	1	
		4

b

		-6
-3		-17
		-7

REASONING	11	11, 12	12–14

11 Write the following as mathematical expressions, e.g. $2 + (-3)$.

a The sum of 3 and 4

b The sum of -2 and -9

c The difference between 5 and -2

d The difference between -2 and 1

e The sum of a and the opposite of b

f The difference between a and the opposite of b

12 An addition number fact like $3 + 4 = 7$ can be turned into two subtraction number facts
($7 - 3 = 4$, $7 - 4 = 3$).

   a Use the number fact $7 + (-2) = 5$ to state two subtraction number facts.

   b Use the number fact $-3 + 7 = 4$ to state two subtraction number facts.

   c Find the value of $-2 + (-3)$ and hence state two subtraction number facts.

   d If you wanted to convince somebody that $1 - (-3) = 4$, how could you do this using an addition
   number fact?

13 Simplify these numbers. (*Hint*: In part **a**, $-(-4)$ is the same as $0 - (-4)$.)

   a $-(-4)$ **b** $-(-(-1))$ **c** $-(-(-(-(-3))))$

14 a If a is a positive number and b is a negative number, decide if each of the following statements is
   always true.

   i $a + b$ is negative   **ii** $a - b$ is positive

   b If a and b are both negative numbers, decide if each of the following statements is *always* true.

   i $a + b$ is negative   **ii** $a - b$ is positive

   c If a and b are both negative numbers and $b < a$, is $a - b$ always positive? Give reasons.

ENRICHMENT: Negative fractions   –   –   15(½)

15 Negative decimals and fractions can be added and subtracted using the same rules as those for integers.
Calculate the answer to these sums and differences of fractions.

   a $2 + \left(-\frac{1}{2}\right)$ **b** $5 + \left(-\frac{4}{3}\right)$ **c** $-\frac{1}{2} + \left(-\frac{3}{2}\right)$ **d** $-\frac{2}{3} + \left(-\frac{10}{3}\right)$

   e $5 - \left(-\frac{1}{3}\right)$ **f** $10 - \left(-\frac{3}{2}\right)$ **g** $-\frac{5}{4} - \left(-\frac{3}{4}\right)$ **h** $-\frac{4}{7} - \left(-\frac{1}{2}\right)$

   i $\frac{9}{2} + \left(-\frac{9}{3}\right)$ **j** $\frac{9}{2} - \left(-\frac{9}{3}\right)$ **k** $4\frac{2}{3} + \left(-1\frac{1}{2}\right)$ **l** $5\frac{5}{7} + \left(-4\frac{4}{5}\right)$

   m $-\frac{3}{2} + \left(-\frac{1}{3}\right)$ **n** $-\frac{7}{4} - \left(-\frac{2}{5}\right)$ **o** $3\frac{2}{7} - \left(-1\frac{1}{2}\right)$ **p** $-5\frac{1}{6} - \left(-3\frac{2}{5}\right)$

The temperature of the Moon's sunlit side is around 125°C and
the dark side temperature is around −175°C. The sunlit side is
$125 - (-175) = 300$°C warmer than the dark side.

6D   Multiplying and dividing integers   EXTENDING

LEARNING INTENTIONS
- To know that the sign of a product or quotient of two negative numbers is positive
- To know that the sign of a product or quotient of a negative and positive number is negative
- To be able to multiply and divide integers

The rules for multiplication and division of integers can be developed by considering repeated addition.

For example: 4 groups of -3 is $-3 + (-3) + (-3) + (-3) = -12$. So, $4 \times (-3) = -12$.

Also, $-3 \times 4 = -12$ since $a \times b = b \times a$.

We also know that if $5 \times 7 = 35$, then $35 \div 7 = 5$, so if $4 \times (-3) = -12$ then $-12 \div (-3) = 4$. This is saying there are 4 groups of -3 in -12, which we know from the repeated addition above.

Also, $-12 \div 4 = -3$.

These examples give rise to the rules governing the multiplication and division of negative numbers.

Lesson starter: Patterns in tables

Complete this table of values for multiplication by noticing the patterns. What does the table of values tell you about the rules for multiplying negative integers?

×	−3	−2	−1	0	1	2	3
−3				0			
−2				0			
−1				0			
0	0	0	0	0	0	0	0
1				0	1		
2				0	2	4	
3				0			

■ To find the product or quotient of two numbers, use their magnitudes to find the magnitude of the answer, and use their signs to decide the sign of the answer.
(For example, to find -3×5, the magnitude of -3 is 3 and the magnitude of 5 is 5, so the product has magnitude 15. The sign is negative since the two numbers are of opposite sign.)

BUILDING UNDERSTANDING

1 State the missing number.

a $2 \times (-3) = -6$, so $-6 \div (-3) = \boxed{}$

b $2 \times (-3) = -6$, so $-6 \div 2 = \boxed{}$

c $-16 \div 4 = -4$, so $\boxed{} \times 4 = -16$

d $16 \div (-4) = -4$, so $\boxed{} \times (-4) = 16$

2 Insert the missing word *positive* or *negative* for each sentence.

a The product (×) of two positive numbers is _____.

b The product (×) of two negative numbers is _____.

c The product (×) of two numbers with opposite signs is _____.

d The quotient (÷) of two positive numbers is _____.

e The quotient (÷) of two negative numbers is _____.

f The quotient (÷) of two numbers with opposite signs is _____.

Example 5   Multiplying and dividing integers

Calculate these products and quotients.

a $5 \times (-6)$ **b** $-3 \times (-7)$ **c** $-36 \div (-4)$ **d** $-18 \div 9$

SOLUTION	EXPLANATION
a $5 \times (-6) = -30$	The two numbers are of opposite sign, so the answer is negative.
b $-3 \times (-7) = 21$	The two numbers are of the same sign, so the answer is positive.
c $-36 \div (-4) = 9$	Both numbers are negative, so the answer is positive.
d $-18 \div 9 = -2$	The two numbers are of opposite sign, so the answer is negative.

Now you try

Calculate these products and quotients.

a -4×8 **b** $-9 \times (-5)$ **c** $21 \div (-3)$ **d** $-50 \div (-10)$

▶

Example 6   Working with multiple operations

Work from left to right to find the answer to $-7 \times 4 \div (-2)$.

SOLUTION

$-7 \times 4 \div (-2) = -28 \div (-2)$
$\qquad\qquad\qquad = 14$

EXPLANATION

First, calculate -7×4.
Then calculate $-28 \div (-2)$.

Now you try

Work from left to right to find the answer to $-12 \div 2 \times (-4)$.

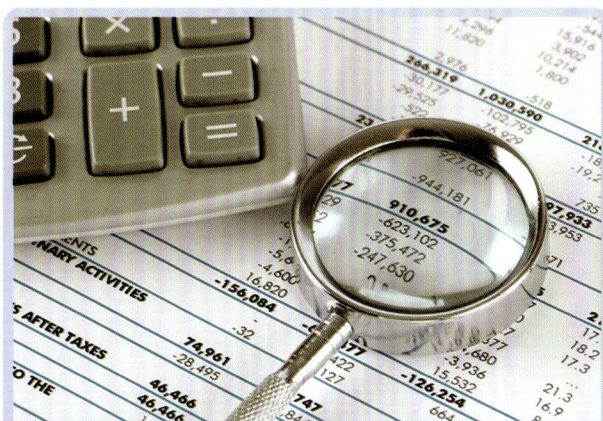

Accountants work with credit (positive amounts) and debit; i.e. debt (negative amounts). When calculating monthly repayments, a debt (e.g. $-\$50\,000$) is divided by the number of months of the loan.

Exercise 6D

FLUENCY	1, 2–6(½)	2–7(⅓)	2–7(¼)

ple 5a

1 State the value of the following.

a $2 \times (-3)$ b -2×3 c $-2 \times (-3)$

d -4×2 e $4 \times (-2)$ f $-4 \times (-2)$

e 5a,b

2 Calculate the answer to these products.

a $3 \times (-5)$ b $1 \times (-10)$ c -3×2 d -9×6

e $-8 \times (-4)$ f $-2 \times (-14)$ g $-12 \times (-12)$ h -11×9

i -13×3 j $7 \times (-12)$ k $-19 \times (-2)$ l -36×3

m $-6 \times (-11)$ n $5 \times (-9)$ o $-21 \times (-3)$ p $-36 \times (-2)$

Example 5c,d

3 Calculate the answer to these quotients.

a $14 \div (-7)$ b $36 \div (-3)$ c $-40 \div 20$ d $-100 \div 25$

e $-9 \div (-3)$ f $-19 \div (-19)$ g $-25 \div 5$ h $38 \div (-2)$

i $84 \div (-12)$ j $-108 \div 9$ k $-136 \div 2$ l $-1000 \div (-125)$

m $-132 \div (-11)$ n $-39 \div (-3)$ o $78 \div (-6)$ p $-156 \div (-12)$

Example 6

4 Work from left to right to find the answer. Check your answer using a calculator.

a $2 \times (-3) \times (-4)$ b $-1 \times 5 \times (-3)$ c $-10 \div 5 \times 2$

d $-15 \div (-3) \times 1$ e $-2 \times 7 \div (-14)$ f $100 \div (-20) \times 2$

g $48 \div (-2) \times (-3)$ h $-36 \times 2 \div (-4)$ i $-125 \div 25 \div (-5)$

j $-8 \div (-8) \div (-1)$ k $46 \div (-2) \times (-3) \times (-1)$ l $-108 \div (-12) \div (-3)$

5 Write down the missing number in these calculations.

a $5 \times \boxed{} = -35$ b $\boxed{} \times (-2) = -8$ c $16 \div \boxed{} = -4$

d $-32 \div \boxed{} = -4$ e $\boxed{} \div (-3) = -9$ f $\boxed{} \div 7 = -20$

g $-5000 \times \boxed{} = -10\,000$ h $-87 \times \boxed{} = 261$ i $243 \div \boxed{} = -81$

j $50 \div \boxed{} = -50$ k $-92 \times \boxed{} = 184$ l $-800 \div \boxed{} = -20$

6 Remember that $\frac{9}{3}$ means $9 \div 3$. Use this knowledge to find the following values.

a $\dfrac{-12}{4}$ b $\dfrac{21}{-7}$ c $\dfrac{-40}{-5}$

d $\dfrac{-124}{-4}$ e $\dfrac{-15}{-5}$ f $\dfrac{-100}{-20}$

g $\dfrac{-900}{30}$ h $\dfrac{20\,000}{-200}$

7 Remember that $3^2 = 3 \times 3 = 9$, and $(-3)^2 = -3 \times (-3) = 9$. Use this knowledge to find the following values.

a $(-2)^2$ b $(-1)^2$ c $(-9)^2$ d $(-10)^2$

e $(-6)^2$ f $(-8)^2$ g $(-3)^2$ h $(-1.5)^2$

PROBLEM-SOLVING   8   8, 9   9, 10

8 List the different pairs of integers that multiply to give these numbers.

a   6   b   16   c -5 d -24

9 Insert a multiplication or division sign between the numbers to make a true statement.

a $2 \boxed{} (-3) \boxed{} (-6) = 1$ b $-25 \boxed{} (-5) \boxed{} 3 = 15$

c $-36 \boxed{} 2 \boxed{} (-3) = 216$ d $-19 \boxed{} (-19) \boxed{} 15 = 15$

10 a There are two distinct pairs of numbers whose product is -8 and difference is 6. What are the two numbers?

b The quotient of two numbers is -11 and their difference is 36. What are the two numbers? There are two distinct pairs to find.

11 Recall that the opposite of a number has the same magnitude but a different sign (e.g. -7 and 7).

   a What number can you multiply by to go from a number to its opposite?

   b How could you get from a number to its opposite using division?

   c Use one of the operations from parts **a** and **b** to explain why you get back to the original number if you take the opposite of an opposite.

12 2^4 means $2 \times 2 \times 2 \times 2$, and $(-2)^4 = -2 \times (-2) \times (-2) \times (-2)$.

   a Calculate:

     i $(-2)^3$ **ii** $(-2)^6$ **iii** $(-3)^3$ **iv** $(-3)^4$

   b Which questions from part **a** give positive answers and why?

   c Which questions from part **a** give negative answers and why?

13 $a \times b$ is equivalent to ab, and $2 \times (-3)$ is equivalent to $-(2 \times 3)$. Use this information to simplify these expressions as much as possible.

   a $a \times (-b)$ **b** $-a \times b$ **c** $-a \times (-b)$

14 $(-1) + (-2) + (-3) + (-4) = -10$ and $(-1) \times (-2) \times (-3) \times (-4) = 24$. Therefore, it is possible to use the numbers $-1, -2, -3$ and -4 to achieve a 'result' of -10 and 24. What other 'results' can you find using those four numbers and any mathematical operations?

   For example: What is $(-1) \times (-2) + (-3) \times (-4)$? Can you find expressions for every integer result from -20 to 20?

15 Calculate the answer to these problems containing fractions. Simplify where possible.

   a $\frac{1}{2} \times \left(-\frac{1}{2}\right)$ **b** $\frac{3}{4} \times \left(-\frac{2}{3}\right)$ **c** $-\frac{5}{7} \times \frac{3}{5}$

   d $-\frac{3}{4} \times \left(-\frac{4}{3}\right)$ **e** $\frac{1}{4} \div \left(-\frac{1}{4}\right)$ **f** $-\frac{5}{8} \div \frac{1}{2}$

   g $-\frac{6}{11} \div \left(-\frac{12}{11}\right)$ **h** $-\frac{3}{2} \div \left(-\frac{1}{4}\right)$ **i** $\frac{a}{b} \times \left(-\frac{b}{a}\right)$

   j $-\frac{b}{a} \times \left(-\frac{a}{b}\right)$ **k** $-\frac{a}{b} \div \frac{a}{b}$ **l** $-\frac{b}{a} \div \left(-\frac{b}{a}\right)$

Progress quiz

6A 1 Draw a number line from -2 to 3, showing all the given integers.

6A 2 Copy and insert the symbol < (less than) or > (greater than) into these statements to make them true.

 a $-2 \boxed{} 4$ b $-9 \boxed{} -12$ c $4 \boxed{} -5$

6A 3 Arrange these numbers in *ascending* order: $-6, 8, -4, 0, 7$.

6B 4 Calculate the answer to these additions and subtractions.

 a $-10 + 12$ b $-4 - 5$ c $26 - 34$ d $-5 - 8 + 9 - 22$

6C 5 Calculate the answer to these additions and subtractions.

 a $9 + (-4)$ b $-8 + (-7)$ c $0 + (-3)$ d $12 - (-8)$

6D 6 Calculate the answer, working from left to right.

 a $-20 - (-10) - (-15)$ b $10 - (-6) + (-4)$

6D 7 Calculate these products and quotients.

 a $4 \times (-3)$ b $-5 \times (-12)$ c $-56 \div 8$ d $-20 \div (-5)$

6D 8 Work from left to right to find the answer.

 a $5 \times (-2) \times (-4)$ b $25 \div (-5) \times 6$

(Ext) c $64 \div (-8) \times (-2)$ d $-40 \div (-4) \div (-5)$

6D 9 Simplify each of the following.

 a $(-5)^2$ b $(-2)^3$

(Ext) c $\dfrac{-72}{-6}$ d $\dfrac{-1260}{4}$

6C 10 Ethan has a debt of $120 on his credit card. He buys another item using his credit card, which adds an extra debt of $90. At the end of the month Ethan paid $140 off his credit card debt.

(Ext) What is the final balance on Ethan's credit card?

6E Order of operations with integers EXTENDING

We have learnt from our study of positive integers that there is a particular order to follow when dealing with mixed operations and brackets. This order also applies when dealing with negative numbers.

For example: $-2 + 3 \times (-4)$ is different from $(-2 + 3) \times (-4)$.

Submarine operators and scuba divers apply the order of operations to calculate a negative height, h metres, relative to sea level. If a diver or submarine at $h = -5$ m descends for 3 minutes at -20 m/min, $h = -5 + 3 \times (-20) = -65$, so the depth is -65 m.

Lesson starter: Brackets or not?

During a classroom debate about truth of the statement $3 \times (-4) - 8 \div (-2) = -8$:

- Lil says that the statement needs to have more brackets to make it true.
- Max says that even with brackets it is impossible to make it true.
- Riley says that it is correct as it is and there is no need for more brackets.

Who is correct and why?

KEY IDEAS

■ When working with more than one operation and with positive and/or negative numbers, follow these rules.
- Deal with brackets first.
- Do multiplication and division next, working from left to right.
- Do addition and subtraction last, working from left to right.

$$-2 \times 3 - (10 + (-2)) \div 4$$
$$\underline{\quad 1st \quad}$$
$$= -2 \times 3 - 8 \div 4$$
$$\underline{2nd} \quad \underline{3rd}$$
$$= \quad -6 \quad - \quad 2$$
$$\underline{\quad last \quad}$$
$$= \quad\quad -8$$

BUILDING UNDERSTANDING

1 Which operation (i.e. brackets, addition, subtraction, multiplication or division) is done first in each of the following problems?

a $-2 \div 2 + 1$

b $-3 + 2 \times (-6)$

c $7 - (-8) \div 4$

d $-6 \div (4 - (-2))$

e $(2 + 3 \times (-2)) + 1$

f $-11 \div (7 - 2 \times (-2))$

2 Classify each of the following statements as true or false.

a $-4 + 2 \times 3 = -4 + (2 \times 3)$

b $-4 + 2 \times 3 = (-4 + 2) \times 3$

c $8 \times (2 - (-2)) = 8 \times 4$

d $8 \times (2 - (-2)) = 8 \times 0$

e $-40 - 20 \div (-5) = (-40 - 20) \div (-5)$

f $-40 - 20 \div (-5) = -40 - (20 \div (-5))$

Example 7   Using order of operations

Use order of operations to evaluate the following.

a $5 + 2 \times (-3)$

b $-6 \times 2 - 10 \div (-5)$

SOLUTION

a $5 + 2 \times (-3) = 5 + (-6)$
$ = -1$

b $-6 \times 2 - 10 \div (-5) = -12 - (-2)$
$ = -12 + 2$
$ = -10$

EXPLANATION

Do the multiplication before the addition.

Do the multiplication and division first.
When subtracting -2, add its opposite.

Now you try

Use order of operations to evaluate the following.

a $10 + (-20) \div 5$

b $5 \times (-7) + (-24) \div 4$

Example 8   Using order of operations with brackets

Use order of operations to evaluate the following.

a $(-2 - 1) \times 8$

b $5 \div (-10 + 5) + 5$

SOLUTION

a $(-2 - 1) \times 8 = -3 \times 8$
$ = -24$

b $5 \div (-10 + 5) + 5 = 5 \div (-5) + 5$
$ = -1 + 5$
$ = 4$

EXPLANATION

Deal with brackets first.

Deal with brackets first. Then do the division before the addition.

Now you try

Use order of operations to evaluate the following.

a $(-10 + 2) \div (3 - 5)$

b $(36 \div (-4) + 2) \times (1 - 3)$

Exercise 6E

FLUENCY · 1, 2, 3–4($\frac{1}{3}$) · 1–4($\frac{1}{2}$) · 3–4($\frac{1}{4}$)

mple 7a 1 Use order of operations to evaluate the following.

a $3 + 2 \times (-4)$

b $5 + 8 \times (-2)$

c $2 + (-3) \times 4$

d $5 + (-2) \times 3$

mple 7a 2 Use order of operations to evaluate the following.

a $10 + 4 \div (-2)$

b $12 + 8 \div (-4)$

c $24 \div (-4) \times 6$

d $40 \div 5 \times (-2)$

ample 7 3 Use order of operations to evaluate the following.

a $2 + 3 \times (-3)$

b $9 + 10 \div (-5)$

c $20 + (-4) \div 4$

d $18 + (-9) \times 1$

e $10 - 2 \times (-3)$

f $10 - 1 \times (-4)$

g $-8 - (-7) \times 2$

h $-2 \times 4 + 8 \times (-3)$

i $-3 \times (-1) + 4 \times (-2)$

j $12 \div (-6) + 4 \div (-2)$

k $-30 \div 5 - 6 \times 2$

l $-2 \times 3 - 4 \div (-2)$

m $8 \times (-2) - (-3) \times 2$

n $-1 \times 0 - (-4) \times 1$

o $0 \times (-3) - (-4) \times 0 + 0$

ample 8 4 Use order of operations to evaluate the following.

a $(3 + 2) \times (-2)$

b $(8 - 4) \div (-2)$

c $-3 \times (-2 + 4)$

d $-1 \times (7 - 8)$

e $10 \div (4 - (-1))$

f $(2 + (-3)) \times (-9)$

g $(24 - 12) \div (16 + (-4))$

h $(3 - 7) \div (-1 + 0)$

i $-2 \times (8 - 4) + (-6)$

j $-2 - 3 \times (-1 + 7)$

k $0 + (-2) \div (1 - 2)$

l $1 - 2 \times (-3) \div (-3 - (-2))$

m $(-3 + (-5)) \times (-2 - (-1))$

n $-3 \div (-1 + 4) \times 6$

o $-5 - (8 + (-2)) + 9 \div (-9)$

PROBLEM-SOLVING · 5, 6 · 6, 7($\frac{1}{2}$) · 7($\frac{1}{2}$), 8

5 A shop owner had bought socks at \$5 a pair but, during an economic downturn, changed the price to sell them for \$3 a pair. In a particular week, 124 pairs are sold and there are other costs of \$280. What is the shop owner's overall loss for the week?

6 A debt of \$550 is doubled and then \$350 of debt is removed each month for 3 months. What is the final balance?

7 Insert brackets to make each statement true.

a $-2 + 3 \times 8 = 8$
b $-10 \div 4 + 1 = -2$
c $-1 + 7 \times 2 - 15 = -3$
d $-5 - 1 \div (-6) = 1$
e $3 - 8 \div 5 + 1 = 0$
f $50 \times 7 - 8 \times (-1) = 50$
g $-2 \times 3 - (-7) - 1 = -21$
h $-3 + 9 \div (-7) + 5 = -3$
i $32 - (-8) \div (-3) + 7 = 10$

8 By inserting only *one* pair of brackets, how many different answers are possible for this calculation? Also include the answers for which brackets are not required.

$-2 + 8 \times (-4) - (-3)$

REASONING	9	9–10(½)	10, 11

9 If brackets are removed from these problems, does the answer change?

a $(2 \times 3) - (-4)$
b $(8 \div (-2)) - 1$
c $(-2 + 3) \times 4$
d $9 \div (-4 + 1)$
e $(9 - (-3) \times 2) + 1$
f $(-1 + 8 \div (-2)) \times 2$

10 State if each of the following is always true or false.

a $(-3 + 1) + (-7) = -3 + (1 + (-7))$
b $(-3 + 1) - (-7) = -3 + (1 - (-7))$
c $(a + b) + c = a + (b + c)$
d $(a + b) - c = a + (b - c)$
e $(a - b) + c = a - (b + c)$
f $(a - b) - c = a - (b - c)$

11 a Is the answer to each of the following positive or negative?

i $-6 \times (-4) \times (-8) \times (-108) \times (-96)$
ii $-100 \div (-2) \div 2 \div (-5)$
iii $(-3)^3$
iv $-1 \times (-2)^3$
v $\dfrac{-6 \times (-3) \times 4 \times 7 \times (-3)}{(-2)^2}$
vi $\dfrac{(-1)^2 \times (-1)}{(-1)^3 \times (-1)}$

b Explain the strategy you used to answer the questions in part **a**.

ENRICHMENT: Powers and negative numbers	–	–	12, 13

12 First, note that:

- $2^4 = 2 \times 2 \times 2 \times 2 = 16$
- $(-2)^4 = -2 \times (-2) \times (-2) \times (-2) = 16$
- $-2^4 = -(2 \times 2 \times 2 \times 2) = -16$

When evaluating expressions with powers, the power is dealt with first in the order of operations.

For example: $\left((-2)^3 - 1\right) \div (-3) = (-8 - 1) \div (-3) = -9 \div (-3) = 3$

Evaluate each of the following.

a 2^2
b $(-2)^2$
c -2^2
d $(-2)^5$
e -2^5
f $(3^2 - 1) \times 4$
g $\left((-3)^3 - 1\right) \div (-14)$
h $30 \div (1 - 4^2)$
i $-10\,000 \div (-10)^4$

13 Kevin wants to raise -3 to the power of 4. He types -3^4 into a calculator and gets -81. Explain what Kevin has done wrong.

The following problems will investigate practical situations drawing upon knowledge and skills developed throughout the chapter. In attempting to solve these problems, aim to identify the key information, use diagrams, formulate ideas, apply strategies, make calculations and check and communicate your solutions.

Sunny's monthly budget

1   Sunny wanted to keep a close track of all the money she earned and spent and decided to keep her own balance sheet, just like at a bank. Below is a copy of Sunny's transaction history for the month of October. Sunny is able to have a negative balance, because her bank is her parents' bank and they are okay if Sunny borrows money from them, as long as she pays them back at a later date.

Date	Transaction Details	Debit	Credit	Balance
4/10	Earned $25 from babysitting		$25	−$30
5/10	Spent $90 on a new pair of shoes	$90		−$120
11/10	Received $15 from Grandma		$15	−$105
18/10	Spent $12 going to the movies	$12		−$117
22/10	Donated $5 to 'Odd Socks' day	$5		−$122
23/10	Earned $60 from babysitting			
27/10	Spent $25 on Holly's birthday present			
30/10	Paid $40 for magazine subscription			

Sunny is interested in managing her money and analysing her earnings and expenditure during the month of October.

a   What was Sunny's balance on 1 October?

b   How much did Sunny owe her parents on 1 October?

c   Complete the last three rows of Sunny's balance sheet.

d   How much did Sunny spend in October?

e   How much did Sunny earn in October?

f   How much does Sunny owe her parents at the end of October?

Body temperature of a polar bear

2   Polar bears are the world's largest land predators and can weigh up to 600 kg. They live in the Arctic where temperatures are regularly below 0°C.
The average winter temperatures in the Arctic (month of January) range from −34°C to −5°C.
The average summer temperatures in the Arctic (month of July) range from −12°C to 10°C.
A polar bear must maintain its body temperature at 37°C and has two coats of fur and a thick layer of fat to help with this task.

You are interested in the various differences between minimum and maximum air temperatures and the body temperature of a polar bear.

a   What is the maximum difference in winter between the outside temperature and a polar bear's body temperature?

b   What is the minimum difference in summer between the outside temperature and a polar bear's body temperature?

c   What would the outside temperature be if there was 100°C difference between the outside temperature and a polar bear's body temperature?

d   The coldest temperature recorded in the Arctic was −69.6°C in Greenland in 1991. What was the difference between the outside temperature and a polar bear's body temperature at this time?

e   Write an expression for the difference between the outside temperature, T°C, and a polar bear's body temperature.

Depth of a scuba dive

3   Alessandro is an experienced scuba diving instructor who teaches groups of adults how to safely scuba dive. During a class, Alessandro travels up and down in the water moving between the different members of his group and constantly checking in on them. Alessandro wears a depth gauge watch and below is a table showing his depths recorded at 2-minute intervals during his most recent 1-hour class.

Time (min)	Depth (m)	Time (min)	Depth (m)	Time (min)	Depth (m)	Time (min)	Depth (m)
0	0	16	−10	32	−15	48	−31
2	−1	18	−8	34	−21	50	−34
4	−3	20	−8	36	−24	52	−30
6	−8	22	−6	38	−28	54	−26
8	−4	24	−12	40	−29	56	−20
10	−9	26	−15	42	−25	58	−12
12	−4	28	−11	44	−22	60	0
14	−5	30	−9	46	−29		

Alessandro is interested in using positive and negative numbers to analyse the change in depth and rate of change of depth over the course of a dive.

a   Using the data provided from the depth gauge watch, what was the total vertical distance Alessandro travelled during the 1-hour class?

b   Scuba divers need to be careful of ascending too quickly as it can cause decompression sickness. It is commonly understood that divers should not exceed an ascent rate of 9 m/minute. From the depth gauge watch data, what was Alessandro's maximum ascent rate and when did this occur?

c   What was Alessandro's average vertical speed over the 1-hour class in m/min?

$$\text{Speed} = \frac{\text{Distance travelled}}{\text{Time taken}}$$

d   A scuba diver instructor assisting a group of beginner scuba divers ended up diving to a depth of d metres and resurfacing on five occasions, and also diving to a depth of $2d$ metres and resurfacing on two occasions, all in the one t minute class. Write an expression for the instructor's average vertical speed in m/min during the class.

6F Substituting integers EXTENDING

The process known as substitution involves replacing a pronumeral (sometimes called a variable) with a number. A car's speed after t seconds could be given by the expression $10 + 4t$. So, after 3 seconds we can calculate the car's speed by substituting $t = 3$ into $10 + 4t$.

So $10 + 4t = 10 + 4 \times 3 = 22$ metres per second.

Lesson starter: Order matters

Two students substitute the values $a = -2$, $b = 5$ and $c = -7$ into the expression $ac - bc$. Some of the different answers received are 21, -49, -21 and 49.

When a vehicle or plane brakes to a stop, its speed is changing at a negative rate, e.g. -5 m/s per second. Aircraft engineers substitute negative numbers into formulas to calculate the stopping distances of various planes.

- Which answer is correct and what errors were made in the calculation of the three incorrect answers?

KEY IDEAS

■ Substitute into an expression by replacing pronumerals (letters representing numbers) with numbers.

$$\begin{aligned} \text{If } a = -3 \text{ then} \\ 3 - 7a &= 3 - 7 \times (-3) \\ &= 3 - (-21) \\ &= 3 + 21 \\ &= 24 \end{aligned}$$

■ Brackets can be used around negative numbers to avoid confusion with other symbols.

BUILDING UNDERSTANDING

1 Which of the following shows the correct substitution of $a = -2$ into the expression $a - 5$?

  A $2 - 5$ **B** $-2 + 5$ **C** $-2 - 5$ **D** $2 + 5$

2 Which of the following shows the correct substitution of $x = -3$ into the expression $2 - x$?

  A $-2 - (-3)$ **B** $2 - (-3)$ **C** $-2 + 3$ **D** $-3 + 2$

3 Rafe substitutes $c = -10$ into $10 - c$ and gets 0. Is he correct? If not, what is the correct answer?

Example 9   Substituting integers

Evaluate the following expressions using $a = 3$ and $b = -5$.

a $2 + 4a$ **b** $7 - 4b$ **c** $b \div 5 - a$

SOLUTION

a $2 + 4a = 2 + 4 \times 3$
$ = 2 + 12$
$ = 14$

b $7 - 4b = 7 - 4 \times (-5)$
$ = 7 - (-20)$
$ = 7 + 20$
$ = 27$

c $b \div 5 - a = -5 \div 5 - 3$
$ = -1 - 3$
$ = -4$

EXPLANATION

Replace a with 3 and evaluate the multiplication first.

Replace the b with -5 and evaluate the multiplication before the subtraction.

Replace b with -5 and a with 3, and then evaluate.

Now you try

Evaluate the following expressions using $x = -7$ and $y = 2$.

a $4 - 5y$ **b** $2x + 5$ **c** $5(y - x)$

Exercise 6F

FLUENCY   1, 2–4(½)   2–5(½)   2–4(⅓), 5

1 Evaluate the following expressions using $a = 4$ and $b = -3$.

Example 9a
a **i** $1 + 2a$ **ii** $5 + 3a$

Example 9b
b **i** $4 - 2b$ **ii** $10 - 7b$

Example 9c
c **i** $b \div 3 - a$ **ii** $b \div 1 - a$

Example 9a,b
2 Evaluate the following expressions using $a = 6$ and $b = -2$.

a $5 + 2a$ **b** $-7 + 5a$ **c** $b - 6$ **d** $b + 10$

e $4 - b$ **f** $7 - 2b$ **g** $3b - 1$ **h** $-2b + 2$

i $5 - 12 \div a$ **j** $1 - 60 \div a$ **k** $10 \div b - 4$ **l** $3 - 6 \div b$

Example 9c
3 Evaluate the following expressions using $a = -5$ and $b = -3$.

a $a + b$ **b** $a - b$ **c** $b - a$ **d** $2a + b$

e $5b + 2a$ **f** $6b - 7a$ **g** $-7a + b + 4$ **h** $-3b - 2a - 1$

Example 9
4 Evaluate these expressions for the given pronumeral values.

a $26 - 4x \, (x = -3)$ **b** $-2 - 7k \, (k = -1)$

c $10 \div n + 6 \, (n = -5)$ **d** $-3x + 2y \, (x = 3, y = -2)$

e $18 \div y - x \, (x = -2, y = -3)$ **f** $-36 \div a - ab \, (a = -18, b = -1)$

5 These expressions contain brackets. Evaluate them for the given pronumeral values. (Remember that ab means $a \times b$.)

a $2 \times (a + b)$ $(a = -1, b = 6)$
b $10 \div (a - b) + 1$ $(a = -6, b = -1)$
c $ab \times (b - 1)$ $(a = -4, b = 3)$
d $(a - b) \times bc$ $(a = 1, b = -1, c = 3)$

PROBLEM-SOLVING	6, 7	6, 7	7, 8

6 The area of a triangle for a fixed base of 4 metres is given by the rule Area $= 2h\,\text{m}^2$, where h metres is the height of the triangle. Find the area of such a triangle with these heights.

a 3 m
b 8 m

7 For a period of time a motorcycle's speed, in metres per second, is modelled by the expression $20 + 3t$, where t is the number of seconds after the motorcycle passes a particular building. The rule applies from 6 seconds before the motorcyclist reached the building.

a Find the motorcycle's speed after 4 seconds.
b Find the motorcycle's speed at $t = -2$ seconds (i.e. 2 seconds before passing the $t = 0$ point).
c Find the motorcycle's speed at $t = -6$ seconds.

8 The formula for the perimeter, P, of a rectangle is $P = 2l + 2w$, where l and w are the length and the width, respectively.

a Use the given formula to find the perimeter of a rectangle with:
  i $l = 3$ and $w = 5$
  ii $l = 7$ and $w = -8$
b What problems are there with part **a ii** above?

REASONING	9	9, 10	10, 11

9 Write two different expressions involving x that give an answer of -10 if $x = -5$.

10 Write an expression involving the pronumeral a combined with other integers, so if $a = -4$ the expression would equal these answers.

a -3
b 0
c 10

11 If a and b are non-zero integers, explain why these expressions will always give the result of zero.

a $a - b + b - a$
b $\dfrac{a}{a} - 1$
c $\dfrac{(a - a)}{b}$
d $\dfrac{ab}{b} - a$

ENRICHMENT: Celsius/Fahrenheit	–	–	12

12 The Fahrenheit temperature scale (°F) is still used today in some countries, but most countries use the Celsius scale (°C). 32°F is the freezing point for water (0°C). 212°F is the boiling point for water (100°C).

The formula for converting °F to °C is °C $= \dfrac{5}{9} \times (°F - 32)$.

a Convert these temperatures from °F to °C.
  i 41°F
  ii 5°F
  iii -13°F
b Can you work out the formula that converts from °C to °F?
c Use your rule from part **b** to check your answers to part **a**.

The temperature of boiling water is 100°C or 212°F.

6G   The Cartesian plane

LEARNING INTENTIONS

• To understand that the Cartesian plane can be extended to include negative numbers on both axes
• To understand what a coordinate pair means if one or both numbers is negative
• To be able to plot a point at a location expressed as x- and y-coordinates

During the seventeenth century, two well-known mathematicians, René Descartes and Pierre de Fermat, independently developed the idea of a number plane. The precise positions of points are illustrated using coordinates, and these points can be plotted using the axes as measuring guides. This invention revolutionised the study of mathematics and provided a vital link between geometry and algebra. The number plane or coordinate plane, is also called the Cartesian plane (named after Descartes). It uses two axes at right angles that extend in both the positive and negative directions.

Mathematician and philosopher René Descartes.

Lesson starter: North, south, east and west

The units for this grid are in metres.

René starts at position O and moves:

• 3 m east
• 4 m south
• 2 m south
• 5 m north.

Pierre starts at position O and moves:

• 1 m west
• 4 m east
• 3 m south
• 5 m north.

Using the number plane, how would you describe René and Pierre's final positions?

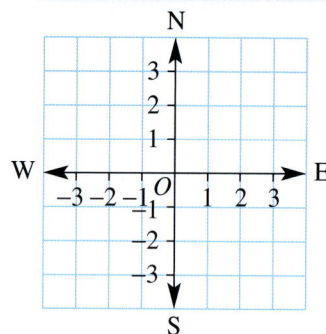

KEY IDEAS

■ The **Cartesian plane** is also called the **number plane**.

■ The diagrams show the two axes (the x-axis and the y-axis) and the four quadrants.

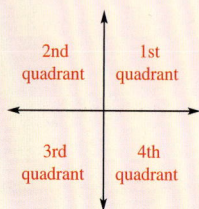

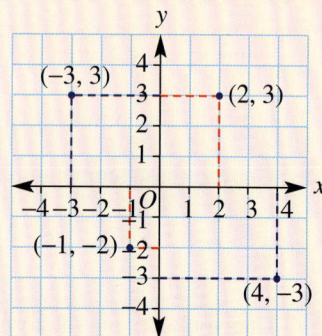

2nd quadrant	1st quadrant
3rd quadrant	4th quadrant

■ A point plotted on the plane has an x-coordinate and y-coordinate, which are written as (x, y).

■ The point $(0, 0)$ is called the origin and labelled O.

■ To plot points, always start at the origin.
  • For (2, 3) move 2 right and 3 up.
  • For (4, −3) move 4 right and 3 down.
  • For (−3, 3) move 3 left and 3 up.
  • For (−1, −2) move 1 left and 2 down.

BUILDING UNDERSTANDING

1 Match the points *A*, *B*, *C*, *D*, *E*, *F*, *G* and *H* with the given coordinates.
  a (−1, 3)
  b (2, −3)
  c (2, 1)
  d (−2, −2)
  e (3, 3)
  f (−3, 1)
  g (1, −2)
  h (−1, −1)

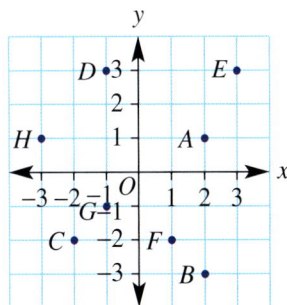

2 Count the number of points, shown as dots, on this plane that have:
  a both *x*- and *y*-coordinates as positive numbers
  b an *x*-coordinate as a positive number
  c a *y*-coordinate as a positive number
  d an *x*-coordinate as a negative number
  e a *y*-coordinate as a negative number
  f both *x*- and *y*-coordinates as negative numbers
  g neither *x* nor *y* as positive or negative numbers.

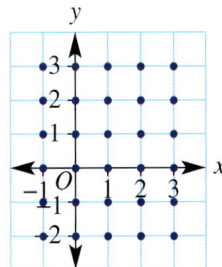

Example 10 Finding coordinates

For the Cartesian plane shown, write down the coordinates of
the points labelled *A*, *B*, *C* and *D*.

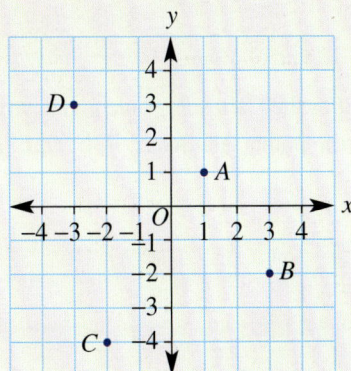

Continued on next page

SOLUTION

$A = (1, 1)$
$B = (3, -2)$
$C = (-2, -4)$
$D = (-3, 3)$

EXPLANATION

For each point, write the x-coordinate first (from the horizontal axis) followed by the y-coordinate (from the vertical axis).

Now you try

For the Cartesian plane shown, write down the coordinates of the points labelled A, B, C and D.

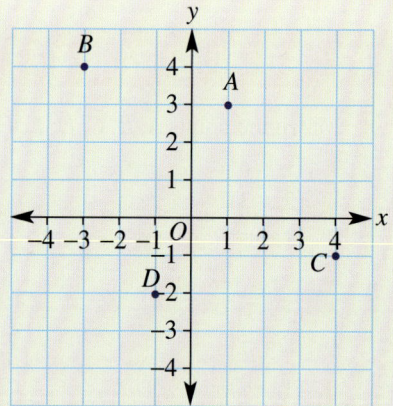

Exercise 6G

FLUENCY

| 1, 3–5 | 2–5 | 3–6 |

Example 10

1   For the Cartesian plane shown, write down the coordinates of the points labelled A, B, C and D.

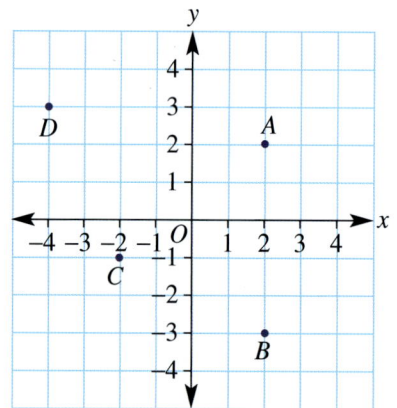

Example 10

2   For the Cartesian plane given, write down the coordinates of the points labelled A, B, C, D, E, F, G and H.

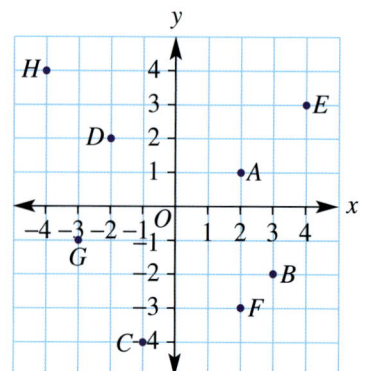

3 a Draw a set of axes using 1 cm spacings. Use −4 to 4 on both axes.

 b Now plot these points.

i (−3, 2)	**ii** (1, 4)	**iii** (2, −1)	**iv** (−2, −4)
v (2, 2)	**vi** (−1, 4)	**vii** (−3, −1)	**viii** (1, −2)

4 For the number plane given, write down the coordinates of the points labelled A, B, C, D, E, F, G and H.

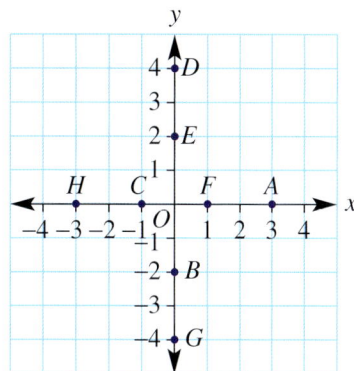

5 Seven points have the following x- and y-coordinates.

x	−3	−2	−1	0	1	2	3
y	−2	−1	0	1	2	3	4

 a Plot the seven points on a Cartesian plane. Use −3 to 3 on the x-axis and −2 to 4 on the y-axis.

 b What do you notice about these seven points on the Cartesian plane?

6 Seven points have the following x- and y-coordinates.

x	−3	−2	−1	0	1	2	3
y	5	3	1	−1	−3	−5	−7

 a Plot the seven points on a Cartesian plane. Use −3 to 3 on the x-axis and −7 to 5 on the y-axis.

 b What do you notice about these seven points on the number plane?

PROBLEM-SOLVING	7, 8	8–10	9–11

7 When plotted on the Cartesian plane, what shape does each set of points form?

 a $A(−2, 0), B(0, 3), C(2, 0)$

 b $A(−3, −1), B(−3, 2), C(1, 2), D(1, −1)$

 c $A(−4, −2), B(3, −2), C(1, 2), D(−1, 2)$

 d $A(−3, 1), B(−1, 3), C(4, 1), D(−1, −1)$

8 Using the origin as one corner, the point $A(3, 2)$ as the opposite corner and the axes as two of the sides, a rectangle can be positioned on a set of axes, as shown opposite. Its area is 6 square units. Find the area of the rectangle if the point A is:

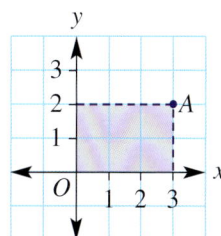

 a (2, 2)

 b (−3, 2)

 c (−1, −4)

 d (3, −5)

9 Karen's bushwalk starts at a point (2, 2) on a grid map. Each square on the map represents 1 km. If Karen walks to the points (2, −7), then (−4, −7), then (−4, 0) and then (2, 0), how far has she walked in total?

10 The points $A(-2, 0)$, $B(-1, ?)$ and $C(0, 4)$ all lie on a straight line. Find the y-coordinate of point B.

11 The points $A(-4, 8)$, $B(-1, ?)$ and $C(2, -2)$ all lie on a straight line. Find the y-coordinate of point B.

REASONING		12	12, 13	12, 13

12 Consider the points $A(-2, 2)$, $B(0, 2)$ and $C(3, -2)$.
  a Which point is closest to (0, 0)?
  b Which point is farthest from (0, 0)?
  c List the given points in order from closest to farthest from the origin, O.

13 A point (a, b) sits on the number plane in one of the four regions 1, 2, 3 or 4, as shown. These regions are called **quadrants**.
  a Name the quadrant or quadrants that include the points where:
    i $a > 0$
    ii $a > 0$ and $b < 0$
    iii $b < 0$
    iv $a < 0$ and $b < 0$
  b Shade the region that includes all points for which $b > a$.

ENRICHMENT: Rules and graphs		–	–	14

14 Consider the rule $y = 2x - 1$.
  a Substitute each given x-coordinate into the rule to find the y-coordinate. Then complete this table.

x	−3	−2	−1	0	1	2	3
y							

  b Draw a Cartesian plane, using −3 to 3 on the x-axis and −7 to 5 on the y-axis.
  c Plot each pair of coordinates (x, y) onto your Cartesian plane.
  d What do you notice about the set of seven points?

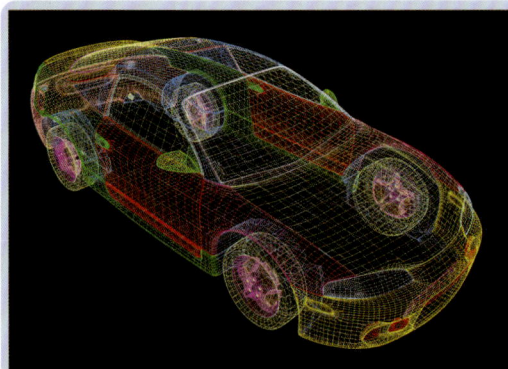

The Cartesian plane was the starting point for the development of computer-generated graphics and design.

Mathematical orienteering

Mathematical orienteering involves hiking in directions defined by two numbers in square brackets giving the horizontal (east/west) and vertical (north/south) distances to travel.

For example, if starting at the origin, then the route defined by [−3, −2] followed by [4, 5] takes the person 3 units left and 2 units down from the origin to the point (−3, −2) then 4 units right and 5 units up to point (1, 3) as shown. The instruction [−1, −3] would then take the person back to the origin as shown. Units are in kilometres and north is up on this map.

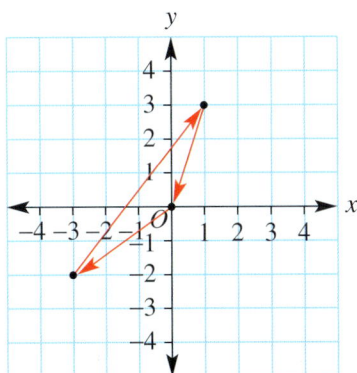

When a course is designed it must meet the following criteria.
- The course must start and finish at the origin (0, 0).
- The total north/south movement must not be more than 20 km.
- The total east/west movement must not be more than 20 km.

Present a report for the following tasks and ensure that you show clear mathematical workings and explanations where appropriate.

Preliminary task

a For the three-component course described in the introduction, find:
  i the total north/south movement (this includes 2 km south, 5 km north and then 3 km south)
  ii the total east/west movement.

b A three-component course starting at (0, 0) is defined by the instructions [4, −2], followed by [−6, −1], followed by [2, 3].
  i   Draw a diagram of this course.
  ii Find the total north/south movement.
  iii Find the total east/west movement.

c Explain why the course from part b satisfies all the criteria for a mathematical orienteering course.

Modelling task

a The problem is to design a mathematical orienteering course where the total north/south and east/west movements are equal to 20 km. Write down all the relevant information that will help solve this problem with the aid of a diagram.

b A mathematical orienteering course with four components is defined by the instructions: [2, 5], [−3, −1], [−1, 6] and [2, 2] and the starting location of (0, 0).

  i Draw a number plane and use arrows to illustrate this course.

  ii Explain whether this course satisfies the criteria for a mathematical orienteering course.

c Another four-component course is defined by the instructions: [−4, 1], [3, 5], [3, −7] and [?, ?]. Determine the instruction [?, ?] to ensure it satisfies all the criteria.

d Construct your own four-component course which starts and ends at the origin and with the north/south and east/west movements each equal to exactly 20 km. Illustrate your course using a number plane.

e For your course from part **d**, write down the four instructions and explain why the total north/south and east/west movements are each equal to exactly 20 km.

f Is it possible to design a four-component course which meets the criteria where one of the instructions is [−11, 2]? Explain why or why not.

g Summarise your results and describe any key findings.

Extension questions

a Design a mathematical orienteering course using six components, with the north/south and east/west movements each exactly 20 km. Try to use each of the four quadrants of a number plane.

b Rather than describing the total north/south distance and the total east/west distance, it is possible to write the conditions for a mathematical orienteering course using total distance north and total distance east. Explain how to do this.

Tracking lift movements

Key technology: Spreadsheets

Negative numbers can be used to describe the position and direction of a lift in a building. Assume the lift starts at level 8. The addition of -3 would mean that the lift travels down three levels. Additionally, a lift stopping at level -2 for example would mean it travels to the floor which is two levels below ground sometimes referred to as Basement 2 or B2.

1 Getting started

Imagine a building where a lift has 4 basement levels, a ground level and 12 floors above ground. Assume that the lift starts at ground level which is level 0. Each movement from one level to a different level will be called an operation. The following table shows the position of the lift after 5 operations.

Operation	Initial	1	2	3	4	5
Position	0	5	−2	3	11	−1

a At what floor is the lift positioned after the following operations?

  i 2   ii 3   iii 5

b What number is **added** to the previous position to obtain the new position after the following operations?

  i 1   ii 2   iii 5

c The number of floors travelled by the lift in the 2nd operation is 7 as it travels from level 5 down to level -2. What is the total number of floors travelled by the lift after the 5 operations?

2 Applying an algorithm

In a scenario using a single lift, we will consider the following type of lift sequence.

- The lift starts at ground level which is level 0.
- A person presses the call button at a random floor level and the lift moves to that level.
- The person enters the lift and presses a desired floor level. The lift moves to that level.
- The person exits the lift and the lift waits for the next call.

  a The following table summarises the position of the lift for a scenario with 5 people and 5 operations. Note the following:

- The lift starts at ground level, level 0.
- The **Entry** level is the level from which the person calls the lift.
- The **Exit** level is the level at which the person exits the lift.
- **Rise/fall – Exit to entry** is the number added to the previous Exit level to travel to the new Entry level.
- **Rise/fall – Entry to exit** is the number added to the Entry level to travel to the new Exit level.

Person	Entry level	Exit level	Rise/fall – Exit to entry	Rise/fall – Entry to exit
1	3	8	3 (starting at 0)	5
2	11	4	3	−7
3	0	8		
4	9		1	−12
5	2	5		

a   Follow the given algorithm to find the missing numbers in the table above.

b   Draw your own table representing a scenario of 7 people and using numbers between −6 and 15 to represent a lift in a building with 6 basement levels and 15 above ground levels. Enter random numbers of your choice in the **Entry level** and **Exit level** columns then calculate the values in both Rise/fall columns.

3 Using technology

We will use a spreadsheet to construct a lift scenario using a special random number function to automatically select our **Entry level** and **Exit level** column values.

a   Create a spreadsheet to represent a scenario of 10 people using random numbers between −4 and 12 to represent a lift in a building with 4 basement levels and 12 above ground levels. Use the following as a guide. Note:

  • The RANDBETWEEN function gives a random integer between the two given values inclusive, in this case −4 and 12.

  • The rules in columns C and D calculate the column values as per the tables in part **2** above.

	A	B	C	D	E
1	Average lift height				
2					
3	Person	Random entry level	Random exit level	Rise/fall - Exit to entry	Rise/fall - Entry to exit
4	1	=RANDBETWEEN(-4,12)	=RANDBETWEEN(-4,12)	=B4	=C4-B4
5	=A4+1			=B5-C4	

b   Fill down at cells A5, B4, C4, D5 and E4 to create a scenario for 10 people.

c   Look at your results. Did your lift ever rise or fall by more than 10 floors?

d   Press Shift F9 to create a new set of numbers and results.

4 Extension

a   Make changes to your spreadsheet so that the scenario of 20 people using random numbers between −7 and 18 to represent a lift in a building with 7 basement levels and 18 above ground levels. Looking at your spreadsheet, is there a time where your lift rises or falls by more than 22 floors? Use Shift F9 to create a new set of numbers.

b   Use the following rules to find the total number of floors that the lift travelled.

  • For total Exit to entry movement, use =SUM(ABS(D4:D23))

  • For total Entry to exit movement, use =SUM(ABS(E4:E23))

c   Use Shift F9 and see if you can create a scenario where the total Exit to entry movement plus the total Entry to exit movement is:

i   greater than 250

ii   less than 100.

Account balance with spreadsheets

If you have money saved in a bank account, your account balance should be positive. If you take out or spend too much money, your account balance may become negative.

a Set up a spreadsheet to record and calculate a bank balance. Enter the given information describing one week of deposits and withdrawals, as shown.

b **i** For the given spreadsheet, what is the balance at the end of May 1st?

   ii On which day does the balance become negative?

c Enter this formula into cell E5: =E4 + C5 – D5

   Fill down to reveal the balance after each day.

d Enter another week of deposits and withdrawals so that the balance shows both positive and negative amounts.

e Now alter your opening balance. What opening balance is needed so that the balance never becomes negative? Is there more than one value? What is the least amount?

f Investigate how positive and negative numbers are used on credit card accounts. Give a brief explanation.

1   Find the next three numbers in these
    patterns.

    a $3, -9, 27,$ _____, _____, _____

    b $-32, 16, -8,$ _____, _____, _____

    c $0, -1, -3, -6,$ _____, _____, _____

    d $-1, -1, -2, -3, -5,$ _____, _____, _____

> Up for a challenge? If you get stuck
> on a question, check out the 'working
> with unfamiliar problems' poster at
> the end of the book to help you.

2   Evaluate the following.

    a $-100 + (-98) + (-96) + \ldots + 98 + 100$

    b $(50 - 53) + (49 - 52) + (48 - 51) + \ldots + (0 - 3)$

    c $2 - 3 + 4 - 5 + 6 - 7 + \ldots - 199 + 200$

3   Insert brackets and symbols $(+, -, \times, \div)$ into these number sentences to make them true.

    a $-3 \boxed{} 4 \boxed{} (-2) = -6$

    b $-2 \boxed{} 5 \boxed{} (-1) \boxed{} 11 = 21$

    c $1 \boxed{} 30 \boxed{} (-6) \boxed{} (-2) = -3$

4   a   The difference between two numbers is 14 and their sum is 8. What are the two numbers?

    b   The difference between two numbers is 31 and their sum is 11. What are the two numbers?

5   If x and y are integers less than 10 and greater than -10, how many different integer pairs (x, y) make
    the equation $x + 2y = 10$ true?

6   In the sequence of numbers $\ldots, e, d, c, b, a, 0, 1, 1, 2, 3, 5, 8, 13, \ldots$ each number is the sum of its two
    preceding numbers, e.g. $13 = 5 + 8$. What are the values of a, b, c, d and e?

7   Given the rule $x^{-2} = \dfrac{1}{x^2}$, evaluate $-(-5)^{-2}$.

8   If $p > q > 0$ and $t < 0$, insert $>$ or $<$ to make each of these a true statement for all values of p, q and t.

    a $p + t \boxed{} q + t$ b $t - p \boxed{} t - q$ c $pt \boxed{} qt$

9   Describe the set of all possible numbers for which the square of the number is greater than the cube of
    the number.

10 A formula linking an object's velocity v m/s with its initial velocity u m/s, acceleration a m/s^2 and its
    change of distance s m is given by $v^2 = u^2 + 2as$. Find:

    a   the velocity if the initial velocity
        is 0 m/s, the acceleration is 4 m/s^2
        and change of distance is 8 m.

    b   the acceleration if the velocity
        is 70 m/s, the initial velocity is
        10 m/s and the change of distance
        is 100 m.

Number line

negative ← → positive

-3 -2 -1 0 1 2 3

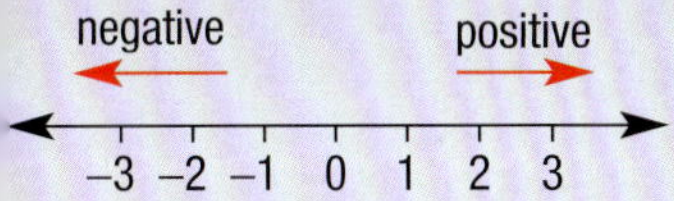

$-3 < 2$ $1 > -1$

Adding and subtracting positive integers

$-3 + 5 = 2$
$-4 + 3 = -1$
$5 - 7 = -2$
$-1 - 10 = -11$

Adding and subtracting negative integers

$2 + (-3) = 2 - 3 = -1$
$-5 + (-4) = -5 - 4 = -9$
$4 - (-3) = 4 + 3 = 7$
$-10 - (-6) = -10 + 6 = -4$

Cartesian plane

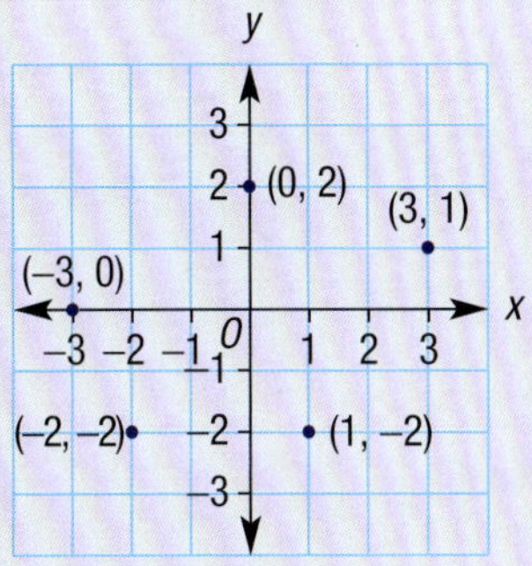

y

3
2 • (0, 2)
1   • (3, 1)
(−3, 0)
O 1 2 3 x
−3 −2 −1 −1
(−2, −2)• −2   • (1, −2)
−3

Integers
$\ldots, -3, -2, -1,$
$0, 1, 2, 3, \ldots$

Multiplication (Ext)

$2 \times 3 = 6$
$2 \times (-3) = -6$
$-2 \times 3 = -6$
$-2 \times (-3) = 6$

Division (Ext)

$10 \div 5 = 2$
$10 \div (-5) = -2$
$-10 \div 5 = -2$
$-10 \div (-5) = 2$

Substitution (Ext)

If $a = -2$ and $b = 4$, then:
$b - a = 4 - (-2) = 6$
$ab + 2a = -2 \times 4 + 2 \times (-2)$
$\qquad = -8 + (-4)$
$\qquad = -12$

Order of operations (Ext)

First brackets, then $\times$ or $\div$ then $+$ or $-$, from left to right.

$3 \times (5 - (-2)) + 8 \div (-4)$
$= 3 \times 7 + (-2)$
$= 21 + (-2)$
$= 19$

Chapter checklist

Chapter checklist with success criteria

A printable version of this checklist is available in the Interactive Textbook ⬇

		✔

6A
1. I can represent integers on a number line.
e.g. Draw a number line showing all integers from -4 to 2.
☐

6A
2. I can compare two integers.
e.g. Insert the symbol < (less than) or > (greater than) into the statement -1 ☐ -6 to make it true.
☐

6B
3. I can add a positive integer to another integer.
e.g. Evaluate $-2 + 3$.
☐

6B
4. I can subtract a positive integer from another integer.
e.g. Evaluate $-3 - 3$.
☐

6C
5. I can add a negative integer to another integer.
e.g. Evaluate $-2 + (-3)$.
☐

6C
6. I can subtract a negative integer from another integer.
e.g. Evaluate $1 - (-3)$.
☐

6D
7. I can multiply two integers.
e.g. Evaluate $-3 \times (-7)$.
(Ext)
☐

6D
8. I can divide two integers.
e.g. Evaluate $-18 \div 9$.
(Ext)
☐

6D
9. I can evaluate expressions involving integers and both multiplication and division.
e.g. Evaluate $24 \div (-3) \times (-1)$
(Ext)
☐

6E
10. I can use order of operations to evaluate expressions involving negative numbers.
e.g. Evaluate $-6 \times 2 - 10 \div (-5)$.
(Ext)
☐

6F
11. I can substitute positive or negative integers into an expression and evaluate.
e.g. Evaluate $b \div 5 - a$ if $a = 3$ and $b = -5$.
(Ext)
☐

6G
12. I can state the coordinates of a point labelled on a number plane.
e.g. State the coordinates of the points labelled A, B, C and D.

☐

6G
13. I can plot a point from a given pair of coordinates.
e.g. Draw a set of axes from -4 to 4 on both axes, and plot the points $(-3, 2)$ and $(-2, -4)$.
☐

Short-answer questions

6A

1 Insert the symbol < (less than) or > (greater than) into each of these statements to make it true.

a $0 \,\square\, 7$ b $-1 \,\square\, 4$ c $3 \,\square\, -7$ d $-11 \,\square\, -6$

6B/C

2 Evaluate:

a $2 - 7$ b $-4 + 2$ c $0 - 15$

d $-36 + 37$ e $5 + (-7)$ f $-1 + (-4)$

g $10 - (-2)$ h $-21 - (-3)$ i $1 - 5 + (-2)$

j $-3 + 7 - (-1)$ k $0 + (-1) - 10$ l $-2 - (-3) - (-4)$

6C

3 Find the missing number for each of the following.

a $-2 + \square = -3$ b $-1 + \square = -10$

c $5 - \square = 6$ d $-2 - \square = -4$

e $-1 - \square = 20$ f $-15 - \square = -13$

g $7 + \square = -80$ h $-15 + \square = 15$

6D

Ext

4 Evaluate:

a $5 \times (-2)$ b -3×7 c $-2 \times (-15)$

d $10 \div (-2)$ e $-36 \div 12$ f $-100 \div (-25)$

g $-3 \times 2 \div (-6)$ h $-38 \div (-19) \times (-4)$

6D

Ext

5 Find the missing number.

a $4 \times \square = -8$ b $\square \div -5 = 10$ c $\square \div 9 = -4$ d $-1 \times \square = 1$

6E

Ext

6 Use order of operations to find the answers to these expressions.

a $-2 + 5 \times (-7)$ b $-1 - 18 \div (-2)$ c $-15 \div (1 + 4)$

d $5 - 4 \times (-3) \div (-3)$ e $(-2 - 5) \times (8 \div (-1))$ f $-7 \times ((-4) - 7) + 3$

6F

Ext

7 Evaluate the following expressions if $a = 7$, $b = -3$ and $c = -1$.

a $a - b$ b $2b - 5a$ c $ab + c$ d $bc - 2a$

6G

8 For the Cartesian plane shown, write down the coordinates of the points labelled A, B, C, D, E and F.

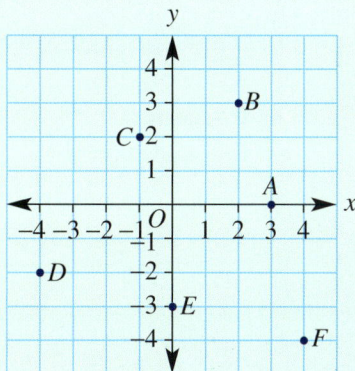

Chapter review *(sidebar)*

Multiple-choice questions

6A

1 When the numbers $-4, 0, -1, 7$ and -6 are arranged from lowest to highest, the correct sequence is:

A $0, -1, -4, -6, 7$
B $0, -4, -6, -1, 7$
C $-6, -4, -1, 0, 7$
D $-1, -4, -6, 0, 7$
E $-6, -1, 0, -4, 7$

6B

2 The difference between -19 and 8 is:

A   152   B -11 C -27 D   11   E   27

6C

3 The missing number in $2 - \square = 3$ is:

A   1   B -1 C   5   D -5 E   2

6C

4 $5 - (-2) + (-7)$ is equal to:

A -4 B   10   C   7   D   0   E   14

6A

5 The temperature inside a mountain hut is initially $-5°C$. After burning a fire for 2 hours the temperature rises to $17°C$. What is the rise in temperature?

A $-12°C$ B $12°C$ C $22°C$ D $-85°C$ E $-22°C$

6D
Ext

6 The product or quotient of two negative numbers is:

A   positive   B   negative   C   zero
D   added   E   different

6D
Ext

7 $-2 \times (-5) \div (-10)$ is equal to:

A -5 B   10   C -20 D   1   E -1

6E
Ext

8 Which operation (i.e. addition, subtraction, multiplication or division) is completed *second* in the calculation of $(-2 + 5) \times (-2) + 1$?

A   addition   B   subtraction   C   multiplication
D   division   E   brackets

6F
Ext

9 If $a = -2$ and $b = 5$, then $ab - a$ is equal to:

A -12 B -8 C   8   D   12   E   9

6G

10 The points $A(-2, 3)$, $B(-3, -1)$, $C(1, -1)$ and $D(0, 3)$ are joined on a number plane. What shape do they make?

A   triangle   B   square   C   trapezium
D   kite   E   parallelogram

Extended-response questions

1 A scientist, who is camped on the ice in Greenland, records the following details in his notepad regarding the temperature over five days. Note that 'min.' stands for minimum and 'max.' stands for maximum.

- Monday: min. = $-18°C$, max. = $-2°C$.
- Decreased $29°C$ from Monday's max. to give Tuesday's min.
- Wednesday's min. was $-23°C$.
- Max. was only $-8°C$ on Thursday.
- Friday's min. is $19°C$ colder than Thursday's max.

a What is the overall temperature increase on Monday?

b What is Tuesday's minimum temperature?

c What is the difference between the minimum temperatures for Tuesday and Wednesday?

d What is the overall temperature drop from Thursday's maximum to Friday's minimum?

e By how much will the temperature need to rise on Friday if its maximum is $0°C$?

2 When joined, these points form a picture on the number plane. What is the picture?
$A(0, 5)$, $B(1, 3)$, $C(1, 1)$, $D(2, 0)$, $E(1, 0)$, $F(1, -2)$, $G(3, -5)$, $H(-3, -5)$, $I(-1, -2)$, $J(-1, 0)$, $K(-2, 0)$, $L(-1, 1)$, $M(-1, 3)$, $N(0, 5)$

7

Geometry

Maths in context: Cable stayed bridges

Skills in geometry are essential for all the practical occupations including animators, architects, astronomers, bricklayers, boilermaker, builders, carpenters, concreters, construction workers, designers, electricians, engineers, jewellers, navigators, plumbers, ship builders and surveyors.

Cable stayed bridges use pylons with attached cables that fan out to support the bridge deck, such as the Langkawi Sky Bridge in Malaysia. Here we can see the application of angles at a point, angles formed by parallel lines and angles in a triangle. The bridge is a 125 m curved pedestrian bridge with steel and concrete panels forming the bridge deck, supported by inverted triangular steel trusses. It is about 100 m above ground and suspended by eight cables from single pylon. The pylon is 81.5 m high and must bear the total load of the bridge via the cables. Engineers had to solve the critical problem of how to balance the immense weight of the bridge from a single point at the top of the pylon.

Cable stayed bridges in Australia include the Anzac Bridge in Sydney, the Eleanor Schonell Bridge and the Kurilpa Bridge in Brisbane, the Seafarers Bridge in Melbourne and the Batman Bridge in Tasmania.

Chapter contents

Victorian Curriculum 2.0

This chapter covers the following content descriptors in the Victorian Curriculum 2.0:

SPACE

VC2M7SP01, VC2M7SP02, VC2M7SP03, VC2M7SP04

MEASUREMENT

VC2M7M04, VC2M7M05

Please refer to the curriculum support documentation in the teacher resources for a full and comprehensive mapping of this chapter to the related curriculum content descriptors.

© VCAA

Online resources

A host of additional online resources are included as part of your Interactive Textbook, including HOTmaths content, video demonstrations of all worked examples, auto-marked quizzes and much more.

7A   Points, lines, intervals and angles   CONSOLIDATING

LEARNING INTENTIONS
- To know the meaning of the terms point, vertex, intersection, line, ray, segment and plane
- To know the meaning of the terms acute, right, obtuse, straight, reflex and revolution
- To understand what collinear points and concurrent lines are
- To be able to name lines, segments, rays and angles in terms of labelled points in diagrams
- To be able to measure angles using protractors
- To be able to draw angles of a given size

The fundamental building blocks of geometry are the point, line and plane. They are the basic objects used to construct angles, triangles and other more complex shapes and objects. Theoretically, points and lines do not occupy any area, but we can represent them on a page using drawing instruments.

Angles are usually described using the unit of measurement called the degree, where 360 degrees (360°) describes one full turn. The idea to divide a circle into 360° dates back to the Babylonians, who used a sexagesimal number system based on the number 60. Because both 60 and 360 have a large number of factors, many fractions of these numbers are very easy to calculate.

Engineers calculate the angles between the straight structural supports used on bridges such as the angles seen here on the Story Bridge, Brisbane.

Lesson starter: Estimating angles

How good are you at estimating the size of angles? Estimate the size of these angles and then check with a protractor.

Alternatively, construct an angle using interactive geometry software. Estimate and then check your angle using the angle-measuring tool.

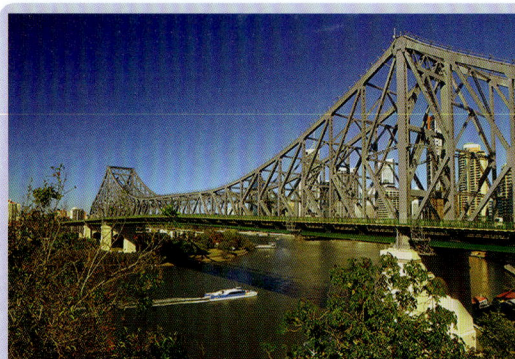

KEY IDEAS

■ A **point** is usually labelled with a capital letter.   • P

■ A **line** passing through two points, A and B, can be called line AB or line BA and extends indefinitely in both directions.
- upper-case letters are usually used to label points.

■ A **plane** is a flat surface and extends indefinitely.

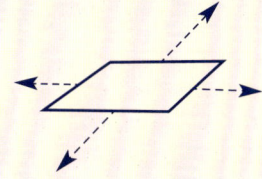

■ Points that all lie on a single line are **collinear**.

■ If two lines meet, an **intersection point** is formed.

■ Three or more lines that intersect at the same point are **concurrent**.

■ A line **segment** (or **interval**) is part of a line with a fixed length and end points. If the end points are A and B then it would be named segment AB or segment BA (or interval AB or interval BA).

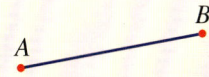

■ A **ray** AB is a part of a line with one end point A and passing through point B. It extends indefinitely in one direction.

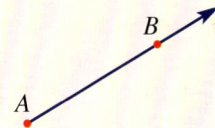

■ When two rays (or lines) meet, an angle is formed at the intersection point called the **vertex**. The two rays are called **arms** of the angle.

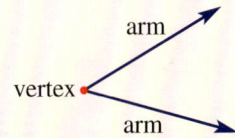

■ An **angle** is named using three points, with the vertex as the middle point. A common type of notation is $\angle ABC$ or $\angle CBA$. The measure of the angle is $a°$.
  • lower-case letters are often used to represent the size of an angle.

■ Part of a circle called an arc is used to mark an angle.

■ These two lines are parallel. This is written $AB \parallel DC$.

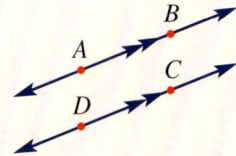

■ These two lines are perpendicular. This is written $AB \perp CD$.

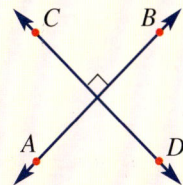

■ The markings on this diagram show that $AB = CD$, $AD = BC$, $\angle BAD = \angle BCD$ and $\angle ABC = \angle ADC$.

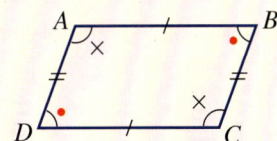

■ Angles are classified according to their size.

Angle type	Size	Examples
acute	between 0° and 90°	
right	90°	
obtuse	between 90° and 180°	
straight	180°	
reflex	between 180° and 360°	
revolution	360°	

■ A **protractor** can be used to measure angles to within an accuracy of about half a degree. Some protractors have increasing scales marked both clockwise and anticlockwise from zero. To use a protractor:

1   Place the centre of the protractor on the vertex of the angle.
2   Align the base line of the protractor along one arm of the angle.
3   Measure the angle using the other arm and the scale on the protractor.
4   A reflex angle can be measured by subtracting a measured angle from 360°.

BUILDING UNDERSTANDING

① Describe or draw the following objects.
   a   a point *P*
   b   a line *AN*
   c   an angle ∠*ABC*
   d   a ray *ST*
   e   a plane
   f   three collinear points *A*, *B* and *C*

② Match the words *line, segment, ray, collinear* or *concurrent* to the correct description.
   a   Starts from a point and extends indefinitely in one direction.
   b   Extends indefinitely in both directions, passing through two points.
   c   Starts and ends at two points.
   d   Three points in a straight line.
   e   Three lines intersecting at the same point.

Why would we use the geometric term *rays* to describe the sunlight showing through the trees?

3 Without using a protractor, draw or describe an example of the following types of angles.

a acute
b right
c obtuse
d straight
e reflex
f revolution

4 What is the size of the angle measured with these protractors?

a

b

c

d

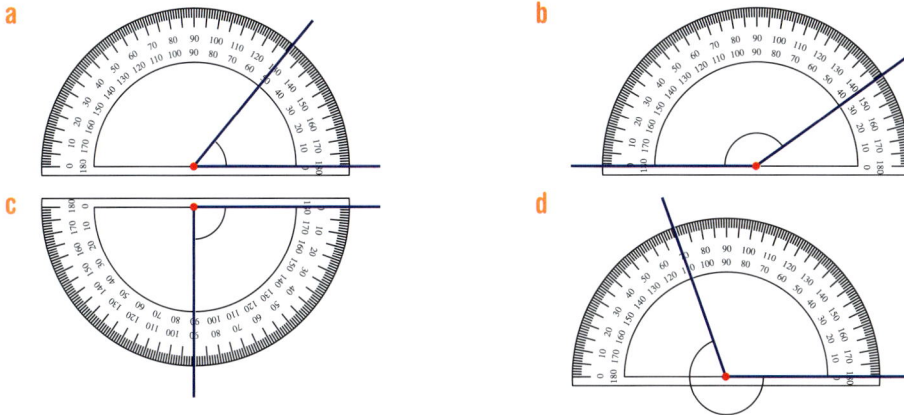

Example 1   Naming objects

Name this line segment and angle.

a

  A   B

b

             P

    Q

                R

SOLUTION

a segment AB

b ∠PQR

EXPLANATION

Segment BA, interval AB or interval BA are also acceptable.

Point Q is the vertex so the letter Q sits in between P and R. ∠RQP is also correct.

Now you try

Name this ray and angle.

a

        A

              B

b B

                        A

           C

Example 2   Classifying and measuring angles

For the angles shown, state the type of angle and measure its size.

a

b

c

SOLUTION

a   acute
$\angle AOB = 60°$

b   obtuse
$\angle EFG = 125°$

c   reflex

obtuse $\angle DOE = 130°$
reflex $\angle DOE = 360° - 130°$
$= 230°$

EXPLANATION

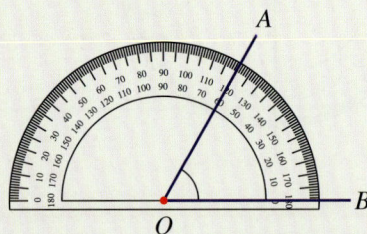

The angle is an acute angle so read from the inner scale, starting at zero.

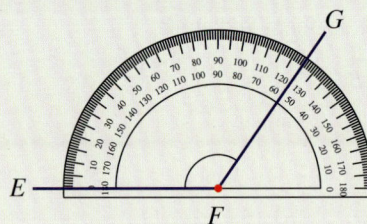

The angle is an obtuse angle so read from the outer scale, starting at zero.

First measure the obtuse angle before subtracting from 360° to obtain the reflex angle.

Now you try

For the angles shown, state the type of angle and measure its size.

a

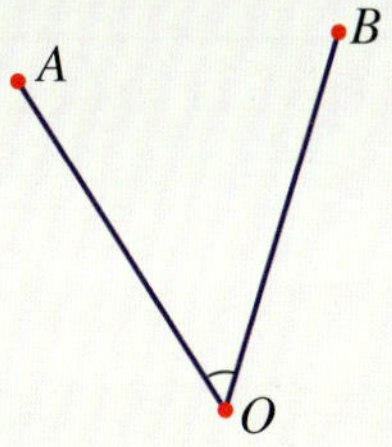

b

c

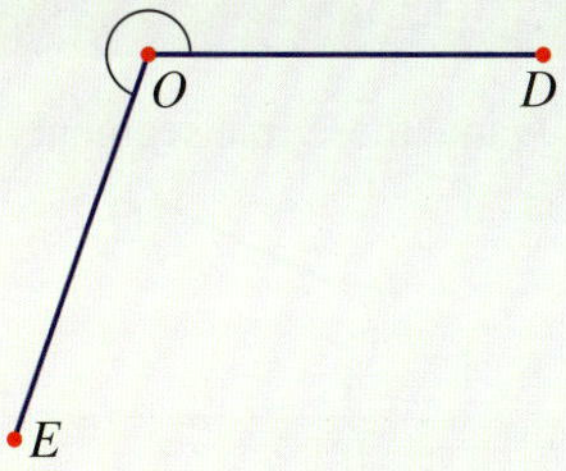

Example 3   Drawing angles

Use a protractor to draw each of the following angles.

a $\angle AOB = 65°$ b $\angle WXY = 130°$ c $\angle MNO = 260°$

SOLUTION

a

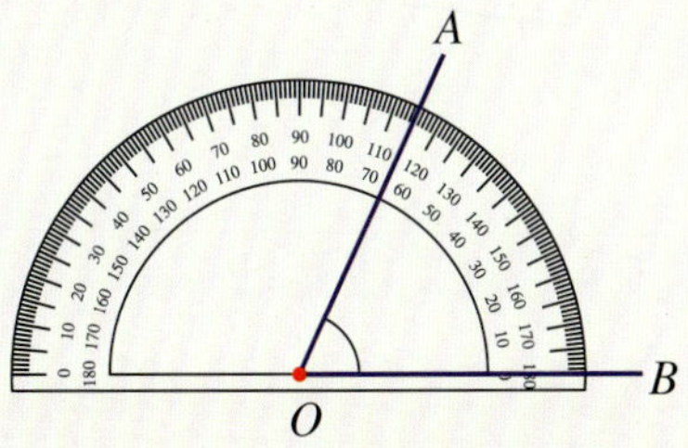

b

c

EXPLANATION

Step 1: Draw a base line OB.
Step 2: Align the protractor along the base line with the centre at point O.
Step 3: Measure 65° and mark a point, A.
Step 4: Draw the arm OA.

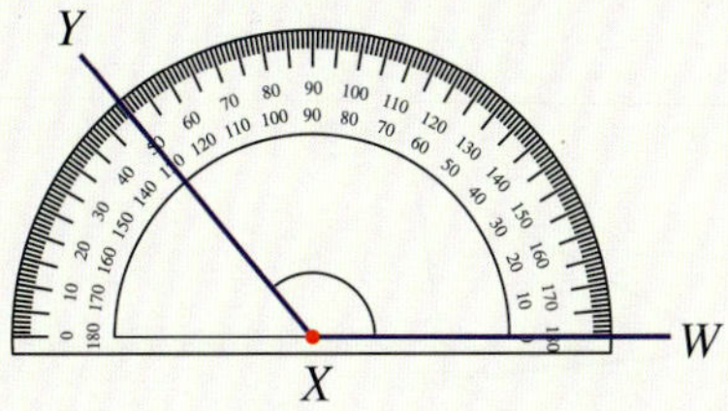

Step 1: Draw a base line XW.
Step 2: Align the protractor along the base line with the centre at point X.
Step 3: Measure 130° and mark a point, Y.
Step 4: Draw the arm XY.

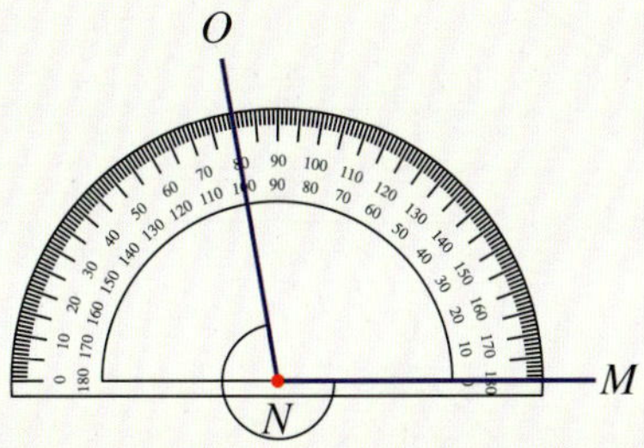

Step 1: Draw an angle of $360° - 260° = 100°$.
Step 2: Mark the reflex angle on the opposite side to the obtuse angle of 100°.
Alternatively, draw a 180° angle and measure an 80° angle to add to the 180° angle.

Now you try

Use a protractor to draw each of the following angles.

a $\angle AOB = 30°$ b $\angle WXY = 170°$ c $\angle MNO = 320°$

Exercise 7A

FLUENCY   1–3, 4–6(½), 7, 8   2, 3, 4–6(½), 7, 8   2, 3–6(½), 7, 8

Example 1a

1   Name these line segments and angles.

a   i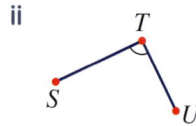

ii   X ————— Y

Example 1b

b   i
A
|
O —— B

ii
        T
    S   U

Example 1

2   Name the following objects.

a   • T

b   C ———— D

c
B
|
A —— C

d
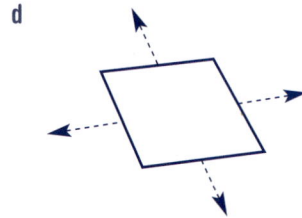

e
    Q
P

f   S
        T

Example 1b

3   Name the angle marked by the arc in these diagrams.

a
A
    B
        C
            D
O

b
            B
    A
            C
    D

c
B
D   E
A   C

d
            O
A   B C   D   E

Example 2 **4** For the angles shown, state the type of angle and measure its size.

a

b

c

d

e

f

g

h

i

Example 3 **5** Use a protractor to draw each of the following angles.

 a 40° b 75° c 90° d 135° e 175°
 f 205° g 260° h 270° i 295° j 352°

6 For each of the angles marked in the situations shown, measure:

 a the angle that this ramp makes with the ground

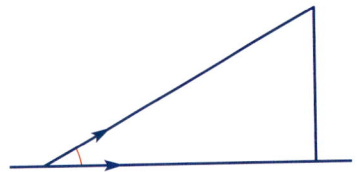

 b the angle the Sun's rays make with the ground

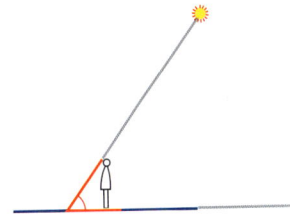

c   the angle or pitch of this roof

d   the angle between this laptop screen and the keyboard.

7   Name the set of three labelled points that are collinear in these diagrams.

a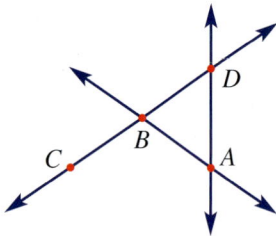

b

8   State whether the following sets of lines are concurrent.

a

b

PROBLEM-SOLVING	9, 10	9–11	11, 12

9   Count the number of angles formed inside these shapes. Count all angles, including ones that may be the same size and those angles that are divided by another segment.

a

b

10 A clock face is numbered 1 to 12. Find the angle the minute hand turns in:

   a   30 minutes   b   45 minutes   c   5 minutes   d   20 minutes
   e   1 minute   f   9 minutes   g   10.5 minutes   h   21.5 minutes

11 A clock face is numbered 1 to 12. Find the angle between the hour hand and the minute hand at:

   a   6:00 p.m.   b   3:00 p.m.   c   4:00 p.m.   d   11:00 a.m.

12 Find the angle between the hour hand and the minute hand of a clock at these times.

   a   10:10 a.m.   b   4:45 a.m.
   c   11:10 p.m.   d   2:25 a.m.
   e   7:16 p.m.   f   9:17 p.m.

REASONING   13   13, 14   14, 15

13 a If points A, B and C are collinear and points A, B and D are collinear, does this mean that points B, C and D are also collinear? Use a diagram to check.

    b If points A, B and C are collinear and points C, D and E are collinear, does this mean that points B, C and D are also collinear? Use a diagram to check.

14 An acute angle $\angle AOB$ is equal to $60°$. Why is it unnecessary to use a protractor to work out the size of the reflex angle $\angle AOB$?

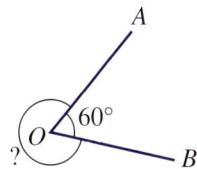

15 The arrow on this dial starts in an upright position. It then turns by a given number of degrees clockwise or anticlockwise. Answer with an acute or obtuse angle.

    a Find the angle between the arrow in its final position with the arrow in its original position, as shown in the diagram opposite, which illustrates part **i**. Answer with an acute or obtuse angle.

i $290°$ clockwise	**ii** $290°$ anticlockwise
iii $450°$ clockwise	**iv** $450°$ anticlockwise
v $1000°$ clockwise	**vi** $1000°$ anticlockwise

    b Did it matter to the answer if the dial was turning clockwise or anticlockwise?

    c Explain how you calculated your answer for turns larger than $360°$.

ENRICHMENT: How many segments?   –   –   16

16 A line contains a certain number of labelled points. For example, this line has three points.

    a Copy and complete this table by counting the total number of segments for the given number of labelled points.

Number of points	1	2	3	4	5	6
Number of segments						

    b Explain any patterns you see in the table. Is there a quick way of finding the next number in the table?

    c If n is the number of points on the line, can you find a rule (in terms of n) for the number of segments? Test your rule to see if it works for at least three cases, and try to explain why the rule works in general.

7B Adjacent and vertically opposite angles

Not all angles in a diagram or construction need to be measured directly. Special relationships exist between pairs of angles at a point and this allows some angles to be calculated exactly without measurement, even if diagrams are not drawn to scale.

Lesson starter: Special pair of angles

By making a drawing or using interactive geometry software, construct the diagrams below. Measure the two marked angles. What do you notice about the two marked angles?

People who calculate angles formed by intersecting lines include: glass cutters who design and construct stained-glass windows; jewellers who cut gemstones at precise angles; and quilt makers who design and sew geometric shapes.

KEY IDEAS

■ **Adjacent** angles are side by side and share a vertex and an arm.
∠AOB and ∠BOC in this diagram are adjacent angles.

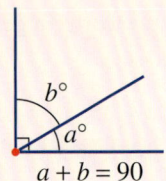

■ Two adjacent angles in a right angle are **complementary**.
They add to 90°.
- If the value of a is 30, then the value of b is 60 because 30° + 60° = 90°.
  We say that 30° is the complement of 60°.

$a + b = 90$

■ Two adjacent angles on a straight line are **supplementary**.
They add to 180°.
If the value of b is 50, then the value of a is 130 because $50° + 130° = 180°$.
We say that 130° is the supplement of 50°.

$a + b = 180$

■ Angles in a **revolution** have a sum of 360°.

$a + b = 360$

■ **Vertically opposite** angles are formed when two lines intersect.
The opposite angles are equal. The name comes from the fact that
the pair of angles has a common vertex and they sit in opposite
positions across the vertex.

■ **Perpendicular** lines meet at a right angle (90°). We write $AB \perp CD$.

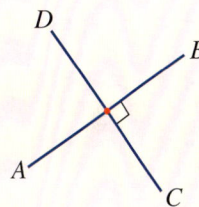

BUILDING UNDERSTANDING

1 a Measure the angles $a°$ and $b°$ in this diagram.
  b Calculate $a + b$. Is your answer 90? If not, check your measurements.
  c State the missing word: $a°$ and $b°$ are _____ angles.

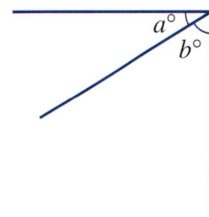

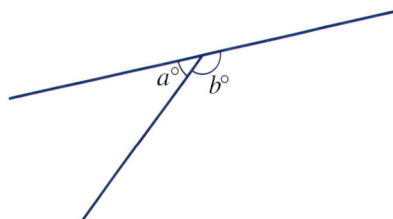

2 a Measure the angles $a°$ and $b°$ in this diagram.
  b Calculate $a + b$. Is your answer 180? If not, check your measurements.
  c State the missing word: $a°$ and $b°$ are _____ angles.

3 a Measure the angles $a°$, $b°$, $c°$ and $d°$ in this diagram.
  b What do you notice about the sum of the four angles?
  c State the missing words: $b°$ and $d°$ are _____ angles.

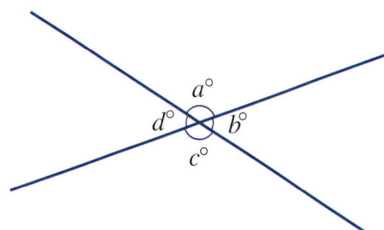

4 **a** Name the angle that is complementary to ∠AOB in this diagram.

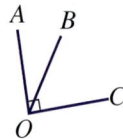

b Name the two angles that are supplementary to ∠AOB in this diagram.

c Name the angle that is vertically opposite to ∠AOB in this diagram.

Example 4   Finding angles at a point using complementary and supplementary angles

Without using a protractor, find the value of the pronumeral a.

a

b

SOLUTION

a $a = 90 - 35$
$\quad = 55$

b $a = 180 - 55$
$\quad = 125$

EXPLANATION

Angles in a right angle add to 90°.
$a + 35 = 90$

Angles on a straight line add to 180°.
$a + 55 = 180$

Now you try

Without using a protractor, find the value of a for the following.

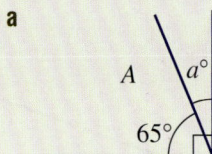

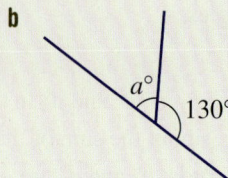

a

b

Example 5 Finding angles at a point using other properties

Without using a protractor, find the value of the pronumeral a.

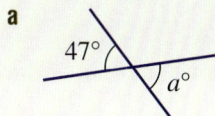

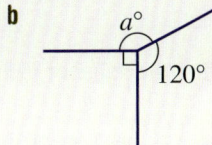

a

47°
$a°$

b

$a°$
120°

SOLUTION

a $a = 47$

b $a = 360 - (90 + 120)$
$= 360 - 210$
$= 150$

EXPLANATION

Vertically opposite angles are equal.

The sum of angles in a revolution is 360°.
$a + 90 + 120 = 360$
a is the difference between 210° and 360°.

Now you try

Without using a protractor, find the value of a for the following.

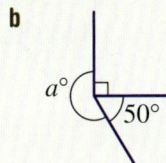

a

$a°$ 116°

b

$a°$ 50°

Exercise 7B

FLUENCY   1, 2–5(½)   1–5(½)   2–6(½)

1 Without using a protractor, find the value of the pronumeral a.

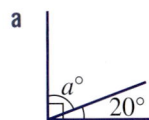

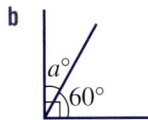

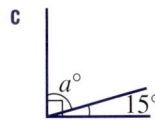

a

$a°$ 20°

b

$a°$ 60°

c

$a°$ 15°

2 Without using a protractor, find the value of the pronumeral a. (The diagrams shown may not be drawn to scale.)

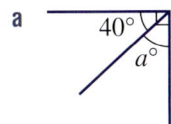

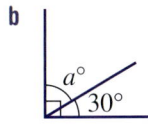

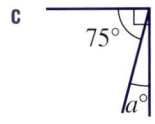

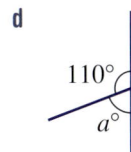

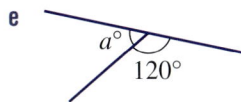

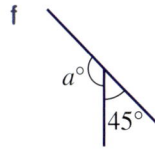

a

40°
$a°$

b

$a°$ 30°

c

75°
$a°$

d

110°
$a°$

e

$a°$ 120°

f

$a°$ 45°

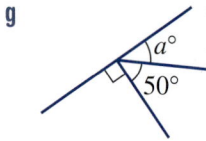

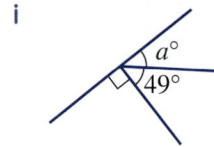

g

$a°$
$50°$

h

$a°$
$60°$

i

$a°$
$49°$

Example 5   **3**   Without using a protractor, find the value of the pronumeral a. (The diagrams shown may not be drawn to scale.)

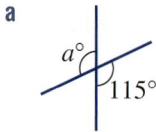

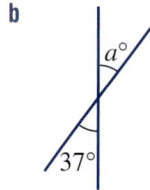

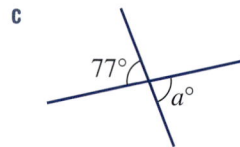

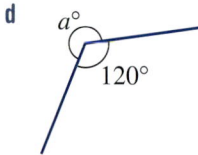

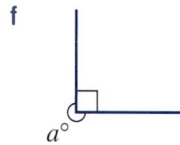

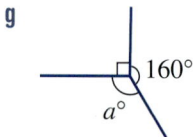

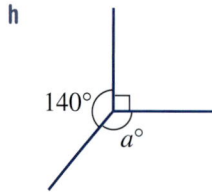

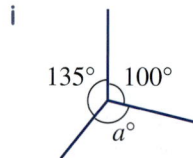

a

$a°$
$115°$

b

$a°$
$37°$

c

$77°$
$a°$

d

$a°$
$120°$

e

$a°$
$220°$

f

$a°$

g

$160°$
$a°$

h

$140°$
$a°$

i

$135°$ $100°$
$a°$

4   For each of the given pairs of angles, write C if they are complementary, S if they are supplementary or N if they are neither.

a $21°, 79°$ **b** $130°, 60°$ **c** $98°, 82°$ **d** $180°, 90°$

e $17°, 73°$ **f** $31°, 59°$ **g** $68°, 22°$ **h** $93°, 87°$

5   Write a statement like $AB \perp CD$ for these pairs of perpendicular line segments.

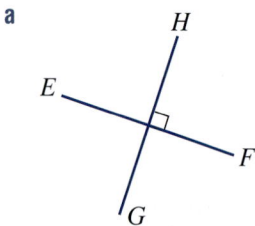

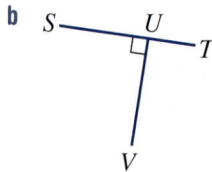

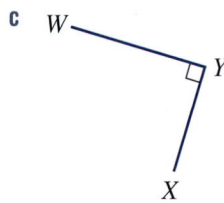

a

H
E
F
G

b

S U T
V

c

W
Y
X

6   Without using a protractor, find the value of a in these diagrams.

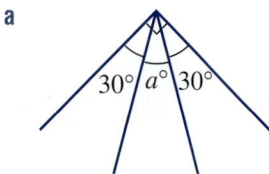

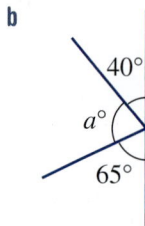

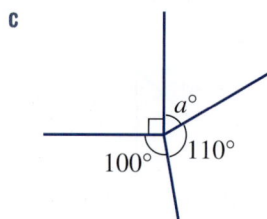

a

$30°$ $a°$ $30°$

b

$40°$
$a°$
$65°$

c

$a°$
$100°$ $110°$

d

e

f

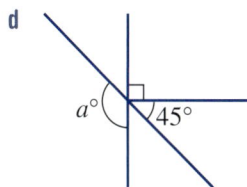

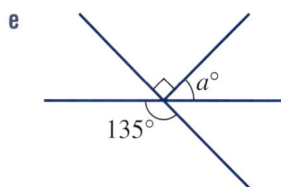

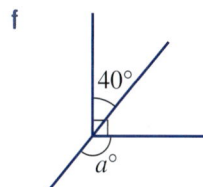

| **PROBLEM-SOLVING** | 7 | 7-8(½) | 8, 9 |

7 Decide whether the given angle measurements are possible in the diagrams below. Give reasons.

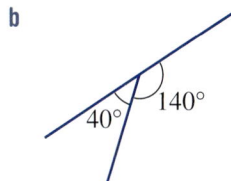

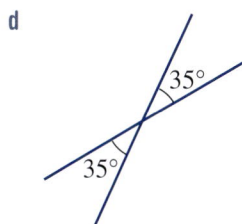

a

b

c

d

e

f

8 Find the value of a in these diagrams.

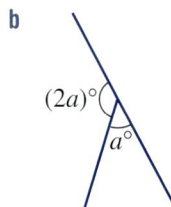

a

b

c

d

e

f

9 A pizza is divided between four people. Bella is to get twice as much as Bobo, who gets twice as much as Rick, who gets twice as much as Marie. Assuming the pizza is cut into slices from the centre outwards, find the angle at the centre of the pizza for Marie's piece.

| **REASONING** | 10 | 10, 11 | 11, 12 |

10 a Is it possible for two acute angles to be supplementary? Explain why or why not.
   b Is it possible for two acute angles to be complementary? Explain why or why not.

11 Write down a rule connecting the letters in these diagrams, e.g. $a + b = 180$.

a 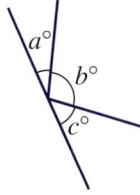   **b**   **c**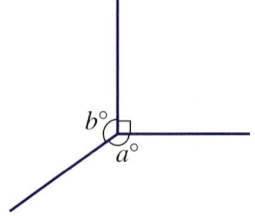

12 What is the minimum number of angles you would need to measure in this diagram if you wanted to know all the angles? Explain your answer.

ENRICHMENT: Pentagon turns   –   –   13

13 Consider walking around a path represented by this regular pentagon. All sides have the same length and all internal angles are equal. At each corner (vertex) you turn an angle of a, as marked.

a How many degrees would you turn in total after walking around the entire shape? Assume that you face the same direction at the end as you did at the start.

b Find the value of a.

c Find the value of b.

d Explore the outside and inside angles of other regular polygons using the same idea. Complete this table to summarise your results.

Regular shape	a	b
Triangle		
Square		
Pentagon		
Hexagon		
Heptagon		
Octagon		

Each of the identical shapes that make up this quilt design is called a rhombus. Four line segments form the sides of each rhombus. How many lines intersect at each vertex? How many angles meet at each vertex? Can you determine the size of the angles in each pattern piece?

7C Transversal and parallel lines

When a line, called a transversal, cuts two or more other lines a number of angles are formed. Pairs of these angles are corresponding, alternate or cointerior angles, depending on their relative position. If the transversal cuts parallel lines, then there is a relationship between the sizes of the special pairs of angles that are formed.

Surveyors use parallel line geometry to accurately measure the angles and mark the parallel lines for angle parking.

Lesson starter: What's formed by a transversal?

Draw a pair of parallel lines using either:

- two sides of a ruler; or
- interactive geometry software (parallel line tool).

Then cross the two lines with a third line (transversal) at any angles.

Measure each of the eight angles formed and discuss what you find. If interactive geometry software is used, drag the transversal to see if your observations apply to all the cases that you observe.

KEY IDEAS

■ A **transversal** is a line passing through two or more other lines that are usually, but not necessarily, parallel.

transversal   transversal

■ A transversal crossing two lines will form special pairs of angles. These are:
  • **corresponding** (in corresponding positions)

  • **alternate** (on opposite sides of the transversal and inside the other two lines)

  • **cointerior** (on the same side of the transversal and inside the other two lines).

■ **Parallel lines** are marked with the same arrow set.
  • If AB is parallel to CD, then we write $AB\|CD$.

■ If a transversal crosses two **parallel** lines, then:
  • corresponding angles are equal
  • alternate angles are equal
  • cointerior angles are supplementary (i.e. sum to 180°).

corresponding   alternate   cointerior

$a = b$ $a = b$ $a = b$ $a + b = 180$ $a + b = 180$

$a = b$

BUILDING UNDERSTANDING

1 Use a protractor to measure each of the eight angles in this diagram.

  a How many *different* angle measurements did you find?

  b Do you think that the two lines cut by the transversal are parallel?

2 Use a protractor to measure each of the eight angles in this diagram.

  a How many *different* angle measurements did you find?

  b Do you think that the two lines cut by the transversal are parallel?

3 Choose the word *equal* or *supplementary* to complete these sentences.

  If a transversal cuts two parallel lines, then:

  a alternate angles are _____.

  b cointerior angles are _____.

  c corresponding angles are _____.

  d vertically opposite angles are _____.

Example 6   Naming pairs of angles

Name the angle that is:

a corresponding to ∠ABF

b alternate to ∠ABF

c cointerior to ∠ABF

d vertically opposite to ∠ABF.

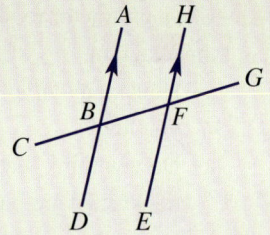

SOLUTION

a ∠HFG (or ∠GFH)

b ∠EFB (or ∠BFE)

c ∠HFB (or ∠BFH)

d ∠CBD (or ∠DBC)

EXPLANATION

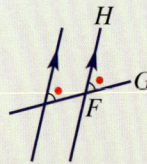

These two angles are in corresponding positions, both above and on the right of the intersection.

These two angles are on opposite sides of the transversal and inside the other two lines.

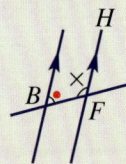

These two angles are on the same side of the transversal and inside the other two lines.

These two angles sit in opposite positions across the vertex B.

Now you try

Using the same diagram as in the example above, name the angle that is:

a corresponding to ∠EFB

b alternate to ∠DBF

c cointerior to ∠EFB

d vertically opposite to ∠GFE.

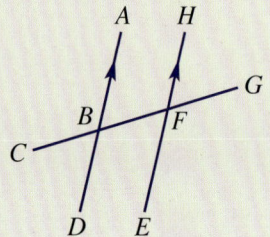

Example 7 Finding angles in parallel lines

Find the value of a in these diagrams and give a reason for each answer.

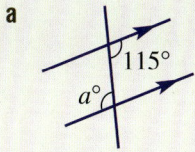

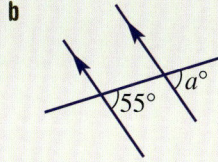

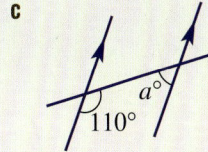

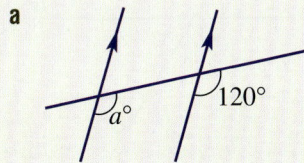

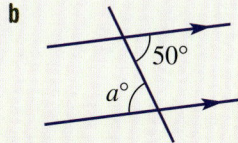

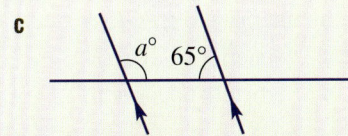

a

$115°$
$a°$

b

$55°$
$a°$

c

$a°$
$110°$

SOLUTION

a $a = 115$
alternate angles in parallel lines

b $a = 55$
corresponding angles in parallel lines

c $a = 180 - 110$
$= 70$

cointerior angles in parallel lines

EXPLANATION

Alternate angles in parallel lines cut by a transversal are equal.

Corresponding angles in parallel lines are equal.

Cointerior angles in parallel lines sum to $180°$.

Now you try

Find the value of a in these diagrams and give a reason for each answer.

a

$a°$
$120°$

b

$50°$
$a°$

c

$a°$ $65°$

Example 8 Determining whether two lines are parallel

Giving reasons, state whether the two lines cut by the transversal are parallel.

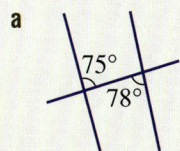

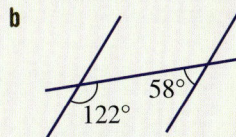

a

$75°$
$78°$

b

$58°$
$122°$

SOLUTION

a not parallel
Alternate angles are not equal.

b parallel
The cointerior angles sum to $180°$.

EXPLANATION

Parallel lines cut by a transversal have equal alternate angles.

$122° + 58° = 180°$
Cointerior angles inside parallel lines are supplementary (i.e. sum to $180°$).

Now you try

Giving reasons, state whether the two lines cut by the transversal are parallel.

a

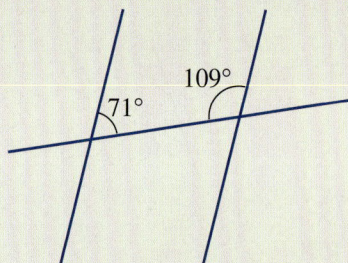

b

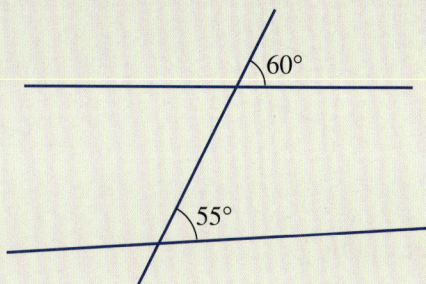

Exercise 7C

Example 6   **1**   Name the angle that is:

    a   corresponding to ∠BGA

    b   alternate to ∠FGH

    c   cointerior to ∠CHG

    d   vertically opposite to ∠FGA.

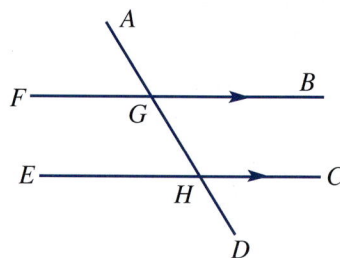

Example 6   **2**   Name the angle that is:

    a   corresponding to ∠ABE

    b   alternate to ∠ABE

    c   cointerior to ∠ABE

    d   vertically opposite to ∠ABE.

Example 6   **3**   Name the angle that is:

    a   corresponding to ∠EBH

    b   alternate to ∠EBH

    c   cointerior to ∠EBH

    d   vertically opposite to ∠EBH.

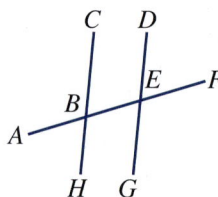

Example 7 **4** Find the value of a in these diagrams, giving a reason.

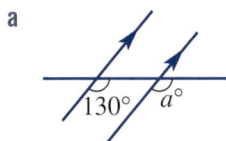

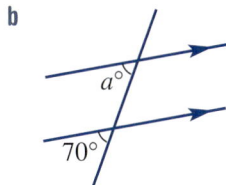

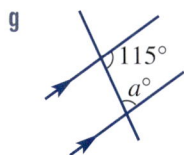

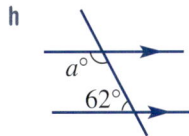

a

130° $a°$

b

$a°$

70°

c

110°

$a°$

d

$a°$

120°

e

$a°$

130°

f

67°

$a°$

g

115°

$a°$

h

$a°$

62°

i

$a°$

100°

j

117°

$a°$

k

64°

$a°$

l

116°

$a°$

Example 7 **5** Find the value of each pronumeral in the following diagrams.

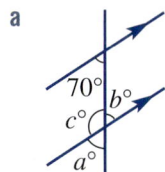

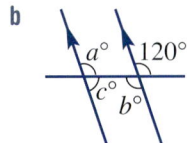

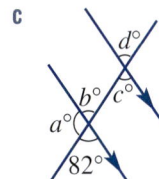

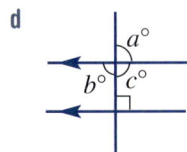

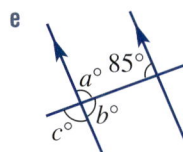

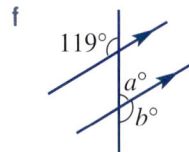

a

70° $b°$

$c°$

$a°$

b

$a°$ 120°

$c°$ $b°$

c

$d°$

$b°$ $c°$

$a°$

82°

d

$a°$

$b°$ $c°$

e

$a°$ 85°

$c°$ $b°$

f

119°

$a°$

$b°$

Example 8 **6** Giving reasons, state whether the two lines cut by the transversal are parallel.

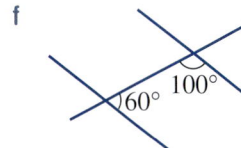

a

59°

58°

b

81°

81°

c

112°

68°

d

132° 132°

e

79° 78°

f

60° 100°

PROBLEM-SOLVING   7–8(½)   7–8(½), 9   8(½), 9, 10

7   Find the value of *a* in these diagrams.

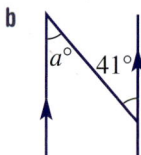

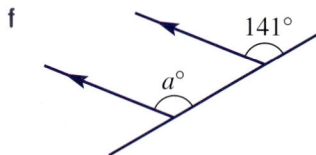

a

b

c

d

e

f

8   Find the value of *a* in these diagrams.

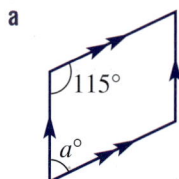

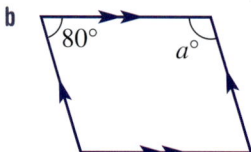

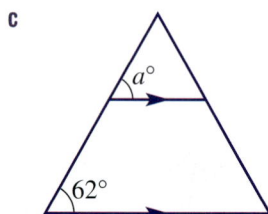

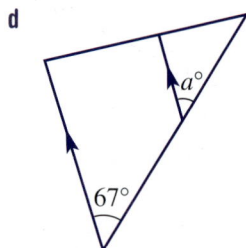

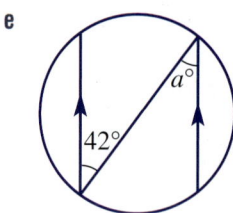

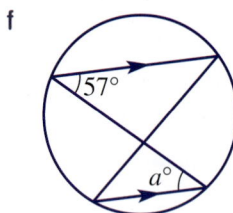

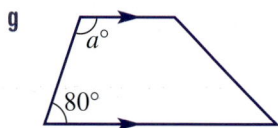

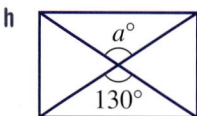

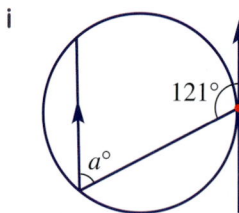

a

b

c

d

e

f

g

h

i

9   A transversal cuts a set of three parallel lines.
   a   How many angles are formed?
   b   How many angles of different sizes are formed if the transversal is *not* perpendicular to the three lines?

10 Two roads merge into a freeway at the same angle, as shown.
   Find the size of the obtuse angle, *a*°, between the parallel roads
   and the freeway.

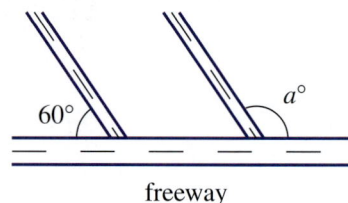

freeway

11 a This diagram includes two triangles with two sides that are parallel.
   Give a reason why:
   i $a = 20$ **ii** $b = 45$.

b Now find the values of a and b in the diagrams below.

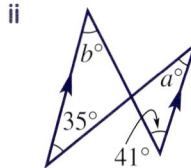

i

ii

iii

12 This shape is a parallelogram with two pairs of parallel sides.
   a Use the 60° angle to find the value of a and b.
   b Find the value of c.
   c What do you notice about the angles inside a parallelogram?

13 Explain why these diagrams do not contain a pair of parallel lines.

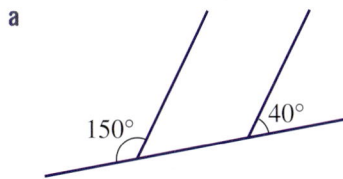

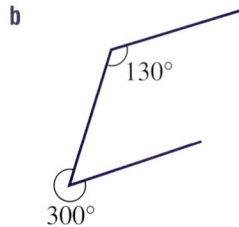

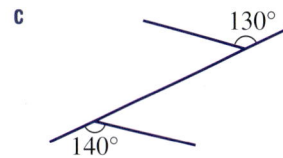

a

b

c

14 Consider this triangle and parallel lines.
   a Giving a reason for your answer, name an angle equal to:
   i $\angle ABD$ **ii** $\angle CBE$.

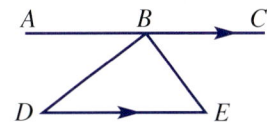

b What do you know about the three angles $\angle ABD$, $\angle DBE$ and $\angle CBE$?
   c What do these results tell you about the three inside angles of the
   triangle BDE? Is this true for any triangle? Try a new diagram to check.

15 Use the ideas explored in Question **14** to show that the angles inside a quadrilateral
   (i.e. a four-sided shape) must sum to 360°. Use this diagram to help.

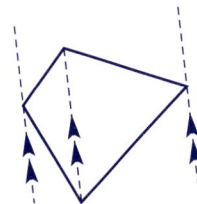

7D Solving compound problems with parallel lines EXTENDING

LEARNING INTENTION
- To be able to combine facts involving parallel lines and other geometric properties to find missing angles in a diagram

Parallel lines are at the foundation of construction in all its forms. Imagine the sorts of problems engineers and builders would face if drawings and constructions could not accurately use and apply parallel lines. Angles formed by intersecting beams would be difficult to calculate and could not be transferred to other parts of the building.

A builder makes sure that the roof rafters are all parallel, the ceiling joists are horizontal and parallel, and the wall studs are perpendicular and parallel.

Lesson starter: Not so obvious

Some geometrical problems require a combination of two or more ideas before a solution can be found. This diagram includes an angle of size $a°$.

- Discuss if it is possible to find the value of a.
- Describe the steps you would take to find the value of a. Discuss your reasons for each step.

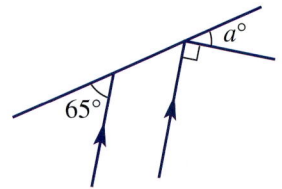

KEY IDEAS

■ Some geometrical problems involve more than one step.
  Step 1: $\angle ABC = 75°$ (corresponding angles on parallel lines)
  Step 2: $a = 360 - 75$ (angles in a revolution sum to $360°$)
  $= 285$

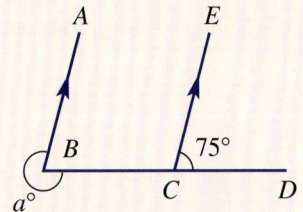

BUILDING UNDERSTANDING

1 In these diagrams, first find the value of a and then find the value of b.

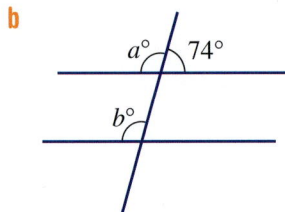

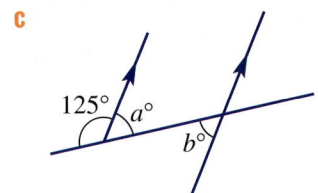

a

b

c

2 Name the angle in these diagrams (e.g. ∠ABC) that you would need to find first before finding the value of *a*. Then find the value of *a*.

a
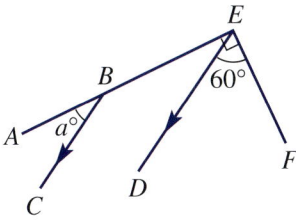

b
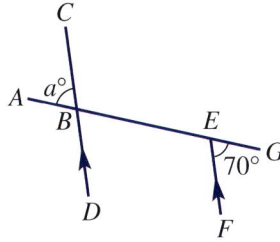

c
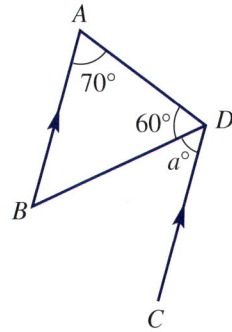

Example 9   Finding angles with two steps

Find the value of *a* in these diagrams.

a
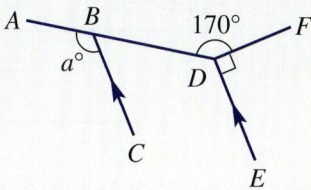

b

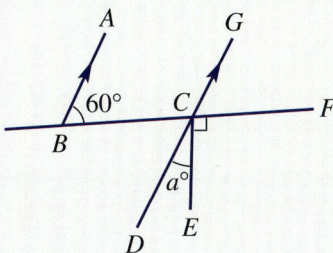

SOLUTION

a ∠BDE = 360° − 90° − 170°
       = 100°
       ∴ a = 100

b ∠ABC = 180° − 70°
       = 110°
       ∴ a = 110 − 60
       = 50

EXPLANATION

Angles in a revolution add to 360°.
∠ABC corresponds with ∠BDE, and
BC and DE are parallel.

∠ABC and ∠BCD are cointerior
angles, with AB and DC parallel.
∠ABC = 110° and a° + 60° = 110°

Now you try

Find the value of *a* in these diagrams.

a
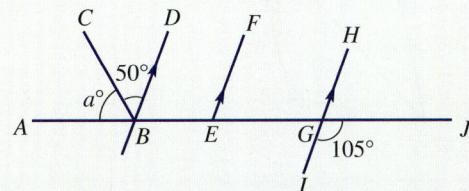

b

Exercise 7D

FLUENCY   1, 2(½), 3, 4(½)   2, 4   2(½), 4(½)

Example 9a

1 Find the value of *a* in these diagrams.

a

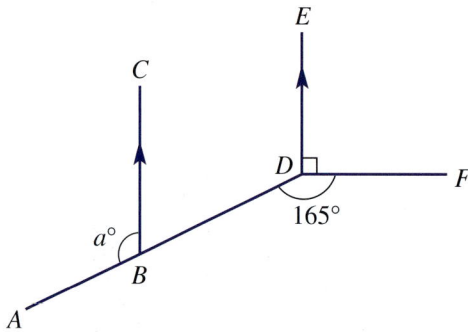

b

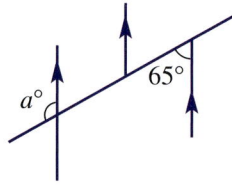

Example 9a

2 Find the value of *a* in these diagrams.

a

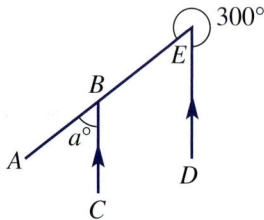

b

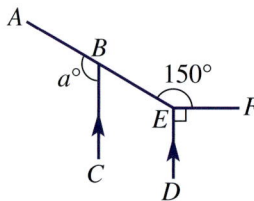

c

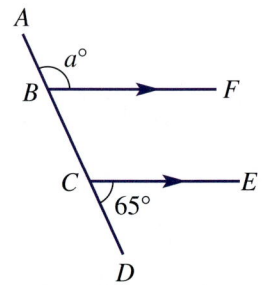

d

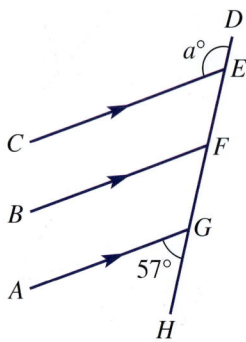

e

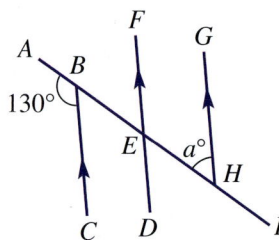

f

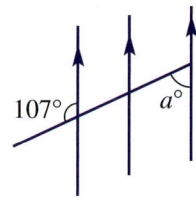

Example 9b

3 Find the value of *a* in these diagrams.

a

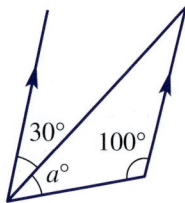

b

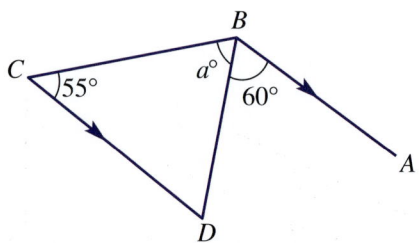

ple 9b

4 **a**
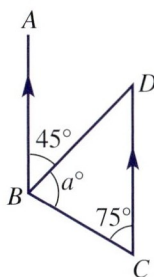

b
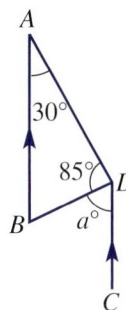

c
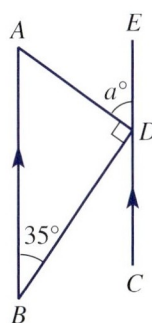

d
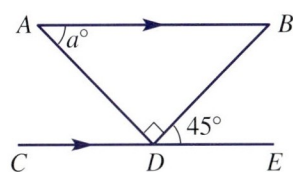

e
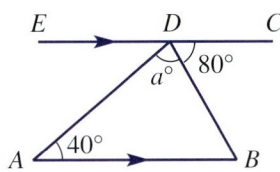

f

5   5   5(½), 6

5   Find the size of ∠ABC in these diagrams.

a
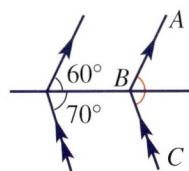

b

c
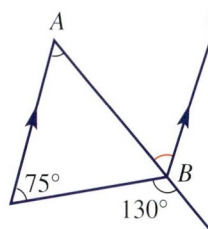

d
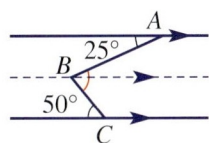

e
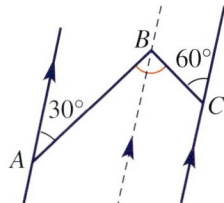

f
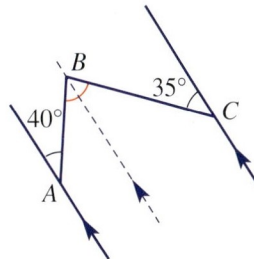

6   Find the value of x in each of these diagrams.

a
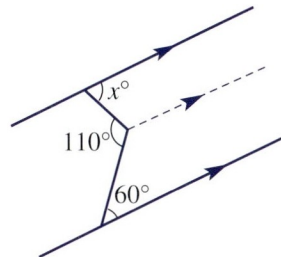

b
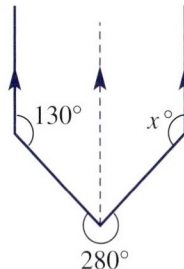

c
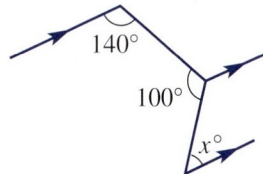

REASONING | 7 | 7, 8(½) | 8, 9

7 What is the minimum number of angles you need to know to find all the angles marked in these diagrams?

a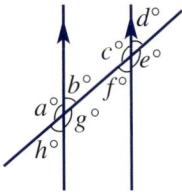

b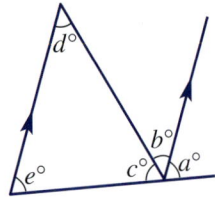

c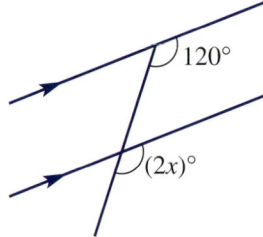

8 In these diagrams, the pronumeral x represents a number and $2x$ means $2 \times x$. Find the value of x in each case.

a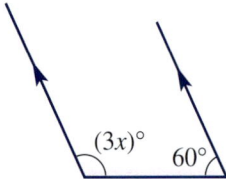

b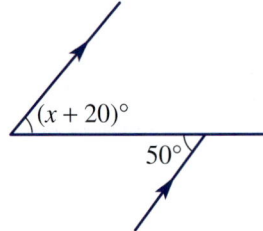

c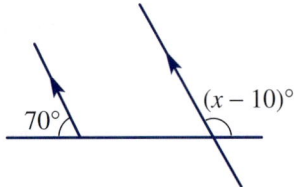

d

e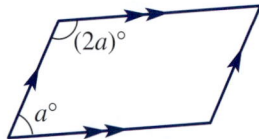

f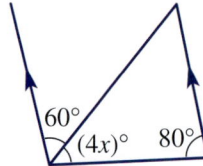

9 Find the value of a in these diagrams.

a

b

c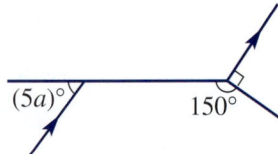

10 Adding extra parallel lines can help to solve more complex geometry problems.

You can see in this problem that the value of $a°$ is the sum of two alternate angles after adding the extra (dashed) parallel line.

Find the value of a in these diagrams.

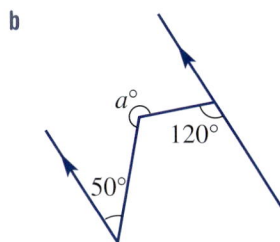

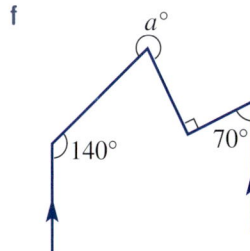

a

b

c

d

e

f

7E   Classifying and constructing triangles

The word 'triangle' (literally meaning 'three angles') describes a shape with three sides. The triangle is an important building block in mathematical geometry. Similarly, it is important in the practical world of building and construction owing to the rigidity of its shape.

In this Melbourne sports stadium, engineers have used triangular structural supports, including equilateral and isosceles triangles. These triangles are symmetrical and evenly distribute the weight of the structure.

Lesson starter: Stable shapes

Consider these constructions, which are made from straight pieces of steel and bolts.

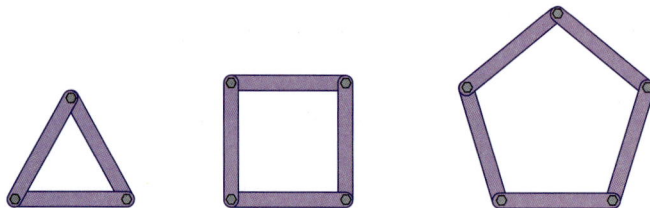

Assume that the bolts are not tightened and that there is some looseness at the points where they are joined.

- Which shape(s) do you think could lose their shape if a vertex is pushed?
- Which shape(s) will not lose their shape when pushed? Why?
- For the construction(s) that might lose their shape, what could be done to make them rigid?

KEY IDEAS

■ **Triangles** can be named using the vertex labels.

triangle *ABC* or △*ABC*

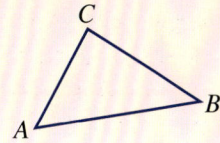

■ Triangles are classified by their **side lengths**.

scalene

3 different sides
3 different angles

isosceles

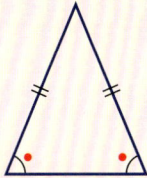

2 equal sides
2 equal angles

equilateral

60°

60°   60°

3 equal sides
3 equal angles (60°)

■ Triangles are also classified by the size of their **interior angles**.

acute

all acute angles

right

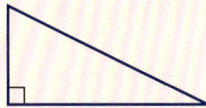

one right angle

obtuse

one obtuse angle

■ The parts of an **isosceles triangle** are named as shown opposite. The base angles are equal and two sides (called the legs) are of equal length. The two sides of equal length are opposite the equal angles.

■ Sides of equal length are indicated by matching markings.

■ **Rulers, protractors** and **arcs** drawn using a pair of compasses can help to construct triangles accurately.

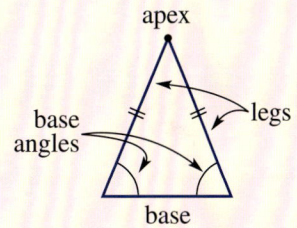

apex

base
angles

legs

base

right triangles

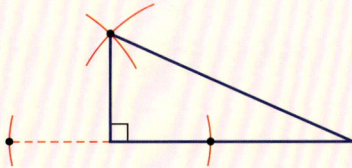

isosceles triangles

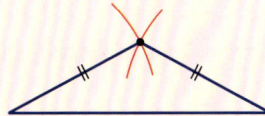

equilateral triangles

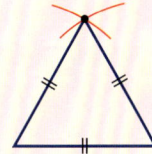

Three side lengths (e.g. constructing a triangle with side lengths 3 cm, 5 cm, 6 cm)

Two sides and the angle between them (e.g. constructing a triangle with side lengths 4 cm and 5 cm with a 40° angle between them)

Two angles and a side (e.g. constructing a triangle with angles 35° and 70° and a side length of 5 cm)

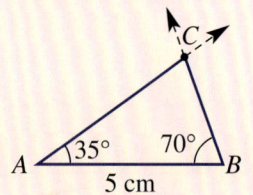

BUILDING UNDERSTANDING

1 Describe or draw an example of each of the triangles given below. Refer back to the **Key ideas** in this section to check that the features of each triangle are correct.

   a scalene   **b** isosceles   **c** equilateral

   d acute   **e** right   **f** obtuse

2 Answer these questions, using the point labels A, B and C for the given isosceles triangle.

   a Which point is the apex?

   b Which segment is the base?

   c Which two segments are of equal length?

   d Which two angles are the base angles?

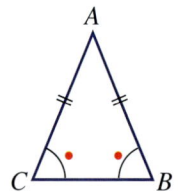

Example 10 Classifying triangles

These triangles are drawn to scale. Classify them by:

   i their side lengths (i.e. scalene, isosceles or equilateral)

   ii their angles (i.e. acute, right or obtuse).

a

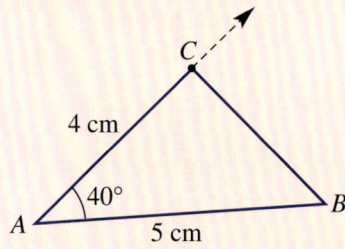

b

SOLUTION	EXPLANATION
a i isosceles	Has 2 sides of equal length.
ii acute	All angles are acute.
b i scalene	Has 3 different side lengths.
ii obtuse	Has 1 obtuse angle.

Now you try

These triangles are drawn to scale. Classify them by:

i   their side lengths

ii   their angles.

a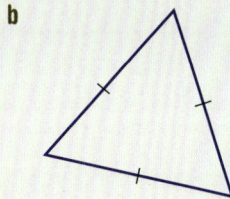

b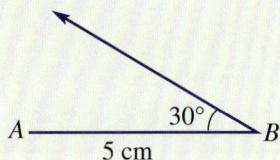

Example 11   Constructing triangles using a protractor and ruler

Construct a triangle ABC with $AB = 5$ cm, $\angle ABC = 30°$ and $\angle BAC = 45°$.

SOLUTION

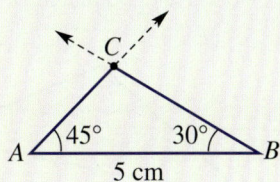

EXPLANATION

First, measure and draw segment AB.
Then use a protractor to form the angle 30° at point B.

Then use a protractor to form the angle 45° at point A.
Mark point C and join with A and with B.

Now you try

Construct a triangle ABC with $AB = 4$ cm, $\angle ABC = 45°$ and $\angle BAC = 60°$.

Example 12   Constructing a triangle using a pair of compasses and ruler

Construct a triangle with side lengths 6 cm, 4 cm and 5 cm.

SOLUTION

6 cm

EXPLANATION

Use a ruler to draw a segment 6 cm in length.

Continued on next page

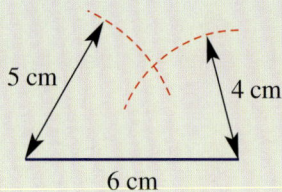

Construct two arcs with radius 4 cm and 5 cm, using each end of the segment as the centres.

Mark the intersection point of the arcs and draw the two remaining segments.

Now you try

Construct a triangle with side lengths 5 cm, 6 cm and 7 cm.

Exercise 7E

FLUENCY	1–8	3–8	3–5, 7, 8

Example 10i

1 Classify each of these triangles according to their side lengths (i.e. scalene, isosceles or equilateral).

a   b   c

Example 10ii

2 These triangles are drawn to scale. Classify them according to their angles (i.e. acute, right or obtuse).

a   b   c

Example 10

3 These triangles are drawn to scale. Classify them by:
  i their side lengths (i.e. scalene, isosceles or equilateral)
  ii their angles (i.e. acute, right or obtuse).

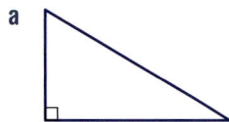

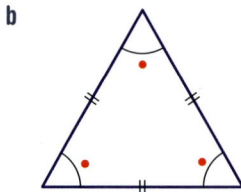

a   b   c

Example 11

4 Use a protractor and ruler to construct the following triangles.
 a triangle ABC with $AB = 5\,\text{cm}$, $\angle ABC = 40°$ and $\angle BAC = 30°$
 b triangle DEF with $DE = 6\,\text{cm}$, $\angle DEF = 50°$ and $\angle EDF = 25°$
 c triangle ABC with $AB = 5\,\text{cm}$, $\angle ABC = 35°$ and $BC = 4\,\text{cm}$

Example 12

5 Construct a triangle with the given side lengths.
 a 7 cm, 3 cm and 5 cm.   b 8 cm, 5 cm and 6 cm.

6 Construct an isosceles triangle by following these steps.
 a Draw a base segment of about 4 cm in length.
 b Use a pair of compasses to construct two arcs of equal radius. (Try about 5 cm but there is no need to be exact.)
 c Join the intersection point of the arcs (apex) with each end of the base.
 d Measure the length of the legs to check they are equal.
 e Measure the two base angles to check they are equal.

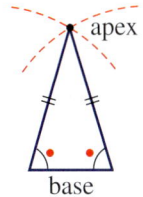

7 Construct an equilateral triangle by following these steps.
 a Draw a segment of about 4 cm in length.
 b Use a pair of compasses to construct two arcs of equal radius.
  Important: Ensure the arc radius is exactly the same as the length of the segment in part a.
 c Join the intersection point of the arcs with the segment at both ends.
 d Measure the length of the three sides to check they are equal.
 e Measure the three angles to check they are all equal and 60°.

8 Construct a right triangle by following these steps.
 a Draw a segment, AB, of about 4 cm in length.
 b Extend the segment AB to form the ray AD. Make AD about 2 cm in length.
 c Construct a circle with centre A and radius AD. Also mark point E.
 d Draw two arcs with centres at D and E, as shown in the diagram. Any radius will do as long as they are equal for both arcs.
 e Mark point C and join with A and B.

PROBLEM-SOLVING   9   9, 10   10, 11

9 Is it possible to draw any of the following? If yes, give an example.
 a an acute triangle that is also scalene
 b a right triangle that is also isosceles
 c an equilateral triangle that is also obtuse
 d a scalene triangle that is also right angled

10 Without using a protractor, accurately construct these triangles. Rulers can be used to set the pair of compasses.
 a triangle ABC with $AB = 5.5\,\text{cm}$, $BC = 4.5\,\text{cm}$ and $AC = 3.5\,\text{cm}$
 b an isosceles triangle with base length 4 cm and legs 5 cm
 c an equilateral triangle with side length 3.5 cm
 d a right triangle with one side 4 cm and hypotenuse 5 cm

11 Copy and complete the following table, making the height of each cell large enough to draw a triangle in each cell. Draw an example of a triangle that fits the triangle type in both the row and column. Are there any cells in the table for which it is impossible to draw a triangle?

Triangles	Scalene	Isosceles	Equilateral
Acute			
Right			
Obtuse			

REASONING   12   12, 13   13, 14

12 a   Is it possible to divide every triangle into two right triangles using one line segment? Explore with diagrams.
    b   Which type of triangle can always be divided into two identical right triangles?

13 Try drawing a triangle with side lengths 4 cm, 5 cm and 10 cm. Explain why this is impossible.

14 a   Is the side opposite the largest angle in a triangle always the longest?
    b   Can you draw a triangle with two obtuse angles? Explain why or why not.

ENRICHMENT: Gothic arches   –   –   15

15 a   The Gothic, or equilateral arch, is based on the equilateral triangle. Try to construct one, using this diagram to help.

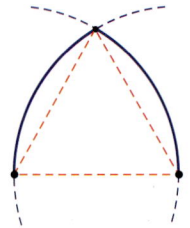

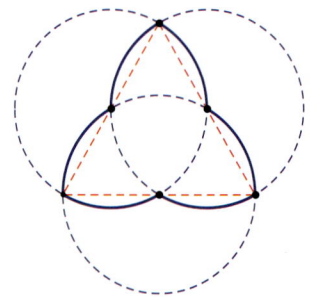

    b   The trefoil uses the midpoints of the sides of an equilateral triangle. Try to construct one, using this diagram to help.

7F Classifying quadrilaterals and other polygons

Polygons are closed plane shapes with straight sides. Each side is a segment and joins with two other sides at points called vertices. The number of sides, angles and vertices are the same for each type of polygon, and this number determines the name of the polygon. The word *polygon* comes from the Greek words *poly* meaning 'many' and *gonia* meaning 'angle'.

Quadrilaterals are polygons with four sides. There are special types of quadrilaterals and these are identified by the number of equal side lengths and the number of pairs of parallel lines.

Architects designed these giant domes for plant greenhouses at the Eden Project, England. Steel hexagons, pentagons and triangles support plastic 'pillows' full of air that insulate plants from the cold.

Lesson starter: Quadrilaterals that you know

You may already know the names and properties of some of the special quadrilaterals. Which ones do you think have:

- 2 pairs of parallel sides?
- all sides of equal length?
- 2 pairs of sides of equal length?

Are there any types of quadrilaterals that you know which you have not yet listed?

KEY IDEAS

- **Polygons** are closed plane figures with straight sides.

- A **vertex** is the point at which two sides of a shape meet. (*Vertices* is the plural form of vertex.)

- **Convex** polygons have all vertices pointing outward and all interior (inside) angles smaller than 180°.

- **Non-convex** (or concave) polygons have at least one vertex pointing inward and at least one interior angle larger than 180°.

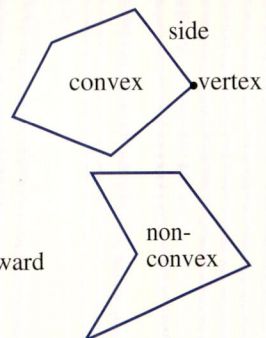

■ Polygons are classified by the number of sides they have.

■ **Regular** polygons have sides of equal length and angles of equal size.

- In a diagram, sides of equal length are shown using markings (or dashes).

Number of sides	Type
3	Triangle or trigon
4	Quadrilateral or tetragon
5	Pentagon
6	Hexagon
7	Heptagon or septagon
8	Octagon
9	Nonagon
10	Decagon
11	Undecagon
12	Dodecagon

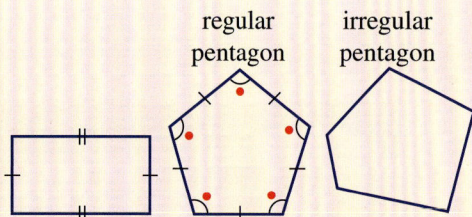

regular pentagon   irregular pentagon

■ Polygons are usually named with capital letters for each vertex and in succession, clockwise or anticlockwise.

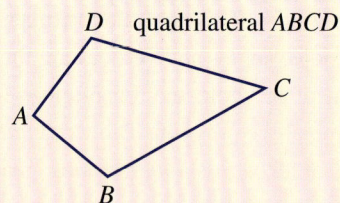

quadrilateral *ABCD*

■ A **diagonal** is a segment that joins two vertices, dividing a shape into two parts.

diagonals

■ Special quadrilaterals

Square

Rectangle

Rhombus

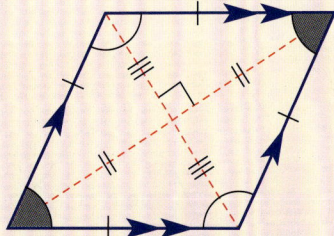

Parallelogram

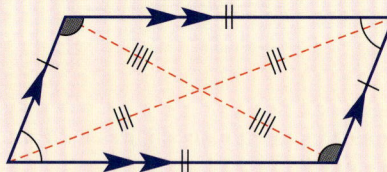

Kite

Trapezium

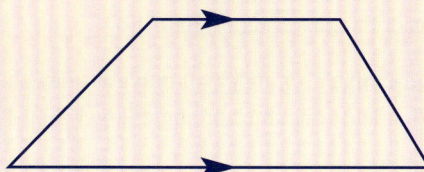

■ Quadrilaterals with parallel sides contain two pairs of cointerior angles.

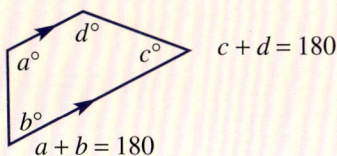

$$c + d = 180$$
$$a + b = 180$$

BUILDING UNDERSTANDING

1 Consider these three polygons.

i 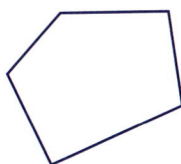　　　ii 　　　iii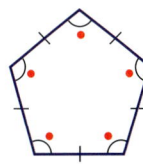

   a The three shapes are examples of what type of polygon?
   b Which shape(s) are convex and why?
   c Which shape(s) are non-convex and why?
   d State the missing words in this sentence. The third shape is called a _____ _____.

2 Draw an example of each of the quadrilaterals listed. Mark any sides of equal length with single or double dashes, mark parallel lines with single or double arrows and mark equal angles using the letters $a°$ and $b°$. (Refer back to the **Key ideas** in this section should you need help.)
   a square　　　　　　**b** rectangle　　　　　　**c** rhombus
   d parallelogram　　　**e** trapezium　　　　　**f** kite

3 **a** Draw two examples of a non-convex quadrilateral.
   b For each of your drawings, state how many interior angles are greater than $180°$.

Example 13　Classifying polygons

a State the type of polygon and whether it is convex or non-convex.
b Is the polygon regular or irregular?

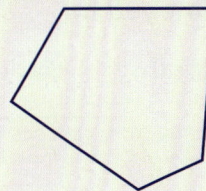

Continued on next page

SOLUTION

a   convex pentagon

b   irregular

EXPLANATION

The polygon has 5 sides and all the vertices are pointing outward.

The sides are not of equal length and the angles are not equal.

Now you try

a   State the type of polygon and whether it is convex or non-convex.

b   Is the polygon regular or irregular?

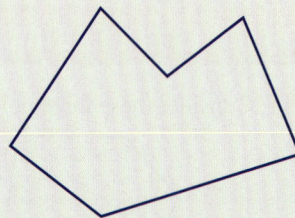

Example 14   Classifying quadrilaterals

State the type of each quadrilateral given below.

a

b

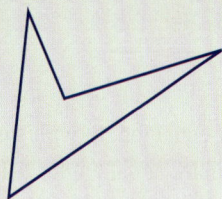

SOLUTION

a   non-convex quadrilateral

b   trapezium

EXPLANATION

One interior angle is greater than 180°.

There is one pair of parallel sides.

Now you try

State the type of each quadrilateral given.

a

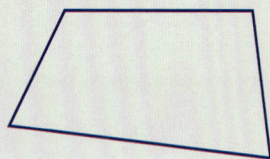

b

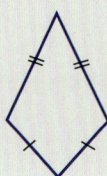

Exercise 7F

FLUENCY   1–6   2–8   2–6, 8

Example 13

1 **a** State the type of polygon shown below and whether it is convex or non-convex.

b Is the polygon shape regular or irregular?

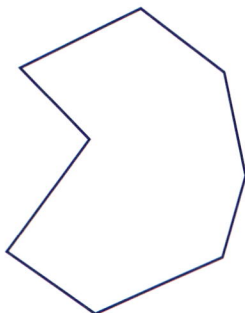

2 How many sides do each of these polygon have?

a pentagon   **b** triangle

c decagon   **d** heptagon

e undecagon   **f** quadrilateral

g nonagon   **h** hexagon

i octagon   **j** dodecagon

Example 13

3 **a** Which of the given shapes are convex?

b State the type of polygon by considering its number of sides.

i   **ii**   **iii**

iv   **v**   **vi**

Example 14a

4 Classify each of these quadrilaterals as either convex or non-convex.

a   **b**   **c**

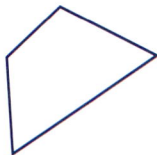   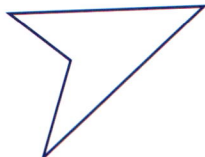   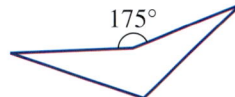

175°

Example 14b   **5**   State the type of special quadrilateral given below.

a 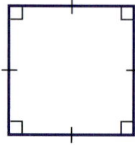   **b** 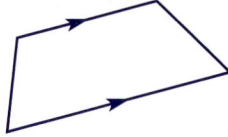   **c**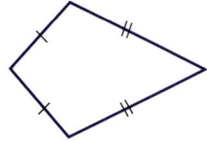

d   **e**   **f**

Example 14b   **6**   List all the types of quadrilateral that have:

    a   2 different pairs of sides of equal length

    b   2 different pairs of opposite angles that are equal in size

    c   2 different pairs of parallel lines

    d   only 1 pair of parallel lines

    e   only 1 pair of opposite angles that are equal in size.

7   State whether the following are polygons (P) or not polygons (N).

    a   circle   **b**   square   **c**   rectangle   **d**   oval

    e   cylinder   **f**   cube   **g**   line   **h**   segment

8   Use your knowledge of the properties of quadrilaterals to find the unknown angles and lengths in each of these diagrams.

a 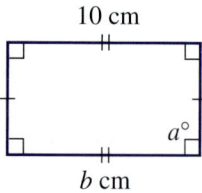   **b** 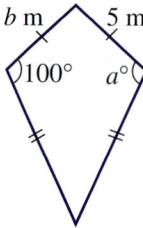   **c**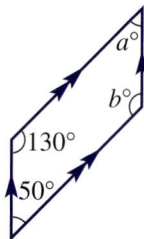

9   Draw line segments to show how you would divide the given shapes into the shapes listed below.

a

two triangles

b

one rectangle and
two triangles

c

three triangles

d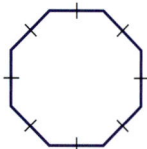

four triangles and
one square

e

two quadrilaterals

f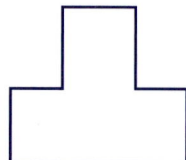

one pentagon
and one heptagon

10 A diagonal between two vertices divides a polygon into two parts.

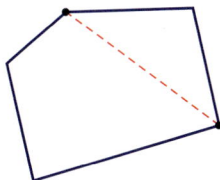

a What is the maximum (i.e. largest) number of diagonals that can be drawn for the following shapes if the diagonals are *not* allowed to cross?

 i convex pentagon

 ii convex decagon

b What is the maximum number of diagonals that can be drawn for the following shapes if the diagonals *are* allowed to cross?

 i convex pentagon

 ii convex decagon

11 Using the given measurements, accurately draw this equilateral triangle onto a piece of paper and cut it into 4 pieces, as shown. Can you form a square with the four pieces?

| REASONING | 12 | 12, 13 | 13, 14 |

12 State whether each of the following statements is true or false.

a A regular polygon will have equal interior (i.e. inside) angles.

b The sum of the angles inside a pentagon is the same as the sum of the angles inside a decagon.

c An irregular polygon must always be non-convex.

d Convex polygons are not always regular.

13 The diagonals of a quadrilateral are segments that join opposite vertices.

a List the quadrilaterals that have diagonals of equal length.

b List the quadrilaterals that have diagonals intersecting at 90°.

14 **a** Are squares a type of rectangle or are rectangles a type of square? Give an explanation.

    b Are rhombuses a type of parallelogram? Explain.

    c Is it possible to draw a non-convex trapezium?

ENRICHMENT: Construction challenge   –   –   15

15 Use a pair of compasses and a ruler to construct these figures. Use the diagrams as a guide, then measure to check the properties of your construction.

    a a rhombus with side length 5 cm

    b a line parallel to segment AB and passing through point P

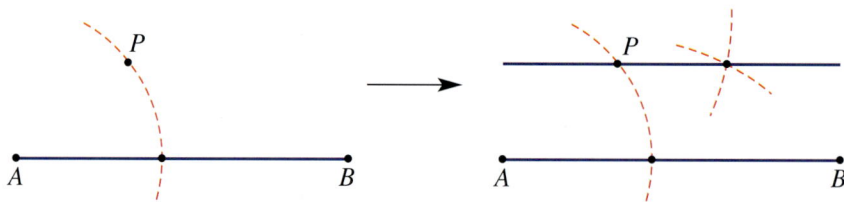

Each trapezium-shaped tabletop is a quadrilateral and two together forms a hexagon. Could these two trapezium-shaped tables be joined to make a parallelogram?

7A **1** Consider the diagram below and answer the following.

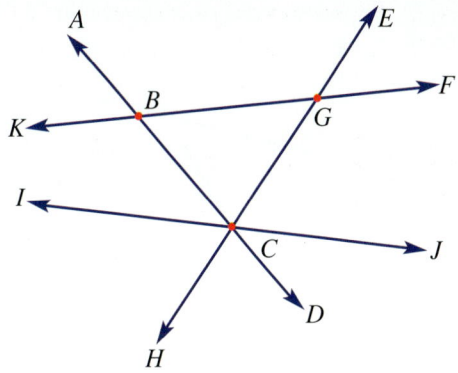

a Name the point where the line *EH* intersects *KF*.

b Name an angle which has its vertex at *G*.

c Name an angle adjacent to ∠*FGH*.

d Name a set of three concurrent lines.

e Name an obtuse angle with its vertex at *B* and use your protractor to measure the size of this angle.

7B **2** Find the value of each pronumeral below and give a reason for each answer.

a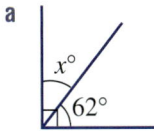

b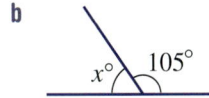

c

d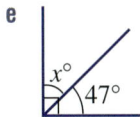

e

f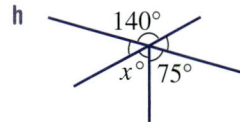

g

h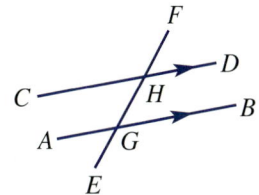

7C **3** Name the angle that is:

a corresponding to ∠*EGB*

b alternate to ∠*AGH*

c vertically opposite to ∠*GHD*

d cointerior to ∠*CHG*.

7C **4** Find the value of *a* in these diagrams and give a reason for each answer.

a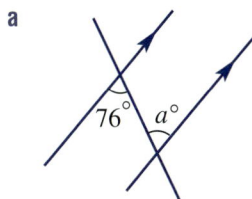

b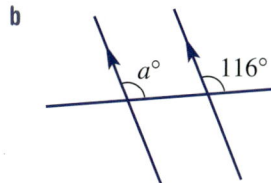

c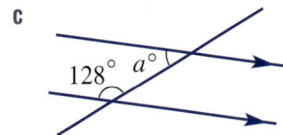

Progress quiz

7C

5 Giving reasons, state whether the two lines cut by the transversal are parallel.

a

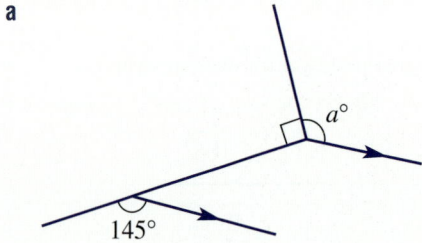

b

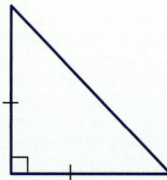

7D

(Ext)

6 Find the value of *a* in these diagrams.

a

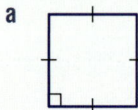

b

7E

7 Classify this triangle by:
a its side lengths
b its angles.

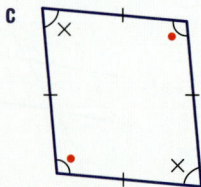

7E

8 Construct an equilateral triangle with each side having a length of 6 cm.

7F

9 State the special type of quadrilateral given in each diagram below.

a

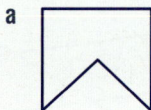

b

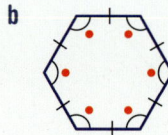

c

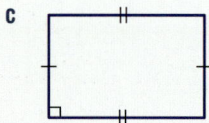

d

7F

10 Name the type of shape stating whether it is concave or convex, regular or irregular.

a

b

c

d

7G Angle sum of a triangle

LEARNING INTENTIONS
- To know that the sum of interior angles in a triangle is 180°
- To know what an exterior angle is
- To be able to find exterior angles in triangles using supplementary angles
- To understand that the angle sum of a polygon can be determined by decomposing into triangles

The three interior angles of a triangle have a very important property. No matter the shape of the triangle, the three angles always add to the same total.

The Millau Viaduct in France is the tallest bridge structure in the world; its tallest pylon is 343 m. The different triangles formed by the bridge's cables all have the same angle sum.

Lesson starter: A visual perspective on the angle sum

Use a ruler to draw any triangle. Cut out the triangle and tear off the three corners. Then place the three corners together.

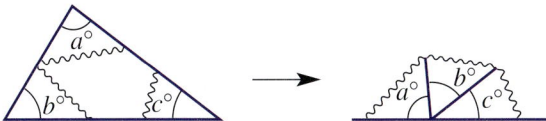

What do you notice and what does this tell you about the three angles in the triangle? Compare your results with those of others. Does this work for other triangles?

KEY IDEAS

■ The **angle sum** of the interior angles of a triangle is 180°.

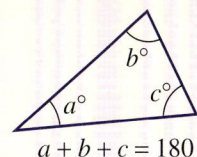

$$a + b + c = 180$$

■ If one side of a triangle is extended, an **exterior** angle is formed. In the diagram shown opposite, ∠DBC is the exterior angle. The angle ∠DBC is supplementary to ∠ABC (i.e. adds to 180°).

■ The angle sum S of a polygon with n sides can be determined by decomposing into triangles.

Quadrilateral ($n = 4$)

Pentagon ($n = 5$)

Angle sum = $3 \times 180° = 540°$

Angle sum = $2 \times 180° = 360°$

BUILDING UNDERSTANDING

1 **a** Use a protractor to measure the three angles in this triangle.

b Add your three angles. What do you notice?

2 For the triangle opposite, give reasons why:

a a must equal 20

b b must equal 60.

3 What is the size of each angle in an equilateral triangle?

4 For the isosceles triangle opposite, give a reason why:

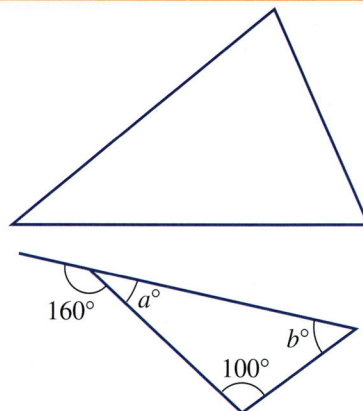

a $a = 70$

b $b = 40$.

Example 15 Finding an angle in a triangle

Find the value of *a* in these triangles.

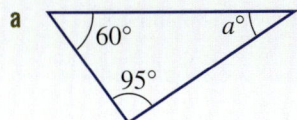

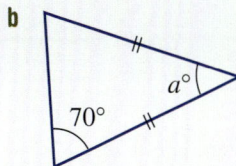

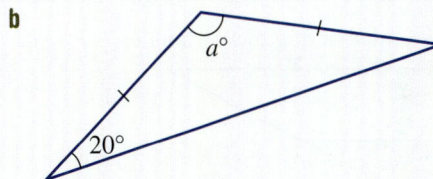

a

b

SOLUTION

a $a = 180 - (60 + 95)$
$= 180 - 155$
$= 25$

b $a = 180 - (70 + 70)$
$= 180 - 140$
$= 40$

EXPLANATION

The sum of angles in a triangle is 180.
Add the two known angles.
Find the difference between 180 and 155.

The two angles opposite the sides of equal length (i.e. the base angles) in an isosceles triangle are equal in size.
Add the two equal angles.
Find the difference between 140 and 180.

Now you try

Find the value of *a* in these triangles.

a

b

Example 16 Finding an exterior angle

Find the size of the exterior angle ($x°$) in this diagram.

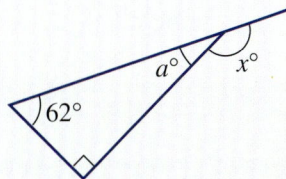

Continued on next page

SOLUTION

$a = 180 - (90 + 62)$
  $= 180 - 152$
  $= 28$

$x = 180 - 28$
  $= 152$

∴ The size of the exterior angle is 152°.

EXPLANATION

The angle sum for a triangle is 180°.
Add the two known angles.
a is the difference between 180 and 152.

Angles of size $x°$ and $a°$ are supplementary
(i.e. they add to 180°).
x is the difference between 180 and 28.

Now you try

Find the size of the exterior angle ($x°$) in this diagram.

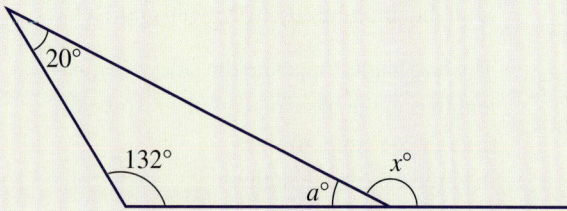

Exercise 7G

FLUENCY

| 1, 2(½), 3, 4–5(½) | 2–5(½) | 2(½), 4–5(½) |

Example 15a

1 Find the value of a in these triangles.

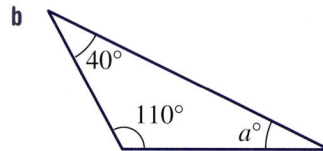

a

b

Example 15a

2 Find the value of a in each of these triangles.

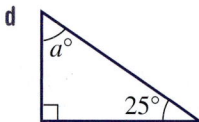

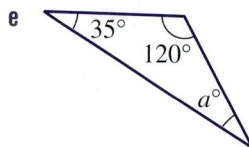

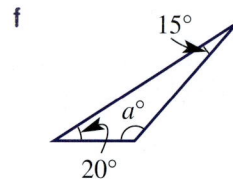

a

b

c

d

e

f

ple 15b **3** Find the value of *a* in each of these isosceles triangles.

a

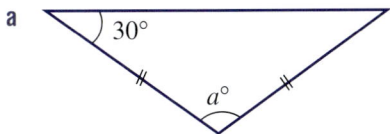

30°

a°

b

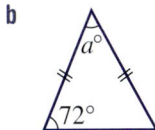

a°

72°

ple 15b **4** Find the value of *a* in each of these isosceles triangles.

a

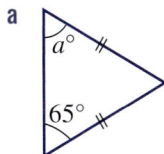

a°

65°

b

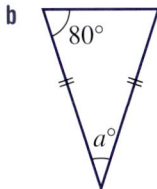

80°

a°

c

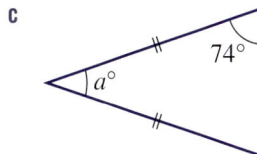

74°

a°

d

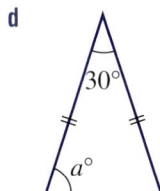

30°

a°

e

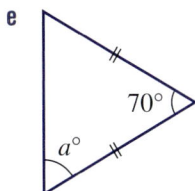

70°

a°

f

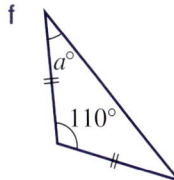

a°

110°

mple 15 **5** The triangles below have exterior angles. Find the value of *x*. For parts **b** to **f**, you will need to first calculate the value of *a*.

a

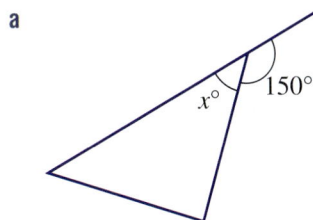

x° 150°

b

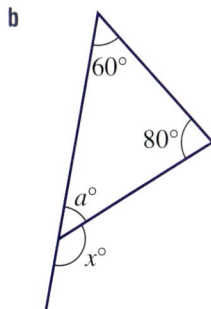

60°

80°

a°

x°

c

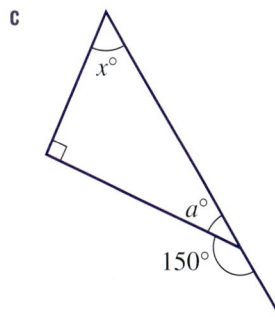

x°

a°

150°

d

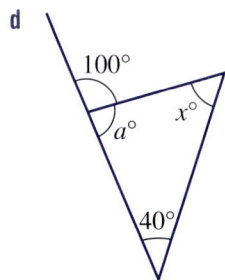

100°

a° *x*°

40°

e

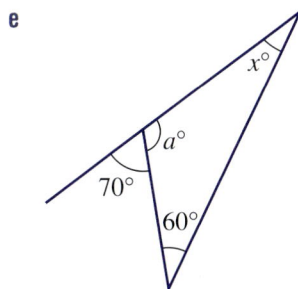

x°

a°

70°

60°

f

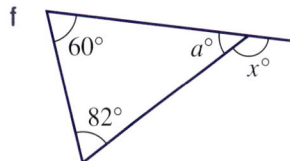

60° *a*° *x*°

82°

PROBLEM-SOLVING | 6(½) | 6–7(½) | 6–7(½), 8

6 Find the value of *a* in each of these triangles.

a

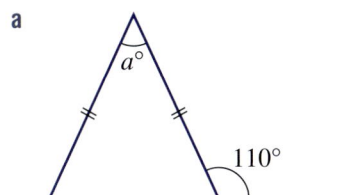

a°

110°

b

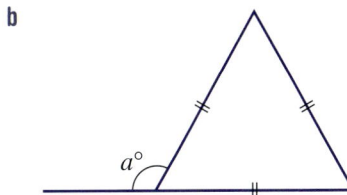

a°

c

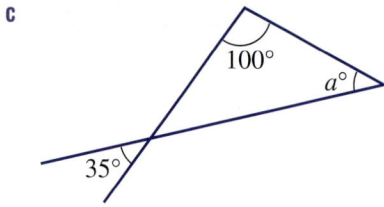

d

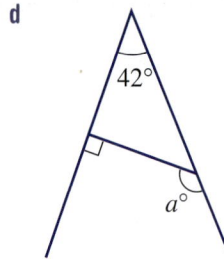

e

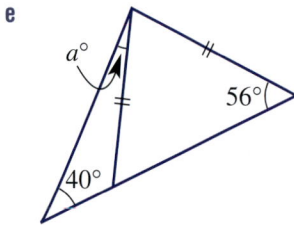

f

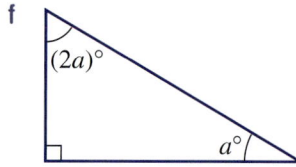

7 Each of these diagrams has parallel lines. Find the value of a.

a

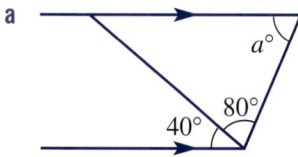

b

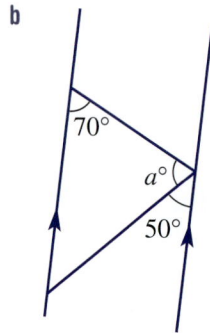

c

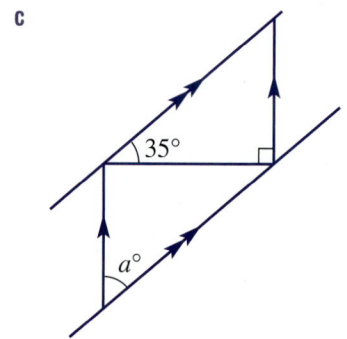

d

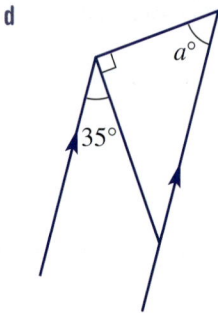

e

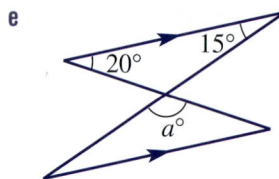

f

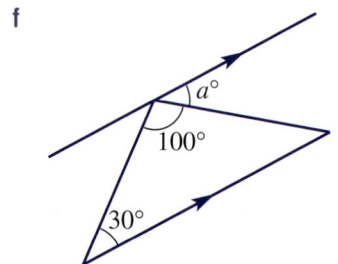

8 A plane flies horizontally 200 m above the ground. It detects two beacons on the ground. Some angles are known, and these are shown in the diagram. Find the angle marked $a°$ between the line of sight to the two beacons.

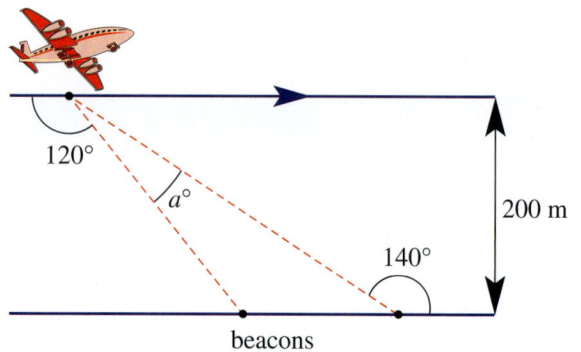

REASONING   9   9, 10   10, 11

9 In the **Key Ideas**, we can see how polygons can be decomposed into triangles.
   For example: A quadrilateral can be decomposed into two triangles without any intersecting diagonals
   so the angle sum of a quadrilateral equals $2 \times 180° = 360°$.
   a By decomposing into triangles, without any intersecting diagonals, how many triangles are formed
   in these polygons?
   i pentagon   **ii** hexagon   **iii** heptagon
   b Using your results from part **a**, determine the angle sum of the following polygons.
   i pentagon   **ii** hexagon   **iii** heptagon

10 Determine the angle sum of the following polygons.
   a octagon   **b** nonagon   **c** decagon

11 If S is the angle sum of a polygon with n sides, find a rule linking S with n.

ENRICHMENT: Exploring triangle theorems   –   –   12–14

12 a Find the sum $75° + 80°$.
   b Find the value of a in the diagram opposite.
   c What do you notice about the answers to parts **a** and **b**?
   d Do you think this would be true for other triangles with different
   angles? Explore.

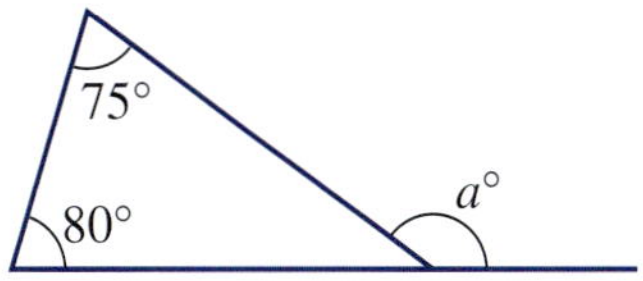

13 This diagram includes two parallel lines.
   a The angles marked $a°$ are always equal. From the list 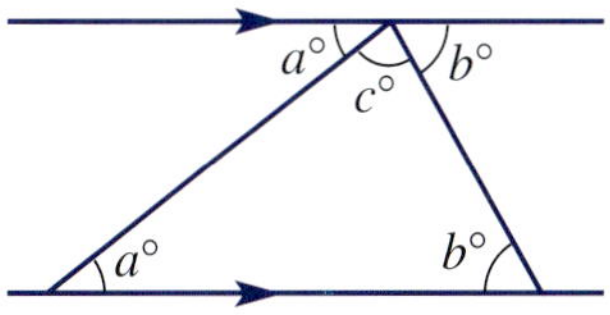
   (corresponding, alternate, cointerior, vertically opposite), give a
   reason why.
   b Give a reason why the angles marked $b°$ are always equal.
   c At the top of the diagram, angles $a°$, $b°$ and $c°$ lie on a straight line. What does this tell you about
   the three angles $a°$, $b°$ and $c°$ in the triangle?

14 Complete these proofs. Give reasons for each step where brackets are shown.
   a The angle sum in a triangle is $180°$.

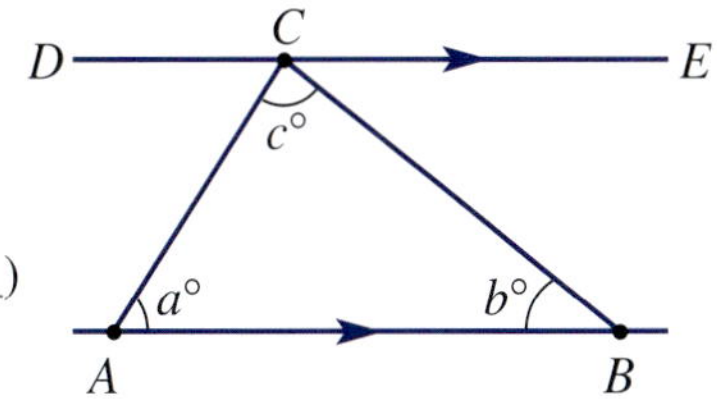

   $\angle DCA = a°$ (Alternate to $\angle BAC$ and DE is parallel to AB.)
   $\angle ECB = \underline{\hspace{1cm}}$ (\underline{\hspace{3cm}})
   $\angle DCA + \angle ACB + \angle ECB = \underline{\hspace{1cm}}$ (\underline{\hspace{3cm}})
   $\therefore a + b + c = \underline{\hspace{2cm}}$

   b The exterior angle outside a triangle is equal to the sum of the
   two interior opposite angles.

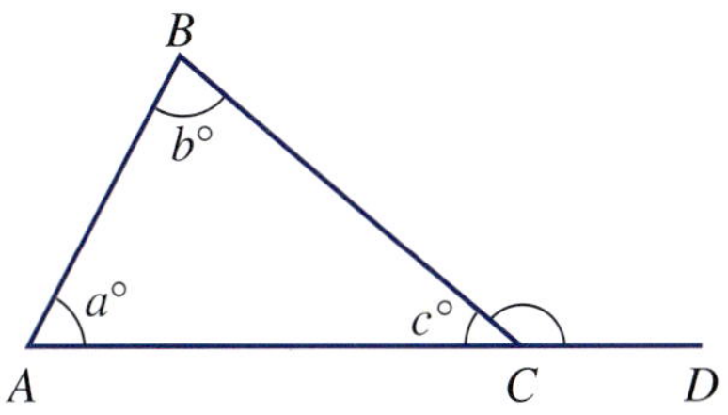

7H Symmetry

You see many symmetrical geometrical shapes in nature. The starfish and sunflower are two examples. Shapes such as these may have two types of symmetry: line and rotational.

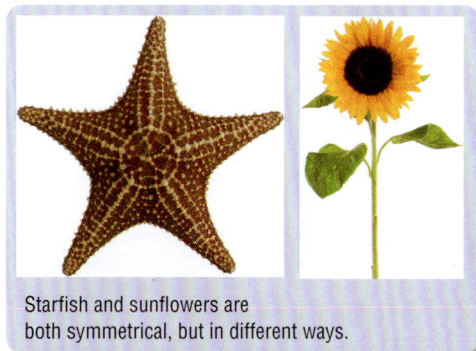

Starfish and sunflowers are both symmetrical, but in different ways.

Lesson starter: Working with symmetry

On a piece of paper, draw a square (with side lengths of about 10 cm) and a rectangle (with length of about 15 cm and width of about 10 cm), then cut them out.

•   How many ways can you fold each shape in half so that the two halves match exactly? The number of creases formed will be the number of lines of symmetry.
•   Now locate the centre of each shape and place a sharp pencil on this point. Rotate the shape 360°. How many times does the shape make an exact copy of itself in its original position? This number describes the rotational symmetry.

KEY IDEAS

■   An axis or **line of symmetry** divides a shape into two equal parts. It acts as a mirror line, with each half of the shape being a reflection of the other.
    •   An isosceles triangle has one line (axis) of symmetry.
    •   A rectangle has two lines (axes) of symmetry.

■   The **order of rotation** is the number of times a shape makes an exact copy of itself (in its original position) after rotating 360°.
    •   We say that there is no rotational symmetry if the order of **rotational symmetry** is equal to 1.

BUILDING UNDERSTANDING

1 How many ways could you fold each of these shapes in half so that the two halves match exactly? (To help you solve this problem, try cutting out the shapes and folding them.)

a square   b rectangle   c equilateral triangle

d isosceles triangle   e rhombus   f parallelogram

2 For the shapes listed in Question **1**, imagine rotating them 360° about their centre. How many times do you make an exact copy of the shape in its original position?

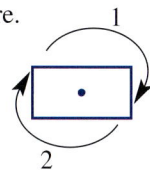

Example 17   Finding the symmetry of shapes

Give the number of lines of symmetry and the order of rotational symmetry for each of these shapes.

a rectangle

b regular pentagon

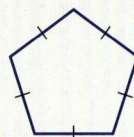

SOLUTION

EXPLANATION

a 2 lines of symmetry

rotational symmetry:
order 2

b 5 lines of symmetry

rotational symmetry:
order 5

Now you try

Give the number of lines of symmetry and the order of rotational symmetry for each of these shapes.

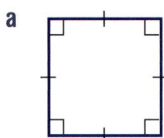

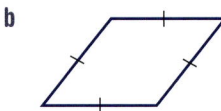

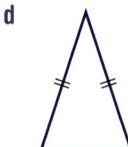

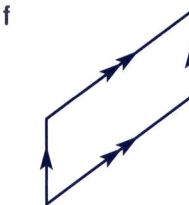

a isosceles trapezium

b equilateral triangle

Exercise 7H

FLUENCY   1–6   2–7   2–4, 6, 7

Example 17

1 Give the number of lines of symmetry and the order of rotational symmetry for this regular hexagon.

Example 17

2 Give the number of lines of symmetry and the order of rotational symmetry for each shape.

a

b

c

d

e

f

3 Name a type of triangle that has the following properties.
  a 3 lines of symmetry and order of rotational symmetry 3
  b 1 line of symmetry and no rotational symmetry
  c no line or rotational symmetry

4 List the special quadrilaterals that have these properties.
  a lines of symmetry:
    i 1   **ii** 2   **iii** 3   **iv** 4
  b rotational symmetry of order:
    i 1   **ii** 2   **iii** 3   **iv** 4

5 State the number of lines of symmetry and the order of rotational symmetry for each of the following.

a

b

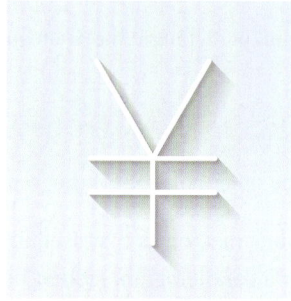

c

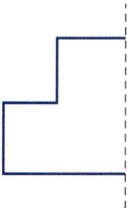

d

6 Of the capital letters of the alphabet shown in the font here, state which have:

a 1 line of symmetry

b 2 lines of symmetry

c rotational symmetry of order 2.

A B C D E F G H I J K L M
N O P Q R S T U V W X Y Z

7 Complete the other half of these shapes for the given axis of symmetry.

a

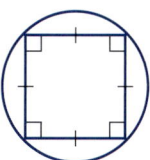

b

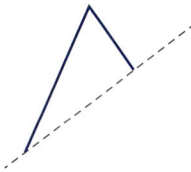

c

| PROBLEM-SOLVING | 8 | 8, 9 | 8, 9 |

8 Draw the following shapes, if possible.

a a quadrilateral with no lines of symmetry

b a hexagon with one line of symmetry

c a shape with line symmetry of order 7 and rotational symmetry of order 7

d a diagram with no line of symmetry but rotational symmetry of order 3

e a diagram with line of symmetry of order 1 and no rotational symmetry

9 These diagrams are made up of more than one shape. State the order of line symmetry and of rotational symmetry.

a

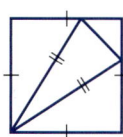

b

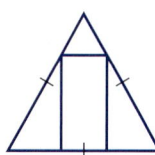

c

10 Many people think a rectangle has four lines of symmetry, including the diagonals.

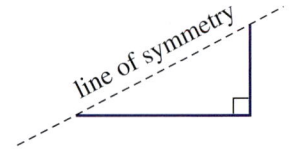

   a Complete the other half of this diagram to show that this is not true.

   b Using the same method as that used in part **a**, show that the diagonals of a parallelogram are not lines of symmetry.

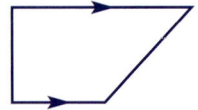

line of symmetry

11 A trapezium has one pair of parallel lines.
   a State whether trapeziums always have:
     i line symmetry
     ii rotational symmetry.
   b What type of trapezium will have one line of symmetry?

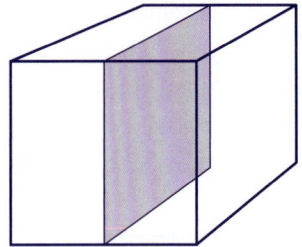

12 Some solid objects also have symmetry. Rather than line symmetry, they have **plane symmetry**. This cube shows one plane of symmetry, but there are more that could be drawn.

State the number of planes of symmetry for each of these solids.
   a cube   **b** rectangular prism   **c** right square pyramid

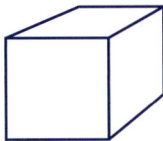
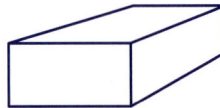
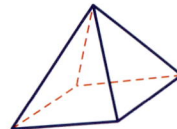

   d right triangular prism   **e** cylinder   **f** sphere

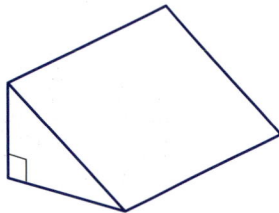
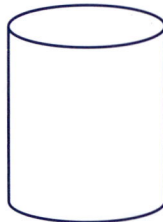
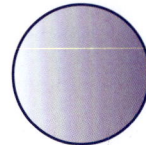

7I   Reflection and rotation

LEARNING INTENTIONS

*   To understand that a shape can be reflected or rotated to give an image
*   To be able to draw the result of a point or shape being reflected in a mirror line
*   To be able to draw the result of a point or shape being rotated about a point

Reflection and *rotation* are two types of transformations that involve a change in position of the points on an object. If a shape is reflected in a mirror line or rotated about a point, the size of the shape is unchanged. Hence, the transformations reflection and rotation are said to be *isometric*.

Lesson starter: Draw the image

Here is a shape on a grid.

*   Draw the image (result) after reflecting the shape in the mirror line *A*.
*   Draw the image (result) after reflecting the shape in the mirror line *B*.
*   Draw the image after rotating the shape about point *O* by $180°$.
*   Draw the image after rotating the shape about point *O* by $90°$ clockwise.
*   Draw the image after rotating the shape about point *O* by $90°$ anticlockwise.

Discuss what method you used to draw each image and the relationship between the position of the shape and its image after each transformation.

When designing 'The Mirrored Staircase' in this picture, the architect has drawn one staircase and then reflected its design across the vertical line that is the axis of symmetry.

KEY IDEAS

■ **Reflection** and **rotation** are **isometric transformations** that give an **image** of an object or shape without changing its shape and size.

■ The **image** of point *A* is denoted *A'*.

■ A reflection involves a mirror line, as shown in the diagram opposite.

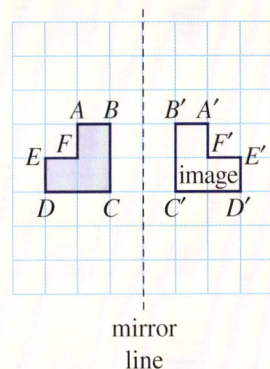

■ A rotation involves a centre point of rotation (C) and an angle of
rotation, as shown.

- A pair of compasses can be used to draw each circle, to help find
  the position of image points.

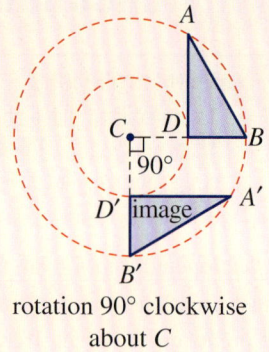

rotation 90° clockwise
about C

BUILDING UNDERSTANDING

1 Use the grid to reflect each shape in the given mirror line.

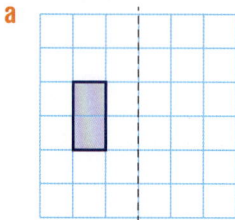

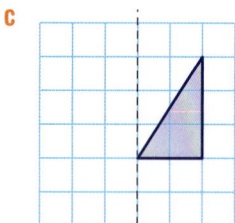

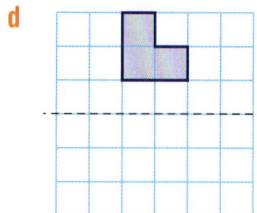

a

b

c

d

e

f

2 Give the coordinates of the image point A′ after the point A(2, 0) is
rotated about point C(0, 0) by the following angles.

a 180° clockwise
b 180° anticlockwise
c 90° clockwise
d 90° anticlockwise

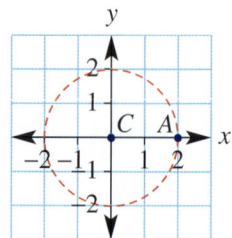

3 a Are the size and shape of an object changed after a reflection?
   b Are the size and shape of an object changed after a rotation?

Example 18   Drawing reflections

Draw the reflected image of this shape and give the
coordinates of A′, B′, C′ and D′. The y-axis is the mirror
line.

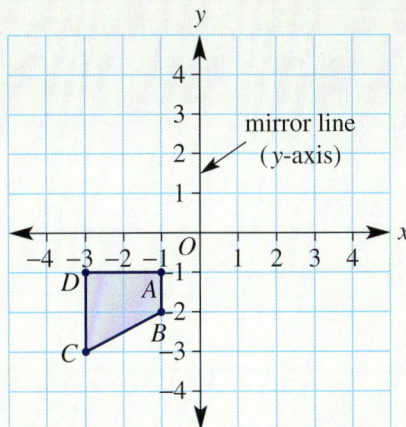

SOLUTION

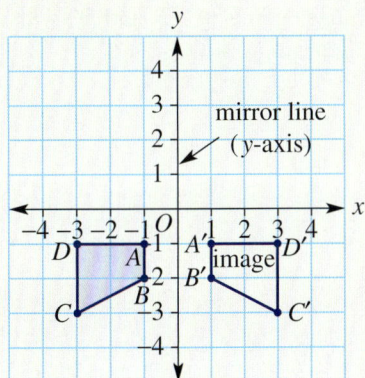

$A' = (1, -1)$, $B' = (1, -2)$, $C' = (3, -3)$, $D' = (3, -1)$

EXPLANATION

Reflect each vertex A, B, C and
D about the mirror line. The line
segment from each point to its image
should be at 90° to the mirror line.

Now you try

Draw the reflected image of this shape and give the coordinates
of A′, B′, C′ and D′. The y-axis is the mirror line.

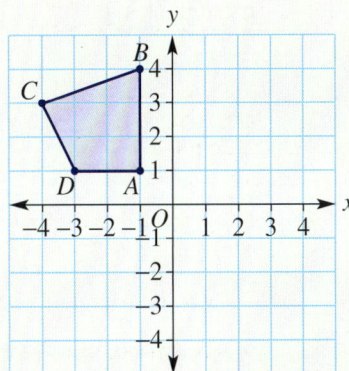

Example 19   Drawing rotations

Draw the image of this shape and give the coordinates
of A', B' and D' after carrying out the following rotations.

a   90° anticlockwise about C

b   180° about C

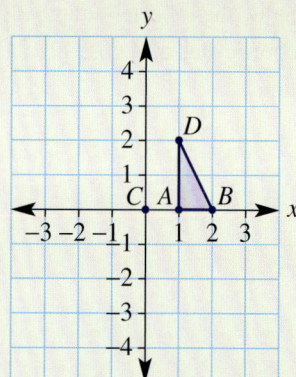

SOLUTION

a

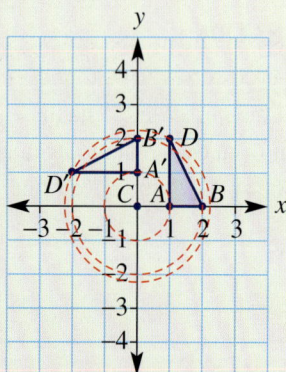

$A' = (0, 1),\ B' = (0, 2),\ D' = (-2, 1)$

b

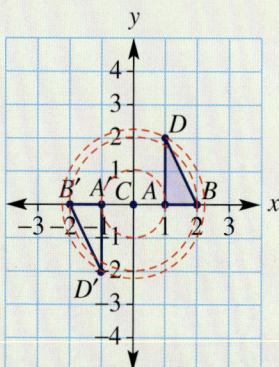

$A' = (-1, 0),\ B' = (-2, 0),\ D' = (-1, -2)$

EXPLANATION

Rotate each point on a circular arc around
point C by 90° anticlockwise.

Join the three image points (A', B' and D') with
line segments to form the result.

Rotate each point on a circular arc around
point C by 180° in either direction.

Join the three image points (A', B' and D') with
line segments to form the result.

Now you try

Draw the image of this shape and give the coordinates of
A', B' and D' after carrying out the following rotations.

a 90° anticlockwise about C

b 180° about C

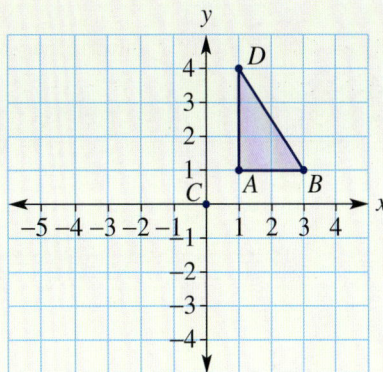

Exercise 7I

FLUENCY 1, 2(½), 3, 4 | 2–3(½), 4, 5 | 2–3(½), 4, 5

1 Draw the reflected image of this shape and give the coordinates of A', B', C' and D'. The y-axis is the mirror line.

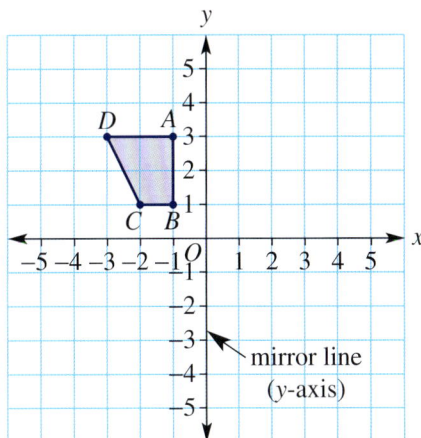

2 Draw the image of each shape in the mirror line and give the coordinates of A', B', C' and D'. Note that the y-axis is the mirror line for parts **a** to **c**, whereas the x-axis is the mirror line for parts **d** to **f**.

a

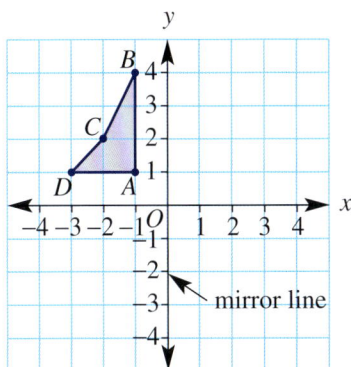

b

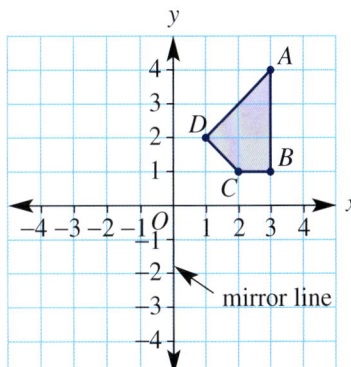

c
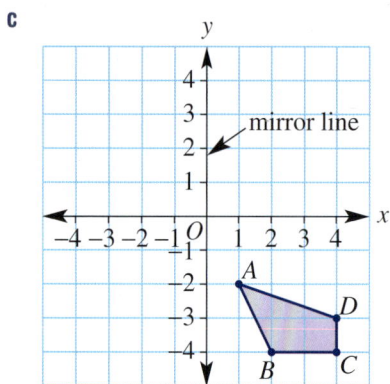

d
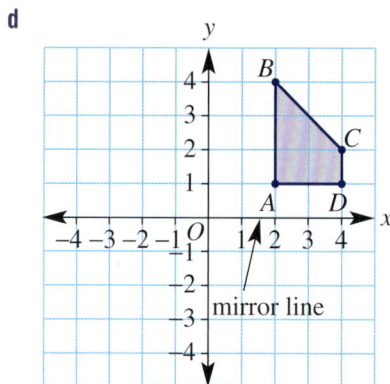

e
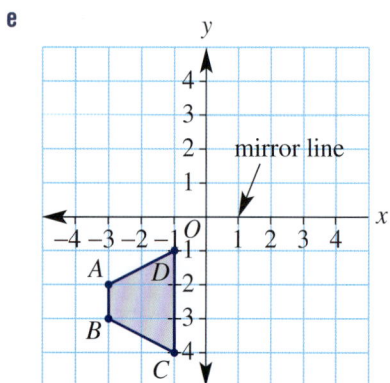

f

3 Give the new coordinates of the image point A' after point A has been rotated around point $C(0, 0)$ by:

a 180° clockwise

b 90° clockwise

c 90° anticlockwise

d 270° clockwise

e 360° anticlockwise

f 180° anticlockwise.

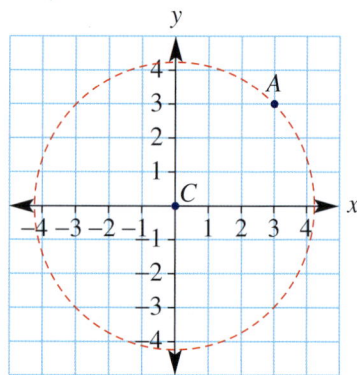

Example 19

4 Draw the image of this shape and give the coordinates of A', B' and D' after the following rotations.

a 90° anticlockwise about C

b 180° about C

c 90° clockwise about C

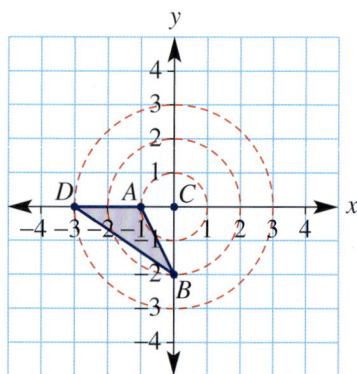

ample 19   **5**   Draw the image of this shape and give the coordinates of A', B' and D'
after the following rotations.

   a   90° anticlockwise about C
   b   180° about C
   c   90° clockwise about C

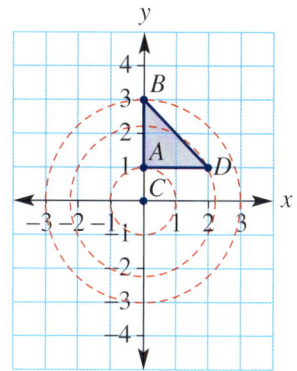

| **PROBLEM-SOLVING** | 6, 7 | 6–8 | 6, 8, 9 |

6   The mirror lines on these grids are at a 45° angle. Draw the reflected image.

   a   **b**   **c**

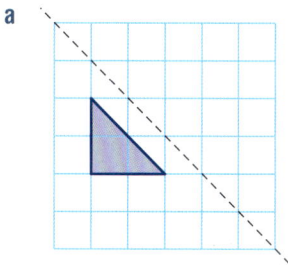   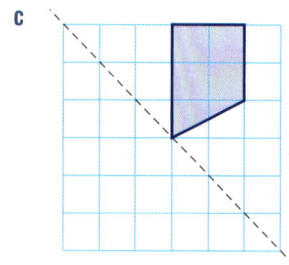

   d   **e**   **f**

7   On the Cartesian plane, the point $A(-2, 5)$ is reflected in the x-axis and this image point is then
reflected in the y-axis. What are the coordinates of the final image?

8   A point, $B(2, 3)$, is rotated about the point $C(1, 1)$. State the coordinates
of the image point B' for the following rotations.

   a   180°
   b   90° clockwise
   c   90° anticlockwise

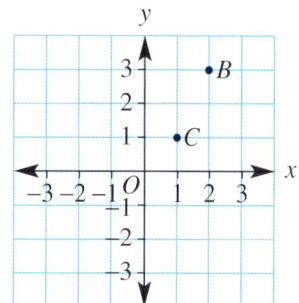

9 For each shape given, by how many degrees has it been rotated and in which direction?

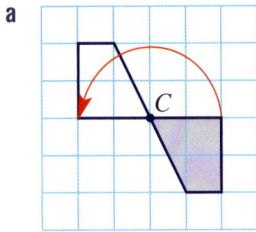

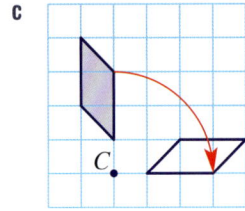

a

b

c

10 a By repeatedly reflecting a shape over a moving mirror line, patterns can be formed. This right-angled triangle for example is reflected 4 times by placing the mirror line vertically and on the right side each time. Create a pattern using these starting shapes by repeatedly placing the vertical mirror line on the right side.

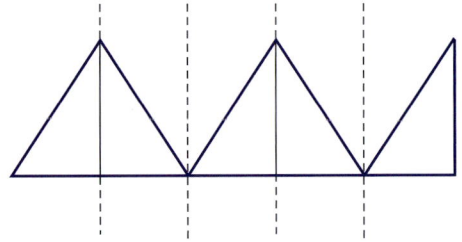

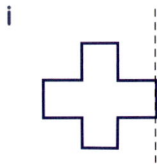

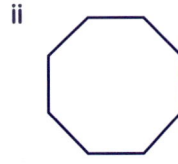

i

ii

iii Create your own using reflection.

b By repeatedly rotating a shape about a point, patterns can be formed. This diagram shows a semicircle rotated by 90° three times about the given point. Create a pattern using three 90° rotations about the given point.

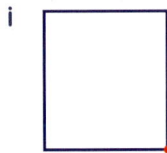

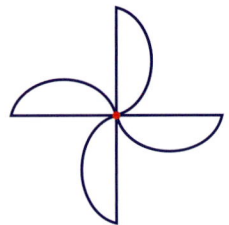

i

ii

iii Create your own using rotation.

c See if you can combine reflections and rotations to create more complex patterns.

11 Write the missing number in these sentences.

a Rotating a point 90° clockwise is the same as rotating a point _____ anticlockwise.

b Rotating a point 38° anticlockwise is the same as rotating a point _____ clockwise.

c A point is rotated 370° clockwise. This is the same as rotating the point _____ clockwise.

12 A point S has coordinates $(-2, 5)$.

a Find the coordinates of the image point S' after a rotation 180° about $C(0, 0)$.

b Find the coordinates of the image point S' after a reflection in the x-axis followed by a reflection in the y-axis.

c What do you notice about the image points in parts **a** and **b**?

d Test your observation on the point $T(-4, -1)$ by repeating parts **a** and **b**.

13 Explore reflecting shapes dynamically, using interactive geometry software.

   a On a grid, create any shape using the polygon tool.

   b Construct a mirror line.

   c Use the reflection tool to create the reflected image about your mirror line.

   d Drag the vertices of your original shape and observe the changes in the image. Also try dragging the mirror line.

14 Explore rotating shapes dynamically, using interactive geometry software.

   a On a grid, create any shape using the polygon tool.

   b Construct a centre of rotation point and a rotating angle (or number).

   c Use the rotation tool to create the rotated image that has your nominated centre of rotation and angle.

   d Drag the vertices of your original shape and observe the changes in the image. Also try changing the angle of rotation.

The following problems will investigate practical situations drawing upon knowledge and skills developed throughout the chapter. In attempting to solve these problems, aim to identify the key information, use diagrams, formulate ideas, apply strategies, make calculations and check and communicate your solutions.

Roof trusses

1   When building a house, the frame to hold the roof up is constructed of roof trusses. Roof trusses come in different designs and define the pitch, or angle, of the external roof and the internal ceiling. The image here shows a roof with W trusses.
    The standard W truss provides an external pitch for the roof and a flat internal ceiling for the plaster.

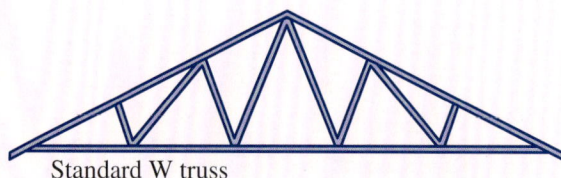

Standard W truss

A builder is interested in how the lengths and angles work together for a standard W roof truss and the overall height of the truss above the ceiling which depends on the pitch angle.

a   Why do you think this design of truss is called a W truss?

b   How many segments of timber are required to construct one W truss?

c   Using the guidelines below, construct an accurate scale of a W truss in your workbook with a roof pitch of 30°.

   i   Draw a horizontal base beam of 12 cm.

   ii   Divide the base beam into five equal segments.

   iii   Measure 30° angles and draw the two sloping roof beams.

   iv   Divide each sloping roof beam into three equal segments.

   v   Draw the internal support beams by connecting lines between the equal segment markings on the roof and base beams.

d   On your accurate diagram, measure and label each of the internal angles formed by the support beams.

e   From your answers in part **d**, label any parallel support beams.

f   From your accurate diagram, what is the vertical height from the top of the roof to the ceiling (base beam)?

g   Investigate the angle (pitch) of either a roof at school or a roof at home. If possible, take a photo of the roof trusses and measure the relevant angles.

The perfect path for a hole-in-one

2   Visualising angles is a key to successfully playing mini-golf. When a golf ball bounces off a straight wall we can assume that the angle at which it hits the wall (incoming angle) is the same as the angle at which it leaves the wall (outgoing angle).

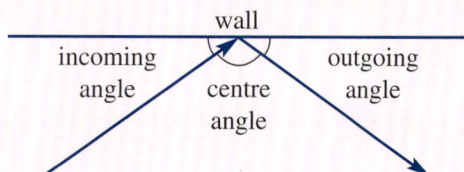

You are interested in drawing a path where incoming angles equal outgoing angles so that you can score a hole-in-one.

A sample mini-golf hole is shown here.

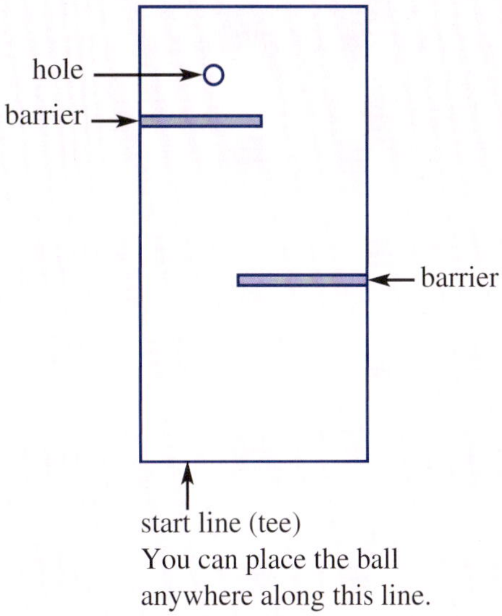

A two-bounce pathway

a   Your first try. You may need to copy the diagram onto paper first. Select a point on the starting line where you choose to tee off from and choose an angle to hit the ball at. Trace this path, ensuring each outgoing angle equals each incoming angle and see how close you end up to going in the hole.

b   Label each of your angles along your path.

c   Can you draw an accurate path for a hole-in-one?

A three-bounce pathway

d   Can you design a three-bounce path for a hole-in-one? Label and measure your angles.

Design your own

e   Design your own mini-golf hole that is possible for someone to score a hole-in-one through bouncing off walls or barriers. Show the correct pathway.
(*Hint:* You may wish to draw the correct pathway first and then place in the barriers to make it challenging for players.)

hole
barrier

barrier

start line (tee)
You can place the ball anywhere along this line.

Tessellating bathroom tiles

3   A tessellation is defined as an arrangement of shapes closely fitted together in a repeated pattern without gaps or overlapping.

Elise is interested in what simple shapes tessellate and how to tile a bathroom using regular and irregular shapes.

a   Name the only three regular polygons that tessellate by themselves.

b   Why can't a regular pentagon or a regular octagon tessellate by themselves?

c   Create your own tessellation using a combination of regular triangles, squares and hexagons. Elise is designing her new bathroom and wishes to have a floor tile pattern involving just pentagons. Elise's builder says that it is impossible to tessellate the bathroom floor with regular pentagons, but he is confident that he can tessellate the floor with irregular pentagons if he can find the right tiles.

d   Suggest what the internal angles of an irregular pentagon tile should be to ensure they tessellate with one another.

e   Draw an irregular pentagon that would tessellate with itself.

f   Create a bathroom floor pattern to show Elise how irregular pentagon tiles can tessellate.

7J   Translation

Translation involves a shift in an object left, right, up or down. The orientation of a shape is unchanged. Translation is another isometric transformation because the size and shape of the image is unchanged.

Lesson starter: Describing a translation

Consider this shape $ABCD$ and its image $A'B'C'D'$.

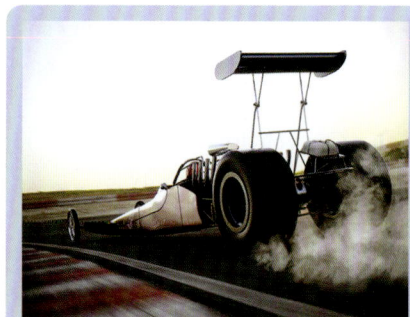

In a dragster race along 300 m of straight track, the main body of the car is translated down the track in a single direction.

- Use the words left, right, up or down to describe how the shape $ABCD$, shown opposite, could be translated (shifted) to its image.
- Can you think of a second combination of translations that give the same image?
- How would you describe the reverse translation?

KEY IDEAS

■ **Translation** is an isometric transformation involving a shift left, right, up or down.

■ Describing a translation involves saying how many units a shape is shifted left, right, up and/or down.

BUILDING UNDERSTANDING

1 Point *A* has coordinates (3, 2). State the coordinates of the image point *A′* when point *A* is translated in each of the following ways.

a 1 unit right
b 2 units left
c 3 units up
d 1 unit down
e 1 unit left and 2 units up
f 3 units left and 1 unit down
g 2 units right and 1 unit down
h 0 units left and 2 units down

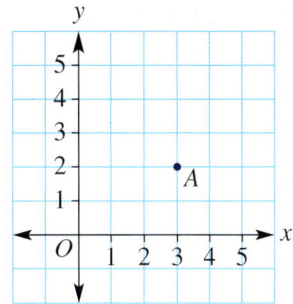

2 A point is translated to its image. State the missing word (i.e. left, right, up or down) for each sentence.

a (1, 1) is translated _____ to the point (1, 3).
b (5, 4) is translated _____ to the point (1, 4).
c (7, 2) is translated _____ to the point (7, 0).
d (3, 0) is translated _____ to the point (3, 1).
e (5, 1) is translated _____ to the point (4, 1).
f (2, 3) is translated _____ to the point (1, 3).
g (0, 2) is translated _____ to the point (5, 2).
h (7, 6) is translated _____ to the point (11, 6).

3 The point (7, 4) is translated to the point (0, 1).

a How far left has the point been translated?
b How far down has the point been translated?
c If the point (0, 1) is translated to (7, 4):
   i How far right has the point been translated?
   ii How far up has the point been translated?

Example 20   Translating shapes

Draw the image of the triangle *ABC* after a translation 2 units to the right and 3 units down.

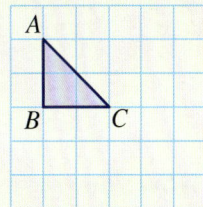

Continued on next page

SOLUTION

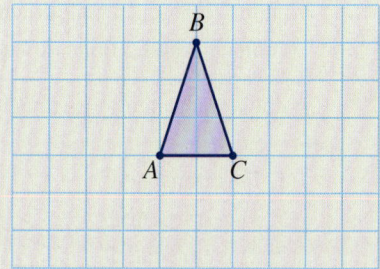

EXPLANATION

Shift every vertex 2 units to the right and 3 units down. Then join the vertices to form the image.

Now you try

Draw the image of the triangle ABC after a translation 1 unit left and 3 units down.

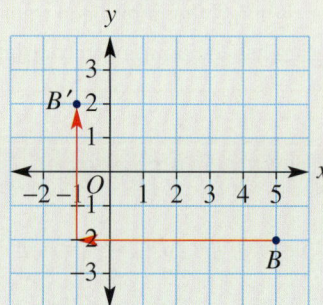

Example 21   Describing translations

A point $B(5, -2)$ is translated to $B'(-1, 2)$. Describe the translation.

SOLUTION

Translation is 6 units left and 4 units up.

EXPLANATION

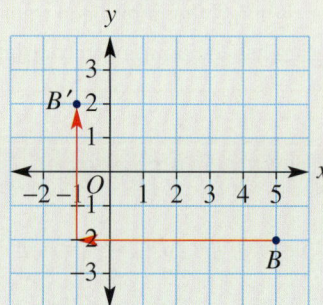

Now you try

A point $B(-2, 5)$ is translated to $B'(4, -3)$. Describe the translation.

Exercise 7J

FLUENCY   1, 2, 3–4(½)   2–4(½)   2(½), 3–4(⅓)

mple 20

1   Draw the image of the triangle *ABC* after a translation 3 units to the left and 2 units down.

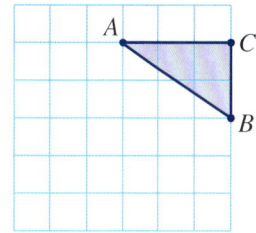

mple 20

2   Draw the image of these shapes after each translation.

   a   3 units left and 1 unit up

   b   1 unit right and 2 units up

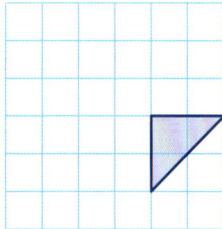

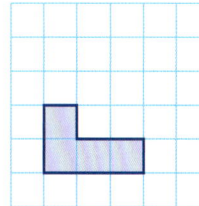

   c   3 units right and 2 units down

   d   4 units left and 2 units down

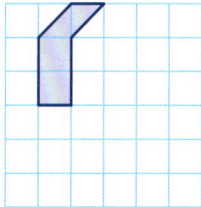

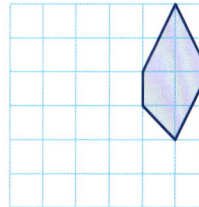

3   Point *A* has coordinates $(-2, 3)$. Write the coordinates of the image point A' when point *A* is translated in each of the following ways.

   a   3 units right
   b   2 units left
   c   2 units down
   d   5 units down
   e   2 units up
   f   10 units right
   g   3 units right and 1 unit up
   h   4 units right and 2 units down
   i   5 units right and 6 units down
   j   1 unit left and 2 units down
   k   3 units left and 1 unit up
   l   2 units left and 5 units down

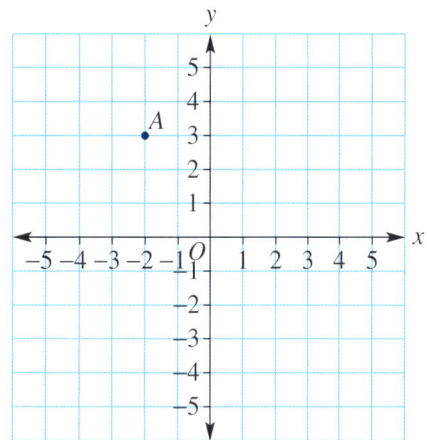

Example 21

4 Describe the translation when each point is translated to its image. Give your answer similar to these examples: '4 units right' or '2 units left and 3 units up'.

a $A(1, 3)$ is translated to $A'(1, 6)$.   **b** $B(4, 7)$ is translated to $B'(4, 0)$.

c $C(-1, 3)$ is translated to $C'(-1, -1)$.   **d** $D(-2, 8)$ is translated to $D'(-2, 10)$.

e $E(4, 3)$ is translated to $E'(-1, 3)$.   **f** $F(2, -4)$ is translated to $F'(4, -4)$.

g $G(0, 0)$ is translated to $G'(-1, 4)$.   **h** $H(-1, -1)$ is translated to $H'(2, 5)$.

i $I(-3, 8)$ is translated to $I'(0, 4)$.   **j** $J(2, -5)$ is translated to $J'(-1, 6)$.

k $K(-10, 2)$ is translated to $K'(2, -1)$.   **l** $L(6, 10)$ is translated to $L'(-4, -3)$.

PROBLEM-SOLVING	5	5, 6	6, 7

5 A point, A, is translated to its image, A'. Describe the translation that takes A' to A (i.e. the reverse translation).

a $A(2, 3)$ and $A'(4, 1)$

b $B(0, 4)$ and $B'(4, 0)$

c $C(0, -3)$ and $C'(-1, 2)$

d $D(4, 6)$ and $D'(-2, 8)$

6 If only horizontal or vertical translations of distance 1 are allowed, how many different paths are there from points A to B on each grid below? No point can be visited more than once.

a

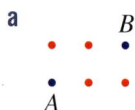

b

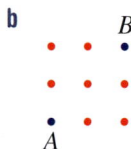

7 Starting at $(0, 0)$ on the Cartesian plane, how many different points can you move to if a maximum of 3 units in total can be translated in any of the four directions of left, right, up or down with all translations being whole numbers? Do not count the point $(0, 0)$.

REASONING	8	8	8, 9

8 A shape is translated to its image. Explain why the shape's size and orientation is unchanged.

9 A combination of translations can be replaced with one single translation. For example, if $(1, 1)$ is translated 3 units right and 2 units down, followed by a translation of 6 units left and 5 units up, then the final image point $(-2, 4)$ could be obtained with the single translation 3 units left and 3 units up. Describe the single translation that replaces these combinations of translations.

a $(1, 1)$ is translated 2 units left and 1 unit up, followed by a translation of 5 units right and 2 units down.

b $(6, -2)$ is translated 3 units right and 3 units up, followed by a translation of 2 units left and 1 unit down.

c $(-1, 4)$ is translated 4 units right and 6 units down, followed by a translation of 6 units left and 2 units up.

d $(-3, 4)$ is translated 4 units left and 4 units down, followed by a translation of 10 units right and 11 units up.

ENRICHMENT: Combined transformations   –   –   10

10 Write the coordinates of the image point after each sequence of transformations. For each part, apply the next transformation to the image of the previous transformation.

a (2, 3)
- reflection in the x-axis
- reflection in the y-axis
- translation 2 units left and 2 units up

b (−1, 6)
- translation 5 units right and 3 units down
- reflection in the y-axis
- reflection in the x-axis

c (−4, 2)
- rotation 180° about (0, 0)
- reflection in the y-axis
- translation 3 units left and 4 units up

d (−3, −7)
- rotation 90° clockwise about (0, 0)
- reflection in the x-axis
- translation 6 units left and 2 units down

e (−4, 8)
- rotation 90° anticlockwise about (0, 0)
- translation 4 units right and 6 units up
- reflection in the x- and the y-axis

Construction material moved onto a building by a modern crane has undergone a combination of transformations.

7K Drawing solids

LEARNING INTENTIONS
- To be able to draw pyramids, cylinders and cones
- To be able to use square or isometric dot paper to accurately draw solids

Three-dimensional solids can be represented as a drawing on a two-dimensional surface (e.g. paper or computer screen), provided some basic rules are followed.

Architects create 3D models of building plans by hand or with computer software.

Lesson starter: Can you draw a cube?

Try to draw a cube. Here are two bad examples.

- What is wrong with these drawings?
- What basic rules do you need to follow when drawing a cube?

KEY IDEAS

■ Draw cubes and rectangular prisms by keeping:
  - parallel sides pointing in the same direction
  - parallel sides the same length.

■ Draw **pyramids** by joining the apex with the vertices on the base.

triangular pyramid (tetrahedron)

apex

triangular base

square pyramid

apex

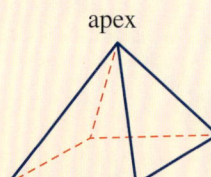

square base

■ Draw **cylinders** and **cones** by starting with an oval shape.

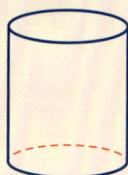

cylinder

cone

■ **Square** and **isometric dot paper** can help to accurately draw solids. Drawings made on isometric dot paper clearly show the cubes that make up the solid.

square dot paper

isometric dot paper

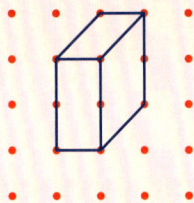

BUILDING UNDERSTANDING

1 Copy these diagrams and add lines to complete the solid. Use dashed line for invisible sides.

a cube

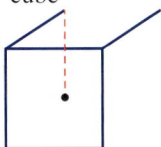

b cylinder

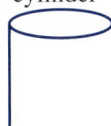

c square pyramid

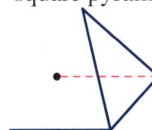

2 Cubes are stacked to form these solids. How many cubes are there in each solid?

a

b

c

Example 22   Drawing solids

Draw these solids.

a a cone on plain paper

b this solid on isometric dot paper

SOLUTION

a

b

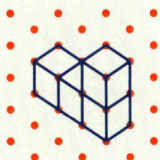

EXPLANATION

Draw an oval shape for the base and the apex point. Dot any line or curve which may be invisible on the solid.
Join the apex to the sides of the base.

Rotate the solid slightly and draw each cube starting at the front and working back.

Now you try

Draw these solids.

a   a square-based pyramid on plain paper

b   this solid on isometric dot paper

Exercise 7K

FLUENCY	1–4	2–4, 5(½)	2, 4, 5(½)

Example 22a

1   Draw a square-based prism on plain paper.

Example 22a

2   On plain paper, draw an example of these common solids.

    a   cube

    b   tetrahedron

    c   cylinder

    d   cone

    e   square-based pyramid

    f   rectangular prism

Example 22b

3   Copy these solids onto square dot paper.

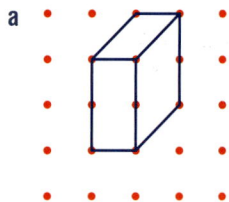

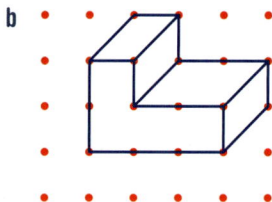

    a

    b

Example 22b

4   Draw these solids onto isometric dot paper.

    a

    b

    c

5   Here is a cylinder with its top view (circle) and side view (rectangle).

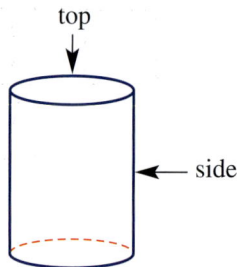

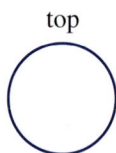

Draw the shapes which are the top view and side view of these solids.

a cube

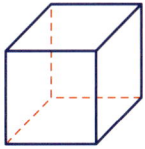

b square prism

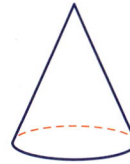

c cone

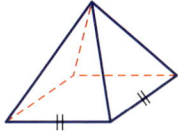

d square pyramid

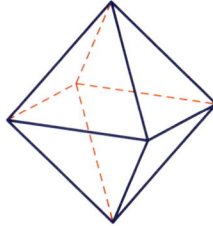

e octahedron

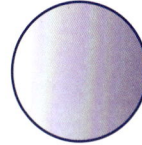

f sphere

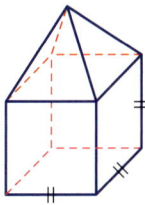

g square pyramid on cube

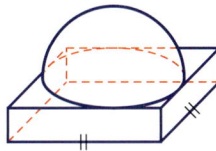

h hemisphere $\left(\frac{1}{2}\text{ sphere}\right)$ on square prism

i cone on hemisphere

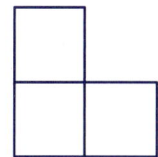

PROBLEM-SOLVING

6   6, 7   7, 8

6 Here is the top (plan or bird's eye) view of a stack of 5 cubes. How many different stacks of 5 cubes could this represent?

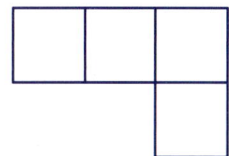

7 Here is the top (plan) view of a stack of 7 cubes. How many different stacks of 7 cubes could this represent?

8 Draw these solids, making sure that:
  i each vertex can be seen clearly
  ii dashed lines are used for invisible sides.
  a tetrahedron (solid with 4 faces)
  b octahedron (solid with 8 faces)
  c pentagonal pyramid (pyramid with pentagonal base)

REASONING   9   9   9, 10

9   Andrea draws two solids as shown. Aiden says that they are drawings of exactly the same solid. Is
Aiden correct? Give reasons.

   and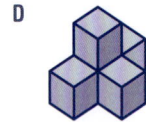

10 Match the solids **a**, **b**, **c** and **d** with an identical solid chosen from **A**, **B**, **C** and **D**.

a 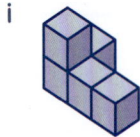   **b**   **c** 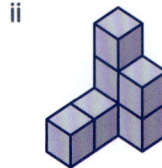   **d**

A 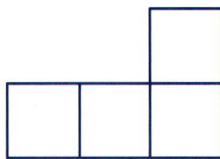   **B** 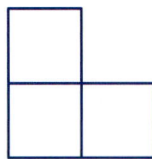   **C**   **D**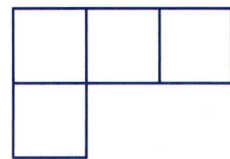

ENRICHMENT: Three viewpoints   –   –   11

11 This diagram shows the front and left sides of a solid.

a Draw the front, left and top views of these solids.

   i   **ii**

b Draw a solid that has these views.

   i   front   left   top

   ii   front   left   top

7L   Nets of solids

LEARNING INTENTIONS
- To understand that a net is a two-dimensional representation of a solid's faces
- To know what a polyhedron is
- To know what the five Platonic solids are
- To be able to draw a net of simple solids

The ancient Greek philosophers studied the properties of polyhedra and how these could be used to explain the natural world. Plato (427–347 BCE) reasoned that the building blocks of all three-dimensional objects were regular polyhedra which have faces that are identical in size and shape. There are five regular polyhedra, called the Platonic solids after Plato, which were thought to represent fire, earth, air, water and the universe or cosmos.

Platonic solids form excellent dice; their symmetry and identical faces provide fair and random results. Platonic dice have 4, 6, 8, 12 or 20 faces and are used in role-playing games such as 'Dungeons and Dragons'.

Lesson starter: Net of a cube

Here is one Platonic solid, the regular hexahedron or cube, and its net.

If the faces of the solid are unfolded to form a net, you can clearly see the 6 faces.

Can you draw a different net of a cube? How do you know it will fold to form a cube? Compare this with other nets in your class.

KEY IDEAS

■ A **net** of a solid is an unfolded two-dimensional representation of all the faces. Here are two examples.

square pyramid

cylinder

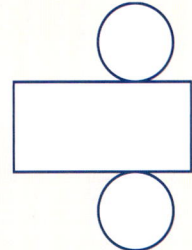

■ A **polyhedron** (plural: polyhedra) is a solid with flat faces.
- They can be named by their number of faces, e.g. tetrahedron (4 faces), hexahedron (6 faces).

■ The five **Platonic solids** are **regular polyhedra** each with identical regular faces and the same number of faces meeting at each vertex.

- regular tetrahedron (4 equilateral triangular faces)

- regular hexahedron or cube (6 square faces)

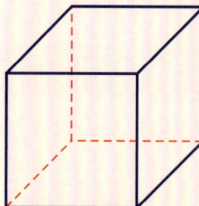

- regular octahedron (8 equilateral triangular faces)

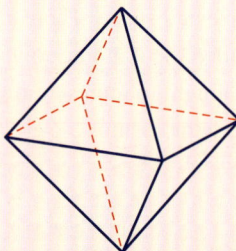

- regular dodecahedron (12 regular pentagonal faces)

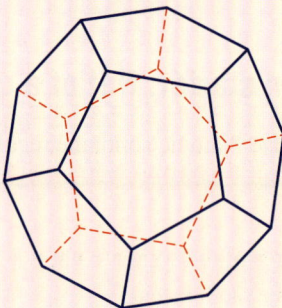

- regular icosahedron (20 equilateral triangular faces)

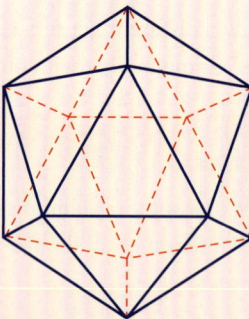

BUILDING UNDERSTANDING

1 State the missing words in these sentences.
  a A regular polygon will have _____ length sides.
  b All the faces on regular polyhedra are _____ polygons.
  c The _____ solids is the name given to the 5 regular polyhedra.

2 Which of the following nets would *not* fold up to form a cube?

A 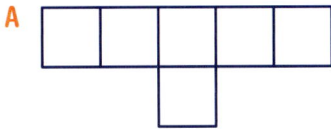 B C

3 Name the type of shapes that form the faces of these Platonic solids.

a tetrahedron   b hexahedron   c octahedron

d dodecahedron   e icosahedron

4 Name the solids that have the following nets.

a 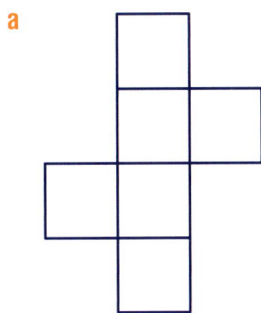   b 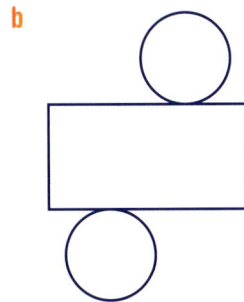   c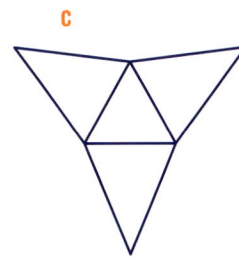

Example 23   Drawing nets

Draw a net for these solids.

a rectangular prism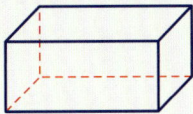

b regular tetrahedron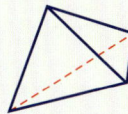

SOLUTION

a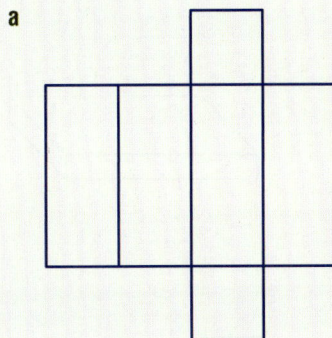

EXPLANATION

This is one possible net for the rectangular prism, but others are possible.

Continued on next page

b

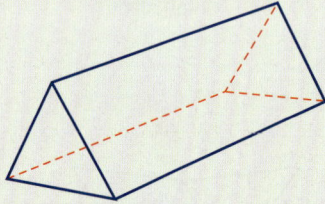

Each triangle is equilateral. Each outer triangle folds up to meet centrally above the centre triangle.

Now you try

Draw a net for these solids.

a triangular prism

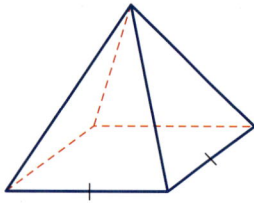

b square-based pyramid

Exercise 7L

FLUENCY   1–5   2–6   3(½), 4–6

Example 23a **1** Draw a net for this rectangular prism.

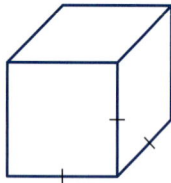

Example 23b **2** Draw a net for this pyramid.

Example 23 **3** Draw one possible net for these solids.

a   **b**   **c**

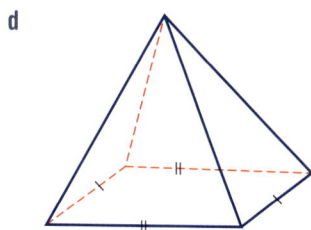

d

e

f

4 Which Platonic solid(s) fit these descriptions? There may be more than one.

   a Its faces are equilateral triangles.

   b It has 20 faces.

   c It has 6 vertices.

   d It is a pyramid.

   e It has 12 sides.

   f It has sides which meet at right angles (not necessarily all sides).

5 Here are nets for the five Platonic solids. Name the Platonic solid that matches each one.

   a

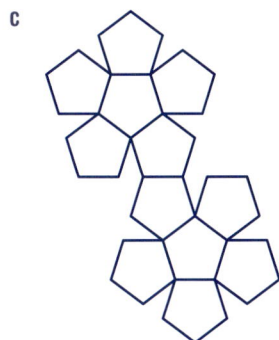

   b

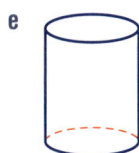

   c

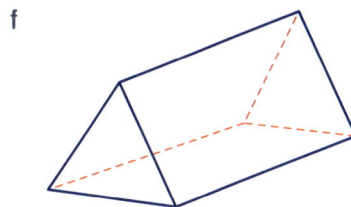

   d

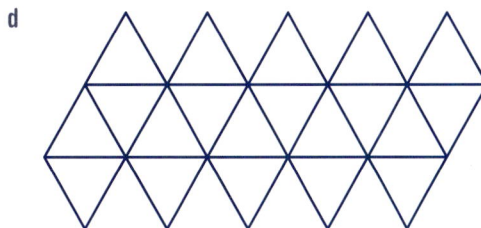

   e

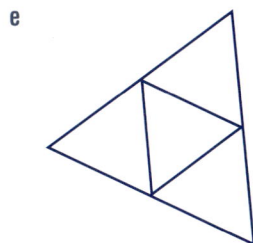

6 How many faces meet at each vertex for these Platonic solids?

   a tetrahedron   **b** hexahedron   **c** octahedron

   d dodecahedron   **e** icosahedron

PROBLEM-SOLVING		7	7	7, 8

7 Try drawing a net for a cone. Check by drawing a net and cutting it out to see if it works. Here are two cones to try.

a

b

8 How many different nets are there for these solids? Do not count rotations or reflections of the same net.

    a regular tetrahedron   **b** cube

REASONING		9	9	9, 10

9 Imagine gluing two tetrahedrons together by joining two faces as shown, to form a new solid.

    a How many faces are there on this new solid?

    b Are all the faces identical?

    c Why do you think this new solid is not a Platonic solid.

        (*Hint:* Look at the number of faces meeting at each vertex.)

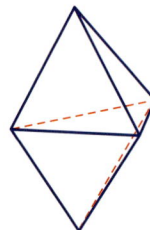

10 Decide if it is possible to draw a net for a sphere.

ENRICHMENT: Number of cubes		–	–	11

11 Consider a number of 1 cm cubes stacked together to form a larger cube. This one, for example, contains $3 \times 3 \times 3 = 27$ cubes.

    a For the solid shown:

        i how many 1 cm cubes are completely inside the solid with no faces on the outside?

        ii how many 1 cm cubes have at least one face on the outside?

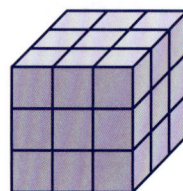

    b Copy and complete this table.

n (side length)	1	2	3	4	5
n^3 (number of 1 cm cubes)	1	8			
Number of inside cubes	0				
Number of outside cubes	1				

    c For a cube stack of side length n cm, $n \geqslant 2$, find the rule for:

        i the number of cubes in total

        ii the number of inside cubes

        iii the number of outside cubes.

BMX ramp

Marion is designing a BMX ramp and wishes to use three equal length pieces of steel for each side of the ramp. Her design is shown in this diagram with the three pieces of equal length steel shown as the line segments AB, BC and CD, shown in green.

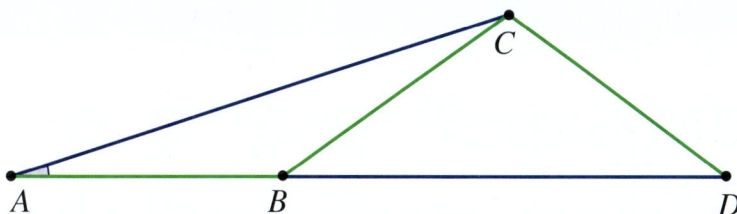

The points A, B and D are on a straight line and represent the base of the ramp. The line segment AC represents the ramp slope.

Present a report for the following tasks and ensure that you show clear mathematical working and explanations where appropriate.

Preliminary task

   a Copy the diagram above, putting dashes on AB, BC and CD to indicate they are the same length.

   b What type of triangle is $\triangle ABC$? Give a reason.

   c If $\angle BAC = 15°$, use your diagram to find the size of:

      i $\angle ACB$ **ii** $\angle ABC$.

   d If $\angle ABC = 140°$, determine the size of all the other angles you can find in the diagram.

Modelling task

rmulate

   a The problem is to find the steepest ramp that Marion can build using the three equal length pieces of steel. Write down all the relevant information that will help solve this problem, including any diagrams as appropriate.

Solve

   b Starting with $\angle BAC = 25°$, determine the following angles giving reasons for each calculation. Illustrate with a diagram.

      i $\angle ACB$ **ii** $\angle ABC$ **iii** $\angle CBD$ **iv** $\angle BDC$ **v** $\angle BCD$

   c Determine the angle $\angle BDC$ for:

      i $\angle BAC = 30°$ **ii** $\angle BAC = 40°$.

   d Describe the problem that occurs when using the steel to make a ramp with $\angle BAC = 45°$ and illustrate with a diagram.

ate and verify

   e Is it possible for Marion to use an angle $\angle BAC$ greater than $45°$? Explain why or why not.

   f If the angle $\angle BAC$ must be a whole number of degrees, determine the slope angle for the steepest ramp possible.

unicate

   g Summarise your results and describe any key findings.

Extension questions

Now Marion has five pieces of equal length steel (*AB*, *BC*, *CD*, *DE* and *EF*) and she uses them to make a ramp, *AE*, in the following way.

a Copy out the diagram and find all the angles if $\angle BAC = 15°$.

b Determine the steepest possible slope angle if all angles in the diagram must be a whole number of degrees.

c Compare your answer to the angle found in the case when she used three pieces of equal length steel.

Classifying shapes

Key technology: Dynamic geometry

Classification systems are used all around the world to help sort information and make it easier for us to find what we are looking for. Similarly, shapes are also classified into subgroups according to their properties, including the number of parallel sides, side lengths and angles.

1 Getting started

Let's start by classifying triangles by using this flowchart.

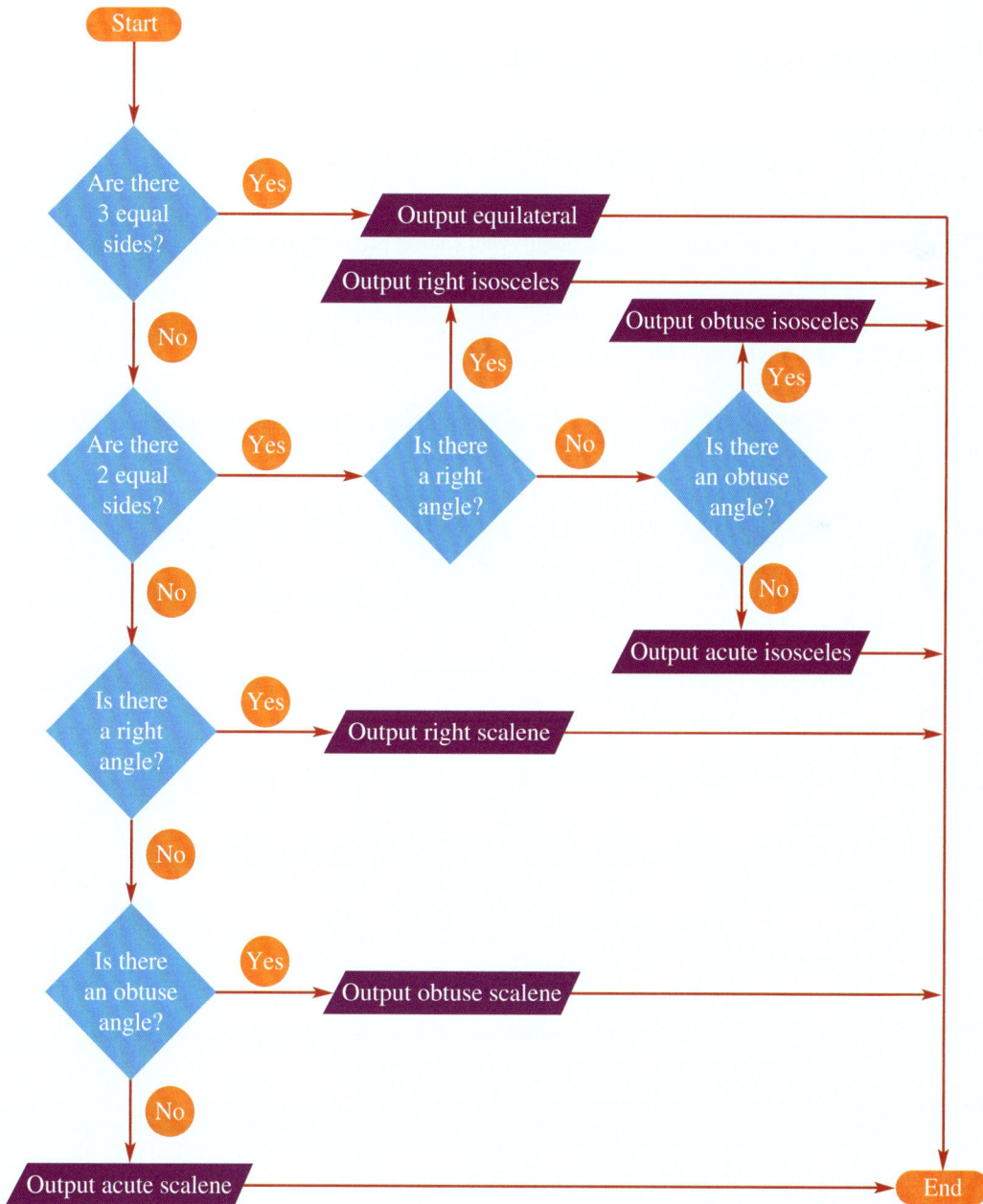

Technology and computational thinking

Work through the flowchart for each of these triangles and check that the algorithm classifies each triangle correctly.

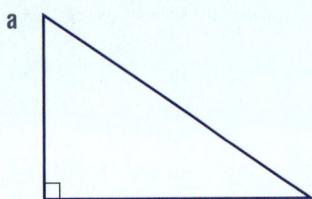

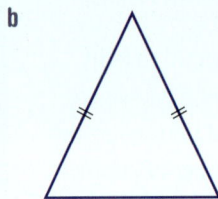

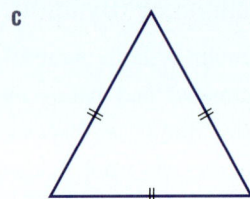

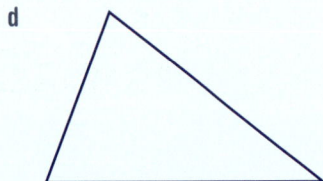

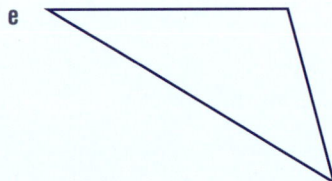

a

b

c

d

e

2 Applying an algorithm

The special quadrilaterals that we consider here are: parallelogram, rectangle, rhombus, square, trapezium and kite.

a Use the definitions in this chapter to think about what shared properties they have. Note the following definitions:

- **Parallelogram**: A quadrilateral with two pairs of parallel sides
- **Rectangle**: A parallelogram with all angles 90 degrees
- **Rhombus**: A parallelogram with all sides equal
- **Square**: A rhombus with all angles 90 degrees OR a Rectangle with all sides equal
- **Trapezium**: A quadrilateral with one pair of parallel sides
- **Kite**: A quadrilateral with two pairs of adjacent equal sides

b Draw a flowchart similar to the one in part **1** for triangles, that helps to classify quadrilaterals. Test your algorithm using a range of special quadrilaterals.

3 Using technology

Construct these shapes using dynamic geometry. The construction for an isosceles triangle is shown in the diagram.

a isosceles triangle
b equilateral triangle
c right-angled triangle

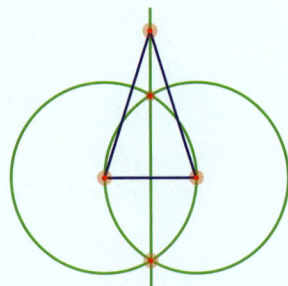

4 Extension

a Construct as many of the special quadrilaterals as you can using dynamic geometry. The construction for a rectangle is shown here. Note that the perpendicular line tool is used in this construction to save having to construct multiple perpendicular lines using circles.

b Test that your construction is correct by dragging one of the initial points. When dragging, the properties of the shape should be retained.

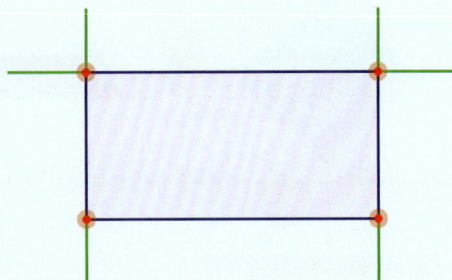

The perfect billiard ball path

When a billiard ball bounces off a straight wall (with no side spin), we can assume that the angle at which it hits the wall (incoming angle) is the same as the angle at which it leaves the wall (outgoing angle). This is similar to how light reflects off a mirror.

Single bounce

Use a ruler and protractor to draw a diagram for each part and then answer the questions.

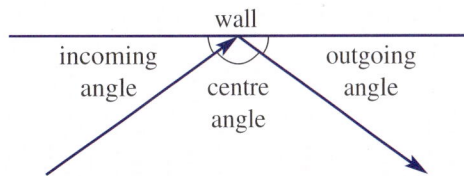

a   Find the outgoing angle if:

   i   the incoming angle is $30°$

   ii the centre angle is $104°$.

b   What geometrical reason did you use to calculate the answer to part **a ii** above?

Two bounces

Two bounces of a billiard ball on a rectangular table are shown here.

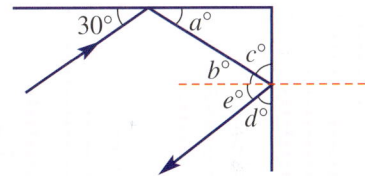

a   Find the values of angles *a, b, c, d* and *e*, in that order. Give a reason for each.

b   What can be said about the incoming angle on the first bounce and the outgoing angle on the second bounce? Give reasons for your answer.

c   Accurately draw the path of two bounces using:

   i   an initial incoming bounce of $20°$
            ii an initial incoming bounce of $55°$.

More than two bounces

a   Draw paths of billiard balls for more than two bounces starting at the midpoint of one side of a rectangular shape, using the starting incoming angles below.

   i $45°$
                              ii $30°$

b   Repeat part **a** but use different starting positions. Show accurate diagrams, using the same starting incoming angle but different starting positions.

c   Summarise your findings of this investigation in a report that clearly explains what you have found. Show clear diagrams for each part of your report.

1 Rearrange six matchsticks to make up four equilateral triangles.

Up for a challenge? If you get stuck on a question, check out the 'Working with unfamiliar problems' poster at the end of the book to help you.

2 How many equilateral triangles of any size are in this diagram?

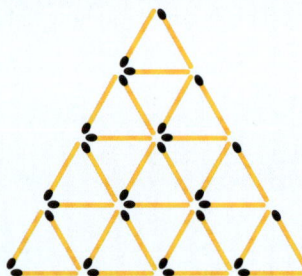

3 What is the angle between the hour hand and minute hand of a clock at 9:35 a.m.?

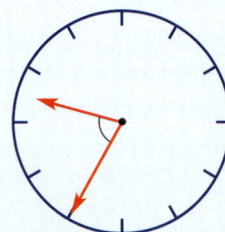

4 Two circles are the same size. The shaded circle rolls around the other circle. How many degrees will it turn before returning to its starting position?

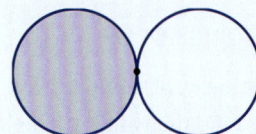

5 A polygon's vertices are joined by diagonals. How many diagonals can be drawn in each of these polygons?
   a decagon (10 sides)
   b 50-gon

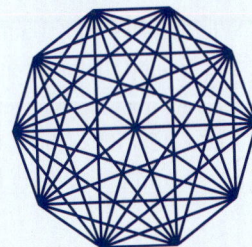

6 This solid is made by stacking 1 cm cubes. How many cubes are used?

Measuring angles

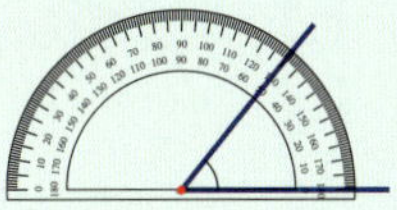

Angles
acute $0°-90°$
right $90°$
obtuse $90°-180°$
straight $180°$
reflex $180°-360°$
revolution $360°$

Angles at a point

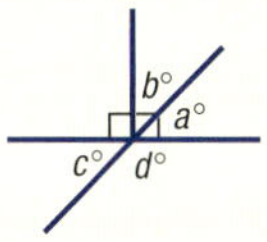

Complementary
$a + b = 90$
Supplementary
$c + d = 180$
Vertically opposite
$a = c$
Revolution
$a + b + 90 + c + d = 360$

Geometrical objects

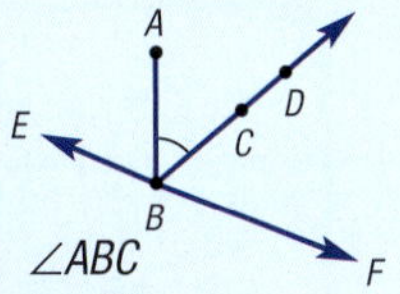

$\angle ABC$
ray BD
line EF
segment AB
collinear points B, C, D
vertex B

Angles and parallel lines

Parallel lines

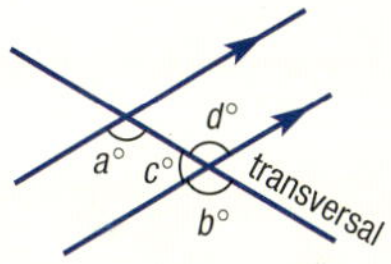

$a = b$ (corresponding)
$a = d$ (alternate)
$a + c = 180$ (cointerior)

If $a = 120$, then $b = 120$,
$d = 120$ and $c = 60$.

Constructions

Three side lengths

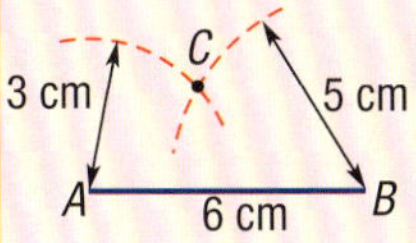

Two sides and the
angle between them

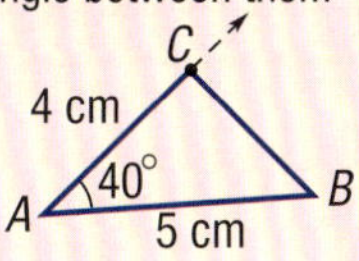

Two angles and a side

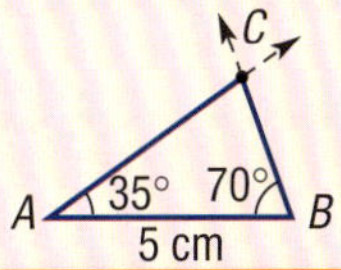

**Compound problems
with parallel lines (Ext)**

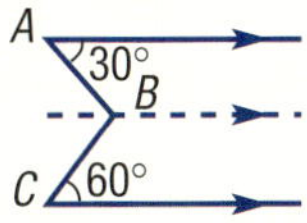

$\angle ABC = 30° + 60° = 90°$

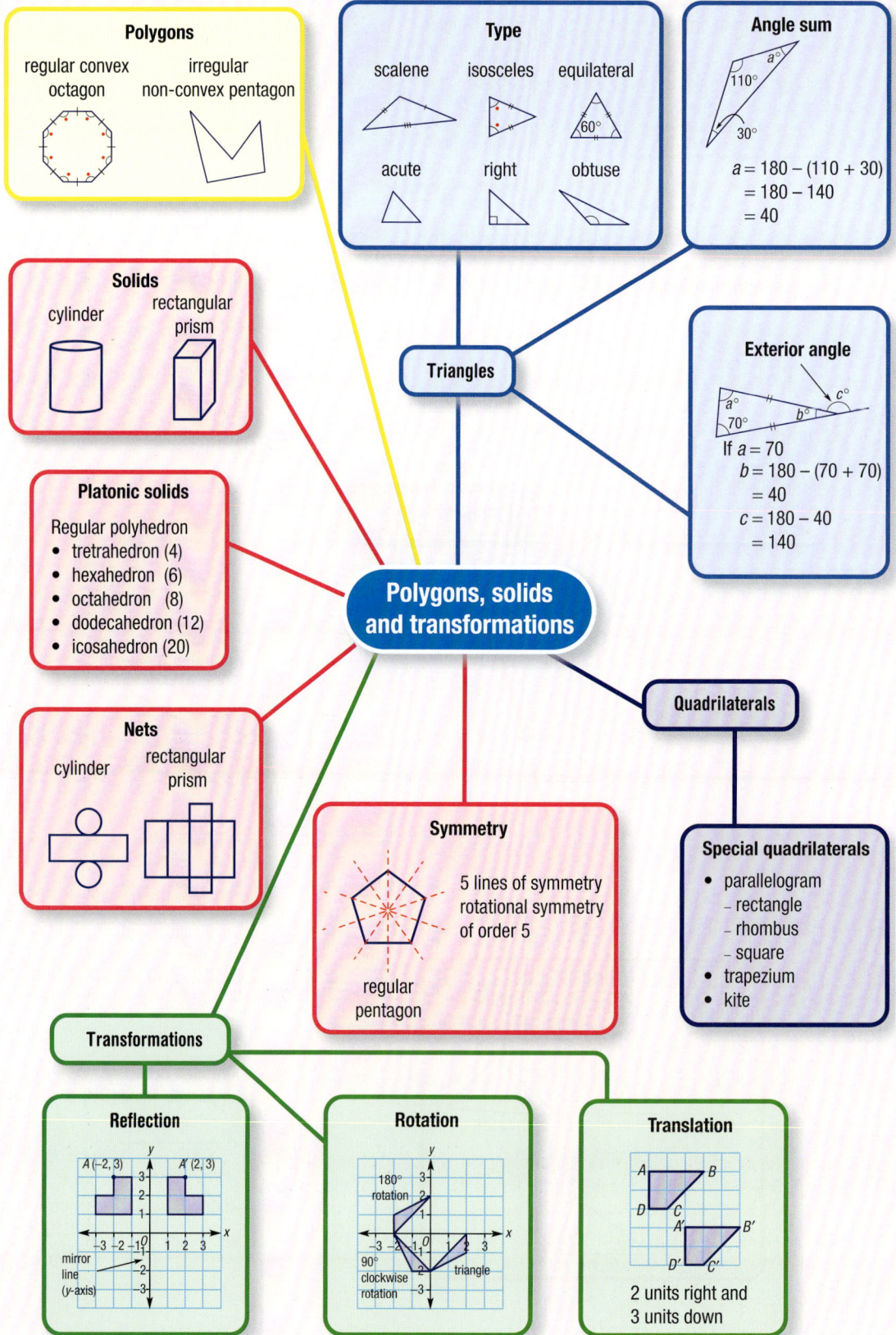

Polygons

regular convex   irregular
octagon   non-convex pentagon

Type

scalene   isosceles   equilateral

acute   right   obtuse

Angle sum

110°   a°

30°

$a = 180 - (110 + 30)$
$= 180 - 140$
$= 40$

Solids

cylinder   rectangular prism

Exterior angle

a°   70°   b°   c°

If $a = 70$
$b = 180 - (70 + 70)$
$= 40$
$c = 180 - 40$
$= 140$

Triangles

Platonic solids

Regular polyhedron
• tretrahedron (4)
• hexahedron (6)
• octahedron (8)
• dodecahedron (12)
• icosahedron (20)

Polygons, solids and transformations

Quadrilaterals

Nets

cylinder   rectangular prism

Symmetry

5 lines of symmetry
rotational symmetry
of order 5

regular pentagon

Special quadrilaterals

• parallelogram
 – rectangle
 – rhombus
 – square
• trapezium
• kite

Transformations

Reflection

$A(-2, 3)$ $A'(2, 3)$

mirror line (y-axis)

Rotation

180° rotation

90° clockwise rotation   triangle

Translation

A   B
D   C
A'   B'
D'   C'

2 units right and
3 units down

Chapter checklist with success criteria

A printable version of this checklist is available in the Interactive Textbook ✔

7A	**1. I can name lines, rays and segments.** e.g. Name this line segment. $A \quad\quad B$	☐
7A	**2. I can name angles.** e.g. Name the marked angle. *P* *Q* *R*	☐
7A	**3. I can classify an angle based on its size.** e.g. Classify 134° as an acute angle, a right angle, an obtuse angle, a straight angle, a reflex angle or a revolution.	☐
7A	**4. I can measure the size of angles with a protractor.** e.g. Use a protractor to measure the angle ∠EFG. *G* *E* *F*	☐
7A	**5. I can draw angles of a given size using a protractor.** e.g. Use a protractor to draw an angle of size 260°.	☐
7B	**6. I can find angles as a point using complementary or supplementary angles.** e.g. Find the value of *a* in these diagrams. **a** $a°$ 130° **b** 65° $a°$	☐
7B	**7. I can find the size of angles without a protractor using other angles at a point.** e.g. Find the value of *a* without a protractor. $a°$ 120°	☐
7C	**8. I can name angles in relation to other angles involving a transversal.** e.g. Name the angle that is (a) alternate to ∠ABF, and (b) cointerior to ∠ABF. *A* *H* *G* *B* *F* *C* *D* *E*	☐

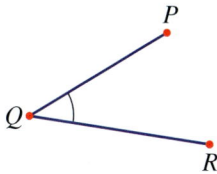

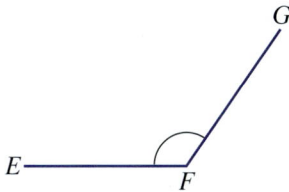

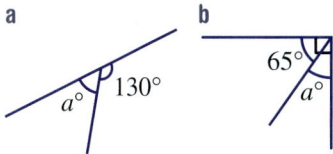

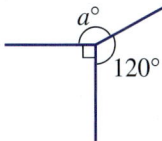

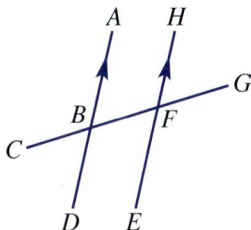

Chapter checklist

		✔

7C

9. I can find the size of unknown angles in parallel lines.
e.g. Find the value of a, giving a reason for your answer.

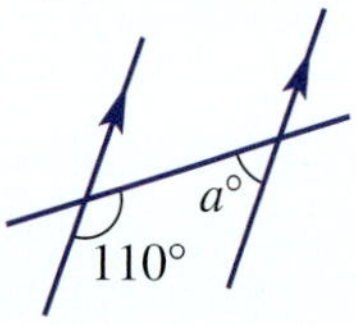

$110°$ $a°$

☐

7C

10. I can determine whether two lines are parallel given a transversal.
e.g. State whether the two lines cut by this transversal are parallel.

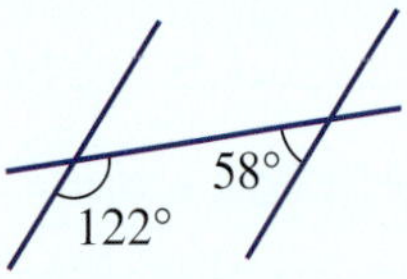

$58°$
$122°$

☐

7D

11. I can solve problems involving parallel lines and angles at a point.   **Ext**
e.g. Find the value of a in this diagram.

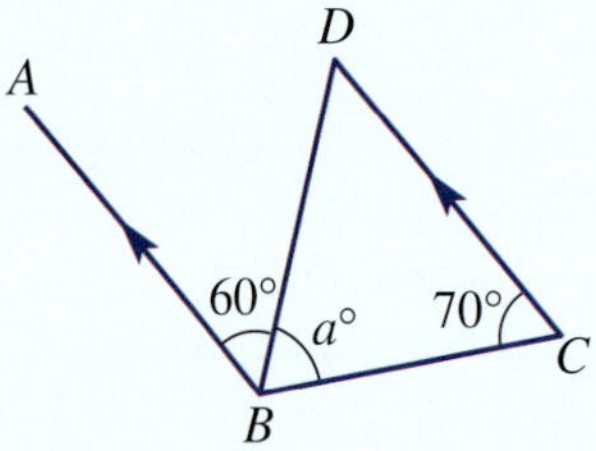

D
A
$60°$ $a°$ $70°$ C
B

☐

7E

12. I can classify a triangle as scalene, isosceles or equilateral.
e.g. Classify this triangle based on the side lengths.

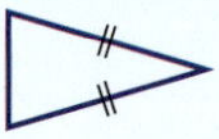

☐

7E

13. I can classify a triangle as acute, right or obtuse.
e.g. Classify this triangle based on the angles.

☐

7E

14. I can construct a triangle with given lengths and angles.
e.g. Construct a triangle ABC with $AB = 5$cm, $\angle ABC = 30°$ and $\angle BAC = 45°$.

☐

7E

15. I can construct a triangle using a ruler and pair of compasses.
e.g. Construct a triangle with side lengths 6 cm, 4 cm and 5 cm.

☐

7F

16. I can name polygons based on the number of sides.
e.g. State the name for a polygon with five sides.

☐

7F

17. I can classify polygons as convex/non-convex and regular/irregular.
e.g. State whether this shape is convex or non-convex, and whether it is regular or irregular.

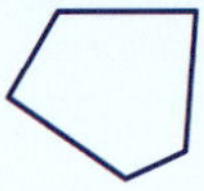

☐

	✔

7F | **18. I can classify quadrilaterals.**
e.g. Determine whether the quadrilateral shown is convex or non-convex and what type(s) of special quadrilateral it is. | ☐

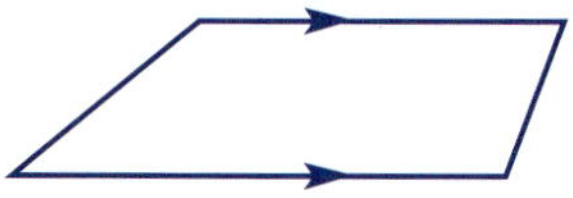

7G | **19. I can use the angle sum of a triangle to find an unknown angle.**
e.g. Find the value of *a* in this triangle.

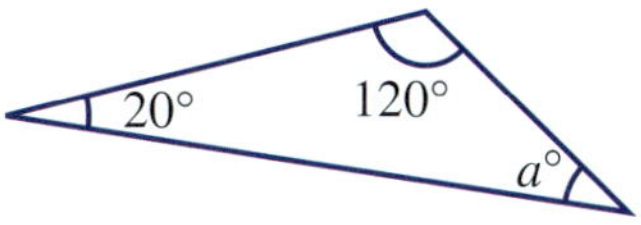

20° 120° *a*° | ☐

7G | **20. I can find an unknown angle within an isosceles triangle.**
e.g. Find the value of *a* in this diagram.

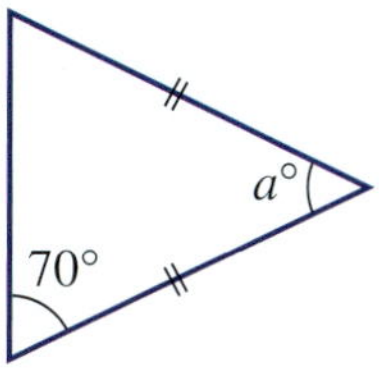

a°
70° | ☐

7G | **21. I can find exterior angles for a triangle.**
e.g. Find the value of *x* in this diagram.

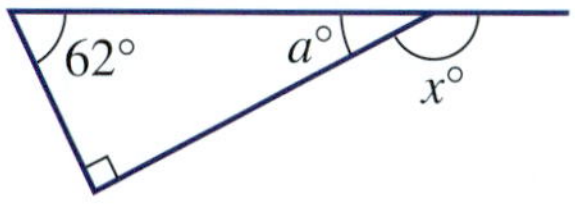

62° *a*° *x*° | ☐

7H | **22. I can determine the line and rotational symmetry of a shape.**
e.g. Give the order of line symmetry and of rotational symmetry for a rectangle. | ☐

7I | **23. I can find the result of a reflection of a point or shape in the coordinate plane.**
e.g. The shape *ABCD* is reflected in the *y*-axis. State the coordinates of *A′*, *B′*, *C′* and *D′* and connect them to draw the image.

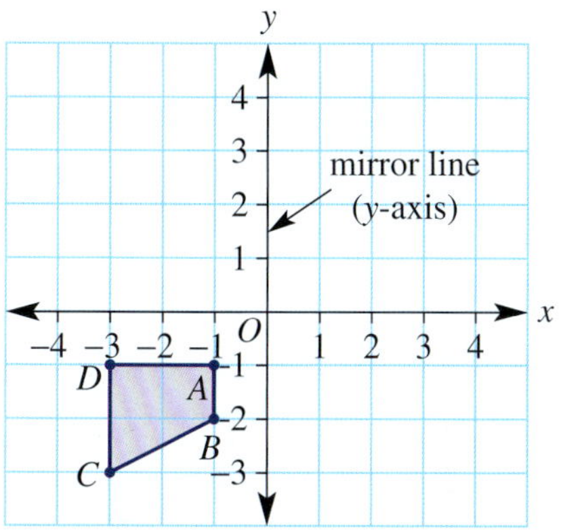

mirror line (*y*-axis)

D *A*
C *B* | ☐

Chapter checklist

		✔
7I	**24. I can find the result of a rotation of a point or shape in the coordinate plane.** e.g. The triangle ABD is rotated 90° anticlockwise about C. State the coordinates of A', B' and D' and hence draw the image. 	☐
7J	**25. I can draw the result of a translation.** e.g. Draw the image of the triangle ABC after a translation 2 units to the right and 3 units down. 	☐
7J	**26. I can describe a translation.** e.g. A point $B(5, -2)$ is translated to $B'(-1, 2)$. Describe the translation.	☐
7K	**27. I can draw simple solids.** e.g. Draw a cone.	☐
7K	**28. I can draw solids on isometric dot paper.** e.g. Draw this solid on isometric dot paper. 	☐
7L	**29. I can draw a net for a solid.** e.g. Draw a net for a rectangular prism and for a regular tetrahedron.	☐

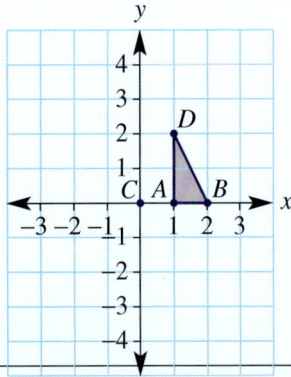

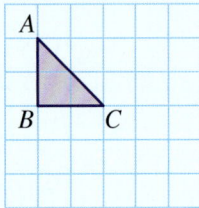

Short-answer questions

7A

1 Name each of these objects.

a

b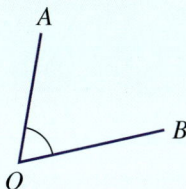

c •P

d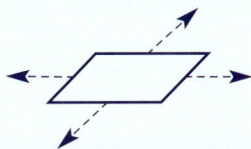

e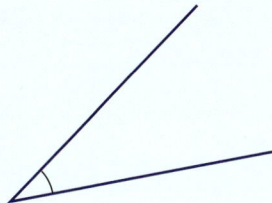

f

7A

2 For the angles shown, state the type of angle and measure its size using a protractor.

a

b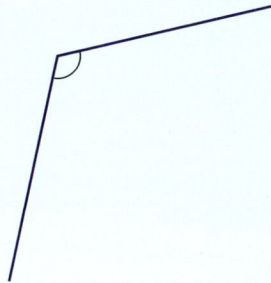

c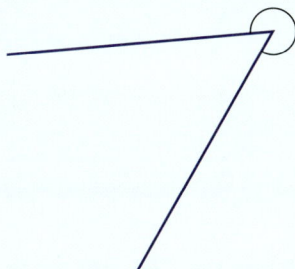

7A

3 Find the angle between the hour and minute hands on a clock at the following times. Answer with an acute or obtuse angle.

a   6:00 a.m.

b   9:00 p.m.

c   3:00 p.m.

d   5:00 a.m.

7B

4 Without using a protractor, find the value of a in these diagrams.

a

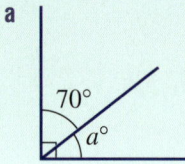

70°
$a°$

b

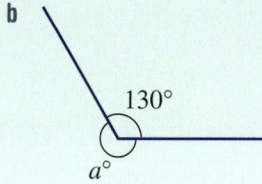

130°
$a°$

c

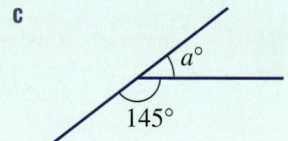

$a°$
145°

d

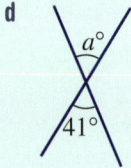

$a°$
41°

e

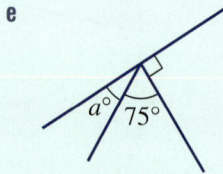

$a°$ 75°

f

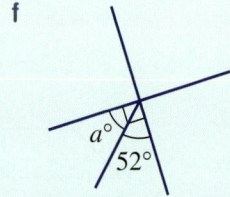

$a°$
52°

g

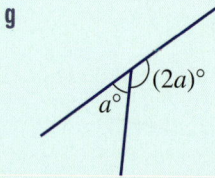

$a°$ $(2a)°$

h

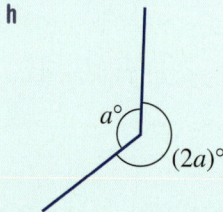

$a°$
$(2a)°$

i

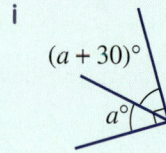

$(a + 30)°$
$a°$

7C

5 Using the pronumerals a, b, c or d given in the diagram, write down a pair of angles that are:

a vertically opposite

b cointerior

c alternate

d corresponding

e supplementary but not cointerior.

$b°$
$a°$
$d°$ $c°$

7C

6 For each of the following, state whether the two lines cut by the transversal are parallel. Give reasons for each answer.

a

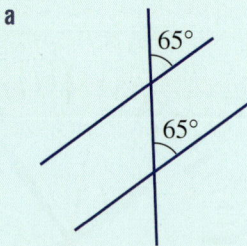

65°
65°

b

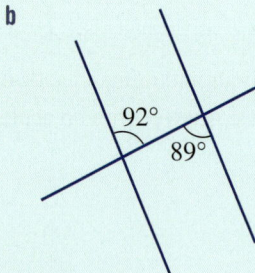

92°
89°

c

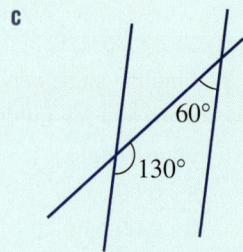

60°
130°

7D

(Ext)

7 Find the value of a in these diagrams.

a

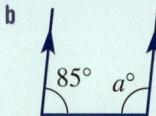

80°
$a°$

b

85°
$a°$

c

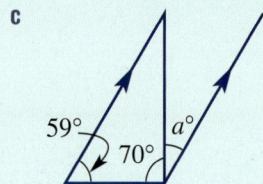

59°
70°
$a°$

d $a°$ $150°$

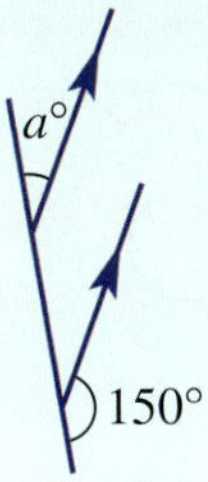

e $a°$ $140°$

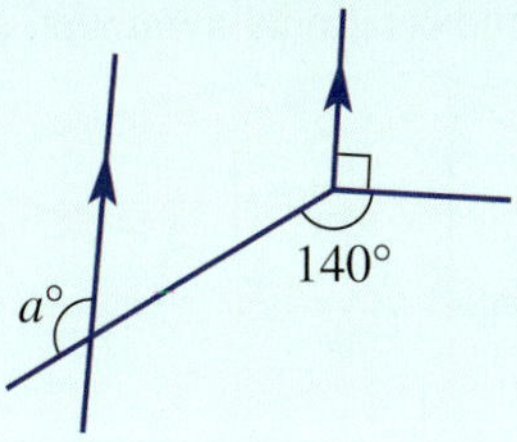

f $70°$ $a°$ $32°$

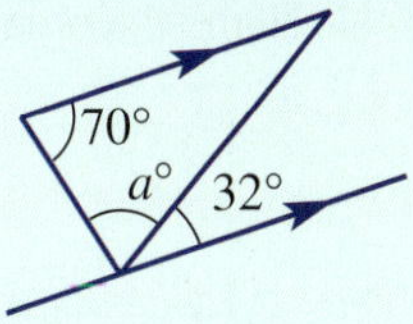

7E 8 Use a protractor and ruler to construct these triangles.
   a   triangle ABC with $AB = 4$ cm, $\angle CAB = 25°$ and $\angle ABC = 45°$
   b   triangle ABC with $AB = 5$ cm, $\angle BAC = 50°$ and $AC = 5$ cm

7E 9 Use a protractor, pair of compasses and a ruler to construct these triangles.
   a   triangle ABC with $AB = 5$ cm, $BC = 6$ cm and $AC = 3$ cm
   b   triangle ABC with $AB = 6$ cm, $BC = 4$ cm and $AC = 5$ cm

7F 10 How many sides do these polygons have?
   a   pentagon   b   heptagon   c   undecagon

7F 11 A diagonal inside a polygon joins two vertices. Find how many diagonals can be drawn inside a quadrilateral if the shape is:
   a   convex   b   non-convex.

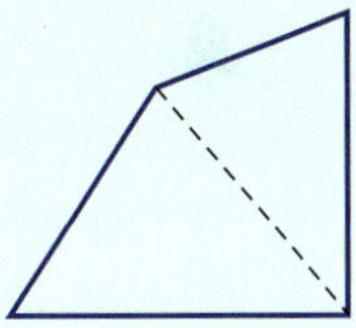

7F 12 Name each of these quadrilaterals.
   a   b 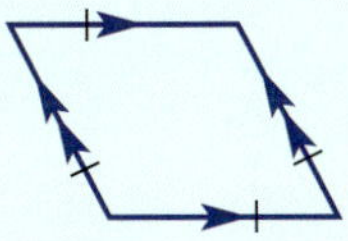   c

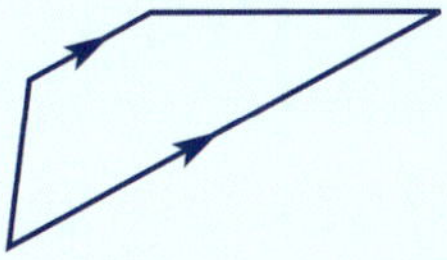

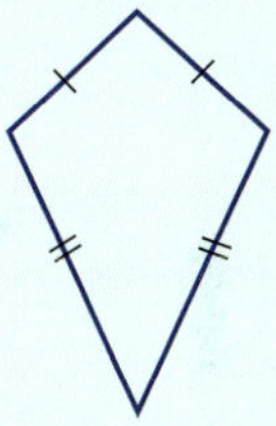

7G 13 Find the value of a in each of these shapes.
   a $80°$ $70°$ $a°$
   b $42°$ $a°$
   c $65°$ $a°$
   d $a°$
   e $20°$ $a°$
   f $40°$ $a°$
   g $a°$ $110°$
   h $a°$ $75°$ $25°$
   i $15°$ $a°$

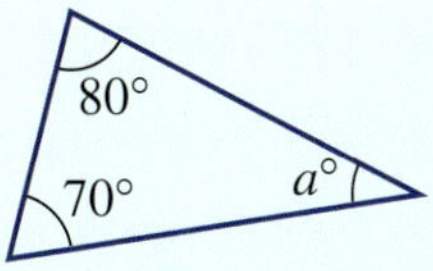

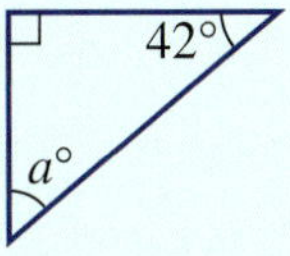

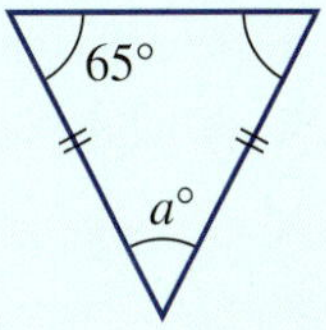

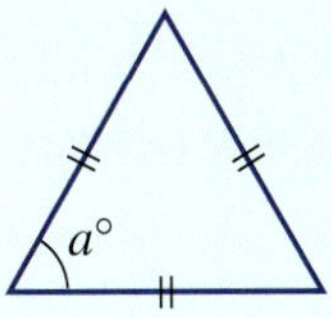

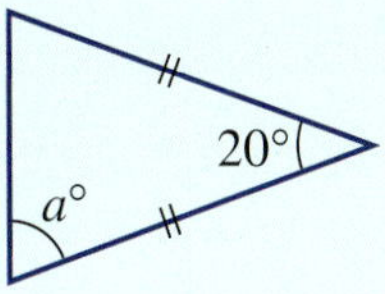

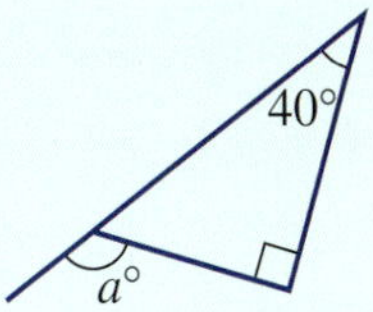

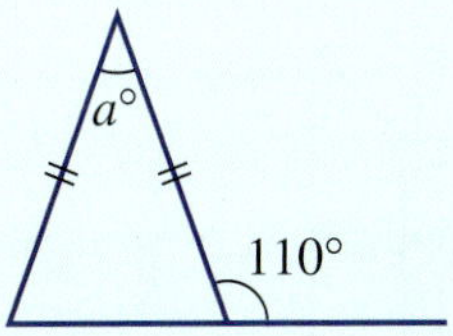

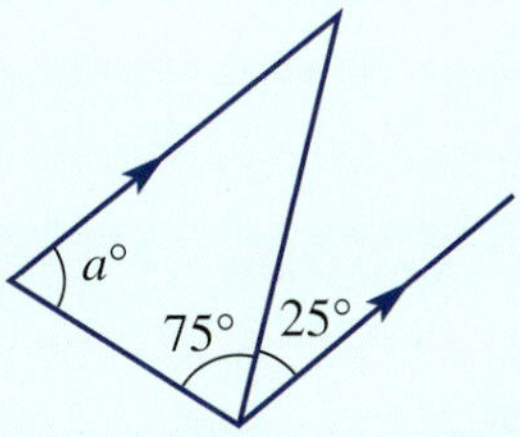

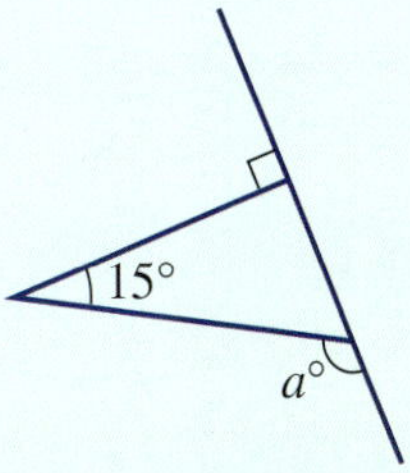

Chapter review

7H 14 Name the order of line and rotational symmetry for each of these diagrams.

a 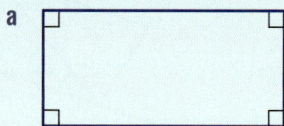   b   c

7I 15 Write the coordinates of A', B' and C' when this shape is reflected in the following mirror lines.

a the y-axis

b the x-axis

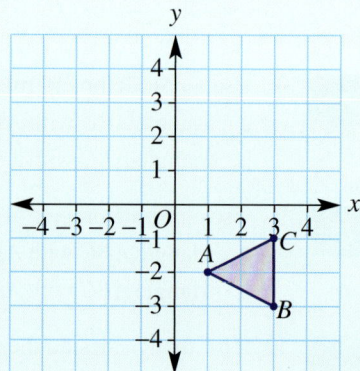

7I 16 Points $A(0, 4)$, $B(2, 0)$ and $D(3, 3)$ are shown here. Write down the coordinates of the image points A', B' and D' after each of the following rotations.

a 180° about $C(0, 0)$

b 90° clockwise about $C(0, 0)$

c 90° anticlockwise about $C(0, 0)$

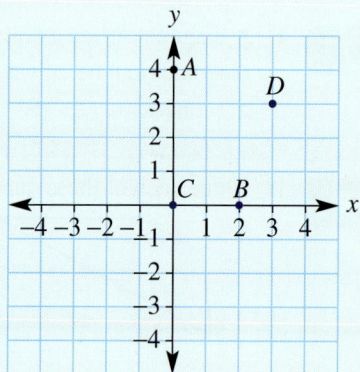

7J 17 Write the coordinates of the vertices A', B' and C' after each of these translations.

a 4 units right and 2 units up

b 1 unit left and 4 units up

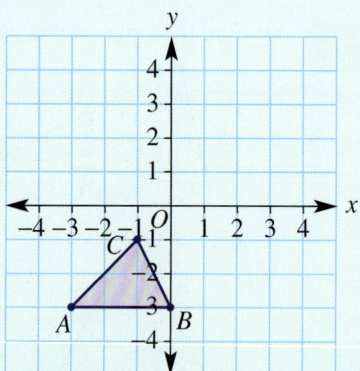

7K 18 Draw a side view, top view and net for each of these solids.

a 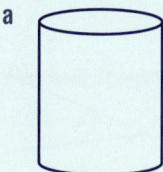   b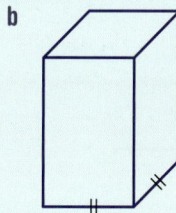

Multiple-choice questions

7A

1 Three points are collinear if:

   A they are at right angles.

   B they form a 60° angle.

   C they all lie in a straight line.

   D they are all at the same point.

   E they form an arc on a circle.

7A

2 The angle shown here can be named:

   A $\angle QRP$ **C** $\angle QPR$ **E** $\angle PQP$

   B $\angle PQR$ **D** $\angle QRR$

7B

3 Complementary angles:

   A sum to 180°   **B** sum to 270°   **C** sum to 360°

   D sum to 90°   **E** sum to 45°

7A

4 A reflex angle is:

   A 90°   **B** 180°   **C** between 180° and 360°

   D between 0° and 90°   **E** between 90° and 180°

7A

5 What is the size of the angle measured by the protractor?

   A 15°   **C** 105°   **E** 195°

   B 30°   **D** 165°

7A

6 The angle a minute hand on a clock turns in 20 minutes is:

   A 72°   **B** 36°   **C** 18°   **D** 144°   **E** 120°

7C

7 If a transversal cuts two parallel lines, then:

   A cointerior angles are equal.

   B alternate angles are supplementary.

   C corresponding angles are equal.

   D vertically opposite angles are supplementary.

   E supplementary angles add to 90°.

7E

8 The three types of triangles all classified by their interior angles are:

   A acute, isosceles and scalene.

   B acute, right and obtuse.

   C scalene, isosceles and equilateral.

   D right, obtuse and scalene.

   E acute, equilateral and right.

7F

9 A non-convex polygon has:
- **A** all interior angles of 90°.
- **B** six sides.
- **C** all interior angles less than 180°.
- **D** all interior angles greater than 180°.
- **E** at least one interior angle greater than 180°.

7F

10 The quadrilateral that has 2 pairs of sides of equal length and 1 pair of angles of equal size is called a:
- **A** kite   **B** trapezium   **C** rhombus   **D** triangle   **E** square

7H

11 A rhombus has line symmetry of order:
- **A** 0   **B** 1   **C** 2   **D** 3   **E** 4

7I

12 The point $T(-3, 4)$ is reflected in the x-axis; hence, the image point T' has coordinates:
- **A** $(3, 4)$ **B** $(-3, 4)$ **C** $(0, 4)$ **D** $(3, -4)$ **E** $(-3, -4)$

7J

13 The translation that takes $A(2, -3)$ to $A'(-1, 1)$ could be described as:
- **A** 3 units left.
- **B** 4 units up.
- **C** 3 units left and 4 units up.
- **D** 1 unit right and 2 units down.
- **E** 1 unit left and 2 units down.

Extended-response questions

1 A factory roof is made up of three sloping sections. The sloping sections are all parallel and the upright supports are at 90° to the horizontal, as shown. Each roof section makes a 32° angle (or pitch) with the horizontal.

factory

- **a** State the size of each of these angles.
  - **i** $\angle EAB$
  - **ii** $\angle GCD$
  - **iii** $\angle ABF$
  - **iv** $\angle EBF$
- **b** Complete these sentences.
  - **i** $\angle BAE$ is _____ to $\angle CBF$.
  - **ii** $\angle FBC$ is _____ to $\angle GCB$.
  - **iii** $\angle BCG$ is _____ to $\angle GCD$.
- **c** Solar panels are to be placed on the sloping roofs and it is decided that the angle to the horizontal is to be reduced by 11°. Find the size of these new angles.
  - **i** $\angle FBC$
  - **ii** $\angle FBA$
  - **iii** $\angle FCG$

2   Two cables support a vertical tower, as shown in the
    diagram opposite, and the angle marked $a°$ is the angle
    between the two cables.
    a   Find $\angle BDC$.
    b   Find $\angle ADC$.
    c   Find the value of a.
    d   If $\angle DAB$ is changed to $30°$ and $\angle DBC$ is changed
        to $65°$, will the value of a stay the same? If not,
        what will be the new value of a?

3   Shown is a drawing of a simple house on a Cartesian
    plane.
    Draw the image of the house after these transformations.
    a   translation 5 units left and 4 units down
    b   reflection in the x-axis
    c   rotation $90°$ anticlockwise about $C(0,0)$

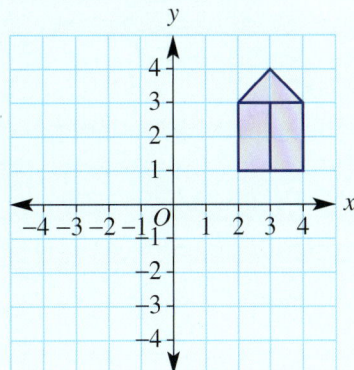

8

Statistics and probability

Maths in context: Collecting all types of data

Statistical calculations, tables, charts and graphs are essential for interpreting all types of data and are widely used, including by governments, hospitals, medical professions, sports clubs, farmers, insurance companies and many businesses.

There are more than one hundred sports played in Australia. Each has a national and state organisation that keeps a record of results, calculates statistical measures such as the mean, median and mode, and provides progress graphs and charts. Australia has sport websites for athletics, basketball, canoeing and kayaking, cricket, cycling, diving, football, hockey, netball, Paralympics, rowing, rugby, sailing, skiing, snowboarding, swimming, volleyball and water polo.

The following Australian government organisations obtain and record data and provide statistical measures and displays.

- ABS (Australian Bureau of Statistics): collects data from samples and also runs the Australian Census every five years. ABS provides the government with population numbers and data on people's health, education levels, employment, and housing.

- BOM (Bureau of Meteorology): records weather data and forecasts the probabilities of rain, storms, wind strengths, temperatures, fires, floods and droughts. This is important information for planning by emergency services, air traffic control, farmers, and even holiday-makers!

- CSIRO (Commonwealth Scientific and Industrial Research Organisation): provides agricultural data, such as water availability, soil types, land use and crop forecasts.

Chapter contents

Victorian Curriculum 2.0

This chapter covers the following content descriptors in the Victorian Curriculum 2.0:

STATISTICS

VC2M7ST01, VC2M7ST02, VC2M7ST03

PROBABILITY

VC2M7P01, VC2M7P02

ALGEBRA

VC2M7A04

Please refer to the curriculum support documentation in the teacher resources for a full and comprehensive mapping of this chapter to the related curriculum content descriptors.

© VCAA

Online resources

A host of additional online resources are included as part of your Interactive Textbook, including HOTmaths content, video demonstrations of all worked examples, auto-marked quizzes and much more.

8A   Collecting and classifying data

LEARNING INTENTIONS

- To know the meaning of the terms primary source, secondary source, census, sample and observation
- To be able to classify variables as numerical (discrete or continuous) or categorical
- To understand that different methods are suitable for collecting different types of data, based on the size and nature of the data

People collect or use data almost every day. Athletes and sports teams look at performance data, customers compare prices at different stores, investors look at daily interest rates, and students compare marks with other students in their class. Companies often collect and analyse data to help produce and promote their products to customers and to make predictions about the future.

A doctor records a patient's medical data to track their recovery. Examples include temperature, which is continuous numerical data, and number of heart beats recorded during a fixed time period, which is discrete numerical data.

Lesson starter: Collecting data

Consider, as a class, the following questions and discuss their implications.

- Have you or your family ever been surveyed by a telemarketer at home? What did they want? What time did they call?
- Do you think that telemarketers get accurate data? Why or why not?
- Why do you think companies collect data this way?
- If you wanted information about the most popular colour of car sold in Victoria over the course of a year, how could you find out this information?

KEY IDEAS

■ In statistics, a **variable** is something measurable or observable that is expected to change over time or between individual observations. It can be numerical or categorical.
  - **Numerical (quantitative)** data can be discrete or continuous:
    - **Discrete numerical** – data that can only be particular numerical values, e.g. the number of TV sets in a house (could be 0, 1, 2, 3 but not values in between such as 1.3125).
    - **Continuous numerical** – data that can take any value in a range. Variables such as heights, weights and temperatures are all continuous. For instance, someone could have a height of 172 cm, 172.4 cm or 172.215 cm (if it can be measured accurately).
  - **Categorical** – data that are not numerical such as colours, gender, brands of cars are all examples of categorical data. In a survey, categorical data come from answers which are given as words (e.g. 'yellow' or 'female') or ratings (e.g. 1 = dislike, 2 = neutral, 3 = like).

■ Data can be collected from primary or secondary sources.
  • Data from a **primary source** are firsthand information collected from the original source by the person or organisation needing the data, e.g. a survey an individual student conducts to answer a question that interests them.
  • Data from a **secondary source** have been collected, published and possibly summarised by someone else before we use it. Data collected from newspaper articles, textbooks or internet blogs represent secondary source data.

■ Samples and populations
  • When an entire population (e.g. a maths class, all the cars in a parking lot, a company, or a whole country) is surveyed, it is called a **census**.
  • When a subset of the population is surveyed, it is called a **sample**. Samples should be randomly selected and large enough to represent the views of the overall population.
  • When we cannot choose which members of the population to survey, and can record only those visible to us (e.g. people posting their political views on a news website), this is called an **observation**.

BUILDING UNDERSTANDING

1 Match each word on the left to its meaning on the right.

a	sample	A	only takes on particular numbers within a range
b	categorical	B	a complete set of data
c	discrete numerical	C	a smaller group taken from the population
d	primary source	D	data grouped in categories like 'blue', 'brown', 'green'
e	continuous numerical	E	data collected firsthand
f	population	F	can take on any number in a range

2 Give an example of:
  a discrete numerical data
  b continuous numerical data
  c categorical data.

Example 1   Classifying variables

Classify the following variables as categorical, discrete numerical or continuous numerical.
a   the Australian state or territory in which a baby is born
b   the length of a newborn baby

SOLUTION	EXPLANATION
a categorical	As the answer is the name of an Australian state or territory (a word, not a number) the data are categorical.
b continuous numerical	Length is a continuous measurement, so all numbers are theoretically possible.

Now you try

Classify the following variables as categorical, discrete numerical or continuous numerical.
a   the number of children a person has
b   the brand of shoes someone wears

Example 2   Collecting data from primary and secondary sources

Decide whether a primary source or a secondary source is suitable for collection of data on each of the following and suggest a method for its collection.
a   a coffee shop wants to know the average number of customers it has each day
b   a detergent manufacturer wants to know the favourite washing powder or liquid for households in Australia

SOLUTION	EXPLANATION
a primary source by recording daily customer numbers	This information is not likely to be available from other sources, so the business will need to collect the data itself, making this a primary source
b secondary data source using the results from a market research agency	A market research agency might collect these results using a random phone survey. Obtaining a primary source would involve conducting the survey yourself but it is unlikely that the sample will be large enough to be suitable.

Now you try

Decide whether a primary source or secondary source is suitable for collection of data on each of the following and suggest a method for its collection.
a   the maximum temperature each year in Australia for the past 100 years
b   the number of pets owned by everyone in a class at school

Exercise 8A

FLUENCY

| 1, 2–3(½), 4 | 2–3(½), 4 | 2–3(½), 4 |

Example 1

1 Classify the following as categorical or numerical.
 a the eye colour of each student in your class
 b the date of the month each student was born, e.g. the 9th of a month
 c the weight of each student when they were born
 d the brands of airplanes landing at Melbourne's international airport
 e the temperature of each classroom
 f the number of students in each classroom period one on Tuesday

Example 1

2 Classify the following variables as categorical, continuous numerical or discrete numerical data.
 a the number of cars in each household
 b the weights of packages sent by Australia Post on Wednesday 20 December 2023
 c the highest temperature of the ocean each day
 d the favourite brand of chocolate of the teachers at your school
 e the colours of the cars in the school car park
 f the brands of cars in the school car park
 g the number of letters in different words on a page
 h the number of advertisements in a time period over each of the free-to-air channels
 i the length of time spent doing this exercise
 j the arrival times of planes at JFK airport
 k the daily pollution levels in the Burnley Tunnel on the City Link Freeway
 l the number of text messages sent by an individual yesterday
 m the times for the 100 m freestyle event at the world championships over the last 10 years
 n the number of Blu-ray discs someone owns
 o the brands of cereals available at the supermarket
 p marks awarded on a maths test
 q the star rating on a hotel or motel
 r the censorship rating on a movie showing at the cinema

3 Is observation or a sample or a census the most appropriate way for a student to collect data on each of the following?
 a the arrival times of trains at Southern Cross Station during a day
 b the arrival times of trains at Southern Cross Station over the year
 c the heights of students in your class
 d the heights of all Year 7 students in the school
 e the heights of all Year 7 students in Victoria
 f the number of plastic water bottles sold in a year
 g the religions of Australian families
 h the number of people living in each household in your class
 i the number of people living in each household in your school
 j the number of people living in each household in Australia

k   the number of native Australian birds found in a suburb

l   the number of cars travelling past a school between 8 a.m. and 9 a.m. on a school day

m   the money spent at the canteen by students during a week

n   the ratings of TV shows

Example 2

4   Identify whether a primary or secondary source is suitable for the collection of data on the following.

a   the number of soft drinks bought by the average Australian family in a week

b   the age of school leavers in far North Queensland

c   the number of soft drinks consumed by school age students in a day

d   the highest level of education by the adults in Australian households

e   the reading level of students in Year 7 in Australia

PROBLEM-SOLVING	5, 6	5, 7–9	8–10

5   Give a reason why someone might have trouble obtaining reliable and representative data using a primary source to find the following.

a   the temperature of the Indian Ocean over the course of a year

b   the religions of Australian families

c   the average income of someone in India

d   drug use by teenagers within a school

e   the level of education of different cultural communities within Victoria

6   Secondary sources are already published data that are then used by another party in their own research. Why is the use of this type of data not always reliable?

7   When obtaining primary source data you can survey the population or a sample.

a   Explain the difference between a 'population' and a 'sample' when collecting data.

b   Give an example situation where you should survey a population rather than a sample.

c   Give an example situation where you should survey a sample rather than a population.

8   A Likert-type scale is for categorical data where items are assigned a number; for example, the answer to a question could be 1 = dislike, 2 = neutral, 3 = like.

a   Explain why the data collected are categorical even though the answers are given as numbers.

b   Give examples of a Likert-type scale for the following categorical data. You might need to reorder some of the options.

   i   strongly disagree, somewhat disagree, somewhat agree, strongly agree

   ii   excellent, satisfactory, poor, strong

   iii never, always, rarely, usually, sometimes

   iv   strongly disagree, neutral, strongly agree, disagree, agree

9   A sample should be representative of the population it reports on. For the following surveys, describe who might be left out and how this might introduce a bias.

a   a telephone poll with numbers selected from a phone book

b   a postal questionnaire

c   door-to-door interviews during the weekdays

d   a *Dolly* magazine poll conducted online via social media

e   a Facebook survey

10 Another way to collect primary source data is by direct observation. For example, the colour of cars travelling through an intersection (categorical data) is best obtained in this way rather than through a questionnaire.
   a Give another example of a variable for which data could be collected by observation.
   b Explain how you could estimate the proportion of black cars parked at a large shopping centre car park without counting every single one.

11 Television ratings are determined by surveying a sample of the population.
   a Explain why a sample is taken rather than conducting a census.
   b What would be a limitation of the survey results if the sample included 50 people nationwide?
   c If a class census was taken on which (if any) television program students watched from 7.30–8.30 last night, why might the results be different to the official ratings?
   d Research how many people are sampled by Nielsen Television Audience Measurement in order to get an accurate idea of viewing habits and stick within practical limitations.

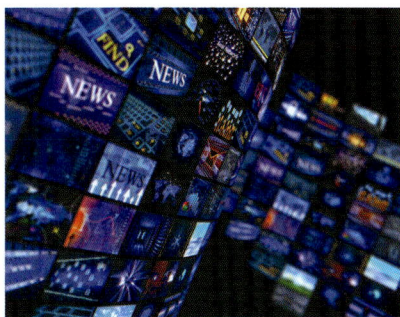

12 Australia's census surveys the entire population every five years.
   a Why might Australia not conduct a census every year?
   b Over 40% of all Australians were born overseas or had at least one of their parents born overseas. How does this impact the need to be culturally sensitive when designing and undertaking a census?
   c The census can be filled out on a paper form or using the internet. Given that the data must be collated in a computer eventually, why does the government still allow paper forms to be used?
   d Why might a country like India or China conduct their national census every 10 years?

13 When conducting research on Indigenous Australians, the elders of the community are often involved. Explain why the elders are usually involved in the research process.

14 Write a sentence explaining why two different samples taken from the same population can produce different results. How can this problem be minimised?

15 a Use a random number generator on your calculator or computer to record the number of times the number 1 to 5 appears (you could even use a die by re-rolling whenever you get a 6) out of 50 trials. Record these data.
   i Tabulate your results.
   ii Compare the results of the individuals in the class.
   iii Explain why differences between different students might occur.
   b Choose a page at random from a novel or an internet page and count how many times each vowel (A, E, I, O, U) occurs. Assign each vowel the following value A = 1, E = 2, I = 3, O = 4, U = 5 and tabulate your results.
   i Why are the results different from those in part a?
   ii How might the results for the vowels vary depending on the webpage or novel chosen?

8B Summarising data numerically

LEARNING INTENTIONS

- To understand that numerical data can be summarised as a single number by finding its range, mean, median or mode
- To be able to find the range of a set of numerical data
- To be able to find the mean, median and mode of a set of numerical data

Although sometimes it is important to see a complete set of data, either as a list of numbers or as a graph, it is often useful to summarise the data with a few numbers.

For example, instead of listing the height of every Year 7 student in a school, you could summarise this by stating the median height and the difference (in cm) between the tallest and shortest people.

Lesson starter: Class summary

For each student in the class, find their height (in cm), their age (in years), and how many siblings they have.

- Which of these three sets of data would you expect to have the largest range?
- Which of these three sets of data would you expect to have the smallest range?
- What do you think is the mean height of students in the class? Can you calculate it?

The median (i.e. middle) height of school students, of relevant ages, is used to determine suitable dimensions for classroom chairs and desks.

KEY IDEAS

■ The **range** of a set of data is given by:
Range = highest number − lowest number.

$$1 \quad 6 \quad 7 \quad 1 \quad 5 \longrightarrow \text{range} = 7 - 1 = 6$$

lowest highest

■ **Mean, median** and **mode** are three different measures that can be used to summarise a set of data. The word **average** is used to refer to the mean.

- These are also called **measures of centre** or **measures of central tendency**.

■ The **mean** of a set of data is given by:

Mean = (sum of all the values) ÷ (total number of values)

$$1 + 6 + 7 + 1 + 5 = 20 \longrightarrow \text{mean} = 20 \div 5 = 4$$

■ The **median** is the middle value when the values are sorted from lowest to highest. If there are two middle values, then add them together and divide by 2.

1 1 ⑤ 6 7   1 3 4 9 10 12

middle ⟶ median = 5   middle ⟶ median = $\frac{1}{2}(4 + 9) = 6.5$

■ The **mode** is the most common value. It is the value that occurs most frequently. We also say that it is the value with the highest frequency. There can be more than one mode.

① ① 5 6 7 ⟶ mode = 1

BUILDING UNDERSTANDING

1 Consider the set of numbers 1, 5, 2, 10, 3.
   a State the largest number.
   b State the smallest number.
   c What is the range?

2 State the range of the following sets of numbers.
   a 2, 10, 1, 3, 9
   b 6, 8, 13, 7, 1
   c 0, 6, 3, 9, 1
   d 3, 10, 7, 5, 10

3 For the set of numbers 1, 5, 7, 7, 10, find the:
   a total of the numbers when added
   b mean
   c median
   d mode.

These people are lined up in order of height. Whose heights are used to calculate: the range? the median? the mean?

Example 3 Finding the range, mean and mode

Consider the ages (in years) of seven people who are surveyed in a shop:
15, 31, 12, 47, 21, 65, 12.
a Find the range of values.
b Find the mean of this set of data.
c Find the mode of this set of data.

SOLUTION

EXPLANATION

a range $= 65 - 12$
$\quad\quad\quad = 53$

Highest number $= 65$, lowest number $= 12$
The range is the difference.

b mean $= 203 \div 7$
$\quad\quad\quad = 29$

Sum of values $= 15 + 31 + 12 + 47 + 21 + 65 + 12 = 203$
Number of values $= 7$

c mode $= 12$

The most common value is 12.

Now you try

Consider the test scores of 5 people: 25, 19, 32, 25, 29.
a Find the range of values.
b Find the mean test score.
c Find the mode test score.

Example 4 Finding the median

Find the median of the following:
a 7, 2, 8, 10, 9, 7, 13
b 12, 9, 15, 1, 23, 7

SOLUTION

EXPLANATION

a Values: 2, 7, 7, 8, 9, 10, 13

median $= 8$

Place the numbers in ascending order. (There is just one middle value, because there is an odd number of values.)
The median is 8, because it is the middle value of the sorted list.

b Values: 1, 7, 9, 12, 15, 23

median $= \dfrac{9 + 12}{2}$

$\quad\quad\quad = \dfrac{21}{2}$

$\quad\quad\quad = 10.5 \quad\quad \left(\text{or } 10\tfrac{1}{2}\right)$

Place the numbers in ascending order and circle the two middle values. (There are two middle values because there is an even numbers of values.)
The median is formed by adding the two middle values and dividing by 2.

Now you try

Find the median of the following.

a 7, 2, 9, 3, 5, 1, 8

b 10, 2, 5, 7, 3, 3, 1, 8

Exercise 8B

FLUENCY	1–6($\frac{1}{2}$)	3–6($\frac{1}{2}$), 7	4–6($\frac{1}{2}$), 7, 8

ple 3a

1 Find the range of the following.

a 3, 6, 7, 10   b 2, 8, 11, 12, 15   c 4, 1, 8, 2, 9   d 3, 12, 20, 2, 4, 11

ple 3b

2 Find the mean of the following.

a 4, 3, 2, 5, 6   b 2, 10, 5, 7   c 2, 2, 7, 1, 4, 2   d 9, 2, 10

mple 3

3 Consider the ages (in years) of nine people who are surveyed at a train station:
18, 37, 61, 24, 7, 74, 51, 28, 24.

a Find the range of values.

b Find the mean of this set of data.

c Find the mode of this set of data.

mple 3

4 For each of the following sets of data, calculate the:

 i   range

 ii mean

 iii mode.

a 1, 7, 1, 2, 4   b 2, 2, 10, 8, 13

c 3, 11, 11, 14, 21   d 25, 25, 20, 37, 25, 24

e 1, 22, 10, 20, 33, 10   f 55, 24, 55, 19, 15, 36

g 114, 84, 83, 81, 39, 12, 84   h 97, 31, 18, 54, 18, 63, 6

ple 4a

5 Find the median of:

a 2, 5, 10, 12, 15   b 1, 7, 8, 10, 11

c 3, 1, 5, 2, 9   d 12, 5, 7, 10, 2

e 12, 18, 31, 15, 19, 10, 12   f 17, 63, 4, 13, 97, 82, 56

ole 4b

6 Find the median of:

a 3, 8, 10, 14, 16, 19   b 2, 7, 8, 10, 13, 18

c 1, 5, 2, 9, 13, 17   d 5, 2, 3, 11, 7, 15

e 3, 2, 3, 1, 8, 7, 6, 9   f 4, 9, 2, 7, 8, 1, 5, 6

mple 4

7 The median for the data set 5 7 7 10 12 13 17 is 10. What would be the new median if the following number is added to the data set?

a 9   b 12   c 20   d 2

8   The number of aces that a tennis player serves per match is recorded over eight matches.

Match	1	2	3	4	5	6	7	8
Number of aces	11	18	11	17	19	22	23	12

    a   What is the mean number of aces the player serves per match? Round your answer to 1 decimal place.

    b   What is the median number of aces the player serves per match?

    c   What is the range of this set of data?

PROBLEM-SOLVING	9, 10	10, 11	10–12

9   Brent and Ali organise their test marks for a number of topics in Maths, in a table.

	Test 1	Test 2	Test 3	Test 4	Test 5	Test 6	Test 7	Test 8	Test 9	Test 10
Brent	58	91	91	75	96	60	94	100	96	89
Ali	90	84	82	50	76	67	68	71	85	57

    a   Which student has the higher mean?

    b   Which student has the higher median?

    c   Which student has the smaller range?

    d   Which student do you think is better at tests? Explain why.

10   Alysha's tennis coach records how many double faults Alysha has served per match over a number of matches. Her coach presents the results in a table.

Number of double faults	0	1	2	3	4
Number of matches with this many double faults	2	3	1	4	2

    a   In how many matches does Alysha have no double faults?

    b   In how many matches does Alysha have 3 double faults?

    c   How many matches are included in the coach's study?

    d   What is the total number of double faults scored over the study period?

    e   Calculate the mean of this set of data, correct to 1 decimal place.

    f   What is the range of the data?

11   A soccer goalkeeper recorded the number of saves he makes per game during a season. He presents his records in a table.

Number of saves	0	1	2	3	4	5
Number of games	4	3	0	1	2	2

    a   How many games did he play that season?

    b   What is the mean number of saves this goalkeeper made per game? Hint: first find the total number of saves made for the season.

    c   What is the most common number of saves that the keeper had to make during a game?

12   The set 1, 2, 5, 5, 5, 8, 10, 12 has a mode of 5 and a mean of 6.

    a   If a set of data has a mode of 5 (and no other modes) and a mean of 6, what is the smallest number of values the set could have? Give an example.

    b   Is it possible to make a data set for which the mode is 5, the mean is 6 and the range is 20? Explain your answer.

13 Evie surveys all the students in her class to find the distance from their homes to school. One of the students is on exchange from Canada and reports a distance of 16 658 km. Would this very large value have a greater effect on the mean or median distance? Explain your answer.

14 Consider the set of values 1, 3, 5, 10, 10, 13.
  a Find the mean, median, mode and range.
  b If each number is increased by 5, state the effect this has on the:
    i mean   **ii** median   **iii** mode   **iv** range
  c If each of the original numbers is doubled, state the effect this has on the:
    i mean   **ii** median   **iii** mode   **iv** range
  d Is it possible to include extra numbers and keep the same mean, median, mode and range? Try to expand this set to at least 10 numbers, but keep the same values for the mean, median, mode and range.

15 a Two whole numbers are chosen with a mean of 10 and a range of 6. What are the numbers?
  b Three whole numbers are chosen with a mean of 10 and a range of 2. What are the numbers?
  c Three whole numbers are chosen with a mean of 10 and a range of 4. Can you determine the numbers? Try to find more than one possibility.

16 Prove that for three consecutive numbers, the mean will equal the median.

17 a Give an example of a set of numbers with the following properties.
    i mean = median = mode   **ii** mean > median > mode
    iii mode > median > mean   **iv** median < mode < mean
  b If the range of a set of data is 1, is it still possible to find data sets for each of parts **i** to **iv** above?

18 Find the mean and median of the fractions $\frac{1}{2}, \frac{1}{3}, \frac{1}{4}, \frac{1}{5}$.

An important aspect of scientific investigation is collecting data and summarising it numerically.

8C Column graphs and dot plots

Categorical data can be counted and presented as a *column graph*. Each column's length indicates the frequency of that category. Column graphs can also be useful for labelled continuous data (e.g. height of people).

Discrete numerical data can be counted and presented as a *dot plot*, with the number of dots representing the frequency.

Consider a survey of students who are asked to choose their favourite colour from five possibilities, as well as state how many people live in their household. The colours could be shown as a column graph, and the number of people shown in a dot plot.

Favourite colour

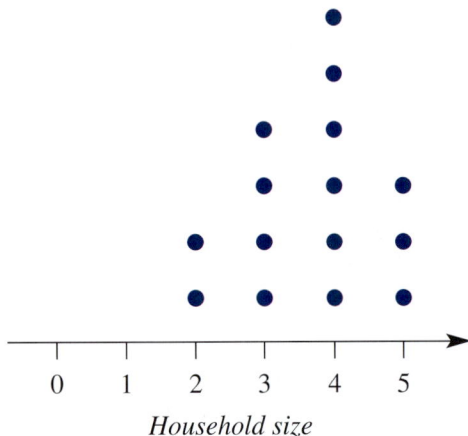

As a column graph (horizontal)

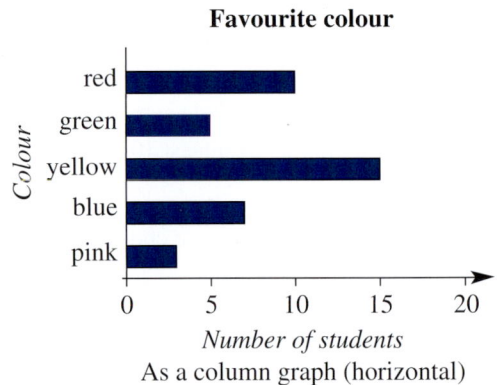

Household size

Favourite colour

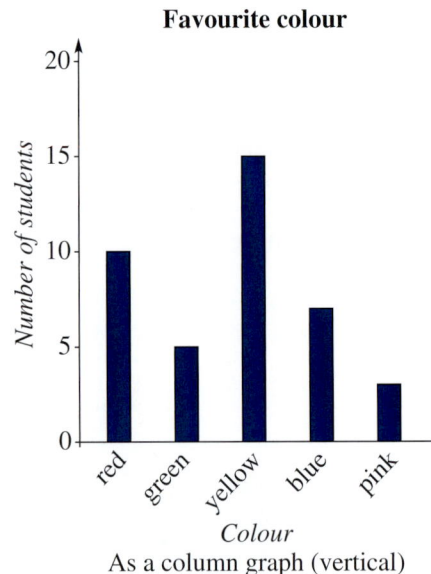

As a column graph (vertical)

Lesson starter: Favourite colours

Survey the class to determine the number of people in each student's family and each student's favourite colour from the possibilities red, green, yellow, blue and pink.

*   Each student should draw a column graph and a dot plot to represent the results.
*   What are some different ways that the results could be presented into a column graph? (There are more than 200 ways.)

KEY IDEAS

■ A **dot plot** can be used to display discrete numerical data, where each dot represents one **datum.**

■ A **column graph** is a way to show data in different categories, and is useful when more than a few items of data are present.

■ Column graphs can be drawn vertically or horizontally. Horizontal column graphs are sometimes also called bar graphs.

■ Graphs should have the following features:

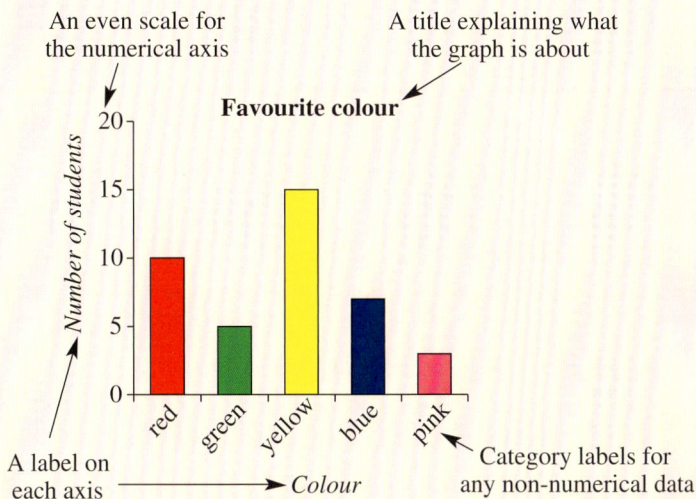

■ Any numerical axis must be drawn to scale.

■ An **outlier** is a value that is noticeably distinct from the main cluster of points.

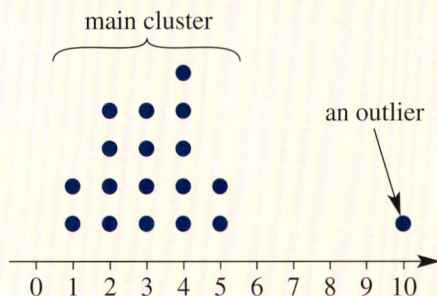

■ Data represented as a dot plot could be described as **symmetrical** or **skewed** (or neither).

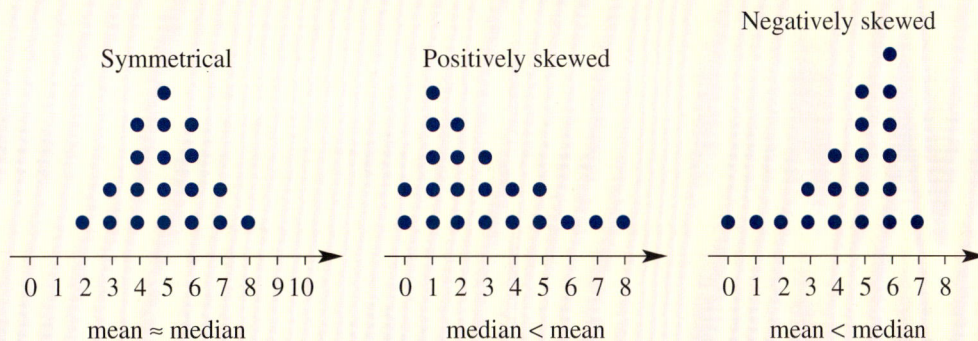

BUILDING UNDERSTANDING

1 The graph opposite shows the height of four boys.

Answer true or false to each of the following statements.
  a Mick is 80 cm tall.
  b Vince is taller than Tranh.
  c Peter is the shortest of the four boys.
  d Tranh is 100 cm tall.
  e Mick is the tallest of the four boys.

Height chart

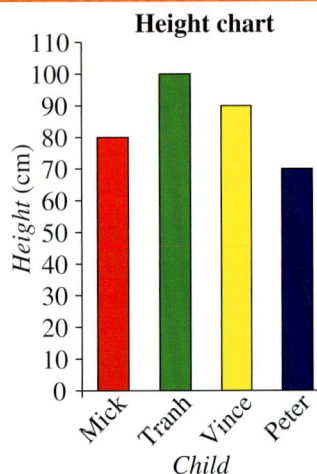

2 The favourite after-school activity of a number of Year 7 students is recorded in the column graph shown opposite.
  a How many students have chosen television as their favourite activity?
  b How many students have chosen social networking as their favourite activity?
  c What is the most popular after-school activity for this group of students?
  d How many students participated in the survey?

After-school activities

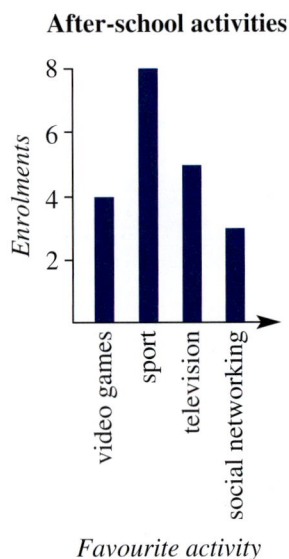

Favourite activity

▶ **Example 5** **Interpreting a dot plot**

The dot plot on the right represents the results of a survey that asked some children how many pets they have at home.
  a Use the graph to state how many children have 2 pets.
  b How many children participated in the survey?
  c What is the range of values?
  d What is the median number of pets?
  e What is the outlier?
  f What is the mode?

Pets at home survey

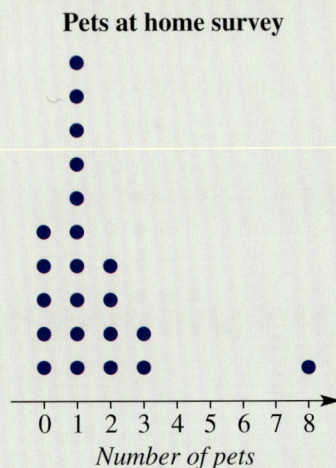

Number of pets

SOLUTION

a   4 children

b   22 children

c $8 - 0 = 8$

d   1 pet

e   the child with 8 pets

f   1 pet

EXPLANATION

There are 4 dots in the '2 pets' category, so 4 children have 2 pets.

The total number of dots is 22.

Range = highest − lowest
In this case, highest = 8, lowest = 0.

As there are 22 children, the median is the average of the 11th and 12th value. In this case, the 11th and 12th values are both 1.

The main cluster of children has between 0 and 3 pets, but the person with 8 pets is significantly outside this cluster.

The most common number of pets is 1.

Now you try

The dot plot shows the number of visits a sample of pet owners have made to the vet in the past year.

a   How many people were surveyed?

b   How many people made more than three visits to the vet in the past year?

c   What is the range?

d   What is the median?

e   What is the outlier?

f   What is the mode?

Visiting the vet

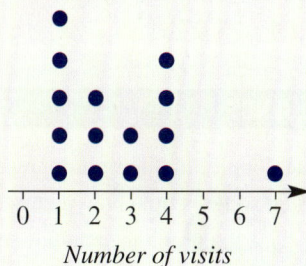

Number of visits

Example 6   Constructing a column graph

Draw a column graph to represent the following people's heights.

Name	Tim	Phil	Jess	Don	Nyree
Height (cm)	150	120	140	100	130

Continued on next page

SOLUTION

Height chart

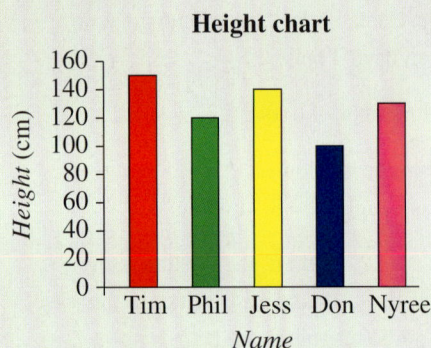

EXPLANATION

First decide which scale goes on the vertical axis.

Maximum height = 150 cm, so axis goes from 0 cm to 160 cm (to allow a bit above the highest value).

Remember to include all the features required, including axes labels and a graph title.

Now you try

Draw a column graph to represent the following people's arm spans.

Name	Matt	Pat	Carly	Kim	Tristan
Arm span (cm)	180	190	150	160	170

Exercise 8C

FLUENCY   1–6   2–7   2, 3, 5–7

Example 5

1   The dot plot on the right represents the results of a survey that asked some people how many times they had flown overseas.

   a   Use the graph to state how many people have flown overseas once.

   b   How many people participated in the survey?

   c   What is the range of values?

   d   What is the median number of times flown overseas?

   e   What is the outlier?

   f   What is the mode?

Overseas flights

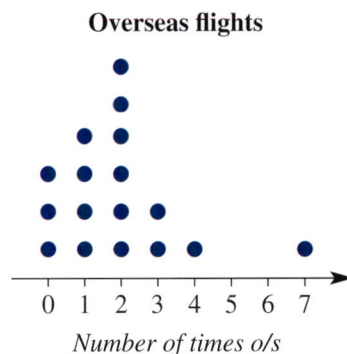

Number of times o/s

Example 5

2   In a Year 4 class, the results of a spelling quiz are presented as a dot plot.

   a   What is the most common score in the class?

   b   How many students participated in the quiz?

   c   What is the range of scores achieved?

   d   What is the median score?

   e   Identify the outlier.

Spelling quiz results

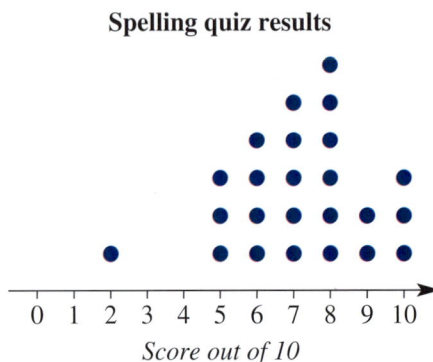

Score out of 10

3 From a choice of pink, blue, yellow, green or red, each student of Year 7B chose their favourite colour. The results are graphed on the right.

a How many students chose yellow?
b How many students chose blue?
c What is the most popular colour?
d How many students participated in the class survey?
e Represent these results as a dot plot.

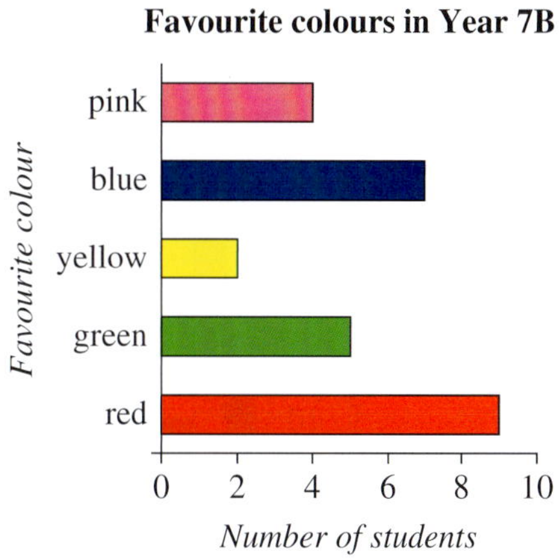

Favourite colours in Year 7B

4 Joan has graphed her height at each of her past five birthdays.

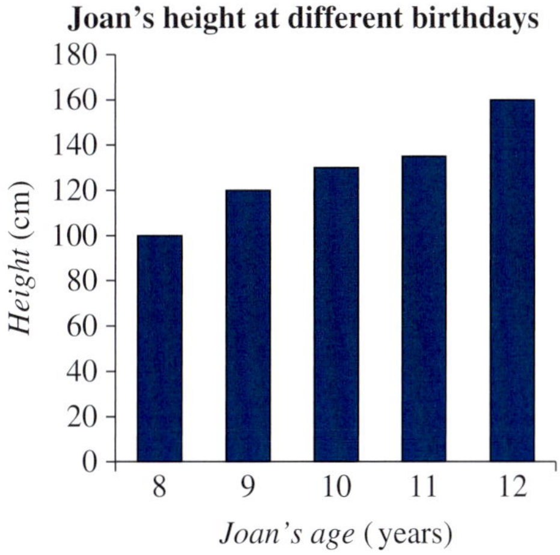

Joan's height at different birthdays

a How tall was Joan on her 9th birthday?
b How much did she grow between her 8th birthday and 9th birthday?
c How much did Joan grow between her 8th and 12th birthdays?
d How old was Joan when she had her biggest growth spurt?

5 Draw a column graph to represent each of these students' heights at their birthdays.

a Mitchell

Age (years)	Height (cm)
8	120
9	125
10	135
11	140
12	145

b Fatu

Age (years)	Height (cm)
8	125
9	132
10	140
11	147
12	150

Example 6

6 Every five years, a company in the city conducts a transport survey of people's preferred method of getting to work in the mornings. The results are graphed below.

Transport methods

a Copy the following table into your workbook and complete it, using the graph.

	1990	1995	2000	2005	2010	2015
Use public transport	30					
Drive a car	60					
Walk or cycle	10					

b In which year(s) is public transport the most popular option?
c In which year(s) are more people walking or cycling to work than driving?
d Give a reason why the number of people driving to work has decreased.
e What is one other trend that you can see from looking at this graph?

7 a Draw a column graph to show the results of the following survey of the number of male and female puppies sold by a commercial dog breeder. Put time (years) on the horizontal axis.

	2010	2011	2012	2013	2014	2015
Number of male puppies born	40	42	58	45	30	42
Number of female puppies born	50	40	53	41	26	35

b During which year(s) were there more female puppies sold than male puppies?
c Which year had the fewest number of puppies sold?
d Which year had the greatest number of puppies sold?
e During the entire period of the survey, were there more male or female puppies sold?

PROBLEM-SOLVING   8   8, 9   9, 10

8 The average (mean) income of adults in a particular town is graphed over a 6-year period.

a Describe in one sentence what has happened to the income over this period of time.
b Estimate what the average income in this town might have been in 2012.
c Estimate what the average income might be in 2028 if this trend continues.

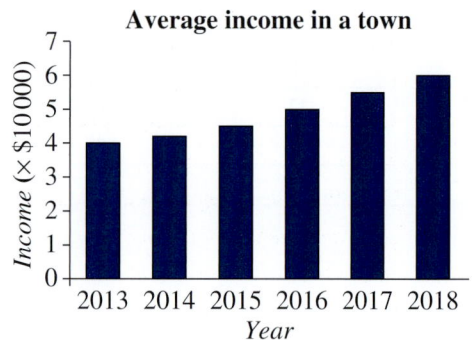

Average income in a town

9 A survey is conducted of students' favourite subjects from a choice of Art, Maths, English, History and Science. Someone has attempted to depict the results in a column graph.

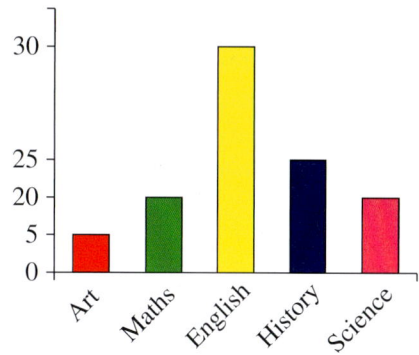

   a What is wrong with the scale on the vertical axis?

   b Give at least two other problems with this graph.

   c Redraw the graph with an even scale and appropriate labels.

   d The original graph makes Maths look twice as popular as Art, based on the column size. According to the survey, how many times more popular is Maths?

   e The original graph makes English look three times as popular as Maths. According to the survey, how much more popular is English?

   f Assume that Music is now added to the survey's choice of subjects. Five students who had previously chosen History now choose Music, and 16 students who had previously chosen English now choose Music. What is the most popular subject now?

10 Mr Martin and Mrs Stevensson are the two Year 3 teachers at a school. For the latest arithmetic quiz, they have plotted their students' scores on a special dot plot called a parallel dot plot, shown opposite.

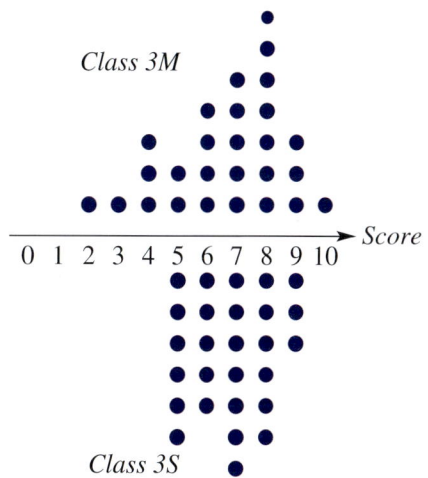

Arithmetic quiz scores

   a What is the median score for class 3M?

   b What is the median score for class 3S?

   c State the range of scores for each class.

   d Based on this test, which class has a greater spread of arithmetic abilities?

   e If the two classes competed in an arithmetic competition, where each class is allowed only one representative, which class is more likely to win? Justify your answer.

REASONING	11	11, 12	12, 13

11 At a central city train station, three types of services run: local, country and interstate. The average number of passenger departures during each week is shown in the stacked column graph.

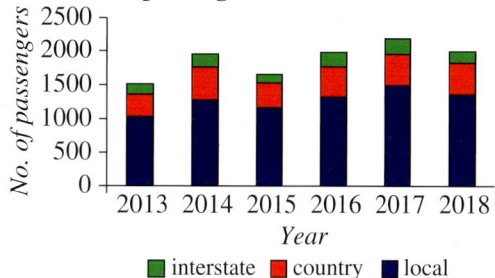

Train passengers at Urbanville Station

   a Approximately how many passenger departures per week were there in 2013?

   b Approximately how many passenger departures were there *in total* during 2018?

   c Does this graph suggest that the total number of passenger departures has increased or decreased during the period 2013–2018?

   d Approximately how many passengers departed from this station in the period 2013–2018? Explain your method clearly and try to get your answer within 10 000 of the actual number.

12 The mean value of data represented in a dot plot can be found by adding the value represented by each dot, then dividing by the number of dots.

Number of children

a Use this method to find the mean number of children per household, shown in this dot plot of 10 households.

b A faster method is to calculate $(2 \times 1) + (3 \times 2) + (4 \times 3) + (1 \times 4)$ and divide by 10. Explain why this also works to find the mean.

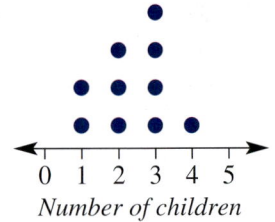

13 Classify the following dot plots as representing symmetrical, positively skewed or negatively skewed data. Find the mean number in each case and compare it to the median.

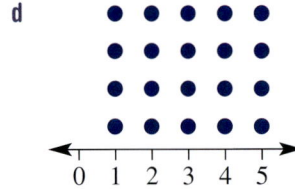

a

b

c

d

ENRICHMENT: How many ways? — — 14

14 As well as being able to draw a graph horizontally or vertically, the order of the categories can be changed. For instance, the following three graphs all represent the same data.

How many different column graphs could be used to represent the results of this survey? (Assume that you can only change the order of the columns, and the horizontal or vertical layout.) Try to list the options systematically to help with your count.

8D Line graphs

A **line graph** is a connected set of points joined with straight line segments. The variables on both axes should be continuous numerical data. It is often used when a measurement varies over time, in which case time is conventionally listed on the horizontal axis. One advantage of a line graph over a series of disconnected points is that it can often be used to estimate values that are unknown.

A business can use line graphs to display data such as expenses, sales and profits, versus time. A line graph makes it easy to visualise trends, and predictions can then be made.

Lesson starter: Room temperature

As an experiment, the temperature in two rooms is measured hourly over a period of time. The results are graphed below.

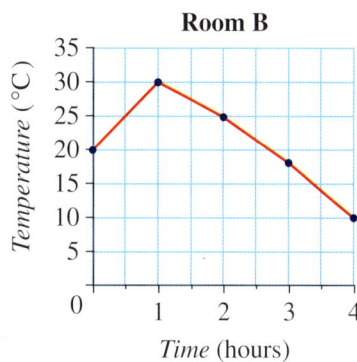

- Each room has a heater and an air conditioner to control the temperature. At what point do you think these were switched on and off in each room?
- For each room, what is the approximate temperature 90 minutes after the start of the experiment?
- What is the proportion of time that room A is hotter than room B?

KEY IDEAS

■ A **line graph** consists of a series of points joined by straight line segments.

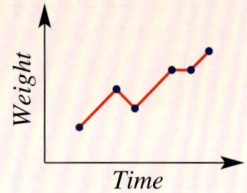

- The variables on both axes should be **continuous** numerical data.

- Time is often shown on the horizontal axis.

■ A common type of line graph is a **travel graph**.
- Time is shown on the horizontal axis.
- Distance is shown on the vertical axis.
- The slope of the line indicates the rate at which the distance is changing over time This is called **speed**.

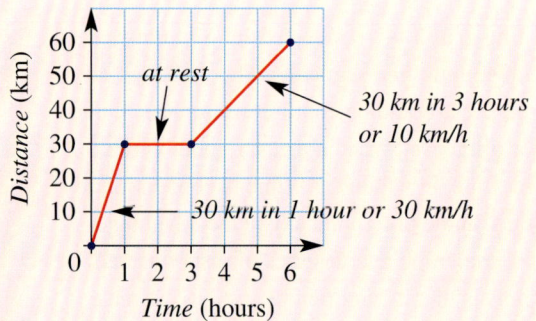

BUILDING UNDERSTANDING

1 The line graph shows the weight of a cat over a 3-month period. It is weighed at the start of each month. State the cat's weight at the start of:

a January

b February

c March

d April

Cat's weight over time

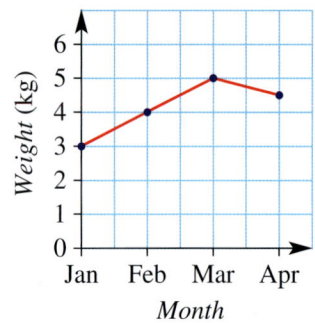

2 The graph shows Lillian's height over a 10-year period from when she was born.

a What was Lillian's height when she was born?

b What was Lillian's height at the age of 7 years?

c At what age did she first reach 130 cm tall?

d How much did Lillian grow in the year when she was 7 years old?

e Use the graph to estimate her height at the age of $9\frac{1}{2}$ years.

Lillian's height

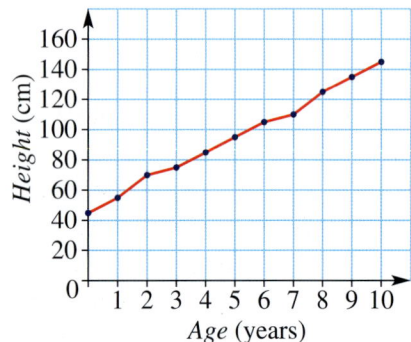

Example 7   Drawing a line graph

The temperature in a room is noted at hourly intervals.

Time	9 a.m.	10 a.m.	11 a.m.	12 p.m.	1 p.m.
Temperature (°C)	10	15	20	23	18

a   Present the results as a line graph.

b   Use your graph to estimate the room temperature at 12:30 p.m.

SOLUTION

a

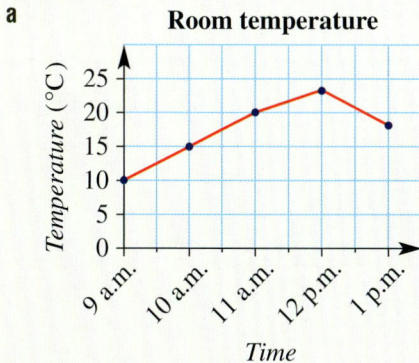

Room temperature

b   About 20°C

EXPLANATION

- The vertical axis is from 0 to 25. The scale is even (i.e. increasing by 5 each time).
- Dots are placed for each measurement and joined with straight line segments.

By looking at the graph halfway between 12 p.m. and 1 p.m., an estimate is formed.

Now you try

The temperature outside is noted at hourly intervals.

Time	4 p.m.	5 p.m.	6 p.m.	7 p.m.	8 p.m.
Temperature (°C)	25	30	20	18	15

a   Present the results as a line graph.

b   Use your graph to estimate the outside temperature at 5:30 p.m.

Example 8   Interpreting a travel graph

This travel graph shows the distance travelled by a cyclist over 5 hours.

a   How far did the cyclist travel in total?

b   How far did the cyclist travel in the first hour?

c   What is happening in the second hour?

d   When is the cyclist travelling the fastest?

e   In the fifth hour, how far does the cyclist travel?

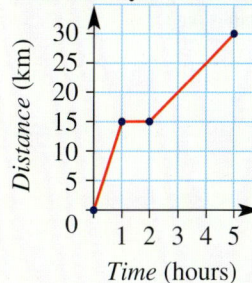

Distance cycled over 5 hours

Continued on next page

SOLUTION	EXPLANATION
a 30 km	The right end point of the graph is at (5, 30).
b 15 km	At time equals 1 hour, the distance covered is 15 km.
c at rest	The distance travelled does not increase in the second hour.
d in the first hour	This is the steepest part of the graph.
e 5 km	In the last 3 hours, the distance travelled is 15 km, so in 1 hour, 5 km is travelled.

Now you try

This travel graph shows the distance travelled by a hiker over 4 hours.

a How far did the hiker travel in total?

b How far did the hiker travel in the first hour?

c When is the hiker stationary?

d When is the hiker travelling the fastest?

e How far was travelled in the fourth hour?

Distance hiked over 4 hours

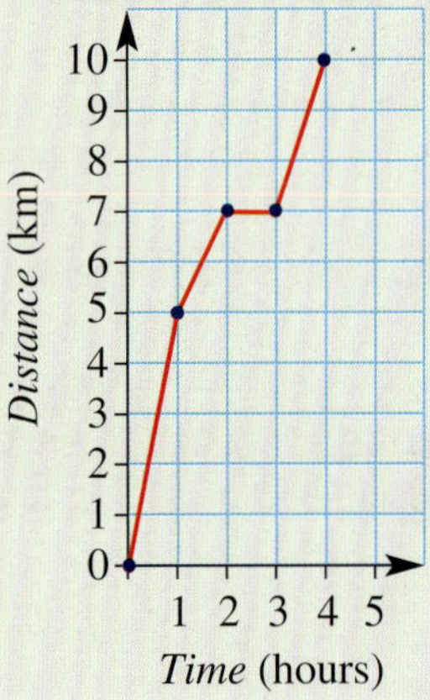

Exercise 8D

FLUENCY

| 1–4 | 2–5 | 2, 4, 5 |

Example 7

1 A dog is weighed at the beginning of each month for five months as shown.

a Draw a line graph of its weight.

Month	Jan	Feb	March	April	May
Weight (kg)	5	6	8	7	6

b Use your graph to estimate the weight of the dog mid April.

2 Oliver measures his pet dog's weight over the course of a year, by weighing it at the start of each month. He obtains the following results.

	Jan	Feb	Mar	Apr	May	Jun	Jul	Aug	Sep	Oct	Nov	Dec
Weight (kg)	7	7.5	8.5	9	9.5	9	9.2	7.8	7.8	7.5	8.3	8.5

a Draw a line graph showing this information, making sure the vertical axis has an equal scale from 0 kg to 10 kg.

b Describe any trends or patterns that you see.

c Oliver put his dog on a weight loss diet for a period of 3 months. When do you think the dog started the diet? Justify your answer.

3 Consider the following graph, which shows the outside temperature over a 24-hour period that starts at midnight.

a What was the temperature at midday?

b When was the hottest time of the day?

c When was the coolest time of the day?

d Use the graph to estimate the temperature at these times of the day:

  i 4:00 a.m.

  ii 9:00 a.m.

  iii 1:00 p.m.

  iv 3:15 p.m.

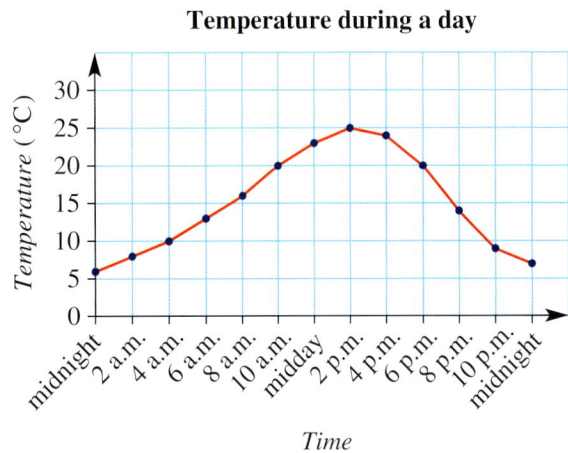

Temperature during a day

Time

4 This travel graph shows the distance travelled by a van over 6 hours.

a How far did the van travel in total?

b How far did the van travel in the first hour?

c What is happening in the fourth hour? (i.e. from $t = 3$ to $t = 4$)

d When is the van travelling the fastest?

e Estimate how far the van travels in the sixth hour?

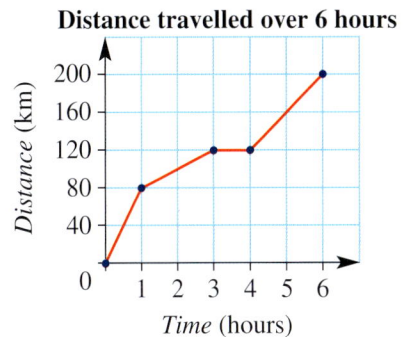

Distance travelled over 6 hours

Time (hours)

5 This travel graph shows the distance travelled by a bushwalker over 5 hours.

a For how long was the bushwalker at rest?

b How far did the bushwalker walk in the second hour?

c During which hour did the bushwalker walk the fastest?

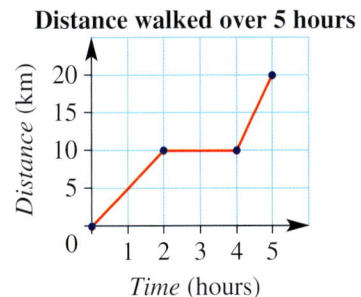

Distance walked over 5 hours

Time (hours)

PROBLEM-SOLVING   6   6   6, 7

6 The water storage levels for a given city are graphed based on the percentage of water available on the first day of each month. For this question, assume that the amount of water used does not change from month to month.

   a During which month did it rain the most in this city?

   b At what time(s) in the year is the water storage below 40%?

   c From August 1 to September 1, if a total of 20 megalitres of water went into storage, how much water was used during this period?

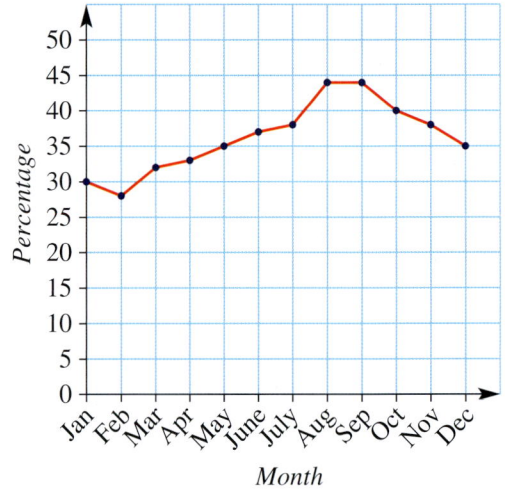

Water storage levels

Percentage vs *Month*

7 The temperature in a living room is measured frequently throughout a particular day. The results are presented in a line graph, as shown below. The individual points are not indicated on this graph to reduce clutter.

   a Twice during the day the heating was switched on. At what times do you think this happened? Explain your reasoning.

   b When was the heating switched off? Explain your reasoning.

   c The house has a single occupant, who works during the day. Describe when you think that person is:

      i waking up

      ii going to work

      iii coming home

      iv going to bed.

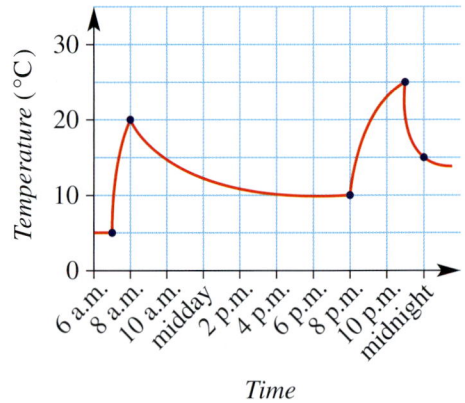

Temperature in a living room

Temperature (°C) vs *Time*

   d These temperatures were recorded during a cold winter month. Draw a graph that shows what the lounge room temperature might look like during a hot summer month. Assume that the room has an air conditioner, which the person is happy to use when at home.

REASONING   8   8, 9   8–10

8 Draw travel graphs to illustrate the following journeys.

   a A car travels:
   - 120 km in the first 2 hours
   - 0 km in the third hour
   - 60 km in the fourth hour
   - 120 km in the fifth hour.

   b A jogger runs:
   - 12 km in the first hour
   - 6 km in the second hour
   - 0 km in the third hour
   - at a rate of 6 km per hour for 2 hours.

9   Explain how the steepness of sections of a travel graph can be used to describe how fast someone or something is travelling.

10 A person records the length (cm) and weight (grams) of newborn babies at a hospital over the course of a year.
    a   Explain what would be wrong with drawing a line graph with length on the horizontal axis and weight on the vertical axis.
    b   Give an example of a possible use of line graphs when dealing with newborn baby length or weight data.

ENRICHMENT: Which hemisphere?   11

11 The following line graph shows the maximum temperature in a city for the first day of each month.

Temperature in a year

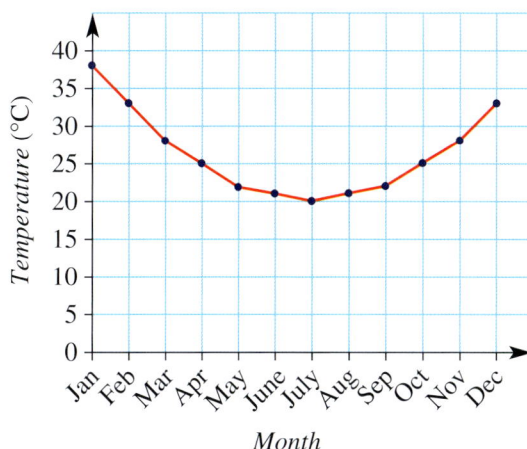

Month

    a   Is this city in the Northern or Southern hemisphere? Explain why.
    b   Is this city close to the equator or far from the equator? Explain why.
    c   Redraw the graph to start the 12-month period at July and finish in June.
    d   Describe how the new graph's appearance is different from the one shown above.
    e   In another city, somebody graphs the maximum temperature over a 12-month period, as shown opposite.
        In which hemisphere is this city likely to be? Explain your answer.

Temperature in a year

Month

8E Stem-and-leaf plots

LEARNING INTENTIONS
- To be able to interpret a stem-and-leaf plot
- To be able to represent data in a stem-and-leaf plot

A stem-and-leaf plot is a useful way of presenting numerical data in a way that allows trends to be spotted easily. Each number is split into a stem (the first digit or digits) and a leaf (the last digit).

	Stem	Leaf
53 is	5	3
78 is	7	8
125 is	12	5

By convention, leaves are shown in increasing order as you work away from the stem, and stems are shown in increasing order going down the page.

The advantage of presenting data like this comes when multiple numbers have the same stem. For example, the list 122, 123, 124, 124, 127, 129 can be represented as shown below.

Stem	Leaf
12	2 3 4 4 7 9

Stem-and-leaf plots are used to display data such as in government, scientific and business reports. This plot lists daily temperatures (e.g. 2|5 means 25°C). The range = 34 − 18 = 16°C. Can you find the median and the mode?

Lesson starter: Test score analysis

In a class, students' most recent test results out of 50 are recorded.

Test 1 results
43, 47, 50, 26, 38, 20, 25, 20, 50, 44, 33, 47, 47, 50, 37, 28, 28, 22, 21, 29

Test 2 results

Stem	Leaf
1	8
2	7 8
3	2 2 4 5 5 7 9
4	0 1 2 3 3 6 8 8
5	0 0

4|3 means 43 out of 50 marks

- For each test, try to find how many students:
  - achieved a perfect score (i.e. 50)
  - failed the test (i.e. less than 25)
  - achieved a mark in the 40s.
- If there are 100 test results that you wish to analyse, would you prefer a list or a stem-and-leaf plot?
- What is it that makes a stem-and-leaf plot easier to work with? Discuss.

KEY IDEAS

■ A stem-and-leaf plot is a way to display numerical data.

■ Each number is usually split into a **stem** (the first digit or digits) and a **leaf** (the last digit).

■ For example:

Stem	Leaf
0	7
3	1
15	2

The number 7 is   0 | 7
The number 31 is   3 | 1
The number 152 is   15 | 2

3|1 means 31

■ A key is usually connected to each stem-and-leaf plot to show the value of the stem and leaf. For example: 4|8 means 48 or 4|8 means 4.8 cm.

■ Leaves should be aligned vertically, listed in ascending order as you move away from the stem.

■ Any outliers can be identified by looking at the lowest value or highest value to see if they are far away from all the other numbers.

■ The **shape** of a distribution can be seen from a stem-and-leaf plot:

Symmetrical

Stem	Leaf
1	3 6
2	1 3 9
3	0 1 2 5
4	0 2 3
5	4 5

Positively Skewed

Stem	Leaf
1	1 2 6
2	4 7 8 8
3	2 5 9
4	3 8
5	4
6	8
7	0

Negatively Skewed

Stem	Leaf
2	9
3	6
4	3
5	1 8
6	2 4 5 7
7	3 5

BUILDING UNDERSTANDING

1 The number 52 is entered into a stem-and-leaf plot.
   a What digit is the stem?   **b** What digit is the leaf?

2 If 8|5 represents 85, what number is represented by the following combinations?
   a 3|9   **b** 2|7   **c** 13|4

3 In this stem-and-leaf plot, the smallest number is 35. What is the largest number?

Stem	Leaf
3	5 7 7 9
4	2 8
5	1 7

3|5 means 35

Example 9   Interpreting a stem-and-leaf plot

Average daily temperatures are shown for some different countries.

Stem	Leaf
1	3 6 6
2	0 0 1 2 5 5 6 8 9
3	0 2

2|5 means 25°C

a   Write out the temperatures as a list.
b   How many countries' temperatures are represented?
c   What are the minimum and maximum temperatures?
d   What is the range of temperatures recorded?
e   What is the median temperature recorded?

SOLUTION

a   13, 16, 16, 20, 20, 21, 22, 25, 25,
     26, 28, 29, 30, 32

b   14

c   minimum = 13°C
     maximum = 32°C

d   range = 19°C

e   median = 23.5°C

EXPLANATION

Each number is converted from a stem and a leaf to a single number. For example, 1|3 is converted to 13.

The easiest way is to count the number of leaves – each leaf corresponds to one country.

The first stem and leaf is 1|3 and the last stem and leaf is 3|2.

Range = maximum − minimum = 32 − 13 = 19.

The middle value is halfway between the numbers 2|2 and 2|5, so median = $\frac{1}{2}(22 + 25) = 23.5$.

Now you try

The age of a number of people is shown in a stem-and-leaf plot.

a   Write out the ages as a list.
b   How many people's ages are represented?
c   What are the youngest and oldest people's ages?
d   Give the range of ages.
e   What is the median age?

Stem	Leaf
1	8
2	1 1 4
3	0 2 8 9
4	3

3|2 means 32 years old

Example 10   Creating a stem-and-leaf plot

Represent this set of data as a stem-and-leaf plot:
23, 10, 36, 25, 31, 34, 34, 27, 36, 37, 16, 33

SOLUTION

Sorted: 10, 16, 23, 25, 27, 31, 33, 34, 34, 36, 36, 37

Stem	Leaf
1	0 6
2	3 5 7
3	1 3 4 4 6 6 7

2|5 means 25

EXPLANATION

Sort the list in increasing order so that it can be put directly into a stem-and-leaf plot.

Split each number into a stem and a leaf. Stems are listed in increasing order and leaves are aligned vertically, listed in increasing order down the page.

Add a key to show the value of the stem and leaf.

Now you try

Represent this set of data as a stem-and-leaf plot:
36, 42, 38, 24, 32, 25, 29, 41, 48, 35.

Exercise 8E

FLUENCY   1–3, 4(½)   2, 3, 4–5(½)   3, 4–5(½)

1   The number of buttons on some calculators are shown in this stem and leaf plot.
   a   Write out all the numbers in a list.
   b   How many calculators are represented?
   c   What are the minimum and maximum number of buttons?
   d   What is the range of the number of buttons recorded?
   e   What is the median number of buttons recorded?

Stem	Leaf
1	3 7
2	0 2 4 8 9
3	1 3 5

2|4 means 24

2   This stem-and-leaf plot shows the ages of people in a group.
   a   Write out the ages as a list.
   b   How many ages are shown?
   c   Answer true or false to each of the following.
      i   The youngest person is aged 10.
      ii   Someone in the group is 17 years old.
      iii Nobody listed is aged 20.
      iv   The oldest person is aged 4.

Stem	Leaf
0	8 9
1	0 1 3 5 7 8
2	1 4

1|5 means 15 years old

Example 9d,e

3 For each of the stem-and-leaf plots below, state the range and the median.

a

Stem	Leaf
0	9
1	3 5 6 7 7 8 9
2	0 1 9

1|8 means 18

b

Stem	Leaf
1	1 4 8
2	1 2 4 4 6 8
3	0 3 4 7 9
4	2

3|7 means 37

c

Stem	Leaf
3	1 1 2 3 4 4 8 8 9
4	0 1 1 2 3 5 7 8
5	0 0 0

4|2 means 42

Example 10

4 Represent each of the following sets of data as a stem-and-leaf plot.
   a 11, 12, 13, 14, 14, 15, 17, 20, 24, 28, 29, 31, 32, 33, 35
   b 20, 22, 39, 45, 47, 49, 49, 51, 52, 52, 53, 55, 56, 58, 58
   c 21, 35, 24, 31, 16, 28, 48, 18, 49, 41, 50, 33, 29, 16, 32
   d 32, 27, 38, 60, 29, 78, 87, 60, 37, 81, 38, 11, 73, 12, 14

Example 10

5 Represent each of the following data sets as a stem-and-leaf plot. (Remember: 101 is represented as 10|1.)
   a 80, 84, 85, 86, 90, 96, 101, 104, 105, 110, 113, 114, 114, 115, 119
   b 120, 81, 106, 115, 96, 98, 94, 115, 113, 86, 102, 117, 108, 91, 95
   c 192, 174, 155, 196, 185, 178, 162, 157, 173, 181, 158, 193, 167, 192, 184, 187, 193, 165, 199, 184
   d 401, 420, 406, 415, 416, 406, 412, 402, 409, 418, 404, 405, 391, 411, 413, 408, 395, 396, 417

PROBLEM-SOLVING	6, 7	7, 8	8–10

6 This back-to-back stem-and-leaf plot shows the ages of all the people in two shops. The youngest person in Shop 1 is 15 (not 51).

For each statement below, state whether it is true in Shop 1 only (1), Shop 2 only (2), both shops (B) or neither shop (N).

Shop 1	Stem	Shop 2
5	1	6 7
7 7 5 3	2	4 5
	3	1
2	4	5

1|5 means 15 years old

   a This shop has a 31-year-old person in it.
   b This shop has six people in it.
   c This shop has a 42-year-old person in it.
   d This shop has a 25-year-old person in it.
   e This shop has two people with the same age.
   f This shop has a 52-year-old person in it.
   g This shop has a 24-year-old person in it.
   h This shop's oldest customer is an outlier.
   i This shop's youngest customer is an outlier.

7 A company recorded the duration (in seconds) that visitors spent on its website's home page.

a How many visitors spent less than 20 seconds on the home page?

b How many visitors spent more than half a minute?

c How many visitors spent between 10 and 30 seconds?

d What is the outlier for this stem-and-leaf plot?

e The company wishes to summarise its results with a single number. 'Visitors spend approximately ____ on our home page.' What number could it use?

Stem	Leaf
0	2 4 6 8 9
1	0 0 1 2 8
2	2 7 9
3	
4	
5	8

2|7 means 27 seconds

8 Two radio stations poll their audience to determine their ages.

a Find the age difference between the oldest and youngest listener polled for:

  i station 1

  ii station 2.

b One of the radio stations plays contemporary music that is designed to appeal to teenagers and the other plays classical music and broadcasts the news. Which radio station is most likely to be the one that plays classical music and news?

c Advertisers wish to know the age of the stations' audiences so that they can target their advertisements more effectively (e.g. to 38 to 57 year olds; note that "38-57" is a 20-year age range, not 19 years, because it starts at 38 years 0 days and extends to 57 years 364.999... days.). Give a 20-year age range for the audience majority who listen to:

  i station 1

  ii station 2.

Station 1	Stem	Station 2
0	1	2 3 3 4 5 6 8 9
8 7	2	0 0 1 2 4 5 8 8
9 7 5 4 3 3	3	1 1 2
7 6 5 5 4 4 1	4	8
9 3 2 0	5	

3|4 means 34 years old

9 A group of students in Year 6 and Year 7 have their heights recorded in a back-to-back stem-and-leaf plot, shown here.

a State the range of heights for:

  i Year 7   ii Year 6.

b Which year level has a bigger range?

c State the median height for:

  i Year 7   ii Year 6.

d Which year level has the larger median height?

e Describe how you might expect this back-to-back stem-and-leaf plot to change if it recorded the heights of Year 1 students on the left, and Year 9 students on the right.

Year 6	Stem	Year 7
	10	
	11	
6 3 1	12	
8 4 3 2	13	8
7 6 5 4 0	14	3 4 7 9
6 4 1	15	0 1 2 4 6
2 0	16	2 3 6 8
3	17	

14|6 means 146 cm

10 A teacher has compiled her students' recent test scores out of 50 as a stem-and-leaf plot. However, some values are missing, as represented by the letters a, b, c and d.

Stem	Leaf
1	5
2	4 5 a 6 7 9
3	b 0 1 5
4	2 8 c
5	d

3|1 means 31

a How many students took the test?

b How many students passed the test (i.e. achieved a mark of 25 or higher)?

c State the possible values for each of the missing digits a to d.

REASONING   11   11, 12   12, 13

11 a Explain why it is important that leaves are aligned vertically. (*Hint*: Consider how the overall appearance could be helpful with a large data set.)

b Why might it be important that data values are sorted in stem-and-leaf plots?

12 a Give an example of positively skewed data in a stem-and-leaf plot, and investigate how the mean and median compare.

b Give an example of negatively skewed data in a stem-and-leaf plot, and investigate how the mean and median compare.

c Give an example of symmetrical data in a stem-and-leaf plot, and investigate how the mean and median compare.

13 A stem-and-leaf plot is constructed showing the ages of all the people who attended a local farmers' market at a certain time of the day. However, the plot's leaves cannot be read.

Stem	Leaf
1	?
2	?
3	? ? ? ? ? ? ? ? ? ?
4	? ? ? ? ? ? ? ? ? ? ? ? ? ? ? ?
5	? ? ?

a For each of the following, either determine the exact answer or give a range of values the answer could take.

   i How many people were at the market?

   ii How many people aged in their 30s were at the market?

   iii How old is the youngest person?

   iv What is the age difference between the youngest and oldest person?

   v How many people aged 40 or over were at the market?

   vi How many people aged 35 or over were at the market?

b Classify each of the following as true or false.

   i The majority of people at the market were aged in their 30s or 40s.

   ii There were five teenagers present.

   iii Exactly two people were aged 29 years or under.

   iv Two people in their 40s must have had the same age.

   v Two people in their 30s must have had the same age.

   vi Two people in their 20s could have had the same age.

c Explain why it is possible to determine how many people were aged 40 or over, but not the number of people who are aged 40 or under.

d It is discovered that the person under 20 years of age is an outlier for this market. What does that tell you about how old the next oldest person is?

ENRICHMENT: Negative stem-and-leaf plots   –   –   14

14 Negative numbers can also be displayed in stem-and-leaf plots. This stem-and-leaf plot gives the average winter temperatures in 15 different cities.

Stem	Leaf
-2	9 4 4
-1	7 5 3 2
-0	8 5
0	3 4 6
1	5 8
2	3

$-1|5$ means $-15°C$

a What are the minimum and maximum temperatures listed?

b Find how many cities had average temperatures:
   i between $-10°C$ and $10°C$
   ii between $-25°C$ and $5°C$
   iii below $5°C$.

c Why is there a 0 row and a -0 row, even though 0 and -0 are the same number?

d What is the average (or mean) of all the listed temperatures in the 15 cities? Give your answer correct to 1 decimal place.

e What is the median of all the listed temperatures? Compare this to the mean found in part d.

8F   Sector graphs and divided bar graphs   EXTENDING

LEARNING INTENTIONS
- To understand that pie charts and divided bar graphs are used to represent proportions of a total
- To be able to draw and interpret a pie chart
- To be able to draw and interpret a divided bar graph

A pie chart (also called a sector graph) consists of a circle divided into different sectors or 'slices of pie', where the size of each sector indicates the proportion occupied by any given category. A divided bar graph is a rectangle divided into different rectangles or 'bars', where the size of each rectangle indicates the proportion of each category.

If a student is asked to describe how much time they spend each evening doing different activities, they could present their results as either type of graph:

From both graphs, it is easy to see that most of the student's time is spent playing sport and the least amount of time is spent using the internet.

Lesson starter: Student hobbies

Rania, Kristina and Ralph are asked to record how they spend their time after school. They draw the following graphs.

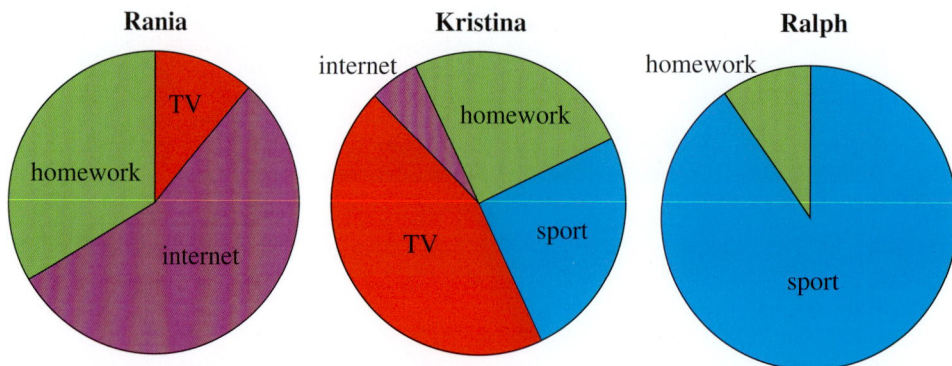

- Based on these graphs alone, describe each student in a few sentences.
- Justify your descriptions based on the graphs.

KEY IDEAS

■ To calculate the size of each section of the graph, divide the value in a given category by the sum of all category values. This gives the category's proportion or fraction.

■ To draw a **sector graph** (also called a **pie chart**), multiply each category's proportion or fraction by 360° and draw a sector of that size.

■ To draw a **divided bar graph**, multiply each category's proportion or fraction by the total width of the rectangle and draw a rectangle of that size.

BUILDING UNDERSTANDING

1 Jasna graphs a sector graph of how she spends her leisure time.

   a What does Jasna spend the most time doing?

   b What does Jasna spend the least time doing?

   c Does she spend more or less than half of her time playing sport?

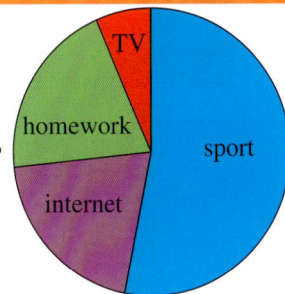

2 Thirty students are surveyed to find out their favourite sport and their results are graphed below.

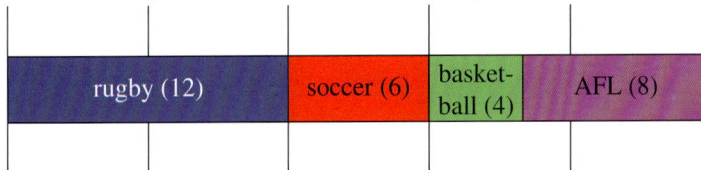

   a What is the most popular sport for this group of students?

   b What is the least popular sport for this group of students?

   c What fraction of the students has chosen soccer as their favourite sport?

   d What fraction of the students has chosen either rugby or AFL?

Example 11   Drawing a sector graph and a divided bar graph

On a particular Saturday, Sanjay measures the number of hours he spends on different activities.

Television	Internet	Sport	Homework
1 hour	2 hours	4 hours	3 hours

Represent the table as:

a a sector graph

b a divided bar graph.

Continued on next page

SOLUTION

a

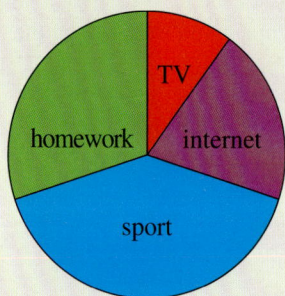

b

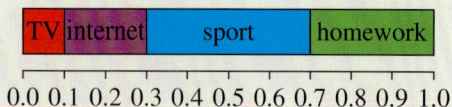

0.0 0.1 0.2 0.3 0.4 0.5 0.6 0.7 0.8 0.9 1.0

EXPLANATION

The total amount of time is
$1 + 2 + 4 + 3 = 10$ hours. Then we can
calculate the proportions and sector sizes:

Category	Proportion	Sector size (°)
Television	$\frac{1}{10}$	$\frac{1}{10} \times 360 = 36$
Internet	$\frac{2}{10} = \frac{1}{5}$	$\frac{1}{5} \times 360 = 72$
Sport	$\frac{4}{10} = \frac{2}{5}$	$\frac{2}{5} \times 360 = 144$
Homework	$\frac{3}{10}$	$\frac{3}{10} \times 360 = 108$

Using the same proportions calculated
above, make sure that each rectangle takes
up the correct amount of space. For example,
if the total width is 15 cm, then sport
occupies $\frac{2}{5} \times 15 = 6$ cm.

Now you try

Consider the following time allocation:

Entertainment	Sport	Homework
5 hours	2 hours	3 hours

Represent this table as:

a a sector graph

b a divided bar graph.

Exercise 8F

FLUENCY   1–3   2–3   3

Example 11 **1** Consider the following results of a study on supermarket shopping habits.

Items	Food	Drinks	Household items	Other
Proportion of money spent	50%	25%	20%	5%

a Represent this information in a divided bar graph.

b Graph this information as a sector graph.

ple 11a **2** A group of passengers arriving at an airport is surveyed to establish which countries they have come from. The results are presented below.

Country	China	United Kingdom	USA	France
No. of passengers	6	5	7	2

a What is the total number of passengers who participated in the survey?

b What proportion of the passengers surveyed have come from the following countries? Express your answer as a fraction.

    i China   ii United Kingdom

    iii USA   iv France

c On a sector graph, determine the angle size of the sector representing:

    i China   ii United Kingdom

    iii USA   iv France

d Draw a pie chart showing the information calculated in part c.

ple 11b **3** A group of students in Years 7 and 8 is polled on their favourite colour, and the results are shown at right.

Colour	Year 7 votes	Year 8 votes
Red	20	10
Green	10	4
Yellow	5	12
Blue	10	6
Pink	15	8

a Draw a sector graph (pie chart) to represent the Year 7 colour preferences.

b Draw a different pie chart to represent the Year 8 colour preferences.

c Describe two differences between the charts.

d Construct a divided bar graph that shows the popularity of each colour across the total number of Years 7 and 8 students combined

PROBLEM-SOLVING	4	4, 5	5, 6

4 A group of Year 7 students was polled on their favourite foods, and the results are shown in this sector graph.

a If 40 students participated in the survey, find how many of them chose:

    i chocolate   ii chips

    iii fruit   iv pies.

b Health experts are worried about what these results mean. They would like fruit to appear more prominently in the sector graph, and to not have the chocolate sector next to the chips. Redraw the sector graph so this is the case.

c Another 20 students were surveyed. Ten of these students chose chocolate and the other 10 chose chips. Their results are to be included in the sector graph. Of the four sectors in the graph, state which sector will:

    i increase in size   ii decrease in size   iii stay the same size.

5 Yakob has asked his friends what is their favourite school subject, and he has created the following divided bar graph from the information.

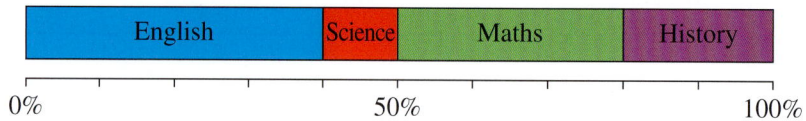

English	Science	Maths	History

0%   50%   100%

a If Yakob surveyed 30 friends, state how many of them like:
  i   Maths best
  ii History best
  iii either English or Science best.

b Redraw these results as a sector graph.

6 Friends Krishna and Nikolas have each graphed their leisure habits, as shown below.

  a Which of the two friends spends more of their time playing sport?

  b Which of the two friends does more intellectual activities in their leisure time?

  c Krishna has only 2 hours of leisure time each day because he spends the rest of his time doing homework. Nikolas has 8 hours of leisure time each day. How does this affect your answers to parts **a** and **b** above?

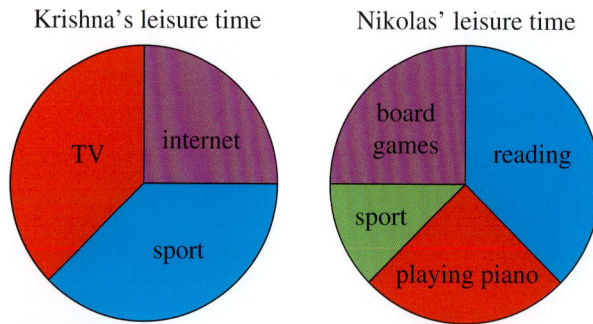

Krishna's leisure time

TV   internet   sport

Nikolas' leisure time

board games   reading   sport   playing piano

When creating a personal budget, people often include a sector graph. The sector sizes show the proportion of income allocated for items such as bills, rent, food, clothing, car expenses and insurance.

7   In two surveys, people were asked what is their favourite pet animal.

   a   If 16 people participated in survey 1, how many chose dog?

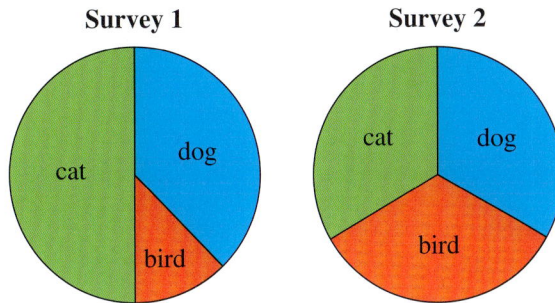

Survey 1   **Survey 2**

   b   If 30 people participated in survey 2, how many chose bird?
   c   Jason claims that 20 people participated in survey 1. Explain clearly why this cannot be true.
   d   Jaimee claims that 40 people participated in survey 2. Explain clearly why this cannot be true.
   e   In fact, the same number of people participated for each survey. Given that fewer than 100 people participated, how many participants were there? Give all the possible answers.

8   **a**   In a sector graph representing three different categories (red, blue and green), it is known that the proportion of red is $\frac{1}{3}$ and the proportion of blue is $\frac{1}{4}$. What is the proportion of green? Answer as a fraction and the number of degrees of this sector.

   b   Explain why it is impossible to create a sector graph where the proportion of red is $\frac{1}{2}$, the proportion of green is $\frac{1}{3}$ and the proportion of blue is $\frac{1}{4}$.

9   Consider the divided bar graph shown below.

   a   Show how this graph will look if the segments are placed in the order C, D, A, B (from left to right).

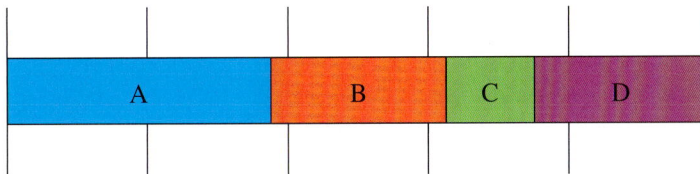

   b   In how many different ways could this divided bar graph be drawn (counting ABCD and CDAB as two different ways)?
   c   If this bar graph is redrawn as a sector graph, how many ways could the segments be arranged? Try to list them systematically. Do not consider two sector graphs to be different if one is just a rotation of another.

8A **1** Classify the following variables as categorical, discrete numerical or continuous numerical.
- **a** eye colour
- **b** animal weight (kg)
- **c** number of siblings
- **d** time to run 100 metres (sec)

8B **2** For each of the following sets of data, calculate the:
- **i** range
- **ii** mean
- **iii** median
- **iv** mode.
- **a** 5, 12, 3, 8, 2, 9, 3
- **b** 15, 24, 22, 28, 16, 15

8C **3** This dot plot represents the number of children in each family of some Year 7 students.
- **a** What is the most common family size in this class? (Family size means the number of children.)
- **b** How many families are shown by this graph, assuming there are no siblings within the class?
- **c** What is the range of family sizes?
- **d** What is the median family size?
- **e** Identify the outlier.

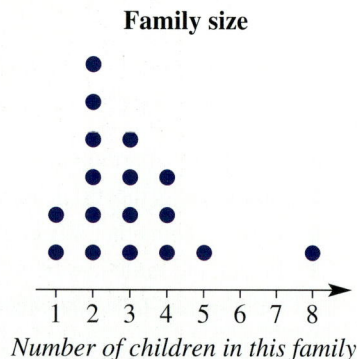

Family size

Number of children in this family

8D **4** The temperature outside a classroom was recorded four times during one school day. The following results were obtained.

Time	9 a.m.	11 a.m.	1 p.m.	3 p.m.
Temperature	15°C	20°C	28°C	25°C

- **a** Draw a line graph showing this information.
- **b** Use your graph to estimate the temperature at noon.

8D **5** This travel graph shows the distance travelled by a cyclist over 5 hours.
- **a** How far did the cyclist travel in total?
- **b** How far had the cyclist travelled after 3 hours?
- **c** What is happening in the fourth hour?
- **d** In the fifth hour, how far did the cyclist travel?
- **e** During what hour was the cyclist travelling the fastest?

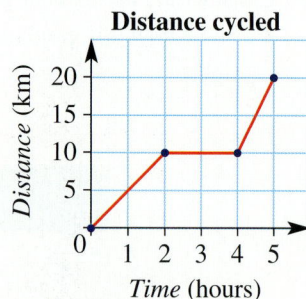

Distance cycled

8E **6** This stem-and-leaf table shows the noon temperatures (in °C) of different towns around Australia on one particular day.

Stem	Leaf
1	4 7 8
2	0 2 4 5 7 8 9
3	0 3 7

2|7 means 27°C

  a How many towns have their temperatures listed in this stem-and-leaf table?

  b What is the maximum and minimum noon temperature recorded?

  c What is the range of temperatures recorded?

  d What is the median temperature recorded?

8E **7** Represent this set of data as a stem-and-leaf plot: 10, 21, 16, 18, 7, 19, 18, 9, 20, 12

8F **8** Some Year 7 students were asked how they travelled to school. The results are shown in this table.

Ext

Public transport	Bicycle	Car
14	2	4

  a Represent the data as a sector graph.

  b Represent the data as a divided bar graph of total length 15 cm.

8G   Describing probability   CONSOLIDATING

LEARNING INTENTIONS
- To understand that we can describe the likelihood of events using phrases such as 'even chance', 'unlikely' and 'certain'
- To be able to describe the likelihood of an event

Often, there are times when you may wish to describe how likely it is that an event will occur. For example, you may want to know how likely it is that it will rain tomorrow, or how likely your sporting team will win this year's premiership, or how likely it is that you will win a lottery. Probability is the study of chance.

Thursday 8 November

Min 20   Max 25
Showers clearing. Windy.

Possible rainfall: **4 to 8 mm**

Chance of any rain: **80%**

The Bureau of Meteorology (BOM) uses percentages to describe the chance of rain. For example: very high (90%) chance; high (70%) chance; medium (50%) chance; slight (20%) chance; near zero chance.

Lesson starter: Likely or unlikely?

Try to rank these events from least likely to most likely. Compare your answers with other students in the class and discuss any differences.

- It will rain tomorrow.
- The Matildas will win the soccer World Cup.
- Tails landing uppermost when a 20-cent coin is tossed.
- The Sun will rise tomorrow.
- The king of spades is at the top of a shuffled deck of 52 playing cards.
- A diamond card is at the bottom of a shuffled deck of 52 playing cards.

KEY IDEAS

■ When using the English language to describe chance, there are a number of phrases that can be used.

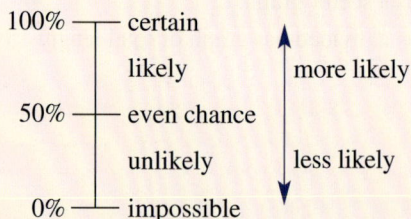

```
100% ── certain
          likely
                        more likely
50% ── even chance
          unlikely
                        less likely
0% ── impossible
```

■ If two events have the same chance of occurring, then we say that it is **equally likely** they will occur.

■ A **fair** coin or die is one for which all outcomes are equally likely. For example, a fair coin has an equal chance of landing heads or tails up and is not biased by being heavier on one side than the other.

BUILDING UNDERSTANDING

1 Match each of the events **a** to **d** with a description of how likely they are to occur (**A** to **D**).

   a A tossed coin landing heads up.

   b Selecting an ace first try from a fair deck of 52 playing cards.

   c Obtaining a number other than 6 if a fair 6-sided die is rolled.

   d Obtaining a number greater than 8 if a fair 6-sided die is rolled.

   A unlikely

   B likely

   C impossible

   D even chance

2 State the missing words in these sentences.

   a If an event is guaranteed to occur, we say it is _____.

   b An event that is equally likely to occur or not occur has an _____ _____.

   c A rare event is considered _____.

   d An event that will never occur is called _____.

Example 12 Describing chance

Classify each of the following statements as either true or false.

a It is likely that children will go to school next year.

b It is an even chance for a fair coin to display tails.

c Rolling a 3 on a 6-sided die and getting heads on a coin are equally likely.

d It is certain that two randomly chosen odd numbers will add to an even number.

SOLUTION	EXPLANATION
a true	Although there is perhaps a small chance that the laws might change, it is (very) likely that children will go to school next year.
b true	There is a 50-50, or an even chance, of a fair coin displaying tails. It will happen, on average, half of the time.
c false	These events are not equally likely. It is more likely to flip heads on a coin than to roll a 3 on a 6-sided die.
d true	No matter what odd numbers are chosen, they will always add to an even number.

Now you try

Classify each of the following statements as true or false.

a It is an even chance that it will rain every day this year.

b It is likely that it will rain some time in the next year.

c Rolling an even number and rolling an odd number on a fair 6-sided die are equally likely.

d It is certain that heads will be flipped at least once on a fair coin if it is flipped 10 times.

Exercise 8G

FLUENCY 1–3   2–4   3, 4

Example 12

1 Classify each of the following statement as either true or false.

   a It is likely that some people will use public transport next week.

   b Getting a tail on a coin and rolling a 6 on a 6-sided die are equally likely.

   c There is a 1 in 5 chance of randomly selecting the letter A from the word MARCH.

   d It is an even chance for a 6-sided die to show a number less than 3.

Example 12

2 Consider a fair 6-sided die with the numbers 1 to 6 on it. Answer true or false to each of the following.

   a Rolling a 3 is unlikely.

   b Rolling a 5 is likely.

   c Rolling a 4 and rolling a 5 are equally likely events.

   d Rolling an even number is likely.

   e There is an even chance of rolling an odd number.

   f There is an even chance of rolling a multiple of 3.

3 Match up each of the events **a** to **d** with an equally likely event **A** to **D**.

   a Rolling a 2 on a 6-sided die

   b Selecting a heart card from a fair deck of 52 playing cards

   c Flipping a coin and tails landing face up

   d Rolling a 1 or a 5 on a 6-sided die

   A Selecting a black card from a fair deck of 52 playing cards

   B Rolling a number bigger than 4 on a 6-sided die

   C Selecting a diamond card from a fair deck of 52 playing cards

   D Rolling a 6 on a 6-sided die

Example 12

4 Consider the spinner shown, which is spun and could land with the arrow pointing to any of the three colours. (If it lands on a boundary, it is spun again until it lands on a colour.)

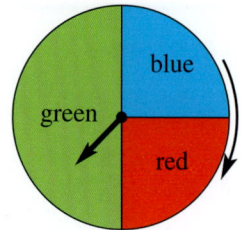

   a State whether each of the following is true or false.

     i There is an even chance that the spinner will point to green.

     ii It is likely that the spinner will point to red.

     iii It is certain that the spinner will point to purple.

     iv It is equally likely that the spinner will point to red or blue.

     v Green is twice as likely to occur as blue.

   b Use the spinner to give an example of:

     i an impossible event

     ii a likely event

     iii a certain event

     iv two events that are equally likely.

5   Three spinners are shown below. Match each spinner with the description.

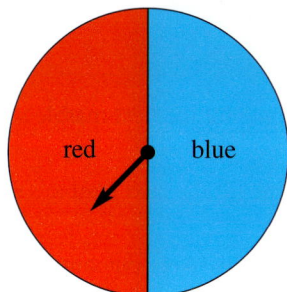

Spinner 1   **Spinner 2**   **Spinner 3**

a   Has an even chance of red, but blue is unlikely.
b   Blue and green are equally likely, but red is unlikely.
c   Has an even chance of blue, and green is impossible.

6   Draw spinners to match each of the following descriptions, using blue, red and green as the possible colours.

a   Blue is likely, red is unlikely and green is impossible.
b   Red is certain.
c   Blue has an even chance, red and green are equally likely.
d   Blue, red and green are all equally likely.
e   Blue is twice as likely as red, but red and green are equally likely.
f   Red and green are equally likely and blue is impossible.
g   Blue, red and green are all unlikely, but no two colours are equally likely.
h   Blue is three times as likely as green, but red is impossible.

7   For each of the following spinners, give a description of the chances involved so that someone could determine which spinner is being described. Use the colour names and the language of chance (i.e. 'likely', 'impossible' etc.) in your descriptions.

a   **b**   **c**

d   **e**   **f**

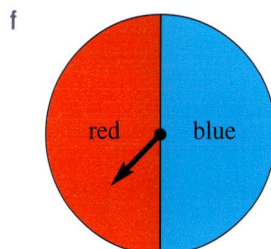

8 A bag contains 4 blue marbles, 4 red marbles and 2 yellow marbles. A single marble is chosen at random.
   a Describe two equally likely events for this situation.
   b Once a marble has been chosen, it is *not* put back into the bag.
   i If the first marble chosen was blue, what is the most likely outcome for the next marble's colour? Explain your answer.
   ii If the first marble chosen was red, what is the most likely outcome for the next marble's colour? Explain your answer.
   iii If a yellow marble was chosen first, explain why there are two equally likely outcomes for the next marble.

9 A coin consists of two sides that are equally likely to occur when tossed. It is matched up with a spinner that has exactly the same chances, as shown below.

heads →

Tossing the coin with heads landing uppermost is equally likely to spinning red on the spinner. Tossing the coin with tails landing uppermost is equally likely to spinning blue on the spinner. Hence, we say that the coin and the spinner are **equivalent**.
   a Draw a spinner that is equivalent to a fair 6-sided die. (*Hint*: The spinner should have six sections of different colours.)
   b How can you tell from the spinner you drew that it is equivalent to a fair die?
   c A die is 'weighted' so that there is an even chance of rolling a 6, but rolling the numbers 1 to 5 are still equally likely. Draw a spinner that is equivalent to such a die.
   d How could you make a die equivalent to the spinner shown in the diagram?
   e Describe a spinner that is equivalent to selecting a card from a fair deck of 52 playing cards.

The game of 'Twister' uses a spinner to determine the positions to be attempted.

–   –   10

10 The language of chance is a bit vague. For example, for each of the following spinners it is 'unlikely' that you will spin red, but in each case the chance of spinning red is different.

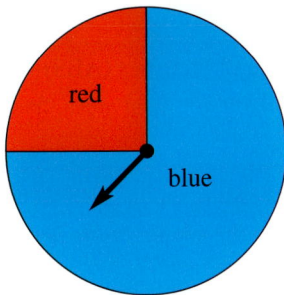
Spinner 1

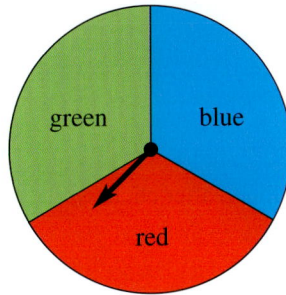
Spinner 2

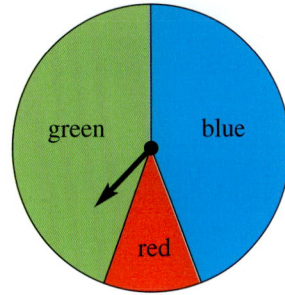
Spinner 3

Rather than describing this in words, we could give the fraction (or decimal or percentage) of the spinner occupied by a colour.

a For each of the spinners above, give the fraction of the spinner occupied by red.

b What fraction of the spinner would be red if it had an even chance?

c Draw spinners for which the red portion occupies:

  i 100% of the spinner

  ii 0% of the spinner.

d For the sentences below, fill in the gaps with appropriate fraction or percentage values.

  i An event has an even chance of occurring if that portion of the spinner occupies _____ of the total area.

  ii An event that is impossible occupies _____ of the total area.

  iii An event is unlikely to occur if it occupies more than _____ but less than _____ of the total area.

  iv An event is likely if it occupies more than _____ of the total area.

e How can the fractions help determine if two events are equally likely?

f Explain why all the fractions occupied by a colour must be between 0 and 1.

The following problems will investigate practical situations drawing upon knowledge and skills developed throughout the chapter. In attempting to solve these problems, aim to identify the key information, use diagrams, formulate ideas, apply strategies, make calculations and check and communicate your solutions.

Using Australian Census data

1   The Australian Census occurs every five years, and the Australian Bureau of Statistics (ABS) website shows key statistics, called QuickStats, which provide Census data available for most areas, from small areas to state, territory and national level.

The QuickStats search button can be found after clicking the 'Census' heading on the ABS website. *You are interested in using this resource to find various statistics about the people in the area in which you live and about the people in particular regions of Australia.*

   a   Using QuickStats on the ABS website, for your local suburb:
   i   find the total number of people who live in your suburb
   ii   find the median age of the people who live in your suburb
   iii   find the average number of people per household in your suburb.

   b   Complete the above questions from part **a** for the state or territory you live in.

   c   Research the median age for each of Australia's six states and two territories and represent this data in an appropriate graph. Which state has the oldest median age? Which state has the youngest median age?

   d   Research a topic of interest, for example: education, language, ancestry, religion, marriage, employment, income, size of family, size of home etc.

   Compare your suburb, region or state for your topic of interest and present your findings using suitable graphs and make appropriate summary comments.

Head-to-head

2   Many media enterprises like to compare elite sport players via the analysis of particular statistics. *You are interested in making a fair comparison between two elite players using statistical data to calculate measures of centre and construct graphs.*

   a   Lionel Messi and Cristiano Ronaldo are two exceptional soccer players, but which one is better?

   The following data compares key statistics for these two players at a particular point in time.

Statistic	Messi	Ronaldo
Matches	784	936
Goals	637	670
Goal assists	264	215

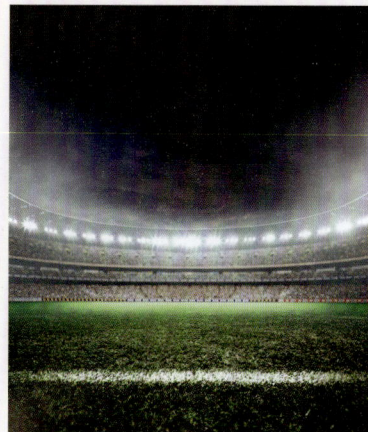

   i Represent this data in appropriate graphs.

   ii Calculate Messi's and Ronaldo's average number of goals per match and show this information in an appropriate graph.

   iii Which player do you think is better? Use your graph to justify your answer.

b Carry out your own research to compare two exceptional players for your chosen sport.

   For example: Emma Kearney vs Daisy Pearce in AFLW, or Serena Williams vs Steffi Graf in tennis

   i Determine which statistics are most important and carry out research on your two individual players.

   ii Present your findings in appropriate graphs, including column, line or pie graphs.

   iii Include numerical values for mean, median, mode and/or range for key statistics.

   iv Conclude with your personal opinion, based on the statistics, on the most valuable player.

Spin for a spin class

3 Chloe loves to exercise, but she quickly becomes bored with the same exercise routine.
To help add variety and fun to her exercise routine she wants to design a spinner that she can spin each day to determine which activity she will do.

Chloe would like to design a spinner that makes it equally likely that she will do a yoga, bike or swim session, but twice as likely that she will do a running session compared to each of the other exercises.

a Design a spinner for Chloe's four possible exercise options.

Chloe is loving the variety and surprise of the exercise spinner and decides to introduce a second spinner related to the duration of her fitness session. She would like a 15 minute, 30 minute and 60 minute session to be equally likely to occur, her favourite 45 minute session to be 1.5 times more likely to occur and her longest and hardest 90 minute session to be half as likely to occur.

b Design a spinner for Chloe's five exercise duration times

c When Chloe uses both spinners, what are the details of her most likely exercise session?

d If Chloe uses the spinners for 100 days, how many 90 minute sessions might she expect to complete?

e If Chloe uses the spinners for n days, how many yoga sessions might she expect to complete?

8H   Theoretical probability in single-step experiments

LEARNING INTENTIONS
- To know the meaning of the terms experiment, trial, outcome, event and sample space
- To understand that the probability of an event is a number between 0 and 1 inclusive representing the chance it will occur
- To be able to calculate probabilities of simple events

The **probability** of an event occurring is a number between 0 and 1 inclusive. This number states precisely how likely it is for an event to occur. It is often written as a fraction and can indicate how frequently the event would occur over a large number of trials. For example, if you toss a fair coin many times, you would expect heads to come up half the time, so the probability is $\frac{1}{2}$. If you roll a fair 6-sided die many times, you should roll a 4 about one-sixth of the time, so the probability is $\frac{1}{6}$.

To be more precise, we should list the possible outcomes of rolling the die: 1, 2, 3, 4, 5, 6. Doing this shows us that there is a 1 out of 6 chance that you will roll a 4 and there is a 0 out of 6 (= 0) chance of rolling a 9.

GENETIC INHERITANCE OF EYE COLOUR

Parent 1   Parent 2

Colour of the child's eyes

50%   12.5%   37.5%

The study of genetics applies theoretical probability calculations to predict the chance of various traits in offspring. The above eye colour probabilities are one example.

Lesson starter: Spinner probabilities

Consider the three spinners shown below.

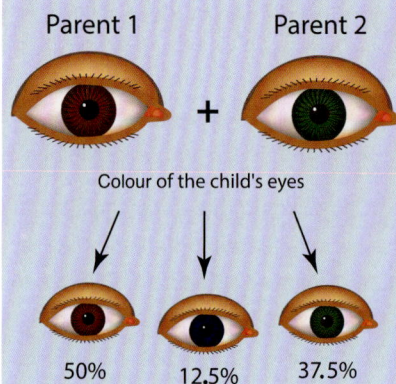

- What is the probability of spinning blue for each of these spinners?
- What is the probability of spinning red for each of these spinners?
- Try to design a spinner for which the probability of spinning green is $\frac{4}{7}$ and the probability of spinning blue is 0.

KEY IDEAS

- A random **experiment** is a chance activity which produces varying results.

- A **trial** is a single component of an experiment such as tossing a coin, rolling a die or spinning a spinner.

- An **outcome** is a possible result of the experiment, like rolling a 5 or a coin showing tails.

- The **sample space** is the set of all possible outcomes of an experiment.

- An **event** is either a single outcome (e.g. rolling a 3) or a collection of outcomes (e.g. rolling a 3, 4 or 5).

- When considering an event, a **favourable outcome** is one of the outcomes we are interested in. (e.g. in considering the event of rolling an even number on a die, the favourable outcomes are 2, 4 and 6.)

- The **probability** of an event is a number between 0 and 1 inclusive, to represent the chance of the event occurring. The probability of an event occurring, if all the outcomes are equally likely, is:

$$\frac{\text{number of outcomes where the event occurs}}{\text{total number of outcomes}}$$

- Probability is often written as a fraction, but it can be written as a decimal or as a percentage.

- We write Pr(green) to mean 'the probability that the outcome is green'.

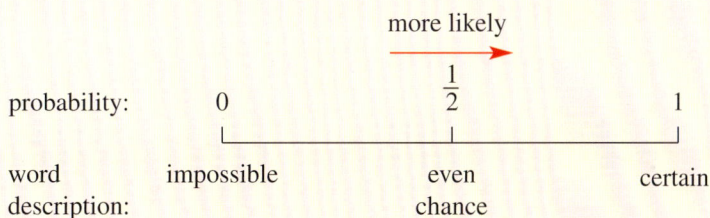

more likely

probability: 0 $\frac{1}{2}$ 1

word description: impossible   even chance   certain

BUILDING UNDERSTANDING

1 Match up each experiment **a** to **d** with the list of possible outcomes **A** to **D**.

   a   tossing a coin   **A**   1, 2, 3, 4, 5, 6
   b   rolling a die   **B**   red, white, blue
   c   selecting a suit from a fair   **C**   heads, tails
      deck of 52 playing cards   **D**   hearts, diamonds,
   d   choosing a colour on the   clubs, spades
      French flag

The French flag is divided into three sections of different colours and equal size.

2 State the missing words in the following sentences.

   a   The _____ _____ is the set of possible outcomes.
   b   An impossible event has a probability of _____.
   c   If an event has a probability of 1, then it is _____.
   d   The higher its probability, the _____ likely the event will occur.
   e   An event with a probability of $\frac{1}{2}$ has an _____ of occurring.

Example 13   Listing sample spaces and favourable outcomes

A spinner with numbers 1 to 7 is spun. The event being considered is 'spinning an odd number'.
a   List the sample space.
b   List the favourable outcomes.

SOLUTION

a   sample space = {1, 2, 3, 4, 5, 6, 7}

b   favourable outcomes = {1, 3, 5, 7}

EXPLANATION

For the sample space, we list all the possible outcomes. Technically, the sample space is {spin a 1, spin a 2, spin a 3 etc.} but we do not usually include the additional words.

Because we are considering the event 'spinning an odd number', we list the outcomes from the sample space that are odd.

Now you try

A spinner with numbers 1 to 5 is spun. The event being considered is 'spinning an even number'.
a   List the sample space.
b   List the favourable outcomes.

Example 14   Calculating probabilities

A fair 6-sided die is rolled.
a   Find the probability of rolling a 3, giving your answer as a fraction.
b   Find the probability of rolling an even number, giving your answer as a decimal.
c   Find the probability of rolling a number greater than 4. Give your answer as a percentage correct to one decimal place.

SOLUTION

a   sample space = {1, 2, 3, 4, 5, 6}
   favourable outcomes = {3}
   $Pr(3) = \frac{1}{6}$

b   sample space = {1, 2, 3, 4, 5, 6}
   favourable outcomes = {2, 4, 6}

   $Pr(even) = \frac{3}{6}$
   $= \frac{1}{2}$
   $= 0.5$

EXPLANATION

The number of possible outcomes is 6. The number of favourable outcomes is 1. We divide to find the probability.

Find the probability as a fraction first, then convert to a decimal.

c sample space = {1, 2, 3, 4, 5, 6}   Find the probability as a fraction first, then
   favourable outcomes = {5, 6}   convert to a percentage and round.

$$Pr(\text{greater than } 4) = \frac{2}{6}$$

$$= \frac{1}{3}$$

$$= 33.3\% \,(1 \text{ decimal place})$$

Now you try

A spinner has the numbers 1, 2, 3, 4 and 5 on it, each with an equal area. It is spun once.

a Find the probability of spinning a 3, giving your answer as a fraction.

b Find the probability of spinning an odd number, giving your answer as a decimal.

c Find the probability of spinning an even number, giving your answer as a percentage.

Exercise 8H

FLUENCY	1–5, 6(½)	2–7	2, 3, 6–8

mple 13a

1 List the sample space for the following experiments.

   a A 6-sided die is rolled.

   b A spinner with numbers 1 to 4 is spun

   c A spinner with colours red, green and blue is spun.

   d A letter is chosen at random from the word LUCK.

mple 13b

2 A 6-sided die is rolled. List the favourable outcomes for the following events.

   a An odd number is rolled.

   b A number less than 4 is rolled.

   c A number other than 6 is rolled.

   d A number other than 3 or 5 is rolled.

ample 13

3 A letter from the word TRACE is chosen at random.

   a List the sample space.

   b The event being considered is choosing a vowel (remember that vowels are A, E, I, O, U). List the favourable outcomes.

   c The event being considered is choosing a consonant (remember that a consonant is any letter that is not a vowel). List the favourable outcomes.

   d The event being considered is choosing a letter that is also in the word MATHS. List the favourable outcomes.

mple 14

4 A fair 4-sided die (numbered 1, 2, 3 and 4) is rolled.

   a List the sample space.

   b Find the probability of rolling a 3, given your answer as a fraction.

   c Find the probability of rolling an odd number, given your answer as a decimal.

   d Find the probability of rolling a number more than 1, giving your answer as a percentage.

Example 14

5 Consider the spinner shown.

a How many outcomes are there? List them.

b Find Pr(red); i.e. find the probability of the spinner pointing to red.

c Find Pr(red or green).

d Find Pr(not red).

e Find Pr(yellow).

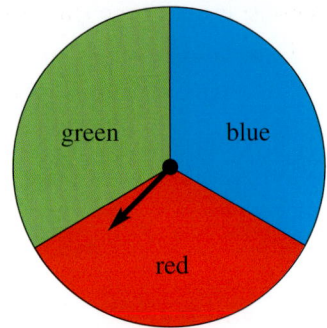

Example 14

6 A spinner with the numbers 1 to 7 is spun. The numbers are evenly spaced.

a List the sample space.

b Find Pr(6).

c Find Pr(8).

d Find Pr(2 or 4).

e Find Pr(even).

f Find Pr(odd).

g Give an example of an event having the probability of 1.

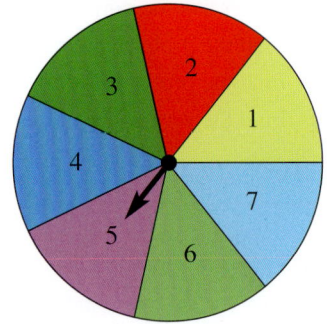

7 The letters in the word MATHS are written on 5 cards and then one is drawn from a hat.

a List the sample space.

b Find Pr(T), giving your answer as a decimal.

c Find Pr(consonant is chosen), giving your answer as a decimal.

d Find the probability that the letter drawn is also in the word TAME, giving your answer as a percentage.

8 The letters in the word PROBABILITY are written on 11 cards and then one is drawn from a hat.

a Find Pr(P).

b Find Pr(P or L).

c Find Pr(letter chosen is in the word BIT).

d Find Pr(not a B).

e Find Pr(a vowel is chosen).

f Give an example of an event with the probability of $\frac{3}{11}$.

PROBLEM-SOLVING	9	9, 10	10, 11

9 A bag of marbles contains 3 red marbles, 2 green marbles and 5 blue marbles. They are all equal in size and weight. A marble is chosen at random.

a What is the probability that a red marble is chosen? (*Hint*: It is not $\frac{1}{3}$ because the colours are not all equally likely.) Give your answer as a percentage.

b What is the probability that a blue marble is chosen? Give your answer as a percentage.

c What is the probability that a green marble is *not* chosen? Give your answer as a percentage.

10 Consider the spinner opposite, numbered 2 to 9.

a List the sample space.

b Find the probability that a prime number will be spun, giving your answer as a decimal. (Remember that 2 is a prime number.)

c Giving your answers as decimals, state the probability of getting a prime number if each number in the spinner opposite is:

i increased by 1

ii increased by 2

iii doubled

(*Hint*: It will help if you draw the new spinner.)

d Design a new spinner with at least three sectors for which Pr(prime) = 1.

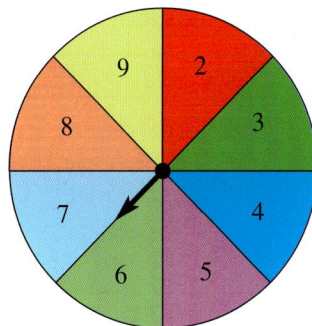

11 A bag contains various coloured marbles – some are red, some are blue, some are yellow and some are green. You are told that Pr (red) = $\frac{1}{2}$, Pr(blue) = $\frac{1}{4}$ and Pr(yellow) = $\frac{1}{6}$. You are not told the probability of selecting a green marble.

a If there are 24 marbles:

i find how many there are of each colour.

ii what is the probability of getting a green marble?

b If there are 36 marbles:

i find how many there are of each colour.

ii what is the probability of getting a green marble?

c What is the minimum number of marbles in the bag?

d Does the probability of getting a green marble depend on the actual number of marbles in the bag? Justify your answer.

REASONING 12 12, 13 13, 14

12 Consider an experiment where a spinner has numbers 1–9 which are each equally likely to be spun.

a Explain why the events 'spinning an even number' and 'spinning an odd number' are not equally likely, by first listing the favourable outcomes in each case.

b Find the probability of spinning a number less than 4 and, hence, give an example of an equally likely event.

c Find the probability of spinning a number less than 10.

d Give an example of an event that has a probability of $\frac{2}{3}$.

13 a State the values of the pronumerals in the following table.

Event	Pr(event occurs)	Pr(event does not occurs)	Sum of two numbers
Rolling a die, get a 3	$\frac{1}{6}$	$\frac{5}{6}$	a
Tossing a coin, get H	$\frac{1}{2}$	b	c
Rolling a die, get 2 or 5	d	$\frac{2}{3}$	e
Selecting a letter from 'HEART', getting a vowel	f	g	h

b If the probability of selecting a vowel in a particular word is $\frac{3}{13}$, what is the probability of selecting a consonant?

c If the probability of spinning blue with a particular spinner is $\frac{4}{7}$, what is the probability of spinning a colour other than blue?

14 A box contains different coloured counters of identical size and shape. A counter is drawn from the box, with $Pr(\text{purple}) = 10\%$, $Pr(\text{yellow}) = \frac{2}{3}$ and $Pr(\text{orange}) = \frac{1}{7}$.

a Is it possible to obtain a colour other than purple, yellow or orange? If so, state the probability.

b What is the minimum number of counters in the box?

c If the box cannot fit more than 1000 counters, what is the maximum number of counters in the box?

ENRICHMENT: Designing spinners   –   –   15

15 a For each of the following, design a spinner using only red, green and blue sectors to obtain the desired probabilities. If it cannot be done, then explain why.

   i $Pr(\text{red}) = \frac{1}{2}$, $Pr(\text{green}) = \frac{1}{4}$, $Pr(\text{blue}) = \frac{1}{4}$

   ii $Pr(\text{red}) = \frac{1}{2}$, $Pr(\text{green}) = \frac{1}{2}$, $Pr(\text{blue}) = \frac{1}{2}$

   iii $Pr(\text{red}) = \frac{1}{4}$, $Pr(\text{green}) = \frac{1}{4}$, $Pr(\text{blue}) = \frac{1}{4}$

   iv $Pr(\text{red}) = 0.1$, $Pr(\text{green}) = 0.6$, $Pr(\text{blue}) = 0.3$

b If $Pr(\text{red}) = x$ and $Pr(\text{green}) = y$, write a formula using x and y to determine what $Pr(\text{blue})$ must equal.

8I   Experimental probability in single-step experiments

LEARNING INTENTIONS
- To understand what experimental probability is and how it is related to the (theoretical) probability of an event for a large number of trials
- To be able to find the expected number of occurrences of an event
- To be able to find the experimental probability of an event given experiment results

Although the probability of an event tells us how often an event should happen in theory, we will rarely find this being exactly right in practice. For instance, if you flip a coin 100 times, it might come up heads 53 times out of 100, which is not exactly $\frac{1}{2}$ of the times you flipped it. Sometimes we will not be able to find the exact probability of an event, but we can carry out an experiment to estimate it.

Flipping a fair coin 100 times does not necessarily mean it will come up heads 50 times.

Lesson starter: Flipping coins

For this experiment, each class member needs a fair coin that they can flip.

- Each student should flip the coin 20 times and count how many times heads occurs.
- Tally the total number of heads obtained by the class.
- How close is this total number to the number you would expect that is based on the probability of $\frac{1}{2}$? Discuss what this means.

KEY IDEAS

■ The **experimental probability** of an event occurring based on a particular experiment is defined as:
$$\frac{\text{number of times the event occurs}}{\text{total number of trials in the experiment}}$$

■ The **expected number** of occurrences = probability × number of trials.

■ If the number of trials is large, then the experimental probability is likely to be close to the actual probability of an event.

BUILDING UNDERSTANDING

1   A 6-sided die is rolled 10 times and the following numbers come up: 2, 4, 6, 4, 5, 1, 6, 4, 4, 3.
  a   What is the experimental probability of getting a 3?
  b   What is the experimental probability of getting a 4?
  c   What is the experimental probability of getting an odd number?

2 When a coin is flipped 100 times, the results are 53 heads and 47 tails.

   a What is the experimental probability of getting a head?

   b What is the experimental probability of getting a tail?

   c What is the theoretical probability of getting a tail if the coin is fair?

Example 15   Working with experimental probability

When playing with a spinner with the numbers 1 to 4 on it, the following numbers come up:
1, 4, 1, 3, 3, 1, 4, 3, 2, 3.

a What is the experimental probability of getting a 3?

b What is the experimental probability of getting an even number?

c Based on this experiment, how many times would you expect to get a 3 if you spin 1000 times?

SOLUTION

a $\frac{2}{5}$ or 0.4 or 40%

b $\frac{3}{10}$ or 0.3 or 30%

c 400 times

EXPLANATION

$\dfrac{\text{number of 3s}}{\text{number of trials}} = \dfrac{4}{10} = \dfrac{2}{5}$

$\dfrac{\text{number of times with even result}}{\text{number of trials}} = \dfrac{3}{10}$

probability $\times$ number trials $= \dfrac{2}{5} \times 1000 = 400$

Now you try

When rolling a die, the following numbers come up: 1, 4, 3, 6, 6, 2, 4, 3.

a What is the experimental probability of rolling a 3?

b What is the experimental probability of rolling an even number?

c Based on this experiment, how many times would you expect to get a 3 if you rolled the die 80 times?

Exercise 8I

FLUENCY		1–6	1–7	3–7

Example 15

1 A spinner with the numbers 1 to 5 on it is spun and the following numbers come up:
2, 5, 5, 3, 4, 4, 1, 2, 3, 5, 3, 3

   a What is the experimental probability of getting a 5?

   b What is the experimental probability of getting an odd number?

   c Based on this experiment, how many times would you expect to get an odd number if you spin 150 times?

2   A survey is conducted on people's television viewing habits.

Number of hours per week	0–4	5–9	10–19	20–29	30+
Number of people	20	10	15	5	0

   a   How many people participated in the survey?

   b   What is the probability that a randomly selected participant watches less than 5 hours of television?

   c   What is the probability that a randomly selected participant watches 20–29 hours of television?

   d   What is the probability that a randomly selected participant watches between 5 and 29 hours of television?

   e   Based on this survey, the experimental probability of watching 30+ hours of television is 0. Does this mean that watching 30+ hours is impossible?

3   A fair coin is flipped.

   a   How many times would you expect it to show tails in 1000 trials?

   b   How many times would you expect it to show heads in 3500 trials?

   c   Initially, you flip the coin 10 times to find the probability of the coin showing tails.

      i   Explain how you could get an experimental probability of 0.7.

      ii   If you flip the coin 100 times, are you more or less likely to get an experimental probability close to 0.5?

4   A fair 6-sided die is rolled.

   a   How many times would you expect to get a 3 in 600 trials?

   b   How many times would you expect to get an even number in 600 trials?

   c   If you roll the die 600 times, is it possible that you will get an even number 400 times?

   d   Are you more likely to obtain an experimental probability of 100% from two throws or to obtain an experimental probability of 100% from 10 throws?

5   Each time a basketball player takes a free throw there is a 4 in 6 chance that the shot will go in. This can be simulated by rolling a 6-sided die and using numbers 1 to 4 to represent 'shot goes in' and numbers 5 and 6 to represent 'shot misses'.

   a   Use a 6-sided die over 10 trials to find the experimental probability that the shot goes in.

   b   Use a 6-sided die over 50 trials to find the experimental probability that the shot goes in.

   c   Working with a group, use a 6-sided die over 100 trials to find the experimental probability that the shot goes in.

   d   Use a 6-sided die over just one trial to find the experimental probability that the shot goes in. (Your answer should be either 0 or 1.)

   e   Which of the answers to parts a to d above is closest to the theoretical probability of 66.67%? Justify your answer.

6 The colour of the cars in a school car park is recorded.

Colour	Red	Black	White	Blue	Purple	Green
Number of cars	21	24	25	20	3	7

Based on this sample:

a What is the probability that a randomly chosen car is white?

b What is the probability that a randomly chosen car is purple?

c What is the probability that a randomly chosen car is green or black?

d How many purple cars would you expect to see in a shopping centre car park with 2000 cars?

7 The number of children in some families is recorded in the table shown.

Number of children	0	1	2	3	4
Number of families	5	20	32	10	3

a How many families have no children?

b How many families have an even number of children?

c How many families participated in the survey?

d Based on this experiment, what is the probability that a randomly selected family has 1 or 2 children?

e Based on this experiment, what is the probability that a randomly selected family has an even number of children?

f What is the total number of *children* considered in this survey?

PROBLEM-SOLVING		8	8, 9	8, 9

8 A handful of 10 marbles of different colours is placed into a bag. A marble is selected at random, its colour recorded and then returned to the bag. The results are shown below.

Red marble chosen	Green marble chosen	Blue marble chosen
21	32	47

a Based on this experiment, how many marbles of each colour do you think there are? Justify your answer in a sentence.

b For each of the following, state whether or not they are possible colours for the 10 marbles.

   i   3 red, 3 green, 4 blue   **ii** 2 red, 4 green, 4 blue   **iii** 1 red, 3 green, 6 blue

   iv 2 red, 3 green, 4 blue, 1 purple   **v** 2 red, 0 green, 8 blue

9 Match each of the experiment results **a** to **d** with the most likely spinner that was used (**A** to **D**).

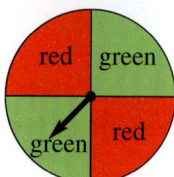

	Red	Green	Blue
a	18	52	30
b	27	23	0
c	20	23	27
d	47	0	53

10 Thomas and his dog Loui have a trick where Thomas throws a ball and Loui catches it with his mouth. Assume that there is a 50% chance that the trick will be successful on any occasion, and they will try four times to see how many catches are successful. This can be simulated with four coin flips (use heads to represent a successful catch).

a Count the number of successful catches in each group of four coin flips and write your 20 results down.

b Copy and complete a table like the one below to summarise your results.

Number of catches	0	1	2	3	4	Total
Frequency						20

c Based on your simulation, what is the experimental probability that there will be just one successful catch?

d Based on your simulation, what is the experimental probability that there will be four catches?

e Explain why you might need to use simulations and experimental probabilities to find the answer to parts **c** and **d** above.

f If you had repeated the experiment only 5 times instead of 20 times, how might the accuracy of your probabilities be affected?

g If you had repeated the experiment 500 times instead of 20 times, how might the accuracy of your probabilities be affected?

11 Classify the following statements as true or false. Justify each answer in a sentence.

a If the probability of an event is $\frac{1}{2}$, then it must have an experimental probability of $\frac{1}{2}$.

b If the experimental probability of an event is $\frac{1}{2}$, then its theoretical probability must be $\frac{1}{2}$.

c If the experimental probability of an event is 0, then the theoretical probability is 0.

d If the probability of an event is 0, then the experimental probability is also 0.

e If the experimental probability is 1, then the theoretical probability is 1.

f If the probability of an event is 1, then the experimental probability is 1.

12 A spinner is spun 500 times. The table opposite shows the tally for every 100 trials.

a Give the best possible estimate for Pr(red), Pr(green) and Pr(blue) based on these trials.

b If your estimate is based on just one set of trials, which one would cause you to have the most inaccurate results?

	Red	Green	Blue
First set of 100 trials	22	41	37
Second set of 100 trials	21	41	38
Third set of 100 trials	27	39	34
Fourth set of 100 trials	25	46	29
Fifth set of 100 trials	30	44	26

c Design a spinner that could give results similar to those in the table. Assume you can use up to 10 sectors of equal size.

d Design a spinner that could give results similar to those in the table if you are allowed to use sectors of different sizes.

Modelling

Water restrictions

A dam near the town of Waterville has received limited flows from its catchment area in recent times. As a percentage of its full capacity, the volume of water in the dam at the start of each of the last 12 months is given in the following table.

Month	Jan	Feb	Mar	Apr	May	Jun	July	Aug	Sep	Oct	Nov	Dec
Water volume for month (%)	75	72	68	65	63	60	59	56	52	49	47	44

The water restrictions policy for Waterville include the following statements.

- Once the volume of water decreases to 60% of full capacity, level 1 restrictions apply.
- Once the volume of water decreases to 50% of full capacity, level 2 restrictions apply.
- Once the volume of water decreases to 35% of full capacity, level 3 restrictions apply.

Present a report for the following tasks and ensure that you show clear mathematical workings and explanations where appropriate.

Preliminary task

a By considering the water volume for the Waterville dam for each of the given 12 months, find:
   i   the mean (round to one decimal place)
   ii   the median
   iii the range.
b Use the given data to construct a line graph for the water volume of the dam near Waterville. Use the following axes on your graph.
   - Time (in months) on the horizontal axis
   - Water volume (%) on the vertical axis

Modelling task

Formulate

a The problem is to estimate how many months it will be until level 3 restrictions apply, based on the current trends. Write down all the relevant information that will help solve this problem.

Solve

b Describe the general trend/pattern that you see in the data.
c Find the volume decrease as a percentage of the full capacity from:
   i   the month of January to the month of July
   ii   the month of May to the month of December.
d Consider the decrease in water volume from one month to the next.
   i   State the 11 different decreases across the 12 months.
   ii   Find the mean percentage decrease using your data from part **d i** above. Round your answer to one decimal place.
e If the trend continued, estimate the water volume (as a percentage of the full capacity) in:
   i   January of the following year
   ii   December of the following year.

uate and verify

f Using the data from above, determine the month when the following were applied:

   i level 1 restrictions

   ii level 2 restrictions.

g Estimate when level 3 water restrictions will apply. Justify your answer with the use of the mean percentage decrease from part **d** and your graph.

municate

h Summarise your results and describe any key findings.

Extension questions

a Determine the mean monthly percentage increase required after December of the given year for the dam to be at 50% capacity in 12 months' time.

b Determine the mean monthly percentage increase required after December of the given year for the dam to be back at 100% capacity in 12 months' time.

c Describe some reasons why it might be unreasonable to expect the volume of water in the dam to increase or decrease by a fixed amount each month.

Technology and computational thinking

Soccer in the rain

Key technology: Spreadsheets

Unfortunately for many sporting clubs, matches are sometimes cancelled due to rain. Frances, a keen soccer player, is interested in the probability of a certain number of matches being cancelled across a 10-match season. To be eligible for state-wide selection, she needs to have played in at least 7 non-cancelled matches, meaning that no more than 3 matches can be cancelled.

1 Getting started

Information provided by Frances's sporting club shows that from the past 100 planned matches, 20 of them were cancelled due to rain.

a   Based on the data provided by the club, what is the experimental probability that any particular match will be cancelled?

b   Out of a 10-match season, what is the expected number of matches that will be cancelled due to rain?

c   Do you think that in her next 10-match season, Frances has a good chance of playing at least 7 matches? Give a reason.

2 Using technology

We will use Excel to simulate the outcomes of Frances's 10-match soccer season.

a   First, use the RANDBETWEEN function as shown to generate a set of random integers between 1 and 10 inclusive.

b   Given that the probability of a wet day is 0.2, we will assign the following:

   • 1 or 2 means that it is wet and the match is cancelled
   • 3 to 10 means that it is dry and the match is not cancelled.

	A
1	Using RANDBETWEEN
2	
3	=RANDBETWEEN(1,10)

Press the F9 key to recalculate your random number. Keep doing this until you record at least two wet days (1 or 2).

c   Upgrade your spreadsheet so it simulates a full 10-match season in one go as shown. Column B will confirm if the day is wet or dry and row 14 counts the total number of wet days in the simulated season.

d   Fill down at cells A4 and B4 to row 13. This should produce results for a 10-match season.

	A	B
1	Soccer simulation	
2		
3	Random number	Wet or Dry
4	=RANDBETWEEN(1,10)	=IF(A4<3,"Wet","Dry")
5		
6		
7		
8		
9		
10		
11		
12		
13		
14	Total days Wet	=COUNTIF(B4:B13,"Wet")

3 Applying an algorithm

a   Press the F9 key to recalculate your random numbers in your 10-match simulation spreadsheet.

b   Keep a record of how many wet days there are for each 10-match season. Use the following table to record your results. If, for example, your next simulation results in 3 wet days, then add a dash in the tally under '3'. Repeat for a total for 20 simulations.

Number of wet days	0	1	2	3	4	5	6	7	8	9	10
Tally											
Frequency											

c   Out of your 20 simulations, what is the frequency corresponding to:

i   0 wet days?

ii   1 wet day?

iii 2 wet days?

iv   3 wet days?

v   no more than 3 wet days?

d   Based on these results, what do you think Frances's chances are of playing in at least 7 matches? Give reasons.

4 Extension

a   To improve your simulation results, increase the total number of simulations completed using your spreadsheet. Update the tally/frequency table to include a total of one hundred 10-match season results.

b   Using your new results, what is the frequency of no more than 3 wet days?

c   Use your result to calculate the probability that Frances will play in at least 7 matches.

d   Compare your result from part c with the theoretical result of 0.88, correct to two decimal places.

Monopoly risk

In the game of Monopoly, two 6-sided dice are rolled to work out how far a player should go forward. For this investigation, you will need two 6-sided dice or a random number simulator that simulates numbers between 1 and 6.

a Roll the two dice and note what they add up to. Repeat this 100 times and complete this table.

Dice sum	2	3	4	5	6	7	8	9	10	11	12	Total
Tally												100

b Represent the results in a column graph. Describe the shape of the graph. Do you notice any patterns?

c Use the results of your experiment to give the experimental probability of two dice adding to:
   i 3   ii 6   iii 8   iv 12   v 15.

d What is the most likely sum for the dice to add to, based on your experiment? Is this the mean, median or mode that you are describing?

e If the average Monopoly game involves 180 rolls, find the expected number of times, based on your experiment, that the dice will add to:
   i 3   ii 6   iii 8   iv 12   v 15.

f Why do you think that certain sums happen more often than others? Explain why this might happen by comparing the number of times the dice add to 2 and the number of times they add to 8.

g What is the mean dice sum of the 100 trials you conducted above?

To conduct many experiments, a spreadsheet can be used. For example, the spreadsheet below can be used to simulate rolling three 6-sided dice. Drag down the cells from the second row to row 1000 to run the experiment 1000 times.

	A	B	C	D
1	Die 1	Die 2	Die 3	=MODE(D2:D1001)
2	=RANDBETWEEN(1,6)	=RANDBETWEEN(1,6)	=RANDBETWEEN(1,6)	=A2+B2+C2

h Investigate what the most likely dice sums are when you roll more than two dice. You should use a spreadsheet like the one above to find the most likely values. (Note: Instead of using the MODE function to help you, you can also use the AVERAGE function.)

1 Six numbers are listed in ascending order and some are removed. The mean and median are both 6, the mode is 2 and the range is 10. Fill in the missing numbers.

> Up for a challenge? If you get stuck on a question, check out the 'Working with unfamiliar problems' poster at the end of the book to help you.

$$?, ?, 5, ?, ?, ?$$

2 A survey is conducted at a school and the results are presented as a pie chart. Find the minimum number of people who participated in the survey if the smallest sector has an angle of:

a   90°   b   36°   c   92°   d   35°

3 In a class of 20 students, a poll was taken of the number of cars owned by each family. The median number of cars owned is 1.5 and the mean number is 1.4 cars. Complete the table of the results, shown below.

Number of cars	0	1	2	3
Number of students	4			

4 Each of the 8 letters of a word is written on a separate card. Given the following probabilities, what is the word?

$$\text{Pr(letter P)} = \text{Pr(letter R)} = 12.5\%, \quad \text{Pr(letter B)} = \frac{1}{4}, \quad \text{Pr(vowel)} = 0.375$$

5 Frank the fisherman enjoys beach fishing on Fraser Island, Qld. One year he kept a count of the fish types that he caught and displayed these numbers as a pie chart in his fish shop. Calculate the answers to these questions, showing all steps.

a   What angle did Frank use to represent his whiting catch?

b   Find the difference between the smallest and largest angles in this pie chart.

c   What is the probability of Frank catching a tailor?

d   Find the probability that Frank does *not* catch a golden trevally.

e   What is the probability of Frank catching a flathead or golden trevally?

flathead, 12
tailor, 75
dart, 160
golden trevally, 3
whiting, 50

6 A circular spinner is made using the colours red, green, purple and yellow in four sectors with two sectors being equal in size. The spinner is spun 120 times and the results obtained are shown in the table below.

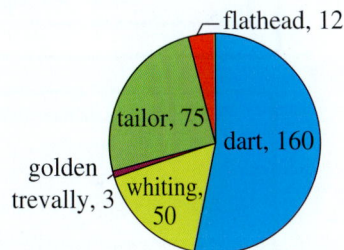

Sector colour	Red	Green	Purple	Yellow
Frequency	40	32	19	29

Design a spinner that is likely to give these results, labelling the sector colours and angles. Explain the mathematical reason for your answer and show relevant calculations.

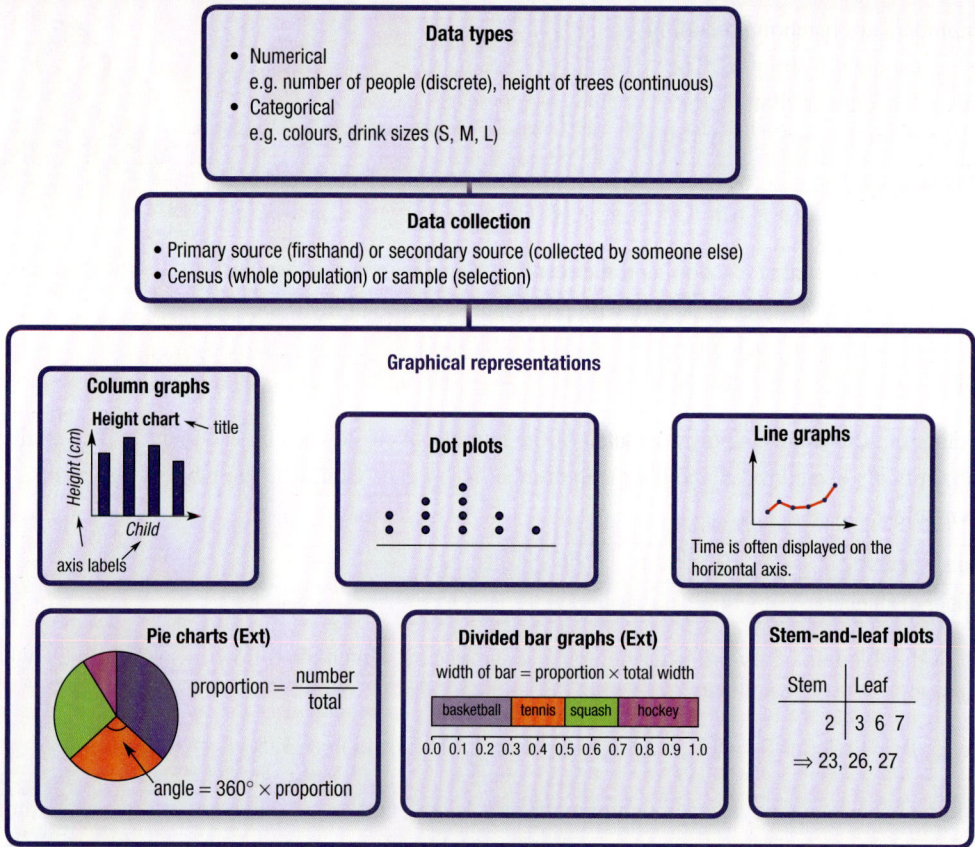

Chapter summary

Data types
- Numerical
  e.g. number of people (discrete), height of trees (continuous)
- Categorical
  e.g. colours, drink sizes (S, M, L)

Data collection
- Primary source (firsthand) or secondary source (collected by someone else)
- Census (whole population) or sample (selection)

Graphical representations

Column graphs

Height chart ← title

axis labels

Dot plots

Line graphs

Time is often displayed on the horizontal axis.

Pie charts (Ext)

$$\text{proportion} = \frac{\text{number}}{\text{total}}$$

$$\text{angle} = 360° \times \text{proportion}$$

Divided bar graphs (Ext)

width of bar = proportion × total width

| basketball | tennis | squash | hockey |

0.0 0.1 0.2 0.3 0.4 0.5 0.6 0.7 0.8 0.9 1.0

Stem-and-leaf plots

Stem	Leaf
2	3 6 7

$\Rightarrow$ 23, 26, 27

Statistics and probability

Summarising data numerically

range = 10 − 1
     = 9

1, 2, 2, 3, 4, 4, 4, 5, 5, 6, 7, 8, 8, 9, 10

mode = 4   median = 5
(most common value) (middle value)

$$\text{mean} = \frac{\text{sum of values}}{\text{number of values}}$$

$$= \frac{78}{15} = 5.2$$

Experimental probability

Use an experiment or survey or simulation to estimate probability.
e.g. Spinner lands on blue 47 times out of 120 $\longrightarrow$
Experimental probability $= \frac{47}{120}$

Outcome: possible result of an experiment
Event: either a single outcome or a collection of outcomes

Probability: how likely an event is

unlikely   likely
0        $\frac{1}{2}$ 1

impossible   even chance   certain
more likely $\longrightarrow$

Experiment/trial: e.g. roll a fair die
Sample space: {1, 2, 3, 4, 5, 6}
Pr(roll a 5) $= \frac{1}{6}$
Pr(roll odd number) $= \frac{3}{6} = \frac{1}{2}$

Expected number is
Pr(event) × number of trials
e.g. Flip coin 100 times,
     expected number of heads
$$= \frac{1}{2} \times 100 = 50$$
e.g. Roll die 36 times,
     expected number of 5s
$$= \frac{1}{6} \times 36 = 6$$

Sample space: e.g.
{red, green, blue}
Pr(spin red) $= \frac{1}{3}$
Pr(don't spin blue) $= \frac{2}{3}$

Chapter checklist with success criteria

A printable version of this checklist is available in the Interactive Textbook ⬇   ✔

8A	**1. I can classify variables.** e.g. Classify the length of a newborn baby as categorical, discrete numerical or continuous numerical.	☐
8A	**2. I can choose a suitable method for collecting data.** e.g. Decide whether a primary or secondary source is suitable for an economist collecting data on the average income of Australian households, and suggest a method for its collection.	☐
8B	**3. I can find the range for a set of data.** e.g. Find the range of 15, 31, 12, 47, 21, 65, 12.	☐
8B	**4. I can find the mean for a set of data.** e.g. Find the mean of 15, 31, 12, 47, 21, 65, 12.	☐
8B	**5. I can find the median for a set of data (including an even number of values).** e.g. Find the median of 15, 31, 12, 47, 21, 65, 12, 29.	☐
8B	**6. I can find the mode for a set of data.** e.g. Find the mode of 15, 31, 12, 47, 21, 65, 12.	☐
8C	**7. I can interpret a column graph and a dot plot.** e.g. Use the dot plot to state how many children have 2 pets, and identify any outliers.	☐

Pets at home survey

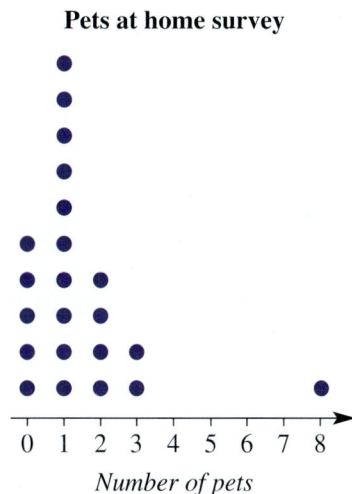

Number of pets

8C	**8. I can construct a column graph and a dot plot from a set of data.** e.g. Construct a column graph to represent the heights of five people: Tim (150 cm), Phil (120 cm), Jess (140 cm), Don (100 cm), Nyree (130 cm).	☐
8D	**9. I can draw a line graph.** e.g. Draw a line graph to represent the temperature in a room at the following times: 9 a.m. (10°C), 10 a.m. (15°C), 11 a.m. (20°C), 12 p.m. (23°C), 1 p.m. (18°C).	☐

		✔

8D

10. I can interpret a travel graph.
e.g. Describe what is happening in the travel graph shown, including stating when the cyclist is travelling fastest and when they are stationary.

Distance cycled over 5 hours

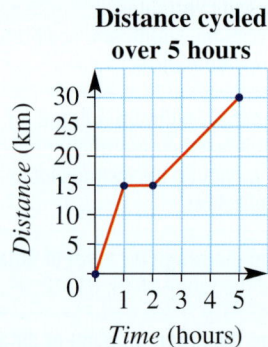

☐

8E

11. I can interpret a stem-and-leaf plot.
e.g. Average daily temperatures (in °C) are shown in the stem-and-leaf plot. Write the temperatures as a list and state the median.

Stem	Leaf
1	3 6 6
2	0 0 1 2 5 5 6 8 9
3	0 2

2|5 means 25°C

☐

8E

12. I can create a stem-and-leaf plot.
e.g. Represent this set of data as a stem-and-leaf plot:
23, 10, 36, 25, 31, 34, 34, 27, 36, 37, 16, 33.

☐

8F

13. I can draw a sector graph (pie chart) with correct sector sizes.   (Ext)
e.g. Draw a pie chart to represent the following allocation of a 10-hour day: Television (1 hour), Internet (2 hours), Sport (4 hours), Homework (3 hours).

☐

8F

14. I can draw a divided bar graph with correct rectangle widths.   (Ext)
e.g. Draw a divided bar graph to represent the following allocation of a 10-hour day: Television (1 hour), Internet (2 hours), Sport (4 hours), Homework (3 hours).

☐

8G

15. I can describe the chance of events using standard English phrases.
e.g. Decide whether rolling a 3 on a 6-sided die and getting heads on a coin are equally likely.

☐

8H

16. I can list the sample space of an experiment and the favourable outcomes of an event.
e.g. If a fair 6-sided die is rolled, list the sample space.
List the favourable outcomes for the event 'roll an odd number'.

☐

8H

17. I can calculate the probability of a simple event, giving an answer as a fraction, decimal or percentage.
e.g. If a fair 6-sided die is rolled, find the probability of getting a number less than 3. Answer as a percentage rounded to one decimal place.

☐

8I

18. I can find the expected number of occurrences of an event.
e.g. If an event has probability 0.4, find the expected number of times the event would occur in 1000 trials.

☐

8I

19. I can calculate the experimental probability of an event.
e.g. When playing with a spinner the following numbers come up: 1, 4, 1, 3, 3, 1, 4, 3, 2, 3.
Find the experimental probability of getting an even number.

☐

Short-answer questions

8C 1 Draw a column graph to represent the following people's ages.

Name	Sven	Dane	Kelly	Hugo	Frankie
Age (years)	20	12	15	22	25

8C 2 A Year 7 group was asked how many hours of television they watch in a week. The results are given in the table.

TV watched (hours)	No. of students
8	5
9	8
10	14
11	8
12	5

a How many students participated in the survey?

b What is the total number of hours of television watched?

c Find the mean number of hours of television watched.

d Show this information in a column graph.

8D 3 The number of students in the library is recorded hourly, as displayed in the graph.

a How many students entered the library when it first opened?

b How many students were in the library at 8 hours after opening?

c If the library opens at 9 a.m, at what time are there the most number of students in the library?

d How many students were in the library at 4 p.m?

Visiting in the library

Number of students vs *Hours after library opening*

8F **Ext** 4 120 people were asked to nominate their favourite take-away food from the list: chicken, pizza, hamburgers, Chinese. The results are given in the table.

Food	Frequency
Chicken	15
Pizza	40
Hamburgers	30
Chinese	35

a If you want to show the data in a pie chart, state the angle needed to represent Chinese food.

b What percentage of people prefer hamburgers?

c Represent the results in a pie chart.

8B 5 Consider the data 1, 4, 2, 7, 3, 2, 9, 12. State the:
a range   b mean   c median   d mode.

8B 6 Consider the data 0, 4, 2, 9, 3, 7, 3, 12. State the:
a range   b mean   c median   d mode.

8E

7 The stem-and-leaf plot shows the price of various items in a shop.

a How many items cost more than $20?

b What is the cost of the most expensive item?

c State the range of the prices.

d If a customer had $20 to spend, how much money would they have left after buying the most expensive item they can afford?

Stem	Leaf
0	1 1 4 5 8
1	0 2 2 2 3 4 7
2	4 5 5
3	1

1|4 means $14

8G

8 For each of the following descriptions, choose the probability from the set $0, \frac{1}{8}, \frac{3}{4}, 1, \frac{19}{20}$ that matches best.

a certain

b highly unlikely

c highly likely

d likely

e impossible

8H

9 List the sample space for each of the following experiments.

a A fair 6-sided die is rolled.

b A fair coin is tossed.

c A letter is chosen from the word DESIGN.

d Spinning the spinner shown opposite.

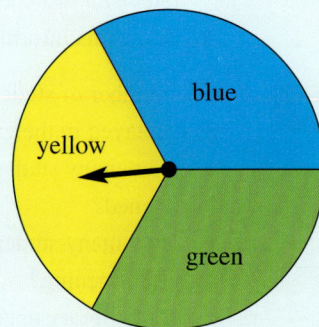

8H

10 Vin spins a spinner with nine equal sectors, which are numbered 1 to 9.

a How many outcomes are there?

b Find the probability of spinning:

i an odd number

ii a multiple of 3

iii a number greater than 10

iv a prime number less than 6

v a factor of 8

vi a factor of 100.

8H

11 One card is chosen at random from a standard deck of 52 playing cards. Find the probability of drawing:

a a red king

b a king or queen

c a jack of diamonds

d a picture card (i.e. king, queen or jack).

8I

12 A coin is flipped 100 times, resulting in 42 heads and 58 tails.

a What is the experimental probability of getting heads? Give your answer as a percentage.

b What is the actual probability of getting heads if the coin is fair? Give your answer as a percentage.

8H

13 Consider the spinner shown.

   a State the probability that the spinner lands in the green section.

   b State the probability that the spinner lands in the blue section.

   c Tanya spins the spinner 100 times. What is the expected number of times it would land in the red section?

   d She spins the spinner 500 times. What is the expected number of times it would land in the green section?

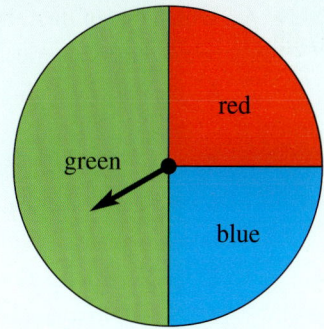

Multiple-choice questions

8C

1 In the column graph shown, the highest income is earned by:

   A Michael   **B** Alice   **C** Dan   **D** Laura   **E** Victoria

Annual income

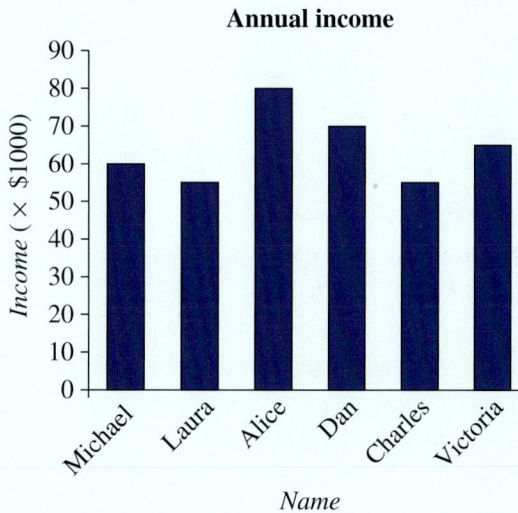

Questions 2 and 3 relate to the following information.

The results of a survey are shown below.

Instrument learned	piano	violin	drums	guitar
Number of students	10	2	5	3

8F

Ext

2 If the results above are presented as a sector graph, then the angle occupied by the drums sector is:

   A 360°   **B** 180°   **C** 120°   **D** 90°   **E** 45°

8I

3 Based on the survey, the experimental probability that a randomly selected person learns the guitar is:

   A $\frac{1}{4}$ **B** $\frac{1}{2}$ **C** 3   **D** $\frac{3}{5}$ **E** $\frac{3}{20}$

8A

4 Which one of the following variables is continuous numerical?
  A the Australian State or Territory in which babies are born
  B the number of babies born in a given year
  C the number of hairs on a baby's head
  D the weight (in kg) of newborn babies
  E the length (in number of letters) of a baby's first name

Questions 5 and 6 relate to the following information.

In a class of 20 students, the number of days each student was absent over a 10-week period is recorded.

1, 0, 1, 2, 2, 3, 2, 4, 3, 0, 1, 1, 2, 3, 3, 3, 2, 2, 2, 2

8B

5 The mode is:
  A 0   **B** 1   **C** 2   **D** 3   **E** 4

8B

6 The mean number of days a student was absent is:
  A 1   **B** 2   **C** 1.95   **D** 3   **E** 39

8B

7 The range of the numbers 1, 5, 3, 9, 12, 41, 12 is:
  A 40   **B** 41   **C** 12   **D** 3   **E** 1

8H

8 Which of the following events has the same probability as rolling an odd number on a fair 6-sided die?
  A rolling a number greater than 4 on a fair 6-sided die
  B choosing a vowel from the word CAT
  C tossing a fair coin and getting heads
  D choosing the letter T from the word TOE
  E spinning an odd number on a spinner numbered 1 to 7

8H

9 Each letter of the word APPLE is written separately on five cards. One card is then chosen at random. Pr(letter P) is:
  A 0   **B** 0.2   **C** 0.4   **D** 0.5   **E** 1

8I

10 A fair 6-sided die is rolled 600 times. The expected number of times that the number rolled is either a 1 or a 2 is:
  A 100   **B** 200   **C** 300   **D** 400   **E** 500

Extended-response questions

1   The number of rainy days experienced throughout a year in a certain town is displayed below.

Month	Jan	Feb	Mar	Apr	May	Jun	Jul	Aug	Sep	Oct	Nov	Dec
No. of rainy days	10	11	3	7	2	0	1	5	6	9	7	5

a   Show this information in a column graph.

b   For how many days of the year did it rain in this town?

c   What is the probability that it will rain in any day during winter (i.e. during June, July and August)?

d   What type of variable (e.g. continuous numerical) is the number of rainy days?

e   What type of variable is the month?

f   What other type of graph could be used to present this data?

2   At a school camp, a survey was conducted to establish each student's favourite dessert.

Ice-cream	Yoghurt	Danish pastry	Jelly	Pudding	Cheesecake
10	5	2	7	4	12

a   How many students participated in the survey?

b   What is the most popular dessert selected?

c   What is the probability that a randomly selected student chooses jelly as their favourite dessert?

d   For each of the following methods listed below, state whether it would be a reasonable way of presenting the survey's results.
   i   column graph
   ii   line graph
   iii sector graph (pie chart)
   iv   divided bar graph

e   If the campers attend a school with 800 students, how many students from the entire school would you expect to choose pudding as their preferred dessert?

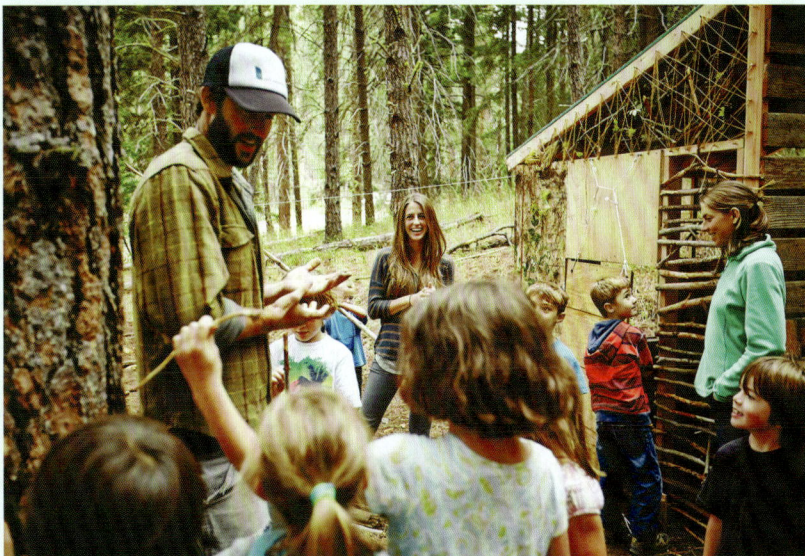

9

Equations

Maths in context: Equations are solved every day in many occupations

Solving equations is an essential skill used in solving problems in a vast number of occupations, including business, agriculture, construction, engineering, financial services, food production, manufacturing, technology and the trades.

It is important for the managers of both the large stores and small independent retailers, such as cafes, fashion boutiques, electronics shops and shoe shops, to keep track of cash flow and ensure a profit. Financial calculations involve using formulas and solving equations to calculate measures such as the number of sales required to break-even (no profit and no loss), and overall profit as a percentage of sales.

Construction workers, such as engineers, builders, concreters, plumbers and roofers, solve equations to find the time a job will take, the cost of materials and possible profit.

Service businesses who have clients, such as dog groomers, fitness and dance instructors, hairdressers, hotel owners, optometrists and physiotherapists must all manage their finances. Equations are solved to find the number of clients needed to make a certain profit per week.

Electronic engineers and electricians require skills in algebra to apply formulas and solve equations related to the power supply in buildings, vehicles, electronic components, appliances and various devices.

Chapter contents

Victorian Curriculum 2.0

This chapter covers the following content descriptors in the Victorian Curriculum 2.0:

ALGEBRA

VC2M7A01, VC2M7A03, VC2M7A06

Please refer to the curriculum support documentation in the teacher resources for a full and comprehensive mapping of this chapter to the related curriculum content descriptors.

© VCAA

Online resources

A host of additional online resources are included as part of your Interactive Textbook, including HOTmaths content, video demonstrations of all worked examples, auto-marked quizzes and much more.

9A   Introduction to equations

LEARNING INTENTIONS
- To understand the difference between an equation and an expression
- To be able to determine if an equation is true or false, substituting for pronumerals if required
- To be able to write an equation given an English description

An equation is a mathematical statement stating that two expressions have the same value. It consists of two expressions that are separated by an equals sign (=).

Sample equations include:

$$3 + 3 = 6$$
$$30 = 2 \times 15$$
$$100 - 30 = 60 + 10$$

which are all true equations.

An equation does not have to be true. For instance, $2 + 2 = 17$ and $5 = 3 - 1$ and $10 + 15 = 12 + 3$ are all false equations.

Many mathematical equations need to be solved to build and launch space stations into orbit.

If an equation contains pronumerals, one cannot generally tell whether the equation is true or false until values are substituted for the pronumerals. For example, $5 + x = 7$ could be true (if x is 2) or it could be false (if x is 15).

Lesson starter: Equations: True or false?

Rearrange the following five symbols to make as many different equations as possible.

$$5, 2, 3, +, =$$

- Which of them are true? Which are false?
- Is it always possible to rearrange a set of numbers and operations to make true equations?

KEY IDEAS

■ An **expression** is a collection of pronumerals, numbers and operators without an equals sign (e.g. $2x + 3$).

■ An **equation** is a mathematical statement stating that two expressions are equal (e.g. $2x + 3 = 4y - 2$).

■ Equations have a left-hand side (LHS), a right-hand side (RHS) and an equals sign in between.

$$\underbrace{2x + 3}_{\text{LHS}} = \underbrace{4y - 2}_{\text{RHS}}$$

- The equals sign indicates that the LHS and RHS have the same numerical value.

■ Equations are mathematical statements that can be true (e.g. $2 + 3 = 5$) or false (e.g. $2 + 3 = 7$).

■ If a pronumeral is included in an equation, you need to know the value to substitute before deciding whether the equation is true. For example, $3x = 12$ would be true if 4 is substituted for x, but it would be false if 10 is substituted.

BUILDING UNDERSTANDING

1 Classify each of these equations as true or false.
   a $2 + 3 = 5$
   b $3 + 2 = 6$
   c $5 - 1 = 6$

2 If $x = 2$, is $10 + x = 12$ true or false?

3 Consider the equation $4 + 3x = 2x + 9$.
   a If $x = 5$, state the value of the left-hand side (LHS).
   b If $x = 5$, state the value of the right-hand side (RHS).
   c Is the equation $4 + 3x = 2x + 9$ true or false when $x = 5$?

Example 1   Identifying equations

Which of the following are equations?
a $3 + 5 = 8$ b $7 + 7 = 18$ c $2 + 12$ d $4 = 12 - x$ e $3 + u$

SOLUTION	EXPLANATION
a $3 + 5 = 8$ is an equation.	There are two expressions (i.e. $3 + 5$ and 8) separated by an equals sign.
b $7 + 7 = 18$ is an equation.	There are two expressions separated by an equals sign. Although this equation is false, it is still an equation.
c $2 + 12$ is not an equation.	This is just a single expression. There is no equals sign.
d $4 = 12 - x$ is an equation.	There are two expressions separated by an equals sign.
e $3 + u$ is not an equation.	There is no equals sign, so this is not an equation.

Now you try

Decide whether the following are equations (E) or not (N).
a $3 + 7$ b $12 = 4 + 8$ c $10 + 3 = 20$ d $2 - 3x$ e $5 + q = 12$

Example 2   Classifying equations

For each of the following equations, state whether it is true or false.

a $7 + 5 = 12$

b $5 + 3 = 2 \times 4$

c $12 \times (2 - 1) = 14 + 5$

d $3 + 9x = 60 + 6$, if $x = 7$

e $10 + b = 3b + 1$, if $b = 4$

f $3 + 2x = 21 - y$, if $x = 5$ and $y = 8$

SOLUTION

a   true

b   true

c   false

d   true

e   false

f   true

EXPLANATION

The left-hand side (LHS) and right-hand side (RHS) are both equal to 12, so the equation is true.

LHS $= 5 + 3 = 8$ and RHS $= 2 \times 4 = 8$, so both sides are equal.

LHS $= 12$ and RHS $= 19$, so the equation is false.

If x is 7, then:
LHS $= 3 + 9 \times 7 = 66$, RHS $= 60 + 6 = 66$

If b is 4, then:
LHS $= 10 + 4 = 14$, RHS $= 3(4) + 1 = 13$

If $x = 5$ and $y = 8$, then:
LHS $= 3 + 2(5) = 13$, RHS $= 21 - 8 = 13$

Now you try

For each of the following equations, state whether it is true or false.

a $4 + 9 = 15$

b $12 - 3 = 5 + 4$

c $4 \times (3 + 2) = 10 + 10$

d $10 + 2x = 16$, if $x = 6$

e $16 - a = 7a$, if $a = 2$

f $3a + b = 2b - a$, if $a = 10$ and $b = 2$

Example 3   Writing equations from a description

Write equations for each of the following scenarios.

a   The sum of x and 5 is 22.

b   The number of cards in a deck is x. In 7 decks there are 91 cards.

c   Priya's age is currently j years. In 5 years' time her age will equal 17.

d   Corey earns \$$w$ per year. He spends $\frac{1}{12}$ on sport and $\frac{2}{13}$ on food. The total amount Corey spends on sport and food is \$15 000.

SOLUTION

a $x + 5 = 22$

b $7x = 91$

EXPLANATION

The sum of x and 5 is written $x + 5$.

$7x$ means $7 \times x$ and this number must equal the 91 cards.

c $j + 5 = 17$ In 5 years' time Priya's age will be 5 more than her current age, so $j + 5$ must be 17.

d $\frac{1}{12} \times w + \frac{2}{13} \times w = 15\,000$ $\frac{1}{12}$ of Corey's wage is $\frac{1}{12} \times w$ and $\frac{2}{13}$ of his wage is $\frac{2}{13} \times w$.

Now you try

Write equations for each of the following.

a The product of 3 and a is 21.

b The sum of p and q is 10.

c Tristan's age is currently t years. Three years ago he was 24.

d John has a marbles and Michael has b marbles. When John combines half of his marble collection with a quarter of Michael's collection, the total is 150 marbles.

Exercise 9A

FLUENCY	1–5(½), 7	2–7(½)	2(½), 5–7(½)

Example 1

1 State whether the following are equations (Yes or No).

a $2 + 6 = 8$ b $1 + 1 = 3$ c $9 - 3$ d $3 = 9 + x$ e $5 - y$

Example 1

2 Classify each of the following as an equation (E) or not an equation (N).

a $7 + x = 9$ b $2 + 2$ c $2 \times 5 = t$

d $10 = 5 + x$ e $2 = 2$ f $7 \times u$

g $10 \div 4 = 3p$ h $3 = e + 2$ i $x + 5$

Example 2a–c

3 For each of the following equations, state whether it is true or false.

a $10 \times 2 = 20$ b $12 \times 11 = 144$ c $3 \times 2 = 5 + 1$

d $100 - 90 = 2 \times 5$ e $30 \times 2 = 32$ f $12 - 4 = 4$

g $2(3 - 1) = 4$ h $5 - (2 + 1) = 7 - 4$ i $3 = 3$

j $2 = 17 - 14 - 1$ k $10 + 2 = 12 - 4$ l $1 \times 2 \times 3 = 1 + 2 + 3$

Example 2d

4 If $x = 3$, state whether each of these equations is true or false.

a $5 + x = 7$ b $x + 1 = 4$ c $13 - x = 10 + x$ d $6 = 2x$

Example 2e

5 If $b = 4$, state whether each of the following equations is true or false.

a $5b + 2 = 22$ b $10 \times (b - 3) = b + b + 2$

c $12 - 3b = 5 - b$ d $b \times (b + 1) = 20$

Example 2f

6 If $a = 10$ and $b = 7$, state whether each of these equations is true or false.

a $a + b = 17$ b $a \times b = 3$ c $a \times (a - b) = 30$

d $b \times b = 59 - a$ e $3a = 5b - 5$ f $b \times (a - b) = 20$

g $21 - a = b$ h $10 - a = 7 - b$ i $1 + a - b = 2b - a$

Example 3a

7 Write equations for each of the following.
- **a** The sum of 3 and x is equal to 10.
- **b** When k is multiplied by 5, the result is 1005.
- **c** The sum of a and b is 22.
- **d** When d is doubled, the result is 78.
- **e** The product of 8 and x is 56.
- **f** When p is tripled, the result is 21.
- **g** One-quarter of t is 12.
- **h** The sum of q and p is equal to the product of q and p.

PROBLEM-SOLVING	8, 9	8, 10	8, 10, 11

Example 3b–d

8 Write true equations for each of these problems. You do not need to solve them.
- **a** Chairs cost $\$c$ at a store. The cost of 6 chairs is $546.
- **b** Patrick works for x hours each day. In a 5-day working week, he works $37\frac{1}{2}$ hours in total.
- **c** Pens cost $\$a$ each and pencils cost $\$b$. Twelve pens and three pencils cost $28 in total.
- **d** Amy is f years old. In 10 years' time her age will be 27.
- **e** Andrew's age is j and Hailey's age is m. In 10 years' time their combined age will be 80.

9 Find a value of m that would make this equation true: $10 = m + 7$.

10 Find two possible values of k that would make this equation true: $k \times (8 - k) = 12$. (*Hint:* Try whole numbers between 1 and 10.)

11 If the equation $x + y = 6$ is true, and x and y are both whole numbers between 1 and 5, what values could they have?

REASONING	12, 13	13, 14(½)	14

12 Explain why the equation $a + 3 = 3 + a$ is always true, regardless of the value of a.

13 Explain why the equation $b = b + 10$ is never true, regardless of the value of b.

14 Equations involving pronumerals can be split into three groups:
A: Always true, no matter what values are substituted.
N: Never true, no matter what values are substituted.
S: Sometimes true but sometimes false, depending on the values substituted.
Classify each of these equations as A, N or S.
- **a** $x + 5 = 11$
- **b** $12 - x = x$
- **c** $a = a$
- **d** $5 + b = b + 5$
- **e** $a = a + 7$
- **f** $5 + b = b - 5$
- **g** $0 \times b = 0$
- **h** $a \times a = 100$
- **i** $2x + x = 3x$
- **j** $2x + x = 4x$
- **k** $2x + x = 3x + 1$
- **l** $a \times a + 100 = 0$

ENRICHMENT: Equation permutations	–	–	15, 16

15 For each of the following, rearrange the symbols to make a true equation.
- **a** $6, 2, 3, \times, =$
- **b** $1, 4, 5, -, =$
- **c** $2, 2, 7, 10, -, \div, =$
- **d** $2, 4, 5, 10, -, \div, =$

16 a How many different equations can be produced using the symbols $2, 3, 5, +, =$?
- **b** How many of these equations are true? List them.
- **c** Is it possible to change just one of the numbers above and still produce true equations by rearranging the symbols? Explain your answer.
- **d** Is it possible to change just the operation above (i.e. +) and still produce true equations? Explain your answer.

9B Solving equations by inspection

Solving an equation is the process of finding the values that pronumerals must take in order to make the equation true. Pronumerals are also called 'unknowns' when solving equations. For simple equations, it is possible to find a solution by trying a few values for the pronumeral until the equation is true. This method does not guarantee that we have found all the solutions (if there is more than one) and it will not help if there are no solutions, but it can be a useful and quick method for simple equations.

A house painter solves an equation to calculate the number of litres of paint needed. If undercoat paint covers $12\,m^2$/L and the total wall area is $240\,m^2$, the painter solves: $12x = 240$, giving $x = 20$, so 20 litres are required.

Lesson starter: Finding the missing value

- Find the missing values to make the following equations true.

$$10 \times \boxed{} - 17 = 13$$

$$27 = 15 + 3 \times \boxed{}$$

$$2 \times \boxed{} + 4 = 17$$

- Can you always find a value to put in the place of $\boxed{}$ in any equation?

KEY IDEAS

■ **Solving** an equation means finding the values of any pronumerals that make the equation true. These values are called **solutions** to the equation.

■ An **unknown** in an equation is a pronumeral whose value needs to be found in order to make the equation true.

■ One method of solving equations is by **inspection** (also called **trial and error**), which involves inspecting (or trying) different values and seeing which ones make the equation true.

BUILDING UNDERSTANDING

1 If the missing number is 5, classify each of the following equations as true or false.

a $\boxed{} + 3 = 8$

b $10 \times \boxed{} + 2 = 46$

c $10 - \boxed{} = 5$

d $12 = 6 + \boxed{} \times 2$

2 For the equation $\boxed{} + 7 = 13$:

a State the value of the LHS (left-hand side) if $\boxed{} = 5$.

b State the value of the LHS if $\boxed{} = 10$.

c State the value of the LHS if $\boxed{} = 6$.

d What value of $\boxed{}$ would make the LHS equal to 13?

3 State the unknown pronumeral in each of the following equations. Note that you do not need to find its value.

a $4 + x = 12$

b $50 - c = 3$

c $4b + 2 = 35$

d $5 - 10d = 2$

Example 4   Finding the missing number

For each of these equations, find the value of the missing number that would make it true.

a $\boxed{} \times 7 = 35$

b $20 - \boxed{} = 14$

SOLUTION

a 5

b 6

EXPLANATION

$5 \times 7 = 35$ is a true equation.

$20 - 6 = 14$ is a true equation.

Now you try

Find the value of the missing number that would make the following equations true.

a $\boxed{} \div 3 = 7$

b $12 + \boxed{} = 27$

Example 5   Solving equations by inspection

Solve each of the following equations by inspection.

a $c + 12 = 30$ **b** $5b = 20$ **c** $2x + 13 = 21$

SOLUTION

EXPLANATION

a $c + 12 = 30$
$$c = 18$$

The unknown variable here is c.

$18 + 12 = 30$ is a true equation.

An alternative method is to 'undo' the operation

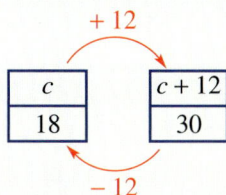

b $5b = 20$
$$b = 4$$

The unknown variable here is b.

Recall that $5b$ means $5 \times b$, so if $b = 4$ then $5b = 5 \times 4 = 20$.

An alternative method is to 'undo' the operation.

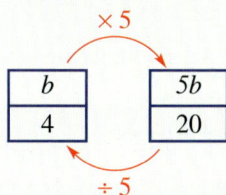

c $2x + 13 = 21$
$$x = 4$$

The unknown variable here is x.

Trying a few values:

$x = 10$ makes LHS $= 20 + 13 = 33$, which is too large.

$x = 3$ makes LHS $= 6 + 13 = 19$, which is too small.

$x = 4$ makes LHS $= 21$.

An alternative method is to 'undo' the operation.

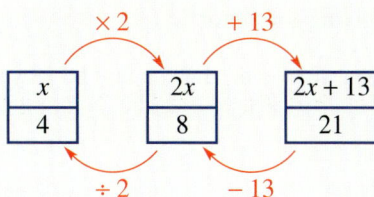

Now you try

Solve the following equations by inspection.

a $q - 5 = 13$ **b** $2x = 16$ **c** $3a + 5 = 35$

Exercise 9B

FLUENCY   1, 2–4($\frac{1}{2}$)   2–5($\frac{1}{2}$)   3–5($\frac{1}{3}$)

Example 4

1 For each of these equations, find the value of the missing number that would make it true.

a $\boxed{} \times 4 = 24$ b $\boxed{} \div 5 = 10$ c $10 - \boxed{} = 2$ d $9 + \boxed{} = 26$

Example 4

2 Find the value of the missing numbers.

a $4 + \boxed{} = 7$ b $2 \times \boxed{} = 12$ c $13 = \boxed{} + 3$ d $10 = 6 + \boxed{}$

e $42 = \boxed{} \times 7$ f $100 - \boxed{} = 30$ g $\boxed{} \times 4 = 80$ h $\boxed{} + 12 = 31$

Example 5a,b

3 Solve the following equations by inspection.

a $8 \times y = 64$ b $6 \div l = 3$ c $l \times 3 = 18$ d $4 - d = 2$

e $l + 2 = 14$ f $a - 2 = 4$ g $s + 7 = 19$ h $x \div 8 = 1$

i $12 = e + 4$ j $r \div 10 = 1$ k $13 = 5 + s$ l $0 = 3 - z$

Example 5c

4 Solve the following equations by inspection.

a $2p - 1 = 5$ b $3p + 2 = 14$ c $4q - 4 = 8$ d $4v + 4 = 24$

e $2b - 1 = 1$ f $5u + 1 = 21$ g $5g + 5 = 20$ h $4(e - 2) = 4$

i $45 = 5(d + 5)$ j $3d - 5 = 13$ k $8 = 3m - 4$ l $8 = 3o - 1$

Example 5c

5 Solve the following equations by inspection. (All solutions are whole numbers between 1 and 10.)

a $4 \times (x + 1) - 5 = 11$ b $7 + x = 2 \times x$ c $(3x + 1) \div 2 = 8$

d $10 - x = x + 2$ e $2 \times (x + 3) + 4 = 12$ f $15 - 2x = x$

PROBLEM-SOLVING   6, 7   6–8   7–11

6 Find the value of the number in each of these examples.

a   A number is doubled and the result is 22.

b   3 less than a number is 9.

c   Half of a number is 8.

d   7 more than a number is 40.

e   A number is divided by 10, giving a result of 3.

f   10 is divided by a number, giving a result of 5.

7 Ezekiel's current age is unknown. In 5 years' time he will be 18 years old.

a   If x is Ezekiel's current age, which of the following equations can be used to describe this situation?

   A $x + 18 = 5$ **B** $x + 5 = 18$ **C** $5x = 18$ **D** $x - 5 = 18$

b   Solve the equation by inspection to find the value of x.

c   How old is Ezekiel?

8   Arabella is paid $10 an hour for x hours. During a particular week, she earns $180.

   a   Write an equation involving x to describe this situation.
   b   Solve the equation by inspection to find the value of x.

9   One bag of sand weighs w kg and another bag which is twice as heavy, weighs 70 kg.

   a   Write an equation involving w to describe this situation.
   b   Solve the equation by inspection to find the value of w.

10   Chloe buys x kg of apples at $4.50 per kg. She spends a total of $13.50.

   a   Write an equation involving x to describe this situation.
   b   Solve the equation by inspection to find x.

11   Yanni's current age is y years. In 12 years' time he will be three times as old.

   a   Write an equation involving y to describe this situation.
   b   Solve the equation by inspection to find y.

REASONING   12   12   12, 13

12   a   Solve the equation $x + (x + 1) = 19$ by inspection.
     b   The expression $x + (x + 1)$ can be simplified to $2x + 1$. Use this observation to solve $x + (x + 1) = 181$ by inspection.

13   There are three consecutive positive integers that add to 45.

     a   Solve the equation $x + (x + 1) + (x + 2) = 45$ by inspection to find the three numbers.
     b   An equation of the form $x + (x + 1) + (x + 2) = ?$ has a positive integer solution only if the right-hand side is a multiple of 3. Explain why this is the case. (*Hint*: Simplify the LHS.)

ENRICHMENT: Multiple pronumerals   –   –   14

14   When multiple pronumerals are involved, inspection can still be used to find a solution. For each of the following equations find, by inspection, one pair of values for x and y that make them true.

   a $x + y = 8$ b $x - y = 2$ c $3 = 2x + y$
   d $x \times y = 6$ e $12 = 2 + x + y$ f $x + y = x \times y$

9C Equivalent equations

LEARNING INTENTIONS
- To understand what it means for two equations to be equivalent
- To be able to apply an operation to both sides of an equation to form an equivalent equation
- To be able to determine that two equations are equivalent by finding an operation that has been applied to both sides

Sometimes, two equations essentially express the same thing. For example, the equations $x + 5 = 14$, $x + 6 = 15$ and $x + 7 = 16$ are all made true by the same value of x. Each time, we have added one to both sides of the equation. The following diagram shows that if we do the same to both sides of an equation such as $x + 5 = 14$, we can make equivalent equations, $x + 2 = 11$, $x + 6 = 15$ and $2x + 10 = 28$.

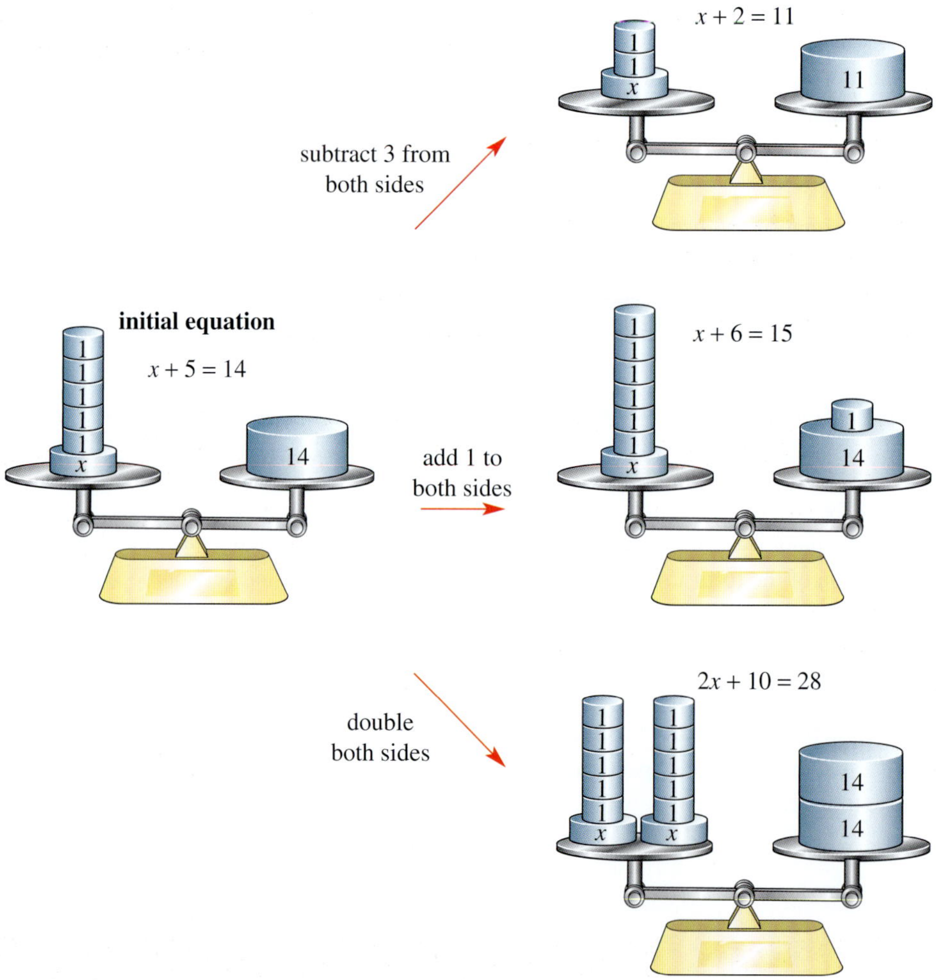

$x + 2 = 11$

subtract 3 from both sides

initial equation

$x + 5 = 14$

add 1 to both sides

$x + 6 = 15$

double both sides

$2x + 10 = 28$

A true equation stays true if we 'do the same thing to both sides', such as adding a number or multiplying by a number. The exception to this rule is that multiplying both sides of any equation by zero will always make the equation true, and dividing both sides of any equation by zero is not permitted because nothing can be divided by zero. Other than this exception, if we do the same thing to both sides we will have an equivalent equation.

Lesson starter: Equations as scales

The scales in the diagram show $2 + 3x = 8$.

- What would the scales look like if two '1 kg' blocks were removed from both sides?
- What would the scales look like if the two '1 kg' blocks were removed just from the left-hand side? (Try to show whether they would be level.)
- Use scales to illustrate why $4x + 3 = 4$ and $4x = 1$ are equivalent equations.

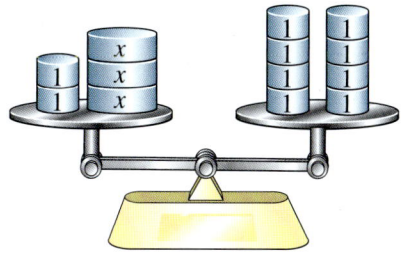

KEY IDEAS

■ Two equations are **equivalent** if substituting pronumerals always makes both equations true or both equations false. For example, "$x + 3 = 10$" and "$10 = x + 3$" are always either both true (if x is 7) or both false (if x is not equal to 7).

■ To show that two equations are equivalent you can repeatedly:
- add the same number to both sides
- subtract the same number from both sides
- multiply both sides by the same number (other than zero)
- divide both sides by the same number (other than zero)
- swap the left-hand side with the right-hand side of the equation

BUILDING UNDERSTANDING

1 Give an equation that results from adding 10 to both sides of each of these equations.

  a $10d + 5 = 20$ b $7e = 31$ c $2a = 12$ d $x = 12$

2 Match up each of these equations (**a** to **e**) with its equivalent equation (i.e. **A** to **E**), where 3 has been added to both sides.

  a $10 + x = 14$ **A** $12x + 3 = 123$

  b $x + 1 = 13$ **B** $x + 13 = 11x + 3$

  c $12 = x + 5$ **C** $13 + x = 17$

  d $x + 10 = 11x$ **D** $x + 4 = 16$

  e $12x = 120$ **E** $15 = x + 8$

Example 6   Applying an operation

For each equation, find the result of applying the given operation to both sides and then simplify.

  a $2 + x = 5$ [$+ 4$]   b $7x = 10$ [$\times 2$]

  c $30 = 20b$ [$\div 10$]   d $7q - 4 = 10$ [$+ 4$]

Continued on next page

SOLUTION	EXPLANATION

a
$$2 + x = 5$$
$$2 + x + 4 = 5 + 4$$
$$x + 6 = 9$$

The equation is written out, and 4 is added to both sides.

Simplify the expressions on each side.

b
$$7x = 10$$
$$7x \times 2 = 10 \times 2$$
$$14x = 20$$

The equation is written out, and both sides are multiplied by 2.

Simplify the expressions on each side.

c
$$30 = 20b$$
$$\frac{30}{10} = \frac{20b}{10}$$
$$3 = 2b$$

The equation is written out, and both sides are divided by 10.

Simplify the expressions on each side.

d
$$7q - 4 = 10$$
$$7q - 4 + 4 = 10 + 4$$
$$7q = 14$$

The equation is written out, and 4 is added to both sides.

Simplify the expressions on each side.

Now you try

Find the result of applying the given operation to both sides and then simplifying.

a $q + 5 = 8$ $[+ 11]$
b $7k = 10$ $[\times 3]$
c $15 = 25b$ $[\div 5]$
d $9 + 3b = 8 + 2a$ $[- 8]$

Example 7   Showing that equations are equivalent

Show that these pairs of equations are equivalent by stating the operation used.
a $2x + 10 = 15$ and $2x = 5$
b $5 = 7 - x$ and $10 = 2(7 - x)$
c $10(b + 3) = 20$ and $b + 3 = 2$

SOLUTION	EXPLANATION

a Both sides have had 10 subtracted.

$$2x + 10 = 15$$
$$-10 \quad \quad -10$$
$$2x = 5$$

$2x + 10 - 10$ simplifies to $2x$, so we get the second equation by subtracting 10.

b Both sides have been multiplied by 2.

$$5 = 7 - x$$
$$\times 2 \quad \quad \times 2$$
$$10 = 2(7 - x)$$

$2(7 - x)$ represents the RHS; i.e. $7 - x$, being multiplied by 2.

c Both sides have been divided by 10.

$$10(b + 3) = 20$$
$$\div 10 \quad \quad \div 10$$
$$b + 3 = 2$$

Remember $10(b + 3)$ means $10 \times (b + 3)$. If we have $10(b + 3)$, we get $b + 3$ when dividing by 10.

Now you try

Show that these pairs of equations are equivalent by showing the operation used.

a $3a - 4 = 10$ and $3a = 14$ **b** $3r = 5 - 4r$ and $6r = 2(5 - 4r)$

c $x - 7 = 9 - 3x$ and $x - 16 = -3x$

Exercise 9C

FLUENCY   1, 2–3($\frac{1}{2}$)   2–4($\frac{1}{2}$)   2–4($\frac{1}{3}$)

1 For each equation, find the result of applying the given operation to both sides and then simplify.

a $3 + x = 7$ [+ 3]

b $4x = 7$ [× 3]

c $15 = 5b$ [÷ 5]

d $5q + 2 = 6$ [− 2]

2 For each equation, show the result of applying the listed operations to both sides.

a $5 + x = 10$ [+ 1]   **b** $3x = 7$ [× 2]   **c** $12 = 8q$ [÷ 4]

d $9 + a = 13$ [− 3]   **e** $7 + b = 10$ [+ 5]   **f** $5 = 3b + 7$ [− 5]

g $2 = 5 + a$ [+ 2]   **h** $12x - 3 = 3$ [+ 5]   **i** $7p - 2 = 10$ [+ 2]

3 Show that these pairs of equations are equivalent by stating the operation used.

a $4x + 2 = 10$ and $4x = 8$

b $7 + 3b = 12$ and $9 + 3b = 14$

c $20a = 10$ and $2a = 1$

d $4 = 12 - x$ and $8 = 2(12 - x)$

e $18 = 3x$ and $6 = x$

f $12 + x = 3$ and $15 + x = 6$

g $4(10 + b) = 80$ and $10 + b = 20$

h $12x = 5$ and $12x + 4 = 9$

4 For each of the following equations, find the equivalent equation that is the result of adding 4 to both sides and then multiplying both sides by 3.

a $x = 5$ **b** $2 = a + 1$ **c** $d - 4 = 2$

d $7 + a = 8$ **e** $3y - 2 = 7$ **f** $2x = 6$

PROBLEM-SOLVING   5   5, 6   6, 7

5 Match up each of these equations (**a** to **e**) with its equivalent equation (i.e. **A** to **E**), stating the operation used.

a $m + 10 = 12$ **A** $7 - m = 6$

b $3 - m = 2$ **B** $5m = 18$

c $12m = 30$ **C** $6m = 10$

d $5m + 2 = 20$ **D** $6m = 15$

e $3m = 5$ **E** $m + 12 = 14$

6 For each of the following pairs of equations, show they are equivalent by listing the two steps required to transform the first equation to the second.

a $x = 5$ and $3x + 2 = 17$

b $m = 2$ and $10m - 3 = 17$

c $5(2 + x) = 15$ and $x = 1$

d $10 = 3x + 10$ and $0 = x$

7 For each of the following equations, write an equivalent equation that you can get in one operation. Your equation should be simpler (i.e. smaller) than the original.

a $2q + 7 = 9$

b $10x + 3 = 10$

c $2(3 + x) = 40$

d $x \div 12 = 5$

REASONING	8	8, 9	8–10

8 Sometimes two equations that look quite different can be equivalent.

a Show that $3x + 2 = 14$ and $10x + 1 = 41$ are equivalent by copying and completing the following.

$$3x + 2 = 14$$

$-2 \Big(\quad \Big) -2$

$$3x = 12$$

$\div 3 \Big(\quad \Big) \div 3$

$$\_\_ = \_\_$$

$\times 10 \Big(\quad \Big) \times 10$

$$\_\_ = \_\_$$

$+1 \Big(\quad \Big) +1$

$$10x + 1 = 41$$

b Show that $5x - 3 = 32$ and $x + 2 = 9$ are equivalent. (*Hint*: Try to go via the equation $x = 7$.)

c Show that $(x \div 2) + 4 = 9$ and $(x + 8) \div 2 = 9$ are equivalent.

9 As stated in the rules for equivalence listed in the **Key ideas**, multiplying both sides by zero is not permitted.

a Write the result of multiplying both sides of the following equations by zero.

i $3 + x = 5$

ii $2 + 2 = 4$

iii $2 + 2 = 5$

b Explain in a sentence why multiplying by zero does not give a useful equivalent equation.

10 Substituting pronumerals into expressions can be done by finding equivalent equations. Show how you can start with the equation $x = 3$ and find an equivalent equation with:

a $7x + 2$ on the LHS

b $8 + 2x$ on the LHS

ENRICHMENT: Equivalence relations	–	–	11

11 Classify each of the following statements as true or false, justifying your answer.

a Every equation is equivalent to itself.

b If equation 1 and equation 2 are equivalent, then equation 2 and equation 1 are equivalent.

c If equation 1 and equation 2 are equivalent, and equation 2 and equation 3 are equivalent, then equation 1 and equation 3 are equivalent.

d If equation 1 and equation 2 are *not* equivalent, and equation 2 and equation 3 are *not* equivalent, then equation 1 is *not* equivalent to equation 3.

9D Solving equations algebraically

A soccer player preparing for a game will put on shin pads, then socks and, finally, soccer boots. When the game is over, these items are removed in reverse order: first the boots, then the socks and, finally, the shin pads. Nobody takes their socks off before their shoes. A similar reversal of procedures occurs with equivalent equations.

Here are three equivalent equations.

$$
\begin{array}{c}
x = 3 \\
\times 2 \left(\right) \times 2 \\
2x = 6 \\
+ 4 \left(\right) + 4 \\
2x + 4 = 10
\end{array}
$$

We can undo the operations around x by doing the opposite operation in the reverse order.

$$
\begin{array}{c}
2x + 4 = 10 \\
- 4 \left(\right) - 4 \\
2x = 6 \\
\div 2 \left(\right) \div 2 \\
x = 3
\end{array}
$$

Because these equations are equivalent, this means that the solution to $2x + 4 = 10$ is $x = 3$. An advantage with this method is that solving equations by inspection can be very difficult if the solution is not just a small whole number.

Lesson starter: Attempting solutions

Georgia, Kartik and Lucas try to solve the equation $4x + 8 = 40$. They present their attempted solutions below.

Georgia

$$
\begin{array}{c}
4x + 8 = 40 \\
\div 4 \left(\right) \div 4 \\
x + 8 = 10 \\
- 8 \left(\right) - 8 \\
x = 2
\end{array}
$$

Kartik

$$
\begin{array}{c}
4x + 8 = 40 \\
- 8 \left(\right) + 8 \\
4x = 48 \\
\div 4 \left(\right) \div 4 \\
x = 12
\end{array}
$$

Lucas

$$
\begin{array}{c}
4x + 8 = 40 \\
- 8 \left(\right) - 8 \\
4x = 32 \\
\div 4 \left(\right) \div 4 \\
x = 8
\end{array}
$$

- Which of the students has the correct solution to the equation? Justify your answer by substituting each student's final answer.
- For each of the two students with the incorrect answer, explain the mistake they have made in their attempt to have equivalent equations.
- What operations would you do to both sides if the original equation was $7x - 10 = 11$?

KEY IDEAS

■ Sometimes it is difficult to solve an equation by inspection, so a systematic approach is required.

■ To solve an equation, find a simpler equation that is equivalent. Repeat this until the solution is found.

■ A simpler equation can be found by applying the opposite operations in reverse order. e.g. for $5x + 2 = 17$, we have:

$$x \xrightarrow{\times 5} 5x \xrightarrow{+2} 5x + 2$$

So we solve the equation by 'undoing' them in reverse order.

$$5x + 2 \xrightarrow{-2} 5x \xrightarrow{\div 5} x$$

This gives the solution:

$$5x + 2 = 17$$
$$-2 \qquad \qquad -2$$
$$5x = 15$$
$$\div 5 \qquad \qquad \div 5$$
$$x = 3$$

■ A solution can be checked by substituting the value to see if the equation is true.

$$\text{LHS} = 5x + 2 \qquad \text{RHS} = 17$$
$$= 5 \times 3 + 2$$
$$= 17$$

BUILDING UNDERSTANDING

1 State whether each of the following equations is true or false.
   a $x + 4 = 7$, if $x = 3$
   b $b - 2 = 7$, if $b = 5$
   c $7(d - 6) = d$, if $d = 7$
   d $g + 5 = 3g$, if $g = 2$
   e $f \times 4 = 20$, if $f = 3$

2 Consider the equation $7x = 42$.
   a State the missing number in the diagram opposite.
   b What is the solution to the equation $7x = 42$?

$$7x = 42$$
$$\div 7 \qquad \qquad \div 7$$
$$x = \underline{\quad}$$

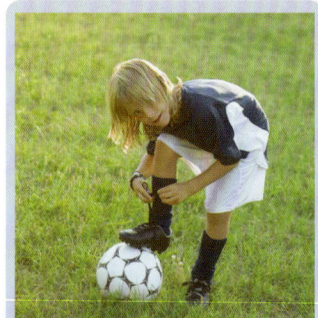

The order in which things are done matters in both sports and maths.

3 The equations $g = 2$ and $12(g + 3) = 60$ are equivalent.
   What is the solution to the equation $12(g + 3) = 60$?

4 State the operation applied in each of the following. Remember that the same operation must be used for both sides.

a
$$5 + a = 30$$
$$a = 25$$

b
$$10b = 72$$
$$b = 7.2$$

c
$$12 = \frac{c}{4}$$
$$48 = c$$

d
$$8 = c - 12$$
$$20 = c$$

Example 8   Solving one-step equations

Solve each of the following equations algebraically.

a $5x = 30$ b $17 = y - 21$ c $10 = \frac{q}{3}$

SOLUTION

a
$$5x = 30$$
$\div 5$ ( ) $\div 5$
$$x = 6$$

So the solution is $x = 6$.

EXPLANATION

The opposite of $\times 5$ is $\div 5$.

By dividing both sides by 5, we get an equivalent equation.

Recall that $5x \div 5$ simplifies to x.

b
$$17 = y - 21$$
$+ 21$ ( ) $+ 21$
$$38 = y$$

So the solution is $y = 38$.

The opposite of -21 is $+21$.

Write the pronumeral on the LHS.

c
$$10 = \frac{q}{3}$$
$\times 3$ ( ) $\times 3$
$$30 = q$$

So the solution is $q = 30$.

Multiplying both sides by 3 gives an equivalent equation that is simpler. Note that $\frac{q}{3} \times 3 = q$.

Write the pronumeral on the LHS.

Now you try

Solve each of the following equations algebraically.

a $10a = 30$ b $23 = 19 + x$ c $7 = \frac{y}{4}$

▷ **Example 9   Solving two-step equations**

Solve each of the following equations algebraically and check the solution.

a $7 + 4a = 23$ **b** $\dfrac{d}{3} - 2 = 4$ **c** $12 = 2(e + 1)$

SOLUTION

a
$$7 + 4a = 23$$
$-7 \quad \quad -7$
$$4a = 16$$
$\div 4 \quad \quad \div 4$
$$a = 4$$

Check:
$$\text{LHS} = 7 + 4a \quad \text{RHS} = 23 \checkmark$$
$$= 7 + 4 \times 4$$
$$= 7 + 16$$
$$= 23$$

b
$$\dfrac{d}{3} - 2 = 4$$
$+2 \quad \quad +2$
$$\dfrac{d}{3} = 6$$
$\times 3 \quad \quad \times 3$
$$d = 18$$

Check:
$$\text{LHS} = \dfrac{d}{3} - 2 \quad \text{RHS} = 4 \checkmark$$
$$= \dfrac{18}{3} - 2$$
$$= 6 - 2$$
$$= 4$$

c
$$12 = 2(e + 1)$$
$\div 2 \quad \quad \div 2$
$$6 = e + 1$$
$-1 \quad \quad -1$
$$5 = e$$

So the solution is $e = 5$.

Check:
$$\text{LHS} = 12 \quad \text{RHS} = 2(e + 1)$$
$$= 2(5 + 1)$$
$$= 2 \times 6$$
$$= 12 \checkmark$$

EXPLANATION

At each step, try to make the equation simpler by applying an operation to both sides.

Choose the opposite operations based on $7 + 4a$:

$$a \xrightarrow{\times 4} 4a \xrightarrow{+7} 7 + 4a$$

Opposite operations: -7, then $\div 4$.

Check that our equation is true by substituting $a = 4$ back into the LHS and RHS. Both sides are equal, so $a = 4$ is a solution.

At each step, try to make the equation simpler by applying an operation to both sides.

The opposite of -2 is $+2$ and the opposite of $\div 3$ is $\times 3$.

Check that our equation is true by substituting $d = 18$ back into the LHS and RHS. Both sides are equal, so $d = 18$ is a solution.

At each step, try to make the equation simpler by applying an operation to both sides.

The opposite of $\times 2$ is $\div 2$ and the opposite of $+1$ is -1.

Write the solution on the LHS.

Check that our equation is true by substituting $e = 5$ back into the equation.

Now you try

Solve each of the following equations algebraically and check the solution.

a $9 + 3x = 15$ **b** $\dfrac{m}{4} - 3 = 2$ **c** $4(p - 2) = 24$

Exercise 9D

FLUENCY   1, 2(½), 3, 4, 5(½)   2(½), 3, 4, 5–7(½)   2(¼), 4, 5–7(⅓)

1 Solve each of the following equations algebraically.

a i $4x = 20$ ii $7x = 56$

b i $5 = y - 2$ ii $38 = y - 26$

c i $20 = \dfrac{q}{2}$ ii $7 = \dfrac{q}{3}$

2 Solve the following equations algebraically.

a $6m = 54$ b $g - 9 = 2$ c $s \times 9 = 81$ d $i - 9 = 1$

e $7 + t = 9$ f $8 + q = 11$ g $4y = 48$ h $7 + s = 19$

i $24 = j \times 6$ j $12 = l + 8$ k $1 = v \div 2$ l $19 = 7 + y$

m $k \div 5 = 1$ n $2 = y - 7$ o $8z = 56$ p $13 = 3 + t$

q $b \times 10 = 120$ r $p - 2 = 9$ s $5 + a = 13$ t $n - 2 = 1$

3 Copy and complete the following to solve the given equations algebraically.

a

b

c

d

4 For each of these equations, state the first operation you would apply to both sides to solve it.

a $2x + 3 = 9$ b $4x - 7 = 33$

c $5(a + 3) = 50$ d $22 = 2(b - 17)$

5 Solve each of the following equations algebraically. Check the solution by substituting the value into the LHS and RHS.

a $6f - 2 = 64$ b $\dfrac{k}{4} + 9 = 10$ c $5x - 4 = 41$ d $3(a - 8) = 3$

e $5k - 9 = 31$ f $\dfrac{a}{3} + 6 = 8$ g $2n - 8 = 14$ h $\dfrac{n}{4} + 6 = 8$

i $1 = 2g - 7$ j $30 = 3q - 3$ k $3z - 4 = 26$ l $17 = 9 + 8p$

m $10d + 7 = 47$ n $38 = 6t - 10$ o $9u + 2 = 47$ p $7 = 10c - 3$

q $10 + 8q = 98$ r $80 = 4(y + 8)$ s $4(q + 8) = 40$ t $7 + 6u = 67$

6 Solve the following equations, giving your solution as fractions.

a $4x + 5 = 8$ b $3 + 5k = 27$ c $22 = (3w + 7) \times 2$

d $10 = 3 \times (2 + x)$ e $3 = (8x + 1) \div 2$ f $3(x + 2) = 7$

7 Solve the following equations algebraically. (Note: The solutions for these equations are negative numbers.)

a $4r + 30 = 2$

b $2x + 12 = 6$

c $10 + \frac{t}{2} = 2$

d $\frac{y}{4} + 10 = 4$

e $-3x = 15$

f $4 = 2k + 22$

g $2x = -12$

h $5x + 20 = 0$

i $0 = 2x + 3$

PROBLEM-SOLVING	8, 9	9–11	10–12

8 For each of the following, write an equation and solve it algebraically.

a   The sum of x and 5 is 12.

b   The product of 2 and y is 10.

c   When b is doubled and then 6 is added, the result is 44.

d   7 is subtracted from k. This result is tripled, giving 18.

e   3 is added to one-quarter of b, giving a result of 6.

f   10 is subtracted from half of k, giving a result of 1.

9 Freddy gets paid $12 per hour, plus a bonus of $50 for each week. In one week he earned $410.

a   Write an equation to describe this, using n for the number of hours worked.

b   Solve the equation algebraically and state the number of hours worked.

10 Eliana buys 12 pencils and 5 pens for the new school year. The pencils cost $1.00 each.

a   If pens cost $x each, write an expression for the total cost.

b   The total cost was $14.50. Write an equation to describe this.

c   Solve the equation algebraically, to find the total cost of each pen.

d   Check your solution by substituting your value of x into $12 + 5x$.

11 Write equations and solve them algebraically to find the unknown value in each of the following diagrams.

a
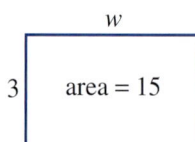

b
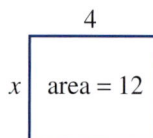

c
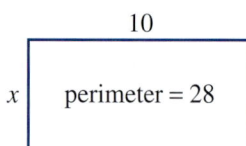

d
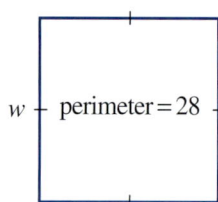

12 Solve the following equations algebraically.

a $7(3 + 5x) - 21 = 210$

b $(100x + 13) \div 3 = 271$

c $3(12 + 2x) - 4 = 62$

REASONING   13   13, 14   14, 15

13 Write five different equations that give a solution of $x = 2$.

14 a Show that $2x + 5 = 13$ and $5x = 20$ are equivalent by filling in the missing steps.

  b Show that $10 + 2x = 20$ and $2(x - 3) = 4$ are equivalent.

  c Two equations are written down and they each have a single solution. If the solution is the same for both equations, does this guarantee the equations are equivalent? Justify your answer.

  d If two equations have different solutions, does this guarantee they are not equivalent? Justify your answer.

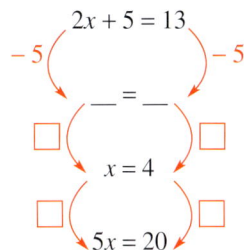

$$2x + 5 = 13$$
$$-5 \quad (\quad) \quad -5$$
$$\_\_ = \_\_$$
$$\square \quad (\quad) \quad \square$$
$$x = 4$$
$$\square \quad (\quad) \quad \square$$
$$5x = 20$$

15 Nicola has attempted to solve four equations. Describe the mistake she has made in each case.

a
$$4x + 2 = 36$$
$$\div 4 \quad (\quad) \quad \div 4$$
$$x + 2 = 9$$
$$-2 \quad (\quad) \quad -2$$
$$x = 7$$

b
$$3x + 10 = 43$$
$$-10 \quad (\quad) \quad -10$$
$$3x = 33$$
$$-3 \quad (\quad) \quad -3$$
$$x = 30$$

c
$$2a + 5 = 11$$
$$-5 \quad (\quad) \quad -5$$
$$2a = 16$$
$$\div 2 \quad (\quad) \quad \div 2$$
$$a = 8$$

d
$$7 + 12a = 43$$
$$-12 \quad (\quad) \quad -12$$
$$7 + a = 31$$
$$-7 \quad (\quad) \quad -7$$
$$a = 24$$

ENRICHMENT: Pronumerals on both sides   –   –   16(½)

16 If an equation has a pronumeral on both sides, you can subtract it from one side and then use the same method as before. For example:

$$5x + 4 = 3x + 10$$
$$-3x \quad (\quad) \quad -3x$$
$$2x + 4 = 10$$
$$-4 \quad (\quad) \quad -4$$
$$2x = 6$$
$$\div 2 \quad (\quad) \quad \div 2$$
$$x = 3$$

Solve the following equations using this method.

a $5x + 2 = 3x + 10$

b $8x - 1 = 4x + 3$

c $5 + 12l = 20 + 7l$

d $2 + 5t = 4t + 3$

e $12s + 4 = 9 + 11s$

f $9b - 10 = 8b + 9$

g $5j + 4 = 10 + 2j$

h $3 + 5d = 6 + 2d$

9A

1 Classify each of the following as an equation (E) or not an equation (N).

    a $4 + w = 9$

    b $x + 12$

    c $3 + 10 = 17$

    d $20 + 6$

9A

2 If $x = 4$, state whether each of these equations is true (T) or false (F).

    a $3x - 4 = 8$

    b $5x + 6 = 25$

    c $9 - x = x + 1$

    d $2x = 5x - 8$

9A

3 Write an equation for each of the following. (You do not need to solve the equations you write.)

    a The sum of 5 and m is equal to 12.

    b When d is doubled, the result is 24.

    c The product of 9 and x is 72.

    d Canaries cost $\$c$ each and budgies cost $\$b$ each. Three canaries and four budgies cost \$190.

9B

4 Solve the following equations by inspection.

    a $a - 5 = 4$

    b $36 = x \times 9$

    c $m \div 5 = 6$

    d $3a + 1 = 7$

9C

5 For each equation, find the result of applying the given operation to both sides. You *do not* need to solve the equation.

    a $4x = 7$ (multiply by 5)

    b $2a + 5 = 21$ (subtract 5)

9C

6 State the operation applied to get from the first to the second equation in each of the following.

    a $\square \left(\begin{matrix} 4x - 8 = 12 \\ 4x = 20 \end{matrix} \right) \square$

    b $\square \left(\begin{matrix} 18 = 6x \\ 3 = x \end{matrix} \right) \square$

    c $\square \left(\begin{matrix} 3a = 5 \\ 6a = 10 \end{matrix} \right) \square$

9D

7 Solve each of the following equations algebraically.

    a $a + 7 = 19$

    b $w - 4 = 27$

    c $k \div 9 = 7$

    d $5m = 40$

9D

8 Solve each of the following equations algebraically and check your solution.

    a $12x = 132$

    b $8 + 3a = 29$

    c $42 = 8m - 6$

    d $100 = 5(y + 12)$

9D

9 For each of the following, write an equation and solve it algebraically.

    a When x is doubled then 2 is added, the result is 12.

    b 5 is subtracted from k. The result is tripled giving 21.

    c 1 less than the product of 5 and y is 19.

9E Equations with fractions EXTENDING

Solving equations that involve fractions is straightforward once we recall that, in algebra, $\frac{a}{b}$ means $a \div b$. This means that if we have a fraction with b on the denominator, we can multiply both sides by b to get a simpler, equivalent equation.

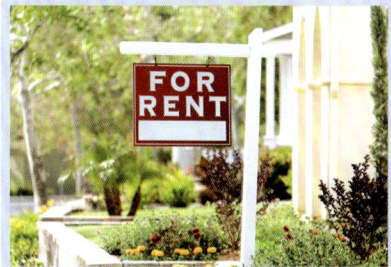

Lesson starter: Fractional differences

Consider these three equations.

a $\dfrac{2x+3}{5} = 7$ b $\dfrac{2x}{5} + 3 = 7$ c $2\left(\dfrac{x}{5}\right) + 3 = 7$

- Solve each of them (by inspection or algebraically).
- Compare your solutions with those of your classmates.
- Why do two of the equations have the same solution?

Fraction equations are solved when a business or a person calculates annual expenses. If rent is \$500/week and the annual rent is \$x, then $\frac{x}{52} = 500$. Solving this equation gives $x = 26\,000$, so rent is \$26 000 p.a.

KEY IDEAS

■ Recall that $\frac{a}{b}$ means $a \div b$.

■ To solve an equation that has a fraction on one side, multiply both sides by the denominator.

$$\times 5 \left(\begin{array}{c} \dfrac{x}{5} = 4 \\ x = 20 \end{array} \right) \times 5$$

■ If neither side of an equation is a fraction, do not multiply by the denominator.

$$\times 3 \left(\begin{array}{c} \dfrac{x}{3} + 5 = 8 \\ \cdots \end{array} \right) \times 3$$

✗ Do not do this because the LHS is not yet a fraction by itself.

$$-5 \left(\begin{array}{c} \dfrac{x}{3} + 5 = 8 \\ \dfrac{x}{3} = 3 \end{array} \right) -5 \qquad ✔ \text{ Do this}$$

$$\times 3 \left(\begin{array}{c} \dfrac{x}{3} = 3 \\ x = 9 \end{array} \right) \times 3$$

■ The expressions $\frac{x}{3} + 2$ and $\frac{x+2}{3}$ are different, as demonstrated in these flow charts.

$$x \xrightarrow{\div 3} \frac{x}{3} \xrightarrow{+2} \frac{x}{3} + 2 \qquad \text{vs} \qquad x \xrightarrow{+2} x + 2 \xrightarrow{\div 3} \frac{x+2}{3}$$

BUILDING UNDERSTANDING

1   Classify each of the following as true or false.

   a $\frac{a}{5}$ means $a \div 5$.   **b** $\frac{q}{12}$ means $12 \div q$.

   c $\frac{4+a}{3}$ means $(4 + a) \div 3$.   **d** $\frac{4+a}{3}$ means $4 + (a \div 3)$.

   e $\frac{12+3q}{4}$ means $(12 + 3q) \div 4$.   **f** $2 + \frac{x}{5}$ means $(2 + x) \div 5$.

2   **a**   If $x = 10$, state the value of $\frac{x+4}{2}$.

   b   If $x = 10$, state the value of $\frac{x}{2} + 4$.

   c   State whether the following is true or false: $\frac{x+4}{2}$ and $\frac{x}{2} + 4$ are equivalent expressions.

3   State the missing parts to solve each of these equations.

   a

$$\times 4 \left(\genfrac{}{}{0pt}{}{\frac{b}{4} = 11}{b = \underline{}} \right) \times 4$$

   b

$$\times 5 \left(\genfrac{}{}{0pt}{}{\frac{d}{5} = 3}{\underline{} = \underline{}} \right) \times 5$$

   c

$$\square \left(\genfrac{}{}{0pt}{}{\frac{h}{4} = 7}{\underline{} = \underline{}} \right) \square$$

   d

$$\square \left(\genfrac{}{}{0pt}{}{\frac{p}{13} = 2}{\underline{} = \underline{}} \right) \square$$

4   For each of the following equations (**a** to **d**), choose the appropriate first step (i.e. **A** to **D**) needed to solve it.

   a $\frac{x}{3} = 10$ **A**   Multiply both sides by 2.

   b $\frac{x}{3} + 2 = 5$ **B**   Multiply both sides by 3.

   c $\frac{x-3}{2} = 1$ **C**   Subtract 2 from both sides.

   d $\frac{x}{2} - 3 = 5$ **D**   Add 3 to both sides.

Example 10   Solving equations with fractions

Solve each of the following equations.

   a $\frac{a}{7} = 3$ **b** $\frac{5y}{3} = 10$ **c** $\frac{3x}{4} + 7 = 13$ **d** $\frac{2x-3}{5} = 3$

SOLUTION

   a

$$\times 7 \left(\genfrac{}{}{0pt}{}{\frac{a}{7} = 3}{a = 21} \right) \times 7$$

EXPLANATION

Multiplying both sides by 7 removes the denominator of 7.

b

$$\frac{5y}{3} = 10$$

$\times 3$ ( ) $\times 3$

$$5y = 30$$

$\div 5$ ( ) $\div 5$

$$y = 6$$

Multiplying both sides by 3 removes the denominator of 3.

The equation $5y = 30$ can be solved normally.

c

$$\frac{3x}{4} + 7 = 13$$

$- 7$ ( ) $- 7$

$$\frac{3x}{4} = 6$$

$\times 4$ ( ) $\times 4$

$$3x = 24$$

$\div 3$ ( ) $\div 3$

$$x = 8$$

First, we subtract 7 because we do not have a fraction by itself on the LHS.
Once there is a fraction by itself, multiply by its denominator (in this case, 4) and solve the equation $3x = 24$ as you would normally.

d

$$\frac{2x - 3}{5} = 3$$

$\times 5$ ( ) $\times 5$

$$2x - 3 = 15$$

$+ 3$ ( ) $+ 3$

$$2x = 18$$

$\div 2$ ( ) $\div 2$

$$x = 9$$

First, multiply both sides by 5 to remove the denominator.

Then solve the equation $2x - 3 = 15$ as you would normally.

Now you try

Solve each of the following equations.

a $\dfrac{p}{10} = 5$

b $\dfrac{2m}{5} = 4$

c $\dfrac{3u}{5} + 8 = 11$

d $\dfrac{2x + 3}{7} = 3$

Exercise 9E

FLUENCY	1, 2–3(½)	2–4(½)	2–4(¼)

1 Solve each of the following equations.

a $\dfrac{a}{4} = 2$

b $\dfrac{a}{10} = 3$

c $\dfrac{x}{5} = 7$

d $\dfrac{x}{2} = 100$

2 Solve the following equations algebraically.

a $\dfrac{m}{6} = 2$

b $\dfrac{c}{9} = 2$

c $\dfrac{s}{8} = 2$

d $\dfrac{r}{5} = 2$

e $\dfrac{3u}{5} = 12$

f $\dfrac{2y}{9} = 4$

g $\dfrac{5x}{2} = 10$

h $\dfrac{3a}{8} = 6$

i $\dfrac{4h}{5} = 8$

j $\dfrac{3j}{5} = 9$

k $\dfrac{5v}{9} = 5$

l $\dfrac{3q}{4} = 6$

Example 10c,d

3 Solve the following equations algebraically. Check your solutions using substitution.

a $\dfrac{h + 15}{12} = 2$

b $\dfrac{y + 5}{11} = 1$

c $\dfrac{j + 8}{11} = 1$

d $\dfrac{b - 2}{2} = 1$

e $\dfrac{7u - 12}{9} = 1$

f $14 + \dfrac{4t}{9} = 18$

g $1 = \dfrac{w + 5}{11}$

h $1 = \dfrac{4r - 13}{3}$

i $\dfrac{2q}{9} + 2 = 4$

j $\dfrac{s + 2}{5} = 1$

k $\dfrac{3l}{2} + 9 = 21$

l $12 = \dfrac{2z}{7} + 10$

m $1 = \dfrac{v - 4}{7}$

n $\dfrac{f - 2}{7} = 1$

o $9 = 4 + \dfrac{5x}{2}$

p $3 = \dfrac{7 + 4d}{9}$

q $\dfrac{7n}{5} + 14 = 21$

r $\dfrac{7m + 7}{4} = 21$

s $3 = \dfrac{7p}{4} - 11$

t $\dfrac{4a - 6}{5} = 6$

Example 10

4 Solve the following equations algebraically. (Note: The solutions to these equations are negative numbers.)

a $\dfrac{y + 4}{3} = 1$

b $\dfrac{a}{10} + 2 = 1$

c $\dfrac{2x}{5} + 10 = 6$

d $\dfrac{x}{4} + 12 = 0$

e $0 = 12 + \dfrac{2u}{5}$

f $\dfrac{3y}{5} + 8 = 2$

g $1 = \dfrac{-2u - 3}{5}$

h $-2 = \dfrac{4d}{5} + 2$

PROBLEM-SOLVING	5	5, 6	6, 7

5 In each of the following cases, write an equation and solve it to find the number.

a A number is halved and the result is 9.

b One-third of q is 14.

c A number, r, is doubled and then divided by 5. The result is 6.

d 4 is subtracted from q and this is halved, giving a result of 3.

e 3 is added to x and the result is divided by 4, giving a result of 2.

f A number, y, is divided by 4 and then 3 is added, giving a result of 5.

6 A group of five people go out for dinner and then split the bill evenly. They each pay $31.50.

a If b represents the total cost of the bill, in dollars, write an equation to describe this situation.

b Solve this equation algebraically.

c What is the total cost of the bill?

7 Lee and Theo hired a tennis court for a cost of x, which they split evenly. Out of his own pocket, Lee also bought some tennis balls for $5.

a Write an *expression* for the total amount of money that Lee paid.

b Given that Lee paid $11 in total, write an equation and solve it to find the total cost of hiring the court.

c State how much money Theo paid for his share of hiring the tennis court.

8 **a** Explain, in one sentence, the difference between $\frac{2x+3}{5}$ and $\frac{2x}{5}+3$.

b What is the first operation you would apply to both sides to solve $\frac{2x+3}{5}=7$?

c What is the first operation you would apply to both sides to solve $\frac{2x}{5}+3=7$?

d Are there any values of x for which $\frac{2x+3}{5}$ and $\frac{2x}{5}+3$ are equal to each other?

9 Sometimes an equation's solution will be a fraction. For example, $2x=1$ has the solution $x=\frac{1}{2}$.

a Give another equation that has $x=\frac{1}{2}$ as its solution.

b Find an equation that has the solution $x=\frac{5}{7}$.

c Could an equation have the solution $x=-\frac{1}{2}$? Justify your answer.

10 Dividing by 2 and multiplying by $\frac{1}{2}$ have the same effect.

For example, $6\div2=3$ and $6\times\frac{1}{2}=3$.

a Show how each of these equations can be solved algebraically.

i $\frac{x}{2}=5$ **ii** $\frac{1}{2}\times x=5$

b Solve the two equations $\frac{x+4}{3}=10$ and $\frac{1}{3}(x+4)=10$ algebraically, showing the steps you would use at each stage clearly.

c How does rewriting divisions as multiplications change the first step when solving equations?

11 Solve each of the following equations, giving your answers as a fraction.

a $\frac{2x+5}{4}=3$ **b** $\frac{3x-4}{6}=\frac{3}{4}$

c $\left(\frac{7+2x}{4}\right)\times3=10$ **d** $\frac{1}{2}=\frac{3x-1}{5}$

12 Consider the equation $\frac{5x-3}{7}=6$. The solution is $x=9$. Change one number or one operator (i.e. $\times$, $-$ or $\div$) in the equation so that the solution will be $x=12$.

9F   Equations with brackets   EXTENDING

> **LEARNING INTENTIONS**
> * To be able to expand brackets and collect like terms in algebraic expressions
> * To understand that expanding brackets and collecting like terms is a useful technique when solving equations involving brackets

Recall from Chapter 4 that expressions with brackets can be expanded using the picture shown to the right about rectangles' areas.

So $3(x + 5)$ is equivalent to $3x + 15$.

When solving $3(x + 5) = 21$, we could first divide both sides by 3 or we could first expand the brackets, giving $3x + 15 = 21$, and then subtract 15. For some equations, the brackets must be expanded first.

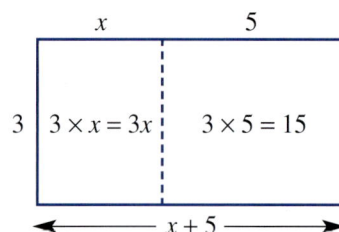

Lesson starter: Removing brackets

a Draw two rectangles, with areas $4(x + 3)$ and $5(x + 2)$.

b Use these to show that $4(x + 3) + 5(x + 2)$ is equivalent to $9x + 22$.

c Can you solve the equation $4(x + 3) + 5(x + 2) = 130$?

KEY IDEAS

■ To expand brackets, use the **distributive law**, which states that:

$a(b + c) = ab + ac$ e.g. $3(x + 4) = 3x + 12$

$a(b - c) = ab - ac$ e.g. $4(b - 2) = 4b - 8$

■ **Like terms** are terms that contain exactly the same pronumerals and can be collected to simplify expressions. For example, $3x + 4 + 2x$ can be simplified to $5x + 4$.

■ Equations involving brackets can be solved by first expanding brackets and collecting like terms.

BUILDING UNDERSTANDING

1 Which of the following is the correct expansion of $5(x + 2)$?

   A $5 \times x + 2$ **B** $5x + 2$ **C** $5x + 10$ **D** $10x$

2 State the missing numbers.

   a $3(x + 2) = 3x + \boxed{}$ **b** $4(3a + 1) = 12a + \boxed{}$

   c $2(b + 1) = \boxed{}b + 2$ **d** $6(2c + 3) = \boxed{}c + 18$

3 Answer true or false to each of the following.

a $4x + 3x$ can be simplified to $7x$.

b $2a + 4b$ can be simplified to $6ab$.

c $6p - 4p$ can be simplified to $2p$.

d $7a + 3 + 2a$ can be simplified to $9a + 3$.

e $2b + 3$ can be simplified to $5b$.

f $20x - 12x + 3y$ can be simplified to $32x + 3y$.

Example 11   Expanding brackets

Expand each of the following.

a $4(x + 3)$

b $6(q - 4)$

c $5(3a + 4)$

SOLUTION

a $4(x + 3) = 4x + 12$

b $6(q - 4) = 6q - 24$

c $5(3a + 4) = 15a + 20$

EXPLANATION

Using the distributive law:

$$4(x + 3) = 4x + 12$$

	x	$+3$
4	$4x$	$+12$

Using the distributive law:

$$6(q - 4) = 6q - 24$$

	q	-4
6	$6q$	-24

Using the distributive law:

$$5(3a + 4) = 5 \times 3a + 20$$

	$3a$	$+4$
5	$15a$	$+20$

Now you try

Expand each of the following.

a $3(x + 7)$

b $8(m - 6)$

c $5(8y + 7)$

Example 12   Simplifying expressions with like terms

Simplify each of these expressions.

a $2x + 5 + x$

b $3a + 8a + 2 - 2a + 5$

SOLUTION

a $2x + 5 + x = 3x + 5$

b $3a + 8a + 2 - 2a + 5 = 9a + 7$

EXPLANATION

Like terms are $2x$ and x.
These are combined to give $3x$.

Like terms are combined:
$3a + 8a - 2a = 9a$ and $2 + 5 = 7$

Now you try

Simplify each of these expressions.

a $4a + 7 + 2a$

b $4a + 9a + 3 - 4a - 6$

Example 13   Solving equations by expanding brackets

Solve each of these equations by expanding brackets first.

a $3(x + 2) = 18$ **b** $7 = 7(4q - 3)$ **c** $3(b + 5) + 4b = 29$

SOLUTION

EXPLANATION

a

$$3(x + 2) = 18$$
$$3x + 6 = 18$$
$$-6 \qquad \qquad -6$$
$$3x = 12$$
$$\div 3 \qquad \qquad \div 3$$
$$x = 4$$

Expand brackets.

	x	$+2$
3	$3x$	$+6$

Solve the equation by performing the same operations to both sides.

b

$$7 = 7(4q - 3)$$
$$7 = 28q - 21$$
$$+21 \qquad \qquad +21$$
$$28 = 28q$$
$$\div 28 \qquad \qquad \div 28$$
$$1 = q$$

so $q = 1$ is the solution.

Expand brackets.

	$4q$	-3
7	$28q$	-21

Solve the equation by performing the same operations to both sides.

c $3(b + 5) + 4b = 29$
$$3b + 15 + 4b = 29$$
$$7b + 15 = 29$$
$$-15 \qquad \qquad -15$$
$$7b = 14$$
$$\div 7 \qquad \qquad \div 7$$
$$b = 2$$

Expand brackets.

	b	$+5$
3	$3b$	$+15$

Collect like terms to simplify the expression.
Solve the equation by performing the same operations to both sides.

Now you try

Solve each of these equations by expanding brackets first.

a $5(m + 4) = 30$ **b** $50 = 10(3x - 1)$ **c** $5(q - 1) + 2q = 23$

Exercise 9F

FLUENCY	1, 2–6($\frac{1}{2}$)	2–7($\frac{1}{2}$)	2–5($\frac{1}{4}$), 6–7($\frac{1}{2}$)

1 Expand each of the following.

Example 11a **a** **i** $3(x + 2)$ **ii** $5(x + 7)$

Example 11b **b** **i** $5(q - 2)$ **ii** $11(q - 4)$

Example 11c **c** **i** $3(2a + 7)$ **ii** $6(4a - 1)$

2 Expand each of the following.

a $2(x + 1)$

b $5(2b + 3)$

c $2(3a - 4)$

d $5(7a + 1)$

e $4(3x + 4)$

f $3(8 - 3y)$

g $12(4a + 3)$

h $2(u - 4)$

3 Simplify these expressions by collecting like terms.

a $3a + a + 2$

b $5 + 2x + x$

c $2b - 4 + b$

d $5a + 12 - 2a$

e $5x + 3 + x$

f $3k + 6 - 2k$

g $7 + 2b - 1$

h $6k - k + 1$

4 Solve the following equations by expanding the brackets first. Check your solutions by substituting them in.

a $2(10 + s) = 32$

b $2(5 + l) = 12$

c $3(p - 7) = 6$

d $8(y + 9) = 72$

e $8(4 + q) = 40$

f $7(p + 7) = 133$

g $8(m + 7) = 96$

h $22 = 2(b + 5)$

i $25 = 5(2 + p)$

j $63 = 7(p + 2)$

k $9(y - 6) = 27$

l $2(r + 8) = 32$

5 Solve these equations by expanding the brackets first.

a $6(3 + 2d) = 54$

b $8(7x - 7) = 56$

c $3(2x - 4) = 18$

d $27 = 3(3 + 6e)$

e $44 = 4(3a + 8)$

f $30 = 6(5r - 10)$

g $10 = 5(9u - 7)$

h $3(2q - 9) = 39$

6 Solve the following equations by first expanding the brackets. You will need to simplify the expanded expressions by collecting like terms.

a $5(4s + 4) + 4s = 44$

b $5i + 5(2 + 2i) = 25$

c $3(4c - 5) + c = 50$

d $3(4 + 3v) - 4v = 52$

e $5(4k + 2) + k = 31$

f $4q + 6(4q - 4) = 60$

g $40 = 4y + 6(2y - 4)$

h $44 = 4f + 4(2f + 2)$

i $40 = 5t + 6(4t - 3)$

7 Solve the following equations algebraically. (Note: The answers to these equations are negative numbers.)

a $3(u + 7) = 6$

b $2(k + 3) = 0$

c $6(p - 2) = -18$

d $16 = 8(q + 4)$

e $5(2u + 3) = 5$

f $3 = 2(x + 4) + 1$

g $4(p - 3) + p = -32$

h $3(r + 4) + 2r + 40 = 2$

i $2(5 + x) - 3x = 15$

PROBLEM-SOLVING | 8 | 8 | 8, 9

8 For each of the following problems:
   i write an equation.
   ii solve your equation by first expanding any brackets.

a 5 is added to x and then this is doubled, giving a result of 14.

b 3 is subtracted from q and the result is tripled, giving a final result of 30.

c A number, x, is doubled and then 3 is added. This number is doubled again to get a result of 46.

d 4 is added to y and this is doubled. Then the original number, y, is subtracted, giving a result of 17.

9   Solve the following equations.

    a $-3(x - 2) = 3$ **b** $-5(4 - 3x) = -35$ **c** $1 - 2(x - 1) = -7$

REASONING		10	10, 11	11, 12(½)

10   For each of the following equations, explain why there are no solutions by first simplifying the LHS.

    a $2(x + 5) - 2x = 7$

    b $3(2x + 1) + 6(2 - x) = 4$

    c $4(2x + 1) - 10x + 2(x + 1) = 12$

11   Consider the equation $2(3x + 4) - 6x + 1 = 9$.

    a   Show that this equation is true if $x = 0$.

    b   Show that this equation is true if $x = 3$.

    c   Explain why this equation is always true.

    d   Give an example of another equation involving brackets that is always true, where one side contains a variable but the other side is just a number.

12   For equations like $4(3x + 2) = 44$, you have been expanding the brackets first. Since $4(3x + 2) = 44$ is the same as $4 \times (3x + 2) = 44$, you can just start by dividing both sides by 4. Without expanding brackets, solve the equations in Question **4** by dividing first.

ENRICHMENT: Expanding multiple brackets		–	–	13(½)

13   Solve each of the following equations by expanding all sets of brackets.

    a $6(2j - 4) + 4(4j - 3) = 20$

    b $3(4a + 5) + 5(1 + 3a) = 47$

    c $2(5a + 3) + 3(2a + 3) = 63$

    d $222 = 3(4a - 3) + 5(3a + 3)$

    e $77 = 2(3c - 5) + 3(4c + 5)$

    f $240 = 4(3d + 3) + 6(3d - 2)$

    g $2(x + 3) + 4(x + 5) = 32$

    h $4(x + 5) + 4(x - 5) = 24$

    i $2(3x + 4) + 5(6x + 7) + 8(9x + 10) = 123$

    j $2(x + 1) + 3(x + 1) + 4(x + 1) = 36$

The following problems will investigate practical situations drawing upon knowledge and skills developed throughout the chapter. In attempting to solve these problems, aim to identify the key information, use diagrams, formulate ideas, apply strategies, make calculations and check and communicate your solutions.

Zana's earning goal

1 Zana helps her uncle at the local garden nursery and gets paid $12 per hour.
   Zana is interested in the total amount of money she can earn for a certain number of hours worked, as well as the time taken for her to reach an earning goal, including and excluding bonuses.

   a   Write an equation for Zana's situation using the pronumerals P to represent Zana's pay (in dollars) and h to represent the number of hours Zana works in a month.

   b   If Zana works for a total of 15 hours for the month of May, how much pay will she receive?

   If Zana works more than 20 hours in a month, she also receives a monthly bonus of $30 from her uncle to thank her for her hard work.

   c   Write an equation for Zana's pay when she works more than 20 hours in a month.
   d   If Zana works 24 hours in June, what would be her total pay for this month?
   e   If Zana wishes to earn $4500 over the course of the year, how many hours will she need to work on average each month? Use your equation from part c and round your answer to the nearest hour.

Local cafe's rent

2 The local cafe is forecasting the profit they will make each day. On average, the cafe owners are confident they can make a profit of $10 for every breakfast ordered, a $15 profit for every lunch ordered and a $3 profit on every drink ordered.
   The cafe wishes to determine if they will be able to pay the rent for their current premises or whether they will need to move to cheaper premises.

   a   Using appropriate pronumerals, write an equation for the total profit the cafe makes per day.
       The cafe kept a record of orders for the week and these are shown below.

Day	Breakfasts	Lunches	Drinks
Monday	36	42	90
Tuesday	30	54	75
Wednesday	28	57	96
Thursday	42	51	99
Friday	35	70	120

b   Using your equation from part **a**, calculate the profit the cafe made on each of the above days.

c   What was the average daily profit for this week?

d   Using this average daily profit, forecast what profit the cafe can make over the course of the year, assuming they are open 5 days per week for 52 weeks of the year.

e   The current rent for the premises is $42 000 per annum. What percentage of the cafe's profit goes towards rent? Give your answer to the nearest per cent.

f   What other expenses do you think the cafe needs to pay out of their profit?

Human heart beat

3   Zachary has a resting heart rate of 70 beats per minute, and a general light activity heart rate of 90 beats per minute.

Zachary is interested in the number of times his heart beats over the course of various time intervals including a whole year.

a   If Zachary is at rest on average 14 hours a day, and in a light activity state on average 10 hours a day, how many times will Zachary's heart beat in:

   i   1 day?

   ii   1 year? (assume a non-leap year)

   iii t years? (assume a leap year every four years)

b   Write an expression for the number of times a heart beats in t years, if the average heart rate is n beats per minute.

c   If an average human heart can beat 4 billion times (4 000 000 000), and Tamara has an average heart rate of 90 beats per minute, how many years can Tamara's heart beat for?

d   Investigate how many times your heart beats in a year.
    Take the following things into account:

   • your average resting heart rate, your average sitting heart rate, your average walking heart rate, your average exercise heart rate

   • the average number of hours you sleep, sit, walk, exercise per day.

e   Set up a spreadsheet that would allow a user to input their different state heart rates and the average number of hours they spend at each state in a day. Using appropriate equations in the spreadsheet, calculate the number of heart beats in a year.

9G Using formulas

Often, two or more pronumerals (or variables) represent related quantities. For example, the speed (s) at which a car travels and the time (t) it takes to arrive at its destination are related variable quantities. A formula is an equation that contains two or more pronumerals and shows how they are related.

The volume, V, of a rugby ball is calculated using the formula:
$$\text{Volume} = \frac{\pi L W^2}{6}$$
where L is the length and W is the width.

Lesson starter: Fahrenheit and Celsius

In Australia, we measure temperature in degrees Celsius, whereas in the USA it is measured in degrees Fahrenheit. A formula to convert between them is $F = \frac{9C}{5} + 32$.

- At what temperature in degrees Fahrenheit does water freeze?
- At what temperature in degrees Fahrenheit does water boil?
- What temperature is $100°$ Fahrenheit in Celsius? What is significant about this temperature?

KEY IDEAS

- A variable is a pronumeral that represents more than one value.

- A **formula** is a **rule** or **equation** that shows the relationship between two or more **variables**. For example:

$$A = l\,w$$

area of rectangle   length   width

- In the example above there are three variables, whereby $A = 6$, $l = 2$ and $w = 3$ is one solution for this formula because $6 = 2 \times 3$.
  - $A = lw$ has three variables: A, l and w. If two variables are known, then the formula can be used to find the unknown variable.
  - The **subject** of an equation is a pronumeral that occurs by itself on the left-hand side. For example: T is the subject of $T = 4x + 1$.
  - To use a formula, first substitute all the known values into the formula, then solve the resulting equation, if possible.

BUILDING UNDERSTANDING

1 State whether each of the following equations is a rule (R) or not a rule (N).

    a $2x + 5 = 10$ **b** $y = 3x + 5$ **c** $F = ma$

    d $5 - q = 3$ **e** $w = 12 - v$ **f** $P = I + k - 3$

2 Substitute:

    a $x = 3$ into the expression $5x$ **b** $x = 7$ into the expression $4(x + 2)$

    c $y = 3$ into the expression $20 - 4y$ **d** $y = 10$ into the expression $\dfrac{y + 4}{7}$

Example 14   Applying a formula

Consider the rule $k = 3b + 2$. Find the value of:

a k if $b = 5$ **b** k if $b = 10$ **c** b if $k = 23$.

SOLUTION

a $k = 3 \times 5 + 2$
      $= 17$

b $k = 3 \times 10 + 2$
      $= 32$

c

$$23 = 3b + 2$$
$$-2 \left(\qquad \right) -2$$
$$21 = 3b$$
$$\div 3 \left(\qquad \right) \div 3$$
$$7 = b$$

Therefore, $b = 7$.

EXPLANATION

Substitute $b = 5$ into the equation.

Substitute $b = 10$ into the equation.

Substitute $k = 23$ into the equation. Now solve the equation to find the value of b.

Write the final solution as an equation with the variable on the left-hand side.

Now you try

Using the formula $B = 5A + 7$, find the value of:

a B if $A = 2$ **b** B if $A = 12$ **c** A if $B = 52$.

Example 15   Applying a formula involving three pronumerals

Consider the rule $Q = w(4 + t)$. Find the value of:

a Q if $w = 10$ and $t = 3$ **b** t if $Q = 42$ and $w = 6$

SOLUTION

a $Q = 10(4 + 3)$
      $= 10 \times 7$
      $= 70$

EXPLANATION

Substitute $w = 10$ and $t = 3$ to evaluate.

b

$$42 = 6(4 + t)$$
$$42 = 24 + 6t$$

$-24 \Big(\qquad \Big) -24$

$$18 = 6t$$

$\div 6 \Big(\qquad \Big) \div 6$

$$3 = t$$

Substitute $Q = 42$ and $w = 6$.
Expand the brackets and then solve the equation.

Therefore $t = 3$.

Write the final solution as an equation with the variable on the left-hand side.

Now you try

Consider the rule $F = mg - 5$. Find the value of:

a F if $m = 7$ and $g = 10$

b m if $F = 93$ and $g = 9.8$.

Exercise 9G

FLUENCY	1–4	2–5	2, 4, 5

1 Consider the rule $k = 5b + 3$. Find the value of:

ple 14a,b

    a **i** k if $b = 2$ **ii** k if $b = 7$

mple 14c

    b **i** b if $k = 23$ **ii** b if $k = 58$

xample 14

2 Consider the rule $h = 2m + 1$. Find:

    a h if $m = 3$

    b h if $m = 4$

    c m if $h = 17$. Set up an equation and solve it algebraically

    d m if $h = 21$. Set up an equation and solve it algebraically.

xample 14

3 Consider the formula $y = 5 + 3x$. Find:

    a y if $x = 6$ **b** x if $y = 17$ **c** x if $y = 26$

ample 15

4 Consider the rule $A = q + t$. Find:

    a A if $q = 3$ and $t = 4$ **b** q if $A = 5$ and $t = 1$ **c** t if $A = 3$ and $q = 3$

ample 15

5 Consider the formula $G = 7x + 2y$. Find:

    a G if $x = 3$ and $y = 3$ **b** x if $y = 2$ and $G = 11$ **c** y if $G = 31$ and $x = 3$

PROBLEM-SOLVING	6, 7	6–8	7–9

6 The formula for the area of a rectangle is $A = l \times w$, where l is the rectangle's length and w is its width.

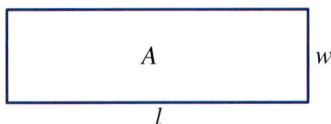

$$A \qquad\qquad w$$

$$l$$

    a Set up and solve an equation to find the width of a rectangle with $A = 20$ and $l = 5$.

    b A rectangle is drawn for which $A = 25$ and $w = 5$.

        i Set up and solve an equation to find l.   **ii** What type of rectangle is this?

7 The perimeter for a rectangle is given by $P = 2(w + l)$. Find the:

   a perimeter when $w = 3$ and $l = 5$

   b value of l when $P = 10$ and $w = 2$

   c area of a rectangle if its perimeter is 20 and width is 5.

8 A formula relating density (d), mass (m) and volume (v) is $d = \frac{m}{v}$.

   a Find the value of d if $m = 12$ and $v = 4$.

   b Find the density of an object with a mass of 12 grams, and a volume of $4\,\text{cm}^3$, giving an answer with the units g/cm^3.

   c Another object has a density of $10\,\text{g/cm}^3$ and a volume of $5\,\text{cm}^3$. Write an equation and solve it to find its mass, m.

9 To convert between temperatures in Celsius and Fahrenheit the rule is $F = \frac{9C}{5} + 32$.

   a Find F if $C = 20$.

   b Find the value of C if $F = 50$.

   c Find the temperature in Celsius if it is 53.6° Fahrenheit.

   d Marieko claims that the temperature in her city varies between 68° Fahrenheit and 95° Fahrenheit. What is the difference, in Celsius, between these two temperatures?

REASONING   10   10, 11   11, 12

10 There are two different formulas that can be used to calculate a person's maximum heart rate (H) from their age (a).

$$\text{Formula 1: } H = 220 - a$$
$$\text{Formula 2: } H = 206.9 - 0.67a$$

   a Find the two values of H that the formulas give for a 10-year-old person by substituting $a = 10$.

   b Find the two values of H that the formulas give for a 100-year-old person.

   c Demonstrate that both formulas give a similar maximum heart rate for a 40-year-old person.

   d Use formula 1 to find the age of someone with a maximum heart rate of 190.

   e Use formula 2 to find the age of someone with a maximum heart rate of 190. Round to the nearest whole number.

11 Rearranging a formula involves finding an equivalent equation that has a different variable on one side by itself. For example, the formula $S = 6g + b$ can be rearranged to make g by itself. Now we have a formula that can be used to find g once S and b are known.

$S = 6g + b$
$-b \quad\quad -b$
$S - b = 6g$
$\div 6 \quad\quad \div 6$
$\frac{S - b}{6} = g$

   a Rearrange $S = 5d + 3b$ to make a rule where d is by itself.

   b Rearrange the formula $F = \frac{9C}{5} + 32$ to make C by itself.

   c Rearrange the formula $Q = 3(x + 12) + x$ to make x by itself.
     (*Hint*: You will need to expand the brackets first.)

12 A taxi company charges different amounts of money based on how far the taxi travels and how long the passenger is in the car. Although the company has not revealed the formula it uses, some sample costs are shown below.

Distance (D) in km	Time (t) in minutes	Cost (C) in dollars
10	20	30
20	30	50

a Show that the rule $C = D + t$ is consistent with the values above.

b Show that the rule $C = 3D$ is not consistent with the values above.

c Show that the rule $C = 2D + 10$ is consistent with the values above.

d Try to find at least two other formulas that the taxi company could be using, based on the values shown.

ENRICHMENT: AFL equations — — 13

13 In Australian Rules Football (AFL), the score, S, is given by $S = 6g + b$, where g is the number of goals scored and b is the number of 'behinds' (i.e. near misses).

a Which team is winning if the Abbotsford Apes have scored 11 goals ($g = 11$) and 9 behinds ($b = 9$), whereas the Brunswick Baboons have scored 12 goals and 2 behinds?

b The Camberwell Chimpanzees have scored 7 behinds and their current score is $S = 55$. Solve an equation algebraically to find how many goals the team has scored.

c In some AFL competitions, a team can score a 'supergoal', which is worth 9 points. If q is the number of supergoals that a team kicks, write a new formula for the team's score.

d For some rare combinations of goals and behinds, the score equals the product of g and b. For example, 4 goals and 8 behinds gives a score of $4 \times 6 + 8 = 32$, and $4 \times 8 = 32$. Find all the other values of g and b that make the equation $6g + b = gb$ true.

9H Using equations to solve problems

Our methods for solving equations can be applied to many situations in which equations occur.

Digital advertisers calculate cost per click, $c. If an ad that cost $2000 had 10 000 clicks, then $10\,000\,c = 2000$. Solving this equation gives $c = 0.2$, i.e. 20 cents per click.

Lesson starter: Stationery shopping

Sylvia bought 10 pencils and 2 erasers for $20.40. Edward bought 5 pencils and 3 erasers for $12.60.

- Use the information above to work out how much Karl will pay for 6 pencils and 5 erasers.
- Describe how you got your answer.
- Is there more than one possible solution?

KEY IDEAS

■ To solve a problem, follow these steps.

Step 1: Use a pronumeral to stand in for the unknown.

Let $p = the cost of a pencil.

Step 2: Write an equation to describe the problem.

$10p + 2 \times 3.5 = 25$.

Step 3: Solve the equation.

This can be done by inspection or algebraically.

Step 4: Make sure that you answer the original question and the solution seems reasonable and realistic.

Don't forget to include the correct units (e.g. dollars, years, cm).

BUILDING UNDERSTANDING

1 For each of the following problems, choose the best pronumeral definition.

a Problem: Monique's age next year is 12. How old is she now?

A Let m = Monique's current age.   **B** Let m = Monique.

C Let m = 12.   **D** Let m = Monique's age next year.

E Let m = this year.

b Problem: Callan has 15 boxes, which weigh a total of 300 kg. How much does each box weigh?

A Let w = 15.

B Let w = 300.

C Let w = the weight in kilograms of one box.

D Let w = the number of boxes.

E Let w = the total weight in kilograms.

c Problem: Jared's family has a farm with cows and sheep. The total number of animals is 200 and there are 71 cows. How many sheep are there?

A Let x = the size of a sheep.   **B** Let x = the total number of animals.

C Let x = the number of sheep.   **D** Let x = the number of cows.

E Let x = Jared's age.

Example 16   Solving a problem using equations

The sum of Kate's current age in years and her age next year is 19. How old is Kate?

SOLUTION

Let k = Kate's current age in years.

$k + (k + 1) = 19$

$$2k + 1 = 19$$
$$-1 \quad \bigg(\qquad \bigg) \quad -1$$
$$2k = 18$$
$$\div 2 \quad \bigg(\qquad \bigg) \quad \div 2$$
$$k = 9$$

Kate is currently 9 years old.

EXPLANATION

Define a pronumeral to stand for the unknown number.

Write an equation to describe the situation. Note that $k + 1$ is Kate's age next year.

Simplify the LHS and then solve the equation algebraically.

Answer the original question.

Now you try

Hiring a cabin costs $80 per day, plus you must pay a $30 cleaning fee. Given that the total cost is $350, how many days was the cabin hired?

Exercise 9H

FLUENCY   1–4   2–5   3–5

Example 16   **1**   The sum of Jerry's current age and his age next year is 43. How old is Jerry?

Example 16   **2**   Launz buys a car and a trailer for a combined cost of $40 000. The trailer costs $2000.
    a   Define a pronumeral for the car's cost.   **b**   Write an equation to describe the problem.
    c   Solve the equation algebraically.   **d**   Hence, state the cost of the car.

Example 16   **3**   Valentina buys 12 pens for a total cost of $15.60.
    a   Define a pronumeral for the cost of one pen.   **b**   Write an equation to describe the problem.
    c   Solve the equation algebraically.   **d**   Hence, state the cost of one pen.

Example 16   **4**   Isabella is paid $17 per hour and gets paid a bonus of $65 each week. One particular week she earned $643.
    a   Define a pronumeral for the number of hours Isabella worked.
    b   Write an equation to describe the problem.
    c   Solve the equation algebraically.
    d   How many hours did Isabella work in that week?

Example 16   **5**   This rectangular paddock has an area of $720 \, \text{m}^2$.
    a   Write an equation to describe the problem, using w for the paddock's width in metres.
    b   Solve the equation algebraically.
    c   How wide is the paddock?
    d   What is the paddock's perimeter?

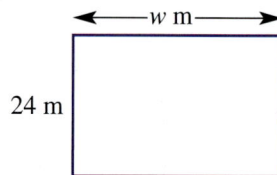

PROBLEM-SOLVING   6, 7   7–10   10–13

6   A number is doubled, then 3 is added and the result is doubled again. This gives a final result of 34. Set up and solve an equation to find the original number, showing all the steps clearly.

7   The perimeter of the shape shown is 30. Find the value of x.

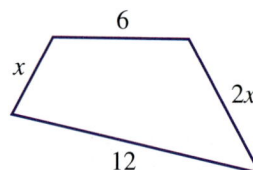

8   Alexa watches some television on Monday, then twice as many hours on Tuesday, then twice as many hours again on Wednesday. If she watches a total of $10\frac{1}{2}$ hours from Monday to Wednesday, how much television did Alexa watch on Monday?

9   Marcus and Sara's combined age is 30. Given that Sara is 2 years older than Marcus, write an equation and find Marcus' age.

10   An isosceles triangle is shown at right. Write an equation and solve it to find $x°$, the unknown angle. (Remember: The sum of angles in a triangle is $180°$.)

11 Find the value of y in the triangle shown here, by first writing an equation.

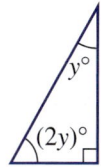

12 A rectangle has width w and height h. The perimeter and area of the rectangle are equal. Write an equation and solve it by inspection to find some possible values for w and h. (Note: There are many solutions to this equation. Try to find a few.)

13 Find the values of x and y in the rectangle shown.

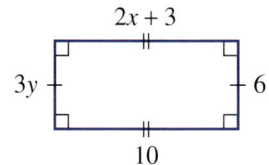

REASONING | 14 | 14, 15 | 15, 16

14 In some situations an equation makes sense, but in other situations it does not make sense. In this question you will consider the equation $3c + 10 = 4$.
   a Theodore set up an equation to be used to find the number of chairs in a room (c). The equation he wrote was $3c + 10 = 4$. Explain why he must have made a mistake.
   b Benedict set up an equation to be used to find the temperature outside in °C. He also wrote the equation $3c + 10 = 4$. Explain why this equation could be used for temperature even though it could not be used for the number of chairs.

15 If photocopying costs 35 cents a page and p is the number of pages photocopied, which of the following equations have possible solutions? Justify your answers. (Note: Fraction answers are not possible because you must still pay 35 cents even if you photocopy only part of a page.)
   a $0.35p = 4.20$ **b** $0.35p = 2.90$ **c** $0.35p = 2.80$

16 Assume that an isosceles triangle is drawn so that each of its three angles is a whole number of degrees. Prove that the angle a must be an even number of degrees.

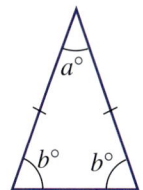

ENRICHMENT: Strange triangles | – | – | 17

17 Recall that the sum of angles in a triangle is 180°.
   a David proposes the following triangle, which is not drawn to scale.
      i Find the value of x.
      ii Explain what makes this triangle impossible.
   b Helena proposes the following triangle, which is also not drawn to scale.
      i Explain why the information in the diagram is not enough to find x.
      ii What are the possible values that x could take?
   c Design a geometric puzzle, like the one in part **a**, for which there can be no solution.

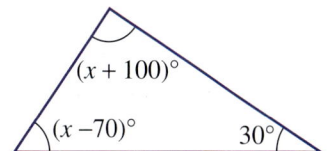

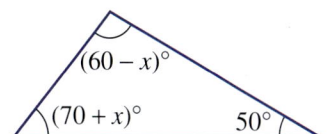

Modelling

100 m Gift handicap

Each year the town of Walpole runs a special race called the Walpole Gift where each runner is assigned a handicap advantage. A runner's handicap advantage is the number of metres provided as a head-start in front of the start line. This means a runner with a 10 metre handicap advantage only has to run the remaining 90 metres. Their handicap advantage is determined by their previous performance.

Three runners, Peter, Jethro and Leonard, compare their given handicap for the upcoming Walpole Gift. They also estimate their average speed for the race in m/s (metres per second).

Runner	Peter	Jethro	Leonard
Handicap advantage	10 m	4 m	0 m
Average speed estimate	7 m/s	8 m/s	9 m/s

Present a report for the following tasks and ensure that you show clear mathematical workings and explanations where appropriate.

Preliminary task

a Complete the following table for Peter where time is in seconds and the distance is measured from the start line. The first two distances are completed for you.

Time (s)	0	1	2	3	4	5	6	7	8	9	10
Distance from start line (m)	10	17									

b Approximately how long does it take for Peter to complete the race? Round to the nearest second.

c How long does it take for Peter to reach the point 6 metres before the finish line?

Modelling task

Formulate

a The problem is to determine who wins the Walpole Gift and how this is affected by the handicaps. Write down all the relevant information that will help solve this problem.

b Using d metres as the distance from the starting line and t for the time in seconds, write rules for the distance covered for:
  i   Peter using his estimated speed of 7 m/s and handicap of 10 m
  ii Jethro using his estimated speed of 8 m/s and handicap of 4 m
  iii Leonard using his estimated speed of 9 m/s with no handicap.

c Use your rules to find the distance from the start line of:
  i   Peter after 5 seconds
  ii Jethro after 8 seconds
  iii Leonard after 6 seconds.

d Use your rules to find when:
  i   Peter reaches the 52 m mark
  ii Jethro reaches the 28 m mark
  iii Leonard reaches the 90 m mark.

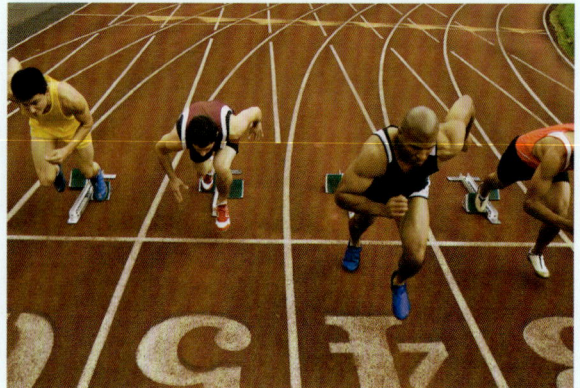

Solve

e   After how many seconds does:

   i   Leonard catch Peter?

   ii   Jethro catch Peter?

   iii Leonard catch Jethro?

f   Determine the placings for the three men.

ate and verify

g   Compare the performance of each of the men in the race. Include a description of when and where on the 100 m track anyone got overtaken.

h   Assume that the three men kept the same speed in next year's race, but their handicaps could change. Give an examples of handicaps that would result in:

   i   Peter beating Leonard

   ii   Jethro beating Leonard.

unicate

i   Summarise your results and describe any key findings.

Extension questions

a   Assume the original handicap advantage stayed the same next year, but that Peter and Jethro could run faster.

   i   At what speed would Peter need to travel so that he beats Leonard?

   ii   At what speed would Jethro need to travel so that he beats Leonard?

b   Assume the original handicap advantage stayed the same next year and all three runners had the same speed as this year, but the track could be longer or shorter than 100 metres. Investigate how this would affect the handicaps required by Peter and Jethro.

Making a pen with 100 metres

Key technology: Spreadsheets

The size and shape of the things we make depend on the amount of material that we have and any restrictions that we might have regarding the shape's dimensions. For example, making a rectangular pen with 100 metres of fencing can result in many different shaped rectangles. Depending on the relationship between the length and the width, we can determine the dimensions of the rectangle using equations.

1 Getting started

Working with 100 metres of fencing, let's consider making a rectangular pen where the length is 10 metres more than the width. Let x metres be the width of the rectangle.

  a Write an expression for the following.

    i length of the rectangle

    ii perimeter of the rectangle

  b Using the fact that there is a total of 100 m of fencing available, write an equation.

  c Simplify and solve your equation to find the width of the pen.

  d Repeat parts **a–c** above if the length of the pen is 5 metres more than the width.

2 Using technology

We will set up a spreadsheet to assist in the calculation of the dimensions of the pen for varying lengths and widths.

  a Construct a spreadsheet as shown including an adjustable amount which is the difference between the length and width of the pen.

  b Fill down at cells A7, B6 and C6 until you find the width and length that give the correct perimeter of 100 m.

  c Now change the length and width difference in cell C3 to 20 metres. What does your spreadsheet say about the dimensions required to produce a rectangular pen using 100 m of fencing?

	A	B	C
1	The 100 m pen		
2			
3	Length and width difference		10
4			
5	width	length	perimeter
6	1	=A6+C$3	=2*A6+2*B6
7	=A6+1		

3 Applying an algorithm

a   Now change the length and width difference to 5 metres. What do you notice about the results in your spreadsheet?

b   Make an adjustment to the formula in cell A7 so that your spreadsheet will show the required width and length to create a pen using 100 m of fencing. Shown here is the formula in cell A7 where the increment has been adjusted to 0.5.

	A	B	C
1	The 100 m pen		
2			
3	Length and width difference		25
4			
5	width	length	perimeter
6	1	=A6+C$3	=2*A6+2*B6
7	=A6+0.5		

c   Now try adjusting the difference in cell C3 to be 25 and write down the dimensions of the pen where the perimeter is 100 m.

d   Describe the shape of the pen if the value entered into cell C3 is 0.

e   Further adjustment of the formula in cell A7 may be needed for non-integer values in cell C3. Use your spreadsheet to find the dimensions of the pen if the difference in the width and length is the following.

   i   12.5 metres

   ii   24.2 metres

   iii   18.7 metres

4 Extension

a   Using the pronumeral d for the difference between the length and the width of the pen, write expressions for the following. Remember that x metres is the width of the pen.

   i   length of the rectangle

   ii   perimeter of the rectangle

b   Using the fact that there is a total of 100 m of fencing available, write an equation using the variables x and d.

c   Simplify and solve your equation to find the width of the pen. Your answer should be an expression in terms of d.

d   Use your result from part **c** to check some of your conclusions from part **3** above. For example, if $d = 12.5$, find the value of x that creates a pen using 100 m of fencing.

Technology and computational thinking

Theme parks

There are thousands of theme parks all over the world which offer a vast array of rides that are built to thrill. By searching the internet, you can discover the longest, tallest, fastest and scariest rides. Although prices are kept competitive, theme parks need to make a profit so that they can maintain safety standards and continue to build new and more exciting rides.

Thrill World and Extreme Park are two theme parks. Both charge different prices for entry and for each ride. Their prices are:

- Thrill World: $20 entry and $5 per ride
- Extreme Park: $60 entry and $3 per ride.

  a   Copy and complete the table below for each theme park. The total cost for the day includes the entry cost and cost of the rides.

Number of rides (n)	1	2	3	4	5	6	7	8	...	20	21	22	23	24	25
Thrill World total cost T	$25								...						
Extreme Park total cost E	$63								...						

  b   Write a formula for:
  i T, the total cost, in dollars, for n rides at Thrill World
  ii E, the total cost, in dollars, for n rides at Extreme Park.

  c   For each of these thrill seekers, use an equation to calculate how many rides they went on.
  i   Amanda, who spent $105 at Thrill World
  ii   George, who spent $117 at Extreme Park

  d   Refer to your completed table to determine the number of rides that will make the total cost for the day the same at each theme park.

  e   A third theme park, Fun World, decides to charge no entry fee but to charge $10 per ride. Find the minimum number of rides that you could go on at Fun World before it becomes cheaper at:
  i   Thrill World
  ii   Extreme Park.

Investigate how much Fun World should charge to attract customers while still making profits that are similar to those of Thrill World and Extreme Park. Provide some mathematical calculations to support your conclusions.

1 Find the unknown number in the following problems.

> Up for a challenge? If you get stuck on a question, check out the 'Working with unfamiliar problems' poster at the end of the book to help you.

  a A number is added to half of itself and the result is 39.
  b A number is doubled, then tripled, then quadrupled. The result is 696.
  c One-quarter of a number is subtracted from 100 and the result is 8.
  d Half of a number is added to 47, and the result is the same as the original number doubled.
  e A number is increased by 4, the result is doubled and then 4 is added again to give an answer of 84.

2 A triangle has sides $2x + 7$, $3x + 4$ and $4(x - 4)$ measured in cm. If the perimeter of the triangle is 220 cm, find the difference between the longest and shortest sides.

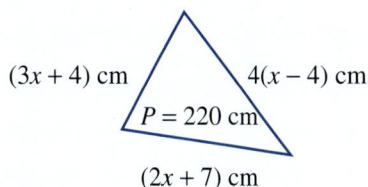

$(3x + 4)$ cm $4(x - 4)$ cm

$P = 220$ cm

$(2x + 7)$ cm

3 For this rectangle, find the values of x and y and determine the perimeter. The sides are measured in cm.

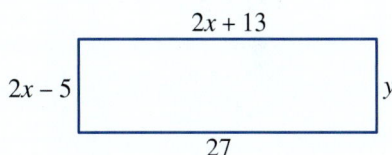

$2x + 13$

$2x - 5$ y

27

4 A rectangular property has a perimeter of 378 m. It is divided up into five identical rectangular house blocks as shown in this diagram. Determine the area of each house block.

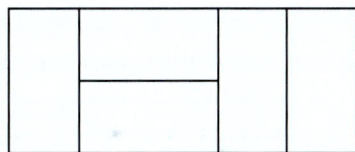

5 Find the values of a, b and c, given the clues:
$5(a + 2) + 3 = 38$ and $2(b + 6) - 2 = 14$ and $3a + 2b + c = 31$

6 Find the values of a and b for each of these geometric figures.

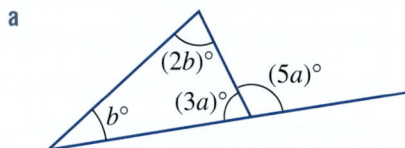

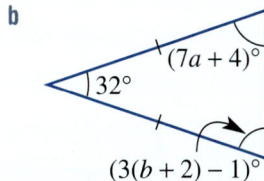

  a

  $(2b)°$ $(5a)°$
  $(3a)°$
  $b°$

  b

  $(7a + 4)°$
  $32°$
  $(3(b + 2) - 1)°$

7 James's nanna keeps goats and chickens in her backyard. She says to James, 'There are 41 animals in this yard'. James says to his nanna, 'There are 134 animal legs in this yard'.
How many goats and how many chickens are in the paddock?

8 Five consecutive numbers have the middle number $3x - 1$. If the sum of these five numbers is 670, find the value of x and list the five numbers.

Chapter summary

Solving an equation

Finding pronumeral values to make equation true
e.g. $15 + x = 20$
solution: $x = 5$

Formulas

Formulas or rules are types of equations.
e.g. $F = ma$, $A = l \times w$,
$P = 4x$

Solving equations

e.g.
$$-5 \left(\begin{array}{c} 3x + 5 = 38 \\ 3x = 33 \\ x = 11 \end{array} \right) -5 \atop \div 3 \quad \div 3$$

e.g.
$$\times 4 \left(\begin{array}{c} \frac{x}{4} = 7 \\ x = 28 \end{array} \right) \times 4$$

e.g.
$$+2 \left(\begin{array}{c} 5x - 2 = 33 \\ 5x = 35 \\ x = 7 \end{array} \right) +2 \atop \div 5 \quad \div 5$$

Equations with fractions (Ext)

Equations with fractions are solved by multiplying by the denominator when fraction is by itself.

e.g.
$$-2 \left(\begin{array}{c} 2 + \frac{x}{7} = 4 \\ \frac{x}{7} = 2 \\ x = 14 \end{array} \right) -2 \atop \times 7 \quad \times 7$$

e.g.
$$\times 4 \left(\begin{array}{c} \frac{3x + 9}{4} = 6 \\ 3x + 9 = 24 \\ 3x = 15 \\ x = 5 \end{array} \right) \times 4 \atop -9 \quad -9 \atop \div 3 \quad \div 3$$

Equations

Equivalent equations

Equivalent equations are obtained by performing the same operation to both sides

e.g.
$$+8 \left(\begin{array}{c} 12 + 3x = 5 \\ 20 + 3x = 13 \end{array} \right) +8$$

To solve algebraically, use equivalent equations and opposite operations.

Main expression	First step
$3x + 5$	-5
$12x$	$\div 12$
$5x - 2$	$+2$
$\frac{x}{4}$	$\times 4$

Equations with brackets (Ext)

Brackets should be expanded and like items collected. Use the distributive law to expand.

e.g.
$$4(x + 2) = 4x + 8$$

e.g.
$$5(x + 3) + 2x = 29$$
$$5x + 15 + 2x = 29$$
$$-15 \left(\begin{array}{c} 7x + 15 = 29 \\ 7x = 14 \\ x = 2 \end{array} \right) -15 \atop \div 7 \quad \div 7$$

Applications

1 Use a pronumeral for the unknown.
2 Write an equation.
3 Solve the equation.
4 Answer the original question.

e.g. John's age in 3 years will be 15. How old is he now?

1   Let j = John's current age in years
2    $j + 3 = 15$
3    $-3 \left(\begin{array}{c} j + 3 = 15 \\ j = 12 \end{array} \right) -3$
4   John is currently 12 years old.

Chapter checklist with success criteria

A printable version of this checklist is available in the Interactive Textbook

9A	**1. I can identify an equation.** e.g. Which of the following are equations? $7 + 7 = 18$, $2 + 12$, $4 = 12 - x$, $3 + u$.	☐
9A	**2. I can classify an equation as true or false, given the value of any pronumerals.** e.g. Decide whether $10 + b = 3b + 1$ is true when $b = 4$.	☐
9A	**3. I can write an equation from an English description.** e.g. Write an equation for "the sum of x and 5 is 22."	☐
9B	**4. I can solve equations by inspection.** e.g. Solve the equation $5b = 20$ by inspection.	☐
9C	**5. I can apply an operation to both sides of an equation.** e.g. State the result of adding 4 to both sides of the equation $7q - 4 = 10$.	☐
9C	**6. I can show that two equations are equivalent.** e.g. Show that $5 = 7 - x$ and $10 = 2(7 - x)$ are equivalent by stating the operation used.	☐
9D	**7. I can solve one-step equations using equivalent equations.** e.g. Solve $5x = 30$ algebraically.	☐
9D	**8. I can solve two-step equations using equivalent equations.** e.g. Solve $7 + 4a = 23$ algebraically.	☐
9D	**9. I can check the solution to an equation using substitution.** e.g. Check that the solution to $12 = 2(e + 1)$ is $e = 5$.	☐
9E	**10. I can solve equations involving fractions.** (Ext) e.g. Solve $\dfrac{3x}{4} + 7 = 13$.	☐
9F	**11. I can expand brackets.** (Ext) e.g. Expand $5(3a + 4)$.	☐
9F	**12. I can collect like terms.** (Ext) e.g. Simplify $3a + 8a + 2 - 2a + 5$.	☐
9F	**13. I can solve equations involving brackets.** (Ext) e.g. Solve $3(b + 5) + 4b = 29$.	☐
9G	**14. I can apply formulas when the unknown is by itself.** e.g. For the rule $k = 3b + 2$, find the value of k if $b = 10$.	☐
9G	**15. I can apply formulas when an equation must be solved.** e.g. For the rule $k = 3b + 2$, find the value of b if $k = 23$.	☐
9H	**16. I can solve problems using equations.** e.g. The sum of Kate's current age and her age next year is 19. Use an equation to determine how old Kate is.	☐

Short-answer questions

9A

1 Classify each of the following equations as true or false.

    a $4 + 2 = 10 - 2$

    b $2(3 + 5) = 4(1 + 3)$

    c $5w + 1 = 11$, if $w = 2$

    d $2x + 5 = 12$, if $x = 4$

    e $y = 3y - 2$, if $y = 1$

    f $4 = z + 2$, if $z = 3$

9A

2 Write an equation for each of the following situations. You do not need to solve the equations.

    a The sum of 2 and u is 22.

    b The product of k and 5 is 41.

    c When z is tripled the result is 36.

    d The sum of a and b is 15.

9B

3 Solve the following equations by inspection.

    a $x + 1 = 4$ **b** $x + 8 = 14$ **c** $9 + y = 10$

    d $y - 7 = 2$ **e** $5a = 10$ **f** $\frac{a}{5} = 2$

9C

4 For each equation, find the result of applying the given operation to both sides and then simplify.

    a $2x + 5 = 13$ $[-5]$

    b $7a + 4 = 32$ $[-4]$

    c $12 = 3r - 3$ $[+3]$

    d $15 = 8p - 1$ $[+1]$

9D

5 Solve each of the following equations algebraically.

    a $5x = 15$

    b $r + 25 = 70$

    c $12p + 17 = 125$

    d $12 = 4b - 12$

    e $5 = 2x - 13$

    f $13 = 2r + 5$

    g $10 = 4q + 2$

    h $8u + 2 = 66$

9E

Ext

6 Solve the following equations algebraically.

    a $\frac{3u}{4} = 6$ **b** $\frac{8p}{3} = 8$ **c** $3 = \frac{2x + 1}{3}$

    d $\frac{5y}{2} + 10 = 30$ **e** $4 = \frac{2y + 20}{7}$ **f** $\frac{4x}{3} + 4 = 24$

9F

Ext

7 Expand the brackets in each of the following expressions.

    a $2(3 + 2p)$

    b $4(3x + 12)$

    c $7(a + 5)$

    d $9(2x + 1)$

9F

Ext

8 Solve each of these equations by expanding the brackets first.

a $2(x - 3) = 10$

b $27 = 3(x + 1)$

c $48 = 8(x - 1)$

d $60 = 3y + 2(y + 5)$

e $7(2z + 1) + 3 = 80$

f $2(5 + 3q) + 4q = 40$

9F

Ext

9 Consider the equation $4(x + 3) + 7x - 9 = 10$.

a Is $x = 2$ a solution?

b Show that the solution to this equation is *not* a whole number.

9F

Ext

10 a Does $3(2x + 2) - 6x + 4 = 15$ have a solution? Justify your answer.

b State whether the following are solutions to $5(x + 3) - 3(x + 2) = 2x + 9$.

i $x = 2$

ii $x = 3$

9G

11 The formula for the area of a trapezium is $A = \frac{1}{2}h(a + b)$, where h is the height of the trapezium, and a and b represent the parallel sides.

a Set up and solve an equation to find the area of a trapezium with height 20 cm and parallel sides of 15 cm and 30 cm.

b Find the height of a trapezium whose area is 55 cm² and has parallel sides 6 cm and 5 cm, respectively.

9G

12 Consider the rule $F = 3a + 2b$. Find:

a F if $a = 10$ and $b = 3$

b b if $F = 27$ and $a = 5$

c a if $F = 25$ and $b = 8$

9H

13 For each of the following problems, write an equation and solve it to find the unknown value.

a A number is added to three times itself and the result is 20. What is the number?

b The product of 5 and a number is 30. What is the number?

c Juanita's mother is twice as old as Juanita. The sum of their ages is 60. How old is Juanita?

d A rectangle has a width of 21 cm and a perimeter of 54 cm. What is its length?

9H

14 Find the value of y for each of these figures.

a

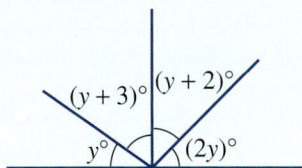

b

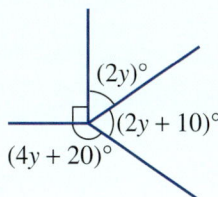

Multiple-choice questions

9A

1 If $x = 3$, which one of the following equations is true?

A $4x = 21$

B $2x + 4 = 12$

C $9 - x = 6$

D $2 = x + 1$

E $x - 3 = 4$

9A

2 When 11 is added to the product of 3 and x, the result is 53. This can be written as:

A $3x + 11 = 53$

B $3(x + 11) = 53$

C $\frac{x}{3} + 11 = 53$

D $\frac{x + 11}{3} = 53$

E $3x - 11 = 53$

9B

3 Which of the following values of x make the equation $2(x + 4) = 3x$ true?

A 2   B 4   C 6

D 8   E 10

9C

4 The equivalent equation that results from subtracting 3 from both sides of $12x - 3 = 27$ is:

A $12x = 24$

B $12x - 6 = 24$

C $12x - 6 = 30$

D $9x - 3 = 24$

E $12x = 30$

9D

5 To solve $3a + 5 = 17$, the first step to apply to both sides is to:

A add 5

B divide by 3

C subtract 17

D divide by 5

E subtract 5

9D

6 The solution to $2t - 4 = 6$ is:

A $t = 1$ B $t = 3$ C $t = 5$

D $t = 7$ E $t = 9$

9E

Ext

7 The solution of $\frac{2x}{7} = 10$ is:

A $x = 35$ B $x = 70$ C $x = 20$

D $x = 30$ E $x = 5$

9E

Ext

8 The solution to the equation $10 = \frac{3p + 5}{2}$ is:

A $p = 5$ B $p = 20$ C $p = 15$

D $p = 7$ E $p = 1$

9F

Ext

9   The solution of $3(u + 1) = 15$ is:

   A $u = 5$ B $u = 4$ C $u = 11$

   D $u = 6$ E $u = 3$

9G

10   A formula relating A, p and t is $A = 3p - t$. If $A = 24$ and $t = 6$, then p equals:

   A   18   B   4   C   30

   D   2   E   10

Extended-response questions

1   Udhav's satellite phone plan charges a connection fee of 15 cents and then 2 cents per second for every call.

   a   How much does a 30-second call cost?

   b   Write a rule for the total cost, C, in cents, for a call that lasts t seconds.

   c   Use your rule to find the cost of a call that lasts 80 seconds.

   d   If a call cost 39 cents, how long did it last? Solve an equation to find t.

   e   If a call cost \$1.77, how long did it last?

   f   On a particular day, Udhav makes two calls – the second one lasting twice as long as the first, with a total cost of \$3.30. What was the total amount of time he spent on the phone?

2   Gemma is paid \$$x$ per hour from Monday to Friday, but earns an extra \$2 per hour during weekends. During a particular week, she worked 30 hours during the week and then 10 hours on the weekend.

   a   If $x = 12$, calculate the total wages Gemma was paid that week.

   b   Explain why her weekly wage is given by the rule $W = 30x + 10(x + 2)$.

   c   Use the rule to find Gemma's weekly wage if $x = 16$.

   d   If Gemma earns \$620 in one week, find the value of x.

   e   If Gemma earns \$860 in one week, how much did she earn from Monday to Friday?

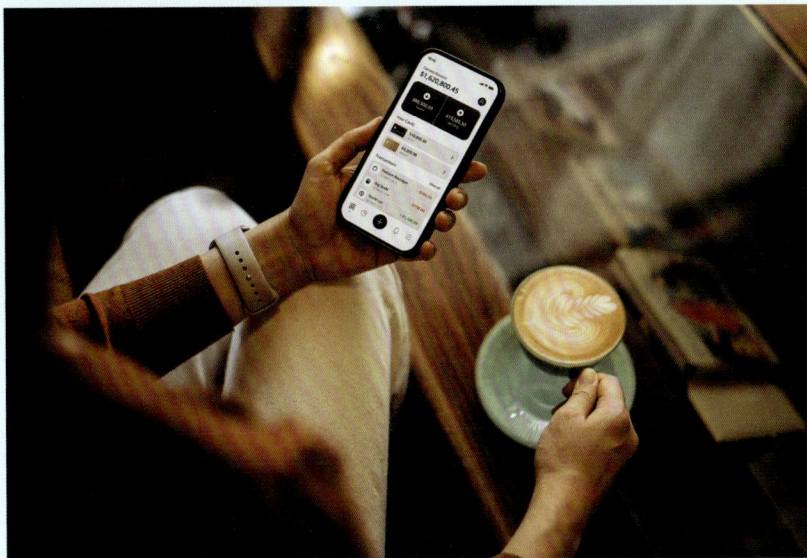

10

Measurement

Maths in context: Measurement is important everywhere

Measurement skills are essential for all practical occupations, including:
- all engineers, architects, auto mechanics, bakers, boiler makers, bricklayers, builders, carpenters and chefs
- construction workers, electricians, farmers, hairdressers, house painters, mechanics, miners and nurses
- pharmacists, plumbers, roboticists, seamstresses, sheet metal workers, surveyors, tilers, vets and welders.

Practical workers use a variety of measurement units, illustrated by these facts.
- The Eiffel Tower in France is painted with 50 tonnes of paint every 7 years.
- The Sydney Harbour Bridge is repainted every 5 years by two robots and 100 painters, using 30 000 litres of paint weighing 140 tonnes.

- The Sydney Harbour Bridge's surface area is 485 000 m^2 (around 60 football fields).
- The volume of water in Sydney Harbour is about 500 gigalitres or five hundred thousand million litres or 0.5 km^3.
- The Great Wall of China is more than 6000 km long.
- Australia's unbroken dingo-proof fence is 5614 km long and runs from South Australia to Queensland.
- The Great Pyramid of Giza, built in 2500 BCE, is made of 2.5 million stone blocks that each weigh about 2300 kg (2.3 tonnes), heavier than a Tesla Model 3 with a mass of 1800 kg or 1.8 tonnes!
- The maximum daytime temperature on Mars is about 20°C, but a freezing −65°C at night.

Chapter contents

Victorian Curriculum 2.0

This chapter covers the following content descriptors in the Victorian Curriculum 2.0:

MEASUREMENT

VC2M7M01, VC2M7M02, VC2M7M03, VC2M7M06

ALGEBRA

VC2M7A01, VC2M7A03, VC2M7A06

Please refer to the curriculum support documentation in the teacher resources for a full and comprehensive mapping of this chapter to the related curriculum content descriptors.

© VCAA

Online resources

A host of additional online resources are included as part of your Interactive Textbook, including HOTmaths content, video demonstrations of all worked examples, auto-marked quizzes and much more.

10A   Metric units of length   CONSOLIDATING

LEARNING INTENTIONS
- To be able to choose a suitable unit for a length within the metric system
- To be able to convert between metric lengths (km, m, cm and mm)
- To be able to read a length shown on a ruler or tape measure

The metric system was developed in France in the 1790s and is the universally accepted system today. The word *metric* comes from the Greek word *metron*, meaning 'measure'. It is a decimal system where length measures are based on the unit called the *metre*. The definition of the metre has changed over time.

Originally, it was proposed to be the length of a pendulum that beats at a rate of one beat per second. It was later defined as $1/10\,000\,000$ of the distance from the North Pole to the equator on a line on Earth's surface passing through Paris. In 1960, a metre became $1\,650\,763.73$ wavelengths of the spectrum of the krypton-86 atom in a vacuum. In 1983, the metre was defined as the distance that light travels in $1/299\,792\,458$ seconds inside a vacuum.

To avoid the use of very large and very small numbers, an appropriate unit is often chosen to measure a length or distance. It may also be necessary to convert units of length. For example, 150 pieces of timber, each measured in centimetres, may need to be communicated as a total length using metres. Another example might be that 5 millimetres is to be cut from a length of timber 1.4 metres long because it is too wide to fit a door opening that is 139.5 centimetres wide.

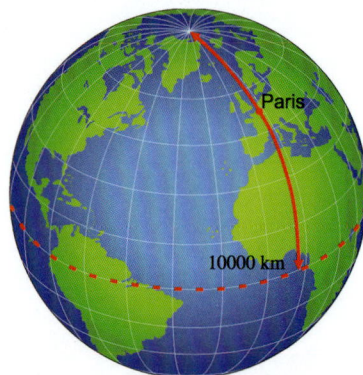

A carpenter may need to measure lengths in metres, centimetres and millimetres. Making accurate measurements and converting units are essential skills for construction workers.

Lesson starter: How good is your estimate?

Without measuring, guess the length of your desk, in centimetres.

- Now use a ruler to find the actual length in centimetres.
- Convert your answer to millimetres and metres.
- If you lined up all the class desks end to end, how many desks would be needed to reach 1 kilometre? Explain how you got your answer.

KEY IDEAS

■ **Metric system**
- 1 centimetre (cm) = 10 millimetres (mm)
- 1 metre (m) = 100 centimetres (cm)
- 1 kilometre (km) = 1000 metres (m)

$$\times 1000 \quad \times 100 \quad \times 10$$

km   m   cm   mm

$$\div 1000 \quad \div 100 \quad \div 10$$

■ **Conversion**
- When converting to a smaller unit, multiply by 10 or 100 or 1000. The decimal point appears to move to the right. For example:

$$2.3\,m = (2.3 \times 100)\,cm \qquad 28\,cm = (28 \times 10)\,mm$$
$$= 230\,cm \qquad\qquad\qquad = 280\,mm$$

- When converting to a larger unit, divide by a power of 10 (i.e. 10, 100, 1000). The decimal point appears to move to the left. For example:

$$47\,mm = (47 \div 10)\,cm \qquad 4600\,m = (4600 \div 1000)\,km$$
$$= 4.7\,cm \qquad\qquad\qquad = 4.6\,km$$

■ When reading scales, be sure about what units are showing on the scale. This scale shows 36 mm.

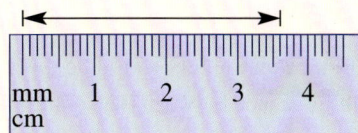

mm   1   2   3   4
cm

BUILDING UNDERSTANDING

1 Use the metric system to state how many:
  a millimetres in 1 centimetre
  b centimetres in 1 metre
  c metres in 1 kilometre
  d millimetres in 1 metre
  e centimetres in 1 kilometre
  f millimetres in 1 kilometre.

2 State the missing number or word in these sentences.
  a When converting from metres to centimetres, you multiply by _____.
  b When converting from metres to kilometres, you divide by _____.
  c When converting from centimetres to metres, you _____ by 100.
  d When converting from kilometres to metres, you _____ by 1000.

3 Calculate each of the following.
  a 100×10
  b 10×100
  c 100×1000
  d $10 \times 100 \times 1000$

4 **a** When multiplying by a power of 10, in which direction does the decimal point move – left or right?
  b When dividing by a power of 10, in which direction does the decimal point move – left or right?

Example 1   Choosing metric lengths

Which metric unit would be the most appropriate for measuring these lengths?
a dimensions of a large room
b thickness of glass in a window

SOLUTION

a metres (m)

b millimetres (mm)

EXPLANATION

Using mm or cm would give a very large number, and using km would give a number that is very small.

The thickness of glass is likely to be around 5 mm.

Now you try

Which metric unit would be the most appropriate for measuring these lengths?
a distance between the centre of the city and a nearby suburb
b height of a book on a bookshelf

Example 2   Converting metric units of length

Convert to the units given in brackets.
a 3 m (cm)
b 25 600 cm (km)

SOLUTION

a 3 m = 3 × 100 cm
        = 300 cm

b 25 600 cm = 25 600 ÷ 100 000
              = 0.256 km

EXPLANATION

1 m = 100 cm
Multiply since you are converting to a smaller unit.

There are 100 cm in 1 m and 1000 m in 1 km and 100 × 1000 = 100 000.

Now you try

Convert to the units given in brackets.
a 2 km (m)
b 3400 mm (m)

Example 3   Reading length scales

Read the scales on these rulers to measure the marked length.

a

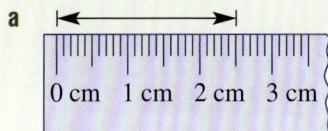

b

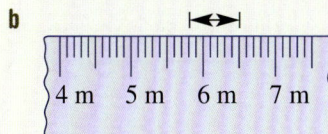

SOLUTION	EXPLANATION
a 25 mm	2.5 cm is also accurate.
b 70 cm	Each division is $\frac{1}{10}$ of a metre, which is 10 cm.

Now you try

Read the scales on these rules to measure the marked length.

a   Answer in millimetres.

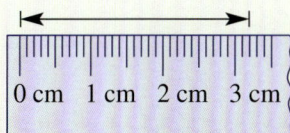

b   Answer in centimetres.

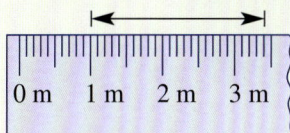

Exercise 10A

FLUENCY	1–3, 4–7(½)	2, 4–7(½), 8	2, 4–7(½), 8, 9

1 Which metric unit would be the most appropriate for measuring the following?

a   the distance between two towns

b   the thickness of a nail

c   height of a flag pole

d   length of a garden hose

e   dimensions of a small desk

f   distance across a city

Example 1

2 Choose which metric unit would be the most suitable for measuring the real-life length indicated in each of these photos.

a

b

c

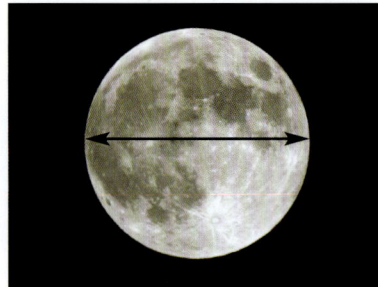

d

e

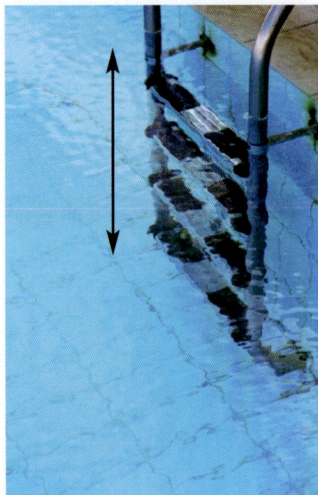

f

Example 2a

3 Convert to the units given in the brackets.

a   4 m (cm)   b   6 km (m)   c   30 mm (cm)   d   700 cm (m)

Example 2a

4 Convert these measurements to the units shown in brackets.

a   5 cm (mm)   b   2 m (cm)   c   3.5 km (m)   d   26.1 m (cm)

e   40 mm (cm)   f   500 cm (m)   g   4200 m (km)   h   472 mm (cm)

i   6.84 m (cm)   j   0.02 km (m)   k   9261 mm (cm)   l   4230 m (km)

5 Add these lengths together and give the result in the units shown in brackets.

a   2 cm and 5 mm (cm)   b   8 cm and 2 mm (mm)   c   2 m and 50 cm (m)

d   7 m and 30 cm (cm)   e   6 km and 200 m (m)   f   25 km and 732 m (km)

Example 2b

6 Convert to the units shown in the brackets.

a 3 m (mm)

b 6 km (cm)

c 2.4 m (mm)

d 0.04 km (cm)

e 47 000 cm (km)

f 913 000 mm (m)

g 216 000 mm (km)

h 0.5 mm (m)

i 0.7 km (mm)

Example 3

7 These rulers show centimetres with millimetre divisions. Read the scale to measure the marked length.

i in centimetres   ii in millimetres

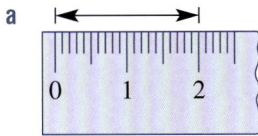

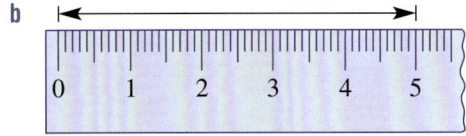

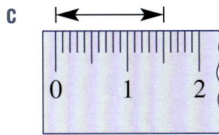

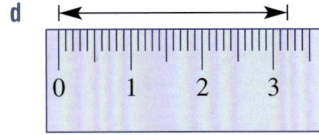

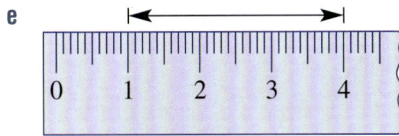

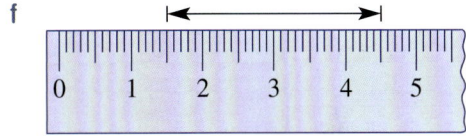

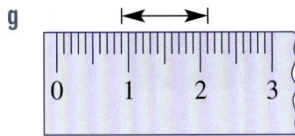

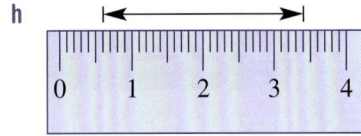

a

b

c

d

e

f

g

h

8 Read the scale on these tape measures. Be careful with the units given!

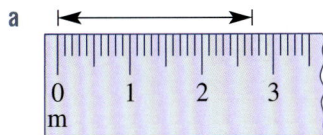

a

b

9 Use subtraction to find the difference between the measurements, and give your answer with the units shown in brackets.

a 9 km, 500 m (km)

b 3.5 m, 40 cm (cm)

c 0.2 m, 10 mm (cm)

PROBLEM-SOLVING	10–12	12–15	14–17

10 Arrange these measurements from smallest to largest.

a 38 cm, 540 mm, 0.5 m

b 0.02 km, 25 m, 160 cm, 2100 mm

c 0.003 km, 20 cm, 3.1 m, 142 mm

d 0.001 km, 0.1 m, 1000 cm, 10 mm

11 Joe widens a 1.2 m doorway by 50 mm. What is the new width of the doorway, in centimetres?

12 Three construction engineers individually have plans to build the world's next tallest tower. The Titan tower is to be 1.12 km tall, the Gigan tower is to be 109 500 cm tall and the Bigan tower is to be 1210 m tall. Which tower will be the tallest?

13 Steel chain costs $8.20 per metre. How much does it cost to buy chain of the following lengths?

    a 1 km   **b** 80 cm   **c** 50 mm

14 A house is 25 metres from a cliff above the sea. The cliff is eroding at a rate of 40 mm per year. How many years will pass before the house starts to fall into the sea?

15 Mount Everest is moving with the Indo-Australian plate at a rate of about 10 cm per year. How many years will it take to move 5 km?

16 A ream of 500 sheets of paper is 4 cm thick. How thick is 1 sheet of paper, in millimetres?

17 A snail slides 2 mm every 5 seconds. How long will it take to slide 1 m?

REASONING   18   18   18, 19

18 Copy this chart and fill in the missing information.

19 Many tradespeople measure and communicate with millimetres, even for long measurements like timber beams or pipes. Can you explain why this might be the case?

ENRICHMENT: Very small and large units   –   –   20

20 When 1 metre is divided into 1 million parts, each part is called a **micrometre** (μm). At the other end of the spectrum, a **light year** is used to describe large distances in space.

    a State how many micrometres there are in:

        i 1 m   **ii** 1 cm   **iii** 1 mm   **iv** 1 km

    b A virus is 0.000312 mm wide. How many micrometres is this?

    c Research the length called the light year. Explain what it is and give example of distance using light years, such as to the nearest star other than the Sun.

10B Perimeter CONSOLIDATING

LEARNING INTENTIONS
- To understand that perimeter is the distance around the outside of a two-dimensional shape
- To understand that marks can indicate two (or more) sides are of equal length
- To be able to find the perimeter of a shape when the measurements are given

The distance around the outside of a two-dimensional shape is called the perimeter. The word *perimeter* comes from the Greek words *peri*, meaning 'around', and *metron*, meaning 'measure'. We associate perimeter with the outside of all sorts of regions and objects, like the length of fencing surrounding a block of land or the length of timber required to frame a picture.

This fence marks the perimeter (i.e. the distance around the outside) of a paddock. Farmers use the perimeter length to calculate the number of posts needed for the fence.

Lesson starter: Is there enough information?

This diagram includes only 90° angles and only one side length is marked. Discuss if there is enough information given in the diagram to find the perimeter of the shape. What additional information, if any, is required?

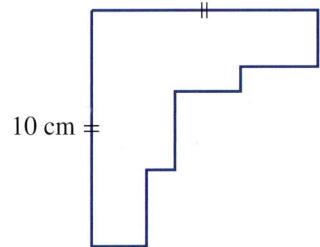

10 cm

KEY IDEAS

■ **Perimeter**, sometimes denoted as P, is the distance around the outside of a two-dimensional shape.

■ Sides with the same markings are of equal length.

■ The unknown lengths of some sides can sometimes be determined by considering the given lengths of other sides.

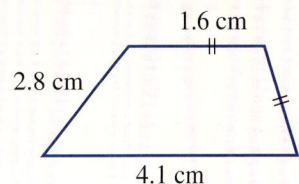

1.6 cm

2.8 cm

4.1 cm

$$P = 1.6 + 1.6 + 2.8 + 4.1$$
$$= 10.1 \text{ cm}$$

BUILDING UNDERSTANDING

1 These shapes are drawn on 1 cm grids. Give the perimeter of each.

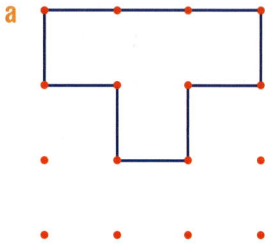

a

b

2 Use a ruler to measure the lengths of the sides of these shapes, and then find the perimeter.

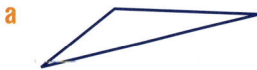

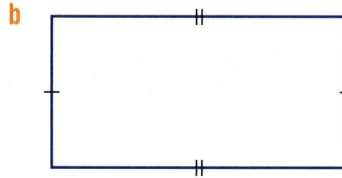

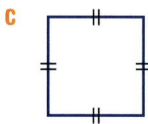

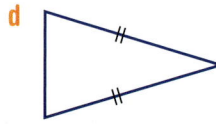

a

b

c

d

Example 4   Finding the perimeter

Find the perimeter of each of these shapes.

a

3 cm

5 cm

b

3 m

6 m   5 m

2 m

SOLUTION

a perimeter $= 2 \times 5 + 3$

$\qquad\qquad = 13\,\text{cm}$

b perimeter $= 2 \times 6 + 2 \times 8$

$\qquad\qquad = 28\,\text{m}$

EXPLANATION

There are two equal lengths of 5 cm and one length of 3 cm.

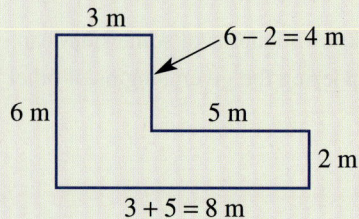

3 m

6 m $6 - 2 = 4$ m

5 m

2 m

$3 + 5 = 8$ m

Now you try

Find the perimeter of each of these shapes.

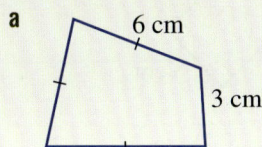

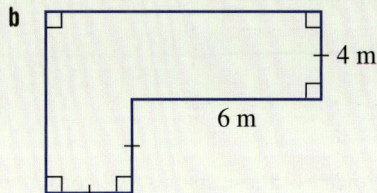

a

6 cm

3 cm

b

4 m

6 m

Exercise 10B

FLUENCY   1–4   2–5   2, 4, 5

1 Find the perimeter of each of the shapes.

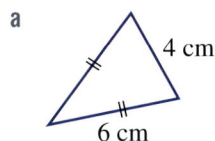

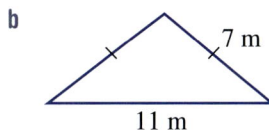

a

4 cm

6 cm

b

7 m

11 m

2 Find the perimeter of these shapes. (Diagrams are not drawn to scale.)

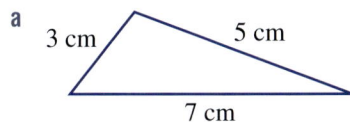

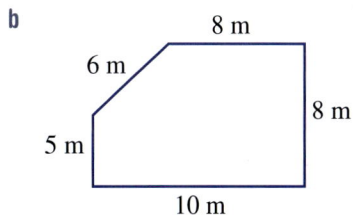

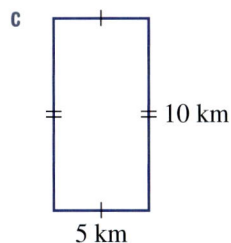

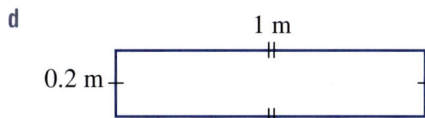

a

3 cm   5 cm

7 cm

b

8 m

6 m

5 m

8 m

10 m

c

10 km

5 km

d

1 m

0.2 m

e

10 cm

6 cm

f

2.5 cm

Example 4b **3** Find the perimeter of each of these shapes.

a

b

Example 4b **4** Find the perimeter of these shapes. All corner angles are 90°.

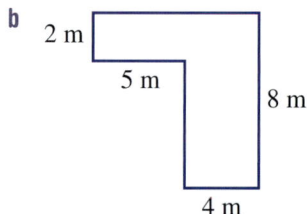

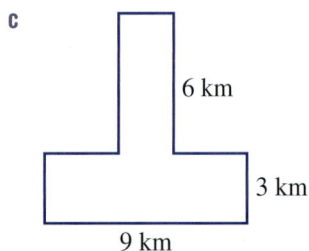

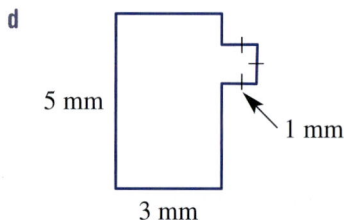

a

b

c

d

5 **a** A square has a side length of 2.1 cm. Find its perimeter.

b A rectangle has a length of 4.8 m and a width of 2.2 m. Find its perimeter.

c An equilateral triangle has all sides the same length. If each side is 15.5 mm, find its perimeter.

PROBLEM-SOLVING		6, 7	7–9	9–12

6 A grazing paddock is to be fenced on all sides. It is rectangular in shape, with a length of 242 m and a width of 186 m. If fencing costs $25 per metre, find the cost of fencing required.

7 The lines on a grass tennis court are marked with chalk. All the measurements are shown in the diagram and given in feet.

a Find the total number of feet of chalk required to do all the lines of the given tennis court.

b There are 0.305 metres in 1 foot. Convert your answer to part **a** to metres.

8 Only some side lengths are shown for these shapes. Find the perimeter. (Note: All corner angles are 90°.)

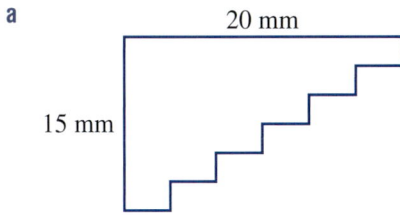

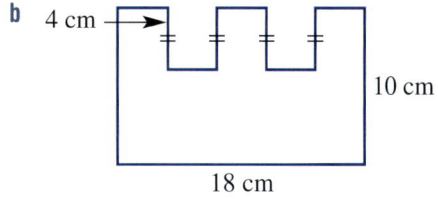

a

20 mm

15 mm

b 4 cm

10 cm

18 cm

9 Find the perimeter of each of these shapes. Give your answers in centimetres.

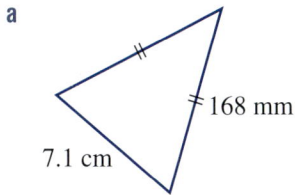

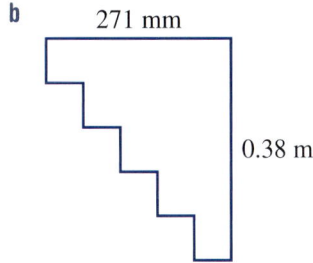

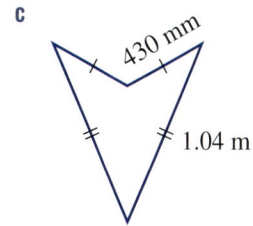

a

168 mm

7.1 cm

b 271 mm

0.38 m

c 430 mm

1.04 m

10 A square paddock has 100 equally-spaced posts that are 4 metres apart, including one in each corner. What is the perimeter of the paddock?

11 The perimeter of each shape is given. Find the missing side length for each shape.

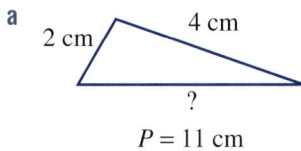

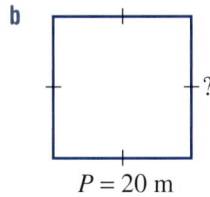

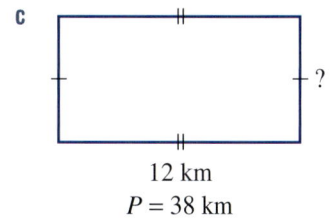

a

2 cm   4 cm

?

$P = 11$ cm

b

?

$P = 20$ m

c

?

12 km

$P = 38$ km

12 A rectangle has a perimeter of 16 cm. Using only whole numbers for the length and width, how many different rectangles can be drawn? Do not count rotations of the same rectangle as different.

REASONING   13   13, 14   14, 15

13 Write an algebraic rule (e.g. $P = 2a + b$) to describe the perimeter of each shape.

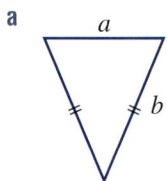

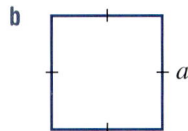

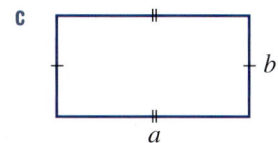

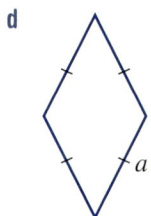

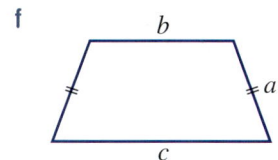

a

a

b

b

a

c

b

a

d

a

e

a

b

f

b

a

c

14 Write an algebraic rule for the perimeter of each given shape.

a

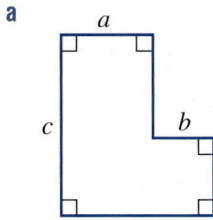

b

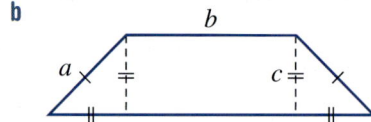

15 a A square has perimeter P. Write an expression for its side length.

b A rectangle has perimeter P and width a. Write an expression for its length.

ENRICHMENT: Picture frames   –   –   16

16 The amount of timber used to frame a picture depends on the outside lengths of the overall frame. Each side is first cut as a rectangular piece, and two corners are then cut at 45° to make the frame.

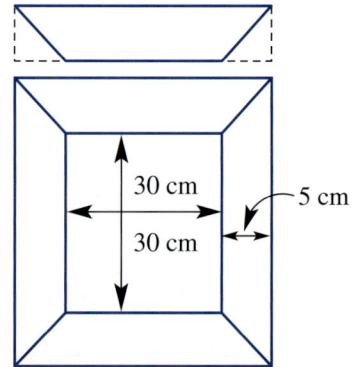

a A square painting of side length 30 cm is to be framed with timber of width 5 cm. Find the total length of timber required for the job.

b A rectangular photo with dimensions 50 cm by 30 cm is framed with timber of width 7 cm. Find the total length of timber required to complete the job.

c Kimberley uses 2 m of timber of width 5 cm to complete a square picture frame. What is the side length of the picture?

d A square piece of embroidery has side length a cm and is framed by timber of width 4 cm. Write an expression for the total length of timber used in cm.

The perimeter of a house is found by adding the lengths of all the outside walls. Scaffolding is required around the perimeter for construction work above ground level.

10C Circles, π and circumference

> **LEARNING INTENTIONS**
> - To know the features of a circle including the radius, diameter and circumference
> - To know that π is the ratio of the circumference of a circle to its diameter
> - To be able to calculate a circle's circumference, diameter or radius if given one of the other two measurements

The special number π, pronounced pi, has fascinated mathematicians, scientists, designers and engineers since the ancient times. This mathematical constant, which connects a circle's circumference to its diameter, is critical in any calculation that involves circular shapes. It also appears in many other areas of mathematics. Evidence suggests that the Egyptians used the approximation $\frac{22}{7}$ to help make calculations and that the Babylonians used the number $\frac{25}{8} = 3.125$. Around 250 AD, the Greek mathematician Archimedes used an algorithm to prove that π was between 3.1410 and 3.1429 and in a similar manner around 265 AD, a Chinese mathematician, Liu Hui, proved that $π \approx 3.1416$. Today we can use computers and complex mathematics to approximate π correct to millions of decimal places.

Lesson starter: How close can you get?

For this activity, you will need some string, scissors, a ruler and a pair of compasses. We know that π is the ratio of a circle's circumference, C, to its diameter, d, and so $π = \frac{C}{d}$. In this activity, we will estimate the value of π by drawing a circle and measuring both its diameter and circumference.

- Use a pair of compasses to construct a circle of any size and draw in a diameter.
- Use a piece of string to trace around the circle and cut to size.
- Measure the length of the string (the circumference) and the circle's diameter.
- Use your measurements to approximate the value of π using $π = \frac{C}{d}$.
- Calculate a class average to see how this approximation compares to an accurate value of π.

> ## KEY IDEAS
>
> ■ Features of a circle
>   - **Diameter** (d) is the distance across the centre of a circle.
>   - **Radius** (r) is the distance from the centre to the circle. Note: $d = 2r$.
>   - **Chord:** A line interval connecting two points on a circle.
>   - **Tangent:** A line that touches the circle at a point.
>   - A tangent to a circle is at right angles to the radius.
>   - **Sector:** A portion of a circle enclosed by two radii and a portion of a circle (arc).
>   - **Segment:** An area of a circle 'cut off' by a chord.

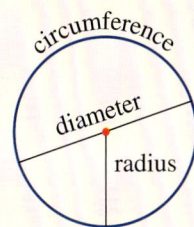

■ **Circumference** (C) is the distance around a circle.

- $C = 2\pi r$ or $C = \pi d$
- Pi (π) is a constant numerical value and is an irrational number, meaning that it cannot be expressed as a fraction.
  - As a decimal, the digits have no pattern and continue forever.
- The ratio of the circumference to the diameter of any circle is equal to pi (π); i.e. $\pi = \dfrac{C}{d}$.
- $\pi = 3.14159$ (correct to 5 decimal places)
  - Common approximations include 3, 3.14 and $\dfrac{22}{7}$.
  - A more precise estimate for pi can be found on most calculators or on the internet.

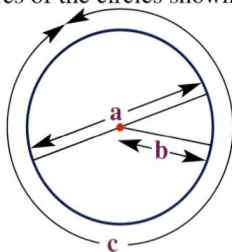

BUILDING UNDERSTANDING

1 State whether the following statements relating features of a circle are true or false.

a $r = 2d$ b $C = 2\pi r$ c $d = \pi C$

d $\pi = \dfrac{C}{d}$ e $\pi = \dfrac{C}{r}$ f $d = 2r$

2 Name the features of the circles shown.

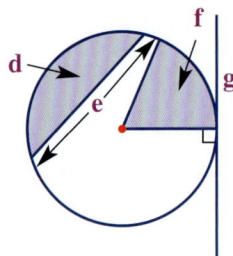

3 The following relate to a circle's radius and diameter.

a   Find a circle's diameter if its radius is 15 mm.

b   Find a circle's radius if its diameter is 8 cm.

Example 5   Approximating π

A common approximation of π is the fraction $\dfrac{22}{7}$.

a   Write $\dfrac{22}{7}$ as a decimal rounded to:

   i   two decimal places

   ii   three decimal places.

b   Decide if $\dfrac{22}{7}$ is a better approximation to π than the number 3.14.

SOLUTION

a i $\frac{22}{7} = 3.14$ (2 d.p.)

ii $\frac{22}{7} = 3.143$ (3 d.p.)

b $\frac{22}{7} = 3.14285...$ and $\pi = 3.14159...$

So, $\frac{22}{7}$ is a better approximation compared to 3.14.

EXPLANATION

$\frac{22}{7} = 3.142...$ so round down for 2 decimal places

$\frac{22}{7} = 3.1428...$ so round up for 3 decimal places

$\frac{22}{7} - \pi = 0.0013$ (4 d.p.) and $\pi - 3.14 = 0.0016$ (4 d.p.)

So, $\frac{22}{7}$ is closer to π.

Now you try

A possible approximation of π is the fraction $\frac{25}{8}$.

a Write $\frac{25}{8}$ as a decimal rounded to:

  i two decimal places

  ii three decimal places.

b Decide if $\frac{25}{8}$ is a better approximation to π than the number 3.14.

Example 6   Calculating the circumference

Calculate the circumference of these circles using a calculator and rounding your answer correct to two decimal places.

a

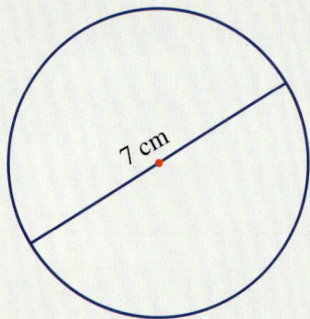

7 cm

b

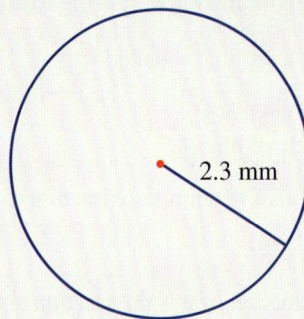

2.3 mm

SOLUTION

a $C = \pi d$
   $= \pi(7)$
   $= 21.99$ cm

EXPLANATION

Since you are given the diameter, use the $C = \pi d$ formula. Substitute $d = 7$ and use a calculator for the value of π. Round as required.

Continued on next page

b $C = 2\pi r$
$= 2\pi(2.3)$
$= 14.45\,\text{mm}$

Since you are given the diameter, use the $C = 2\pi r$ formula. Substitute $r = 2.3$ and use a calculator for the value of π. Round as required.

Now you try

Calculate the circumference of these circles using a calculator and rounding your answer correct to two decimal places.

a

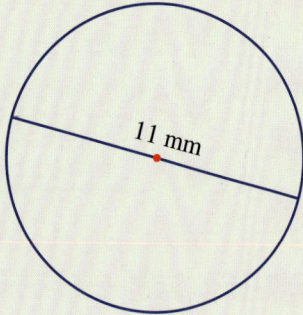

11 mm

b

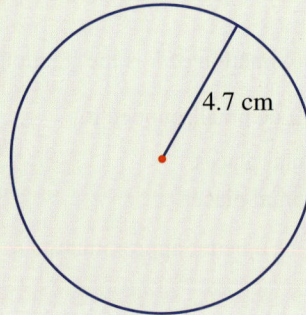

4.7 cm

Exercise 10C

FLUENCY   1, 2, 3–5(½)   2, 3–5(½)   2, 3–5(¼)

Example 5

1 A reasonable approximation of π is the fraction $\dfrac{28}{9}$.

    a Write $\dfrac{28}{9}$ as a decimal rounded to:

        i   two decimal places

        ii three decimal places.

    b Decide if $\dfrac{28}{9}$ is a better approximation to π than the number 3.14.

Example 5

2 A good approximation of π is the fraction $\dfrac{355}{113}$.

    a Write $\dfrac{355}{113}$ as a decimal rounded to:

        i   three decimal places

        ii four decimal places.

    b Decide if $\dfrac{355}{113}$ is a better approximation to π than the number 3.142.

The Ancient Greek mathematician and astronomer Archimedes was able to prove that π was between $\dfrac{223}{71}$ and $\dfrac{22}{7}$.

ample 6a

3 Calculate the circumference of these circles using $C = \pi d$ and round your answer correct to two decimal places.

a

5 cm

b

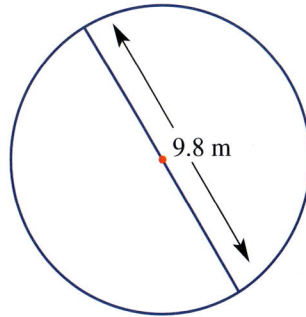

13 cm

c

4.6 m

d

9.8 m

mple 6b

4 Calculate the circumference of these circles using $C = 2\pi r$ and round your answer correct to two decimal places.

a

4 mm

b

21 cm

c

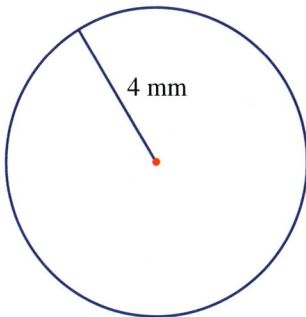

8.3 mm

d

16.2 m

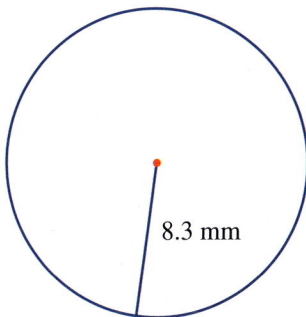

5 Estimate the circumference of these circles using the given approximation of π.

a

2 cm

$\pi = 3$

b

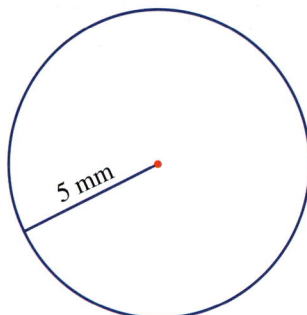

5 mm

$\pi = 3.14$

c

14 m

$\pi = \dfrac{22}{7}$

d

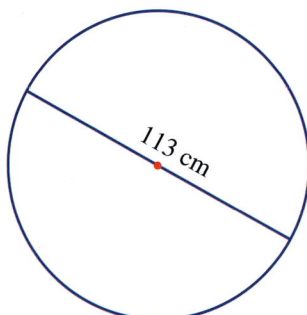

113 cm

$\pi = \dfrac{355}{113}$

PROBLEM SOLVING   6, 7   6–8   7–9

6 A log in a wood yard has a diameter of 40 cm. Find its circumference, correct to one decimal place.

7 We know that the rule $C = \pi d$ can be rearranged to give $d = \dfrac{C}{\pi}$. Use this rearranged rule to calculate the following, correct to two decimal places.
   a a circle's diameter if the circumference is 10 cm
   b a circle's diameter if the circumference is 12.5 m
   c a circle's radius if the circumference is 7 mm
   d a circle's radius if the circumference is 37.4 m

8 A circular pond has radius 1.4 metres. Find its circumference, correct to one decimal place.

9 A bicycle wheel completes 1024 revolutions while on a Sunday ride. Find the distance travelled by the bicycle if the wheel's diameter is 85 cm. Round to the nearest metre.

REASONING   10   10, 11   11, 12

10   The following are four fractions which ancient cultures used to approximate π.

   • Egyptian $\frac{22}{7}$

   • Babylonians $\frac{25}{8}$

   • Indian $\frac{339}{108}$

   • Chinese $\frac{142}{45}$

   a   Which one of these ancient historical approximations is closest to the true value of π? Note that π written to five decimal places is 3.14159.

   b   In more recent times, $\frac{22}{7}$ has been a very popular approximation throughout many countries. Explain why you think this is the case.

   c   Find your own simple fraction which is a reasonable approximation of π. Write your fraction as a decimal and compare it with π written in decimal form with at least five decimal places.

11   If $C = \pi d$, find a rule for the radius of a circle, r, in terms of its circumference, C, and use it to find the radius of a circle if its circumference is 25 cm. Round to two decimal places.

12   A professor expresses the circumference of a circle with diameter 5 cm using the exact value, 5π cm. Use an exact value to give the circumference of a circle with the given diameter or radius.

   a   Diameter 7 cm

   b   Radius 3 mm

ENRICHMENT: Planetary circumnavigation   –   –   13

13   While not being perfect spheres, the circumference of the planets in our solar system can be approximated by using a circle. Here are some planetary facts with some missing details. Calculate the missing numbers, rounding to the nearest integer.

Part	Planet	Diameter (km approx.)	Circumference (km approx.)
a	Earth	12 750	
b	Mars	6 780	
c	Jupiter		439 260
d	Mercury		15 330

10D   Arc length and perimeter of sectors and composite shapes   EXTENDING

Whenever a portion of a circle's circumference is used in a diagram or construction, an arc is formed. To determine the arc's length, the particular fraction of the circle is calculated by considering the angle at the centre of the circle that defines the arc.

Lesson starter: The rule for finding an arc length

Complete this table to develop the rule for finding an arc length (l).

Angle	Fraction of circle	Arc length	Diagram
180°	$\frac{180}{360} = \frac{1}{2}$	$l = \frac{1}{2} \times \pi d$	
90°	$\frac{90}{360} = $ _____	$l = $ _____ $\times$ _____	
45°			
30°			
150°			
θ			

KEY IDEAS

■ A circular **arc** is a portion of the circumference of a circle.
In the diagram:
r = radius of circle
$a°$ = number of degrees in the angle at the centre of a circle
l = **arc length**
Formula for arc length:

$$l = \frac{a°}{360} \times 2\pi r \text{ or } l = \frac{a°}{360} \times \pi d$$

■ The sector also has two straight edges, each with length of r.
Formula for perimeter of **sector**:

$$P = \frac{a°}{360} \times 2\pi r + 2r \text{ or } P = \frac{a°}{360} \times \pi d + d$$

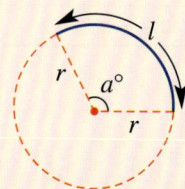

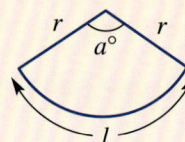

■ Common circle portions

quadrant   **semicircle**

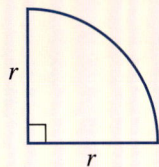

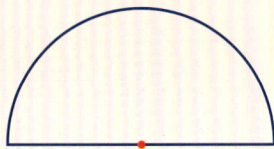

$$P = \frac{1}{4} \times 2\pi r + 2r \qquad P = \frac{1}{2} \times 2\pi r + 2r$$

■ A **composite figure** is made up of more than one basic shape.

BUILDING UNDERSTANDING

1 What fraction of a circle is shown in these diagrams? Name each shape.

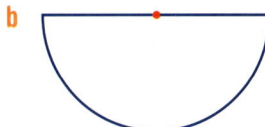

a   b

2 What fraction of a circle is shown in these sectors? Simplify your fraction.

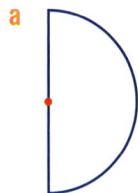

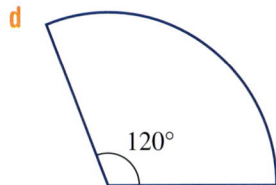

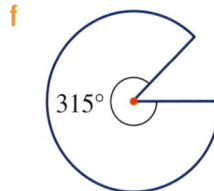

a   b   c 60°

d 120°   e   f 315°

3 Name the two basic shapes that make up these composite figures.

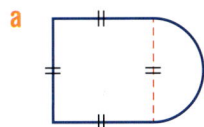

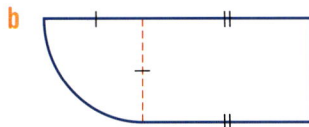

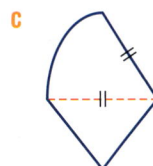

a   b   c

Example 7 Finding an arc length

Find the length of each of these arcs for the given angles, correct to two decimal places.

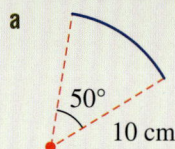

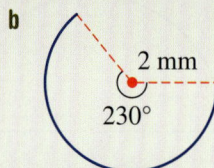

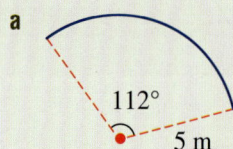

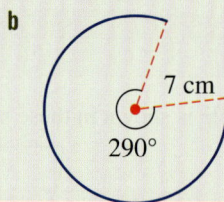

a

50°
10 cm

b

2 mm
230°

SOLUTION

a $l = \dfrac{50}{360} \times 2\pi \times 10$

$= 8.73\,\text{cm}$

b $l = \dfrac{230}{360} \times 2\pi \times 2$

$= 8.03\,\text{mm}$

EXPLANATION

The fraction of the full circumference is $\dfrac{50}{360}$ and the full circumference is $2\pi r$, where $r = 10$.

The fraction of the full circumference is $\dfrac{230}{360}$ and the full circumference is $2\pi r$, where $r = 2$.

Now you try

Find the length of each of these arcs for the given angles, correct to two decimal places.

a

112°
5 m

b

7 cm
290°

Example 8 Finding the perimeter of a sector

Find the perimeter of each of these sectors, correct to one decimal place.

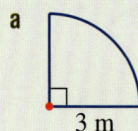

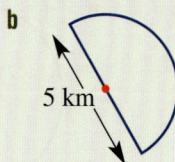

a

3 m

b

5 km

SOLUTION

a $P = \dfrac{1}{4} \times 2\pi \times 3 + 2 \times 3$

$= 10.7\,\text{m}$

b $P = \dfrac{1}{2} \times \pi \times 5 + 5$

$= 12.9\,\text{km}$

EXPLANATION

The arc length is one-quarter of the circumference and included are two radii, each of 3 m.

A semicircle's perimeter consists of half the circumference of a circle plus a full diameter. In this case, the whole circle's circumference is found using $\pi \times d$ since we have the diameter.

Now you try

Find the perimeter of each of these sectors, correct to one decimal place.

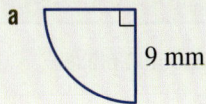

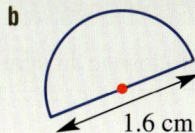

a

9 mm

b

1.6 cm

Example 9   Finding the perimeter of a composite shape

Find the perimeter of the following composite shape, correct to one decimal place.

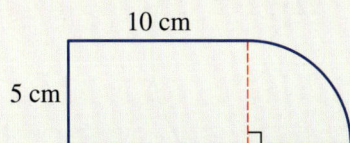

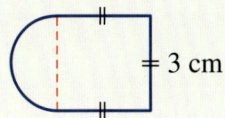

10 cm

5 cm

SOLUTION

$P = 10 + 5 + 10 + 5 + \frac{1}{4} \times 2\pi \times 5$

$= 37.9\,\text{cm}$

EXPLANATION

There are two straight sides of 10 cm and 5 cm shown in the diagram. The radius of the circle is 5 cm, so the straight edge at the base of the diagram is 15 cm long. The arc is a quarter circle.

Now you try

Find the perimeter of the following composite shape, correct to one decimal place.

3 cm

Exercise 10D

FLUENCY

| 1,(½), 2–4 | 1–4(½) | 1(⅓), 2–4(½) |

Example 7

1 Find the length of each of the following arcs for the given angles, correct to two decimal places.

a

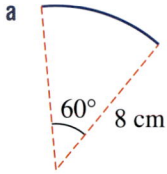

60° 8 cm

b

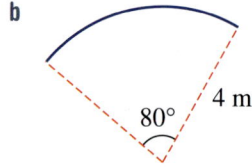

80° 4 m

c

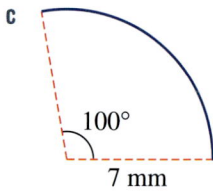

100°
7 mm

d

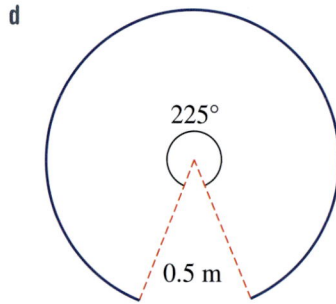

225°
0.5 m

e

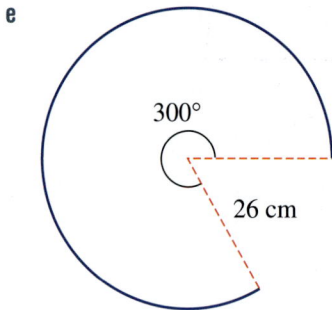

300°
26 cm

f

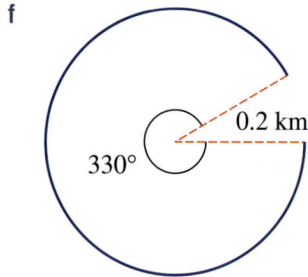

330° 0.2 km

Example 8a

2 Find the perimeter of each of these quadrants, correct to one decimal place.

a

4 cm

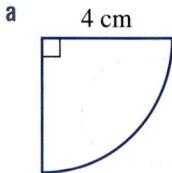

b

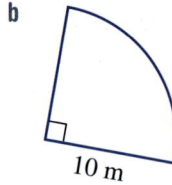

10 m

c

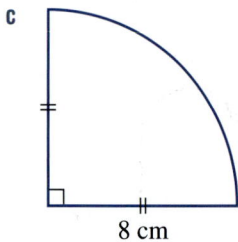

8 cm

d

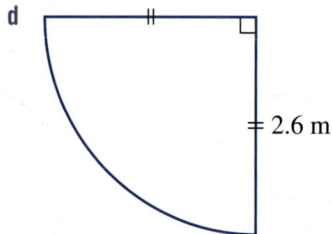

2.6 m

3 Find the perimeter of these semicircles, correct to one decimal place.

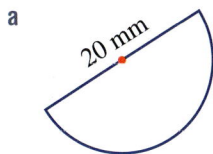

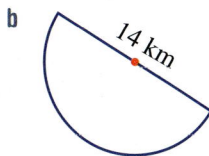

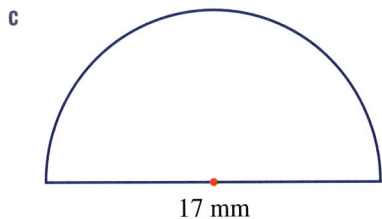

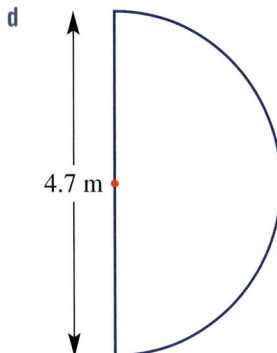

a 20 mm

b 14 km

c 17 mm

d 4.7 m

4 Find the perimeter of these sectors, correct to one decimal place. Include the two radii in each case.

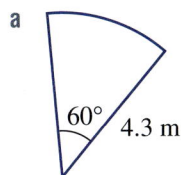

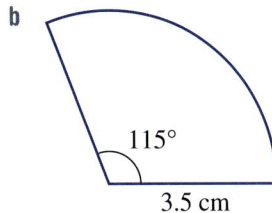

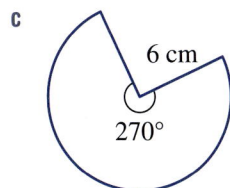

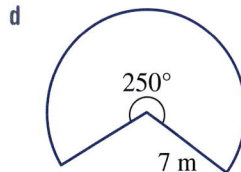

a 60° 4.3 m

b 115° 3.5 cm

c 6 cm 270°

d 250° 7 m

PROBLEM-SOLVING   5, 6   5–7   5–8

5 Find the perimeter of each of these composite shapes, correct to one decimal place.

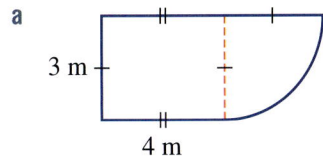

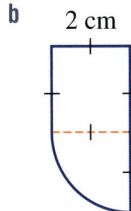

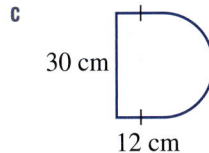

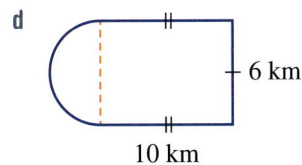

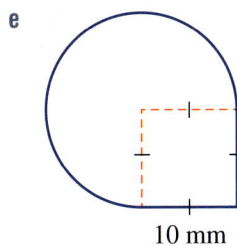

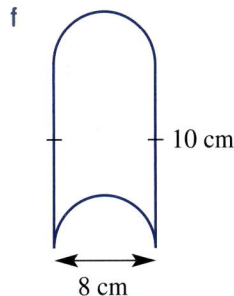

a 3 m 4 m

b 2 cm

c 30 cm 12 cm

d 6 km 10 km

e 10 mm

f 10 cm 8 cm

6   A window consists of a rectangular part of height 2 m and width 1 m, with a semicircular top having a diameter of 1 m. Find its perimeter, correct to the nearest 1 cm.

7   For these sectors, find only the length of the arc, correct to two decimal places.

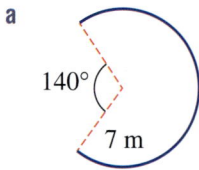

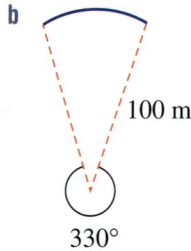

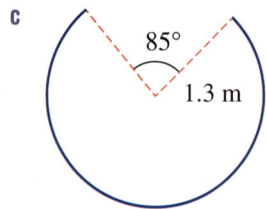

a

140°

7 m

b

100 m

330°

c

85°

1.3 m

8   Calculate the perimeter of each of these shapes, correct to two decimal places.

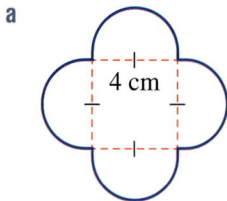

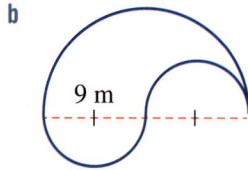

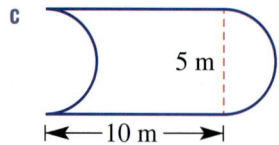

a

4 cm

b

9 m

c

5 m

10 m

REASONING   9   9, 10   9–11

9   Give reasons why the circumference of this composite shape can be found by simply using the rule $P = 2\pi r + 4r$.

r

10   Explain why the perimeter of this shape is given by $P = 2\pi r$.

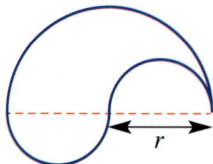

r

11 Find the radius of each of these sectors for the given arc lengths, correct to one decimal place.

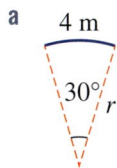

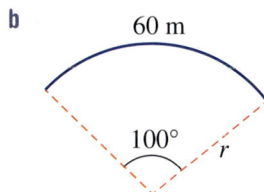

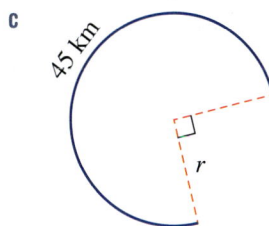

a

4 m

30° r

b

60 m

100° r

c

45 km

r

ENRICHMENT: Exact values and perimeters　　—　　　—　　　12, 13

12 The working to find the exact perimeter of this composite shape is given by:

$$P = 2 \times 8 + 4 + \frac{1}{2}\pi \times 4$$
$$= 20 + 8\pi \, \text{cm}$$

4 cm

8 cm

Find the exact perimeter of each of the following composite shapes.

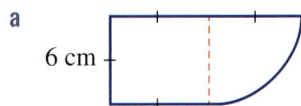

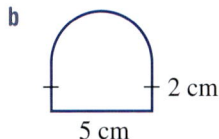

a

6 cm

b

2 cm

5 cm

13 Find the exact answers for Question **8** in terms of π.

10E   Units of area and area of rectangles

LEARNING INTENTIONS

• To understand what the area of a two-dimensional shape is
• To be able to convert between metric areas (square millimetres, square centimetres, square metres, square kilometres, hectares)
• To be able to find the area of squares and other rectangles

Area is measured in square units. It is often referred to as the amount of space contained inside a flat (i.e. plane) shape; however, curved three-dimensional (3D) solids also have surface areas.

The amount of paint needed to paint a house and the amount of chemical needed to spray a paddock are examples of when area would be considered.

Agricultural pilots fly small planes that spray crops with fertiliser or pesticide. The plane is flown up and down the paddock many times, until all the area has been sprayed.

Lesson starter: The 12 cm² rectangle

A rectangle has an area of 12 square centimetres $(12\,\text{cm}^2)$.

• Draw examples of rectangles that have this area, showing the length and width measurements.
• How many different rectangles with whole number dimensions are possible?
• How many different rectangles are possible if there is no restriction on the type of numbers allowed to be used for length and width?

KEY IDEAS

■ The metric units of area include:
  • 1 square millimetre $(1\,\text{mm}^2)$
  • 1 square centimetre $(1\,\text{cm}^2)$
    $1\,\text{cm}^2 = 100\,\text{mm}^2$

  • 1 square metre $(1\,\text{m}^2)$
    $1\,\text{m}^2 = 10\,000\,\text{cm}^2$

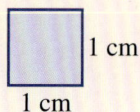
□ 1 mm
1 mm

1 cm
1 cm

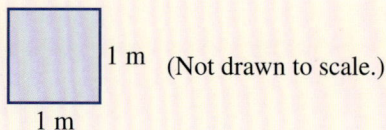
1 m   (Not drawn to scale.)
1 m

- 1 square kilometre $(1\,\text{km}^2)$
  $1\,\text{km}^2 = 1\,000\,000\,\text{m}^2$

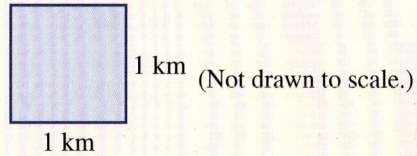

1 km (Not drawn to scale.)

1 km

- 1 hectare $(1\,\text{ha})$
  $1\,\text{ha} = 10\,000\,\text{m}^2$

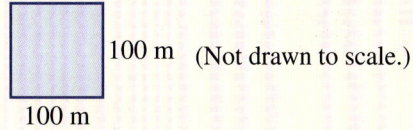

100 m (Not drawn to scale.)

100 m

■ The dimensions of a rectangle are called length (l) and width (w).

■ The area of a rectangle is given by the number of rows multiplied by the number of columns. Written as a formula, this looks like: $A = l \times w$. This also works for numbers that are not integers.

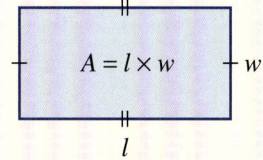

■ The area of a square is given by: $A = l \times l = l^2$

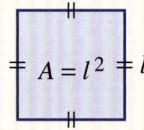

BUILDING UNDERSTANDING

1 For this rectangle drawn on a 1 cm grid, find each of the following.
   a the number of single 1 cm squares
   b the length and the width
   c length × width

2 For this square drawn on a centimetre grid, find the following.
   a the number of single 1 cm squares
   b the length and the width
   c length × width

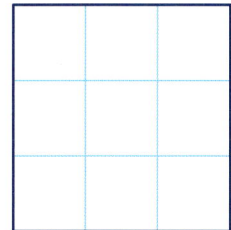

3 Count the number of squares to find the area in square units of these shapes.

   a 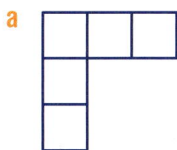   **b** 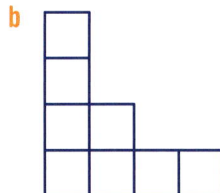   **c**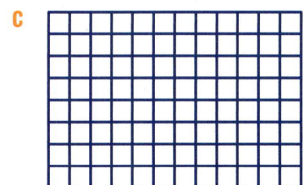

4   Which unit of area (mm^2, cm^2, m^2, ha or km^2) would you choose to measure these areas? Note that 1 km^2 is much larger than 1 ha.

 a   area of an A4 piece of paper
 b   area of a wall of a house
 c   area of a small farm
 d   area of a large desert
 e   area of a large football oval
 f   area of a nail head

Example 10   Counting areas

Count the number of squares to find the area of the shape drawn on this centimetre grid.

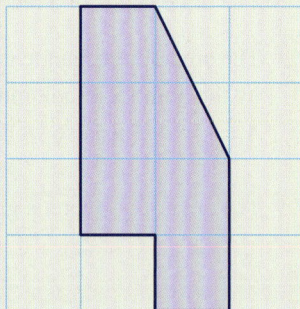

SOLUTION

6 cm^2

EXPLANATION

There are 5 full squares and half of 2 squares in the triangle, giving 1 more.

$\frac{1}{2}$ of 2 = 1

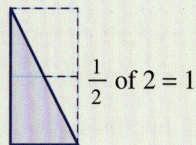

Now you try

Count the number of squares to find the area of the shape drawn on this centimetre grid.

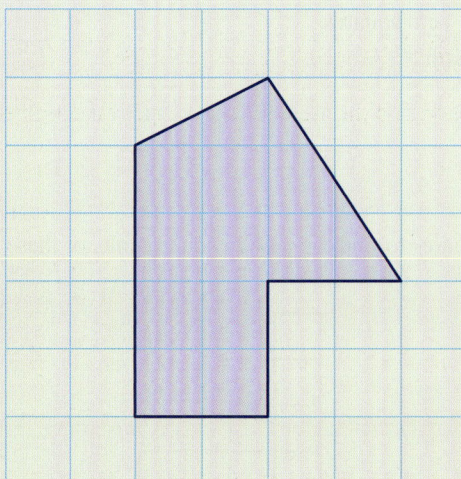

Example 11   Finding areas of rectangles and squares

Find the area of this rectangle and square.

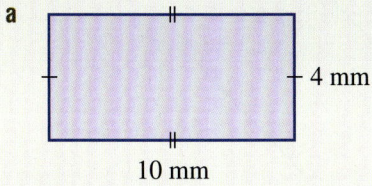

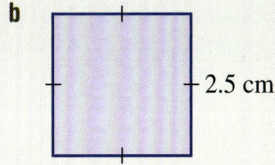

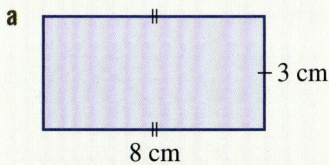

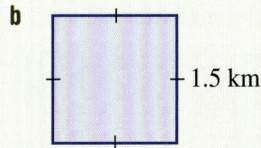

a

4 mm

10 mm

b

2.5 cm

SOLUTION

a   Area $= l \times w$
$= 10 \times 4$
$= 40\,\text{mm}^2$

b   Area $= l^2$
$= 2.5^2$
$= 6.25\,\text{cm}^2$

EXPLANATION

The area of a rectangle is the product of the length and width.

The width is the same as the length, so
$A = l \times l = l^2$
$(2.5)^2 = 2.5 \times 2.5$

Now you try

Find the area of this rectangle and square.

a

3 cm

8 cm

b

1.5 km

Exercise 10E

FLUENCY   1, 2, 3(½), 4–6   2, 3(½), 4, 5, 7   2–3(½), 4, 5, 7, 8

Example 10

1   Count the number of squares to find the area of these shapes on centimetre grids.

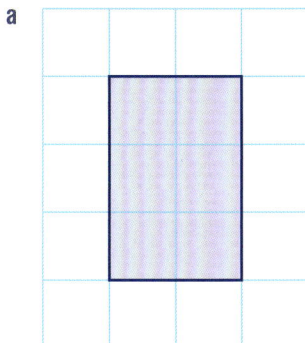

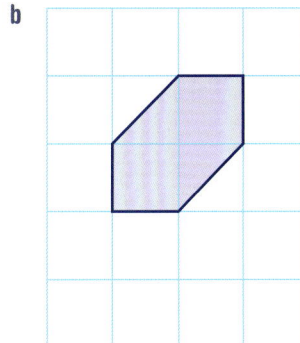

a

b

Example 10   **2** Count the number of squares to find the area of these shapes on centimetre grids.

a

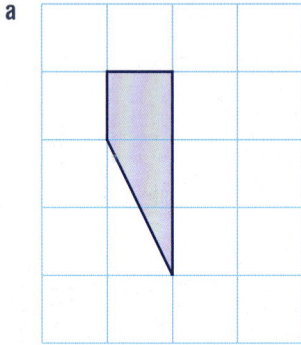

b

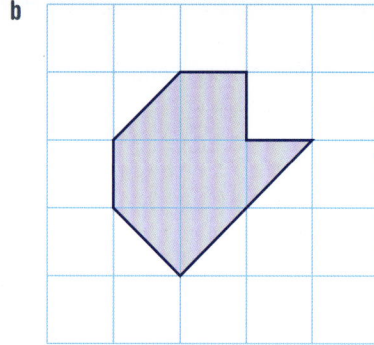

c

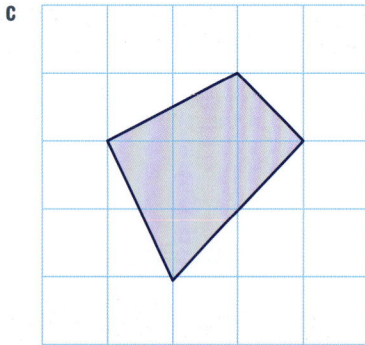

d

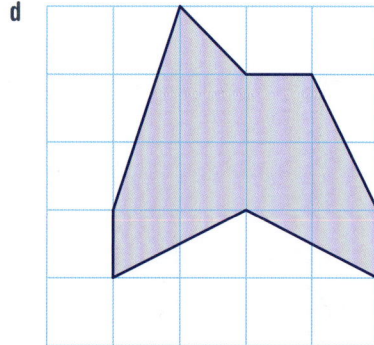

Example 11   **3** Find the area of these rectangles and squares. Diagrams are not drawn to scale.

a

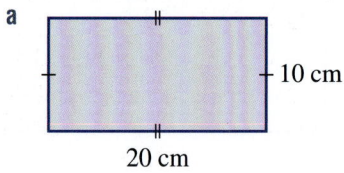

10 cm

20 cm

b

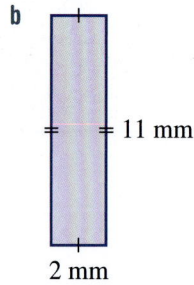

11 mm

2 mm

c

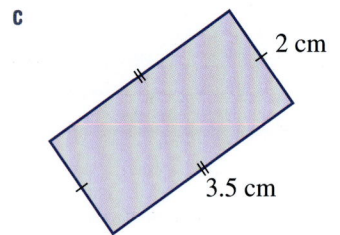

2 cm

3.5 cm

d

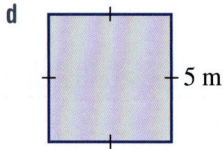

5 m

e

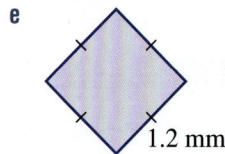

1.2 mm

f

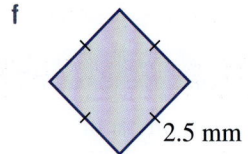

2.5 mm

g

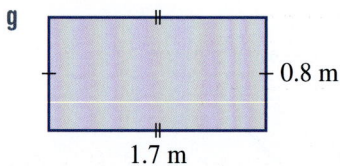

0.8 m

1.7 m

h

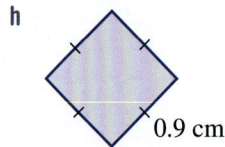

0.9 cm

i

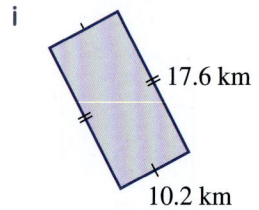

17.6 km

10.2 km

4 Find the side length of a square with each of these areas. Use trial and error if you are unsure.

a $4\,\text{cm}^2$ **b** $25\,\text{m}^2$ **c** $144\,\text{km}^2$

5 There are $10\,000\,\text{m}^2$ in one hectare (ha). Convert these measurements to hectares.

   a $20\,000\,\text{m}^2$ **b** $100\,000\,\text{m}^2$ **c** $5000\,\text{m}^2$

6 A rectangular soccer field is to be laid with new grass. The field is $100\,\text{m}$ long and $50\,\text{m}$ wide. Find the area of grass to be laid.

7 Glass is to be cut for a square window of side length $50\,\text{cm}$. Find the area of glass required for the window.

8 Two hundred square tiles, each measuring $10\,\text{cm}$ by $10\,\text{cm}$, are used to tile an open floor area. Find the area of flooring that is tiled.

PROBLEM-SOLVING   9, 10   9–11   9, 11, 12

9 **a** A square has a perimeter of $20\,\text{cm}$. Find its area.

   b A square has an area of $9\,\text{cm}^2$. Find its perimeter.

   c A square's area and perimeter are the same number. How many units is the side length?

10 The carpet chosen for a room costs $70 per square metre. The room is rectangular and is $6\,\text{m}$ long by $5\,\text{m}$ wide. What is the cost of carpeting the room?

11 Troy wishes to paint a garden wall that is $11\,\text{m}$ long and $3\,\text{m}$ high. Two coats of paint are needed. The paint suitable to do the job can be purchased only in whole numbers of litres and covers an area of $15\,\text{m}^2$ per litre. How many litres of paint will Troy need to purchase?

12 A rectangular area of land measures $200\,\text{m}$ by $400\,\text{m}$. Find its area in hectares.

REASONING   13   13, 14   14–16

13 **a** Find the missing length for each of these rectangles.

   i   **ii**

      $A = 50\,\text{cm}^2$ $5\,\text{cm}$ $A = 22.5\,\text{mm}^2$ $2.5\,\text{mm}$

            ?   ?

   b Explain the method that you used for finding the missing lengths of the rectangles above.

14 Explain why the area shaded here is exactly $2\,\text{cm}^2$.

                                            $1\,\text{cm}$

                                       $4\,\text{cm}$

15 A square has perimeter P cm.

   a If $P = 44$, find the area of the square.

   b If P is unknown, write an expression for the area of the square, using P.

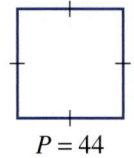

$P = 44$

16 A square has all its side lengths doubled. How does this change the area? Investigate and justify your answer.

ENRICHMENT: Area conversions   17

17 a Use this diagram or similar to help answer the following.

   i How many mm^2 in 1 cm^2?

   ii How many cm^2 in 1 m^2?

   iii How many m^2 in 1 km^2?

10 mm

10 mm

$A = 1$ cm^2

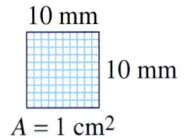

   b Complete the diagram below.

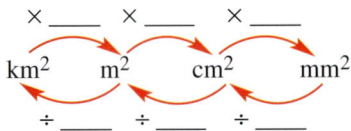

$$\times \underline{\quad} \quad \times \underline{\quad} \quad \times \underline{\quad}$$

km^2 m^2 cm^2 mm^2

$$\div \underline{\quad} \quad \div \underline{\quad} \quad \div \underline{\quad}$$

   c Convert these units to the units shown in brackets.

   i 2 cm^2 (mm^2)

   ii 10 m^2 (cm^2)

   iii 3.5 km^2 (m^2)

   iv 300 mm^2 (cm^2)

   v 21 600 cm^2 (m^2)

   vi 4 200 000 m^2 (km^2)

   vii 0.005 m^2 (mm^2)

   viii 1 km^2 (ha)

   ix 40 000 000 cm^2 (ha)

Working with different units of area is important in the division of land.

10F   Area of parallelograms

LEARNING INTENTIONS
* To understand that the area of a parallelogram is related to the area of a rectangle
* To be able to find the area of a parallelogram given its base and height

Recall that a parallelogram is a quadrilateral with two pairs of parallel sides. Opposite sides are of the same length and opposite angles are equal.

Like a triangle, the area of a parallelogram is found by using the length of one side (called the base) and the height (which is perpendicular to the base.)

Whenever pairs of parallel straight lines meet a parallelogram is formed, including an area which can be calculated using a base length and a perpendicular height.

Lesson starter: Developing the rule

Start this activity by drawing a large parallelogram on a loose piece of paper. Ensure the opposite sides are parallel and then use scissors to cut it out. Label one side as the base and label the height, as shown in the diagram.

* Cut along the dotted line.
* Now shift the triangle to the other end of the parallelogram to make a rectangle.
* Now explain how to find the area of a parallelogram.

KEY IDEAS

■ A **parallelogram** is a quadrilateral with both pairs of opposite sides parallel.
- For parallelograms, the dimensions are called base (b) and perpendicular height (h).
- The base can be *any* side of the parallelogram.
- The height is perpendicular to the base.

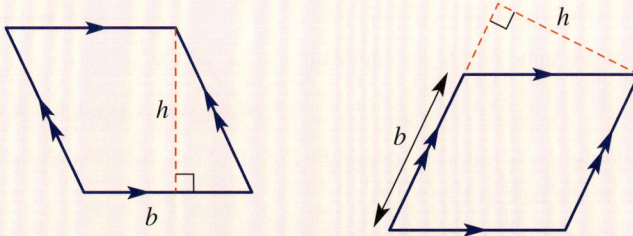

- The area of a parallelogram is base × perpendicular height.

■ The formula for the area of a parallelogram is:

$A = b \times h$

A = area
b = length of the base
h = perpendicular height

BUILDING UNDERSTANDING

1 State the missing numbers, using the given values of b and h.

a $b = 5, h = 7$
$A = bh$
$= \underline{} \times \underline{}$
$= 35$

b $b = 20, h = 3$
$A = \underline{}$
$= 20 \times \underline{}$
$= \underline{}$

c $b = 8, h = 2.5$
$A = \underline{}$
$= 8 \times \underline{}$
$= \underline{}$

2 For each of these parallelograms, state the side length of the base and the height that might be used to find the area.

a
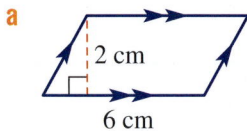
2 cm
6 cm

b
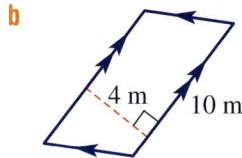
4 m
10 m

c
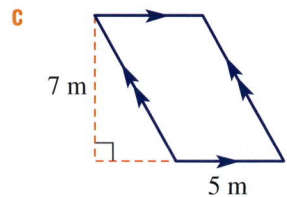
7 m
5 m

d
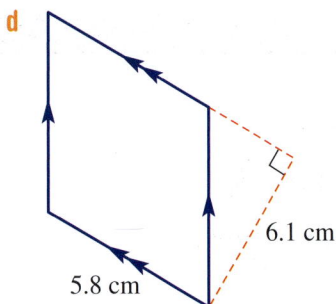
6.1 cm
5.8 cm

e
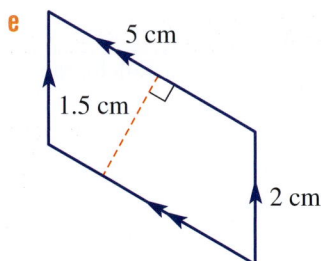
5 cm
1.5 cm
2 cm

f
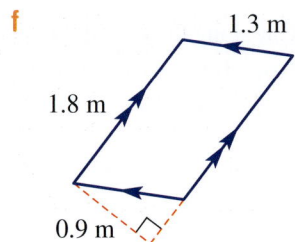
1.3 m
1.8 m
0.9 m

Example 12   Finding the area of a parallelogram

Find the area of these parallelograms.

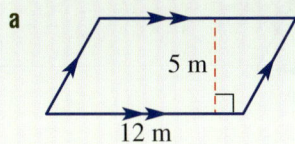

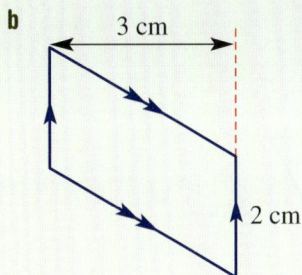

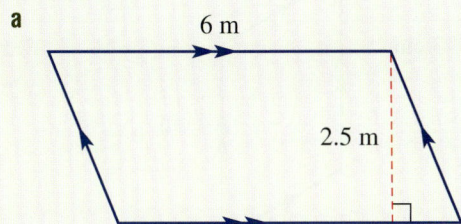

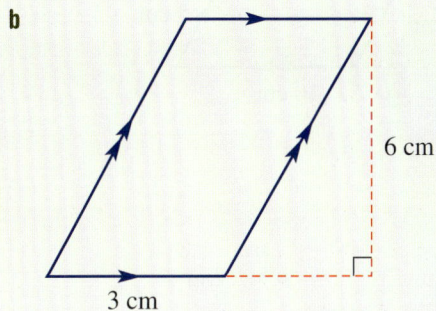

a

5 m
12 m

b

3 cm
2 cm

SOLUTION

a $A = bh$
   $= 12 \times 5$
   $= 60$ m^2

b $A = bh$
   $= 2 \times 3$
   $= 6$ cm^2

EXPLANATION

Choose the given side as the base (12 m) and note the perpendicular height is 5 m.

Use the given side as the base (2 cm), noting that the height is 3 cm.

Now you try

Find the area of these parallelograms.

a

6 m
2.5 m

b

6 cm
3 cm

Exercise 10F

FLUENCY   1, 2(½), 3, 4(½), 5   2, 4, 5   2(½), 4(½), 5, 6

ple 12a   **1**   Find the area of these parallelograms.

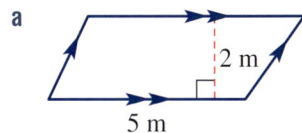

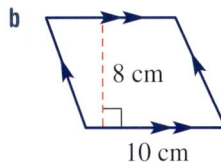

a   2 m   5 m

b   8 cm   10 cm

Example 12a   **2**   Find the area of these parallelograms.

a

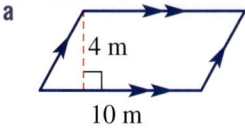

4 m
10 m

b

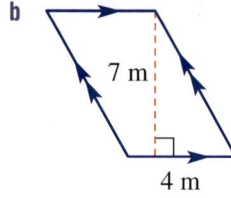

7 m
4 m

c

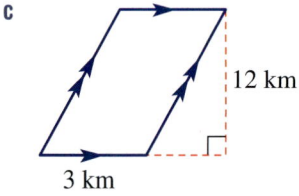

12 km
3 km

d

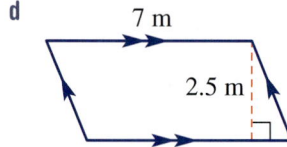

7 m
2.5 m

Example 12b   **3**   Find the area of these parallelograms.

a

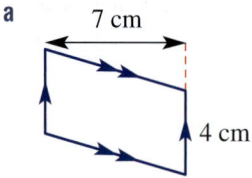

7 cm
4 cm

b

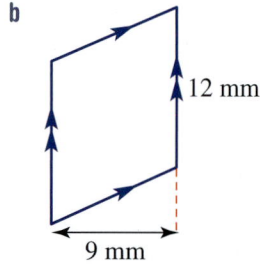

12 mm
9 mm

Example 12b   **4**   Find the area of these parallelograms. Note that you will need to consider which dimensions are the base and the height.

a

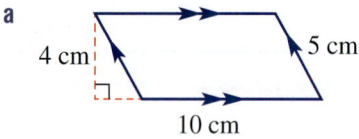

4 cm
5 cm
10 cm

b

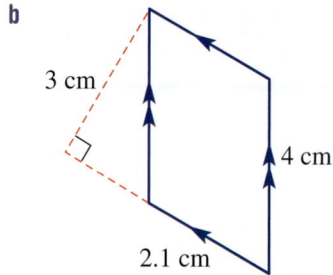

3 cm
4 cm
2.1 cm

c

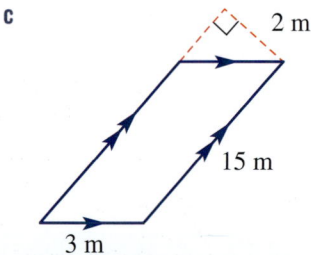

2 m
15 m
3 m

d

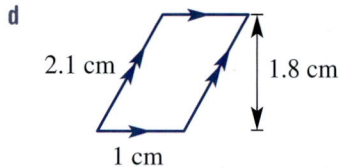

2.1 cm
1.8 cm
1 cm

5   These parallelograms are on 1 cm grids (not to scale). Find their area.

a

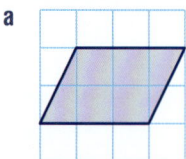

b

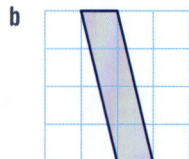

c

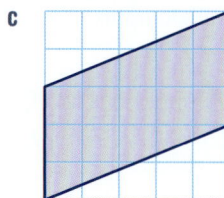

d

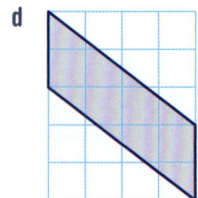

6 The floor of an office space is in the shape of a parallelogram. The longest sides are 9 m and the perpendicular distance between them is 6 m. Find the area of the office floor.

PROBLEM-SOLVING   7, 8   8, 9   8–10

7 Find the height of a parallelogram when its:
   a area = 10 m² and base = 5 m
   b area = 28 cm² and base = 4 cm
   c area = 2.5 mm² and base = 5 mm

8 Find the base of a parallelogram when its:
   a area = 40 cm² and height = 4 cm
   b area = 150 m² and height = 30 m
   c area = 2.4 km² and height = 1.2 km

9 A large wall in the shape of a parallelogram is to be painted with a special red paint, which costs $20 per litre. Each litre of paint covers 5 m². The wall has a base length of 30 m and a height of 10 m. Find the cost of painting the wall.

10 A proposed rectangular flag for a new country is yellow with a red stripe in the shape of a parallelogram, as shown.
   a Find the area of the red stripe.
   b Find the yellow area.

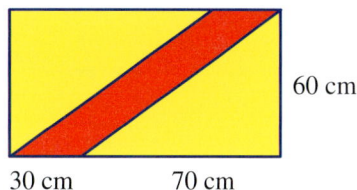

60 cm

30 cm   70 cm

REASONING   11   11, 12   12, 13

11 Explain why this parallelogram's area will be less than the given rectangle's area.

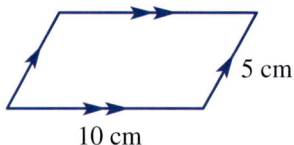

5 cm

10 cm

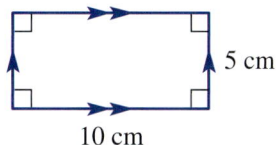

5 cm

10 cm

12 A parallelogram includes a green triangular area, as shown. What fraction of the total area is the green area? Give reasons for your answer.

13 The area of a parallelogram can be thought of as twice the area of a triangle. Use this idea to complete this proof of the rule for the area of a parallelogram.

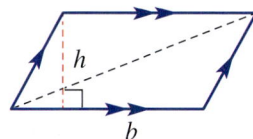

h

b

Area = twice triangle area
   = 2 × _____
   = _____

14 The Puerta de Europa (Gate of Europe) towers are twin office buildings in Madrid, Spain. They look like normal rectangular glass-covered skyscrapers but they lean towards each other at an angle of 15° to the vertical. Two sides are parallelograms and two sides are rectangles. Each tower has a vertical height of 120 m, a slant height of 130 m and a square base of side 50 m.

All four sides are covered with glass. If the glass costs $180 per square metre, find the cost of covering *one* of the towers with glass. (Assume the glass covers the entire surface, ignoring the beams.)

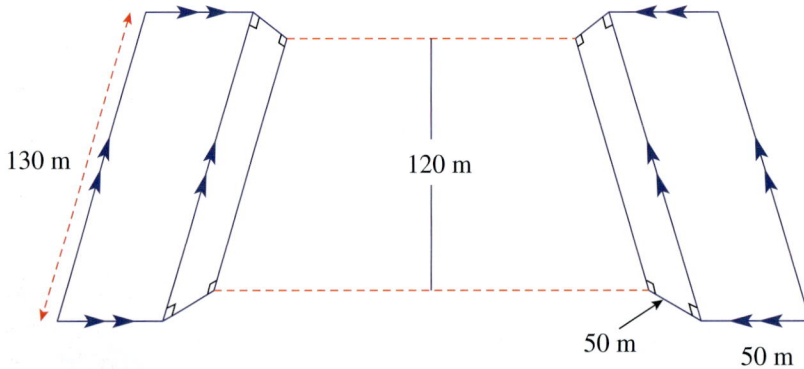

10G Area of triangles

In terms of area, a triangle can be considered to be half a parallelogram, which is why the formula for the area of a triangle is the same as for a parallelogram but with the added factor of $\frac{1}{2}$. One of the sides of a triangle is called the base (b), and the height (h) is the distance between the base and the opposite vertex. This is illustrated using a line that is perpendicular (i.e. at 90°) to the base.

Any shape with all straight sides (i.e. polygons) can be divided up into a combination of rectangles (or squares) and triangles. This can help to find areas of such shapes.

The Flatiron Building, New York City, was built in 1902 on a triangular block of land. Each of its 22 floors is an isosceles triangle, like the triangular shape of an iron.

Lesson starter: Half a parallelogram

Consider a triangle which is duplicated, rotated and joined to the original triangle as shown.

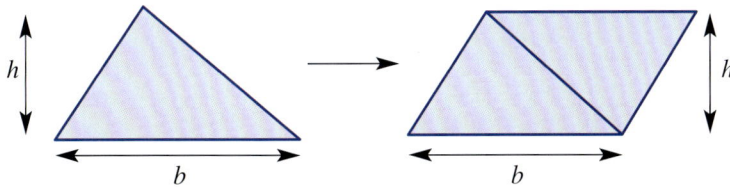

- What type of shape is the one to the right?
- What is the rule for the area of the shape to the right?
- What does this tell you about the rule for the original triangle?

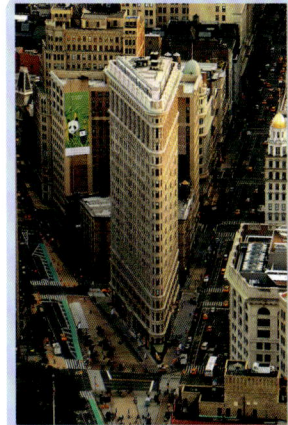

KEY IDEAS

■ A triangle's dimensions are called the **base** (b) and **height** (h).
- The base can be any side of the triangle.
- The height is **perpendicular** to the base.

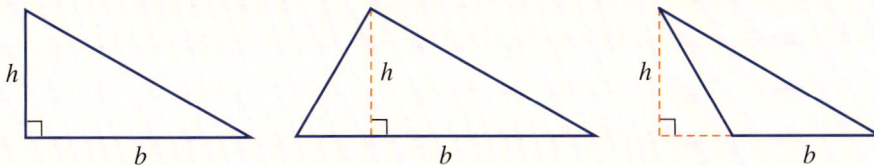

■ The area of a triangle is given by the formula:

$$A = \frac{1}{2} bh = \frac{1}{2} \times \text{base} \times \text{height}$$

Note that $\frac{1}{2} bh$ is equivalent to $\frac{bh}{2}$ or $b \times h \div 2$.
- The area of triangle is half the area of a parallelogram.

BUILDING UNDERSTANDING

1 For each of these triangles, what length would be used as the base?

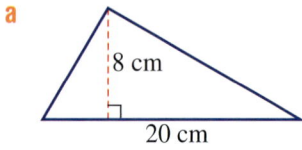

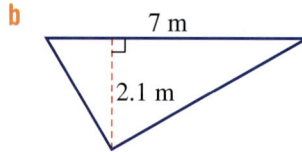

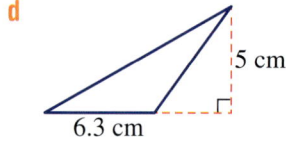

a

8 cm

20 cm

b

7 m

2.1 m

c

2 m

3 m

d

5 cm

6.3 cm

2 For each of these triangles, what length would be used as the height?

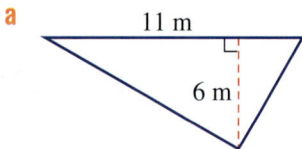

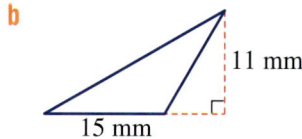

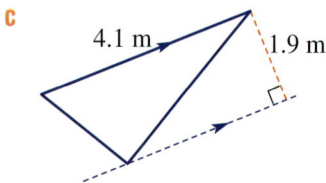

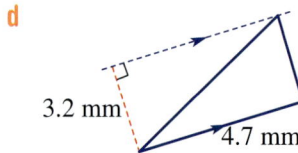

a

11 m

6 m

b

11 mm

15 mm

c

4.1 m   1.9 m

d

3.2 mm

4.7 mm

3 State the value of A in $A = \frac{1}{2}bh$ if:

a $b = 5$ and $h = 4$ **b** $b = 7$ and $h = 16$ **c** $b = 2.5$ and $h = 10$

Example 13   Finding areas of triangles

Find the area of each given triangle.

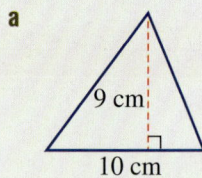

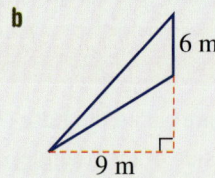

a

9 cm

10 cm

b

6 m

9 m

SOLUTION

a area $= \frac{1}{2}bh$

$= \frac{1}{2} \times 10 \times 9$

$= 45 \text{ cm}^2$

b area $= \frac{1}{2}bh$

$= \frac{1}{2} \times 6 \times 9$

$= 27 \text{ m}^2$

EXPLANATION

Use the formula and substitute the values for base length and height.

The length measure of 9 m is marked at 90° to the side marked 6 m. So 6 m is the length of the base and 9 m is the perpendicular height.

Now you try

Find the area of each given triangle.

a

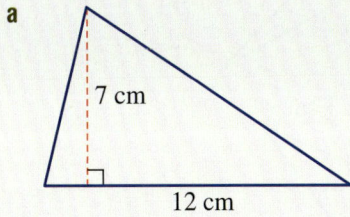

7 cm

12 cm

b

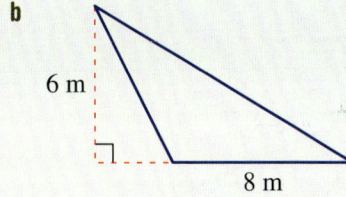

6 m

8 m

Exercise 10G

FLUENCY   1, 2(½), 3, 4(½), 5   2(½), 4(½), 5, 6   2(½), 4–5(½), 7

ple 13a **1** Find the area of each triangle given.

a

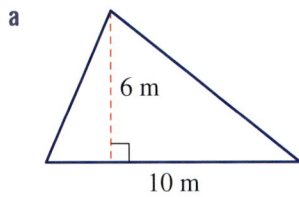

6 m

10 m

b   8 cm

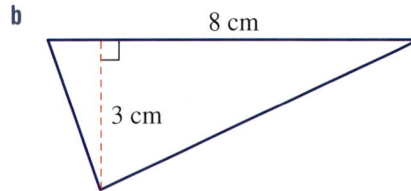

3 cm

ple 13a **2** Find the area of each triangle given.

a

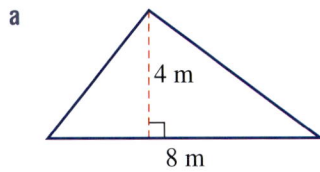

4 m

8 m

b   12 cm

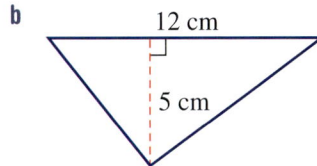

5 cm

c

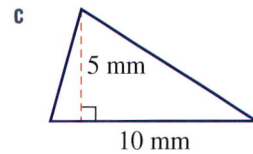

5 mm

10 mm

d

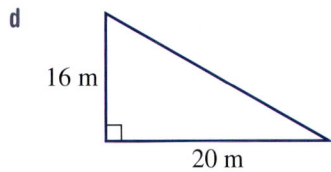

16 m

20 m

e

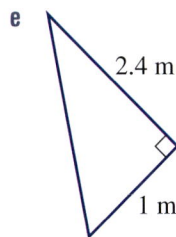

2.4 m

1 m

f   2.5 cm

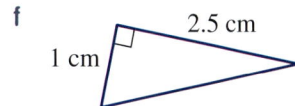

1 cm

ple 13b **3** Find the area of each triangle given.

a

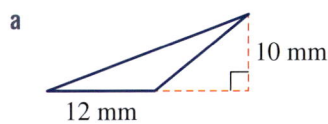

10 mm

12 mm

b

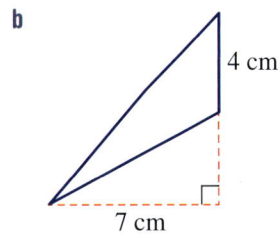

4 cm

7 cm

Example 13b

4 Find the area of each of the following triangles.

a

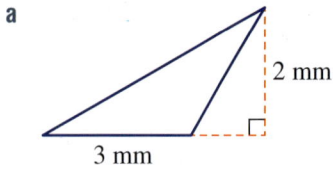

2 mm

3 mm

b   7 km

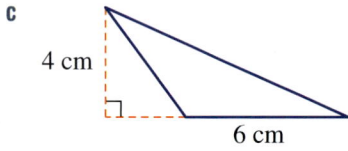

7 km

c

4 cm

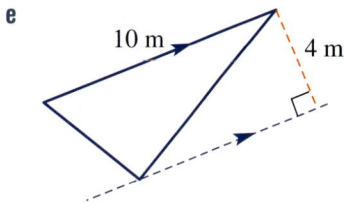

6 cm

d   1.3 cm

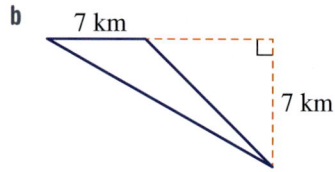

2 cm

e

10 m   4 m

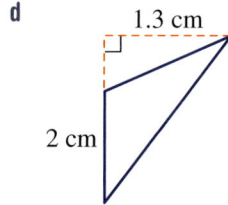

f   1.7 m

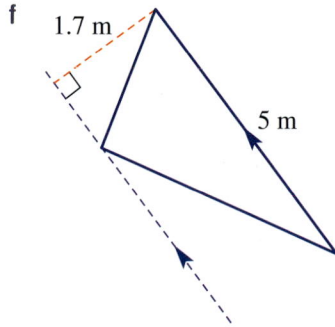

5 m

5 Find the area of these triangles, which have been drawn on 1 cm grids. Give your answer in cm^2.

a

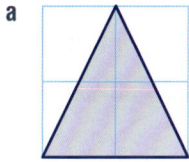

b

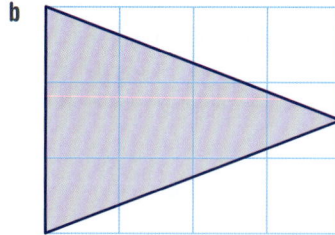

c

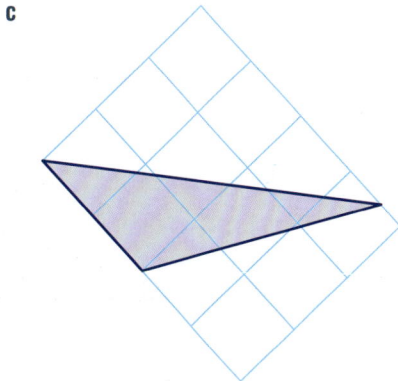

d

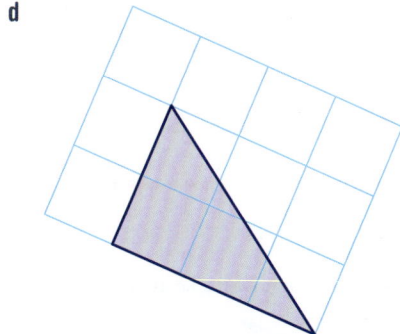

6 A rectangular block of land measuring 40 m long by 24 m wide is cut in half along a diagonal. Find the area of each triangular block of land.

7 A square pyramid has a base length of 120 m and a triangular face of height 80 m. Find the area of one triangular face of the pyramid.

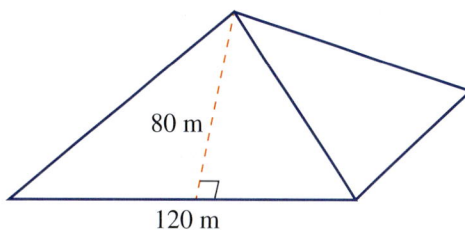

80 m
120 m

PROBLEM-SOLVING　　　8, 9　　　9, 10　　　9–11

8 Each face of a 4-sided die is triangular, with a base of 2 cm and a height of 1.7 cm. Find the total area of all 4 faces of the die.

9 A farmer uses fencing to divide a triangular piece of land into two smaller triangles, as shown. What is the difference in the two areas?

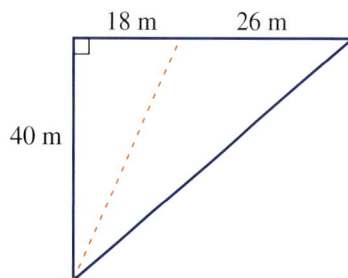

18 m　　26 m

40 m

10 A yacht must have two of its sails replaced as they have been damaged by a recent storm. One sail has a base length of 2.5 m and a height of 8 m and the bigger sail has a base length of 4 m and a height of 16 m. If the cost of sail material is $150 per square metre, find the total cost to replace the yacht's damaged sails.

11 **a** The area of a triangle is 10 cm^2 and its base length is 4 cm. Find its height.
　　 b The area of a triangle is 44 mm^2 and its height is 20 mm. Find its base length.

REASONING　　　12　　　12, 13　　　13, 14

12 The midpoint, M, of the base of a triangle joins the opposite vertex. Is the triangle area split in half exactly? Give reasons for your answer.

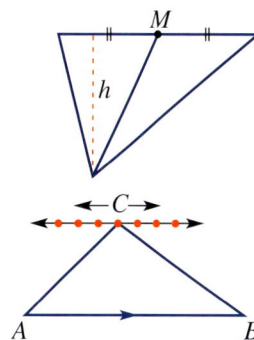

M
h

13 If the vertex C for this triangle moves parallel to the base AB, will the area of the triangle change? Justify your answer.

$\leftarrow C \rightarrow$

14 The area of a triangle can be found using the formula $A = \frac{1}{2}bh$. Write down the formula to find the base, b, if you are given the area, A, and height, h.

A　　　B

ENRICHMENT: Estimating areas with curves　　　–　　　–　　　15

15 This diagram shows a shaded region that is $\frac{1}{2}$ of 3 cm^2 = 1.5 cm^2.

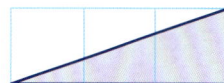

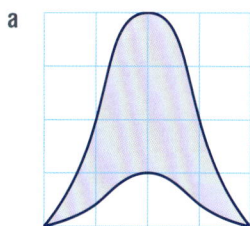

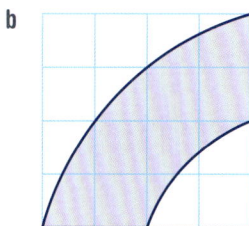

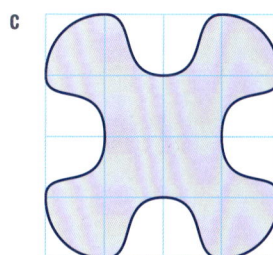

Using triangles like the one shown here, and by counting whole squares also, estimate the areas of these shapes below.

a　　　　**b**　　　　**c**

Progress quiz

10A

1 Which metric unit would be most appropriate for measuring the lengths of:
   a the height of the classroom?
   b the width of your thumb
   c the distance from Sydney to Canberra?

10A

2 Convert to the units given in brackets.
   a 4 m (cm)
   b 2 m (mm)
   c 3.5 cm (mm)
   d 3 km (m)
   e 1.45 km (m)
   f 23 000 m (km)

10B

3 Find the perimeter of each of these shapes.
   a

   46 mm, 5 cm, 5 cm

   b

   4 m, 1.2 m

   c

   70 cm, 25 cm, 32 cm, 52 cm

10C 🖩

4 A good approximation of π is the fraction $\frac{69}{22}$.

   a Write $\frac{69}{22}$ as a decimal, rounded to three decimal places.

   b Decide if $\frac{69}{22}$ is a better approximation to π than the number 3.14.

10C 🖩

5 Calculate the circumference of these circles using a calculator and rounding your answer correct to two decimal places.
   a

   9 mm

   b

   6 cm

10D 🖩

6 Find the perimeter of these shapes, correct to one decimal place.
   a

   74°, 5 cm

   b

   12 cm

   c

   6 cm, 10 cm

10E

7 Find the area of this rectangle and square.

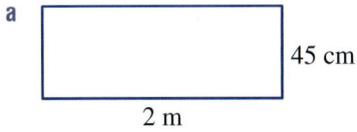

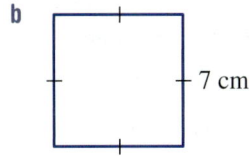

a

45 cm

2 m

b

7 cm

10F

8 Find the area of these parallelograms.

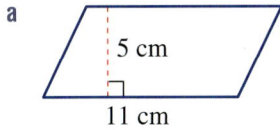

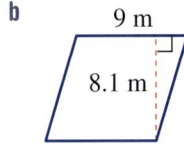

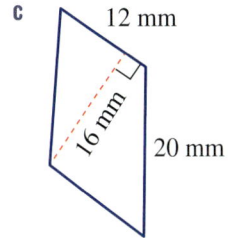

a

5 cm

11 cm

b

9 m

8.1 m

c

12 mm

16 mm

20 mm

10G

9. Find the area of these triangles.

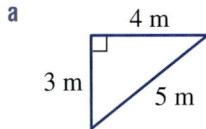

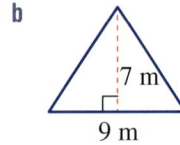

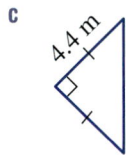

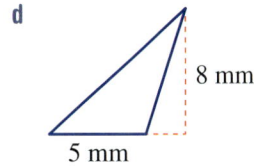

a

4 m

3 m

5 m

b

7 m

9 m

c

4.4 m

d

8 mm

5 mm

10B/E

10 The perimeter of a square made of thin wire is 60 cm. Find:

a the area of this square

b the area of a rectangle made with this wire, if its length is twice its width

c the number of smaller squares that can be made from this wire if each square has an area of 4 square centimetres.

10G

11 What fraction of the entire shape is the shaded region?

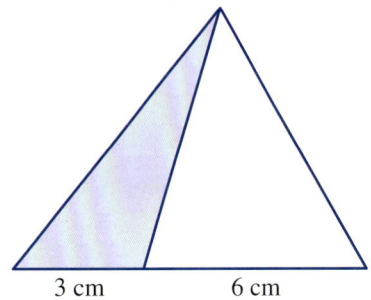

3 cm   6 cm

10H   Area of composite shapes   EXTENDING

LEARNING INTENTIONS
- To understand what a composite shape is
- To be able to identify simple shapes that make up a composite shape
- To be able to find the area of a composite shape

The areas of more complicated shapes can be found by dividing them up into more simple shapes, such as the rectangle and triangle. We can see this in an aerial view of any Australian city. Such a view will show that many city streets are not parallel or at right angles to each other. As a result, this causes city blocks to form interesting shapes, many of which are composite shapes made up of rectangles and triangles.

Streets, parks and buildings form complex shapes that can be made up of triangles and rectangles.

Lesson starter: Dividing land to find its area

Working out the area of this piece of land could be done by dividing it into three rectangles, as shown.

- Can you work out the area using this method?
- What is another way of dividing the land to find its area? Can you use triangles?
- What is the easiest method to find the area? Is there a way that uses subtraction instead of addition?

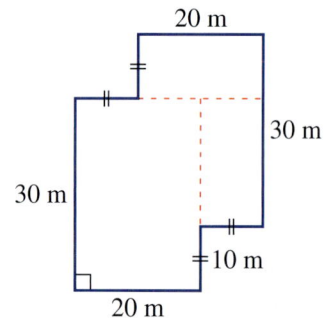

20 m

30 m

30 m

10 m

20 m

KEY IDEAS

■ **Composite shapes** are made up of more than one simple shape.

■ The area of composite shapes can be found by adding or subtracting the areas of simple shapes.

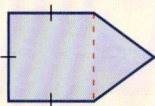

A square plus a triangle   A rectangle minus a triangle

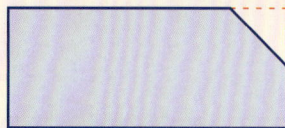

BUILDING UNDERSTANDING

1 Describe where you would draw a dotted line to divide these shapes into two more simple shapes.

a

b

c

2 To find the area of each of the following shapes, decide if the easiest method would involve the *addition* of two shapes or the *subtraction* of one shape from another.

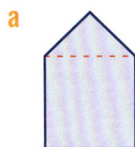

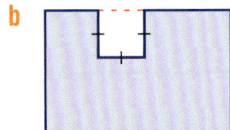

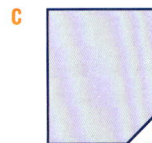

a

b

c

3 State the missing numbers to complete the solutions for the areas of these shapes.

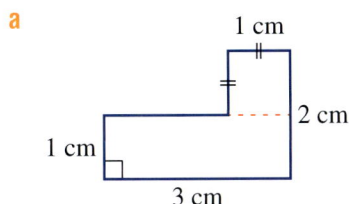

a

1 cm

2 cm

1 cm

3 cm

$A = l^2 + \underline{\quad}$
$= 1^2 + 3 \times \underline{\quad}$
$= \underline{\quad} + \underline{\quad}$
$= \underline{\quad} \text{ cm}^2$

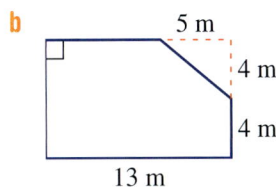

b

5 m

4 m

4 m

13 m

$A = lw - \underline{\quad}$
$= \underline{\quad} \times 8 - \frac{1}{2} \times \underline{\quad} \times \underline{\quad}$
$= \underline{\quad} - \underline{\quad}$
$= \underline{\quad} \text{ m}^2$

Example 14   Finding the area of composite shapes using addition

Find the area of each of these composite shapes.

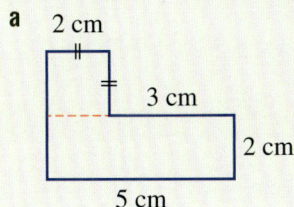

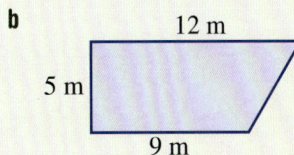

a

2 cm

3 cm

2 cm

5 cm

b

12 m

5 m

9 m

SOLUTION

a $A = l \times w + l^2$
$= 5 \times 2 + 2^2$
$= 10 + 4$
$= 14 \text{ cm}^2$

EXPLANATION

The shape is made up of a rectangle of length 5 cm and width 2 cm and a square with side length 2 cm.

Continued on next page

b $\quad A = l \times w + \frac{1}{2}bh$

$\quad = 9 \times 5 + \frac{1}{2} \times 3 \times 5$

$\quad = 45 + 7.5$

$\quad = 52.5 \, \text{m}^2$

Divide the shape into a rectangle and triangle and find the missing lengths.

Now you try

Find the area of these composite shapes.

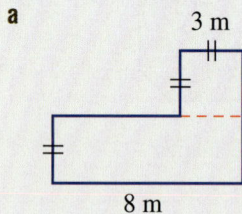

a

b

Example 15   Finding the area of composite shapes using subtraction

Find the area of each of these composite shapes.

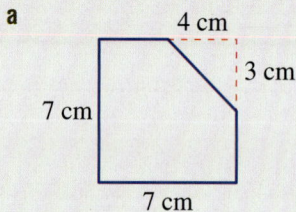

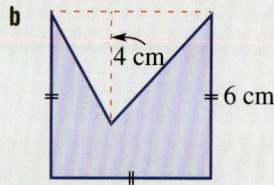

a

b

SOLUTION

a $\quad A = l^2 - \frac{1}{2}bh$

$\quad = 7^2 - \frac{1}{2} \times 4 \times 3$

$\quad = 49 - 6$

$\quad = 43 \, \text{cm}^2$

EXPLANATION

Subtract the triangle $\left(\frac{1}{2} \times 4 \times 3\right)$ from the square (7×7).

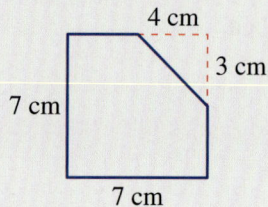

b $A = l^2 - \frac{1}{2}bh$

   $= 6^2 - \frac{1}{2} \times 6 \times 4$

   $= 36 - 12$

   $= 24\,cm^2$

Subtract the triangle $\left(\frac{1}{2} \times 6 \times 4\right)$ at the top of the shape from the larger square (6×6).

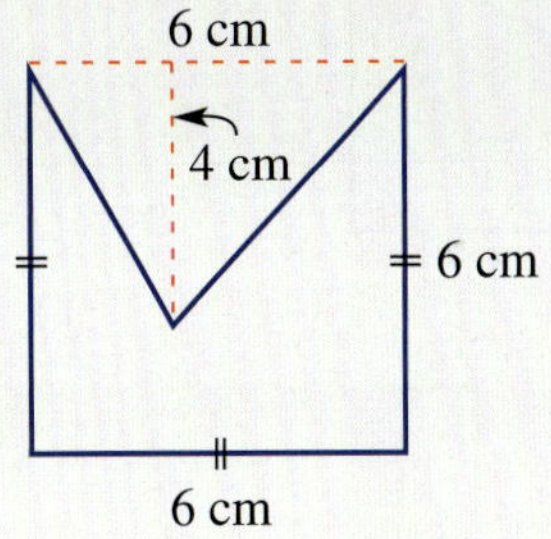

6 cm

4 cm

6 cm

6 cm

Now you try

Find the area of each of these composite shapes.

a 7 cm, 8 cm, 10 cm, 2 cm

b 5 cm, 3 cm, 2 cm

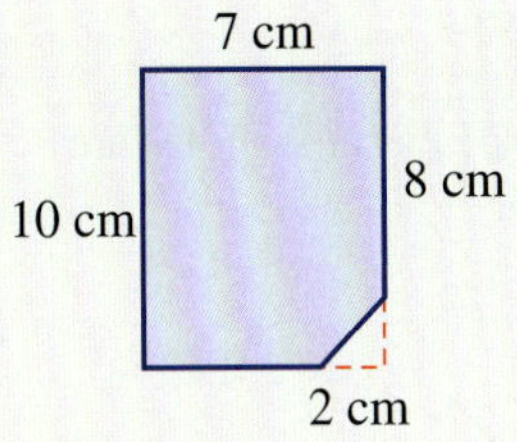

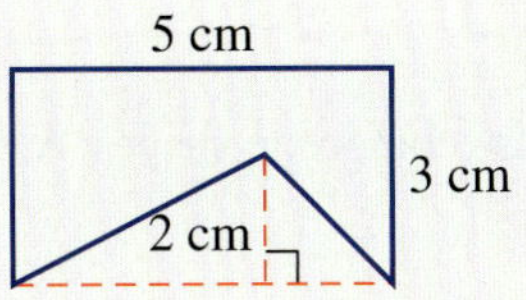

Exercise 10H

FLUENCY   1, 2(½), 3, 4(½)   2(½), 4(½)   2(½), 4(½)

Example 14

1 Find the area of these composite shapes. Assume that all angles that look like right angles are right angles.

a 11 cm, 4 cm, 7 cm, 4 cm

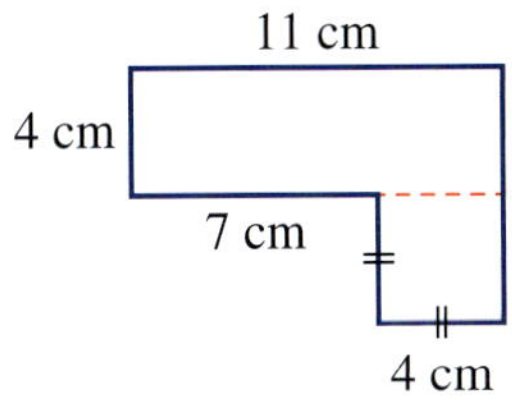

b 10 m, 4 m, 6 m

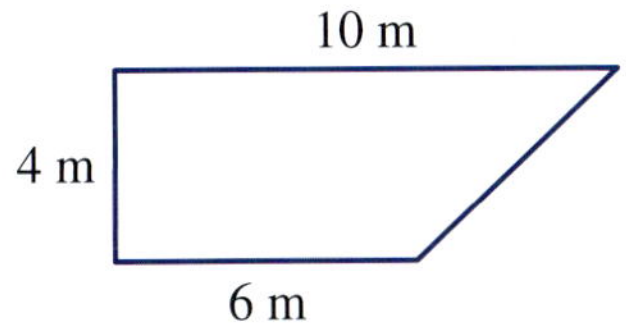

Example 14

2 Find the area of these composite shapes by adding together the area of simpler shapes. Assume that all angles that look like right angles are right angles.

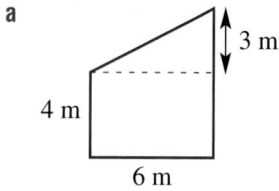

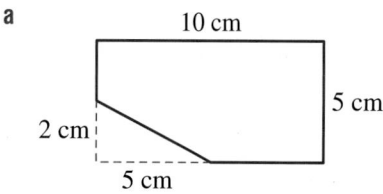

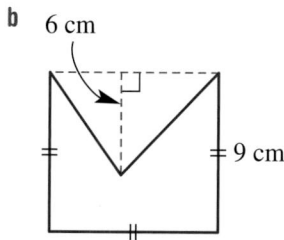

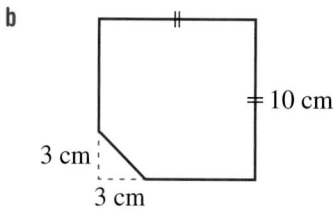

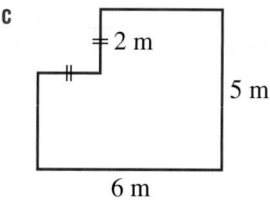

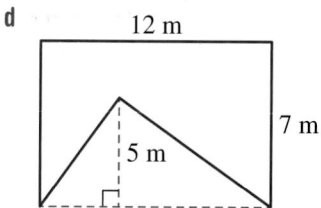

a

3 m
4 m
6 m

b

10 mm
10 mm
40 mm

c

2 m
8 m
3 m

d

5 m
3 m
9 m

e

21 cm
9 cm
17 cm

f

6 km
3 km
10 km

Example 15

3 Find the area of these composite shapes. Assume that all angles that look like right angles are right angles.

a

10 cm
5 cm
2 cm
5 cm

b

6 cm
9 cm

Example 15

4 Use subtraction to find the area of these composite shapes. Assume that all angles that look like right angles are right angles.

a

3 m
2 m
6 m
7 m

b

10 cm
3 cm
3 cm

c

2 m
5 m
6 m

d

12 m
7 m
5 m

e

20 cm
14 cm

f

1 m
2.5 m
4 m

PROBLEM-SOLVING   5, 6   5–7   6–8

5 Find the areas of these composite shapes. Assume that all angles that look like right angles are right angles.

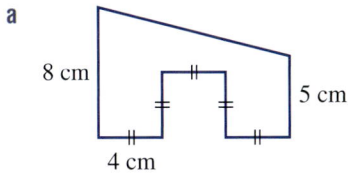

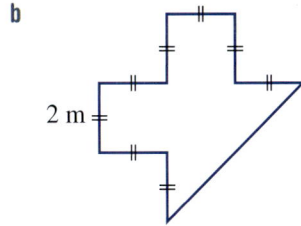

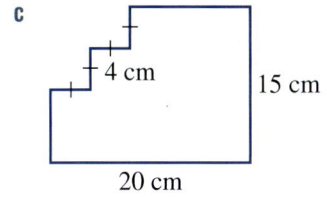

a
8 cm

5 cm

4 cm

b
2 m

c
4 cm

15 cm

20 cm

6 By finding the missing lengths first, calculate the area of these composite shapes.

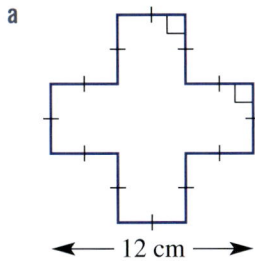

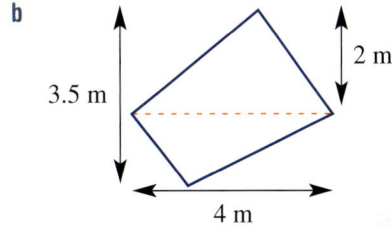

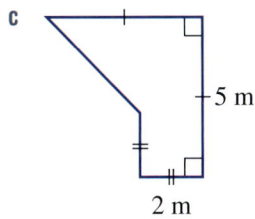

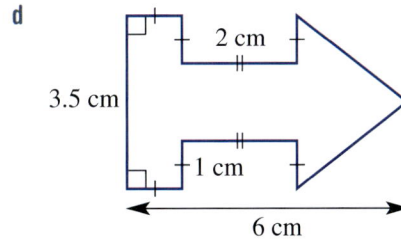

a
12 cm

b
3.5 m

2 m

4 m

c
5 m

2 m

d
2 cm

3.5 cm

1 cm

6 cm

7 A wall has three square holes cut into it to allow for windows, as shown. Find the remaining area of the wall.

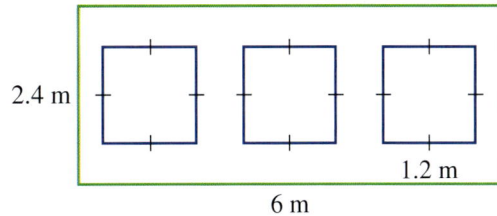

2.4 m

6 m

1.2 m

8 A factory floor, with dimensions shown opposite, is to be covered with linoleum. Including underlay and installation, the linoleum will cost $25 per square metre. The budget for the job is $3000. Is there enough money in the budget to cover the cost?

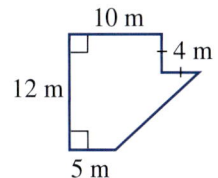

10 m

4 m

12 m

5 m

REASONING   9   10   9, 10

9   Explain why using subtraction is sometimes quicker than using addition to find the
    area of a composite shape. Refer to the diagram as an example.

10 The 4-sided shape called the trapezium has one pair of parallel sides.

    a   For the trapezium shown opposite, is it possible to find the base
        length of each triangle on the sides? Justify your answer.

    b   Can you come up with a method for finding the area of this
        trapezium using the rectangle and triangles shown in the
        diagram? Use diagrams to explain your method.

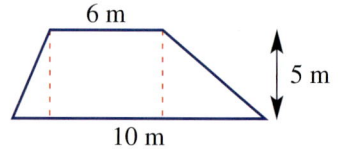

ENRICHMENT: Adding to infinity   –   –   11

11 The square given opposite, which has an area of 1 unit, is divided to show

    the areas of $\frac{1}{2}, \frac{1}{4}, \frac{1}{8}, \ldots$

    a   Similar to the one shown opposite, draw your own square, showing
        as many fractions as you can. Try to follow the spiral pattern shown.
        (Note: The bigger the square you start with, the more squares you will
        be able to show.)

    b   i   Write the next 10 numbers in this number pattern.

            $\frac{1}{2}, \frac{1}{4}, \frac{1}{8}, \ldots$

        ii Will the pattern ever stop?

    c   What is the total area of the starting square?

    d   What do your answers to parts **b ii** and **c** tell you about the answer to the sum below?

        $\frac{1}{2} + \frac{1}{4} + \frac{1}{8} + \frac{1}{16} + \ldots$ (continues forever)

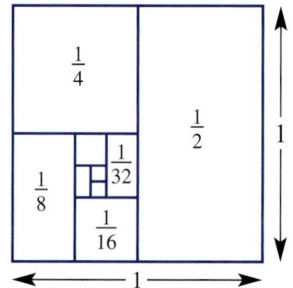

Architects and engineers calculate the areas of many geometric shapes
when designing and constructing modern multistorey towers, such as
the 182 m high Hearst Tower in New York City.

10I Volume of rectangular prisms

The amount of space inside a three-dimensional (3D) object is called volume. Volume is measured in cubic units such as the cubic centimetre, which is 1 cm long, 1 cm wide and 1 cm high.

Just like the topics of length and area, different units can be selected, depending on the size of the volume being measured. For example, the volume of water in the sea could be measured in cubic kilometres and the volume of concrete poured from a cement mixing truck could be measured in cubic metres.

The Pacific Ocean contains around 700 million cubic kilometres of water.

Lesson starter: Volume

We all know that there are 100 cm in 1 m, but do you know how many cubic centimetres are in 1 cubic metre?

- Try to visualise 1 cubic metre: 1 metre long, 1 metre wide and 1 metre high. Guess how many cubic centimetres would fit into this space.
- Describe a method for working out the exact answer. Explain how your method works.

KEY IDEAS

■ **Volume** is measured in cubic units.

■ The common metric units for volume include:
  • cubic millimetres (mm^3)

  (Not drawn to scale.)

1 mm
1 mm
1 mm

  • cubic centimetres (cm^3)

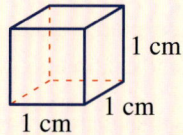
1 cm
1 cm
1 cm

  • cubic metres (m^3)

  (Not drawn to scale.)

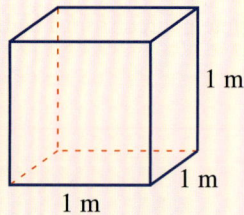
1 m
1 m
1 m

  • cubic kilometres (km^3)

  (Not drawn to scale.)

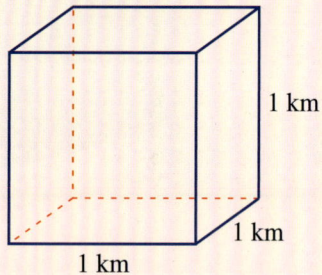
1 km
1 km
1 km

■ The volume of a **rectangular prism** is given by the formula:

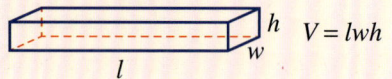
h
l
w
$V = lwh$

  $V = $ length $\times$ width $\times$ height
  $ = lwh$

  • A rectangular prism is also called a **cuboid**.

■ The volume of a **cube** is given by:

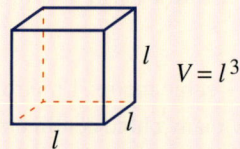
l
l
l
$V = l^3$

  $V = l \times l \times l$
  $ = l^3$

BUILDING UNDERSTANDING

1 For each of these solids, count the number of cubic units to find its volume.

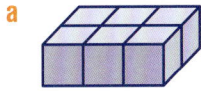

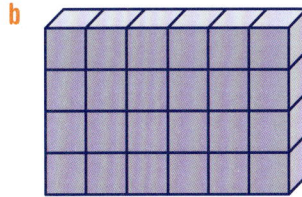

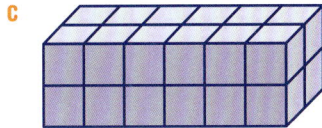

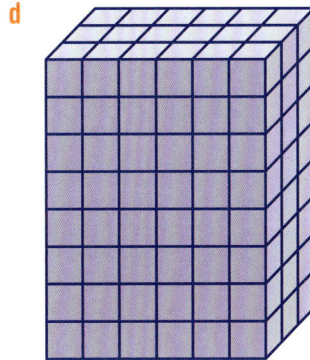

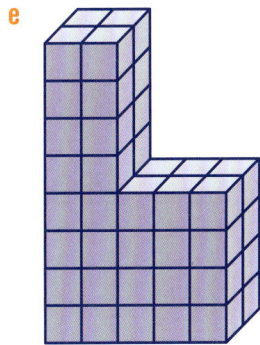

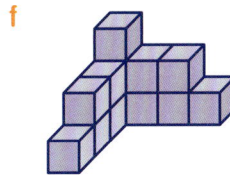

a

b

c

d

e

f

2 State the missing numbers to complete the working shown for each of these solids.

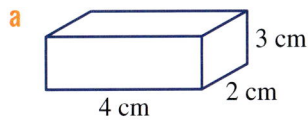

a

3 cm
2 cm
4 cm

b

6 m
3 m
1 m

c

2 km
2 km
2 km

$V = lwh$
$= 4 \times \underline{\quad} \times \underline{\quad}$
$= \underline{\quad} \text{cm}^3$

$V = lwh$
$= 1 \times \underline{\quad} \times \underline{\quad}$
$= \underline{\quad}\,\underline{\quad}$

$V = lwh$
$= 2 \times \underline{\quad} \times \underline{\quad}$
$= \underline{\quad} \text{km}^3$

Example 16   Finding the volume of a cuboid

Find the volume of this rectangular prism.

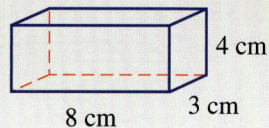

4 cm
8 cm
3 cm

SOLUTION

$V = lwh$
$\quad = 8 \times 3 \times 4$
$\quad = 96\,\text{cm}^3$

EXPLANATION

Use the formula for the volume of a rectangular prism, then substitute the three lengths into the formula.

Now you try

Find the volume of this rectangular prism.

2 cm
4 cm
6 cm

Exercise 10I

FLUENCY

| 1, 2(½), 3–5 | 2(½), 3–6 | 2(½), 4–6 |

Example 16

1 Find the volume of these rectangular prisms.

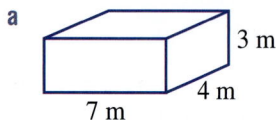

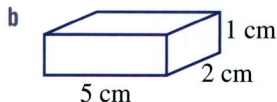

a
3 m
4 m
7 m

b
1 cm
2 cm
5 cm

Example 16

2 Find the volume of these rectangular prisms.

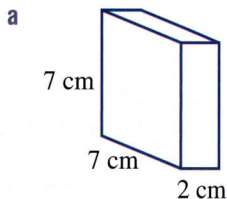

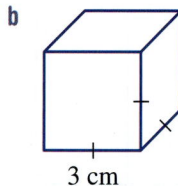

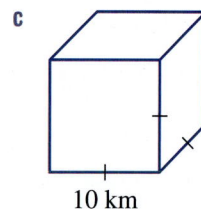

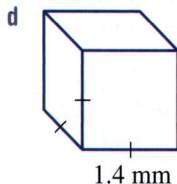

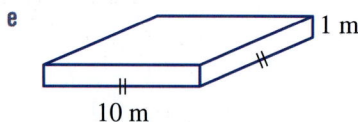

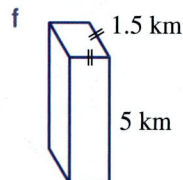

a
7 cm
7 cm
2 cm

b
3 cm

c
10 km

d
1.4 mm

e
1 m
10 m

f
1.5 km
5 km

3 A fruit box is 40 cm long, 30 cm wide and 20 cm high. Find its volume.

4 A shipping container is 3 m wide, 4 m high and 8 m long. Find its volume.

5 A short rectangular ruler is 150 mm long, 40 mm wide and 2 mm thick. Find its volume.

6 There is enough ice on Earth to fill a cube of side length 300 km. Find the approximate volume of ice on Earth.

PROBLEM-SOLVING	7(½), 8	7–9	7(½), 9, 10

7 These solids are made up of more than one rectangular prism. Use addition or subtraction to find the volume of the composite solid.

a

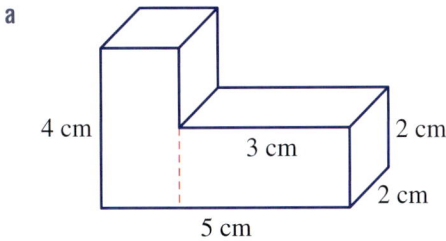

4 cm   3 cm   2 cm   2 cm   5 cm

b

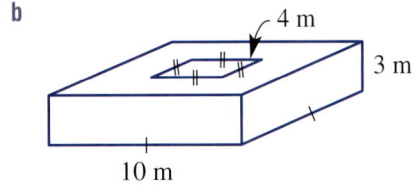

4 m   3 m   10 m

c

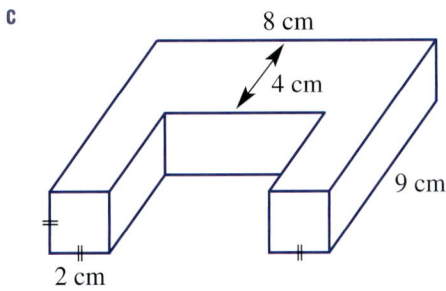

8 cm   4 cm   9 cm   2 cm

d

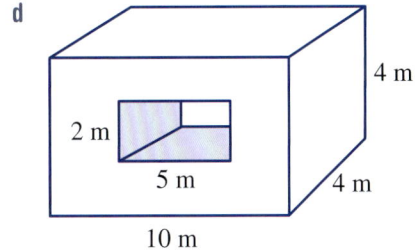

2 m   5 m   4 m   4 m   10 m

8 A box measuring 30 cm long, 20 cm high and 30 cm wide is packed with matchboxes, each measuring 5 cm long, 2 cm high and 3 cm wide. How many matchboxes will fit in the box?

9 The outside dimensions of a closed wooden box are 20 cm by 20 cm by 20 cm. If the box is made of wood that is 2 cm thick, find the volume of air inside the box.

10 a The area of one face of a cube is 25 cm^2. Find the cube's volume.
   b The perimeter of one face of a cube is 36 m. Find the cube's volume.

REASONING	11	11	11, 12

11 We can find the area of this shaded triangle by thinking of it as half a rectangle. Use the same idea to find the volume of each of these solids.

a

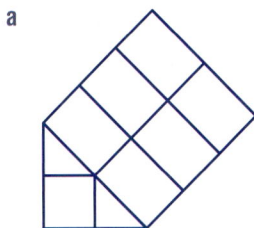

b

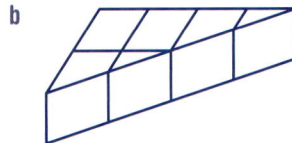

c

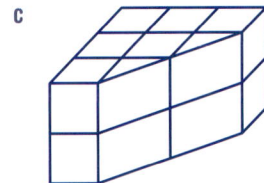

12 a Find the height of these rectangular prisms with the given volumes. Use trial and error, or set up and solve an equation.

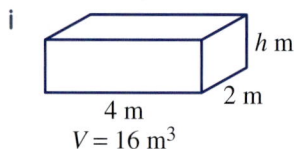

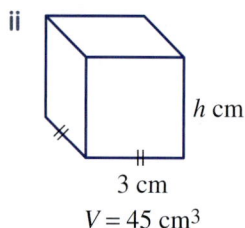

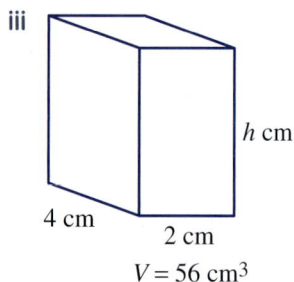

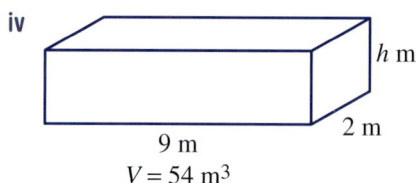

i

4 m
2 m
h m
$V = 16$ m^3

ii

h cm
3 cm
$V = 45$ cm^3

iii

h cm
4 cm
2 cm
$V = 56$ cm^3

iv

h m
9 m
2 m
$V = 54$ m^3

b Can you explain a method that always works for finding the height of a rectangular prism?

c Use V, l and w to write a rule for h.

ENRICHMENT: Cubic conversions   –   –   13

13 a The diagram shows a 1 cm^3 block that is divided into cubic millimetres.

  i How many mm^3 are there along one side of the cube?

  ii How many mm^3 are there in one layer of the cube? (*Hint:* How many cubes sit on the base?)

  iii How many layers of mm^3 are there in the cube?

  iv Use your answers from parts **i** to **iii** above to now calculate how many mm^3 there are in 1 cm^3.

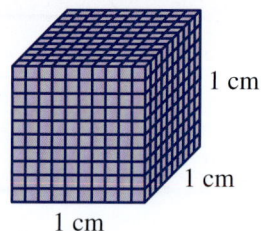

1 cm
1 cm
1 cm

b Use a similar method to calculate the number of:

  i cm^3 in 1 m^3

  ii m^3 in 1 km^3

c Complete the diagram shown.

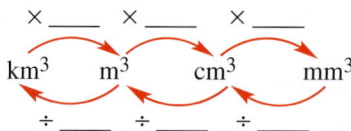

$$\times \underline{\quad} \qquad \times \underline{\quad} \qquad \times \underline{\quad}$$

km^3 \qquad m^3 \qquad cm^3 \qquad mm^3

$$\div \underline{\quad} \qquad \div \underline{\quad} \qquad \div \underline{\quad}$$

The following problems will investigate practical situations drawing upon knowledge and skills developed throughout the chapter. In attempting to solve these problems, aim to identify the key information, use diagrams, formulate ideas, apply strategies, make calculations and check and communicate your solutions.

Painting a bedroom

1   Braxton wishes to redesign his bedroom and wants to start by painting the walls and the ceiling. Braxton measures his room to be $4.5\,\text{m} \times 3.0\,\text{m}$, and the height of his ceiling to be $2.4\,\text{m}$.
Braxton wants to calculate the total wall and ceiling area of his room in order to determine the number of litres of paint to purchase.

a   What is the area of Braxton's ceiling?

b   What is the total area of Braxton's walls (assuming there are no doors or windows)?

c   Braxton does have three doors (one entry door and two wardrobe doors) each measuring $800\,\text{mm} \times 2.1\,\text{m}$, and one window measuring $1500\,\text{mm} \times 1.8\,\text{m}$ in his bedroom. What is the total area of Braxton's doors and window?

d   Using your answers to parts b and c, what is the actual total area of Braxton's walls?

e   Braxton decides to paint the walls and ceiling with two coats of paint. What is the total area Braxton will be painting?

f   Braxton decides to use the same colour paint for both the walls and the ceiling. He has chosen his colour and the paint tin says that the coverage for the paint is $12\,\text{m}^2$ per litre of paint. How many litres of paint does Braxton need to buy?

Building a sponge pit

2   The Year 7 Student Representative Council (SRC) at Ashwelling Secondary College wish to build a 'sponge pit' as a fun activity where students can connect and interact.
They would like the sponge pit to be big enough to have four students sit comfortably in there to ask one another questions. They decide to make the sponge pit in the shape of a cube with side length $1.5\,\text{m}$.
Materials:

- $45\,\text{mm} \times 90\,\text{mm}$ pine for the sponge pit frame at $3.89 per linear metre
- $18\,\text{mm}$ Marine plywood ($1500\,\text{mm} \times 750\,\text{mm}$) for the bottom and sides of the sponge pit at $58.95 per sheet
- $5\,\text{cm}$ length foam sponge cubes at $7.95 for a pack of 100

The SRC need to determine the quantity and cost of the materials needed for the school's maintenance team to build the sponge pit.

a   How many metres of pine is required for the sponge pit frame?

b   How many sheets of marine plywood (1500 mm × 750 mm) are required to line the bottom and the sides of the sponge pit?

c   What is the volume of the sponge pit? Give your answer in $3\,cm^3$.

d   For the 'balls', the SRC actually decide to use blue cubes of a dense sponge material. The side length of the cube is 5 cm. What is the volume of one blue sponge cube?

e   While there always will be some space between cubes in the sponge pit, assuming that there are no gaps, what is the maximum number of sponge cubes needed to fill the empty pit?

f   Given that students need to sit in the sponge pit, and that there will be some gaps, a decision is made to order only 75% of the maximum number of sponge cubes. How many packs of 100 sponge cubes need to be ordered?

g   What is the total cost of materials for the sponge pit? Round your answer to the nearest dollar.

h   If the school decides to build a sponge pit, but they only have $1000 for the total budget for materials, what would be the maximum side length of the pit that could be built?

Planting pine trees on a farm

3   A farmer has a vacant rectangular paddock which is 50 m long and 30 m wide. She would like to plant a pine plantation on the paddock to be harvested every 15 years. She decides all pine trees must be planted at least 2 m away from the paddock fence, so the trees do not overhang the paddock boundary or damage her fences.

   • Pine trees planted 4 m apart will generally reach their maximum growth height.
   • Pine trees planted 3 m apart will generally reach only 70% of their maximum growth height.
   • Pine trees planted 2 m apart will generally reach only 35% of their maximum growth height.

   The farmer is interested in how many trees to plant depending on how far apart they should be and how to maximise the harvest which depends on the planting arrangements.

a   How many trees can the farmer plant in their vacant paddock if they decide to plant them 4 m apart?

b   How many trees can the farmer plant in their vacant paddock if they decide to plant them 3 m apart?

c   How many trees can the farmer plant in their vacant paddock if they decide to plant them 2 m apart?

d   Given the different growth heights that will be achieved, how far apart should the farmer plant the pine trees to maximise their harvest?

10J Volume of triangular prisms

LEARNING INTENTIONS

- To understand that the volume of a prism can be calculated using the area of the cross-section and the perpendicular height
- To know what a triangular prism is
- To be able to find the volume of a triangular prism

We know that the rule for the volume of a rectangular prism, $V = l \times w \times h$, includes the product $l \times w$ which represents the area of the base. So, $V = l \times w \times h$ could be rewritten as $V = A \times h$ where A is the area of the base. The area of the base also tells us how many cubes fit on one layer inside the solid. Multiplying by the height gives the total number of cubes in the solid and hence the volume. This rule $V = A \times h$ can therefore be applied to other prisms, including a triangular prism provided that the area of the base (cross-section) can be calculated.

h
A
l
w

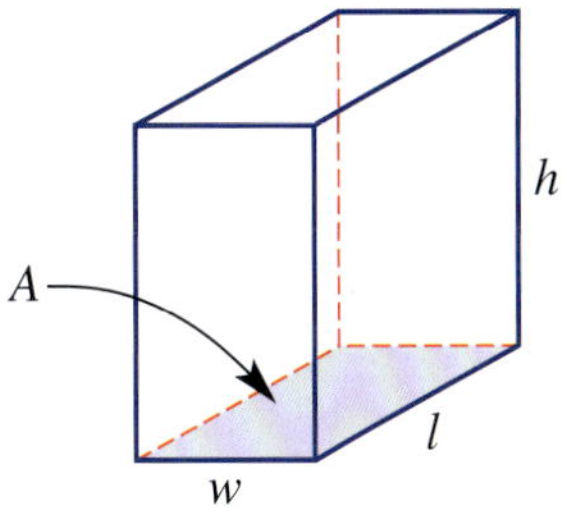

Lesson starter: A trio of triangular prisms

We know that the volume of a prism is given by $V = A \times h$ and for the triangular prisms shown below, that area A corresponds to the cross-section which is a triangle.

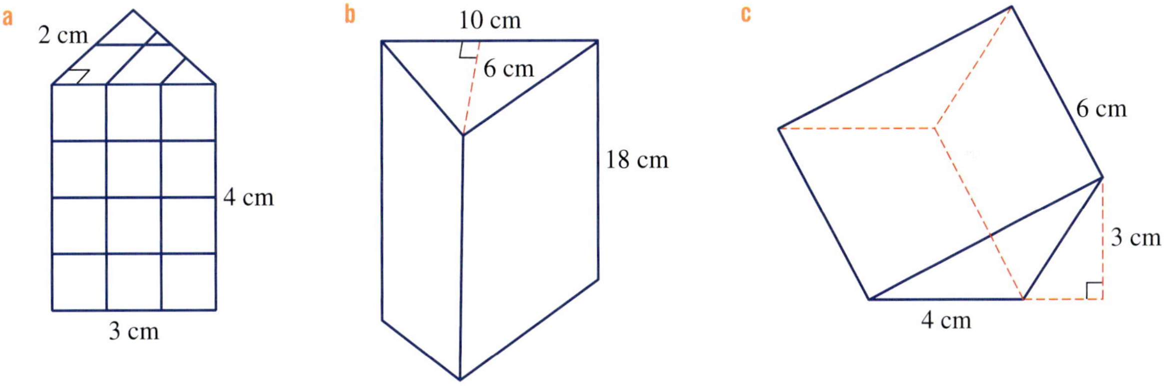

a
2 cm
4 cm
3 cm
b
10 cm
6 cm
18 cm
c
6 cm
3 cm
4 cm

- Draw a two-dimensional representation of the triangular cross-sections of the three prisms labelling the base and the height.
- Calculate the area, A of the triangular cross sections.
- Use $V = A \times h$ to find the volume of each prism by firstly deciding what measurement represents the height.
- Discuss the shape and orientation of the triangular cross-sections of the three prisms and the direction of the height (h) used in the formula $V = A \times h$.

KEY IDEAS

■ A **right triangular prism** has:
  • a uniform (constant) triangular cross-section (base)
  • three rectangular faces
  • a height measured perpendicular (at 90°) to the base.

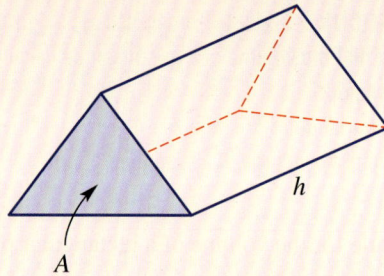

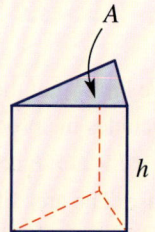

■ The volume of a triangular prism is given by the formula $V = A \times h$, where:
  • V is the volume
  • A is the area of the triangular cross-section (base)
  • h is the height of the prism which is perpendicular (at 90°) to the base
  • the area of the cross-section A can be found using the formula for the area of a triangle $A = \frac{1}{2}bh$.

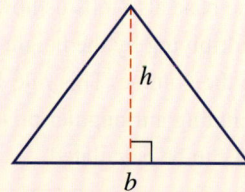

BUILDING UNDERSTANDING

1 For each triangular prism decide which measurement would be used as the height, h, in the formula $V = A \times h$.

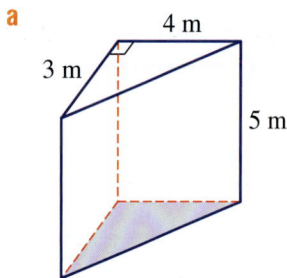

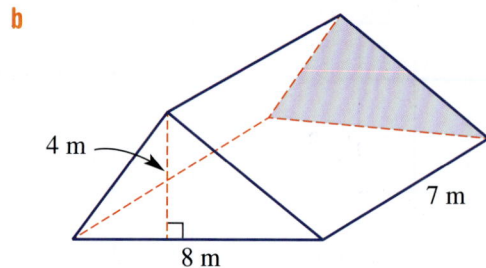

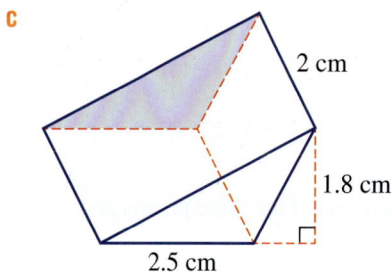

a

b

c

2 For the triangular prisms in question 1 above, find the area of the triangular cross-section using $A = \frac{1}{2}bh$.

3 For the triangular prisms in question 1 above, find the volume using $V = A \times h$.

⊙

Example 17 Finding the volume of a triangular prism

Find the volume of these triangular prisms.

a

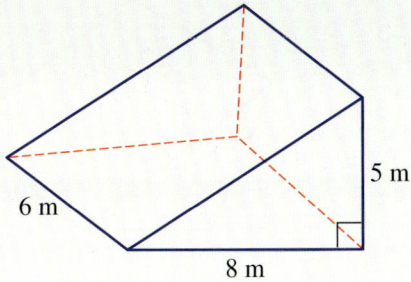

6 m
8 m
5 m

b

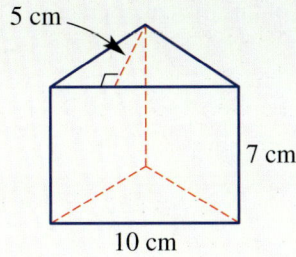

5 cm
7 cm
10 cm

SOLUTION

a $A = \frac{1}{2}bh$

$\quad = \frac{1}{2} \times 8 \times 5$

$\quad = 20\,\text{m}^2$

$V = A \times h$

$\quad = 20 \times 6$

$\quad = 120\,\text{m}^3$

b $A = \frac{1}{2}bh$

$\quad = \frac{1}{2} \times 10 \times 5$

$\quad = 25\,\text{cm}^2$

$V = A \times h$

$\quad = 25 \times 7$

$\quad = 175\,\text{cm}^3$

EXPLANATION

First find the area of the triangular cross-section.

The height used for the prism is 6 cm and is perpendicular to the cross-section.

First find the area of the triangular cross-section with base 10 cm and height 5 cm.

Use the rule for the volume of a prism noting that the height is 7 cm.

Now you try

Find the volume of these triangular prisms.

a

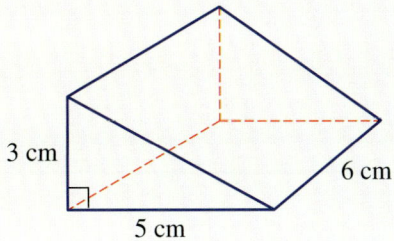

3 cm
5 cm
6 cm

b

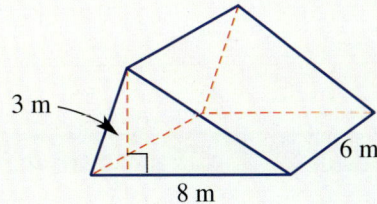

3 m
8 m
6 m

▷

Example 18   Finding the volume of a triangular prism with an obtuse angled triangular cross-section

Find the volume of this triangular prism.

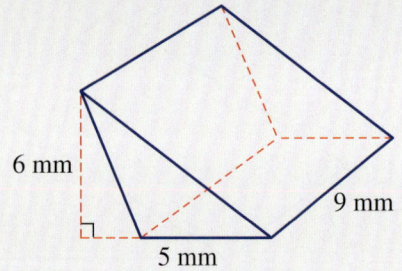

SOLUTION

$A = \frac{1}{2}bh$

$\quad = \frac{1}{2} \times 5 \times 6$

$\quad = 15 \, \text{mm}^2$

$V = A \times h$

$\quad = 15 \times 9$

$\quad = 135 \, \text{mm}^3$

EXPLANATION

First find the area of the triangular cross-section.

The height used for the prism is 9 mm and is perpendicular to the cross-section.

Now you try

Find the volume of this triangular prism.

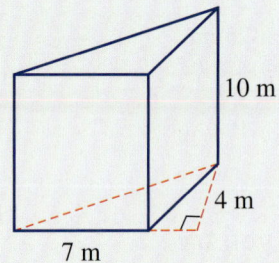

Exercise 10J

FLUENCY   1–4   2–5   2(⅓), 4(⅓), 6

Example 17

1 Find the volume of these triangular prisms.

a

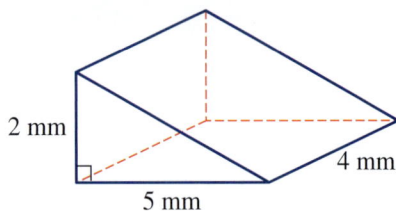

b

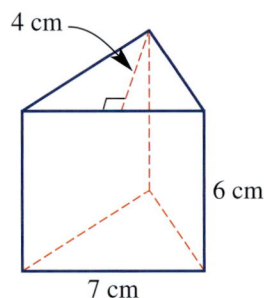

2 Find the volume of these triangular prisms.

a

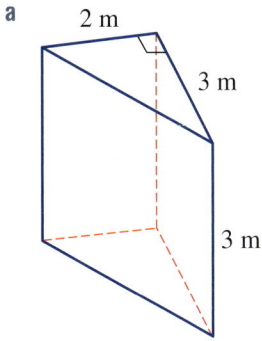
2 m
3 m
3 m

b

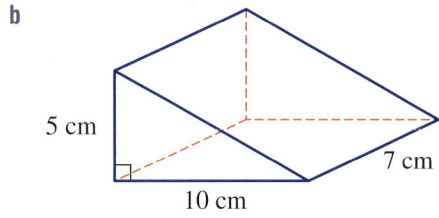
5 cm
7 cm
10 cm

c

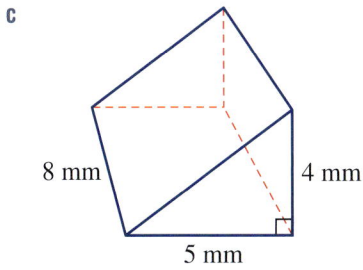
8 mm
4 mm
5 mm

d

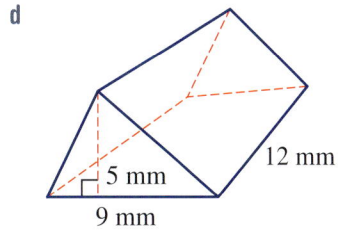
12 mm
5 mm
9 mm

e

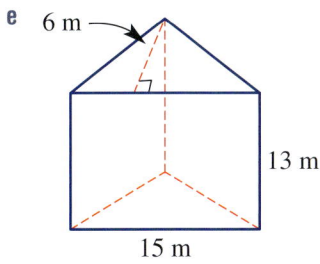
6 m
13 m
15 m

f

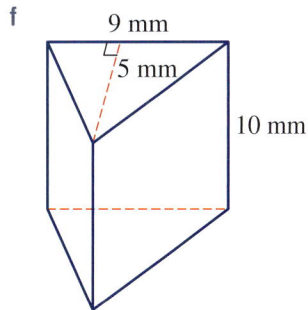
9 mm
5 mm
10 mm

3 Find the volume of these triangular prisms.

a

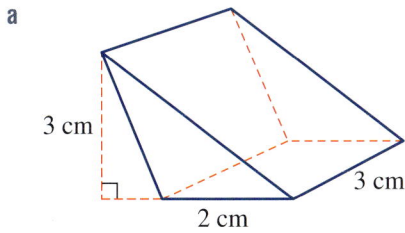
3 cm
2 cm
3 cm

b

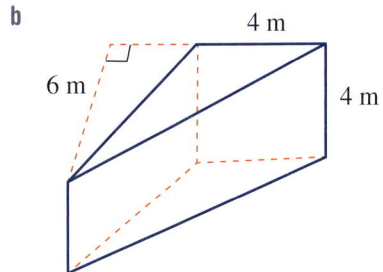
4 m
6 m
4 m

Example 18

4 Find the volume of these triangular prisms.

a

3 m
5 m
4 m

b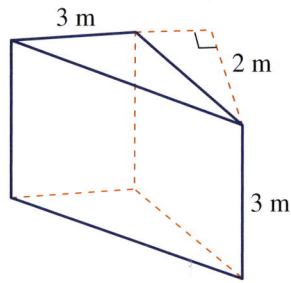

3 m
2 m
3 m

c

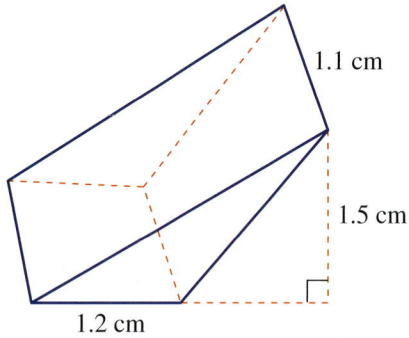

1.1 cm
1.5 cm
1.2 cm

5 A simple tent is in the shape of a triangular prism as shown. Find the tent's volume.

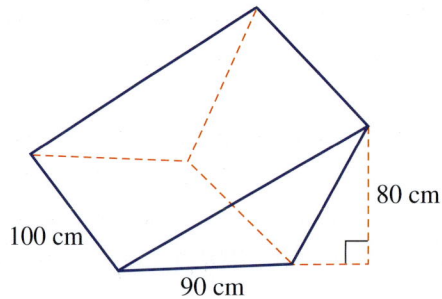

1.4 m
3 m
2 m

6 A concrete ramp is in the shape of a triangular prism as shown. Find the volume of concrete in cm^3.

100 cm
90 cm
80 cm

7, 8(½)   7, 8   8, 9

7 A chocolate bar is in the shape of a triangular prism. The triangular cross-section has base 3 cm and height 2 cm. Its total length is 12 cm. Find the volume of the chocolate in the bar.

8 The following composite solids combine rectangular and triangular prisms. Find the volume.

a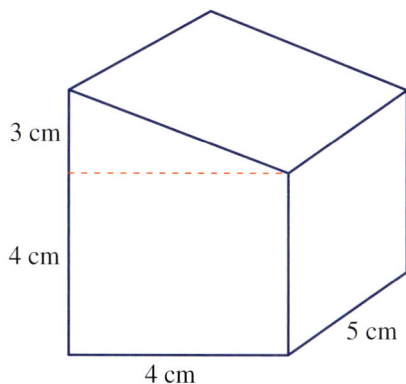

b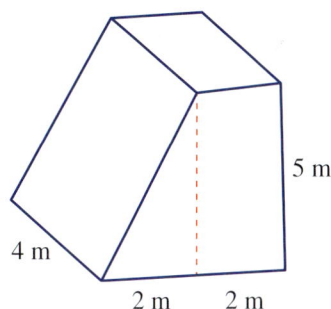

c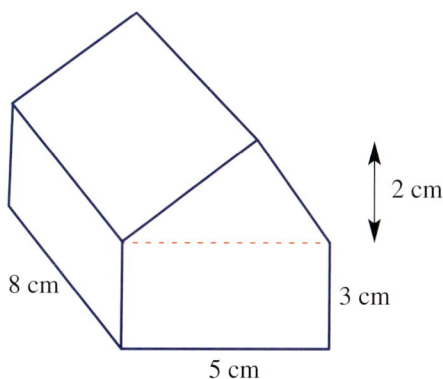

d

9 A box in the shape of a cube has side length 20 cm. It contains 400 small metal wedges, each of which is a triangular prism with cross-sectional area 2.8 cm^2 and length 3.5 cm. Find the volume of air space remaining in the box.

10   10, 11   10(½), 11, 12

10 The following refer to triangular prisms with given volumes and unknown cross-sectional areas or height measurements.
   a If the volume is 40 cm^3 and the cross-sectional area is 10 cm^2, find its height.
   b If the volume is 8.2 m^3 and the cross-sectional area is 1.6 m^2, find its height.
   c If the volume is 125 mm^3 and the height is 20 mm, find its cross-sectional area.
   d If the volume is 4000 cm^3 and the height is 400 cm, find its cross-sectional area.

11 A triangular prism has volume 24 cm^3 and height 8 cm. The height of the triangular cross-section is 2 cm. Find the base length of the triangular cross-section.

12 A triangular prism has volume 100 mm^3 and height 20 mm. The base of the triangular cross-section is 4 mm. Find the height of the triangular cross-section.

13 The given triangular prism has volume V, height h_2 and the triangular cross-section has base b and height h_1.

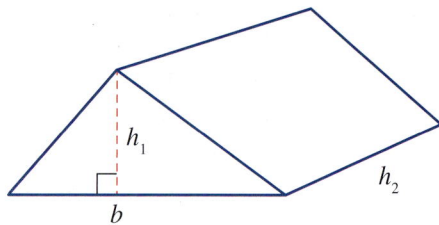

   a Write a rule for the volume V in terms of b, h_1, and h_2.

   b Write a rule for the volume h_2 in terms of V, b and h_1.

   c Write a rule for the volume h_1 in terms of V, b and h_2.

   d Write a rule for the volume b in terms of V, h_1 and h_2.

   e Use one of your rules above to find:

     i h_2 if $V = 12$, $b = 4$ and $h_1 = 4$.

     ii h_1 if $V = 20$, $b = 5$ and $h_2 = 8$.

     iii b if $V = 80$, $h_1 = 20$ and $h_2 = 10$.

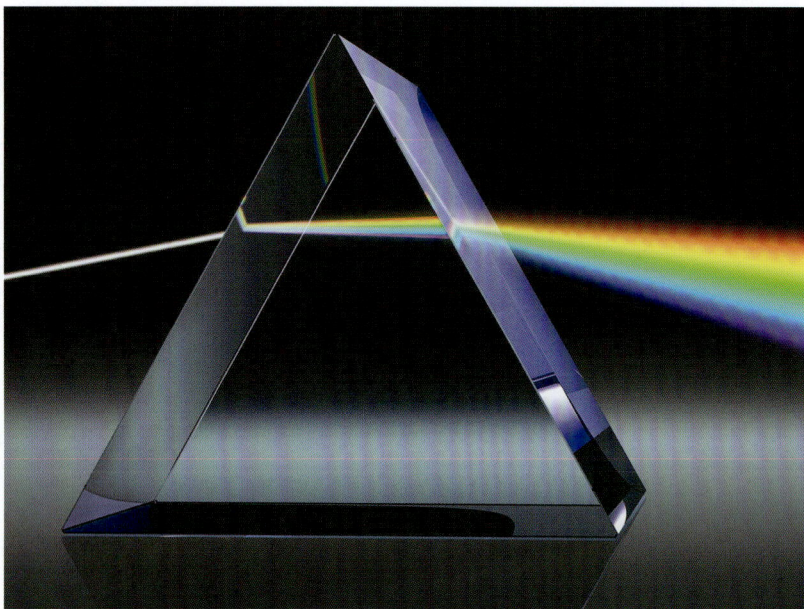

10K Capacity CONSOLIDATING

> **LEARNING INTENTIONS**
> - To understand that capacity is the volume of fluid or gas that an object can hold
> - To know that common metric units include millilitres, litres, kilolitres and megalitres
> - To be able to convert between common units for capacity
> - To be able to convert between the volume and capacity of a container

Capacity relates to the volume of fluid or gas that a container can hold. For example, the capacity of a water tank may be 5000 litres, or a farmer's water allocation might be 300 megalitres (meaning 300 million litres). The basic unit is the litre, which contains $1000\,\text{cm}^3$ of space. Other common metric units for capacity include the millilitre, kilolitre and megalitre. There is a clear link between capacity and volume, as they both relate to the space occupied by a three-dimensional object.

The space that a surfboard occupies is given in litres, as it is measured by the volume of water it displaces when submerged in a bath. Boards with a higher litre capacity float higher in the water.

Lesson starter: Water containers

Will, Tony and Ethan each bring a container to collect some water from a fountain.

- Will says his container holds 2 litres.
- Tony says his container holds $2000\,\text{cm}^3$.
- Ethan says his container holds 2000 millilitres.

Who can collect the most water? Give reasons for your answer.

> **KEY IDEAS**
>
> ■ **Capacity** is the volume of fluid or gas that an object can hold.
>
> ■ Common metric units include:
> - 1 litre (L) = 1000 millilitres (mL)
> - 1 kilolitre (kL) = 1000 litres (L)
> - 1 megalitre (ML) = 1000 kilolitres (kL)
>
> ■ Relating volume and capacity
> - $1\,\text{cm}^3 = 1\,\text{mL}$
> - $1\,\text{m}^3 = 1000\,\text{L} = 1\,\text{kL}$

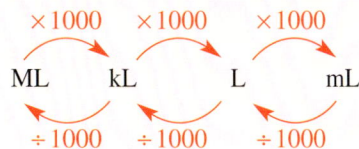

$$\times 1000 \qquad \times 1000 \qquad \times 1000$$

$$\text{ML} \quad \text{kL} \quad \text{L} \quad \text{mL}$$

$$\div 1000 \qquad \div 1000 \qquad \div 1000$$

MILK
1 L
(1000 mL)

MILK
$1000\,\text{cm}^3$

BUILDING UNDERSTANDING

1 State the missing number.

    a 1 mL contains the volume of _____ cm^3.

    b 1 L contains _____ mL.

    c 1 L contains _____ cm^3.

    d 1 kL contains _____ L.

    e 1 ML contains _____ kL.

2 State which volumes are the same.

    a 1 L, 10 kL, 1000 mL, 1 m^3, 1000 cm^3

    b 1 m^3, 100 L, 1000 L, 1000 ML, 1 kL

3 From options **A** to **F**, choose the capacity that best matches the given container.

a	teaspoon	**A**	18 L
b	cup	**B**	250 mL
c	bottle	**C**	10 kL
d	kitchen sink	**D**	20 mL
e	water tank	**E**	45 ML
f	water in a lake	**F**	0.8 L

Example 19   Converting units for capacity

Convert to the units shown in brackets.

a 500 mL (L)   **b** 4 kL (L)

SOLUTION

a 500 mL $= 500 \div 1000$ L

           $= 0.5$ L

b 4 kL $= 4 \times 1000$ L

        $= 4000$ L

EXPLANATION

When converting to a larger unit, divide. There are 1000 mL in 1 L.

When converting to a smaller unit, multiply. There are 1000 L in 1 kL.

Now you try

Convert to the units shown in brackets.

a 7200 mL (L)   **b** 7 ML (kL)

Example 20 Converting units for capacity using multiple steps

Convert to the units shown in the brackets.

a 8 400 000 mL (kL)

b 3 ML (L)

SOLUTION

a $8\,400\,000\,\text{mL} = 8\,400\,000 \div 1000\,\text{L}$
$= 8400 \div 1000\,\text{kL}$
$= 8.4\,\text{kL}$

b $3\,\text{ML} = 3 \times 1000\,\text{kL}$
$= 3 \times 1000 \times 1000\,\text{L}$
$= 3\,000\,000\,\text{L}$

EXPLANATION

There are 1000 mL in 1 L and 1000 L in 1 kL.

There are 1000 kL in 1 ML and 1000 L in 1 kL.
So, 1 ML is 1 million litres.

Now you try

Convert to the units shown in the brackets.

a 67 000 000 L (ML)

b 9 kL (mL)

Example 21 Converting cm³ to litres

Find the capacity of this container, in litres.

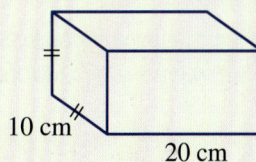

SOLUTION

$V = 20 \times 10 \times 10$
$= 2000\,\text{cm}^3$
$= 2000\,\text{mL}$
$= 2000 \div 1000\,\text{L}$
$= 2\,\text{L}$

EXPLANATION

$V = lwh$
$1\,\text{cm}^3 = 1\,\text{mL}$
There are 1000 mL in 1 litre.

Now you try

Find the capacity of this container, in litres.

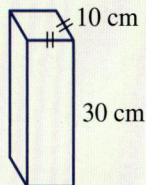

Exercise 10K

FLUENCY   1, 2(½), 3, 5, 7(½)   2(½), 3–5, 7(½)   2(¼), 4–6, 7(½)

1 Convert to the units shown in the brackets.

Example 19a
  a 700 mL (L)   **b** 8000 mL (L)   **c** 60 mL (L)

Example 19b
  d 2 kL (L)   **e** 5 kL (L)   **f** 7.5 kL (L)

Example 19
2 Convert to the units shown in brackets.

  a 2 L (mL)   **b** 0.1 L (mL)   **c** 6 ML (kL)   **d** 24 kL (L)

  e 2000 L (kL)   **f** 3500 mL (L)   **g** 70 000 mL (L)   **h** 2500 kL (ML)

  i 0.257 L (mL)   **j** 9320 mL (L)   **k** 3.847 ML (kL)   **l** 47 000 L (kL)

  m 0.5 kL (L)   **n** 91 000 kL (ML)   **o** 0.42 L (mL)   **p** 170 L (kL)

3 Read these scales to determine the amount of water in each of the containers.

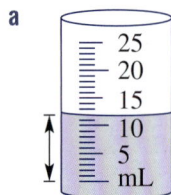

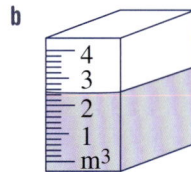

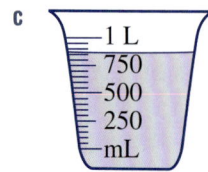

  a   **b**   **c**

4 A cup of 200 mL of water is added to a jug already containing 1 L of water. Find the total volume in:

  a mL   **b** L.

5 Convert to the units shown in brackets.

Example 20a
  a 4 700 000 mL (kL)   **b** 260 000 mL (kL)   **c** 5 000 000 L (ML)   **d** 3 840 000 L (ML)

Example 20b
  e 9 ML (L)   **f** 0.4 ML (L)   **g** 0.2 kL (mL)   **h** 0.005 kL (mL)

6 A farmer purchases 3.3 ML of water for her apple orchard. How many litres is this?

Example 21
7 Find the capacity of each of these rectangular prism containers, in litres.

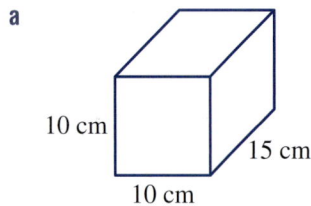

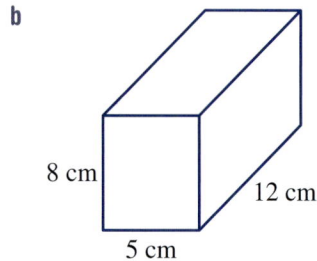

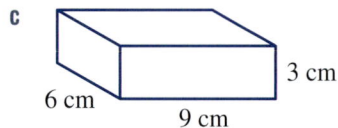

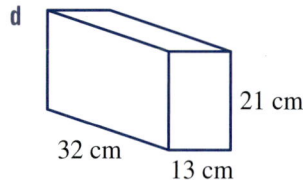

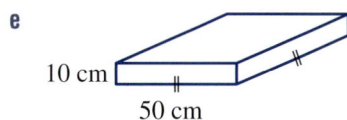

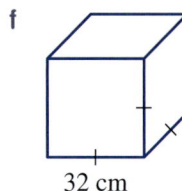

  a   **b**

  c   **d**

  e   **f**

PROBLEM-SOLVING   8, 9   9, 10   10–12

8 A swimming pool in the shape of a rectangular prism has length 50 m, width 25 m and depth 2 m. Find the swimming pool's:

    a volume, in m^3.   **b** capacity, in L.

9 A dripping tap leaks about 10 mL every minute.

    a If there are 50 drips per minute, find the volume of one drip.

    b Find the approximate volume of water, in litres, that has leaked from a tap after the following time periods.

       i 100 minutes   **ii** 1 hour   **iii** 1 day   **iv** 1 year

10 A dose of 12 mL of medicine is to be taken twice each day from a 0.36 L bottle. How many days will it take to finish the medicine?

11 A gas bottle contains 50 L of liquid gas. If the liquid gas is used at a rate of 20 mL per minute, how many hours will the gas bottle last?

12 A city's dams have 2 million megalitres of water and the average daily consumption of the city's people is 400 L per day per person. If the city's population is 5 million people, how long will the dam supply last without further water catchment?

REASONING   13   13   13, 14

13 If x is any number, then x litres is the same as $1000 \times x = 1000x$ millilitres because there are 1000 mL in 1 L. Write expressions for x L in the following units.

    a cm^3 **b** m^3 **c** kL   **d** ML

14 **a** A rectangular prism has length l cm, width w cm and height h cm. Write an expression for the capacity of the container measured in:

       i cm^3 **ii** mL   **iii** L   **iv** kL

    b A rectangular prism has length l m, width w m and height h m. Write an expression for the capacity of the container measured in:

       i m^3 **ii** L   **iii** kL   **iv** ML

ENRICHMENT: Added depth   –   –   15

15 A container is 10 cm long, 5 cm wide and 8 cm high.

    a Find the depth of water when the following amounts of water are poured in. (Remember: $1 \text{ mL} = 1 \text{ cm}^3$.)

       i 400 mL   **ii** 200 mL   **iii** 160 mL

8 cm   10 cm   5 cm

    b After adding 200 mL, a further 30 mL is added. What is the increase in depth?

    c A 1-litre container of milk has a base area of 8 cm by 7 cm. After 250 mL of milk is poured out, what is the depth of the milk remaining in the container? Give your answer to the nearest mm.

10L Mass and temperature CONSOLIDATING

LEARNING INTENTIONS
- To know that common metric units for mass are milligrams, grams, kilograms and tonnes
- To know that temperatures are commonly measured in degrees Celsius, where 0°C is the freezing point of water and 100°C is the boiling point of water
- To be able to convert between common units of mass

The scales for both mass and temperature are based on the properties of water. In France in 1795, the gram was defined as being the weight of $1\,cm^3$ of water at 0°C. Later it was redefined to be the weight at 4°C, as this is considered to be the temperature at which water is the most dense. So, 1 litre of water is very close to 1 kilogram, which is the basic unit for mass. Up until 2018, the kilogram was defined as the weight of a platinum-based ingot stored in Paris but recently the kilogram has been redefined in terms of an electric current. Other units for mass include the tonne, gram and milligram. A small car has a mass of about 1 tonne and a 20-cent coin has a mass of about 11 grams.

A small car has a mass of about 1 tonne. A vehicle ferry operator must keep the ship stable by balancing the mass of vehicles as the ferry is loaded and unloaded.

Temperature tells us how hot or cold something is. Anders Celsius (1701–1744), a Swedish scientist, worked to define a scale for temperature. After his death, temperature was officially defined by:

- 0°C (0 degrees Celsius) – the freezing point of water.
- 100°C (100 degrees Celsius) – the boiling point of water (at one standard unit of pressure).

This is still the common understanding of degrees Celsius. As mentioned in Chapter 9, Fahrenheit is another scale used for temperature. This is investigated further in the Enrichment questions.

Lesson starter: Choose a unit of mass

Choosing objects for given masses
Name five objects of which their mass would commonly be measured in:

- tonnes
- kilograms
- grams
- milligrams.

Choosing places for given temperatures
Is it possible for the temperature to drop below 0°C? How is this measured and can you give examples of places or situations where this might be the case?

Ice melts at 0°C.

KEY IDEAS

■ The basic unit for mass is the **kilogram** (kg). 1 litre of water has a mass that is very close to 1 kilogram.

■ Metric units for mass include:
  • 1 **gram** (g) = 1000 **milligrams** (mg)
  • 1 **kilogram** (kg) = 1000 **grams** (g)
  • 1 **tonne** (t) = 1000 **kilograms** (kg)

$$\times 1000 \qquad \times 1000 \qquad \times 1000$$

$$t \qquad kg \qquad g \qquad mg$$

$$\div 1000 \qquad \div 1000 \qquad \div 1000$$

■ The common unit for temperature is **degrees Celsius** (°C).
  • 0°C is the freezing point of water.
  • 100°C is the boiling point of water.

BUILDING UNDERSTANDING

1 Choose the pair of equal mass measurements.
  a 1 kg, 100 g, 1000 g, 10 t
  b 1000 mg, 10 kg, 1 g, 1000 t

2 From options **A** to **F**, choose the mass that best matches the given object.
  a human hair   **A** 300 g
  b 10-cent coin   **B** 40 kg
  c bottle   **C** 100 mg
  d large book   **D** 1.5 kg
  e large bag of sand   **E** 13 t
  f truck   **F** 5 g

3 From options **A** to **D**, choose the temperature that best matches the description.
  a temperature of coffee   **A** 15°C
  b temperature of tap water   **B** 50°C
  c temperature of oven   **C** −20°C
  d temperature in Antarctica   **D** 250°C

Example 22   Converting units of mass

Convert to the units shown in brackets.
a 2.47 kg (g)   **b** 170 000 kg (t)

SOLUTION

a 2.47 kg = 2.47 × 1000 g
           = 2470 g

EXPLANATION

1 kg = 1000 g
Multiply because you are changing to a smaller unit.

Continued on next page

b   170 000 kg = 170000 ÷ 1000 t   1 t = 1000 kg
                    = 170 t   Divide because you are changing to a
                                                         larger unit.

Now you try

Convert to the units shown in brackets.

a   32.5 kg (g)   **b**   9500 kg (t)

Exercise 10L

FLUENCY	1, 2(½), 3–7	2(½), 3, 4(½), 5, 7, 8	2(½), 6–9

1   Convert to the units shown in the brackets.

Example 22a   **a   i**   4.29 kg (g)   **ii**   7500 g (kg)

Example 22b   **b   i**   620 000 kg (t)   **ii**   5.1 t (kg)

Example 22   **2**   Convert to the units shown in brackets.

   a   2 t (kg)   **b**   70 kg (g)
   c   2.4 g (mg)   **d**   2300 mg (g)
   e   4620 mg (g)   **f**   21 600 kg (t)
   g   0.47 t (kg)   **h**   312 g (kg)
   i   27 mg (g)   **j** $\frac{3}{4}$ t (kg)
   k $\frac{1}{8}$ kg (g)   **l**   10.5 g (kg)
   m   210 000 kg (t)   **n**   0.47 t (kg)
   o   592 000 mg (g)   **p**   0.08 kg (g)

3   What mass is indicated on these scales?

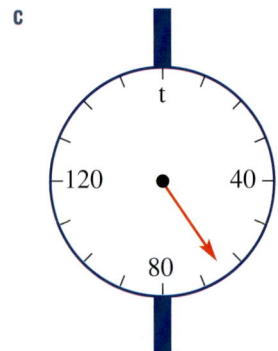

   a   **b**   **c**

4   What temperature is indicated on these scales?

a
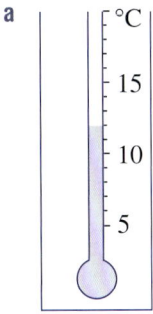

b
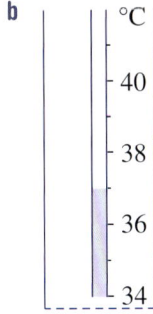

c
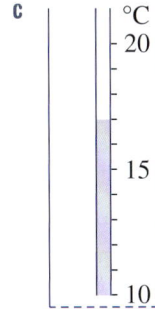

d
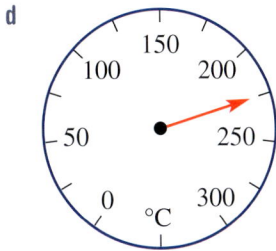

e
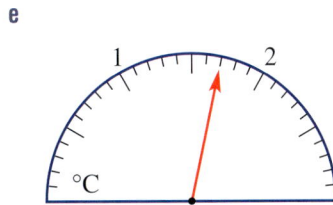

f
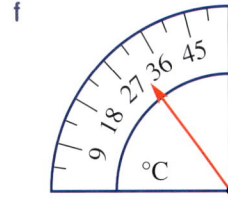

5   A small truck delivers 0.06 t of stones for a garden. Write the mass of stones using these units.
   a   kg
   b   g
   c   mg

6   A box contains 20 blocks of cheese, each weighing 150 g. What is the approximate mass of the box in the following units?
   a   g
   b   kg

7   The temperature of water in a cup is initially 95°C. After half an hour, the temperature is 62°C. What is the drop in temperature?

8   An oven is initially at a room temperature of 25°C. The oven dial is turned to 172°C. What is the expected increase in temperature?

9   Add all the mass measurements and give the result in kg.
   a   3 kg, 4000 g, 0.001 t
   b   2.7 kg, 430 g, 930 000 mg, 0.0041 t

PROBLEM-SOLVING	10,11	11,12	12–14

10   Arrange these mass measurements from smallest to largest.
   a   2.5 kg, 370 g, 0.1 t, 400 mg
   b   0.00032 t, 0.41 kg, 710 g, 290 000 mg

11   The highest and lowest temperatures recorded over a 7-day period are as follows.

Day	1	2	3	4	5	6	7
Lowest temperature (°C)	8	6	10	9	7	8	10
Highest temperature (°C)	24	27	31	32	21	19	29

   a   Which day had the largest temperature range?
   b   What is the largest temperature drop from the highest temperature on one day to the lowest temperature on the next day?
   c   What would have been the final temperature on Day 7 if the temperature increased from the minimum by 16°C?

12 A 10 kg bag of flour is used at a rate of 200 g per day. How many days will the bag of flour last?

13 A boat has a weight limit of 3.5 t carrying capacity. Loaded onto the boat are 1500 tins of coffee at 500 g each, 36 bags of grain at 20 kg each, 190 boxes of mangoes at 5.5 kg each and 15 people, averaging 80 kg each. Is the load too much for the weight limit of the boat?

14 A truck tare mass (i.e. mass with no load) is 13.2 t. The truck's gross mass is 58.5 t. This is the total maximum mass allowed, including the load.
a   What is the maximum load the truck can carry?
b   The truck is loaded with 120 timber beams at 400 kg each. Will it exceed its gross weight limit?

REASONING	15	15,16	16,17

15 Water weighs 1 kg per litre. What is the mass of these volumes of water?
a   1 mL   b   1 kL   c   1 ML

16 The containers shown below are in the shape of rectangular prisms and are filled with water. Calculate the mass of water in each container, in kg.

a

15 cm
40 cm
20 cm

b

1 m

c

2 m
12 m
15 m

17 The kelvin (K) is a temperature unit used by many scientists, where 273 K is approximately 0°C. (The kelvin used to be called the 'degree kelvin' or °K.) An increase in 1 K is the same as an increase in 1°C.
a   Write the following temperatures in °C.
  i   283 K   ii   300 K   iii   1000 K
b   Write the following temperatures in kelvins.
  i   0°C   ii   40°C   iii   −273°C

ENRICHMENT: Fahrenheit	–	–	18

18 Daniel Fahrenheit (1686–1736) proposed the Fahrenheit temperature scale in 1724. It was commonly used in Australia up until the mid-twentieth century, and is still used today in the United States.
32°F is the freezing point of water.
212°F is the boiling point of water.
a   What is the difference between the temperature, in Fahrenheit, for the boiling point of water and the freezing point of water?
b   An increase of temperature by 1°F is the same as an increase by what amount in °C?

Liquid nitrogen freezes at −210°C and boils at −196°C.

c   An increase of temperature by 1°C is the same as an increase by what amount in °F?
d   To convert from °F to °C, we use the formula $C = (F - 32) \times \frac{5}{9}$. Convert these Fahrenheit temperatures to °C.
  i   32°F   ii   68°F   iii   140°F   iv   221°F
e   Find the rule to convert from °C to °F. Test your rule to see if it works and write it down.

Estimating park lake area

A local shire wants to estimate the volume of water in its local lake. The bird's-eye view of the lake is shown here and each grid square represents 10 metres by 10 metres. The average depth of water in the lake is 3 metres.

Present a report for the following tasks and ensure that you show clear mathematical workings and explanations where appropriate.

Preliminary task

a   Estimate the area of the shaded region in the following grids. Each grid square represents an area of one square metre.

i 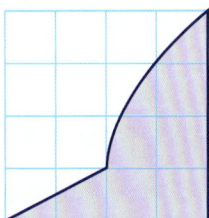   ii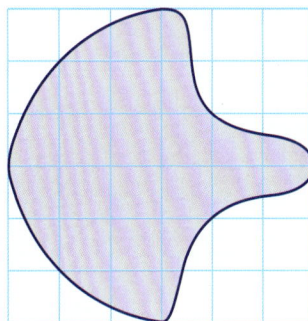

b   A body of water has a surface area of $2000\,\text{m}^2$. The volume of water can be found using the formula: Volume = Surface Area × Depth.
   If the average depth of the water is 3 metres, find:
   i   the volume of water in cubic metres
   ii the volume of water in litres. Use the fact that $1\,\text{m}^3 = 1000\,\text{L}$.

Modelling task

rmulate

a   The problem is to estimate the volume of water in the shire lake. Write down all the relevant information that will help solve the problem.

b   Outline your method for estimating the surface area of the lake shown above.

Solve

c   Estimate the area of the lake in square metres. Explain your method, showing any calculations.

d   Estimate the volume of water in the lake. Give your answer in both m^3 and in litres.

ate and verify

e   Compare your results with others in your class and state the range of answers provided.

f   Review your method for estimating the surface area of the lake and refine your calculation.

g   Explain how you improved your method to find the surface area of the lake.

unicate

h   Summarise your results and describe any key findings. You should also describe any methods you could use to obtain a better estimate of the volume.

Extension questions

a   Use the internet to find a map or satellite view of a lake in your local area, then estimate its area.

b   Compare how your estimates and methods would change if the lake's depth is no longer assumed to be a constant 3 metres.

Dynamic area formulas

(Key technology: Dynamic geometry)
In many industries like architecture, design and construction, it is common to calculate areas of shapes. To do this we use formulas including two or more variables. An understanding of how these formulas work helps to make calculations and solve more complex problems involving composite shapes and three-dimensional solids.

1 Getting started

Consider the formula for the area of a triangle, $A = \frac{1}{2}bh$.

a   Use the formula to find the area of these triangles.

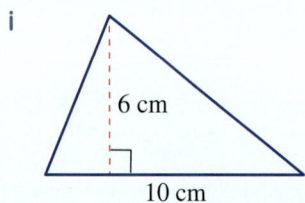

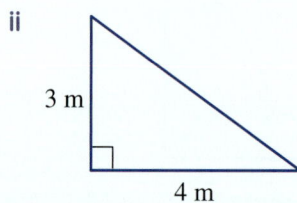

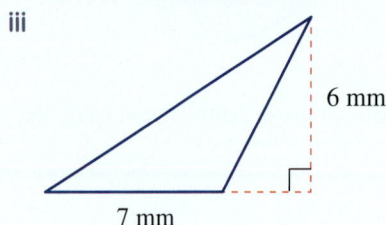

i

6 cm

10 cm

ii

3 m

4 m

iii

6 mm

7 mm

b   By redrawing the above triangles and adding other line segments, show that it is possible to view all of the above three triangles as half of a parallelogram.

c   Explain how the area formula for a triangle is connected to the area of a parallelogram.

2 Applying an algorithm

a   Open a dynamic geometry program or website and follow these steps to construct a triangle with fixed height.

- Construct a line AB.
- Construct a line parallel to AB and passing through D.
- Place a point C on the parallel line.
- Construct a line perpendicular to AB passing through C and construct point E.
- Construct the triangle ABC by constructing AB, BC and AC.
- Construct the segment CE.
- Construct the triangle ABC using the polygon tool.
- Measure the lengths of the segments AB and CE and the area of triangle ABC.

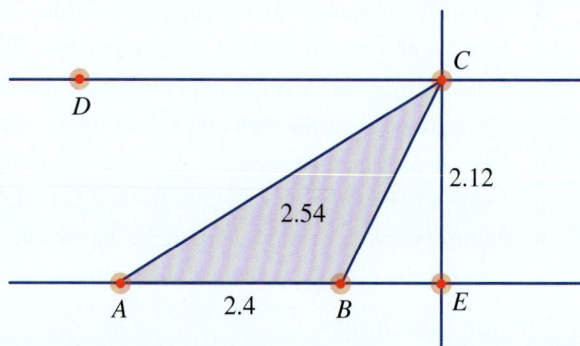

D

C

2.54

2.12

A   2.4   B

E

b Drag the point C on the constructed parallel line. What do you notice about the three measurements? Do your observations remain the same for an acute, a right and an obtuse triangle?

c Adjust one of the points A or B to change the base length, then repeat part **b** above. What do you notice?

3 Using technology

a Explore the formula for the area of a parallelogram using a dynamic geometry, by following these steps.

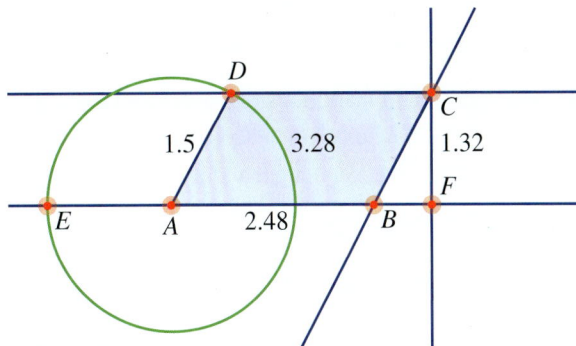

- Construct a line AB and segment AB.
- Construct a circle with centre A and radius AE with E on line AB.
- Construct point D on the circle.
- Construct a line parallel to AB passing through D.
- Construct the line segment AD.
- Construct a line parallel to AD passing through B.
- Construct point C.
- Construct a line perpendicular to AB passing through C.
- Construct the point F and line segment CF.
- Construct the quadrilateral ABCD using the polygon tool.
- Measure the lengths AB, CF and AD and the area of ABCD.

b By dragging point D on the circle, the length AD does not change. Drag point D to change the area of the parallelogram. What do you notice?

c As you drag point D, what do you notice about the length CF? When the length CF is close to zero, what is the area of the parallelogram?

d Drag the point E or B to change the size of the parallelogram. Then repeat parts **b** and **c** above.

e What do your observations tell you about the formula for the area of a parallelogram?

4 Extension

a Use dynamic geometry to construct a circle. Calculate the circumference and diameter. Show that regardless of the size of the circle, the circumference divided by the diameter is equal to π.

b Construct a quadrilateral of your choice using dynamic geometry and calculate its area. Explore how the area depends on the lengths corresponding to the variables in the area formula.

Investigation

Opal mining

Greg, Sally and Alston apply for a mining licence to look for opals at Coober Pedy in South Australia. They are required to choose an area and mark it out with special orange tape so that others will know which areas are already taken. Their length of tape is 200 m.

Square mining areas

They first decide to mark out an area as a square.

a   Make a drawing of their square area.

b   Calculate the side length and area and show this on your diagram. Also show any working.

Rectangular mining areas

They then change the mining area and experiment with different side lengths.

a   Show three possible lengths and areas for rectangular mining sites.

b   Complete a table similar to the one below. Fill in the missing numbers for the side lengths given, then add your own rectangle measurements from part a above.

Length	Width	Perimeter	Area
10		200	
20		200	
35		200	
		200	
		200	
		200	

c   Are there any rectangles that give a larger area than the square mining area from above?

Circular mining areas

They now decide to try to arrange the tape to form a circle. For this section, you will need the rule to calculate the distance around a circle (circumference). The circumference C is given by $C = 2 \times \pi \times r$ where r is the length of the radius and $\pi \approx 3.14$.

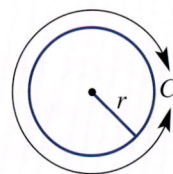

a   Calculate the radius of the circle correct to one decimal place. Use a trial and error (guess and check) technique and remember that the circumference will be 200 m. Explain and show your method using a table of values.

b   Calculate the area of the circular mining area correct to the nearest square metre. Use the special rule for the area of a circle A which is given by $A = \pi \times r^2$.

The largest area

Compare the areas marked out with the 200 m tape by Greg, Sally and Alston. Comment on any differences. Which shape gives the largest area for the given perimeter? Would your answer be the same if any shape were allowed to be used? Explain.

1   Without measuring, state which line looks longer: A or B? Then measure to check your answer.

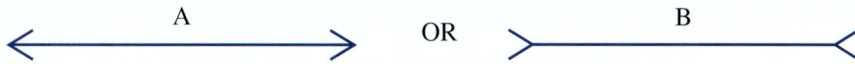

> Up for a challenge? If you get stuck on a question, check out the 'Working with unfamiliar problems' poster at the end of the book to help you.

A   OR   B

2   You have two sticks of length 3 m and 5 m, both with no scales. How might you mark a length of 1 m?

3   Count squares to estimate the area of these circles if each grid square is 1 cm across.

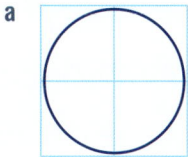

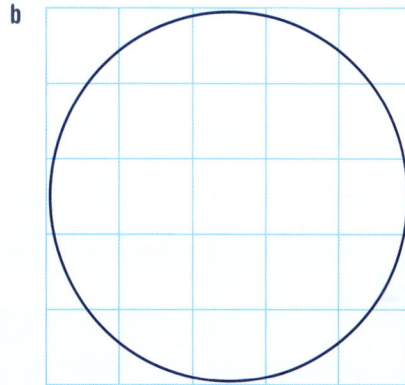

a

b

4   A house roof has 500 m^2 of area. If there is 1 mm of rainfall, how much water, in litres, can be collected from the roof?

5   Work out the volume of this rectangular prism with the given face areas.

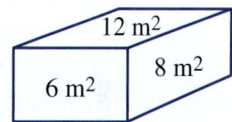

12 m^2
8 m^2
6 m^2

6   Find the area of the shaded region in the diagram shown at right.

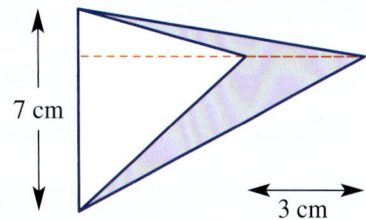

7 cm

3 cm

7   A cube of side length 20 cm contains 5 L of water.
   a   What is the depth of water in the cube?
   b   What is the increase in depth if 1.5 L is added to the cube of water?

8   These two rectangles overlap, as shown. Find the total area of the shaded region.

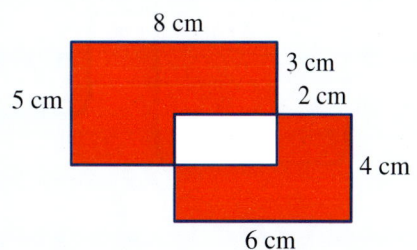

8 cm
3 cm
5 cm
2 cm
4 cm
6 cm

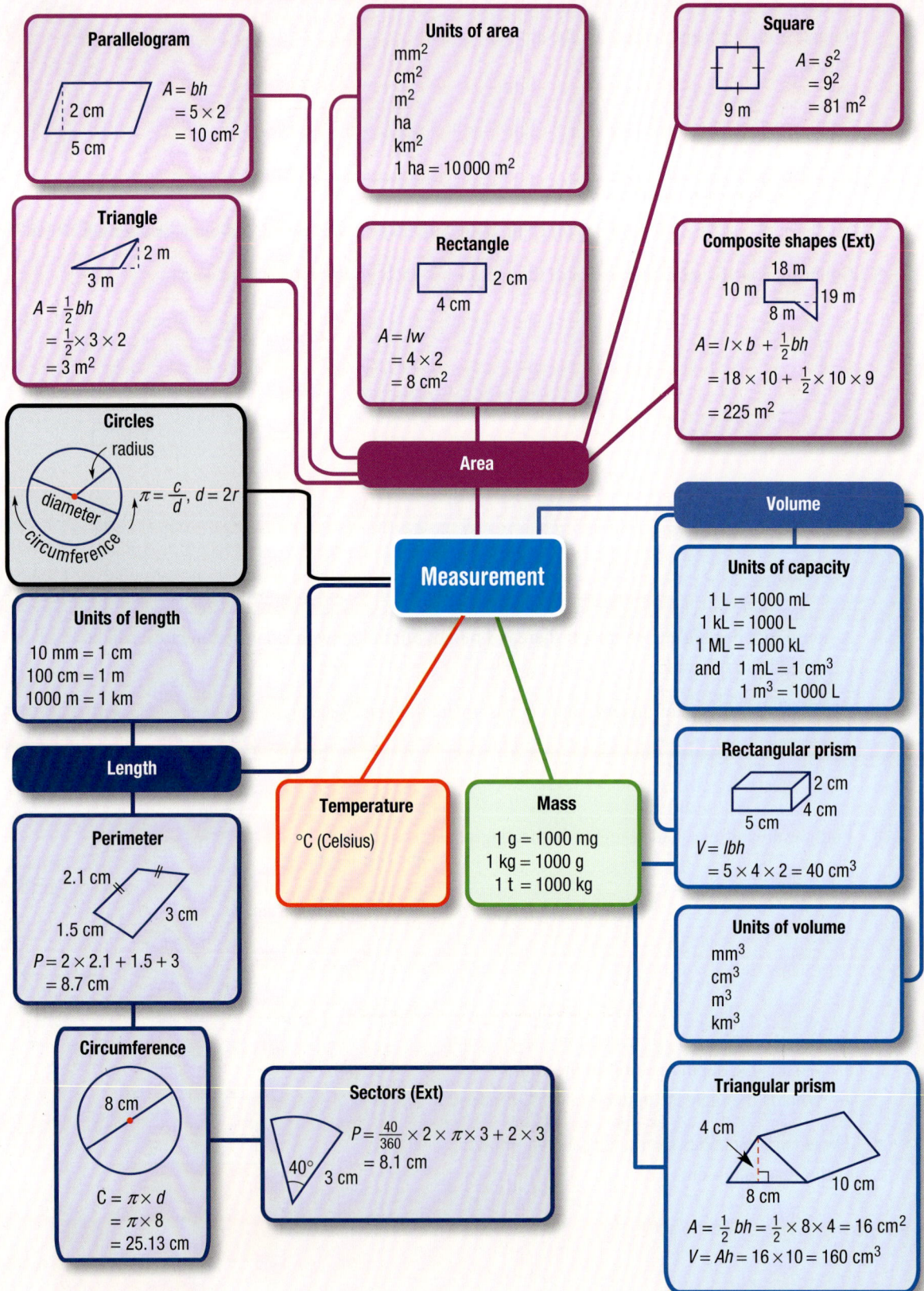

Chapter summary

Parallelogram

$A = bh$
$= 5 \times 2$
$= 10 \text{ cm}^2$

2 cm
5 cm

Units of area

mm^2
cm^2
m^2
ha
km^2
$1 \text{ ha} = 10\,000 \text{ m}^2$

Square

$A = s^2$
$= 9^2$
$= 81 \text{ m}^2$

9 m

Triangle

2 m
3 m

$A = \frac{1}{2}bh$
$= \frac{1}{2} \times 3 \times 2$
$= 3 \text{ m}^2$

Rectangle

2 cm
4 cm

$A = lw$
$= 4 \times 2$
$= 8 \text{ cm}^2$

Composite shapes (Ext)

18 m
10 m   19 m
8 m

$A = l \times b + \frac{1}{2}bh$
$= 18 \times 10 + \frac{1}{2} \times 10 \times 9$
$= 225 \text{ m}^2$

Circles

radius
diameter
circumference

$\pi = \frac{c}{d}, \; d = 2r$

Area

Measurement

Volume

Units of length

$10 \text{ mm} = 1 \text{ cm}$
$100 \text{ cm} = 1 \text{ m}$
$1000 \text{ m} = 1 \text{ km}$

Units of capacity

$1 \text{ L} = 1000 \text{ mL}$
$1 \text{ kL} = 1000 \text{ L}$
$1 \text{ ML} = 1000 \text{ kL}$
and $1 \text{ mL} = 1 \text{ cm}^3$
$1 \text{ m}^3 = 1000 \text{ L}$

Length

Temperature

°C (Celsius)

Mass

$1 \text{ g} = 1000 \text{ mg}$
$1 \text{ kg} = 1000 \text{ g}$
$1 \text{ t} = 1000 \text{ kg}$

Rectangular prism

2 cm
5 cm   4 cm

$V = lbh$
$= 5 \times 4 \times 2 = 40 \text{ cm}^3$

Perimeter

2.1 cm
1.5 cm   3 cm

$P = 2 \times 2.1 + 1.5 + 3$
$= 8.7 \text{ cm}$

Units of volume

mm^3
cm^3
m^3
km^3

Circumference

8 cm

$C = \pi \times d$
$= \pi \times 8$
$= 25.13 \text{ cm}$

Sectors (Ext)

40°   3 cm

$P = \frac{40}{360} \times 2 \times \pi \times 3 + 2 \times 3$
$= 8.1 \text{ cm}$

Triangular prism

4 cm
8 cm   10 cm

$A = \frac{1}{2}bh = \frac{1}{2} \times 8 \times 4 = 16 \text{ cm}^2$
$V = Ah = 16 \times 10 = 160 \text{ cm}^3$

Chapter checklist with success criteria

A printable version of this checklist is available in the Interactive Textbook   ✔

10A	**1. I can choose a suitable metric unit for measuring a length.** e.g. Which metric unit would be most appropriate for measuring the width of a large room?	☐
10A	**2. I can convert metric units of length.** e.g. Convert 25 600 cm to km.	☐
10A	**3. I can read a length scale.** e.g. Measure the marked length on the scale. 4 m 5 m 6 m 7 m	☐
10B	**4. I can find the perimeter of a shape.** e.g. Find the perimeter of this shape. 3 m 6 m 5 m 2 m	☐
10C	**5. I can approximate π using a fraction.** e.g. Round $\frac{25}{8}$ using three decimal places and decide if $\frac{25}{8}$ is a better approximation to π than the number 3.14.	☐
10C	**6. I can calculate the circumference of a circle.** e.g. Calculate the circumference of this circle, rounding your answer correct to two decimal places. 8 cm	☐
10D	**7. I can find the perimeter of a sector.** e.g. Find the perimeter of this sector, correct to two decimal places. 100° 4 m **Ext**	☐
10D	**8. I can find the perimeter of a composite shape.** e.g. Find the perimeter of this composite shape, correct to two decimal places. 5 m 8 m **Ext**	☐
10E	**9. I can find the area of a shape by considering squares on a grid.** e.g. Count the number of squares to find the area of the shape drawn on this centimetre grid.	☐

Chapter checklist

		✔
10E	**10. I can find the area of squares and other rectangles.** e.g. Find the area of this rectangle. 4 mm 10 mm	☐
10F	**11. I can find the area of parallelograms.** e.g. Find the area of this parallelogram. 5 m 12 m	☐
10G	**12. I can find the area of triangles.** e.g. Find the area of this triangle. 9 cm 10 cm	☐
10H	**13. I can find the area of composite shapes.** **Ext** e.g. Find the area of this composite shape. 4 cm 6 cm	☐
10I	**14. I can find the volume of rectangular prisms (cuboids).** e.g. Find the volume of this cuboid. 4 cm 8 cm 3 cm	☐
10J	**15. I can find the volume of triangular prisms.** e.g. Find the volume of this triangular prism. 2 cm 5 cm 4 cm	☐
10K	**16. I can convert between units of capacity.** e.g. Convert 500 mL to litres.	☐
10K	**17. I can convert between volumes and capacities.** e.g. A container has a volume of 2000 cubic centimetres. Find its capacity in litres.	☐
10L	**18. I can convert between units of mass.** e.g. Convert 2.47 kg to grams.	☐

Short-answer questions

10A

1 Using the metric system, state how many:
  a millimetres in 1 cm   **b** metres in 1 km   **c** centimetres in 1 km.

10A

2 Convert to the units shown in brackets.
  a 5 cm (mm)   **b** 200 cm (m)   **c** 3.7 km (m)   **d** 421 000 cm (km)
  e 7.1 kg (g)   **f** 24 900 mg (g)   **g** 28 490 kg (t)   **h** 0.009 t (g)
  i 4000 mL (L)   **j** 29 903 L (kL)   **k** 0.4 ML (kL)   **l** 0.001 kL (mL)
  m 1 day (min)   **n** 3600 s (min)   **o** 84 h (days)   **p** 2.5 h (s)

10A

3 Read these scales.

a

b

c
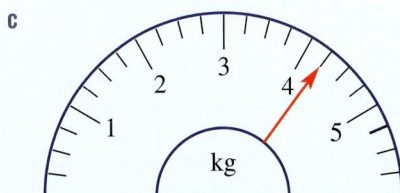

d
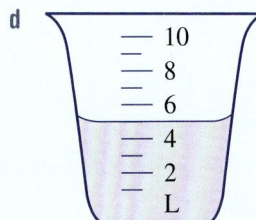

10B

4 Find the perimeter of these shapes. Assume that all angles that look like right angles are right angles.

a
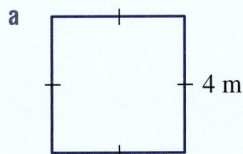
4 m

b
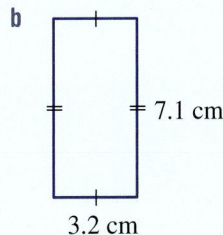
7.1 cm
3.2 cm

c
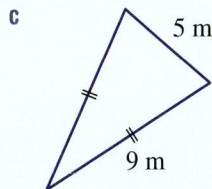
5 m
9 m

d
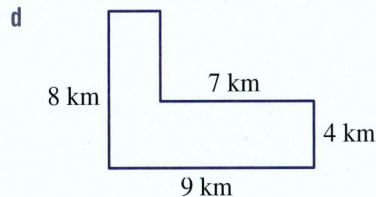
8 km
7 km
4 km
9 km

e
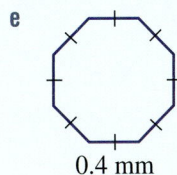
0.4 mm

f
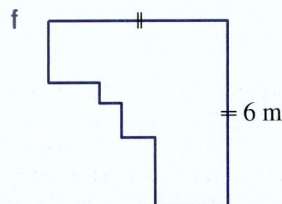
6 m

10C

5 A common approximation to π is $\frac{22}{7}$.

a Write $\frac{22}{7}$ rounded to three decimal places.

b Decide if $\frac{22}{7}$ is a better approximation to π than the number 3.14.

10C

6 Calculate the circumference of these circles using a calculator and rounding your answer correct to two decimal places.

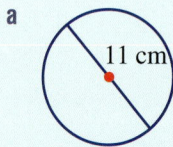

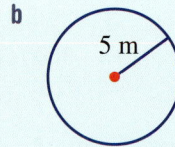

a

11 cm

b

5 m

10D

Ext

7 Find the perimeter of these shapes, correct to one decimal place.

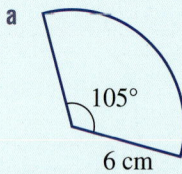

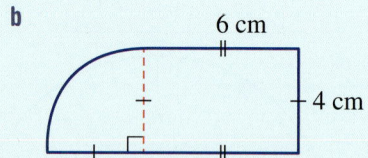

a

105°

6 cm

b

6 cm

4 cm

10F/G

8 Find the area of each of the following shapes. Assume that all angles that look like right angles are right angles.

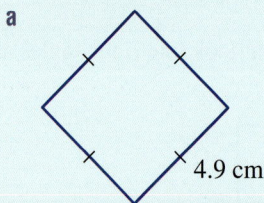

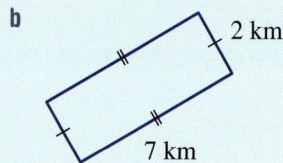

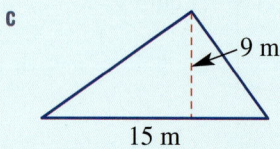

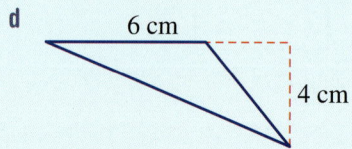

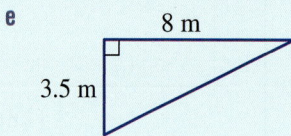

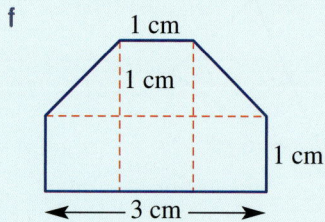

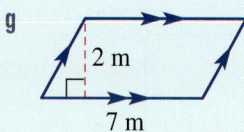

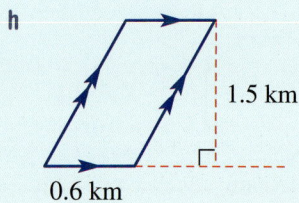

a

4.9 cm

b

2 km

7 km

c

9 m

15 m

d

6 cm

4 cm

e

8 m

3.5 m

f

1 cm

1 cm

1 cm

3 cm

g

2 m

7 m

h

1.5 km

0.6 km

10H

(Ext) ▦

9 Find the area of these composite shapes. Assume that all angles that look like right angles are right angles.

a

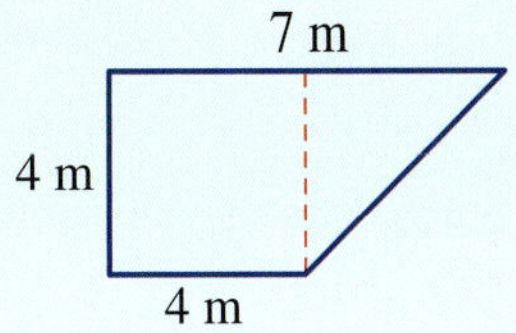

7 m

4 m

4 m

b

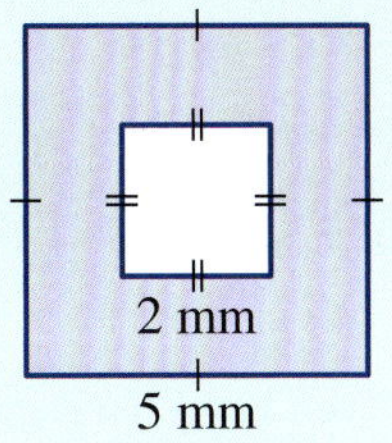

2 mm

5 mm

c

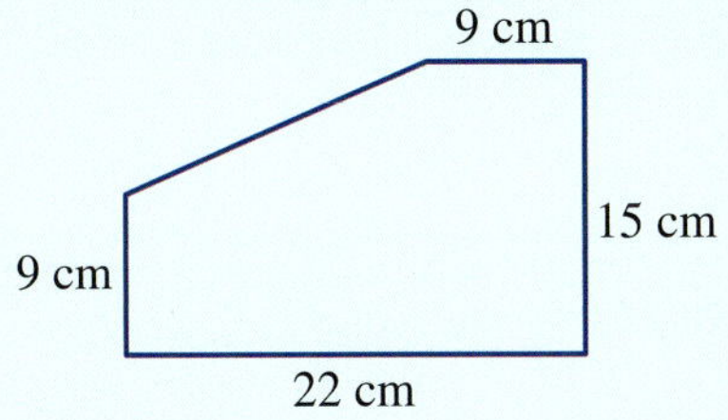

9 cm

9 cm

15 cm

22 cm

d

2 m

6 m

4 m

12 m

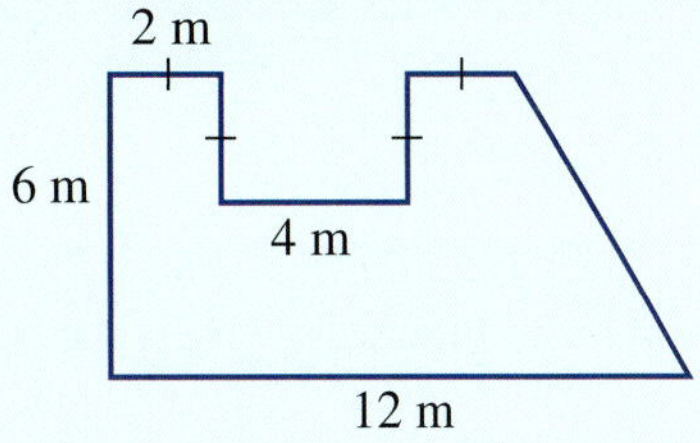

10I

▦

10 Find the volume contained in each of these rectangular prisms.

a

1 cm cubes

b

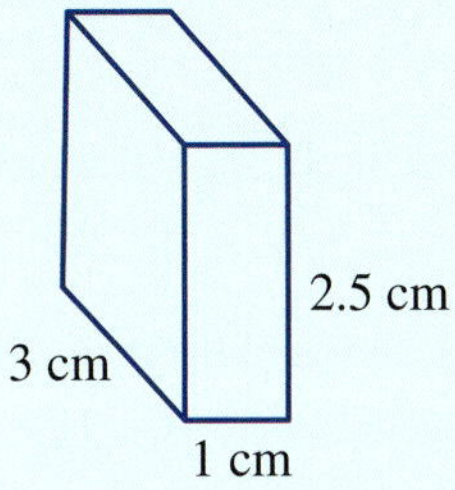

2.5 cm

3 cm

1 cm

c

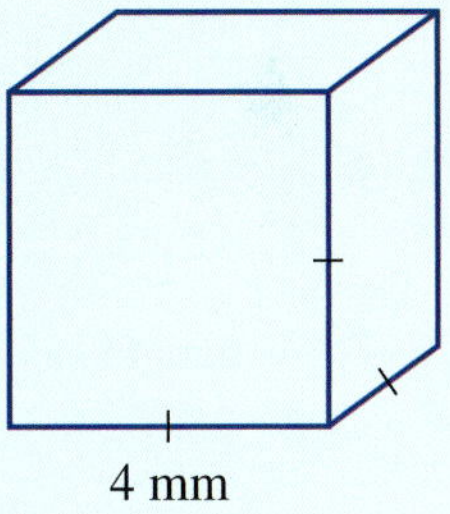

4 mm

10J

11 Find the volume of these triangular prisms.

a

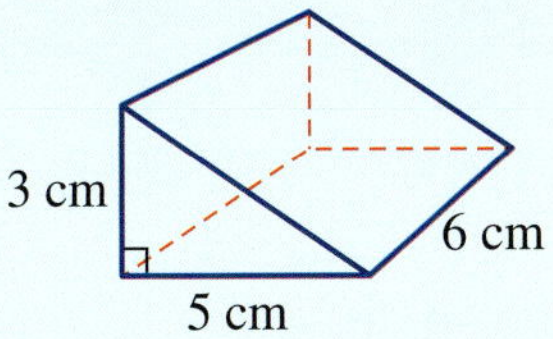

3 cm

5 cm

6 cm

b

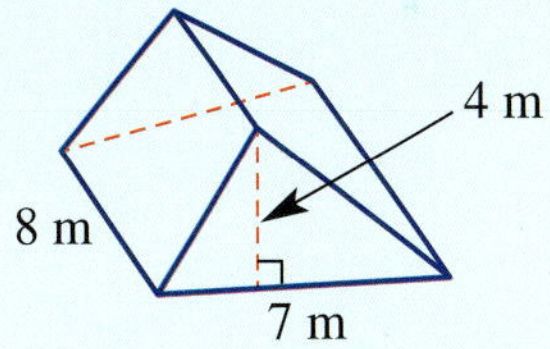

8 m

4 m

7 m

c

6 mm

7 mm

10 mm

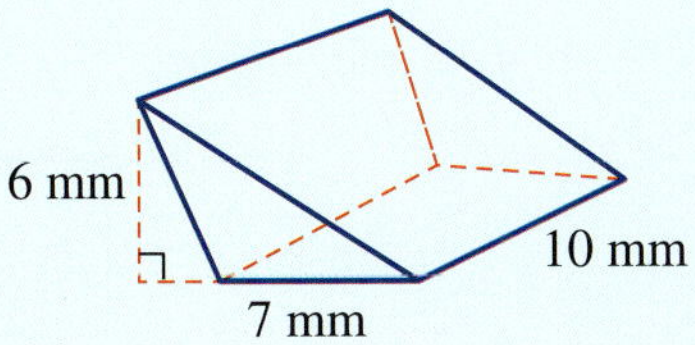

10K

▦

12 A rectangular fish tank is of length 60 cm, width 40 cm and height 30 cm. Give the tank's capacity in:

a cm^3 **b** mL   **c** L.

10L

▦

13 Arrange these measurements from smallest to largest.

a 3 t, 4700 kg, 290 000 g, 45 mg

b 50 000 mL, 1 ML, 51 L, 0.5 kL

Chapter review

Multiple-choice questions

10A

1 How many millimetres are there in 1 m?

A 1   B 10   C 100   D 1000   E 10000

10A

2 Shonali buys 300 cm of wire that costs $2 per metre. How much does she pay for the wire?

A $150   B $600   C $1.50   D $3   E $6

10B

3 The triangle given has a perimeter of 20 cm. What is the missing base length?

A 6 cm   B 8 cm   C 4 cm

D 16 cm   E 12 cm

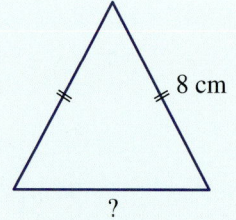

10C

4 Which of the following is the best approximation of π?

A $\frac{61}{20}$ B $\frac{41}{12}$ C $\frac{20}{7}$ D $\frac{10}{3}$ E $\frac{16}{5}$

10D

(Ext) (calc)

5 The length of the arc only on a sector with a centre angle of 160° and radius 7 cm is closest to:

A 19.0 cm   B 20.1 cm   C 19.5 cm   D 9.8 cm   E 33.5 cm

10E

6 The area of a rectangle with length 2 m and width 5 m is:

A 10 m^2 B 5 m^2 C 5 m   D 5 m^3 E 10 m

10G

(calc)

7 A triangle has base length 3.2 cm and height 4 cm. What is its area?

A 25.6 cm^2 B 12.8 cm   C 12.8 cm^2 D 6 cm   E 6.4 cm^2

10H

(Ext) (calc)

8 The total area of this composite shape is:

A 56 km^2 B 45.5 km^2 C 35 km^2

D 10.5 km^2 E 24.5 km^2

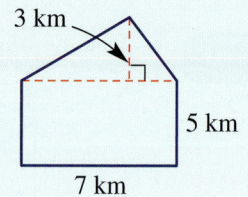

10I

9 A cube has a side length of 3 cm. Its volume is:

A 27 cm^3 B 9 cm^2 C 3 cm   D 9 cm^3 E 36 cm^3

10J

10 A triangular prism has cross-sectional area A cm^2, height 4 cm and volume 36 cm^3. The value of A is:

A 3   B 18   C 9

D 4.5   E 27

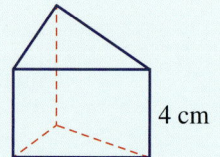

10K

11 2000 cm^3 is the same as:

A 2 m^3 B 2 L   C 2 kL   D 2 mL   E 2 t

10L

(calc)

12 9 tonnes of iron ore is being loaded onto a ship at a rate of 20 kg per second. How many minutes will it take to load all of the 9 tonnes of ore?

A 0.75 min   B 45 min   C 7.3 min   D 450 min   E 7.5 min

10G

13 The base length of a parallelogram is 10 cm and its area is 30 cm^2. The parallelogram's height is:

A 10 cm   B 3 cm   C 30 cm   D 3 cm^2 E 10 m^2

Extended-response questions

1 A truck carries a large rectangular container of dimensions 6 m long, 3 m wide and 2 m high. The truck weighs 15.4 tonnes without its load.

   a Find the area of the base of the container in:

      i m^2 **ii** cm^2.

   b Find the volume of the container in m^3.

   c How many litres of water could the truck hold in the container?

   d Since 1 L of water weighs 1 kg, give the weight of the truck if the container was filled with water. Give your answer in tonnes.

   e The truck completes three journeys, which take, on average, 1 hour, 17 minutes and 38 seconds per trip. What is the total time for the three journeys?

Ext **2** Lachlan builds a race track around the outside of his family house block. The block combines rectangular and triangular areas, as shown in the diagram.

   a How far is one complete circuit of the track?

   b Lachlan can jog 10 laps at about 33 seconds each. What is the total time, in minutes and seconds, that it takes him to complete the 10 laps?

   c What is the total area of the block?

   d The house occupies $100\,m^2$ and the rest of the block is to have instant turf, costing \$12 per square metre. What will be the cost for the instant turf?

   e The house sits on a concrete slab that is 50 cm deep. What is the volume of concrete, in m^3?

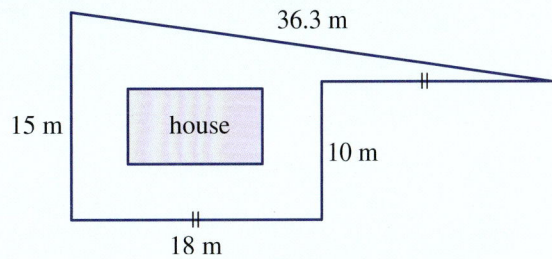

Negative numbers

Short-answer questions

1 For each of the following, insert =, > or <.

    a $-3\_\_3$ **b** $-10 \div 2\_\_5$ **c** $-20 \times (-1)\_\_\dfrac{-40}{-2}$

2 Calculate:

    a $-5 + (-8)$ **b** $12 - 96$ **c** $-12 - 96$

    d $-4 - 8 - 9$ **e** $-12 + 96$ **f** $-7 - (-7)$

(Ext) 3 Find:

    a -6×4 **b** $-9 \times 8 \times (-1)$ **c** $(-12)^2$

    d $\dfrac{-9 \times (-7)}{3}$ **e** $-150 \div (-2 - 3)$ **f** $-10 + 7 \times (-3)$

(Ext) 4 State whether the answer to each of the following is positive or negative.

    a $-3 \times (-3) \times (-3)$ **b** $-109 \times 142 \times (-83)$ **c** $-2 \times (-1 - (-3))$

(Ext) 5 Copy and complete.

    a $\_\_ + 9 = -6$ **b** $\_\_ \times (-3) = -6 \times (-4)$ **c** $16 \times \_\_ = -64$

(Ext) 6 If $a = 6$ and $b = -4$, find the value of:

    a $-a + b$ **b** $a - b$ **c** $2(b - a)$

    d $-ab^2$ **e** $a^2 + b^2$ **f** $24 \div (ab)$

Multiple-choice questions

1 Which of the following statements is incorrect?

    A $-2 > -4$ **B** $0 < 5$ **C** $0 < -10$ **D** $-9 < -8$ **E** $-5 < 3$

2 $12 + (-9) - (-3)$ is the same as:

    A $12 + 9 + 3$ **B** $12 - 9 + 3$ **C** $12 - 9 - 3$ **D** $12 - 12$ **E** 12

(Ext) 3 If $a = -3$, the value of $a^2 \times -2$ is:

    A 36 **B** -36 **C** 18 **D** -18 **E** 12

4 The point that is 3 units below $(3, 1)$ has coordinates:

    A $(0, 1)$ **B** $(0, -2)$ **C** $(0, -1)$ **D** $(3, 4)$ **E** $(3, -2)$

(Ext) 5 $12 \times (-4 + (-8) \div 2)$ equals:

    A -96 **B** 72 **C** -72 **D** 60 **E** 96

Extended-response question

Refer to the given Cartesian plane when answering these questions.

a Name any point that lies in the first quadrant.

b Name any point(s) with a y-value of zero. Where does each point lie?

c Which point has coordinates $(-1, -2)$?

d Find the distance between points:

    i A and B **ii** D and E.

e What shape is formed by joining the points $IDAG$?

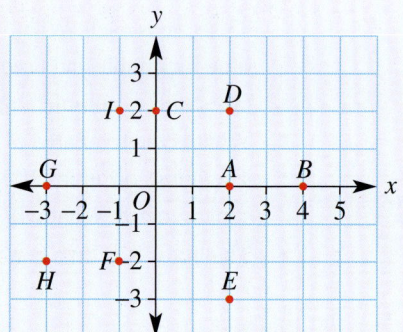

f   What is the area of *IDAG*?

g   *ABXD* are the vertices of a square. What are the coordinates of *X*?

h   Decode: (2, 2), (2, −3), (0, 2), (−1, 2), (2, 2), (2, −3)

Geometry

Short-answer questions

1 **a**   Name two pairs of parallel lines.

    b   Name a pair of perpendicular lines.

    c   List any three lines that are concurrent. At what point do they cross?

    d   Name two points that are collinear with point *C*.

    e   Name the point at which line *BE* and line *FD* intersect.

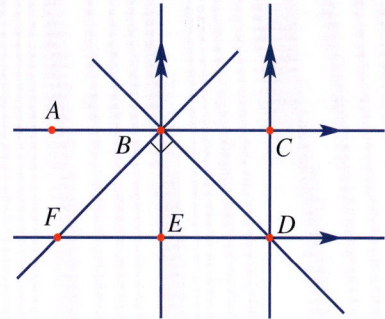

2   Measure these angles.

    a

    b

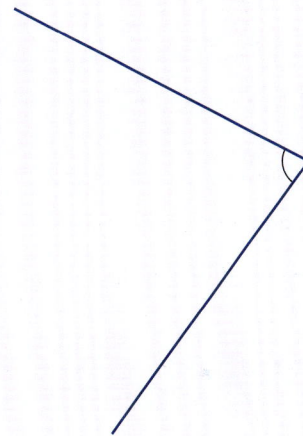

    c

3   What angle is complementary to 65°?

4   What angle is supplementary to 102°?

5   Find the value of *a* in each of the following angles.

    a

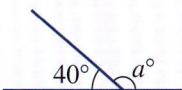

    b

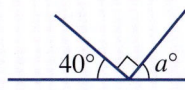

    c

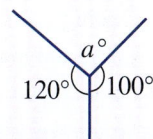

    d

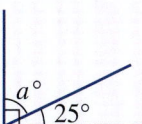

    e

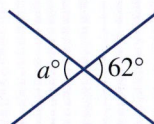

    f

6 Find the value of each angle formed when these two parallel lines are crossed by the transversal, as shown.

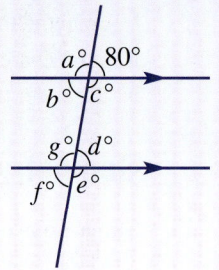

7 Name each of the following shapes.

a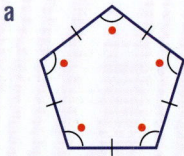

b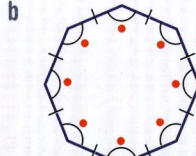

c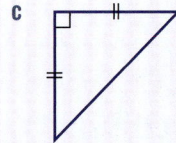

d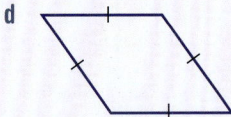

e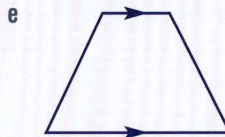

f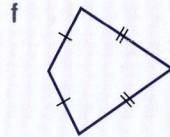

8 Find the value of a in these diagrams.

a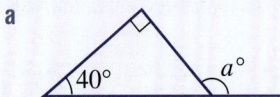

b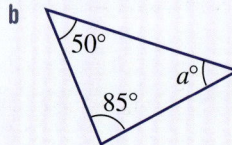

c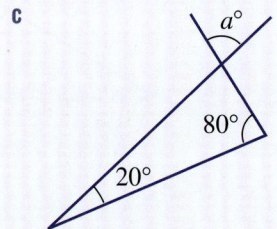

9 For each of the following, find the value of every pronumeral.

a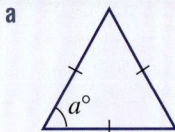

b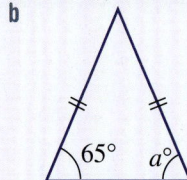

c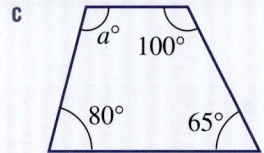

d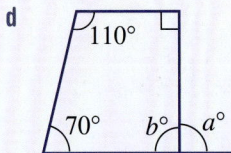

e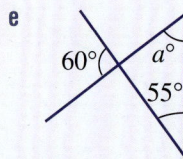

f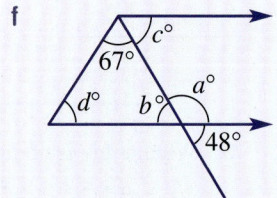

10 State the coordinates of the vertices of the image triangle (A', B' and C') if triangle ABC is transformed in the following ways.

a reflected in the x-axis

b reflected in the y-axis

c rotated about $O(0, 0)$ by 90° clockwise

d rotated about $O(0, 0)$ by 90° anticlockwise

e rotated about $O(0, 0)$ by 180°

f translated 4 units to the left and 1 unit up

g translated 3 units to the left and 2 units down

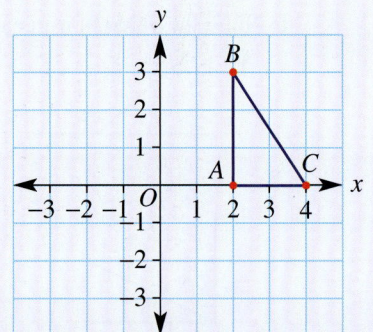

Multiple-choice questions

1   Which statement is correct?
    A   Line m is perpendicular to line l.
    B   Line m bisects line l.
    C   Line m is parallel to line l.
    D   Line m is shorter than line l.
    E   Line m is longer than line l.

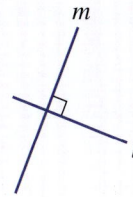

2   An angle of $181°$ is classified as:
    A   acute   **B**   reflex   **C**   straight   **D**   obtuse   **E**   sharp

3   Which two angles represent alternate angles?
    A $a°$ and $e°$
    B $d°$ and $f°$
    C $a°$ and $f°$
    D $g°$ and $b°$
    E $c°$ and $f°$

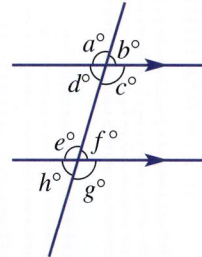

4   Which of the following shows a pair of supplementary angles? Assume that lines which look parallel are parallel.
    A   **B**   **C**

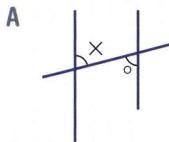

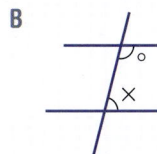

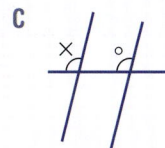

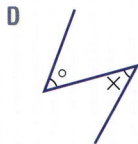

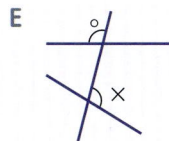

    D   **E**

5   The order of rotation of a parallelogram is:
    A   2   **B**   4   **C**   3   **D**   0   **E**   1

Extended-response question

a   Draw any triangle in your workbook and extend each side, as shown below.
b   Measure the angles a, b and c. What should they add to?
c   Find the values of x, y and z (i.e. the exterior angles of the triangle).
d   What is the total of angles $x + y + z$?
e   Repeat for any quadrilateral, as shown below. What is the value of $w + x + y + z$?

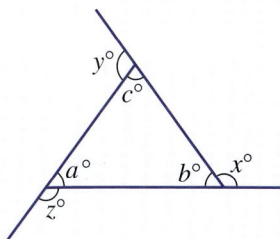

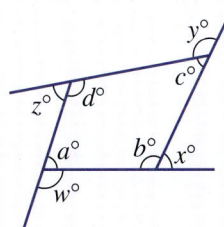

Statistics and probability

Short-answer questions

1 Consider the set of numbers 1, 2, 5, 5, 8, 9, 10, 5, 3, 8.
  a List them in ascending order.
  b How many numbers are in the set?
  c Calculate the:
    i mean   **ii** mode
    iii median   **iv** range.
  d If each number in the set is doubled, what is the new mean?

2 A spinner is designed with different numbers in each sector. Consider spinners **A** to **D** shown below.

A

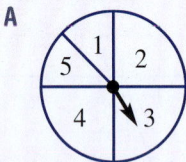

B

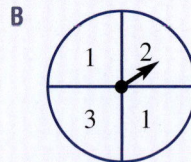

C

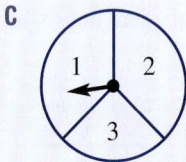

D

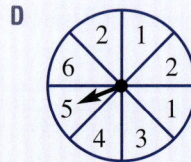

  a Which spinner has the lowest probability of landing on the number 1 in a single spin?
  b Which spinner has a 50% probability of landing on the number 1 in a single spin?
  c List the spinners in order, from the most likely to land on the number 1 to the least likely.

3 One card is randomly selected from a standard deck of 52 playing cards. Find the probability that the selected card is:
  a red   **b** black   **c** a heart
  d an ace   **e** a king   **f** a red 7.

4 This stem-and-leaf plot shows the ages of a group of people in a room.
  a How many people are in the room?
  b What are the ages of the youngest and oldest people?
  c For the data presented in this plot, find the:
    i range   **ii** median   **iii** mode.

Stem	Leaf
0	3 5
1	1 7 9
2	0 2 2 3
3	6 9
4	3 7

2|3 means 23 years old

5 A set of six scores is given as 17, 24, 19, 36, 22 and ☐.
  a Find the value of ☐ if the mean of the scores is 23.
  b Find the value of ☐ if the median of the scores is 22.
  c If the value of ☐ is 14, and the score of 17 is removed from the set, calculate the new mean and median of the group.

Multiple-choice questions

The following information is relevant for Questions 1 and 2.

A survey asked 60 participants their favourite colour. The results are shown below.

Blue	Pink	Green	Purple	Black
12	20	6	12	10

(Ext) 1 If a divided bar graph 10 cm long is constructed to display the data, the length required for purple would be:

   A 12 cm   **B** 2 cm   **C** 1 cm   **D** 5 cm   **E** 3 cm

(Ext) 2 If the results are shown as a sector graph, the size of the smallest sector would be:

   A 36°   **B** 6°   **C** 10°   **D** 60°   **E** 30°

3 For the set of numbers 1, 5, 2, 10, 1, 6, the difference between the mode and median is:

   A 5.5   **B** 2.5   **C** 3.5   **D** 3.2   **E** 2

4 For the set of numbers 3, 2, 1, 5, 7, 3, 1, 3, the mean is:

   A 3   **B** 5   **C** 6   **D** 22.375   **E** 3.125

5 Which of the following sets of numbers has a mode of 3 and a mean of 2?

   A 1, 1, 2, 2, 3   **B** 2, 2, 2, 4, 5   **C** 1, 2, 3, 4, 5   **D** 1, 3, 3, 3, 0   **E** 1, 2, 3, 3, 3

Extended-response question

A pack of playing cards includes 13 cards for each suit: hearts, diamonds, clubs and spades. Each suit has an ace, king, queen, jack, 2, 3, 4, 5, 6, 7, 8, 9 and 10. One card is drawn at random from the pack. Find the following probabilities.

a Pr(heart)   **b** Pr(club)

c Pr(diamond or spade)   **d** Pr(ace of hearts)

e Pr(number less than 4 and not an ace)   **f** Pr(king)

g Pr(ace or heart)   **h** Pr(queen or club)

Equations

Short-answer questions

1 Solve:

   a $x + 9 = 12$ **b** $\dfrac{x}{9} = 12$ **c** $x - 9 = 12$ **d** $9x = 12$

2 Solve:

   a $3x + 3 = 9$ **(Ext) b** $\dfrac{x}{2} + 6 = 12$ **(Ext) c** $3(m - 1) = 18$

3 If $y = mx + b$, find:

   a y when $m = 3$, $x = 4$ and $b = 8$ **b** b when $y = 20$, $m = 4$ and $x = 4$

   c m when $y = 36$, $x = 3$ and $b = 12$

4 If $P = S - C$, find:

   a P when $S = 190$ and $C = 87$ **b** S when $P = 47.9$ and $C = 13.1$

   c C when $P = 384$ and $S = 709$.

5 Use your knowledge of geometry and shapes to find the value of x in each of the following.

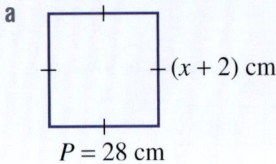

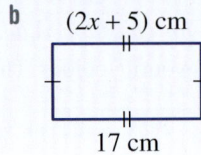

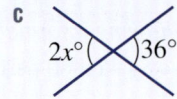

a

$(x + 2)$ cm

$P = 28$ cm

b

$(2x + 5)$ cm

17 cm

c

$2x°$ $36°$

6 The perimeter of this triangle is 85 cm. Write an equation and then solve it to find the value of x.

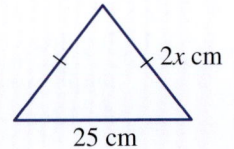

$2x$ cm

25 cm

Multiple-choice questions

1 The solution to the equation $x - 3 = 7$ is:

   A 4   **B** 10   **C** 9   **D** 11   **E** 3

(Ext) **2** The solution to the equation $2(x + 3) = 12$ is:

   A 4.5   **B** 2   **C** 7   **D** 6   **E** 3

3 $m = 4$ is a solution to:

   A $3m + 12 = 0$ **B** $\dfrac{m}{4} = 16$ **C** $10 - 2m = 2$

   D $m + 4 = 0$ **E** $3m - 6 = 2$

4 The solution to $2p - 3 = 7$ is:

   A $p = 4$ **B** $p = 5$ **C** $p = 2$ **D** $p = 10$ **E** $p = 3$

5 Ying thinks of a number. If he adds 4 to his number and then multiplies the sum by 5, the result is 35. What equation represents this information?

   A $y + 9 = 35$ **B** $5y - 4 = 35$ **C** $5y + 4 = 35$

   D $5(y + 4) = 35$ **E** $y + 20 = 35$

Extended-response question

The cost of hiring a hall for an event is $200 plus $40 per hour.

a What is the cost of hiring the hall for 3 hours?

b What is the cost of hiring the hall for 5 hours?

c What is the cost of hiring the hall for n hours?

d If the cost of hiring the hall totals $460, for how many hours was it hired?

Measurement

Short-answer questions

1 Complete these conversions.

   a $5\,m = $ __ cm   **b** $6\,km = $ __ m   **c** $1800\,mm = $ __ m

   d $1.7\,cm = $ __ m   **e** $180\,cm = $ __ m   **f** $5\tfrac{1}{2}\,L = $ __ mL

2 Find the perimeter of each of the following.

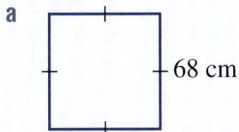

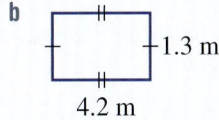

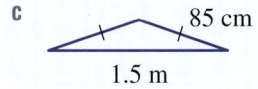

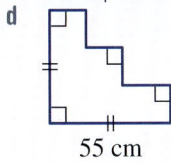

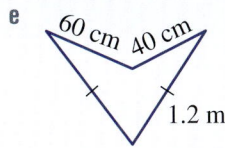

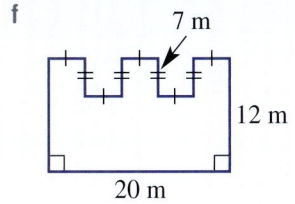

a

68 cm

b

1.3 m
4.2 m

c

85 cm
1.5 m

d

55 cm

e

60 cm   40 cm
1.2 m

f

7 m
12 m
20 m

3 Find the area of each of the following.

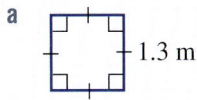

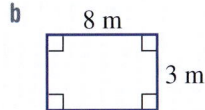

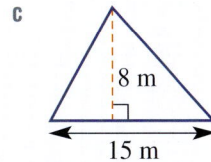

a

1.3 m

b

8 m
3 m

c

8 m
15 m

(Ext) **d**

4.5 m
7 m
12 m

e

12 m
7 m
12 m

f

7 m
8 m
10 m
12 m

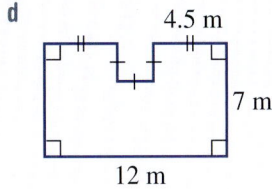

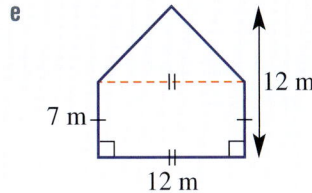

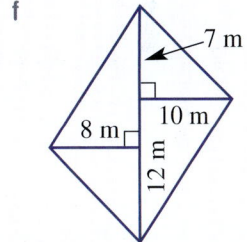

4 Calculate the volume of these solids.

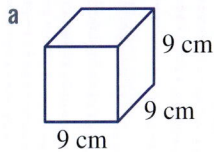

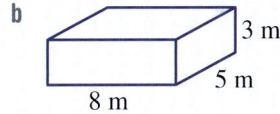

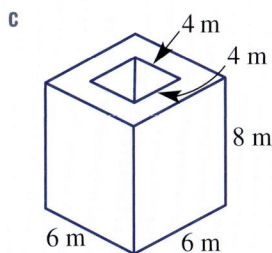

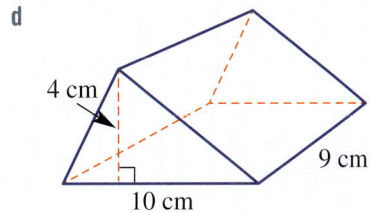

a

9 cm
9 cm
9 cm

b

3 m
5 m
8 m

c

4 m
4 m
8 m
6 m   6 m

d

4 cm
9 cm
10 cm

5 Convert:

a $5 L = \_\_ mL$

b $7 cm^3 = \_\_ mL$

c $\frac{1}{4} L = \_\_ mL$

d $3 kL = \_\_ L$

e $8 m^3 = \_\_ kL$

f $25\,000 mL = \_\_ L$

6 Find the capacity of a fish tank in litres if it is a rectangular prism 50 cm long, 40 cm wide and 30 cm high.

Semester review 2

7   Find the circumference of a circle with radius 3 cm. Round to two decimal places.

8   A collection of objects have the following individual masses: 220 kg, 0.05 t and 67000 g. What is their total combined mass in kg?

9   A factory freezer is installed in a warehouse and is at an initial temperature of 28°C. After it is switched on, the temperature drops by 31°C. What is the new temperature?

Multiple-choice questions

1   17 mm is the same as:
   A   0.17 m   B   0.17 cm   C   0.017 m   D   170 cm   E   1.7 m

2   0.006 L is the same as:
   A   6 mL   B   36 mL   C   10 mL   D   60 mL   E   600 mL

3   Which of the following shapes has the largest perimeter?

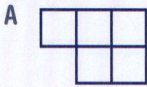

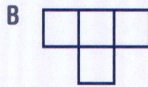

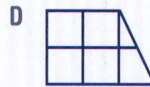

   A   B   C   D   E

4   The perimeters of the two shapes shown here are equal. The area of the square is:
   A   30 m^2 B   7.5 m^2 C   56.25 m^2
   D   120 m^2 E   60 m^2

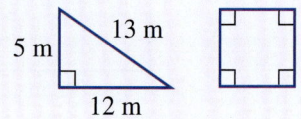

5   Which of the following rectangular prisms holds exactly 1 litre?

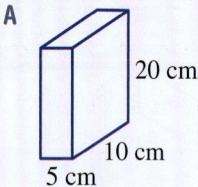

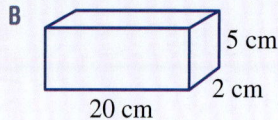

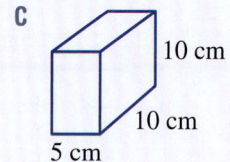

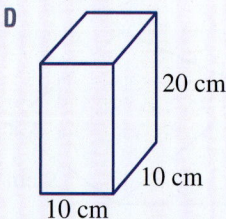

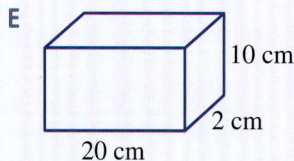

Extended-response question

Robert has been given 36 m of fencing with which to build the largest rectangular enclosure that he can, using whole number side lengths.

a   Draw three possible enclosures and calculate the area of each one.

b   What are the dimensions of the rectangle that gives the largest possible area?

c   If Robert chooses the dimensions in part b and puts a post on each corner, and then posts every metre along the boundary, how many posts will he need?

d   If it takes 15 minutes to dig each hole for each post, how many hours will Robert spend digging?

Index

Working with unfamiliar problems: Part 1

1 14, 27
2 123456787654321
3 625
4 60
5 431×52
6 $490
7 16
8 150°
9 270
10 Discuss: e.g. count how many times 'the' appears on one page and multiply by the number of written pages in the book.
11 Varies: e.g. 7.5 km for an average step of 75 cm
12 a $1 + 2 + 3 + 4 + 5 + 6 + 7 + 8 \times 9 = 100$
   b Many solutions e.g. $123 - 45 - 67 + 89 = 100$
13 2.5 cm, 75 cm (answers vary if thickness of glass considered)
14 $110, $130, $170
15 7 trips
16 $2\frac{2}{3}$ days

Working with unfamiliar problems: Part 2

1 17, 26, 35, 44, 53, 62, 71, 80
2 60°, 155°
3 12, 18, 20, 24, 30, 36 and 40
4 12 arrangements possible, 8 open box nets

5 25
6 231
7 2520
8 15
9 7
10 1200 approximately $240
11 41°
12 7
13 7200°
14 99
15 e
16 204

Chapter 1

1A

Building understanding

1 a Babylonian   b Roman   c Egyptian
2 a I   b ∩   c ℓ   d ⸀
3 a ▼   b ◀   c ▼
4 a I   b V   c X   d L   e C
5 $5 - 1 = 4$

Now you try

Example 1

a 4 is II
   23 is ∩∩III
   142 is ℓ∩∩ ∩∩II

b 4 is ▼▼
   23 is ◀▼▼▼
   142 is ▼▼ ◀◀ ▼ ▼

c 4 is IV
   23 is XXIII
   142 is CXLII

Exercise 1A

1 ∩II II, ℓ∩∩∩I

2 ◀▼▼ ▼▼, ▼▼▼◀▼

3 XIV, CXXXI

4 a i III   ii ∩∩I
     iii ℓ∩II II   iv ℓℓℓ∩∩∩ ∩∩II
   b i ▼▼   ii ◀◀◀▼▼
     iii ▼ ▼▼   iv ▼▼ ◀▼▼
   c i II   ii IX   iii XXIV   iv CLVI
5 a i 33   ii 111   iii 213   iv 241
   b i 12   ii 24   iii 71   iv 205
   c i 4   ii 8   iii 16   iv 40
6 a XXXVI   b ℓ∩∩∩∩ ∩∩∩ I
   c ◀◀ ◀◀▼▼   d DCLXXVIII

7 ◀◀▼ (21)
8 CLXXXVIII (188)
9 ∩∩∩∩II ∩∩∩ II (74)
10 a Roman   b Babylonian   c Roman
11 a IV   b IX   c XIV
   d XIX   e XXIX   f XLI
   g XLIX h LXXXIX i XCIX
   j CDXLIX k CMXXII l MMMCDI
12 A separate picture is to be used for each 1, 10, 100 etc. The number 999 uses 27 pictures.
13 a i ◀▼▼   ii ▼ ◀▼▼
     iii ▼▼ ......   iv ▼▼▼ ◀▼
     v ▼ ▼ ▼   vi ▼▼ ...... ◀◀▼▼
   b third position $= 60 \times 60 = 3600$
   c 216 000
14 Answers may vary.

1B

Building understanding

1 a Hundreds   **b** Thousands
   c Tens   **d** Ones
2 a B   b E   c C   d H
3 a B   b E   c D   d A
   e C   f F   g G
4 a True   b False   c True   d True
   e False   f True   g False   h True

Now you try

Example 2
a $7 \times 10 = 70$ b $7 \times 1000 = 7000$

Example 3
a $2715 = 2 \times 1000 + 7 \times 100 + 1 \times 10 + 5 \times 1$
b $40\,320 = 4 \times 10\,000 + 3 \times 100 + 2 \times 10$

Example 4
a $370 = 3 \times 10^2 + 7 \times 10^1$
b $20\,056 = 2 \times 10^4 + 5 \times 10^1 + 6 \times 1$

Exercise 1B

1 a 40   b 400
2 a 7   b 70   c 70   d 700
   e 700 f 7000 g 700   h 70\,000
3 a 20   b 2000 c 200   d 200\,000
4 a $1 \times 10 + 7 \times 1$
   b $2 \times 100 + 8 \times 10 + 1 \times 1$
   c $9 \times 100 + 3 \times 10 + 5 \times 1$
   d 2×10
5 a $4 \times 1000 + 4 \times 100 + 9 \times 10 + 1 \times 1$
   b $2 \times 1000 + 3 \times 1$
   c $1 \times 10\,000 + 1 \times 1$
   d $5 \times 10\,000 + 5 \times 1000 + 5 \times 100 + 5 \times 10 + 5 \times 1$
6 a $3 \times 10^3 + 8 \times 10^1$
   b $4 \times 10^2 + 5 \times 10^1$
   c $9 \times 10^4 + 3 \times 10^1$
   d $4 \times 10^4 + 7 \times 10^3 + 5 \times 10^2$
7 a $4 \times 10^4 + 2 \times 10^3 + 9 \times 1$
   b $3 \times 10^3 + 6 \times 10^2 + 4 \times 1$
   c $2 \times 10^2 + 4 \times 10^1 + 5 \times 1$
   d $7 \times 10^5 + 3 \times 10^2 + 6 \times 1$
8 a 347   b 9416   c 7020
   d 600\,003   e 4\,030\,700   f 90\,003\,020
9 a 44, 45, 54, 55
   b 29, 92, 279, 729, 927
   c 4, 23, 136, 951
   d 345, 354, 435, 453, 534, 543
   e 12\,345, 31\,254, 34\,512, 54\,321
   f 1001, 1010, 1100, 10\,001, 10\,100
10 a 6   b 6   c 24
11 27
12 a $A \times 10 + B \times 1$
   b $A \times 1000 + B \times 100 + C \times 10 + D \times 1$
   c $A \times 100\,000 + A \times 1$

13 Position gives the place value and only one digit is needed for each place. There is also a digit for zero.
14 a You do not need to write the zeros.
   b i 41×10^2
      ii 37×10^4
      iii 2177×10^4
   c i 38\,100
      ii 7\,204\,000
      iii 1\,028\,000\,000
   d i 1×10^6
      ii 1×10^9
      iii 1×10^{12}
      iv 1×10^{100}
      v 1×10^{googol}

1C

Building understanding

1 a Add, plus, sum
   b Minus, take away, difference
2 a 10   b 69   c 12   d 20
3 a 27   b 16
4 a True   b True   c True
   d False   e True   f False
5 a 18   b 19   c 32
   d 140   e 21   f 9

Now you try

Example 5
a 796   b 174   c 23   d 148

Exercise 1C

1 a 64   b 97   c 579
   d 748   e 948   f 5597
2 a 11   b 36   c 112
   d 4   e 3111   f 10\,001
3 a 24   b 75   c 95
   d 133   e 167   f 297
4 a 24   b 26   c 108
   d 222   e 317   f 5017
5 a 51   b 128   c 244
   d 119   e 242   f 502
6 a 268   b 65   c 19   d 111
7 a 12   b 27   c 107
   d 133   e 14   f 90
   g 1019   h 0   i 3
8 38 hours
9 107 runs
10 32 cows
11 29 marbles
12 107 cards
13 a i

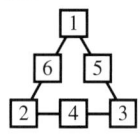

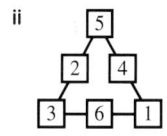

b i

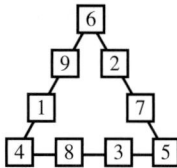

ii

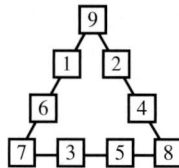

14 a Because $3 + 9$ is more than 10, so you have to carry.

b Because $8 - 6$ is easy, but $1 - 6$ means you have to carry.

15 a $c - b = a$ **b** $b - a = c$

16 a Four ways (totals are 9, 10, 11 and 12)

b Answers may vary.

17 a

6	1	8
7	5	3
2	9	4

b

10	15	8
9	11	13
14	7	12

c

15	20	13
14	16	18
19	12	17

d

1	15	14	4
12	6	7	9
8	10	11	5
13	3	2	16

18 29 and 58

1D

Building understanding

1 a 101   **b** 110   **c** 1005   **d** 1105

2 a 27   **b** 84   **c** 15   **d** 979

3 a 1   **b** 6   **c** 1   **d** 3

Now you try

Example 6

a 92   **b** 735

Example 7

a 46   **b** 1978

Exercise 1D

1 a 51   **b** 462

2 a 87   **b** 99   **c** 41   **d** 86

   e 226   **f** 745   **g** 1923   **h** 5080

3 a 161   **b** 225   **c** 2229   **d** 1975

4 a 77   **b** 192   **c** 418

   d 4208   **e** 1223   **f** 1982

5 a 31   **b** 20   **c** 19   **d** 58

   e 36   **f** 112   **g** 79   **h** 72

6 a 16   **b** 47   **c** 485   **d** 166

7 1854 sheep

8 576 kilometres

9 a 1821 students   **b** 79 students

10 a
$$\begin{array}{r} 3\,\boxed{8} \\ +5\;\;3 \\ \hline \boxed{9}\;\;1 \end{array}$$
b
$$\begin{array}{r} 1\,\boxed{1}\,4 \\ +\;\;7\,\boxed{7} \\ \hline \boxed{1}\,9\;\;1 \end{array}$$
c
$$\begin{array}{r} \boxed{6}\,\boxed{7} \\ +\boxed{8}\,4\;\;7 \\ \hline 9\;\;1\;\;4 \end{array}$$

11 a
$$\begin{array}{r} 6\,\boxed{2} \\ -\;\;2\;\;8 \\ \hline \boxed{3}\,4 \end{array}$$
b
$$\begin{array}{r} 2\,\boxed{6}\,5 \\ -\boxed{1}\,8\,\boxed{4} \\ \hline 8\;\;1 \end{array}$$
c
$$\begin{array}{r} 3\,\boxed{0}\,\boxed{9}\,2 \\ -\;\;9\,2\,\boxed{7} \\ \hline \boxed{2}\,1\,6\;\;5 \end{array}$$

12 a i 29   **ii** 37

   b Yes

   c No

   d The balance of $-19 + 20$ is $+1$, so add 1 to 36.

13 a Answers may vary.

   b Different combinations in the middle column can be used to create the sum.

14 a

62	67	60
61	63	65
66	59	64

b

101	115	114	104
112	106	107	109
108	110	111	105
113	103	102	116

15 452 and 526

16 Answers may vary.

1E

Building understanding

1 a 20, 24, 28   **b** 44, 55, 66   **c** 68, 85, 102

2 a True   **b** True   **c** False   **d** True

   e True   **f** True   **g** False   **h** False

3 a 3   **b** 0   **c** 5   **d** 2

Now you try

Example 8

a 32   **b** 126   **c** 76

d 210   **e** 300

Example 9

a 294   **b** 2976

Exercise 1E

1 a 15   **b** 32   **c** 36   **d** 27

   e 28   **f** 36   **g** 56   **h** 40

2 a 105   **b** 124   **c** 252   **d** 159

   e 57   **f** 174   **g** 112   **h** 266

3 a 96   **b** 54   **c** 96   **d** 72

4 a 56   **b** 52   **c** 87

   d 108   **e** 126

5 a 66 **b** 129 **c** 432 **d** 165
  e 258 **f** 2849 **g** 2630 **h** 31581
6 a 235 **b** 4173 **c** 3825 **d** 29190
7 $264
8 1680 metres
9 116 cards
10 No
11 a
$$\begin{array}{r} 3\;9 \\ \times \;\; 7 \\ \hline 2\boxed{7}3 \end{array}$$
  b
$$\begin{array}{r} 2\;5 \\ \times \;\boxed{5} \\ \hline 1\,2\,5 \end{array}$$
  c
$$\begin{array}{r} 7\;9 \\ \times \;\boxed{3} \\ \hline \boxed{2}3\,7 \end{array}$$
  d
$$\begin{array}{r} 1\;3\;2 \\ \times \;\;\;\boxed{8} \\ \hline 10\boxed{5}6 \end{array}$$
  e
$$\begin{array}{r} 2\boxed{7} \\ \times \;\; 7 \\ \hline \boxed{1}8\,9 \end{array}$$
  f
$$\begin{array}{r} \boxed{3}\boxed{9} \\ \times \;\; 9 \\ \hline 3\,5\,1 \end{array}$$
  g
$$\begin{array}{r} 2\;3\boxed{2} \\ \times \;\;\;\; 5 \\ \hline 1\boxed{1}6\,0 \end{array}$$
  h
$$\begin{array}{r} \boxed{3}\boxed{1}\,4 \\ \times \;\;\;\;\boxed{7} \\ \hline \boxed{2}\,1\;9\,8 \end{array}$$
12 12 ways
13 a 3×21 **b** 9×52 **c** 7×32
  d 5×97 **e** $a \times 38$ **f** $a \times 203$
14 Three ways: (0, 1), (1, 5), (2, 9). You cannot carry a number to the hundreds column.
15 a Answers may vary; e.g.
$$\begin{array}{r} \boxed{2}1\boxed{7} \\ \times \;\;\;\;\; 7 \\ \hline \boxed{1}5\boxed{1}9 \end{array}$$
  b Answers may vary; e.g.
$$\begin{array}{r} 2\;9\;\boxed{5} \\ \times \;\;\;\;\; 3 \\ \hline 8\boxed{8}5 \end{array}$$
16 6, 22

Progress quiz

1 a ∩ ‖
      ℮∩∩‖
  b CXXXIV
  c ▼▼ ◀▼▼▼
2 $5 \times 10\,000 + 8 \times 100 + 6 \times 10 + 2 \times 1$
3 a 375 **b** 64 **c** 57 **d** 71
4 a 62 **b** 78
5 a 28 **b** 72 **c** 108 **d** 45
6 a 84 **b** 195
7 a 252 **b** 948 **c** 15022
8 a 1973 students **b** 77 students
9 a T **b** T **c** F **d** T **e** T **f** S

1F

Building understanding

1 a 2 **b** 0 **c** 0 **d** 4
2 a 100 **b** 10 **c** 10000
3 a Incorrect, 104 **b** Incorrect, 546
  c Correct **d** Incorrect, 2448

Now you try

Example 10
a 23000 **b** 2920 **c** 17296

Exercise 1F

1 a 400 **b** 290 **c** 1830
  d 4600 **e** 50000 **f** 63000
  g 14410 **h** 29100000
2 a 340 **b** 1440 **c** 6440
  d 22500 **e** 41400 **f** 460000
  g 63400 **h** 9387000
3 a 407 **b** 1368 **c** 1890
  d 9416 **e** 18216 **f** 40768
  g 18620 **h** 33858
4 a i 430 **ii** 72000
  b i 1420 **ii** 7800
  c i 1488 **ii** 5730
5 a 209 **b** 546 **c** 555 **d** 2178
6 $2176
7 $6020
8 86400 seconds
9 a
$$\begin{array}{r} 2\boxed{3} \\ \times \;\; 1\;7 \\ \hline 1\;\boxed{6}\,1 \\ 2\;\boxed{3}\,0 \\ \hline \boxed{3}\boxed{9}\,1 \end{array}$$
  b
$$\begin{array}{r} 1\boxed{4}\,3 \\ \times \;\;\; 1\boxed{3} \\ \hline \boxed{4}\,2\,9 \\ 1\;\boxed{4}\boxed{3}\,0 \\ \hline \boxed{1}\boxed{8}5\,9 \end{array}$$
  c
$$\begin{array}{r} \boxed{4}\boxed{9} \\ \times \;\;\;\; 3\;7 \\ \hline 3\;4\;3 \\ \boxed{1}\,4\boxed{7}\boxed{0} \\ \hline \boxed{1}\boxed{8}\boxed{1}\,3 \end{array}$$
  d
$$\begin{array}{r} \boxed{1}\,2\,\boxed{6} \\ \times \;\;\;\; 2\boxed{1} \\ \hline 1\;2\;6 \\ \boxed{2}\,5\,\boxed{2}\,0 \\ \hline \boxed{2}\,6\,4\boxed{6} \end{array}$$
10 60480 degrees
11 One number is a 1.
12 a 39984 **b** 927908
  c 4752188 **d** 146420482
13 a 1600 **b** 780 **c** 810 **d** 1000
14 a 84000 **b** 3185
15 123, 117

1G

Building understanding

1 a 2 **b** 3 **c** 7 **d** 12
2 a 1 **b** 2 **c** 2 **d** 5
3 a 1 **b** 1 **c** 5 **d** 5

Now you try

Example 11
a 4 **b** 121 **c** 65
Example 12
a 23 and 1 remainder **b** 72 and 3 remainder

Exercise 1G

1 a 4   **b** 3   **c** 6   **d** 5
   e 7   **f** 9   **g** 8   **h** 11

2 a 21   **b** 22   **c** 32   **d** 103
   e 41   **f** 21   **g** 301   **h** 61

3 a 22   **b** 31   **c** 17   **d** 7

4 a 12   **b** 9   **c** 21   **d** 21   **e** 30   **f** 16

5 a 26   **b** 1094   **c** 0   **d** 0

6 a 23 rem. 2 = $23\frac{2}{3}$ **b** 13 rem. 1 = $13\frac{1}{7}$

   c 69 rem. 1 = $69\frac{1}{2}$ **d** 41 rem. 1 = $41\frac{1}{6}$

   e 543 rem. 1 = $543\frac{1}{4}$ **f** 20 333 rem. 2 = $20\,333\frac{2}{3}$

   g 818 rem. 3 = $818\frac{3}{5}$ **h** 10 001 rem. 0 = 10 001

7 a 131 rem. 1 = $131\frac{1}{4}$ **b** 241 rem. 4 = $241\frac{4}{7}$

   c 390 rem. 5 = $390\frac{5}{6}$ **d** 11 542 rem. 1 = $11\,542\frac{1}{8}$

8 4 packs

9 107 packs

10 a $243   **b** $27

11 67 posts

12 15 taxis

13 19 trips; any remainder needs 1 more trip

14

2	9	12
36	6	1
3	4	18

15 a 1, 12   **b** 13, 7   **c** 4, 5

16 $68

17 a 1   **b** 0   **c** a

18 8 or 23

19 $a = b$ or $a = -b$

20 a 33 rem. 8 = $33\frac{8}{11}$ **b** 54 rem. 8 = $54\frac{8}{17}$

   c 31 rem. 1 = $31\frac{1}{13}$ **d** 108 rem. 1 = $108\frac{1}{15}$

   e 91 rem. 16 = $91\frac{16}{23}$ **f** 123 rem. 25 = $123\frac{25}{56}$

21

1	6	20	56
40	28	2	3
14	5	24	4
12	8	7	10

22 a 37   **b** 43   **c** 75
   d 91   **e** 143   **f** 92

1H

Building understanding

1 a Up   **b** Down   **c** Up
   d Up   **e** Down   **f** Down

2 a Larger   **b** Smaller
   c Smaller   **d** Larger

Now you try

Example 13
a 70   **b** 6400

Example 14
a 480   **b** 8000

Example 15
a 360 000   **b** 42

Exercise 1H

1 a i 70   **ii** 40   **iii** 150
   b i 400   **ii** 700   **iii** 1800

2 a 60   **b** 30   **c** 120
   d 190   **e** 200   **f** 900
   g 100   **h** 600   **i** 2000

3 a 20   **b** 30   **c** 100
   d 900   **e** 6000   **f** 90 000
   g 10 000   **h** 10

4 a 130   **b** 80   **c** 150   **d** 940
   e 100   **f** 1000   **g** 1100   **h** 2600
   i 1000   **j** 7000

5 a 120   **b** 160   **c** 100   **d** 12
   e 40   **f** 2000   **g** 4000   **h** 100

6 a 1200   **b** 6300   **c** 20 000
   d 8 000 000   **e** 5   **f** 16
   g 10   **h** 25

7 ≈ 2100 scoops

8 Answers may vary.

9 ≈ 1200 sheep

10 ≈ 8 people

11 a 200   **b** 100 000
   c 800   **d** 3 000 000 or 4 000 000

12 a i Larger   **ii** Larger
   b i Larger   **ii** Larger
   c i Smaller   **ii** Smaller
   d i Larger   **ii** Larger

13 a i 9   **ii** 152   **iii** 10   **iv** 448
   b One number is rounded up and the other is rounded down.
   c i 3   **ii** 3   **iii** 1   **iv** 2
   d If the numerator is decreased, then the approximation will be smaller. If the denominator is increased then the approximation will also be smaller. If the opposite occurs the approximation will be larger.

1I

Building understanding

1 a Addition   **b** Division   **c** Multiplication
   d Multiplication   **e** Division   **f** Addition
   g Division   **h** Multiplication   **i** Division
   j Subtraction   **k** Multiplication   **l** Division

2 a True   **b** False   **c** False   **d** True

Now you try

Example 16
a 34   **b** 40

Example 17
a 12   **b** 76

Exercise 1I

1 a 11   b 17   c 4   d 0
2 a 8   b 17   c 14   d 11
3 a 12   b 21   c 19   d 8
4 a 20   b 18   c 14   d 6
5 a 23   b 21   c 0   d 18
  e 32   f 2   g 22   h 22
  i 38   j 153   k 28   l 200
6 a 10   b 3   c 2   d 22
  e 2   f 9   g 18   h 3
  i 10   j 121   k 20   l 1
7 a 27   b 10   c 8   d 77
  e 30   f 21   g 192
8 a 48   b 18   c 13   d 28   e 22
9 75 books
10 45 TV sets
11 a $(4 + 2) \times 3 = 18$
  b $9 \div (12 - 9) = 3$
  c $2 \times (3 + 4) - 5 = 9$
  d $(3 + 2) \times (7 - 3) = 20$
  e $(10 - 7) \div (21 - 18) = 1$
  f $(4 + 10) \div (21 \div 3) = 2$
  g $[20 - (31 - 19)] \times 2 = 16$
  h $50 \div (2 \times 5) - 4 = 1$
  i $(25 - 19) \times (3 + 7) \div 12 + 1 = 6$
12 First prize $38, second prize $8
13 a No   b Yes   c No   d Yes   e Yes
  f No   g No   h Yes   i Yes
14 a No   b Yes   c No   d Yes
15 a b b 0   c $a + 1$ d b
16 a Multiply by 2 and add 1.
  b Multiply by 3 and subtract 3, or subtract 1 and then multiply by 3.
  c Multiply by itself and add 1.

Problems and challenges

1 The two people pay $24 each, which is $48 in total. Of that $48 the waiter has $3, leaving a balance of $45 for the bill.
2
3 5
4 One way is $(2 + 7) \times 11 + 4 - 3$
5 a 22 L/day   b 7900 L/year
6 21, 495

Chapter checklist with success criteria

1   ∩∩II, ▼▼ ⟨▼▼ ⟨▼▼; CXLIV
2 40 000
3 $5 \times 100 + 1 \times 10 + 7 \times 1$; $5 \times 10^2 + 1 \times 10^1 + 7 \times 1$
4 288; 38

5 611
6 519
7 116
8 124; 1379
9 3700
10 8596
11 31
12 quotient 27, remainder 6
13 4100
14 30 000
15 200
16 14
17 94

Chapter review

Short-answer questions

1 a i III   ii ∩∩∩I
  iii ℮℮∩∩ |||
           |||
  b i ⟨▼▼   ii ▼......
  iii ▼▼ ⟨▼▼
  c i XIV   ii XL   iii CXLVI
2 a 50   b 5000   c 50 000
3 a 459   b 363   c 95   d 217
4 a 128   b 2324   c 191   d 295
5 a 95   b 132   c 220
  d 41   e 33   f 24
  g 29 000   h 10 800   i 14 678
6 a 1413   b 351
  c 46 rem. 5   d 7540 rem. 2
7 a
```
   2 2 3
 +7 3 8
 ──────
   9 6 1
```
  b
```
   7 2 9
 −4 7 3
 ──────
   2 5 6
```
  c
```
      5 3
    × 2 7
   ──────
      3 7 1
    1 0 6 0
   ────────
    1 4 3 1
```
  d
```
        1 8 3
  5)9 1⁴1⁵5
```
8 a 70   b 3300   c 1000
9 a 800   b 400   c 5000   d 10
10 a 24   b 4   c 14   d 20   e 0   f 13

Multiple-choice questions

1 B   2 C   3 E   4 A   5 B
6 A   7 D   8 C   9 B   10 A

Extended-response questions

1 a 646 loads   b 9044 kilometres
  c $36 430   d $295
2 a 3034 sweets   b 249
  c Liquorice sticks, 6   d Yes (124)

Chapter 2

2A

Building understanding

1 a M   b N   c F   d N
   e F   f F   g M   h F
   i N   j M   k N   l F
2 a F   b N   c M   d N
   e N   f N   g N   h M
   i F   j M   k F   l N

Now you try

Example 1
a 1, 3, 7, 21   b 1, 2, 3, 5, 6, 10, 15, 30

Example 2
a 4, 8, 12, 16, 20, 24   b 26, 52, 78, 104, 130, 156

Example 3
$165 = 11 \times 15$

Exercise 2A

1 a 1, 2, 3, 4, 6, 12
   b 1, 2, 3, 4, 6, 8, 12, 16, 24, 48
2 a 1, 2, 5, 10
   b 1, 2, 3, 4, 6, 8, 12, 24
   c 1, 17
   d 1, 2, 3, 4, 6, 9, 12, 18, 36
   e 1, 2, 3, 4, 5, 6, 10, 12, 15, 20, 30, 60
   f 1, 2, 3, 6, 7, 14, 21, 42
   g 1, 2, 4, 5, 8, 10, 16, 20, 40, 80
   h 1, 29
   i 1, 2, 4, 7, 14, 28
3 a 5, 10, 15, 20, 25, 30
   b 8, 16, 24, 32, 40, 48
   c 12, 24, 36, 48, 60, 72
   d 7, 14, 21, 28, 35, 42
   e 20, 40, 60, 80, 100, 120
   f 75, 150, 225, 300, 375, 450
   g 15, 30, 45, 60, 75, 90
   h 100, 200, 300, 400, 500, 600
   i 37, 74, 111, 148, 185, 222
4 a 3, 18
   b 5
   c 1, 4, 6, 9, 12, 24
   d 3, 4, 5, 8, 12, 15, 24, 40, 120
5 a 22   b 162   c 21   d 117
6 a 24   b 1   c 1, 4, 9, 16, 25
7 a 12×16
   b 21×15
   c 12×15
   d 11×11
   e 12×28 or 24×14 or 21×16
   f 19×26 or 38×13
8 a 20 min   b 5 laps   c 4 laps

9 a 25
   b 0
   c 23
   d 2, 7, 12, 17, 37, 47, 62, 87, 137, 287
   e 2
10 a False   b True   c False
    d False   e True
11 a 840   b 2520
12 a 1, 2, 4, 5, 10, 20, 25, 50, 100
    b 1, 2, 4, 5, 10, 20, 25, 50, 100
13 Answers may vary, but they should be multiples of 9.
14 1, 2, 3, 5, 10, 30 must also be factors.
15 Check the output each time.

2B

Building understanding

1 a 1, 2, 4   b 4
2 Factors of 18 are 1, 2, 3, 6, 9 and 18.
   Factors of 30 are 1, 2, 3, 5, 6, 10, 15 and 30.
   Therefore, the HCF of 18 and 30 is 6.
3 a 24, 48   b 24
4 Multiples of 9 are 9, 18, 27, 36, 45, 54, 63, 72, 81 and 90.
   Multiples of 15 are 15, 30, 45, 60, 75, 90, 105 and 120.
   Therefore, the LCM of 9 and 15 is 45.

Now you try

Example 4
6

Example 5
a 28   b 30

Exercise 2B

1 a 5   b 10
2 a 1   b 1   c 2   d 3
   e 4   f 15   g 50   h 24
   i 40   j 25   k 21   l 14
3 a 10   b 3   c 1
   d 1   e 8   f 12
4 a 36   b 21   c 60   d 110
   e 12   f 10   g 36   h 18
   i 60   j 48   k 132   l 105
5 a 30   b 84   c 12
   d 45   e 40   f 36
6 a HCF = 5, LCM = 60   b HCF = 12, LCM = 24
   c HCF = 7, LCM = 42   d HCF = 9, LCM = 135
7 312
8 9
9 LCM = 780, HCF = 130
10 a 12 min
    b Andrew 9 laps, Bryan 12 laps, Chris 6 laps
    c 3 times (including the finish)
11 a 8, 16   b 24, 32

12 1 and 20; 2 and 20; 4 and 20; 5 and 20; 10 and 20; 4 and 5; 4 and 10.

13 No

14 a 2520

   b 2520

   c Identical answers; 2520 is already divisible by 10, so adding 10 to list does not alter LCM.

   d $27\,720\,(2^3 \times 5 \times 7 \times 9 \times 11)$

2C

Building understanding

1 a Not even

   b Digits do not sum to a multiple of 3

   c 26 is not divisible by 4

   d Last digit is not 0 or 5

   e Not divisible by 3 (sum of digits is not divisible by 3)

   f 125 is not divisible by 8 and it is not even

   g Sum of digits is not divisible by 9

   h Last digit is not 0

2 a 2   **b** 2   **c** 0   **d** 0

3 3, 6 and 9

4 2, 5 and 10

Now you try

Example 6

a Yes, digit sum is 24, which is divisible by 3.

b No, 82 is not divisible by 4.

Example 7

2, 3, 5, 6, 9 and 10 (all except 4 and 8).

Exercise 2C

1 a No   **b** Yes   **c** Yes   **d** No

2 a Yes   **b** No   **c** Yes   **d** Yes

3 a No   **b** Yes   **c** No   **d** Yes

4 a No   **b** Yes   **c** No   **d** Yes

5 a Yes   **b** No   **c** Yes   **d** No

6 a Yes   **b** No   **c** Yes   **d** Yes

   e No   **f** Yes   **g** No   **h** Yes

   i No   **j** Yes   **k** No   **l** Yes

8 a No   **b** $38

9 a 10, 15, 20, 25, 30

   b 12, 15, 18, 21, 24

   c 10, 12, 14, 16, 18

   d 12, 18, 24, 30, 36

   e 16, 24, 32, 40, 48   (other answers possible)

   f 18, 27, 36, 45, 54

   g 10, 20, 30, 40, 50

   h 12, 16, 20, 24, 28

10 2, 4, 8, 11, 22, 44

11 200

12 15

13 36

14 966

15 a Yes, because it is divisible by 3 and 5.

   b No, because it is not divisible by 3.

   c As many as possible from:

      22 470, 25 470, 28 470, 20 475, 23 475, 26 475, 29 475.

16 a Yes

   b Multiples of 3; adding a multiple of 3 does not change the result of the divisibility test for 3.

   c 18

17 a 0, 4, 8   **b** 2, 6

18 a 11, 22, 33, 44, 55, 66, 77, 88, 99

   b 0

   c 110, 121, 132, 143, 154, …

   d Equals the centre digit or 11 plus the centre digit

   e Difference is 0 or 11

   f Sum the odd- and even-placed digits. If the difference between these two sums is 0 or is divisible by 11, then the number is divisible by 11.

   g i Yes   **ii** Yes   **iii** No

     iv Yes   **v** Yes   **vi** Yes

   h Answers may vary.

2D

Building understanding

1 No

2 Yes

3 2, 3, 5, 7, 11, 13, 17, 19, 23, 29

4 4, 6, 8, 9, 10, 12, 14, 15, 16, 18

5 101

6 201 is divisible by 3.

7

Number	Divisible by 2	Divisible by 3	Divisible by 4	Divisible by 5	Divisible by 6	Divisible by 8	Divisible by 9	Divisible by 10
243 567	✗	✓	✗	✗	✗	✗	✓	✗
28 080	✓	✓	✓	✓	✓	✓	✓	✓
189 000	✓	✓	✓	✓	✓	✓	✓	✓
1 308 150	✓	✓	✗	✓	✓	✗	✓	✓
1 062 347	✗	✗	✗	✗	✗	✗	✗	✗

Now you try

Example 8
Prime: 13, 19, 79
Composite: 32, 57, 95

Example 9
2, 3, 7

Exercise 2D

1 a P   b C   c P
2 a C   b P   c C   d P   e C   f C
   g P   h P   i C   j C   k C   l P
   m P   n P   o C   p P   q P   r P
3 a 2, 3, 7   b 3, 13   c 2, 3, 5
   d 5   e 2, 7   f 2, 3
4 a 32, 33, 34, 35, 36, 38, 39, 40, 42, 44, 45, 46, 48, 49
   b 51, 52, 54, 55, 56, 57, 58, 60, 62, 63, 64, 65, 66, 68, 69
   c 81, 82, 84, 85, 86, 87, 88, 90, 91, 92, 93, 94, 95, 96, 98, 99
5 a 5, 11   b 7, 13   c 11, 13
   d 11, 17   e 5, 73   f 7, 19
6 16
7 5 and 7, 11 and 13, 17 and 19, as well as other pairs
8 17 and 71, as well as other pairs such as 37 and 73, 79 and 97, 11 and 11.
9 $30 = 13 + 17$, $32 = 29 + 3$, $34 = 29 + 5$, $36 = 29 + 7$, $38 = 31 + 7$, $40 = 37 + 3$, $42 = 31 + 11$, $44 = 41 + 3$, $46 = 41 + 5$, $48 = 41 + 7$, $50 = 19 + 31$
   (other answers are possible)
10 $2 + 3 = 5$ and $2 + 5 = 7$. All primes other than 2 are odd and two odds sum to give an even number that is not a prime. So, any pair that sums to a prime must contain an even prime, which is 2.
11 (5, 7, 11), as well as other groups
12 Check your spreadsheet using smaller primes.

2E

Building understanding

1 E   2 D
3

Value	Base number	Index number	Basic numeral
2^3	2	3	8
5^2	5	2	25
10^4	10	4	10000
2^7	2	7	128
1^{12}	1	12	1
12^1	12	1	12
0^5	0	5	0

Now you try

Example 10
a 7^5 b $5^4 \times 11^3$

Example 11
a 125   b 800

Example 12
a 16   b 47

Exercise 2E

1 a 3^3 b 2^5 c 15^4
   d 10^4 e 6^2 f 1^6
2 a $4^2 \times 5^3$ b $3^4 \times 7^2$ c $2^3 \times 5^2$
3 a $3^2 \times 5^2$ b $2^2 \times 7^3$ c $9^2 \times 12^2$
   d $5^3 \times 8^2$ e $3^3 \times 6^3$ f $7^4 \times 13^2$
   g $4^3 \times 7^1 \times 13^1$ h $9^3 \times 10^2$ i $2^3 \times 3^2 \times 5^2$
4 $2^6 \times 3^5 \times 5^4$
5 a $2 \times 2 \times 2 \times 2$
   b 17×17
   c $9 \times 9 \times 9$
   d $3 \times 3 \times 3 \times 3 \times 3 \times 3 \times 3$
   e $14 \times 14 \times 14 \times 14$
   f $8 \times 8 \times 8 \times 8 \times 8 \times 8 \times 8 \times 8$
   g $10 \times 10 \times 10 \times 10 \times 10$
   h $54 \times 54 \times 54$
6 a $3 \times 3 \times 3 \times 3 \times 3 \times 2 \times 2 \times 2$
   b $4 \times 4 \times 4 \times 3 \times 3 \times 3 \times 3$
   c $7 \times 7 \times 5 \times 5 \times 5$
   d $4 \times 4 \times 4 \times 4 \times 4 \times 4 \times 9 \times 9 \times 9$
   e $5 \times 7 \times 7 \times 7 \times 7$
   f $2 \times 2 \times 3 \times 3 \times 3 \times 4$
   g $11 \times 11 \times 11 \times 11 \times 11 \times 9 \times 9$
   h $20 \times 20 \times 20 \times 30 \times 30$
7 a 32   b 64   c 1000   d 72
   e 10000   f 1000   g 64   h 121
8 a 25   b 1   c 10
   d 64   e 128   f 8
   g 22   h 900   i 8
9 a 4   b 2   c 3   d 6
   e 3   f 2   g 2   h 4
10 a <   b >   c =   d <
   e >   f >   g <   h <
11 125
12 a $1 + 5 + 5^2 + 5^3 = 156$
   b 55 mins
   c 305 175 781 people
   d 75 mins
   e Approx. 75 000 000 000 000 000
13 a +   b $\times$ c −
   d ÷   e $\times$ f −
14 a 1, 3, 9, 27, 81, 243, 729
   b 1, 5, 25, 125, 625
   c i 1, 2, 4, 8, 16, 32, 64, 128, 256
      ii It is the powers of 2.
   d i 2, 6, 18, 54, 162, 486
      ii They are being multiplied by 3 each time. This sequence is double the powers of 3.
15 $a = 2$, $b = 4$
16 a 1, 2, 6, 24, 120, 720
   b i $2^4 \times 3^2 \times 5 \times 7$ ii $2^7 \times 3^2 \times 5 \times 7$
      iii $2^7 \times 3^4 \times 5 \times 7$ iv $2^8 \times 3^4 \times 5^2 \times 7$

c 0

d 0

e It is the index number on the base 5.

   i 1   **ii** 1   **iii** 3   **iv** 6

f e.g. $23! \times 4!$

2F

Building understanding

1 Composite: 15, 8, 9, 27, 4, 12; Prime: 13, 7, 5, 23, 11, 2

2 **a** 5, 4   **b** 6, 2   **c** 10, 2, 5

3 **a** 3, 3, 2, 5   **b** 2, 2, 2, 7   **c** 5, 11, 2, 2

4 **a** $2^3 \times 3^2$ **b** $3^4 \times 5^2$

  c $2^2 \times 3 \times 7^2$ **d** $2^2 \times 3^2 \times 11^2$

Now you try

Example 13

$180 = 2^2 \times 3^2 \times 5$

Exercise 2F

1 **a** $2^2 \times 3^2$ **b** $2^2 \times 5^2$

2 **a** $2^3 \times 3^2$ **b** $2^3 \times 3$ **c** 2×19 **d** $2^2 \times 11$

  e $2^2 \times 31$ **f** $2^4 \times 5$ **g** $2^5 \times 3$ **h** 2^4

  i 3×5^2 **j** 3×37 **k** 2^6 **l** $2^3 \times 7$

3 **a** $2^3 \times 3 \times 5^2$ **b** $2^5 \times 5^2$

  c $2^3 \times 5^4$ **d** $2^5 \times 3 \times 5^2$

  e $2^6 \times 5^6$ **f** $2^3 \times 3^2 \times 5^4$

  g $2^2 \times 5 \times 41$ **h** $2 \times 3 \times 5 \times 23$

4 **a** D   **b** A   **c** C   **d** B

5 2310

6 **a** $144 = 2^4 \times 3^2$, $96 = 2^5 \times 3$

  b HCF $= 2^4 \times 3 = 48$

7 **a** $25\,200 = 2^4 \times 3^2 \times 5^2 \times 7$, $77\,000 = 2^3 \times 5^3 \times 7 \times 11$

  b HCF $= 2^3 \times 5^2 \times 7 = 1400$

8 **a** $2 \times 3 \times 7 = 42$

  b $3 \times 5 \times 11 = 165$

  c $2^2 \times 3 \times 5 \times 7 = 420$

9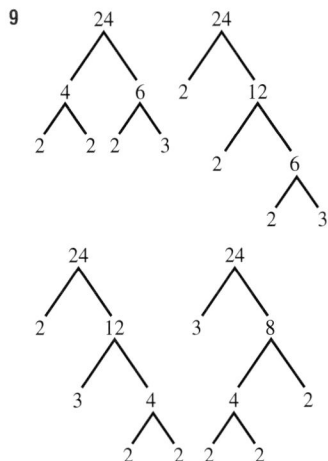

10 **a** 424 cannot have a factor of 5.

  b 8 is not a prime number.

  c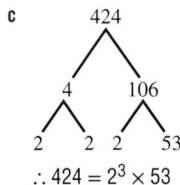

  $\therefore 424 = 2^3 \times 53$

11 **a** **i** $5 \times 10 \neq 60$

    ii 6 is not a prime number.

    iii A 2 has been left off the prime factor form.

  b $60 = 2^2 \times 3 \times 5$

12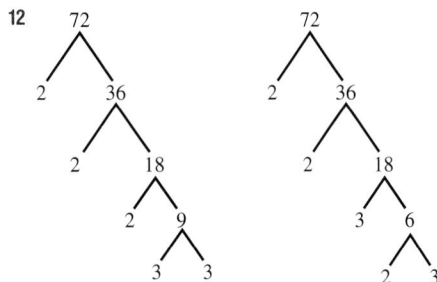

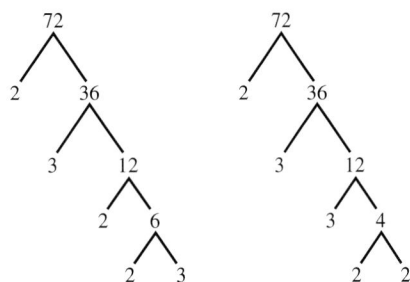

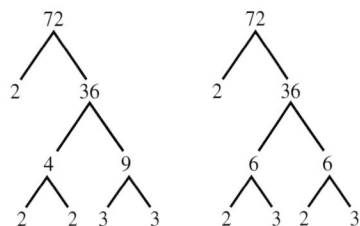

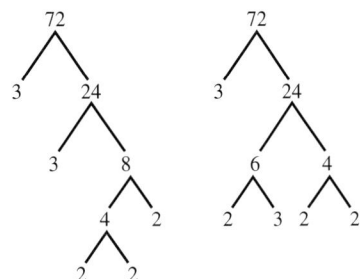

Answers

Ch2 Progress quiz

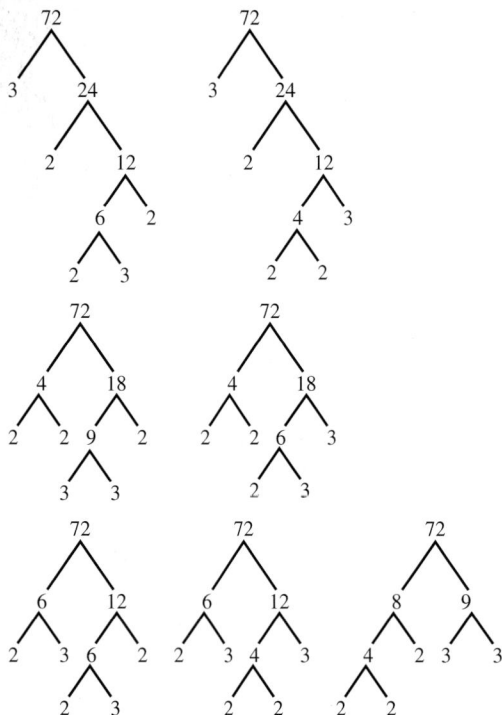

13

$2 \times 3 \times 5 \times 7 = 210$	$2 \times 3 \times 7 \times 11 = 462$
$2 \times 3 \times 5 \times 11 = 330$	$2 \times 3 \times 7 \times 13 = 546$
$2 \times 3 \times 5 \times 13 = 390$	$2 \times 3 \times 7 \times 17 = 714$
$2 \times 3 \times 5 \times 17 = 510$	$2 \times 3 \times 7 \times 19 = 798$
$2 \times 3 \times 5 \times 19 = 570$	$2 \times 3 \times 7 \times 23 = 966$
$2 \times 3 \times 5 \times 23 = 690$	$2 \times 5 \times 7 \times 11 = 770$
$2 \times 3 \times 5 \times 29 = 870$	$2 \times 5 \times 7 \times 13 = 910$
$2 \times 3 \times 5 \times 31 = 930$	$2 \times 3 \times 11 \times 13 = 858$

14 Check with your teacher.

15 Answers may vary.

Progress quiz

1 a 16:1, 2, 4, 8, 16
  b 70:1, 2, 5, 7, 10, 14, 35, 70
2 a 7, 14, 21, 28   **b** 20, 40, 60, 80
3 a 5   **b** 18
4 a 24   **b** 45
5 a No, Last 2 digits not $\div$ 4
  b Yes, Sum of 21 $\div$ 3
  c Yes, Sum of 24 $\div$ 3, and even $\div$ 2
  d Yes, Sum of 27 $\div$ 9
6 2, 3, 4, 5, 6, 10, 12, 20, 24, 30, 40, 60
7 a C : large number of factors
  b N : only one factor
  c P : only two factors, 1 and itself
  d N
8 a 5, 7   **b** 2, 3
9 a 5^4 **b** $3^2 \times 7^5$

10 a $3 \times 3 \times 3 \times 3 = 81$
  b $1 \times 1 \times 1 \times 1 \times 3 \times 3 = 9$
  c $5 \times 10 \times 10 \times 10 \times 10 = 50\,000$
  d $4 \times 4 = 16$
  e $9 \times 9 - 3 \times 3 \times 3 \times 2 = 81 - 54$
            $= 27$
11 a $24 = 2 \times 2 \times 2 \times 3$
        $= 2^3 \times 3$
  b $180 = 2^2 \times 3^2 \times 5$

2G

Building understanding

1 36 cm^2, a square number
2 $1^2 = 1$, $2^2 = 4$, $3^2 = 9$, $4^2 = 16$, $5^2 = 25$, $6^2 = 36$, $7^2 = 49$, $8^2 = 64$, $9^2 = 81$, $10^2 = 100$, $11^2 = 121$, $12^2 = 144$, $13^2 = 169$, $14^2 = 196$, $15^2 = 225$
3 a A square is not possible.
  b Draw a 4 by 4 square.
4 a 36   **b** 25   **c** 121
  d 100   **e** 49   **f** 144
5 a 5   **b** 4   **c** 10   **d** 7 cm

Now you try

Example 14
a 81   **b** 6   **c** 70
Example 15
a 3 and 4   **b** 10 and 11
Example 16
a 60   **b** 3

Exercise 2G

1 a 16   **b** 49   **c** 9   **d** 100
2 a 64   **b** 4   **c** 1   **d** 144
  e 36   **f** 225   **g** 25   **h** 0
  i 121   **j** 10 000   **k** 400   **l** 2500
3 a 5   **b** 3   **c** 1   **d** 11
  e 0   **f** 9   **g** 7   **h** 4
  i 2   **j** 12   **k** 20   **l** 13
4 a 50   **b** 80   **c** 90   **d** 27
5 a 5 and 6   **b** 6 and 7   **c** 8 and 9
  d 7 and 8   **e** 9 and 10   **f** 10 and 11
  g 2 and 3   **h** 1 and 2
6 a 30   **b** 64   **c** 65
  d 36   **e** 4   **f** 0
  g 81   **h** 4   **i** 13
7 a Because $\sqrt{64} = 8$
  b 32 tile lengths
  c 36 tile lengths
8 a 8   **b** 9   **c** 5   **d** 5
9 121, 144, 169, 196
10 a 4 and 81, or 36 and 49
  b 36 and 121; other answers possible
11 a 1156   **b** 6561   **c** 10 609

12 a 144
  b 144
  c $a = 3, b = 4$
  d Answers may vary; e.g. $4^2 \times 5^2$ and 20^2
13 a 121 and 12 321
  b 1 234 321
  c 1 234 321
14 a 8
  b

n	1	2	3	4	5	6	7	8	9	10	11	12	13	14	15	16	17	18	19	20
n^2	1	4	9	16	25	36	49	64	81	100	121	144	169	196	225	256	289	324	361	400
Difference	–	3	5	7	9	11	13	15	17	19	21	23	25	27	29	31	33	35	37	39

  c The difference between consecutive square numbers increases by 2 each time.
  d Answers may vary.

2H

Building understanding

1 a 8, 11, 14, 17, 20
  b 32, 31, 30, 29, 28
  c 52, 48, 44, 40, 36
  d 123, 130, 137, 144, 151
2 a 3, 6, 12, 24, 48
  b 5, 20, 80, 320, 1280
  c 240, 120, 60, 30, 15
  d 625, 125, 25, 5, 1
3 a Ratio of 3
  b Difference subtracting 2
  c Difference adding 11
  d Neither
  e Ratio of $\frac{1}{2}$
  f Neither
  g Neither
  h Difference subtracting 3

Now you try

Example 17
a 19, 22, 25
  b 131, 117, 103
Example 18
a 135, 405, 1215
  b 80, 40, 20

Exercise 2H

1 a i 26, 33, 40
    ii 59, 68, 77
  b i 22, 17, 12
    ii 55, 43, 31
2 a 23, 28, 33
  b 44, 54, 64
  c 14, 11, 8
  d 114, 116, 118
  e 27, 18, 9
  f 5, 4, 3
  g 505, 606, 707
  h 51, 45, 39
3 a 32, 64, 128
  b 80, 160, 320
  c 12, 6, 3
  d 45, 15, 5
  e 176, 352, 704
  f 70 000, 700 000, 7 000 000
  g 16, 8, 4
  h 76, 38, 19
4 a 50, 32, 26
  b 25, 45, 55
  c 32, 64, 256
  d 9, 15, 21
  e 55, 44, 33
  f 333, 111
  g 70, 98, 154
  h 126, 378, 3402

5 a 17, 23, 30
  b 16, 22, 29
  c 36, 49, 64
  d 17, 12, 6
  e 17, 19, 23
  f 47, 95, 191
  g 5, 7, 6
  h 32, 40, 38
6 a 49, 64, 81; square numbers
  b 21, 34, 55; Fibonacci numbers
  c 216, 343, 512; cubes (i.e. powers of 3)
  d 19, 23, 29; primes
  e 16, 18, 20; composite numbers
  f 161, 171, 181; palindromes (or increasing by 10)
7 a 115, 121, 128
  b 24, 48, 16
  c 42, 41, 123
  d 9, 6, 13
8 1, 2, 3, 4, 5, 6, 7, 8, 9, 10 (total = 55)
9 a 39
  b 57
  c 110
  d 192
10 1, 0, 0, 1, 2
11 Difference is 0, ratio is 1.
12 a 55
  b 100
  c 2485
  d 258
13 a 3
  b 10
  c 45
  d 276
  e $n \times (n - 1) \div 2$
14 a 135
  b 624
  c 945

2I

Building understanding

1 a

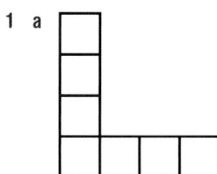

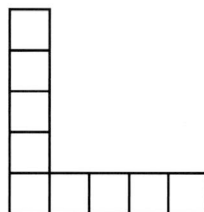

  b

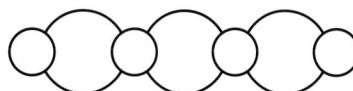

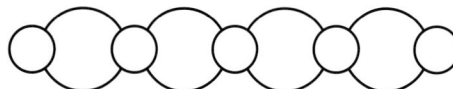

2 a

and

b

and

c

and

Now you try

Example 19

a

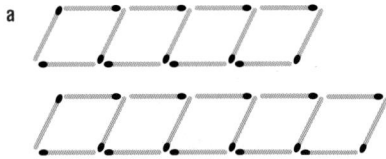

b 4, 7, 10, 13, 16
c 4 matchsticks are required to start the pattern, and an additional 3 matchsticks are required to make the next term in the pattern.

Example 20

a

b

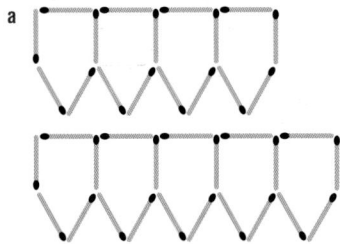

Number of shapes	1	2	3	4	5
Number of sticks required	5	9	13	17	21

c Number of sticks = 1 + 4 × number of shapes

d 81

Exercise 21

1 a

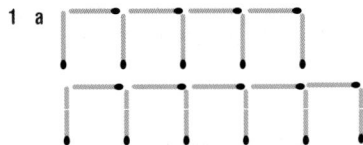

b 3, 5, 7, 9, 11
c 3 sticks are required to start, then 2 are added.

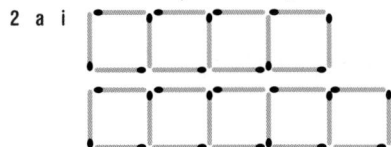

2 a i

ii 4, 7, 10, 13, 16
iii 4 sticks are required to start, then 3 are added.

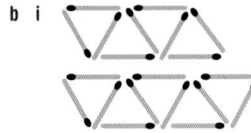

b i

ii 3, 5, 7, 9, 11
iii 3 sticks are required at the start, then 2 are added.

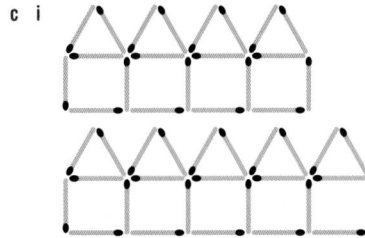

c i

ii 6, 11, 16, 21, 26
iii 6 sticks are required to start, then 5 are added.

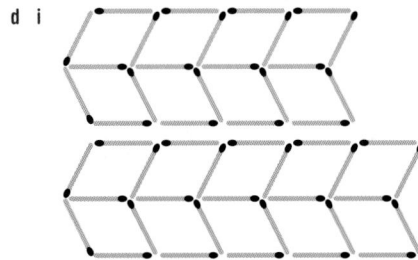

d i

ii 7, 12, 17, 22, 27
iii 7 sticks are required to start, then 5 are added.

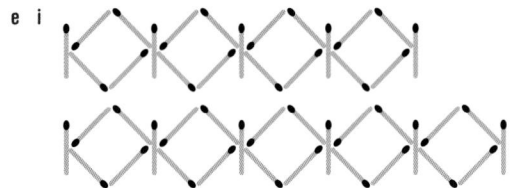

e i

ii 6, 11, 16, 21, 26
iii 6 sticks are required to start, then 5 are added.

f i

ii 4, 7, 10, 13, 16
iii 4 sticks are required to start, then 3 are added.

3 a

b

No. of crosses	1	2	3	4	5
No. of sticks required	4	8	12	16	20

c Number of sticks = 4 × number of crosses
d 80 sticks

4 a

b

No. of fence sections	1	2	3	4	5
No. of planks required	4	7	10	13	16

c Number of planks = 3 × number of fence sections + 1
d 61 planks

5 a

No. of tables	1	2	3	4	5
No. of students	5	8	11	14	17

b Number of students = 3 × number of tables + 2
c 23 students
d 21 tables

6 a

Spa length	1	2	3	4	5	6
No. of tiles	8	10	12	14	16	18

b Number of tiles = 2 × spa length + 6
c 36 tiles
d 12 units

7 A
8 A
9 Answers may vary, examples below.

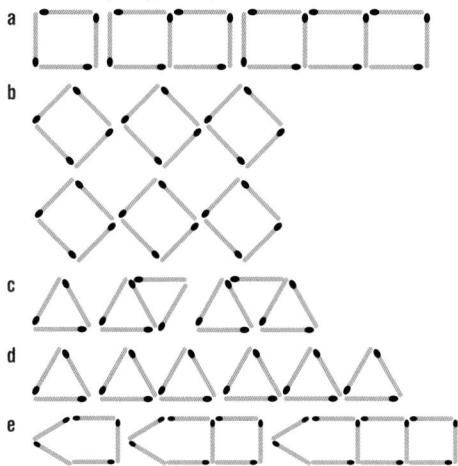

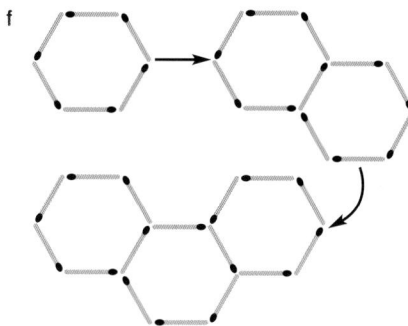

a
b
c
d
e

f

10 a 5   **b** 41   **c** $4g + 1$ **d** 16
11 a $m + n$
b Number of pieces for each new panel
c

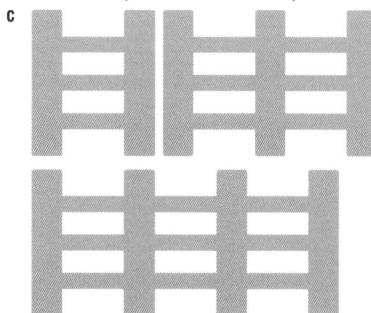

12 a

Number of straight cuts	1	2	3	4	5	6	7
Maximum number of sections	2	4	7	11	16	22	29

b 56
c 211

2J

Building understanding

1 a True   **b** False   **c** True   **d** True
2 a A   **b** D   **c** B   **d** C

Now you try

Example 21

a

input	3	5	7	12	20
output	7	9	11	16	24

b

input	1	2	5	7	10
output	3	11	35	51	75

Example 22
a $output = input - 5$
b $output = input \times 6$ (or $output = 6 \times input$)

Exercise 2J

1 a

input	1	3	5	10	20
output	6	8	10	15	25

b

input	3	9	1	10	6
output	6	18	2	20	12

2 a

input	4	5	6	7	10
output	7	8	9	10	13

b

input	5	1	3	9	0
output	20	4	12	36	0

c

input	11	18	9	44	100
output	3	10	1	36	92

d

input	5	15	55	0	100
output	1	3	11	0	20

3 a

input	1	2	3	4	5
output	7	17	27	37	47

b

input	6	8	10	12	14
output	7	8	9	10	11

c

input	5	12	2	9	14
output	16	37	7	28	43

d

input	3	10	11	7	50
output	2	16	18	10	96

4 a output = input + 1
b output = 4 × input
5 a output = input + 11
b output = input ÷ 6
6 a output = 2 × input

b

input	1	2	3	7	10	15	50	81
output	2	4	6	14	20	30	100	162

7 a output = 3 × input

input	4	10	13	6	8	3	5	11	2
output	12	30	39	18	24	9	15	33	6

b output = input − 9

input	12	93	14	17	21	10	43	9	209
output	3	84	5	8	12	1	34	0	200

8 a

input	3	6	8	12	2
output	7	34	62	142	2

b

input	6	12	1	3	8
output	5	3	25	9	4

c

input	5	12	2	9	0
output	30	156	6	90	0

d

input	3	10	11	7	50
output	15	190	231	91	4950

9 a $y = x + 6$
b $y = 3x$
c $y = x - 2$
d $y = x^2 + 1$

10 a output = 2 × input + 1 ; output = 3 × input − 2
b Infinitely many
11 a output = input − 7
b output = input + 4
c output = input ÷ 4
d output = (input − 1) ÷ 2
e output = (input − 4) × 2
12 a i output = 2 × input − 3
ii output = 4 × input + 1
iii output = 5 × input − 1
iv output = input ÷ 6 + 2
v output = 10 × input + 3
vi output = 4 × input − 4
b Answers may vary.

2K

Building understanding

1 C
2 a x-axis **b** y-axis **c** origin
d first **e** y-coordinate **f** x, y, x, y

Now you try

Example 23

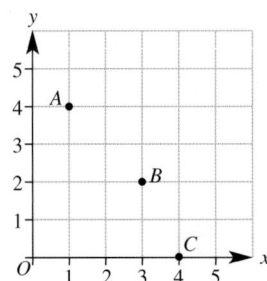

Example 24

a

input (x)	output (y)
0	4
1	5
2	6
3	7

b

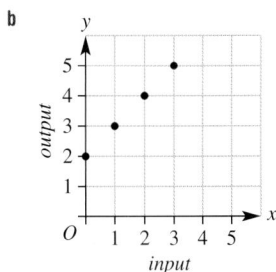

c Yes

Exercise 2K

1 a–d

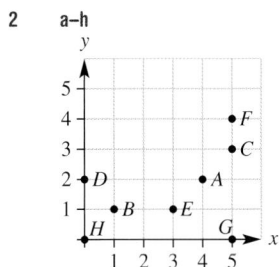

2 a–h

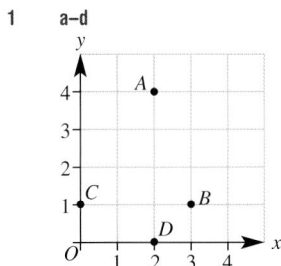

3 a $A(1, 4)$, $B(2, 1)$, $C(5, 3)$, $D(2, 6)$, $E(4, 0)$, $F(6, 5)$, $G(0, 3)$, $H(4, 4)$

b $M(1, 2)$, $N(3, 2)$, $P(5, 1)$, $Q(2, 5)$, $R(2, 0)$, $S(6, 6)$, $T(0, 6)$, $U(5, 4)$

4 a

input (x)	output (y)
0	2
1	3
2	4
3	5

b

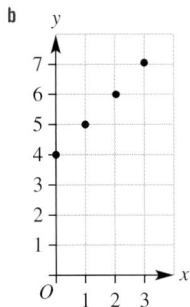

c Yes

5 a

input (x)	output (y)
1	0
2	1
3	2
4	3

b

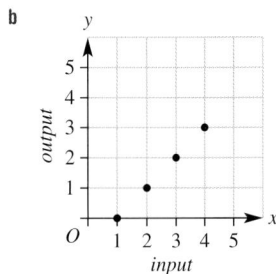

c Yes

6 a

input (x)	output (y)
0	0
1	2
2	4
3	6

b

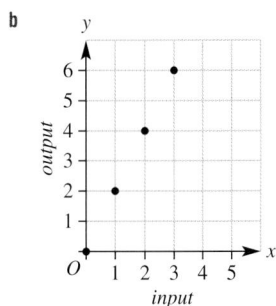

c Yes

7 a

input (x)	output (y)
0	0
1	1
2	4
3	9

2K

b Points at (0, 0), (1, 1), (2, 4), (3, 9)

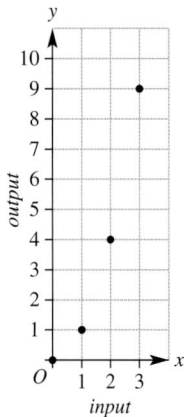

c No

8 a

input (x)	output (y)
1	6
2	3
3	2
6	1

b Points at (1, 6), (2, 3), (3, 2), (6, 1)

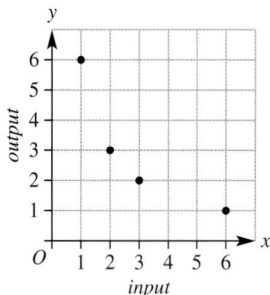

c No

9

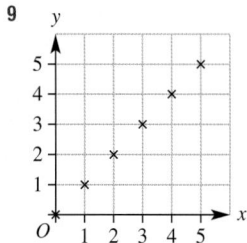

10

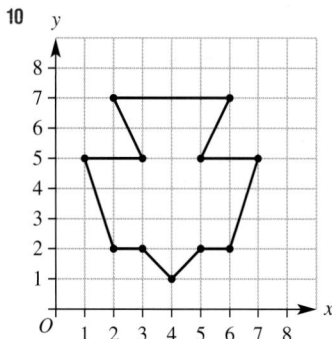

11 a

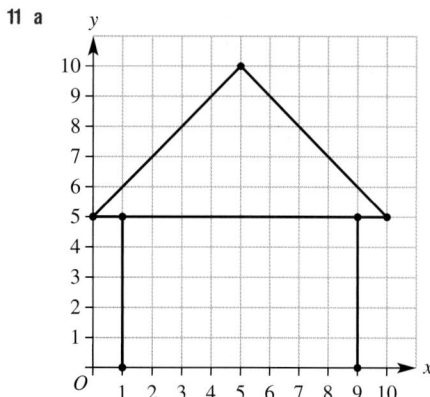

b (4, 0), (4, 3), (6, 3), (6, 0), but answers may vary.
c Answers may vary.
d Answers may vary.

12 a

length (x)	perimeter (y)
1	4
2	8
3	12
4	16

b Points at (1, 4), (2, 8), (3,12), (4, 16)
c Yes

13 a HELP
b (4, 4), (5, 1), (3, 1), (3, 4), (5, 1), (5, 4)
c KEY UNDER POT PLANT
d 215100325134510011540044512551 43

14 a $D(4, 5)$
b $D(4, 1)$
c $D(0, 0)$
d $D(1, 5)$

15 a output = input + 2
b output = input $\times$ 3
c output = input $\div$ 2

16 a (3, 6) or any with $x = 3$
b Any point on a vertical line with $x = 3$
c (3, 5)

17 a $M(3, 2)$
b (1, 2)
c Find the average of the x-values, then the average of the y-values.
d (4, 2)
e (2.5, 3.5)
f ($-0.5, -0.5$)
g (5, 3)

Problems and challenges

1 101
2 a 28 (1, 2, 4, 7, 14)
  b 1, 2, 4, 8, 16, 31, 62, 124, 248
3 a 18 tulips per bunch
  b 7 red, 6 pink and 8 yellow bunches
4 14 + 18 = 32

5 $5^2 = 4^2 + 9$, $6^2 = 5^2 + 11$

6 Answers may vary. Check that the answer is the whole number that you are looking for.

7 602

8 1, 5, 7, 11, 13, 17, 19, 23, 25, 29, 31, 35

Chapter checklist with success criteria

1 1, 2, 4, 5, 8, 10, 20, 40

2 11, 22, 33, 44, 55, 66

3 12×11

4 12

5 30

6 2, 3, 4 and 6

7 17 has exactly two factors (1 and 17), but 35 has more than two factors (1, 5, 7, 35)

8 2, 3, 5

9 $2^2 \times 3^4$

10 13

11 $60 = 2^2 \times 3 \times 5$

12 36

13 40

14 6 and 7

15 $\dfrac{1}{2}$

16 54, 66, 78

17 Start with 5 sticks, add three sticks each time.

18 number of sticks = 3 × number of triangles; 60 sticks required for 20 triangles

19

input	4	2	9	12	0
output	13	7	28	37	1

20 output = input × 7

21

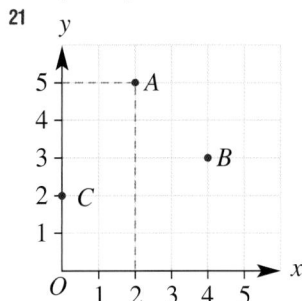

22

input (x)	output (y)
0	1
1	2
2	3
3	4

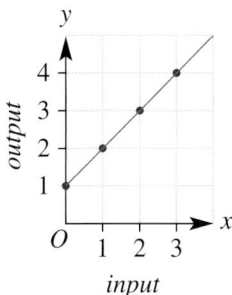

Chapter review

Short-answer questions

1 a 1, 2, 3, $\boxed{4}$, 5, $\boxed{6}$, $\boxed{8}$, $\boxed{10}$, $\boxed{12}$, $\boxed{15}$, $\boxed{20}$, $\boxed{24}$, $\boxed{30}$, $\boxed{40}$, $\boxed{60}$, $\boxed{120}$

  b For example, 1200, 1440, 1800

2 a 8, 16, 24, 32, 40, 48, 56, 64, 72, 80, 88, 96
$\boxed{7}$, 14, $\boxed{21}$, 28, $\boxed{35}$, 42, $\boxed{49}$, 56, $\boxed{63}$, 70, $\boxed{77}$, 84

  b 7, 13

3 a i 5

    ii 2

    iii 24

  b i 65

    ii 18

    iii 88

4 a Composite 21, 30, 16; prime 11, 7, 3, 2

  b Only one, 13

5 a 2, 5, 7, 11

  b 30, 42, 70

6 a 6^8

  b $5^4 \times 2^5$

7 a 2^5

  b $2^3 \times 5^2$

  c $3^2 \times 5^2$

8 a 10

  b 3

  c 4

9 a 16

  b 7

  c 397

  d 131

10 a No

  b Yes

  c No

11 a

Number	Divisible by 2	Divisible by 3	Divisible by 4	Divisible by 5
84 539 424	✓	✓	✓	✗

Number	Divisible by 6	Divisible by 8	Divisible by 9	Divisible by 10
84 539 424	✓	✓	✗	✗

Explanation:
84 539 424 is an even number, therefore is divisible by 2.
84 539 424 has a digit sum of 39, therefore is divisible by 3, but not by 9.
84 539 424 is divisible by 2 and 3, therefore is divisible by 6.
The last two digits are 24, which is divisible by 4.
The last three digits are 424, which is divisible by 8.
The last digit is a 4, therefore not divisible by 5 or 10.

  b Answers may vary.

  c Any six-digit number ending in 0 with sum of digits which is divisible by 9.

12 a i 5 **ii** 50 **iii** 13
   iv 18 **v** 14 **vi** 20
   b i 4 and 5 **ii** 8 and 9 **iii** 7 and 8
13 a 36, 39, 42
   b 43, 35, 27
   c 112, 70, 28
14 a 280, 560, 1120
   b 900, 300, 100
   c 1000, 2500, 6250
15 a 168, 51, 336, 46, 672, 41
   b 212, 307, 421, 554, 706, 877
16 a

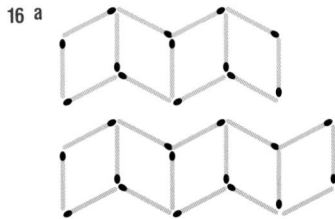

b

No. of rhombuses	1	2	3	4	5
No. of sticks required	4	7	10	13	16

   c Four sticks are required to start the pattern, and an additional three sticks are required to make each next term in the pattern.
17 a 5
   b 32
   c $3g + 2$
   d 21 windows
18 a

input	3	5	7	12	20
output	8	10	12	17	25

   b

input	4	2	9	12	0
output	15	11	25	31	7

19 a output = input + 9
   b output = 12 × input + 8
   c output = 2 × input + 1
   d output = 10 − input
20 a $A(1, 3), B(3, 4), D(2, 1)$
   b $C(4, 2)$
   c $E(5, 0)$
21 a 36, 49, 64; square the counting numbers
   b 125, 216, 343; cube of the counting numbers
   c (4, 6), (5, 7), (6, 8); each y-value is 2 more than the x-value
   d 31, 31, 30; days of the month in a leap year
   e $\sqrt{5}, \sqrt{6}, \sqrt{7}$; square root of the counting numbers
   f 7, 64, 8; two sequences: 1, 2, 3, 4, … and 1, 2, 4, 8, 16, …

Multiple-choice questions

1 B	**2** E	**3** C	**4** E	**5** B	**6** B
7 D	**8** A	**9** C	**10** E	**11** B	**12** D

Extended-response questions

1 a i Width 3^3 cm, length 5^3 cm
   ii Area = $3^3 \times 5^3$ cm^2, perimeter = $2 \times 3^3 + 2 \times 5^3$ cm
   b i 2^6
   ii Area = 16^3 or 4^6 or 2^{12}, perimeter = 16^2 or 4^4 or 2^8
   c $5^4 \times 7^3$ **d** 16^2 or 4^4 or 2^8
2 a i 1 **ii** 2
   b

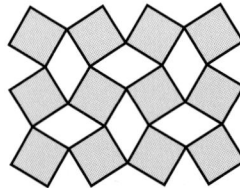

   c

Rows	1	2	3	4	5	6
Desks per row	4	4	4	4	4	4
Total no. of desks	4	8	12	16	20	24
Total no. of rhombuses	0	3	6	9	12	15

   d Number of rhombuses = 3 × (number of rows − 1)
     = $3(n - 1)$

   e

Rows	1	2	3	4	5	6	7	8
Desks per row	5	5	5	5	5	5	5	5
Total desks	5	10	15	20	25	30	35	40
Rhombuses	0	4	8	12	16	20	24	28

Rows	1	2	3	4	5	6	7	8
Desks per row	6	6	6	6	6	6	6	6
Total desks	6	12	18	24	30	36	42	48
Rhombuses	0	5	10	15	20	25	30	35

Rows	1	2	3	4	5	6	7	8
Desks per row	7	7	7	7	7	7	7	7
Total desks	7	14	21	28	35	42	49	56
Rhombuses	0	6	12	18	24	30	36	42

Rows	1	2	3	4	5	6	7	8
Desks per row	8	8	8	8	8	8	8	8
Total desks	8	16	24	32	40	48	56	64
Rhombuses	0	7	14	21	28	35	42	49

   f No. of rhombuses = (no. of desks − 1)× (no. of rows − 1)
     = $(d - 1)(n - 1)$

   g 10 201 desks

Chapter 3

3A

Building understanding

1 a 9   b 7
2 Proper: b, e, f
  Improper: a, c
  Whole numbers: d
3 c, e, f

Now you try

Example 1
a 10   b 7
c i 10   ii 7   iii $\frac{7}{10}$

Example 2

Example 3 (Answers may vary.)

Exercise 3A

1 a 5   b 2
  c i 5   ii 2   iii $\frac{2}{5}$
2 A a 4   b 1
    c i 4   ii 1   iii $\frac{1}{4}$
  B a 8   b 7
    c i 8   ii 7   iii $\frac{7}{8}$
  C a 3   b 2
    c i 3   ii 2   iii $\frac{2}{3}$
  D a 12   b 5
    c i 12   ii 5   iii $\frac{5}{12}$
3 a

b

c

d

e

f

4 Answers may vary.
a

b

c

5 a $\frac{7}{5}, \frac{8}{5}, \frac{9}{5}$ b $\frac{9}{8}, \frac{10}{8}, \frac{11}{8}$
  c $\frac{5}{3}, \frac{6}{3}, \frac{7}{3}$ d $\frac{7}{7}, \frac{6}{7}, \frac{5}{7}$
  e $\frac{5}{2}, \frac{3}{2}, \frac{1}{2}$ f $\frac{23}{4}, \frac{28}{4}, \frac{33}{4}$
6 a $1\frac{1}{2}, \frac{3}{2}, 3\frac{1}{2}, \frac{7}{2}, 5, \frac{10}{2}$ b $\frac{1}{5}, \frac{4}{5}, 2\frac{1}{5}, \frac{11}{5}$
  c $\frac{3}{7}, 1\frac{4}{7}, \frac{11}{7}, 2\frac{2}{7}, \frac{16}{7}$ d $3\frac{1}{3}, \frac{10}{3}, 3\frac{2}{3}, \frac{11}{3}, 4\frac{2}{3}, \frac{14}{3}$

7 Division

8 a $\frac{6}{11}$ **b** $\frac{4}{8} = \frac{1}{2}$ **c** $\frac{7}{12}$

d $\frac{5}{6}$ **e** $\frac{3}{12} = \frac{1}{4}$ **f** $\frac{5}{9}$

9 a $\frac{12}{43}$ **b** $\frac{13}{15}$ **c** $\frac{11}{12}$ **d** $\frac{1}{12}$ **e** $\frac{2}{11}$

f $\frac{144}{475}$ **g** $\frac{7}{20}$ **h** $\frac{1}{4}$ **i** $\frac{3}{7}$

10 a

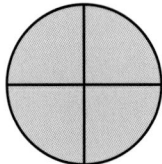

Four quarters makes up one whole, so $\frac{4}{4} = 1$. A similar diagram can be used for sixths.
(This could also be shown on a number line.)

b $\frac{6}{3}, \frac{10}{5}, \frac{40}{20}$ (other answers possible).

11 C

12 a $\frac{1}{5}$ **b** 50 mL

c 40 mL   **d** $\frac{4}{25}$

e 32 mL   **f** $\frac{16}{125}$

g 90 mL   **h** $\frac{9}{25}$

i 122 mL   **j** $\frac{61}{125}$

k Approximately, yes they will.

3B

Building understanding

1 $\frac{3}{6}, \frac{2}{4}, \frac{11}{22}, \frac{5}{10}$

2 $\frac{4}{10}, \frac{16}{40}, \frac{2}{5}, \frac{80}{200}$

3 $\frac{4}{6}, \frac{6}{9}, \frac{8}{12}$

4 a $\frac{1}{5}$ **b** $\frac{1}{6}$ **c** $\frac{2}{3}$

Now you try

Example 4
a $\frac{3}{5} = \frac{6}{10}$ **b** $\frac{18}{24} = \frac{9}{12}$ **c** $\frac{5}{6} = \frac{20}{24}$

Example 5
a $\frac{4}{5}$ **b** $\frac{1}{4}$

Example 6
a $=$ **b** $\neq$

Exercise 3B

1 a $\frac{6}{8}$ **b** $\frac{3}{6}$ **c** $\frac{4}{10}$ **d** $\frac{12}{20}$

2 a $\frac{1}{2}$ **b** $\frac{3}{5}$ **c** $\frac{3}{4}$ **d** $\frac{4}{6}$

3 a $\frac{6}{15}$ **b** $\frac{6}{8}$ **c** $\frac{20}{40}$ **d** $\frac{30}{40}$

4 a 9   **b** 50   **c** 33   **d** 56
e 8   **f** 2   **g** 12   **h** 39
i 35   **j** 200   **k** 105   **l** 2

5 a $\frac{3}{4}$ **b** $\frac{2}{3}$ **c** $\frac{1}{3}$ **d** $\frac{4}{11}$

e $\frac{2}{5}$ **f** $\frac{1}{11}$ **g** $\frac{1}{7}$ **h** $\frac{1}{3}$

i $\frac{7}{9}$ **j** $\frac{3}{8}$ **k** $\frac{5}{6}$ **l** $\frac{5}{1} = 5$

6 a $\neq$ **b** $=$ **c** $=$ **d** $\neq$ **e** $=$
f $=$ **g** $=$ **h** $=$ **i** $=$

7 a $\frac{7}{14} = \frac{1}{2}$ **b** $\frac{12}{16} = \frac{3}{4}$ **c** $\frac{4}{42} = \frac{2}{21}$ **d** $\frac{7}{63} = \frac{1}{9}$

8 a 35   **b** 45   **c** 30   **d** 24

9 $\frac{2}{9}$

10 Justin 4, Joanna 3, Jack 5

11 a 75   **b** $\frac{1}{3}$ **c** 150

12 a $\frac{6}{10}, \frac{30}{50}, \frac{36}{60}$ (other answers possible)

b 3 and 5 are both multiplied by the same value, so the new sum of numerator and denominator will be $8 \times$ that value, which is even (because 8 is even).

13 Answers may vary.
a

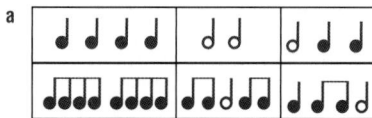

b 12 quavers (eighth notes) to a bar
c

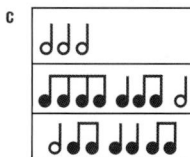

d

Note	British name / American name	Rest
	Breve / Double whole note	
	Semibreve / Whole note	
	Minim /Half note	
	Crotchet / Quarter note	Or—
	Quaver / Eighth note For notes of this length and shorter, the note has the same number of flags (or hooks) as the rest has branches.	
	Semiquaver / Sixteenth note	

e Each dot increases the length of the note by another 50%.

e.g. ♩• $= \frac{3}{4}$ note (value = 3 beats)

= half note + 50%

= half note + quarter note

3C

Building understanding

1 a   2 and 3   b   11 and 12   c   36 and 37
2 a   24   b   360   c   60   d   24
3 a

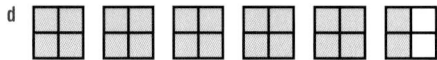

   b

   c

   d

4 a   8   b   12   c   28   d   44
   e   17   f   7   g   10   h   24
5 a $7\frac{1}{2}$, $10\frac{1}{2}$

   b $1\frac{2}{3}$, $2\frac{1}{3}$, $4\frac{2}{3}$

   c $23\frac{1}{5}$, $24\frac{2}{5}$, $25\frac{4}{5}$, $26\frac{1}{5}$

Now you try

Example 7
$\frac{17}{6}$

Example 8
$3\frac{2}{7}$

Example 9
$4\frac{1}{2}$

Exercise 3C

1 a $\frac{5}{3}$ b $\frac{11}{5}$ c $\frac{7}{2}$ d $\frac{7}{4}$

2 a $\frac{11}{5}$ b $\frac{10}{3}$ c $\frac{29}{7}$ d $\frac{5}{2}$
   e $\frac{14}{3}$ f $\frac{42}{5}$ g $\frac{55}{9}$ h $\frac{42}{8}$
   i $\frac{23}{12}$ j $\frac{53}{12}$ k $\frac{115}{20}$ l $\frac{643}{10}$

3 a $1\frac{2}{5}$ b $1\frac{2}{3}$ c $3\frac{2}{3}$ d $2\frac{2}{7}$
   e $1\frac{5}{7}$ f $6\frac{2}{3}$ g $4\frac{3}{8}$ h $6\frac{6}{7}$
   i $3\frac{1}{12}$ j $9\frac{3}{10}$ k $2\frac{31}{100}$ l $12\frac{3}{11}$

4 a $2\frac{1}{2}$ b $2\frac{4}{5}$ c $1\frac{1}{3}$ d $1\frac{1}{3}$
   e $1\frac{1}{8}$ f $3\frac{1}{3}$ g $2\frac{2}{3}$ h $2\frac{2}{5}$

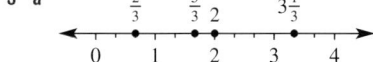

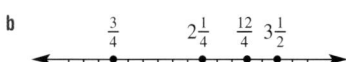

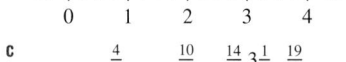

5 a

   b

   c

6 a   5 and 6   b   7 and 8   c   6 and 7
7 a   15   b $1\frac{7}{8}$ c   9   d $1\frac{1}{8}$
8 Answers may vary.
9 a   11   b   9   c $4x - 1$
   d $3y - 1$ e mn

10 $2\frac{1}{8}$, $2\frac{3}{7}$, $2\frac{5}{6}$

11 a   i $1\frac{2}{3}$, $2\frac{1}{3}$, $3\frac{1}{2}$ ii $1\frac{5}{6}$

    b   i $2\frac{3}{4}$, $3\frac{2}{4}$, $4\frac{2}{3}$ ii $1\frac{11}{12}$

    c   i $3\frac{4}{5}$, $4\frac{3}{5}$, $5\frac{3}{4}$ ii $1\frac{19}{20}$

    d $1\frac{29}{30}$

    e   A mixed numeral with a whole number part equal to 1.
        Denominator equal to product of two largest numbers,
        numerator is one less than denominator.

    f, g   Answers may vary.

3D

Building understanding

1 a $\frac{5}{7}$ b $\frac{7}{3}$ c $\frac{9}{11}$ d $\frac{8}{5}$

2 a   10   b   20   c   6   d   12
   e   30   f   12   g   24   h   30

3 a   15   b   20   c   21   d   10
   e   24   f   60   g   12   h   12

4 a   6   b   8   c   4   d   6   e   15   f   15

Now you try

Example 10
a   >   b   <   c   =   d   <

Example 11

a $\frac{2}{6}$, $\frac{1}{2}$, $\frac{3}{4}$

b $\frac{3}{4}$, $\frac{5}{4}$, $1\frac{7}{8}$, $\frac{9}{4}$, $2\frac{1}{2}$, $\frac{23}{8}$

Exercise 3D

1 a   >   b   <   c   >   d   <
2 a   >   b   <   c   >   d   =
3 a   >   b   <   c   >   d   <
4 a   >   b   =   c   <   d   >
   e   <   f   >   g   <   h   =
   i   >   j   >   k   <   l   >

5 a $\frac{3}{5}$, $\frac{7}{5}$, $\frac{8}{5}$ b $\frac{2}{9}$, $\frac{1}{3}$, $\frac{5}{9}$

   c $\frac{2}{5}$, $\frac{3}{4}$, $\frac{4}{5}$ d $\frac{3}{5}$, $\frac{2}{3}$, $\frac{5}{6}$

6 a $2\frac{1}{4}$, $\frac{5}{2}$, $\frac{11}{4}$, $3\frac{1}{3}$ b $\frac{5}{3}$, $\frac{7}{4}$, $\frac{11}{6}$, $1\frac{7}{8}$

   c $\frac{11}{5}$, $\frac{9}{4}$, $2\frac{1}{2}$, $2\frac{3}{5}$, $2\frac{7}{10}$ d $4\frac{1}{6}$, $4\frac{10}{27}$, $4\frac{4}{9}$, $4\frac{2}{3}$, $\frac{15}{3}$

7 a $\frac{4}{5}$, $\frac{7}{10}$, $\frac{3}{5}$, $\frac{1}{2}$, $\frac{3}{10}$ b $\frac{3}{4}$, $\frac{5}{8}$, $\frac{1}{2}$, $\frac{3}{8}$, $\frac{1}{4}$

   c $\frac{5}{6}$, $\frac{2}{3}$, $\frac{1}{2}$, $\frac{5}{12}$, $\frac{1}{3}$

8 a $\frac{3}{5}, \frac{3}{6}, \frac{3}{7}, \frac{3}{8}$ **b** $\frac{1}{10}, \frac{1}{15}, \frac{1}{50}, \frac{1}{100}$

c $10\frac{2}{3}, 8\frac{3}{5}, 7\frac{1}{11}, 5\frac{4}{9}$ **d** $2\frac{1}{3}, 2\frac{1}{5}, 2\frac{1}{6}, 2\frac{1}{9}$

9 $\frac{1}{4}, \frac{1}{8}, \frac{1}{11}$

10 Andrea, Rob, Dean, David

11 a $\frac{5}{9}, \frac{6}{9}$ **b** $\frac{11}{4}, \frac{14}{4}$ **c** $\frac{5}{6}, \frac{3}{6}$ **d** $\frac{10}{14}, \frac{11}{14}$

12 Answers may vary.

a $\frac{13}{20}$ **b** $\frac{1}{3}$ **c** $\frac{5}{21}$

d $\frac{3}{4}$ **e** $2\frac{1}{4}$ **f** $8\frac{29}{40}$

13 a $\frac{3}{4}, \frac{7}{8}$, 1 can be written $\frac{6}{8}, \frac{7}{8}, \frac{8}{8}$, which is in ascending order.

b $\frac{15}{16}$

c If you keep doubling the numerator and denominator, then add 1 to the numerator you will generate a new 'second largest' value each time, e.g. $\frac{15}{16}, \frac{31}{32}, \frac{63}{64}, \ldots$

14 a 7, 8 **b** 16

15 a i $\frac{1}{4}$ **ii** $\frac{3}{8}$ **iii** $\frac{1}{2}$ **iv** $\frac{1}{3}$

b Answers may vary.

3E

Building understanding

1 a Denominator

b Denominator, numerators

c Denominators, lowest common denominator

d Check, simplified

2 a 15 **b** 6 **c** 24 **d** 48

3 a ✓ **b** ✗ **c** ✓ **d** ✗

Now you try

Example 12

a $\frac{5}{7}$ **b** $1\frac{2}{9}$

Example 13

a $\frac{8}{15}$ **b** $1\frac{9}{20}$

Example 14

a $4\frac{1}{5}$ **b** $3\frac{17}{20}$

Exercise 3E

1 a $\frac{7}{9}$ **b** $\frac{7}{12}$ **c** $\frac{7}{15}$ **d** $\frac{5}{9}$

2 a $1\frac{2}{7}$ **b** $1\frac{3}{10}$ **c** $1\frac{4}{5}$ **d** $1\frac{4}{19}$

3 a $\frac{3}{4}$ **b** $\frac{14}{15}$ **c** $\frac{2}{3}$ **d** $\frac{7}{12}$

e $\frac{13}{20}$ **f** $\frac{19}{20}$ **g** $\frac{13}{21}$ **h** $\frac{23}{40}$

4 a $1\frac{13}{30}$ **b** $1\frac{9}{28}$ **c** $1\frac{13}{33}$ **d** $1\frac{5}{12}$

5 a $3\frac{4}{5}$ **b** $7\frac{3}{7}$ **c** $12\frac{3}{4}$ **d** $5\frac{5}{9}$

e $10\frac{1}{3}$ **f** $21\frac{1}{6}$ **g** $19\frac{3}{11}$ **h** $12\frac{2}{5}$

6 a $4\frac{5}{12}$ **b** $7\frac{7}{30}$ **c** $12\frac{1}{6}$ **d** $13\frac{9}{28}$

e $15\frac{1}{10}$ **f** $19\frac{1}{9}$ **g** $25\frac{21}{44}$ **h** $15\frac{5}{24}$

7 a $\frac{1}{2}$ **b** $\frac{5}{9}$ **c** $1\frac{3}{8}$ **d** $2\frac{1}{20}$

e $1\frac{5}{6}$ **f** $1\frac{29}{44}$ **g** $7\frac{7}{10}$ **h** 3

8 a $\frac{14}{15}$ **b** $\frac{1}{15}$

9 $8\frac{3}{20}$ km

10 a $\frac{3}{4}$ **b** 400 **c** $\frac{1}{4}$, 250 pieces

11 a $\frac{47}{60}$ **b** $\frac{13}{60}$ **c** 39

12 Jim $\left(\frac{36}{60}\right)$, Vesna $\left(\frac{37}{60}\right)$, Juliet $\left(\frac{38}{60}\right)$, Mikhail $\left(\frac{39}{60}\right)$

13 a 5, 2

b 2, 4, 8 or 2, 3, 24

c 5, 1 or 30, 3

14 a Maximum: $\frac{6}{1} + \frac{5}{2} + \frac{4}{3} = 9\frac{5}{6}$

Minimum: $\frac{1}{4} + \frac{2}{5} + \frac{3}{6} = 1\frac{3}{20}$

b Maximum: $\frac{8}{1} + \frac{7}{2} + \frac{6}{3} + \frac{5}{4} = 14\frac{3}{4}$

Minimum: $\frac{1}{5} + \frac{2}{6} + \frac{3}{7} + \frac{4}{8} = 1\frac{97}{210}$

c Answers may vary.

d Maximum: Largest numbers as numerators, smallest numbers as denominators; combine largest numerator available with smallest denominator available to produce the fractions.

Minimum: Smallest numbers as numerators, largest numbers as denominators; combine smallest numerator available with smallest denominator available to produce the fractions.

3F

Building understanding

1 a Denominator **b** Multiply

c Simplify **d** Multiply

2 a 12 **b** 18 **c** 24 **d** 63

3 a ✓ **b** ✗ **c** ✗ **d** ✓

Now you try

Example 15

a $\frac{5}{11}$ **b** $\frac{3}{20}$ **c** $\frac{1}{6}$

Example 16

a $1\frac{5}{12}$ **b** $1\frac{13}{20}$

Exercise 3F

1 a $\frac{2}{7}$ **b** $\frac{3}{11}$ **c** $\frac{7}{18}$ **d** $\frac{1}{3}$

2 a $\frac{4}{9}$ **b** $\frac{3}{19}$ **c** 0 **d** $\frac{8}{23}$

3 a $\frac{5}{12}$ **b** $\frac{1}{10}$ **c** $\frac{13}{30}$ **d** $\frac{9}{28}$

4 a $\frac{2}{3}$ **b** $\frac{2}{5}$ **c** $\frac{1}{2}$ **d** $\frac{1}{4}$

e $\frac{1}{2}$ **f** $\frac{1}{2}$ **g** $\frac{1}{6}$ **h** $\frac{1}{4}$

5 a $1\frac{3}{5}$ **b** $8\frac{3}{7}$ **c** $1\frac{1}{7}$ **d** $3\frac{2}{9}$

e $2\frac{5}{12}$ **f** $3\frac{5}{28}$ **g** $4\frac{7}{18}$ **h** $7\frac{1}{20}$

6 a $2\frac{2}{3}$ **b** $4\frac{3}{5}$ **c** $4\frac{2}{3}$ **d** $4\frac{8}{9}$

e $4\frac{2}{3}$ **f** $\frac{37}{45}$ **g** $9\frac{37}{44}$ **h** $2\frac{29}{60}$

7 $\frac{11}{20}$ L

8 $\frac{3}{5}$

9 $\frac{1}{6}$

10 $\$7\frac{3}{4}$, $\$7.75$

11 a Ice-cream $\frac{3}{4}$, chocolate $\frac{3}{4}$, sponge $\frac{7}{8}$

b Ice-cream $\frac{1}{4}$, chocolate $\frac{1}{4}$, sponge $\frac{1}{8}$

c $2\frac{3}{8}$ **d** $\frac{5}{8}$

12 a 3, 4. Other answers possible.
b 3, 1. Other answers possible.
c 1, 2. Other answers possible.
d 4, 3; 1, 6; or 2, 4.

13 a $\frac{1}{4}$ **b** 4 years   **c** 10 years

14 a i $\frac{8}{15}$: 'Converting to an improper fraction' is quick and efficient for this question.

ii $3\frac{36}{55}$: 'Borrowing a whole number' keeps the numbers smaller and easier to deal with for this question.

15 Answers may vary.

3G

Building understanding

1 a 0, 1   **b** 1
c Whole number, proper fraction
2 You get a smaller answer because you are multiplying by a number that is less than 1.
3 a

b

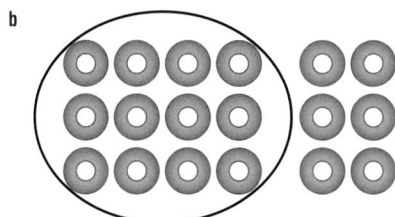

c

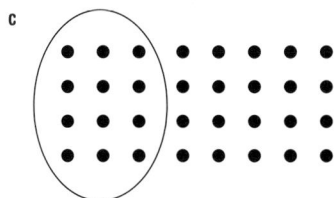

4 D

Now you try

Example 17

a $\frac{2}{35}$ **b** $\frac{3}{4}$ **c** $\frac{5}{12}$

Example 18

a 14   **b** $13\frac{1}{3}$

Example 19

a $1\frac{19}{21}$ **b** 21

Example 20

a $9\frac{9}{10}$ **b** 12

Exercise 3G

1 a $\frac{1}{6}$ **b** $\frac{1}{15}$ **c** $\frac{10}{21}$ **d** $\frac{6}{35}$

e $\frac{3}{20}$ **f** $\frac{2}{21}$ **g** $\frac{5}{24}$ **h** $\frac{4}{45}$

2 a $\frac{1}{7}$ **b** $\frac{1}{3}$ **c** $\frac{2}{5}$ **d** $\frac{2}{7}$

3 a $\frac{2}{5}$ **b** $\frac{5}{22}$ **c** $\frac{6}{11}$ **d** $\frac{4}{11}$

e $\frac{6}{35}$ **f** $\frac{3}{10}$ **g** $\frac{2}{7}$ **h** $\frac{1}{6}$

4 a 6   **b** 9   **c** 16   **d** 15

e 12   **f** 4   **g** 80   **h** 33

5 a $5\frac{5}{6}$ **b** $1\frac{31}{35}$ **c** $3\frac{3}{10}$ **d** $4\frac{7}{8}$

e $5\frac{1}{3}$ **f** 7   **g** 6   **h** $3\frac{1}{3}$

6 a $3\frac{11}{15}$ **b** $1\frac{25}{63}$ **c** $7\frac{4}{5}$ **d** 24

7 a $\frac{3}{5}$

b 48 in Year 7, 72 in Year 8.

8 $11\frac{2}{3}$ L

9 7 cups of self-raising flour, 3 cups of cream
10 7 games

11 a $\times\frac{7}{12}$ **b** $\times\frac{7}{12}$ **c** $\times\frac{1}{12}$

d ✓   **e** ✓   **f** $\times\frac{1}{12}$

12 D; e.g. $\frac{2}{7}\times\frac{3}{5}=\frac{6}{35}$. The two numerators will always multiply to give a smaller number than the two larger denominators. Hence, the product of two proper fractions will always be a proper fraction.

13 Answers may vary.
a $\frac{2}{5}\times\frac{3}{2}$ **b** $\frac{5}{4}\times\frac{3}{5}$ **c** $\frac{3}{7}\times\frac{2}{6}$

14 a $\frac{2}{7}, \frac{3}{8}$

Progress quiz

1 a A square with 4 equal parts, 3 of which are shaded; answers may vary.

b 4
c 3

d

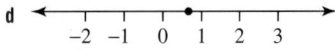

e Proper fraction

2 $1\frac{2}{3}$ or $\frac{5}{3}$ or $1\frac{4}{6}$ or $\frac{10}{6}$

3 $\frac{2}{5} = \frac{4}{10}, \frac{6}{15}, \frac{20}{50}, \frac{10}{25}, \frac{8}{20}$ … (Answers may vary.)

4 a $\frac{2}{5}$　　**b** $\frac{1}{2}$　　**c** $\frac{7}{3} = 2\frac{1}{3}$　　**d** 3

5 $\frac{8}{5}$

6 $3\frac{1}{4}$

7 a >　　**b** =　　**c** =　　**d** <

8 $\frac{4}{9}, \frac{1}{2}, \frac{2}{3}, \frac{9}{4}$

9 a $\frac{6}{7}$　　**b** $\frac{7}{10}$　　**c** $1\frac{3}{20}$　　**d** $5\frac{1}{4}$

10 a $\frac{1}{12}$　　　　**b** $\frac{7}{12}$　　　　**c** $2\frac{3}{10}$

11 a \$336　　**b** $\frac{14}{33}$　　**c** $\frac{3}{5}$　　**d** $\frac{3}{4}$

3H

Building understanding

1 A

2 a $\frac{5}{11} \times \frac{5}{3}$　**b** $\frac{1}{3} \times \frac{5}{1}$　**c** $\frac{7}{10} \times \frac{5}{12}$　**d** $\frac{8}{3} \times \frac{1}{3}$

3 a $\frac{5}{2} \div \frac{4}{3}, \frac{5}{2} \times \frac{3}{4}$　　　**b** $24 \div \frac{16}{5}, \frac{24}{1} \times \frac{5}{16}$

　　c $\frac{47}{11} \div \frac{21}{4}, \frac{47}{11} \times \frac{4}{21}$　　**d** $\frac{8}{3} \div \frac{80}{7}, \frac{8}{3} \times \frac{7}{80}$

4 a less　　　**b** more　　　**c** more

　　d more　　　**e** less　　　**f** less

Now you try

Example 21

a $\frac{7}{6}$　　　　**b** $\frac{1}{3}$　　　　**c** $\frac{3}{11}$

Example 22

a $\frac{3}{20}$　　　　　　**b** $1\frac{4}{5}$

Example 23

a 40　　　　　　**b** 45

Example 24

a $1\frac{1}{15}$　　　　　　**b** $1\frac{19}{23}$

Exercise 3H

1 a $\frac{5}{2}$　　**b** $\frac{7}{5}$　　**c** $\frac{5}{3}$　　**d** $\frac{9}{4}$

2 a $\frac{1}{2}$　　**b** $\frac{1}{6}$　　**c** $\frac{1}{10}$　　**d** $\frac{1}{4}$

3 a $\frac{6}{11}$　　**b** $\frac{3}{8}$　　**c** $\frac{2}{7}$　　**d** $\frac{3}{26}$

4 a $\frac{3}{8}$　　**b** $\frac{5}{33}$　　**c** $\frac{2}{5}$　　**d** $\frac{5}{7}$

5 a $\frac{3}{4}$　　**b** $1\frac{1}{3}$　　**c** $1\frac{3}{5}$　　**d** $\frac{3}{14}$

6 a 20　　**b** 21　　**c** 100　　**d** 120

　　e 30　　**f** 40　　**g** 4　　**h** $6\frac{2}{3}$

7 a $\frac{5}{7}$　　**b** $\frac{4}{5}$　　**c** $\frac{11}{14}$　　**d** $\frac{3}{4}$

　　e $1\frac{11}{16}$　　**f** $1\frac{3}{11}$　　**g** $3\frac{1}{3}$　　**h** $\frac{3}{4}$

8 a $\frac{3}{40}$　　**b** 30　　**c** $1\frac{13}{35}$　　**d** $\frac{1}{3}$

　　e 28　　**f** $\frac{4}{15}$　　**g** $6\frac{4}{7}$　　**h** $2\frac{1}{10}$

9 $\frac{3}{4}$

10 9

11 $\frac{9}{10}$ metres (or 90 cm)

12 8

13 22 km

14 a

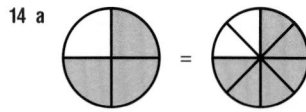

So $\frac{3}{4} = \frac{6}{8}$, so dividing the shaded region in half gives three eighths, i.e. $\frac{3}{8}$

b

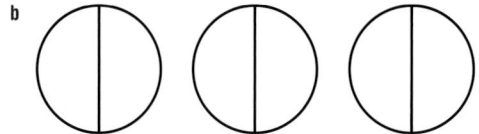

You can fit six halves into three wholes, so $3 \div \frac{1}{2} = 6$.

15 $\frac{1}{2}$ of 8 and $\frac{1}{2} \div \frac{1}{8} = 4$, $12 \div 4$ and $12 \times \frac{1}{4} = 3$, $10 \times \frac{1}{2}$ and $10 \div 2 = 5$, $3 \div \frac{1}{2}$ and $3 \times 2 = 6$

16 a 240 km　　　　　　**b** 160 km

17 Answers may vary.

3I

Building understanding

1 a 70, 70　　　**b** 60, 60　　　**c** 40, 40

2 a $\frac{1}{4} = 25\%, \frac{2}{4} = 50\%, \frac{3}{4} = 75\%, \frac{4}{4} = 100\%$

　　b $\frac{1}{5} = 20\%, \frac{2}{5} = 40\%, \frac{3}{5} = 60\%, \frac{4}{5} = 80\%, \frac{5}{5} = 100\%$

　　c $\frac{1}{3} = 33\frac{1}{3}\%, \frac{2}{3} = 66\frac{2}{3}\%, \frac{3}{3} = 100\%$

3 86%

Now you try

Example 25

a $\frac{39}{100}$　　　　**b** $\frac{21}{50}$　　　　**c** $2\frac{1}{5}$

Example 26
a 9%   b 55%

Example 27
a $17\frac{1}{2}\%$ b 225%

Exercise 3I

1 a i $\frac{19}{100}$ ii $\frac{29}{100}$ iii $\frac{57}{100}$

   b i $\frac{7}{10}$ ii $\frac{9}{20}$ iii $\frac{12}{25}$

2 a $\frac{11}{100}$ b $\frac{71}{100}$ c $\frac{43}{100}$ d $\frac{49}{100}$

   e $\frac{1}{4}$ f $\frac{3}{10}$ g $\frac{3}{20}$ h $\frac{22}{25}$

3 a $1\frac{1}{5}$ b $1\frac{4}{5}$ c $2\frac{37}{100}$ d $4\frac{1}{100}$

   e $1\frac{3}{4}$ f $1\frac{1}{10}$ g $3\frac{4}{25}$ h $8\frac{2}{5}$

4 a 8%   b 15%   c 97%   d 50%
   e 35%   f 32%   g 86%   h 90%
   i 112%   j 135%   k 400%   l 160%

5 a $12\frac{1}{2}\%$ b $33\frac{1}{3}\%$ c $26\frac{2}{3}\%$ d $83\frac{1}{3}\%$

   e 115%   f 420%   g 290%   h $32\frac{1}{2}\%$

6 a $\frac{3}{4}$ b 75%   c $\frac{1}{4}$ d 25%

7 $12\frac{1}{2}\%$

8 70%
9 70%, 80%

10 a $\frac{18}{25}$ b 72%

11 4 (they are 10%, 30%, 70%, 90%)

12 $\frac{55}{1000} = \frac{11}{200}$

13 For example, $8\frac{1}{2}\%$, which is $\frac{85}{1000} = \frac{17}{200}$. Other answers
    possible.

14 Answers may vary.

3J

Building understanding

1 a 10   b 100   c 2
   d 1   e 5   f 4
2 a ii   b ii   c i   d i

Now you try

Example 28
a 36   b 60

Example 29
In Shop B the jumper is cheaper by $2.

Exercise 3J

1 a 10   b 20   c 6   d 16
2 a 70   b 36   c 10   d 27
   e 10   f 7   g 150   h 200
   i 4   j 48   k 44   l 190
   m 22   n 84   o 36   p 63
3 a 96   b 600   c 66   d 100
   e 15   f 72   g 73   h 600
4 10% of $200 = $20
   20% of $120 = $24
   10% of $80 = $8
   50% of $60 = $30
   20% of $200 = $40
   5% of $500 = $25
   30% of $310 = $93
   10% of $160 = $16
   1% of $6000 = $60
   50% of $88 = $44
5 a $42   b 24 mm   c 9 kg
   d 90 tonnes   e 8 min   f 400 cm
   g 1.5 g   h 3 hectares   i 144 seconds
6 35
7 No (red $45, striped $44)
8 240
9 12
10 a 120   b 420   c 660
11 a $80/week   b $2080   c $4160
12 a Computer games 30 min, drums 24 min, outside 48 min,
      reading 12 min
   b 5% time remaining
   c Yes, with 1 min to spare
13 80 min
14 a 20   b 90   c 20   d 64
15 They are the same

16 $37\frac{1}{2}\%$

17 a $140   b $1.50
18 a i 1200
      ii 24%, 22%, 20%, 18%, 16%
      iii 2%
   b i 30%
      ii Week 1: 30%, 2400 pieces; week 2: 25%, 2000 pieces;
          week 3: 20%, 1600 pieces; week 4: 15%, 1200 pieces;
          week 5: 10%, 800 pieces
      iii

Week	Cumulative %	Pieces completed
Week 1	30%	2400
Week 2	55%	4400
Week 3	75%	6000
Week 4	90%	7200
Week 5	100%	8000

3K

Building understanding

1 a B   b C
  c False   d True
2 a 8   b C   c False
  d True   e False

Now you try

Example 30
a i 2:5   ii 5:2
b i 3:7   ii 3:4:7   iii 4:3

Example 31
a 3:1   b 1:2:4   c 3:1

Exercise 3K

1 a i 5:3   ii 3:5
  b i 3:7   ii 3:7:4   iii 4:3
2 a i 8:5   ii 5:8
  b i 7:5   ii 6:7:5   iii 5:6
3 a 4:3   b 3:7   c 1:4
  d 3:1   e 7:4:3   f 1:3:4:7
4 a 1:2   b 1:4   c 2:1   d 3:1
  e 4:3   f 7:9   g 4:3   h 11:9
  i 6:7   j 9:7   k 9:2   l 11:6
5 a 1:2:5   b 1:2:6   c 2:1:3
  d 4:2:3   e 3:4:1   f 1:45:8
  g 5:3:2   h 6:3:4
6 a 2:1   b 1:4   c 4:3   d 8:5
  e 1:2   f 4:5   g 3:2:5   h 1:2:4
7 a 1:2   b 1:1   c 1:2
  d 1:1   e 3:2   f 5:7
8 a 2   b 10   c 21
  d 18   e 3   f 300
9 a 3:4   b 5:3   c 9:4   d 7:13
  e 2:3   f 3:5   g 3:7   h 2:1
  i 4:1   j 5:18   k 15:16   l 7:12

10 a $1\frac{2}{3}:2 = \frac{5}{3}:\frac{6}{3} = 5:6$

   b i 1:2   ii 8:3
      iii 2:3   iv 57:40
11 2:1. His answer should use whole numbers only.
12 a 4 litres to 6 litres is the ratio 4:6 = 2:3
   b i More red
     ii More yellow
     iii More yellow
13 a 1:4   b 3:5   c 8:5
   d 4:5   e 3:8   f 4:3
14 $n:n^2 = n:n \times n = 1:n$ (by dividing both sides by n) So, $n:n^2$ is not equal to 1:2, except in the case where $n = 2$ where $n:n^2 = 2:4 = 1:2$.
15 a i Orange   ii Green   iii Violet
   b i Yellow orange
     ii Blue violet
     iii Yellow green
   c i 1:3   ii 3:1
   d 2:3

3L

Building understanding

1 a 1:9   b 10   c $\frac{1}{10}$ d $\frac{9}{10}$
   e i 40 mL   ii 360 mL
2 a 5   b $\frac{2}{5}$ c $\frac{3}{5}$
   d i $60   ii $90

Now you try

Example 32
a i $\frac{2}{9}$ ii $\frac{7}{9}$
b 1:4
c 450 mL

Example 33
45:15

Exercise 3L

1 a i $\frac{2}{5}$ ii $\frac{3}{5}$
   b i $\frac{1}{6}$ ii $\frac{5}{6}$
   c i $\frac{3}{7}$ ii $\frac{4}{7}$
2 a i $\frac{4}{7}$ ii $\frac{3}{7}$
   b 2:1
   c 40 g
3 a $\frac{5}{8}$ b 3:1   c 10
   d $\frac{7}{9}$ e 3:2   f 4
4 6 kg, 18 kg
5 15 L, 20 L
6 a $16, $24   b $30, $70
   c 12 kg, 20 kg   d 60 kg, 12 kg
   e 30 L, 24 L   f 12 L, 54 L
   g 56 m, 40 m   h 80 m, 70 m
7 a i 2 L   ii 6 L   iii 16 L
   b 150 L   c 6 L   d 8 L
8 a $12   b $36
9 a $40, $40, $100   b 250 g, 150 g, 350 g
   c 22 L, 110 L, 33 L   d 140 kg, 490 kg, 210 kg
10 a 175   b 24   c 154   d 220
11 90°
12 2
13 No, 134 ÷ 7 = 19 remainder 1
14 8
15 4
16 a i 1:4   ii 3:1
   b i 54 m   ii 8 km
   c 41:11

Problems and challenges

1 22.5
2 Answers will vary, but possible answers are:
   a 6, 7, 8, 9   b 4, 5, 6, 7, 8   c 2, 3, 4, 6, 7, 8
   d 1, 2, 3, 4, 5, 6, 9 or 1, 2, 3, 4, 5, 7, 8

3

$\frac{2}{5}$	$A = \frac{9}{10}$	$\frac{4}{5}$
$B = \frac{11}{10}$	$C = \frac{7}{10}$	$D = \frac{3}{10}$
$E = \frac{3}{5}$	$\frac{1}{2}$	1

4 a $\frac{1}{6} + \frac{1}{5} \times \frac{1}{3}$ b $\frac{1}{3} \div \frac{1}{4} - \frac{1}{6}$ c $\frac{1}{6} + \frac{1}{4} - \frac{1}{5}$

5 Because the final 20% reduction is off the original $50 plus also off the $10 increase, the 20% reduction will be $12 overall.

6 $260

Chapter checklist with success criteria

1 $\frac{3}{8}$; numerator = 3; denominator = 8

2

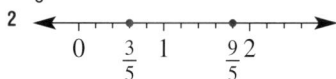
$0 \quad \frac{3}{5} \quad 1 \quad \frac{9}{5} \; 2$

3

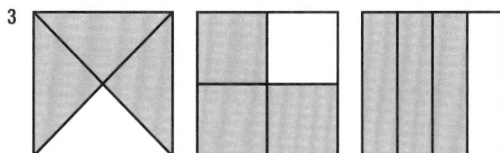

4 8; 15

5 $\frac{3}{5}$

6 Yes, multiplying numerator and denominator by 5 shows they are equivalent.

7 $\frac{16}{5}$

8 $2\frac{3}{4}; 3\frac{1}{3}$

9 $\frac{2}{3}$ is bigger; $\frac{2}{3} > \frac{3}{5}$

10 $\frac{2}{3}, \frac{3}{4}, \frac{4}{5}$

11 $\frac{19}{12} = 1\frac{7}{12}$

12 $\frac{25}{3} = 8\frac{1}{3}$

13 $\frac{7}{12}$

14 $\frac{29}{12} = 2\frac{5}{12}$

15 $\frac{2}{3}$

16 15; 7

17 $\frac{7}{10}$

18 $\frac{8}{5} = 1\frac{3}{5}$

19 $\frac{3}{2} = 1\frac{1}{2}$

20 $\frac{9}{25}$

21 44%; 37.5%

22 60

23 4:3

24 2:5

25 12 litres

26 10kg and 5kg

Chapter review

Short answer questions

1 $\frac{1}{14}, \frac{1}{10}, \frac{1}{8}, \frac{1}{6}, \frac{1}{5}, \frac{1}{4}, \frac{1}{3}, \frac{1}{2}$

2 $\frac{3}{5} = \frac{6}{10} = \frac{9}{15} = \frac{12}{20} = \frac{15}{25}$ etc

Multiplying by the same number in the numerator and denominator is equivalent to multiplying by 1, and so does not change the value of the fraction.

3 a $\frac{3}{5}$ b $\frac{2}{7}$ c $\frac{5}{7}$

4 a $1\frac{1}{2}$ b $1\frac{3}{4}$ c $1\frac{2}{3}$ d $3\frac{1}{2}$

5 a $\frac{2}{7}$ $<$ $\frac{4}{7}$ b $\frac{3}{8}$ $>$ $\frac{1}{8}$

  c $1\frac{2}{3}$ $>$ $1\frac{3}{5}$ d $3\frac{1}{9}$ $<$ $\frac{29}{9}$

6 a $\frac{5}{7}$ b $\frac{5}{8}$

7 a 10 b 21 c 24

8 a 10 b 21 c 24

9 a $2\frac{1}{5}, \frac{9}{5}, 1\frac{3}{5}$ b $\frac{9}{4}, \frac{11}{6}, \frac{14}{8}, \frac{5}{3}$

  c $5\frac{2}{3}, 5\frac{7}{18}, 5\frac{1}{3}, \frac{47}{9}, 5\frac{1}{9}$

10 a $\frac{1}{2}$ b $\frac{5}{6}$ c $1\frac{5}{24}$

  d $5\frac{23}{30}$ e $\frac{1}{2}$ f $2\frac{1}{2}$

  g $1\frac{9}{40}$ h $6\frac{5}{36}$ i $12\frac{3}{5}$

11 a 7 b 80 c 12

  d 5 e $\frac{1}{6}$ f $7\frac{1}{2}$

12 a $\frac{4}{3}$ b $\frac{12}{7}$ c $\frac{4}{11}$ d $\frac{3}{16}$

13 a $\frac{1}{5}$ b 20 c 4 d $\frac{1}{5}$

14

Percentage form	Fraction
36%	$\frac{9}{25}$
220%	$2\frac{1}{5}$
5%	$\frac{5}{100}$
140%	$1\frac{2}{5}$
44%	$\frac{11}{25}$
18%	$\frac{9}{50}$

15 a ii b i

16 a 3:5 b 5:4 c 4:3 d 5:4:3

17 a 3:1 b 16:3 c 23:5

18 a $70, $10 b $32, $48

Multiple-choice questions

1 B	**2** C	**3** A	**4** C	**5** D
6 B	**7** D	**8** D	**9** A	**10** C

Extended-response questions

1 a $7\frac{5}{8}$ b $5\frac{11}{24}$ c $10\frac{17}{80}$ d $6\frac{2}{21}$

2 a 126 cm b $52\frac{1}{2}$ cm, $22\frac{1}{2}$ cm, 51 cm

3 a $176 b $24

4 a $550 b 264 L c $99 d $200

5 a $12\frac{1}{2}\%$ b $208

6 $55\frac{2}{3}\%$

Chapter 4

4A

Building understanding

1 a $4x, 3y, 24z, 7$ **b** 7
c 4 **d** z
2 a F **b** A **c** D
d B **e** C **f** E

Now you try

Example 1
a $4q, 10r, s, 2t$
b 6
c The coefficient of q is 4, the coefficient of r is 10, the coefficient of s is 1 and the coefficient of t is 2.

Example 2
a $p + 10$ **b** ab **c** $3k$
d $\frac{1}{2}z$ or $\frac{z}{2}$ **e** $b - 4$

Example 3
a $3m + 5$ **b** $\frac{a+b}{2}$ or $\frac{1}{2}(a+b)$
c $pq - 3$ **d** $7(m - 5)$

Exercise 4A

1 a $3x, 2y$ **b** $4a, 2b, c$
c $5a, 3b, 2$ **d** $2x, 5$
2 a 5 **b** 6 **c** 8 **d** 1
3 a The coefficient of a is 2, the coefficient of b is 3 and the coefficient of c is 1.
b The coefficient of a is 4, the coefficient of b is 1, the coefficient of c is 6 and the coefficient of d is 2.
4 a i 2 **ii** 17
b i 3 **ii** 15
c i 3 **ii** 21
d i 4 **ii** 2
e i 2 **ii** 1
f i 4 **ii** 12
5 a $x + 1$ **b** $5 + k$ **c** $2u$ **d** $4y$
e $\frac{p}{2}$ **f** $\frac{q}{3}$ **g** $r - 12$ **h** $9n$
i $10 - t$ **j** $\frac{y}{8}$
6 a $2(x + 5)$ **b** $3a + 4$ **c** $8k - 3$ **d** $8(k - 3)$
e $6(x + y)$ **f** $\frac{7x}{2}$ **g** $\frac{p}{2} + 2$ **h** $12 - xy$
7 a The product of 7 and x.
b The sum of a and b.
c The sum of x and 4 is doubled.
d a is tripled and subtracted from 5.
8 a 70 **b** $10n$
9 a $8x$ **b** $x + 3$ **c** $8(x + 3)$
10 a $1000x$ **b** $100x$ **c** $100\,000x$
11 a $\frac{\$A}{4}$ **b** $\frac{\$A}{n}$ **c** $\frac{\$A - 20}{n}$
12 'One-quarter of the sum of a and b.' (Answers may vary.)

13 a True **b** True **c** False
d True **e** False
14 a False **b** False
c True **d** True
15 $c \div 2, c - 4, c + 1, 2c, 3c, 3c + 5, 4c - 2, c \times c$
16 'The sum of 2 and twice the value of x is taken from 3' becomes $3 - (2x + 2)$. (Answers may vary.)

4B

Building understanding

1 a 14 **b** 1 **c** 10 **d** 8
2 13
3 15
4 3
5 a 17 **b** 20 **c** 72 **d** 12

Now you try

Example 4
a 12 **b** 5 **c** 7

Example 5
a 4 **b** 42

Example 6
a 36 **b** 91 **c** 6

Exercise 4B

1 a 7 **b** 4 **c** 10 **d** 15
2 a 4 **b** 12 **c** 14 **d** 70
3 a 13 **b** 5 **c** 6 **d** 4
4 a 19 **b** 9 **c** 7 **d** 20
e 3 **f** 1 **g** 47 **h** 20
i 35 **j** 86 **k** 8 **l** 6
5 a 5 **b** 9 **c** 4 **d** 45
e 5 **f** 24 **g** 0 **h** 8
6 a 27 **b** 22 **c** 41
d 8 **e** 10 **f** 70
7 a

n	1	2	3	4	5	6
$n + 4$	5	6	7	8	9	10

b

x	1	2	3	4	5	6
$12 - x$	11	10	9	8	7	6

c

b	1	2	3	4	5	6
$2(b - 1)$	0	2	4	6	8	10

d

q	1	2	3	4	5	6
$10q - q$	9	18	27	36	45	54

8 a 75 **b** 45 **c** 54 **d** 11
e 12 **f** 5 **g** 33 **h** 19
9 5
10 x is between 4 and 33 inclusive.

11

x	5	9	12	1	6	7
$x + 6$	11	15	18	7	12	13
$4x$	20	36	48	4	24	28

12 a 1 and 24, 2 and 12, 3 and 8, 4 and 6

b Infinitely many answers; e.g. $x = \dfrac{1}{5}$, $y = 120$.

13 Because $5 \times (a + a)$ is $5 \times 2 \times a$, which is $10a$. Every multiple of 10 ends with 0.

14 a $x = 10$, $y = 45$ (other answers possible)

b 300

c Because if $x + 2y = 100$, then multiplying both sides by 3 results in $3x + 6y = 300$.

15 a

x	5	10	7	9	5	8
y	3	4	2	5	2	0
$x + y$	8	14	9	14	7	8
$x - y$	2	6	5	4	3	8
xy	15	40	14	45	10	0

b 2 and 2, 3 and $1\dfrac{1}{2}$, 6 and $1\dfrac{1}{5}$; answers may vary.

4C

Building understanding

1 a

	$x = 0$	$x = 1$	$x = 2$	$x = 3$
$2x + 2$	2	4	6	8
$(x + 1) \times 2$	2	4	6	8

b equivalent

2 a

	$x = 0$	$x = 1$	$x = 2$	$x = 3$
$5x + 3$	3	8	13	18
$6x + 3$	3	9	15	21

b No

Now you try

Example 7
$2a + 6$ and $(a + 3) \times 2$ are equivalent

Example 8
a $10 \times x \times 10 = 100x$
b $ab = ba$

Exercise 4C

1 a N **b** E **c** E
2 a $2x + 3$, $x + 3 + x$ **b** $5x - 2$, $3x - 2 + 2x$
c $2x + 4$ and $x + 4 + x$ **d** $5a$ and $4a + a$
e $2k + 2$ and $2(k + 1)$ **f** $b + b$ and $4b - 2b$
3 a $x + x + x = 3x$ **b** $2x \times 2 = 4x$
c $x + 99 = x - 1 + 100$ **d** $2(10 + x) = 20 + 2x$
4 a $10(a + b) = 10a + 10b$
b $a + 100 + b = b + 100 + a$

c $(a + b)(a - b) = a^2 - b^2$
d $ab + ba = 2ab$
5 a C **b** A **c** E
d F **e** B **f** D

6

	$6x + 5$	$4x + 5 + 2x$
$x = 1$	11	11
$x = 2$	17	17
$x = 3$	23	23
$x = 4$	29	29

They are equivalent because they are always equal.
7 $2x + 2 + 2x$, $2(2x + 1)$; answers may vary.
8 $2(w + l)$; answers may vary.
9 $9a + 4b$; answers may vary (must have 2 terms).
10 If $x = 8$, all four expressions have different values.
11 b ab and ba
c $a \times (b + c)$ and $a \times b + a \times c$
d $a - (b + c)$ and $a - b - c$
e $a - (b - c)$ and $a - b + c$
f $a \div b \div c$ and $a \div (b \times c)$
12 a $3 + 12 = 12 + 3$, $17 + 12 = 12 + 17$, $58 + 12 = 12 + 58$ (other answers possible)
b $2(8 + 1) = 2 + 2 \times 8$, $2(100 + 1) = 2 + 2 \times 100$, $2(3 + 1) = 2 + 2 \times 3$ (other answers possible)
c $(3 + 8)^2 = 3^2 + 2 \times 3 \times 8 + 8^2$, $(5 + 9)^2 = 5^2 + 2 \times 5 \times 9 + 9^2$, $(7 + 7)^2 = 7^2 + 2 \times 7 \times 7 + 7^2$, (other answers possible)

13 a

	$4 \times (a + 2)$	$8 + 4a$
$x = 1$	12	12
$x = 2$	16	16
$x = 3$	20	20
$x = 4$	24	24

b $5(2 + a)$
c $24 + 6a$
14 $2a + a + 5b$, $3a + 12b - 7b$; answers may vary.
15 a Yes; for any value of x, expressions A and B are equal, and expression B and C are equal, so expressions A and C are equal.
b No; e.g. if expression A is $7x$, expression B is $3x$ and expression C is $5x + 2x$.

4D

Building understanding

1 a x and y **b** a, b and c
c k **d** p and q
2 a like
b like terms
c terms
d $15a$ (Answers may vary.)
e equivalent
f $5x + 4$ (Answers may vary.)

Now you try

Example 9
a Not like terms   b Like terms   c Not like terms
d Like terms   e Like terms   f Not like terms

Example 10
a $15a + 4$ b $4q$ c $6x + 18y + 3$
d $7a + b$ e $8uv + 10u + 2v$

Exercise 4D

1 a L   b N   c L   d N
2 a N   b L   c L   d N
   e N   f L   g N   h L
   i L   j L   k L   l N
3 a $2a$ b $5x$ c $7b$ d $8d$
   e $12u$ f $12ab$ g $11ab$ h xy
4 a $3a + 5b$ b $7a + 9b$ c $x + 6y$
   d $7a + 2$ e $7 + 7b$ f $6k - 2$
   g $5f + 12$ h $4a + 6b - 4$ i $6x + 4y$
   j $8a + 4b + 3$ k $7h + 4$ l $14x + 30y$
   m $2x + 9y + 10$ n $8a + 13$ o $12b$
5 a $9ab + 4$ b $6xy + 5x$
   c $7cd - 3d + 2c$ d $9uv + 7v$
   e $11pq + 2p - q$ f $6ab + 36$
6 a $27n$ b $31n$ c $58n$
7 a $3a + 4$ b 19
8 a $4x$ b $7x$ c $11x$ d $3x$
9 a $12xy$ b $6ab + 5$ c $10ab$
   d $6xy + 3$ e $5xy + 14$ f $10cde$
   g $6xy + 6x + 4$ h $9ab + 9$ i $7xy - 2y$
10 a

	$3x + 2x$	$5x$
$x = 1$	5	5
$x = 2$	10	10
$x = 3$	15	15

   b For example, if $x = 5$ and $y = 10$, then $3x + 2y = 35$ but $5xy = 250$.

11 a

	$5x + 4 - 2x$	$3x + 4$
$x = 1$	7	7
$x = 2$	10	10
$x = 3$	13	13

   b For example, if $x = 10$, $5x + 4 - 2x = 34$ but $7x + 4 = 74$.
   c For example, if $x = 1$, $5x + 4 - 2x = 7$ but $7x - 4 = 3$.
12 a $18x - 15x = 3x$
   b Calculate 3×17 instead, because that will equal $18 \times 17 - 15 \times 17$.
   c $3 \times 17 = 51$.
13 a $2a + a + 3b$, $b + 3a + 2b$ (Answers may vary.)
   b 12

Progress quiz

1 a 4   b $7a, 4b, c, 9$
   c 4   d 9

2 a $m \times p$ or mp b $a + k$
   c $t + 8$ d $w - 4$
3 a $\dfrac{m}{2} + 7$ b $\dfrac{m + 7}{2}$ c $\dfrac{a + k}{3}$
   d $a + \dfrac{k}{3}$ e $3(d - 12)$ f $3d - 12$
4 a 19   b 3   c 9
5 a 24   b 11   c 5
   d 22   e 3
6 $3a + 4$ and $4 + 3a$
7 a $x + 10 = 10 + x$
   b $2(a + b) = 2a + 2b$
8 a L   b N   c N   d L
9 a $8a + 5b + 5$ b $7cd + 3c + 8d + 4$
10 $8x + 8y$, $8(x + y)$ (Answers may vary.)

4E

Building understanding

1 a Both are 21   b Both are 35
   c Both are 56   d Yes
2 a True   b True   c False
   d True   e False   f False
3 a $\dfrac{2}{3}$ b $\dfrac{2}{3}$ c $\dfrac{2}{3}$
4 a C   b E   c B
   d A   e D

Now you try

Example 11
a $5def$ b $30xyz$ c $10a^2$

Example 12
a $\dfrac{3x + 2}{2x + 1}$ b $\dfrac{4q}{5}$

Exercise 4E

1 a $2ab$ b $5xyz$ c $8qr$ d $12stuv$
   e $2x$ f $5p$ g $8ab$ h $6a$
   i $28f$ j $10ab$ k $10b$ l $28xz$
2 a $36a$ b $63d$ c $8e$
   d $15a$ e $12ab$ f $63eg$
   g $8abc$ h $28adf$ i $12abc$
   j $8abc$ k $60defg$ l $24abcd$
3 a w^2 b a^2 c $3d^2$ d $2k^2$
   e $7p^2$ f $3q^2$ g $12x^2$ h $36r^2$
4 a $\dfrac{x}{5}$ b $\dfrac{z}{2}$ c $\dfrac{a}{12}$ d $\dfrac{b}{5}$
   e $\dfrac{2}{x}$ f $\dfrac{5}{d}$ g $\dfrac{x}{y}$ h $\dfrac{a}{b}$
   i $\dfrac{4x + 1}{5}$ j $\dfrac{2x + y}{5}$ k $\dfrac{2 + x}{1 + y}$ l $\dfrac{x - 5}{3 + b}$
5 a $\dfrac{2}{5}$ b $\dfrac{5}{9}$ c $\dfrac{9a}{4}$ d $\dfrac{2b}{5}$
   e $\dfrac{x}{2}$ f $\dfrac{3x}{4}$ g $\dfrac{2}{3}$ h $\dfrac{3}{4}$
   i $2a$ j 3   k $2y$ l $\dfrac{3}{y}$

6 a $3k$ **b** $6x$ **c** $12xy$

7 a $4x$ g   **b** nx g   **c** $2nx$ g

8 a $20   **b** $\dfrac{\$C}{5}$

9 a $3a$ **b** $7c$ **c** $7b$

  d $12y$ **e** $10x$

10 a $6p$

  b $3 \times 2p$ also simplifies to $6p$, so they are equivalent.

11 a

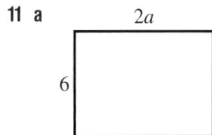

  b $12a$

  c $\dfrac{12a}{3a}$ simplifies to 4. It has four times the area.

  d Area is multiplied by 9.

12 a $100\,abc$

  b 4200

  c Multiplying a number by 100 is simpler than multiplying by 4 or 5.

13 a $16\,ab$ **b** $14\,ab$ **c** 0

14 a $38 \times a \times b \times b$ **b** $7x^2y^3$

  c $1200\,a^3b^2c^2$ **d** $24\,a^3b^2c^2$

4F

Building understanding

1 a $3a + 6$

  b $x + y + x + y = 2x + 2y$

  c $p + 1 + p + 1 + p + 1 + p + 1 = 4p + 4$

  d $4a + 2b + 4a + 2b + 4a + 2b = 12a + 6b$

2 a $4x$ **b** 12   **c** $4x + 12$

3 a 60, 3, 63

  b 30, 4, 210, 28, 238

  c 20, 1, 100, 5, 95

4 a

	4(x + 3)	**4x + 12**
$x = 1$	16	16
$x = 2$	20	20
$x = 3$	24	24
$x = 4$	28	28

  b equivalent

Now you try

Example 13

a Using brackets: $6(7 + x)$, without brackets: $42 + 6x$

b Using brackets: $7(r + 5)$, without brackets: $7r + 35$

Example 14

a $4b + 28$ **b** $9k - 45$

c $10p + 25$ **d** $27xz - 18x$

Exercise 4F

1 a $2(x + 4)$ and $2x + 8$ **b** $2(a + 1)$ and $2a + 2$

  c $12(x + 4)$ and $12x + 48$ **d** $8(z + 9)$ and $8z + 72$

2 a $6y + 48$ **b** $7l + 28$ **c** $8s + 56$

  d $8 + 4a$ **e** $7x + 35$ **f** $18 + 3a$

3 a $4x - 12$ **b** $5j - 20$ **c** $8y - 64$

  d $8e - 56$ **e** $18 - 6e$ **f** $80 - 10y$

4 a $60g - 70$ **b** $15e + 40$ **c** $35w + 50$

  d $10u + 25$ **e** $56x - 14$ **f** $27v - 12$

  g $7q - 49$ **h** $20c - 4v$ **i** $4u + 12$

  j $48l + 48$ **k** $5k - 50$ **l** $9o + 63$

5 a $6it - 6iv$ **b** $2dv + 2dm$ **c** $10cw - 5ct$

  d $6es + 6ep$ **e** $dx + 9ds$ **f** $10ax + 15av$

  g $5jr + 35jp$ **h** $in + 4iw$ **i** $8ds - 24dt$

  j $2fu + fv$ **k** $14kv + 35ky$ **l** $4em + 40ey$

6 a $5(x + 3) = 5x + 15$ **b** $2(b + 6) = 2b + 12$

  c $3(z - 4) = 3z - 12$ **d** $7(10 - y) = 70 - 7y$

7 a $t + s$

  b $2(t + s) = 2t + 2s$

8 $3(4x + 8y)$ and $2(6x + 12y)$ (Answers may vary.)

9 $2l + 2w$

10 a 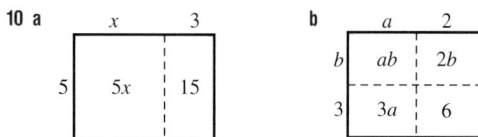   **b**

  c $ab + 3b + 5a + 15$

11 $a \times 99$ is the same as $a \times (100 - 1)$, which expands to $100a - a$.

12 a 4 ways, including $1(10x + 20y)$

  b Infinitely many ways

13 a Rosemary likes Maths and Rosemary likes English.

  b Priscilla eats fruit and Priscilla eats vegetables.

  c Bailey likes the opera and Lucia likes the opera.

  d Frank plays video games and Igor plays video games.

  e Pyodir likes fruit and Pyodir likes vegetables and Astrid likes fruit and Astrid likes vegetables.

4G

Building understanding

1 a 35   **b** 20

2 a 24 cm   **b** 40 m

3 a $3x$ **b** 36

Now you try

Example 15

a 35   **b** 120 cm^2

Example 16

a $2n$

b $20 + 5k$

c $80 + 110n$ for n days, so $850 total.

Exercise 4G

1 a 28   b 44 cm
2 a 13   b 18 m
3 $2n$
4 a $10x$ b $15x$ c kx
5 a 180 km   b 30 km   c $70n$
6 a $200   b $680   c $50 + 80x$
7 a B   b A   c D   d E   e C
8 a

Hours	1	2	3	4	5
Total cost ($)	150	250	350	450	550

   b $100t + 50$
   c $3050
9 a $25   b $(10x + 5)$ c $75
10 a 90 cents   b $6.30   c $0.3 + 0.6t$
11 a 33
   b $g = 8, b = 5$
   c $g = 3$ and $b = 2$, $g = 1$ and $b = 14$, $g = 0$ and $b = 20$
12 a $(5b + 2c + 6d)$ b $(5b + 4c + 3d)$
   c $8
13 a cn b $3cn$ c $6cn$
14 a $10 + 30x$
   b 2 h 20 min
   c Because you don't pay the booking fee twice.
   d $32
   e It will get closer to $30.
15 a $(0.2 + 0.6t)$ b $(0.8 + 0.4t)$
   c Emma's   d 3 min
   e Answers may vary.

Problems and challenges

1 25
2 a $P = 10m$ b $P = 20(x + 3)$ c $P = 5(w + y)$
3 Largest $18x + 70$, smallest $12x + 44$, difference
   $6x + 26 = 86$ cm
4 $15a + 10$, $5(3a + 2)$
5 a $a = 4, b = 12, c = 16, d = 8, e = 36$
   b $a = 6, b = 3, c = 5, d = 10, e = 15$
6 5050
7 Because $2(x + 5) - 12 - x + 2$ simplifies to x.

Chapter checklist with success criteria

1 13
2 $3a, b, 13$; there is no constant term.
3 $a + b$
4 40
5 17
6 48
7 $3x + 4$ and $2x + 4 + x$ are equivalent.
8 $x + x = 2x$

9 $2ab$ and $5ba$ are like terms; the pronumerals are the same, even though they are written in a different order (one a and one b).
10 $9a + 4b + 3$
11 $24abc$
12 $\frac{2a}{3}$
13 $3a + 6b$
14 $22cm$
15 $30 + 60n$ (dollars)

Chapter review

Short-answer questions

1 a $5a, 3b, 7c, 12$ b 12   c 7
2 a $u + 7$ b $3k$ c $7 + \frac{r}{2}$
   d $h - 10$ e xy f $12 - x$
3 a 15   b 24   c 2   d 32
4 a 15   b 8   c 4   d 27
5 a 16   b 200   c 5   d 20
6 a E   b N   c E   d N
7 a L   b N   c L   d L
   e N   f L   g N   h L
8 a $7x + 3$ b $11p$
   c $7a + 14b + 4$ d $3m + 17mn + 2n$
   e $1 + 7c + 4h - 3o$ f $4u + 3v + 2uv$
9 a $12ab$ b $6xyz$ c $36fgh$ d $64klm$
10 a $\frac{3}{2}$ b $\frac{3}{5}$ c $\frac{a}{3}$ d $\frac{4x}{3z}$
11 a $3x + 6$ b $4p - 12$
   c $14a + 21$ d $24k + 36l$
12 $2(6b + 9c)$, $6(2b + 3c)$ (Answers may vary.)
13 $9t$
14 $c + d$
15 $3x$

Multiple-choice questions

1 B   2 A   3 C   4 D   5 D
6 D   7 C   8 A   9 E   10 A

Extended-response questions

1 a i $24.50   ii $45.50   iii $213.50
   b $3.5 + 2.1d$
   c $87.50
   d If $d = 40$, $2.1 + 3.5d = 142.10$, not 87.50.
   e $6 + 1.2d$
2 a 26   b $78
   c $4x + 2y + 10$ d $12x + 6y + 30$
   e $x(x + 5) + 3y$ (Answers may vary.)

Chapter 5

5A

Building understanding

1 a $\dfrac{2}{10}$ b $\dfrac{3}{100}$ c $\dfrac{7}{1000}$

2 a 5   b 6   c 7   d 37

3 a 7.6   b 12.9   c 33.04
   d 26.15   e 8.42   f 99.012

Now you try

Example 1

a $\dfrac{3}{100}$ b $\dfrac{3}{10}$

Example 2

a 0.9   b 0.03   c 4.307

Example 3

a 8.7 > 8.4
b 10.184 < 10.19
c 0.0401 > 0.00928

Exercise 5A

1 a $\dfrac{3}{10}$ b $\dfrac{3}{1000}$ c $\dfrac{3}{100}$

2 a $\dfrac{6}{10}$ b $\dfrac{6}{100}$ c $\dfrac{6}{1000}$ d $\dfrac{6}{10}$

   e 6   f $\dfrac{6}{100}$ g $\dfrac{6}{100}$ h $\dfrac{6}{1000}$

3 a 0.3   b 0.8   c 0.15   d 0.23
   e 0.9   f 0.02   g 0.121   h 0.074

4 a 6.4   b 5.7   c 212.3   d 1.16
   e 14.83   f 7.51   g 5.07   h 18.612

5 a >   b <   c >   d <
   e <   f >   g >   h <
   i >   j >   k >   l <

6 a False   b False   c True   d False
   e True   f True   g False   h True
   i True   j True   k True   l False

7 a 0.1   b 0.03   c 0.02   d 0.5
   e 0.001   f 0.01   g 0.15   h 0.11

8 a 3.05, 3.25, 3.52, 3.55
   b 3.06, 3.6, 30.3, 30.6
   c 1.718, 1.871, 11.87, 17.81
   d 22.69, 22.96, 26.92, 29.26, 29.62

9 a Waugh, Border, Gilchrist, Taylor, Hughes
   b First

10 a Day 6   b Day 4
    c Days 2, 5 and 6

11 When you insert it at the start or end you do not change the place value of any other digits, but when you insert the '0' in the middle somewhere, you do change the place value. For example, in 12.34, the value of 4 is $\dfrac{4}{100}$, but in 12.304 it is now $\dfrac{4}{1000}$. Similarly, 102.34 changes the value of the digit 1 from 10 to 100.

12 a C.C, C.A, B.C, B.A, A.C, A.B
    b C.BC, C.AB, B.CA, B.BB, A.CA, A.BC, A.AA, BA.CA, AB.AB

13 a 0.A   b 0.0A   c 0.AA   d A.A0A

14 a i 0.1, 1.0 (2 ways)
       ii 0.12, 0.21, 1.02, 1.20, 2.01, 2.10, 10.2, 12.0, 20.1, 21.0 (10 ways)
       iii 0.123, 0.132, 0.213, 0.231, 0.312, 0.321, 1.023, 1.032, 1.203, 1.230, 1.302, 1.320, 2.013, 2.031, 2.103, 2.130, 2.301, 2.310, 3.012, 3.021, 3.102, 3.120, 3.201, 3.210, 10.23, 10.32, 12.03, 12.30, 13.02, 13.20, 20.13, 20.31, 21.03, 21.30, 23.01, 23.10, 30.12, 30.21, 31.02, 31.20, 32.01, 32.10, 102.3, 103.2, 120.3, 123.0, 130.2, 132.0, 201.3, 203.1, 210.3, 213.0, 230.1, 231.0, 301.2, 302.1, 310.2, 312.0, 320.1, 321.0 (60 ways)
    b 408 ways

5B

Building understanding

1 a 5.8   b 6.78
2 a i 1   ii 7   iii 4   iv 8
   b i 25.8   ii 25.82
      iii 25.817   iv 26

Now you try

Example 4

a 53.7   b 4.2

Example 5

a 18.62   b 3.1416   c 0.140

Exercise 5B

1 a i 32.5   ii 57.4
   b i 19.7   ii 46.1

2 a 14.8   b 7.4   c 15.6   d 0.9
   e 6.9   f 9.9   g 55.6   h 8.0

3 a 3.78   b 11.86   c 5.92   d 0.93
   e 123.46   f 300.05   g 3.13   h 9.85
   i 56.29   j 7.12   k 29.99   l 0.90

4 a 15.9   b 7.89   c 236   d 1
   e 231.9   f 9.4   g 9.40   h 34.713

5 a 24.0   b 14.90   c 7   d 30.000

6 a 28   b 9   c 12   d 124
   e 22   f 118   g 3   h 11

7 a $13   b $31   c $7   d $1567
   e $120   f $10   g $1   h $36

8 a $51   b $44   c Very accurate

9 a 0 s   b 0.4 s   c 0.34 s   d 52.825 s

10 a $49.58
    b $49.61
    c $90.60
    d 22 cents more, as 52.8 × 1.72 = 90.82 to two decimal places.

11 2.25, 3 decimal places

12 Samara: Round to 2 decimal places = 0.45, then round this to 1 decimal = 0.5. Cassandra: Rounding to 1 decimal place, critical digit is the second 4, which is less than 5, therefore rounded to 1 decimal place = 0.4.
Samara has a flaw of rounding an already rounded number. Cassandra is correct.
13 Depends on your calculator.
14 Depends on your software package.

5C

Building understanding

1 C   **2** B

Now you try

Example 6
a 36.37   **b** 12.332
Example 7
a 5.32   **b** 6.884

Exercise 5C

1 a 5.75   **b** 4.75   **c** 34.177   **d** 7.918
  e 7.41   **f** 7.09   **g** 12.74   **h** 10.531
2 a 16.06   **b** 21.33   **c** 7.71
  d 9.85   **e** 343.75   **f** 37.567
  g 21.592   **h** 340.0606
3 a 12.1   **b** 114.13   **c** 6.33   **d** 70.79
4 a 12.3   **b** 131.4   **c** 22.23
  d 13.457   **e** 43.27   **f** 4947.341
5 a 7, 8   **b** 6, 5, 1, 4
  c 0, 1, 0, 2   **d** 7, 5, 1, 6, 1
6 186.19
7 $54.30
8 49.11 mm
9

+	0.01	0.05	0.38	1.42
0.3	0.31	0.35	0.68	1.72
0.75	0.76	0.80	1.13	2.17
1.20	1.21	1.25	1.58	2.62
1.61	1.62	1.66	1.99	3.03

10 $2036.10
11 a 8.15 − 3.2 = 4.95, 8.15 − 4.95 = 3.2
  b 6.5 − 3.7 = 2.8, 6.5 − 2.8 = 3.7
  c 10.1 − 8.3 = 1.8, 10.1 − 1.8 = 8.3
  d 6.31 − 3.8 = 2.51, 6.31 − 2.51 = 3.8
12 a Yes, e.g. 2.3 + 1.7 = 4, 3.81 + 1.19 = 5
  b Yes, e.g. 4.8 − 1.8 = 3, 7.92 − 2.92 = 5
13 a Answers may vary; e.g. 3.57 + 4.15 + 3.44
  b Answers may vary; e.g. 1.35 + 2.87 + 6.94 = 11.16
14 Always end up with $10.89 unless the starting value has the same first digit, in which case we end up with zero. The 8 forms as it comes from adding two 9s. This produces a 1 to be carried over, which results in the answer being a $10 answer, rather than a $9 answer.

5D

Building understanding

1 a 100   **b** 100
2 a 1000   **b** 10
3 a i Right 2 places   **ii** Right 6 places
    iii Left 3 places   **iv** Left 7 places
  b Left 2 places

Now you try

Example 8
a 51 094.2   **b** 390
Example 9
a 39.2807   **b** 0.0812
Example 10
a 289 000   **b** 0.0078
Example 11
877.8

Exercise 5D

1 a 2432.7   **b** 436.1   **c** 1840
2 a 48.7   **b** 352.83   **c** 4222.7
  d 1430.4   **e** 5699.23   **f** 125.963
  g 12 700   **h** 154 230   **i** 3400
  j 2132   **k** 86 710 000   **l** 516 000
3 a 4.27   **b** 35.31   **c** 2.4422
  d 56.893   **e** 12.13518   **f** 9.32611
  g 0.029   **h** 0.001362   **i** 0.00054
  j 0.367   **k** 0.000002   **l** 0.0100004
4 a 2291.3   **b** 31.67   **c** 0.49
  d 0.222   **e** 63 489 000   **f** 0.0010032
5 a 15 600   **b** 43 000   **c** 225.1
  d 0.016   **e** 213 400   **f** 21.34
  g 0.007   **h** 9 900 000   **i** 0.0034
6 a 158.4   **b** 3.36   **c** 85.4   **d** 7054
  e 71.06   **f** 7.5   **g** 2.037   **h** 21.7
7 $187
8 a 1 200 000 mL   **b** 12 000
9 3000 cents, $30
10 $21 400
11 225 kg
12 Answers may vary.

Starting number	Answer	Possible two-step operations
12.357	1235.7	× 1000, ÷10
34.004 5	0.034004 5	÷100, ÷10
0.003601	360.1	× 100, × 1000
BAC.DFG	BA.CDFG	÷100, × 10
D.SWKK	DSWKK	× 100 000, ÷10
FWY	F.WY	÷1000, × 10

13 ÷1 000 000

14 a i 5×10^{13} **ii** 4.2×10^7
     iii 1.23×10^{16}
  b i 2×10^{19} **ii** 1.08×10^{21}
  c, d   Answers may vary.
  e 3.5×10^{-11}
  f i 1×10^{-6} **ii** 9×10^{-10}
     iii 7.653×10^{-12}

5E

Building understanding

1 a 1   **b** 2   **c** 3   **d** 3   **e** 5   **f** 9
2 a 19.2   **b** 1.92   **c** 0.192
3 It helps you check the position of the decimal point in the answer.
4 a The decimal point is the actual 'dot'; decimal places are the numbers after the decimal point.
  b 1 decimal point, 4 decimal places
5 in the question; decimal places

Now you try

Example 12
a 12   **b** 77

Example 13
a 289.35   **b** 4.628

Example 14
a 158 700   **b** 4.27

Exercise 5E

1 a 8   **b** 40   **c** 70   **d** 24
2 a 94.57 **b** 17.04   **c** 30.78   **d** 21.645
3 a 20.84   **b** 26.6   **c** 183.44
  d 100.8   **e** 218.46   **f** 15.516
  g 23.12   **h** 12.42   **i** 5.44
  j 311.112   **k** 0.000966 **l** 1.32131
4 a 100.8   **b** 483   **c** 25 400
  d 9800   **e** 14 400   **f** 364 550
  g 0.68   **h** 371   **i** 90.12
5 a $31.50, $32·   **b** $22.65, $23
  c $74.80, $75   **d** $17.40, $17
  e $145.20, $145   **f** $37 440, $37 440
  g $88.92, $89   **h** $4.41, $4
  i $18.0625, $18
6 a 29.47 m   **b** 3.56 kg   **c** 165.85 km
7 a 67.2 m   **b** $198.24
8 $1531.25
9 a 738.4 km   **b** Yes
  c 1.57 L left in the tank
10 a 3.92 is less than 4, 6.85 is less than 7, so 3.92 × 6.85 is less than 4 × 7.
  b 4.21 is greater than 4, 7.302 is greater than 7, so 4.21 × 7.302 is greater than 4 × 7.
  c Answer may vary, e.g. 3.9 × 7.4 = 28.86 is greater than 4 × 7 = 28.

11 Answers may vary; 0.25, 0.26
12 Answers may vary; 0.0043
13 a 38.76   **b** 73.6   **c** 0.75   **d** 42, 0.42

Progress quiz

1 a 6 hundredths   **b** 6 ones
2 a 0.9   **b** 0.019   **c** 3.25
3 a <   **b** >   **c** >   **d** >
4 a 16.88   **b** 2.350   **c** 0.7
5 a 5.4   **b** 17.031 **c** 3.52   **d** 5.78
6 a 3450   **b** 0.65345
7 a 15   **b** 18   **c** 20
8 a 90 000 **b** 119   **c** 1.912 **d** 136 800
9 a 8.011   **b** 197.44
10 a $10.15 **b** $179.55

5F

Building understanding

1 B
2 Directly above the decimal point in the dividend
3 a 60   **b** 60   **c** 60   **d** 60
  e An identical change has occurred in both the dividend and the divisor.
4 a 32.456, 3   **b** 12 043.2, 12
  c 34.5, 1   **d** 1 234 120, 4

Now you try

Example 15
a 3.796   **b** 0.0826

Example 16
a 1179.7   **b** 83.8

Example 17
0.0214

Example 18
9.765

Exercise 5F

1 a 3.51   **b** 5.19   **c** 4.37   **d** 9.113
2 a 4.2   **b** 6.1   **c** 21.34
  d 0.7055   **e** 1.571   **f** 0.308
  g 3.526   **h** 124.3   **i** 0.0024
  j 117.105   **k** 0.6834   **l** 0.0025625
3 a 30.7   **b** 77.5   **c** 26.8
  d 8.5   **e** 645.3   **f** 980
  g 800.6   **h** 2 161 000
4 a 44.4   **b** 0.08
  c 0.050425   **d** 0.79
5 a 1.1807   **b** 8.267   **c** 0.0123748
  d 0.00423   **e** 0.096487   **f** 0.0007825
6 a 11.83 kg   **b** $30.46   **c** 304.33 m
  d 239.17 g   **e** 965.05 L   **f** $581.72
7 a 20.84   **b** 93.36   **c** 10.93
  d 18.49   **e** 67.875   **f** 158.35

8 a 8, 9   **b** 9   **c** 1, 5, 5   **d** 7, 7, 0

9 $1.59/L

10 238 frames

11 26.67, 26 can be filled

12 a $66.35   **b** $21.90

13 Apples $3.25/kg; bananas $3.10/kg; hence, bananas are better value.

14 a 24.5 m/s   **b** 88.2 km/h   **c** Yes

15 a 24.53   **b** 19.7   **c** 2453

    d 1.97   **e** 2.453   **f** 197

16 a 0.5   **b** 0.3   **c** 0.01   **d** 1.1   **e** 4.8

    f Answers may vary.

5G

Building understanding

1 a 5   **b** 100   **c** 75, 7   **d** 5, 4

2 a 2   **b** 15, 20   **c** 10, 4   **d** 16

3 a False   **b** True   **c** True

    d False   **e** True   **f** True

Now you try

Example 19

a $\frac{407}{1000}$ **b** $7\frac{9}{20}$

Example 20

a 0.123   **b** 19.75

c 0.83333... or 0.8$\dot{3}$

Exercise 5G

1 a $\frac{3}{10}$ **b** $\frac{41}{100}$ **c** $\frac{201}{1000}$ **d** $\frac{7}{100}$

2 a $\frac{2}{5}$ **b** $\frac{11}{50}$ **c** $\frac{3}{20}$ **d** $\frac{3}{4}$

3 a $\frac{1}{2}$ **b** $6\frac{2}{5}$ **c** $10\frac{3}{20}$ **d** $18\frac{3}{25}$

    e $3\frac{1}{4}$ **f** $\frac{1}{20}$ **g** $9\frac{3}{40}$ **h** $5\frac{24}{125}$

4 a 0.7   **b** 0.9   **c** 0.31   **d** 0.79

    e 1.21   **f** 3.29   **g** 0.123   **h** 0.03

5 a $\frac{8}{10}=0.8$ **b** $\frac{5}{10}=0.5$ **c** $\frac{35}{100}=0.35$

    d $\frac{46}{100}=0.46$ **e** $\frac{95}{100}=0.95$ **f** $3\frac{25}{100}=3.25$

    g $\frac{25}{10}=2.5$ **h** $\frac{375}{1000}=0.375$

6 a 0.5   **b** 0.5   **c** 0.75

    d 0.4   **e** 0.$\dot{3}$ **f** 0.375

    g 0.41$\dot{6}$ **h** 0.$\overline{428571}$

7 a 0, 0.5, 1

    b 0, 0.$\dot{3}$, 0.$\dot{6}$, 0.9(0.9999999... = 1)

    c 0, 0.25, 0.5, 0.75, 1

    d 0, 0.2, 0.4, 0.6, 0.8, 1.0

8 a $\frac{1}{4}$, 0.4, $\frac{1}{2}$, $\frac{5}{8}$, 0.75, 0.99   **b** $\frac{1}{9}$, 0.13, $\frac{3}{7}$, 0.58, $\frac{4}{5}$, 0.84

9 a Tan: $\frac{11}{37}=0.\overline{297}$; Lillian: $\frac{6}{21}=0.\overline{285714}$; hence, Tan is the better chess player.

    b Two or more

10 0.11 mm, $\frac{11}{100}$ mm

11 2, $\frac{4}{7}=0.\overline{571428}$, repeating pattern

12 a 0.5, 0.$\dot{3}$, 0.25, 0.2, 0.1$\dot{6}$, 0.$\overline{142857}$, 0.125, 0.$\dot{1}$, 0.1

    b, c Answers may vary.

13 a $\frac{1}{10}$, $\frac{1}{5}$, $\frac{1}{4}$, $\frac{2}{5}$, $\frac{1}{2}$, $\frac{3}{5}$, $\frac{3}{4}$, $\frac{4}{5}$, $\frac{9}{10}$

    b, c Answers may vary.

14 Answers may vary; $2\frac{4}{9}$, $2\frac{45}{100}$, $2\frac{3}{7}$

15 a No, for example, $\frac{1}{3}$ is 0.$\dot{3}$, which is recurring.

    b Yes, by writing the decimal places as a numerator with a suitable power of 10, e.g. 0.3701 is $\frac{3701}{10000}$.

16 Answers may vary.

5H

Building understanding

1 C

2 B

3 A

4 a 50   **b** 50%

    c i 5   **ii** 100   **iii** 20   **iv** 1

    d i 50%   **ii** 50%   **iii** 50%   **iv** 50%

5 a 100, ÷, 100, .   **b** 35, 100, 35, 0

Now you try

Example 21

a 0.92   **b** 0.04   **c** 1.5

d 0.076   **e** 0.0005

Example 22

a 70.3%   **b** 2310%

Exercise 5H

1 a 0.7   **b** 0.4   **c** 0.5   **d** 0.2

    e 0.48   **f** 0.32   **g** 0.71   **h** 0.19

2 a 0.08   **b** 0.02   **c** 0.03   **d** 0.05

3 a 0.32   **b** 0.27   **c** 0.68   **d** 0.54

    e 0.06   **f** 0.09   **g** 1   **h** 0.01

    i 2.18   **j** 1.42   **k** 0.75   **l** 1.99

4 a 0.225   **b** 0.175   **c** 0.3333   **d** 0.0825

    e 1.1235   **f** 1.888   **g** 1.50   **h** 5.20

    i 0.0079   **j** 0.00025   **k** 0.0104   **l** 0.0095

5 a 80%   **b** 30%   **c** 45%   **d** 71%

6 a 41.6%   **b** 37.5%   **c** 250%   **d** 231.4%

    e 2.5%   **f** 0.14%   **g** 1270%   **h** 100.4%

7 a 86%, 0.78, 75%, 0.6, 22%, 0.125, 2%, 0.5%

    b 50, 7.2, 2.45, 1.8, 124%, 55%, 1.99%, 0.02%

8 35%

9 a 25%   **b** 78%

10 24 gigalitres

11 a AB.CD%   **b** AAC%   **c** ABDC%

    d D.D%   **e** CDB.A%   **f** CC.CDDD%

12 a 0.0AB   **b** B.CD   **c** 0.AC

    d 0.00DA   **e** AB.BB   **f** 0.DDD

13 a No

  b Answers may vary. Examples include: percentage score on a Maths test, percentage of damaged fruit in a crate, percentage of spectators wearing a hat, percentage of the day spent sleeping.

  c Answers may vary. Examples include: percentage profit, percentage increase in prices, percentage increase in the price of a house, percentage score on a Maths test with a bonus question.

14 a $F \div A \times 100$

  b F: points scored for the team; A: points scored against the team

  c 100%

  d 158 points

  e Yes; Hawthorn 90.60%, Port Adelaide 91.32%

5I

Building understanding

1 a 4   **b** 4   **c** $\frac{1}{2}$

  d 50%   **e** $\frac{1}{2}$ **f** 50%

2 a 10   **b** $\frac{1}{5}$ **c** $\frac{4}{5}$

  d 20%   **e** 80%

3 a $\frac{3}{10}$ **b** 0.3   **c** 30%

Now you try

Example 23

a $\frac{1}{4}$ **b** 0.25   **c** 25%

Example 24

a $\frac{2}{5}$ **b** 0.6   **c** 60%

Example 25

Millie (35%), Adam (40%), Yoe (39%) so Adam has completed the most.

Exercise 5I

1 a $\frac{2}{5}$ **b** $\frac{1}{4}$ **c** $\frac{1}{10}$ **d** $\frac{3}{5}$

2 a 0.3   **b** 0.7   **c** 0.29   **d** 0.05

3 a 25%   **b** 70%   **c** 46%   **d** 65%

4 a $\frac{3}{10}$, 0.3, 30%

  b $\frac{3}{5}$, 0.6, 60%

  c $\frac{1}{5}$, 0.2, 20%

  d $\frac{3}{4}$, 0.75, 75%

  e $\frac{1}{20}$, 0.05, 5%

  f $\frac{3}{20}$, 0.15, 15%

5 a 0.6, 60%   **b** 0.5, 50%

  c 0.25, 25%   **d** 0.4, 40%

  e 0.75, 75%   **f** 0.8, 80%

6 a $\frac{1}{10}$ **b** 0.1   **c** 10%

7 a $\frac{1}{5}$ **b** 20%   **c** 0.8

8 Val (70%), Mel (67%), Wendy (69%) so Val scored the highest.

9 Wally (58%), Su (55%), Drew (53%) so Wally has walked the most.

10 a $1500 \, m^2$

  b i $\frac{1}{20}$, 5%   **ii** $\frac{3}{5}$, 60%   **iii** $\frac{1}{8}$, 12.5%

  c $\frac{29}{40}$

  d 27.5%

11 95%, 0.95

12 a $\frac{1}{25}$, 4%, 0.04

  b $\frac{2}{5}$, 40%, 0.4

  c $\frac{1}{20}$, 5%, 0.05

  d $\frac{1}{100}$, 1%, 0.01

  e $\frac{1}{50}$, 2%, 0.02

  f $\frac{1}{40}$, 2.5%, 0.025

13 a $\frac{1}{5}$

  b 40%

14 Ross 75%, Maleisha 72% or Ross 0.75, Maleisha 0.72

15 Hatch 15%, 4WD 16%; hence, 4WD has larger price reduction.

16 Yellow 20%, blue 19%; hence, blue has least percentage of sugar.

17 a $\frac{a}{a+b}$ **b** $\frac{100b}{a+b}$

18 a 3   **b** $\frac{1}{30}$ **c** $\frac{1}{6}$

  d $\frac{17}{30}$ **e** 20%   **f** $96\frac{2}{3}\%$

Problems and challenges

1 a 2

  b $100A$

  c 0.2

  d $\frac{479}{330}$ or $\frac{1437}{990}$

  e $2 \times \$1$ coins, 3×50-cent pieces and 3×20-cent pieces

2 Height of rungs: 0.18 m, 0.36 m, 0.54 m, 0.72 m, 0.9 m, 1.08 m, 1.26 m, 1.44 m, 1.62 m, 1.8 m

3 a A = 1, B = 7, C = 8

  b A = 7, B = 5, C = 1, D = 9

  c A = 4, B = 2

  d A = 3, B = 7

4 a i 1.96   **ii** 2.25   **iii** 2.1025

  b i 1.73   **ii** 1.732

5 a $\frac{4}{9}$ **b** $3\frac{2}{9}$ **c** $\frac{17}{99}$ **d** $4\frac{728}{999}$

Chapter checklist with success criteria

1 $\dfrac{8}{1000}$

2 3.17

3 2.37

4 23.53⑨8

5 0.44

6 73.752

7 66.85

8 43100

9 0.00782

10 0.023

11 32

12 25.047; 19.2

13 2.0̇9̇ and 0.00838

14 $10\dfrac{7}{20}$

15 10.6

16 0.583̇ (or 0.58 3̄)

17 0.125

18 4.5%

19 $\dfrac{1}{5}$; 0.2; 20%

20 As percentages they are 80%, 78% and 82%, so the largest is 82%.

Chapter review

Short-answer questions

1 a 0.44, 0.4, 0.04
   b 2.16, 2.026, 2.016
   c 0.98, 0.932, 0.895

2 a 8.1   b 0.81   c 8.01   d 0.801

3 a 3 hundredths = $\dfrac{3}{100}$ b 3 thousandths = $\dfrac{3}{1000}$
   c 3 ones = 3

4 a False   b False   c True
   d True   e False   f True

5 45.265, 45.266, 45.267, 45.268, 45.269, 45.270, 45.271, 45.272, 45.273, 45.274

6 a 423.5   b 15.89   c 7.3   d 70.000
   e 2.8   f 0.67   g 0.455
   h 0.0123456790123456790123456790123456790123456 8

7 a 9.53   b 4.137   c 43.35
   d 240.49857   e 83.497   f 205.22

8 a True   b False   c False
   d False   e True

9 a 137   b 790   c 22.51
   d 0.096208   e 696.956   f 360.5
   g 563 489.3

10 a 28   b 45   c 14
    d 30   e 45   f 9

11 a 19.2   b 63.99   c 19.32
    d 0.95   e 1.52   f 6
    g 16   h 3   i 3.1̇09̇

12

Decimal	Fraction	Percentage
0.45	$\dfrac{45}{100} = \dfrac{9}{20}$	45%
0.7	$\dfrac{70}{100} = \dfrac{7}{10}$	70%
0.32	$\dfrac{32}{100} = \dfrac{8}{25}$	32%
0.06	$\dfrac{6}{100} = \dfrac{3}{50}$	6%
0.79	$\dfrac{79}{100}$	79%
1.05	$\dfrac{105}{100} = \dfrac{21}{20}$	105%
0.35	$\dfrac{35}{100} = \dfrac{7}{20}$	35%
0.65	$\dfrac{65}{100} = \dfrac{13}{20}$	65%
0.125	$\dfrac{125}{1000} = \dfrac{1}{8}$	12.5%

13 a $\dfrac{3}{10}$, 0.3, 30%

    b $\dfrac{4}{5}$, 0.8, 80%

    c $\dfrac{3}{4}$, 0.75, 75%

    d $\dfrac{9}{50}$, 0.18, 18%

14 Dillon (75%), Judy (80%), Jon (78%) so Judy scored the highest.

Multiple-choice questions

1 D
2 B
3 C
4 E
5 A
6 D
7 D
8 B
9 A
10 C

Extended-response questions

1 a Jessica $12.57; Jaczinda $13.31; hence, Jaczinda earns higher pay rate by 74 cents per hour.
   b $37.47, $37.45 to the nearest 5 cents
   c $40.56
   d $48.34

2 a $30.40
   b $18 240.30

3 32 minutes and 26 seconds, on average

Semester review 1

Computation with positive integers

Short-answer questions

1 a ▾ ⟨⟨▾▾   b LXXIV   c ∩∩∩‖∣ / ∩∩∩‖∣

2 a 67849   b 700850

3 a 99323   b 6867
  c 441   d 196000
  e 1644   f $764\frac{3}{4}$

4 a False
  b True
  c True

5 36

6 a 30   b 56
  c 48   d 160
  e 16   f 42

7 a False
  b True
  c False
  d True
  e True
  f True

8 $18 \times (7 + 3)$

9 9 times

10 a 3859640
   b 3860000
   c 4000000

Multiple-choice questions

1 E   2 B   3 D   4 C   5 A

Extended-response question

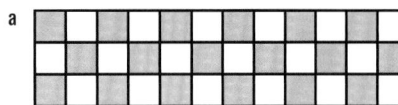

a 28   b $700   c $1000   d 12 h

Number properties and patterns

Short-answer questions

1 a 1, 3, 5, 15
  b 1, 2, 3, 5, 6, 10, 15, 30
  c 1, 2, 4, 5, 10, 20, 25, 50, 100

2 a 3, 6, 9, 12, 15
  b 7, 14, 21, 28, 35
  c 11, 22, 33, 44, 55

3 1, 2, 3 and 6

4 4

5 a 121   b 144   c 25

6 120

7 False

8 a 1   b 1   c 1

9 a 61   b 17

10

input	4	5	6	9	11	100
output	19	23	27	39	47	403

11 $A(1, 0)$, $B(4, 1)$, $C(3, 2)$, $D(1, 3)$, $E(3, 4)$

Multiple-choice questions

1 C   2 A   3 B   4 E   5 D

Extended-response question

a

b 18

c 9th

d $61

Fractions and percentages

Short-answer questions

1 $\frac{3}{10}, \frac{1}{3}, \frac{2}{5}, \frac{1}{2}$

2 $\frac{17}{3}$

3 a $\frac{11}{12}$

  b $2\frac{2}{3}$

  c $6\frac{1}{4}$

  d $\frac{1}{5}$

  e 4

  f $\frac{1}{2}$

4 $\frac{3}{20}$

5 $120

6 $60

7 a True
  b True
  c True
  d False

8 a 1:3
  b 1:3:4
  c 12:5

9 a $50, $10
  b $24, $36

Multiple-choice questions

1 B   2 C   3 E   4 D   5 A

Extended-response question

a 6

b $\dfrac{8}{9}$

c 9

d Last dose on Sunday week

Algebraic techniques

Short-answer questions

1 a 4
   b Yes
   c 9
   d 7

2 a $x + 3$
   b $12a$
   c $2x + 3y$
   d $\dfrac{w}{6}$
   e $y - 2x$

3 a $100m$
   b $24x$
   c $1\,000\,000p$
   d $\dfrac{y}{24}$

4 a 13
   b 11
   c 39
   d 6
   e 6
   f 24

5 36

6 a $10a$
   b $4x$
   c $12a$
   d m
   e $6 + 5a$
   f $4x + 2y$

7 a $2x + 14$
   b $3(x + 4) = 3x + 12$

8 a $6bc$
   b $5b$
   c p

9 a $2a + 6$
   b $12a - 12b$
   c $24m + 32$

10 $12xy$

Multiple-choice questions

1 B
2 A
3 C
4 E
5 D

Extended-response question

a i $12
   ii $(3x + 6)$
   iii $(3x + 2y)$
b $(50 - 3x - 2y)$

Decimals

Short-answer questions

1 a 0.2
   b 0.13
   c 1.7

2 a 6 units
   b $\dfrac{4}{1000}$
   c 136.1

3 a 18
   b 18.4
   c 18.40

4 a 4.07
   b 269.33
   c 19.01
   d 0.24
   e 0.09
   f 60

5 a 0.833   b 3   c 36

6 a 4.5387   b 0.045387   c 1.23

7 a 36490
   b 0.018
   c 3886

8 a $\dfrac{4}{5}$ b 1.1   c $\dfrac{2}{3}$

9 a True
   b False
   c False
   d True
   e False
   f True

Multiple-choice questions

1 E
2 C
3 D
4 A
5 B

Extended-response question

a $64.08
b $64.10
c $64.35
d 25c
e It becomes $63.90 rather than $63.80.

Chapter 6

6A

Building understanding

1 a $-2, 2$ b $-7, -5$
2 a -2 b 7 c -21 d 1071
3 a greater   b less   c greater   d less

Now you try

Example 1

Example 2
a $5 > -7$ b $-4 < -1$

Exercise 6A

1

2 a

b

3 a $-2, -1, 0, 1, 2, 3, 4$
  b $-2, -1, 0, 1$
  c $-4, -3, -2, -1, 0$
  d $-9, -8, -7, -6, -5, -4$
4 a $<$ b $>$ c $>$ d $<$
  e $<$ f $<$ g $<$ h $>$
  i $<$ j $>$ k $<$ l $>$
5 a $4°C$ b $-1°C$ c $-7°C$ d $-25°C$
6 a $-1\frac{1}{2}$ b $-\frac{2}{3}$ c $-4\frac{3}{5}$
  d $-9\frac{1}{4}$ e $-11\frac{1}{4}$ f $-19\frac{4}{7}$
7 a $-10, -6, -3, -1, 0, 2, 4$
  b $-304, -142, -2, 0, 1, 71, 126$
8 a $0, -1, -2$ b $-2, 0, 2$
  c $-5, -10, -15$ d $-44, -46, -48$
  e $-79, -75, -71$ f $-101, -201, -301$
9 a 5 b $-\$10$
10 a $-50\,m$ b $-212.5\,m$ c $0\,m$
11 a 2 b 4 c 4
   d 7 e 3 f 3
   g 6 h 44
12 a
   difference $= 8$
   b $4\frac{1}{2}\left(\text{or} -4\frac{1}{2}\right)$
   c The opposites are reflected to the other side of 0 on a number line, so if the originals are listed left-to-right (ascending) then their opposites will be right-to-left (descending).

13 a -2 b 1 c -1
   d -7 e -51 f 357

6B

Building understanding

1 a Right   b Right   c Left   d Left
2 a D   b A   c B   d C

Now you try

Example 3
a 3 b -5 c -4 d -10

Exercise 6B

1 a 3 b -4 c -1 d 5
2 a 1 b 3 c 2 d 1
  e -1 f -3 g -2 h -2
  i -4 j -8 k -1 l 2
  m 2 n -9 o 6 p -31
3 a -2 b -1 c -8 d -19
  e -4 f -10 g -15 h -7
  i -41 j -12 k -22 l -47
  m -300 n -100 o -93 p -634
4 a 5 b 9 c 5 d 2
  e 5 f 7 g 3 h 10
  i 5 j 16 k -4 l -5
  m -6 n -13 o -30 p -113
5 a 5 b -9 c 1 d -13
  e 1 f -22 g -32 h -4
6 a $\$145$ b $\$55$ c $\$5250$
7 a $3°C$ b $-3°C$ c $-46°C$
8 $69°C$
9 a $59\,m$ b $56\,m$
10 Answers may vary.
11 a i Positive   ii Positive
     iii Negative   iv Zero
   b i No   ii Yes
12 Answers may vary.
   a $-, +$ b $+, -, -$
   c $+, +, -, +$ d $-, +, +, +, -$
   e $+, +, -$ or $-, +, +$ f $-, +, -, -$

6C

Building understanding

1 b $6, -3$ c $-3, 1$ d $-11, -7$ e $3, 5$
  f $6, -2$ g $-3, 7$ h $-11, -7$
2 a 4 b Subtracting   c -5
  d Subtracting   e 2 f Adding
3 a False   b True   c True
  d False   e False   f True
  g False   h False

Answers

6C

Now you try

Example 4
a 6   b −9   c 10   d −5

Exercise 6C

1 a 2   b 3   c −2   d −4
2 a 1   b 5   c 6   d 2
   e −3   f −5   g −2   h −4
   i −3   j −22   k −35   l −80
   m −10   n −29   o −50   p −112
3 a 5   b 11   c 50   d 90
   e −4   f −3   g −5   h −34
   i 2   j 1   k 0   l 8
   m 28   n 34   o −12   p −76
4 a −3   b −10   c −4   d 4
   e −1   f 4   g −1   h −5
   i −4   j 4   k 2   l −24
   m −6   n −5   o 2   p 4
5 a 0   b −5   c 8   d 12
   e −9   f 5   g −6   h −91
   i −15   j 6   k 17   l 11
6 −143 m
7 −$35 000
8 −$30
9 a i $8000   ii −$6000
   b $2000
10 a

−2	0	5
8	1	−6
−3	2	4

   b

−13	−11	−6
−3	−10	−17
−14	−9	−7

11 a $3 + 4$ b $-2 + (-9)$
   c $5 - (-2)$ d $(-2) - 1$
   e $a + (-b)$ f $a - (-b)$

12 a $5 - 7 = -2$
     $5 - (-2) = 7$
   b $4 - 7 = -3$
     $4 - (-3) = 7$
   c $-2 + (-3) = -5$,
     so $-5 - (-2) = -3$,
         $-5 - (-3) = -2$
   d Either from $-3 + 4 = 1$ or $4 + (-3) = 1$, you can rearrange to get $1 - (-3) = 4$.
13 a 4   b −1   c −3
14 a i No   ii Yes
   b i Yes   ii No
   c Yes, if $b < a$, then subtracting b takes the result to a number bigger than zero.

15 a $\frac{3}{2}$ b $\frac{11}{3}$ c −2   d −4
   e $\frac{16}{3}$ f $\frac{23}{2}$ g $-\frac{1}{2}$ h $-\frac{1}{14}$
   i $\frac{3}{2}$ j $\frac{15}{2}$ k $\frac{19}{6}$ l $\frac{32}{35}$
   m $-\frac{11}{6}$ n $-\frac{27}{20}$ o $\frac{67}{14}$ p $-\frac{53}{30}$

6D

Building understanding

1 a 2   b −3   c −4   d −4
2 a Positive   b Positive   c Negative
   d Positive   e Positive   f Negative

Now you try

Example 5
a −32   b 45   c −7   d 5

Example 6
24

Exercise 6D

1 a −6   b −6   c 6
   d −8   e −8   f 8
2 a −15   b −10   c −6   d −54
   e 32   f 28   g 144   h −99
   i −39   j −84   k 38   l −108
   m 66   n −45   o 63   p 72
3 a −2   b −12   c −2   d −4
   e 3   f 1   g −5   h −19
   i −7   j −12   k −68   l 8
   m 12   n 13   o −13   p 13
4 a 24   b 15   c −4   d 5
   e 1   f −10   g 72   h 18
   i 1   j −1   k −69   l −3
5 a −7   b 4   c −4   d 8
   e 27   f −140   g 2   h −3
   i −3   j −1   k −2   l 40
6 a −3   b −3   c 8   d 31
   e 3   f 5   g −30   h −100
7 a 4   b 1   c 81   d 100
   e 36   f 64   g 9   h 2.25
8 a $(1, 6), (2, 3), (-1, -6), (-2, -3)$
   b $(1, 16), (2, 8), (4, 4), (-1, -16),$
     $(-2, -8), (-4, -4)$
   c $(-1, 5), (-5, 1)$
   d $(-1, 24), (-24, 1), (-2, 12), (-12, 2),$
     $(-3, 8), (-8, 3), (-4, 6), (-6, 4)$
9 a ×, ÷   b ÷, ×   c ×, ×   d ÷, ×
10 a $(4, -2), (-4, 2)$ b $(33, -3), (-33, 3)$
11 a −1
   b Divide by (-1)
   c If the original number is x then its opposite is $x \times (-1)$, and the opposite of that is $x \times (-1) \times (-1)$. But $(-1) \times (-1) = 1$, so you end up with $x \times 1$ which is the original number, x.
12 a i −8   ii 64   iii −27   iv 81
   b Parts ii and iv, even number of negative factors
   c Parts i and iii, odd number of negative factors
13 a $-ab$ b $-ab$ c ab
14 Answers will vary.

15 a $-\dfrac{1}{4}$ **b** $-\dfrac{1}{2}$ **c** $-\dfrac{3}{7}$ **d** 1

e -1 **f** $-\dfrac{5}{4}$ **g** $\dfrac{1}{2}$ **h** 6

i -1 **j** 1 **k** -1 **l** 1

Progress quiz

1

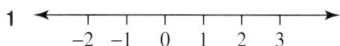

2 a $-2 < 1$ **b** $-9 > -12$ **c** $4 > -5$

3 $-6, -4, 0, 7, 8$

4 a 2 **b** -9 **c** -8 **d** -26

5 a 5 **b** -15 **c** -3 **d** 20

6 a 5 **b** 12

7 a -12 **b** 60 **c** -7 **d** 4

8 a 40 **b** -30 **c** 16 **d** -2

9 a 25 **b** -8 **c** 12 **d** -315

10 Debt of $70 or $-$70

6E

Building understanding

1 a Division **b** Multiplication **c** Division
d Subtraction **e** Multiplication **f** Multiplication

2 a True **b** False **c** True
d False **e** False **f** True

Now you try

Example 7
a 6 **b** -41

Example 8
a 4 **b** 14

Exercise 6E

1 a -5 **b** -11 **c** -10 **d** -1

2 a 8 **b** 10 **c** -36 **d** -16

3 a -7 **b** 7 **c** 19 **d** 9
e 16 **f** 14 **g** 6 **h** -32
i -5 **j** -4 **k** -18 **l** -4
m -10 **n** 4 **o** 0

4 a -10 **b** -2 **c** -6 **d** 1
e 2 **f** 9 **g** 1 **h** 4
i -14 **j** -20 **k** 2 **l** -5
m 8 **n** -6 **o** -12

5 $528

6 $-$50

7 a $(-2 + 3) \times 8 = 8$
b $-10 \div (4 + 1) = -2$
c $(-1 + 7) \times 2 - 15 = -3$
d $(-5 - 1) \div (-6) = 1$
e $(3 - 8) \div 5 + 1 = 0$
f $50 \times (7 - 8) \times (-1) = 50$
g $-2 \times (3 - (-7)) - 1 = -21$

h $(-3 + 9) \div (-7 + 5) = -3$
i $(32 - (-8)) \div (-3 + 7) = 10$

8 Three answers $(-10, -21, -31)$

9 a No **b** No **c** Yes
d Yes **e** No **f** Yes

10 a True **b** True **c** True
d True **e** False **f** False

11 a i Negative **ii** Negative **iii** Negative
iv Positive **v** Negative **vi** Negative
b If there is an even number of negative factors the result will be positive, if odd then negative

12 a 4 **b** 4 **c** -4
d -32 **e** -32 **f** 32
g 2 **h** -2 **i** -1

13 Kevin should have typed $(-3)^4$ to raise -3 to the power of 4. -3^4 is -1×3^4.

6F

Building understanding

1 C **2** B **3** No, 20

Now you try

Example 9
a -6 **b** -9 **c** 45

Exercise 6F

1 a i 9 **ii** 17
b i 10 **ii** 31
c i -5 **ii** -7

2 a 17 **b** 23 **c** -8 **d** 8
e 6 **f** 11 **g** -7 **h** 6
i 3 **j** -9 **k** -9 **l** 6

3 a -8 **b** -2 **c** 2 **d** -13
e -25 **f** 17 **g** 36 **h** 18

4 a 38 **b** 5 **c** 4
d -13 **e** -4 **f** -16

5 a 10 **b** -1 **c** -24 **d** -6

6 a $6\,\text{m}^2$ **b** $16\,\text{m}^2$

7 a 32 metres per second
b 14 metres per second
c 2 metres per second

8 a i 16 **ii** -2
b A negative dimension is not possible.

9 Answers may vary.

10 Answers may vary.

11 a $a - a = 0$ and $-b + b = 0$
b $\dfrac{a}{a} = 1$
c $a - a = 0$
d $\dfrac{ab}{b}$ cancels to simply give a.

12 a i $5°C$ **ii** $-15°C$ **iii** $-25°C$
b $F = \dfrac{9C}{5} + 32$

6G

Building understanding

1 a D b B c A d C
   e E f H g F h G
2 a 9   b 18   c 15   d 6
   e 10   f 2   g 1

Now you try

Example 10
$A = (1, 3)$
$B = (-3, 4)$
$C = (4, -1)$
$D = (-1, -2)$

Exercise 6G

1 $A(2, 2), B(2, -3), C(-2, -1), D(-4, 3)$
2 $A(2, 1), B(3, -2), C(-1, -4), D(-2, 2), E(4, 3),$
   $F(2, -3), G(-3, -1), H(-4, 4)$
3 a, b

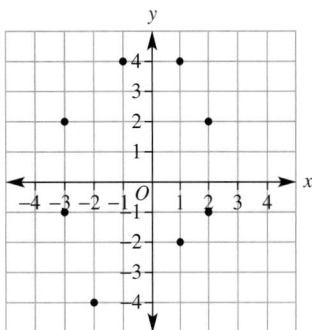

4 $A(3, 0), B(0, -2), C(-1, 0), D(0, 4),$
   $E(0, 2), F(1, 0), G(0, -4), H(-3, 0)$

5 a

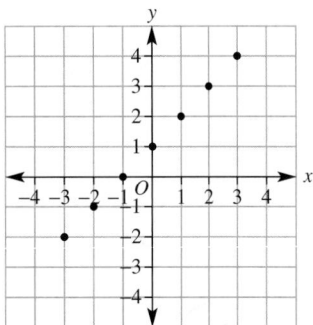

   b They lie in a straight line.

6 a

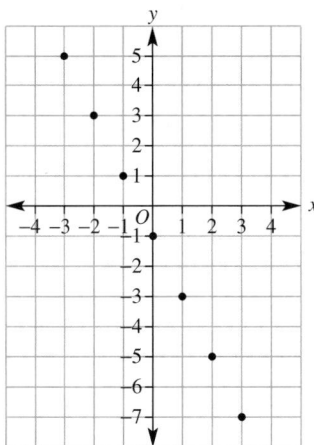

   b They lie in a straight line.
7 a Triangle (isosceles)   b Rectangle
   c Trapezium   d Kite
8 a 4 square units   b 6 square units
   c 4 square units   d 15 square units
9 28 km
10 $y = 2$
11 $y = 3$
12 a B b C c B, A, C
13 a i   1 and 4   ii 4
       iii 3 and 4   iv 3
   b

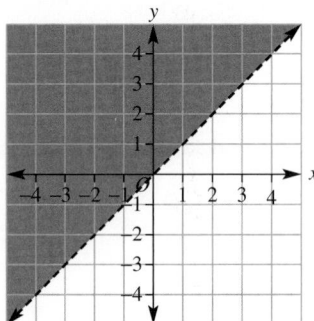

14 a $y = \{-7, -5, -3, -1, 1, 3, 5\}$
    b, c

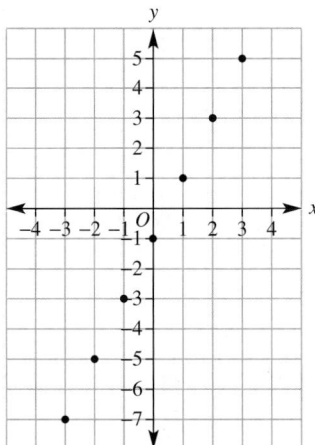

    d They are in a straight line.

Problems and challenges

1 a −81, 243, −729
  b 4, −2, 1
  c −10, −15, −21
  d −8, −13, −21
2 a 0
  b −153
  c 101
3 a $-3 \times (4 + (-2)) = -6$
  b $-2 \times 5 \times (-1) + 11 = 21$
     or $-2 \times 5 \div (-1) + 11 = 21$
  c $1 \times 30 \div (-6) - (-2) = -3$
4 a 11 and −3
  b 21 and −10
5 9 pairs
6 $a = 1, b = -1, c = 2, d = -3, e = 5$
7 $-\dfrac{1}{25}$
8 a $p + t > q + t$
  b $t - p < t - q$
  c $pt < qt$
9 All numbers less than 1 except 0
10 a 8 m/s   b 24 m/s^2

Chapter checklist with success criteria

1
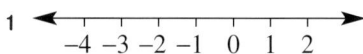
   $-4\ -3\ -2\ -1\ \ 0\ \ 1\ \ 2$
2 $-1 > -6$
3 1
4 −6
5 −5
6 4
7 21
8 −2
9 8
10 −10
11 −4
12 $A = (1, 1); B = (3, -2); C = (-2, -4); D = (-3, 3)$
13
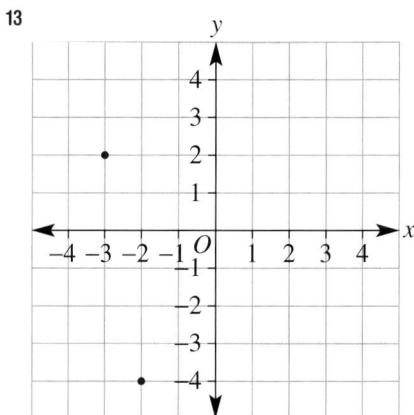

Chapter review

Short-answer questions

1 a <   b <
  c >   d <
2 a −5   b −2
  c −15   d 1
  e −2   f −5
  g 12   h −18
  i −6   j 5
  k −11   l 5
3 a −1   b −9
  c −1   d 2
  e −21   f −2
  g −87   h 30
4 a −10   b −21
  c 30   d −5
  e −3   f 4
  g 1   h −8
5 a −2   b −50
  c −36   d −1
6 a −37   b 8
  c −3   d 1
  e 56   f 80
7 a 10   b −41
  c −22   d −11
8 $A(3, 0), B(2, 3), C(-1, 2), D(-4, -2), E(0, -3), F(4, -4)$

Multiple-choice questions

1 C
2 E
3 B
4 D
5 C
6 A
7 E
8 C
9 B
10 C

Extended-response questions

1 a 16°C   b −31°C   c 8°C
  d 19°C   e 27°C

2 Rocket

Chapter 7

7A

Building understanding

1 **a** •P

b

c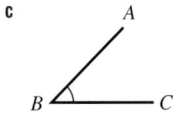

d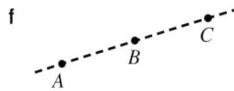

e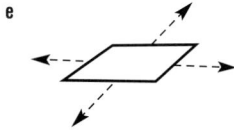

f

2 **a** Ray   **b** Line   **c** Segment

   d Collinear   **e** Concurrent

3 Answers may vary.

4 **a** 50°   **b** 145°   **c** 90°   **d** 250°

Now you try

Example 1

a Ray BA

b $\angle BCA$ or $\angle ACB$

Example 2

a Acute, $\angle AOB = 50°$

b Straight, $\angle EFG = 180°$

c Reflex $\angle EOD = 250°$

Example 3

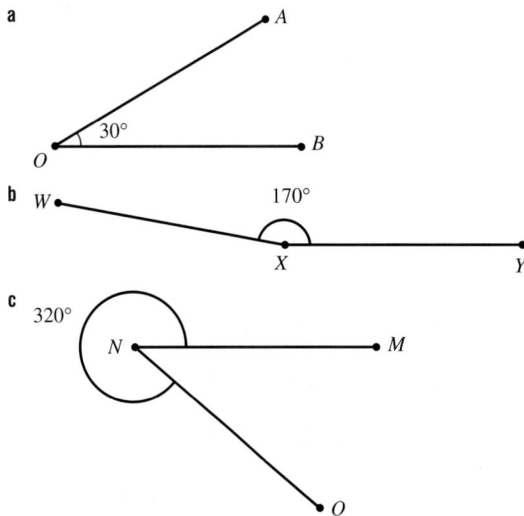

Exercise 7A

1 **a** **i** Segment PQ **ii** Segment XY

   b **i** $\angle AOB$ or $\angle BOA$ **ii** $\angle STU$ or $\angle UTS$

2 **a** Point T **b** Line CD

   c $\angle BAC$ or $\angle CAB$ **d** Plane

   e Ray PQ **f** Segment ST

3 **a** $\angle BOC$ or $\angle COB$ **b** $\angle BAC$ or $\angle CAB$

   c $\angle BEA$ or $\angle AEB$ **d** $\angle AOC$ or $\angle COA$

4 **a** Acute, 40°   **b** Acute, 55°   **c** Right, 90°

   d Obtuse, 125°   **e** Obtuse, 165°   **f** Straight, 180°

   g Reflex, 230°   **h** Reflex, 270°   **i** Reflex, 325°

5 **a** 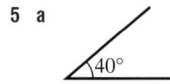   **b**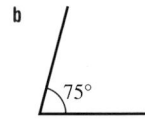

   c 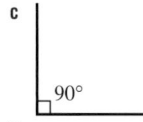   **d**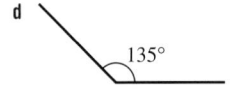

   e 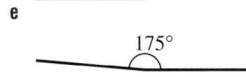   **f**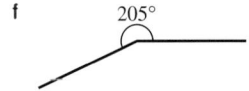

   g 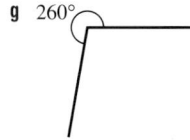   **h**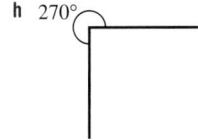

   i 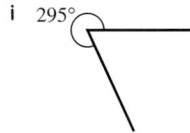   **j**

6 **a** 29°   **b** 55°   **c** 35°   **d** 130°

7 **a** C, B and D **b** A, C and D

8 **a** No   **b** Yes

9 **a** 8   **b** 14

10 **a** 180°   **b** 270°   **c** 30°   **d** 120°

   e 6°   **f** 54°   **g** 63°   **h** 129°

11 **a** 180°   **b** 90° or 270°

   c 120° or 240°   **d** 30° or 330°

12 **a** 115°   **b** 127.5°   **c** 85°   **d** 77.5°

   e 122°   **f** 176.5°

13 **a** Yes   **b** No

14 Use the revolution to get $360° - 60° = 300°$.

15 **a** **i** 70°   **ii** 70°   **iii** 90°

     iv 90°   **v** 80°   **vi** 80°

   b No

   c Subtract 360° until you have a number that is less than 180°, then change the sign if it is negative.

16 **a** Missing numbers are 0, 1, 3, 6, 10, 15.

   b For 5 points, add 4 to the previous total; for 6 points, add 5 to the previous total, and so on.

   c Number of segments $= \frac{n}{2}(n - 1)$

7B

Building understanding

1 **a, b** Angles should add to 90°
  c Complementary
2 **a, b** Angles should add to 180°
  c Supplementary
3 **a, b** Angles should add to 360°
  c Vertically opposite angles
4 **a** $\angle BOC$ or $\angle COB$
  b $\angle AOD$ or $\angle DOA$ and $\angle BOC$ or $\angle COB$
  c $\angle COD$ or $\angle DOC$

Now you try

Example 4
a $a = 25$ **b** $a = 50$

Example 5
a $a = 116$ **b** $a = 220$

Exercise 7B

1 **a** 70   **b** 30   **c** 75
2 **a** 50   **b** 60   **c** 15
  d 70   **e** 60   **f** 135
  g 40   **h** 30   **i** 41
3 **a** 115   **b** 37   **c** 77
  d 240   **e** 140   **f** 270
  g 110   **h** 130   **i** 125
4 **a** N   **b** N   **c** S   **d** N
  e C   **f** C   **g** C   **h** S
5 **a** $EF \perp GH$ **b** $ST \perp UV$ **c** $WY \perp XY$
6 **a** 30   **b** 75   **c** 60   **d** 135
  e 45   **f** 130
7 **a** No, should add to 90°.   **b** Yes, they add to 180°.
  c Yes, they add to 360°.   **d** Yes, they are equal.
  e No, they should be equal.   **f** No, should add to 360°.
8 **a** 30   **b** 60   **c** 60   **d** 45
  e 180   **f** 36
9 24°
10 **a** No, if both are less than 90° they cannot add to 180°
   b Yes, e.g. 20° and 70°.
11 **a** $a + b = 90$ **b** $a + b + c = 180$
   c $a + b = 270$
12 Only one angle – the others are either supplementary or vertically opposite.
13 **a** 360°   **b** 72   **c** 108
   d

Regular shape	a	b
Triangle	120	60
Square	90	90
Pentagon	72	108
Hexagon	60	120
Heptagon	≈ 51	≈ 129
Octagon	45	135

7C

Building understanding

1 **a** 4   **b** No
2 **a** 2   **b** Yes
3 **a** Equal   **b** Supplementary
  c Equal   **d** Equal

Now you try

Example 6
a $\angle DBC$ (or $\angle CBD$)   **b** $\angle BFH$ (or $\angle HFB$)
c $\angle DBF$ (or $\angle FBD$)   **d** $\angle HFB$ (or $\angle BFH$)

Example 7
a $a = 120$, corresponding angles in parallel lines
b $a = 50$, alternate angles in parallel lines
c $a = 115°$, cointerior angles in parallel lines

Example 8
a Parallel, because the cointerior angles sum to 180°
b Not parallel, because the corresponding angles are not equal

Exercise 7C

1 **a** $\angle CHG$ or $\angle GHC$ **b** $\angle CHG$ or $\angle GHC$
  c $\angle BGH$ or $\angle HGB$ **d** $\angle BGH$ or $\angle HGB$
2 **a** $\angle DEH$ or $\angle HED$ **b** $\angle BEF$ or $\angle FEB$
  c $\angle DEB$ or $\angle BED$ **d** $\angle CBG$ or $\angle GBC$
3 **a** $\angle FEG$ or $\angle GEF$ **b** $\angle DEB$ or $\angle BED$
  c $\angle GEB$ or $\angle BEG$ **d** $\angle ABC$ or $\angle CBA$
4 **a** 130, corresponding   **b** 70, corresponding
  c 110, alternate   **d** 120, alternate
  e 130, vertically opposite   **f** 67, vertically opposite
  g 65, cointerior   **h** 118, cointerior
  i 100, corresponding   **j** 117, vertically opposite
  k 116, cointerior   **l** 116, alternate
5 **a** $a = 70, b = 70, c = 110$
  b $a = 120, b = 120, c = 60$
  c $a = 98, b = 82, c = 82, d = 82$
  d $a = 90, b = 90, c = 90$
  e $a = 95, b = 85, c = 95$
  f $a = 61, b = 119$
6 **a** No, corresponding angles should be equal.
  b Yes, alternate angles are equal.
  c Yes, cointerior angles are supplementary.
  d Yes, corresponding angles are equal.
  e No, alternate angles should be equal.
  f No, cointerior angles should be supplementary.
7 **a** 35   **b** 41   **c** 110
  d 30   **e** 60   **f** 141
8 **a** 65   **b** 100   **c** 62
  d 67   **e** 42   **f** 57
  g 100   **h** 130   **i** 59
9 **a** 12 angles   **b** 2 angles
10 120
11 **a** **i** The angle marked $a°$ is alternate to the 20° angle.
     ii The angle marked $b°$ is alternate to the 45° angle.
   b **i** $a = 25, b = 50$
     ii $a = 35, b = 41$
     iii $a = 35, b = 25$

Answers

7D

12 a $a = 120, b = 120$
  b 60
  c Opposite angles are equal.
13 a The two angles do not add to 180°.
  b The cointerior angles do not add to 180°.
  c Alternate angles are not equal.
14 a i ∠*BDE*, alternate   **ii** ∠*BED*, alternate
  b Add to 180°
  c Three inside angles of a triangle add to 180°, which is always true.
15 The angles of each triangle add to 180°, so the total is 360°.

7D

Building understanding

1 a $a = 65, b = 115$ **b** $a = 106, b = 106$
  c $a = 55, b = 55$
2 a ∠*BED*, $a = 30$ **b** ∠*EBD*, $a = 70$
  c ∠*ADC* or ∠*ABD*, $a = 50$

Now you try

Example 9
a $a = 30$ **b** $a = 55$

Exercise 7D

1 a 105   **b** 115
2 a 60   **b** 120   **c** 115   **d** 123
  e 50   **f** 73
3 a 50   **b** 65
4 a 80   **b** 60   **c** 65   **d** 45
  e 60   **f** 55
5 a 130°   **b** 120°   **c** 55°   **d** 75°
  e 90°   **f** 75°
6 a 50   **b** 150   **c** 60
7 a 1   **b** 2   **c** 2
8 a 30   **b** 60   **c** 40   **d** 30
  e 120   **f** 10
9 a 60   **b** 45   **c** 12
10 a 110   **b** 250   **c** 40   **d** 110
  e 40   **f** 300

7E

Building understanding

1 a 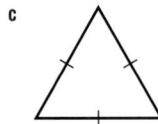   **b**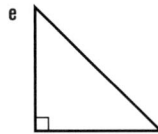

c 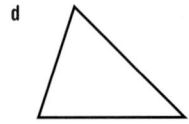   **d**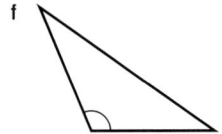

e 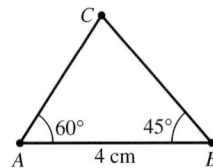   **f**

2 a *A*   **b** *BC*
  c *AC* and *AB*   **d** ∠*ACB* and ∠*ABC*

Now you try

Example 10
a i Isosceles   **ii** Right
b i Equilateral   **ii** Acute

Example 11

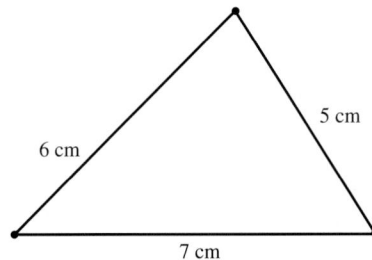

Example 12

Exercise 7E

1 a Equilateral   **b** Isosceles
  c Scalene
2 a Right   **b** Obtuse
  c Acute
3 a i Scalene   **ii** Right
  b i Equilateral   **ii** Acute
  c i Isosceles   **ii** Obtuse
4 Check measurements with a ruler and protractor.
5 Check your answer by measuring the lengths of the sides.
6 Check by doing parts **d** and **e**.
7 Check by doing parts **d** and **e**.
8 Check that ∠*CAB* = 90°.

9 a Yes

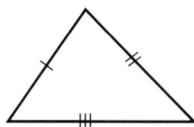

b Yes

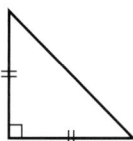

c No

d Yes

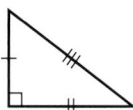

e

f

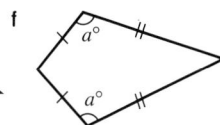

3 a

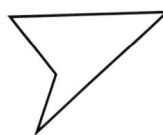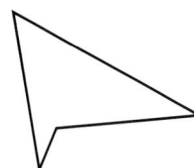

b 1

10 a Start with one side and the intersection of two arcs to give the other two lengths.
b Start with the base and use two arcs of equal radius.
c Start with the base and use two arcs with the same radius as the base.
d Start with the 4 cm segment, construct a right angle (see Q7), then the hypotenuse.

Now you try

Example 13
a Hexagon, non-convex
b Irregular

Example 14
a Convex quadrilateral
b Convex kite

11

Triangles	Scalene	Isosceles	Equilateral
Acute			
Right			
Obtuse			

Exercise 7F

1 a Octagon, non-convex
b Irregular

2 a 5   **b** 3   **c** 10   **d** 7
e 11   **f** 4   **g** 9   **h** 6
i 8   **j** 12

3 a i, iv and vi
b **i** Quadrilateral   **ii** Pentagon
   iii Hexagon   **iv** Octagon
   v Octagon   **vi** Triangle

4 a Convex   **b** Non-convex
c Non-convex

5 a Square   **b** Trapezium
c Kite   **d** Rhombus
e Rectangle   **f** Parallelogram

6 a Rectangle, kite, parallelogram
b Rhombus, parallelogram
c Square, rectangle, rhombus, parallelogram
d Trapezium
e Kite

12 a Yes
b Isosceles
13 The two shorter sides together must be longer than the longest side.
14 a Yes
b No, the three sides will not join.
15 a Check that the dashed lines form an equilateral triangle.
b Use the diagram to assist.

7 a N   **b** P   **c** P   **d** N
e N   **f** N   **g** N   **h** N

8 a $a = 90, b = 10$ **b** $a = 100, b = 5$
c $a = 50, b = 130$

9 Answers may vary. Some possibilities are given.

a
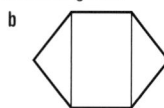

b
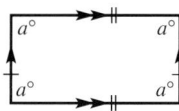

7F

Building understanding

1 a Pentagon
b i and iii; all interior angles are less than $180°$
c ii; there is one interior angle greater than $180°$
d Regular pentagon

2 a
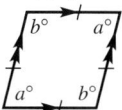

b
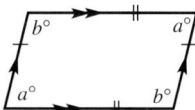

c

d

c
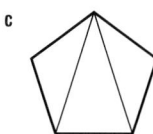

d
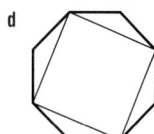

e
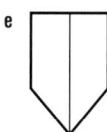

f

10 a i 2   **ii** 7
    b i 5   **ii** 35

11 Forming a square is possible.

12 a True   **b** False
    c False   **d** True

13 a Square, rectangle
    b Square, rhombus, kite

14 a A square is a type of rectangle because a rectangle can be constrained to form a square.
    b Yes, a parallelogram can be constrained to be a rhombus.
    c No

15 a Use given diagram and check that all sides are the same length.
    b Use given diagram and check that the distance between the lines are always equal.

Progress quiz

1 a G
    b Angle EGF or FGH or EGK or KGH and other names
    c Angle EGF or KGH and other names
    d AD, IJ and EH
    e Angle ABF or angle KBD measures $125°$

2 a $x = 28$ (angles in a right angle add to $90°$)
    b $x = 75$ (angles on a straight line add to $180°$)
    c $x = 64$ (vertically opposite)
    d $x = 23$ (angles in a straight line add to $180°$)
    e $x = 43$ (angles in a right angle add to $90°$)
    f $x = 60$ (revolution)
    g $x = 150$ (revolution)
    h $x = 65$ (vertically opposite)

3 a $\angle GHD$ **b** $\angle DHG$
    c $\angle FHC$ **d** $\angle AGH$

4 a $a = 76$ (alternate angles in parallel lines)
    b $a = 116$ (corresponding angles in parallel lines)
    c $a = 52$ (cointerior angles in parallel lines)

5 a No, corresponding angles are not equal.
    b Yes, cointerior angles add to $180°$.

6 a 125
    b 79

7 a Isosceles triangle
    b Right-angled triangle

8

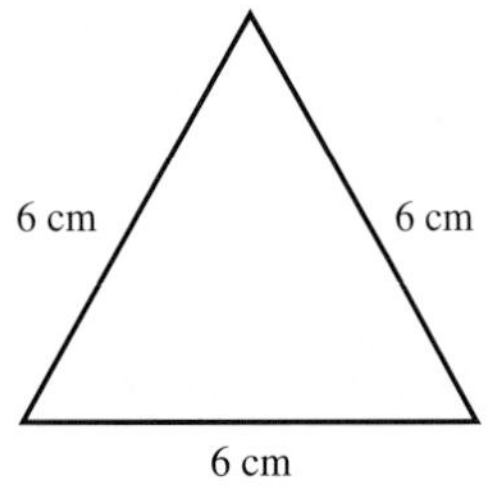

6 cm   6 cm

6 cm

9 a Square   **b** Trapezium
    c Rhombus   **d** Parallelogram

10 a Concave irregular pentagon
    b Convex regular hexagon
    c Convex irregular rectangle
    d Non-convex irregular decagon

7G

Building understanding

1 The three angles should add to $180°$.

2 a The $160°$ angle and a are on a straight line, which should add to $180°$.
    b $a + b + 100 = 180$; so if $a = 20$, b must be 60.

3 $60°$

4 a The two base angles in an isosceles triangle are equal.
    b The sum must be $180°$ (i.e. $70° + 70° + 40° = 180°$).

Now you try

Example 15
a $a = 25$ **b** $a = 140$

Example 16
$x = 152$

Exercise 7G

1 a 40   **b** 30
2 a 60   **b** 30   **c** 55
    d 65   **e** 25   **f** 145
3 a 120   **b** 36
4 a 65   **b** 20   **c** 32
    d 75   **e** 55   **f** 35
5 a 30   **b** 140   **c** 60
    d 60   **e** 10   **f** 142
6 a 40   **b** 120   **c** 45
    d 132   **e** 16   **f** 30
7 a 60   **b** 60   **c** 55
    d 55   **e** 145   **f** 50
8 $20°$
9 a i 3   **ii** 4   **iii** 5
    b i $540°$ **ii** $720°$ **iii** $900°$
10 a $1080°$ **b** $1260°$ **c** $1440°$
11 $S = 180(n - 2)$
12 a $155°$ **b** 155
    c They are the same.   **d** Yes, always true
13 a Alternate angles in parallel lines
    b Alternate angles in parallel lines
    c They must add to $180°$.
14 a $\angle DCA = a$ (Alternate to $\angle BAC$ and DE is parallel to AB.)

     $\angle ECB = b$ (Alternate to $\angle ABC$ and DE is parallel to AB.)

     $\angle DCA + \angle ACB + \angle ECB = 180°$ (Angles on a line add to $180°$.)
     $\therefore a + b + c = 180$
    b $a + b + c = 180$ (Angles in a triangle sum to $180°$.)
     $a + b = 180 - c$ (1)
     Also $\angle ACB + \angle BCD = 180°$ (Angles in a straight line sum to $180°$.)
     $c + \angle BCD = 180°$
     $\angle BCD = (180 - c)°$ (2)
     From (1) and (2) we have $\angle BAC = a° + b°$.

7H

Building understanding

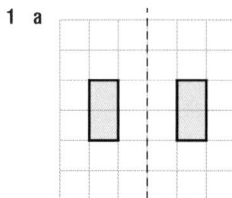

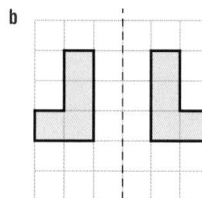

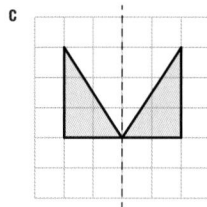

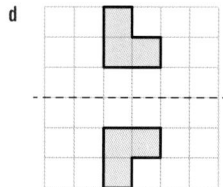

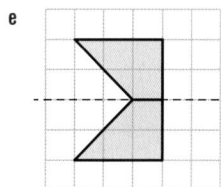

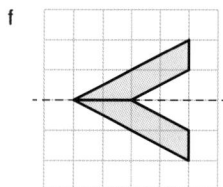

1 a 4 ways   b 2 ways   c 3 ways
  d 1 way   e 2 ways   f 0 ways
2 a 4   b 2   c 3
  d 1   e 2   f 2

Now you try

Example 17
a Line symmetry: order 1 and rotational symmetry: order 1
b Line symmetry: order 3 and rotational symmetry: order 3

Exercise 7H

1 6 and 6
2 a 4 and 4   b 2 and 2   c 2 and 2
  d 1 and 1   e 1 and 1   f 0 and 2
3 a Equilateral   b Isosceles   c Scalene
4 a i Kite   ii Rectangle, rhombus
   iii None   iv Square
  b i Trapezium, kite
   ii Rectangle, rhombus, parallelogram
   iii None
   iv Square
5 a 5, 5
  b 1, 1
  c 1, 1
  d 4, 4
6 a A, B, C, D, E, M, T, U, V, W, Y. K is almost symmetric but not quite.
  b H, I, O, X
  c H, I, N, O, S, X, Z
7 a   b
  c
8 a   b
  c   d
  e

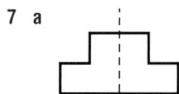

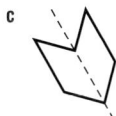

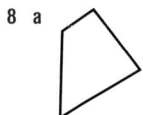

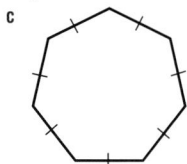

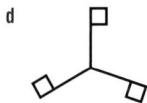

9 a 4 and 4   b 1 and 1
  c 1 and 1
10 a   b
11 a i No   ii No
  b Isosceles trapezium
12 a 9   b 3   c 4
  d 1   e Infinite   f Infinite

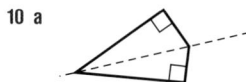

7I

Building understanding

1 a   b   c   d   e   f

2 a $(-2, 0)$ b $(-2, 0)$
  c $(0, -2)$ d $(0, 2)$
3 a No   b No

Now you try

Example 18

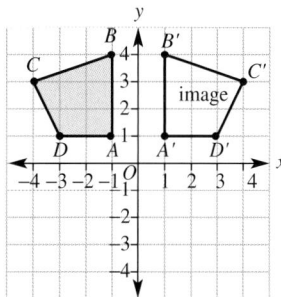

$A' = (1, 1)$
$B' = (1, 4)$
$C' = (4, 3)$
$D' = (3, 1)$

Answers

71

Example 19

a

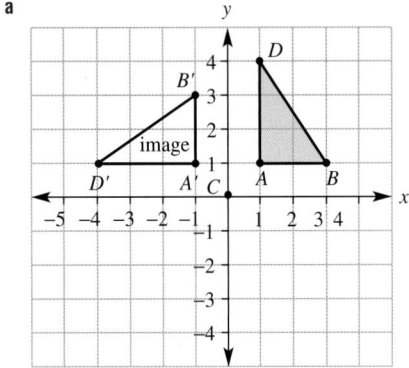

$A' = (-1, 1)$, $B' = (-1, 3)$, $D' = (-4, 1)$

b

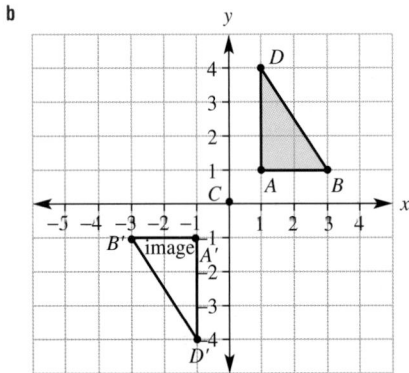

$A' = (-1, -1)$, $B' = (-3, -1)$, $D' = (-1, -4)$

Exercise 7I

1 $A'(1, 3)$, $B'(1, 1)$, $C'(2, 1)$, $D'(3, 3)$

2 a $A'(1, 1)$, $B'(1, 4)$, $C'(2, 2)$, $D'(3, 1)$
  b $A'(-3, 4)$, $B'(-3, 1)$, $C'(-2, 1)$, $D'(-1, 2)$
  c $A'(-1, -2)$, $B'(-2, -4)$, $C'(-4, -4)$, $D'(-4, -3)$
  d $A'(2, -1)$, $B'(2, -4)$, $C'(4, -2)$, $D'(4, -1)$
  e $A'(-3, 2)$, $B'(-3, 3)$, $C'(-1, 4)$, $D'(-1, 1)$
  f $A'(-3, -4)$, $B'(-1, -4)$, $C'(-1, -1)$, $D'(-2, -3)$

3 a $(-3, -3)$ **b** $(3, -3)$ **c** $(-3, 3)$
  d $(-3, 3)$ **e** $(3, 3)$ **f** $(-3, -3)$

4 a $A'(0, -1)$, $B'(2, 0)$, $D'(0, -3)$
  b $A'(1, 0)$, $B'(0, 2)$, $D'(3, 0)$
  c $A'(0, 1)$, $B'(-2, 0)$, $D'(0, 3)$

5 a $A'(-1, 0)$, $B'(-3, 0)$, $D'(-1, 2)$
  b $A'(0, -1)$, $B'(0, -3)$, $D'(-2, -1)$
  c $A'(1, 0)$, $B'(3, 0)$, $D'(1, -2)$

6 a   **b**

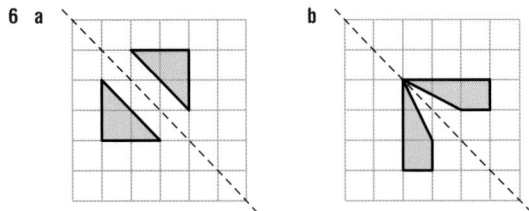

c   **d**

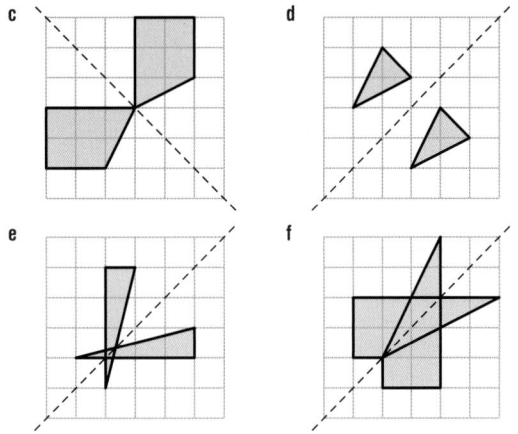

e   **f**

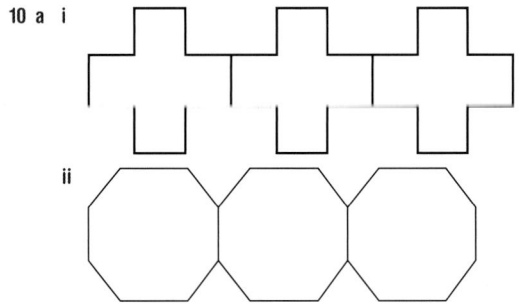

7 $(2, -5)$

8 a $(0, -1)$ **b** $(3, 0)$ **c** $(-1, 2)$

9 a 180° anticlockwise   **b** 90° anticlockwise
  c 90° clockwise

10 a i

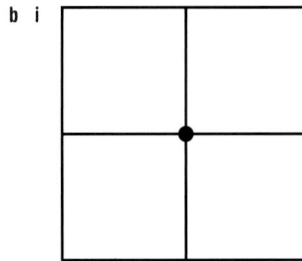

ii

iii Answers may vary.

b i

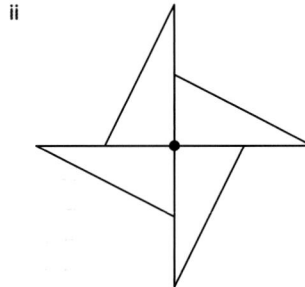

ii

iii Answers may vary.
  c Answers may vary.

11 a 270° **b** 322° **c** 10°
12 a (2, −5) **b** (2, −5)
  c The same point **d** (4, 1) for both
13 Check with your teacher.
14 Check with your teacher.

7J

Building understanding

1 a (4, 2) **b** (1, 2) **c** (3, 5) **d** (3, 1)
  e (2, 4) **f** (0, 1) **g** (5, 1) **h** (3, 0)
2 a up **b** left **c** down **d** up
  e left **f** left **g** right **h** right
3 a 7 units
  b 3 units
  c i 7 units **ii** 3 units

Now you try

Example 20

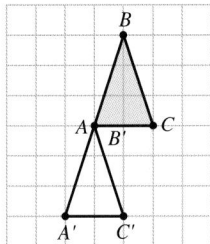

Example 21
Translation is 6 units right and 8 units down.

Exercise 7J

1

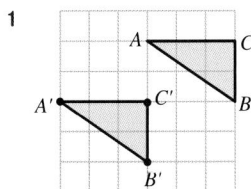

2 a **b**

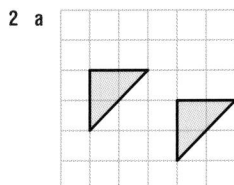 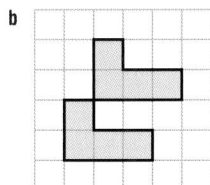

c **d**

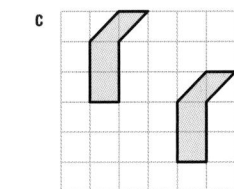 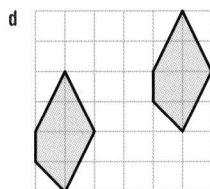

3 a (1, 3) **b** (−4, 3) **c** (−2, 1)
  d (−2, −2) **e** (−2, 5) **f** (8, 3)
  g (1, 4) **h** (2, 1) **i** (3, −3)
  j (−3, 1) **k** (−5, 4) **l** (−4, −2)
4 a 3 units up
  b 7 units down
  c 4 units down
  d 2 units up
  e 5 units left
  f 2 units right
  g 1 unit left and 4 units up
  h 3 units right and 6 units up
  i 3 units right and 4 units down
  j 3 units left and 11 units up
  k 12 units right and 3 units down
  l 10 units left and 13 units down
5 a 2 units left and 2 units up
  b 4 units left and 4 units up
  c 1 unit right and 5 units down
  d 6 units right and 2 units down
6 a 4 **b** 12
7 24 points
8 It is neither rotated nor enlarged.
9 a 3 right and 1 down **b** 1 right and 2 up
  c 2 left and 4 down **d** 6 right and 7 up
10 a (−4, −1) **b** (−4, −3)
  c (−7, 2) **d** (−13, −5)
  e (4, −2)

7K

Building understanding

1 a **b**

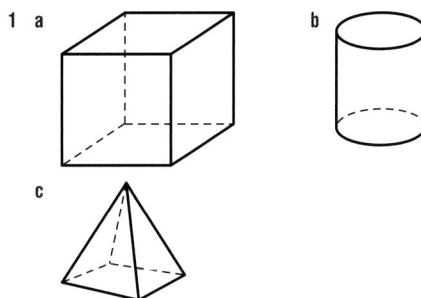

c

2 a 2 **b** 4
  c 6

Now you try

Example 22
a **b**

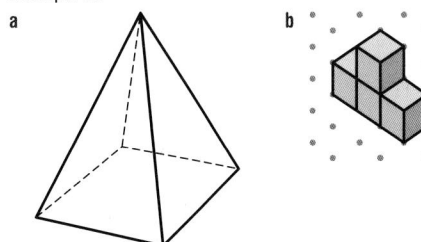

Exercise 7K

1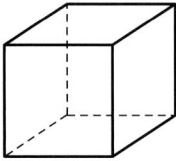

2 a 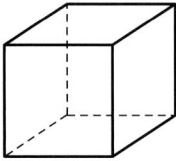   b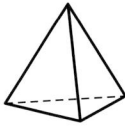

c    d

e    f

3 See given diagrams.

4 a    b

c

5 a 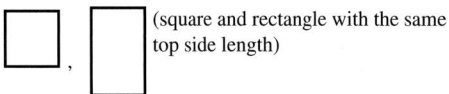 (two squares)

b 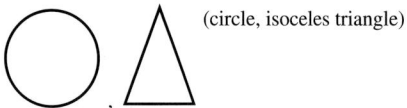 (square and rectangle with the same top side length)

c 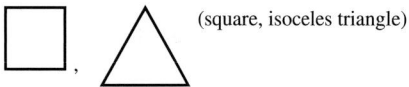 (circle, isoceles triangle)

d 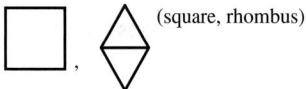 (square, isoceles triangle)

e (square, rhombus)

f  (2 circles)

g 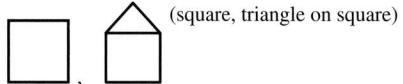 (square, triangle on square)

h 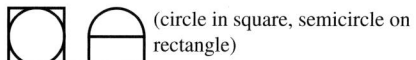 (circle in square, semicircle on rectangle)

i 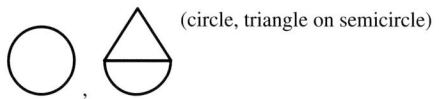 (circle, triangle on semicircle)

6 6
7 20
8 a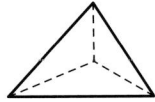

(4-faced pyramid)

b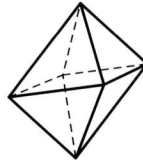

(8-faced double pyramid)

c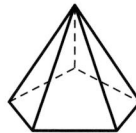

(pyramid with 5-sided base)

9 Yes, one can be rotated to match the other.

10 a C   b A   c B   d D

11 a i   front   left   top

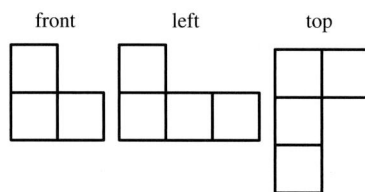

ii   front   left   top

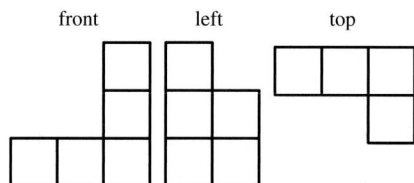

b i **ii**

7L

Building understanding

1 a Equal **b** Regular
  c Platonic
2 A and C
3 a Equilateral triangle **b** Square
  c Equilateral triangle **d** Regular pentagon
  e Equilateral triangle
4 a Cube **b** Cylinder
  c Triangular pyramid

Now you try

Example 23
a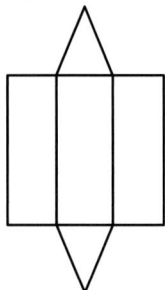

b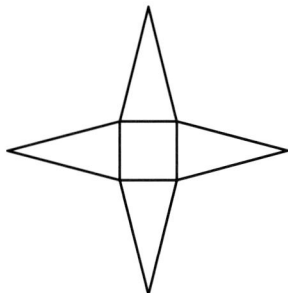

Exercise 7L

1 Answers may vary.
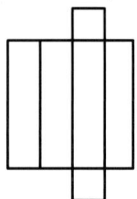

2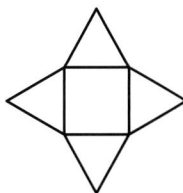

3 Answers may vary.
a 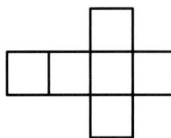 **b**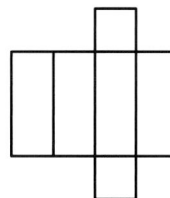
c 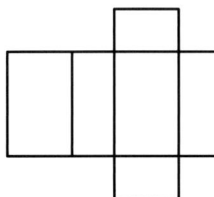 **d**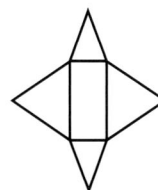
e 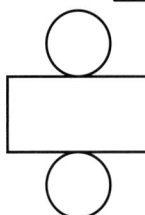 **f**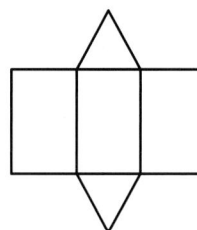

4 a Tetrahedron, octahedron, icosahedron
  b Icosahedron
  c Octahedron
  d Tetrahedron
  e Hexahedron, octahedron
  f Hexahedron, octahedron
5 a Octahedron **b** Hexahedron
  c Dodecahedron **d** Icosahedron
  e Tetrahedron
6 a 3 **b** 3 **c** 4
  d 3 **e** 5
7 a **b**
8 a 2 **b** 11
9 a 6
  b Yes
  c There is not the same number of faces meeting at each vertex.
10 No
11 a i 1 **ii** 26

b

n (side length)	1	2	3	4	5
n^3 (number of 1 cm cubes)	1	8	27	64	125
Number of inside cubes	0	0	1	8	27
Number of outside cubes	1	8	26	56	98

c i n^3
  ii $(n-2)^3$
  iii $n^3 - (n-2)^3$

Problems and challenges

1 Tetrahedron

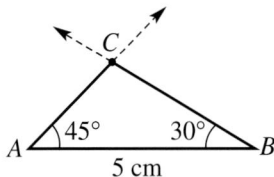

2 27
3 77.5°
4 720°
5 a 35
  b 1175
6 161

Chapter checklist with success criteria

1 Segment AB
2 ∠PQR (or ∠RQP)
3 Obtuse
4 125°
5

260°

6 a 50
  b 25
7 150°
8 (a) ∠EFB (or ∠BFE); (b) ∠HFB (or ∠BFH)
9 $a = 70$ (cointerior angles are supplementary)
10 Yes, the two lines are parallel since $122 + 58 = 180$, cointerior angles are supplementary in parallel lines.
11 $a = 50$
12 Isosceles
13 Obtuse
14

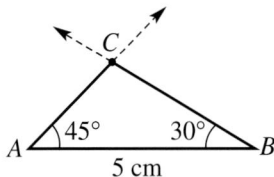

15

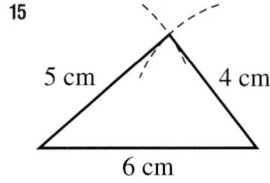

16 Pentagon
17 Convex; irregular
18 Convex; trapezium
19 40°
20 $a = 40$
21 $x = 152$
22 Line symmetry order = 2; rotational symmetry order = 2
23 $A' = (1, -1), B' = (1, -2), C' = (3, -3), D' = (3, -1)$

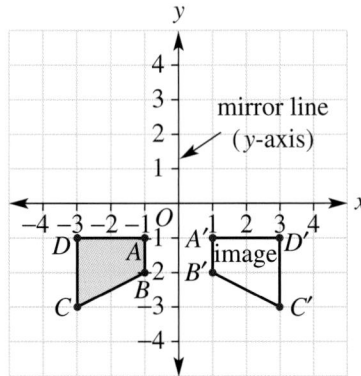

24 $A' = (0, 1), B' = (0, 2), D' = (-2, 1)$

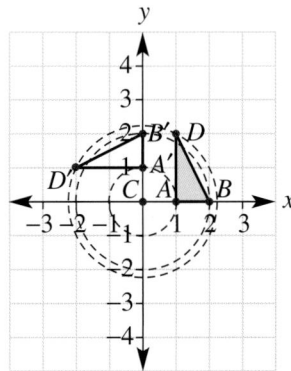

25

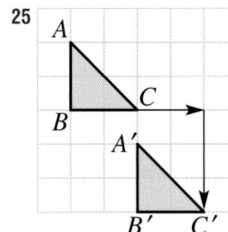

26 Translation is 6 units left and 4 units up.

27

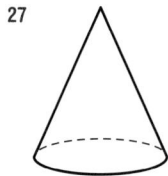

28

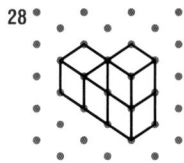

29

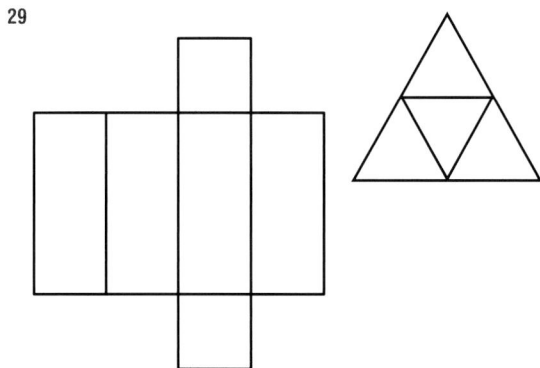

Chapter review

Short-answer questions

1 a Segment CD **b** $\angle AOB$ or $\angle BOA$
   c Point P **d** Plane
   e Ray AC **f** Line ST
2 a Acute, $35°$ **b** Obtuse, $115°$
   c Reflex, $305°$
3 a $180°$ **b** $90°$ **c** $90°$ **d** $150°$
4 a 20   **b** 230   **c** 35   **d** 41
   e 15   **f** 38   **g** 60   **h** 120
   i 30
5 a a and b **b** a and d
   c a and c **d** b and c
   e c and d or b and d
6 a Yes, corresponding angles are equal.
   b No, alternate angles should be equal.
   c No, cointerior angles should be supplementary.
7 a 100   **b** 95   **c** 51
   d 30   **e** 130   **f** 78
8 Check lengths and angles with a ruler and pair of compasses.
9 Check lengths and angles with a ruler and pair of compasses.
10 a 5   **b** 7   **c** 11
11 a 2   **b** 1
12 a Trapezium   **b** Rhombus
   c Kite
13 a 30   **b** 48   **c** 50
   d 60   **e** 80   **f** 130
   g 40   **h** 80   **i** 105
14 a 2, 2   **b** 1, 1   **c** 0, 2

15 a $A'(-1, -2), B'(-3, -3), C'(-3, -1)$
   b $A'(1, 2), B'(3, 3), C'(3, 1)$
16 a $A'(0, -4), B'(-2, 0), D'(-3, -3)$
   b $A'(4, 0), B'(0, -2), D'(3, -3)$
   c $A'(-4, 0), B'(0, 2), D'(-3, 3)$
17 a $A'(1, -1), B'(4, -1), C'(3, 1)$
   b $A'(-4, 1), B'(-1, 1), C'(-2, 3)$
18 a

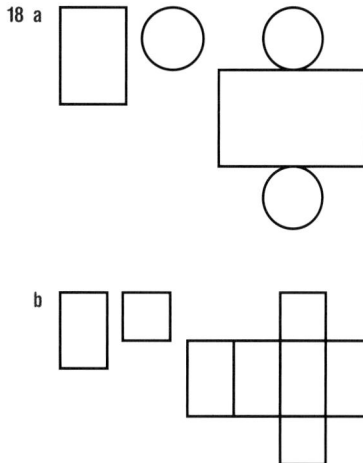

   b

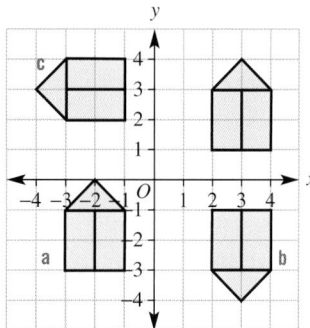

Multiple-choice questions

1 C   **2** B   **3** D   **4** C
5 D   **6** E   **7** C   **8** B
9 E   **10** A   **11** C   **12** E
13 C

Extended-response questions

1 a i $32°$ **ii** $32°$ **iii** $148°$ **iv** $58°$
   b i Corresponding   **ii** Cointerior
     iii Supplementary
   c i $21°$ **ii** $159°$ **iii** $69°$
2 a $30°$ **b** $65°$
   c 35   **d** It stays the same.
3

Chapter 8

8A

Building understanding

1 a C   b D   c A
  d E   e F   f B
2 Answers may vary.

Now you try

Example 1
a Discrete numerical
b Categorical

Example 2
a Secondary, e.g. find the results published in a magazine or journal.
b Primary, e.g. run a survey of everyone in the class.

Exercise 8A

1 a Categorical   b Numerical   c Numerical
  d Categorical   e Numerical   f Numerical
2 a Discrete numerical   b Continuous numerical
  c Continuous numerical   d Categorical
  e Categorical   f Categorical
  g Discrete numerical   h Discrete numerical
  i Continuous numerical   j Continuous numerical
  k Continuous numerical   l Discrete numerical
  m Continuous numerical   n Discrete numerical
  o Categorical   p Discrete numerical
  q Discrete numerical   r Categorical
3 a Observation
  b Sample of days using observation or secondary source records within each day
  c Census of the class
  d Sample
  e Sample
  f Sample using secondary source data
  g Census (this question appears on the population census)
  h Census of the class
  i Sample
  j Results from the population census
  k Observation
  l Observation
  m Sample
  n Sample
4 a Secondary – a market research company
  b Secondary – department of education data
  c Primary data collection via a sample
  d Secondary source using results from the census
  e Secondary source using NAPLAN results or similar
5 a Proximity to the Indian Ocean makes first hand collection of the data difficult and size of the ocean makes it hard to get representative data.
  b Too many people to ask and a sensitive topic means that using the census results as your source would be better.

c Extremely large population makes primary data difficult to collect.
d Sensitive topic might make students less keen to give honest and reliable answers.
e Cultural issues and the different cultural groups that exist in the community make collection difficult.
6 The data is often collected by a market research company. It is not always possible to know how the data is collected, the areas it is collected from and whether there was a bias introduced in the surveys.
7 a Population is the entire group of people but a sample is a selection from within it.
  b If the population is small enough (e.g. a class) or there is enough time/money to survey the entire population (e.g. national census).
  c When it is too expensive or difficult to survey the whole population, e.g. television viewing habits of all of Victoria
8 a The answers stand for different categories and are not treated as numbers. They could have been A–E rather than 1–5.
  b i 1 = strongly disagree, 2 = somewhat disagree, 3 = somewhat agree, 4 = strongly agree.
    ii 1 = poor, 2 = satisfactory, 3 = strong, 4 = excellent.
    iii 1 = never, 2 = rarely, 3 = sometimes, 4 = usually, 5 = always.
    iv 1 = strongly disagree, 2 = disagree, 3 = neutral, 4 = agree, 5 = strongly agree.
9 a Excludes people who have only mobile numbers or who are out when phone is rung; could bias towards people who have more free time.
  b Excludes people who do not respond to these types of mail outs; bias towards people who have more free time.
  c Excludes working parents; bias towards shift workers or unemployed.
  d Excludes anyone who does not read this magazine; bias towards girls; bias towards those who use social media.
  e Excludes people who do not use Facebook; bias towards specific age groups or people with access to technology.
10 a For example, number of babies at a local playground. Other answers possible.
  b Count a sample, e.g. just one floor of one car park.
11 a Too expensive and difficult to measure television viewing in millions of households.
  b Not enough people – results can be misleading.
  c Programs targeted at youth are more likely to be watched by the students.
  d Research required.
12 a Too expensive and people might refuse to respond if it came too often.
  b English as a second language can impact the collection of data (simple, unambiguous English is required). Some people from particular cultures may not be keen to share information about themselves.
  c Some people cannot access digital technologies and they would be excluded from the results.
  d Larger populations and a greater proportion of people in poverty can make census data harder to obtain.

13 It gives ownership and establishes trust where there may not have been any. It also ensures a deeper understanding of the process and need for honesty in the collection and use of any data.

14 Different people are chosen in the samples. Larger, randomly selected samples give more accurate guides.

15 a i Answers may vary.
  ii Answers may vary.
  iii Random processes give different results.
 b i Different vowels have different frequencies of occurring.
  ii If a high frequency word has an unusual range of vowels, e.g. a web page about Mississippi.

8B

Building understanding

1 a 10   **b** 1   **c** 9
2 a 9   **b** 12   **c** 9   **d** 7
3 a 30   **b** 6   **c** 7   **d** 7

Now you try

Example 3
a 13   **b** 26   **c** 25

Example 4
a 5   **b** 4

Exercise 8B

1 a 7   **b** 13   **c** 8   **d** 18
2 a 4   **b** 6   **c** 3   **d** 7
3 a 67   **b** 36   **c** 24
4 a i 6   **ii** 3   **iii** 1
 b i 11   **ii** 7   **iii** 2
 c i 18   **ii** 12   **iii** 11
 d i 17   **ii** 26   **iii** 25
 e i 32   **ii** 16   **iii** 10
 f i 40   **ii** 34   **iii** 55
 g i 102   **ii** 71   **iii** 84
 h i 91   **ii** 41   **iii** 18
5 a 10   **b** 8   **c** 3
 d 7   **e** 15   **f** 56
6 a 12   **b** 9   **c** 7
 d 6   **e** $4.5 \text{ or } 4\frac{1}{2}$ **f** $5.5 \text{ or } 5\frac{1}{2}$
7 a 9.5   **b** 11   **c** 11   **d** 8.5
8 a 16.6   **b** 17.5   **c** 12
9 a Brent   **b** Brent   **c** Ali   **d** Brent
10 a 2   **b** 4   **c** 12
 d 25   **e** 2.1   **f** 4
11 a 12   **b** 2   **c** 0 saves
12 a 3 values; e.g. {5, 5, 8}
 b Yes, e.g. {0, 0, 5, 5, 5, 7, 20}
13 The mean distance is increased by a large amount (the median is basically unaffected).

14 a Mean: 7, median: 7.5, mode: 10, range: 12
 b i Increases by 5   **ii** Increases by 5
  iii Increases by 5   **iv** No effect
 c i Doubles   **ii** Doubles
  iii Doubles   **iv** Doubles
 d Yes; e.g. if the set were duplicated: 1, 1, 3, 3, 5, 5, 10, 10, 10, 10, 13, 13.
15 a 7 and 13
 b 9, 10, 11
 c They must be 8, 10 and 12.
16 Numbers are: $x, x + 1, x + 2$;
$$\text{mean} = \frac{(3x + 3)}{3} = x + 1 = \text{median}$$
17 a i 4, 4, 4; answers may vary.
  ii 1, 4, 3, 9, 1; answers may vary.
  iii 2, 3, 8, 10, 10; answers may vary.
  iv 1, 2, 3, 4, 4, 16; answers may vary.
 b It is possible. (Hint: Divide every number by the current range.)
18 $\text{mean} = \dfrac{77}{240}$, $\text{median} = \dfrac{7}{24}$

8C

Building understanding

1 a True   **b** False   **c** True
 d True   **e** False
2 a 5   **b** 3   **c** Sport   **d** 20

Now you try

Example 5
a 15   **b** 5   **c** 6
d 2   **e** 7   **f** 1

Example 6

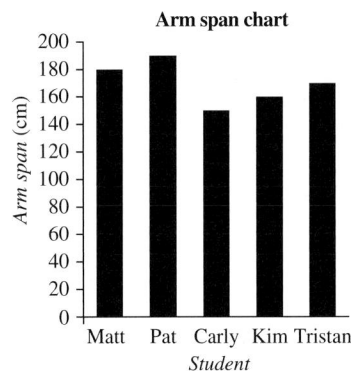

Arm span chart

Exercise 8C

1 a 4   **b** 17
 c 7   **d** 2
 e Person with 7 trips   **f** 2 trips
2 a 8   **b** 24   **c** 8   **d** 7   **e** 2

3 a 2 **b** 7 **c** Red **d** 27

e Favourite colour in 7B

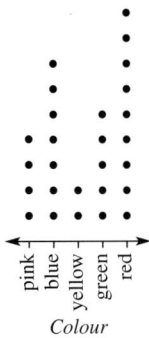

Colour

4 a 120 cm **b** 20 cm
c 60 cm **d** 11 years old

5 a

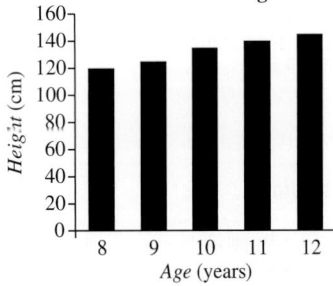

Mitchell's height

b

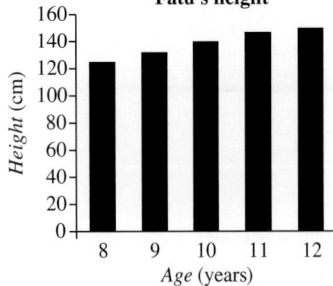

Fatu's height

6 a

	1990	1995	2000	2005	2010	2015
Using public transport	30	25	40	50	60	55
Driving a car	60	65	50	40	20	20
Walking or cycling	10	20	15	15	25	60

b 2005 and 2010
c 2010 and 2015
d Environmental concerns; answers may vary.
e Public transport usage is increasing; answers may vary.

7 a

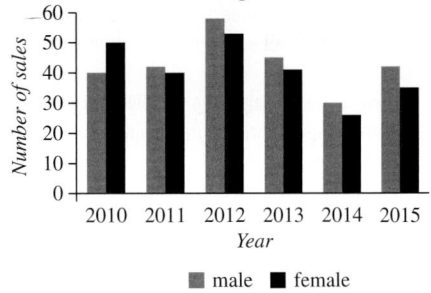

Dogs sold

■ male ■ female

b 2010 **c** 2014 **d** 2012 **e** Male
8 a It has increased steadily.
b Approx. $38 000
c Approx. $110 000 – $130 000
9 a It is unequal.
b The axes have no labels and the graph does not have a title.
c

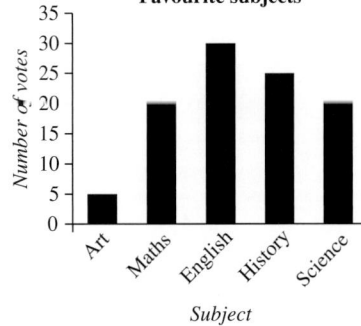

Favourite subjects

d Four times as popular
e One and a half times as popular
f Music
10 a 7
b 7
c 3M : 8, 3S : 4
d 3M
e 3M because best student got 10.
11 a 1500
b 104 000
c Increased
d Approx. 590 000 passengers
12 a 2.4
b Because 1 + 1 + 2 + 2 + 2 + 3 + 3 + 3 + 3 + 4 can be thought of as $(2 \times 1) + (3 \times 2) + (4 \times 3) + (1 \times 4)$ to calculate the total number of children.
13 a Symmetric, with a mean of 4.5, equal to the median of 4.5
b Negatively showed, with a mean of 4.25, less than the median of 4.5.
c Positively showed, with a mean of 4.85, greater than the median of 4.5.
d Symmetric, with a mean of 3, equal to median of 3.
14 240

8D

Building understanding

1 a 3 kg   b 4 kg   c 5 kg   d 4.5 kg
2 a 45 cm   b 110 cm   c 8 years
   d 15 cm   e 140 cm

Now you try

Example 7

a

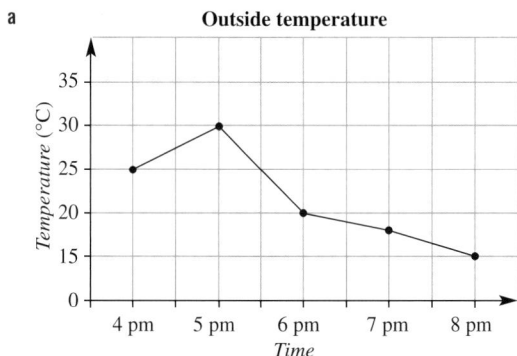

Outside temperature

b 25°C

Example 8

a 10 km
b 5 km
c In the third hour (from 2 to 3 hours)
d In the first hour
e 3 km

Exercise 8D

1 a

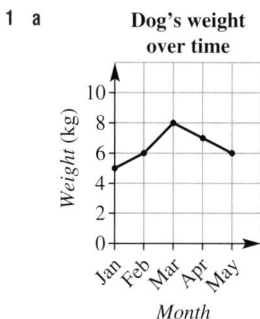

Dog's weight over time

b 6.5 kg

2 a

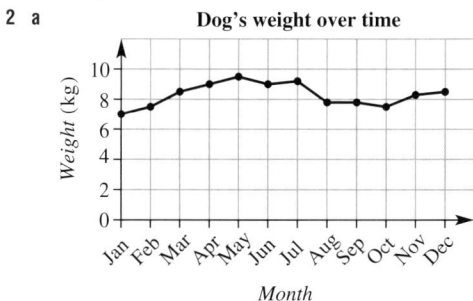

Dog's weight over time

b Weight increases from January until July, then goes down suddenly.
  c July
3 a 23°C
  b 2:00 pm
  c 12:00 am
  d i 10°C   ii 18°C
    iii 24°C   iv 24.5°C
4 a 200 km   b 80 km
  c At rest   d In the first hour
  e 40 km
5 a 2 hours   b 5 km   c Fifth hour
6 a July
  b Jan to July and Oct to Dec
  c 20 megalitres because the level stayed the same
7 a At 7 am and 8 pm
  b At 8 am and 11 pm
  c i Around 7 am (heater goes on)
    ii Around 8 am (turns heater off)
    iii Around 8 pm (heater put back on)
    iv Around 11 pm (heater turned off)
  d Answers may vary.
8 a

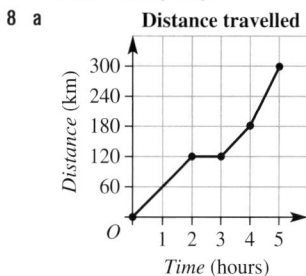

Distance travelled

b

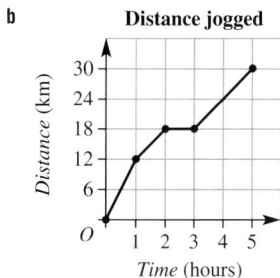

Distance jogged

9 The steeper sections of graph correspond to the person/object travelling faster. Horizontal section correspond to stationary periods.
10 a Time should be on the horizontal axis, not length; in practice, this would be a meaningless graph with a number of dots and lines going in each direction.
  b Length of new born babies over time, or weight over time. Possibly you could calculate the average (mean) length or weight month by month so it is easier to see on the graph if these are trends.
11 a The city is in the Southern hemisphere because it is hot in January–December.
  b The city is quite close to the equator because the winter temperatures are reasonably high.

Temperature in a year

Month

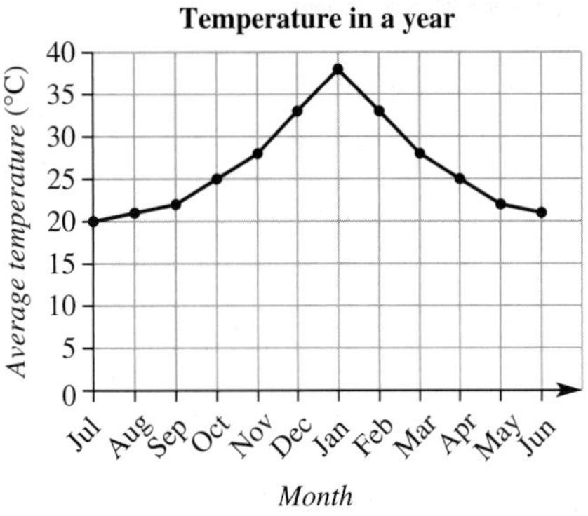

d Maximum occurs in the middle.
e The city is in the Northern hemisphere because it is hot in June–July.

8E

Building understanding

1 a 5   b 2
2 a 39   b 27   c 134
3 57

Now you try

Example 9

a 18, 21, 21, 24, 30, 32, 38, 39, 43
b 9
c Youngest is 18 years old. Oldest is 43 years old.
d 25 years
e 30 years old

Example 10

Stem	Leaf
2	4 5 9
3	2 5 6 8
4	1 2 8

3|2 means 32

Exercise 8E

1 a 13, 17, 20, 22, 24, 28, 29, 31, 33, 35
   b 10
   c 13, 35
   d 22
   e 26
2 a 8, 9, 10, 11, 13, 15, 17, 18, 21, 24
   b 10
   c i False   ii True   iii True   iv False
3 a Range = 20, median = 17
   b Range = 31, median = 26
   c Range = 19, median = 40.5

4 a

Stem	Leaf
1	1 2 3 4 4 5 7
2	0 4 8 9
3	1 2 3 5

2|8 means 28

b

Stem	Leaf
2	0 2
3	9
4	5 7 9 9
5	1 2 2 3 5 6 8 8

4|7 means 47

c

Stem	Leaf
1	6 6 8
2	1 4 8 9
3	1 2 3 5
4	1 8 9
5	0

3|5 means 35

d

Stem	Leaf
1	1 2 4
2	7 9
3	2 7 8 8
4	
5	
6	0 0
7	3 8
8	1 7

6|0 means 60

5 a

Stem	Leaf
8	0 4 5 6
9	0 6
10	1 4 5
11	0 3 4 4 5 9

10|4 means 104

b

Stem	Leaf
8	1 6
9	1 4 5 6 8
10	2 6 8
11	3 5 5 7
12	0

11|5 means 115

c

Stem	Leaf
15	5 7 8
16	2 5 7
17	3 4 8
18	1 4 4 5 7
19	2 2 3 3 6 9

16|2 means 162

d

Stem	Leaf
39	1 5 6
40	1 2 4 5 6 6 8 9
41	1 2 3 5 6 7 8
42	0

41|3 means 413

6 a 2   **b** B   **c** 1   **d** B   **e** 1
   f N   **g** 2   **h** 1   **i** N
7 a 10   **b** 1   **c** 8
   d 58   **e** 10 seconds
8 a i 49 years   **ii** 36 years
   b Radio station 1
   c i 33 to 52 years
     ii 12 to 31 years, or 13 to 32 years
9 a i 30   **ii** 52
   b Year 6
   c i 151.5 cm   **ii** 144.5 cm
   d Year 7
   e The difference between the two plots would increase, with the median on the left going down and median on the right going up.
10 a 15
   b 13
   c a is 5 or 6, b is 0, c is 8 or 9, d is 0.
11 a Easier to compare sizes of different stems visually.
   b Helps in noticing trends and calculating the median.
12 a Answers may vary, but the mean should be greater than the median.
   b Answers may vary, but the mean should be less than the median.
   c Answers may vary but the mean and median should be approximately equal.
13 a i 30
     ii 10
     iii Between 10 and 19 years old

     iv Between 31 and 49 years
     v 18
     vi Between 18 and 28
   b i True   **ii** False   **iii** True
     iv True   **v** False   **vi** False
   c Cannot determine how many people are exactly aged 40 years.
   d Close to 30 years
14 a Minimum: $-29°C$, maximum: $23°C$
   b i 5   **ii** 10   **iii** 11
   c Because -05 and 05 are different numbers
   d $-5.2°C$
   e $-8°C$; it is $2.8°C$ lower than the mean.

8F

Building understanding

1 a Playing sport   **b** Watching television
   c More
2 a Rugby   **b** Basketball
   c $\frac{1}{5}$ **d** $\frac{2}{3}$

Now you try

Example 11
a

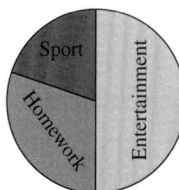

b

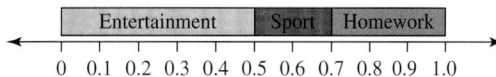

Exercise 8F

1 a

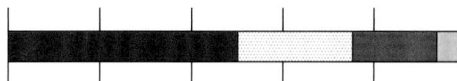

■ food ☐ drinks ■ household items ☐ other

b

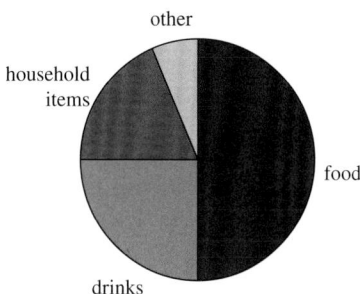

2 a 20
   b i $\frac{3}{10}$ **ii** $\frac{1}{4}$
     iii $\frac{7}{20}$ **iv** $\frac{1}{10}$
   c i $108°$ **ii** $90°$
     iii $126°$ **iv** $36°$

d

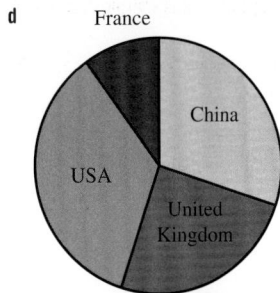

France, China, USA, United Kingdom

3 a

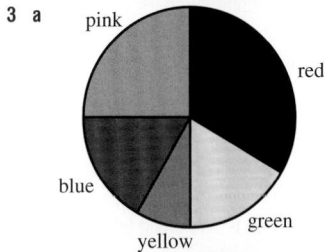

pink, red, blue, green, yellow

b

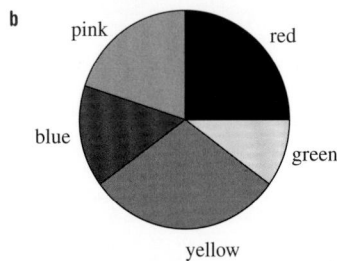

pink, red, blue, green, yellow

c Higher proportion of Year 7s like red; higher proportion of Year 8s likes yellow.

d

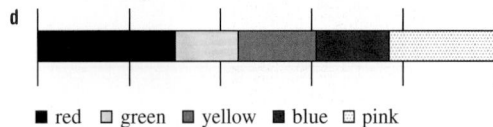

■ red　□ green　■ yellow　■ blue　□ pink

4 a i 20　　**ii** 10　　**iii** 6　　**iv** 4

b

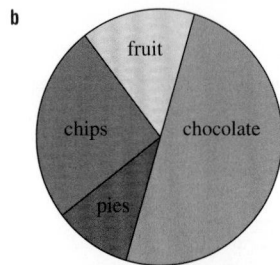

fruit, chips, chocolate, pies

c i Chips　　　　**ii** Fruits and pies
iii Chocolate

5 a i 9　　　**ii** 6　　　**iii** 15
b

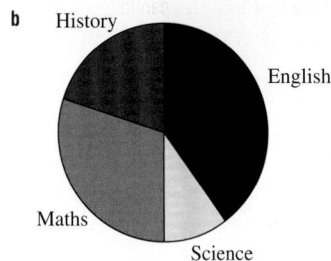

History, English, Maths, Science

6 a Krishna
b Nikolas
c It means Nikolas spends more time playing sport.
7 a 6
b 10
c Bird was chosen by $\frac{1}{8}$, which would be 2.5 people.

d Each portion is $\frac{1}{3}$, but $\frac{1}{3}$ of 40 is not a whole number.

e 24, 48, 72 or 96 people participated in each survey.

8 a $\frac{5}{12}$, 150°

b Because $\frac{1}{2} + \frac{1}{3} + \frac{1}{4} = 1\frac{1}{12}$, which is greater than 100%.

9 a

C　D　A　B

b 24
c 6

Progress quiz

1 a Categorical
b Continuous numerical
c Discrete numerical
d Continuous numerical
2 a i 10　　**ii** 6　　**iii** 5　　**iv** 3
b i 13　　**ii** 20　　**iii** 19　　**iv** 15
3 a 2 children　　**b** 17 families　　**c** 7
d 3 children　　**e** 8 children
4 a

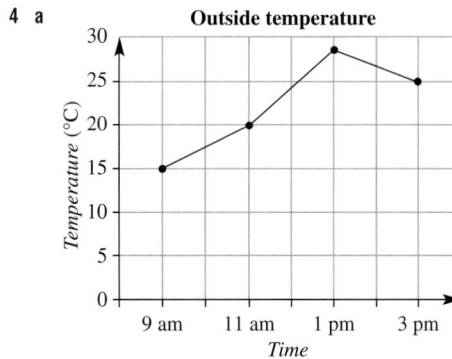

Outside temperature

b Around 24°C
5 a 20 km　　**b** 10 km　　**c** At rest
d 10 km　　**e** 5th hour
6 a 13 towns
b Maximum 37°C, minimum 14°C
c 23°C
d 25°C

7

Stem	Leaf
0	7　9
1	0　2　6　8　8　9
2	0　1

1|6 means 16

8 a

b
Methods of transport

8G

Building understanding

1 **a** D **b** A **c** B **d** C
2 **a** Certain **b** Even chance
  c Unlikely **d** Impossible

Now you try

Example 12
a False **b** True **c** True **d** False

Exercise 8G

1 **a** True **b** False **c** True **d** False
2 **a** True **b** False **c** True
  d False **e** True **f** False
3 **a** D **b** C **c** A **d** B
4 **a** **i** True **ii** False **iii** False
    iv True **v** True
  b **i** Spinner landing on yellow (other answers possible)
    ii Spinner not landing on red
    iii Spinner landing on green, blue or red
    iv Spinner landing on blue or on red
5 **a** Spinner 3 **b** Spinner 2 **c** Spinner 1
6 Answers may vary.
7 **a** Blue, red and green are equally likely.
  b Red and green both have an even chance.
  c Green and blue are equally likely; red and blue are not
    equally likely.
  d Blue is certain.
  e Blue, red and green are all possible, but no two colours are
    equally likely.
  f Red and blue both have an even chance.
8 **a** Choosing a red marble and choosing a blue marble
  b **i** Red, because there are still 4 red marbles (and only
      3 blue).

  ii Blue, because there are still 4 blue marbles (and only
    3 red).
  iii Red and blue are equally likely because there are still 4
    of each colour present.
9 **a**

  b All sectors have the same size; i.e. 60°.
  c

  d By replacing the 5 with a 6 (so that there are two faces
    with 6).
  e With 52 equal segments
10 **a** Spinner 1: $\frac{1}{4}$, spinner 2: $\frac{1}{3}$, spinner 3: $\frac{1}{9}$

  b $\frac{1}{2}$

  c **i**

  ii

Other answers possible

  d **i** 50% **ii** 0%
    iii 0%,50% **iv** 50%
  e If the two fractions are equal, the two events are equally
    likely.
  f The proportion of the spinner's area cannot exceed 100%
    (or 1) and must be greater than or equal to 0%.

8H

Building understanding

1 **a** C **b** A **c** D **d** B
2 **a** Sample space **b** Zero **c** Certain
  d More **e** Even chance

Now you try

Example 13
a {1, 2, 3, 4, 5} b {2, 4}

Example 14
a $\frac{1}{5}$ b 0.6 c 40%

Exercise 8H

1 a {1, 2, 3, 4, 5, 6} b {1, 2, 3, 4}
   c {red, green, blue} d {L, U, C, K}
2 a {1, 3, 5} b {1, 2, 3}
   c {1, 2, 3, 4, 5} d {1, 2, 4, 6}
3 a {T, R, A, C, E} b {A, E}
   c {T, R, C} d {T, A}
4 a {1, 2, 3, 4} b $\frac{1}{4}$
   c 0.5 d 75%
5 a 3: red, green, blue b $\frac{1}{3}$
   c $\frac{2}{3}$ d $\frac{2}{3}$
   e 0
6 a {1, 2, 3, 4, 5, 6, 7} b $\frac{1}{7}$
   c 0 d $\frac{2}{7}$
   e $\frac{3}{7}$ f $\frac{4}{7}$
   g Number chosen is less than 10; answers may vary.
7 a {M, A, T, H, S} b 0.2
   c 0.8 d 60%
8 a $\frac{1}{11}$ b $\frac{2}{11}$ c $\frac{5}{11}$ d $\frac{9}{11}$ e $\frac{4}{11}$
   f Choosing a letter in the word ROPE; answers may vary.
9 a 30% b 50% c 80%
10 a {2, 3, 4, 5, 6, 7, 8, 9}
   b 0.5
   c i 0.375 ii 0.375 iii 0
   d Possible spinner:

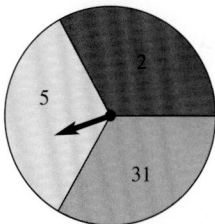

11 a i 12 red, 6 blue, 4 yellow, 2 green
      ii $\frac{1}{12}$
   b i 18 red, 9 blue, 6 yellow, 3 green
      ii $\frac{1}{12}$
   c 12
   d No, because it is always $1 - \frac{1}{2} - \frac{1}{4} - \frac{1}{6}$.
12 a Even = {2, 4, 6, 8} with probability $\frac{4}{9}$, odd = {1, 3, 5, 7, 9}
      with probability $\frac{5}{9}$
   b $\frac{1}{3}$, spinning a number greater than 6 (other answers possible)

c 1
d Spinning a number less than 7. Other answers are possible.
13 a $a = 1, b = \frac{1}{2}, c = 1, d = \frac{1}{3}, e = 1, f = \frac{2}{5}, g = \frac{3}{5}, h = 1$
   b $\frac{10}{13}$
   c $\frac{3}{7}$
14 a Yes, $\frac{19}{210}$ b 210 c 840
15 a i

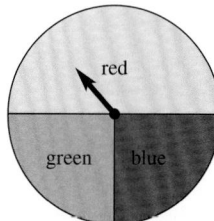

   ii Cannot be done because adds to more than 1.
   iii Cannot be done because adds to less than 1.
   iv

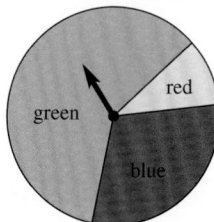

   b $1 - x - y$. Also x, y and $1 - x - y$ must all be between 0 and 1.

8I

Building understanding

1 a $\frac{1}{10}$ b $\frac{2}{5}$ c $\frac{3}{10}$
2 a $\frac{53}{100}$ b $\frac{47}{100}$ c $\frac{1}{2}$

Now you try

Example 15
a $\frac{1}{4}$ or 0.25 or 25% b $\frac{5}{8}$ or 0.625 or 62.5%
c 20

Exercise 8I

1 a $\frac{1}{4}$ or 0.25 or 25%
   b $\frac{2}{3}$
   c 100
2 a 50 b $\frac{2}{5}$
   c $\frac{1}{10}$ d $\frac{3}{5}$
   e No, just that nobody did it within the group surveyed.
3 a 500
   b 1750
   c i 7 tails ii More

4 a 100

b 300

c Yes (but this is very unlikely)

d From 2 throws

5 Answers may vary.

6 a $\frac{1}{4}$ **b** $\frac{3}{100}$ **c** $\frac{31}{100}$ **d** 60

7 a 5   **b** 40   **c** 70

d $\frac{26}{35}$ **e** $\frac{4}{7}$ **f** 126

8 a 2 red, 3 green and 5 blue

b i Yes   **ii** Yes   **iii** Yes

iv Yes   **v** No

9 a C   **b** D   **c** B   **d** A

10 a Answers may vary.

b Answers may vary.

c Answers may vary.

d Answers may vary.

e No technique for finding theoretical probability has been taught yet.

f Less accurate

g More accurate

11 a False; there is no guarantee it will occur exactly half of the time.

b False; e.g. in two rolls, a die might land 3 one time. The theoretical probability is not $\frac{1}{2}$, though.

c False; perhaps the event did not happen yet but it could.

d True; if it is theoretically impossible it cannot happen in an experiment.

e False; experiment might have been lucky.

f True; if it is certain, then it must happen in an experiment.

12 a Red: 25%, green: 42.2%, blue: 32.8%

b Fifth set is furthest from the final estimate.

c Have 4 green sectors, 3 blue and 3 red sectors

d Red: 90°, green: 150°, blue: 120°

Problems and challenges

1 2, 2, 5, 7, 8, 12

2 a 4   **b** 10   **c** 90   **d** 72

3

No. of cars	0	1	2	3
No. of students	4	6	8	2

4 PROBABLE (or PEBBLIER)

5 a 60°

b $192 - 3.6 = 188.4°$

c $\frac{1}{4}$ or 25%

d $\frac{99}{100}$ or 99%

e $\frac{1}{20}$ or 5%

6 A spinner with these sector angles has actual probabilities close to the experimental probabilities.

Sector colour	Red	Green	Purple	Yellow
Sector angle	120°	90°	60°	90°
Actual probability	$\frac{40}{120}$	$\frac{30}{120}$	$\frac{20}{120}$	$\frac{30}{120}$
Experimental probability	$\frac{40}{120}$	$\frac{32}{120}$	$\frac{19}{120}$	$\frac{29}{120}$

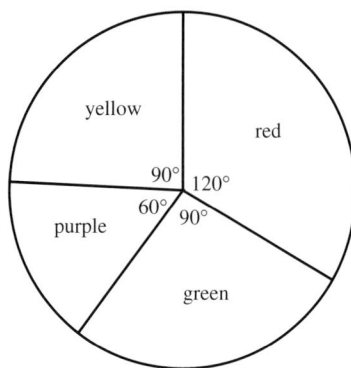

Chapter checklist with success criteria

1 Continuous numerical

2 Secondary source by looking at the census data

3 53

4 29

5 25

6 12

7 4 children have 2 pets; 8 pets is an outlier.

8

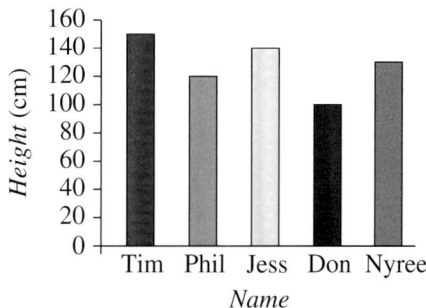

Height chart

9

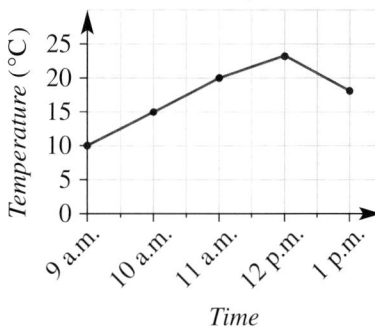

Room temperature

10 The cyclist travels 15 km in the first hour, is at rest during the second hour and travels 15 km between the second and fifth hour. The cyclist is travelling fastest during the first hour.

11 13, 16, 16, 20, 20, 21, 22, 25, 25, 26, 28, 29, 30, 32; median = 23.5(°C)

12

Stem	Leaf
1	0 6
2	3 5 7
3	1 3 4 4 6 6 7

2|5 means 25

13

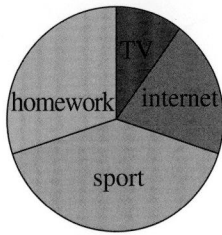

14

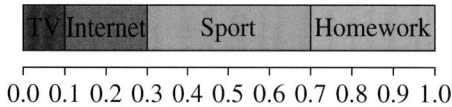

15 These events are not equally likely. It is more likely to flip heads on a coin than to roll a 3 on a 6-sided die.

16 Sample space {1, 2, 3, 4, 5, 6}; favourable outcomes {1, 3, 5}

17 33.3%

18 400

19 $\frac{3}{10}$ (or 0.3, or 30%)

Chapter review

Short-answer questions

1

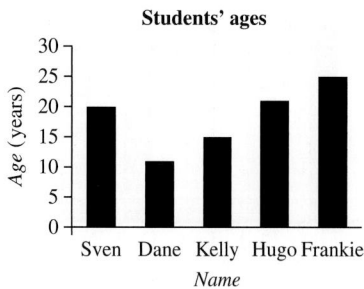

2 a 40 **b** 400 **c** 10 hours

d

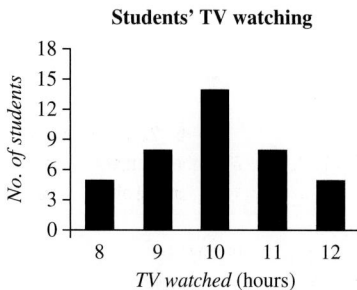

3 a 4 students **b** 2 students
c 1 pm **d** 6 students

4 a 105° **b** 25%

c

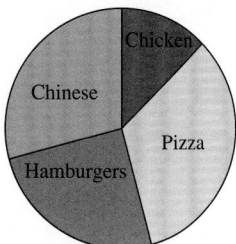

5 a 11 **b** 5 **c** 3.5 **d** 2
6 a 12 **b** 5 **c** 3.5 **d** 3
7 a 4 **b** $31 **c** $30 **d** $3

8 a 1 **b** $\frac{1}{8}$ **c** $\frac{19}{20}$ **d** $\frac{3}{4}$ **e** 0

9 a {1, 2, 3, 4, 5, 6} **b** {heads, tails}
c {D, E, S, I, G, N} **d** {blue, yellow, green}

10 a 9

b i $\frac{5}{9}$ **ii** $\frac{1}{3}$ **iii** 0

iv $\frac{1}{3}$ **v** $\frac{4}{9}$ **vi** $\frac{4}{9}$

11 a $\frac{1}{26}$ **b** $\frac{2}{13}$ **c** $\frac{1}{52}$ **d** $\frac{3}{13}$

12 a 42% **b** 50%

13 a $\frac{1}{2}$ **b** $\frac{1}{4}$ **c** 25 **d** 250

Multiple-choice questions

1 B **2** D **3** E **4** D **5** C
6 C **7** A **8** C **9** C **10** B

Extended-response questions

1 a

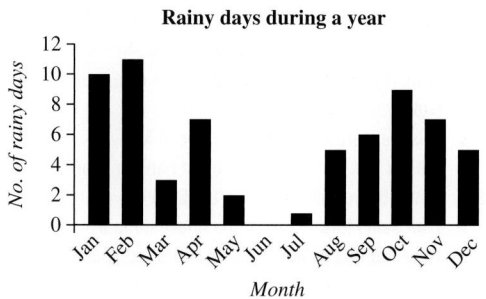

b 66

c $\frac{6}{92} = \frac{3}{46}$

d Discrete numerical
e Categorical
f Line graph

2 a 40
b Cheesecake
c $\frac{7}{40}$
d i Yes **ii** No **iii** Yes **iv** Yes
e 80

Chapter 9

9A

Building understanding

1 a True   **b** False   **c** False
2 True
3 a 19   **b** 19   **c** True

Now you try

Example 1
a N   **b** E   **c** E   **d** N   **e** E

Example 2
a False   **b** True   **c** True
d False   **e** True   **f** False

Example 3
a $3a = 21$ **b** $p + q = 10$

c $t - 3 = 24$ **d** $\frac{1}{2} \times a + \frac{1}{4} \times b = 150$

Exercise 9A

1 a Yes   **b** Yes   **c** No   **d** Yes   **e** No
2 a E   **b** N   **c** E   **d** E   **e** E
   f N   **g** E   **h** E   **i** N
3 a True   **b** False   **c** True   **d** True
   e False   **f** False   **g** True   **h** False
   i True   **j** True   **k** False   **l** True
4 a False   **b** True   **c** False   **d** True
5 a True   **b** True   **c** False   **d** True
6 a True   **b** False   **c** True   **d** True
   e True   **f** False   **g** False   **h** True
   i True
7 a $3 + x = 10$ **b** $5k = 1005$ **c** $a + b = 22$
   d $2d = 78$ **e** $8x = 56$ **f** $3p = 21$
   g $\frac{t}{4} = 12$ **h** $q + p = q \times p$
8 a $6c = 546$ **b** $5x = 37.5$
   c $12a + 3b = 28$ **d** $f + 10 = 27$
   e $j + 10 + m + 10 = 80$
9 $m = 3$
10 $k = 2, k = 6$
11 $x = 1$ and $y = 5$, $x = 2$ and $y = 4$, $x = 3$ and $y = 3$, $x = 4$ and $y = 2$, $x = 5$ and $y = 1$
12 Because it does not make a difference what order you add, so the value of $a + 3$ will always equal the value of $3 + a$.
13 Because for any value of b, the two sides will differ by 10 (and therefore never be equal.)
14 a S   **b** S   **c** A   **d** A
   e N   **f** N   **g** A   **h** S
   i A   **j** S   **k** N   **l** N
15 a $6 = 2 \times 3$; answers may vary.
   b $5 - 4 = 1$; answers may vary.
   c $10 \div 2 = 7 - 2$; answers may vary.
   d $4 - 2 = 10 \div 5$; answers may vary.

16 a 12
   b 4, (e.g. $2 + 3 = 5$, $3 + 2 = 5$, $5 = 2 + 3$, $5 = 3 + 2$)
   c Yes; if 5 is changed to 1, then $1 + 2 = 3$ is a true equation.
   d Yes; if $+$ is changed to $-$, then $5 - 3 = 2$ is a true equation.

9B

Building understanding

1 a True   **b** False   **c** True   **d** False
2 a 12   **b** 17   **c** 13   **d** 6
3 a x **b** c **c** b **d** d

Now you try

Example 4
a 21   **b** 15

Example 5
a $q = 18$ **b** $x = 8$ **c** $a = 10$

Exercise 9B

1 a 6   **b** 50   **c** 8   **d** 17
2 a 3   **b** 6   **c** 10   **d** 4
   e 6   **f** 70   **g** 20   **h** 19
3 a $y = 8$ **b** $l = 2$ **c** $l = 6$ **d** $d = 2$
   e $l = 12$ **f** $a = 6$ **g** $s = 12$ **h** $x = 8$
   i $e = 8$ **j** $r = 10$ **k** $s = 8$ **l** $z = 3$
4 a $p = 3$ **b** $p = 4$ **c** $q = 3$ **d** $v = 5$
   e $b = 1$ **f** $u = 4$ **g** $g = 3$ **h** $e = 3$
   i $d = 4$ **j** $d = 6$ **k** $m = 4$ **l** $o = 3$
5 a $x = 3$ **b** $x = 7$ **c** $x = 5$
   d $x = 4$ **e** $x = 1$ **f** $x = 5$
6 a 11   **b** 12   **c** 16
   d 33   **e** 30   **f** 2
7 a B   **b** $x = 13$
   c 13 years old
8 a $10x = 180$ **b** $x = 18$
9 a $2w = 70$ **b** $w = 35$
10 a $4.5x = 13.5$ **b** $x = 3$
11 a $y + 12 = 3y$ **b** $y = 6$
12 a $x = 9$ **b** $2x + 1 = 181$ so $x = 90$
13 a $x = 14$, so 14, 15 and 16 are the numbers.
   b LHS is $3x + 3$ or $3(x + 1)$, which will always be a multiple of 3.
14 a $x = 2$ and $y = 6$; answers may vary.
   b $x = 12$ and $y = 10$; answers may vary.
   c $x = 1$ and $y = 1$; answers may vary.
   d $x = 12$ and $y = 0.5$; answers may vary.
   e $x = 10$ and $y = 0$; answers may vary.
   f $x = 2$ and $y = 2$; answers may vary.

9C

Building understanding

1 a $10d + 15 = 30$ **b** $7e + 10 = 41$
   c $2a + 10 = 22$ **d** $x + 10 = 22$
2 a C   **b** D   **c** E   **d** B   **e** A

Now you try

Example 6

a $q + 16 = 19$ **b** $21k = 30$
c $3 = 5b$ **d** $1 + 3b = 2a$

Example 7

a 4 is added to both sides
b Both sides are doubled
c 9 is subtracted from both sides

Exercise 9C

1 a $6 + x = 10$ **b** $12x = 21$
   c $3 = b$ **d** $5q = 4$

2 a $6 + x = 11$ **b** $6x = 14$ **c** $3 = 2q$
   d $6 + a = 10$ **e** $12 + b = 15$ **f** $0 = 3b + 2$
   g $4 = 7 + a$ **h** $12x + 2 = 8$ **i** $7p = 12$

3 a Subtracting 2   **b** Adding 2
   c Dividing by 10   **d** Multiplying by 2
   e Dividing by 3   **f** Adding 3
   g Dividing by 4   **h** Adding 4

4 a $3(x + 4) = 27$ **b** $18 = 3(a + 5)$
   c $3d = 18$ **d** $3(11 + a) = 36$
   e $3(3y + 2) = 33$ **f** $3(2x + 4) = 30$

5 a E (+2)   **b** A (+4)   **c** D (÷2)
   d B (−2)   **e** C (× 2)

6 a × 3 then +2   **b** × 10 then −3
   c ÷5 then −2   **d** −10 then ÷3

7 a $2q = 2$ **b** $10x = 7$
   c $3 + x = 20$ **d** $x = 60$

8 a

b

c

9 a i $0 = 0$ **ii** $0 = 0$ **iii** $0 = 0$
   b Regardless of original equation, will always result in $0 = 0$.

10 a

b

11 a True; you can +3 to both sides and then −3 to get the
original equation again.
   b True; simply perform the opposite operations in the reverse
order, so +4 becomes −4.
   c True; use the operations that take equation 1 to equation 2
and then the operations that take equation 2 to equation 3.
   d False; e.g. equation 1: $x = 4$, equation 2: $x = 5$, equation 3:
$2x = 8$.

9D

Building understanding

1 a True   **b** False   **c** True   **d** False   **e** False
2 a 6   **b** $x = 6$
3 $g = 2$
4 a −5   **b** ÷10   **c** × 4   **d** +12

Now you try

Example 8

a $a = 3$ **b** $x = 4$ **c** $y = 28$

Example 9

a $x = 2$ **b** $m = 20$ **c** $p = 8$

Exercise 9D

1 a i $x = 5$ **ii** $x = 8$
   b i $y = 7$ **ii** $y = 64$
   c i $q = 40$ **ii** $q = 21$

2 a $m = 9$ **b** $g = 11$ **c** $s = 9$ **d** $i = 10$
   e $t = 2$ **f** $q = 3$ **g** $y = 12$ **h** $s = 12$
   i $j = 4$ **j** $l = 4$ **k** $v = 2$ **l** $y = 12$
   m $k = 5$ **n** $y = 9$ **o** $z = 7$ **p** $t = 10$
   q $b = 12$ **r** $p = 11$ **s** $a = 8$ **t** $n = 3$

3 a

b

c

d

4 a Subtract 3   **b** Add 7
c Divide by 5   **d** Divide by 2

5 a $f = 11$ **b** $k = 4$ **c** $x = 9$ **d** $a = 9$
e $k = 8$ **f** $a = 6$ **g** $n = 11$ **h** $n = 8$
i $g = 4$ **j** $q = 11$ **k** $z = 10$ **l** $p = 1$
m $d = 4$ **n** $t = 8$ **o** $u = 5$ **p** $c = 1$
q $q = 11$ **r** $y = 12$ **s** $q = 2$ **t** $u = 10$

6 a $x = \dfrac{3}{4}$ **b** $k = \dfrac{24}{5}$ **c** $w = \dfrac{4}{3}$

d $x = \dfrac{4}{3}$ **e** $x = \dfrac{5}{8}$ **f** $x = \dfrac{1}{3}$

7 a $r = -7$ **b** $x = -3$ **c** $t = -16$
d $y = -24$ **e** $x = -5$ **f** $k = -9$
g $x = -6$ **h** $x = -4$ **i** $x = -\dfrac{3}{2}$

8 a $x + 5 = 12 \rightarrow x = 7$ **b** $2y = 10 \rightarrow y = 5$
c $2b + 6 = 44 \rightarrow b = 19$ **d** $3(k - 7) = 18 \rightarrow k = 13$
e $\dfrac{b}{4} + 3 = 6 \rightarrow b = 12$ **f** $\dfrac{k}{2} - 10 = 1 \rightarrow k = 22$

9 a $12n + 50 = 410$ **b** $n = 30 h$

10 a $12 + 5x$ **b** $12 + 5x = 14.5$
c $x = 0.5$, so pens cost 50 cents.

11 a $3w = 15 \rightarrow w = 5$ **b** $4x = 12 \rightarrow x = 3$
c $2(10 + x) = 28 \rightarrow x = 4$ **d** $4w = 28 \rightarrow w = 7$

12 a $x = 6$ **b** $x = 8$ **c** $x = 5$

13 Examples include:
$x + 1 = 3, 7x = 14, 21 - x = 19, \dfrac{4}{x} = x, \dfrac{x}{2} = 1.$

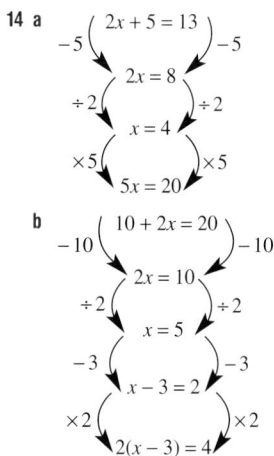

14 a

$$-5 \Big(\begin{matrix} 2x + 5 = 13 \\ 2x = 8 \end{matrix} \Big) -5$$
$$\div 2 \Big(\begin{matrix} 2x = 8 \\ x = 4 \end{matrix} \Big) \div 2$$
$$\times 5 \Big(\begin{matrix} x = 4 \\ 5x = 20 \end{matrix} \Big) \times 5$$

b

$$-10 \Big(\begin{matrix} 10 + 2x = 20 \\ 2x = 10 \end{matrix} \Big) -10$$
$$\div 2 \Big(\begin{matrix} 2x = 10 \\ x = 5 \end{matrix} \Big) \div 2$$
$$-3 \Big(\begin{matrix} x = 5 \\ x - 3 = 2 \end{matrix} \Big) -3$$
$$\times 2 \Big(\begin{matrix} x - 3 = 2 \\ 2(x - 3) = 4 \end{matrix} \Big) \times 2$$

c Yes
d Yes

15 a First step, should have subtracted 2 first.
b Second step, LHS divided by 3, RHS has 3 subtracted.
c First step, RHS has 5 added not subtracted.
d First step, LHS has $11a$ subtracted, not 12.

16 a $x = 4$ **b** $x = 1$ **c** $l = 3$ **d** $t = 1$
e $s = 5$ **f** $b = 19$ **g** $j = 2$ **h** $d = 1$

Progress quiz

1 a E   **b** N   **c** E   **d** N
2 a T   **b** F   **c** T   **d** F
3 a $5 + m = 12$ **b** $2d = 24$
c $9x = 72$ **d** $3c + 4b = 190$

4 a $a = 9$ **b** $x = 4$ **c** $m = 30$ **d** $a = 2$
5 a $20x = 35$ **b** $2a = 16$
6 a $+ 8$ **b** $\div 6$ **c** $\times 2$
7 a $a = 12$ **b** $w = 31$ **c** $k = 63$ **d** $m = 8$
8 a $x = 11$ **b** $a = 7$ **c** $m = 6$ **d** $y = 8$
9 a $x = 5$ **b** $k = 12$ **c** $y = 4$

9E

Building understanding

1 a True   **b** False   **c** True
d False   **e** True   **f** False
2 a 7   **b** 9   **c** False
3 a $b = 44$ **b** $d = 15$
c $\times 4, h = 28$ **d** $\times 13, p = 26$
4 a B   **b** C   **c** A   **d** D

Now you try

Example 10
a $p = 50$ **b** $m = 10$ **c** $u = 5$ **d** $x = 9$

Exercise 9E

1 a $a = 8$ **b** $a = 30$
c $x = 35$ **d** $x = 200$
2 a $m = 12$ **b** $c = 18$ **c** $s = 16$ **d** $r = 10$
e $u = 20$ **f** $y = 18$ **g** $x = 4$ **h** $a = 16$
i $h = 10$ **j** $j = 15$ **k** $v = 9$ **l** $q = 8$
3 a $h = 9$ **b** $y = 6$ **c** $j = 3$ **d** $b = 4$
e $u = 3$ **f** $t = 9$ **g** $w = 6$ **h** $r = 4$
i $q = 9$ **j** $s = 3$ **k** $l = 8$ **l** $z = 7$
m $v = 11$ **n** $f = 9$ **o** $x = 2$ **p** $d = 5$
q $n = 5$ **r** $m = 11$ **s** $p = 8$ **t** $a = 9$
4 a $y = -1$ **b** $a = -10$ **c** $x = -10$ **d** $x = -48$
e $u = -30$ **f** $y = -10$ **g** $u = -4$ **h** $d = -5$
5 a $\dfrac{t}{2} = 9 \rightarrow t = 18$ **b** $\dfrac{q}{3} = 14 \rightarrow q = 42$

c $\dfrac{2r}{5} = 6 \rightarrow r = 15$ **d** $\dfrac{q - 4}{2} = 3 \rightarrow q = 10$

e $\dfrac{x + 3}{4} = 2 \rightarrow x = 5$ **f** $\dfrac{y}{4} + 3 = 5 \rightarrow y = 8$

6 a $\dfrac{b}{5} = 31.50$ **b** $b = 157.5$ **c** \$157.50

7 a $\dfrac{x}{2} + 5$

b $\dfrac{x}{2} + 5 = 11 \rightarrow x = \$12$

c \$6

8 a The different order in which 3 is added and the result is multiplied by 5.
b Multiply by 5
c Subtract 3
d No, the difference between them is always 2.4 for any value of x.

9 a $4x = 2$ (other solutions possible)
b $7x = 5$
c Yes, e.g. $2x + 1 = 0$

10 a i Multiply by 2   **ii** Divide by $\frac{1}{2}$

  b $x = 26$ for both of them.

  c Makes the first step a division (by a fraction) rather than multiplication.

11 a $x = \frac{7}{2}$ **b** $x = \frac{17}{6}$ **c** $x = \frac{19}{6}$ **d** $x = \frac{7}{6}$

12 Answers will vary. Substitute $x = 12$ into your equation to ensure it is a valid solution.

9F

Building understanding

1 C

2 a 6   **b** 4   **c** 2   **d** 12

3 a True   **b** False   **c** True

  d True   **e** False   **f** False

Now you try

Example 11

a $3x + 21$ **b** $8m - 48$ **c** $40y + 35$

Example 12

a $6a + 7$ **b** $9a - 3$

Example 13

a $m = 2$ **b** $x = 2$ **c** $q = 4$

Exercise 9F

1 a i $3x + 6$ **ii** $5x + 35$

  b i $5q - 10$ **ii** $11q - 44$

  c i $6a + 21$ **ii** $24a - 6$

2 a $2x + 2$ **b** $10b + 15$ **c** $6a - 8$

  d $35a + 5$ **e** $12x + 16$ **f** $24 - 9y$

  g $48a + 36$ **h** $2u - 8$

3 a $4a + 2$ **b** $5 + 3x$ **c** $3b - 4$ **d** $3a + 12$

  e $6x + 3$ **f** $k + 6$ **g** $2b + 6$ **h** $5k + 1$

4 a $s = 6$ **b** $l = 1$ **c** $p = 9$ **d** $y = 0$

  e $q = 1$ **f** $p = 12$ **g** $m = 5$ **h** $b = 6$

  i $p = 3$ **j** $p = 7$ **k** $y = 9$ **l** $r = 8$

5 a $d = 3$ **b** $x = 2$ **c** $x = 5$ **d** $e = 1$

  e $a = 1$ **f** $r = 3$ **g** $u = 1$ **h** $q = 11$

6 a $s = 1$ **b** $i = 1$ **c** $c = 5$

  d $v = 8$ **e** $k = 1$ **f** $q = 3$

  g $y = 4$ **h** $f = 3$ **i** $t = 2$

7 a $u = -5$ **b** $k = -3$ **c** $p = -1$

  d $q = -2$ **e** $u = -1$ **f** $x = -3$

  g $p = -4$ **h** $r = -10$ **i** $x = -5$

8 a i $2(5 + x) = 14$ **ii** $x = 2$

  b i $3(q - 3) = 30$ **ii** $q = 13$

  c i $2(2x + 3) = 46$ **ii** $x = 10$

  d i $2(y + 4) - y = 17$ **ii** $y = 9$

9 a $x = 1$ **b** $x = -1$ **c** $x = 5$

10 a LHS simplifies to 10, but $10 = 7$ is never true.

  b LHS simplifies to 15, not 4.

  c LHS simplifies to 6, not 12.

11 a LHS = 9, RHS = 9, therefore true.

  b LHS = 9, RHS = 9, therefore true.

  c LHS simplifies to 9.

  d For example $2(x + 5) - 3 - 2x = 7$. (Answers may vary.)

12 a $s = 6$ **b** $l = 1$ **c** $p = 9$ **d** $y = 0$

  e $q = 1$ **f** $p = 12$ **g** $m = 5$ **h** $b = 6$

  i $p = 3$ **j** $p = 7$ **k** $y = 9$ **l** $r = 8$

13 a $j = 2$ **b** $a = 1$ **c** $a = 3$

  d $a = 8$ **e** $c = 4$ **f** $d = 8$

  g $x = 1$ **h** $x = 3$ **i** $x = 0$

  j $x = 3$

9G

Building understanding

1 a N   **b** R   **c** R

  d N   **e** R   **f** R

2 a 15   **b** 36   **c** 8   **d** 2

Now you try

Example 14

a $B = 17$ **b** $B = 67$ **c** $A = 9$

Example 15

a $F = 65$ **b** $m = 10$

Exercise 9G

1 a i $k = 13$ **ii** $k = 38$

  b i $b = 4$ **ii** $b = 11$

2 a $h = 7$ **b** $h = 9$ **c** $m = 8$ **d** $m = 10$

3 a $y = 23$ **b** $x = 4$ **c** $x = 7$

4 a $A = 7$ **b** $q = 4$ **c** $t = 0$

5 a $G = 27$ **b** $x = 1$ **c** $y = 5$

6 a $20 = w \times 5, w = 4$

  b i $25 = 5l, l = 5$ **ii** Square

7 a $P = 16$ **b** $l = 3$

  c 25 units squared

8 a $d = 3$ **b** 3g/cm^3

  c $10 = \frac{m}{5}$

    $m = 50$ grams

9 a $F = 68$ **b** $C = 10$ **c** $12°C$ **d** $15°C$

10 a $H = 210, H = 200.2$

  b $H = 120, H = 139.9$

  c The formulas give 180 and 180.1 respectively, which are close.

  d 30 years old

  e 25 years old

11 a $d = \frac{S - 3b}{5}$ **b** $C = \frac{5(F - 32)}{9}$

  c $x = \frac{Q - 36}{4}$

12 a Check by substituting values back into equation.

  b If $D = 20$, C should equal 60 not 50, as in row 2.

  c Check by substituting values back into equation.

  d For example, $C = 2t - 10$, $C = \frac{Dt}{20} + 20$. (Answers may vary.)

13 a Abbotsford Apes

  b 8 goals

  c $S = 9q + 6g + b$

  d 0 goals and 0 behinds, 2 goals and 12 behinds, 3 goals and 9 behinds, 7 goals and 7 behinds.

9H

Building understanding

1 a A   b C   c C

Now you try

Example 16
4 days

Exercise 9H

1 21 years
2 a Let c = car's cost   b $c + 2000 = 40\,000$
   c $c = 38\,000$ d \$38\,000
3 a Let p = cost of one pen   b $12p = 15.6$
   c $p = 1.3$ d \$1.30
4 a Let h = number of hours worked
   b $17h + 65 = 643$ c $h = 34$ d 34 hours
5 a $24w = 720$ b $w = 30$
   c 30 m   d 108 m
6 $2(2x + 3) = 34 \rightarrow x = 7$
7 $x = 4$
8 1.5 h
9 14 years old
10 $2x + 154 = 180 \rightarrow x = 13$
11 $3y = 90 \rightarrow y = 30$
12 Examples include: $h = 3$, $w = 6$ or $h = 12$, $w = 2.4$.
    (Answers may vary.)
13 $x = 3.5$, $y = 2$
14 a Solution is $c = -2$ but you cannot have a negative number
       of chairs.
    b Solution of $c = -2$ means the temperature is $-2°C$, which
       is possible although unpleasant.
15 a Possible ($p = 12$)
    b Not possible because solution is not a whole number.
    c Possible ($p = 8$)
16 $a + 2b = 180$, so $a = 180 - 2b = 2(90 - b)$ is always even.
17 a i $x = 60$
       ii One angle is $-10°$, which is impossible.
    b i $60 - x + 70 + x + 50$ is always 180, regardless of the
           value of x.
       ii Any value less than 60 and greater than -70.
    c Answers may vary.

Problems and challenges

1 a 26   b 29   c 368   d $31\frac{1}{3}$ e 36
2 27 cm
3 $x = 7$, $y = 9$, $P = 72$ cm
4 1458 m^2
5 $a = 5$, $b = 2$, $c = 12$
6 a $a = 22.5$, $b = 37.5$ b $a = 10$, $b = 23$
7 26 goats, 15 chickens
8 $x = 45$; 132, 133, 134, 135, 136

Chapter checklist with success criteria

1 $7 + 7 = 18$ and $4 = 12 - x$ are both equations.
2 It is false because the LHS is 14 and the RHS is 13.
3 $x + 5 = 22$
4 $b = 4$
5 $7q = 14$

6 Both sides have been multiplied by 2.

$$\times 2 \left(\begin{array}{c} 5 = 7 - x \\ 10 = 2(7 - x) \end{array} \right) \times 2$$

7 $x = 6$
8 $a = 4$
9 Yes, the solution is $e = 5$ because $2(5 + 1)$ equals 12.
10 $x = 8$
11 $15a + 20$
12 $9a + 7$
13 $b = 2$
14 $k = 32$
15 $b = 7$
16 $k + k + 1 = 19$; Kate is currently 9 years old

Chapter review

Short-answer questions

1 a False   b True   c True
   d False   e True   f False
2 a $2 + u = 22$ b $5k = 41$
   c $3z = 36$ d $a + b = 15$
3 a $x = 3$ b $x = 6$ c $y = 1$
   d $y = 9$ e $a = 2$ f $a = 10$
4 a $2x = 8$ b $7a = 28$ c $15 = 3r$ d $16 = 8p$
5 a $x = 3$ b $r = 45$ c $p = 9$ d $b = 6$
   e $x = 9$ f $r = 4$ g $q = 2$ h $u = 8$
6 a $u = 8$ b $p = 3$ c $x = 4$
   d $y = 8$ e $y = 4$ f $x = 15$
7 a $6 + 4p$ b $12x + 48$
   c $7a + 35$ d $18x + 9$
8 a $x = 8$ b $x = 8$ c $x = 7$
   d $y = 10$ e $z = 5$ f $q = 3$
9 a No
   b Solution is $x = \frac{7}{11}$, which is not whole.
10 a No; LHS simplifies to 10.
    b i   Is a solution.   ii Is a solution.
11 a Area = 450 cm^2 b Height = 10 cm
12 a 36   b 6   c 3
13 a 5   b 6   c 20   d 6 cm
14 a $y = 35$ b $y = 30$

Multiple-choice questions

1 C   2 A   3 D   4 B   5 E
6 C   7 A   8 A   9 B   10 E

Extended-response questions

1 a 75 cents   b $C = 15 + 2t$
   c \$1.75   d 12 seconds
   e 81 seconds
   f 2.5 min in total (50 seconds for the first call, then
      100 seconds)
2 a \$500
   b 30 hours at \$$x$/hour, and 10 hours at \$$(x + 2)$/hour.
   c \$660
   d $x = 15$
   e $x = 21$, so Gemma earned \$630 from Monday to Friday.

Chapter 10

10A

Building understanding

1 a 10   **b** 100   **c** 1000
  d 1000   **e** 100 000   **f** 1 000 000
2 a 100   **b** 1000
  c divide   **d** multiply
3 a 1000   **b** 1000
  c 100 000   **d** 1 000 000
4 a Right   **b** Left

Now you try

Example 1
a Kilometres (km)   **b** Centimetres (cm)

Example 2
a 2000 m   **b** 3.4 m

Example 3
a 32 mm   **b** 240 cm

Exercise 10A

1 a Kilometres   **b** Millimetres   **c** Metres
  d Metres   **e** Centimetres   **f** Kilometres
2 a Metres   **b** Millimetres   **c** Kilometres
  d Kilometres   **e** Centimetres   **f** Centimetres
3 a 400 cm   **b** 6000 m
  c 3 cm   **d** 7 m
4 a 50 mm   **b** 200 cm   **c** 3500 m
  d 2610 cm   **e** 4 cm   **f** 5 m
  g 4.2 km   **h** 47.2 cm   **i** 684 cm
  j 20 m   **k** 926.1 cm   **l** 4.23 km
5 a 2.5 cm   **b** 82 mm   **c** 2.5 m
  d 730 cm   **e** 6200 m   **f** 25.732 km
6 a 3000 mm   **b** 600 000 cm   **c** 2400 mm
  d 4000 cm   **e** 0.47 km   **f** 913 m
  g 0.216 km   **h** 0.0005 m   **i** 700 000 mm
7 a i 2 cm   **ii** 20 mm
  b i 5 cm   **ii** 50 mm
  c i 1.5 cm   **ii** 15 mm
  d i 3.2 cm   **ii** 32 mm
  e i 3 cm   **ii** 30 mm
  f i 3 cm   **ii** 30 mm
  g i 1.2 cm   **ii** 12 mm
  h i 2.8 cm   **ii** 28 mm
8 a 2.7 m   **b** 0.4 km
9 a 8.5 km   **b** 310 cm   **c** 19 cm
10 a 38 cm, 0.5 m, 540 mm
   b 160 cm, 2100 mm, 0.02 km, 25 m
   c 142 mm, 20 cm, 0.003 km, 3.1 m
   d 10 mm, 0.1 m, 0.001 km, 1000 cm
11 125 cm
12 Bigan tower

13 a $8200   **b** $6.56   **c** 41 c
14 625 years
15 50 000 years
16 0.08 mm
17 2500 s
18

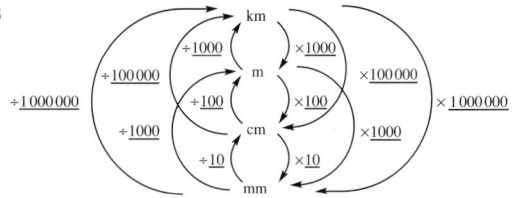

19 So that only one unit is used, and mm deliver a high degree of accuracy.
20 a i 1 million   **ii** 10 000   **iii** 1000
      iv 1 billion (1 000 000 000)
   b 0.312 μm
   c The distance you travel in 1 year at the speed of light

10B

Building understanding

1 a 10 cm   **b** 12 cm
2 a 6.3 cm   **b** 12 cm
  c 5.2 cm   **d** 6.4 cm

Now you try

Example 4
a 21 cm   **b** 36 m

Exercise 10B

1 a 16 cm   **b** 25 m
2 a 15 cm   **b** 37 m   **c** 30 km
  d 2.4 m   **e** 26 cm   **f** 10 cm
3 a 20 m   **b** 22 cm
4 a 42 cm   **b** 34 m   **c** 36 km   **d** 18 mm
5 a 8.4 cm   **b** 14 m   **c** 46.5 mm
6 $21 400
7 a 516 ft   **b** 157.38 m
8 a 70 mm   **b** 72 cm
9 a 40.7 cm   **b** 130.2 cm   **c** 294 cm
10 400 m
11 a 5 cm   **b** 5 m   **c** 7 km
12 4, including a square
13 a $P = a + 2b$ **b** $P = 4a$
   c $P = 2a + 2b$ **d** $P = 4a$
   e $P = 2a + 2b$ **f** $P = 2a + b + c$
14 a $P = 2a + 2b + 2c$ or $2(a + b + c)$
   b $P = 2a + 2b + 2c$ or $2(a + b + c)$
15 a $\dfrac{P}{4}$ **b** $\dfrac{(P - 2a)}{2}$
16 a 160 cm   **b** 216 cm
   c 40 cm   **d** $4a + 32$ or $4(a + 8)$

10C

Building understanding

1 a False   b True   c False
   d True   e False   f True
2 a Diameter   b Radius
   c Circumference   d Segment
   e Chord   f Sector
   g Tangent
3 a 30 mm   b 4 cm

Now you try

Example 5
a i 3.13   ii 3.125
b 3.14 is closer

Example 6
a 34.56 mm   b 29.53 cm

Exercise 10C

1 a i 3.11   ii 3.111
   b 3.14 is closer
2 a i 3.142   ii 3.1416
   b $\frac{355}{113}$ is closer
3 a 15.71 cm   b 40.84 cm
   c 14.45 m   d 30.79 m
4 a 25.13 mm   b 131.95 cm
   c 52.15 mm   d 101.79 m
5 a 12 cm   b 31.4 mm
   c 44 m   d 355 cm
6 125.7 cm
7 a 3.18 cm   b 3.98 m
   c 1.11 mm   d 5.95 m
8 8.8 m
9 2734 m
10 a $\frac{22}{7}$
   b It is a relatively simple fraction and also quite accurate.
   c Answers will vary.
11 $r = \frac{C}{2\pi}$, 3.98 cm
12 a 7π cm   b 6π mm
13 a 40 055 km   b 21 300 km
   c 139 821 km   d 4880 km

10D

Building understanding

1 a $\frac{1}{4}$ quadrant   b $\frac{1}{2}$ semicircle
2 a $\frac{1}{2}$ b $\frac{1}{4}$ c $\frac{1}{6}$
   d $\frac{1}{3}$ e $\frac{3}{4}$ f $\frac{7}{8}$
3 a square, semicircle   b quadrant, rectangle
   c sector, triangle

Now you try

Example 7
a 9.77 m   b 35.43 cm

Example 8
a 32.1 mm   b 4.1 cm

Example 9
13.7 cm

Exercise 10D

1 a 8.38 cm   b 5.59 m   c 12.22 mm
   d 1.96 m   e 136.14 cm   f 1.15 km
2 a 14.3 cm   b 35.7 m
   c 28.6 cm   d 9.3 m
3 a 51.4 mm   b 36.0 km
   c 43.7 mm   d 12.1 m
4 a 13.1 m   b 14.0 cm
   c 40.3 cm   d 44.5 m
5 a 18.7 m   b 11.1 cm   c 101.1 cm
   d 35.4 km   e 67.1 mm   f 45.1 cm
6 657 cm
7 a 26.88 m   b 52.36 m   c 6.24 m
8 a 25.13 cm   b 56.55 m   c 35.71 m
9 The four arcs make one full circle ($2\pi r$) and the four radii make $4r$.
10 The perimeter includes one large semicircle $\left(\frac{1}{2} \times 2\pi r = \pi r\right)$ and the two smaller semicircles. Which make one full smaller circle ($\pi \times r$). So the total is $2\pi r$.
11 a 7.6 m   b 34.4 m   c 9.5 km
12 a $24 + 3\pi$ cm   b $9 + 2.5\pi$ cm
13 a 8π cm   b 18π m   c $5\pi + 20$ cm

10E

Building understanding

1 a 8   b 4 cm and 2 cm
   c 8 cm^2
2 a 9   b 3 cm and 3 cm
   c 9 cm^2
3 a 5 square units   b 8 square units
   c 96 square units
4 a cm^2 b m^2 c ha
   d km^2 e ha   f mm^2

Now you try

Example 10
12 cm^2

Example 11
a 24 cm^2 b 2.25 km^2

Exercise 10E

1 a 6 cm^2 b 3 cm^2
2 a 2 cm^2 b 5 cm^2 c 4.5 cm^2 d 9 cm^2
3 a 200 cm^2 b 22 mm^2 c 7 cm^2
   d 25 m^2 e 1.44 mm^2 f 6.25 mm^2
   g 1.36 m^2 h 0.81 cm^2 i 179.52 km^2

4 a 2 cm   b 5 m   c 12 km

5 a 2 ha   b 10 ha   c 0.5 ha

6 $5000 \, m^2$

7 $2500 \, cm^2$

8 $20\,000 \, cm^2$

9 a $25 \, cm^2$ b 12 cm   c 4 units

10 $2100

11 5 L

12 8 ha

13 a i 10 cm   ii 9 mm

     b Divide the area by the given length.

14 Half of a rectangle with area $4 \, cm^2$

15 a $121 \, cm^2$ b $\left(\dfrac{P}{4}\right)^2$

16 Area is quadrupled ($\times 4$).

17 a i 100   ii 10 000   iii 1 000 000

     b $\times 1\,000\,000$ $\times 10\,000$ $\times 100$

$$km^2 \quad m^2 \quad cm^2 \quad mm^2$$

         $\div 1\,000\,000$ $\div 10\,000$ $\div 100$

     c i $200 \, mm^2$ ii $100\,000 \, cm^2$

        iii $3\,500\,000 \, m^2$ iv $3 \, cm^2$

        v $2.16 \, m^2$ vi $4.2 \, km^2$

        vii $5000 \, mm^2$ viii 100 ha

        ix 0.4 ha

10F

Building understanding

1 a $A = bh$ b $A = bh$ c $A = bh$

       $= 5 \times 7$ $= 20 \times 3$ $= 8 \times 2.5$

       $= 35$ $= 60$ $= 20$

2 a $b = 6 \, cm, h = 2 \, cm$ b $b = 10 \, m, h = 4 \, m$

     c $b = 5 \, m, h = 7 \, m$ d $b = 5.8 \, cm, h = 6.1 \, cm$

     e $b = 5 \, cm, h = 1.5 \, cm$ f $b = 1.8 \, m, h = 0.9 \, m$

Now you try

Example 12

a $15 \, m^2$ b $18 \, cm^2$

Exercise 10F

1 a $10 \, m^2$ b $80 \, cm^2$

2 a $40 \, m^2$ b $28 \, m^2$ c $36 \, km^2$ d $17.5 \, m^2$

3 a $28 \, cm^2$ b $108 \, mm^2$

4 a $40 \, cm^2$ b $6.3 \, cm^2$

     c $30 \, m^2$ d $1.8 \, cm^2$

5 a $6 \, cm^2$ b $4 \, cm^2$ c $15 \, cm^2$ d $8 \, cm^2$

6 $54 \, m^2$

7 a 2 m   b 7 cm   c 0.5 mm

8 a 10 cm   b 5 m   c 2 km

9 $1200

10 a $1800 \, cm^2$ b $4200 \, cm^2$

11 Because height must be less than 5 cm.

12 Half; area (parallelogram) $= bh$ and area (triangle) $= \dfrac{1}{2} bh$

13 Area $=$ twice triangle area

           $= 2 \times \dfrac{1}{2} bh$

           $= bh$

14 $4 500 000

10G

Building understanding

1 a 20 cm   b 7 m   c 2 m   d 6.3 cm

2 a 6 m   b 11 mm   c 1.9 m   d 3.2 mm

3 a 10   b 56   c 12.5

Now you try

Example 13

a $42 \, cm^2$ b $24 \, m^2$

Exercise 10G

1 a $30 \, m^2$ b $12 \, cm^2$

2 a $16 \, m^2$ b $30 \, cm^2$ c $25 \, mm^2$

     d $160 \, m^2$ e $1.2 \, m^2$ f $1.25 \, cm^2$

3 a $60 \, mm^2$ b $14 \, cm^2$

4 a $3 \, mm^2$ b $24.5 \, km^2$ c $12 \, cm^2$

     d $1.3 \, cm^2$ e $20 \, m^2$ f $4.25 \, m^2$

5 a $2 \, cm^2$ b $6 \, cm^2$ c $3 \, cm^2$ d $3 \, cm^2$

6 $480 \, m^2$

7 $4800 \, m^2$

8 $6.8 \, cm^2$

9 $160 \, m^2$

10 $6300

11 a 5 cm   b 4.4 mm

12 Yes, the base and height for each triangle are equal.

13 No, the base and height are always the same.

14 $b = \dfrac{2A}{h}$

15 a $7 \, cm^2$ b $8 \, cm^2$ c $11 \, cm^2$

Progress quiz

1 a Metres   b Millimetres   c Kilometres

2 a 400 cm   b 2000 mm   c 35 mm

     d 3000 m   e 1450 m   f 23 km

3 a 14.6 cm   b 10.4 m   c 354 cm

4 a 3.136   b No

5 a 28.27 mm   b 37.70 cm

6 a 16.5 cm   b 30.8 cm   c 41.4 cm

7 a $0.9 \, m^2$ b $49 \, cm^2$

8 a $55 \, cm^2$ b $72.9 \, m^2$ c $192 \, mm^2$

9 a $6 \, m^2$ b $31.5 \, m^2$ c $9.68 \, m^2$ d $20 \, mm^2$

10 a $225 \, cm^2$ b $200 \, cm^2$ c 7

11 $\dfrac{1}{3}$

10H

Building understanding

1 a   b

     c

2 a Addition

     b Subtraction

     c Subtraction

3 a $A = l^2 + lw$
$= 1^2 + 3 \times 1$
$= 1 + 3$
$= 4\,cm^2$

b $A = lw - \dfrac{1}{2}\,bh$
$= 13 \times 8 - \dfrac{1}{2} \times 5 \times 4$
$= 104 - 10$
$= 94\,m^2$

Now you try

Example 14
a $33\,m^2$ b $30\,cm^2$

Example 15
a $68\,cm^2$ b $10\,cm^2$

Exercise 10H

1 a $60\,cm^2$ b $32\,m^2$
2 a $33\,m^2$ b $600\,mm^2$ c $25\,m^2$
   d $21\,m^2$ e $171\,cm^2$ f $45\,km^2$
3 a $45\,cm^2$ b $54\,cm^2$
4 a $39\,m^2$ b $95.5\,cm^2$ c $26\,m^2$
   d $54\,m^2$ e $260\,cm^2$ f $4\,m^2$
5 a $53\,cm^2$ b $16\,m^2$ c $252\,cm^2$
6 a $80\,cm^2$ b $7\,m^2$
   c $14.5\,m^2$ d $11.75\,cm^2$
7 $10.08\,m^2$
8 Yes, with $100 to spare.
9 Subtraction may involve only two simple shapes.
10 a No; bases could vary depending on the position of the top side.
   b Yes, $40\,m^2$; take out the rectangle and join the triangles to give a base of $10 - 6 = 4$.
11 a See given diagram in Chapter 10, Exercise 10G, Question 11.
   b i $\dfrac{1}{16}, \dfrac{1}{32}, \dfrac{1}{64}, \dfrac{1}{128}, \dfrac{1}{256}, \dfrac{1}{512}, \dfrac{1}{1024}, \dfrac{1}{2048}, \dfrac{1}{4096}, \dfrac{1}{8192}$
     ii No
   c 1 square unit
   d Total must equal 1.

10I

Building understanding

1 a 6   b 24   c 24
   d 144   e 56   f 13
2 a $V = lwh$
     $= 4 \times 2 \times 3$
     $= 24\,cm^3$
   b $V = lwh$
     $= 1 \times 3 \times 6$
     $= 18\,m^3$
   c $V = l^3$
     $= 2 \times 2 \times 2$
     $= 8\,km^3$

Now you try

Example 16
$48\,cm^3$

Exercise 10I

1 a $84\,m^3$ b $10\,cm^3$
2 a $98\,cm^3$ b $27\,cm^3$ c $1000\,km^3$
   d $2.744\,mm^3$ e $100\,m^3$ f $11.25\,km^3$
3 $24\,000\,cm^3$
4 $96\,m^3$
5 $12\,000\,mm^3$
6 $27\,000\,000\,km^3$
7 a $28\,cm^3$ b $252\,m^3$ c $104\,cm^3$ d $120\,m^3$
8 600
9 $4096\,cm^3$
10 a $125\,cm^3$ b $729\,m^3$
11 a 6 cubic units   b 4 cubic units   c 14 cubic units
12 a i 2 m   ii 5 cm   iii 7 cm   iv 3 m
   b Use: Volume ÷ area of base
   c $h = V \div (l \times w)$
13 a i 10   ii 100   iii 10   iv 1000
   b i $1\,000\,000$ ii $1\,000\,000\,000$
   c $\times 1\,000\,000\,000$ $\times 1\,000\,000$ $\times 1000$

     km^3 m^3 cm^3 mm^3

     $\div 1\,000\,000\,000$ $\div 1\,000\,000$ $\div 1000$

10J

Building understanding

1 a 5 m   b 7 m   c 2 cm
2 a $6\,m^2$ b $16\,m^2$ c $2.25\,cm^2$
3 a $30\,m^3$ b $112\,m^3$ c $4.5\,cm^3$

Now you try

Example 17
a $45\,cm^3$ b $72\,m^3$

Example 18
$140\,m^3$

Exercise 10J

1 a $20\,mm^3$ b $84\,cm^3$
2 a $9\,m^3$ b $175\,cm^3$ c $80\,mm^3$
   d $270\,mm^3$ e $585\,m^3$ f $225\,mm^3$
3 a $9\,cm^3$ b $48\,m^3$
4 a $30\,m^3$ b $9\,m^3$ c $0.99\,cm^3$
5 $4.2\,m^3$
6 $360\,000\,cm^3$
7 $36\,cm^3$
8 a $110\,cm^3$ b $60\,m^3$ c $160\,cm^3$ d $140\,cm^3$
9 $4080\,cm^3$
10 a 4 cm   b 5.125 m
   c $6.25\,mm^2$ d $10\,cm^3$

11 3 cm
12 2.5 mm

13 a $V = \dfrac{b h_1 h_2}{2} = \dfrac{1}{2} b h_1 h_2$ **b** $h_2 = \dfrac{2V}{b h_1}$

    c $h_1 = \dfrac{2V}{b h_2}$ **d** $b = \dfrac{2V}{h_1 h_2}$

    e i 1.5   **ii** 1   **iii** 0.8

10K

Building understanding

1 a 1   **b** 1000   **c** 1000
   d 1000   **e** 1000
2 a 1 L, 1000 mL, 1000 cm³   **b** 1 m³, 1000 L, 1 kL
3 a D   **b** B   **c** F   **d** A   **e** C   **f** E

Now you try

Example 19
a 7.2 L   **b** 7000 kL

Example 20
a 67 ML   **b** 9 000 000 ml

Example 21
3 L

Exercise 10K

1 a 0.7 L   **b** 8 L   **c** 0.06 L
   d 2000 L   **e** 5000 L   **f** 7500 L
2 a 2000 mL   **b** 100 mL   **c** 6000 kL   **d** 24 000 L
   e 2 kL   **f** 3.5 L   **g** 70 L   **h** 2.5 ML
   i 257 mL   **j** 9.32 L   **k** 3847 kL   **l** 47 kL
   m 500 L   **n** 91 ML   **o** 420 mL   **p** 0.17 kL
3 a 12 mL   **b** 2.5 m³   **c** 875 mL
4 a 1200 mL   **b** 1.2 L
5 a 4.7 kL   **b** 0.26 kL
   c 5 ML   **d** 3.84 ML
   e 9 000 000 L   **f** 400 000 L
   g 200 000 mL   **h** 5000 mL
6 3 300 000 L
7 a 1.5 L   **b** 0.48 L   **c** 0.162 L
   d 8.736 L   **e** 25 L   **f** 32.768 L
8 a 2500 m³   **b** 2 500 000 L
9 a 0.2 mL
   b i 1 L   **ii** 0.6 L
    iii 14.4 L   **iv** 5256 L
10 15 days
11 41 h 40 min
12 1000 days
13 a $1000x$ cm³   **b** $0.001x$ m³
   c $0.001x$ kL   **d** $0.000001x$ ML
14 a i lwh **ii** lwh
    iii $\dfrac{lwh}{1000}$ **iv** $\dfrac{lwh}{1000000}$
   b i lwh m³   **ii** $1000 lwh$ L
    iii lwh kL   **iv** $\dfrac{lwh}{1000}$ ML

15 a i 8 cm   **ii** 4 cm   **iii** 3.2 cm
   b 0.6 cm   **c** 13.4 cm

10L

Building understanding

1 a 1 kg, 1000 g   **b** 1000 mg, 1 g
2 a C   **b** F   **c** A   **d** D   **e** B   **f** E
3 a B   **b** A   **c** D   **d** C

Now you try

Example 22
a 32 500 g   **b** 9.5 t

Exercise 10L

1 a i 4290 g   **ii** 7.5 kg
   b i 620 t   **ii** 5100 kg
2 a 2000 kg   **b** 70 000 g   **c** 2400 mg
   d 2.3 g   **e** 4.620 g   **f** 21.6 t
   g 470 kg   **h** 0.312 kg   **i** 0.027 g
   j 750 kg   **k** 125 g   **l** 0.0105 kg
   m 210 t   **n** 470 kg   **o** 592 g
   p 80 g
3 a 4 kg   **b** 12 g   **c** 65 t
4 a 12°C   **b** 37°C   **c** 17°C
   d 225°C   **e** 1.7°C   **f** 31.5°C
5 a 60 kg   **b** 60 000 g   **c** 60 000 000 mg
6 a 3000 g   **b** 3 kg
7 33°C
8 147°C
9 a 8 kg   **b** 8.16 kg
10 a 400 mg, 370 g, 2.5 kg, 0.1 t
   b 290 000 mg, 0.00032 t, 0.41 kg, 710 g
11 a 4th day   **b** 25°C   **c** 26°C
12 50 days
13 Yes, by 215 kg
14 a 45.3 t   **b** Yes, by 2.7 t
15 a 1 g   **b** 1 t   **c** 1000 t
16 a 12 kg   **b** 1000 kg   **c** 360 000 kg
17 a i 10°C   **ii** 27°C   **iii** 727°C
   b i 273 K   **ii** 313 K   **iii** 0 K
18 a 180°F   **b** $\dfrac{5}{9}$°C   **c** $\dfrac{9}{5}$°F or $1\dfrac{4}{5}$°F
   d i 0°C   **ii** 20°C
    iii 60°C   **iv** 105°C
   e $F = \dfrac{9C}{5} + 32$

Problems and challenges

1 Both line segments are the same length.
2 Mark a length of 5 m, then use the 3 m stick to reduce this to 2 m. Place the 3 m stick on the 2 m length to show a remainder of 1 m.
3 a 3 cm²   **b** 20 cm²
4 500 L

5 $24\,\text{m}^3$
6 $10.5\,\text{cm}^2$
7 **a** 12.5 cm   **b** 3.75 cm
8 $48\,\text{cm}^2$

Chapter checklist with success criteria

1 Metres (m)
2 0.256 km
3 0.7 m (or 70 cm)
4 28 m
5 3.125; it is a less accurate approximation than 3.14 (both are less than π but 3.14 is closer).
6 25.13 cm
7 14.980 m
8 28.85 m
9 $6\,\text{cm}^2$
10 $40\,\text{mm}^2$
11 $60\,\text{m}^2$
12 $45\,\text{cm}^2$
13 $24\,\text{cm}^2$
14 $96\,\text{cm}^3$
15 $20\,\text{cm}^3$
16 0.5 L
17 2 L
18 2470 g

Chapter review

Short-answer questions

1 **a** 10
   b 1000
   c 100 000
2 **a** 50 mm
   b 2 m
   c 3700 m
   d 4.21 km
   e 7100 g
   f 24.9 g
   g 28.49 t
   h 9000 g
   i 4 L
   j 29.903 kL
   k 400 kL
   l 1000 mL
   m 1440 min
   n 60 min
   o 3.5 days
   p 9000 s
3 **a** 2.5 cm
   b 2.3 cm
   c 4.25 kg
   d 5 L

4 **a** 16 m   **b** 20.6 cm
   c 23 m   **d** 34 km
   e 3.2 mm   **f** 24 m
5 **a** 3.143   **b** Yes
6 **a** 34.56 cm   **b** 31.42 m
7 **a** 23.0 cm   **b** 26.3 cm
8 **a** $24.01\,\text{cm}^2$
   b $14\,\text{km}^2$
   c $67.5\,\text{m}^2$
   d $12\,\text{cm}^2$
   e $14\,\text{m}^2$
   f $5\,\text{cm}^2$
   g $14\,\text{m}^2$
   h $0.9\,\text{km}^2$
9 **a** $22\,\text{m}^2$
   b $21\,\text{mm}^2$
   c $291\,\text{cm}^2$
   d $52\,\text{m}^2$
10 **a** $18\,\text{cm}^3$
    b $7.5\,\text{cm}^3$
    c $64\,\text{mm}^3$
11 **a** $45\,\text{cm}^3$
    b $112\,\text{m}^3$
    c $210\,\text{mm}^3$
12 **a** $72\,000\,\text{cm}^3$
    b 72 000 mL
    c 72 L
13 **a** 45 mg, 290 000 g, 3 t, 4700 kg
    b 50 000 mL, 51 L, 0.5 kL, 1 ML

Multiple-choice questions

1 D
2 E
3 C
4 E
5 C
6 A
7 E
8 B
9 A
10 C
11 B
12 E
13 B

Extended-response questions

1 **a** **i** $18\,\text{m}^2$ **ii** $180\,000\,\text{cm}^2$
   b $36\,\text{m}^3$ **c** 36 000 L
   d 51.4 t   **e** 3 h 52 min 54 s
2 **a** 97.3 m   **b** 5 min 30 s   **c** $270\,\text{m}^2$
   d $2040   **e** $50\,\text{m}^3$

Semester review 2

Negative numbers

Short-answer questions

1 a $<$ b $<$ c $=$
2 a -13 b -84 c -108
  d -21 e 84 f 0
3 a -24 b 72 c 144
  d 21 e 30 f -31
4 a Negative   b Positive   c Negative
5 a -15 b -8 c -4
6 a -10 b 10 c -20
  d -96 e 52 f -1

Multiple-choice questions

1 C   2 B   3 D   4 E   5 A

Extended-response question

a D
b A, B, O and G, all lie on the x-axis.
c F
d i 2 units   ii 5 units
e Trapezium
f 8 square units
g $X(4, 2)$
h DECIDE

Geometry

Short-answer questions

1 a $AC \parallel FD$ or $EB \parallel DC$
  b BF and BD
  c CD, ED, BD at D or any three of AC, BD, BE or BF at B
  d A and B
  e E
2 a $30°$ b $80°$ c $150°$
3 $25°$
4 $78°$
5 a $a = 140$ b $a = 50$ c $a = 140$
  d $a = 65$ e $a = 62$ f $a = 56$
6 $a = 100, b = 80, c = 100, d = 80, e = 100, f = 80, g = 100$
7 a Regular pentagon   b Regular octagon
  c Isosceles right triangle   d Rhombus
  e Trapezium   f Kite
8 a 130 b 45 c 80
9 a $a = 60$
  b $a = 65$
  c $a = 115$
  d $a = 90, b = 90$
  e $a = 65$
  f $a = 132, b = 48, c = 48, d = 65$

10 a $A'(2, 0), B'(2, -3), C'(4, 0)$
   b $A'(-2, 0), B'(-2, 3), C'(-4, 0)$
   c $A'(0, -2), B'(3, -2), C'(0, -4)$
   d $A'(0, 2), B'(-3, 2), C'(0, 4)$
   e $A'(-2, 0), B'(-2, -3), C'(-4, 0)$
   f $A'(-2, 1), B'(-2, 4), C'(0, 1)$
   g $A'(-1, -2), B'(-1, 1), C'(1, -2)$

Multiple-choice questions

1 A   2 B   3 B   4 B   5 A

Extended-response question

a Answers may vary.
b $a + b + c = 180°$
c Answers may vary.
d $x + y + z = 360°$
e $360°$

Statistics and probability

Short-answer questions

1 a $1, 2, 3, 5, 5, 5, 8, 8, 9, 10$
  b 10
  c i 5.6 ii 5 iii 5 iv 9
  d 11.2
2 a A   b B   c B, C, D, A
3 a $\dfrac{1}{2}$ b $\dfrac{1}{2}$ c $\dfrac{1}{4}$
  d $\dfrac{1}{13}$ e $\dfrac{1}{13}$ f $\dfrac{1}{26}$
4 a 13
  b $3, 47$
  c i 44 ii 22 iii 22
5 a 20
  b 22
  c Mean is 23, median is 22

Multiple-choice questions

1 B   2 A   3 B   4 E   5 D

Extended-response question

a $\dfrac{1}{4}$ b $\dfrac{1}{4}$ c $\dfrac{1}{2}$
d $\dfrac{1}{52}$ e $\dfrac{2}{13}$ f $\dfrac{1}{13}$
g $\dfrac{4}{13}$ h $\dfrac{4}{13}$

Equations

Short-answer questions

1 a $x = 3$ b $x = 108$ c $x = 21$ d $x = \dfrac{4}{3}$

2 a $x = 2$ b $x = 12$ c $m = 7$
3 a $y = 20$ b $b = 4$ c $m = 8$
4 a $P = 103$ b $S = 61$ c $C = 325$
5 a $x = 5$ b $x = 6$ c $x = 18$
6 $4x + 25 = 85$; $x = 15$

Multiple-choice questions

1 B   2 E   3 C   4 B   5 D

Extended-response question

a $320   b $400
c $(200 + 40n)$ d $6\frac{1}{2}h$

Measurement

Short-answer questions

1 a 500   b 6000   c 1.8
   d 0.017   e 1.8   f 5500
2 a 272 cm   b 11 m   c 3.2 m
   d 220 cm   e 3.4 m   f 92 m

3 a $1.69 \, \text{m}^2$ b $24 \, \text{m}^2$ c $60 \, \text{m}^2$
   d $75 \, \text{m}^2$ e $114 \, \text{m}^2$ f $171 \, \text{m}^2$
4 a $729 \, \text{cm}^3$ b $120 \, \text{m}^3$
   c $160 \, \text{m}^3$ d $180 \, \text{cm}^3$
5 a 5000   b 7   c 250
   d 3000   e 8   f 25
6 60 L
7 18.85 cm
8 337 kg
9 $-3°C$

Multiple-choice questions

1 C   2 A   3 E   4 C   5 A

Extended-response question

a Answers may vary; e.g. $8 \, \text{m} \times 10 \, \text{m}$, $4 \, \text{m} \times 14 \, \text{m}$, $15 \, \text{m} \times 3 \, \text{m}$
b 9 m by 9 m (area = $81 \, \text{m}^2$)
c 36 posts
d 9 h

Working with unfamiliar problems

What am I asked to find?

1

Identify the problem

- Underline or highlight important words and phrases (if permitted).
- Summarise what you are **told** (the facts).
- Write out what you are **asked** (the question).

Does my solution make sense?

4

Check and Communicate

- Check that you have answered the question.
- Does your answer make **sense**?
- Can you **explain** (justify) your answer?
- Is what you have presented easy to follow, **reads well**, mathematically correct in its content and its setting out?

You can try more than one strategy. Remember it is OK to make a mistake before trying again!

Trying different strategies can help uncover a useful pathway to the correct solution.